lonely planet

Morocco

**Matt Fletcher
Joyce Connolly
Frances Linzee Gordon
Dorinda Talbot**

LONELY PLANET PUBLICATIONS
Melbourne • Oakland • London • Paris

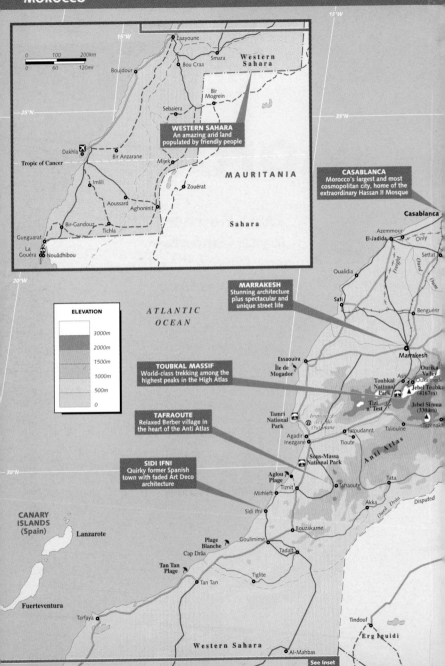

MOROCCO

WESTERN SAHARA
An amazing arid land populated by friendly people

CASABLANCA
Morocco's largest and most cosmopolitan city, home of the extraordinary Hassan II Mosque

MARRAKESH
Stunning architecture plus spectacular and unique street life

TOUBKAL MASSIF
World-class trekking among the highest peaks in the High Atlas

TAFRAOUTE
Relaxed Berber village in the heart of the Anti Atlas

SIDI IFNI
Quirky former Spanish town with faded Art Deco architecture

ELEVATION

3000m
2000m
1500m
1000m
500m
0

See Inset

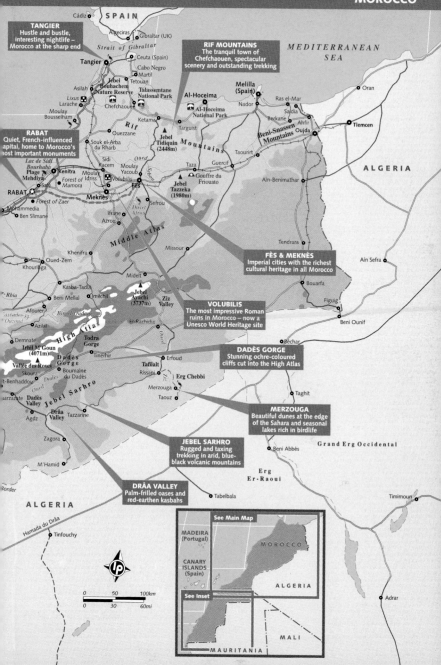

TANGIER
Hustle and bustle, interesting nightlife – Morocco at the sharp end

RIF MOUNTAINS
The tranquil town of Chefchaouen, spectacular scenery and outstanding trekking

RABAT
Quiet, French-influenced capital, home to Morocco's most important monuments

FÈS & MEKNÈS
Imperial cities with the richest cultural heritage in all Morocco

VOLUBILIS
The most impressive Roman ruins in Morocco – now a Unesco World Heritage site

DADÈS GORGE
Stunning ochre-coloured cliffs cut into the High Atlas

MERZOUGA
Beautiful dunes at the edge of the Sahara and seasonal lakes rich in birdlife

JEBEL SARHRO
Rugged and taxing trekking in arid, blue-black volcanic mountains

DRÂA VALLEY
Palm-frilled oases and red-earthen kasbahs

SPAIN

MEDITERRANEAN SEA

ALGERIA

Cádiz
Algeciras · Gibraltar (UK)
Strait of Gibraltar
Tangier
Ceuta (Spain)
Cabo Negro
Martil
Tetouan
Asilah
Jebel Bouhachem Nature Reserve
Talassemtane National Park
Al-Hoceima
Melilla (Spain)
Oran
Lixus
Larache
Chefchaouen
Al-Hoceima National Park
Nador
Ras el-Mar
Saïdia
Moulay Bousselham
Ketama
Targuist
Berkane
Ahfir
Oujda
Tlemcen
Ouezzane
Rif Mountains
Beni-Snassen Mountains
Souk el-Arba du Rharb
Jebel Tidiquin (2448m)
Taza
Taourirt
Sidi Kacem
Oued
Guercif
Aïn-Benimathar
Plage Mehdiya
Kenitra
Moulay Yacoub
Gouffre du Friouato
Salé
Moulay Idriss
Volubilis
Fès
Jebel Tazzeka (1980m)
RABAT
Forest of Mamora
Meknes
Sefrou
Forest of Zaer
Mohammedia
Ifrane
Ben Slimane
Azrou
Dayet Aoua
Middle Atlas
Missour
Tendrara
Khenifra
Oued-Zem
Midelt
Aïn Sefra
Khouribga
Bouarfa
'Rbia
Kasba-Tadla
Figuig
Beni Mellal
Imilchil
Jebel Ayachi (3737m)
Ziz Valley
Afourer
Bin el Ouidane
Beni Ounif
Azilal
Er-Rachidia
Béchar
Demnate
High Atlas
Todra Gorge
Irhil M'Goun (4071m)
Dadès Gorge
Tinerhir
Taghit
Vallée des Roses
Skoura
Boumalne du Dadès
Tafilalt
Erfoud
Erg Chebbi
t-Benhaddou
Ourd
Dadès Valley
Jebel Sarhro
Rissani
Merzouga
Taouz
arzazate
Dráa Valley
Agdz
Tazzarine
Grand Erg Occidental
Zagora
Beni Abbès
Erg Er-Raoui
M'Hamid
Tabelbala
Timimoun
ALGERIA
Hamada du Dráa
Tinfouchy
Adrar

See Main Map

See Inset

MADEIRA (Portugal)
CANARY ISLANDS (Spain)
MOROCCO
ALGERIA
MALI
MAURITANIA

0   50   100km
0   30   60mi

Morocco
5th edition – March 2001
First published – July 1989

Published by
Lonely Planet Publications Pty Ltd ABN 36 005 607 983
90 Maribyrnong St, Footscray, Victoria 3011, Australia

Lonely Planet Offices
Australia Locked Bag 1, Footscray, Victoria 3011
USA 150 Linden St, Oakland, CA 94607
UK 10a Spring Place, London NW5 3BH
France 1 rue du Dahomey, 75011 Paris

Photographs
All of the images in this guide are available for licensing from
Lonely Planet Images.
email: lpi@lonelyplanet.com.au

Front cover photograph
Family caravan on Agadir beach, Agadir, Morocco (Izzet Keribar)

ISBN 0 86442 762 X

text & maps © Lonely Planet Publications Pty Ltd 2001
photos © photographers as indicated 2001

Printed by Craft Print International Ltd, Singapore

Contents – Text

Contents – Maps

The Authors

Matt Fletcher After travelling on and off during and after Art College, Matt started writing and taking pictures seriously in 1996 while in East Africa and Southern Africa. A brief spell as a staff writer on an adventure sports magazine soon passed and Matt has been freelancing ever since, travelling and trekking in Europe, Australia and Africa. Matt is a contributor to Lonely Planet's *Walking in Spain* and *Walking in Australia* guides, as well as the *Kenya* and *East Africa* guides. This was his second trip to Morocco, and the wild mountains look set to keep dragging him back.

Joyce Connolly Born in Edinburgh, Scotland, Joyce has been on the move since an early age, including time in Germany and the Netherlands where she developed an appreciation of fine beers. Fuelled by the travel bug (and, of course, beer) she studied to become a professional tourist but instead stumbled into publishing in Oxford. In 1995 she set off to Australia in pursuit of Jason Donovan who obligingly moved in round the corner from her in Bondi. Having satisfied that urge she moved to Melbourne to woo LP; she became an editor and was entrusted with updating the Gippsland chapter of the *Victoria* guide. Since then she's flown the editorial coop to update Zimbabwe for *Southern Africa* and more recently *Morocco*. She's now back in the UK trying to come to terms with the British weather and no longer being the most beautiful girl in the world.

Frances Linzee Gordon Frances grew up in the Highlands of Scotland, but later went to London University, where she read Latin, but later decided modern languages might be the thing, and worked in Spain, Germany and Belgium. Frances has travelled in nearly 40 different countries and has qualifications in nine languages. She is a Fellow of the Royal Geographical Society in London and holds a licentiateship of the Royal Photographical Society. Frances has contributed to LP's guides to *Mediterranean Europe*, *Western Europe*, *Africa* and *Ethiopia, Eritrea & Djibouti*.

Dorinda Talbot Born in Melbourne, Australia, Dorinda began travelling when 18 months old and has since seen a fair slice of the world, including South-East Asia, the USA and Europe. After studying journalism at Deakin University in Victoria, Dorinda worked as a reporter in Alice Springs before embarking on the traditional Aussie sojourn to London. She has worked for numerous magazines in London and has contributed to LP's *Mediterranean Europe* and *Canada* guides.

Damien Simonis With a degree in languages and several years' reporting and sub-editing on several Australian newspapers, Sydney-born Damien left the country in 1989. He has lived, worked and travelled extensively in Europe, the Middle East and North Africa. Since 1992, LP has kept him busy with guides to *Jordan & Syria*, *Egypt & the Sudan*, *Morocco*, *North Africa*, *Italy*, the *Canary Islands* and *Spain*.

FROM THE AUTHORS

Matt Fletcher Thanks firstly to Clare Irvin who again helped tremendously. Big thanks also to Dr Jaouad Berrada for the welcome in Rabat and to Joyce for all her hard work in Morocco – I know it wasn't easy. Thanks also to Lorna and Akim in Mohammedia; Harvey Palmer, Cathy Myers and Robert Drechsler for laughs at the *mort de mouton;* Azi Mnii at the London Moroccan tourist office; Adel Nouayba, the genial director of Centre de Hassan II in Asilah; Harrak Abdeslm in Tetouan; Abdel Aziz al-Mouden, his very knowledgeable big brother Abdeslam and jokers Jaouad Achagra and Rabie Taleb Alami for a great trek in the Rif. In the High Atlas thanks to Aït Hammou al-Housssaïn and to Jerry le Ferve and Mustapha Ahitass of Explore. Hamish Brown provided maps and wise words, while Chris Bowden and Jorge Fernández-Orueta added birding tips. In Tangier Debbi Hamida, Stephanie Sweet, Thor Kuniholm and particularly Matt Schofield were a great help. Thanks also to Hazel Reeves, Chris Lawrence, Ag, Blob, Fleur and the staff at the British Embassy, plus Leila Mourad and John Shackleton at the British Council. Thanks Geoff for fielding insane phone calls, to Verity and Michelle for their patience and encouragement, Damien Simonis and John Noble for Spanish info and Dorinda Talbot for her great work in the High Atlas. Lastly, thanks to Bando for being such a good cleaner.

Joyce Connolly I couldn't have done this job without the help and company of Jason Rankin (aka Cowboy Surfer) who came to the end of the road and resisted the urge to throw my bag on the floor, and Benjamin Villand who always drove safely and taught me much about the true value of beer, wine and carpets. Big mint tea cheers to Joanne Vella and Clare Irvin who made sense of all the readers letters for me, and Matt Fletcher for all the words of encouragement and not letting me take the worming tablets. More really big thanks goes to all the travellers who willingly became drinking partners and kept me sane. They include my mum – Mary Leggat – & Alan Campbell; Verity Campbell, Jan Campbell & Josef; Bob O'Sullivan, Paul Maxwell & James Schultz; Angelina & Amy; Estaban, Frankie & Abby; Christoff Reinecke; Angela Pugh & Steven Buckler; Elly Fattore; Agnes Pottier; Didier Heberli; Hartley Wynberg, Matt Hargest & Marcel Mettelseifen; Monique & Bas; Michael & Justine; Daniella & David; Brahim Bahri; and Phil, Clive & Justin. I'd also like to thank the following Moroccans for unerring hospitality: the Bazar Zougagh Fatima family; Nemri Sala Heddine; Malek in Safi; Ben Zitoun Youness; and every Mohammed I met for boosting my ego.

Back on the work-front those who gave me invaluable assistance with my research include Fiona Cameron & Preben Kristensen; Aziz Mnii at the Moroccan National Tourist Office, London; Youssef Lafquih at the Marrakesh Syndicat d'Initiative; and Amina Zakkari, Fès' female guide extraordinaire. To those who kept the emails flowing – Lucienne Cooper & Jennifer Smith in particular – thanks, I couldn't have done it without you. I also would have been lost without the girl power I got from singing Spice Girls' songs. Finally an apology to the innocent tourists who heard far too much from me on the Agadir Berber dinner bus.

This Book

This book started life as one-third of the *Morocco, Tunisia & Algeria* guide, which was written and updated by Geoff Crowther and Hugh Finlay. The third edition was expanded and revised by Damien Simonis. The fourth edition was further expanded and updated by Frances Linzee Gordon and Dorinda Talbot. This fifth edition was revised by Matt Fletcher and Joyce Connolly. Dorinda Talbot's original research was used for substantial parts of the High Atlas section of the Trekking chapter, particularly the treks in the Jebel Toubkal region. Matt updated these treks and compiled the rest of this new chapter.

From the Publisher

The fifth edition of *Morocco* was edited and proofread in Lonely Planet's Melbourne office by Brigitte Ellemor, with the assistance of Susan Holtham, Russell Kerr, Michelle Glynn, Julia Taylor, Bethune Carmichael, Justin Flynn, John Hinman and Hilary Rogers. Mapping and design were coordinated by Brett Moore and then by Hunor Csutoros, who also designed chapter ends and compiled the climate charts. Mapping assistance was provided by Sarah Sloane, Kieran Grogan, Csanad Csuturos, Katie Butterworth, Andrew Smith, Heath Comrie and Ann Jeffree. Daniel New designed the cover and Mick Weldon and Martin Harris supplied the illustrations. Quentin Frayne and Emma Koch compiled the Language chapter. Michael Sklovsky provided extra information for the colour section 'Moroccan Arts & Crafts' and generously allowed Lonely Planet staff to photograph items from his Ishka Handcrafts stores in Melbourne.

Acknowledgement

Grateful acknowledgment is made for reproduction permission:
Flamingo/HarperCollins Australia: Excerpt from *Café Royal*
© *Larry Buttrose* (1987)

THANKS
Many thanks to the travellers who used the last edition and wrote to us with helpful hints, advice and interesting anecdotes. Your names appear in the back of this book.

Foreword

ABOUT LONELY PLANET GUIDEBOOKS

The story begins with a classic travel adventure: Tony and Maureen Wheeler's 1972 journey across Europe and Asia to Australia. Useful information about the overland trail did not exist at that time, so Tony and Maureen published the first Lonely Planet guidebook to meet a growing need.

From a kitchen table, then from a tiny office in Melbourne (Australia), Lonely Planet has become the largest independent travel publisher in the world, an international company with offices in Melbourne, Oakland (USA), London (UK) and Paris (France).

Today Lonely Planet guidebooks cover the globe. There is an ever-growing list of books and there's information in a variety of forms and media. Some things haven't changed. The main aim is still to help make it possible for adventurous travellers to get out there – to explore and better understand the world.

At Lonely Planet we believe travellers can make a positive contribution to the countries they visit – if they respect their host communities and spend their money wisely. Since 1986 a percentage of the income from each book has been donated to aid projects and human rights campaigns.

Updates Lonely Planet thoroughly updates each guidebook as often as possible. This usually means there are around two years between editions, although for more unusual or more stable destinations the gap can be longer. Check the imprint page (following the colour map at the beginning of the book) for publication dates.

Between editions up-to-date information is available in two free newsletters – the paper *Planet Talk* and email *Comet* (to subscribe, contact any Lonely Planet office) – and on our Web site at www.lonelyplanet.com. The *Upgrades* section of the Web site covers a number of important and volatile destinations and is regularly updated by Lonely Planet authors. *Scoop* covers news and current affairs relevant to travellers. And, lastly, the *Thorn Tree* bulletin board and *Postcards* section of the site carry unverified, but fascinating, reports from travellers.

Correspondence The process of creating new editions begins with the letters, postcards and emails received from travellers. This correspondence often includes suggestions, criticisms and comments about the current editions. Interesting excerpts are immediately passed on via newsletters and the Web site, and everything goes to our authors to be verified when they're researching on the road. We're keen to get more feedback from organisations or individuals who represent communities visited by travellers.

Lonely Planet gathers information for everyone who's curious about the planet – and especially for those who explore it first-hand. Through guidebooks, phrasebooks, activity guides, maps, literature, newsletters, image library, TV series and Web site we act as an information exchange for a worldwide community of travellers.

Research Authors aim to gather sufficient practical information to enable travellers to make informed choices and to make the mechanics of a journey run smoothly. They also research historical and cultural background to help enrich the travel experience and allow travellers to understand and respond appropriately to cultural and environmental issues.

Authors don't stay in every hotel because that would mean spending a couple of months in each medium-sized city and, no, they don't eat at every restaurant because that would mean stretching belts beyond capacity. They do visit hotels and restaurants to check standards and prices, but feedback based on readers' direct experiences can be very helpful.

Many of our authors work undercover, others aren't so secretive. None of them accept freebies in exchange for positive write-ups. And none of our guidebooks contain any advertising.

Production Authors submit their raw manuscripts and maps to offices in Australia, USA, UK or France. Editors and cartographers – all experienced travellers themselves – then begin the process of assembling the pieces. When the book finally hits the shops, some things are already out of date, we start getting feedback from readers and the process begins again …

WARNING & REQUEST

Things change – prices go up, schedules change, good places go bad and bad places go bankrupt – nothing stays the same. So, if you find things better or worse, recently opened or long since closed, please tell us and help make the next edition even more accurate and useful. We genuinely value all the feedback we receive. A well-travelled team reads and acknowledges every letter, postcard and email and ensures that every morsel of information finds its way to the appropriate authors, editors and cartographers for verification.

Everyone who writes to us will find their name in the next edition of the appropriate guidebook. They will also receive the latest issue of *Planet Talk*, our quarterly printed newsletter, or *Comet*, our monthly email newsletter. Subscriptions to both newsletters are free. The very best contributions will be rewarded with a free guidebook.

Excerpts from your correspondence may appear in new editions of Lonely Planet guidebooks, the Lonely Planet Web site, *Planet Talk* or *Comet*, so please let us know if you *don't* want your letter published or your name acknowledged.

Send all correspondence to the Lonely Planet office closest to you:

Australia: Locked Bag 1, Footscray, Victoria 3011
USA: 150 Linden St, Oakland, CA 94607
UK: 10A Spring Place, London NW5 3BH
France: 1 rue du Dahomey, 75011 Paris

Or email us at: talk2us@lonelyplanet.com.au

For news, views and updates see our Web site: www.lonelyplanet.com

HOW TO USE A LONELY PLANET GUIDEBOOK

The best way to use a Lonely Planet guidebook is any way you choose. At Lonely Planet we believe the most memorable travel experiences are often those that are unexpected, and the finest discoveries are those you make yourself. Guidebooks are not intended to be used as if they provide a detailed set of infallible instructions!

Contents All Lonely Planet guidebooks follow roughly the same format. The Facts about the Destination chapters or sections give background information ranging from history to weather. Facts for the Visitor gives practical information on issues like visas and health. Getting There & Away gives a brief starting point for researching travel to and from the destination. Getting Around gives an overview of the transport options when you arrive.

The peculiar demands of each destination determine how subsequent chapters are broken up, but some things remain constant. We always start with background, then proceed to sights, places to stay, places to eat, entertainment, getting there and away, and getting around information – in that order.

Heading Hierarchy Lonely Planet headings are used in a strict hierarchical structure that can be visualised as a set of Russian dolls. Each heading (and its following text) is encompassed by any preceding heading that is higher on the hierarchical ladder.

Entry Points We do not assume guidebooks will be read from beginning to end, but that people will dip into them. The traditional entry points are the list of contents and the index. In addition, however, some books have a complete list of maps and an index map illustrating map coverage.

There may also be a colour map that shows highlights. These highlights are dealt with in greater detail in the Facts for the Visitor chapter, along with planning questions and suggested itineraries. Each chapter covering a geographical region usually begins with a locator map and another list of highlights. Once you find something of interest in a list of highlights, turn to the index.

Maps Maps play a crucial role in Lonely Planet guidebooks and include a huge amount of information. A legend is printed on the back page. We seek to have complete consistency between maps and text, and to have every important place in the text captured on a map. Map key numbers usually start in the top left corner.

Although inclusion in a guidebook usually implies a recommendation we cannot list every good place. Exclusion does not necessarily imply criticism. In fact there are a number of reasons why we might exclude a place – sometimes it is simply inappropriate to encourage an influx of travellers.

Introduction

Morocco has been drawing travellers in search of adventure and the exotic for centuries. For many travellers, Morocco provides the first taste of Africa, Islamic culture and the developing world. It can be quite a shock, as Morocco is, and always has been, a fascinating and often bewildering place – full of contrasting images, exotic sights, strange smells and wild experiences. For those travellers wanting a different sort of trip, full of variety and life, Morocco provides a wonderful assault on the senses.

Morocco was known to the ancient Arabs as Al-Maghreb al-Aqsa, the 'Farthest Land of the Setting Sun', and stands at the western extremity of the Arab and Muslim world. On a good day you can see Spain from Tangier and Morocco has long been a gateway for Europeans into Africa and for Africans and Arabs into Europe. Today the pull in both directions is as strong as ever – economic opportunity lures ever increasing numbers of Africans into the European Union, while a new generation of travellers are discovering Morocco, which has again become a very popular and hip travel destination.

However, Morocco's image is changing. The old romantic notions of a conservative nation steeped in Islamic and feudal history now jars against the contemporary reality. The medieval labyrinthine medinas of Marrakesh, Fès and Meknès are for many, what Morocco is all about, but don't be surprised to hear the shrill ring of a cellphone or a sign pointing down some darkened alley to the nearest Internet cafe. The young King Mohammed VI may be a direct descendant of the Prophet Mohammed and have absolute power, but he's also President of Oudayas Surf Club in Rabat.

Morocco has a wealth of experiences to offer, starting with an astonishingly rich architectural tradition and deep cultural history. Medieval cities, Roman ruins, Berber fortresses and beautiful Islamic monuments await. The country's numerous mountain ranges exert an enormous pull over adventure sports freaks, trekkers and climbers, whether

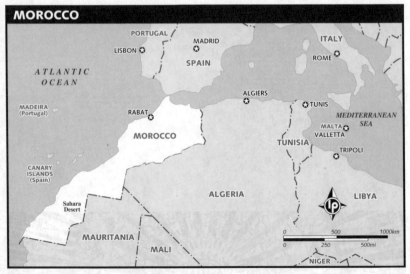

MOROCCO

they be after the icy snow-covered ridges of the High Atlas Mountains in winter or the rocky semi-desert of the Jebel Sarhro.

Huge sections of Morocco's isolated mountain regions still remain the sole preserve of the Berber tribespeople and their animals. Whatever hassles may be thrown at you in the hectic towns and cities, don't doubt the legendary genuine hospitality of these people.

The Atlantic and Mediterranean coastlines illustrate brilliantly the tumultuous history of Morocco, with fortified cities constructed by a host of nationalities and dynasties waiting to be explored. The coast also offers fine sandy beaches (some developed, some not), numerous surfing breaks and windsurfing spots, while the estuaries and lagoons support a tremendous diversity of wildlife – and they're just one piece in the jigsaw of habitats that makes Morocco such a great bird-watching destination.

Dropping off the back of the vast High Atlas (which lie across the heart of the country) and sweeping towards the vast Saharan emptiness of Algeria, are some of the most stunning arid and desert landscapes in North Africa. Among them, the kasbahs of the Drâa Valley; the classic rolling sand dunes at Merzouga; and the endless arid beauty of the coastal drive into the Western Sahara. Get off the beaten track and out into these places – they can be explored on foot, by 4WD or on the back of a camel.

Once off the beaten track Morocco can arguably become a warmer, more welcoming place. Get out into the unknown because for many, encounters with local communities form the most enduring memories of all.

Morocco is not necessarily a country you can gracefully glide through and see everything with the minimum of fuss. Sometimes it's a demanding, frustrating place that confronts you at every turn. But what it offers is a unique experience of totally differing cultures and wildly varied landscape. Take a deep breath and dive in.

Facts about Morocco

HISTORY

The early history of the area now known as Morocco remains largely shrouded in mystery. Perched on the very edge of the known world in ancient times, only scant shreds of evidence throw any light on the societies that inhabited this territory. Even after the arrival of the Phoenicians, hotly followed by the Romans, Vandals, Byzantines and Arabs, much of what we know of the original inhabitants remains obscure. Modern historians, relying on the limited and often unreliable accounts of contemporary writers, have offered us little more than broad assumptions.

This applies not only to Morocco, but also to the rest of North Africa, known to the Arabs as the Maghreb, meaning 'Sunset' or 'West'. The invaders of the region rarely made great inroads and in Morocco this was particularly the case.

The Berbers, as the local peoples came to be known, were notoriously difficult to subdue. When threatened by invasion, they simply recoiled into the relative safety of the vast Sahara Desert. This split between Berber native and urban invader has remained a constant throughout Morocco's history. Central rulers, even of Berber tribes themselves, have rarely managed to exercise real power over the entire reach of the country.

Prehistory

Morocco's early history tends to be lumped together with that of the rest of the Maghreb. Archaeological evidence indicating the presence of *Homo erectus* dates back at least 200,000 years (although some scholars believe it may go back still further). At this time, much of the Sahara was covered by forest, scrub and savanna grasses, and was teeming with animals. From around 6000 BC, rainfall began to fall off dramatically and the grasslands began to give way to an inhospitable desert.

Evidence suggests that two different races appeared in North Africa between about 15,000 and 10,000 BC. The first, the Oran-ian branch, is named after the city and important archaeological area of Oran in Algeria; the second, the Capsian line, is named after Gafsa (ancient Capsa) in Tunisia.

The origins of both remain obscure and the cause of much speculation. It appears that a kind of fusion took place with the indigenous peoples, the long-term result of which was a spread of Neolithic (New Stone Age) culture. Rock paintings, particularly in the Hoggar in modern Algeria, are the best source of knowledge about this period, although there have been several finds in Morocco too.

It's from these peoples that the Berbers are thought to owe their descent. Although little is known about them for certain, they were probably pastoralists who also practised hunting and land cultivation. By the time the Phoenicians appeared (the first of the invaders from the east), the local inhabitants were well established.

Carthage

First on the scene in a long series of foreign invaders were the powerful and wealthy Phoenician traders. Sailing from their capital in Tyre (in modern-day Lebanon), they patrolled the North African coast in search of suitable staging posts for the lucrative trade in raw metals from Spain. The foundation of the first of these places has been positively dated to the 8th century BC. Carthage, in today's Tunisia, became their principal and most powerful base, but the Phoenicians also had posts in Sicily, the Balearic Islands and all the way along the North African coast to the Atlantic.

In Morocco, they were ensconced in Tamuda (near present-day Tetouan), Tingis (Tangier), Lixus and Mogador (Essaouira). However, these possessions remained in Phoenician hands only until the end of the 3rd century BC.

By the 4th century BC Carthage had become one of the richest cities in the Mediterranean world. It attracted the avaricious eye

Morocco's Timeline

BC

200,000+ years ago *Homo erectus* emerges.

15,000–10,000 Two different races appear in North Africa: Oranian branch and Capsian line.

6000 Annual rainfall drops and land becomes arid.

8th–3rd century Phoenician traders establish staging posts along North African coast including Carthage in modern-day Tunisia. Carthage becomes one of the richest cities in the Mediterranean and in the 3rd century clashes with the Greeks and Romans.

146 Carthage destroyed by Rome.

25 King Juba II increases Rome's influence in Africa.

AD

44 Mauretanian kingdom is bequeathed to Rome and split into Mauretania Caesariensis and Mauretania Tingitana; Roman colonies established at Lixus and Volubilis.

249–53 Rome withdraws from Ceuta.

200-300 Mauretania Tingitana abandoned by Rome to local tribes.

4th century Constantine converts to Christianity in 313. Christianity then spreads in Romanised Africa.

429 King Gaeseric leads the Vandals into Morocco from Spain.

533 Byzantine emperor Justinian fails to retake the core of North Africa.

535 Vandals defeated by Byzantines.

640 Islam's influence spreads through Egypt.

649 Byzantines are defeated by Islamic armies.

710 Musa bin Nusayr gains a foothold in Spain.

740 Arab rulers expelled from the Maghreb.

780s Moulay Idriss establishes the first Moroccan state with Fès as the capital.

791 Moulay Idriss murdered.

803 Moulay Idriss' son Idriss II assumes power.

829 Idriss II dies.

1062 Almoravid leader, Youssef ben Tach-fin founds Marrakesh.

1415 Portugal takes Ceuta.

1465 Merinid dynasty crumbles.

1471 Portugal takes Tangier.

1492 Spain captures Granada from the Moors.

1497 Spain takes Melilla.

1524 Marrakesh becomes Saadian dynasty capital.

1542 Portuguese expelled from Agadir and Safi.

1578 Battle of the Three Kings.

1660s Moulay ar-Rashid secures the sultanate.

1672–1727 Moulay Ismail makes Meknès his capital.

1859 Spain occupies Tetouan.

1873–94 Moulay al-Hassan rules Morocco.

1904 Spain to send troops to the northern Morocco.

1907 France occupies Casablanca.

1909 Moulay Abd al-Hafiz became sultan.

1911 France occupies Fès; Spain occupies Larache.

1912 Morocco becomes a French protectorate on 30 March.

1914–18 WWI; France occupies Taza.

1921–26 Abd al-Krim leads resistance against the Spanish.

1923 Tangier becomes an international zone.

1934 France crushes Berber resistance.

1939–45 WWII.

1939 Franco comes to power in Spain.

1940 Hitler overruns France.

1943 Allied landings in North Africa.

1953 Mohammed V deposed by French.

1955 Mohammed V returns to Morocco.

1956 Morocco gains independence on 2 March.

1961 Mohammed V dies and is succeeded by his son Hassan II.

1975 Green March into the Western Sahara.

1989 Morocco joins Maghreb Arab Union.

1996 Morocco signs EU free trade agreement which comes into effect in 2000.

1999 Hassan II dies and is succeeded by his son Mohammed VI.

Hanno the Navigator

In the 5th century BC, as Carthage, the base for Phoenician traders in modern-day Tunisia, approached the zenith of its power, some of its more illustrious sons set out on voyages of discovery. Hanno the Navigator is probably the most famous, and tales abound of his fleet's exploration down Morocco's Atlantic coast. He's credited with founding several towns including Thymiaterion (Kenitra), Acra (Agadir) and Carian Fortress (perhaps Essaouira).

However, the exact extent of Hanno's exploration is debatable. Some believe he only ventured to the edge of the Sahara, while others think he reached the shores of the Gambia or Sierra Leone and perhaps as far as Cameroon. Historians also debate the purpose of his travels. Some believe he intended to locate new and valuable sources of fish, but he is said to have returned with stories of a fabulous and legendary gold route up from West Africa, suggesting that his motives were more lucrative than simply finding new food sources. Much later, his golden tales were confirmed as Morocco became a lucrative source of both gold and slaves.

of the Greeks and later the Romans. Mighty clashes between these rival powers soon followed and Rome was almost destroyed by Hannibal, the most famous Carthaginian leader. However, it was the Romans who came out on top, completely destroying Carthage in 146 BC.

In Africa, Carthage treated indigenous people particularly harshly, conscripting many into what was almost a slave army and collecting huge taxes. This caused huge resentment.

The 'Libyans' formed the majority of their African subjects – this was a collective term for those people inhabiting the areas to the south and east of Carthage. Fed up with Carthaginian control over large tracts of the land of modern Tunisia, the Libyans, together with the formidable Numidian forces to the west (led by the powerful king, Massinissa), carried on a steady campaign

of harassment against their Carthaginian overlords.

It's difficult to gauge with certainty the impact of the Carthaginian legacy on its subjects. By the time the Arabs appeared on the scene some eight centuries later, the Libyans, Numidians and, in the far west, the Mauri (Mauretanians or Moors), had all come to be known by outside observers as the 'Berbers'.

The Carthaginian regime also resulted in the marginalisation of certain groups of the indigenous population, forcing some into a semi-nomadic lifestyle in the hinterland of the Sahara Desert and Atlas Mountains. From these wild and inaccessible regions in the heart of what is now Morocco, they launched a continual wave of attacks upon whichever unsuspecting foreign power was foolhardy enough to arrive on the coast.

Rome

During the first hundred or so years of Rome's occupation of Morocco after the fall of Carthage, Rome remained content to maintain the garrisons posted there to protect the ports and trade routes. It also kept a watchful and suspicious eye on events unrolling in the interior of the country.

Towards the end of the pre-Christian era, however, Rome's interest in North Africa grew keener. Colonists arrived, local agricultural production was cranked up, and increasingly direct control was sought.

Beyond the cluster of small trading enclaves on the coast, the Mauretanian kingdom (including what's now Morocco and much of northern Algeria) had remained largely untainted by either Carthaginian or Roman influence. In 33 BC, however, Bocchus II of Mauretania died, bequeathing his entire kingdom to Rome. The Romans, not wishing to expend unnecessary energy and resources, preferred to foster local rule.

In AD 44 the kingdom was split into two provinces: Mauretania Caesariensis, with its capital in Caesarea (in present-day Algeria), and Mauretania Tingitana, with its capital at Tingis (Tangier). Several Roman colonies were also established including Lixus, where they succeeded the Phoenicians, and Volubilis. The latter became a minor centre of Graeco-Roman culture (see the special section 'Volubilis' in the Middle Atlas & the East chapter).

On the whole, however, Morocco remained virtually cut off from the rest of Roman North Africa, largely due to the extensive and imposing presence of the Rif and Atlas mountain ranges – access was always easier by sea to ports like Tingis. The proud tribes of the Rif Mountains, in particular, retained their independence and occasionally launched small but wearing campaigns against the imperial power.

During the first three centuries AD, Roman North Africa was comparatively stable and wealthy. It provided 60% of the empire's grain needs and other commodities such as olive oil. Rich, Romanised North Africans gradually began to enter the Roman administration and eventually provided an emperor, the Libyan Septimius Severus, who took power in AD 193.

The latter half of the 3rd century brought strife to the empire, and Rome's African possessions did not remain untouched. Parts of Tunisia, northern Algeria, Libya and Egypt were all maintained, while Mauretania Tingitana was abandoned to local tribes. The exception was the city of Tingis, which remained a Romanised enclave protecting the strategic crossing between Spain and North Africa. In the 4th century Christianity spread rapidly through what was left of the empire, though by then it was weakened beyond repair.

Vandals & Byzantium

In AD 429, King Gaeseric (or Genseric), who had been busy marauding in southern Spain, decided to take the entire Vandal people (about 80,000 men, women and children) across to Africa. Bypassing Tingis, he managed within a few years to scupper the Roman forces and wring hefty concessions from them. By the middle of the 5th century he controlled almost the entire western Mediterranean. Rome was all but a spent force.

Vandal control over the former Roman provinces in Morocco was never cast-iron, and their unbridled exploitation of the local economy only served to accelerate their decline. In addition, tribes from the surrounding areas, including the Atlas Mountains, kept up a campaign of continual harassment.

Eventually, the emperor Justinian sent an army to retake the core of North Africa in 533. However, his dream of a Roman renaissance was not fulfilled and the empire split in two.

Subsequent Byzantine rule in North Africa appears to have been both ineffectual and uneventful with very little impact on the unfettered tribes of the Maghreb. A more powerful force was about to unleash itself upon the world.

The Coming of Islam

Islam appeared on the distant peninsula of Arabia in the early 7th century and within a hundred years, the destiny of North Africa was altered forever. By 640, Islam's green banner was flying over the towns of Egypt and in 649 the Islamic armies defeated the Byzantines and took control of the coast west of Egypt into modern-day Tunisia. With depleted forces, however, the Arabs were unable to capitalise on their successes. Another attempt was made in the 660s, but divided by internal conflicts over who should be caliph (successor of the Prophet and effectively secular and spiritual leader of the Muslim world), they were weakened and defeated.

It wasn't until Uqba bin Nafi al-Fihri began his campaign of conquest of North Africa that the full military force of Islam was brought to bear. From 669, in a highly successful three-year campaign, he swept across the top of the continent.

Islam's first great city in the Maghreb, Kairouan (Qayrawan) in modern-day Tunisia, was founded. With an army of Arab cavalry and Islamised Berber infantry from Libya, Uqba marched into the Atlas and is said to have conquered land as far afield as the Atlantic coast.

A lull ensued, but in 681 Uqba went on the rampage again, mostly in Morocco. Things began well, but finished disastrously, and in 683 he was defeated by the Berber chieftain, Qusayla. This led to the eviction of the Arabs from the entire region of the Maghreb as far east as Libya. Qusayla occupied Kairouan.

The Byzantine cities that still existed sat tight, careful not to provoke trouble on either side, but their days were numbered. By 698 the Arabs had succeeded in evicting the Byzantines from North Africa. Various Berber tribes continued to resist, including those led by the legendary princess, Al-Kahina.

It was then Musa bin Nusayr's turn to take command of the conquering armies. Succeeding eventually in gaining a foothold in Morocco, he went about befriending, rather than alienating, the local Berber population. This wise policy and the new religion were well received by the tribal peoples. Islam, with its roots in a tough desert and tribal environment, probably appealed to Berber sensibilities.

By 710, Musa considered his work in Morocco done. His wandering eye now fell on Europe and, with his lieutenant Tariq (the name 'Gibraltar' is a bastardisation of Jebel Tariq – 'Tariq's Mountain') he set about conquering Spain. By 732 they had made their deepest advance, reaching Poitiers in France.

Moroccan Dynasties

Islam had arrived in Morocco, but the Arab invaders who had introduced it were not so warmly received. Treating Berbers, including Islamic converts, as second-class citizens, the Arab overlords began to be deeply resented. A wave of religious fervour, issuing from the East and inspired by the proselytising behaviour of the Kharijite heresy, suddenly swept across the Islamic world. Taken up zealously by the Berbers and moulded to their cause, it resulted in the Arab governors being completely evicted.

Although a substantial population of Arab citizens remained, by 740 all effective Arab rulers had been expelled from the Maghreb. Tunisia and Algeria would again succumb to Arab control and, in the 15th century, fall into the hands of the Ottomans, but Morocco was never again to come under the direct sway of the eastern Arab dynasties.

Moulay Idriss, an Arab noble fleeing persecution from the ruling Abbasid dynasty in Baghdad, arrived in Morocco in the 780s. Winning the respect of enough Berber tribes, he established a dominant dynasty in northern Morocco. This is generally considered to be the first Moroccan state.

Idriss is also credited with founding Fès, and his rapid rise to power was sufficiently alarming for the caliph in Baghdad, Harun ar-Rashid, to send a mission to kill him. Idriss was finally dispatched in 791 with a draught of poison. His son, just a baby on his father's death, assumed power in 803 at the tender age of 11. By the time he died in 829, a stable Idrissid state that dominated all of northern Morocco had been established.

This state of affairs did not last long. By the middle of the following century, the Idrissids had been reduced to one of a number of bit players on a wider stage. Among them, the Fatimid dynasty had managed to install itself in Tunisia, in Cairo and even in Fès for a short period. This rival dynasty

The Berbers

Morocco is still populated by the descendants of an ancient race that has inhabited Morocco since Neolithic times. The Berbers, famous throughout history as warriors, were notoriously resistant to being controlled by any system beyond the tribe.

Phoenicians, Romans, Arabs and even the French and Spanish felt the full fury of their wrath, and the Moroccan sultans also failed to gain full allegiance from all the clans of the mountain tribes.

In the Rif, until comparatively recently, a deadly insult was, 'your father died in his bed', an illustration of their warrior status.

Many Berbers have quite distinctive features, such as light skin, blue eyes, and in some cases blond or red hair. Their ethnic origin remains obscure and the subject of hot debate, though many claim they are Caucasian people.

Though the country has long been dominated by the Arabs, Berbers have managed to hang onto their culture with amazing tenacity.

Berber dialects are still spoken by many, the tradition of Berber crafts remain alive and the strong tribal structure still predominates. Some tribes will marry only within the clan.

was responsible for encouraging the so-called invasion of the Maghreb by the Beni Hillal Arab tribesmen from the East.

Long at odds with the Fatimids were the Umayyad Muslims of Al-Andalus who, in their turn, had become increasingly meddlesome in the affairs of northern Morocco.

Into this general chaos came a new force from a new direction. Inspired by the Quranic teacher, Abdallah bin Yasin, the Sanhaja confederation of Berber Saharan tribes began to wage war throughout southern and central Morocco. Because of their dress, they were known as *Al-Mulathamin*, 'the Veiled Ones' and later as the *Al-Murabitin* 'People of the Monastery' – the Almoravids.

In 1062 their leader, Youssef ben Tachfin, founded Marrakesh as his capital and led troops on a march of conquest that, at its height, saw a unified empire stretching from Senegal in Africa to Saragossa in northern Spain.

This brilliant flash was just that, for as quickly as they had risen, the Almoravids crumbled in the face of another Moroccan dynasty. These new Muslim overlords were strictly conservative and became known as 'Those who Proclaim the Unity of God' *(Al-Muwahhidin)* – the Almohads.

Inspired by the teachings of Mohammed ibn Tumart against the growing religious laxness of the Almoravids, Abd al-Mu'min, his successor, began a campaign against them. In the 30 years to 1160, the Almohads successfully conquered all of Almoravid Morocco, as well as what are now Algeria, Tunisia and parts of Libya. In the following years, Muslim Spain also fell.

The greatest of his successors, Yacoub al-Mansour (the Victorious), continued the fight against dissidents in the Maghreb and the Reconquista in Spain. By his death in 1199, Morocco's greatest dynasty was at the height of its power. Many of the empire's cities flourished in this golden age of Moroccan cultural development. Trouble was never far away, however.

The Almohads tended to treat most of their subjects as conquered enemies and drained them of their wealth. Marrakesh was the principal beneficiary. The empire was expanding too quickly, however, and suddenly it began to crumble under its own weight.

As it caved in, the Maghreb divided into three parts: Ifriqiyya (Tunisia) came under the Hafsids; Algeria under the Banu Abd al-Wad; and Morocco under the Merenids. Although borders have changed and imperial rulers have come and gone, this division has remained more or less intact until today.

The Merenids ruled until 1465 (although a rival family, the Wattasids, held effective power from as early as 1420). The mid-14th century marked the pinnacle of Merenid rule. Many of the monuments that survive to this day, especially *medersas* (theological colleges) were built by the Merenids. They also built Fès el-Jdid (New Fès) as their capital.

As the dynasty declined, Morocco slid into chaos. Spotting an opportunity, the adventurous maritime power of Portugal took Ceuta (Sebta) in 1415. Only a few years earlier, a Spanish force had debarked in northern Morocco to sack Tetouan in reprisal for piracy.

The Wattasids then took over as the next ruling dynasty. By the early 16th century, however, Morocco was effectively divided into two shaky kingdoms: that of the Wattasids in Fès and the Saadians in Marrakesh.

Growing European interference caused Morocco to turn in on itself. Portugal's seizure of Sebta had symbolised the beginning; by 1515 Lisbon possessed a string of bases along the Moroccan coast. Spain took Melilla in 1497.

The rise of the Saadian dynasty, originally from Arabia, was largely due to the popularity that they won by their determination to turf out the Portuguese. After winning back some of the coastal bases from Lisbon, they began expanding northwards. Marrakesh became their capital from 1524 and they wrested Fès from the Wattasids in 1554.

Ottoman & European Threats

The next threat to Moroccan independence was the rapidly expanding Ottoman Empire. It eventually came to control all the Maghreb up to Tlemcen in present-day Algeria. War and empire-building create strange bedfellows and Mohammed ash-Sheikh, the Saadian sultan, entered into an alliance with Spain to check the Turkish advance. It proved an uneasy arrangement, but probably helped to keep Morocco out of Turkish hands.

No sooner did the Turkish threat recede than a Portuguese army, headed by King Dom Sebastian, arrived in northern Morocco. They had come to help Mohammed al-Mutawwakil regain his throne, after his Saadian uncle had deposed him with Turkish intervention.

The ensuing Battle of the Three Kings in 1578 finally put an end to Portuguese pretensions in Morocco, although by this stage many of their coastal footholds had been lost anyway. Not long after the Battle of the Three Kings, the Saadian sultan Ahmed al-Mansour undertook a foreign campaign of his own, looting Timbuktu and taking home a rich booty of gold and slaves.

With the Christian reconquest of the peninsula at the turn of the century, the Spanish Catholic monarchy began to pursue a violent policy of national and religious unity. This led to waves of Muslim and Jewish refugees seeking asylum in Morocco. A whole community of these exiles set up shop in Salé and Rabat, and soon acquired de facto autonomy as a base for the highly successful and infamous Sallee Rovers (or corsairs).

Like those before it, the Saadian dynasty eventually collapsed and was succeeded by one that has been in charge, sometimes only nominally, right up until today – the Alawites (or Alaouites). Like the Saadians before them, they are of Arab origin and claim descent from the Prophet and therefore the right to be considered sherifs.

Alawite Rule

From early in the 17th century, the notion of central rule in Morocco had hardly existed. The Saadians had found themselves continually preoccupied with putting down local rebellions, and into this growing vacuum stepped the Alawites.

It took Moulay ar-Rashid some 30 years before he finally managed to secure the sultanate in the early 1660s. His successor, Moulay Ismail, made Meknès his capital, which he set about turning into a kind of Moroccan Versailles.

Ismail's reign, from 1672 to 1727, was largely spent pacifying tribes inside Morocco. It is said that he accomplished this with boundless and legendary cruelty. As a result of his military efforts, Portugal was left with just one base in Morocco, Mazagan (modern-day El-Jadida), and Spain had only four small bases on the north coast.

At the time of Ismail's death, Morocco was relatively stable and independent, but his demise saw a degeneration into chaos. The following century was characterised by phases of stagnation, periodically rocked by internal strife.

European Interference

As Moulay Abd ar-Rahman and Mohammed bin Abd ar-Rahman continued to grapple with internal problems, powerful European powers began taking an increasingly keen interest in all the countries of North Africa. These concerns materialised in 1830 with France's occupation of neighbouring Algeria. The most alarming element of all was the sultan's total inability to do anything.

As Europe's big players moved to secure advantages over each other, the competition for influence in Morocco grew.

Moulay al-Hassan (1873–94) began some economic, administrative and military reforms and managed to keep Europe at arm's length, but could not prevent attempts by Spain and Britain to get a foothold along the coast (at Río de Oro, Sidi Ifni and Cap Juby). Europeans stepped up trade and set up industries in Morocco, but the benefit to the Moroccan people was minimal.

Al-Hassan's successor, Moulay Abd al-Aziz, came to the throne ill-prepared to cope with the problems in store for him. An attempt at tax reform and repeated French military intervention caused uproar. France bought off Italy (by offering it a free hand in Libya), Spain (with the promise of a northern sphere of interest in Morocco), and Great Britain (allowing it free reign in Egypt and the Sudan). In 1905 France hoped to pull off the establishment of a protectorate with a so-called 'plan of reforms'. Moulay Abd al-Hafiz became sultan in 1909, but the situation had already slipped beyond the Moroccans' control.

Germany (who had been left out of the colonial carve up) was given concessions in the Congo in 1911 (though not until sending a gunboat to Agadir and pushing Germany and France to the brink of war), leaving the way free for France to move in. Spain had already sent troops to the northern zone allocated to it by agreement in 1904.

The French Protectorate

The treaty of Fès, by which Morocco became a French protectorate, was signed on 30 March 1912. The sultan became a figurehead and effective control rested firmly with the governor, or resident-general, General Lyautey, and his successors. Spain controlled the northern tranche of the country and Tangier was made an international zone in 1923.

The Moroccan people were not impressed. As usual, it was the Berber mountain tribes who reacted most strongly and remained beyond colonial control. After WWI the Berber leader Abd al-Krim marshalled a revolt in the Rif and Middle Atlas Mountains, and for five years had the Spaniards and French on the run. Spain came close to a massive and embarrassing defeat, and France only managed to end all effective Berber resistance in 1934.

The process of colonisation in the French zone was rapid. From a few thousand people before 1912, the number of foreigners living in Morocco rose to more than 100,000 by 1929. Thereafter, the Great Depression put a dampener on significant growth.

The French contribution was threefold: it built roads and railways, developed the port of Casablanca virtually from scratch and moved the political capital to Rabat. In the French zone, *villes nouvelles* (new towns) were built next to the old medinas. This was largely a result of an enlightened policy on Lyautey's part – in Algeria he had witnessed the wholesale destruction of many old cities by his countrymen. The Spaniards followed suit in their zone, but on a much more modest scale.

During WWII the number of Europeans in Morocco virtually doubled. After Franco

came to power in Spain in 1939 and Hitler overran France in 1940, Spanish Morocco became a seat of Nazi propaganda, which tended, curiously, to foment Moroccan nationalist aspirations in the rest of the country.

Various local opposition groups began to form, but the French administration ignored pleas for reform. The Allied landings in North Africa in 1943 further muddied the waters. However, the Free French Forces, in spite of US President Roosevelt's sympathy for the nationalists' cause, were adamant that nothing in Morocco should change. In January 1944 the Istiqlal (Independence) party led by Allal al-Fasi, one of Morocco's most intractable nationalists, demanded full independence.

When the war ended, nationalist feeling grew and the French became increasingly inflexible. Moroccans boycotted French goods and terrorist acts against the administration multiplied. The sultan, Mohammed V, sympathised with the nationalists – so much so that the French authorities in Rabat had him deposed in 1953 and deported to Madagascar. This act served only to make him a hero in the people's eyes. In 1955, Paris allowed his return and talks finally began on handing power to the Moroccans.

Madrid's administration of the Spanish zone after the war was considerably less heavy-handed than that of the French. In fact the area even became something of a haven for Moroccan nationalists. Spain had not been consulted on the expulsion of the sultan and continued to recognise him. By this time there was virtually no cooperation between the French and Spanish zones.

Independence

Mohammed V returned to Morocco in November 1955 to a tumultuous welcome. On 2 March 1956 the French protectorate formally came to an end. Shortly afterwards, Spain pulled out of the north, but hung on to the enclaves of Ceuta, Melilla and Sidi Ifni. It abandoned the latter in 1970, but has shown no desire to give up the other two.

The sultan resumed virtually autocratic rule over an optimistic country; he became a king in August 1957 and prime minister in May

Western Sahara

After various about-faces, Madrid abandoned the phosphate-rich territory of the Spanish Sahara in 1974. During the 1970s political opinion in Morocco united against the Spanish occupation and the last Spanish troops pulled out shortly after the Green March of November 1975, in which 350,000 Moroccans walked over the border in a politically orchestrated move to claim the region.

Mauritania dropped its claims to part of the territory in 1979 in exchange for Rabat's renouncing plans to absorb Mauritania, but by the late 1960s it had already become clear that the 100,000 or so inhabitants of the territory wanted independence. The Popular Front for the Liberation of Saguia al-Hamra and Río de Oro (Polisario), initially set up to harass the Spaniards, did not take kindly to Moroccan intervention and embarked on a 16-year guerrilla war against it in an attempt to establish the Saharawi Arab Democratic Republic.

Backed by Libya and Algeria, Polisario scored occasional successes against far superior Moroccan forces. The building of sand and rock defence lines by Morocco in 1981 was a turning point. Embedded with electronic sensors to warn of attack, they stretched about 1600km along the Algerian and Mauritanian frontiers. In 1984 Morocco and Libya proclaimed a 'union' in Oujda that resulted in the latter withdrawing its support for Polisario. As Algeria's internal problems grew in the late 1980s and early '90s, support for its Saharan proteges lessened.

In 1991 the United Nations brokered a cease-fire on the understanding that a referendum would be held in 1992 to allow the people of the Western Sahara to decide between independence and integration with Morocco.

For Hassan II the territory had proved a useful internal exile for the troublesome military and the late king's favourable relationship with the West enabled him to constantly defer a referendum on the region's autonomy.

Both sides exchanged prisoners in 1996, and there were the first direct talks between palace officials and Polisario. These were followed by talks between representatives from Morocco, Algeria, Mauritania and Polisario.

However, little progress has been made on the actual referendum and fundamental problems still remain despite the intervention of UN secretary-general Kofi Annan and his special envoy for Western Sahara, former US secretary of state, James Baker.

The fundamental problem is with voter eligibility. The criteria set by the UN is that voters must have been present in the disputed territory in 1974 for them and their descendants to have the right to vote. Since 1975 thousands of Moroccans have moved to the Western Sahara, and these government supporters also claim the right to vote. Polisario, on the other hand, wants only those registered as citizens in the Spanish population census prior to the Green March to be eligible to vote.

The upshot of this is that 150,000 people lodged appeals when the UN announced its voting register, while another 65,000 Moroccans came forward and claimed the right to vote.

Despite the delays, all parties still publicly support a referendum supervised by the UN. However, thanks to further Moroccan diplomatic manoeuvring it's unlikely any vote will take place until 2002. And privately, many observers believe that a vote will never take place, despite the flexibility the late Hassan II showed and the ascension of his son Mohammed VI, a reformer. However, it's likely that the Western Sahara, will remain in limbo for the next few years. Also in limbo will be the tens of thousands of Saharans still living in UN-administered refugee camps in the territory. Once Morocco established control of the region, tens of thousands of Saharans left the territory and headed east to Algeria, while thousands more remain in refugee camps.

For the traveller these political problems are almost impossible to detect, with the overwhelming welcome from the Saharawis being far more apparent. Morocco has done much to improve the region's infrastructure and the region's inhabitants enjoy better education facilities than in Morocco itself. Things are calmer and incidents few (and certainly not publicised). For their part the Sawaharis remain ever optimistic, waiting patiently for their day to come.

1960. He died suddenly in February 1961 and was succeeded by his son, Hassan II.

The Reign of Hassan II

The new king inherited a country with a weak economy and weakened administration (few technocrats were trained by the French). In 1962 the first democratic constitution was formed giving Hassan II extensive powers to appoint or dismiss ministers. The first parliamentary elections were held in 1963 and six months later the king relinquished the post of prime minister. The student and worker riots in Casablanca in 1965 caused Hassan II to declare a state of emergency, dissolve parliament and reappoint himself prime minister.

The state of emergency was finally lifted in 1970 and a revised constitution introduced in 1972. A coup attempt in 1971 had delayed its promulgation. Another attempted takeover in 1972 led him to suspend much of the consti-

tution. A general election was finally held in 1977; it ended 12 years of direct rule and supporters of the king won a big majority.

The 1980s were marked by economic stagnation and hardship. In 1984 there was rioting over bread price rises in Fès, which troops dealt with severely – at least 100 people died. A harsh crackdown on Islamist and radical left-wing opposition organisations followed, with hundreds of trade union and opposition leaders and activists being detained.

However, in the late 1980s Hassan granted a series of amnesties to both political and nonpolitical detainees and in 1988 the Organisation Marocaine des Droits de l'Homme, a human rights organisation, received official recognition.

Hassan II's pro-allied position during the Gulf War in 1990–91 did him little harm. Although popular sentiment tended to side with Iraq's Saddam Hussein, Hassan man-

Relations with Israel

Although full diplomatic relations between Israel and Morocco may still be some way away, strong ties between the countries enable Morocco to maintain a unique position in Arab-Israeli relations. Its conciliatory stance on Israel has made allies in the West while keeping faith with Arab leaders.

Many Jews came to Morocco having been expelled from Spain with the Moors after the fall of Granada in 1492. During WWII the monarchy resisted pressure from Vichy France and protected 300,000 Moroccan Jews while acting as a gateway for Jews travelling to the USA and Canada to escape persecution in Europe. Many Jews left Morocco when the state of Israel was established in 1947 and more left during the Suez crisis of 1956.

There are 700,000 Jews of Moroccan origin living in Israel, and around 30,000 Jews still living in Morocco. Israeli Jews have long been allowed to holiday in Morocco and, officially at least, there is little bad blood between the resident Jews and the rest of the Moroccan population.

Even though Moroccan troops supported Egypt and Syria in the Arab-Israeli wars of 1967–73, Hassan continued behind-the-scenes negotiations that smoothed the way for the Camp David Agreement long before Egypt's President Anwar Sadat went to Israel in 1977.

At a peace plan meeting of Arab leaders in Fès in 1982, Hassan II, while calling for a Palestinian state, also recognised Israel's right to exist. In 1986 Shimon Peres, Israel's former foreign minister, openly visited Morocco, to the shock of many Arab states. Official contact continued and after signing a peace accord with the Palestinian Liberation Organisation (PLO) in Washington in September 1993, Yitzhak Rabin, the then Israeli prime minister, stopped by Rabat on his way home to thank Hassan II for his discreet work as intermediary.

Hassan II's enormous influence over the Middle East peace talks was vividly illustrated at his funeral. It brought together Israeli prime minister, Ehud Barak, and Palestinian leader, Yassar Arafat, and saw the first official exchange of pleasantries between President Bouteflika of Algeria and Barak, the leaders of the two countries that are technically still at war.

Relations with Algeria

In the early 1990s Morocco's traditionally stormy relations with Algeria seemed to be on the mend. The Algerian president, Mohammed Boudiaf, lent a sympathetic ear to the Moroccan campaign for the Western Sahara and indicated his desire for a prompt settlement, but after his assassination in 1992 relations deteriorated, culminating in the closure of the border in August 1994. (The two nations, once allies against French occupation, fought a brief border war in the Sahara in 1963 and huge sections of the frontier are still disputed.)

Algeria was accused of meddling in Western Saharan affairs in 1996 and, in protest, Hassan II called for the total suspension of the Arab Maghreb Union (AMU), which also includes Libya, Mauritania and Tunisia. Slowly, relations between the two countries began to thaw. When President Bouteflika took office in April 1999 the Moroccan government hinted that Algeria could revive the AMU, was willing to consider reopening the border and adopted a neutral stance towards the Algerian conflict. In return, Morocco hoped to gain Algeria's lasting neutrality towards the Western Sahara issue.

The positive dialogue continued when President Bouteflika attended Hassan II's funeral in July 1999, but inexplicably turned sour when, in September 1999, President Bouteflika accused Morocco of harbouring Islamic insurgents who were destabilising Algeria.

Even though a genuine settlement between Morocco and Algeria appears distant at present, many hope the ascendancy of Mohammed VI may help move negotiations forward. In the meantime, Algeria's sad and brutal civil war rages on.

aged to keep in with the West and the Gulf States in a low-profile fashion that aroused little rancour among his subjects.

Strikes and riots over low wages and poor social conditions saw unions clashing with the authorities again in the early and mid-1990s. In 1995, the death sentence on Mohammed Basri, the leader of the Union Socialiste des Forces Populaires, was overturned and he was allowed to return from a 30-year exile.

The years 1996 and 1997 were characterised above all by an upsurge in violent confrontation between the Islamist national student union (now controlled by the radical Islamist Al-Adel wal-Ihssan party) and government security forces. The trouble ignited at Casablanca University and rapidly spread to other universities, particularly Marrakesh and Mohammedia.

In 1996 and 1997 there were also high-profile demonstrations by unemployed graduates. A petition was even presented to Hassan II. This caused the government major embarrassment and led to some over-reaction. In January 1997 three protesters, part of a group of 30 students staging peaceful demonstrations in Marrakesh, were sentenced to six months in prison.

The end of Hassan II's reign saw a gradual improvement in human rights and greater political openness. The Socialist Union of Popular Forces and the Istiqlal Party were brought into government in the elections of 1997. Despite constitutional changes Hassan II remained an absolute ruler until his death on 23 July 1999, aged 70.

The Present

In 1999 the West lost three of its strongest allies in the Arab world with the deaths of Hassan II of Morocco, King Hussein of Jordan and Sheikh Isa bin Sulman al-Khalifa of Bahrain. Mohammed VI ascended the Moroccan throne just before his 35th birthday, and as young Middle Eastern leaders took control of Jordan, Bahrain and, later, Syria.

Mohammed VI is the latest in a long dynastic line of Alawites. He claims a double role as temporal leader (king) and spiritual and moral guide (Emir al-Mu'mineen, or Commander of the Faithful), thanks to his family's claim of direct descent from Hussein ibn Ali, the grandson of the Prophet Mohammed.

The religious significance of Mohammed VI's ancestry should not be underestimated and goes part of the way to explaining how his family has stayed in power so long, when other traditional rulers in the Arab and wider Muslim world have been toppled.

Since assuming power Mohammed VI has shown a more liberal hand than his father, who managed to create a climate of fear during his reign (most Moroccans would never criticise him publicly) and whose regime was responsible for thousands of political arrests and hundreds of 'disappearances'. The sacking of his father's much-feared interior minister, Driss Basri, in November 1999, brought an end to this chapter and was widely welcomed. Mohammed VI has made moves to tackle the bloated civil service and corruption. He has promised widespread reform of the business and banking sectors and plans to give women more fundamental and equal rights.

However, despite being an obvious moderniser, and understanding that he must carry the people with him, he retains tight political control. He immediately appointed several of his close associates to key posts in the army, government and media.

GEOGRAPHY & GEOLOGY

Morocco presents by far the most varied geological smorgasbord in North Africa and boasts some of the most beautiful countryside in the continent. With its long Atlantic and Mediterranean coasts it has remained to some degree shielded from the rest of the continent by the Atlas Mountains to the east and the Sahara desert to the south.

If you include the Western Sahara, the kingdom covers 710,850 sq km; more than a third of it is disputed territory.

There are four distinct mountain ranges or massifs in Morocco that are considered geologically unstable and leave Morocco subject to earthquakes, such as the one that devastated Agadir in 1960.

In the north, the Rif Mountains (sometimes confusingly known as the Rif Atlas) forms an arc of largely impenetrable limestone and sandstone mountain territory, shooting steeply back from the Mediterranean to heights of about 2200m. The local population is largely made up of Berbers, many of whom are happily engaged in the cultivation of kif (the local name for marijuana).

Running north-east to south-west from the Rif is the Middle Atlas range (Moyen Atlas), which rises to an altitude of 3340m. It is separated from the Rif by the only real access route linking Atlantic Morocco with the rest of North Africa, the Taza Gap.

The low hills east of Agadir rise to form the highest of the mountain ranges, the High Atlas, which more or less runs parallel to the south of the Middle Atlas. Its tallest peak, Jebel Toubkal, is 4167m high and, like much of the surrounding heights, is covered in a mantle of snow through the winter and into spring. Further south again, the lower slopes of the Anti Atlas drop down into the arid wastes of the Sahara.

The rivers (known as *oued*, from the Arabic *wadi*) are mostly torrential and depend on seasonal rainfall and melting snows. The Drâa, Ziz and Dadès Rivers, among others, drain off into the Sahara, although occasionally the Drâa completes its course all the way to the Atlantic coast north of Tan Tan.

Among other rivers draining into the Atlantic are the Sebou, which rises south of Fès and empties into the ocean at Mehdiya about 40km north of Rabat, and the Oum er-Rbia, which has its source in the Middle Atlas, north-east of Khenifra, and reaches the Atlantic at Azemmour just north of El-Jadida.

Between each of the mountain ranges and the Atlantic lie plains and plateaus, which are generally well watered and, in places, quite fertile.

South of the Anti Atlas, the dry slopes, riven by gorges, trail off into the often stony desert of the Western Sahara. This sparsely populated and unforgiving region is bounded to the east and south by Algeria and Mauritania.

CLIMATE

The geological variety is mirrored by wide-ranging climatic conditions.

Weather in the coastal regions is generally mild, but can become cool and wet, particularly in the north. Average daily temperatures in Tangier and Casablanca range from about 12°C (54°F) in winter

(December to March) to 25°C (77°F) and above in summer (June to September). Rainfall is highest in the Rif and northern Middle Atlas, where only the summer months are almost dry. The Atlantic coast remains agreeable year round, cooled by sea breezes. The southern Atlantic coast is more arid.

Marrakesh and the interior of Morocco can become stiflingly hot in summer, easily exceeding 40°C, particularly when the desert

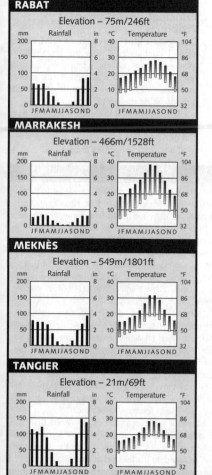

RABAT
Elevation – 75m/246ft

MARRAKESH
Elevation – 466m/1528ft

MEKNÈS
Elevation – 549m/1801ft

TANGIER
Elevation – 21m/69ft

winds from the Sahara (known as the *sirocco* or *chergui,* from the Arabic *ash-sharqi* meaning 'the easterly') are blowing. The chergui can occur at any time of the year, but is most common in spring. Even in winter, these lowlands can be quite hot during the day, with the mercury hitting 30°C, but temperatures drop quickly in the evening. In the desert, the dry atmosphere means that temperatures can swing wildly from baking days to freezing (quite literally) nights.

The rainy season is from November to January, but can go on as late as April. This cooler spell is the best time to visit the desert and oases. However, recent years have been typified by drought. Drought years seem to now rotate on a two-year cycle, with devastating effects on agriculture.

In winter the mountains can get as cold as -20°C (without taking the wind-chill factor into account), with snow often blocking mountain passes, so take enough warm clothing to cope with an unwelcome night stuck in an unheated bus.

In oases, the heat is intense during the day, but during the night in winter, it can drop below zero.

ECOLOGY & ENVIRONMENT

The first-time visitor to Morocco may be struck by the amount of green encountered in a country more popularly associated with vast stretches of desert. Travellers arriving in northern Morocco after crossing the arid *meseta* (high plateau) of central and southern Spain are surprised by the comparative lushness they find across the Strait of Gibraltar.

Until the first century or so of the Christian era, sweeping savanna and good pasture covered much of the Maghreb. But the process of desertification that had already been under way for thousands of years gradually forced the mainly Berber population to seek refuge in the Atlas Mountains.

Desertification and, on a larger scale, deforestation continue apace. Like most other countries in North Africa, demographic pressures have caused increasing environmental havoc. Nineteen species of birds and animals found in Morocco at the turn of the 20th century have disappeared. A recent victim, and a great loss for bird enthusiasts, was the slender-billed curlew, which was last recorded in 1995. Other extinct species include the famous Barbary lion, as well as various species of gazelle and oryx, and the red-necked ostrich (though these have since been reintroduced). Among the further 34 bird and animal species said to be in acute danger are leopards, monk seals and bald ibis.

The conservation movement in Morocco is relatively well developed, particularly in comparison with other North African countries. This has more to do with pragmatic, economic reasons than issues of equity. Like many African countries, people and the environment in Morocco are much more mutually dependent than in more developed, industrialised countries. Morocco is particularly dependent on its forests for its wellbeing.

These woodland areas are crucial to the countryís manufacturing industries, and supply the paper, construction, sawing, mining and crafts industries. They also provide raw materials such as cork, tannin, rubber, medicinal products and fuel. On a local level, the forests are an important source of food, and poorer rural communities depend on them for game meat, mushrooms and berries.

Apart from their well-cited functions of regulating the climate and purifying the air, trees are essential in Morocco to prevent soil erosion and as a key habitat for Moroccoís rich wildlife, including species that are already extinct in other parts of the world.

Principal Environmental Problems

Overgrazing In many regions of Morocco, animal husbandry forms the basis of the local economy. Often, when cultivation is restricted by climate or space (in arid or mountainous zones for example), this is the only possible means of living.

Livestock, when not controlled, can have a devastating impact on the environment and out-compete native wild animals when food and water supplies are limited.

The Marvellous Argan Tree

AMERENS HEDWICH

They may look cute, but goats damage argan trees by eating the leaves.

The drought-resistant argan tree is endemic to southern Morocco. Ancient forests, found in the area from Essaouira to Tiznit and out to Taroudannt, are a haven for wildlife and important to local economies. The fruits are collected by hand and the inner nuts (often having passed through a goat's digestive systems first) are pressed to release the valuable oil that is used in cooking and cosmetics. Efforts are now under way to expand the marketability of the oil and to create a sustainable industry.

Overgrazing and wood collection is now threatening many argan forests. The adaptable domestic goat is able to feed on almost anything, anywhere, and can cause tremendous damage by climbing into the branches of the argan trees and stripping them bare. Certain areas in the Souss Valley are now characterised by shrivelled dead trees that are known locally as *rochers verts*. Argan trees are so overgrazed that they are said to resemble 'green rocks'.

So unique is the argan forests' ecosystem that Unesco has declared a huge area north of Agadir a biosphere reserve. More information on the argan tree can be found on the Internet at www.gtz.org.ma.

During very dry periods, the situation is aggravated by hungry herds congregating on a single area of land and exhausting it. The new seedlings are trampled underfoot and any chance of natural regeneration is scuppered. Overgrazing reduces the number and diversity of plant and animal species. This stripping of the land is the first step towards desertification.

Deforestation Poorer tribal populations who inhabit the remoter regions of Morocco pose the greatest threat to forests. Huge tracts of forest are being cleared to satisfy their ever-expanding needs for fuel, fodder, construction materials and arable land.

During the two world wars and shortly before independence, much forest was lost in this way in the north of the country. In certain mountain regions, such as the Rif and the High Atlas, illegal felling greatly exceeds authorised felling. It often takes place in isolated regions, little surveyed by forest rangers.

However, on a more positive note, the widespread use of bottled gas, even in the most remote villages, has slowed the rate of deforestation in some areas, though much still needs to be done.

Forest Fires Forest fires are relatively rare in Morocco, but when they do occur, they can be devastating. In the north, particularly in the Rif area, huge populations of cork, thuya, cedar and, above all, pine tree have been lost in this way.

In this region almost all felling of trees is carried out with the aid of 'controlled' fires. During the season of the chergui, these can quickly spread out of control. Land is also cleared in this way for the extension of roads or the cultivation of crops.

Land Mismanagement Ironically, it is the Moroccan forestry department that has often been guilty of misguided practices. Methods intended for forests of temperate climes have been applied to forests in Morocco, often with disastrous results.

The widespread practice of thinning is carried out to accelerate the tree's growth by removing the competition from surrounding vegetation. One of the principal causes of deforestation has been the thinning of Moroccan holm oaks, cork oaks and argan trees. In the Forest of Mamora near Rabat, for example, broom was thinned from under cork oaks. This led to serious soil erosion and the oaks later died from dehydration. Hoping to bring aid to local farmers, agricultural organisations have cleared much argan forest on the Souss Plain for the purpose of large-scale market gardening. The land is ill-adapted to cultivation and after three successive years without the necessary replenishment of the soil by fertiliser, the land becomes sterile. The replanting of foreign species such as the canary pine, again ill-adapted to the soil, has had a similar effect.

Hunting Whether legal or illegal, hunting continues to be the single most important cause of animal extinction. The last wild Barbary lion, for example, was shot in 1936 in the region of Taza. Leopards, cheetahs, hyaenas, jackals and desert foxes have all become extremely rare.

Lion King

The last Barbary lion, a species indigenous to Morocco and used in amphitheatres across the Roman Empire for disposing of Christians, died in captivity in the 1960s, while the last wild specimen had been shot 30 years earlier.

However, legend has it that the King of Morocco had been himself happily feeding wrongdoers to his personal collection of felines as late as 1914. The last dissident to meet this fate was apparently offered a short reprieve by the king, but instead retorted that: 'It's better to be eaten by lions than bitten by a dog', and was dispatched *toute suite*.

The Parc Zoologique National in Rabat, Port Lympne in the UK, and various other organisations, have established a small captive breeding program with the descendants of the king's man eaters, now about 80% pure Barbary lion. There is even hushed talk of a release program, but this is unlikely to be very popular with the Moroccan public.

The disappearance or scarcity of these carnivores has subsequently caused an imbalance of other species. In the Middle Atlas, for example, populations of macaque monkeys (Barbary ape) and wild boars (also not hunted for food) have grown disproportionately.

Animals most under threat are those hunted for their meat or skin. Common in Morocco until quite recently were partridges, bustards, rabbits, hares, gazelles and moufflons (a type of mountain sheep). Some are now endangered. The Barbary deer has recently disappeared from Morocco, although a reintroduction program is currently under way in certain forests of the north.

Outlook

Despite various measures undertaken by the government and backed by international organisations, the situation remains grave. One-third of all of Morocco's ecosystems have been seriously damaged and are in danger of disappearing, 10% of vertebrates are considered endangered, and each year 25,000 hectares of forest are lost forever.

Forests that have already disappeared include those made up of the Atlantic pistachio and the wild olive. Those in real danger of disappearing include the forests of Moroccan pine, thuya and Atlas cedar. Considered seriously degraded are the forests of argan, red juniper, holm oak, canary oak *(Quercus canariensis)* and tauzin oak *(Quercus pyrenaica)*.

With the disappearance of so much forest, soil erosion becomes a serious problem eventually leading to a loss of agricultural yield because of the impoverishment of the land. In addition, dams silt up and flooding becomes more common.

Morocco's program of large-scale agriculture has also been criticised. Dams have been constructed to divert water to these vast, cultivated areas. This has led to the lowering of the water table and many ecosystems (such as the valleys in the arid lands close to the Sahara) are no longer able to sustain the animal life that depended on them.

FLORA & FAUNA

God begot living things from water,
Some of them creep, others crawl,
and there are some who crouch.
God creates what he wants.
God is almighty in all things.
Quran, sura XXIV, verse 45

The biodiversity found in Morocco is among the greatest in the Mediterranean basin, the rich landscape providing a diverse habitat for vegetation, animals and birds.

The country can be divided roughly into three ecological zones: the coastal regions, consisting of both the Atlantic and Mediterranean littorals; the mountainous regions, encompassing the three ranges of the High, Middle and Anti Atlas; and the desert region that includes the Moroccan steppe area.

Within these zones, more than 40 different ecosystems have been identified, home to some 4000 species of plants, over 100 species of reptiles and 460 species of birds. The remarkable forests of Morocco provide perhaps the richest habitat. This ecosystem shelters two-thirds of the country's plants and at least one-third of its animal species, including many species unique to Morocco.

While travelling in any region of Morocco, it's worth keeping a look out for the holy shrines, marabouts (mausolea of holy men or saints). These are dotted throughout the countryside and recognisable by their domed roofs and whitewashed walls. They are often surrounded by little islands of vegetation that have been protected over the years, sometimes centuries, because of their sacred significance.

Coastal Regions

Stretching for more than 3500km from the Algerian border to the Mauritanian frontier, Morocco's vast coastal region teems with life.

The Mediterranean littoral, extending from Algeria to the Spanish enclave of Ceuta, is made up of wild and jagged rocky scree. Among the plants you might find here are various types of algae, sea holly and sea stock. Fish include tuna, swordfish and mullet, although over-fishing continues to deplete this area. Porpoises and dolphins are commonly spotted around the Strait of Gibraltar.

The Atlantic coast is made up of low sandstone cliffs with intermittent, but extensive, beaches of fine sand. Fish include sea bream, tarpon and conger eel, and there are also dolphins. The shoreline is home to abundant marine life including various types of sea urchin, mudskipper, limpet and small octopus. These, along with the shellfish marooned in the pools at low tide, attract an excellent variety of seabirds, including the Moroccan cormorant, white-eyed gull, turnstone and sandwich tern. The area is also known for the diversity of anemone and, particularly, mussel species. Just inland, and planted along the humid coastal belts, are eucalyptus and olive groves, plus some cereal crops.

Further south lying on a fertile strip of land between Agadir and Tiznit, is the inland lagoon of Oued Massa, home of the famous Souss-Massa National Park, generally considered the country's premier habitat for birds (see under Around Agadir in the South Atlantic Coast chapter).

Just inland from the coast, and stretching between the towns of Kenitra, Rabat and Meknès, is the Forest of Mamora. The woodland is made up principally of cork oaks, but is also home to pine, acacia and eucalyptus plantations. You may come across the rare Mamora wild pear and chameleons hunting insects in the thick undergrowth. The forests provide a rich habitat for many species of resident and migratory birds, including the white stork, colourful roller, spotted flycatcher and black-shouldered kite.

Mountainous Regions

Of the four mountainous regions dividing the country, the Rif is the lowest, but also the wettest, with up to 1000mm of rainfall every year. It's home to the wild olive, holm oak, cedar and various species of pine. Foxes, monkeys and wild boars abound.

The Middle Atlas has been called (somewhat generously) the Switzerland of Morocco, with its villages of wooden chalets with steep-pitched roofs set amid vast forests of cedar, juniper, oak, conifer and ash. Flowers typically found include pit trefoil and broom and among the flowers scamper various lizards including the blue- and green-eyed variety, the Algerian sand lizard and Berber skink. A good place to see Barbary apes is around Azrou.

The High Atlas boasts the most diverse habitats of the mountain chains, with rocky peaks and enormous plateaus, as well as deep gorges and steep-sided valleys accessible only on foot. The northern slopes are characterised by forests of cedar trees, holm oaks, thuyas and Aleppo pines. At higher altitudes, thuriferous juniper is found. This increasingly rare shrub also features on the southern slopes of the High Atlas, along with red cedar forests.

Flowers in the High Atlas region include thyme, convolvulus and pit trefoil. If you're very lucky, you might come across the painted frog that loves high altitudes and inhabits the riverbeds of this region. Also preferring higher habitats are mountain gazelles, most commonly seen at altitudes above 2000m. Bird life includes horned larks and the garrulous red-billed choughs.

The higher mountain ranges are the undisputed domain of some of the most impressive raptors in Morocco, including the lammergeyer, the beautiful golden eagle (distinguished by its large wingspan) and the acrobatic booted eagle.

Among the mammals inhabiting the region are populations of Barbary sheep and very rarely seen leopards. To the south, on the same latitude as the Canary Islands, are the Anti Atlas, which protect the Souss Plain from the dry wind of the desert.

The large and ancient cedar forests that characterise these ranges provide a rich habitat for a significant number of species, including the famous and sociable macaque monkey (Barbary ape) that is usually easily spotted. Other mammals, though they're rarely sighted, include leopards, now close to extinction; nocturnal common genets; polecats; pine and beach martens; red foxes; and lynxes.

Birds inhabiting the area include red crossbills, fire crests, various species of woodpeckers and treecreepers, and short-toed eagles. Of the plant life, the Atlas species of cedar grows at altitudes of 1200m to 2700m, and in the cedar glades, orchids, geranium, campanula and scarlet dianthus are commonly found. The area is also home to Morocco's only species of peony.

Many people choose to visit Morocco when the spring flowers are in bloom. On the slopes of the Atlas Mountains, common flowers include the Barbary nut iris and the germander. In the cedar forests, species include viburnum, campanula and, later in spring, yellow broom.

Spring (particularly from April to May) is also an excellent period for butterflies. Species common to the area include the scarlet cardinal and bright yellow Cleopatra; less frequently seen are the Spanish marbled white, hermit and Larquin's blue. Later in the summer, the cedar forests of the Middle Atlas are known for their several species of fritillary butterfly.

Other kinds of forests found in the Anti Atlas, and in the eastern foothills of the High Atlas (as well as in the region between Agadir and Essaouira), are the smaller, less dense plantations of the indigenous argan tree (see the boxed text 'The Marvellous Argan Tree' earlier). These are home to the Barbary squirrel (which feeds on argan nuts), honey badgers, hares, the Moussier's redstart, and a very rare visitor, the dark chanting goshawk.

Moroccan Steppe

Continuing south of the Atlas into the hot, arid region of the Moroccan steppe, the landscape changes dramatically. Forests give way to plains of alfalfa grass dotted with the occasional juniper, acacia and sage bushes.

Harsh and inhospitable as the region appears, it is in fact home to a large number of animal species, including the golden jackal, desert fox, Dorcas gazelle and numerous small rodents.

Thousands of species of insects also inhabit the area, as well as the galeode spider and several species of lizard, including the mastigure and the nocturnal gecko. Hunted almost to extinction in some parts of the world (including eastern Morocco), but still seen in this area, is the houbara bustard.

Desert Region

Finally there is the inhospitable, desert region of the south, made up of a wide variety of habitats including the famous *ergs* (sand dunes), the *hammada* (stony desert) which stretches to the Mauritanian border, and the extensive plains of tussock grass.

In the oases, lush and productive orchards and gardens are cultivated. This diverse area is home to a large number of species that tend to either be nocturnal or only active in the cool of dusk and dawn. The erg is home to Fennec foxes (frequently illegally trapped and sold as pets) and genets. Reptiles include Berber skinks and sand vipers that prey on rodents like jerboas and sand rats.

The hammada has several species of reptiles, scorpions and a vast number of insects. Spiny-tailed lizards are commonly seen out in the midday sun but other reptiles including horned vipers, horseshoes and Montpelier snakes are more shy. Mammals include porcupines, striped hyaenas, Edmi gazelles and much rarer Addax antelopes.

Egyptian vultures circle over the plains. Flowers include daisies and the pink asphodels, a member of the lily family.

Apart from the date palms (that have become virtually a monoculture), the oases are home to Mauritanian toads and numerous birds including common bulbuls and trumpeter finches. They also act as important food and watering spots for migrating European swallows on their journey to and from South Africa.

National Parks

Genuinely worried about the loss of habitat and the resulting disappearance of plant and animal species, Morocco has begun to demark certain areas for protection. Toubkal National Park in the Atlas Mountains was the first to be created (in 1942) and covers an area of 36,000 hectares. Tazzeka followed in 1950, and more recently the park of Souss-Massa in 1991. Other parks in the Atlas Mountains and the Moroccan Sahara are expected to be created in the next few years, while parks that exist in name are starting to be viewed by the authorities as possible tourist areas, not simply semi-protected areas.

As in many African countries, the greatest obstacle to overcome is local opposition. Antagonised by the loss of their grazing land, lack of compensation, and unsympathetic and harsh policing, local communities are often unwilling to cooperate. In an effort to win support, park guides are recruited from local communities. New industry has also been encouraged, such as craft production for the lucrative tourist industry. There are hopes that some of the revenue gained from tourism in the parks will eventually be returned to the community for the development of clinics, schools and skill training centres.

There is also a move for some national parks to become self-supporting and actually charge tourists for entry. Souss-Massa National Park near Agadir is likely to be the first to do so.

Environmental Programs

Extensive plantation programs are also under way, some with international backing. The area of the Rif Mountains, in particular, has been the centre of much activity, and fire prevention measures have been widely introduced. In the south, particularly in the area around Agadir and Essaouira, and in the Sahara Desert near Erfoud, Zagora and Laayoune, work has been carried out to fight the desertification that is threatening the palm groves and some of the inhabited areas. Every year, two million fruit trees are distributed throughout these regions.

Other protective measures include the plantation of wind breaks, natural screens and green belts around built-up areas.

A program of reintroduction of wild animal species, including the Barbary deer, partridges, several types of gazelles and pheasants, is also under way. In November 1995 around 40 gazelles and oryx were introduced into the Souss-Massa National Park in a joint international effort involving 16 zoos in France, Germany, Denmark and the Czech Republic.

In 1996 24 Addax antelopes and Mediterranean monk seals were reintroduced following a French-Moroccan initiative.

Perhaps the most ambitious and publicised effort was the PNR plan (national plan of replanting), which promised to meet the demand for timber of all national industries by the year 2000. However, the project has been widely criticised for its policy of planting rapidly growing trees – most often of foreign varieties such as pines, eucalypts and acacias – without taking into account the suitability of the species for their environment.

Although these foreign varieties have initially shown high yields, in recent times there have been several major disasters around the country. Entirely because of the unsuitability of the tree species, huge losses caused by the cold, drought and by insect plagues have occurred. In the Gharb, the area north and east of Rabat, yields from the 100,000 eucalyptus plantations have fallen dramatically.

Cold-Blooded Capitalism

Your first encounter with Morocco's reptiles is likely to be in a souq. Snake charmers, stalls selling various reptiles (or parts of reptiles) for use in folk medicine and magic, and tortoise shells turned into decorative fire-bellows or banjo-like musical instruments for souvenir-hungry tourists, can all be found.

Take a close look at the snakes and you'll discover that often the snake's mouth is stitched closed leaving a tiny gap for their tongue to flicker though. The snakes frequently develop fatal mouth infections and are unable to feed so need to be replaced by freshly caught specimens (see Treatment of Animals under Society & Conduct later in this chapter for other animal welfare issues).

At present an estimated 10,000 tortoises are killed annually for the tourist trade which, when combined with large-scale habitat loss, helps explain why one of Morocco's tortoises (Testudo graeca graeca) is on the UN's Convention on the International Trade of Endangered Species (Cites) list. Current legislation doesn't prohibit their sale (or the sale of their shells) within Morocco, but try and take it out of the country and you'll be in big trouble. Don't do it.

GOVERNMENT & POLITICS

The kingdom of Morocco is ruled by Mohammed VI who ascended the throne in July 1999. During the reign of his father, Hassan II, the country's constitution was considerably modernised and moved closer to becoming a parliamentary democracy – in a superficial sense at least.

Morocco remains an absolute monarchy. The king appoints or dismisses the prime minister and members of the cabinet and can dissolve the legislature. The king is responsible for religious affairs, foreign policy, defence and internal security. Elected politicians deal with economic and social questions.

The government is supported by the 325 members of the Majlis an-Nuwab (Chamber of Representatives) who are directly elected for five years, and the 270 members of the Chamber of Advisers, who are chosen for nine years from professional associations, trade unions and local councils. However, in reality these chambers remain little more than forums for debate as their power is still severely limited.

Long Live the King

King Hassan II owed much of his popularity to his apparent *baraka* (good grace) in narrowly surviving two assassination attempts. During his 42nd birthday party army cadets stormed his palace, but the rebel leader is reported to have crumbled when the king read the opening verse of the Quran.

A year later, in 1972, Defence Minister General Mohammed Oufkir organised an attempt to shoot the royal Boeing 727 from the sky. Hassan II is said to have ordered the pilot to radio that the king was dead, fooling the attackers and allowing a safe landing.

Hassan II became one of the West's closest allies in the Arab world and his funeral brought together a fascinating mix of over 30 world leaders. As a mark of respect and an effort to pull the country together at a potentially volatile time, President Clinton of the USA and President Chirac of France walked behind his coffin through the crowds.

Constitution

Hassan II reigned for 38 years and carried out several reforms including the introduction of an elected chamber and a system of multiparty politics. His son, Mohammed VI has now taken over the delicate game of presenting an image of steady democratisation to the West – while maintaining absolute power over the political life of the country.

Under a constitution established in 1972, several political parties, trade unions and professional bodies were to take an active part in the country's administration. However, the king retained the right to name his prime minister and ministers, control the armed forces and to dissolve the Chamber of Representatives.

In September 1992 Hassan II, keen to sustain his reputation for reform, declared that the constitution should be altered to form a *gouvernement d'alternance*. Although this would mean handing over some power to the opposition parties, the major ministries of finance, foreign and internal affairs would remain firmly in the hands of the loyalists. Similarly, the king would renounce his right to appoint ministers, but retain the right to appoint the prime minister. In this way, the government would be more representative of public opinion superficially, but in reality all policy-making would remain the preserve of the monarch.

The opposition rejected the offer since it failed to rectify the gross imbalance of power. In a large demonstration, it used the 50th anniversary of the Istiqlal party's demand for independence in 1944, to call for greater democracy in modern Morocco.

Frustrated by unsuccessful attempts to entice the opposition parties into government, Hassan II abandoned his proposals and, in February 1995, a centre-right alliance of five pro-monarchy parties was put into power.

In September 1996 a ground-breaking plan was finally announced for the formation of a bicameral legislature. Deputies to the lower Chamber of Representatives would be elected directly while deputies to the upper Chamber of Advisers would come from local and regional government, professional bodies and trade unions.

In February 1997 all the main political parties signed a joint declaration pledging co-operation on reform of the political process. Local elections took place in June 1997 and the Koutla (the alliance of opposition parties including the Istiqlal and USFP parties) nearly doubled their number of seats, although there were widespread reports of excessive government interference, influence and vote rigging. Elections for the Chamber of Representatives were held in November 1997. The Bloc Démocratique party won 102 seats, pro-monarchy parties known as Entente Nationale won 100, centrist parties took 97. Abdelillah Benkirane's Al-Islah wal-Tajdid (Unification and Reform) merged with the Mouvement Populaire Démocratique et Constitutionel and won nine seats. This secured parliamentary representation for the Islamists for the first time.

In February 1998 Hassan II appointed Abderrahmane al-Youssoufi as prime minister, Morocco's first socialist prime minister since independence. Significantly, his coalition government does not include any members of the pro-monarchy Entente Nationale. As yet Mohammed VI has done little to change the constitution.

Political Parties

The left and centre-left parties forming the Bloc Démocratique are a ragbag of groups, including Parti Istiqlal, the Union Socialiste des Forces Populaires, Parti du Renouveau et du Progrès, the former Communist Parti du Progrès du Socialisme and the smaller Organisation de l'Action Démocratique et Populaire.

Ranged against them are the five main pro-monarchy parties. These include the Mouvement Populaire, which is the biggest and attracts most of its support from the rural Berber population. The others are: the liberal Union Constitutionelle, the Rassemblement National des Indépendants, the Mouvement Nationale Populaire and the Parti National Démocratique.

The Islamists are represented by the Parti de la Justice et du Dévelop pement (formerly the Mouvement Populaire Constitutionnel et Démocratique).

Tiers of Government

For administrative purposes, the country is divided into 39 *wilayat* (provinces), four of them making up the territory of the Western Sahara. The provinces are subdivided into eight *préfectures* (Casablanca is made up of five), which are further subdivided into *qaidates*, under the direction of *qaids*.

Qaids (or *caids*) are appointed by the Ministry of the Interior and have similar powers to those of pashas (who are responsible for administering urban municipalities). Other local government officials go by the name of *moqadams*.

Outlook

Human rights steadily improved throughout the 1990s and, upon coming to power, Mohammed VI accelerated the release of political prisoners and apologised for past political disappearances. While Moroccans now live in a more politically tolerant state (the climate of fear that many maintain existed under Hassan II has largely disappeared) and most political prisoners are free, political detentions continue (especially related to the Western Sahara) and insulting the king remains a widely interpreted criminal offence. However, the government continues a dialogue with pressure groups such as Amnesty International. Heavy-handed government practices are likely to be slower to disappear than many optimistic commentators first thought.

The king's position as head of the government seems secure and although Morocco is disturbed by the troubles plaguing neighbouring Algeria, few believe the country will experience the same difficulties. However, Islamism remains a challenge for the monarchy. There is widespread frustration among opposition parties anxious to win representation in government and although there has been a reduction of media censorship, freedom of speech remains restricted (through official and self-censorship).

A number of illegal opposition parties have sprung up, especially among the so-called Islamic dissidents. The government is nervous of these groups and has adopted an ambivalent policy towards them. While maintaining a steady and strict surveillance of all dissident political activity, it has dealt harshly with university-based groups, but has allowed limited expression to more established and respected radical elements.

Another challenge to the country's stability is the disputed territory of the Western Sahara. A resolution seems a long way off and the simmering conflict remains a barrier to the greater integration of North African economies (see the boxed text 'Western Sahara' earlier in this chapter).

The ascendancy of Mohammed VI has brought a new feeling of optimism; he has raised Morocco's expectations of increased freedom of speech and a far higher standard of living. To hold on to power he needs to meet the growing population's demands for a higher standard of living. It remains to be seen whether growing unemployment can be remedied by economic modernisation through increased privatisation and greater integration into the Western economies.

ECONOMY

After years of mishaps and International Monetary Fund (IMF) imposed austerity measures, there are signs that Morocco has turned a difficult corner. The economy is now in fairly good shape. Inflation is around 2%. Continued public spending cuts and privatisation have made the economy leaner and fitter, but at the high social cost of increased unemployment. However, while the economy grew by an impressive 6.8% in 1998 it contracted by 1.5% in 1999 because of drought. The pressures of a soaring population, a top-heavy public sector, disappointing progress in most industries and low foreign investment remain considerable obstacles.

Gross Domestic Product (GDP) was predicted to have been US$41.3 billion in 2000, or US$1430 per person. The informal (black) 'sector' of the economy is reckoned conservatively to make up 30% of GDP, while government expenditure accounts for 26.4%. The mainstays of the economy are agriculture, mining, tourism, manufacturing and remittances from Moroccans abroad.

One of Morocco's biggest problems remains an over-dependence on (unpredictable) rain-fed agriculture, which makes up 18% of GDP. In drought years production can drop by 50%. Substantial investment in irrigation is needed and a fund of US$200 million has been created for irrigation projects and to tackle problems of rural communities locked into poverty due to drought.

An estimated 40% of the possible workforce is currently unemployed. Over the last decade the economy has grown by an average 3.5% per year, but needs to grow by 6% to create enough jobs for the growing population. In July 2000 the World Bank initiated a three-year program to help Morocco hit this target and the government is expected to use the US$1.1 billion windfall from the sale of the second GSM cellphone licence (see the boxed text 'Getting Mobile' in the Facts for the Visitor chapter) to increase foreign and domestic investment.

Government figures put the number of people below the poverty line (by World Bank definitions) at around four million. Opposition politicians claim real figures are higher and that the gap between wealthy and poor is widening. An average farm or factory worker earns around Dr1000 a month.

Recent privatisations have enabled the private sector to expand. Since 1993 government stakes in 60 companies have been sold off, but the state remains a dominant player in the economy. Recently the pace of privatisation has slowed, but the sale of stakes in Maroc Télécom and Royal Air Maroc are likely. Of the 55 companies on Morocco's stock exchange, 3% are foreign-owned. Many of the largest companies in Morocco are family-owned and do not trade on the stock market. Some people allege that this is because many Moroccan companies do not wish to expose themselves to the rigorous accounting scrutiny stock exchange membership entails. Tax evasion is common.

Morocco borrows heavily but has managed its foreign debt well and is a 'good client' for the World Bank. In 1999 foreign debt amounted to US$18.9 billion. Debt-swap, which enables Morocco to exchange foreign debt for foreign investment, was increased from 20% to 30%. Spain, Italy and France (Morocco's largest trading partner) are keen to take up these favourable investment terms.

Overall, the economy is expected to grow further, particularly with the spin-offs of continuing economic expansion in Europe. The dirham is likely to remain tied to the dollar and other currencies and will not be traded on foreign exchanges. The main economic hope for Morocco is the free trade agreement signed with the European Union (EU) that came into force in March 2000. By 2012 all trade barriers between Morocco and the EU will be removed. The payoff for Europe should be a tighter clamp on the flow of illegal immigrants and access to new markets. However, for Morocco to benefit from free trade much economic modernisation is needed and the country needs to progress from an agricultural to industrial economy. A huge billion dollar EU-sponsored investment program in Morocco's infrastructure and development is planned for the next decade.

European Connections

Europe sees Morocco as a useful ally among Arab states and a bulwark against the diffusion of Islamic fundamentalism.

Hassan II first unsuccessfully applied for Morocco to join the EU in 1987. In 1996 the free trade zone agreement was signed between the EU and Morocco.

Many Mediterranean EU members fear that a flood of cheap agricultural produce from Morocco will provide unwelcome competition. As it is, the trade balance between the EU and Morocco only moderately favours Europe. Considerable economic modernisation is needed to prepare Morocco for free trade and programs are being undertaken to increase the competitiveness of Moroccan goods and to expand nonagricultural exports.

The government has moved to halt illegal immigration to Europe and to tackle the flourishing smuggling business in all sorts of consumer items via the Spanish enclaves in the north of the country. In return, the EU has promised US$1 billion to help persuade farmers in the Rif Mountains to grow crops other than kif (Morocco is said to supply 60% to 80% of Europe's dope). Annually, there are 80,000 hectares of kif in cultivation, producing around 2500 tonnes of resin with an estimated value of US$1.5 billion (European street value is at least 60% more than this).

Morocco is also becoming an important transit point for heroin and cocaine headed for Europe. The stakes are high and the drugs issue gives Rabat leverage when bargaining with the EU.

To preserve dwindling fish stocks, Morocco has not renewed the Spanish fishing licence that expired in November 1999. This, coupled with the issue of Moroccan immigration to Spain and the enclaves of Melilla and Ceuta, continues to sour relations with Spain, one of Morocco's most important trading partners.

Such strong ties to Europe also have a down side. Morocco still exports too much to too few countries (France takes 30% of the total), making it vulnerable to recession in Europe.

Resources

Agriculture employs about 40% of the population and although Morocco doesn't produce enough grain and cereal to meet its own needs, food exports (mainly fruits and vegetables) make up about 30% of the total exports.

There has been massive investment in fish processing plants recently in an effort to conserve valuable fishstocks that will benefit Morocco in the long-term.

At the top of its mineral assets are phosphates. If you include the Western Sahara, Morocco is said to have 75% of the planet's reserves and a 40% share of the world's market. World prices have recovered from their depression in the early 1990s and phosphates now form a major foreign exchange earner. Phosphate mining is controlled by the Office Chérifien des Phosphates, a state monopoly.

Other mineral exports include fluorite, barytes, manganese, iron ore, lead, zinc, cobalt, copper and antimony, but with phosphates accounting for 90% of mineral exports, these are relatively insignificant.

Morocco's search for oil continues. The hydrocarbons law has been amended to cap state involvement in any concession at 25% (previously it was 50%) in an effort to encourage foreign investment. Foreign oil exploration companies are currently investigating the viability of oil deposits offshore. There are two refineries for processing imported oil; these are at Mohammedia and Sidi Kacem.

Remittances from the 1.7 million Moroccans living abroad (most of whom live in Europe and half in France) are the biggest source of foreign income.

Tourism, hit hard by the effects of the Gulf War in 1990–91, picked up in 1992, then recovered strongly again in 1996 after a three-year recession. It remains the second largest hard-currency earner and makes up 7.8% of GDP.

Visitors to Morocco in 1999 numbered 2.35 million (up 11.9% from 1998); a little over a third of them are Europeans and a growing majority of them are French. Likewise, the numbers of tourists from Spain, the UK and Italy have increased, but the number of visitors from Germany has fallen.

Tourism is worth an estimated US$1.8 billion per year and provides jobs, both formal and 'informal', for half the working population of cities like Marrakesh.

POPULATION & PEOPLE

The population of Morocco in 2000 was estimated to be just under 29 million. About 70% of the population is under 30 years old. With a growth rate of 2.2%, the population threatens to become a destabilising factor in a country where a great rift separates the well-off minority from the growing legions of unemployed youth.

As the rural flight to the cities continues and is exacerbated by droughts, urban populations continue to expand; it's estimated that well over half the people live in the cities. The largest is the Atlantic port and commercial centre of Casablanca, with 3.2 million people officially. The capital, Rabat, numbers 1.75 million people if Salé is included. Fès has more than one million people and Marrakesh over 500,000, with Meknès, Oujda and Agadir not far behind.

Arabs, Berbers & Moors

The bulk of the population is made up of Berbers or Arabs, although the distinction is not always easily made. The numbers of ethnic Arabs who came to Morocco with the first Islamic invasion of the 7th century, or 400 years later with the Beni Hillal, were comparatively small. Bigger numbers came from Spain as the Catholics evicted the Muslims in the course of the Reconquista. They have to a large degree mixed with Berbers, who in turn have been significantly Arabised.

When it is said that most of the inhabitants of the northern coastal areas and big cities are Arabic, what is usually meant is that they are Arabic-speaking. Probably less than 25% of the population is now monolingual in Berber and bilingualism has increased thanks to modern communications and transport.

Little is known of the racial origins of the Berbers. The word Berber comes from an Arabic word possibly borrowed from the Latin (and ultimately ancient Greek) *barbari*, signifying the non-Latin speaking peoples of the Maghreb. The antiquated name for this area of North Africa, Barbary, has the same origins.

Marble for Sugar

In the 16th century a thriving sugar industry existed in Morocco. Located to the south of the High Atlas, the plantations were watered by a complex and sophisticated system of irrigation. Owned by the state, managed by entrepreneurial Europeans and worked by slaves, the 14 or so factories produced large amounts of sugar that were exported all over the world.

The highest quality sugar was reserved for European countries, particularly Italy and France. Britain was considered to be the greatest connoisseur. So valued was the product, and so in demand, that the Saadian sultans, with a taste for luxury and keen to embellish their palaces, would exchange it gram for gram for the best Carraran marble from Italy.

The decline of the factories eventually came with competition from the Americas, though many may have been damaged by rival dynasties trying to undermine the economy. According to historian Al-Oufrani, some factories may have been destroyed by locals protesting against slavery.

The Berbers inhabit the mountain regions and parts of the desert, and are generally divided into three groups identified by dialect. Those speaking Riffian are, not surprisingly, found mainly in the Rif.

The dominant group in the Middle Atlas speaks Amazigh (also known as Tamazight or Braber), while in the High Atlas the predominant dialect is known as Chleuh. In reality, the tribal structure is much more fractured.

Europeans have long used the term Moors as a generic description for the whole populace of the Maghreb and even for the whole Muslim world. The name probably more justly refers to a group of people living in the south of Morocco, but who also spread out across Mauritania, Algeria and Mali. Moor was probably derived from the Greek word *mauros*, which was used to describe these people. Only a small proportion of them, also known as the 'blue people' because of the colour of their attire and the fact that the fabric dye lends a bluish hue to their skin, live on Moroccan soil. They are sometimes roughly lumped together with the Tuaregs of southern Algeria. In spite of tourist hype, however, few if any actual Tuaregs live in Morocco.

Jews

Morocco once hosted a large population of Jews, roughly divided into those of obscure Berber origin and Arabic speakers who found themselves compelled to leave Andalusian Spain in the face of the Reconquista. By the end of the 1960s this number had dropped significantly, as most Jews opted to migrate to the state of Israel after 1947. The ancient *mellah*, or Jewish quarter, of many Moroccan towns can still often be identified. Nevertheless, there is still a sizable Jewish population of around 30,000 in Morocco.

Other Ethnic Groups

Growing commercial links with the interior of Africa over the centuries has attracted a population of black Africans from various parts of sub-Saharan Africa into the south of Morocco, particularly into the southern oases and desert settlements. Many originally came as slaves.

Setting apart the more recent arrivals, Europeans that have been absorbed into the general population include Iberians who came to Morocco when the Muslims were forced out of Spain. They were joined in later times by Spanish traders and workers, many of whom have also assimilated into the Moroccan populace. The population of Europeans living in Morocco numbers around 60,000, down from around half a million at independence. Most expats are French, Spanish and Italian. Conversely, there are an estimated 1.7 million Moroccans living abroad, mostly in Europe and particularly France and Spain.

EDUCATION

Morocco faces the dual problems of high illiteracy and graduate unemployment. It spends a lot on educating its young – as much as 27% of the national budget according to some claims – but still has a long way to go. In spite of enrolments of nearly four million children in schools and some 230,000 students in the country's 11 universities, estimates are that 34% of Moroccan men are illiterate. The figure among women is much higher still – around 62%.

Literacy figures highlight the gulf between the urban and rural populations. In some rural areas illiteracy rates can be as high as 63% for men and 78% for women. For social reasons and economic growth the government recognises that it's important to educate girls and women, but there's a long way to go. Between 1994 and 1998 illiteracy rates among women fell by 5.5%.

National service, which applies to males, lasts up to 18 months.

ARTS
Dance

Talk of dance in the Middle East or North Africa and the first thing to pop into most Western minds is the belly-dance. This is something you can see (for a price) at plenty of the more expensive tourist hotels (and occasionally in quite sleazy 'nightclubs' in the bigger cities), although it is not essentially a Moroccan art.

You may also get a chance to see so-called folk dancing, which is usually a poor hotel imitation of the real thing out in the Berber backblocks.

Some of the kinds of dance you may be lucky enough to encounter outside the hotels include the following:

Ahidous This is a complex circle dance seen in the Middle Atlas. Usually associated with harvest rites, it is an occasion for the whole community to join in. Alternating circles of men and women dance and sing antiphonally around musicians, usually playing *bendirs* (single-headed drum) only, but sometimes other instruments.

Ahouach This is linked to the ahidous of the Atlas Mountains, but is performed in the kasbahs of the south. The dancing is done by women alone, again in a circle around musicians.

Gnaoua This term describes a spiritual brotherhood of descendants from slaves brought to Morocco from Central and West Africa. Gnaoua is also a type of music. *L'fraja* describes the musical show they put on for the public, and *lila* is a much more private ritual where the dancers go into a trance to invoke spirits.

Guedra The term takes its name from a kind of drum commonly used to accompany a dance performed solely by women (see also the boxed text 'Musical Instruments' later).

Music

Invasion and cultural cross-fertilisation have bequeathed several musical traditions to Morocco. Popular cassettes (the choice of CDs is limited) can be brought for Dr15 to Dr20 at music stands throughout the country. If you are interested in buying recordings of various types of Moroccan music, try Le Comptoir Marocain de Distribution de Disques in Casablanca. The Ministry of Culture in Rabat sells compilation cassettes and CDs.

In Paris, the Institute de Monde Arab has a good selection of recordings of groups working in France and the Arab world. If you are after musical instruments have a look around the medinas but also try specialist music shops in major towns.

Arab-Andalusian Music In addition to the more 'standard' musical patrimony from Arab lands further to the east, Morocco knows another classical tradition that developed in Muslim Spain under the guidance of a man called Ziryeb, a musician who settled in Granada in the 9th century.

He developed a suite system known as the *nawba,* which played on the alternate use of rhythm and nonrhythm, and vocals and instrumental. In all, there are 24 *nawbat;* they are tightly structured and correspond to the 24 harmonic modes of Andalusian music. Each is purportedly in tune with an hour of the day.

Another musical system that emerged under the guidance of Ziryeb aligned music with the Ptolemaic system of viewing medicine and human health as determined by humours, the four chief fluids of the body (blood, phlegm, choler and melancholy).

As the Muslims were forced out of Spain by the end of the 15th century, the music moved and took root in Morocco. The palaces of Rabat and Oujda, among others, became havens for the preservation of the Andalusian tradition. The tradition is still going strong and the orchestras of Casablanca, Fès and Marrakesh remain popular. Of modern exponents of the art, Sheikh Salah was one of the best. Also worth a listen is *Juan Pena Lebrijand & the Orquestra Andalusi.*

Berber Music Long before the Arabs even knew of the existence of Morocco, the Berber tribes had been developing their own music, which was later enhanced by the arrival of various Arab instruments and styles.

Music is not just entertainment – it is also the medium for storytelling and the passing on of oral culture from generation to generation. It can still be heard at *moussems* (pilgrimages or festivals in honour of a local saint), wedding ceremonies, public town or tribal gatherings and festivals, as well as at private celebrations.

The music of any tribe is often also a reflection of the musicality of the local dialect. Instrumental pieces can be heard, but often the music is accompanied by songs and dancing that can involve men *and* women, something that occasionally raises the hackles of some city (generally ortho-dox Arab) Muslims.

Storytelling is a big part of the musical repertoire of the Berbers. The *heddaoua* (wandering minstrels) move from one small town to another and recite poetry and the like, often in a hazy allusive style sometimes attributable to the effects of kif. They usually provide musical accompaniment, but dance is not necessarily part of the performance.

Master Musicians of Jajouka featuring Bachir Attar and *Maroc Moyen-Atlas: Musique Sacree et Profane* are albums that are great introductions to Berber music.

Raï This originated in the Algerian city of Oran and grew in popularity in the 1960s. The lyrics were considered subversive by the authorities and Raï was banned on Al-gerian state radio until the mid-1980s. Some of the leading musicians moved to France to avoid persecution.

Algerian Raï is one of the strongest in-fluences on Moroccan contemporary music. Raï has retained its distinctly Arab-African rhythms and continues to evolve. Using a variety of modern electrical instruments it now incorporates elements of jazz, hip hop and rap, and can be heard in music stores as far east as Egypt and Jordan.

Morocco's leading exponents include Cheb Khaled, Cheb Mimoun, Raïs Mohand and Chaba Zahouniacan.

Contemporary Music Various Moroccan musicians have experimented with moves to combine aspects of their heritage and Western influences. Hassan Erraji, an *oud* (Arab lute) player who moved to Belgium and studied European as well as Arab clas-sical music, has put out several CDs, in-cluding *Marhaba, La Dounia* and *Nikriz*. Although the Arab roots of his music pre-vail, he introduces other elements that are well removed from the Oriental tradition, such as saxophone, into some of his pieces.

Aisha Kandisha goes several steps further, taking traditional sounds and infusing these with a meld of modern Western music rang-ing from soul to rock to produce an almost

---

Musical Instruments

Some of the instruments you will see being played all over the country include the following:

Amzhad A single-chord violin, made of wood and a goatskin cover, and played with a horse-hair bow; it is a specifically Berber instrument.

Andir A long, narrow trumpet, most often used for celebrations during Ramadan.

Bendir A single-headed oriental drum; other Berber names are *tagnza* and *allun.*

Darbuka A generic term for a form of drum typical throughout the Arab world; it is usually made of terracotta in the form of a jug, with a goatskin cover on one side.

Ghaita A reed oboe, in wide use throughout Morocco.

Guedra Another kind of drum most commonly used by the so-called 'blue people' to accompany a dance performed solely by women; the dance is one you're less and less likely to see, except per-haps in a hotel's watered-down floor show version.

Guimbri An instrument with two or three strings stretched over an animal skin.

Kanza Loosely resembling a guitar, this three-stringed instrument has a rectangular base.

Kemenja A typical Arab instrument, not unlike the Western viola.

Nira (or Lira) A generic Arabic term for various types of reed flute.

Oud Arab lute.

Qarqba Large, metal castanets (plural *qaraqib*).

Tbel (or Tabala) A cylindrical wooden drum hung around the neck, or held under the arm.

Tebilat Two different sized and shaped drums fastened together with leather lacing and covered in skin

Zmar An odd-looking double clarinet.

overwhelming but infectious mix – the title of one CD, *Jarring Effects*, is a good example.

Hassan Hakmoun and Nass Marrakech both fuse the infectious rhythms of traditional Gnaoua music with modern jazz.

Umm Deleila is one of the most famous Saharawi singers to highlight the continuing problems of the disputed territory of the Western Sahara.

Literature

A gentleman without reading is like a dog without training.

Moroccan proverb

Far from the heart of Muslim Arab civilisation and great seats of power and learning such as Cairo, Damascus, Baghdad and Jerusalem, Morocco has never really been at the forefront of Arab letters, although several greats spent some time in Morocco.

They include Ibn Khaldun and the philosopher Averroes (or Ibn Rushd). The former, who lived in the 14th century, is considered the foremost Arab historian and is best known for his remarkable *Histoire Universelle* and philosophical treatise *Muqqaddima*. Born in Algeria, he spent some time in Fès, but his travels took him on to Spain, Cairo and Syria.

Averroes, as he was known in the West, was equally known for his medical treatises and commentaries on Aristotle. Born in Cordoba, in Muslim Spain, he spent his last years in Marrakesh.

Moroccan literary genres such as the novel and drama, long taken for granted as an integral part of Western culture, are a comparatively recent development in the Arab world. Until the late 19th century, the bulk of literature consisted of traditional poetry, much of it in imitation of older classics (for a full treatment of literature in the Arab world, past and present, see the three-volume *Cambridge History of Arabic Literature*).

Egypt has tended to lead the way over the past 100 years, but Morocco, too, has seen a growth of modern talent.

Many Moroccan authors still write in French, although more and more are turning to their native tongue, even at the risk of not gaining wider recognition for want of translation into French.

Much of the literature emerging from Morocco over the last century has appeared more political than literary, and has been concerned almost exclusively with the independence movement and the construction of a post-colonial society.

Two writers of the extreme left, Abraham Serfaty and Mohammed Khaïr-Eddine, were arrested for their political writing in 1972, and the works of one of Morocco's most famous and talented writers, Driss Chraïbi (see later in this entry), were banned for a long time.

Until very recently, the bulk of Moroccan literature was not known beyond France and the Maghreb. Gradually, Moroccan writers are getting better known and, in 1987, one of the most outspoken of the country's writers and critics, Tahar Ben Jelloun, won the prestigious French *Prix Goncourt* for his novel *La Nuit Sacrée* (The Sacred Night).

Another well-known writer and international prize winner is the poet Abdu Elaraki who, in 1988, won the Gold Medal at the European Academy of Arts awards for his collection of poems entitled *Rêe de Poème* (Dream of Poetry). In 1990 Mohammed al-Haloui won the Kuwaiti prize for his poem *A Sebta*.

Unfortunately, few of these titles have been translated into English. The following books are a recommended selection of Moroccan literature, most of which have been translated. Note that most books are published in different editions by different publishers in different countries. As a result, a book might be a hardcover rarity in one country while it's readily available in paperback in another. Fortunately, bookshops and libraries search by title or author, so your bookshop or library is best placed to advise you on their availability.

Year of the Elephant, written in English by Leila Abouzeid, is one of a series of stories that recount the life of Zahra, a Moroccan woman. In the face of an unsympathetic society she carves out a degree of independence for herself without abandoning the pillars of her upbringing, including the Islamic faith.

In *Si Yussef*, Anouar Majid evokes Moroccan life through the eyes of a man who looks back on his life in Tangier. The character was a bookkeeper who started his apprenticeship in survival, as did most of the port city's urchins, as a guide for foreigners.

Tahar ben Jelloun has been resident in France since 1971. At least two of his works, which he writes in French, have appeared in English. *Solitaire* explores the seemingly insurmountable difficulties encountered by a Moroccan migrant in France. In *Silent Day in Tangier*, an elderly and bedridden man ruminates over his past. It is largely a personal exploration and the many allusions to the history of Tangier and Morocco from about the time of the Rif war onwards are unobtrusively woven into the observations of an old and angry man.

Abdel Krim Ghallab, editor in chief of *Al-'Alam* newspaper, is considered one of Morocco's finer modern writers. Although he writes in Arabic, some of his works, including *Le Passé Enterré*, have been translated into French.

Ahmed Sefrioui, a writer of Berber origin who grew up in Fès, aims to relate the life of ordinary Moroccans through the eyes of his characters, such as little Mohammed in *La Boite à Merveilles*. Here is all the hubbub and local colour of the Fès of half a century ago.

An important representative of Moroccan *émigré* (emigrant) literature is Driss Chraïbi, who was born in El-Jadida and now lives in France. A prolific writer, his novels tend to be political, which sets him at odds with Sefrioui, who prefers to deal with more essential human issues. His works include *Le Passé Simple* and *Mort au Canada*. One work that appears in English translation is *Heirs to the Past*. A couple of other novels have also been translated into English, but are hard to come by.

Mohammed Khaïr-eddine, who died in 1999, wrote in French and Arabic, and was one of Morocco's ground-breaking authors. His poems, novels and other writings express a desire for revolt and change, not only in the context of Moroccan society and traditions, but in his own methods of writing. One of the better known anthologies is *Ce Maroc!*

For something closer to the pulse of traditional society, *Contes Berbères de l'Atlas de Marrakesh*, a series of Berber tales edited by Alphonse Lequil, might be worth perusing.

The famous American novelist and Tangier resident, Paul Bowles, translated a series of oral tales from Moroccan Arabic into English. The tales were compiled by Mohammed Mrabet, Mohammed Choukri and Larbi Layachi (whose work was published under the pseudonym Driss ben Hamed Charhadi). Among Mrabet's works are *Love with a Few Hairs* and *M'Hashish*. His is an uncompromising account of the life of Tanjawi street lads and the sometimes irksome activities they undertook to earn a crust.

In Choukri's main work, *For Bread Alone: An Autobiography,* he describes the seemingly unbearable saga of his family, one of many families forced by drought in the Rif during the early 1940s to seek opportunities in Tangier, only to be largely crushed by its indifference.

Layachi's best-known work is *A Life Full of Holes*. As humble in origin as the other two, Layachi is said to have wanted to use a pseudonym because he didn't want anyone to know who he was: jobless and living in 'a rotten country in rotten times'.

Architecture

Classical Period Situated at one of the furthest boundaries of the Roman Empire, Morocco is not as rich in classical remains as more centrally placed countries such as Algeria or Tunisia. It still boasts, however, some important sites spread mainly around the north-east of the country. Volubilis (the most impressive), Banusa and Thamusida were excavated by the French in the first half of the 19th century, and Cotta and Lixus by the Spanish in the second half.

Islamic Period In the 11th century the Almoravid dynasty, whose empire included Andalusia, introduced the Hispano-Moorish style into Morocco. The beautiful prayer hall of the Kairaouine Mosque in Fès owes a great deal to the art of the caliphs of Cordoba in Spain.

With the succession of the Almohads in the second half of the 12th century, the Spanish influence reached its peak.

Under Abd al-Mu'min some magnificent mosques were built – the most famous of which is the Koutoubia in Marrakesh. His son, Abu Yacoub, was responsible for the Giralda in Seville (which once formed part of an enormous mosque) and the Great Mosque at Salé.

The greatest of Al-Mu'min's successors, his grandson Yacoub al-Mansour (r. 1184–99), finished the kasbah at Marrakesh and added to it the Great Mosque. He was responsible for the enormous Almohad wall with its famous gates at Rabat. Yacoub also began work on what was intended to be the greatest mosque in all of the Muslim west, if not the world, the Hassan Mosque, which was never completed.

Much work was continued under the Merenids. Abu Youssef Yacoub, the second of their sultans, founded a new town, Fès el-Jdid, next to Fès el-Bali, where he set up his palace complex. In the last quarter of the 13th century many mosques were built in towns throughout the country, including Fès, Meknès, Marrakesh and Salé. Medersas (religious schools) were also built, including the two stunning examples at Fès: the Bou Inania and el-Attarine. The royal necropolis at Chellah was also constructed during this time.

As the Merenid dynasty waned, so too did the fortunes of the empire and the artistic output. A brief period of expansion occurred at the end of the 17th century under the Saadian dynasty, which included an incursion into Sudan by the sultan Moulay Ahmed al-Mansour.

Enormous booty was brought back from the wealthy city of Timbuktu and used to embellish Moulay Ahmed's capital city of Marrakesh, particularly the el-Badi palace.

Unfortunately only the ruins remain, but the Saadian tombs give some idea of the former richness of the palace.

Of the sultans of the Alawite dynasty (which continues to this day) the second,

Moulay Ismail (1672–1727), was the most prolific. He dotted his empire with kasbahs where he housed the famous black regiments and prepared for his campaigns. Meknès, his chosen capital, was encircled by more than 40km of walls and embellished with a palace, barracks and enormous stables. The extraordinary Bab Mansour gate is the archetypal monument of the period.

European-Style Architecture In the 16th century the lucrative trade in spices, slaves and gold that flourished along the Mediterranean and Atlantic coasts attracted the greedy eyes of the Spanish and Portuguese.

Having seized these coastal towns, they constructed many Christian fortresses in order to maintain control. These were characterised by vast, fortified walls topped by towers and monumental gateways flanked by square bastions. Examples of this style can be seen at Agadir, Essaouira, Safi and Mazagan.

Towards the end of the 18th century, Sultan Sidi Mohammed ben Abdallah used the captive French architect, Cornut, to completely redesign the walls and street plan of the city of Essaouira. The new fortifications, characterised by *skalas* (fortresses) and batteries, were a defence later adopted by many ports along the Atlantic coast. Sidi ben Mohammed, along with many of the sultans who followed him, also built a series of public buildings at Fès, Marrakesh and Meknès which were influenced by the Moorish styles prevalent in Europe.

Contemporary Architecture During the French protectorate, the construction of the villes nouvelles in many of the cities not only left those cities intact, but also provided an opportunity for new architectural expression.

For several years, two French town planners, Prost and Ecochard (administrators appointed by General Lyautey), oversaw a new 'rational' policy of town planning that eventually gave rise in 1917 to a whole new school.

Initially (from around 1912 to 1920), the aims of the school were to try to marry

[Continued on page 59]

Moroccan Architecture

History

From the 7th century onwards, Morocco - like the rest of North Africa, the Middle East, northern India and Spain - fell under the control of Islam. The impact on the country's culture was enormous and Morocco's architecture, like many of its arts, was dominated by Islamic influence.

Over the course of time, however, Morocco developed its own style influenced by its climate, history, social structure, natural resources and its location on the major trade routes - this brought it into contact with other foreign influences. The angular, austere style of the Moroccan mosque, for example, is in stark contrast to both the opulent buildings of the Ottoman Turks and the decorative, Persian-influenced structures found in Iraq.

Nevertheless, much of the philosophy and the basic principles behind Islamic construction remained the same throughout the Arab world, including North Africa and Morocco.

Religious Architecture

Mosques

Embodying the Islamic faith and representing one of its predominant architectural features is the mosque, or masjid, also known as *jamaa, jami', djemaa, 'jama or jemaa*. The building was developed in the very early days of the religion and takes its form from the simple, private houses where believers would customarily gather for worship.

The plan of the Prophet Mohammed's first house can be seen in almost all mosques. The courtyard has become the *sahn*, the portico is now the arcaded *riwaqs* and the houses are the haram or prayer hall.

Divided into a series of aisles that segregate the sexes, this hall can reach immense proportions in the larger mosques. Running down the centre is a broader aisle that leads to the mihrab, the vaulted niche in the qibla. Built to face Mecca, this wall indicates the direction of prayer.

It is also the site of the minbar, a kind of pulpit raised above a narrow staircase. As a rule, only the main community mosque contains a minbar. In grander mosques, the minbar is often ornately and beautifully decorated. They are less commonly found in the smaller local mosques.

On Friday, the minbar is also the place from where the *khutba*, or the weekly sermon,

All mosques have a mihrab, a niche carved into the wall facing Mecca.

Title page: The 16th-century Borj Nord, Fès (photo by Christopher Wood)

Inset: Ceiling decoration at Medersa Bou Inania, built from 1350 to 1357, Fès (photo by Amerens Hedwich)

is delivered to the congregation. Islam does not recognise priests as such, but the closest equivalent is the imam, a learned man, schooled above all in Islam and the Islamic law. Often he will double as the mosque's muezzin, who calls the faithful to prayer each day.

Before entering the haram and participating in the communal worship, Muslims must perform a ritual ablution in the mosque's fountain or basin.

Beyond its obvious religious function, the mosque also serves as a kind of community centre, school and point of social contact. You'll often see groups of children or adults, sitting cross-legged on reed mats, being versed in some text (usually the Quran); people in quiet discussion; or seeking all sorts of advice from the imam. Others just

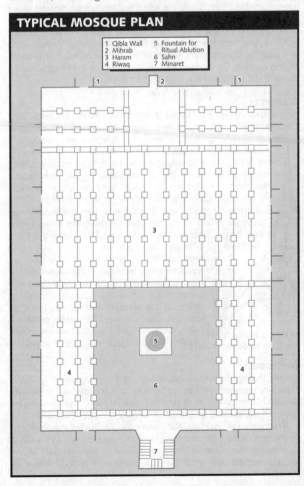

TYPICAL MOSQUE PLAN

1	Qibla Wall	5	Fountain for Ritual Ablution
2	Mihrab		
3	Haram	6	Sahn
4	Riwaq	7	Minaret

choose to shelter here or pause for thought in the cool, peaceful tranquillity that the mosque invariably provides.

Minarets

The minaret (from the word *menara*, meaning lighthouse) is often at one corner of the mosque.

In the Maghreb and Spain the dominant style of minaret is square-based all the way to the top. Only one rather small but beautiful minaret, built in 1939 in the sacred town of Moulay Idriss near Meknès, departs from the standard - it's cylindrical. Most minarets have internal staircases for the muezzins to climb; the microphone now saves them the effort. There are also a few hexagonal minarets in the Rif, the best example being the Great Mosque in Chefchaouen.

The greatest mosque in Morocco is the Kairaouine (Qayrawin) mosque in Fès. Dating from the 9th century, it has elaborate interior decoration and vaulting. Unfortunately, like most mosques in Morocco, it is closed to non-Muslims. The one exception to this rule is the huge Hassan II Mosque in Casablanca; it should not be missed.

Medersas

Although the mosques are closed, there are many *medersas* open to view that are greatly rewarding. Originating in 10th century Persia, these beautiful buildings served as residential colleges where theology and Muslim law were taught. Some also functioned as early universities. Morocco's first medersa was built in the 13th century, following the traditional design. Salé has a stunning Merenid medersa and those at Meknès and Bou Inania in Fès are also impressive.

An open-air courtyard, with an ablution fountain in the centre and a main prayer hall at the far end, is surrounded by an upper gallery of student cells. Generally the most impressive of them were built by the sultans of the Merenid dynasty between the 14th and 16th centuries.

The medersas are remarkable not so much for their architecture, but for their incredibly elaborate decoration, which includes detailed carving, *zellij* (tilework), Kufic script and *muqarna* (stalactite-type decoration used to decorate doorways and window recesses) stucco work. The master craftsmen who designed them liked to challenge visitors to find a single square inch free of artwork.

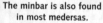

VERITY CAMPBELL

The minbar is also found in most medersas.

Marabouts

Dotted throughout the towns, villages and countryside of Morocco, these whitewashed, earthen-walled huts mark the tombs of marabouts, Muslim holy men. The word *koubba* (dome) is also used to describe the shrine of a marabout, and these are usually covered by a cupola.

Widespread as they are, the marabouts play a very important role in the lives of the local communities. They serve not just as the site of pilgrimages (for those in search of *baraka*, a blessing), but also as weekly markets and charitable and community centres. Above all,

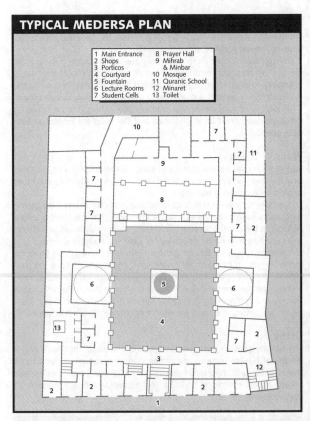

TYPICAL MEDERSA PLAN

1 Main Entrance
2 Shops
3 Porticos
4 Courtyard
5 Fountain
6 Lecture Rooms
7 Student Cells
8 Prayer Hall
9 Mihrab
  & Minbar
10 Mosque
11 Quranic School
12 Minaret
13 Toilet

once a year, a *moussem* (pilgrimage or festival) is held in honour of the name-saint, often an occasion of very exuberant festivals.

Mausoleums

Similar to marabouts, but on a much grander scale, are mausoleums. Although Islam forbids the building of elaborate tombs, mausoleums erected in the memory of great sultans or kings became, after mosques and palaces, the most important structures in Islam.

For a powerful leader, a building constructed after his death was as important as one built during his life: they symbolised, above all, his great power.

Although Morocco has nothing in the same league as India's extraordinary Mughal tomb, the Taj Mahal, there are several tombs very much worth a visit. Unusually they are open to non-Muslims. Among them are the Mausoleum of Moulay Ismail in Meknès and the more modern Mausoleum of Mohammed V in Rabat.

Medina Architecture

Three major elements - walls, gates and citadels (kasbahs) - form the basis of the old fortified town, the medina.

Initially, such fortifications were only erected in frontier towns. From the late 9th and 10th centuries, however, and right up until the advent of artillery rendered them useless, vast fortified walls, mighty towers, and elaborate gates became a crucial feature of almost every city and town.

As central control weakened, political power began to be seized by the large number of local dynasties and the need for protection was paramount.

Walls & Towers

Vast city ramparts are a feature of many towns in Morocco, particularly the imperial cities. Undistinguished architecturally, they are more impressive for their sheer size.

Typically, they were constructed of pisé (wet clay baked hard by the sun), and square towers that served as barracks, granaries, and arsenals. At Meknès the fortifications also contained water cisterns and vast stables ź so providing everything necessary for long and rigorous defence.

Other features characterising the walls include crenellations (opening in the upper part of a parapet), walkways, and machicolations (projecting wall or parapet allowing floor openings through which missiles were dropped on the enemy below). Measuring more than 16km in circumference and defended by 200 gates, the red pisé walls surrounding Marrakesh are among the most impressive of Morocco's town defences.

Gates

The Islamic gate, or *bab*, was designed above all to impress. It was a symbol of power, security and riches, and an assertion of the sultan's status far beyond any functional need. For historians, the gates are also a very useful gauge of building techniques and building materials available at the time.

CHRISTOPHER WOOD

Bottom: The fortified walls at Tangier feature crenellations and turrents through which missiles were launched.

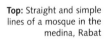

Top: Straight and simple lines of a mosque in the medina, Rabat

Bottom left: One of the few examples of a hexagonal minaret in Morocco: the Great Mosque, Chefchaouen

Bottom right: Column featuring *zellij* (tilework) in the *medersa* (theological college), Salè

CHRIS BARTON

CHRISTOPHER WOOD

CHRISTINE OSBORNE

Top: Traditional patterns of Merenid artisanship visible in tilework and carved wooden shutters in the Medersa el-Attarine, Fès

Middle: The interior of the Koubba Ba'adiyn, a domed sanctuary built in the early 12th century, Marrakesh

Bottom: Exterior view of the Koubba Ba'diyin, the smallest and oldest monument in the city

Top: Plain, arched doorways, Essaouira – decoration is reserved for the internal elements of the house

Middle: The sturdy Bab Bou Jeloud, the main entrance to the medina in Fès el Bali, Fès

Right: The pale blue wash now used on houses in Chefchaouen was introduced by Jewish residents in the 1930s.

CHRISTOPHER WOOD

MATT FLETCHER

DORINDA TALBOT

Top: The kasbah of Aït Benhaddou in the High Atlas is one of the most exotic and best-preserved kasbahs in the Atlas region.

Middle: Berber houses in Aït Igrane, in the Toubkal Massif, High Atlas, take a similar form to the defensive kasbah structure.

Bottom: Stalls line the walls of the interior of the *funduq* (caravanserai) in the Souq an-Nejjarine, Fès.

In general, two crenellated, stone-block towers flank the central bay in which the gate is set. The arch itself most frequently takes the horse-shoe form and encloses, or is enclosed by, several multifoil curves. The gates are usually highly decorated with friezes, tracery (ornamental patternwork in stone) or brightly coloured glazed tiles, and the span-drels (the space enclosed by the curve of an arch), lintels (architrave) and crenellations are ornamented with motifs of geometrical, foliated or shell-based design.

One of the best known babs in Morocco is the Almohad Bab Oudaia in Rabat. Built in the 12th century, it is considered one of the masterpieces of Moorish architecture. The monumental Bab el-Mansour in Meknès was begun in the 17th century by the megalomaniac sultan Moulay Ismail, and is famous for the outrageously rich decoration which covers it.

Kasbahs

The kasbah, as it's commonly known in the western region of the Islamic world, or citadel, was usually constructed at the same time as the city walls and gates. It is regarded as one of the most original de-velopments of Islamic architecture, and served as the fortified urban residence of the king, sultan or feudal lord. From the 10th century almost every town of any significance had one.

Initially, the kasbah's function was strictly military, serving to house the army away from the city's population. Gradually, feudal rulers chose kasbahs as their homes and installed amenities such as reception rooms and baths. Later established as official palaces, they became a symbol of dynastic authority.

Usually the kasbah was built astride the city's walls, or positioned in a commanding corner. Its location was designed to dominate both practically and symbolically the city it overlooked.

Domestic Architecture
Royal Palaces

Also built to impress were the royal palaces. Remarkably austere on the outside, their status as symbols of power lay not so much in their archi-tectural magnificence as in their physical presence: the huge walled en-closures separated a world of luxury within from the base world without.

Brilliance was reserved for the inside of the palace. Lavish furnish-ings and lofty spaces made the palace, not the artificial, architectural features of the exterior.

For centuries, the extraordinary decoration and luxury of these palaces far surpassed any European vision of good living. One of the most famous palaces was the 16th-century Palais el-Badi, 'the Incom-parable' in Marrakesh. Although in ruins now, it became a legend in its time in Europe.

A typical feature of the palaces was the *mechouar* or judgement hall, a large open space used for ceremonies, parades, games and public ex-ecutions. It was overlooked by an *iwan* (platform), from where the sultan would receive homage from, and dispense justice to, his people.

Inside the palace, and well protected from intruders and prying eyes, was the harem. It was often housed in particularly luxurious and spacious apartments, and decorated with beautiful examples of geometrical zellij designs and stucco muqarna work. The Palais de la Bahia in Marrakesh is a good example of this. Also reserved for the ladies of the house were the gardens of the harem where exercise could be taken. These gardens are often fine monuments to the use of enclosed, sheltered space.

The Dar el-Makhzen (Royal Palace) in Fès is considered one of the finest palaces in Morocco. Its 80 hectares are covered with pavilions, gardens, a private mosque and medersa. Although it's not open to the public, many smaller, former palaces are.

Some house museums, such as the Dar Jamaï museum in Meknès, others now serve as restaurants or luxury hotels, such as the Palais Jamaï in Fès. The palaces in Marrakesh, in particular, can give visitors an idea at least of former lavishness and splendour.

Town Houses

The Moroccan town house (riad) has remained largely unaltered for five centuries. Known as the dar (interior courtyard house), it is typical of the Islamic dwellings of the Middle East and Mediterranean.

The principal feature is a central courtyard, around which are grouped suites of rooms in a symmetrical pattern. In the wealthier houses, service areas are often tacked on to one side, and these in turn might have their own courtyard as necessity and means dictate.

The interior courtyard serves a very important function as a modifier of the climate in hot, dry regions. With very few exterior windows, the courtyard functions as a kind of 'light well' into which the light penetrates during the day, and an 'air well', into which the cool, dense air of evening sinks at night.

One of the great advantages of this set-up is that it permits outdoor activities, with protection from the wind, dust and sun. The system also allows natural ventilation because the sun's rays cannot reach the courtyard until later in the afternoon.

Rooms in Muslim houses are multipurpose and can be used interchangeably for eating, relaxing and sleeping. This flexible use of living space is also reflected in the absence of awkward furniture such as tables and cupboards. Many Muslims take their meals sitting on rugs, mats or cushions. When the meal is over, these can be rolled up and squirreled away.

The function of interiors can also change with the time of day. The hottest part of the day is spent in the cool of the courtyard, and at night the roof terrace is used as a sleeping area.

Decoration is reserved for the internal elements such as the courtyard. The street facade is usually just a plain wall, and the only opening is the entrance door.

Sometimes the doors of houses can be elaborately decorated, marking the symbolic importance of the house entrance - the vulnerable threshold between the private world and the public world. Auspicious symbols, designs and colours are often used, such as the stylised design of the hand of Fatima, seen so commonly in the medinas of Morocco.

The importance of domestic privacy is also extended into the interior of the house. The word haram (harem), meaning sacred or forbidden area, which, far removed from its Western connotations, denotes the family living quarters.

The harem, or domestic area of the house, is primarily the women's domain; the husband usually has his own room just outside this area. In the interiors of some houses, *mashrabiyya* (latticed wooden screens), are sometimes erected in front of a harem that opens onto the reception room. This allows women to observe men's gatherings and festivities without being observed themselves.

Forming an essential part of the wealthier town houses are the interior gardens. These can be elaborately paved with ceramic tiles and richly planted. Usually the centre of the garden is dominated by a fountain or pool ź even the poorer houses may contain some focal point such as a tree, shrub or ornamental object. This design is closely connected to the climate: the evaporation of water and the presence of plants both raise the humidity and keep the air cool.

The garden also has a strongly symbolic and recreational function. To the Muslim, the beauty of creation and of the garden is held to be a reflection of God.

The aim of many Muslim gardens is to create harmony through a combination of scent and colour provided by plants, with music provided by tinkling fountains and bird song. Fruit trees, laurel and cypress provide the essential shade; jasmine, rose and geranium, the scents.

Traditional gardens that are open to the public include the Dar Jamaï museum in Meknès, the Dar Batha museum in Fès and the Dar el-Makhzen museum in Tangier.

Urban Architecture

Unlike European urban centres, Islamic villages, towns and cities rarely conform to any geometric symmetry of town planning. More commonly, cities are divided into town quarters.

This ancient system is found throughout the Islamic world, and is thought to originate in 8th-century Baghdad. Again, in contrast to Western towns, quarters are not divided by social status; instead, the

Bottom: Traditional structural elements such as arches were also adapted for use as decorative features on a smaller scale.

CHRISTOPHER WOOD

CHRISTOPHER WOOD

mosque, *hammam* (traditional bathhouse) fountain, oven and school are shared by all residents, rich and poor.

Despite their chaotic appearance, the old, Islamic towns are carefully adapted to the rigours of the climate. Like the domestic house, the deep, narrow streets of the medina keep the sun's rays from the centre during the day, and draw in the cool, dense evening air during the night. The massing of multistoreyed structures sharing partée walls also reduces the total surface area exposed to the sun.

Souqs

The souq or bazaar, along with the mosque and possibly the hammam, make up the quintessential elements of a Muslim town. The souq is also the commercial backbone of the city.

At first sight, it appears a hotchpotch of houses randomly erected wherever the tiniest space allows. In reality, a very particular order governs the layout of the souq. This pattern is amazingly constant, and can be found repeating itself from North Africa to India.

The standard plan consists of a network of streets covered with vaults, domes or awnings. The streets are lit by openings in the central bays that allow light to penetrate, but keep the interior cool and well ventilated. The design owes much in its form to the classical precedent with the agora and its surrounding buildings and colonnaded market place.

The congregational mosque provides the focal point to the souq, and around it the shops are grouped in a strict hierarchy. First come the vendors of candles, incense and other objects used in the rites of worship. Next to them are the booksellers, long venerated by Muslim cultures, and the vendors of small leather goods. These are followed by the general clothing and textile stalls, the domain of the richest and most powerful merchants.

The hierarchy then descends through furnishings, domestic goods and utensils, until, with the most ordinary wares, the walls and gates of the city are reached.

Here, on the city perimeters, where the caravans often used to assemble, are the ironmongers, blacksmiths and the other craftsmen and vendors serving the caravan trade.

Furthest afield are the potteries and the tanneries, usually exiled to beyond the city walls because of the noxious odours and smoke they produce.

Top: Multistoreyed houses in the *mellah* (Jewish quarter), Fès

MATT FLETCHER

Qissaria

Another feature of the Islamic souq is the *qissaria*, generally found at the heart of the medina. Its form is said to derive from the classical basilica, and consists of an oblong and colonnaded covered hall, with a large door at one end that is securely locked at night.

The qissaria serves as an internal strong-room housing the trade in valuable objects such as precious textiles, furs, gems and metals, similar to a certain degree to the covered arcades in London's Piccadilly. In recent times, this term also seems to have been revived to describe the covered shopping centres in the *ville nouvelle* (new town).

Funduqs

Muslim civilisations have always been mobile. With the harsh climate of some parts of Morocco and the difficult and often dangerous terrain, many merchants and pilgrims required rest and shelter for the night. This led to the creation of caravanserais, known in North Africa as *funduqs*, which sprang up at regular intervals along the major trade routes of the entire Islamic world.

Top: The busy carpet souq under cover in the *qissaria* (covered market) in the Rabat medina

CHRISTOPHER WOOD

Their function can be compared to modern-day motels or motorway cafes, providing food and accommodation for both traveller and their transport, usually camels, mules or horses.

In general, they were unremarkable architecturally. An unadorned facade provided a doorway wide enough to allow camels or heavily laden beasts to enter. The central courtyard was usually open to the sky and was surrounded by a number of similar stalls for various purposes, including shops and stabling. Accommodation was on the 2nd floor.

Funduqs can be seen in many of the larger cities, including one that is still used in Chefchaouen and the Souq an-Nejjarine in Fès, now used as an arts centre. However, many of them have fallen into a sad state of decay.

Hammams

Another essential feature of Islamic towns and societies is the hammam or public bath. Although serving a mundane function, the hammam can be a surprisingly impressive architectural structure. Most commonly, however, they are identifiable only by the smoking chimney and low, glass-studded dome and are rarely as grand as those in Turkey.

The Muslim hammam is directly descended from the classical bath, although with time the emphasis altered from social and sporting purposes to the Muslim concern with ritual and cleanliness. In modern Morocco, the hammam plays an extremely important role in the social life of women. Mothers frequently use them as catching pens for potential wives for their sons.

Traditionally, the hammam consists of a spacious, domed disrobing room, with a pool in the centre. Next in the bathing sequence is the 'cold room', an elongated room with three domes, so named because of its position furthest from the heating room. Afterwards comes the warm room, larger and more elaborately constructed and decorated than the cold room, with niches in the four corners of the chamber where the bather can recline.

The hot or steam room is the next stop and is the simplest room with a low, domed ceiling. A final stop is made in the warm room where the bather can be cleansed and massaged, soaped and shampooed, and rinsed by bath attendants.

Later, after returning to the disrobing room, the bather can recline and rest on couches before being served tea, coffee or sherbet.

Top: The entrance to the Merinid *funduq* (caravanserai), Fès, is large enough for beasts of burden to pass through.

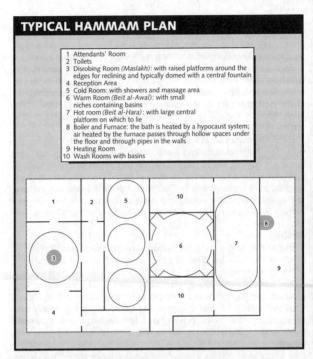

TYPICAL HAMMAM PLAN

1 Attendants' Room
2 Toilets
3 Disrobing Room *(Maslakh)*: with raised platforms around the
 edges for reclining and typically domed with a central fountain
4 Reception Area
5 Cold Room: with showers and massage area
6 Warm Room *(Beit al-Awal)*: with small
 niches containing basins
7 Hot room *(Beit al-Hara)*: with large central
 platform on which to lie
8 Boiler and Furnace: the bath is heated by a hypocaust system;
 air heated by the furnace passes through hollow spaces under
 the floor and through pipes in the walls
9 Heating Room
10 Wash Rooms with basins

Berber Architecture

In the central and southern regions of Morocco the climate, geography and social conditions have also largely dictated the forms of architecture.

As recently as the late 1930s it was considered highly dangerous to travel in these areas of Morocco because of the difficulty of policing and communication and the prevalence of tribal feuds and banditry. Born of these conditions, the buildings of the region - even the very poor ones - were primarily structures of defence.

In the southern valleys of the Drâa, Dadès and Ziz, the indigenous Berber communities have built large numbers of both communal and private defensive structures.

Rising out of the desert landscape, the impression is of massive, powerful and uncompromising strength, and some of these buildings number among Morocco's most imposing sights. Throughout the centuries, these Berbers have adhered to their own, austere building style, unmoved by contact with other traditions, most notably those of Islam and the Arabs.

Ksar

One of the earliest forms of Berber architecture was the fortified village, the *ksar* (from the Arabic *qasr*, meaning castle or palace).

The basic structure consists of a square or rectangular enclosure wall with four, square corner towers and a single entrance leading into a central, covered alley. The space between this street and the wall is filled with warren-like courtyard houses and alleys, a mosque and a well.

As the village expands, more quarters are constructed around this structure, with new exterior ramparts erected along with entrance ways. The towers are used as granaries, food stores or arsenals. One of the best examples of the ksar (plural *ksour*) is the spectacular Aït Benhaddou in the valley of the Assif Mellah, which has been the setting of many Hollywood films.

Individual houses are built along these same lines, with the basic courtyard plan, high ramparts and corner towers. Both the village and the house are constructed of pisé. The lower half of the defensive walls is earthen and the upper storeys are made of baked brick and feature characteristic mud-brick decoration. The towers taper a little towards the top, and slit windows let the light in and missiles out. However, these are extremely fragile, and rain would destroy the building within 50 years.

Kasbah

Similar in style to the ksar is the kasbah, which is a rural as well as urban fortification. This building is most commonly found in southern Morocco, particularly along the Route des Kasbahs in the Dadès Valley.

The kasbahs were usually erected by some local potentate at key places in the region under his rule in order to give protection for his small garrisons. Like their cousins in the cities, they are generally fortified, square, pisé buildings with just a few openings on the outside.

Agadir

One of the most curious structures of North African architecture is the agadir, or fortified communal granary. It is generally found among the indigenous Berber communities in isolated mountain areas, and its development grew out of the social needs of these people. The sedentary agriculturists of the valleys needed a strong defensive structure where they could safely keep food reserves, arms and valuables from the ravages of marauding tribesmen.

CHRISTINE OSBORNE

Bottom: The kasbah at Telouet, near Ouarzazate, was once the residence and palatial headquarters of the powerful Glaoui tribe.

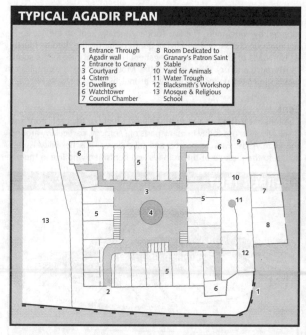

TYPICAL AGADIR PLAN

1 Entrance Through Agadir wall
2 Entrance to Granary
3 Courtyard
4 Cistern
5 Dwellings
6 Watchtower
7 Council Chamber
8 Room Dedicated to Granary's Patron Saint
9 Stable
10 Yard for Animals
11 Water Trough
12 Blacksmith's Workshop
13 Mosque & Religious School

These requirements led to communal building efforts, in which walls, fortifications and water cisterns were built by the whole tribe. Within the walls, each family then built their individual storehouses. These fortifications also provide a refuge for women, children and valuable livestock in times of battle. In times of peace, the agadirs on trade routes and strategic crossings serve as market places and caravanserais.

As a result of this tribal, group effort, the building came to represent both physically and symbolically the survival and identity of the group. Unfortunately, because of these strong cultural connotations, a large number of granaries were systematically destroyed by the Glaoui overlords during their expansion in southern Morocco at the beginning of the 20th century.

Other features of agadirs may include a miniature mosque, and, in the granaries of the Anti Atlas and western High Atlas, a council chamber, reception room and blacksmith's workshop. Some anthropologists interpret the granary as an early, but intermediate, stage of urban organisation among the Berbers; the next evolutionary stage of which is the ksar.

Generally there are two basic forms of agadir: those with an interior courtyard; and those where storehouse cells are aligned along either side of a long narrow alley. Both types follow a common plan: there are usually two to four tiers of small storage chambers grouped around the central courtyard or alley, which is entered through a narrow door set in the bleak and impregnable exterior facade. This single entrance is guarded by watchmen. The livestock is generally kept on the 1st floor, the grain on the second and living quarters are on the third or fourth.

The walls of the granaries are generally made of pisé in the south of Morocco and dry stone in the Atlas Mountains. Good examples of agadirs in Morocco include the one at Imilchil.

Tent

The tent has existed as a form of shelter throughout Islamic history and is still widely in use today in many parts of Morocco, particularly around the High Atlas. Easy to put up and take down, this flexibility is well suited to the lifestyle of the nomads and herdsmen who live in them.

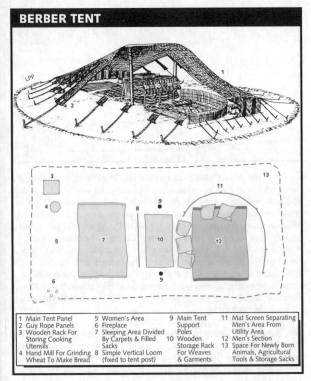

BERBER TENT

1 Main Tent Panel	5 Women's Area	9 Main Tent	11 Mat Screen Separating
2 Guy Rope Panels	6 Fireplace	Support	Men's Area From
3 Wooden Rack For	7 Sleeping Area Divided	Poles	Utility Area
Storing Cooking	By Carpets & Filled	10 Wooden	12 Men's Section
Utensils	Sacks	Storage Rack	13 Space For Newly Born
4 Hand Mill For Grinding	8 Simple Vertical Loom	For Weaves	Animals, Agricultural
Wheat To Make Bread	(fixed to tent post)	& Garments	Tools & Storage Sacks

As in the domestic house, space is divided into separate areas for the women, men and their guests. There is also space inside the exterior wall of the tent for animals and for the storage of food. The tent is made of a weave of wool and hair and is surprisingly resistant to the elements.

Frances Linzee Gordon

[Continued from page 42]

modern living requirements with the classic Hispano-Moorish style, while keeping in check the increasing numbers of unscrupulous architects and speculators.

In the 1930s a Moroccan variant of Art Deco was developed, the best examples of which can be seen in Casablanca. Although new town-planning departments have been set up in different towns across the country – most recently in Fès and Agadir in 1989 – Casablanca continues to lead the way in architectural innovation (see the boxed text 'Casablanca Is Beautiful' in the North Atlantic Coast chapter).

Painting

Prehistoric Art Most evidence for prehistoric art exists in the form of multiple (and still largely unstudied) Neolithic rock engravings. The best sites are found in the central region of the High Atlas and in southern Morocco, notably in the area between the Anti Atlas and the Drâa Valley.

Difficult to date accurately, the majority seem to come from a period between 4000 and 2000 BC, and resemble similar finds south of Oran in Algeria. Geometric or symbolic signs are the most commonly occurring motif and are difficult to interpret. People and animals feature in later engravings and this has allowed the classification of three stylistic periods: 'the hunters', 'the animal carriers' and 'the daggers of the Atlas'.

European Artists in Morocco Since the Renaissance in the West, the common Western perception of Oriental society was one of harems, opulent palaces and all-powerful sultans. The imagination of many had been fired by the tales of explorers and travellers such as the 19th-century writer, Mariano Fortuny.

With the expansion of colonialism and development of transport in the 19th century, this fascination came to a head and many artists, rejecting the traditional 'grand tour' of Italy and Greece, crossed the Mediterranean in search of the exotic.

One of the first artists of this period to visit Morocco was the French romantic painter Eugene Delacroix (1798–1863). The official court painter to Louis-Philippe, Delacroix first arrived in Morocco as part of a diplomatic mission to the Sultan Abd ar-Rahman. During the five months he spent in Morocco he discovered pristine countryside, a way of life unchanged since the Middle Ages and an intensity of light and brilliance of colours he had never imagined.

After a visit to Meknès, the artist observed: 'There are paintings to be made at every street corner…which would make the fortunes of 20 generations of painters'.

The countless notebooks he filled with watercolours, sketches and minute descriptions of colour and tone were to inspire him and influence his painting for the rest of his life.

Ironically, it was Delacroix's work – and one painting in particular, the *Jewish Wedding* exhibited in the Palais du Luxembourg in Paris – which would inspire countless other French artists to visit Morocco. Some of them, including Emile Vernet-Lecomte and Alfred Dehodencq, both contemporaries of Delacroix, even reworked his Jewish wedding theme.

Two other painters greatly influenced by Delacroix's work were the French artists Henri Regnault and Georges Clairin. Visiting Tangier for the first time in 1863, they too became responsible for perpetuating the myth of the Oriental dream.

Initially, artists continued to paint purely imaginative compositions based on classical themes. Gradually a note of realism crept in as they tried to embellish their pictures with authentic and decorative detail and local colour.

By the end of the 19th century artists were recording, often straight onto the canvas, the people and the culture they came across, albeit still in rather a romanticised way.

Public squares, ceremonies, street scenes and souqs, combined with the legendary painterly qualities of the Moroccan light – its clarity, intensity and continual interplay – all provided endless inspiration for the artists who visited the country.

Other famous painters to visit Morocco included the Russian painter Elie-Anatole, the Belgian Jean-François Portaels, the Frenchman Adolphe Gumery, the Spaniard José Gallegos y Arnosa, Edmund Aubrey Hunt and James McBey, plus in 1912, the father of Fauvism, Matisse.

Matisse spent two periods in Tangier experimenting and developing techniques that would characterise his mature style: the use of bold, non-naturalistic and expressive colour; the abstraction rather than strict representation of the image through pure colour, flat shape and strong pattern; and the creation (rather than imitation) of light through colour. His aim was to 'express spirituality through the tangible'. Matisse was also greatly influenced by the abstract quality, subtle harmony and pure colour found in traditional Moroccan art.

Moroccan Artists Although Moroccan naive (self-taught) artists such as Hamri in Tangier and Ben Allal in Marrakesh were exhibiting their work in the 1940s, it was not until the 1960s that anything like a school of painting began to develop.

Several movements resulted, with little in common except for a tendency to abstraction, which has traditionally dominated Moroccan painting. This is partly explained by the fact that Islam has for centuries frowned upon the representation of living things in artwork.

Other common characteristics include inspiration sought from rural life, a return to one's roots, and the recurring theme of the conflict between ancient tradition and modern life.

One of the best-known of Morocco's painters is the semiotic artist Ahmed Cherkaoui, whose works are dominated by signs and symbols. Other well-known artists include Rabi, who tries through his compositions to 'synthesise spiritual meditation with the act'; Hassani, whose pictures are a celebration of the colours of his country; Alaoui, who examines through abstraction the play of Moroccan light; and Boutaleb, Saladi and Ahardan, whose strongly imaginative work borders on surrealism.

Crafts

Morocco has a rich and varied tradition of handicraft production, and the better souqs are crawling with items to keep the avid souvenir-hunter well occupied. See the special section 'Arts & Crafts' and under Shopping in some of the major city sections.

Cinema

Morocco's first exposure to the world of cinema was as the setting for many pre-independence films, particularly French productions. However, as a film-making country, Morocco is a relative newcomer, with its first efforts (which were little more than shorts and documentaries) not produced until the 1960s.

The first feature film was made in 1968, but during the 1970s a period of stagnation occurred. In the 1980s the Cinema Support Fund, tax benefits and film festivals at Rabat and Casablanca were set up in order to encourage production. Films are being made again, but cinema remains a very small industry in Morocco.

In contrast to Western directors who are drawn to Morocco for its exotic locations, local film makers are more interested in the exploration of contemporary issues and, in particular, the conflict that arises between ancient tradition and modern life.

The film *El-Chergui* (1970) by Moumem Smihi is a good example of this last theme. Other films include *Le Coiffeur du Quartier des Pauvres* (1985) by Mohammed Reggab, which deals with the plight of the poor in a working class suburb of Casablanca, and *Le Grand Voyage* (1980) by Abd er-Rahmane Tazi, in which the geographical and social gap between the north and the south of the country is emphasised.

Other contemporary film makers include Souheil Ben Barka, Latif Lahlou, Hassan Benjelloun, Abdellah Mesbahi and Hakim Noury.

Morocco is also keen to win back foreign directors put off in the past by Morocco's notorious bureaucracy, lack of facilities and absence of any cohesive organisation with which to deal. Tunisia continues to net far more custom than Morocco and provides the classic desert location for scenes such as those in the film *The English Patient* in 1996.

For more information on foreign films shot in Morocco, see Films in the Facts for the Visitor chapter.

Theatre

Morocco is one of the most theatrical places in the world. Storytellers, acrobats, clowns, musicians, dancers, and mime artists have been found for centuries in public squares, private houses and palaces, transmitting from generation to generation an important part of the country's artistic heritage.

The Djemaa el-Fna in Marrakesh is considered the cradle of popular Moroccan theatre and is a good place to watch it in action.

In contrast to Western theatre, the Moroccan *halqa* (meaning circle and in reference to the crowds it attracts) is itinerant, spontaneous, relies on audience participation and does not confine itself to one genre. It is a mixture of farce, tragedy and history, and is often accompanied by music and dancing.

The second form of Moroccan theatre is the more classic *el-bsat* (entertainment). It enjoyed a golden age during the reign of the Alawite sultan, Sidi Mohammed ben Abdallah, at the end of the 18th century and was essentially a piece of critical theatre that took contemporary social and political issues as its themes.

Most performances were staged before the sultan inside the walls of the Dar el-Makhzen palace in Fès. Various companies would perform a series of short sketches, after which the second part would start. A theme was chosen and all the companies would be expected to contribute to an improvised performance.

Actors traditionally took advantage of this occasion to denounce the abuses of the administration or the injustices committed by even the most powerful official. It was also a place for settling accounts or for the enactment of revenge through the ultimate public mortification.

Egyptian troupes touring Morocco in the 1920s inspired a revival of this art form and it once again became a mouthpiece for popular protest, this time against the colonial powers.

Ironically, in order to escape censorship, the plays of Molière were chosen, using particular characters to symbolise the anti-colonial struggle.

There are a tremendous number of other forms of Moroccan theatre, including the travelling puppet shows, poetry recitations of the Ilizlan, the itinerant Berber artists from the Middle Atlas, the Tuaregs from the Sahara and the 'ceremonial theatre' (consisting of ecstatic dancing and mysterious chanting) of the Zaouias.

Despite the recent onslaught of satellite television, the Moroccan theatrical tradition is still thriving.

SOCIETY & CONDUCT
Traditional & Modern Culture

For the first-time visitor to a Muslim country, the curious mix of conservatism and westernised 'liberalism' never ceases to confuse. At the one end of the spectrum is the Muslim fundamentalist clad in a *jellaba* (flowing garment), who rejects all things European (particularly French), new and modern. At the other end, is the very westernised Muslim, donning baseball cap and sneakers and renouncing all things Islamic, traditional and old.

However liberal some Moroccans may wish to seem, travellers will still be treated and judged by the very definite social code that governs Muslim societies. Many travellers may find this judgmental attitude a little difficult to adjust to initially. The key is trying to understand it.

For most Moroccans the family is the most important single element in life and comes before work, friendship and sometimes even marriage. Many Moroccans live with their families before and after marriage, and some of the worst insults question one's parentage. Although strongly resembling nosiness in Western eyes, it's perfectly normal for a Moroccan to inquire in detail about family relationships.

Sole women travellers are particularly prone to inquisitive interrogation. Most Moroccans simply cannot understand why any woman would either attempt to, or want to, travel unaccompanied by a member of her family or spouse. Some Moroccan women won't even visit the souq without a family member and never venture outside the home after nightfall.

Marriage Coming also under close scrutiny is the traveller's conjugal status. Marriage remains an extremely well respected institution in Morocco and very few women would consider life without it. For some Moroccans, it is the woman's only purpose in life and there are abundant Moroccan proverbs to confirm this: 'a women without a husband is like a bird without a nest', for example.

For this reason, it is not considered in the least rude or presumptive to inquire about marital status and women will find that questions of this nature occur very early on in a conversation, often preceded only by: 'What's your name, where are you from?'

Although the average age for marriage has gone up, most men still marry before reaching 30 years of age and women are generally married before 25. Unmarried Moroccan women above this age are often treated with much patronising sympathy (and sometimes even suspicion of having lost the all-essential virginity). Western women above the accepted age for brides will often be asked bluntly why they are not married, or even (much to the chagrin of the thirty-somethings), if they are in fact widowed!

In Moroccan society marriage is seen less as the culmination of a romance and more as the signing of a business contract. Many marriages continue to be arranged, particularly in the rural areas, and parents play an important role in the negotiations which, like a major commercial deal, can take months to set up. Bridegrooms pay a *sedaq* (bride price) and the brides come with a dowry. The aspiration of a young couple is to produce children who will continue the family line and bring it prestige and respect.

Consequently, single women travellers should not be overly shocked or surprised by the number of marriage proposals they may attract. It wouldn't even occur to most Moroccan men that a single (and particu-larly older) woman, possibly with her virginity in doubt, wouldn't utterly jump at the chance to be married to him.

The fact that some women may choose not to marry at all would not occur to most Moroccans, and probably wouldn't be believed anyway.

On the business side, a marriage to a westerner has become the longed-for solution for many Moroccans hoping to escape high unemployment with a passport and visa. Interestingly, each year many of them manage it.

Religion Islam is also a very important element in life, and one that Moroccans love to discuss. Unlike Western societies where atheism or just apathy are acceptable or even fashionable, for the Moroccan a life without God would be unthinkable and blasphemous. The term *haji* (for men) or *haja* (for women), given to those who have made the journey to Mecca, is highly respected and often aspired to, even among the young. Muslims see Islam as the last and most perfect of all religions and are proud of it.

Because of the strength of feeling involved, it may be wise for travellers to adopt an ambivalent stance on religion if they have any views on it. By the same token, Moroccans very rarely become pedantic or aggressive on the subject and will be surprised and delighted if you show even the most minimal knowledge of Islam, or any interest in learning about it. Sometimes foreigners are even encouraged to convert, such is the kudos surrounding the religion. A surprising number of expats do convert for convenience in order to become a better accepted member of society.

Conversation Moroccans love to talk. For the men, particularly, conversation forms a major part of life and hours are spent every day arguing about current issues over a coffee in the towns' abundant cafes. Foreigners are often alarmed at the intensity and emotion of these arguments. A squabble on a bus can seem to degenerate into a life-threatening feud.

This public display of emotion is perfectly normal and is often accompanied by dramatic shouting, gestures and lots of acting. If you should ever become the target of these displays, you should ignore it and quietly leave.

Women in Society

One of the features of Moroccan society that strikes the traveller most is the strict segregation of the sexes in public life. The role of women remains firmly in the home. Public areas, by contrast, such as the cafes, streets, cinemas and bars, are firmly the domain of men. Any woman seen in these areas (although allowances are obviously made for foreigners) is still assumed to be a prostitute.

Considered to be 'women's areas' are the women's public baths, the cemeteries on Friday and the flat roofs of the medina, where many domestic tasks are carried out. Both sexes greatly respect the 'spaces' of the other and tension can arise when the boundaries are crossed. Women travellers can feel extremely uncomfortable in the seedy, male preserve of the bars, for example, and may wish to stick to the hotel bars.

These unwritten social rules do not apply uniformly across the country, however, and Arab and Berber traditions can vary widely. While women of Arab descent are generally discouraged from, for example, selling produce in shops and markets, Berber women have no trouble with this. Arab women are, theoretically, not supposed to dance, especially in public. It is not, however, uncommon for Berber women to participate in communal dances with men.

The lot of women is definitely improving in Morocco. For many, the turning point – symbolically at least – came in 1947 on the occasion of the opening of a school in Tangier, when the eldest daughter of King Mohammed V appeared in public without a veil. It was not until the constitution of 1972, however, that women won the right to vote. Twenty-one years later two women were elected to parliament for the first time. In the municipal elections of the following year, 77 women candidates were selected.

Despite these advances on the political front, women still remain inferior to men in the eyes of the law. A woman's inheritance, for example, is still half that of a man's.

Women are now entitled to maternity benefits, widow's pension and, in theory at least, equal opportunity in the workplace. Women are entering the workforce in greater numbers (although married women still have to seek their husband's permission) and are beginning to hold important professional positions such as company directors, doctors, judges and pilots.

In the last 25 years the number of working women has risen dramatically, up from a figure of just 8% in 1973 to around 25% today. However, although entitled to equal pay in theory, women in practice earn a salary 15% to 40% less than a man's.

Judges trained in Sharia'a (Islamic law) enforce family law and the government is working to reform it. Reforms of the legal code now ensure that divorce is only possible with the consent of both parties. This at last combats the vicious situation in which women, often with children but without means to support themselves, could be divorced by their husbands by verbal repudiation. They have little chance of finding a new husband and don't have training or the opportunity to work.

Women in Morocco, like their European neighbours, are choosing to marry later and, outside the very conservative rural areas, there is now more freedom to choose a husband. Polygamy has been on the decrease for some years and the minimum age of marriage has been increased to 16 years and it may be raised to 18 years. However, domestic violence is common and many poorer women continue to turn to prostitution.

Child labour remains a problem in Morocco. Many young girls from rural area are sent by their families to work as domestic servants and end up with abusive and exploitative employers.

In the school room there are signs of improvement, with increasing numbers of girls receiving education at both primary and secondary levels, although they are still outnumbered by their male counterparts by a ratio of around 1:3.

During the 1960s centres and clubs were set up by the state for women across the country. Their establishment sprang less from altruism, however, and more from the pragmatism of a government anxious to bridle the galloping birth rate. Nevertheless, these centres have been instrumental in teaching women about health, child care and family planning. An estimated 42% of Moroccans are using contraceptives, including the pill. Even so, a large number of women will have their first child before they are 20. Access to safe termination of unwanted pregnancy is extremely limited. An estimated 330 women die per 100,000 births.

The media has started to acknowledge women and their influence and importance in society. Radio stations now broadcast programs for women to disseminate knowledge about preventative and curative medicine, and widespread access to the Internet and satellite TV is becoming extremely influential.

Recently established organisations include needlework workshops for widowed or divorced women, kindergartens, multi-purpose work cooperatives and vocational centres.

At the Los Angeles Olympic Games of 1984, Nawal al-Moutawakil became Morocco's first female gold medallist for her performance in the 400m hurdles. She managed to break out of the traditional gender role and become an idol for African and Moroccan woman alike. At the Ministry of Youth and Sport, a special department now exists to encourage women's participation in sport.

Economic necessity is a catalyst and changes are occurring slowly, but it will take several decades for any significant progress to be achieved. For the present, the large majority of women remain in low status, menial jobs and are victims of considerable social prejudices, at least by Western standards.

Social change begun in Hassan II's reign has been continued by King Mohammed VI. His sympathy for social issues has earned him respect in Morocco and abroad but has met a fair amount of opposition from the Islamists who object to these reforms and see them as an unhealthy influence of the Western world on an Arab country.

If you want to read more about women in Morocco, see Books in the Facts for the Visitor chapter. Among the more famous feminist writers of Morocco is Fatima Mernissi.

Dos & Don'ts

Hospitality One of the most attractive aspects of the country is the warmth, openness and complete lack of inhibition of the people. 'To a Moroccan, a guest is a gift from Allah' – the same rings true for all Muslims.

Arab hospitality is legendary and invitations may well be extended to the home. This is perfectly normal in Morocco and you may find that an invitation is earned after just a brief conversation with the driver of a taxi, with a young man or woman in the hammam, or sitting next to an old man on the bus. This is a tremendous opportunity to experience something of real Moroccan culture.

'Dine and feed your guests even if you are starving' goes the proverb, and the generosity you are shown can be nothing short of astonishing.

It is customary in Muslim countries to remove your shoes if there is a carpet in the house, and your compliance with this custom will be greatly appreciated.

Handshakes are always exchanged between guests and hosts and, if you can manage it, a greeting in Arabic will go down well. Sometimes a short tour of the house will follow or you will be shown to the bathroom.

Conversation over tea and (usually) pastries then follows and, quite some time later and while still seated, you will be invited to carry out the pre-dinner ablution ritual. Water from a kettle is poured over your hands, which are held over a basin.

Meals are usually eaten at a knee-high table. Food is served in common dishes and eaten with the hands, and you should only eat what is placed nearest to you. Stretching is considered very bad form.

The first course usually consists of various 'Moroccan salads', which are more like pickles and relishes with warm, freshly baked bread. A large main course is generally served next, such as a couscous or *tajine* (meat and vegetable stew). You will probably find that all the 'choice' morsels (often little more than gristle or fat among the poorer households) are pushed firmly and persistently towards you. It is considered impolite to decline these, but if you're really stuck, a claim to be vegetarian may alleviate the situation a little, although it should be said that vegetarianism is a completely alien notion to most Moroccans. Meat, including goat or camel, remains a luxury.

Several more courses may appear, so don't feel obliged, as in the West, to finish everything on your plate. Moroccans tend to encourage, even bully, their guests into eating as much as they can and wouldn't dream of sending you home anything less than stuffed. Pacing is the secret. Guests should remember to keep their left hand firmly out of the communal dish (see Taboos later).

Body contact plays an important role in Moroccan social interaction and friendship is much more physical than westerners are used to. Handshakes, kisses and hugs are all common forms of greeting and Moroccans

Body Language

One of the most common sounds you will probably hear coming from the mouths of Moroccans will be a hiss. This is an all-purpose noise that can easily get on a new-comer's nerves. It is perhaps most commonly used by people riding bicycles or pushing carts to warn people to move out of the way; you will also often here the word *ba'alak!*, which means the same thing.

A hiss can also simply be a means of getting your attention. Sometimes there is little doubt that it is the equivalent of the wolf whistle.

When well-acquainted people meet on the street, they will often shake hands and then fleetingly kiss the back of their fingers. It is not recommended you try this one out for yourself, as it requires a depth of acquaintance travellers are unlikely to build up with locals.

If someone draws a finger up and down their chin while trying to explain something to you, they are almost certainly telling you something about Berbers (nine times out of 10 it'll be some fellow telling you there is a Berber market on today, and that this is the only chance you'll have to see it – a tale not to be believed).

of the same sex can often be seen walking down the street or sitting side by side with hands interlocked.

Avoiding Offence As a rule, a high degree of modesty is demanded of both sexes in dress as well as behaviour. None of the rules are adhered to uniformly and, in the bigger cities, especially Casablanca, the veil and head scarf are more the exception than the rule. Nevertheless, for the outsider it pays to err on the side of modesty, particularly in the more conservative countryside.

Stricter Muslims consider excessive display of flesh, whether male or female, offensive. Women, in particular, are well advised to avoid tight or revealing clothing. Even in the height of summer, cover the shoulders, upper arms and opt for long trousers or skirts. Western women needn't cover their heads and doing so tends to point you out as a 'green' tourist attracting more attention from men.

Women who disregard such considerations risk causing genuine offence and attracting unwanted attention (see Women Travellers in the Facts for the Visitor chapter). Obviously a little common sense goes a long way so take your cues from local women. You can get away with a lot more on the beaches of Agadir than in a Berber village in the Atlas Mountains.

Public displays of affection, although very common among friends of the same sex, is frowned upon between couples, even married ones.

Taboos Unfortunately, mosques in active use, including some of the most impressive, are off limits to non-Muslims. You may be able to get the odd glimpse through the doors, but don't push it if people make it known that your curiosity is not appreciated. The same applies to most other religious monuments in use. Cemeteries are also close to being no-go areas and many Muslims don't appreciate westerners taking short-cuts through them.

As much as Moroccans love to talk, there are certain subjects that, if not outright taboo, are best left alone, particularly in group discussion. One of these is the royal family.

With the possible exception of the more radical students, Moroccans are incredibly averse to criticising, or even discussing, their royal family. Although many may in reality feel antimonarchist, it's not the done thing to be seen to be so. It may even be foolish and dangerous – insulting the monarchy is a criminal offence, and one that's widely interpreted.

Photos and posters of the royal family are displayed, almost big-brother-like, in every public space and place, as is the striking, red Moroccan flag.

Many Moroccans feel genuinely patriotic and, with the king's claim to direct descent from the Prophet, criticism of him could be regarded as blasphemous. This may well explain the Moroccans' reluctance to discuss their royals.

Other taboo subjects include Islam and the Prophet, Israel and Palestine, the issue of the Western Sahara (see History earlier in this chapter) and the topic of sex and sexual etiquette (although you may find that Moroccans of the same gender will quiz you in private and with great relish about this).

The left hand in Muslim societies is also taboo as it is used for personal hygiene after visiting the toilet. It should not be used to eat with or to touch any common source of food or water, nor to hand over money or presents or for unnecessary contact with others, such as patting children on the head.

Treatment of Animals

Pets are a luxury not often seen in Morocco. Animals are kept for their utilitarian benefits, as draught animals or as sources of food, and have few rights.

Cats are the exception; you'll see them everywhere, often snoozing on the rooftops of the medinas. Generally they are left in peace and sometimes offered plates of food, since this is the animal that the Prophet Mohammed singled out for kind treatment.

Dogs are not so lucky and are considered dirty by Islam – if you pat a dog you must wash seven times before entering the mosque. Consequently they are treated as outcasts, even by shepherds in the High Atlas who rely on them to protect the flock.

They are fed sporadically, if at all, are very hostile to outsiders and can carry rabies.

Donkeys, the archetypal beast of burden, have the roughest deal. You will see them being hurried through the medina weighed down with merchandise. The Arabic word *hmar,* meaning donkey, is often used as a term of abuse, usually implying stupidity or mental slowness. Appropriately, the donkey is the logo adopted by Societé Protectrice des Animaux et de la Nature (Spana), one of Morocco's few animal welfare organisations.

A British mother and daughter founded Spana in 1959. Their original aim was to educate the owners of mules, donkeys and horses in the training and care of their charges. Although now Moroccan-run, the organisation is still partly funded by its mother charity in Britain, the Society for the Protection of Animals Abroad. Its main objectives include the setting up and running of animal hospitals where abandoned or mistreated animals (the large majority of which are donkeys, mules or horses) can be brought.

In the souqs, mobile hospitals are set up and the merchants treat these almost like garages. They also provide shelter and new homes for abandoned animals; conduct surveillance and health checks on other working animals, and campaign to limit unwanted populations of cats and dogs through sterilisation and, sometimes, destruction. Spana inspects and kits out the mules at Imlil for trekking up Jebel Toubkal, and in Marrakesh they inspect and license the carriage horses used in calèches and distribute more humane harnessing equipment. The horse's hooves are branded so if you witness any problems you can report these to the police and/or Mr Al-Morsli at the Centre Hospitalier pour Animaux (☎ 04-303110), Cite Mohammadi, Daoudiat, Marrakesh. Visitors are welcome.

Spana has 10 hospitals, including ones in Rabat, Meknès, Tangier and Midelt and other places. For more information or to visit them, contact Spana (☎ 07-747209, fax 747493, @ spana@mtds.net.ma) at 41 Résidence Zohra, Harhoura, Temara 12000.

RELIGION
Islam

'Allahu akbar, Allahu akbar…Ashhadu an la Ilah ila Allah…Ashhadu an Mohammedan rasul Allah…Haya ala as-sala…Haya ala as-sala…'.

Of all the sounds that assault the ears of the first-time visitor to Morocco, perhaps the call to prayer leaves the most indelible impression. Five times a day Muslims are called, if not to enter a mosque to pray, at least to take the time to pray where they are. The midday prayers on Friday, when the imam (prayer leader) of the mosque delivers his weekly *khutba* (sermon), are considered the most important.

Islam shares its roots with the great monotheistic faiths that sprang from the harsh land of the Middle East – Judaism and Christianity – but is considerably younger than both.

The holy book of Islam is the Quran. Its pages carry many references to the earlier prophets of both the older religions – Adam, Abraham (Ibrahim), Noah, Moses and others – but there the similarities begin to end. Jesus is seen merely as another in a long line of prophets that ends definitively with Mohammed.

For Muslims, Islam can only be the apogee of the monotheistic faiths from which it derives so much. Muslims traditionally attribute a place of great respect to Christians and Jews as *Ahl al-Kitab*, the People of the Book. However, the more strident will claim Christianity was a new and improved version of the teachings of the Torah and Islam was the next logical step and therefore 'superior'. Do not be surprised if you occasionally run into someone wanting you to convert!

Mohammed was born into one of the trading families of the Arabian city of Mecca (in present-day Saudi Arabia) in AD 570. He began to receive revelations in AD 610 and, after a time, started imparting the content of Allah's message to the Meccans. The essence was a call to submit to God's will (the word Islam means submission), but not all Meccans thought much of it.

Mohammed gathered quite a following in his campaign against Meccan idolaters, but the powerful families of the city became so angry with him that he felt forced to flee to Medina (Islam's second most holy city, also in Saudi Arabia) in 622. Mohammed's flight from Mecca or *Hejira* (migration) marks the beginning of the Muslim calendar.

In Medina he continued to preach and increased his power base. Soon he and his supporters began to clash with the Meccans, led by powerful elements of the Quraysh tribe, possibly over trade routes.

By 632 Mohammed had been able to revisit Mecca and many of the tribes in the surrounding area had sworn allegiance to him and the new faith. Mecca became the symbolic centre of the faith, containing as it did the Kaaba, which housed the Black Stone supposedly given to Abraham by the archangel Gabriel. Mohammed determined that Muslims should face Mecca when praying outside the city.

Upon his death in 632, the Arabs exploded into the Syrian desert, quickly conquering all of what makes up modern Syria, Iraq, Lebanon, Israel and the Palestinian Territories. This was accomplished under the caliphs (successors), or Companions of Mohammed, of whom there were four. They in turn were succeeded by the Umayyad (661–750) dynasty in Damascus and then the Abbasid line (749–1258) in the newly built city of Baghdad.

Islam quickly spread west, first taking in Egypt and then fanning out across North Africa. By the end of the 7th century the Muslims had reached the Atlantic and thought themselves sufficiently in control of the Gezirat al-Maghreb (the Island of the West, or North Africa beyond Egypt) to consider marching on Spain in 710.

Islam is now the religion of about 99% of Moroccans. In order to live a devout life, the Muslim is expected to carry out at least the Five Pillars of Islam:

Shahada This is the profession of faith, the basic tenet of the Muslim faith: 'There is no God but Allah, and Mohammed is His Prophet'. It is a phrase commonly heard as part of the call to prayer and at many other events, such as births and deaths. The first half of the sentence has virtually become an exclamation – useful for any time of life or situation. People can often be heard muttering it to themselves, as if seeking a little strength to get through the trials of the day.

Sala Sometimes written 'salat', this is the obligation of prayer, ideally performed five times a day, when muezzins call the faithful to pray. Although Muslims can pray anywhere, it is considered more laudable to pray together in a masjid (mosque). The important midday prayers are on Friday and are held in a special kind of mosque, the *jami'*.

Zakat Alms-giving to the poor was, from the start, an essential part of the social teaching of Islam. It was later developed in some parts of the Muslim world into various forms of tax to redistribute funds to the needy. The moral obligation towards one's poorer neighbours continues to be emphasised at a personal level, and exhortations to give are often posted up outside mosques.

Sawm Ramadan, the ninth month of the Muslim calendar, commemorates the revelation of the Quran to Mohammed. In a demonstration of the Muslims' renewal of faith, they are asked to abstain from sex and from letting anything pass their lips between dawn and dusk every day of the month. This includes smoking. For more on the month of fasting (Ramadan), see Public Holidays & Special Events in the Facts for the Visitor chapter.

Haj The pinnacle of a devout Muslim's life is the pilgrimage to the holy sites in and around Mecca. Ideally, the pilgrim should go to Mecca in the last month of the year, Zuul-Hijja, and join Muslims from all over the world in the pilgrimage and the subsequent feast. The returned pilgrim can be addressed as Haji and, in some villages, it is still quite common to see the word Al-Haji and simple scenes painted on the walls of houses showing that its inhabitants have made the pilgrimage.

Islam & The West

Ignorance abounds in the West about the nature of Islam and Muslims, who are associated all too readily with a fearful image of unpredictable, gun-toting, unreasonable terrorists. Ever since the Crusades, this sort of image has tended to stick in the Western subconscious, and has been fuelled by the intractable conflict in the Middle East between Israel and its Arab neighbours, and the determined campaign of demonisation of Arab leaders who are considered a menace to Western interests.

Many Muslims point to conflicts in the heart of the West, such as the horrors perpetrated in Northern Ireland, and ask whether they make everyone living in Ireland and the UK bloodthirsty extremists.

It also has to be said that, although perhaps more familiar with Western ways than westerners are with Arab ways, people in the Arab world, Muslims or otherwise, sometimes have a startlingly contorted picture of the West and what makes it tick.

A combination of grudging respect for, and envy of, its wealth and technological advantages, and occasionally a disdain for its perceived moral decadence, colour the way many Muslims, including Moroccans, deal with westerners. The soap-operatic drivel of Western TV does little to help.

For all this, visitors to Morocco find – hustlers, hasslers and touts aside – the reality could not be further from the truth. That a gulf separates East and West in terms of mentality and world view few would dispute, but the warmth accorded to outsiders by the average Moroccan belies any stereotypes of the typical Muslim. After all, Islam demands of its faithful a sense of community and hospitality to strangers.

Much is made of religious fundamentalism in Muslim countries, but this should be considered in the light of the role that religion plays in these countries. Islam is not just a religion that can be separated from daily life and government, as is now the case with the Christian churches in the West. Islam is, for want of a better word, more holistic in that it provides a framework for both secular and spiritual life. Calls for an Islamic state therefore do not sound as strange to Muslims as they do to westerners.

Having said that, it is probably fair to observe that the majority of ordinary Muslims do not favour such a development, and that the popular following of fundamentalist groups is not as great as some imagine. Much of the success they do have is less a result of religious fervour than a reflection of the frustrated hopes of many classes in countries grappling with severe economic difficulties.

Morocco is not exempt from this, although neither the social stresses nor the fundamentalist movements are as great an issue as in, say, neighbouring Algeria.

Sunnis & Shiites The power struggle between Ali, Mohammed's son-in-law and the last of the four caliphs of Mohammed, and the emerging Umayyad dynasty in Damascus, caused a great schism at the heart of the new religion.

The succession to the caliphate had been marked by considerable intrigue and bloodshed. Ali, the father of Mohammed's male heirs, lost his struggle and the Umayyad leader was recognised as the legitimate successor to the caliphate. Those who favoured the Umayyad caliph became known as the Sunnis. They are the majority of Muslims and are considered the orthodox mainstream of Islam.

The Shiites, on the other hand, recognise only the successors of Ali. Most of the Shiites are known as Twelvers, because they believe in 12 imams, the last of whom has been lost from sight, but who will appear some day to create an empire of the true faith. The rest are called the Seveners because they believe that seven imams will succeed Ali.

The Sunnis have divided into four schools of religious thought, each lending more or less importance to various aspects of doctrine. In Morocco, where the population is virtually entirely Sunni, it is the Maliki school that predominates. The Malikis, along with the Hanafi school, are somewhat less rigid in their application and interpretation of the Quran than the other schools. An illustration of this emerged by the 15th century, when *qaids* (community judges) were recorded as having applied Sharia'a in accordance with local custom rather than to the letter.

Saints & Mysticism Morocco is not alone in the Muslim world in hosting a strongly mystical offshoot of Islam, but perhaps is unique in the weight that this carries with a large part of the population.

From an early point in the life of Islam, certain practitioners sought to move closer to God through individual effort and spiritual devotion, rather than simply living by God's laws. These people came to be known as Sufis (from *suf,* meaning wool and referring to the simple woollen cord they tended

to wear as a belt for their garments). Various orders of Sufis emerged throughout the lands where Islam held sway, and this was as true of Morocco as of anywhere else.

Orthodox Muslims regarded (and still regard) such groups with suspicion, particularly as the orders tend to gather in the name of a holy man (or *wali,* which has come to be loosely translated as 'saint', although saints in the Christian sense play no role in Islam). Public gatherings take many forms, from the dances of the 'whirling dervishes' to more ecstatic and extreme demonstrations of self-mutilation (where participants may, for instance, push skewers into their cheeks without feeling any pain).

The orders generally gather at the mosque or tomb of their 'saint' and follow a particular *tariqa* (path), or way of worshipping. Various orders acquired permanence over the centuries. 'Membership' might run through generations of the same families, who trace their lineage back to the original saint or spiritual master and through him to the Prophet; the veracity of such links is of secondary importance.

This mystic tendency found particularly fertile ground in the traditions and superstitions of the Berbers. There is little doubt that the cults that prosper in Morocco do so mostly in rural Berber areas. The focal point of gatherings of such groups is generally a *zawiyya,* which could be a small meeting place or a big complex grouping the mosque, school and hostels around the tomb of the saint, or *marabout.* Marabout, from the Arabic *muraabit,* is a word used more by French scholars than the locals and has come to designate the saint and the tomb.

For orthodox Muslims, veneration of a saint is tantamount to worship of an idol, although Sufis would not see it that way. According to them, the wali is a 'friend' (the more literal meaning of wali) of God and so an intermediary, and marabouts are regarded in a similar fashion. The great moussems to the tombs of such saints are as much a celebration of the triumph of the spirit as an act of worship of a particular saint.

Possibly the best known of these saints in Morocco is Moulay Idriss, whose tomb stands in the town of the same name outside Meknès. He died in 791 and is one of a number of equally venerated figures across the Muslim world. They also include Ahmed al-Badawi in Tanta (Egypt) and Abdal Qadir in Baghdad (Iraq).

In Morocco as elsewhere, such cults and their individualistic approach to Islam were considered by the mainly city-dwelling orthodox Muslims as deviant and by their leaders as politically dangerous.

And so, armed with imprecations against heresy, various attempts have been made to put an end to the phenomenon in Morocco, starting with the Almoravids. In more recent times, concerted efforts were made again in the 1930s, but there are two obstacles to such campaigns: the territory of the rural Berbers is difficult to control, and the people who follow the cults make up a big chunk of the total populace – you cannot simply get rid of them all!

Islamic Customs When a baby is born, the first words uttered to it are the call to prayer. A week later this is followed by a ceremony in which the baby's head is shaved and an animal is sacrificed.

The major event of a boy's childhood is circumcision, which normally takes place between the ages of seven and 12 years.

Marriage ceremonies are colourful and noisy affairs that usually take place in summer. One of the customs is for all the males to get in their cars and drive around the streets in a convoy making as much noise as possible. The ceremony usually takes place in either the mosque or the home of the bride or groom. After that, the partying goes on until the early hours of the morning, often until sunrise.

The death ceremony is simple: a burial service is held at the mosque and the body is then buried with the feet facing Mecca.

When Muslims pray, they must follow certain rituals. First they must wash their hands, arms, feet, head and neck in running water before praying; all mosques have an area set aside for this purpose. If they are not in a mosque and there is no water available, clean sand suffices; where there is no sand, they must go through the motions of washing.

They must always face towards Mecca – all mosques are oriented so that the mihrab (prayer niche) faces the correct direction – and follow a set pattern of gestures and genuflections. Photos of rows of Muslims kneeling in the direction of Mecca with their heads touching the ground are legion. You regularly see Muslims praying by the side of the road or in the street, as well as in mosques.

In everyday life, Muslims are prohibited from drinking alcohol and eating pork, which is considered unclean, and must refrain from gambling, fraud, usury, and slander.

Christianity

There are few Moroccan Christians and the existence of the occasional church is due more to the presence of Europeans over the centuries than local need. Nevertheless, there is evidence that Christianity made some inroads in North Africa during the time of Roman rule. How far it went beyond the Roman or Romanised population and upper classes is a matter of debate, although it appears that some Berber tribes turned, for a time at least, to the imported faith.

For whatever reason, the departure of the Romans and later of the Byzantines was followed by the virtual disappearance of Christianity from North Africa.

LANGUAGE

The official language in Morocco is Arabic, although French, the legacy of the protectorate, is still widely used in the cities (much less so among rural Berbers). Morocco's close ties to France help to explain its continued importance in education, business and the press.

There are three main Berber dialects in use, mainly in the Rif and Atlas Mountains. Modern means of communication have left only a minority of Berbers monolingual – most speak at least some Arabic.

To a lesser extent than French, Spanish has maintained some hold in northern parts of the country, where Spain exercised administrative control until 1956. You may also come across it in the territory of the former Spanish Sahara, over which Madrid relinquished control in 1975, and the former enclave of Sidi Ifni. In towns like Tetouan, for instance, Spanish is more likely to be understood than French.

Reforms to the education system include the introduction of English into the curriculum for younger students, so it may become more widely spoken. However at present English speakers will find a smattering of basic French (and a little Spanish) can be a great asset. In the main cities and towns you will find plenty of people, many of them touts you may not necessarily want to hang around with, who speak a variety of languages, including English, German and Italian. See the Language chapter at the back of this book for some handy words and phrases in Arabic and French.

Facts for the Visitor

SUGGESTED ITINERARIES

There is much to see in Morocco, and deciding on what to see and what to skip can be hard (see the boxed text 'The Best of Morocco' later).

Moroccans are some of the most hospitable and helpful people you're likely to meet, and getting around is straightforward, whether you're using public or private transport. However, there are people who think that tourists automatically owe them a living, and if you're moving quickly between popular tourist centres, you are likely to bump into a fair few of them.

While these hustlers and touts need not be a serious problem (smiles and polite but firm refusals of offers of 'guiding services' or 'something special' usually do the trick), being the new face in a town can be wearing. However, after a few days in a place this unwanted attention often dissipates. So, take your time travelling around Morocco and don't be afraid to concentrate on just a handful of places – getting to know a place well can be very rewarding and by doing so you're more likely to meet normal, genuinely friendly Moroccans without an interest in your tourist dollars.

That said, depending on how much time is available, you might want to consider some of the following options.

One Week

Marrakesh Loop Start in Marrakesh, then head west to the relaxed port of Essaouira. Continue south to the modern resort of Agadir and take a day trip to Immouzzer des Ida Outanane. Go on to Taroudannt before crossing the breathtaking Tizi n'Test back to Marrakesh (don't miss the beautiful Tin Mal Mosque en route).

The Rif & Fès After buzzing through Tangier, head south via Tetouan to Chefchaouen and the wild Rif Mountains. Continue south to Fès or Meknès, taking in the remarkable Roman ruins of Volubilis if possible.

Two Weeks

Imperial Cities Tour Flying into Casablanca and taking a tour of Morocco's fascinating Imperial Cities (Rabat, Meknès, Fès and Marrakesh) could easily take up two weeks (it's not something to be rushed in seven days). You may also be able to spend a day or two in the High Atlas.

North Coast Trip Fly into Casablanca and head north to Rabat. Take in the bird sanctuaries of Lac de Sidi Bourhaba and Moulay Bousselham, and continue up the coast to the old Spanish town of Larache (and Lixus ruins) and the picturesque port of Asilah. Tangier is worth some time before relaxing in Chefchaouen. You could then do some trekking around the Jebel Tazekka circuit south of Taza, or take in Fès and Meknès.

Southern Oasis & the Sahara From Marrakesh, head south-east to Ouarzazate, visiting the fabulous kasbah (fort) of Aït Benhaddou en route. Continue south along the Drâa Valley to Zagora, then track back and explore east along the Dadès Valley to Erfoud, stopping to explore the Vallée des Roses and the Dadès and Todra Gorges. A short drive east of Erfoud is the village of Merzouga and Erg Chebbi, an area of real Saharan dunes.

From Erfoud, you could head back west to Ouarzazate via the villages of Rissani and Tazzarine, skirting south of the volcanic peaks of Jebel Sarhro before heading back to Marrakesh.

One Month

Atlas Mountains It wouldn't be difficult to spend a month exploring the High Atlas, walking and travelling by local *camionette* (pick-up trucks) between the villages. Taroudannt, inland from Agadir, is a good base for treks into the western High Atlas and Azilal is a good launching point for treks into the central High Atlas. Tafraoute is the base for walks in the Anti Atlas.

The South & Imperial Cities In four weeks you could comfortably combine a tour of the Imperial Cities with a trip around the southern river valleys and the edge of the Sahara. You could also contemplate a trek into the rugged Jebel Sarhro, or from the Dadès or Todra Gorges you could head up into the High Atlas. Alternatively, from Zagora or M'Hamid, you could organise a camel trek through the desert.

Southern Coast & Inland Starting at Casablanca, snake down the Atlantic coast, stopping at the former Portuguese port of El-Jadida and Oualidia for some beach life. Continue south on through Safi, famous for its pottery, easy-going Essaouira, Agadir, Tiznit and even Sidi Ifni. You could then continue into the Western Sahara, going as far south as Tan Tan, Laayoune and with time, Dakhla. Or, head east into the Anti Atlas and spend your time wandering through picturesque villages and oases.

PLANNING

If you're a first-time visitor to Africa, consider checking out Lonely Planet's *Read This First: Africa* for lots of helpful advice.

When to Go

The most pleasant time to explore Morocco is spring (March to May), when there should be enough water around to keep the country green and the dust down. Next best is autumn (September to October) after the worst of the summer heat (it can be lovely on the coast midsummer, but viciously hot in the interior). Likewise, winter can be idyllic in Marrakesh and further south during the day, but you can be chilled to the bone at night (a light sleeping bag is a very handy item to carry at this time of year).

Don't underestimate the extremes of heat in the summer and cold in the winter, particularly in the High Atlas, where some peaks can remain snowcapped from November to July. Along the north coast and in the Rif Mountains, it can get very chilly and is frequently wet and cloudy in winter and early spring. For weather information (24-hour answering machine), call ☎ 02-364242 in Casablanca.

Also bear in mind that during Ramadan, the traditional month of fasting and purification, some restaurants and cafes close during the day and general business hours are usually reduced (see Public Holidays & Special Events later in this chapter for more details).

What Kind of Trip

Travelling solo is often cited as a sure-fire way of meeting fellow travellers and getting to know local people, not to mention being invited to share some of the best food to be had in the country. However, out of high season other travellers can be difficult to meet, and travelling solo tends to attract more attention from hustlers and touts. Women travelling alone will attract much more attention than solo men, and probably more than two women travelling on their own. Though Morocco is just as physically safe as the average Western city, you're likely to experience a few rather forward proposals and the occasional wandering hand (see Women Travellers later in this chapter).

Travelling with a small group of friends opens up a huge range of possibilities in Morocco. Hotel costs will be substantially lower if sharing a room; hiring a car or taxi becomes economical; and if you decide to go trekking, costs and the weight of equipment can be shared. By travelling in a group, you may be able to get off the beaten track a little more.

There are numerous travel companies offering cultural tours and adventure-based holidays (mostly mountain trekking and desert expeditions) in Morocco. Prices vary, but are generally more expensive than arranging a trip yourself, though for solo travellers some make good economic sense. If you're pushed for time, organised holidays also make sense. They take away the hard work of hiring guides, finding accommodation and so on, leaving you free to enjoy some of the most fabulous parts of the country. For more information, see Organised Tours in the Getting There & Away chapter.

Maps

Few decent maps of Morocco are available in the country itself, so you are advised to get one before leaving home.

The Best of Morocco

	region	comments
ACTIVITIES		
Bird-Watching Besides the abundant resident species, Morocco boasts vast numbers and species of migratory birds.	Everywhere, particularly the Atlantic coast	The best times for bird viewing are from late March to April, and September to October.
Desert Safaris Excursions with 4WDs, camels, tents and bivouacs are easily organised around Er-Rachidia	Central Morocco	Many towns offer trips but wait until you're close to the desert; shop around as there's plenty of competition.
Skiing Ski in the Rif Mountains and Middle Atlas, but the most popular spot is Oukaïmeden in the Ourika Valley.	High Atlas	Many mountain guides specialise in ski-trekking. Long cross-country trips are possible.
Surfing Agadir has the best surfing in the country and there are also good breaks north and south of Rabat.	Atlantic coast	There's a great surf club at Rabat.
Trekking All Morocco's mountains are relatively unexplored and offer dramatic peaks and fertile valleys where traditional Berber village life continues.	Rif Mountains, Atlas Mountains & Jebel Sarhro	Short walks and excursions are possible. For lengthy treks you may need to hire guides and mules.
Windsurfing The top spot is Essaouira, also known as 'Windy City'.	Central Atlantic coast	It's possible to hire gear in Essaouira for around Dr120 an hour.
NATURAL BEAUTY SPOTS		
Anti Atlas Pink mountains and pretty valleys surround the Berber village of Tafraoute.	South-east of Agadir	This area is best visited in the spring and autumn.
Drâa, Dadès & Ziz Valleys Rich river valleys full of *palmeraies* (oases) and beautiful ruined kasbahs.	Central Morocco	If you can, this is the time to hire a car.
Erg Chebbi An alluring landscape of drifting Saharan dunes near Merzouga.	Central Morocco	There's plenty of cheap accommodation by the sand dunes.
Middle Atlas Ancient, beautiful cedar forests around Azrou, Midelt and Ifrane are home to rich bird and animal life.	South of Fès & Meknès	A car is almost essential.
Rif Mountains Wild, isolated and very unexplored landscapes.	Around Chefchaouen	Drive along the mountains' backbone for a dramatic landscape.

The Best of Morocco

	region	comments
HOLY PLACES		
Hassan II Mosque This mosque was inaugurated in 1993 and is the biggest in the world after Mecca.	Casablanca	The interior decoration is living proof that Morocco's famous craftsmen have lost none of their ancient mastery.
Moulay Idriss The holiest town in Morocco is home to the tomb of the country's most revered saint – Moulay Idriss – and the focus of a huge annual pilgrimage.	Near Meknès	For centuries the town was strictly out of bounds to non-Muslims; officially, 'infidels' still cannot stay the night here.
Tin Mal Mosque Built c.1155 as a memorial for the founder of the Almohad dynasty, Mohammed ibn Toumert.	Tizi n'Test	Non-Muslims are allowed to visit the mosque every day except Friday, when prayers are held.
MUSEUMS & MEDERSAS		
Archaeological Museum One of the best museums in Morocco, it contains the most important finds from excavations at Roman sites across the country. The highlight is the Bronze collection.	Rabat	Don't miss the two stunning bronze busts of Cato and Juba II.
Medersa Bou Inania This former theological college is considered the most extravagant, elaborate and perfect of the monuments built under the Merenid dynasty.	Fès	If there's just one monument you visit, it should be this. It provides stunning evidence of Morocco's decorative tradition, including *zellij* (tilework), carved cedar ceilings and sculpted plaster.
Dar Batha Museum Housed in a former palace, the museum contains a good collection of antique Moroccan crafts, including Fassi embroidery and tribal carpets. It's best known for its collection of ceramics.	Fès	The pottery room contains some excellent examples of the famous blue pottery of Fès. It's a good place to see the 'real thing' before embarking on a shopping trip to the medina.
Dar Jamaï Palace This beautiful palace now houses an excellent collection of Moroccan artefacts.	Meknès	An attractive overgrown Andalusian garden in the grounds is a pleasant place to spend some time.
School of Traditional Arts & Crafts Set up to preserve craftsmanship, it has taught ancient professions such as painting, woodwork, weaving and zellij-making for 50 years.	Rabat	This is a wonderful opportunity to observe Moroccan craftsmen at work. The techniques they employ have remained almost unchanged since the 14th century.

The Best of Morocco

	region	comments
CULTURAL EXPERIENCES		
A Visit to the Doctor Every souq has an apothecary who dispenses ancient remedies for every illness of the body, mind and soul, including charms and aphrodisiacs.	Any Moroccan souq	Many travellers swear by the carob fruit commonly prescribed by apothecaries for unhappy stomachs.
Culinary Treats Many believe that Moroccan cuisine is among the best in the world. If you can, indulge, and have at least one good splurge.	Marrakesh	Though expensive by Moroccan standards, a meal in an exclusive restaurant will cost no more than a pizza and a bottle of wine in London.
Entertainers Morocco has a rich selection of artists, from brilliant musicians and singers to spectacular acrobats and spell-binding storytellers.	Marrakesh	Many of Morocco's best entertainers were born into their trades, and practise an art passed down from father to son for generations.
Henna Hands Women travellers may like to go local and have their feet or hands decorated with henna.	Herb & spice markets	This traditional mark of newlyweds might even throw off-scent any Moroccan admirers you have collected.
Hot from the Hammam A vestige of classical times, the public baths still play an important role in people's lives and offer a fascinating insight into society. For women travellers they're a rare opportunity to meet local women.	All towns & cities	Many of the budget hotels are without showers so travellers find the local hammam most welcome, and will soon get into the habit of using them.
Moroccan Hospitality Don't pass up a chance to share a cup of tea with locals.	Anywhere	If invited into a home, remove your shoes and drink at least three cups.
Music Enjoy exciting Berber music in informal surroundings.	Central Morocco	The hypnotic music of the Berbers is an ancient tradition.
Oases Amid the Wilderness The Andalusian gardens of Morocco provide an escape from the noise and chaos of the medina, you'll find incredible peace amid tinkling fountains, bird song, scented flowers and lush greenery.	Fès, Meknès & Chefchaouen	These places make a great spot for a picnic.
Roman Morocco Even if you're not normally into Roman remains, those at Volubilis are worth the effort. The buildings are remarkably well preserved and, unusually, the beautiful mosaics are in their original settings.	North of Meknès	For a memorable experience, try to catch the ruins in the last rays of the setting sun.

There are several reasonable maps covering all of north-western Africa and taking in parts of Egypt and the Sudan in the east. Kümmerley & Frey publishes *Africa, North and West* on a scale of 1:4,000,000; the Michelin map No 953 covers much the same area.

There are several maps of Morocco. Michelin's No 959 map is arguably the best. In addition to the 1:4,000,000 scale map of the whole of Morocco, including the disputed territory of Western Sahara, there is a 1:1,000,000 enlargement of Morocco and 1:600,000 enlargements of Marrakesh and the High Atlas, Middle Atlas and Meknès areas. Sites of weekly markets, kasbahs and marabouts (holy mausolea of local saints) are also shown. You can buy these in major Moroccan cities.

Preferred by many and with similar, often clearer, detail (and occasionally available in Morocco) is the GeoCenter World Map *Morocco*, which shows the country at a handy 1:800,000 scale. Hildebrand's *Morocco* covers the entire country at a scale of 1:900,000 and includes seven small city maps. Kümmerley & Frey's *Morocco* includes six small city maps, but its main 1:1,000,000 scale map doesn't cover all of the Western Sahara. Hallwag's *Morocco* is distinguished by its comparatively detailed maps of the Canary Islands. The main map is on a scale of 1:1,000,000.

Survey Maps & Air Charts The Cartography Division of the Conservation & Topography Department in Rabat stocks a range of maps, including topographical sheets, which are useful for hiking.

It's also possible to get hold of 1:200,000 Russian survey maps and air charts of Morocco from good map shops worldwide.

See the Trekking chapter for more information about maps.

What to Bring

Pack the minimum. There is nothing worse than having to lug loads of excess stuff around. If it's not essential, leave it at home.

A backpack is far more practical than an overnight bag and more likely to stand up to the rigours of Moroccan travel. It is worth getting a good one, as buckles and straps soon start falling off cheap backpacks.

In summer a hat, sunglasses and sunscreen are a must. For women, a large cotton scarf is useful (though there are plenty to buy in Morocco). Shorts are a bit of a no-no for men and women – they may be OK on the beach, but elsewhere you're better off wearing long, loose, lightweight skirts or trousers and cotton shirts that cover the shoulders and upper arms. Moroccan men only wear shorts for sport – male travellers will feel more comfortable and will be a lot better received if they do likewise.

If you plan to hike in the Atlas Mountains it really is worth having decent hiking clothes. Sturdy walking boots are essential and a water bottle and purification tablets are recommended. Trekking above the snow level requires more specialised equipment. For more information, see the Trekking chapter.

Other handy items include a Swiss army knife, a universal washbasin plug or tennis ball cut in half (even moderately expensive hotels are often devoid of plugs), a torch (flashlight), a small calculator (for bargaining in markets), a few metres of nylon cord, a handful of clothes pegs, earplugs (for successful sleeping in the noisier cheapies), a small sewing kit, any special medication you need and a medical kit (see Health later in this chapter).

Condoms, the pill and other contraceptives are available in the big cities (you can buy the pill and other medicinal drugs over the counter), but you are better off bringing your own.

RESPONSIBLE TOURISM

Dress code is important all over Morocco, but especially in the deeply conservative hill-tribe societies. Many of the inhabitants have had little or no exposure either to modernisation from inside their country or foreign customs from without. Travellers will feel most comfortable in buttoned shirts (rather than T-shirts, which are seen by some villagers as underwear) and trousers or long skirts (rather than shorts). The importance of dress in the villages cannot be overemphasised. An effort to respect tradition will bring greater rewards for the traveller. You are much more likely to attract a friendly reception, generous hospitality, reasonable prices in the souqs (markets) and help or assistance.

Again, as in other parts of Morocco, photographers should be aware that cameras can cause offence and, in some cases, extreme upset, particularly when pointed at women. Always ask in advance and, if you do find a cooperative subject, it's polite to leave a very small 'consideration' (donation) for them.

It's not a good idea to distribute sweets or pens among children, however great the temptation. It engenders a grossly distorted image of the westerner as a do-gooder of limitless resources that will affect the image of all tourists who come after you. It can also lead to truancy at school as families send out their children to solicit whatever seemingly innocent gift you care to bestow on them. If you really want to help, visit a local school and ask the teachers what you could donate.

The environmental cost of nonbiodegradable rubbish is taking its toll on beaches and 'beauty spots'. Plastic bags and water bottles are two of the biggest culprits. Save shopkeepers money by refusing plastic bags, and invest in water purification tablets (though tap water is drinkable in many places).

Be careful not to buy souvenirs made with endangered animals or plants.

For more information see Responsible Trekking in the Trekking chapter.

TOURIST OFFICES
Local Tourist Offices

The national tourism body, ONMT (Office National Marocain du Tourisme), has offices (usually called Délégation Régionale du Tourisme) in the main cities. The head office (☎ 07-730562), Web site www.tourism-in-morocco.com/indexa.htm, is in Rabat on Rue al-Abtal in Agdal. A few cities also have local offices called Syndicat d'Initiative, which dispense brochures and simple maps.

Tourist Offices Abroad

The ONMT also has offices abroad. They generally stock brochures, some glossy

maps and lists of tour operators running trips to Morocco.

Australia c/o Moroccan Consulate (☎ 02-9922 4999, fax 9923 1053) 11 West St, North Sydney, NSW 2060

Canada (☎ 1514-842 8111, fax 842 5316) Place Montréal Trust 1800, Rue Mac Gill, Suite 2450, Montréal, Quebec H3A 3J6

France (☎ 01 42 60 63 50, fax 01 40 15 97 34) 161 Rue Saint Honoré, Place du Théâtre Français, 75001 Paris

Japan (☎ 03-3403 0070, fax 3403 0072) Suite 303-219 Sendagaya, Shibuya-ku, Tokyo 151

Spain (☎ 341-542 7431) Ventura Rodriguez No 24, 1 ezq 28008 Madrid

UK (☎ 020-7437 0073, fax 7734 8172) 205 Regent St, London W1R 7DE

USA (☎ 212-557 2520, fax 949 8148) Suite 1201, 20 East 46th St, New York 10017

VISAS & DOCUMENTS
Passport

To enter Morocco, your passport must be valid for six months from the date of entry. If you need to renew your passport, allow plenty of time, as it can take anything from an hour to several months. Renewing it in person is usually far quicker, but check first what you need to take with you: photos of a certain size, birth certificate, exact payment in cash etc.

Holders of British Visitors passports should note that the Moroccan authorities do *not* accept them. All British citizens, no matter how young, must now have their own passports.

Visas

A visa is a stamp in your passport or on a separate piece of paper permitting you to enter the country and stay for a specific period of time. Most visitors to Morocco do not require visas and are allowed to remain in the country for 90 days on entry. Exceptions to this include nationals of Israel, South Africa and Zimbabwe, who can apply for a three-month, single-entry visa (about US$15) or a three-month, double-entry visa (about US$25).

Moroccan embassies have been known to insist that you get a visa from your country of origin, unless you have a working

Visas for Neighbouring Countries

Algeria

Since early 1994, and due to the civil war, total confusion has reigned and it may prove next to impossible to get a visa. At the time of writing, it was possible to get a tourist visa, but only from your country of origin. If normal embassy operations resume in Rabat, or if you can persuade officials that it's impossible for you to get a visa from home, you may be able to get one from inside Morocco. Applications must be supported by four photos, a photocopy of your passport details and a letter of invitation or a hotel reservation. Costs at the time of writing were as uncertain as everything else. A one-month visa is likely to cost US$30 to US$40. The land border with Morocco remains closed.

Mali

Visas are required for everyone except French nationals and are valid for one month (US$20), but are renewable. Two photographs and a Yellow Fever Vaccination Certificate are required.

Mauritania

This awkwardly located embassy produces some confusing information. Everyone needs a visa, which is valid for a one-month stay. These can be issued the same day if you apply before noon. Visas cost US$10 and you need two photos. Until recently, officially at least, no visas were being issued for overland travel, or without the presentation of a *return* air ticket. However, many people travelling with their own vehicles have been issued with visas. Though these state 'Entry by air only', no-one seems to mind. However, the current line from embassies in Europe is that overland visas can be issued, but only in Rabat. And in Rabat they are very guarded about this. You *must* check with your 'home' Mauritanian embassy before starting out. Good up-to-date information is also available online at www.sahara-overland.com.

To get to the Rabat embassy, take a petit taxi (about Dr17) or bus No 1, 2, 4 or 8 from the main city bus station to Ave John Kennedy. The embassy is on a small street parallel to the avenue (to your right if you're coming from town).

Senegal

About the only Western nationals to require visas are citizens of Australia, New Zealand, Switzerland and Iceland. You need to bring three passport photos and complete a form. Visas valid for three months cost US$25 and applications take 24 hours to process.

Spain

Nationals of various countries require visas to enter Spain (this also means Ceuta and Melilla), including Australians, South Africans and Israelis. Under the 1995 Schengen agreement, one visa now covers all EU member countries except the UK, the Republic of Ireland and Denmark, and replaces those previously issued by individual nations. In addition to supplying three photos, you may also be asked for photocopies of passport details, credit cards and/or bank statements. The Spaniards prefer you to apply for a visa in your country of residence – an awkward requirement, so be prepared for some diplomatic haggling. If they go along with your request, a visa takes at least 24 hours to issue. Apply between 9 am and noon and pick it up the following day (1 to 2 pm). The consulate is open weekdays.

Tunisia

EU, US and Japanese citizens are among those who do not require a visa for Tunisia. Australians and New Zealanders are among those who do, though it's easy to apply for a visa upon arrival at the airport. A standard one-month visa costs Dr52, though you can request a three-month visa. It can take up to a week to issue. You need two photos and two photocopies of your passport.

visa or residency for the country you're applying in. This can mean some bureaucratic haggling and a long wait for your visa – it can take weeks. However, applications are normally processed in 48 hours.

In Spain, visas are available at consulates in Barcelona, Algeciras, Las Palmas in the Canary Islands and Madrid. In Algeria, it's possible to get a Moroccan visa at Morocco's consulates in Algiers or Oran.

Visa requirements change, so check with the Moroccan embassy in your country or a reputable travel agent before travelling.

Visa Extensions Should the standard 90-day stay be insufficient, it is possible to apply for an extension or even for residence (but the latter is difficult to get). Go to the nearest police headquarters (Préfecture de Police) with your passport, three photos and, preferably, a letter from your embassy requesting a visa extension on your behalf.

However, applications can take hours or days, and different police headquarters use slightly different red tape. Although travellers on visas are advised to go for an extension, it's probably easier to head up to Spain and try to re-enter after a few days. Some travellers have reported difficulties in re-entering by the same route, though this is not always the case.

Visas for Ceuta & Melilla These two Spanish enclaves have the same visa requirements as mainland Spain (see the boxed text 'Visas for Neighbouring Countries' earlier, and the section on Embassies & Consulates in Morocco).

Travel Insurance
You should seriously consider taking out travel insurance for medical cover at the very least – the national health service in Morocco cannot be recommended and the few good private hospitals are expensive. Moreover, most insurance policies not only cover you for medical expenses, but also for luggage theft or loss, ticket loss and cancellation, or delays in your travel arrangements. Cover depends on your insurer, the insurance and your type of ticket, so ask

both your insurer and the ticket-issuing agency to explain where you stand.

Buy travel insurance as early as possible. If you buy it the week before you fly, you may find, for instance, that you're not covered for delays to your flight caused by strikes or other industrial action that may have started or been threatened before you took out the insurance.

Paying for your airline ticket with a credit card often provides limited travel accident insurance and you may be able to reclaim the payment if the operator doesn't deliver. Ask your credit card company what it's prepared to cover.

Some policies offer lower and higher medical expense options, and some specifically exclude 'dangerous activities', which can include scuba diving, motorcycling and even trekking. A locally acquired motorcycle licence is not valid under some policies.

You may prefer a policy that pays doctors or hospitals direct rather than you having to pay on the spot and claim later. If you have to claim later, make sure you keep all documentation. Some policies ask you to call back (reverse charges) to a centre in your home country where an immediate assessment of your problem is made – for reverse-charge calls, you'll need to find the country-specific access code. However, it's worth finding out which private medical service your insurer uses in Morocco so you can call them direct in the event of an emergency.

Check that the policy covers ambulances or an emergency flight home.

Driving Licence & Permits
Although technically you need an International Driving Permit to drive in Morocco, most national licences are recognised, including those held by EU nationals. If bringing your own car, you will need all the appropriate documentation, including a Green Card (see Land in the Getting There & Away chapter).

Hostel & Student Cards
You can stay at most Hostelling International (HI) hostels without a membership card, usually for a couple of dirham extra.

To get a HI card, ask at any hostel or contact your local or national hostelling office.

International student cards do not seem to open many magic doors (eg, museum discounts) in Morocco. However, if you're under age 30, they do entitle you to up to a 60% discount on internal travel (plus some flights *out* of the country) with Royal Air Maroc (RAM). Student rail cards are also available (see Train in the Getting Around chapter).

International Health Certificate

If you're coming to Morocco from certain parts of Asia, Africa and South America where outbreaks of yellow fever or cholera have been reported, you'll need this yellow booklet.

It is a record of your recent vaccinations and is available from your physician or government health department. A Yellow Fever Vaccination Certificate is sometimes a separate document. See Health later in this chapter for general information on immunisations.

Photocopies

The hassles created by losing your passport can be greatly reduced if you have a photocopy of the pages displaying its number, issue date and your photograph. A copy of your birth certificate can also be useful.

Also keep a record of the serial numbers of your travellers cheques (cross them off as you cash them) and photocopies of your credit cards, airline ticket and other travel documents. Keep all this emergency material separate from your passport, cheques and cash, and leave extra copies with someone you can rely on back home. You can also store these details in Lonely Planet's free online Travel Vault. Your password-protected Travel Vault is accessible online – create it at www.ekno.lonelyplanet.com.

Add some emergency cash, say US$100, to this separate stash as well (sewing this into a back trouser pocket is a good wheeze). If you do lose your passport, notify the police immediately (make sure you get a statement for insurance purposes) and contact your nearest consulate.

EMBASSIES & CONSULATES
Moroccan Embassies & Consulates

Morocco has diplomatic representation in the following countries, among others:

Algeria (☎ 02-607408) 8 Rue des Cèdres, Parc de la Reine, Algiers
  Consulate: (☎ 02-243470) 5 Ave de l'ANP, Sidi Bel Abbès, Algiers
Australia (☎ 02-9922 4999) Suite 2, 11 West St, North Sydney, NSW 2060
Canada (☎ 416-236 7391) 38 Range Rd, Ottawa, Ont KIN 8J4
Egypt (☎ 02-340 9677) 10 Sharia Salah ad-Din, Zamalek, Cairo
France (☎ 01 45 20 69 35) 5 Rue Le Tasse, Paris 75016
Germany (☎ 0228-35 50 44) Gotenstrasse, 7-9-5300, Bonn 2
Japan (☎ 03-3478 3271) Silva Kingdom 3-16-3 Sendagaya, Shibuya-ku, Tokyo 151
Mauritania (☎ 02-51411) Tevragh Zeina 634, BP 621, Nouakchott
Netherlands (☎ 070-346 9617) Oranjestraat 9, 2514 JB, The Hague
Spain (☎ 91 563 1090) Calle Serrano 179, 28002 Madrid
Tunisia (☎ 01-782 775) 39 Ave du 1er Juin, Mutuelleville, Tunis
UK (☎ 020-7581 5001) 49 Queen's Gate Gardens, London SW7 5NE
USA (☎ 202-462 7979) 1601 21st St NW, Washington, DC 20009

Embassies & Consulates in Morocco

Rabat is the political and diplomatic capital of Morocco, so most embassies and diplomatic representation is there. The following embassies and consulates can be found in Morocco:

Algeria (☎ 07-765474, fax 632237) 46-8 Ave Tariq ibn Zayid, Rabat; open from 8.30 am to 4 pm weekdays.
  Consulate in Oujda: (☎ 06-683740 or 683741) 11 Blvd Bir Anzarane; open weekday mornings.
Australia
  The Australian embassy in Paris has full consular responsibility for Morocco. Consular services to Australian citizens in Morocco are provided by the Canadian embassy.
Belgium (☎ 02-223049) 13 Blvd Rachidi, Casablanca; open weekday mornings.

Your Own Embassy

As a tourist, it's important to realise what your own embassy – the embassy of the country of which you are a citizen – can and can't do.

Generally speaking, they won't be much help in emergencies if the trouble you're in is remotely your own fault. Remember that you are bound by the laws of the country you're in. Embassies will not be sympathetic if you end up in jail after committing a crime locally, even if such actions are legal in your own country.

In genuine emergencies you might get some assistance, but only if other channels have been exhausted. For example, if you need to get home urgently, a free ticket home is exceedingly unlikely – the embassy would expect you to have insurance. If you have all your money and documents stolen, they might assist with getting a new passport, but a loan for onward travel is out of the question.

On the more positive side, if you are heading into very remote or politically volatile areas, you might consider registering with your embassy so they know where you are, but make sure you tell them when you come back, too. Some embassies post useful warning notices about local dangers or potential problems. The US embassies are particularly good for providing this information and it's worth scanning their notice boards for 'travellers advisories' about security, local epidemics, dangers to lone travellers and so on.

If you are planning to stay more than three months in Morocco, it's a good idea to register with your embassy.

Consulate in Agadir: (☎ 08-824080) Ave Hassan II.
Consulate in Tangier: (☎ 09-227939) 3rd floor, 41 Blvd Mohammed V; open weekday mornings.
Canada (☎ 07-672880) 13 Rue Jaafar as-Sadiq, Agdal, Rabat; open from 8 am to noon and 1.30 to 5.30 pm Monday to Thursday, and Friday to 1.30 pm.
Denmark (☎ 09-938183) 3 Rue ibn Rochd, Tangier; open weekday mornings.
France (☎ 07-689700) Rue Sahnoun, Agdal
Service de Visas: (☎ 07-702404) Rue ibn al-Khatib; open for applications from 8.30 to

11.30 am and for pick-up from 1.30 to 3 pm weekdays.
Consulate in Agadir: (☎ 08-840826) Blvd Mohammed Cheikh Saadi.
Consulate in Casablanca: (☎ 02-489300) Rue Prince Moulay Abdallah; open from 8.45 to 11.45 am and 2.45 to 4.45 pm weekdays.
Consulate in Oujda: (☎ 06-684404) 3 Rue de Berkane; open weekday mornings.
Consulate in Tangier: (☎ 09-932039, 932040) 2 Place de France; open weekday mornings
Germany (☎ 07-709662, fax 706851) 7 Zankat Madnine, Rabat.
Consular Section: (☎ 653605, fax 653649) 12 Ave Mehdi ben Barka (formerly ben Snassen), Rabat; open from 9 am to noon weekdays.
Italy (☎ 07-706598) 2 Rue Idriss el-Azhar, Rabat; open from 9 am to noon weekdays.
Consulate in Agadir: (☎ 08-843093) Rue de Souvenir.
Consulate in Casablanca: (☎ 02-277558) corner of Rue Jean Jaures and Ave Hassan Souktani; open weekday mornings.
Consulate in Tangier: (☎ 09-931064, fax 936647) 35 Rue Assad ibn al-Farrat; open weekday mornings.
Japan (☎ 07-631782) 39 Ave Ahmed Balafrej Souissi, Rabat; open from 9 am to 1 pm weekdays.
Mali (☎ 07-759125) 56 Souissi II, OLM, Rabat.
Mauritania (☎ 07-656678) 266 Souissi II, OLM, Rabat; open from 8.30 am to 3 pm Monday to Thursday and to noon Friday.
New Zealand
The closest embassy is in Madrid, Spain. The UK embassy provides consular support in Morocco.
Netherlands (☎ 07-733512, fax 733333) 40 Rue de Tunis, Rabat; open from 9 am to noon weekdays.
Senegal (☎ 07-754171) 17 Rue Cadi Amadi, Rabat; open from 8 am to 4 pm weekdays.
Spain (☎ 07-768989) 3-5 Zankat Madnine, Rabat.
Consulate in Agadir: (☎ 08-822126) 41 Rue ibn Batouta.
Consulate in Casablanca: (☎ 02-220752, fax 205048) 31 Rue d'Alger; open weekday mornings.
Consulate in Larache: (☎ 09-913302) 1 Rue Casablanca; open 8 am to 1 pm weekdays and 10 am to 12.30 pm Saturday.
Consulate in Rabat: (☎ 07-704147, 704148, fax 704694) 57 Rue du Chellah; open weekdays.
Consulate in Tangier: (☎ 09-935625, fax 932381) 85 Ave Président Habib Bourghiba; open weekday mornings.

Consulate in Tetouan: (☎ 09-703534), Place Moulay el-Mehdi; open weekday mornings.
Tunisia (☎ 07-730636, 730637, fax 727866) 6 Ave de Fès, Rabat; open from 9 am to noon and 2 to 5.30 pm weekdays.
UK (☎ 07-729696, fax 704531) 17 Blvd de la Tour Hassan; consular services available from 8 am to 12.30 pm weekdays and staff will help citizens of the Republic of Ireland and some Commonwealth countries without representation in Morocco.
Consulate in Agadir: (☎ 08-827741) Rue des Administrations Publiques.
Consulate in Casablanca: (☎ 02-221653, fax 265779) 3rd floor, 60 Blvd d'Anfa; open from 8 am to 4.30 pm Monday to Thursday and to 1 pm Friday.
Consulate in Tangier: (☎ 09-941557, fax 942284) 2nd floor, 41 Blvd Mohammed V; open weekday mornings.
USA (☎ 762265, fax 765661) 2 Ave de Marrakesh, Rabat; open from 8.30 am to 12.30 pm and 2.30 to 6.30 pm weekdays.
Consulate: (☎ 02-264550, fax 204127) 8 Blvd Moulay Youssef, Casablanca; open from 8 am to 6 pm weekdays.

CUSTOMS

Duty-free allowances are up to either 200 cigarettes or 50 cigars or 440 grams of tobacco plus 1L of spirits and one bottle of wine.

MONEY
Currency

The Moroccan currency is the dirham (Dr), which is divided into 100 centimes. You will find notes in denominations up to Dr200 and coins of Dr1, Dr2, Dr5 and Dr10, as well as 10, 20 and 50 centimes, though these are becoming rarer.

Exchange Rates

country	unit		dirham
Algeria	AD100	=	Dr14.55
Australia	A$1	=	Dr5.98
Canada	C$1	=	Dr7.37
euro	€1	=	Dr9.52
France	1FF	=	Dr1.45
Germany	DM1	=	Dr4.87
Japan	Y100	=	Dr10.31
Mauritania	UM100	=	Dr4.51
New Zealand	NZ$1	=	Dr4.43
Spain	100ptas	=	Dr5.72
UK	UK£1	=	Dr16.14
USA	US$1	=	Dr11.11

Exchanging Money

The importation or exportation of Moroccan currency is prohibited, but any amount of foreign currency – cash or cheques – may be brought into the country. In the Spanish enclaves of Ceuta and Melilla, the currency is the Spanish peseta (pta).

Most currencies are readily accepted, but the Irish punt, Scottish pound and Australian, Canadian and New Zealand dollars are not recognised. This goes for cash and cheques.

Banking services are reasonably quick and efficient. Rates vary little from bank to bank, but it can't hurt to look around. Almost all banks charge commission on travellers cheques (around Dr10 per cheque), though at the time of writing Wafa Bank was charging Dr10 per transaction.

You'll need your passport to change travellers cheques (plus the travellers cheque receipt in some places) and to get cash advances; some banks want to see it when you change cash, too.

Branches of BMCE (Banque Marocaine du Commerce Extérieur) and Crédit du Maroc are often the most convenient, and often have separate *bureau de change* (foreign exchange) sections that are open on weekends. Major branches of the main banks open on Saturday morning.

If you are arriving from, or heading for, the enclaves of Ceuta and Melilla, the Moroccan banks on the border will exchange cash only. It is difficult to obtain Moroccan currency in mainland Spain and not worth the effort. However, the banks in Melilla and Ceuta deal in dirham at rates inferior to those in Morocco. Another option in the enclaves and on the borders is the black market (see Black Market later in this section) – check the bank rates first, which are usually just as good.

Importing and exporting Moroccan currency is illegal (though it's unlikely anyone will bother you if you take out a little as a souvenir), so the best thing is to wind down to nothing as you approach the end of your trip. Hang on to all exchange receipts, you sometimes need them to re-exchange leftover dirham at most Moroccan banks (including on the borders and at the airports).

Travellers Cheques The main reason for carrying travellers cheques rather than cash is the protection that they offer from theft, although they are losing their popularity as more travellers opt to simply withdraw money from ATMs or get cash advances on credit cards as they go.

American Express (AmEx) and Thomas Cook cheques are widely accepted and have efficient replacement policies, though commission is still often charged when changing both. Keeping a record of the cheque numbers and those you have used is vital when it comes to replacing lost travellers cheques. Make sure you keep this record separate from the cheques themselves. Before changing cheques, ask the bank whether it charges a commission. AmEx is represented by the travel agency Voyages Schwartz, which can be found in Rabat, Casablanca, Marrakesh and Tangier. However, they do not sell or cash travellers cheques.

Credit Cards & ATMs If you're not familiar with the options, ask your bank to explain the workings and relative merits of credit, credit/debit, charge and cash cards. Some banks will charge you every time you make a withdrawal from a foreign cash machine and some do not. Ask your bank.

A major advantage of credit cards is that they allow you to pay for expensive items (eg, airline tickets) without having to carry great wads of cash around. Major credit cards are widely accepted in the main tourist centres, although their use often attracts a surcharge of around 5% from Moroccan businesses. ATMs – automatic teller machines *(guichets automatiques)* – are now a common sight and many accept Visa, MasterCard, Electron, Cirrus, Maestro and InterBank systems. BMCE and Crédit du Maroc ATMs are usually your best bet. The amount of money you can withdraw from an ATM generally depends on the conditions attached to your particular card, although the daily ATM limit on most cards is around Dr3000. ATMs sometimes run dry on weekends, so stock up during the working week.

You can get cash advances on Visa and MasterCard in various banks, including the Banque Populaire, the BMCE, the BMCI and Wafa Bank.

If you want to rely on plastic cards, the best bet is to take two different cards (one Visa, one Maestro/MasterCard is ideal). Better still is a combination of credit card and travellers cheques so you have something to fall back on if an ATM swallows your card or the banks in the area are closed.

International Transfers Most of the banks charge a minimum of around US$30 to send money by telegraphic transfer and it can take up to 14 working days (possibly longer if there are cock-ups) to reach you. A better service (which takes about 10 minutes once all the formalities are taken care of) is offered by two specialist companies.

MoneyGram can be sent through a variety of outlets worldwide (often main post offices) and costs around US$53 to send US$800. The MoneyGram agency in Morocco (where you pick up your cash) is Crédit du Maroc.

A Western Union money transfer can be arranged through its agencies worldwide (ring your local free-call number) and costs around US$60 for US$800. Call Western Union in Morocco (☎ 07-261559 in Rabat or ☎ 02-208080 in Casablanca) for details of agents (often Wafa Bank or the post office).

Black Market The near convertibility of the dirham leaves little room for a black market, but you will find people in the streets asking if you want to exchange money, especially in Tangier and Casablanca. It is wiser to avoid these characters; there is no monetary benefit to be had from such transactions unless you are desperate for cash when the banks are closed. Always check bank rates before dealing with black marketers, who are always on the scam, even in Ceuta and Melilla.

There is also a frontier black market. You will find plenty of Moroccans dealing in dirham and hard currency on the Ceuta frontier and inside the Melilla enclave. In Ceuta itself and on the actual Melilla border there seems to be less activity.

In Oujda and Figuig it is possible to buy and sell Algerian dinar for dirham (in Oujda you can also get hard currency). Discretion is the word, though the authorities seem to turn a blind eye to such transactions. When dealing in dinar, shop around before concluding an exchange. You can get dinar in Melilla too, though the rates are unlikely to be as good as in the two Moroccan frontier towns.

Security
Nothing beats cash for convenience...or risk. If you lose it, it's gone forever and very few travel insurers will come to the rescue. Nonetheless, you'll certainly need to carry some cash with you. Keep a handful of small denomination notes in your wallet (but never carry it in a back pocket) for day-to-day transactions and put the rest in a moneybelt or another safe place. If you're travelling in out-of-the-way places, make sure you have enough cash to last you until you get to a decent-sized town.

Having a secret stash of small denomination US dollars is a good idea too.

Costs
For westerners, Moroccan prices are refreshingly reasonable. With a few small tips here and there, plus entry charges to museums and the like, you can get by on US$20 to US$25 a day per person as long as you stay in cheap unclassified hotels (without star ratings) for around Dr30 per night, eat at cheap restaurants and are not in a hurry. Cooking for yourself and buying fresh foods from local markets will stretch your budget.

If you'd prefer some of life's luxuries such as hot showers, European newspapers, the occasional splurge at a good restaurant and a few taxi rides, plan on US$35 to US$45 a day.

The following prices will give you some idea of what to expect. There's not much difference in price between trains and buses. Local buses can be 20% cheaper than trips with Compagnie de Transports Marocains (CTM), the main national carrier. A 100km bus or train journey costs about Dr17.

A meal in a lower-end restaurant costs as little as Dr25. In a medium-range restaurant you'd pay up to Dr70 and in a more upmarket place, around Dr150, including wine (there's a 10% tax at upmarket places).

Stall food can provide a filling meal for about Dr15. A loaf of bread costs just over Dr1, 1kg of olives around Dr12, 1kg of tomatoes about Dr6 and 1kg of bananas about Dr10. When in season, strawberries cost just Dr6 a kilogram in the north-east.

A pot of mint tea is worth Dr3 to Dr4 – more in very touristy places. Coffee tends to be around Dr5. A 500ml bottle of Coca-Cola will set you back around Dr6. Juice stands can be good value – a big, freshly squeezed orange juice goes for as little as Dr2.50.

The two main local brands of beer, Flag Spéciale and Stork, cost about Dr13 and Dr15 respectively in restaurants and bars, but about half that from liquor stores.

A packet of imported cigarettes costs Dr25. You can, as many locals do, buy them one at a time for Dr1. Local brands, such as Marquise, cost Dr10 for 20.

Although you can buy many foreign newspapers and magazines in the bigger cities, they're not cheap; papers often start at Dr25. The exception is the French press; eg, *Le Monde* costs Dr10, and often arrives on the same day.

Local telephone calls are cheap, but a call to Europe will cost at least Dr17 per minute. Practically all museums and monuments charge a standard Dr10 entry fee.

If you're aged under 26, an international student card (see Hostel & Student Cards under Visas & Documents earlier in this chapter) can get you big reductions on internal flights (and some international flights) and international rail fares departing from Morocco. It will also enable you to purchase a student rail card for reduced internal fares.

Tipping & Bargaining
Tipping and bargaining are integral parts of Moroccan life. Practically any service can warrant a tip, but don't be railroaded. The judicious distribution of a few dirham for a service willingly rendered can, however, make your life a lot easier.

A tip of between 5% and 10% of a restaurant bill is about right (unless the service has been poor, of course), and a dirham or so suffices at a cafe. Museum guides, *gardiens de voitures* (car park attendants), porters,

Kilim Compulsion

Kathryn admired a small amber jewellery case, and again inquired after a price. This time, after some protestation, a price, rather a high one, was quoted. She put the object down then, still regarding it with warm admiration but saying sadly she could never afford such beautiful things.

The elder man smiled benignly. 'If you want it, then you shall have it, dear lady.'

And so began a good hour of negotiation. At the same time, the younger man, seeing me notice the especially intricate pattern in the kilim upon which I sat, began a carpet show, tossing down rug after rug with terrific pomp and seriousness. The dramatic structure of these routines is always the same. First there is the showing itself, each rug tossed down with a flourish, sometimes accompanied by a little sigh from the dealer at the loveliness of the piece; then, a simple inquiry as to one's favourites. To the protestation that one does not want to buy, that one is only looking, there is merely a repetition: 'Yes, please, and what are your favourite pieces?' Finally, one nominates some favourites, and then, by a process of elimination, chooses a favourite. Then you are asked to name a price. You may refuse, in which case the dealer nominates a price. If you make any counter-offer to this inflated opening price, you are already bargaining. A deal of some form is then hard to avoid. You have as good as bought another carpet.

When we finally returned to the car in the declining afternoon, Kathryn had the amber case and two long, indigo-dyed Tuareg scarves – and I had a new carpet. A big one. I was full of sweet tea and vexation.

'What an utter scam! That bullshit out on the road!'

'You didn't have to buy the carpet. No-one forced me to buy these things,' Kathryn said patiently. 'And anyway, they're lovely.'

'It's more subtle than that. They're just very good, that's all. They know every trick of how to get money out of you.'

Perhaps it was all the sugar and the hapless sitting and the chat, or perhaps it was the late afternoon sun, which was still strong. Perhaps it was just us and our predicament, the interpersonal predicament we rarely mentioned, as if it could be filed away until our month here was up.

'I mean, it's late. We're driving on narrow roads we've never driven on before. It's stupid! And why is it me who always ends up buying carpets?'

'I don't know,' she said, peering into the fading light. 'You've just got a weakness for them. Come on, it's a nice carpet. And I love my amber thingamy.'

It was our sixth carpet so far. Sixth. Was I taking leave of my senses? I couldn't afford it and I didn't have the floor-space at home anyway. And 'home'? Kathryn had recently bought her own flat and was moving into it on her return to Sydney. Was not this, truly, the end?

'Come on, just drive,' she said.

'Well if we have an accident, it's your bloody fault.'

From Larry Buttrose *The Blue Man*, published by Lonely Planet; published by Flamingo/HarperCollins in Australia under the title *Café Royale* © Larry Buttrose 1987

baggage handlers and petrol pump attendants expect to be tipped (between Dr3 and Dr5) and it's polite to offer the same to people for permission to take their photograph.

Try to judge each situation on its merits, and pay accordingly. It's also worth bearing in mind that many Moroccans earn the equivalent of about US$3.25 a day.

Some people love it, others hate it, but whatever your view, bargaining is a central part of Morocco's commercial culture. Bargaining applies mainly to the souqs. Taxi fares can sometimes be negotiated. Prices are generally fixed for hotels, restaurants and transport, but it's prudent to check out prices before you commit to buying.

Just about everyone has a personal modus operandi for dealing with merchants. The best advice is to enter into the spirit of the situation and *enjoy* the process. By refusing to bargain where it is expected, you almost appear to be robbing the vendor of one of the pleasures of the trade (and yourself of cash). For Moroccans, bargaining is quite a performance, and even though both parties know the routine is inevitable, they also realise an accommodation will be eventually found.

When on the hunt for souvenirs, look around, indulge in the banter over prices and get a feel for what people are asking. Decide beforehand how much you are prepared to spend – a visit to the Ensemble Artisanal in the major cities will give you an idea of the upper range of prices.

Never embark on a discussion of prices if you are not really interested, as Moroccans attach a good deal of importance to your last word. If they accept a price you name, they can get understandably shirty if you turn around and say you're not interested.

You'll be invited for tea, and countless samples of wares will be laid out before you, along with countless reasons for buying them. Do not allow yourself to be intimidated into buying anything you don't want at a price you don't like. Whatever they tell you, no-one can *make* you buy.

Be aware that some vendors often start with hugely inflated prices. If this is so, wait until the price has reduced considerably before making your first (low) offer, then approach your limit slowly. See the boxed text 'Kilim Compulsion' earlier for author Larry Buttrose's experience and the boxed text 'The Carpet Buying Ritual' in the Middle Atlas & the East chapter for descriptions of some of the practicalities.

You may not have to part with any money at all. A lot of Western goods, such as decent jeans and printed T-shirts, can easily be traded for local products. It's up to you what value you attach to whatever you're trading and to haggle accordingly.

Begging

Whatever advances Morocco may be making economically, great chunks of the population are still being left behind. You will often see Moroccans giving money to beggars; alms-giving is an integral part of Muslim culture and it is hard to find a reason for not giving the elderly and infirm a dirham or two.

You'll see a fair number of women of all ages, apparently abandoned by their husbands, begging on the streets. They're in a difficult position and needless to say, there is no such thing as a single-mother's benefit in Morocco.

Wherever you go, children will hound you for dirham, *bonbons* (sweets) and *stylos* (pens). The best policy is not to encourage them at all. If you'd like to provide children in a poor village with something, go to the local school and ask the teacher if the school needs a supply of pens or notebooks.

POST & COMMUNICATIONS

Post offices are distinguished by the 'PTT' sign or the 'La Poste' logo. You can sometimes buy stamps at *tabacs*, the small tobacco and newspaper kiosks you see scattered about the main city centres.

The postal system is fairly reliable, but not terribly fast. It takes about a week for letters to get to their European destinations, and two weeks or so to get to Australia and North America. About the same period of time is required going in the other direction. Sending post from Rabat or Casablanca is a lot quicker.

Postal Rates

The table 'Postal Rates' later gives sample rates in dirham for airmail postcards weighing up to 5g, letters (up to 25g), airmail parcels (weighing up to 1kg) and surface parcels (up to 1kg).

Sending Mail

The parcel office, indicated by the sign 'Colis postaux', is generally in a separate part of the post office building. Take your parcel unwrapped for customs inspection. Some post offices sell five sizes of tough, self-sealing cardboard boxes. These range in dimension from the small 20x13x7cm (Dr6) to the hefty 50x30x22cm (Dr20). It's not compulsory to use the boxes and it may

Postal Rates

country	postcard 5g (Dr)	letter 25g (Dr)	airmail 1kg (Dr)	surface 1kg (Dr)
Australia	7.50	22.10	202	155
Belgium	6.50	14.10	150	143
Canada	6.70	18.10	127	96
France	6	13.10	143	138
Germany	6.50	14.10	113	146
Hong Kong	7	19.60	184	150
Ireland	6.50	14.10	119	114
Japan	7.50	19.60	186	151
Netherlands	6.50	14.10	113	129
New Zealand	7.50	22.10	244	178
Norway	6.50	14.10	122	117
South Africa	6.50	17.10	175	143
Spain	6	13.10	91	89
Switzerland	6.50	14.10	111	105
UK	6.50	14.10	122	141
USA	6.70	18.10	123	97

work out cheaper to bring your own wrapping materials. There is a 20kg limit and parcels should not be wider, longer or higher than 1.5m.

There is usually an Express Mail Service (EMS), also known as Poste Rapide, in the same office as parcel post. Your letter or package should arrive within 24 hours in Europe and within two to three days elsewhere.

Receiving Mail

Having mail addressed to 'Poste Restante, La Poste Principale' of any big town should not be a problem. However, some offices don't hang on to parcels for more than a couple of weeks before returning them to the sender. Take your passport to claim mail. There's a small charge for collecting letters.

Possibly a more reliable way to receive mail is through AmEx, which is represented by the travel agency Voyages Schwartz and has branches in Rabat, Casablanca, Marrakesh and Tangier. To qualify for the client mail service, you are supposed to have AmEx travellers cheques or an AmEx card. In practice, you are usually asked only to produce a passport for identification. There is no charge for any letters you receive.

Telephone

The telephone system in Morocco is excellent, thanks to the hundreds of millions of dollars that have been invested in recent years.

A few cities and towns still have public phone offices, often next to the post office, but with the privatisation of the telecommunication industry these are becoming increasingly rare.

There are numerous private sector *téléboutiques* throughout the country that are open till late. They are slightly more expensive than public phones. Attendants can provide as much change as you might need and they sell *télécartes* (phonecards). These télécartes cannot be used in other téléboutiques or in public phones.

Télécartes for public phones are available at post offices, some tabacs and a few top-end hotels. You can buy télécartes for Dr62.50 (50 units), Dr87.50 (70 units) and Dr150 (120 units).

Domestic Dialling The domestic operator can be reached on ☎ 10.

To make a local call with a coin-operated phone you must insert a minimum of Dr1.50. Costs are worked out in units (one unit equals 80 centimes) and your initial Dr1.50

Changes to Telephone Numbers

Just before this book went to press, telephone numbers in Morocco changed overnight with little warning. Six-digit numbers now have nine digits, with the addition of the previous area code and an extra digit to the front of the number. All nine digits must be dialled to make local and national calls within Morocco, and to make an international call to Morocco.

In addition, the country's eight area codes have been consolidated into four. See Maroc Telecom's Web site (www.iam.net.ma/plan3.asp) for extra details in French.

While this book uses the old telephone numbers and area codes, the following information will help you dial the right number. For example:

In Casablanca:
old: ☎ 02-787878
new: ☎ 022 787878

In Rabat:
old: ☎ 07-787878
new: ☎ 037 787878

Cellphone numbers are also affected. All old cellphone numbers must be preceded by 06, and the 0 before the old code must be dropped. For example:

old: ☎ 01-787878   new: ☎ 061 787878

To make an international call to Morocco, use the complete number but drop the first 0, for example, to call Rabat:

old: international access code + country code (212) + 7 787878
new: international access code + country code (212) + 37 787878

You'll also need to know which codes cover the town you want to call. Following is a list of towns and regions covered in this guide.

02 – Casablanca & Settat Region
Azemmour, Azilal, Ben Slimane, Beni Mellal, Casablanca, Dar Bouazza, El-Jadida, Khouribga, Mohammedia, Settat, Sidi Bouzid

03 – Rabat & Tangier Region
Al-Hociema, Arbaoua, Azilah, Cabo Negro, Cap Malabata, Cap Spartel, Chefchaouen, Fnideq, Kenitra, Ketama, Ksar el-Kebir, Ksar el-Seghir, Larache, Lixus, Martil, M'diq, Moulay Bousselham, Oued Laou, Oued Loukkos Dam, Ouezzane, Rabat, Salé, Sidi Kacem, Souk el-Arba du Rharb, Tangier, Targa, Temara, Tetouan

04 – Marrakesh & Agadir Region
Abainou, Agadir, Agdz, Aglou Plage, Aït Bekkou, Aït Benhaddou, Amezrou, Benguérir, Boujdour, Boumalne du Dadès, Cascades d'Ouzoud, Dakhla, Demnate, Diabat, El-Kelaâ du Straghna, El-Kelaâ M'Gouna, Essaouira, Fort Bou Jerif, Goulimime, Id-Aïssa, Immouzzer des Ida Outanane, Inezgane, Laayoune, Marrakesh, Merzouga, M'Hamid, Mirhleft, Ouarzazate, Oukaïmeden, Ouled Taima, Safi, Sidi Ifni, Sidi Kaouki, Skoura, Smara, Tafraoute, Taghjicht, Taliouine, Tamegroute, Tan Tan, Tarfaya, Taroudannt, Tata, Tinerhir, Tinfou, Tioute, Tiznit, Youssoufia, Zagora

05 – Fès & Oujda Region
Ahfir, Ain Leuh, Azrou, Berkane, Bouarfa, Boulemane, Er-Rachidia, Erfoud, Fès, Figuig, Guerchif, Ifrane, Immouzzer, Khenifra, Meknès, Midelt, Mischliffen, Moulay Idriss, Moulay Yacoub, Nador, Oujda, Rissani, Saidia, Sefrou, Sidi Yahia Oasis, Taza

Getting Mobile

When Méditel (the Spanish-led consortium that paid US$1.1 billion for Morocco's second GSM cellphone licence in 1999) opened its stores to the public in April 2000, people fought to be the first through the door. Still relatively new, Morocco's two cellphone networks (Maroc Telecom operates the other one) are already having a great influence on how average people communicate in Morocco.

Moroccans love to chat, which partly explains the success of cellphone telephony, but the main reason for the rise of the cellphone is access – it's estimated that landlines only cover 6% of the population, while the cellphone networks cover 85% of the population (and increasing). In addition, cellphones using prepaid cards have been heavily marketed (so it's easy to budget for a cellphone, as opposed to a landline) and they are cheap by anyone's standards. At the time of writing, a standard GSM phone plus a card with 30-minutes' talk time (valid for six months) cost Dr495 (around US$45).

Prices are likely to fall, giving millions of Moroccans the chance to leapfrog a generation of communications technology. Indeed it's estimated that by 2001 the number of cellphone telephone connections will outnumber those of normal phones. And it's not just the BMW-driving chic elite of Rabat or Casablanca who own cellphones. Savvy guides in Fès and Marrakesh have cellphones; people who ride mules are starting to buy cellphones.

The development of the Internet in Morocco has been equally impressive (there are hundreds of Internet Service Providers) and it's hoped that these new industries will help force economic liberalisation and promote growth.

gets you about six minutes. Local calls are half-price on weekends and on public holidays and from 8 pm to 8 am on weekdays.

For long-distance calls within Morocco, one unit gets you from two minutes (35km or under) to 30 seconds (over 35km). Long-distance calls are half-price on weekends and from 8 pm to 8 am weekdays. Call prices are cut by 70% on the first day of a national or religious holiday and by 50% on the second day.

International Dialling When calling overseas from Morocco, dial ☎ 00, your country code and then the city code and number. If you have a problem getting through, you can ask the international operator (☎ 12) to connect you for a fee. To call Morocco from abroad, dial the international access code, then 212 (Morocco's country code), the regional code (minus the zero) and the local number.

International calls from Morocco are fairly expensive. The cheap rate (20% off) operates on weekends and public holidays, and from 8 pm to 8 am weekdays.

International call rates are listed in *Annuaire des Abonnés au Téléphone* – you may be able to look at a copy in major post offices. Per-minute rates to the following countries are: Italy, France and Spain (Dr5); Germany and England (Dr7); Sweden (Dr8); Ireland, Denmark, Belgium, Netherlands and Switzerland (Dr9); USA and Canada (Dr9); Syria and Egypt (Dr10); and Australia, New Zealand, Hong Kong and Japan (Dr20).

Reverse Charges It is possible to make reverse-charge (collect) calls from Morocco, but it can involve painfully long waits in phone offices. If you want to do this, say 'Je voudrais téléphoner en PCV' (pronounced peh-seh-veh) – the French expression for this service.

Many telephone companies outside Morocco operate international services that allow you to dial a toll-free number that connects you with operators in your home country, through whom you can then request reverse-charge and credit-card calls. Countries where this service is available include the UK, France, Spain and the Netherlands.

Calling from Hotels You can make local calls from hotels, but you will generally be charged a minimum of about Dr5. The bigger hotels usually offer international phone and fax services, but they can easily cost double the normal amount and are really only for the desperate or those on expense accounts.

Telephone Directories There is one standard phone book for all Morocco in French – the *Annuaire des Abonnés au Téléphone*. Most phone offices and larger post offices may have a copy. There is a slimmer volume containing fax numbers only. Look up the city first and then the person you want.

A kind of Yellow Pages, *Télécontact,* is available in some bookshops. If your French is OK, you could dial ☎ 16 for information *(renseignements)*.

Cellphones Morocco now has two GSM cellphone networks, which now cover 85% of the population. There's excellent coverage in major towns and cities, and reception is generally good in the north-western and western parts of the country. South and east of the High Atlas, reception is not quite so good, but things are improving all the time.

Ask your cellphone operator about using your phone in Morocco. However, these 'roaming' services are very expensive and rarely as user-friendly or international as the cellphone companies make out.

A cheaper alternative may be a prepaid Moroccan cellphone (see the boxed text 'Getting Mobile' opposite).

Fax
Most téléboutiques offer fax services, but they're often ridiculously expensive. Average prices per page are as follows: local (Dr8); countywide (Dr15); Europe and North Africa (Dr50); Scandinavia, Southern Africa, Asia, Australia, New Zealand, Canada and North America (Dr70).

Email & Internet Access
Email access is widely available, efficient and cheap (usually about Dr10 an hour). See individual destination entries for addresses.

INTERNET RESOURCES
The World Wide Web is a good resource for travellers heading to Morocco, not only for tracking down cheap air fares, but also for information on hotels, activities in-country and all aspects of Moroccan culture.

There's no better place to start surfing than at the Lonely Planet Web site (www.lonely planet.com). Here you'll find updates of current titles, postcards from other travellers and the Thorn Tree bulletin board, where you can post questions before you go or dispense advice when you get back. There are also a number of hotlinks to other useful travel resources.

While running a specific search on the topic you are interested in is usually the best way to get the information you're after, the sites at www.morocco.com and www.maroc .net are excellent starting points. Both contain a wealth of information, up-to-date news stories and Morocco-specific search engines.

The Moroccan government's Web site (www.mincom.gov.ma) is a little light on useful information, but you can download a few Moroccan music files.

Good for news, but crap for practical information, is www.arab.net.

Other useful, more specialised Web sites are listed throughout this book.

BOOKS
Most books are published in different editions by different publishers in different countries. As a result, a book might be a hard-cover rarity in one country while it's readily available in paperback in another. Fortunately, bookshops and libraries search by title or author, so your local bookshop or library is best placed to advise you on the availability of the following selections.

Because of Morocco's colonial heritage under the French, and the continued importance of French in Moroccan society, works in French have been added to the suggested reading list that follows. For information on Moroccan literature, see Arts in the Facts about Morocco chapter.

Lonely Planet
Lonely Planet's *Moroccan Arabic phrasebook* is an introduction to the complexities of the language, and *World Food Morocco* is an intimate insight into Moroccan cuisine from spiced couscous to sweet mint tea.

Larry Buttrose's experiences of Morocco in *The Blue Man* (Journeys series) are those that many travellers will identify with.

For an armchair glimpse of the splendours that await, contact your nearest Lonely Planet office and find out where you can buy the *Morocco Experience* video, or get your local bookshop to order it.

Guidebooks

Michelin's *Guide de Tourisme – Maroc* is an excellent route guide to Morocco. The bad news is that it's only available in French.

Chris Scott's *Sahara Overland*, and to a lesser extent *The Adventure Motorbiking Handbook*, are just about essential companions to any trans-Saharan driving adventures. There's advice on planning a trip and preparing your vehicle or bike, driving or riding off-road and a selection of travellers tales to keep you inspired. Both are published by Trailblazer.

Also available are the *Sahara Handbook* by Simon Glen and *Africa Overland* by the same publishers.

Travel

Morocco – The Traveller's Companion by Margaret & Robin Bidwell is a compilation of writing by westerners who have come into contact with Morocco. The line-up ranges from the likes of Leo Africanus to Samuel Pepys and George Orwell.

By Bus to the Sahara by Gordon West tells of an eventful journey made by the author and his wife, Mary, across Spanish Morocco in the 1930s. Their travels take them to Rabat, Meknès and Marrakesh, and tiny oases villages where they are met and befriended by fire-eaters, sorcerers, slave dealers, holy men and descendants of the Prophet.

Edith Wharton's *In Morocco* chronicles the three years she spent in the country from 1917.

An entertaining account of a westerner's travails in Morocco more than a century ago is *Morocco – Its People & Places* by Edmondo de Amicis, which first appeared in 1882. Equally interesting, but potentially irritating for modern readers, is Frances Macnab's *A Ride in Morocco*, a British woman's rather strident account of her adventures on horseback from Tangier to Marrakesh at the beginning of the 20th century.

Islamic, Arab & North African History

For those wanting to become generally acquainted with the wider Arabic-speaking world, there are several books to recommend. Philip Hitti's very readable *History of the Arabs* is regarded as a classic.

A more recent, but equally acclaimed, work is Albert Hourani's *A History of the Arab Peoples*. It is as much an attempt to convey a feel for evolving Muslim Arab societies as a straightforward history, with extensive, if largely generalised, treatment of various aspects of social, cultural and religious life.

If you want a more comprehensive reference on the whole Muslim world (although it's weak on more recent history), try delving into *A Cambridge History of Islam*. Volume 2A has a section devoted to North African history.

Maghreb: Histoire et Société is one of a number of studies by Jacques Berque, who is regarded as one of the better historians of the region in the French language.

In an attempt to get away from a French interpretation of Maghreb history, Abdallah Laroui wrote *The History of the Maghreb* (translated from the French by Ralph Manheim). He strives to assert an indigenous view and is regarded by some Moroccans as the best there is. Unfortunately, the book is out of print and hard to track down. It is as much an analysis of how historians have dealt with Maghreb history as an account of events, so it is not as useful an introduction to the country.

Gabriel Camps has written several works dealing with various aspects of Maghreb history – *L'Afrique du Nord au Féminin* presents stories of famous women of the Maghreb and the Sahara from 6000 BC to the present.

History

Histoire du Maroc by Bernard Lugan is a reasonable potted history of the country, although it leans back into the category Abdallah Laroui was combating.

Les Almoravides by Vincent Lagardare traces the history of this great Berber dynasty from 1062 to 1145.

The Conquest of the Sahara by Douglas Porch describes France's attempts to gain control of the Sahara and subdue the Tuaregs. His *Conquest of Morocco* examines the takeover of Morocco by Paris, which led to the establishment of the protectorate.

A Country with a Government and a Flag by CR Pennell is an account of the anti-colonial struggle in the Rif from 1921 to 1926 that threatened the French and Spanish hold over their respective protectorates.

In *Lords of the Atlas – The Rise and Fall of the House of Glaoua 1893–1956* Gavin Maxwell recounts the story of Thami al-Glaoui, the Pasha of Marrakesh. The book relates some of the more extraordinary events linked with this local despot, who even after WWII ordered that the heads of his enemies be mounted on the city gates. It's an excellent book.

The Western Sahara desert region, which Morocco claims and for all intents and purposes now controls, remains a contentious issue. If you want to read the Moroccan government's side of the story, you could try *Hassan II présente la Marche Verte*. The title refers to the Green March, when Moroccan troops and civilians moved in to take control of the territory in 1975 as Spain pulled out.

The Western Saharans by Virginia Thompson & Richard Adloff takes a less government-friendly view of the conflict.

Other books on the issue include *Conflict in North-West Africa – The Western Sahara Dispute* by John Damis, *Spanish Sahara* by John Mercer and *Western Sahara – The Roots of a Desert War* by Tony Hedges.

On contemporary Morocco, the French writer Gilles Perrault caused a diplomatic storm with his none-too-complimentary *Notre Ami Le Roi*. Don't be seen carrying this one around with you in Morocco!

People & Society

Patience and Power – Women's Lives in a Moroccan Village by Susan Davies is a fascinating and very readable book that does away with much of the myth surrounding women in Islamic society.

Further insights into the lives of Moroccan women can be found in Elizabeth Warnock Fernea's personal view of women, *A Street in Marrakesh,* and Leonora Peets's *Women of Marrakesh,* which has been translated from the Estonian. Although she is not Muslim, Peets became very close to the women she met in the 40 years she spent in Morocco from 1930.

Moroccan Dialogues by Kevin Dwyer discusses various sociological issues, including marriage and circumcision, in a series of interviews with Moroccans of different generations, backgrounds and social positions.

Peter Mayne's highly readable *A Year in Marrakesh,* first published in 1953, is his account of time spent living among the people of the city and his observations about their lives.

The House of Si Abdallah – The Oral History of a Moroccan Family, recorded, translated and edited by Henry Munson Jr, gives a unique insight into the daily lives and thoughts of Moroccans, mainly seen through the eyes of a traditional peddler in Tangier and his westernised cousin, a woman living in the USA. Munson's *Religion and Power in Morocco* provides an equally good insight into Islam in Morocco.

The Structure of Traditional Moroccan Rural Society by Bernard Hoffman is a good title for detailed information about the Berber population of Morocco. *Les Berbères* by Gabriel Camps and *Berbères Aujourd'hui* by Salem Chaker cover the same subject.

The Mellah Society by Shlomo Deshen looks at Jewish community life in Morocco.

Foreign Writers

Iain Finlayson's *Tangier – City of the Dream* is an intriguing look at some of the Western literati who found a new home in Morocco at one time or another. The single greatest entry deals with Paul and Jane Bowles and those around them, but there is interesting material on William Burroughs, Beat writers, Truman Capote, Joe Orton and others. It is a highly readable account of the life of this 'seedy, salacious, decadent, degenerate' city.

Elias Canetti, a foremost novelist in the German language and Nobel Prize winner, ended up in Marrakesh in 1954 with a film team. He penned his recollections in a slim but moving volume of short and elegantly simple stories entitled *Die Stimmen von Marrakesch*. It has appeared in English as *The Voices of Marrakesh*.

From the 1890s to the early 1930s, *The Times'* correspondent Walter Harris lived through the period in which Morocco fell under the growing influence of France. His whimsical and highly amusing, if not always totally believable, *Morocco that Was* first appeared in 1921.

At the beginning of the 20th century, Budgett Meakin made one of the first serious attempts by a westerner at an overall appraisal of Moroccan society and history. First published in 1901, Darf Publishers in London thought *The Land of the Moors* interesting enough to bring out again in 1986.

If the writing on Morocco from this period appeals, another book of casual interest, mainly for its reflection on the ideas of the more zealous westerners living in the Orient, is Donald Mackenzie's *The Khalifate of the West,* first printed in 1911.

Arts & Architecture

A Practical Guide to Islamic Monuments in Morocco by Richard Parker is exactly what its title suggests, and is full of town maps, pictures and ground plans of important monuments.

Titus Burckhardt's *Fès, City of Islam* is a pictorial treasure, including many of the art historian's own black-and-white shots of the city from his visits in the 1930s.

Casablanca, Mythes et Figures d'Une Aventure Urbaine by Jean-Louis Cohen & Monique Eleb takes an historical look at the architectural evolution of Morocco's biggest city.

Islamic Architecture – North Africa by Antony Hutt is a pictorial overview of the great buildings of the Maghreb.

Rome in Africa by Susan Raven discusses all the Roman sites of Morocco.

Zillij – The Art of Moroccan Ceramics by John Hedgecoe & Salma Sanar Damluji is a decent study of this important aspect of Moroccan decoration.

Les Tapis has all you ever wanted to know (in French) about Moroccan carpets and rugs.

Living in Morocco by Lisl & Landt Dennis is a sumptuous coffee-table book with a lot of material on Moroccan arts and crafts.

Arts and Crafts of Morocco by James Jereb provides excellent information on textiles, jewellery, leatherwork, woodwork, metalwork and ceramics. There is also a good section on collecting Moroccan arts and crafts.

For an aerial approach, get hold of *Maroc Vu d'en Haut* by Anne & Yann Arthus-Bertrand.

If traditional Moroccan dancing fascinates you, *Danses du Maghreb* by Viviane Lièvre will give you a deeper insight into the meaning and history behind it (in French).

Musique du Maroc by Ahmed Aydoun and *La Musique Arabo-Andalouse* by C Poché, both in French, deal with the rich traditions of music in Morocco.

Food

As well as LP's *World Food Morocco* (a mouth-watering introduction to the country's cuisine; see Lonely Planet earlier in this section) there's *The Taste of Morocco* by Robert Carrier, also an excellent illustrated guide to Moroccan cuisine.

Also worth dipping into is *Good Food from Morocco* by Paula Wolfert. The best way to learn the joys of the cuisine, she writes, is to try home-cooking or get invited to a banquet. And she's right.

There are several good cookery books in French, including *Ma Cuisine Marocaine* by Mina al-Glaoui, *Gestes et Saveurs du Maroc* by Fatima Hal and *La Cuisine Marocaine Familiale* by Khadidja Kfita.

Wildlife

A reasonable cross between a coffee-table book and a wildlife guide is *Morocco Fauna & Wide Open Spaces* by Philippe Ploquin & Francoix Peuriot. It is published in French and English.

Mediterranean Wild Flowers by M Blamey & C Grey-Wilson and the *Alternative Holiday Guide to Exploring Nature in North Africa* by J Cremona & R Chote cover some of the country's flora and habitats.

Birds of the Middle East and North Africa by Hollom, Porter, Christensen &

Willis is the definitive guide to the region. *Birds of Europe with North Africa and the Middle East* by Lars Jonsson is superbly illustrated and covers all species likely to be found in Morocco.

Very useful guides to birding locations and finding birds in Morocco include *A Bird-Watchers' Guide to Morocco* by Patrick and Fedora Bergier, and two booklets by David Gosney, *Finding Birds in Northern Morocco* and *Finding Birds in Southern Morocco*.

Bookshops

Morocco is not exactly bursting with good bookshops and you will certainly be much better served if you can read French, as the better stores have a far wider French-language selection on Morocco and general subjects.

Branches of the American Language Center in Rabat, Marrakesh and Casablanca have small bookshops dedicated mainly to English literature and learning the English language (the one in Rabat has a very good selection).

In addition, there is an English Bookshop in Rabat. Rabat probably has the best general bookstores, both for English (limited) and French (loads of choice), although you'll only find the occasional book on Morocco in English. There are also a few good bookshops in Casablanca, Tangier, Marrakesh and Fès. For details, see the relevant chapters.

FILMS

Morocco has been the setting, both real and imagined, for countless films. The most famous is probably *Casablanca*, starring Humphrey Bogart and Ingrid Bergman (shot completely on location in Hollywood). Others having little to do with the country itself and more to do with Western images of exotic North Africa include the hilarious *Road to Morocco* starring Bing Crosby and Bob Hope, the Marx Brothers' *One Night in Casablanca* and *Ali Baba & The Forty Thieves* starring Yul Brynner.

Orson Welles shot much of his acclaimed *Othello* in the former Portuguese ports of Essaouira, Safi and El-Jadida, while Alfred Hitchcock chose the chaotic medinas of Marrakesh for *The Man Who Knew Too Much*, which starred James Stewart and Doris Day.

Lawrence of Arabia, directed by David Lean in 1962 and starring Peter O'Toole, Alec Guinness, Anthony Quinn, Anthony Quayle and Omar Sharif, includes scenes filmed on location in the fabulous kasbah of Aït Benhaddou (much of the village was later rebuilt for the making of *Jesus of Nazareth*). Recently restored to its full glory, 'Lawrence' contains some stupendous shots of central Morocco.

The country features strongly in Bernardo Bertolucci's *The Sheltering Sky* (1990), based on Paul Bowles' famous novel. John

Orson Welles' Othello

As Othello lies dead, a horrified Iago is hoisted above the crowd in an iron cage and the play begins.

Orson Welles filmed much of his adaptation of Shakespeare's classic tale of jealousy and retribution in Essaouira, including this opening scene; a dramatic panoramic shot of the town's ramparts, where Iago is suspended above the rocks and sea.

Considered by many as Welles' most dazzling visual work, *Othello* includes the murder of Rodrigo in a local *hammam* (traditional bathhouse) and a riot scene in the Citerne Portugaise in El-Jadida. The reflection of the roof and the 25 arched pillars in the water covering the citerne's floor created a stunning and memorable effect.

Othello was perhaps Welles' most chaotic shooting schedule, with production spanning three years in the early 1950s. Despite being hampered by a host of difficulties – he left the set regularly to traipse around Europe to borrow money, and during the course of the film went through four Desdemonas (including his fiancee, who then had an affair with one of the crew) – *Othello* won the Grand Prix (now Palme d'Or) at Cannes in 1952.

At the time of Welles' death, *Othello* was the only one of his films he owned. In 1992 it was restored by his daughter and re-released to huge acclaim.

At an open-air performance in Essaouira, a square on the seafront was officially renamed Place Orson Welles in his honour.

Malkovich and Debra Winger star as the American couple wandering ever further from the familiar in post-war North Africa. The early stages of the film were shot in Morocco, although in the novel the action takes place in Oran (Algeria). At one point, we see the 80-year-old Bowles watching his characters from a seat in a Tangier cafe. The 1970 film *In the Land Where the Jumblies Live* is an interview with Bowles at home in Tangier (Bowles died in Tangier in 1999; see the boxed text 'Paul Bowles' in the Mediterranean Coast & the Rif chapter). For information on Moroccan films, see Cinema under Arts in the Facts about Morocco chapter.

NEWSPAPERS & MAGAZINES

Morocco possesses a diverse press in both Arabic and French. The bulk of the daily papers owe their allegiance to one or other political party or grouping. Although censorship decreased after the death of King Hassan II, papers still practice self-censorship and never rock the boat too much. Even those run by opposition parties rarely, if ever, say anything that could be construed as antimonarchist. It is quite all right for the parties to attack one another, and for the opposition to criticise the government, but the country's real power – the royal family – is another kettle of fish.

None of the newspapers make riveting reading and none has a huge circulation.

The pro-government French-language daily *Le Matin du Sahara et du Maghreb* (which also appears in Arabic and Spanish) is an extremely turgid read, yet sometimes manages a print run of 100,000 (many papers publish fewer than 50,000 copies). Many people simply buy it for the crossword, though some enterprising folks simply produce thousands of photocopies of the crossword and send young boys out to sell it in cafes.

Among the French papers (most of which have an Arabic equivalent), *l'Opinion,* which is based in Rabat and attached to the opposition Istiqlal party, is perhaps the most interesting for getting an idea of some of the points of contention in Moroccan society.

Libération, the Union Socialiste des Forces Populaires' daily, produced in

Casablanca, is similar if less punchy. *Al Bayane*, another opposition daily, is not too bad for foreign news. All have listings for the Casablanca and Rabat cinemas, airport shuttle timetables, Royal Air Maroc arrivals and departures, and a list of late-night pharmacies that work on a rotating roster.

For readers of French who are learning Arabic, the monthly *La Tribune du Maroc* is worth getting hold of. It culls the local Arabic and French language press to cover the main events of the month and runs articles in both languages.

There is a plethora of sports papers, fashion magazines and the like, and a surprising number of weeklies dedicated to economics, as well as political and social themes.

There is virtually nothing produced locally in English. A tiny monthly put out in Fès, *The Messenger of Morocco* (Dr3), is of minimal interest.

Foreign Press

In the main cities, a reasonable range of foreign press is available (for a price) at central newsstands and in some of the big hotels. News magazines such as *Time* are usually fairly easy to find, along with the *International Herald Tribune* and a range of UK papers, including the *International Guardian*, and their Continental European equivalents. The French press (including a whole host of magazines) is about as up to date and easy to obtain as it is in France itself, and is by far the cheapest.

Tourist Publications

La Quinzaine du Maroc is a useful (free) booklet loaded with practical information and listings; it appears every fortnight. Look in the bigger hotels and tourist offices in main cities.

RADIO & TV
Local Radio

Moroccan radio is an odd mix. There is only a handful of local AM and FM stations, the bulk of which broadcast in Arabic and French.

Midi 1 at 97.5 FM covers northern Morocco, Algeria and Tunisia, and plays quite reasonable contemporary music, broadcasting in French and Arabic.

Foreign Radio

Throughout northern Morocco and along much of the Atlantic coast, you can pick up a host of Spanish stations, especially on the AM band.

You can usually tune into Spanish radio just about anywhere in Morocco; although reception can be patchy it gives you a choice of music.

On the Mediterranean coast around Tangier and across to Ceuta, you can often pick up English language broadcasts from Gibraltar, while in the east you can occasionally pick up hip Algerian rap broadcasts on Algerian Radio.

The Voice of America (VOA) has long had a presence just outside Tangier, and in September 1993 opened its biggest transmitter outside the USA at a cost of US\$225 million. You can find VOA on many short-wave frequencies, including 6040MHz, 9095MHz, 11,805MHz and 15,205MHz.

The other short-wave option in English is the BBC. It broadcasts on 15,070MHz, 12,095MHz and 9410MHz, and several other frequencies. The bulk of the programs are broadcast from about 8 am to 11 pm.

TV

Satellite dishes are everywhere in Morocco, from the modern cities to the tiny rural villages reliant on small generators. The attraction seems to be the number of free channels that Moroccans seem to be able to get after a single one-off fee. Dozens of foreign stations can be picked up in Arabic, French, German and English (Canal+, CNN, NBC and even Cartoon Network).

Algerian terrestrial TV can be watched throughout Morocco, and Spanish networks dominate in the north of the country due to the proximity to the Iberian Peninsula – the more risque stations like Télé 5 are extremely popular.

There are two government-owned stations. TVM and 2M broadcast in Arabic and French (TVM also has news in Spanish at 7 pm). TV5, basically a European satellite import

from the Francophone world, has shows from France, Belgium, Switzerland and Canada.

VIDEO SYSTEMS

If you want to record or buy video tapes to play back home, you won't get a picture if the image registration systems are different. Morocco and France use the SECAM system, which is incompatible with both the PAL system used in Australia and most of Western Europe, and the NTSC system used in north America and Japan.

PHOTOGRAPHY & VIDEO
Film & Equipment

Kodak and Fuji colour negative film (35mm and APS), as well as video tapes, are readily available in the big cities and towns, but are marginally more expensive than in Europe. Slide film (particularly good quality film) is more difficult to come by. If you buy film in Morocco, be sure to check expiry dates.

A 36-frame roll of Kodak 100 ASA (ISO) 35mm print film will cost around Dr35 to Dr45 and APS film is about Dr40 for 25 shots. A 36-frame roll of Kodak Ektachrome slide film (100 ASA) goes for about Dr80.

There are quite a few processing shops in the cities and larger towns. Photo labs offer the most professional services. It costs around Dr70 to have a 36-frame roll of colour prints developed, and as little as Dr60 to have unmounted slides done. APS film is expensive to develop: it costs Dr35 for developing and then Dr3 per photo.

Technical Tips

Photography For most daylight outdoor shooting, 100 ASA is quite sufficient. Generally, it is best to shoot in the morning and afternoon, as the light in the middle of the day is harsh and can give your pictures a glary, washed-out look.

It is worth keeping a few rolls of 200 ASA and even 400 ASA handy for lousy weather (especially in the north in winter), shots in the medinas (which tend to let in a minimum of sunlight) or if you're using long zoom and telephoto lenses.

For more tips, *Travel Photography: A Guide to Taking Better Pictures* is written by internationally renowned travel photographer, Richard I'Anson and published by Lonely Planet. It's full colour throughout and has been designed to take on the road.

Video A video camera can give a fascinating record of your holiday. As well as videoing the obvious things – sunsets, spectacular views – remember to record some of the ordinary, everyday details of life in the country. Often the most interesting things occur when you're intent on filming something else.

Video cameras have amazingly sensitive microphones and you might be surprised how much sound will be picked up. This can be a problem if there is a lot of ambient noise – filming by the side of a busy road might seem OK when you do it, but viewing it back home might simply give you a deafening cacophony of traffic noise.

One good rule to follow for beginners is to try to film in long takes and not to move the camera around too much. Otherwise, your video could well make your viewers seasick! If your camera has a stabiliser, you can use it to obtain good footage while travelling on various means of transport, even on bumpy roads.

Make sure you keep the batteries charged and have the necessary charger, plugs and transformer for Morocco's electrical system. It is usually worth buying a few extra cartridges duty-free to start off your trip. If you have a LCD display on your camera, using it when shooting will wear down the battery in double-quick time.

Photographing People

It is common courtesy to ask permission before taking photographs of people. Urban Moroccans are generally easy-going about it, but in the countryside locals are not so willing to have cameras pointed at them. In particular, women and older people very often do *not* want to be photographed. Respect their right to privacy and don't take photos.

Taking photographs of your new-found friends is usually a different story, and sending copies back to Morocco will be greatly appreciated.

Restrictions

Morocco is full of photo opportunities, but don't point your camera at anything that is vaguely military or that could be construed as 'strategic'. This includes airports, bridges, government buildings and members of the police or armed forces.

Airport Security

Moroccan airports use X-ray scanning machines for security, which should pose no problems for most films. However, any roll should not be scanned more than half a dozen times to be on the safe side. For some specialised film, eg, film with an ASA rating of 400 or higher, X-ray damage is a danger.

If you do not want to take a chance with any film, good camera shops sell lightweight lead-lined pouches that can hold several rolls and provide total protection.

TIME

Morocco is on GMT/UTC year-round. So (not taking account of daylight-saving time elsewhere) when it's noon in Morocco, it's 8 pm in Perth and Hong Kong, 10 pm in Sydney, midnight in Auckland, 4 am in Los Angeles, 7 am in New York, noon in London and 1 pm in Western Europe. Remember that Spain and the Spanish enclaves of Ceuta and Melilla are two hours ahead in summer, which can affect plans for catching ferries and the like.

Moroccans are not in nearly as much of a hurry to get things done as westerners. Rather than getting frustrated by this, learn to go with the flow a little. It may even lengthen your life. Moroccans are fond of the saying, 'He who hurries has one foot in the grave!'.

ELECTRICITY

Throughout most of the country, electricity supply is 220V at 50Hz AC, although in some places you'll still find 110V; check before plugging in appliances. Sockets are the same as the European round two-pin variety.

WEIGHTS & MEASURES

Morocco uses the metric system. There is a standard conversion table at the back of this book.

LAUNDRY

Unfortunately, self-service laundrettes are few and far between. The best option is to do your washing by hand; most hotels have roof terraces where you can hang it to dry.

Establishments called *pressings* are really more like dry-cleaners. Some will happily wash and iron a pile of backpacker's kit. They take about 48 hours to do the job and a load of washing is priced per item (ranging from about Dr2 for socks up to Dr15 for jackets), so it can work out to be an expensive option. Pressings are usually open from 8 am to 12.30 pm and 2.30 to 7.30 pm daily.

Even in the most basic hotels someone will do washing for you. Clothes invariably will be washed by hand and dried in the sunshine, so allow plenty of time and be sure to agree on a price first!

TOILETS

Outside the major cities, public toilets are rare and usually require your own paper *(papier hygiénique),* a tip for the attendant, stout-soled shoes and very often a nose clip. They are mostly of the 'squatter' variety with a tap and container for sluicing. Flush toilets are a luxury in a country struggling with water shortages.

If you get caught short, duck into the nearest hotel or cafe to use the toilet. People are very unlikely to refuse you. Basic hotels and cafes often don't have toilet paper either, so keep a supply with you.

HEALTH

Travel health depends on your predeparture preparations, your daily health care while travelling and how you handle any medical problem that does develop. While the potential dangers can seem quite frightening, in reality few travellers experience anything more than an upset stomach.

Hospitals, Doctors & Pharmacies

Standards of health care in Morocco vary considerably and some hospitals are quite off-putting. Casablanca and Rabat have the best hospitals, but those in Tangier cannot be recommended. The best advice is to ask foreign consulates for up-to-date lists of recommended doctors and medical specialists.

The Croissant Rouge (the Islamic version of the Red Cross) often has bases close to bus stations in major towns. They are usually open 24 hours and are run by qualified nurses, with doctors on stand-by overnight.

Large towns often have a *pharmacie de nuit,* or night pharmacy, which is open from around 9 pm to 9 am. Normal pharmacies also stay open in the evenings (till about 9 pm) on a rotational basis (inquire at any local pharmacy for details).

French-language newspapers publish lists of hospitals with 24-hour emergency services *(les urgences)* in the major cities. Rabat and Casablanca get the most coverage (see Casablanca and Rabat in the North Atlantic Coast chapter for further details).

Predeparture Planning

Immunisations Plan ahead for getting your vaccinations: some of them require more than one injection, and some vaccinations should not be given together. Note that certain vaccinations should not be given during pregnancy or in people with allergies – discuss with your doctor.

It is recommended that you seek medical advice at least six weeks before travel. Be aware that there is often a greater risk of disease for children and during pregnancy.

No immunisations are officially required for Morocco but discuss your requirements with your doctor. Vaccinations you should consider for this trip include the following (for more details about the diseases themselves, see the individual disease entries later in this section). Carry proof of your vaccinations, especially yellow fever, as this is sometimes needed to enter some countries.

Diphtheria & Tetanus Vaccinations for these two diseases are usually combined and are recommended for everyone. After an initial course of three injections (usually given in childhood), boosters are necessary every 10 years.

Polio Everyone should keep up to date with this vaccination, which is usually given in childhood. A booster every 10 years maintains immunity.

Hepatitis A The vaccine (eg, Avaxim, Havrix 1440 or VAQTA) provides long-term immunity

Medical Kit Check List

Following is a list of items you should consider including in your medical kit – consult your pharmacist for brands available in your country.

- [ ] **Aspirin or paracetamol (acetaminophen in the USA)** – for pain or fever
- [ ] **Antihistamine** – for allergies, eg, hay fever; to ease the itch from insect bites or stings; and to prevent motion sickness
- [ ] **Cold and flu tablets, throat lozenges and nasal decongestant**
- [ ] **Multivitamins** – consider for long trips, when dietary vitamin intake may be inadequate
- [ ] **Antibiotics** – consider including these if you're travelling well off the beaten track; see your doctor, as they must be prescribed, and carry the prescription with you
- [ ] **Loperamide or diphenoxylate** – 'blockers' for diarrhoea
- [ ] **Prochlorperazine or metaclopramide** – for nausea and vomiting
- [ ] **Rehydration mixture** – to prevent dehydration, which may occur, for example, during bouts of diarrhoea; particularly important when travelling with children
- [ ] **Insect repellent, sunscreen, lip balm and eye drops**
- [ ] **Calamine lotion, sting relief spray or aloe vera** – to ease irritation from sunburn and insect bites or stings
- [ ] **Antifungal cream or powder** – for fungal skin infections and thrush
- [ ] **Antiseptic (such as povidone-iodine)** – for cuts and grazes
- [ ] **Bandages, Band-Aids (plasters) and other wound dressings**
- [ ] **Water purification tablets or iodine**
- [ ] **Scissors, tweezers and a thermometer** – note that mercury thermometers are prohibited by airlines
- [ ] **Sterile kit** – in case you need injections in a country with medical hygiene problems; discuss with your doctor

dose. It's not a vaccine, but a ready-made antibody collected from blood donations. It's reasonably effective and, unlike the vaccine, it is protective immediately. However, because it is a blood product, there are concerns about its long-term safety. Hepatitis A vaccine is also available in a combined form, Twinrix, with hepatitis B vaccine. Three injections over a six-month period are required, the first two providing substantial protection against hepatitis A.

Typhoid Vaccination against typhoid may be required if you are travelling for more than a couple of weeks where hygiene is a problem. It's available either as an injection or as capsules to be taken orally. A combined hepatitis A/typhoid vaccine was launched recently but its availability is still limited – check with your doctor to find out its status in your country.

Meningococcal Meningitis Although throughout most of Morocco it is not a problem, sub-Saharan Africa is within the 'meningitis belt'. A single injection gives good protection against the major epidemic forms of the disease for three years. Protection may be less effective in children under two years of age.

Hepatitis B Travellers who should consider vaccination against hepatitis B include those on a long trip, as well as those visiting countries where there are high levels of hepatitis B infection, where blood transfusions may not be adequately screened or where sexual contact or needle sharing is a possibility. Vaccination involves three injections, with a booster at 12 months. More rapid courses are available if necessary.

Yellow Fever Yellow fever vaccination is not required for Morocco but vaccination is recommended for travel in some parts of Africa. A yellow fever vaccine is now the only vaccine that is a legal requirement for entry into certain countries, usually only enforced when coming from an infected area. You may have to go to a special yellow fever vaccination centre.

Rabies Vaccination should be considered by those who will trek or spend a month or longer in Morocco, where rabies is relatively common, especially in dogs which often run semi-wild in remote rural areas. Travellers who are also cycling, handling animals, caving or travelling to remote areas, as well as children (who may not report a bite) should seriously consider getting the shots. Pretravel rabies vaccination involves three injections over 21 to 28 days. If someone who has been vaccinated is bitten or scratched by an animal, they will require two booster injections of vaccine; those not vaccinated require considerable and swift treatment.

(possibly more than 10 years) after an initial injection and a booster at six to 12 months. Alternatively, an injection of gamma globulin can provide short-term protection against hepatitis A – for two to six months, depending on the

Tuberculosis The risk of TB to travellers is usually very low. Vaccination against TB (BCG) is recommended for children and young adults living with or closely associated with local people in high risk areas for three months or more.

Health Insurance

Make sure that you have adequate health insurance (see Travel Insurance under Visas & Documents earlier in this chapter for details).

Travel Health Guides

Lonely Planet's handy pocket size *Healthy Travel Africa* is packed with useful information including pretrip planning, emergency first aid, immunisation and disease information and what to do if you get sick on the road.

Travellers' Health by Dr Richard Dawood is easy to read, authoritative and highly recommended, although it's rather large to lug around.

Even bigger is David Werner's *Where There is No Doctor*. This is a very detailed guide intended for someone, such as a long-term development worker or volunteer, going to work in an underdeveloped country.

Travel with Children by Maureen Wheeler and published by Lonely Planet, includes advice on travel health for younger children.

There are also a number of excellent travel health sites on the Internet. From the Lonely Planet homepage there are links at www .lonelyplanet.com/weblinks to the World Health Organization (WHO) and the US Centers for Disease Control & Prevention.

Other Preparations

Make sure you're healthy before you start travelling. If you are going on a long trip, make sure your teeth are OK. If you wear glasses, take a spare pair and your prescription so you can have another pair made up.

If you require a particular medication take an adequate supply, as it may not be available locally. Take part of the packaging showing the generic name rather than the brand, which will make getting replacements easier. It's a good idea to have a legible prescription or letter from your doctor to show that you legally use the medication to avoid any problems.

Basic Rules

Food There is an old colonial adage that says: 'If you can cook it, boil it or peel it you can eat it…otherwise, forget it'. Vegetables and fruit should be washed with purified water or peeled. Beware of ice cream that is sold in the street or anywhere it might have been melted and refrozen; if there's any doubt (eg, a power cut in the last day or two), steer well clear. Shellfish such as mussels, oysters and clams should be avoided, as should undercooked meat, particularly in the form of mince. Steaming does not make shellfish safe for eating.

If a place looks clean and well run and the vendor also looks clean and healthy, then the food is probably safe. In general, places that are packed with travellers or locals will be fine, while empty restaurants are questionable. The food in busy restaurants is cooked and eaten quite quickly with little standing around, and is probably not reheated.

Water The number one rule is *be careful of the water* and especially ice. If you don't know for certain that the water is safe, assume the worst. Tap water in Morocco's larger towns and cities is usually fine, but check locally. Also remember that water with an unusual or strong mineral content is sometimes enough to upset some delicate stomachs.

Reputable brands of bottled water or soft drinks are generally fine, although in some places bottles may be refilled with tap water. Only use water from containers with a serrated seal – not tops or corks. Take care with fruit juice, particularly if water may have been added.

Sealed plastic bags of pasteurised milk are widely available, though in rural areas milk should be treated with suspicion because it is often unpasteurised. Boiled milk is fine if it is kept hygienically. Tea or coffee should also be OK, since the water should have been boiled.

Water Purification The simplest way of purifying water is to boil it thoroughly. Vigorous boiling should be satisfactory; however,

Nutrition

If your diet is poor or limited in variety, if you're travelling hard and fast and therefore missing meals or if you simply lose your appetite, you can soon start to lose weight and place your health at risk.

Make sure your diet is well balanced. Cooked eggs, tofu, beans, lentils and nuts are all safe ways to get protein. Fruit you can peel (bananas, oranges or mandarins, for example) is usually safe and a good source of vitamins. Melons can harbour bacteria in their flesh and are best avoided. Try to eat plenty of grains (including rice) and bread. Remember that although food is generally safer if it is cooked well, overcooked food loses much of its nutritional value. If your diet isn't well balanced or if your food intake is insufficient, it's a good idea to take vitamin and iron pills.

In hot climates make sure you drink enough – don't rely on feeling thirsty to indicate when you should drink. Not needing to urinate or voiding small amounts of very dark yellow urine is a danger sign. Always carry a water bottle with you on long trips. Excessive sweating can lead to loss of salt and therefore muscle cramping. Salt tablets are not a good idea as a preventative, but in places where salt is not used much, adding salt to food can help.

at high altitude, water boils at a lower temperature, so germs are less likely to be killed. Boil it for longer in these environments.

Consider purchasing a water filter for a long trip. There are two main kinds of filter. Total filters take out all parasites, bacteria and viruses and make water safe to drink. They are often expensive, but they can be more cost-effective than buying bottled water. Simple filters (which can even be a nylon mesh bag) take out dirt and larger foreign bodies from the water so that chemical solutions work much more effectively; if water is dirty, chemical solutions may not work at all. It's very important when buying a filter to read the specifications so that you know exactly what it removes from the water and what it doesn't.

Simple filtering will not remove all dangerous organisms, so if you cannot boil water, it should be treated chemically. Chlorine tablets will kill many pathogens, but not some parasites like giardia and amoebic cysts. Iodine is more effective in purifying water and is available in tablet form. Follow the directions carefully and remember that too much iodine can be harmful.

Medical Problems & Treatment

Self-diagnosis and treatment can be risky, so you should always seek medical help. An embassy, consulate or five-star hotel can usually recommend a good local doctor or clinic. Although we do give drug dosages in this section, they are for emergency use only. Correct diagnosis is vital. In this section we have used the generic names for medications – check with a pharmacist for brands available locally.

Note that antibiotics should ideally be administered only under medical supervision. Take only the recommended dose at the prescribed intervals and use the whole course, even if the illness seems to be cured earlier. Stop immediately if there are any serious reactions, and don't use the antibiotic at all if you are unsure that you have the correct one. Some people are allergic to commonly prescribed antibiotics such as penicillin; carry this information (eg, on a bracelet) when travelling.

Environmental Hazards

Altitude Sickness Lack of oxygen at high altitudes (over 2500m) affects most people to some extent. In Morocco, people trekking in the High Atlas are most likely to be affected, although there are mountains in the Middle and Anti Atlas ranges that reach high enough for altitude sickness, or Acute Mountain Sickness (AMS), to be a problem.

There is no hard-and-fast rule as to what is too high: AMS has been fatal at 3000m, although 3500m to 4500m is the usual range. The effect may be mild or severe and occurs because less oxygen reaches the muscles and the brain at high altitude, requiring the heart and lungs to compensate by working harder.

Symptoms of AMS usually develop during the first 24 hours at altitude but may be delayed up to three weeks. Mild symptoms include headache, lethargy, dizziness, difficulty sleeping and loss of appetite. AMS may become more severe without warning and can be fatal. Severe symptoms include breathlessness, a dry and irritative cough (which may progress to the production of pink, frothy sputum), severe headache, lack of coordination and balance, confusion, irrational behaviour, vomiting, drowsiness and unconsciousness.

Treat mild symptoms by resting at the same altitude until recovery, usually a day or two. Paracetamol or aspirin can be taken for headaches. If symptoms persist or become worse, however, *immediate descent is necessary;* even 500m can help. Drug treatments should never be used to avoid descent or to enable further ascent.

The drugs acetazolamide and dexamethasone are recommended by some doctors for the prevention of AMS; however, their use is controversial. They can reduce the symptoms, but they may also mask warning signs; severe and fatal AMS has occurred in people taking these drugs. In general we do not recommend them for travellers.

To prevent acute mountain sickness:

- Ascend slowly – have frequent rest days, spending two to three nights at each rise of 1000m. If you reach a high altitude by trekking, acclimatisation takes place gradually and you are less likely to be affected than if you fly directly to high altitude.
- It is always wise to sleep at a lower altitude than the greatest height reached during the day if possible. Also, once above 3000m, care should be taken not to increase the sleeping altitude by more than 300m per day.
- Drink extra fluids. The mountain air is dry and cold, and moisture is lost as you breathe. Evaporation of sweat may occur unnoticed and result in dehydration.
- Eat light, high-carbohydrate meals for more energy.
- Avoid alcohol, as it may increase the risk of dehydration.
- Avoid sedatives.

Heat Exhaustion Dehydration and salt deficiency can cause heat exhaustion. Take time to acclimatise to high temperatures,

---

Everyday Health

Normal body temperature is up to 37°C (98.6°F); more than 2°C (4°F) higher indicates a high fever. The normal adult pulse rate is 60 to 100 per minute (children 80 to 100, babies 100 to 140). As a general rule the pulse increases about 20 beats per minute for each 1°C (2°F) rise in fever.

Respiration (breathing) rate is also an indicator of illness. Count the number of breaths per minute: Between 12 and 20 is normal for adults and older children (up to 30 for younger children, 40 for babies). People with a high fever or serious respiratory illness breathe more quickly than normal. More than 40 shallow breaths a minute may indicate pneumonia.

---

drink sufficient liquids and do not do anything too physically demanding.

Salt deficiency is characterised by fatigue, lethargy, headaches, giddiness and muscle cramps; salt tablets may help, but adding extra salt to your food is better.

Anhidrotic heat exhaustion is a rare form of heat exhaustion that is caused by an inability to sweat. It tends to affect people who have been in a hot climate for some time, rather than newcomers. It can progress to heatstroke. Treatment involves removal to a cooler climate.

Heatstroke This serious and occasionally fatal condition can occur if the body's heat-regulating mechanism breaks down and the body temperature rises to dangerous levels. Long, continuous periods of exposure to high temperatures and insufficient fluids can leave you vulnerable to heatstroke.

The symptoms are feeling unwell, not sweating very much (or at all) and a high body temperature (39°C to 41°C or 102°F to 106°F). Where sweating has ceased, the skin becomes flushed and red. Severe, throbbing headaches and lack of coordination will also occur, and the sufferer may be confused or aggressive. Eventually, the victim will become delirious or convulse. Hospitalisation is essential but in the interim, get victims out of the sun, remove their clothing, cover them with a wet sheet or towel and then fan continually. Give fluids if they are conscious.

Hypothermia Too much cold can be just as dangerous as too much heat. If you are trekking at high altitudes or simply taking a long bus trip over mountains, particularly at night, be prepared.

Hypothermia occurs when the body loses heat faster than it can produce it and the core temperature of the body falls. It is surprisingly easy to progress from very cold to dangerously cold due to a combination of wind, wet clothing, fatigue and hunger, even if the air temperature is above freezing. It is best to dress in layers; silk, wool and some of the new artificial fibres are all good insulating materials. A hat is important, as a lot of heat is lost through the head. A strong, waterproof outer layer (and a 'space' blanket for emergencies) is essential. Carry basic supplies, including food containing simple sugars, to generate heat quickly, and fluid to drink.

Symptoms of hypothermia are exhaustion, numb skin (particularly toes and fingers), shivering, slurred speech, irrational or violent behaviour, lethargy, stumbling, dizzy spells, muscle cramps and violent bursts of energy. Irrationality may take the form of sufferers claiming they are warm and trying to take off their clothes.

To treat mild hypothermia, first get the person out of the wind and/or rain, remove their clothing if it's wet and replace it with dry, warm clothing. Give them hot liquids – not alcohol – and some high-kilojoule, easily digestible food. Do not rub victims: instead, allow them to slowly warm themselves. This should be enough to treat the early stages of hypothermia. The early recognition and treatment of mild hypothermia is the only way to prevent severe hypothermia, which is a critical condition.

Jet Lag Jet lag is experienced when a person travels by air across more than three time zones (each time zone usually represents a one-hour time difference). It occurs because many of the functions of the human body (such as temperature, pulse rate and emptying of the bladder and bowels) are regulated by internal 24-hour cycles. When we travel long distances rapidly, our bodies take time to adjust to the 'new time' of our destination, and we may experience fatigue, disorientation, insomnia, anxiety, impaired concentration and loss of appetite. These effects will usually be gone within three days of arrival, but to minimise the impact of jet lag:

- Rest for a couple of days prior to departure.
- Try to select flight schedules that minimise sleep deprivation; arriving late in the day means you can go to sleep soon after you arrive. For very long flights, try to organise a stopover.
- Avoid excessive eating (which bloats the stomach) and alcohol (which causes dehydration) during the flight. Instead, drink plenty of noncarbonated, nonalcoholic drinks such as fruit juice or water.
- Avoid smoking.
- Make yourself comfortable by wearing loose-fitting clothes and perhaps bringing an eye mask and ear plugs to help you sleep.
- Try to sleep at the appropriate time for the time zone you are travelling to.

Motion Sickness Eating lightly before and during a trip will reduce the chances of motion sickness. If you are prone to motion sickness, try to find a place that minimises movement – near the wing on aircraft, close to midships on boats, near the centre on buses. Fresh air usually helps; reading and cigarette smoke don't. Commercial motion-sickness preparations, which can cause drowsiness, have to be taken before the trip commences. Ginger (available in capsule form) and peppermint (including mint-flavoured sweets) are natural preventatives.

Prickly Heat Prickly heat is an itchy rash caused by excessive perspiration trapped under the skin. It usually strikes people who have just arrived in a hot climate. Keeping cool, bathing often, drying the skin and using talcum or prickly heat powder or resorting to air-conditioning may help.

Sunburn In the tropics, the desert or at high altitude, you can get sunburnt surprisingly quickly, even through cloud. Use sunscreen, a hat, and a barrier cream for your nose and lips. Calamine lotion or a commercial after-sun preparation is good for mild sunburn. Protect your eyes with quality sunglasses, especially if you'll be near water, sand or snow.

Infectious Diseases

Diarrhoea Simple things like a change in water, food or climate can all cause a mild bout of diarrhoea, but a few rushed toilet trips with no other symptoms is not indicative of a major problem. Dehydration is the main danger with any diarrhoea, particularly in children or the elderly, as dehydration can occur quite quickly. Under all circumstances *fluid replacement* is the most important thing to remember. Weak black tea with a little sugar, soda water, or soft drinks allowed to go flat and diluted 50% with clean water are all good.

With severe diarrhoea, a rehydrating solution is preferable to replace minerals and salts lost. Commercially available oral rehydration salts (ORS) are very useful; add them to safe (boiled, bottled or purified) water. In an emergency you can make up a solution of six teaspoons of sugar and a half teaspoon of salt to a litre of safe water. You need to drink at least the same volume of fluid that you are losing in bowel movements and vomiting. Urine is the best guide to the adequacy of replacement – if you have small amounts of concentrated urine, you need to drink more. Keep drinking small amounts often. Stick to a bland diet as you recover.

Gut-paralysing drugs such as loperamide or diphenoxylate can be used to bring relief from the symptoms, although they do not actually cure the problem. Only use these drugs if you do not have access to toilets, eg, if you *must* travel. Note that these drugs are not recommended for children under 12 years.

In certain situations antibiotics may be required: diarrhoea with blood or mucus (dysentery), any diarrhoea with fever, profuse watery diarrhoea, persistent diarrhoea not improving after 48 hours and severe diarrhoea. These suggest a more serious cause of diarrhoea and gut-paralysing drugs should be avoided.

In these situations a stool test may be necessary to diagnose what bug is causing your diarrhoea, so you should seek medical help urgently. Where this is not possible, the recommended drugs for bacterial diarrhoea (the most likely cause of severe diarrhoea in travellers) are norfloxacin 400mg twice daily for three days or ciprofloxacin 500mg twice daily for five days. These are not recommended for children or pregnant women. The drug of choice for children would be co-trimoxazole, with dosage dependent on weight. A five-day course is given. Ampicillin or amoxycillin may be given in pregnancy, but medical care is necessary.

Two other causes of persistent diarrhoea in travellers are giardiasis and amoebic dysentery.

Giardiasis is caused by a common parasite, *Giardia lamblia*. Symptoms include stomach cramps, nausea, a bloated stomach, watery, foul-smelling diarrhoea and frequent gas. Giardiasis can appear several weeks after you have been exposed to the parasite. The symptoms may disappear for a few days and then return; this can go on for several weeks.

Amoebic dysentery, caused by the protozoan *Entamoeba histolytica,* is characterised by a gradual onset of low-grade diarrhoea, often with blood and mucus. Cramping abdominal pain and vomiting are less likely than in other types of diarrhoea, and fever may not be present. It will persist until treated and can recur and cause other health problems.

You should seek medical advice if you think you have giardiasis or amoebic dysentery, but where this is not possible, tinidazole or metronidazole are the recommended drugs. Treatment is a 2g single dose of tinidazole or 250mg of metronidazole three times daily for five to 10 days.

Fungal Infections Fungal infections occur more commonly in hot weather and are usually found on the scalp, between the toes (athlete's foot) or fingers, in the groin and on the body (ringworm). You get ringworm (which is a fungal infection, not a worm) from infected animals or other people. Moisture encourages these infections.

To prevent fungal infections wear loose, comfortable clothes, avoid artificial fibres, wash frequently and dry yourself carefully. If you do get an infection, wash the infected area at least daily with a disinfectant or medicated soap and water, and rinse and dry well. Apply an antifungal cream or powder like tolnaftate. Try to expose the infected area to air or sunlight as much as possible and wash all towels and underwear in hot water, change them often and let them dry in the sun.

Hepatitis Hepatitis is a general term for inflammation of the liver. It is a common disease worldwide. There are several different viruses that cause hepatitis, and they differ in the way that they are transmitted. The symptoms are similar in all forms of the illness and include fever, chills, headache, fatigue, feelings of weakness and aches and pains, followed by loss of appetite, nausea, vomiting, abdominal pain, dark urine, light-coloured faeces, jaundiced (yellow) skin and yellowing of the whites of the eyes. People who have had hepatitis should avoid alcohol for some time after the illness, as the liver needs time to recover.

Hepatitis A is transmitted by contaminated food and drinking water. You should seek medical advice, but there is not much you can do apart from resting, drinking lots of fluids, eating lightly and avoiding fatty foods. Hepatitis E is transmitted in the same way as hepatitis A; it can be particularly serious in pregnant women.

There are almost 300 million chronic carriers of **hepatitis B** in the world. It is spread through contact with infected blood, blood products or body fluids, eg, through sexual contact, unsterilised needles and blood transfusions, or contact with blood via small breaks in the skin. Other risk situations include having a shave, tattoo or body piercing with contaminated equipment.

The symptoms of hepatitis B may be more severe than type A and the disease can lead to long term problems such as chronic liver damage, liver cancer or a long-term carrier state. Hepatitis C and D are spread in the same way as hepatitis B and can also lead to long-term complications.

There are vaccines against hepatitis A and B, but there are currently no vaccines against the other types of hepatitis. Following the basic rules about food and water (hepatitis A and E) and avoiding risk situations (hepatitis B, C and D) are important preventative measures.

HIV & AIDS Infection with the human immunodeficiency virus (HIV) may lead to acquired immune deficiency syndrome (AIDS), which is fatal. Any exposure to blood, blood products or body fluids may put the individual at risk. The disease is often transmitted through sexual contact or dirty needles – vaccinations, acupuncture, tattooing and body piercing can be potentially as dangerous as intravenous drug use. HIV/AIDS can also be spread through infected blood transfusions; some developing countries cannot afford to screen blood used for transfusions.

AIDS (or SIDA in French) is an increasing problem in Morocco, as everywhere. In 2000 some 33.4 million people in Africa were infected with HIV (up nearly six million on the previous year) while 7.7 million people were suffering from full-blown AIDS.

As yet there is little public awareness of the disease in Morocco, and despite the efforts of the medical profession, there's considerable ignorance. Although the number of cases of HIV in Morocco is very low (less than two cases per 100,000 head of population) compared even to Europe, it's still a serious problem among high-risk groups.

If you do need an injection, ask to see the syringe unwrapped in front of you, or take a needle and syringe pack with you.

Fear of HIV infection should never preclude treatment for serious medical conditions.

Intestinal Worms These parasites are most common in poor and rural areas. Different worms have different ways of infecting people. Some may be ingested with food such as unwashed fruit and vegetables and undercooked meat (eg, tapeworms) and others enter through your skin (eg, hookworms).

Infestations may not show up for some time, and although they are generally not serious, if left untreated some can cause severe health problems later. Moroccan chemists can recommend treatment, though if you're feeling unwell, consider having a stool test when you return home. The precise parasite can then be identified and eliminated.

Meningococcal Meningitis This serious disease can be fatal. There are recurring epidemics in sub-Saharan Africa and the meningitis season falls at the time most people would be attempting the overland trip across the Sahara – the northern winter before the rains come.

Although in most of Morocco it is not an issue, people penetrating to the very south of the country or going beyond should be aware of the potential danger. The disease is spread through close contact with people who carry it in their throats and noses and spread it through coughs and sneezes, although they may not be aware that they are carriers.

A fever, severe headache, sensitivity to light and neck stiffness that prevents forward bending of the head are the first symptoms. There may also be purple patches on the skin. Death can occur within a few hours, so urgent medical treatment is required.

Treatment is large doses of penicillin given intravenously, or chloramphenicol injections.

Schistosomiasis Also known as bilharzia, this disease is transmitted by minute worms. They infect certain varieties of freshwater snails found in rivers, streams, lakes and particularly behind dams. The worms multiply and are eventually discharged into the water.

The worm enters through the skin and attaches itself to your intestines or bladder. The first symptom may be a general feeling of being unwell, or a tingling and sometimes a light rash around the area where it entered. Weeks later a high fever may develop. Once the disease is established, abdominal pain and blood in the urine are other signs. The infection often causes no symptoms until the disease is well established (several months to years after exposure) and damage to internal organs is irreversible.

The main method of preventing the disease is to avoid swimming or bathing in fresh water where bilharzia is present. Even deep

water can be infected. If you do get wet, dry off quickly and dry your clothes as well.

A blood test is the most reliable way to diagnose the disease, but the test will not show positive until a number of weeks after exposure.

Sexually Transmitted Infections HIV/AIDS and hepatitis B can be transmitted through sexual contact – see the relevant entries earlier for more details. Other sexually transmitted infections (STIs) include gonorrhoea, herpes and syphilis; sores, blisters or rashes around the genitals and discharges or pain when urinating are common symptoms.

In some STIs, such as wart virus or chlamydia, symptoms may be less marked or not observed at all, especially in women. Chlamydia infection can cause infertility in men and women before any symptoms have been noticed.

Syphilis symptoms eventually disappear completely but the disease continues and can cause severe problems in later years. While abstinence from sexual contact is the only 100% effective prevention, using condoms is also effective. The treatment of gonorrhoea and syphilis is with antibiotics. The different sexually transmitted diseases each require specific antibiotics.

Typhoid Typhoid fever is a dangerous gut infection caused by contaminated water and food. Medical help must be sought.

In its early stages sufferers may feel they have a bad cold or flu on the way, as early symptoms are a headache, body aches and a fever that rises a little each day until it is around 40°C (104°F) or more. The victim's pulse is often slow relative to the degree of fever present – unlike the situation with a normal fever where the pulse increases. There may also be vomiting, abdominal pain, diarrhoea or constipation.

In the second week the high fever and slow pulse continue and a few pink spots may appear on the body; trembling, delirium, weakness, weight loss and dehydration may occur. Complications such as pneumonia, perforated bowel or meningitis may occur.

Cuts, Bites & Stings

See Less Common Diseases later in this section for details of rabies and malaria.

Cuts & Scratches Wash well and treat any cut with an antiseptic such as povidone-iodine.

Bedbugs & Lice Bedbugs live in various places, but particularly in dirty mattresses and bedding, evidenced by spots of blood on bedclothes or on the wall. Bedbugs leave itchy bites in neat rows. Calamine lotion or a sting relief spray may help.

All lice cause itching and discomfort. They make themselves at home in your hair (head lice), your clothing (body lice) or in your pubic hair (crabs). You catch lice through direct contact with infected people or by sharing combs, clothing and the like. Powder or shampoo treatment will kill the lice, and infected clothing should then be washed in very hot, soapy water and left in the sun to dry.

Stings Bee and wasp stings are usually painful rather than dangerous. However, in people who are allergic to them, severe breathing difficulties may occur and require urgent medical care. Calamine lotion or a sting relief spray will give relief and ice packs will reduce the pain and swelling.

Ticks Always check all over your body if you have been walking through a potentially tick-infested area, as ticks can cause skin infections and other more serious diseases. If a tick is found attached, press down around the tick's head with tweezers, grab the head and gently pull upwards. Smearing chemicals on the tick will not make it let go and is not recommended.

Snakes To minimise your chances of being bitten, always wear boots, socks and long trousers when walking through undergrowth where snakes may be present. When hopping over logs or rocks, always look down to where your feet will land – snakes love these sheltered spots. Don't put your hands into holes and crevices, and be careful when collecting firewood.

Snake bites do not cause instantaneous death and antivenins are usually available. Immediately wrap the bitten limb tightly, as you would for a sprained ankle, and then attach a splint to immobilise it. Keep the victim still and seek medical help, if possible have the dead snake for identification. However, don't attempt to catch the snake if there is any possibility of being bitten again. Tourniquets and sucking out the poison are now comprehensively discredited.

The huge majority of snake bites in Morocco are nonfatal, though the nastier species inhabit the drier areas south-east of the High Atlas.

Scorpions Five species of scorpion inhabit arid regions of Morocco – be careful to shake out shoes and clothing before getting dressed. Their stings are notoriously painful and the best treatment is a local anaesthetic.

Women's Health

Gynaecological Problems Antibiotic use, synthetic underwear, sweating and contraceptive pills can lead to fungal vaginal infections, especially when travelling in hot climates. Thrush or vaginal candidiasis is characterised by a rash, itch and discharge. Nystatin, miconazole or clotrimazole pessaries are the usual treatment, but some people use a more traditional remedy involving vinegar or lemon juice douches, or yogurt. Maintaining good personal hygiene and wearing loose-fitting clothes and cotton underwear may help prevent these infections.

Sexually transmitted infections are a major cause of vaginal problems. Symptoms include a smelly discharge, painful intercourse and sometimes a burning sensation when urinating. Medical attention should be sought and male sexual partners must also be treated. For more details see the earlier entry on Sexually Transmitted Infections. Besides abstinence, the best thing is to practise safer sex using condoms.

Pregnancy Travelling to Morocco while pregnant does pose some problems. First, the use of some vaccinations normally used to prevent serious diseases are not advisable during pregnancy. Also, some diseases are much more serious for the mother during pregnancy and may increase the risk of damage to the unborn child.

Most miscarriages occur during the first three months of pregnancy. Miscarriage is not uncommon and can occasionally lead to severe bleeding. The last three months should also be spent within reasonable distance of good medical care (not always easy in Morocco).

A baby born as early as 24 weeks stands a chance of survival, but only in a good modern hospital. Pregnant women should avoid all unnecessary medication, although vaccinations and malarial prophylactics should still be taken where needed. Additional care should be taken to prevent illness, and particular attention should be paid to diet and nutrition. Alcohol and nicotine, for example, should be avoided.

Less Common Diseases

The following diseases pose a small risk to travellers in Morocco and so are only mentioned in passing. Seek medical advice if you think you may have any of these diseases.

Cholera This is the worst of the watery diarrhoeas and medical help should be sought. Outbreaks of cholera are generally widely reported, so you can avoid such problem areas. *Fluid replacement is the most vital treatment* – the risk of dehydration is severe, as you may lose up to 20L a day. If there is a delay in getting to hospital, begin taking tetracycline. The adult dose is 250mg four times daily. It is not recommended for children under nine years or for pregnant women. Tetracycline may help shorten the illness, but adequate fluids are required to save lives.

Filariasis This is a mosquito-transmitted parasitic infection found in many parts of Africa, including Morocco, and also in Asia, Central and South America and the Pacific. Possible symptoms include fever, pain and swelling of the lymph glands; inflammation of lymph drainage areas; swelling of a limb or the scrotum; skin rashes; and blindness. Treatment is available to eliminate the parasites from the body, but some of the damage already caused may not be reversible. Medical advice should be obtained promptly if the infection is suspected.

Leishmaniasis This is a group of parasitic diseases transmitted by sandflies, which are found in some areas of Morocco. *Cutaneous leishmaniasis* affects the skin tissue, causing ulceration and disfigurement, and visceral leishmaniasis affects the internal organs.

Seek medical advice, as laboratory testing is required for diagnosis and correct treatment. Avoiding sandfly bites is the best precaution. Bites from these tiny flies are usually painless but itchy, and another reason to cover up and apply repellent.

Malaria Malaria is a minimal problem in Morocco and highly unlikely to affect travellers. A program to drain wetlands in the 1960s virtually eradicated the disease from the country. Annually only a handful of people in the south of Morocco contract a mild variant of the disease. If you expect to be in the extreme south of Morocco during high summer, or plan to continue moving south into the 'malaria belt' of equatorial Africa, get expert advice on antimalarial drugs.

If you are travelling in endemic areas, it is extremely important to avoid being bitten by mosquitoes and to take tablets to prevent this disease. Symptoms range from fever, chills and sweating, headache, diarrhoea and abdominal pains to a vague feeling of ill-health. Seek medical help immediately; without treatment malaria can rapidly become more serious and can be fatal.

Travellers are advised to prevent mosquito bites at all times. The main messages are:

- Wear light-coloured clothing.
- Wear long trousers and long-sleeved shirts.
- Use mosquito repellents containing the compound DEET on exposed areas (prolonged overuse of DEET may be harmful, especially to children, but its use is considered preferable to being bitten by disease-transmitting mosquitoes).
- Avoid perfumes or aftershave.
- Use a mosquito net impregnated with mosquito repellent (permethrin) – it may be worth taking your own.

• Impregnating clothes with permethrin effectively deters mosquitoes and other insects.

Rabies According to a recent newspaper report, there are more than 500,000 stray dogs in Morocco, and a good few have rabies. Reports of rabies have been recently confirmed in the cities of Oujda, Nador, Khouribga, Casablanca and Marrakesh. While the chance of contracting rabies is small, give any dog a wide berth. Vicious, snapping, barking dogs attached to farms and remote homesteads will bite given half a chance, and you should be doubly careful around these beasts.

However, many animals can be infected (such as cats, bats and monkeys) with rabies and it's their saliva which is infectious. Any bite, scratch or even lick from an animal should be cleaned immediately and thoroughly. Scrub the bite thoroughly with soap and running water, apply alcohol or iodine. Medical help should be sought promptly to receive a course of injections to prevent the onset of symptoms and death.

Tetanus This disease is caused by a germ which lives in soil and in the faeces of horses and other animals. It enters the body via breaks in the skin (dog bites are a common cause). The first symptom may be discomfort in swallowing or stiffening of the jaw and neck; this is followed by painful convulsions of the jaw and whole body. The disease can be fatal. It can be prevented by vaccination.

Tuberculosis (TB) TB is a bacterial infection usually transmitted from person to person by coughing but which may be transmitted through consumption of unpasteurised milk. Milk that has been boiled is safe to drink, and the souring of milk to make yogurt or cheese also kills the bacilli.

Travellers are usually not at great risk as close household contact with the infected person is usually required before the disease is passed on. You may need to have a TB test before you travel, as this can help diagnose the disease later if you become ill.

Typhus This disease is spread by ticks, mites or lice. It begins with fever, chills, headache and muscle pains followed a few days later by a body rash. There is often a large painful sore at the site of the bite and nearby lymph nodes are swollen and painful. Typhus can be treated under medical supervision. Seek local advice on areas where ticks pose a danger and always check your skin carefully for ticks after walking in a danger area such as a tropical forest. An insect repellent can help, and walkers in tick-infested areas should consider having their boots and trousers impregnated with benzyl benzoate and dibutylphthalate.

WOMEN TRAVELLERS
Attitudes Towards Women

Prior to marriage, Moroccan men have little opportunity to meet and get to know women, which is why Western women receive so much attention. Not bounded by the Moroccan social structure and Islamic law, these women are seen as excitingly independent, somewhat exotic and generally available!

Around 70% of Morocco's population is under the age of 30 and by the end of their trip most women may think they've met every male in this group and have barely even said hello to a female. The constant attention soon becomes wearing, and no matter the tactic employed, impossible to shake off. There are very few places to be alone; men will seek you out wherever you are and while some of the moves they employ, such as circling for a while before directly approaching you, can be intimidating and overwhelming, they are rarely threatening. One traveller offers this advice:

When trying to rid ourselves of unwanted attention, my sister and I, as unaccompanied women, reacted assertively and then, when this didn't work, aggressively, saying 'f*** off' etc. Moroccan men find this very hard to deal with, often they will react violently with aggressive outbursts and sometimes they will spit on you.

In the end, we discovered the magic word was respect. We would say calmly and firmly, 'I would like to be alone right now and spend time with my sister. Please respect my wishes and leave now'. Because you have made it clear that if they stay they are not respecting you, they run a mile. It was fantastic and quite a relief to discover this.

Megan Brayne

It will soon become clear that there is a prevailing attitude that Western women (and men) are walking visas out of a country where unemployment is rife. Bored youngsters (and the not so young) have everything to gain, and little to lose, by wooing anyone who may be able to offer them an opportunity in another country. That's not to say this is the basis for all mixed nationality relationships (of which there are many success stories), but be aware that some hedge their bets and could be juggling several relationships at any one time. Even if you do take it all with a sack full of salt, you still may end up believing you *must* be the most beautiful woman in the world – it's a great ego-booster.

As a woman travelling alone in Morocco, your first few days are going to be quite intimidating. Everywhere you walk you are likely to be accompanied by tag-teams of men wishing to 'just talk'; walking into coffee shops and restaurants will be difficult as the stares that follow a single female burn through you. Take a few days to acclimatise to the surroundings and then just go with the flow. Talk to the guys, they're a good source of local information – maybe even go for tea where you know there will be other women and/or children – just don't be stupid.

As for those times you do want to be alone, you can try to brazen it out in a cafe or look for the ever increasing number of places accustomed to single Moroccan women's business. *Hammams* (traditional bathhouses) are good male-free zones for a relaxing reprieve; here the stares tend to be innocent and inquisitive rather than penetrating and leery. Hotel terraces too can be extremely relaxing and hassle free – you can even get breakfast up there. Don't be shy of approaching other travellers who will appreciate the hassle you're receiving and may be grateful for someone new to talk to. If that's not enough, consider retreating to a destination such as Marrakesh, Essaouira, Chefchaouen or Agadir, where women can mix with other travellers and fade into relative obscurity.

Women travelling with male companions are likely to encounter a different problem altogether – being invisible. Conversation and transactions will be directed towards the man or men in the party, leaving any woman involved feeling superfluous, to say the least.

Safety Precautions

Moroccans have to be among the most hospitable people in the world. Genuinely welcoming, they are eager to help any traveller and being a woman is a distinct advantage, especially when lost or in some form of distress. Raised according to strict moral codes and with the belief that women have a specific role in society, Moroccans tend to be genuinely concerned for the 'weaker sex' and will offer protection and support if you feel you are in a potentially dodgy situation.

Although drugs and alcohol are having an increasing effect in Morocco, crimes against women remain rare. Only slightly more common is verbal abuse from both men and women, and in extreme circumstances physical harassment such as being stoned. While there's no need for paranoia, it's always a good idea to take a few sensible precautions.

- Don't hitchhike.
- Be aware that some budget hotels double as brothels; don't compromise your safety for the sake of economy.
- On public transport try to sit next to a woman – especially in grand taxis where you're squeezed in far too closely for comfort, and trains where you could potentially be trapped in a compartment.
- Don't wander about alone at night as there's an attitude that, all 'good women' should be at home after dark – take a taxi.
- Avoid walking in remote areas alone such as isolated beaches, forests and sand dunes.
- If you need a drink, head for a large hotel rather than a 'bunker-style' all-male preserve – any woman here is without doubt a prostitute, but then so are many of those in the posher places.

A wedding ring is a very useful accessory. Moroccans of both sexes wear these (someone once defined a prostitute as a 'woman without a wedding ring'). A photo of your 'husband' and 'child' will help immeasurably, although the fact that you're travelling without them will attract suspicion.

Wearing dark glasses is good for avoiding eye contact and a good humoured *'non mercie'* or *'la shukran'* is much more effective than abuse.

Always dress modestly (see Dos & Don'ts under Society & Conduct in the Facts about Morocco chapter) and be aware that hotel and public swimming pools usually attract groups of men, whether they be swimming themselves or drinking at a pool-side bar. Skimpy bikinis will attract attention. At the other end of the scale, sporting a *jellaba* (flowing garment) will earn you respect as well as a million questions as to why you're wearing it: Are you Muslim? Are you Moroccan? Are you married to a Moroccan?

MEN TRAVELLERS

If you're travelling with your wife or girlfriend, Moroccan men will expect you, like them, to put up a good macho display. You must play very protective and jealous; if you don't, some Moroccans will assume that your friend or wife is available for all to appreciate.

All 'decent' women are safely at home by nightfall. Consequently, almost all the women in bars, discos, cafes and nightclubs are working as prostitutes. They are young, attractive and often soberly dressed. It is frequently impossible to differentiate between 'those who are and those who are not', but any woman who approaches you is certainly a prostitute. Even if you just chat, you will be expected to pay for her drinks.

In the main, Moroccans dress conservatively and it's wise for travellers – men included – to cover themselves up. Day-to-day transactions, serious bargaining sessions and general conversation will go better if you slip those hairy legs into a pair of trousers.

GAY & LESBIAN TRAVELLERS

Homosexual acts are officially illegal in Morocco – in theory you can go to jail and/or be fined. However, although not openly admitted or shown, male homosexuality remains relatively common. Male homosexuals are advised to be discreet – aggression towards gay male travellers is not unheard of.

It's really hard, and unhelpful, to categorise the 'gay' places in Morocco. Tangier was once popular, and still is to a lesser extent in summer, but gay travellers follow the same itineraries as everyone else, the most popular destinations being Fès and Marrakesh. 'Gay' bars can be found here and there, but Moroccan nightlife tends to include something for everybody.

Lesbians shouldn't encounter any particular problems, though it's commonly believed by Moroccans that there are no lesbians in their country. Announcing that you're gay probably won't make would-be Romeos magically disappear. For Moroccan men it may simply confirm their belief that Western men don't measure up in the sexual department.

Platonic affection is freely shown in Morocco. You'll see men, more so than women, holding hands. But heterosexual public affection isn't freely shown – it's difficult for single men and women even to meet.

The *Spartacus International Gay Guide*, published annually, includes information about Morocco and lists 'gay' bars and clubs in the bigger cities, as well as health clinics and places to stay.

In the USA, *QT Magazine* (www.qtmagazine.com) is a travel magazine for gays and lesbians, while www.gay-travel.com and www.gaywired.com are both excellent general travel resources.

DISABLED TRAVELLERS

Morocco has few facilities for the disabled. But that doesn't necessarily make it out of bounds for those who do have a physical disability (and a sense of adventure). Not all hotels have lifts (and certainly very few of the cheaper ones), so booking ground-floor hotel rooms ahead of time would be essential. Travelling by car is probably the best transport, though you'll be able to get assistance in bus and train stations (though a tip will be required).

Get in touch with your national support organisation (preferably the 'travel officer' if there is one) before leaving home. They often have travel literature to help with holiday planning and can put you in touch with travel agents who specialise in tours for the disabled.

In the UK, the Royal Association for Disability & Rehabilitation (☎ 020-7250 3222, fax 7250 0212), 12 City Forum, 250 City Rd, London EC1V 8AF, produces three holiday fact packs for disabled travellers. They cost UK£2 each and cover planning, insurance, useful organisations, transport, equipment and specialised accommodation.

Also in the UK, contact Holiday Care Service (☎ 01293-774535, minicom 776943), which prints a fact sheet on Morocco; Web site www.holidaycare.org.uk.

In the USA, Access-Able Travel Source (☎ 303-232 2979, e carol@access-able .com), PO Box 1796, Wheatridge, Co. Its Web site is at www.access-able.com.

Australians could try contacting Wheelchair Travel (☎ 1800-674 468, e sales@ travelability.com), 29 Ranelagh Dr, Mount Eliza, Victoria 3930; its Web site is at www .travelability.com.

In France, contact the CNFLRH (☎ 01 53 80 66 66) at 236 bis Rue de Tolbiac.

Many regular tour operators can tailor-make trips to suit your requirements.

TRAVEL WITH CHILDREN

Moroccan people are generally very friendly, helpful and protective towards children (and their mothers), and there are no particular reasons for not taking young children on holiday with you. The exotic sights and scents of the country will more than make up for any extra planning and complicated arrangements.

Most hotels will not charge children under two years of age. For those between two and 12 years sharing the same room as their parents, it's usually 50% of the adult rate. If you want reasonable toilet and bathroom facilities, you'll need to stay in mid-range hotels.

If you look hard enough, you can buy just about anything you need for young children, though at a price. Large supermarkets in major towns are the best hunting ground.

However, bring as much as possible from home, including any special foods required and high-factor sunscreen. Unfortunately, disposable nappies are a practical solution when travelling despite the environmental drawbacks. International brands are readily available and cost about Dr18 for 10.

To avoid stomach upsets, stick to purified or bottled water. UHT, pasteurised and pow-

dered milk are also widely available. Be extra careful about choosing restaurants, steer clear of salads and stick to piping hot tajines, couscous, soups and omelettes. Moroccan markets are full of delicious fruit and vegies, but be sure to wash and peel them.

It's probably wise to avoid travelling in the interior of the country during midsummer, when temperatures rise to 40°C plus. Always be careful about dehydration and sunburn, even on cloudy days. When travelling, try to break journeys into four- to five-hour stretches, and avoid the hottest time of day. Morocco has a great rail infrastructure and travel by train may be the easiest, most enjoyable option – and children will be able to stretch their legs. The fold-down tables are also handy for drawing and games.

Grand taxis (shared long-distance taxis) and buses can be a real squeeze with young children who don't count as passengers in their own right, but as wriggling luggage – kids have to sit on your lap. The safety record of buses and shared taxis is poor, and many roads are potholed.

Hire-car companies rarely have child seats, so bring your own, and check that they clip into the seat belts.

One reader has reported that letting your kids run amok in carpet shops proved to be an excellent bargaining technique.

For further invaluable advice, see Lonely Planet's *Travel with Children* by Maureen Wheeler.

DANGERS & ANNOYANCES

When all is said and done, Morocco is a comparatively safe place to travel and the great majority of people are friendly and honest. Nevertheless, the country does have a few traps for the unwary.

Theft & Violence

On the whole, theft is not a huge problem in Morocco. Travellers can minimise any risk, however, by being particularly vigilant in the major cities and by generally following a few basic precautions.

When wandering around the streets, keep the valuables you must carry to a minimum and keep what you must carry around with you well hidden. External money pouches attract attention, but neck pouches or moneybelts worn under your clothes do not; that's where you should keep your money, passport and other important documents. Pouches made of cotton are much more comfortable than nylon ones. Pouches can also be customised and sewn into the inside of garments.

In some of the medinas (old parts of town) – such as in Marrakesh and Tangier, which have a particular reputation for petty theft – a common tactic is for one guy to distract you while another cleans out your pockets. Another increasingly common ploy is the dancing pickpocket, who'll sidle up to you, grab you tight and try to do a sort of cancan with you while emptying your pockets (it's popular in Casablanca). There is no point walking around in a state of permanent alert, but keep your eyes open.

Other valuables such as cameras can be left with the hotel reception when you don't want to use them. If you prefer to keep things in your room, nine times out of 10 you'll have no trouble. Where you can, lock everything up. Leaving anything in a car, even out of sight, is asking for grief.

In places like Tangier, physical attacks on foreigners are not entirely unheard of. There are some desperate people in the bigger cities and some feel no compunction about trying to extract money from tourists. Treat the medinas with particular caution at night.

Drugs & Dealers

Morocco's era as a hippie paradise, riding the Marrakesh Express and all that, is long past. Plenty of fine dope (known as kif) may be grown in the Rif Mountains, but drug busts are common and Morocco is not a good place to investigate local prison conditions.

The vast majority of all Moroccan stories of extortion and rip-offs are drug related. A common ploy is to get you stoned, force you to buy a piece the size of a house brick and then turn you over to (or at least threaten to) the police. Or course, once you've been tainted with a little hash, you are unlikely to call the cops, and the hustlers know it.

Associating with Tangier's lowlife is for the initiated only. New arrivals should ignore late-night offers of hashish and grass – these dealers have a sixth sense for greenness, and won't miss an opportunity to squeeze ridiculous amounts of money out of frightened people. Tetouan is another popular venue, but watch out for similar scams in Asilah, Casablanca and Marrakesh. It doesn't matter where you go – offers are a part of the daily routine. Hashish is sometimes referred to as 'chocolate', the Spanish slang, or more often just as 'something special'. You may also have offers of 'shit', which Moroccan dealers apparently feel refers to the same substance.

.. If Sir could just read this letter..

MICK WELDON

With friends like these who needs enemies!

Munching Majoun

You may occasionally come across someone offering you *majoun*, a kind of sticky, pasty mass (not unlike molasses) made of crushed seeds of the marijuana plant.

A small ball of this can send your head into a bit of a spin (see Paul Bowles' *Their Heads Are Green* or *Let It Come Down* for descriptions).

Anyone with a slight tendency to paranoia when smoking dope should be aware that this is a common reaction among first-time majoun-munchers.

Gauche, Green & Gullible

Many Moroccans genuinely believe that 'westerners', though perhaps more sophisticated than themselves, are more naive, gullible and even plain stupid. Some, including the notorious *faux guides* (unofficial guides), may try to exploit this.

Very early on in your encounter with these guides, you will be sized up for what you're worth. Apart from the physical indications, such as your watch, shoes, haircut and clothes, you will be assessed from a series of questions: how long you've been in the country, whether it's your first visit, what your job is, whether you have a family (an indication of wealth) etc.

Considered to be the most lucrative nationalities, in descending order, are the Japanese, Americans, Canadians, Australians, northern Europeans, southern Europeans, and Middle-Eastern Arabs. Considered the least lucrative are sub-Saharan Africans and Arabs from other North African countries.

Always pretend that you know the city or country well. A few words of Arabic will convince them of this.

If you feel you're being categorised, you can always cause confusion by pretending you're from some very obscure land. Sometimes it's useful just to play plain stupid and control the situation that way. Be warned though, Moroccans have a real aptitude for languages and it could be you who looks stupid as your new friend starts spouting away in the language you were convinced you'd catch them out with.

Ketama and the Rif Mountains are kif-growing heartland but also offer fantastic scenery and some great trekking opportunities. However, Ketama is a bag-load of trouble and best avoided unless you're accompanied by a reliable guide. The standard game consists of going to great lengths (including forcing your car to stop) to sell vast amounts of the stuff to people. The buyers then find themselves at the mercy of the next police roadblock.

Large numbers of westerners are doing time for trafficking in Morocco. Some people have been found guilty 'by association' – this includes drivers giving lifts to people carrying cannabis in their hand luggage.

Always bear in mind that it is illegal to sell or consume hashish in Morocco – this usually means little if you're discreet. Smoking it in public is inviting trouble.

According to a recent report by the UK NGO (nongovernmental organisation) the Fair Trials Abroad Trust (☎ 020-8332 2800, fax 8332 2810, e f-t-a@freeserve.org), FTA, Bench House, Ham St, Richmond, London TW10 7HR, any possession of drugs leads to automatic conviction. There are currently about 600 EU citizens imprisoned in Morocco and at least 95% are alleged to have committed offences concerning the trafficking or possession of cannabis. Furthermore, the trust, which provides assistance and legal advice to EU nationals imprisoned overseas, believes that up to 10% of those imprisoned may be innocent. Fair Trials has a Web site at www.fairtrialsabroad. org.

If you get in any trouble, your first phone call should always be to your consulate; remember that it's not unknown for the local police to be in on the scam. If you find yourself arrested by the Moroccan police, you won't have much of a legal leg to stand on. Unless you speak fluent Arabic, it is unlikely that any interpreter on hand will be of sufficient standard to translate an accurate statement. Any statement obtained will play a vital part in subsequent judicial proceedings. According to Fair Trials, physical abuse while in custody is commonplace.

As for taking personal supplies of drugs through customs into Spain – plenty of people take the risk, but it is hardly recommended.

Although the police attitude in Spain is relaxed in respect to small amounts of cannabis, Spanish customs will come down hard on people entering the country from Morocco if they find any. If you're taking a car across, the chances that it will be searched are high.

Touts, Guides & Hustlers

The legendary hustlers of Morocco remain an unavoidable part of the Moroccan experience.

A few years ago special *brigade touristique* (tourist police) were set up in the principal tourist centres to clamp down on Morocco's notorious *faux guides* (unofficial guides) and hustlers. Any person suspected of trying to operate as an unofficial guide could face jail and/or a huge fine.

This has reduced, but not eliminated, the problem of faux guides. These people are often desperate to make a living, and they can be persistent and sometimes very unpleasant. You'll still find plenty hanging around the entrances to the big city's medinas and outside bus and train stations. Those disembarking (and embarking) the ferry in Tangier should expect at least some hassle from touts and hustlers trying to pull you one way or the other (usually to a hotel or ferry ticket office where they can expect a commission). Ceuta and Melilla are far more pleasant ports of entry.

To avoid being hounded to within an inch of your life and to help prevent nervous breakdowns and embarrassing incidents of 'medina rage', try the following advice:

How to Spot a Faux Guide

For many travellers in Morocco, it is a constant puzzle how to tell a good Moroccan from a bad one – or rather, one interested in you from one more interested in your wallet.

In general, be suspicious of anyone who approaches you unasked. A real give-away are those who claim to be students. Unfortunately, knowledge of English is often also an unfavourable indication. English is not widely taught at schools and some have learned it in order to exploit what are considered the most lucrative nationalities.

Apart from the more obvious approaches to start up a friendship, such as showing you around town, taking you to a cheap shop, helping you find a hotel etc, other classic approaches include wanting to practise English, help with the reading or deciphering of official documents, medical prescriptions and, more commonly, letters from friends abroad.

Motorists should look out for false hitchhikers and false breakdowns.

- Politely decline all offers of help and exchange a few good-humoured remarks (preferably in Arabic), but don't shake hands or get involved in lengthy conversation.
- Give the impression that you know exactly where you're going or explain that you employed a guide on your first day and now you'd like to explore the town on your own.
- Wear dark sunglasses and retreat to a cafe, restaurant or taxi if you're beginning to lose your cool. In extreme situations, use the word 'police' and look like you mean it.

However, there's no point having a siege mentality. When arriving in a place for the first time, you might even benefit from the services of a guide – official or otherwise (in bus stations this is particularly true). Faux guides are not necessarily complete impostors. Many are very experienced and speak half a dozen languages, and sometimes their main interest is the commission gained from certain hotels or on articles sold to you in the souqs. Be sure to agree on a guiding price before setting off. They charge around Dr50 per day; a few dirham will suffice if you want to be guided to a specific location (like a medina exit). Whatever you give, you'll often get the you-can't-possibly-be-serious look. The best reply is the I've-just-paid-you-well-over-the-odds look. Maintain your good humour and after a couple of days in a place, the hassle tends to lessen. People will recognise you and probably leave you alone content to prey on new arrivals.

Official guides can be engaged through tourist offices and some hotels at the fixed price of Dr150 per half day (plus tip). It's well worth taking a guide when exploring the intricate and confusing medinas of Fès and Marrakesh. Their local knowledge is extensive and they'll save you from being hassled by other would-be guides. If you don't want a shopping expedition included in your tour, make this clear beforehand (all guides, official and faux, take commission from shops).

Drivers should note that motorised hustlers operate on the approach roads to Fès and Marrakesh. These motorcycle nuisances are keen to find you a hotel, camp site and so on, and can be just as persistent as their colleagues on foot.

Streets & Medinas

A minor irritation is the ever-changing street names in Moroccan cities. For years, there's been a slow process of replacing old French and Spanish names with Arabic ones. The result so far is that, depending on whom you talk to, what map you use or which part of the street you are on, you are likely to see up to three different names.

The general Arabic word for street is *sharia* (*zankat* for smaller ones). In the north you'll still find the Spanish *calle* and *avenida,* and more commonly, the French *avenue, boulevard* or *rue.*

In some cases the Arabic seems to have gained the upper hand. This is reflected in this guidebook, in which some streets appear as 'sharia' or 'zankat' if local usage seems to justify it.

Street names won't help much in the labyrinthine medinas, but if you feel you are getting lost, stick to the main paths (which generally have a fair flow of people going either way) and you'll soon reach a landmark or exit.

It's really only when you dive into the maze of little alleys that it becomes more difficult – some would say more fun!

False Hitchhikers

On some of the more popular tourist routes, in particular the road between Marrakesh and Ouarzazate, you may come across professional hitchhikers and people pretending that their cars have broken down. Once you stop to assist them various scams unfold.

See Car & Motorcycle in the Getting Around chapter for more details.

Moroccan Plumbing

Patience is required when it comes to Moroccan plumbing. In the cheap, unclassified hotels that don't have star ratings, cold water is often the norm.

Sometimes hot water is enthusiastically promised, but doesn't come close to the steaming, powerful shower you'd hoped for, and is often only available at certain times of the day. In country areas, water is sometimes heated by a wood fire – but wood is expensive and water is often in short supply.

EMERGENCIES

The police can be reached on ☎ 19, fire brigade on ☎ 15 and the highway emergency service on ☎ 177. French-speaking police can be contacted in Rabat, Casablanca and Tangier on ☎ 172. Another option is to call the emergency number of your embassy.

BUSINESS HOURS

Although it's a Muslim country, for business purposes Morocco adheres to the Western Monday to Friday working week.

In Muslim countries, Friday is the main prayer day, so many businesses have an extended lunch break on Friday afternoon. Business hours are generally adhered to in the main centres, but should be taken with a pinch of a salt.

During Ramadan, office hours are generally from 8 am to 3 or 4 pm.

Banks

In the bigger centres at least, banks tend to be open from 8.30 to 11.30 am and 2.30 to 4.30 pm weekdays, with Friday lunch lasting from 11.15 am and 3 pm to accommodate the main Friday prayers. These times can vary a little. In some of the main tourist cities, bureaus de change keep longer hours and open over the weekend.

The Banque Populaire, BMCE, BMCI and Crédit du Maroc usually maintain a bureau de change open outside normal banking hours at their main branches in the big cities. These booths are good for currency exchange and cash advances on Visa and MasterCard. Times vary from bank to bank, but you can usually change money until 8 pm daily.

Offices

Should you have any need to tangle with Moroccan bureaucracy, government offices are generally open from 8.30 am to noon and 2 to 6.30 pm Monday to Thursday. On Friday, the midday break lasts from about 11.30 am to 3 pm.

Post offices generally keep similar hours, but close around 6 pm. Téléboutiques and Internet cafes are open until around 10 pm.

Museums & Monuments

Most museums are closed on Tuesday and on other days they loosely follow office hours, which means they are usually closed from about noon to 3 pm. Not all of the sights follow this rule, however. Some of the *medersas* (theological colleges) close at noon on Friday.

Shops & Souqs

Shops tend to be open from about 8 am to 6 pm, often closing for a couple of hours in the middle of the day, but there are no strict rules about this. Most shops, apart from grocery stores and the like, close over the weekend.

Medina souqs and produce markets in the *villes nouvelles* (new towns) of the bigger cities tend to wind down on Thursday afternoon and are usually dead on Friday. Souqs in small villages start early and usually wind down before the heat of the afternoon.

PUBLIC HOLIDAYS & SPECIAL EVENTS

All banks, post offices and most shops are shut on the main public holidays. The 10 national secular holidays are:

New Year's Day 1 January
Independence Manifesto 11 January
Labour Day 1 May
National Day 23 May
Young People's Day 9 July
Feast of the Throne 13 July
Allegiance of Wadi-Eddahab 14 August
Anniversary of the King's and People's Revolution 20 August
Anniversary of the Green March 6 November
Independence Day 18 November

Islamic Holidays

Of more significance to the majority of people are the principal religious holidays. Some are celebrated countrywide, but others are local events and all are tied to the lunar Hejira calendar. The word *hejira* refers to the flight of Mohammed from Mecca to Medina in AD 622, which marks the first year of the Islamic calendar (so the year AD 622 is the year 1 AH).

The calendar is about 11 days shorter than the Gregorian calendar, meaning that the holidays fall on different days each year (see the table 'Islamic Holidays'). Although most business hours and daily life are organised around the Gregorian calendar, the religious rhythms of Muslim society are firmly tied to the lunar calendar. Predicting the exact day the holidays will begin is impossible, as this depends on when the new moon is sighted – the decision rests with the religious authorities in Fès.

Ras as-Sana This means New Year's day and is celebrated on the first day of the Hejira calendar year, 1 Moharram.
Achoura A day of public mourning observed by Shiites on 10 Moharram. It commemorates the assassination of Hussein ibn Ali, the grandson of the Prophet Mohammed and pretender to the caliphate, which led to the schism between Sunnis and Shiites. However, for children it can be a joyous occasion. They receive toys and sweets and parade through the streets to the beating of drums.

Mawlid an-Nabi Achoura A lesser feast celebrating the birth of the Prophet Mohammed on 12 Rabi al-Awal. For a long time it was not celebrated at all in the Islamic world. In the Maghreb this is generally known as Mouloud.

Ramadan & Eid al-Fitr Most Muslims, albeit not all with equal rigour, take part in the fasting that characterises the month of Ramadan, a time when the faithful are called upon to renew their relationship with god as a community.

Ramadan is the month in which the Quran was first revealed. From dawn until dusk, Muslims are expected to refrain from eating, drinking, smoking and sex. This can be a difficult discipline and only people in good health are asked to participate. Children, pregnant women and people who are travelling or are engaged in exacting physical work are considered exempt.

Every evening is, in a sense, a celebration. *Iftar* or *ftur*, the breaking of the day's fast, is a time of animated activity when the people of the local community come together to eat and drink and to pray. The Arabic for fasting is *sawm*. You may find yourself being asked *'Inta sa'im?'* ('Are you fasting?') and encouraged to do so if your answer is *'La, ana faatir'* ('No, I am breaking the fast'). Non-Muslims are not expected to participate, even if more pious Muslims suggest you do. Sharing the suffering involved is an important symbolic social element of Ramadan. The peer pressure on unenthusiastic Muslims is considerable.

Restaurants and cafes that are open during the day may be harder to come by and, at any rate, you should try to avoid openly flouting the fast.

The end of Ramadan – or more accurately the first days of the following month of Shawwal – mark Eid al-Fitr, the Feast of the Breaking of the Fast (also known as Eid as-Sagheer, the Small Feast). It generally lasts four or five days, during which just about everything grinds to a halt. This is not a good time to travel, but it can be a great experience if you are invited to share in some of the festivities with a family. It is a very family-oriented feast, much in the way Christmas is for Christians.

The Haj & Eid al-Adha The fifth pillar of Islam, the sacred duty of all who can afford it, is to make the pilgrimage to Mecca – the *haj*. It can be done at any time, but at least once it should be accomplished in Zuul-Hijja, the 12th month of the Muslim year. At this time, thousands of Muslims from all over the world converge on Islam's most holy city. The high point is the visit to the Kaaba, the construction housing the stone of Ibrahim (Abraham) in the centre of the haram, the sacred area into which non-Muslims are forbidden to enter. The faithful, dressed only in a white robe, circle the Kaaba seven times and kiss the black stone. This is one of a series of acts of devotion carried out by pilgrims.

In the past, great caravans set out from Cairo and Damascus, their ranks swollen by pilgrims from all over the Muslim world, to converge on Mecca amid great circumstance and fanfare. Now the national airlines of Muslim countries put on hundreds of extra flights to jet in the faithful, although many Arabs still head for the sacred city overland. Moroccans often drive or take the bus all the way across North Africa to Cairo and the Red Sea, where they take a boat to Aqaba in Jordan and then continue on into Saudi Arabia. Some get boats direct to Jeddah from Suez. It can be a long and frustrating journey.

The haj culminates in the ritual slaughter of a lamb (in commemoration of Ibrahim's sacrifice) at Mina. This marks the end of the pilgrimage and the beginning of Eid al-Adha, or Feast of the Sacrifice (also known as the 'grand feast' or Eid al-Kabeer). Throughout the Muslim world the act of sacrifice is repeated and the streets of towns and cities seem to run with the blood of slaughtered sheep. The holiday runs from 10 to 13 Zuul-Hijja.

Islamic Holidays

Hejira Year	New Year	Prophet's Birthday	Ramadan begins	Eid al-Fitr	Eid al-Adha
1421	06.04.00	14.06.00	27.11.00	27.12.00	06.03.01
1422	26.03.01	03.06.01	16.11.01	16.12.01	23.02.02
1423	15.03.02	23.05.02	05.11.02	05.12.02	12.02.03
1424	04.03.03	12.05.03	25.10.03	24.11.03	01.02.04
1425	22.02.04	01.05.04	14.10.04	13.11.04	21.01.05
1426	11.02.05	20.04.05	03.10.05	02.11.05	10.01.06

CULTURAL EVENTS

Festivals or *moussems* are commonly held in honour of marabouts (local saints). Sometimes no more than an unusually lively market day, quite a few have taken on regional and even national importance. These festivals are common among the Berbers and are usually held during the summer months.

This is one of those religious frontiers where orthodoxy and local custom have met and compromised. The veneration of saints is frowned upon by orthodox Sunni Muslims, but Islam (no less than Christianity) is made up of many parts and sects (see Religion in the Facts about Morocco chapter). Thus these festivals, which take some of their inspiration from a mix of pre-Islamic Berber tradition and Sufi mystic thought, continue.

Some of the more excessive manifestations, such as self-mutilation while in an ecstatic trance, were once not an unusual sight at such gatherings. Today they have all but disappeared in the face of official disapproval of such 'barbarism'.

It's worth making inquiries at tourist offices to determine when moussems and other such festivals are due to happen. Some of the most important, in chronological order, are as follows:

February
Almond Blossom Festival Held in villages near Tafraoute over several days at the end of February.

March
Cotton Harvest Held in Beni Mellal.
Moussem of Moulay Abdallah ben Brahim Held in Ouezzane in late March.

May/June
Essaouira Festival A week-long art and music festival in the seaside town of Essaouira.
Festival of World Sacred Music Held in Fès at the end of June to start of July.
Fête des Cerises (Cherry Festival) Held in June in Sefrou.
Fête des Roses (Rose Festival) Held in late May at El-Kelaâ M'Gouna in the Dadès Valley.
Moussem & Camel Market Held in June at Goulimime; with its big camel market, this is as much a trade affair as a religious get-together.
Moussem of Ben Aissa One of the largest moussems, held at Meknès' Koubba of Sidi Ben Aissa.

Moussem of Moulay Abdallah ben Brahim Held in Ouezzane in May.
Moussem of Moulay Abdelkader Brings the town of Zagora to life during the period of Mouloud.
Moussem of Moulay Abdeslam ben M'chich Alama Held at Beni Arous near Larache.
Moussem of Sidi Bousselham Held in Moulay Bousselham near Larache; this festival sometimes takes place in June.
Moussem of Sidi Ifni Held in the second week in June.
Moussem of Sidi Mohammed Ma al-Ainin Held at Tan Tan, this is an occasion where you may see the so-called 'blue people', the Tuareg nomads from the Sahara. It also acts as a commercial gathering of tribes and usually happens at the end of May or in early June.
National Folklore Festival Held in Marrakesh, this colourful festival runs for 10 days and occurs around the end of May or early June. Although it is essentially a tourist event, it's well worth attending. It attracts groups of dancers, musicians and other entertainers from all over the country.

July
Fête du Miel (Honey Festival) Held at Immouzzer des Ida Outanane, 60km from Agadir.
Moussem at M'diq Held north-west of Tetouan, this festival takes place early in the month.
Sea Harvest Held at Al-Hoceima.

August
International Arts Festival Held in Asilah.
Moussem of Moulay Abdallah Held south of El-Jadida, the festival takes place late in the month.
Moussem of Moulay Idriss Held in Zerhoun, near Meknès.
Moussem of Sidi Ahmed Held in Tiznit, this celebration of prayer occurs towards the end of the month.
Moussem of Sidi Daoud Held in Ouarzazate.
Moussem of Setti Fatma Held in the Ourika Valley, south of Marrakesh.

September
Fête des Fiancés Held in Imilchil, late in the month. Thousands of people gather for three days and women choose prospective husbands.
Marriage Festival Held at Imilchil, this is a kind of marriage market where the women do the choosing.
Moussem of Moulay Idriss II Held in Fès, sometimes in early October.
Moussem of Sidi Allal al-Hadh Held in Chefchaouen.

Moussem of Sidi Moussa or Quarquour Held near El-Kelaa du Straghna, north of Marrakesh.
Moussem of Sidi Yahia Held at Sidi Yahia Oasis, near Oujda, this moussem is one of the bigger celebrations of its type in Morocco.

October
Fête des Dattes (Date Festival) Held in Erfoud in late October.
Fête du Cheval (Horse Festival) Held in Tissa, north-east of Fès, in early October.

ACTIVITIES
Bird-Watching
Morocco is a bird-watchers' paradise. A startling array of species inhabits the country's diverse ecosystems and varied environments. Around 460 species have been recorded in Morocco, many of them migrants passing through in spring and autumn. Some migrate between sub-Saharan Africa and breeding grounds in Scandinavia, Greenland and northern Russia, while others fly to Morocco to avoid the harsh north European winters.

For details of specialist bird-watching books see Books earlier in this chapter.

A possible 'Top Ten' of birding sites are:

Souss-Massa National Park Fantastic birding in estuarine, lagoon and arid environments. Ideal for sea birds, waders and bald ibis.
Essaouira Islands Including Île de Mogador, these are the famed breeding grounds of the rare Eleanora's falcon.
Dayet Aoua This mountain lake in the Middle Atlas is good for viewing water birds, plus short-toed treecreeper, firecrest and the rare Levaillant's woodpecker in the surrounding woods.
Lac de Sidi Bourhaba Beautiful lake and marsh good for spoonbills, marsh harriers, crested coots, marbled teal and African marsh owls.
Merzouga & Erfoud Numerous desert species; in spring a shallow lake appears north-west of Merzouga, attracting flocks of pink flamingos and other water birds.
Strait of Gibraltar Tens of thousands of migratory storks and birds of prey cross the strait in spring and autumn.
Oued Mouloya & Ras el-Mar Excellent for waders, osprey and sea-bird breeding colonies.
Tamri Great spot for seeing the rare bald ibis.
Moulay Bousselham A coastal lagoon holding thousands of wintering waterfowl, waders and flamingos.

Basic Bird-Watching Tips

- A good quality pair of binoculars is essential.
- Birds are generally most active just after dawn and before dusk.
- Do not disturb birds unnecessarily and never handle or disturb eggs or young birds in a nest.
- Dress in drab clothing and approach birds slowly. Avoid sudden movements or loud talk.
- Always ask permission before birding on private property and be careful not to alarm guards when bird-watching near royal residences or government buildings!

Jebel Toubkal & Oukaïmeden Great for raptors, including the lammergeier vulture.

More information on all these sites is given in the relevant chapters.

Camel Treks
For those prepared to sacrifice their bottoms for the ultimate desert experience, several places in the south of the country offer camel expeditions ranging from a couple of days to two weeks.

Autumn (September to October) and winter (November to February) are the only seasons worth considering. Prices start at around Dr150 to Dr300 per person, but vary depending on the number of people involved, the length of the trek and your negotiating skills.

Places to head for include Zagora and Tinfou in the Drâa Valley; M'Hamid, 95km further south; and the Saharan dunes of Merzouga, south-east of Rissani. See the entries under individual towns for more information.

Climbing
As yet, rock climbing is an undeveloped activity in Morocco but there are some sublime opportunities for the vertically inclined.

Anyone contemplating routes should have plenty of experience under their belt and be prepared to bring all their own equipment.

The Todra Gorge is one of the most popular spots and climbing competitions, run by the Royal Moroccan Ski and Mountaineering Federation (☎/fax 02-474979 in Casablanca), are held here. The beautiful Dadès Gorge is also worth exploring.

Areas in the Anti Atlas and High Atlas offer everything from bouldering to very severe routes, and there is some reasonable rock about 12km south-east of the village of Ben Slimane, which is close to Casablanca. Another possible spot is around Âfin Belmesk (branch off the P7 between Settat and Marrakesh at Mechra Benâbbou and head east).

Fishing

In the Mediterranean and Atlantic you'll find bonito, sea perch, mullet, chad and sea bream. Recommended beach fishing areas are around Dakhla, and south of Rabat at Marmoura Beach and Sidi el-Abed.

Saltwater fishing is free. For details on deep-sea fishing, contact the National Fisheries Office (☎ 02-240551, fax 242305), BP 20300, Casablanca.

Freshwater fish found in Morocco include trout, pike, black bass, perch, roach and carp. Some of the creeks around Marrakesh provide good fishing, as does the Oued Bou Regreg; the artificial lake created by the Moulay Youssef Dam is stocked with fish. Many fishers maintain that the best fishing is to be had in the lakes of the Middle Atlas, which are stocked with trout and black bass.

Unfortunately, the situation on freshwater permits seems unclear. Some offices of Eaux et Forêts (the ministry responsible for fishing) state that nonresidents can buy an annual pass covering all the rivers and lakes in Morocco (Dr400; you need two passport photos, a stamp and an address in Morocco), while others claim that only day passes are available to nonresidents (Dr50; one photo and a passport as ID). Apply to Eaux et Forêts in Casablanca (☎ 02-271589), 25 Blvd Brahim Roudani; or Rabat (☎ 07-703325), 11 Rue Moulay Abdel Aziz. The freshwater fishing season is from April to November.

Golf

Golf is high on the list of Morocco's advertised attractions and was a favourite pastime of the late King Hassan II (who was the honorary president of the Moroccan Golf Federation). There are now 17 courses in the country and many more on the drawing board. Some are excellent, some OK, but almost all are well maintained and landscaped.

The oldest course, laid out in 1917, is the Royal Country Club of Tangier (☎ 09-944484, fax 945450), an 18-hole course that one golfing writer has described as 'adventurous'. The Royal Dar es-Salaam (☎ 07-755864, fax 757671), 10km out of central Rabat, is the best and most modern course. It was rated in the top 100 golf courses in the world by *Golf Magazine* and hosts international competitions – the Hassan II Challenge Cup is held here annually.

Some of the other courses are to be found in Marrakesh (Royal Golf Club; ☎ 04-444341, fax 430084), Ben Slimane, Casablanca (Royal Golf d'Anfa; ☎ 02-365355, fax 393374), Mohammedia and Agadir (12km out of town).

A round usually costs Dr300 to Dr400, plus around Dr100 for a caddy (compulsory) and club hire; dress reasonably smartly.

For further information contact the Royal Moroccan Golf Federation (☎ 07-755960, fax 751026) at the Royal Dar es-Salaam club in Rabat. The national tourist office publishes a brochure on golf.

Mountain Biking Ordinary cycling is possible in Morocco, but mountain biking opens up the options considerably. Roads are well maintained, although very often narrow. For the very fit, the vast networks of *pistes* (dirt tracks) and even the footpaths of the High Atlas offer the most rewarding biking. Any bike tour should be well planned, and you'll need to ensure that you have enough supplies, particularly water, for each leg of the journey.

Some adventure holiday companies outside Morocco and a few operators in Marrakesh and elsewhere offer organised mountain-bike trips.

Skiing

Although somewhat rough and ready in comparison to Europe's alpine offerings, skiing is a viable option from November to April.

The opportunities for ski-trekking *(ski randonne)* tend to vary from area to area, but between late December and February tend to be the best times. The area around Azurki (close to Ifrane) in the central High Atlas is worth exploring, and there are hundreds of opportunities in the Middle Atlas and Toubkal Massif (where the higher slopes and peaks usually have a decent cover of snow from January to early April) and the Tichka Plateau in the western High Atlas.

Oukaïmeden, about 70km south of Marrakesh, is a popular downhill ski station that boasts the highest ski lift in North Africa. A one-day lift pass costs around Dr50 and full equipment hire is usually around Dr70 a day. There are a few other spots dotted around the Middle Atlas equipped for snow sport, the best known and equipped being Mischliffen near Ifrane.

For more information, contact the Federation of Ski and Trekking in Le Ministere de la Jeunesse et Sport (☎/fax 02-474979), Boite Postal 15899, Parc de la Ligue Arabe, Casablanca.

Surfing
With thousands of kilometres of ocean coastline, Morocco isn't a bad place to take your board. Surfing has had little attention in Morocco, but you wouldn't be the first to abandon the chill of the European Atlantic for something a little warmer.

The beaches around Kenitra are a safe bet; Plage Mehdiya, just a few kilometres north of Rabat, is said to have a reliable year-round break, and there are a few other places further up the coast towards Larache.

Anchor Point in Agadir has been recommended, although it can be very inconsistent. Taghazout, close by, is a laid-back spot popular with surfers and there are other excellent beaches north of Agadir, close to Tamri.

Essaouira, too, has been singled out by some surfers, though it's a far better windsurfing destination.

For more information contact Oudayas Surf Club (☎ 07-260683, fax 260684) in Rabat. They're friendly and run surfing courses and competitions. The *Storm Rider Guide to Europe* has more detailed listings.

Trekking
Morocco is a superb destination for mountain lovers, offering a variety of year-round trekking possibilities. There are quite a number of adventure travel companies outside Morocco that organise treks in Morocco to suit all abilities (see Organised Tours in the Getting There & Away chapter). If you'd rather do it on your own, it's relatively straightforward to arrange guides, porters and mules for a more independent adventure. Look at paying a minimum of Dr300 per person plus food.

Jebel Toubkal (4167m), the highest peak in the High Atlas mountain range, tends to attract the lion's share of visitors, but great possibilities exist throughout the country. See the Trekking chapter for further details.

White-Water Rafting
A few specialist adventure companies organise rafting trips. The stunning scenery makes the rivers in the High Atlas near Bin el-Ouidane Dam in the area around Azilal and Afourer popular spots.

Windsurfing
The windy conditions at Essaouira make it an even better spot for windsurfers than for their wax-and-board colleagues. You can hire gear on the beach and there's a reasonable windsurfing community here year-round.

Dar Bouazza, south of Casablanca, is another popular spot for windsurfing.

COURSES
Arabic
The business of learning Arabic is fairly undeveloped in Morocco and the possibilities for doing so are strictly limited.

Apart from possible summer courses at the university in Rabat, your best bet would be to head for the Arabic Language Institute (☎ 03-624850, e alifmbox.azure.net) at 2 Rue Ahmed Hiba in Fès.

The institute has been going since 1983 and is affiliated with the American Language Center. Classes are generally quite small, so each student can expect a reasonable amount of individual attention. The institute offers courses over three and six weeks that cost

Dr4150 or Dr7800 (Dr4350 or Dr8200 in the summer). Individual tuition is available for Dr165 per hour. The institute can also help with accommodation, either in hotels or on a homestay basis with Moroccan families.

Some branches of the Institut Français (formerly the Centre Culturel Français) run Arabic courses – this is the case in Tangier. The École Assimil-Formation (☎ 02-312567) is a private school offering language courses in Casablanca.

WORK

Morocco is not the most fruitful ground for digging up work opportunities. A good command of French is usually a prerequisite and a knowledge of Arabic would certainly not go astray. If you do secure a position, your employer will have to help you get a work permit and arrange residency, which can be an involved process. There is some very limited scope for teaching English and volunteer work.

Teaching English

There are a few possibilities of teaching English as a foreign language in Morocco, and Rabat is one of the best places to start looking. First, you could approach the British Council, but you need to be well qualified (an RSA Diploma in Teaching English as a Foreign Language – TEFLA – will do it) and openings are not all that frequent – a few teachers are also recruited directly from the UK.

Another possible source of work is the American Language Center (☎ 07-767103, fax 766255, [e] alcrabat@mtds.com), at 4 Rue Tanger in Rabat. It prefers to take people with experience, and teachers are offered free Arabic and French classes. The separate library (☎ 07-733331) is on the corner of Ave Fès and Ave Meknès.

The American Language Center has schools in Rabat, Casablanca, Kenitra, Tetouan, Marrakesh, Tangier and Fès. Don't get your hopes up, though. These are all fairly small operations and the chances of just walking into a job are not high. Obviously, qualified TEFLA teachers will have a better chance. You could also try your luck

at the International Language Centre (☎ 07-709718) at 2 Rue Tihama, also in Rabat.

The best time to try is around September to October (the beginning of the academic year) and, to a lesser extent, early January. Casablanca has about half a dozen outfits and is also a good hunting ground.

Volunteer Work

There are many organisations in Morocco that organise voluntary work on regional development projects. They generally pay nothing, sometimes not even lodging, and are aimed at young people looking for something different to do for a few weeks over the summer period. Sometimes these organisations are really summer camps and international exchange programs. Chantiers Sociaux Marocains (☎ 07-297184, fax 698950, [e] csm@planete.co.ma), BP 456, Rabat, is one such organisation with international links. However, it is possible to take Arabic courses and there's some scope for teaching English.

Your embassy may be able to put you onto other projects and NGOs, but unless you have a working knowledge of Arabic or Berber, many will not be interested unless you have specific specialist skills.

You could also try these Web sites: www.workingabroad.com and www.idealist.org.

ACCOMMODATION

Camping

You can camp anywhere in Morocco if you have permission from the site's owner, and there are also many official camp sites. Most of the bigger cities have camp sites, often located well out of town and of more use to people with their own transport. Some are worth the extra effort to get to them, but many offer little shade and are hardly worth what you pay. Most have water, electricity, a small restaurant and grocery store. At official sites you'll pay around Dr10 per person, plus Dr10 to pitch a tent; there are extra charges for vehicles. Electricity generally costs another Dr10 and a hot shower is about Dr5.

Hostels

There are hostels (*auberges de jeunesse*) at Asni, Azrou, Casablanca, Chefchaouen,

Fès, Marrakesh, Meknès, Rabat and Tangier. Some hostels have kitchens and family rooms. If you're travelling alone, they are among the cheapest places to stay (between Dr20 to Dr30 a night).

Hotels

You'll find cheap, unclassified hotels (that don't have a star rating) clustered in certain parts of the medinas of the bigger cities. Some of these places are bright and spotless, others haven't seen a mop for years. It's always worth looking around, especially in high season when they tend to crank up prices as high as they think possible. Singles/doubles cost from Dr30/50 and showers are often cold. Don't get too excited by claims of hot water, as this sometimes amounts to little more than a warm trickle. Occasionally, there is an excellent gas heated shower, which costs around Dr5. Where there is no hot water at all, hotel staff can point you in the direction of a local public shower *(douche)* or hammam (see the boxed text 'Hammams').

For a little more, you can often find better, unclassified or one-star hotels outside the medinas. In one-star hotels rooms with shower start at around Dr60/120; rooms in two-star hotels start at around Dr150/200.

The additional stars in the three- and four-star category (from Dr200 to Dr250) get you a TV and a telephone. You'll come across beautiful, older hotels from an elegant era.

Hotels in the five-star category (from Dr1000 for a double) range from rather sterile modern places to former palaces. A third bed in these rooms costs from around Dr45 (one-star) to Dr100 (four- or five-star).

Prices can include breakfast, which is hardly ever a good deal – coffee and a croissant is Dr7 to Dr10 in a cafe.

You'll need to record your passport details and so on when filling in a hotel register. There's also a tourist tax, plus daily government and local taxes. Combined, these range from Dr3 to Dr35 per pseron, per day. Often they're built into the quoted room tariff.

If you are resident in Morocco, you are entitled to a 25% discount on the classified hotel rates in some establishments.

Self-Catering Apartments

If you're travelling in a small group or as a family, it's worth considering self-catering options, particularly in low season, when prices can drop substantially. Agadir and the bigger tourist centres along the Mediterranean and Atlantic coasts have a fair number of apartments with self-catering facilities.

Houses can sometimes be rented, but these tend to be pretty basic. Official prices for self-catered apartments start at Dr110 per person, going up to hundreds of dollars

Hammams

Visiting a *hammam* (traditional bathhouse) is an excellent alternative to cursing under a cold shower in a cheap hotel. They're busy, social places where you'll find gallons of hot water and staff available to scrub you squeaky clean and massage your travel-weary bod. They're good places to chat to the locals, and especially for women, somewhere to relax for as long as you like away from the street hassle.

Every town has at least one hammam, usually tucked away in the medina. Often there are separate hammams for men and women, while others are open to either sex at different hours or on alternate days. They can be difficult to find; some are unmarked and others simply have a picture of a man or woman stencilled on the wall outside. Local people will be happy to direct you to one. Most hammams are very welcoming, but a few (often those close to mosques) are unwilling to accept foreign visitors.

Bring your own towels (in a waterproof bag), a plastic mat or something to sit on, and flip-flops (thongs). Modesty is important: keep your pants or swimming costume on. You'll be given a bucket and scoop – remember to use the communal bucket when filling yours with hot or cold water. Toiletries can be bought at some hammams, as can handfuls of clay called *ghassoul*, which is used to remove grease and for washing the hair.

Hammams usually cost Dr5, with a massage costing an extra Dr15 or so. Most hammams also have showers costing Dr6.

per person for a beautiful *riad* (traditional, lavish Moroccan town house) in Marrakesh.

Village Accommodation

If you are trekking in the High Atlas or travelling off the beaten track elsewhere, you may be offered accommodation in village homes. Many won't have running water or electricity, but you'll generally find them to be a great deal more comfortable than basic hotels (and even mid-range and top-end hotels when it comes to warmth and hospitality).

You should be prepared to pay what you would in an unclassified hotel or mountain refuge.

FOOD

Moroccan cuisine very much reflects the country's rich cultural heritage. The Berber influence remains strong – many standard Moroccan dishes, such as couscous, *tajines* (meat and vegetable stews) and *harira* (spicy lentil soup), are Berber in origin.

The Bedouin Arabs introduced dates, milk, grains and bread, which have remained staples. They are also credited with inventing dried pasta as a way of preserving flour on their long caravan treks across the desert.

The Moors introduced Andalusian foods (olives, olive oil, nuts, fruits and herbs), and the Arabs brought back a wealth of spices from the Spice Islands (modern Indonesia). Added to all this is the more recent influence of the French (a common breakfast, particularly in the cities, is milky coffee with a croissant).

The best cooking is to be enjoyed in the palace restaurants of the major cities and in private homes throughout the country. Moroccans are extremely hospitable and most travellers will find themselves invited to share in a home-cooked meal at least once.

There may be little variety of dishes in out-of-the-way places, but almost everywhere you'll find plenty of deliciously fresh bread, tajines, fruits and nuts. Budget travellers should look out for the weekly markets, which are excellent for stocking up on picnic foods. It's also possible to buy fresh meat or fish and have it cooked for you in a local restaurant.

It's usual in many restaurants to order your meal an hour or two in advance, particularly if you'd like couscous. Moroccans tend to eat their main meal at lunch time. In the evenings they eat fairly early, so if you're outside the major cities and set out for a feed after 8 or 9 pm, you may not find a great deal of choice.

Menus are generally in French and/or Arabic, so a smattering of either or both will be useful in the eating department.

A cheap meal in a cafe/restaurant can cost as little as Dr20. A good three-course meal in a mid-range restaurant will set you back about Dr60 to Dr80. Moving up a little or indulging in non-Moroccan cuisine (at the occasional Italian or Asian spot) will generally cost around Dr80 to Dr100.

If you want to eat in one of the cavernous restaurants decorated like some of the monuments you have visited – and be treated to a folk music show or Egyptian-style belly dancing – the bill per person will be Dr200 plus. Alcohol will substantially up your bill.

As far as styles of eating places go, there are a few options. Compared to cafes, a *salon de thé* is a more gentile place for a drink (and not just tea; coffee, hot chocolate and soft drinks are also available). These are usually light, airy places that serve a good selection of patisseries and often have seating areas inside (often upstairs) that are mainly used by women. Sometimes places that call themselves cafes have a separate upstairs section that is labelled 'salon de thé'.

Grand cafes are male-dominated, smoke-filled and full of character, but women may feel happier to take their coffee at the tables outside. These are based on the huge cafes of France and often consist of a large, open-plan area filled with tables, and pavement seating. The selection of pastries is sometimes limited but most cafes are happy for you to consume those bought elsewhere at their tables.

Grocery Stores

In cities, towns and even villages you will come across tiny grocery stores brimming with all sorts of foods and household necessities. You'll find fresh bread, biscuits, French processed cheese, tins of sardines and packets of teabags. They are good places to buy a little basic food for bus journeys.

Grocery stores generally also stock toilet paper, soap, shampoo, washing powder and sanitary towels. They tend to be open every day until late in the evening.

Street Food

Morocco's cities and bigger towns offer an array of cheap, food stalls where dishes are freshly cooked and eaten outdoors at simple wooden tables (dining at night among the musicians and fire eaters of the Djemaa el-Fna in Marrakesh is a treat).

You'll also find basic snack stands selling fresh baguette-style sandwiches and wandering vendors selling various Moroccan finger foods.

A good, popular meal-in-itself consists of brochettes of *kefta* (seasoned mince lamb) or lamb with salad, fried potatoes and hot sauce all wrapped in bread (about Dr15).

In some places you'll see people selling little pots of steaming snails and others offering hard-boiled eggs, hot chick peas or fava beans served with salt and cumin.

In coastal places, the catch of the day is cooked at stalls in the port area.

Markets

The outdoor street markets of Morocco are a wonderland of fresh fruit and vegetables, mouth-watering preserves and colourful, vital spices. Look out for the following typically Moroccan foods and ingredients.

Ras el-hanout is a warming mixture of many spices added to winter tajines – ingredients include cardamom, mace and nutmeg. Salt-preserved lemons, sold in tall jars, are often used in Moroccan cooking. *Limouns,* which look like limes, are small green Moroccan lemons.

Among the amazing variety of olives on display you'll discover delicious violet-coloured olives preserved with the juice of bitter oranges.

Rich, golden argan oil, found mainly in the Anti Atlas region, is high in vitamin E and has a distinctive peppery flavour. The Berber people use it for cooking; it is said to be good for the skin and for treating infertility.

Soups & Starters

Harira, a thick soup made from lamb stock, lentils, chick peas, onion, garlic, chopped tomatoes, fresh herbs and spices, is popular as a 1st course in the evening, but is substantial enough to make a meal on its own.

During Ramadan, harira (accompanied by dates or honey cakes) is the dish Moroccans traditionally break the day's fast with. There are variations on the traditional harira, including *marrakchia* harira, which is made without meat. Other soups you may be offered include couscous soup, vegetable soup (usually made with lamb broth) and chicken soup with vermicelli.

Mid-range restaurants generally offer a choice of salads as a first course. A typical Moroccan salad you'll come across is one made from finely diced green peppers, tomatoes and garlic. This is sometimes served as a side dish with grilled brochettes or fish.

Briouats – which you'll probably only find in smart city restaurants – are small envelopes of flaky pastry stuffed with fillings such as minced meat, fish, nuts and rice cooked in milk.

Main Dishes

Couscous and tajines are the staples and you'll find them everywhere. Couscous is a dish traditionally consisting of coarsely ground wheat, but today it is more usually made with rolled grains of semolina pasta.

The grains are steamed in the top container of a *couscoussier* (a large, two-tiered pot used specifically to make couscous), while underneath, in the bottom container, meat or vegetables (or both) simmer away for hours in an aromatic broth. Couscous is often served on huge wooden or ceramic platters (to enable large groups to share in the meal) with the tender stew served on the mounded pile of fluffy semolina, accompanied by a fiery hot sauce called *harissa* (see the boxed text 'Harissa' later in this section).

The preparation of couscous is a long and laborious process, so the dish tends to be served only in the family home. It is often only served on Friday and for authentic (and good) couscous in restaurants, you may need to order hours in advance.

Tajines, delicious slow-cooked stews of meat and vegetables flavoured with herbs and spices, are named after the pot they are cooked in – a round, shallow earthernware dish with a tall conical lid. The stew is usually cooked over an individual charcoal brazier and is served piping hot in the tajine. Typically, it's placed in the centre of the table and everyone dips into this with small pieces of bread rather than using knives and forks. The juice is mopped up first, then the vegetables are gathered up and finally the meat is divided up and eaten with the fingers.

There are endless varieties of tajines; some are very simple, others come with the addition of olives or eggs, prunes and almonds or other dried fruits. A Berber speciality is *m'choui,* a whole lamb roasted in the open air, often seasoned with saffron and hot red pepper, and traditionally served with brochettes of lamb's heart and liver. It's often cooked to celebrate festivals.

The most fabulous Moroccan dish of all may well be *pastilla* (*bastaila* in Arabic), a delicious and incredibly rich mixture of pigeon meat and lemon-flavoured eggs, plus almonds, cinnamon, saffron and sugar, encased in layer upon layer of very fine *ouarka* pastry. Even though pastilla is difficult to find outside the major cities (it's common in Fès, where you can buy it from stalls as well as restaurants), try not to leave Morocco without tasting it.

A much simpler dish, popular just about everywhere, is roast chicken served with crispy chips (the chips are often served cold), fresh bread and sometimes a Moroccan salad.

Brochettes (kebabs) are also available everywhere and are usually very good.

You'll find a wealth of seafood, (straight from the day's catch) along the coast, particularly in El-Jadida, Oualidia, Essaouira, Safi and Agadir. The culinary traditions of Portugal and Spain have long been assimilated into the art of preparing seafood, so you're looking at something more exotic than plain fish and chips. Seafood you're likely to be offered includes sardines, sole, sea bass, prawns, calamari (squid), oysters, mussels and occasionally lobster.

No Moroccan meal is complete without a round or two of fresh bread, the 'staff of life'. In the countryside, you can't beat a breakfast of bread dipped in olive oil and washed down with hot, sweet mint tea. A delicious alternative is bread dipped in argan or almond oil (nicer than the standard offering of bread with margarine and apricot jam!). In Berber homes you'll sometimes be offered bread with a bowl of oil and honey – the oil sits on top of the thick sweet honey creating the ultimate dunking experience.

If you're lucky enough to be invited into a Berber home, you'll find the women of the house busy in the smoky kitchen kneading dough and attending to a simmering tajine. The leftover dough is sometimes pressed onto the back wall of the brick fireplace and comes out crispy and boat shaped.

Bread-making is a central activity in most Moroccan homes, and you may see children carrying the uncooked loaves through medina streets. Bread is made each

---

Harissa

A condiment made from hot red peppers, olive oil and garlic, harissa is widely used throughout the Maghreb for flavouring tajines, couscous and soups. Try making your own!

- Remove the seeds and stems from 100g of hot, dried red chilli peppers and soak them in hot water until soft.
- Meanwhile, peel six cloves of garlic and pound with two tablespoons of coarse salt in a mortar and pestle until smooth.
- Set aside and then do likewise with the drained peppers and another two tablespoons of salt.
- Add to the garlic paste.
- Put six tablespoons of coriander seeds and four tablespoons of cumin seeds in the mortar and pound to a powder.
- Add the garlic and pepper paste and a little olive oil and pound until smooth.
- Continue this process, adding up to 10 tablespoons of olive oil, until the sauce is well blended.

[Continued on page 145]

Since the 16th century, merchant ships have been leaving Moroccan shores laden with exotic goods bound for Europe. *Maroquinerie* (leatherware) was the single most prized item and the word became synonymous with quality leather goods throughout the fashionable courts and houses of Europe.

That tradition lives on, accompanied by a rich heritage in the production of all sorts of goods ź from carpets to richly decorated pottery, heavy silver jewellery to elegant woodwork. Although much of this work is now decorative and aimed at tourists, it has its roots in the satisfaction of the everyday needs of people. Some pieces in the souq are obvious garbage, but items of real quality (and items used by Moroccan families everyday) can be found.

The government goes to some lengths to keep these arts, and small-scale businesses alive. As far back as 1918, at the beginning of the French protectorate, the Office des Industries d'Art Indigène was established to promote craft sales abroad.

Many of the products that attract visitors, such as rugs and chased (embossed) brass and copperware, owe at least some of their visual appeal to a meeting of religious precept and traditional tribal design. Considering the depiction of all living beings an affront to God, Islam imposed strictures on the artist. Consequently, Moroccan public art follows an abstract and decorative path often using seemingly endlessly repeated and interlaced motifs.

Geometry is fundamental to much Islamic design and artisans have, over the centuries, perfected the creation of intricate geometrical patterns, many of which are elaborations on tribal themes long known in Morocco.

Added to this is Arabic calligraphy, which in itself is an artistic medium. The calligraphy you see in great religious buildings in Morocco is generally composed of extracts from the Quran or such ritual declarations as *la illah illa Allah* (There is no god but Allah).

Title page: Decorated bellows, Tinerhir

Inset: Detail of a water seller's hat, Marrakesh

Left: A weaver at work in the silk district of Fès

(All photos on this page and title page by Christopher Wood)

An artistic peak was reached in the 13th century under the Merenids who built richly decorated *medersas* (theological colleges). The base of the medersa walls are covered in *zellij*: fragments of ceramic tiles in hues of green, blue and yellow, interspersed with black, on a white background.

Above these tiles is lacework stucco, topped finally by carved wooden (often cedar) panels, which are continued on the ceiling.

Although the predominant artistic style in Morocco is of Arabic-Islamic descent, the origins of many Berber designs, especially in textiles and jewellery, predate the emergence of Islam. However, depictions of animals and other figurative representations have nothing to do with either artistic tradition. This imagery is borrowed from other African traditions and added to more modern works to make it more attractive to tourists.

Shopping in the Souq

The most useful tool when hunting for crafts is patience. Morocco is crawling with craft souqs, and tourists often find themselves subjected to heavy sales pressure, or you will, in the best circumstances, be caught up in the age-old mint tea ritual, in which gentle but persistent sales pressure is applied.

Before buying anything, you should look around. Every big city has an Ensemble Artisanal, a government-run craft shop with fixed prices (though more expensive than in the souq) and good-quality goods. These are excellent places in which to get a feel for the market. Museums will also give you an idea of the quality to look for.

Right: A cobbler creates custom-built *babouches* (slippers) for a buyer in the Djemaa el-Fna, Marrakesh

CHRISTOPHER WOOD

Carpets & Rugs

Carpet shops. The words themselves evoke for many the sum total of their Moroccan experience. All Moroccan touts seem to assume the first (and only) thing tourists want is a carpet.

The selling of carpets is usually men's business, but making them is women's work, a big difference from other crafts. It can take months to make a good quality Rabat-style carpet, while some small, flat-weave Berber rugs only take a couple of days to complete. However, middlemen take most of the profit either way, so buy direct from the producers whenever possible.

The heavy woollen carpets and throw rugs vary greatly in design and colouring from region to region. Rabat is the centre of the Moroccan urban Islamic carpet-making tradition, which is inspired by the carpet-makers of the Middle East and very formal in style. Rich yarns and lustrous colours are used. The design usually includes a central motif and intricate border – the wider and more complicated the border, the more the carpet is worth. Modern designs are emerging and animal motifs are creeping in.

Chemical colours are commonly used but tend to fade. Vegetable dyes are still used, and tend to fade more slowly – almond leaves, bark, iron sulphate and cow urine are all used.

For the locals, carpets are utilitarian as much as works of art, and the brilliant colours of a new rug are not expected to retain their intensity. You can only rely on the older rugs (aged at least 40 years) *not to* change colour significantly.

The value of a carpet is based not only on the intricacy of design, but also on its age, the number of knots and, perhaps most importantly, the strength of the wool. Many Moroccan soft-wool carpets will not stand up well to much foot traffic.

Well-made, antique carpets are hard to come by and fetch high prices. A square metre of carpet contains tens of thousands of knots

AMERENS HEDWICH

Left: The design and colouring of Moroccan carpets and rugs varies across the country.

and it's basically a case of the more the better, as they indicate a product is more likely to last. The very best examples can have 360,000 to 380,000 knots per square metre but these are rare. Glib claims that the item in front of you has several hundred thousand knots per sq metre can, as a rule, be confidently discounted.

Prices often start ridiculously high. Dr800 to Dr1200 per sq metre is not a bad price to pay. Insistent bargaining can bring prices down to Dr600 to Dr1000, perhaps less depending on the quality and the eagerness of the shopkeeper to sell. If you hold out and the item is not of great quality, the price will come down.

Tribal Rugs Outside Rabat, most of the carpets and rugs are the work of hundreds of different Berber and Arab tribal groups. There is a huge variety of designs and techniques.

Most of the rugs made by these tribal groups are flatwoven (though many do make pile rugs) and feature zigzag, diamond and lozenge designs as well as strong, simple geometrical patterning, such as deep horizontal bands or abstract symbols of the evil eye. Colours are more natural than in Rabat rugs of the Islamic urban style and the best have little repetition of design.

The Moroccan flatweaves used as blankets, coverings for the floor or for general domestic use are called **hanbels**, or **kilims**. Prices will start around Dr300 per square metre.

A **zanafi** or **glaoua** is a rug with a combination of flatweave and deep fluffy pile. Prices start around Dr700 per square metre.

A **shedwi** is a flatwoven rug of black and white bands, tapestry weave and twining.

Other Wool Products

Plenty of other good woollen purchases can be made. Chefchaouen and Ouezzane are in flourishing wool country in the north-west and, in the former especially, all manner of garments can be found. Perhaps the

Right: An example of Berber carpet patterns in the Ensemble Artisanal, Rabat

MATT FLETCHER

best are thick sweaters, which cost from around Dr80 to Dr100 (depending on quality and thickness). Jackets, head gear and woven bags are also available. Inspect the goods closely as quality varies greatly.

Another popular item is the *burnouse* (heavy, hooded cloak), worn by Berbers from all over the country. They are practical in the cold mountain weather, but westerners can look a little silly in them.

Textiles

Although Morocco does not have Egypt's reputation for producing cotton products, many visitors are tempted by *jellaba*, the full-length cotton garments traditionally worn by men, though similar items for women are worn.

Various materials are used to produce a whole range of blankets (as little as Dr80), 'throws' or bed spreads (Dr140 to Dr260) and a host of

CHRISTOPHER WOOD

Left: The colourful and textured attire of a Berber singer, Marrakesh

other attractive textiles. Fès is reputedly Morocco's great silk and brocade centre, but both these art forms are apparently heading for extinction and so are increasingly hard to find.

Leatherwork

The bulk of contemporary leatherwork is aimed solely at tourists. The famous tanneries of Fès provide raw material for about half the country's total production in leather goods.

The most 'authentic' of these items are *babouches* (around Dr60), slippers that are still the most common footwear among Moroccans of both sexes. Men wear yellow or white ones, while other bright, vibrant colours and ornate styles are reserved for women.

There is a whole range of products designed for westerners in search of leather goods more affordable than in the designer stores at home. They can be found all over Morocco. Leather stools are a genuinely

CHRISTOPHER WOOD

traditional item and made of goat leather. If camel saddles are your thing, try Marrakesh.

Some of the best shoulder bags are made in the Rif – check out the souqs of Tetouan and Chefchaouen. Standard lawyer-style satchels go for between Dr80 and Dr200 depending on quality. Tiny bags designed to carry around personal copies of the Quran are popular souvenir items.

The leather is often of a high quality, and to this extent the fame of maroquinerie remains justified. Unfortunately, the artisanship of many items leaves a lot to be desired.

Pottery & Ceramics

The potteries of Safi have long been touted as the main centre of ceramic production in Morocco, but smaller cooperatives are springing up in other parts of the country and the cities of Fès and Meknès have a centuries-old heritage of ceramics production. A lot of it is prosaic, such as the ubiquitous green roof tiles that are largely made in these two Middle Atlas cities and to some extent in Safi.

Right: A shoe shop in Fès sells the commonly worn babouches.

Stages in the pottery making process

Top left: The potter turn a *tajine* (meat and vegetable stew) dish

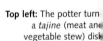

Top right: Pots drying i the sun

Middle left: Twigs and leaves are used to fire the pots

Middle right: A woman carefully paints the fired po

Bottom: Finished prod ucts for sale in a Mar rakesh pottery stall are colourfully decorated particularly for the tourist trade

Safi's pottery-makers have taken their inspiration from the ceramics once produced in Málaga (southern Spain), which are identified by a characteristic metallic sheen. The arrival of many potters from Fès has led to an increasing mixture of that city's traditional designs, which were mostly handed down by artisans exiled from Al-Andalus.

Fès' ceramics are dominated by browns, blues or yellows and greens on white backgrounds. You can see excellent examples of jars, pots and other household items (for wealthy households!) in most of the museums of Moroccan art in the big cities. Meknès, now famous for its chrome green pottery, inherited much of its skills from Fès, and its pottery industry only began to flourish in the 18th century.

CHRISTOPHER WOOD

Right: Rustic Berber pottery, Chefchaouen

Among the easiest to pack, commercially available souvenirs are decorative ceramic plates or coffee and tea sets. The rougher examples can sell for as little as Dr80, but expect to pay several hundred dirham for a well-made plate.

Great and highly functional Moroccan souvenirs are *tajine* (meat and vegetable stew) dishes, a casserole dish with a conical cover. Decorative tajine dishes (and bright and gaudy ceramics generally) are aimed at the tourist, while the locally used product can cost as little as Dr20 (for a two-person dish) or Dr40 (for a dish serving up to nine people).

More precious pottery tends to be muted in colour, decoration and finish. This doesn't make the gaudy stuff intrinsically bad, but it *does* mean you should not pay an arm and a leg for it.

In contrast to the largely urban and sophisticated pottery are the rougher, rustic products of the Berbers. Although simpler, they have their own charm and are characteristic of the regions in which they are

Top: Copper pots and pans in the copperwork district, Fès

Bottom: Gleaming copper pots, Chefchaouen

(Both photos by Christopher Wood)

made. In the High Atlas south and east of Marrakesh, ochre is the dominant colour, the exception being down by Zagora, where you can find pots, jars and cups with a green finish. Water vessels are often decorated with a mysterious black substance that is said to purify the water.

Brass & Copperware

One of the best things about brass and copperware is that it is comparatively hard to cheat on quality. Prices start at about Dr15 for a low-quality, saucer-sized decorative plate, rising to around Dr600 for a large, heavy tray. The latter are lavishly decorated and embossed.

There are plenty of other souvenirs. Candlesticks and lamp bases come in all shapes and sizes, and are best sought in Marrakesh, Fès and Tetouan. Also worth buying are brass mirror frames, often with patterns and designs reminiscent of those found in the best Moroccan Islamic architecture.

For hammered rather than chased copper items, Taroudannt is about the best place.

Jewellery

Much of the jewellery around is not what it is claimed to be. Gold and silver are more often than not plated, and amber is plastic (put a lighted match to it and smell). Unless you are sure of your stuff, you should be cautious about what you buy and be prepared for disappointment.

This is not to say that genuinely good jewellery cannot be found, but you have to look for it. The making of jewellery in Morocco was once the preserve of the Jewish population, and it is said that Muslims at one stage had a superstitious aversion to metalwork. Whatever the truth of that, silverwork was not the exclusive preserve of Jews in Morocco over the past couple of centuries.

Gold Fès is traditionally the place to buy gold jewellery, as much because of the sophisticated, urban and well-off clientele as anything else.

Gold markets are to be found in various other big cities too ź the one in Meknès, which is not overwhelmed by gold-hunting tourists, is worth investigating.

Classic jewellery made in Fès and Tangier remains largely faithful to Andalusian *recherché* (refined) lines, and is often ostentatious and beyond the means of most. The Meknès products are generally more modest.

Essaouira, apart from the contribution made by the jewellers from Fès, boasts a local style dominated by floral designs and enamel work, although little of the jewellery produced has any gold content.

Silver You can find cheap silver-plated jewellery just about anywhere. If you're looking for slightly more valuable and characteristically Moroccan items, you should head south to Tiznit, Tan Tan or Taroudannt or east to Rissani.

Silver has long been highly prized by Berber women – a look in some of the museums of Moroccan art will soon convince you of that. The reason for this is that few peasant families, however powerful in their own stamping ground, could afford the luxury of gold.

MATT FLETCHER

Silver necklaces, bracelets, rings and earrings are invariably quite chunky, and often enlivened with pieces of amber or comparatively cheap precious stones. A particular item you will see in jewellery souqs is the hand of Fatima. The open palm is supposed to protect its wearer from ill fortune.

Other Metalwork

While down around Tiznit and Taroudannt, you might be interested in other silverwork. Specialities in both towns are silver-encrusted sabres and muskets. You can also come across silver daggers and silver (or silver-plated) scabbards.

For wrought iron (the craft was probably imported from Muslim Spain) the place to hunt around is the ironsmiths' souq in Marrakesh. Here you can find frames for mirrors, fire screens, lanterns and the like. Prices are low – between Dr30 and Dr80 for a lantern, depending on the size. However, in recent years craft ironworking has become more common outside Marrakesh.

Left: Silver teapot on show in the Rabat medina

Woodwork

The artisans of Tetouan, Salé and Meknès continue to produce veritable works of art in wood. Painted and sculpted panels for interior decoration are commonplace, and the infinitely more intricate work required to produce the stalactite-like decoration that graces the interior of various medersas, religious buildings and the private homes of the rich also survives. If you're dreaming of taking an elaborate antique door back home prices start around Dr1500.

Nor has the *mashrabiyya* (or *mous-harabiyya*) been consigned to history. These screens were and are designed to allow women to observe the goings-on in the street without being seen themselves. Fès and Meknès are the main centres of production.

CHRISTOPHER WOOD

Right: A wood turner uses an age-old method and a simple lathe, Marrakesh

Pleasantly perfumed cedar is used for most woodwork, and in some of the better workshops you will find beautiful bowls, candlesticks, painted cribs, chests, jewellery boxes and the like. Fès is particularly good for this sort of work. Tetouan produces some interesting pieces too.

For marquetry, inlaid chessboards, caskets and all sorts of wooden trinkets, Essaouira is the centre of production. Thuya wood *(Tris articuta)* is used (the roots of which are truly beautiful) but the once common tree of Essaouira's hinterland is now endangered, though production of all kinds of trinkets continues.

Stone & Precious Stones

In Taroudannt you can pick up lamps, paperweights and boxes made of stone. Various kinds of softer stone are also sculpted into all sorts of shapes and sold for a pittance.

Throughout the Middle and High Atlas you'll pass roadside stands with people offering clumps of all sorts of semiprecious stones such as quartz and amethyst.

In the desert around Erfoud are black marble quarries that furnish the base element for that town's souvenir industry. There are several stores there selling everything from statues to paperweights in black marble, as well as plenty of kids trying to unload more modest trinkets.

Fossils in rock (especially ammonite) are sometimes offered alongside the semiprecious stones. Morocco is full of fossils, and enterprising merchants convert them into all sorts of things, including bowls and superb table-top sections.

Basketware

Throughout Morocco you will come across basketware, a wide term that covers everything from the Rif-style straw hats of the north to

CHRISTOPHER WOOD

Left: A basket merchant is dwarfed by his work, Fès

AMERENS HEDWICH

baskets with cone-shaped covers used by Berbers to carry dates and other merchandise. They make cheap souvenirs (Dr10 to Dr20) and are obviously not made to last forever.

Musical Instruments

It is possible to pick up traditional Moroccan instruments in various places. One good place to look around is in the Bab el-Jedid area of the Meknès medina, where you'll find various string, wind and percussion instruments.

Probably the best place, however, is the medina of Fès (see Shopping under Fès in the Middle Atlas & the East chapter), where small, medium and large drum sets go for around Dr20, Dr50 and Dr80 respectively. For more information on Moroccan music and instruments see Music under Arts in the Facts about Morocco chapter.

CHRISTOPHER WOOD

Top: Huge baskets and tajines, Safi

Right: Long cylindrical drums, Essaouira

CHRISTINE OSBORNE

CHRISTOPHER WOOD

Top: Playing a traditional string instrument at the Fès Festival of World Sacred Music

Bottom: Drums for sale in Fès, one of the best places to buy instruments

[Continued from page 128]

morning and baked in wood-fired ovens by the neighbourhood baker for a small fee; if the household can't pay, they give the baker a loaf that he will sell in market.

Desserts & Pastries

Dessert often consists of a platter of fresh fruit. In summer there is a huge variety to choose from – all sorts of melons, fresh dates and figs, yellow and red plums, peaches, grapes, pears, bananas, Barbary figs (the fruit of the prickly pear cactus), pomegranates, mandarins, tangerines and oranges.

Beghrir (very light pancakes cooked on a griddle or earthenware dish) and *rghaif* (flaky pancakes deep-fried in oil) are sometimes served in restaurants as a dessert with melted butter and honey, but are more traditionally eaten for breakfast.

The delicious deep-fried doughnuts called *sfenj* are more like a snack food – you'll often find them sold at little booths at the centre of a souq or near open markets or bus stations.

Those with a sweet tooth are in for a double treat – in cities and bigger towns, you'll find both Moroccan and French pastries. Moroccan patisseries tend to be family-run and have often been going for generations.

Two famous sweets are *kaab el-ghzal* (gazelle's horns), crescent-shaped pastries stuffed with delicately flavoured almond paste and coated with icing sugar, and *m'hancha* (coiled serpent cake), a flat round of baked almond-stuffed pastry coated with icing sugar and cinnamon.

DRINKS
Tea & Coffee

Morocco's national beverage, sometimes referred to as 'Moroccan whisky', is freshly brewed mint tea (*atay* in Arabic, *thé à la menthe* in French) made with Chinese green gunpowder tea, sprigs of fresh mint *(nanaa')* and vast quantities of sugar. Moroccans adore it and tend to drink it all day long, at every opportunity.

Traditionally, it's served in elegant Moroccan teapots and poured (from a height to make it frothy on top) into small glasses. In restaurants it may be just served by the glass. English tea is usually served black and is invariably known as *thé Lipton*.

Coffee is available everywhere and is generally very good. It's made in varying strengths depending on how much milk is added.

You can order black coffee (*qahwa kehla/cafe noir*), coffee 'broken' with a spot of milk (*qahwa mherresa/cafe cassé*), half coffee and half milk *(ness-ness)*, standard coffee with milk (*qahwa hleeb/café au lait*) and very weak coffee which is mostly milk 'broken' with a little coffee (*hleeb mhers*). If you ask simply for coffee, you'll get café au lait.

Coffee served in Moroccan homes is sometimes flavoured with cinnamon, cardamom, black pepper, ginger or other spices.

Juices

The best places to get freshly squeezed juices are in the occasional small shops that do nothing else, although most cafes and restaurants can make them for you. Orange juice is popular, but you may also come across pomegranate, watermelon and grape juice. Drinks are also made with a mixture of milk or buttermilk and the juices of fresh fruits and almonds.

Soft Drinks & Bottled Water

Coca-Cola and other soft drinks are well established in Morocco, but remember that in hot weather, they don't do an awful lot to quench your thirst.

Several brands of bottled water are available, including Sidi Harazem (still) and Oulmes (sparkling). These cost about Dr5 a litre. However, these plastic bottles are nonbiodegradable and are not recycled. Instead, they seem to accumulate at beauty spots.

Alcohol

Islam forbids the drinking of alcoholic beverages, but they are nonetheless widely available. Some of the better (or at least more expensive) restaurants are licensed, but many are not. The cheapest places are rarely licensed unless they have a bar attached, and alcohol is not sold in medinas.

There are more bars around than is obvious. They tend not to advertise and most are quite basic set-'em-up-and-knock-'em-down places. The bigger cities have the occasional liquor store, where you can get beer, wine and spirits for considerably less than in the bars or restaurants.

Beer The two main locally produced beers, Flag Spéciale (brewed in Tangier) and Stork (brewed in Fès and Casablanca) are quite drinkable without being anything to write home about. Smallish bottles cost between Dr6 and Dr8 in the liquor stores. Bottles in bars and restaurants cost from Dr12 to Dr15 but 'une pression', or 'a glass of beer', often works out cheaper.

Amstel and Heineken are also produced in Morocco under licence and you can come across the odd imported brand, such as US Budweiser, in the liquor stores.

Wine Some quite reasonable wines are produced in Morocco. Vieux Papes is the best known red table wine and Valpierre, made near Rabat, is a popular dry white wine.

Recommended reds include the approachable cabernet Cuvée du President from the Meknès region, Guerrouane and Aït Souala, and the more expensive Beau Vallon. Sémillant white is worth trying. Toulal, both red and white, has received favourable reviews and a good rosé is Gris de Boulaouane. In the liquor stores, wine prices start at about Dr35.

Spirits Various spirits can be bought, although they are hardly cheap. There is a French emphasis, especially in the northern half of the country.

If you like the aniseed-based pastis, one of the more well-known brands costs around Dr120.

ENTERTAINMENT

Morocco isn't exactly the last word in nightlife. The major cities do have some good cinemas, and there are bars, discos and nightclubs (though prostitution features heavily in these places).

You may find the best Moroccan nightlife in the countryside – it's difficult to beat listening to the hypnotic music of the Berbers or drinking in the immense desert sky of the sub-Sahara.

Cinemas

The best cinemas are in Rabat and Casablanca. It's pretty cheap entertainment, with seats costing from Dr7 to Dr30, depending on where you sit.

The better cinemas get some quite up-to-date films, but if they're not French films, they are almost invariably dubbed into French. Most large towns have at least one cinema specialising in kung fu movies and the Indian equivalent of the genre.

Bars

These come in two varieties. The majority are pretty basic; they tend to be discreet about their existence and close fairly early. Many are distinguished by little more than a Flag Spéciale sign outside. The local punters will probably be surprised to see you – particularly if you are a woman.

The other version is the hotel bar. These stay open a little later and are considerably more expensive. Some mid-range hotels and a few of the top-end places have comfortable bars that are worth seeking out.

Discos & Nightclubs

Discos and nightclubs (the words are interchangeable in Morocco) are often filled with prostitutes. Generally, you'll have to pay at least Dr50 to get in, which usually includes a drink, and subsequent drinks cost an average of Dr50.

Some of the sleazier nightclubs, particularly in central Casablanca, put on a cabaret or floor show, usually of the belly-dancing variety. A couple of the more chic jobs in the Casablanca suburbs are better, but very expensive.

Cultural Shows

Some of the big hotels and tourist restaurants put on folk performances. Those in the restaurants are probably preferable, since the settings are often quite sumptuous. The shows themselves can be a mixed bag, but they are entertaining enough if reasonable musicians have been engaged to play traditional Andalusian or Berber music. The dancing is usually Egyptian-style belly dancing (it is not really a Moroccan genre). A few of the top hotels opt for Western-style cabarets.

SPECTATOR SPORT
Football

Sport plays a large role in Moroccan life. Moroccans' biggest passion by far is football (soccer), which seems to be played at every opportunity. You won't have to go far to find a game in progress and you'll know when a big match (local or international) is on because the streets are deserted and every male worth his salt is sitting in a cafe glued to the television. This is not just for Moroccan games – support for Spanish, French, Dutch and German teams is just as fanatical and viewing of Champions League games is essential.

Morocco was unsuccessful in its bid to host the 2006 World Cup, but hopes are high that many of the stadiums due to be built for that competition will be realised. Throughout the country, patches of flat ground (and hectares of beach) are turned into football pitches, even if the ball is just a bundle of rags tied together. It's just a shame that this kind of enthusiasm for the game cut no ice with the decision makers at Federation Internationale de Football Association (FIFA).

There are some 320 football stadiums across the country, with the biggest being the Complexe Mohammed V in Casablanca and the Complexe Moulay Abdellah in Rabat. The country's biggest teams are Raja Casablanca, Wydad Casablanca, MAS Fès and Fath de Rabat. It costs just a few dirham to see a game, and Moroccan papers are filled with fixtures and news. If you can get along to a game, do so.

The Moroccan national team, nicknamed the Lions of the Atlas, play to crowds of 80,000 or more and regularly make it to the World Cup finals. In the 1986 competition, the Lions became the first Arab and African national team to qualify for the second round. With so much enthusiasm and so many kids playing, the team can only get better. As it is, the best players play for big European clubs in France, Portugal, Holland, England and the Arab Gulf States.

Athletics

Morocco began to distinguish itself in the field of athletics in the mid-1980s, when Said Aouita (a native of Kenitra) and Nawal al-Moutawakil burst on to the international scene. At the 1984 Los Angeles Olympics, al-Moutawakil won the gold medal in the 400m hurdles and became the first Arab woman to achieve gold. See Women in Society under Society & Conduct in the Facts about Morocco chapter for information on the impact al-Moutawakil's win had on the status of women in Morocco.

The most famous Moroccan athlete is the young Hicham al-Guerrouj. In 1996 he established two world indoor records by a large margin, but at the 1996 Los Angeles Olympic Games he fell in the 1500m race and lost. In the 2000 Olympics in Sydney he was a hot gold medal favourite, but misjudged the race and ran second. Another Moroccan athletics star, Salah Hissou, won the world championships in the 5000m.

One of the most gruelling marathons in the world, Le Marathon des Sables, takes places every April across the desert terrain of the Moroccan sub-Sahara. Held over seven days, the course covers 220km altogether – 78 of them nonstop in one leg. Participants also carry everything they need for the week, including their food.

The 1997 marathon attracted a field of 370 participants, 34 of them women, and included competitors from as far away as Hong Kong, Japan and New Zealand. The youngest runner was Jallal Sefraoui, a Moroccan student aged 16, and the eldest participant was a 74-year-old retired osteopath, Claude Compain.

Other Sports

Golf is becoming increasingly popular, thanks largely to the Royal Moroccan Golf Federation. The Hassan II Challenge Cup is held annually at the Dar es-Salaam golf course in Rabat and is one of the biggest competitions in the world (see Golf under Activities earlier in this chapter).

Morocco boasts a handful of tennis players who are making a name for themselves on the international circuit. One player, Karim Alami, has beaten big names like Pete Sampras and Boris Becker. The best Moroccan female tennis player is Bahia Mouhtacine, who won the recent African championships.

Other popular sports in Morocco include cycling, basketball and handball.

SHOPPING

A souvenir hunter could spend weeks trawling through the souqs of Morocco. From silver jewellery to copper and brassware, and myriad rugs and carpets, there is an enormous choice. Obviously, items of inferior quality are produced as well as higher quality objects – it pays to take your time before buying. For information on what to look for, see the colour section 'Moroccan Arts & Crafts'.

For some people the big attraction is the herbs and spices. Besides the cumin, saffron, ginger and so on that are usually displayed in huge colourful mounds, you'll find all sorts of obscure things for medicinal purposes.

The Djemaa el-Fna in Marrakesh is a good place for this. If you've got a cough, cold or other ailment, point to the part that hurts and you'll soon have a small plastic bag filled with the wonder herb in your hand.

Directions for use vary, so try to get an explanation of how to take your herbal remedy. The locals swear by these 'ashaab (herbs).

Markets

In common with most African and Middle Eastern countries, Moroccan towns and villages have a weekly market (sometimes twice a week) when people from the surrounding area come to sell their wares and buy goods they do not produce themselves.

These markets are different from the permanent covered markets you'll find in most towns, and usually provide a lively opportunity to observe the distinctive customs and clothing of local tribespeople.

All types of markets are called souqs. Some of the most interesting weekly or twice-weekly souqs include:

location	market days
Agadir	Saturday, Sunday
Chefchaouen	Monday, Thursday
Figuig	Saturday
Ifrane	Sunday
Larache	Sunday
M'Hamid	Monday
Midelt	Sunday
Moulay Idriss	Saturday
Ouarzazate	Sunday
Ouezzane	Thursday
Oujda	Wednesday, Sunday
Sefrou	Thursday
Tafraoute	Wednesday
Taroudannt	Friday
Tinerhir	Monday
Tinzouline	Monday
Zagora	Wednesday, Sunday

Getting There & Away

AIR
Airports & Airlines

For flights to Morocco, the high seasons are from July to the end of August, and mid-December to the end of December. The low seasons are November to mid-December, and January to mid-February.

Direct flights are possible from cities across Europe, the Middle East, West Africa and North America, and they mostly arrive in Casablanca. Air France and Morocco's national carrier, Royal Air Maroc (RAM), take the lion's share of flights. Other carriers include Lufthansa Airlines, KLM-Royal Dutch Airlines, Iberia, British Airways, Swissair, TAP Portugal, Sabena, Alitalia, Air Algérie, Royal Jordanian, EgyptAir, Tunis Air and Regional Air Lines (a small Moroccan carrier).

Mohammed V International Airport

Morocco's main international entry point is the Mohammed V international airport, 30km south-east of Casablanca. It's conveniently linked by regular shuttle trains to Casablanca and Rabat.

Passport control and customs formalities are straightforward. In the arrivals hall you'll find representatives of many international and local car rental agencies, plus people from some of the bigger hotels. The small tourist information desk is open daily from 8.30 am to 7 pm.

BMCE has a *bureau de change* (foreign exchange office; with ATMs) in arrivals and departures. Wafa Bank (with ATM) and Banque Populaire are also represented.

There are several cafes and newsstands dotted around the airport, plus a *téléboutique* (privately operated telephone service) and small *tabac* (tobacconist and newsagency) selling stamps just in front of departures.

Other Airports Daily flights from Paris with Air France and RAM also land at Rabat-Salé airport, 10km east of Salé (Dr150 taxi ride), while Tangier's Ibn Batouta airport (18km south of the city; Dr150 by taxi) has direct flights to Amsterdam, Brussels, London, Madrid, Málaga and Paris. There are also direct flights into Ménara airport, 6km south-west of Marrakesh, from London, Geneva, Granada, Málaga and Paris.

Numerous charter flights arrive at Agadir's new Al-Massira airport, 22km south of the city, along with direct flights to Las Palmas in the Canary Islands.

Laayoune, capital of the Western Sahara, also has flights to the Canary Islands, plus departures to Abidjan (Côte d'Ivoire) and Libreville (Gabon).

There are also occasional international flights to/from Fès, Ouarzazate, Nador and Al-Hoceima, while Oujda is linked to Paris, several other French cities, Amsterdam, Brussels, Dusseldorf and Frankfurt.

Buying Tickets

Your plane ticket will probably be the single most expensive item in your budget, and buying it can be an intimidating business. It is worth putting aside a few hours to research the state of the market. Start early: some of the cheapest tickets have to be bought months in advance and popular

Air Travel Glossary

Cancellation Penalties If you have to cancel or change a discounted ticket, there are often heavy penalties involved; insurance can sometimes be taken out against these penalties. Some airlines impose penalties on regular tickets as well, particularly against 'no-show' passengers.

Courier Fares Businesses often need to send urgent documents or freight securely and quickly. Courier companies hire people to accompany the package through customs and, in return, offer a discount ticket which is sometimes a phenomenal bargain. However, you may have to surrender all your baggage allowance and take only carry-on luggage.

Full Fares Airlines traditionally offer 1st class (coded F), business class (coded J) and economy class (coded Y) tickets. These days there are so many promotional and discounted fares available that few passengers pay full economy fare.

Lost Tickets If you lose your airline ticket an airline will usually treat it like a travellers cheque and, after inquiries, issue you with another one. Legally, however, an airline is entitled to treat it like cash and if you lose it then it's gone forever. Take good care of your tickets.

Low-Cost Airlines These cheapest of scheduled airlines typically don't issue tickets – just reference numbers and reusable boarding passes. There's no free in-flight food or drink and passengers are packed in. You usually book directly with the airline, by telephone or over the Internet.

Onward Tickets An entry requirement for many countries is that you have a ticket out of the country. If you're unsure of your next move you can buy the cheapest onward ticket to a nearby country or a ticket from a reliable airline that can later be refunded if you don't use it.

Open-Jaw Tickets These are return tickets where you fly out to one place but return from another. If available, this can save you backtracking to your arrival point.

Overbooking Since every flight has some passengers who fail to show up, airlines often book more passengers than they have seats. Usually excess passengers make up for the no-shows, but occasionally somebody gets 'bumped' onto the next available flight. Guess who it is most likely to be? The passengers who check in late.

Promotional Fares Officially discounted fares are available from travel agencies or airlines.

Reconfirmation If you don't reconfirm your flight at least 72 hours before departure the airline may drop you from the passenger list. Call to find out if your airline requires reconfirmation.

Restrictions Discounted tickets often have various restrictions on them – such as needing to be paid for in advance and incurring a penalty to be altered. Others are restrictions on the minimum and maximum period you must be away.

Round-the-World Tickets RTW tickets give you a limited period (usually a year) in which to circumnavigate the globe. You can go anywhere the carrying airlines go, as long as you don't backtrack. The number of stopovers or total number of separate flights is decided before you set off and they usually cost a bit more than a basic return flight.

Transferred Tickets Airline tickets cannot be transferred between people. Travellers sometimes try to sell the return half of their ticket, but officials can ask you to prove that you are the person named on the ticket. On an international flight tickets are compared with passports.

Travel Periods Ticket prices vary with the time of year. There is a low (off-peak) season and a high (peak) season, and often a low-shoulder season and a high-shoulder season as well. Usually the fare depends on your outward flight – if you depart in the high season and return in the low season, you pay the high-season fare.

flights sell out early. However, competition between European carriers, who all wish to transport you through their own hubs, is bringing widespread discounting and there are some great deals out there.

Talk to other travellers, look at the ads in newspapers and magazines, consult reference books and watch for special offers. The Internet is becoming an increasingly good place to search for cheap flights, but Morocco is a small market and established travel agents (who often have the best Web sites anyway) may still be cheapest.

When flying from outside of Morocco, airlines are good for information on routes, timetables and ticket restrictions, but rarely supply the cheapest tickets.

Inside Morocco things are different. Despite the numbers of travel agencies, little or no discounting takes place and trawling around the airline offices can often turn up a good deal – prices offered by travel agencies and airlines rarely differ anyway. Oddly, the cheapest fares are not one-way tickets, but one-month returns. In either direction the bulk of traffic is with RAM.

Direct flights will almost always cost you more. Many airlines have code-share agreements with one another and the cheapest deals can often entail a change of plane (and carrier) in a European city. As a rule, the cheapest fares are into Casablanca, though there is little flexibility on some of these tickets. Cheaper student and under-26 tickets are sometimes available.

The fares quoted in this book are intended as a guide only. They are approximate and based on the rates advertised by travel agencies at the time of research. These quoted airfares do not necessarily constitute a recommendation for the particular carrier.

Travellers with Special Needs

If you have special needs of any sort – you have a broken leg, you're a vegetarian, are travelling in a wheelchair, taking the baby or terrified of flying – let the airline know as soon as possible so that they can make arrangements accordingly.

Remind them when you reconfirm your booking (at least 72 hours before departure) and again when you check in. Ring around the airlines before booking a ticket and find out how they can handle your particular needs.

Airports and airlines can be surprisingly helpful, but they do need advance warning. Most international airports will provide escorts from the check-in desk to the plane if necessary and there should be ramps, lifts and accessible toilets and phones.

Toilets within the aircraft, on the other hand, are likely to present a problem. Travellers should discuss this with the airline at an early stage and, if necessary, with their doctor.

Guide dogs for the blind will often have to travel in a specially pressurised baggage compartment with other animals, away from their owner, although smaller guide dogs may be admitted into the cabin. All guide dogs will be subject to the same quarantine laws (six months in isolation etc) as any other animal when entering or returning to countries currently free of rabies, such as Britain or Australia. The recent 'Pets Passport' initiative in the UK doesn't apply to Morocco.

Deaf travellers can ask for airport and in-flight announcements to be written down for them.

Children under two years of age travel for 10% of the standard fare (or free, on some airlines) as long as they don't occupy a seat. They don't get a baggage allowance. 'Skycots' should be provided by the airline if requested in advance; these take a child weighing up to about 10kg. Children aged between two and 12 can usually occupy a seat for half to two-thirds of the full fare, and do get a baggage allowance. Pushchairs can often be taken as hand luggage.

North America

The *New York Times*, the *LA Times*, the *Chicago Tribune* and the *San Francisco Examiner* produce weekly travel sections containing numerous travel agencies' ads.

In the USA, Council Travel (☎ 800-226 8624) and STA Travel (☎ 800-777 0112) have offices in major cities nationwide. Their Web sites are at www.ciee.org and www.statravelgroup.com respectively.

In Canada, Travel CUTS (☎ 800-667 2887) has offices in all major cities; Web site www.travelcuts.com. The *Toronto Globe & Mail* and the *Vancouver Sun* carry travel agencies' ads.

Travel Web sites at www.expedia.com and www.travelocity.com are useful and reliable North American online booking agencies, but there are plenty of others.

Often the cheapest way from North America to Morocco is a return flight to London, Paris or Madrid and an onward ticket from there. Flying to Paris is usually the best value (see France entry later in this chapter) – return tickets from New York to Paris start at around US$460.

However, RAM and TWA fly direct from New York to Casablanca (roughly between US$820 and US$1000 return). Other carriers offer similarly priced deals with a stopover or transfer in Europe. From Los Angeles a range of code-sharing partners can get you to Casablanca for between US$1100 and US$1400, depending on the season. From Vancouver and Montreal, you're looking at between US$900 and US$1220 via New York or a European city. Youth fares are 25% cheaper, but the length of stay varies between airlines.

From Morocco, RAM charges Dr6356 to New York City (two-month return) and Dr6555 to Montreal. However, at the time of writing, British Airways was offering flights to New York (via London) from Dr3960 one way and Air France was offering one-way flights to Montreal (via Paris) for Dr4999, so it's worth shopping around in Casablanca.

The UK

For the latest fares, check out the travel ads in the Sunday newspapers, plus *Time Out* and *TNT*.

Two of the most reliable UK agents, and specialists in student travel, are STA Travel (☎ 020-7361 6262), 86 Old Brompton Rd, London SW7 3LQ, Web site www.statravel.co.uk; and Usit Campus (☎ 0870-240 1010), 52 Grosvenor Gardens, London SW1W 0AG; Web site www.usitcampus.co.uk. Both have offices around the country.

Other good travel agencies are Trailfinders (☎ 020-7937 5400), at www.trailfinders.com on the Web; Travelbag (☎ 020-7287 5535), with a Web site at www.travelbag.co.uk; and Flightbookers (☎ 020-7757 2000).

Reliable online flight-booking sites include www.cheapflights.com, www.airnet.co.uk and www.travelocity.co.uk.

At the time of writing, the cheapest return fares to Casablanca, from regional airports around the UK, were with KLM and Air France (UK£230/290, low/high season) via Amsterdam and Paris. British Airways offered direct flights from London Gatwick to Tangier (three times per week) or Casablanca (daily) for UK£232, while RAM had return flights to Marrakesh (four times a week) for UK£250. British Airways also flies to Marrakesh four times a week and RAM occasionally offers cheap youth tickets, so shop around. Only Air France was offering reasonably priced, three-month return fares at the time of writing.

Package-holiday operator Panorama Holidays (☎ 01273-427777) has charter flights from Manchester and Gatwick to Agadir, but seat-only deals are rare.

Leaving Morocco, fares are usually around Dr4500 return with RAM or British Airways.

Via Spain Often the most cost-efficient way to get to Morocco from the UK and northern Europe is by flying into Málaga in southern Spain and then catching a ferry to Tangier, Nador or the Spanish enclaves of Melilla or Ceuta (see Sea later in this chapter for information).

EasyJet (☎ 0870-600 0000, ☎ 902 299992 in Spain) flies from London's Luton airport and Liverpool to Spanish destinations including Madrid, Barcelona and Málaga; its Web site is at www.easyjet.com. One-way fares start at around UK£40!

Providing direct competition is the BA-run Go (☎ 0845-605 4321, ☎ 901 333500 in Spain), which flies to the same destinations from London's Stanstead airport. It has a Web site at www.go-fly.com. Flights are generally a little more expensive (around UK£50 to UK£60 one way).

Online Booking

Thanks to the combination of ticketless airlines, online booking agencies and abundant Internet cafes, you can buy a flight home from Spain before crossing the Strait of Gibraltar. However, Web browsers used in some Internet cafes are old and do not always support the latest encryption software that allows credit-card purchases. Hackers sometimes 'listen in' on Internet cafes, but this is very rare in Morocco.

Virgin Express (☎ 020-7744 0004, ☎ 02-752 0505 in Brussels, ☎ 91 662 5261 in Spain) has daily flights to Barcelona and Madrid from London Gatwick via Brussels. Its Web site is at www.virgin-express.com. Prices start at UK£49 one way.

Málaga is a very popular destination for charter flights and occasionally there are some amazing bargains (like UK£69 return). Try The Charter Flight Centre (☎ 020-7565 6755), 15 Gillingham St, London SW1 V1HN; or for last-minute flights, check the Avro (☎ 01293-579222) and Flightbookers (☎ 01293-568300) offices at Gatwick airport.

Coming the other way, standby flights from Málaga airport are around 17,000 ptas (cruise the airline offices in the departure lounge).

Continental Europe

In addition to the huge number of charter flights to southern Spain from northern Europe, it's worth considering charter flights into Morocco (at Agadir) itself. Flight-only deals are available.

Due largely to the number of Moroccans working in European cities, RAM also has direct flights between smaller European and Moroccan cities. You're looking at between Dr4000 and Dr4500 for a flight back to northern Europe from Morocco.

France There's no shortage of flights from Paris (and many other French cities) to Casablanca, Agadir, Rabat, Tangier, Fès, Marrakesh, Oujda and Ouarzazate. Most travel agencies can do deals, and fly-drive

arrangements are an attractive option. Given the sheer volume of traffic from France, deals here are often better than in London or Amsterdam.

Both RAM and Air France operate at least three flights a day from Paris to Casablanca (2338FF to 4400FF), while RAM also has similarly priced flights to Tangier and Agadir (four times a week to both). RAM and Air France also have similarly priced flights from Marseille to Casablanca and Lyon to Casablanca.

Various agencies sometimes offer charter flights at very low prices and it's possible to get one-way flights or deals including accommodation. At the time of research, the cheapest charters from Paris were to Agadir (1500FF), Ouarzazate (1400FF) and Tangier (1600FF), with a maximum stay of four weeks; Marseille to Marrakesh was 1390FF.

The student travel agency OTU Voyages (☎ 01 44 41 38 50) has a central Paris office at 39 Ave Georges Bernanos and another 42 offices around the country; Web site www.otu.fr. Usit-Voyages (☎ 01 42 44 14 00) has four addresses in Paris, including 85 Blvd St Michel, and other offices around the country. STA Travel's Paris agent is Voyages Wasteels (☎ 01 43 25 58 35), while Nouvelles Frontières (☎ 08 03 33 33 33) can also be recommended; Web site www.nouvelles-frontieres.com.

Despite the plethora of travel agencies in central Casablanca, there is little discounting on flights from Morocco. At the time of writing the cheapest flight to Paris (return) was Dr4450 and to Marseille Dr2950, both with RAM.

Air France has twice daily flights from Rabat-Salé airport and daily services between Marrakesh and Paris (Dr5165 return).

Spain Despite its proximity, Spain is not the ideal place from which to fly to Morocco. A return flight with RAM from Madrid to Casablanca is around 49,800 ptas (55,600 ptas to Marrakesh). Occasionally, better deals crop up and in high season there are flights from numerous Spanish cities direct to Agadir.

Travels in Spain & Gibraltar

Many people pass through Spain before or after travelling in Morocco: the two countries share many centuries of history and culture; it's cheaper to fly into Spain than to Morocco; and combined the two countries make for an excellent trip.

The following information should make navigating between some of Spain's great cities and its southern ports a little easier. Lonely Planet's *Andalucia* or *Spain* guides offer more comprehensive companions to the area.

Cádiz

This beautiful, historic city has good transport links, and it's well worth exploring the grand 18th-century city centre before moving on.

The municipal tourist office (☎ 956 241001) is on Plaza de San Juan de Dios 11.

Getting There & Away Near the port east of the old city on Plaza de Sevilla is the train station (☎ 956 254301); the main *estación de autobuses* (bus station) of the Comes (☎ 956 211763) line is 800m north-west on Plaza de la Hispanidad. Ten buses leave daily for Seville (1385 ptas) and Algeciras (1270 ptas, two hours). Six Secorbus (☎ 956 257415) services to Madrid (3105 ptas, six hours) leave from Plaza Elios, 2km south-east of the old city.

There are 12 *regionales* (slow, long-distance) trains to/from Seville (1290 ptas), four to Córdoba (2415 to 3900 ptas) and two each for Madrid and Barcelona.

Tarifa

A great, laid-back little town and place of pilgrimage for windsurfers – it blows almost year-round.

The tourist office (☎ 956 680993) is on Paseo de la Alameda west of the old town.

Getting There & Away There are seven Comes buses to Cádiz and Algeciras. The bus stop and office (☎ 956 684038) is on Calle Batallo del Salado. There are also a few buses to La Línea on the Gibraltar frontier.

Algeciras

It ain't pretty, it's functional. The main tourist office (☎ 956 572636) is on Calle Juan de la Cierva. Watch your back around the port, bus station and market; there are legions of moneychangers (a complete rip-off), touts and hustlers.

Getting There & Away From the main bus station (☎ 956 653456) on Calle San Bernardo, numerous buses leave for La Línea (the Gibraltar border), Tarifa and Cádiz (1260 ptas), plus five to Seville (2100 ptas) and three to Madrid (3375 ptas). In addition, Portillo (☎ 956 651055) at Avenida Virgen del Carmen 15 operates six daily buses to Málaga (1990 ptas, 1¾ hours) and four to Granada (2595 ptas). Bacoma (☎ 956 665067), inside the port, has services to Alicante, Valencia and Barcelona, plus Morocco and northern Europe.

Train services from the train station (☎ 956 630202) close by include two daily to/from Madrid (9300 ptas or 5200 ptas, six or 11 hours) and one to/from Granada (2665 ptas, four hours).

Gibraltar

Definitely a place that captures the imagination. There's enough to see and do on the giant limestone rock for a least a couple of days.

The main tourist office (☎ 45000) is in Duke of Kent House, Cathedral Square.

If you're telephoning from outside Gibraltar, the international code is ☎ 350.

Travels in Spain & Gibraltar

Visas & Documents To enter Gibraltar you need a passport or EU identity card. Australia, Canada, EU, Israel, New Zealand, Singapore, South Africa and US passport-holders are among those who do *not* need visas for Gibraltar. For further information, contact Gibraltar's Immigration Department (☎ 46411).

Getting There & Away There are flights to the UK. No 9 buses from Casemates Square head out to the Spanish border, from where it's a five-minute walk to La Línea bus station, which services numerous Spanish destinations.

Málaga

Málaga has excellent national and international transport connections, but take a look around this lively and interesting Spanish town before moving on.

The main municipal tourist office (☎ 95 260 4410) is on Avenida de Cervantes 1.

Getting There & Away The main bus station (☎ 95 235 0061) at Paseo de los Tilos and train station (☎ 95 236 0202) at Explanada de la Estación are within a five-minute walk of each other, 1km west of the town centre.

Of the frequent coastal buses, three go as far as Cádiz and six to Algeciras (1990 ptas, 1¾ hours). Other services include Seville (1900 ptas, 10 daily), Córdoba (1570 ptas, five daily), Granada (1185 ptas, 16 daily), Barcelona (8495 ptas, 15 hours) and Madrid (2650 ptas, at least seven daily, six hours).

Eurolines (☎ 95 2232300), in conjunction with Enatcar (☎ 95 2318828), services numerous international destinations, including England, Italy and Morocco; Eurolines has a Web site at www.eurolines.es (in Spanish).

For trains to destinations within Spain, there are services to/from Córdoba (2100 ptas to 2800 ptas), Seville (2130 ptas), Valencia and Barcelona (6400 ptas to 8400 ptas; three trains, two overnight; 13 to 14 hours), plus four fast Talgo 200 trains (7000 ptas to 8200 ptas) and three slow trains (4700 ptas to 5500 ptas) to Madrid.

To get to the airport (☎ 95 224 8804), take bus No 19 (135 ptas) from the western end of Paseo del Parque outside the stations. Alternatively, you could use the Málaga-Fuengirola train line (135 ptas) between the Málaga and Aeropuerto stations. A taxi to/from the airport will cost around 1300 ptas.

Almería

Almería, the economic hub of the area, is a pleasant place and has a few attractions. The regional tourist office (☎ 950 274355) is at Parque de Nicolás Salmerón.

Getting There & Away The train station (☎ 950 251135) on Plaza de la Estación is a 10-minute walk off to the right from the port. The bus station (☎ 950 210029) on Plaza Barcelona is about a five-minute walk further north.

There are five or more buses to Granada (1300 ptas), eight to Málaga (1945 ptas, 3¼ hours) and at least one bus to Madrid, Valencia and Barcelona.

Four trains run daily to/from Granada (1610 ptas to 1775 ptas), three to/from Seville and two to/from Madrid.

For the airport, 9km east of the city, take the No 14 Aeropuerto bus (110 ptas, every 45 minutes) from the west end of Calle del Doctor Gregorio Marañón.

Travel agencies in Madrid tend to be clustered in the vicinity of the Gran Vía. Budget travellers should try Viajes Zeppelin (☎ 91 542 5154) at Plaza Santo Domingo 2; or TIVE (☎ 91 543 7412), Calle Fernando el Católico 88, the student and youth travel organisation.

Options from southern Spain are greater and often cheaper. Regional Air Lines flies direct from Casablanca and Tangier to Málaga (Dr1508 one way), while Spanish airline Binter Mediterráneo (essentially part of Iberia airlines) has numerous daily flights between Melilla and Granada, Melilla and Málaga (12,225 ptas one way) and Melilla and Almería (12,025 ptas one way) – add around 4000 ptas for return fares. It also has three flights per week between the enclave and Madrid (29,225 ptas) and twice-weekly flights to Marrakesh from Granada and Málaga (30,000 ptas return; Dr2495/2960 one way/return from Morocco).

If you're in Ceuta feeling flush and flash, Helicopteros del Sureste (☎ 956 504974 at Ceuta Ferry Port, ☎ 95 204 8700 at Málaga airport) links Ceuta and Málaga international airport four times daily (15,500 ptas one way, 35 minutes). It has a Web site at www.helisureste.com.

From Casablanca (and Tangier), the cheapest one-way flight to Madrid is around Dr3000, or Dr2300 to Málaga. In addition, Regional Air Lines (☎ 02-538020) has daily services to/from Las Palmas and Agadir (Dr2925 one way) and a weekly flight from Essaouira to Las Palmas, as well as a service to Lisbon in Portugal.

Gibraltar Few travellers want to fork out large sums of money to fly from 'the Rock' across the strait, but it can be done. Regional Air Lines has six flights per week between Casablanca and Gibraltar (Dr2338 one way, UK£104 return).

British Airways has daily flights from London's Gatwick airport (UK£175 return), while Monarch Airlines flies daily to/from Luton (UK£100 to UK£250 return).

Germany In Munich, a great source of travel information and equipment is the Darr Travel Shop (☎ 089-282032) at Theresienstrasse 66. In Berlin, try STA Travel (☎ 030-311 09 50) at Goethestrasse 73. It also has offices in Frankfurt, including one at Bockenheimer Landstrasse 133 (☎ 069-70 30 35), and in 16 other cities across the country. Its Web site is at www.statravel.de.

Agadir is a popular German charter flight destination and seat-only deals from many German cities are often available.

There are RAM flights from Casablanca, Nador and Oujda to Frankfurt and from Nador to Dusseldorf.

Netherlands & Belgium Amsterdam is a popular departure point. The student travel agency NBBS (☎ 020-624 09 89) at Rokin 66 offers reasonably low fares, comparable to those from London. NBBS has branches throughout the city and in Brussels, Belgium.

Brussels is the main hub for Virgin Express (see the earlier UK entry), which flies to Madrid.

Australasia

There are no direct flights between Australia or New Zealand and Morocco. All flights go via the Middle East or Europe. In the low season, return fares start at A$1849, climbing to A$2649 in high season. It can make more sense to fly to Paris or Madrid (A$1499 to A$2279) and make your own way down.

STA Travel (☎ 03-9349 2411 in Melbourne, ☎ 131 766 Australia-wide) is a reliable travel agency with branches around Australia and New Zealand, including Auckland (☎ 09-309 0458) at 10 High St. Its Web site is at www.statravel.com.au. Flight Centre (☎ 131 600 Australia-wide) is also widespread; the main branches are at 82 Elizabeth St, Sydney and at National Bank Towers in Auckland (☎ 09-309 6171). It's at www.flightcentre.com.au on the Web.

In addition, IB Tours (☎ 612-9560 6722), with a Web site at www.ib-tours.com.au; and Ibertours Travel (☎ 613-9670 8388), at www.ibertours.com.au on the Web, are Morocco specialists.

Asia

Hong Kong, Bangkok and Singapore are the main centres for cheap air tickets in South-East Asia, although Morocco is not a huge market. You're unlikely to find anything direct, but reasonable tickets via London, Amsterdam and Paris do crop up. Alternatively, get a cheap ticket to Europe and then head south.

From Morocco the major carriers sometimes offer special fares (eg, Tokyo for Dr7200 with British Airways), but don't hold your breath.

Africa

RAM has direct flights between Casablanca and South Africa (Dr6297 one way), Mali (Dr5006 return), Mauritania (Dr4283 one way), Egypt (Dr4627 return) and Senegal (Dr4440 return). Flights into Algeria from Casablanca cost Dr1658 one way or Dr2401 return, and to Tunisia Dr2788 return (for Tunis) and Dr3598 return (for Jerba, ideal for those heading east into Libya).

Strangely, for the cheapest deals from Morocco to Southern Africa, you'll probably have to go via London, Paris or Amsterdam.

Middle East

RAM has direct flights to Dubai (Dr5455 return) and has recently commenced a service to Gaza in the Palestinian Territories (Dr5455 for one-month return). Gulf Air has the cheapest flights to Abu Dhabi (Dr5455 return).

For Israel, take a flight into Europe first, though at the time of writing Iberia was offering returns to Tel Aviv for Dr4500.

LAND

Taking your own vehicle to Morocco is comparatively straightforward. In addition to your vehicle registration document and an International Driving Permit (although many foreign, including European Union, licences are acceptable), a Green Card is required from the car's insurer. These are relatively inexpensive (say, UK£30 per month) though often only provide third-party, fire and theft protection. Not all insurers cover Morocco.

If you cannot get a Green Card, temporary insurance can be arranged at Spanish or Moroccan ferry ports, but cover is not always adequate. It's therefore advisable to arrange more comprehensive and reliable cover before you leave. Campbell Irvine Ltd (☎ 020-7937 9903, @ ci@netcomuk.co.uk), 48 Earls Court Rd, London, W8 6EJ, can be recommended for foreign insurance. On a UK£5000 vehicle you're looking at more than UK£100 per month for comprehensive cover.

There is no need for a *carnet de passage en doune* when taking your car to Morocco, Algeria or Tunisia, but one is required in many other African countries. Effectively, carnets are customs guarantee documents for the temporary importation of a vehicle in a foreign country. Without it your vehicle could be liable for customs and other taxes upon entering a foreign country – in some African countries this is up to 150% of the vehicle's value! The period of guarantee is not indefinite and varies from country to country.

In the UK, the Automobile Association (☎ 01256-493806) and Royal Automobile Club (☎ 01454-208000) offer carnets, as do similar motoring organisations throughout the world. The carnet itself is relatively cheap. You're looking at about UK£55 to UK£75 for between five and 25 pages – each country where a carnet is required will take up one page. In addition, both organisations require applicants to be members and to take out a financial guarantee or indemnity against any possible claim for duty (eg, should the vehicle be abandoned and become liable for duty). This is commonly arranged by bank guarantee, cash deposit or insurance.

It's essential to ensure that the carnet is filled out properly at each border crossing, or you could be up for a lot of money. The carnet may also need to list any expensive spares you plan to carry, such as a gearbox.

The UK & Europe

Bus It's possible to get a bus ticket to destinations in Morocco from as far away as London, but unlike train tickets, coach fares are all through-tickets. With Eurolines (☎ 01582-726545), at www.eurolines.co.uk on the Web, single/return tickets from London to Tangier, Casablanca and Marrakesh cost UK£93/166, rising to UK£116/192 in high season. Coaches to Fès are fractionally more expensive. Services to Casablanca (32½ hours) and Marrakesh (35½ hours) leave Victoria Coach Station (☎ 020-7730 3466) on Tuesday and Sunday at 8.30 pm. Services to Tangier (25 hours) and Fès (31½ hours) depart on Tuesday and Thursday at 8.30 pm.

Services are run in conjunction with the Compagnie de Transports Marocains (CTM), Morocco's national line.

Busabout (☎ 020-7950 1661), a UK-based hop-on, hop-off bus service, will get you to southern Spain. You buy a pass valid for between 15 days (UK£155) and seven months (UK£659) and travel as often as you like between Western European cities including Madrid, Granada, Málaga, La Línea (handy for Gibraltar) and Tarifa. Buses run on a set route. Busabout is at www.busabout.com on the Web.

From France there are departures from most major cities to numerous destinations in Morocco. Fares vary according to the final destination and season. Eurolines has an office in Paris (☎ 01 49 72 51 51) at 3–5 Ave Porte de la Villette). There's a more central office (☎ 01 43 54 11 99) at Rue St Jacques 55, off Blvd St Michel. Its Web site is at www.eurolines.fr.

Return fares include from Paris to Casablanca or Tangier (1350FF) and Marrakesh (1650FF), from Lyon to Casablanca or Tangier (1500FF), and Marseille to Tangier (1320FF) and Casablanca (1560FF).

There are a large number of Eurolines services (from Germany, Italy, France and the UK) to Málaga, from where there's a hydrofoil service to Ceuta (90 minutes).

From Morocco, CTM (☎ 02-458824 in Casablanca) operates buses from Casablanca and most other main cities to France, Belgium, Spain, Germany and Italy. Most leave from or go via Casablanca and cross at Tangier, but some cross Nador to Almeria.

From Casablanca there are bus services to Paris (Dr1200; via Bordeaux Dr950), Nice (Dr1040), Marseille (Dr1220), Strasbourg (Dr1040), Brussels (Dr1250; via Lille), Frankfurt (Dr1050) and Bologna (Dr1350; via Turin Dr1250).

Buses to Spain leave Casablanca daily except Sunday. Algeciras (Dr450), Málaga (Dr615), Granada (Dr645), Madrid (Dr715), Valencia (Dr890), Barcelona (Dr1100) and Bilbao (Dr920) are among the destinations.

Book at least a week in advance.

There are CTM agents in Barcelona (☎ 932 458856), Madrid (☎ 91 530760), Paris (☎ 01 49 72 51 51) and Brussels (☎ 02-538861).

SAT (☎ 02-444470), 56 Ouled Ziane in Casablanca, also runs reliable services to Europe starting from Tiznit, Casablanca, Fès, Oujda and Nador.

Train A two-zone Inter-Rail pass (UK£235, or UK£169 if aged under 26) allows unlimited rail travel in France, Spain and Morocco for one month. However, you need to have lived in Europe for at least six months (take your passport along as ID).

A single zone Inter-Rail pass covers Morocco and Spain, is valid for 22 days and costs UK£179/129 for those over/under 26 years of age.

For non-EU residents, a Eurail Pass lets you travel in 17 European countries, so will get you as far as Algeciras, but it's not valid in Morocco. Unlimited travel passes are available from 15 days (UK£415/290) up to three months (UK£1165/815). Eurail Flexipasses are slightly different, allowing either 10 days (UK£485/345) or 15 days (UK£645/450) unlimited travel within a two-month period.

Europasses allow between five (UK£260/170) and 15 days (UK£545/380) travel within a two-month period in five European countries.

Eurail passes are supposed to be purchased before arrival in Europe. In the USA, contact Rail Europe (☎ 800 4-EURAIL); Web site www.raileurope.com. However, passes can be bought in London at Drifters Travel Centre (☎ 020-7402 9171), 22 Craven Terrace, W2 3QH, with a Web site at www.driftersclub.com; or Rail Europe (☎ 0990-848848), French Railway House, 179 Piccadilly, WIV OBA.

Train travel is inexpensive in Morocco, so Morocco-only Inter-Rail passes are not good value. Discount rail cards are available in Morocco in any case (see Train in the Getting Around chapter).

Taking a direct train for France is not a bad option. From Paris, your best bet is probably to take the TGV from La Gare Montparnasse to Algeciras or Málaga via Madrid (874/1748FF one way/return 2nd-class, plus 90FF for a couchette; 25 hours).

Heading out of Morocco, standard one-way fares to European cities are only a bit more expensive than the coach – Madrid is Dr730, Paris Dr1570, Brussels Dr1830, Frankfurt Dr2180 and London Dr2220. There are significant reductions for students and those under aged 26.

You can book international tickets in Morocco up to two months ahead.

Mauritania

Although a UN ceasefire has kept the Western Sahara quiet since September 1991, crossing the border into Mauritania isn't straightforward. However, hundreds of adventurous souls in 4WDs and on motorbikes do it every year. Specific overland

visas are required and issued in Rabat and at other Mauritanian embassies in Europe. It's a journey for the thoroughly well prepared, and hitchhiking is near impossible.

The safest route into Mauritania is currently from Dakhla south along the coast (in a military convoy) to Nouâdhibou on the border and then south along the coast to Nouakchott. Vehicles and small convoys, including parts of the Paris-Dakar Rally, have been robbed at gunpoint along other inland routes. The border is heavily mined, so stay on the *piste* (dirt track). In Dakhla you'll need to present yourself to the police, army and customs before getting into the convoy.

Entering Morocco from Mauritania is not officially possible, though guides illicitly lead the way through the border minefields at night.

For the trip to Mauritania and trans-Saharan travel generally, Chris Scott's *Sahara Overland* is just about indispensable. Information is also available at www.sahara-overland.com.

SEA

Catching the ferry from Sète in France, or from Spain and the Spanish enclaves of

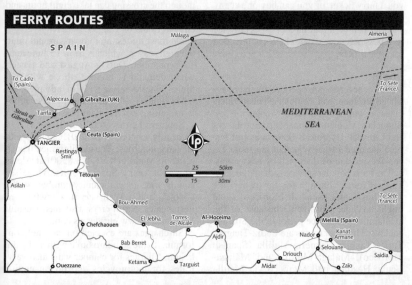

Prepare for Tangier

If you're arriving at or leaving from Tangier, be aware of the shenanigans associated with the port – hustlers with colourful stories (see Dangers & Annoyances under Tangier in the Mediterranean Coast & the Rif chapter). Ceuta or Melilla make better first points of entry for the uninitiated. To avoid some of the hassles when leaving, get your ticket in Tangier's *ville nouvelle* (new town) or from the row of ticket offices just before the space-age-looking ferry terminal port-side (there are also some ticket booths inside the terminal itself, but they're often closed). All the ferry companies are represented here, just a five-minute walk inside the Port Gate.

The latter option is ideal for foot passengers who can turn up (taxis will drop you) with packed bags, buy a ticket and jump on the next available ferry. However, vehicle owners travelling in high season (July to August and the Easter holidays) and those looking for passage on routes with limited services are advised to book in advance.

Make sure that you're given an exit form with your ticket – it must be filled out before your passport is stamped – and allow more than 90 minutes before ferry departure for ticket purchase and passport control.

Opposite the ticket booths, below Tangier's ferry terminal, are a row of bank-run *bureau de change* (foreign exchange offices).

Reductions for students, Inter-Rail or Eurail pass holders and EU pensioners may be possible when buying your ticket in Spain and the Spanish enclaves of Ceuta and Melilla, but in Morocco knowledge of these discounts is denied. Make a point of asking for them. Though the Spanish take credit cards, you must pay in cash in Morocco.

All tickets sold in Morocco are subject to Dr20 tax.

Ceuta and Melilla, is relatively straightforward. Numerous travel agencies will sell you a ferry ticket, or you can buy one at any of the ports. However, arriving at or leaving Tangier can be a real hassle, especially for foot passengers, and can't be recommended for first-timers.

Spain

Various car ferries are operated by the Spanish government-run company Trasmediterránea, as well as by Islena de Navegación SA, Buquebus, Comarit, Comarship, EuroFerrys and Limadet. Hydrofoils (known as fast ferries) are used extensively, but are more expensive and can be disrupted by heavy seas.

The most popular service is the Algeciras-Tangier route, although for car owners the Algeciras-Ceuta (Spanish Morocco) route might be more worthwhile because of the availability of tax-free petrol in the Spanish enclave. The other routes are Cadiz-Tangier, Tarifa-Tangier, Almería-Melilla (Spanish Morocco), Málaga-Melilla and Málaga-Ceuta. Heading into Morocco via Melilla

(and then Nador) is easily the most painless way to arrive from the Spanish mainland, though the crossing can take eight hours and costs twice as much as crossing from Algeciras to Ceuta or Tangier.

On most routes, more boats are put on in the high season, which is from 15 June until 15 September. During August and Easter, when demand is highest, those with vehicles should book well in advance. At other times you're unlikely to have problems getting a convenient passage.

Southern Ferries (☎ 020-7491 4968), 179 Piccadilly, London W1V 9DB, can help with all ferry inquiries; Trasmediterránea has an office in Madrid (☎ 91 423 8500) at Alcalá 61 and at many Spanish ports. There's a countrywide general inquiry number (☎ 902 454645) and a Web site at www.trasmed iterranea.es. EuroFerrys also has a useful Web site at www.euroferrys.com.

Surcharges are exacted on cars not conforming to the standard 6m length and 1.8m height. Charges for camper vans also vary. Rates for motorcycles depend on engine capacity, while bicycles are charged the minimum motorcycle rate.

Spanish passport control is quite straightforward, but customs can be slow if you're coming from Morocco.

Algeciras-Tangier Between Trasmediterránea, EuroFerrys, Comarit and Limadet (who all have identical fares) there's a ferry to and from Tangier at least every 1½ hours between 7 am and 9.30 pm daily. In high season, services run hourly between 6 am and 9 pm, and 24 hours a day upon peak demand (usually in August). Passengers pay 3200 ptas (or Dr210) one way. Children up to four years old travel free, while children four to 12 pay 50%. Cars are 9900 ptas (Dr648) and camper vans are 16,400 ptas (Dr1070); motorcyles and bikes cost 3000 ptas (Dr200). Some ferry companies offer '1st class' for an extra 20%.

All companies cooperate to create one master timetable and also sell tickets on each other's boats. This makes things relatively straightforward, though the Trasmediterránea and Limadet-Ferry ticket offices are usually your best bet.

There's a Trasmediterránea office in Algeciras (☎ 956 651755) at Recinto del Puerto, or buy your ticket port-side.

The crossing takes 2½ hours.

Algeciras-Ceuta (Spanish Morocco) There are 22 fast-ferry crossings (35 minutes) from Ceuta between 6.30 am and 11.30 pm, and the same number from Algeciras between 5.30 am and 10.30 pm. In addition, EuroFerrys puts on at least six ferries (90 minutes) from either end between 8 am to 8.30 pm weekdays, three services on Saturday and two on Sunday. Extra services are added upon demand.

At the time of writing, EuroFerrys was charging 2945 ptas per person (1801 ptas on the normal ferry), 8223 ptas per car, 15,020 ptas for camper vans and from 1860 ptas to 2801 ptas for motorcycles. Some companies offer expensive Club Class tickets.

On EuroFerrys services, children aged between four and 12 pay half fare, and those under four travel free. With other compa-

nies, only children under two years of age travel free.

In Ceuta, there are dozens of private ticket offices close to and inside the ferry terminal (Estación Marítima). The ferry companies themselves have offices around to the left as you walk in the main building – this is often the best place to get tickets (from specific companies only) at the last minute.

Málaga-Ceuta (Spanish Morocco) From Ceuta, Buquebus (in Ceuta ☎ 956 505353; in Málaga ☎ 952 227905; throughout Spain ☎ 902 414242) runs hydrofoil services at 7 am and 7.30 pm, while hydrofoils leave Málaga at 9.15 am and 10 pm. On Friday, the evening departures are at 5 pm (Ceuta) and 8 pm (Málaga).

The journey takes 90 minutes and is ideal for those with flight connections to/from Málaga international airport. An extra daily service is put on when required.

There are two classes of passenger ticket, Club and Turista, which relate directly to the amount of seat padding you'll have under your backside. Club tickets cost 5900 ptas and Turista 4995 ptas. Children aged between four and 12 pay half price, while students and those under 26 get substantial discounts. Cars cost 14,900 ptas, small camper vans around 17,900 ptas and motorbikes from 2700 to 3150 ptas.

It's important to book this hydrofoil service well in advance (even for foot passengers) at peak times.

Cadiz-Tangier The International Maritime Transport Corporation (IMTC) runs a ferry between Cadiz and Tangier once every morning and early evening, in either direction, every day (three hours). Costs for vehicles and bikes are identical to those for the Algeciras-Tangier ferries, but adults are charged 3900 ptas (Dr250) and children 1950 ptas (Dr125).

Buy your tickets port-side or from Vapores Suardiaz Andalucia (☎ 956 282111), Avda Del Puerto, 1-6, 11006 in Cadiz; or from Comarship (☎ 09 336002), 2 Rue Pasteur, in Tangier's ville nouvelle, or its ticket booth in Tangier Port.

Tarifa-Tangier This (one hour) service had just begun at the time of writing, departing from Tarifa at 9 am and Tangier at 3 pm (Moroccan time). Additional sailings are planned. Check at the harbour, or at Marruecotur (☎ 956 684751) at Calle de la Constitución 5/6, opposite Paseo de la Alameda in Tarifa. Fares are 3200 ptas for passengers, 9900 ptas for driver and car, and 3000 ptas for a bike/motorcycle.

Almería-Melilla (Spanish Morocco) Far fewer ferries ply the route between Almería and Melilla (and to and from Melilla generally), and Trasmediterránea offers them all. In the low season there is generally a ferry every day except Saturday from Almería at 11.30 am. Going the other way, there's a departure from Melilla every weekday at 2.30 pm and one at 11.30 pm on Saturday.

The trip takes 6½ to eight hours. The cheapest fare (*butaca turista*, or deck fare) is 4020 ptas each way. You can also get beds in two- or four-person cabins, some with toilets. Prices per person range from 6710 ptas to 11,540 ptas for single occupation of a twin berth.

Children aged from two to 12 travel for half-price (infants go free).

A normal-sized car costs 10,500 ptas, camper vans 16,930 ptas and motorcycles 4295 ptas to 6330 ptas. You can buy tickets at the Estación Marítima (about a 10- to 15-minute walk from the train and bus stations), from travel agencies or from the Trasmediterránea office in the centre of town.

Services are added upon demand in the high season, when fares rise slightly.

Málaga-Melilla (Spanish Morocco) Also operated by Trasmediterránea, ferries leave Málaga in the low season at 1 pm from Tuesday to Saturday, 5 pm on Monday and at 11 pm on Sunday. From Melilla, the ferry departs at 11 pm Wednesday to Saturday and at 8.30 am on Monday. There are departures at 2 am and 11 pm on Tuesday.

Fares are the same as for the Almería-Melilla ferry. The trip takes 7½ to 10 hours.

As in Almería, you can purchase tickets most easily at the Estación Marítima, which

is more or less directly south of the town centre.

Almería-Nador It's also possible to travel directly into/out of Morocco via Nador's own port, 15km north of the city and 1km short of the Spanish enclave of Melilla. However, skip Melilla and you'll miss out on duty-free fuel and booze. Between them, Ferrimaroc (☎ 950 274800 in Almería, ☎ 06-348100 in Morocco) and Limadet (☎ 950 271280) put on six services per week in either direction during the winter and up to three ferries daily during the summer. Ferrimaroc has a Web site at www.ferrimaroc.com.

It's a six- to seven-hour crossing and cabins are available (Dr371 to Dr590). Other prices are similar to the Almería crossing, but prices rise by roughly 15% in high season.

Gibraltar

Gibraltar-Tangier Bland Shipping runs a thrice-weekly passenger-only service between the British outpost and Morocco. The small ferry leaves Gibraltar on Wednesday at 9.30 am, Saturday at 9.30 am and Sunday at 4 pm, and from Tangier on Wednesday at 3.30 pm, Thursday at 5.30 pm and Sunday at 9.30 am. The two-hour voyage costs Dr260/Dr510 or UK£18/35 one way/return.

In Gibraltar, buy your tickets at Bland Travel (☎ 77012) at 81 Irish Town or Tourafrica (☎ 77666), ICC Bldg, Main St. In Tangier, go to Agence Med (☎ 935875), 3 Rue ibn Rochd or Med Travel (☎ 322335), 22 Ave Mohammed V.

There is also talk of a vehicle ferry plying this route, so inquire in advance.

France

Sète-Tangier With a swimming pool and nightclub (of sorts) on board, this car-ferry service is considerably more luxurious than those linking Spain and Morocco, and commensurately more expensive.

It's operated by the Compagnie Marocaine de Navigation (Comanav). The crossing is made six or seven times a month, usually once every four to five days. As a rule, the *Marrakesh* leaves Sète at 7 pm and Tangier at 6 pm (local time).

The trip takes 36 to 38 hours and the fare ranges from 1500FF (Dr1210) for the cheapest four-bed cabin in low season to 3630FF (Dr2920) for a plush two-bed cabin in high season. Children aged between two and 12 travel for half-price.

It'll cost between 1780FF (Dr1440) and 2515FF (Dr2030) to transport your car, and 580FF (Dr470) to 1300FF (Dr1050) for motorcycles.

There are special reduced fares, per passenger and vehicle, for students and people under 26.

You can book tickets for this service at Southern Ferries (see Spain under Sea) or in France at the SNCM Ferry-terranée office (☎ 04 91 56 30 30, fax 04 91 56 36 66) at 61 Blvd des Dames, Marseille 13226; or the Sète office (☎ 04 67 46 68 00, fax 67 74 93 05), 4 Quai d'Alger, Sète 34202.

In Morocco, Comanav's main office (☎ 02-302412, fax 300790) is in Casablanca at 7 Blvd de la Résistance. In Tangier, the office (☎ 09-940488, fax 944022) is at 43 Ave Abou al-Alaâ el-Maâri.

Sète-Nador From June to September, Comanav (see the previous Sète-Tangier entry) also runs a ferry from Sète to Nador in northern Morocco. There are three or four departures in either direction during June and September and a sailing roughly every four days in July and August. Details and prices are much the same as the Sète-Tangier crossing, though about eight hours quicker.

DEPARTURE TAXES

There is no departure tax upon leaving Morocco, and departure formalities are quite straightforward. You must fill in an exit card and have your passport stamped before exiting.

ORGANISED TOURS

A growing number of foreign operators are running organised trips to Morocco. More than 50 agencies operate out of the UK. The Office National Marocain Tourisme (ONMT), in your country is a good place to begin, and it should be able to provide you with a comprehensive list of tour operators.

Possibilities range from the more traditional tours of the Imperial Cities (Rabat, Marrakesh, Fès and Meknès) to beach holidays, golf trips, trekking, bird-watching and desert safaris.

The following information is intended as a guide only, and not as a recommendation of these over other operators.

Remember that the programs on such trips are usually tight, leaving little room for roaming around on your own, but they do remove much of the hassle. It is also possible to join some of these tours after making your own way to Morocco. Some trips, such as trekking Jebel Sarhro, can be as economical as trying to organise it yourself.

Shop around and check itinerary details, accommodation, insurance and tour conditions carefully. Also find out who will arrange the ticketing, visas and other documentation.

Tours from The UK

Best of Morocco (☎ 01380-828533, fax 828630) One of the best-established tour operators for Morocco, with over 30 years experience. Tailor-made tours and holidays include everything from camel trekking and skiing to cultural tours and beach holidays.
Web site: www.morocco-travel.com

Cadogan Holidays (☎ 023-8082 8300, fax 8022 8601) Slightly upmarket package tours to coastal resorts and the Imperial Cities.
Web site: www.cadoganholidays.com

Encounter Overland (☎ 020-7370 6845, e ad venture@encounter.co.uk) One of many adventure companies offering lengthy trans-African expeditions that include Morocco, plus a two-week Morocco-only trip.
Web site: www.encounter-overland.com

Exodus Travels (☎ 020-8675 5550, e sales@ exodustravels.co.uk) An excellent operator offering short or long treks in the High Atlas, Central Atlas, Anti Atlas and Jebel Sarhro, as well as trips to the Sahara and the Imperial Cities.
Web site: www.exodus.co.uk

Explore Worldwide (☎ 01252-760000, e info@ explore.co.uk) Specialises in year-round mountain trekking trips, tours of the Imperial Cities and the Sahara.
Web site: www.explore.co.uk

Far Frontiers (☎/fax 01985-850926, e info@ farfrontiers.com) Tailor-made 4WD, trekking and adventure expeditions.

Naturetrek (☎ 01962-733051, e info@naturetrek .co.uk) Specialist wildlife tours (mostly bird-watching) in winter and High Atlas trekking with a wildlife emphasis in summer.
Web site: www.naturetrek.co.uk

Panorama (☎ 01273-427777, fax 427111) Slightly upmarket package tours to coastal resorts and the Imperial Cities.
Web site: www .panoramaholidays.co.uk

Sherpa Expeditions (☎ 020-8577 2717, e sales@ sherpa-walking-holidays.co.uk) A well-respected trekking company that organises treks in the High Atlas and Jebel Sarhro.
Web site: www.sherpa-walking-holidays.co.uk

Tribes (☎ 01728-685971, e info@tribes.co.uk) Trekking, activity and cultural tours on a strong ethical and environmental basis. Winner of Tourism Concern's 'Responsible Tour Operator' award.
Web site: www.tribes.co.uk

Wildwings (☎ 0117-984 8040, fax 967 4444), International House, Bank Rd, Kingswood, Bristol BS15 2LX. Tailor-made bird-watching trips.

Getting Around

AIR

If time is limited, it might be worth considering the occasional internal flight offered by Royal Air Maroc (RAM). Several reductions are available. If you buy a return international ticket (valid for no longer than a month and including a Saturday night stay), you are entitled to discounts on normal one-way fares.

If you're under 26 or a student under 30, you're entitled to between 25% and 60% off all fares. For example, the student one-way fare from Casablanca to Agadir is Dr323 (Dr908 full fare), to Laayoune it's Dr518 (Dr1463 full fare) and Fès to Agadir (via Casablanca) is around Dr360 (Dr1042 one way). There are group reductions and children aged two to 12 travel at half-price. These discounts are normally only available through RAM.

Internal airports serviced by RAM are Agadir, Al-Hoceima, Casablanca, Dakhla, Er-Rachidia, Essaouira, Fès, Laayoune, Marrakesh, Nador, Ouarzazate, Oujda, Rabat, Tangier, Tan Tan and Tetouan. About the longest flight you could take is the twice-weekly Dakhla-Tangier run via Casablanca and Laayoune or Agadir, which is just over four hours flying time, but can take over seven hours. The bulk of internal flights involve making a connection in Casablanca, from where Marrakesh, Tangier and Agadir are the most popular destinations (with at least daily flights). You can pick up a free timetable at most RAM offices or look it up on the Web (www.royalairmaroc.com).

Regional Air Lines (☎ 02-538080 in Casablanca) offers a more business orientated (and more expensive) service, again using Casablanca as a central hub. Destinations include Agadir, Essaouira, Laayoune, Oujda and Tangier, but their external network is probably more useful (see the Air entry in the Getting There & Away chapter).

BUS

A dense network of buses operates throughout Morocco, with many private companies competing for business alongside the main national carrier, Compagnie de Transports Marocains (CTM). CTM is the only firm to have a truly national service. In most cities or towns there's a single central bus station *(gare routière)*, but in some places CTM maintains a separate terminal. Occasionally, there are other stations for a limited number of fairly local destinations.

Some Moroccan bus stations are like madhouses, with touts running around screaming out any number of destinations for buses about to depart. Occasionally, you will find would-be guides anxious to help you to the right ticket booth – for a small consideration of course – but often touts can actually be of help. They're walking, talking timetables and will happily guide you to the ticket booth (and take a small commission from the company) for the next departing bus *tout suite* (whether it's the most comfortable or quickest service is a different matter!).

Bus (and train) stations in the main cities have left-luggage depots, which are sometimes open 24 hours. All bags must be padlocked. You can also transport bikes on buses, but it'll be charged as freight (around Dr20 for an average journey).

Supratours runs buses in conjunction with trains (see Train later in this chapter).

Compagnie de Transports Marocains (CTM)

CTM (☎ 02-458824 in Casablanca) is the best and most secure bus company in Morocco and serves most destinations of interest to travellers. The company offers both 1st- and 2nd-class buses, but the distinction seems to be made mostly on longer routes away from the big centres (more often than not it will be a 1st-class bus you're getting on). On CTM buses, children four years old and up pay full fare, which tends to be 15% to 30% more expensive than other lines (fares work out to about Dr1 for every four or 5km) and are comparable to 2nd-class fares on normal trains.

Where possible, and especially if services are infrequent or do not originate in the place you want to leave, it's best to book ahead.

Many CTM buses are fairly modern and comfortable (though there are a few dogs out there) and some 1st-class buses have videos (a mixed blessing), air-conditioning and heating (they sometimes overdo both).

Some 1st-class CTM fares are as follows:

from	to	fare (Dr)	hours
Agadir	Laayoune	200	11
	Tangier	237	14
Casablanca	Agadir	140	10
	Fès	80	5
	Marrakesh	65	5
	Tangier	110	7
Marrakesh	Fès	128	8
	Ouarzazate	52	5
Tangier	Fès	85	6
	Tiznit	260	15

There is an official baggage charge on CTM buses (Dr5 per pack). Once you have bought your ticket you get a baggage tag, which you should hang on to, as you'll need it when you arrive.

CTM also operates international buses (in conjunction with Eurolines) from all the main Moroccan cities to Spain, France, Italy and northern Europe. Check out its Web site (www.ctm.co.ma) and see the Land entry in the Getting There & Away chapter for more information.

Other Companies

The other bus companies are all privately owned and only operate regionally. The biggest of them is SATAS, which operates from Casablanca south and is just as good as CTM. Other companies offering '1st-class' services between the major cities usually use modern, comfortable buses.

At the cheaper end of the scale, and on shorter or local routes, there is a fair number of two-bit operations with one or two well-worn buses, so don't expect comfortable seats or air-conditioning. Unlike CTM, these buses tend to stop an awful lot.

Some companies offer 1st and 2nd class, although the difference in fare and comfort is rarely great. On the secondary runs you

Traveller's Code of Etiquette

When travelling on public transport, it's considered both selfish and bad manners to eat while those around you go without. Always buy a little extra that can be offered to your neighbours. A bag of fruit makes a great choice.

Next comes the ritual. If you have offered food, etiquette dictates that your fellow passengers should decline it. It should be offered a second time, this time a little more persuasively, but again it will be turned down. On a third more insistent offer, your neighbours are free to accept the gift if they wish to.

If, conversely, you are offered food, but you don't want it or it even repulses you, it's good manners to accept a small piece anyway. At the same time, you should pat your stomach contentedly to indicate that you are full.

In return, for participating in this elaborate ritual, you will be accorded great respect, offered protection and cared for like a friend, which means fewer worries about leaving your luggage when going to the toilet.

can often buy your tickets on the bus, but if you do, you'll probably have to stand.

More often than not you'll be charged for baggage handling by someone, especially if it's going on top of the bus – Dr3 is about right.

These buses rarely have heating in winter, even when crossing the High Atlas, so make sure you have plenty of warm clothing with you. Occasionally, buses are held up by snowdrifts in mountain passes; then you'll really feel the cold. The Marrakesh-Ouarzazate road is prone to this.

TRAIN

Morocco's Office National des Chemins de Fer (ONCF) is one of the most modern rail systems in Africa, linking most of the main centres. The trains, mostly Belgian-made, are generally comfortable, fast and preferable to buses. Present lines go as far south as Marrakesh.

Buses run by Supratours link up with trains to further destinations with no rail line, so that the ONCF can get you as far south as Dakhla.

Classes

There are three types of train: *ordinaire*, *rapide* and shuttle (TNR). There are different 1st- and 2nd-class fares on all these trains, though 2nd-class fares on rapide and shuttle services are identical.

The main difference between ordinaire and rapide trains is not, as the name suggests, speed (though there's a slight difference), but comfort and air-conditioning. Ordinaire trains are the cheapest on the network, but have now been reduced to one or two late-night services along the main routes. Second-class is more than adequate on any journey.

Tickets & Fares

You are advised to buy tickets at the station, as a supplement is charged for doing so on the train.

A ticket is technically valid for five days, so that you can use it to get off at intermediate stops before reaching your final destination. You need to ask for a *bulletin d'arrêt* at the intermediate stop. Always hang on to tickets, as inspectors check them on the trains and they are collected at the station on arrival.

Children aged under four travel free. Those up to 12 years old get a reduction of 10% to 50%, depending on the service.

Couchettes are available on the overnight ordinaire trains between Marrakesh and Tangier, and Oujda and Casablanca. The compartments fold up into six bunks (couchettes) and they're well worth the extra Dr50. There's also a more expensive overnight rapide train from Oujda.

Some sample 2nd-class fares in ordinaire/rapide trains are as follows:

from	to	fare (Dr)	hours
Casablanca	Fès	73/94	4½
	Marrakesh	56/73	3½
	Rabat	21/27	1
Tangier	Casablanca	87/114	5½
	Fès	72/93	6
	Marrakesh	143/186	9½

Two rail discount cards are available in Morocco. The Carte Fidelité (Dr149) is for those aged over 26 and gives you 50% reductions on eight return or 16 one-way journeys. If you're under 26, the Carte Jeune (Dr99) will give you the same discounts on fares for one year. To apply you need one passport-sized photo and a photocopy of your passport.

It is also possible to transport your bike on ordinaire trains, if they travel in the goods wagon. Prices depend on the distance. For example, Casablanca to Tangier is Dr45 and Casablanca to Marrakesh is Dr32. You'd be lucky to get your bike on any train without a goods wagon.

Shuttles

These express services (TNRs) operate regularly between Kenitra, Rabat, Casablanca and Mohammed V airport, and supplement the rapide services on this line. There are 12 daily services between Casablanca and the airport, roughly between 5.15 am and 8.45 pm, making them a convenient way to catch most flights. For more details, see the Getting Around sections under Casablanca and Rabat.

Supratours Buses

The ONCF runs buses through Supratours to widen its network. Thus Nador, near Melilla on the Mediterranean coast, is linked to the Oujda-Casablanca lines by a special bus to Taourirt station.

Tetouan is linked to the main line from Tangier by bus to Tnine Sidi Lyamani. Train passengers heading further south than Marrakesh link up with buses at Marrakesh station for Essaouira, Agadir, Smara, Laayoune and Dakhla.

Supratours buses are excellent and you don't have to have a train connection to use them – the services from Marrakesh are particularly useful.

Timetables

Timetables for the whole system are posted in French at most stations. A handy pocketbook timetable called the *Horaires des Trains*, covering all destinations, can usually be picked up at train stations.

You can also get timetable and price information from ONCF's simple but efficient Web site (www.oncf.org.ma).

TAXI

The elderly Mercedes you'll see belting along Moroccan roads and gathered in great flocks near bus stations are shared taxis (*grand taxis* in French or *taxiat kebira* in Arabic). They're a big feature of Morocco's public transport system and link towns to their nearest neighbours in a kind of leapfrogging system. Taxis sometimes ply longer routes when there's demand, but these services are few and usually leave first thing in the morning. Grand taxis take six passengers (two in the front, four in the back) and leave when full.

The fixed-rate fares (listed in individual city entries) are generally a little higher than bus fares, but are still very reasonable. Attempts to extract more from foreigners, however, do sometimes occur – try to see what other passengers are paying.

When asking about fares, make it clear you want to pay for *une place* in a *taxi collectif* (shared taxi). Another expression that helps explain that you don't want to hire a taxi for yourself is that you wish to travel *ma'a an-nas* (with other people). Touts and taxi drivers sometimes try and bounce tourists into hiring the whole taxi. Smile and stand your ground if you're not interested, but from some routes hiring an entire grand taxi can be a great way to travel, especially if you're travelling with a small group – you can take your time on the road and stop whenever you want.

Before setting off, negotiate patiently for a reasonable fare (if you're hiring the whole taxi, aim for six times the fare for one place) and make sure plans for stopping en route are clear. The Ziz and Drâa Valleys and the Tizi n'Test are particularly good to visit in a shared taxi.

Taxis are much faster than buses because they travel at a greater rate of knots and don't make as many stops.

PICK-UP TRUCK & 4WD

In the more remote parts of the country, especially in the Atlas Mountains, the way locals get around from village to village is by Berber *camionettes* (pick-up trucks), old vans or in the back of a truck. This is a bumpy but adventurous way to get to know the country and people a little better, but can mean waiting a considerable time (even days) for the next lift. When travelling between remote towns and villages, the best time to travel is early on market days (generally once or twice a week). It's common for 4WD taxis to operate on more remote *pistes* (dirt tracks) that would destroy normal taxis.

CAR & MOTORCYCLE

The roads connecting the main centres of Morocco are generally very good, there's an expanding motorway network, and increasing numbers of visitors are bringing their own cars and motorcycles into the country. There are many places that you simply cannot reach without private transport, so a vehicle can be an enormous advantage.

Road Rules & Hazards

Renting a car does bring its own problems, however, as this reader's experience shows.

In the *hammada* (stony desert), for example, decent roads may stretch for several kilometres before inexplicably evaporating. Taking their place are blotchy pot-holed strings of tar, about the width of a sidewalk. At the same time, the straightness of the road, the flatness of the terrain and the relatively sparse traffic encourages high speeds (110km/h to 120km/h). Thus when an oncoming lorry or grand taxi does arrive, it's a game of chicken that the tourist (in the rented car) must surely lose, flying onto a shoulder lower than the road itself, filled with large, sharp stones...I'm not sure prospective car renters know what they're getting into.

Timothy Brennan, Pittsburg, USA

In Morocco you drive on the right, as in Continental Europe. Daylight driving is generally no problem and not too stressful, though in the bigger cities getting constantly cut off is par for the course. Keep your wits about you at all times – the traffic accident rate in Morocco is high.

Night driving is particularly hazardous: It's legal for vehicles travelling under 20km/h to

Moroccans at work and play: mint vendor with a trolley piled high of the vital ingredient for tea, Essaouira (top); falconer, Marrakesh (middle left); Berber girl with her donkey, Aït Benhaddou (middle right); surfers check out the waves at Oudayas Surf Club (where King Mohammmed VI is the president), Rabat (bottom)

Head to the souq if you're in the market for refreshment from a tired water seller in Fès (top left), some musical entertainment in Casablanca (top right), or beans to prepare your own *harira* (spicy lentil soup) in Chefchaouen (bottom).

Road Distances (km)

	Agadir	Al-Hoceima	Casablanca	Dakhla	Er-Rachidia	Essaouira	Fès	Figuig	Marrakesh	Meknès	Nador	Ouarzazate	Oujda	Rabat	Safi	Smara	Tan Tan	Tangier	Tarfaya	Tetouan
Agadir	---																			
Al-Hoceima	1091	---																		
Casablanca	511	536	---																	
Dakhla	1173	2264	1684	---																
Er-Rachidia	681	616	545	1854	---															
Essaouira	173	887	351	1346	745	---														
Fès	756	275	289	1920	364	640	---													
Figuig	1076	669	920	2249	395	1081	719	---												
Marrakesh	273	758	238	1448	510	176	483	905	---											
Meknès	740	335	229	1913	346	580	60	741	467	---										
Nador	1095	175	628	2260	510	979	339	516	822	399	---									
Ouarzazate	375	992	442	1548	306	380	687	701	204	652	816	---								
Oujda	1099	293	632	2272	514	983	343	326	826	403	104	820	---							
Rabat	602	445	91	1775	482	442	198	877	321	138	535	528	541	---						
Safi	294	792	256	1467	683	129	545	1078	157	486	884	361	888	347	---					
Smara	551	1642	1062	746	1232	724	1307	1627	824	1291	1646	926	1650	1153	845	---				
Tan Tan	331	1422	842	842	1012	504	1087	1407	504	1071	1426	705	1430	933	625	220	---			
Tangier	880	323	369	2053	608	720	303	988	598	287	1086	811	609	278	625	1431	1211	---		
Tarfaya	544	1635	1055	633	1225	517	1300	1620	817	1284	1639	919	1643	1146	838	331	213	1424	---	
Tetouan	892	278	385	2065	604	736	281	931	675	258	437	820	555	294	641	1443	1223	57	1436	---

drive without lights, and in the early evening roads are often very busy with pedestrians (including large groups of schoolchildren), bicycles, horse-and-carts, donkeys and so on.

In towns, you should give way to traffic entering a roundabout from the right when you're already on one (quite a departure from prevailing rules in Europe). Speed limits in built-up areas range from 40km/h to 60km/h.

Outside the towns there is a national speed limit of 100km/h, rising to 120km/h on the motorways. There are two main sections, from Settat up the west coast to Asilah (it should reach Tangier by 2001) and from Rabat to Fès via Mèknes. There are plans to expand the network down to Marrakesh and Agadir from Casablanca and from Fès to Oujda. These projects should be complete by 2002. Tolls must be paid on all journeys. For example, Rabat to Fès is Dr27, Kenitra to Larache is Dr30 and Rabat to Casablanca is Dr17. You take a ticket upon joining the motorway and then pay at the end.

It is compulsory for drivers and passengers to wear seat belts in cars, but no-one does and you'll be lucky to find one in a grand taxi.

Many minor roads are too narrow for normal vehicles to pass without going onto the shoulder. You'll find yourself hitting the dirt a lot in this way. Stones thrown up by oncoming vehicles present a danger for windscreens.

Driving across the mountain ranges in winter can easily involve driving through snow and ice. This kind of driving is obviously dangerous. If a strong *chergui* (dry, easterly desert wind) is blowing and carrying a lot of dust, you'll have to wait until it eases off if you don't want to do your car considerable damage.

The High Atlas passes can often be closed altogether due to snow in the winter: Check the road conditions with the police or call the Service des Travaux Publiques (☎ 07-711717 in Rabat) before travelling.

Some of the pistes in Morocco can be negotiated by ordinary car, many are passable in a Renault 4 and some are 4WD territory only. Whatever vehicle you have, the going will be slow. Many stretches of mountain piste will be impassable in bad weather: The Michelin 959 map generally has these sections marked.

Whatever the season, inquire about road conditions with locals before setting off, check your tyres, take a usable spare and carry an adequate supply of water and petrol.

Rental

Renting a car in Morocco isn't cheap, but it is possible to strike very good bargains with some of the smaller dealers, and if there are four of you it becomes affordable.

Numerous local (and international) agencies exist and many have booths beside each other at airports – this is an excellent place to haggle, playing one company off against another until reaching a price that suits you.

Most of the international rental companies also have representatives throughout Morocco, including Hertz, Avis, Budget and Europcar, but note that rates can vary substantially between them and there is little room for bargaining.

The best cities in which to hire cars are Casablanca and Agadir, where the competition is greatest. There are also many agencies in Marrakesh, Tangier and Fès. The cheapest car is the Fiat Uno, though older Renault 4s are sometimes available. Both are well adapted to tackling Moroccan pistes.

Addresses of the international companies appear under individual city entries. They do not necessarily offer better vehicles than local companies but usually provide better service in the event of a breakdown or accident, as they have a network of offices around the country. Often a replacement car can be sent out to you from their nearest depot. In any event, make an effort to get a look at the car yourself before you sign up.

In many cases you can hire the car in one place and leave it elsewhere, although this usually involves a fee if you want to leave it in a city where the company has no branch.

You should take out Collision Damage Waiver insurance (between Dr50 to Dr100 a day); otherwise, you'll be liable for the first Dr3000 to Dr5000 (depending on the company) in the event of an accident. It's also a good idea to take out personal insurance (around Dr30 a day). When bargaining, make sure that prices include collision damage, insurance and tax.

Most companies demand a (returnable) cash deposit (Dr3000 to Dr5000) unless you pay by credit card, in which case the deposit is waived. However, travellers using smaller, less reputable firms have been stung after paying by credit, realising they've been charged 10 times the agreed fee after returning home.

The minimum age for drivers is usually 21 years (this varies depending on the make of car), with at least one year's driving experience. An International Driving Permit is technically required, but most agencies will accept your national licence.

All companies charge per hour (Dr35 to Dr100 is common) for every hour that you go over time on the return date. If you intend to drive from Morocco to the Spanish enclaves of Ceuta or Melilla, you must have a letter from the car-hire company authorising you to

Car Rental Prices

model	per day (Dr)	per km (Dr)	three days unlimited km (Dr)	seven days unlimited km (Dr)
Fiat Uno	250	2.50	1850	3300
Renault Clio	270	2.80	2250	4500
Fiat Tipo	330	3.30	2800	4900
Peugeot 306	440	4.40	3300	6300
Ford Feroza 4x4	660	6.50	5520	9660

take the car out of the country. Most cars now take unleaded *(sans plomb)* petrol. Keep receipts for oil changes and any mechanical repairs, as these costs should be reimbursed.

Some companies offer motorcycle (Dr200 per day for a DT 125cc Yamaha) and scooter (Dr160 per day) hire. Agadir is a good place to look – you'll find plenty of rental booths in among the big hotels.

The boxed text 'Car Rental Prices' is intended as a general guide only and does not include the 20% government tax that you must pay on all rentals.

Neither is there any point differentiating between international and local companies. Advertised rates vary hugely – some are more expensive than the biggies, others are cheaper. Bargaining means that the price you end up will generally bear little relation to advertised rates.

Fuel
Petrol is readily available in all the main centres. If you're travelling off the beaten track, however, fill up the tank at every opportunity. Super (leaded) and unleaded cost around Dr8.2 per litre and Diesel is around Dr5.3.

Costs rise the further you go from the north-west of the country. The big exception is the territory of Western Sahara, where petrol here is sold by the Atlas Sahara service station chain and is tax-free (that's about 30% less than in the rest of Morocco).

Heading south, the first of these stations is just outside Tarfaya, on the road to Laayoune. If you're heading north, stock up as much as you can here.

The same situation applies in the Spanish enclaves of Ceuta and Melilla, so drivers heading to Morocco and mainland Spain via the enclaves should do their best to arrive there with a near-empty tank.

Roadblocks
Morocco's roads are festooned with police and customs roadblocks. Be sure to stop at all of them and put on your best smile – with luck you should be waved through in about half the time. Generally you'll need to show your passport, state your profession, the pur-

---

Warning

When driving into Fès, Marrakesh and one or two other spots, you are likely to be accosted by hustlers on motorbikes. They will try to direct you to hotels and the like and are every bit as persistent as their colleagues on foot; dodging around these guys can be downright dangerous.

There have been reports of hitchhiking hustlers too. You pick them up and they try to lead you to their 'home' – a carpet factory or the like. The road south from Ouarzazate is particularly bad, as is the road from Asni to Imlil in the High Atlas.

In the Rif Mountains around Ketama, stories abound of tourists being stopped and having large wodges of hash foisted on them by particularly unpleasant characters, only to land in the poo when they reach the next police road block.

---

pose of your visit, the place you are travelling from and your destination.

Occasionally, a dubious fine may be levied, but this is rare. However, foreign number plates in the north of the country do arouse suspicion. Take care.

Parking Attendants
In many towns, parking zones are watched by *gardiens de voitures*. The going rate is Dr6 for a few hours and Dr10 overnight. The parking attendants are not a guarantee of safety, but they do provide some peace of mind and will no doubt offer to wash your car for you.

However, in an increasing number of big city centres, parking tickets are issued from simple kerb-side machines (Dr2 per hour for a maximum stay of two hours).

Mechanics & Repairs
Moroccan mechanics are generally extremely good and all decent-sized towns will have at least one garage. If you need replacement parts and can fit them yourself, get a Moroccan sufficiently well-disposed towards you to help with buying parts, such as replacement tyres, as this may help to keep the price closer to local levels.

BICYCLE

Mountain biking is becoming an increasingly popular way of travelling in Morocco.

There's plenty of opportunity for getting off the beaten track, with thousands of kilometres of remote pistes to be explored. You do need to be pretty fit, though. Distances are great and you'll need to carry all supplies with you (including any spare parts you may need, food and plenty of drinking water). Surfaced roads are generally well-maintained, but they tend to be narrow and dusty and the traffic none too forgiving. You can transport bikes on both buses and trains (see the earlier Bus and Train sections). Most camp sites charge between Dr3 and Dr5 for bicycles.

Moroccan cities and towns are better explored on foot, though you will find bicycles for hire in the bigger places (from around Dr40 per day) and cycle parks where your bike can be parked and watched over for the day.

Quite a few external tour operators (and some hotels in Marrakesh) offer organised mountain-biking trips.

Unfortunately, cyclists in remote areas have reported being besieged by gangs of stone-throwing children, so watch your back.

HITCHING

Hitching is never entirely safe in any country in the world, and we certainly don't recommend it. Travellers who decide to hitch should understand that they are taking a small, but potentially serious risk. However, many people do choose to hitch, and the advice that follows should help to make their journeys as fast and safe as possible.

Hitching in Morocco is possible, but demands a thick skin and considerable diplomatic expertise in the north because of aggressive hustlers. They simply won't take no for an answer and feign outrage if you express lack of interest in whatever they're trying to sell you – usually drugs.

The situation is particularly bad on the road between Tetouan and Tangier. Giving lifts to hustlers acting as hitchhikers in these areas is similarly a bad idea. See also the boxed text 'Warning' under Car & Motorcycle earlier in this chapter.

Drivers usually expect some money for picking you up, so it's as well to offer a little – it may be refused, but it's more likely not to be. Keep public transport fares in mind so that, should you strike someone trying to extort silly amounts from you, you'll know what not to give.

WALKING

The beautiful mountains of Morocco offer almost endless possibilities for walking and trekking. For those with plenty of time, it's worth considering a combination of trekking and travelling by the local trucks that ply regularly between villages on market days. There are endless possibilities for this kind of travel and it ensures that you'll get thoroughly off the beaten track. See the Trekking chapter for an idea of the regions to head to.

LOCAL TRANSPORT

Bus

The bigger cities, such as Casablanca, Rabat, Marrakesh, Fès and Meknès have public bus services. They are especially good for crossing from the *ville nouvelle* (new town) of a city to the medina (old town), and there are usually a few other useful runs. Tickets cost around Dr2.50 to Dr3.50.

Taxi

Cities and bigger towns have local *petit taxis*, which are a different colour in every city. They are licensed to carry up to three passengers and should be metered. They are not permitted to go beyond the city limits. Where they are not metered, agree to a price before hand. If they refuse to use the meter or won't give you a price, ask them to stop and get out. It's like everything else: Many drivers are perfectly honest and some are rotten.

Multiple hire is the rule rather than the exception, so you can get half-full cabs if they are going your way. From 8 pm there is a 50% surcharge.

North Atlantic Coast

From Tangier to the Mauritanian border, Morocco boasts an Atlantic seaboard of some 2500km (including the still-disputed territory of the Western Sahara).

Just as Tangier is a unique mix of Moroccan and European influences, the cities and towns of the coast present a very different face from those of the interior. Most of Morocco's coastal towns and cities were occupied, or even founded, by European powers, and this is reflected in their appearance and feel.

Long used to the sight of foreigners, the people of the coastal cities have been handed down a legacy quite different from that of the often xenophobic interior. Rabat and Casablanca, the political and economic capitals since the French installed their protectorate in 1912, are cosmopolitan centres at the heart of modern Morocco. They are flanked up and down the coast by towns that at one time or another served as bridge-heads for European merchant empires.

What remains is a curious combination of European and Moroccan fortifications, ancient medinas and modern colonial-built cities. While many travellers prefer to head further south, to Essaouira and Agadir, the region has hundreds of kilometres of beaches, many of them crowded in summer and some with reasonable surfing breaks.

CASABLANCA

☎ 02 • pop 3.2 million

With an official population of 3.2 million (though locals argue the figure is anywhere between five and eight million) Casablanca is by far Morocco's largest city, industrial centre and port. This growth is a fairly recent phenomenon, dating from the early days of the French protectorate, when Casablanca (Dar el-Baïda in Arabic and popularly known as Casa) was chosen to become the economic heart of the country.

The dimensions of the modest medina give some idea of just how small the place was when the French embarked on a mas-

Highlights

Asilah p225
Lixus p222
Larache p220

ATLANTIC OCEAN

Salé p211 • Kenitra p216
Rabat p194-5
Mohammedia p192 Central Rabat p202-3
• Casablanca p175
Central Casablanca p183

North Atlantic Coast p174

- Touring some of Morocco's most important monuments in the easy-going capital of Rabat

- Soaking up the picturesque coastal town of Asilah with its Portuguese ramparts, whitewashed houses and great history

- Peeking inside Casablanca's extraordinary new Hassan II Mosque and wonderful colonial architecture

- Chilling out at Moulay Bousselham, a peaceful coastal town with a remarkable lagoon bird habitat and great beach

- Stepping back a few centuries in Salé to inspect the stunning Merenid *medersa* (theological college)

! Telephone numbers in Morocco have changed. For new codes and complete numbers, see the boxed text 'Changes to Telephone Numbers' on page 89.

sive building program, laying out a new city in grand style with wide boulevards, public parks and fountains, as well as imposing Hispano-Moorish civic buildings.

The port handles almost 60% of Morocco's total sea traffic – the lion's share of

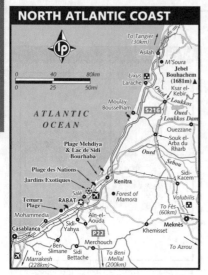

NORTH ATLANTIC COAST

exports are phosphate. Some 20 million tonnes of goods are processed here each year. As this is not a natural haven, ships docked here are protected from the Atlantic by a 3180m-long jetty.

With all this economic activity, Casa became, and to some extent remains, the place to which Moroccans aspiring to fame, fortune or simply a better standard of living tended to gravitate.

The influx of hopefuls from the countryside in search of a job has fuelled the creation of *bidonvilles* (slums), as in any other conurbation, and though efforts have been made to stem the flow, recent droughts have led to renewed influx. Many of those who arrived hopeful have ended up broken – the parade of well-heeled Casablancans who have made it stands in stark contrast to the beggars, prostitutes and other less fortunate residents.

Amid the striking white medium-rise prewar colonial architecture – and there are some Art Deco and modernist jewels – it is the people who make the greatest impression. You hardly ever see women wearing the veil and it's a surprise to see so many women in natty suits, designer sunglasses and high heels.

Men and women mix more easily here than in other Moroccan cities, while on the beaches and in the clubs, the bright young things strut their stuff much like the beautiful youth of many affluent European countries.

Casablanca has all the hallmarks of a brash Western European metropolis, with a hint of the decadent languor that marks many of the southern European cities it so closely resembles. But elements of traditional Morocco remain; if you were in any doubt, laying eyes upon one of the marvels of modern religious architecture – the enormous Hassan II Mosque – should set you straight.

History

Settlement of the Casablanca area has a long history. Prior to the Arab conquest, what is now the western suburb of Anfa was the capital of a Berber state set up by the Barghawata tribe. The Almoravids failed to bring this state into their orbit and it was not until 1188, during the time of the Almohads, that it was finally conquered.

Some 70 years later, Anfa was taken by the Merenids, but when that dynasty became weak, the inhabitants of the area reasserted their independence, taking to piracy and trading directly with England and Portugal.

By the second half of the 15th century, the Anfa pirates had become a serious threat to the Portuguese. A military expedition, consisting of some 10,000 men and 50 ships, was launched from Lisbon. Anfa was sacked and left in ruins. However, in 1515 the Portuguese had to repeat the operation and sixty years later they arrived to stay, renaming the port Casa Branca and erecting fortifications.

Although harried by the tribes of the interior, the Portuguese stayed until 1755, when the colony was abandoned following a devastating earthquake (which also destroyed Lisbon). Sultan Sidi Mohammed ben Abdallah subsequently had the area resettled and fortified, but its importance declined rapidly and by 1830 it was little more than a village, with some 600 inhabitants.

Around the mid-1800s industrialised Europe, looking for ever-increasing quantities of grain and wool, began to focus on the Chaouia hinterland, a wool-producing area

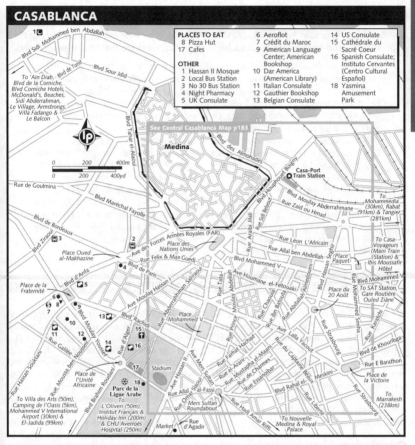

CASABLANCA

PLACES TO EAT
8 Pizza Hut
17 Cafes

OTHER
1 Hassan II Mosque
2 Local Bus Station
3 No 30 Bus Station
4 Night Pharmacy
5 UK Consulate

6 Aeroflot
7 Crédit du Maroc
9 American Language
Center; American
Bookshop
10 Dar America
(American Library)
11 Italian Consulate
12 Gauthier Bookshop
13 Belgian Consulate

14 US Consulate
15 Cathédrale du
Sacré Coeur
16 Spanish Consulate;
Instituto Cervantes
(Centro Cultural
Español)
18 Yasmina
Amusement
Park

around Casablanca. To secure these commodities, European agents established themselves in the city, renamed Casablanca by Spanish merchants.

Prosperity began to return, but the activities and influence of the Europeans caused much resentment among the indigenous population. In 1907, this spilled over into violence: European workers on a quarry railway that crossed a Muslim cemetery in the town were killed.

This was the pretext for intervention that pro-colonialist French politicians had been waiting for. A French warship, along with a

company of marines, was dispatched to Casablanca and proceeded to bombard the town.

Accounts of what followed vary wildly, but it appears that French troops, tribes from the interior and locals collapsed into an orgy of violence. The Jews of the *mellah* (Jewish quarter in the medina) suffered in particular and many of the town's 20,000 inhabitants died in the upheaval.

The incident led to a campaign to subdue the Chaouia hinterland and, later, to the dethronement of the sultan, Moulay Abd al-Aziz; his replacement by Moulay Abd

The Bombing of Casablanca

Walter Harris, the London *Times'* man in Morocco at the turn of the 20th century, was quickly on the spot after the French bombarded Casablanca. His report appears in *Morocco That Was* (now out of print):

A French warship arrived on the scene, and an armed party landed for the protection of the European population of the town. The forts and native quarters were at the same time bombarded. Scenes of the wildest confusion ensued, for not only was the town under the fire of the cannon of the warship, but the tribes from the interior had taken advantage of the panic to invade and pillage the place. Every sort of atrocity and horror was perpetrated, and Casablanca was a prey to loot and every kind of crime.

The European force was sufficient to protect the Consulates, and the greater part of the Christian population escaped murder. When order was restored, the town presented a piti-ful aspect. I saw it a very few days after the bombardment, and the scene was indescrib-able – a confusion of dead people and horses, while the contents of almost every house seemed to have been hurled into the streets and destroyed...Many of the houses had been burned and gutted. Out of dark cellars, Moors and Jews, hidden since the first day of the bombardment, many of them wounded, were creeping, pale and terrified...Blood was everywhere. In what had once been the poorer quarter of the town...I only met one living soul, a mad woman – dishevelled, dirty but smiling – who kept calling, 'Ayesha, my little daughter; my little son Ahmed, where are you: I am calling you'.

It was the beginning of the French occupation of Morocco.

al-Hafiz; and the declaration of the French protectorate in 1912. General Lyautey, pre-viously the French commander of Oran, was appointed as first French resident-general.

Lyautey pursued a program aimed at ex-panding Casablanca as the main port and economic centre of the new protectorate. It was largely his ideas on public works and the layout of the new city that made Casablanca what it is today.

Orientation

Casablanca is a huge, modern metropolis. However, with few of the complications posed by the arcane medinas of the cities of the interior, it is easy enough to find your way around.

The heart of the city is Place des Nations Unies. From this large traffic roundabout at the southern end of the medina, the city's main streets branch out: Ave des Forces Ar-mées Royales (FAR), Ave Moulay Hassan I, Ave Hassan II, Blvd Mohammed V and Blvd Houphouet Boigny.

Casa-Port train station lies about 600m north-east of this main square, on Blvd Houphouet Boigny, while the main train sta-tion, Casa-Voyageurs, is about 2km east of the town centre off Blvd Mohammed V. The main bus station, Gare Routière Ouled Ziane, is about 4km to the south-east on Route Ouled Ziane; the CTM bus station is about 800m east of the square on Rue Léon L'Africain.

The city's main administrative buildings are clustered around Place Mohammed V. Just to the south-west are the carefully main-tained lungs of the city centre – the Parc de la Ligue Arabe. The main consulates are in the area to the west and south of Place Mo-hammed V (see Embassies & Consulates in the Facts for the Visitor chapter).

West of the gardens lies the exclusive suburb of Anfa, the site of the original medi-eval Berber town.

Most of Casablanca's budget and mid-range hotels are in the area bounded by Ave des FAR, Ave Hassan II, Ave Lalla Yacout and Blvd Hassan Seghir (see Dangers & Annoyances later).

Street Names Casablanca's streets are undergoing a name-changing nightmare, and it is not uncommon to encounter three different names for the one street. The changes are largely a matter of Arabisation, but there are a few other factors at work.

The two main squares – Place des Nations Unies and Place Mohammed V (on Ave Hassan II) – have had their names swapped by royal decree. Worse, what is now known as Place des Nations Unies sometimes seems to take the name of the street linking it to Casa-Port train station (Houphouet Boigny) – itself a fairly recent change.

Where possible, the latest names (or what seem to be the latest names) appear on the maps in this book, but be aware of the problem if you buy local street directories.

Information
Tourist Offices The Office National Marocain Tourisme (ONMT; ☎ 271177), 55 Rue Omar Slaoui, south of the city centre, can provide some useful information and not just about Casablanca. It's open 8.30 am to noon and 2.30 to 6.30 pm weekdays.

The tourist office of Syndicat d'Initiative (☎ 221524), 98 Blvd Mohammed V, is less helpful, but is also open 3 to 5 pm Saturday and 9 am to noon Sunday.

You can book half-day city tours (Dr450 for up to three people) at both offices.

Money There are plenty of banks (with ATMs) in Casablanca. Crédit du Maroc's separate *bureau du change* (foreign exchange office) at 48 Blvd Mohammed V is very central. It's open weekdays from 8.30 am to noon and 2.30 to 6.30 pm, plus Saturday mornings. American Express (AmEx) travellers cheques are cashed free of charge. The AmEx representative, Voyages Schwartz (☎ 222947, e schwartz@ mbox.azure.net), 112 Rue Prince Moulay Abdallah, doesn't cash or sell travellers cheques.

If you're stuck for money outside regular banking hours, try one of the big hotels, such as the Hyatt Regency Hôtel or Hôtel Royal Mansour.

Post & Communications The main post office and the place to collect poste restante, at the junction of Blvd de Paris and Ave Hassan II, is open from 8.30 am to 6.30 pm weekdays. The parcel office is to the left of the main entrance. Another post office can be found near the Youth Hostel in the town.

There are several Internet cafes dotted around town. They all charge about Dr20 per hour and open until about 10 pm daily. Try First Cyber, 62 Rue Allah ben Abdellah; EuroNet, 51 Rue Tata; or Haloui Cyber Club, 206 Blvd Mohammed V.

Travel Agencies There are innumerable travel agencies squeezed into the same area as the bulk of the hotels.

Carlson Wagonlits (☎ 203051) 60-62 Rue el-Araibi Jilali; a respected and widespread group of travel agencies
Comanav (☎ 312050, e comanav.voyages@open .net.ma) 43 Ave des FAR; takes bookings for boats from Tangier to Sete, France
Supratours Office (☎ 220577) 98 Blvd Mohammed V; organises rail and bus connections
Trasmediterránea & Intercona (☎ 221737) Place du 16 Novembre; both are ferry companies
Voyages Schwartz (☎ 222947, e schwartz@ mbox.azure.net) 12 Rue Prince Moulay Abdallah; the AmEx representative
Wasteels (☎ 314060) 26 Rue Léon L'Africain, by the CTM bus station; a good place for cheap intercontinental rail tickets

Bookshops & Newsstands Casablanca is a little disappointing for the bibliophile. For books in English, the best bet is the American Bookshop (☎ 279559, e alc.casa@ casanet.net.ma) west of the centre on Blvd Moulay Youssef, just down from the US consulate. It has a reasonable selection of history and guidebooks. The English Forum Bookshop (☎ 269846), 27 Rue Mouftaker Abdelkader, is aimed mainly at students of English, but has a reasonable selection of novels (mainly classics, some sci-fi and a few romances). Otherwise, try Librairie Livre Servile, next to the cinema on Rue Tata. It has a wide range of French and Moroccan books, including a few guidebooks and coffee-table books, as well as a small selection in English.

West of the town centre, the upmarket Gauthier Livres (☎ 264426), 12 Rue Moussa ben Nousseir, has a good selection of French and Moroccan writing, as well as road maps.

If you're after foreign newspapers and magazines, there are several reasonable newsstands set up along Blvd Mohammed V, around Place des Nations Unies, in Casa-Port and Casa-Voyageurs train stations and at the big hotels. French titles are easier to find than English titles.

Casablanca is also the easiest place to find *La Quinzaine du Maroc*, a reasonable booklet of useful names and numbers covering Morocco's main cities.

Film & Photography There are quite a few places where you can buy film or have it developed. Try along Blvd Mohammed V. For decent slide film head to Imaphotos (☎ 470894), 44 Rue Tahar Sebti, which is the Fuji distributor in town. Faugra (☎ 261585), 32–42 Ave Mers Sultan, stocks a wide range of equipment and also does camera repairs.

Cultural Centres Several countries maintain cultural centres in Casablanca.

Dar America (☎ 221460) 10 Place Bel Air. This is the US information service and library. It's open 9.30 am to 12.30 pm and 4 to 6 pm weekdays. Video shows and cultural events are held, but you'll need ID to get in.
Goethe Institut (☎ 200445) right on Place du 16 Novembre. This is a modest affair, open Tuesday to Saturday. It conducts German classes and puts on the occasional film and exhibition. Web site: www.goethe.de
Institut Français (☎ 259078) 121 Blvd Mohammed Zerktouni, south of the city centre. It has a good library, plus it puts on films, lectures and other events. It's open from 9 am to 2.30 pm Tuesday to Saturday. Web site: www.ambafrance-ma.org
Instituto Cervantes (Centro Cultural Español) (☎ 267337) 31 Rue d'Alger, next door to the Spanish consulate. It puts on films and cultural events and has a library. Web site: www.cervantes.es

Medical Services & Emergencies There are several decent hospitals in Casablanca. Among them is the CHU Averroès Hospital (☎ 224109), south of the city centre.

There's a night pharmacy on the corner of Place Oued al-Makhazine and Blvd d'Anfa. The local French-language newspapers list other pharmacies.

In the event of a medical emergency, ring SOS Médecins Maroc (☎ 444444). These private doctors operate around the clock and can come to your hotel for about Dr350. The police can be contacted on ☎ 19.

Dangers & Annoyances In the darkened corners of the central area bounded by Ave des FAR, Ave Hassan II, Ave Lalla Yacout and Blvd Hassan Seghir street prostitution is common. This is an unaccustomed sight in Muslim countries and travellers (particularly women) should take care walking in these areas after dark.

Medina

The medina, although rather small when compared with other medinas in Morocco, is definitely worth a little time and is a pleasant, bright place to stroll around. For things to buy in the medina see Shopping later in this section.

Even though it's the oldest part of the city, the medina looks newer than the medinas in other Moroccan cities, and feels more like an European town than a medieval medina.

If you want to get to the **Chleuh Mosque**, the old city's main Friday Mosque, you just have to follow Rue Chakab Arsalane and its continuation.

A pleasant spot for a cup of coffee is the cafe down on Place de l'Amiral Philibert, where the Youth Hostel is located.

When you coming through the main entrance from Place des Nations Unies beware of the chancers trying to flog you everything from fake Rolex to opium.

Nouvelle Medina & Royal Palace

About 1km south-east of town is the 'nouvelle medina', also known as the Quartier Habous. It was built by the French in the 1930s in an attempt to sort out the housing crisis.

The French architects tried to marry the best features of traditional Moroccan architecture with modern techniques and facilities. The result is a kind of idealised French

[Continued on page 181]

HASSAN II MOSQUE

North of the medina and rising up above the Atlantic ocean, the Hassan II Mosque is the third-largest religious monument in the world. It was finished in August 1993 (in time for the then King Hassan II's 60th birthday) after 10,000 Moroccan craftsmen worked on it for five years.

Designed by the French architect Michel Pinseau, the mosque can hold 25,000 worshippers. Up to 80,000 more can be accommodated in the esplanades around it. Hassan wanted his mosque to have the highest minaret in the world and, at 210m, it is visible from miles around. At night the powerful laser beams projected from the top of the minaret in the direction of Mecca form quite a spectacle.

No less high-tech is the interior of the mosque, fitted out with a centrally heated floor, electric doors and a sliding roof.

The vast prayer hall is said to be large enough to house Notre Dame or St Peter's comfortably and, if the exterior is French-inspired, the interior is all Moroccan. Cedar wood was brought in from the Middle Atlas, marble from Agadir and granite from Tafraoute. The best master craftsmen in the country were assembled and put to work on it, producing astonishing wood-carving, *zellij* (tilework) and stucco moulding.

The mosque is said to have cost around US$600 million and, remarkably, was paid for largely by public subscription. Although you will occasionally hear mutterings about how this vast sum might have been better spent, most Moroccans, particularly those from Casablanca, are very proud of their modern monument. For many it's living proof that the world-famous Moroccan craftsmen have lost none of their ancient mastery. In many homes and shops you will see little certificates displayed as a testimony to their personal contribution.

The mosque is well worth a visit and has the added attraction of being one of the very few religious buildings open to non-Muslims. It also provides a welcome breath of fresh, sea air away from the noise and pollution of the city.

Guided Tours

To see the interior of the mosque you have to take a guided tour. Visitors must be 'decently and respectfully dressed' and, once inside, don't forget to remove your shoes.

There are tours at 9, 10 and 11 am and 2 pm (2.30 pm during summer), every day except Friday. Tours are

Inset: Detail of a domed area inside the mosque (photo by Christopher Wood)

Bottom: Gently curving arcaded colonnade supported by slender marble columns, with views to the Atlantic Ocean and Casablanca

ADAM McCROW

usually in French, but if you arrive at the same time as a large tour group you may be able to tag along to a Spanish, German or English commentary. The circuit lasts about an hour and takes in the prayer hall, ablution rooms, the *hammam* (traditional bathhouse) and the Turkish baths (not yet open). It costs Dr100 (Dr50 for school and university students with a card).

The easiest way to the mosque is along Blvd des Almohades (which turns into Blvd Sidi Mohammed ben Abdallah) from near Casa-Port train station. It's about a 20 minute walk.

You may run into the occasional kid asking for pens. Try to resist the temptation to oblige them, and keep a keen eye on your belongings. A *petit taxi* (local taxi) from the centre should cost around Dr10. Bus No 15 leaves from Place Oued al-Makhazine (Dr3).

CHRISTINE OSBORNE

MATT FLETCHER

Top: The striking zellij workmanship in the fountain forecourt

Bottom: The 200m-high minaret soars above the mosque.

[Continued from page 178]

version of a Moroccan medina and, while a bit twee, is nevertheless attractive.

For the souvenir hunter, the nouvelle medina houses a large collection of bazaars and craft shops. Although it lacks the vitality of the old medina, the nouvelle medina does have a good selection of wares. Bordering the boulevard to the north of the nouvelle medina is the Royal Palace (closed to the public).

To get to the nouvelle medina, take bus No 4 or 40 from the local bus station west of the centre on Place Oued al-Makhazine.

Casablanca Is Beautiful

Casablanca has some wonderful architecture so once you have orientated yourself, take some time to look upwards occasionally. Behind the grime and modern clutter, exuberant carved friezes and beautiful tilework decorate apartment and office blocks, and ornate wrought-iron balconies adorn shabby hotels.

Casablanca was expanded under the sympathetic eye of French Resident-General Lyautey. He pursued a program aimed at expanding Casablanca as the main port and economic centre of *Maroc utile* (what the French considered to be the useful bit of the country). It was largely his policies that gave Casablanca its wide boulevards, public parks and imposing civic buildings.

From 1912 Casablanca began to grow beyond the old walls of the medina. In the 1930s Mauresque architecture developed: a blend of French colonial and traditional Moroccan styles inspired by Art Deco.

Some of Morocco's best Mauresque architecture was designed by Henri Prost and Robert Marrast and is clustered around Place Mohammed V at the heart of Casablanca's *ville nouvelle* (new town). The most accessible is the **Grande Poste** (main post office; 1918), a wonderful building fronted by arches and stone columns and decorated with bold mosaics. The building, erected in 1918, merits a look as part of the impressive array of Moorish administrative edifices that face onto Place Mohammed V.

Close by is the **Palais de Justice** (law courts; 1925), the huge main door and entrance was inspired by the Persian *iwan* (vaulted hall, usually opening into the central court of the medersa of a mosque). The **Ancienne Préfecture** (old police headquarters; 1930) is topped with a modernist clock tower that chimes on the hour and sounds a siren to mark the end of the daily fast during the month of Ramadan.

More in the style of traditional Moroccan architecture is the **Banque D'Etat**. Fronted with decorative stonework, it was the last building constructed on the square. Further away on the edge of the Parc de la Ligue Arabe is the extraordinary but shamefully neglected **Cathédrale du Sacré Coeur**, designed by Paul Tornon in 1930. The striking exterior is dominated by three rows of descending buttresses and gargoyles.

Since the 1940s, Casablanca has been the site of further experiments in town planning, including the use of aerial photography and revolutionary building techniques such as prefabricated concrete. Among the most famous disciples of the new style of post-war architecture are the architects Bodiansky and Candilis.

Bodiansky created three different styles of 'progressive housing' on the outskirts of Casablanca; Candilis, attempting to tackle the serious housing problem among the poor Muslim population, developed the concept of low-rent, 'culture-specific' housing for the masses. Some of these can be seen when entering the town by train.

The pace of architectural innovation slowed considerably after independence, but Casablanca continues to lead the way. In 1993, the great **Hassan II Mosque** was inaugurated, a superb and confident affirmation that Morocco has lost none of its tradition of craftsmanship.

If you want to learn more, *Casablanca, Mythes et Figures d'Une Aventure Urbaine* by Jean-Louis Cohen & Monique Eleb, is an excellent book (in French) examining the architectural evolution of Morocco's biggest city.

Parc de la Ligue Arabe

The biggest park in the city, the Parc de la Ligue Arabe, has an essentially French lay-out, although the flora is more faithful to its location in Africa. It's a pleasant place to walk during the day, take a leisurely coffee or enjoy the diversions of the **Yasmina amusement park** (entry is Dr2).

Cathédrale du Sacré Coeur, built in 1930, is a somewhat neglected former cathedral. It's also an unexpected sight in the heart of a Muslim city and is symbolic of modern Casablanca's essentially European genesis. Sitting on the edge of the Parc de la Ligue Arabe, it reflects the best of the more adventurous architectural products of the Art Deco era. Deconsecrated some time ago, it has been converted into a school, but now it looks like squatters have moved in. Take care around this area as people have been mugged here.

Beaches

Casablanca's beaches are west of town along Blvd de la Corniche, at the end of which (where it becomes Blvd de Biarritz) begins the affluent beachside suburb of 'Ain Diab. This is a trendy area, lined with four-star hotels, upmarket restaurants, bars, coffee shops and nightclubs, and you may feel a little out of place unless you dress accordingly and have a wallet to match.

In high summer the beaches are generally covered wall-to-wall with chic Casablancans, but for the rest of the year you can usually find some space pretty much to yourself at the southern end of 'Ain Diab. When they're not crowded, the beaches are perfectly all right, although they're better suited to a lazy afternoon than a 'beach holiday'. For the latter, you're better off heading further south-west towards Essaouira.

Bus No 9 takes you along the southern end of the beaches at 'Ain Diab. Catch it from the local bus station at Place Oued al-Makhazine.

Sidi Abderrahman

A few kilometres south of the 'Ain Diab beaches, atop a tiny rocky outcrop jutting into the Atlantic, is the small marabout (holy shrine) and settlement of Sidi Abder-rahman. At high tide, it's cut off from the mainland, but otherwise you can stumble across the rocks.

Non-Muslims are not allowed into the shrine itself, but you can walk past the handful of houses and sit down to look out over the ocean. It's about a half-hour walk along the beach down from the No 9 bus station at 'Ain Diab.

Language Courses

If you want to learn Arabic, there are a number of private schools in the city. One with a good reputation, offering private tuition, is École Assimil-Formation (☎ 312567) at 71 Rue Allah ben Abdellah. Another is the Centre International d'Etude de Langues, on the Place de la Victoire, which teaches a host of foreign languages, including Arabic.

Places to Stay – Budget

Camping A place popular with camper vans is *Camping de l'Oasis* (☎ 234257) on Ave Mermoz, 5km out on the P8 road to El-Jadida, south-west of the centre. It charges Dr10 per person, per car and per tent; camper vans cost Dr15. Bus No 31 (Dr2.50) from the centre runs past it, while a *petit taxi* (local taxi) should be around Dr10.

Hostels The *Youth Hostel* (☎ 220551, fax 227677, 6 Place Ahmed el-Bidaoui), faces a small square just inside the medina, in from Blvd des Almohades. It's a large, comfortable and clean place and the director, Hariss, manages it efficiently and with great pride. A dorm bed costs Dr45 with a HI membership card, doubles/triples cost Dr120/180. This includes breakfast, hot showers and use of the kitchen facilities. It's open from 8 to 9.30 am and noon to 11 pm (midnight in summer). From Casa-Port train station, walk out to the first major cross-roads and then turn right along Blvd des Almohades. Turn left when you get to the second opening in the medina wall. Go through it and you'll see the hostel on the right.

Hotels – Medina None of the hotels in the medina have star ratings. The majority are cheap (around Dr40), uninviting, very

CENTRAL CASABLANCA

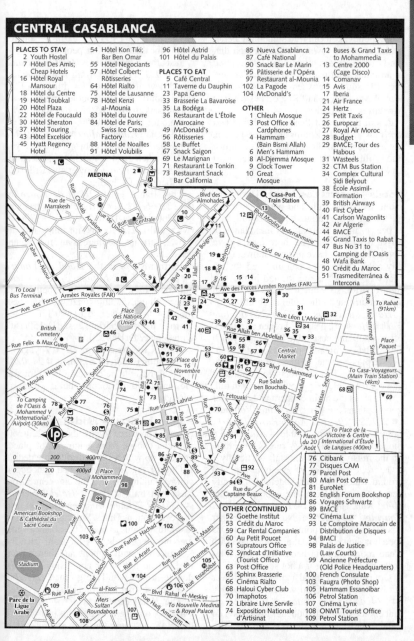

PLACES TO STAY
2 Youth Hostel
7 Hôtel Des Amis;
  Cheap Hotels
16 Hôtel Royal
  Mansour
18 Hôtel du Centre
19 Hôtel Toubkal
20 Hôtel Plaza
22 Hôtel de Foucauld
30 Hôtel Sheraton
37 Hôtel Touring
43 Hôtel Excelsior
45 Hyatt Regency
  Hotel

54 Hôtel Kon Tiki;
  Bar Ben Omar
55 Hôtel Negociants
57 Hôtel Colbert;
  Rôtisseries
64 Hôtel Rialto
75 Hôtel de Lausanne
78 Hôtel Kenzi
  al-Mounia
83 Hôtel du Louvre
84 Hôtel de Paris;
  Swiss Ice Cream
  Factory
88 Hôtel de Noailles
91 Hôtel Volubilis

96 Hôtel Astrid
101 Hôtel du Palais

PLACES TO EAT
5 Café Central
11 Taverne du Dauphin
23 Papa Geno
33 Brasserie La Bavaroise
35 La Bódega
36 Restaurant de L'Étoile
  Marocaine
49 McDonald's
56 Rôtisseries
58 Le Buffet
67 Snack Saigon
69 Le Marignan
71 Restaurant Le Tonkin
73 Restaurant Snack
  Bar California

96 Hôtel Astrid
85 Nueva Casablanca
87 Café National
90 Snack Bar Le Marin
95 Pâtisserie de l'Opéra
97 Restaurant al-Mounia
102 La Pagode
104 McDonald's

OTHER
1 Chleuh Mosque
3 Post Office &
  Cardphones
4 Hammam
  (Bain Bismi Allah)
6 Men's Hammam
8 Al-Djemma Mosque
9 Clock Tower
10 Great
  Mosque

12 Buses & Grand Taxis
  to Mohammedia
13 Centre 2000
  (Cage Disco)
14 Comanav
15 Avis
17 Iberia
21 Air France
24 Hertz
25 Petit Taxis
26 Europcar
27 Royal Air Maroc
28 Budget
29 BMCE; Tour des
  Habous
31 Wasteels
32 CTM Bus Station
34 Complex Cultural
  Sidi Belyout
38 École Assimil-
  Formation
39 British Airways
40 First Cyber
41 Carlson Wagonlits
42 Air Algerie
44 BMCE
46 Grand Taxis to Rabat
47 Bus No 31 to
  Camping de l'Oasis
48 Wafa Bank
50 Crédit du Maroc
51 Trasmediterránea &
  Intercona

OTHER (CONTINUED)
52 Goethe Institut
53 Crédit du Maroc
59 Car Rental Companies
60 Au Petit Poucet
61 Supratours Office
62 Syndicat d'Initiative
  (Tourist Office)
63 Post Office
65 Sphinx Brasserie
66 Cinéma Rialto
68 Haloui Cyber Club
70 Imaphotos
71 Librairie Livre Servile
74 Exposition Nationale
  d'Artisinat

76 Citibank
77 Disques CAM
79 Parcel Post
80 Main Post Office
81 EuroNet
82 English Forum Bookshop
86 Voyages Schwartz
89 BMCE
92 Cinéma Lux
93 Le Comptoir Marocain de
  Distribution de Disques
94 BMCI
98 Palais de Justice
  (Law Courts)
99 Ancienne Préfecture
  (Old Police Headquarters)
100 French Consulate
103 Faugra (Photo Shop)
105 Hammam Essanoibar
106 Petrol Station
107 Cinéma Lynx
108 ONMT Tourist Office
109 Petrol Station

basic, pretty grubby and noisy. For a little more money, you can find something better in the centre of town. For the medina die-hards, there are a number of hotels clustered in an interesting part of the medina around the little square between Rue Centrale (or Rue al-Markiziya) and Rue de Fès (or Rue Mohammed al-Hansaly).

About the best of these is the *Hôtel Des Amis* (☎ 475899). Rooms are at least clean, but as is usual in these places, there is just one cold shower. Singles/doubles cost Dr40/60.

Hotels – Central Casablanca

During the months of June, July and particularly August, a lot of the budget hotels are full, so it is best to make reservations in advance or arrive before noon. The more inexpensive hotels frequently have just one shower (usually cold) shared between up to 25 rooms. Many of the hotels are located in the red-light district, so women should be careful when returning to the hotel at night.

Hôtel du Palais (☎ 276121, 68 Rue Farhat Hachad), near the French consulate, offers about the best value for money you'll find. It has clean and spacious singles/doubles/triples, some with balconies, for Dr62/76/111. The showers are communal and cold. The place is popular and often full.

If price is the main concern and the other good options are gone, try *Hôtel Volubilis* (☎ 207789, 20-2 Rue Abdel Karim Diouri). Singles/doubles with a table, washbasin and bidet cost Dr60/90. They're OK, if a little on the musty side but the staff is friendly.

There's a cluster of cheapies on and around Rue Allah ben Abdellah. Virtually across the road from one another are the *Hôtel Kon Tiki* (☎ 314927) and the *Hôtel Touring* (☎ 310216) at No 87. The former has nice but small rooms for Dr72/110 (Dr5 for a hot shower). The latter is adequate with clean rooms and big beds. Singles/doubles cost Dr62/78 (Dr7 for a hot shower).

Opposite the central market and flower stalls is the friendly *Hôtel Colbert* (☎ 314241, 38 Rue Chaouia). It's an excellent choice (but still not better than Hôtel du Palais) and has hot showers (Dr10). Sin-gles/doubles cost Dr63/83. With bath it's Dr84/100 (add Dr36 per extra person for rooms for three and four people).

Just around the corner is *Hôtel Negociants* (☎ 314023, 116 Rue Allah ben Abdellah) brand new at the time of writing and tiled throughout! Singles/doubles/triples with washbasins go for Dr85/120/160, rooms with bath go for Dr150/210/270.

The small *Hôtel Rialto* (☎ 275122, 9 Rue Salah ben Bouchaib) is bright and well run with a touch (just a touch) of style. Sin-gles/doubles with hot shower cost Dr84/120 and there's a TV lounge.

The slightly seedy *Hôtel de Foucauld* (☎ 222666, 52 Rue Araibi Jilali) has sin-gles/doubles for Dr70/100 and Dr120/150 (with bath). The rooms are dingy but the showers are hot and there is an amazing en-trance hall.

Further south is the *Hôtel du Louvre* (☎ 273747, 36 Rue Nationale). It's not bad, but some rooms are definitely better than others. Singles/doubles start at Dr60/120; rooms with a shower cost Dr90/130. Three or four people sharing costs Dr150/180, with shower Dr180/220.

Across the road from Casa-Voyageurs train station is *Hôtel Terminus* (☎ 240025). It's a bit basic to be charging Dr60 for sin-gles and Dr90 for doubles, but it's pleasant enough.

Places to Stay – Mid-Range

If you're prepared to pay about Dr220/260, you can choose from a number of places and end up with a very comfortable deal.

One of the first hotels you'll notice if you're walking towards the city centre from Casa-Port train station is *Hôtel Excelsior* (☎ 200263, 2 Rue el-Amraoui Brahim) near Place de Nations Unies. Still cashing in on its fast-fading status as one of Casablanca's for-mer premier hotels, it's far from friendly. Rooms come with a phone and there's heat-ing, but no hot water apparently. Singles/doubles/triples with bath go for Dr218/260/339; you pay more for breakfast.

The *Hôtel du Centre* (☎ 446180, fax 446178), on Rue Sidi Belyout just off Ave des FAR and near the train station, offers

Tombs and ruins of the North Atlantic Coast: cemetery, Salé (top); Rabat's most famous landmark, the 44m-high minaret Le Tour Hassan, built in the 12th century (bottom left); the 13th-century Merenid necropolis of Chellah, Rabat (bottom right)

ZELLIJ

One of the most captivating and enduring of Morocco's artistic traditions is *zellij* – the intricate mosaic designs using hand-cut tiles that adorn the walls and floors of mosques and palaces throughout Morocco.

The art of zellij is believed to have been influenced originally by the mosaics of the Byzantines, as well as techniques from Moorish Spain, but Arab influences shaped the craft in a unique Moroccan style.

Moroccan zellij is distinguished by an extraordinary colour palette and by a complex mathematical geometry. Islamic tradition forbids any depiction of living things – considered a decadent pagan tradition – and creativity relies on geometry as its expression, with spectacular results.

There are more than 360 *fourmah* (shapes) available to the *zlayiyyah* (craftsman) who spends the first few years of his apprenticeship endlessly drawing the multitudes of geometric configurations and committing them to memory.

Although zellij enjoyed its greatest popularity between the 10th and 14th centuries, this painstaking and expensive art form remains popular in modern Morocco. The government has helped preserve the tradition by commissioning zellij-makers to decorate public buildings and mosques. Recent examples include the Hassan II Mosque in Casablanca, one of the largest and most elaborate mosques in the world.

Martin Hughes

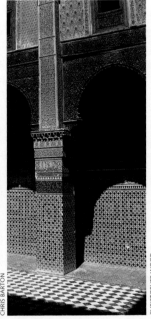

Inset: Intricate tilework, Medersa es-Sahriji, Fès (photo by Christopher Wood)

Left: Zellij base typical c Merenid design, Medersa el-Attarine, Fès

Right: Inlay detail, Hassan II Mosque, Casablanca

CHRIS BARTON

CHRISTOPHER WOOD

better value than the Excelsior. It smells a little damp, but has clean, modern rooms with bath and phone for Dr158/195.

Along the same lines as the Hôtel du Centre, and with a lift, is the **Hôtel de Lausanne** (☎ 268690, 24 Rue Tata), tucked between two tea houses. Unexceptional rooms with bath and phone cost Dr213/250.

There is one surprise packet tucked away south of the city centre just east of Place de Mohammed V. The **Hôtel Astrid** (☎ 277803, fax 293372, 12 Rue 6 Novembre), off Rue Prince Moulay Abdallah, has good, clean and quiet rooms with bath, phone and TV. Some rooms have balconies and there's a lift. Singles/doubles cost Dr224/263.

Moving into the three-star bracket, there is the well-situated and friendly **Hôtel de Paris** (☎ 274275, fax 298069, 2 Rue Ech-Cherie Amziane) in the pedestrian zone off Rue Prince Moulay Abdallah. Pleasant, clean rooms with phone and TV cost Dr338/400.

A little cheaper is **Hôtel de Noailles** (☎ 202554, fax 220589, 22 Blvd du 11 Janvier). Elegant rooms cost Dr218/260 and the teahouse (salon de thé) on the 1st floor, open until 9.30 pm, is very civilised indeed. A reasonable alternative is the **Hôtel Métropole** (☎ 301213, fax 305801, 89 Rue Mohammed Smiha). Singles/doubles with bath and TV cost Dr300/370.

Just outside Casa-Voyageurs train station is the **Ibis Moussafir** (☎ 401984, fax 400799). Modern, comfortable rooms go for Dr351/402. The bar and restaurant (breakfast is Dr38) are open to nonguests.

The **Hôtel Kenzi al-Mounia** (☎ 260727, fax 223314, 24 Blvd de Paris), has a bar and restaurant (open to hotel guests only) and singles/doubles for Dr537/654 (some are better than others; get one away from the noisy lift).

Some other mid-range hotels overlook the beaches along Blvd de la Corniche. They include the **Hôtel de la Corniche** (☎ 362782, fax 391110) charging Dr439/542 for singles/doubles and **Hôtel Suisse** (☎ 396061, fax 367758) charging Dr398/516 (including breakfast).

The four-star **Hôtel Toubkal** (☎ 311414, fax 311146, 9 Rue Sidi Belyout) is at the top-end of the mid-range section. It has singles/doubles from Dr617/749 that are quite good value, although some travellers have complained of the service.

Places to Stay – Top End

Most of Casablanca's top-end hotels are on Ave des FAR.

Pick of the crop, and done out in traditional style is **Hôtel Royal Mansour** (☎ 313011, fax 312583, e rmansour-com@marocnet.ma, 27 Ave des FAR). Rooms start at Dr2800. Just down the road at No 100 is the similarly priced **Hôtel Sheraton** (☎ 439494, fax 315136).

The **Holiday Inn** (☎ 488000, fax 293035) is just off the Ave Hassan II roundabout. Singles/doubles cost Dr2132/2364.

Right on Place des Nations Unies is the five-star **Hyatt Regency Hôtel** (☎ 261234, fax 204446) with singles/doubles from Dr2600/2700. It has a pool open to nonguests (Dr50 per day) and a very expensive bar.

Hôtel Riad Salam (☎ 391313, fax 391345) overlooking Blvd de la Corniche, charges Dr1364/1528, but unfortunately rooms aren't as clean as they should be at this price. Facilities include a pool, health club and thalassotherapy (seawater bathing) centre.

Places to Eat

Restaurants Casablanca has the greatest variety of places to eat in Morocco. Restaurants range from cheap and cheerful seafood places to gastronomic French tables, with a whole host of African, Middle Eastern and Oriental places in between.

Prices, even at the more expensive tables, are reasonable by Western standards and even on the tightest budget you shouldn't go hungry.

Central Casablanca A good place to find cheap restaurants, particularly rotisseries (roast chicken places), is opposite the central market on Rue Chaouia. Restaurants are cheek-by-jowl so it's easy to take your pick. Most restaurants stay open until 2 am and for around Dr15 to Dr25, you can get a generous sandwich with meat, chips and salad to take away. A quarter of chicken, chips and a Coke will cost you around Dr30.

The next restaurant is bit of an odd man out at the top of the row. **Restaurant Amine** opposite the central market near Hôtel Colbert is slightly more upmarket and concentrates on seafood. A huge plate of fried fish costs Dr43 and if you get there early enough try the *pastilla* (rich pigeon pie with fine pastry) for Dr40.

Snack Bar Le Marin on the corner of Ave Lalla Yacout and Rue Chaouia is clean, women-friendly and also a good place to go for nice fried fish (Dr35) and delicious dips. Plates of *crevettes* (shrimp) cost Dr25. There's another branch at 69-71 Rue Allal Fassi near the Mers Sultan roundabout.

The food at **Restaurant Snack Bar California** (*19 Rue Tata*) remains good, which is just as well as outside there's a sign displaying LP's previous recommendation. *Harira* (spicy lentil soup) costs Dr6, delicious *tajine* (meat and vegetable stew) starts at Dr30 and brochettes (skewered meat) served with two types of vegetables plus chips costs Dr30. There is also vegetarian couscous or tajine (Dr30). It's a peaceful and relaxing place for women travellers.

The tiny **Snack Saigon** (*Rue Salah ben Bouchaib*), is a small, simple hole-in-the-wall place. Tajine and salad is about the limit of the menu, but the tajines (about Dr25) are world-class.

Nueva Casablanca, just down from the Café National on Ave Lalla Yacout, is easy to spot (thanks to a garish pink frontage), relaxed and friendly. A good plate of brochettes, chips and salad costs Dr30.

Le Buffet (*99 Blvd Mohammed V*) is a bright, licensed place that is popular for lunch and dinner. The service is good and portions generous. The three-course set meal is Dr75.

If you're after excellent Moroccan food in traditional surroundings, the **Restaurant al-Mounia** (☎ *222669, 95 Rue Prince Moulay Abdallah*) is the place for a splurge. There is a lovely, cool garden at the front where you can dine under the shade of an ancient *faux-poire* (false pear) tree. Main courses cost from Dr85 to Dr140 and vegetarian dishes are available.

For those on a tighter budget, the unlicensed **Restaurant de l'Étoile Marocaine** (☎ *314100, 107 Rue Allah ben Abdellah*) is an excellent alternative to the Al-Mounia. It serves decent Moroccan food including a delicious pastilla for Dr60 or *Mechoui d'Agneau* (roast lamb) for Dr70. It's a friendly little place with sumptuous traditional decor. The restaurant is open until 10 pm.

If you're hankering after South-East Asian food, you could head for **Restaurant Le Tonkin** (☎ *291913, 34 Rue Prince Moulay Abdallah*) on the pedestrian mall. The set menu is Dr85. Another Asian option is **La Pagode** (☎ *277185, 98 Rue Farhat Hachad*), south of the centre. A main course costs around Dr70. Or try **Le Marignan** (☎ *316199, 69 Rue Mohammed Smiha*), on the corner of Blvd Mohammed V. It serves a mixture of Asian food to eat in or take away (they will deliver). Main courses cost around Dr50 and the house speciality is food cooked *sur plaques* (Japanese style) in front of guests. It's open until midnight every day.

For a little more money, you could have an excellent French meal at the **Brasserie La Bavaroise** (☎ *311760, 129 Rue Allah ben Abdellah*). There's a good *plat du jour* (dish of the day), which ranges from pheasant pâté to duck conserve and wild boar stew (all are around Dr70 to Dr100). Desserts include profiteroles and chocolate mousse – heavenly if you haven't seen them for a while.

One of *the* places at which you can see – and be seen with – well-heeled Casablancans (male and female) is **La Bodéga** (☎ *541842, 129 Rue Allah ben Abdellah*), a tapas bar and restaurant north of the central market. It's expensive, but good fun and there's live music. It's open from 12.30 to 3 pm and 7 pm to midnight daily.

For seafood, head straight for the **Taverne du Dauphin** (☎ *221200, 115 Blvd Houphouet Boigny),* open Monday to Saturday. It was founded in 1958 by a French lady from Marseilles and is now run by her grandson, the charming Jean-Claude and his wife. It may not look much from the outside but the food is fresh, beautifully cooked and not overly expensive. A fish fillet costs around Dr65, calamari costs Dr45 and unbelievably delicious grilled Dublin prawns costs Dr48 per 100g (enough for a starter). They also have a good selection of beer, spirits and wine. If you don't fancy a full meal, pop in for a snack at the bar, which is a good place for a relaxed drink.

'Ain Diab For seafood in a totally different atmosphere, you could head out west to the beaches and 'Ain Diab. *Le Cabestan*, *La Mer* and *La Petite Roche* are three of the more upmarket restaurants gathered around the El-Hank Lighthouse. A meal costs around Dr250.

The splurge of the city would have to be *A Ma Bretagne* (☎ 362112), a few hundred metres down the coast from Sidi Abderrahman along the coastal road. It is run by a French *maitre cuisinier* (master chef) and the menu is based around seafood specialities. It also has an excellent wine cellar. If you're going to eat here you're looking at Dr500 per head.

Cafes There are a few cafes in the medina; perhaps the most pleasantly located is the *Café Central* on Place de l'Amiral Philibert.

The city centre is filled with French-style cafes – some of them interesting examples of the Art Deco style.

The grand cafes at the prime locations in town are still the preserve of men, and women may feel uncomfortable. However, recently a couple of chic, Western-style cafes have opened on Rue Allah ben Abdellah, just around the corner from Hôtel Colbert.

A very pleasant spot for a coffee is at one of the string of cafes in the northern part of the Parc de la Ligue Arabe, also an excellent spot for a picnic. There are also teahouses opposite the park.

Patisseries, Ice-Cream Parlours & Fruit-Juice Bars Women on their own may prefer to avoid the male-dominated cafes and drink at one of Casablanca's excellent patisseries instead. *Pâtisserie de l'Opéra* (*50 Blvd du 11 Janvier*) is a civilised, tranquil place, great for a quiet coffee or tea. Fresh bread is baked on the premises.

L'Oliveri (*132 Ave Hassan II*) south of the city centre, is a sophisticated *glacier* (ice-cream parlour) and a haven from the heat and traffic. There is not a huge selec-

tion of flavours – about 10 – but the quality is high. A tub costs Dr25.

The Swiss Ice Cream Factory next to the Hôtel de Paris is a women-friendly place and popular with the young and trendy. The ice cream is home-made and as good as, if not better than, L'Oliveri's. It's open every day from 7 am to 9.30 pm.

There's a good *fruit-juice bar* in Centre 2000 and an even better one next to the Hôtel Kon Tiki: *Bar Ben Omar* serves a wide selection of juices from Dr5 to Dr8.

Fast Food *Papa Geno* (*Rue Allah ben Abdellah*) is a clean and bright fast-food joint; the chef is a complete professional. It's Dr24 for *kefta* (seasoned minced lamb), chips and salad.

If you can't do without a Big Mac, then Casablanca is a good place to be. *McDonald's* is doing very well in Morocco among middle-class families. There are branches at 6 Blvd de la Corniche (the continuation of Blvd Sidi Mohammed ben Abdallah, heading west); off the roundabout at 53 Ave Mers Sultan, east of Parc de la Ligue Arabe; and at 8 Blvd Mohammed V.

There are five *Pizza Huts* scattered all over Casablanca (they all deliver) the most central is at Place de la Fraternité (☎ 473636, *67 Blvd Moulay Youssef*).

Self-Catering The best place for a do-it-yourself lunch is the excellent central market, between Blvd Mohammed V and Rue Allah ben Abdellah. It's a bit expensive but the fresh produce is excellent and a couple of good delis sell delicious pâté and ham.

The numerous tiny general stores dotted around town offer less upmarket food and the cheapest fruit and veg is for sale on stalls wheeled about town.

Entertainment
Nightlife in Casablanca can seem rather disappointing. Basically, there are three alternatives. First you've got the seedy cabaret joints in downtown Casablanca where the cheap hotels are found. Second, there are the more upmarket places that are concentrated out in the 'Ain Diab, but they are expensive

(at least Dr100 to get in, the same for a drink), less accessible and can be picky about dress code. The last option for a night out is at the hotel bars, but they're also on the expensive side and can be a bit predictable.

Prostitutes work all of these places, particularly the cabarets, and men will be expected to pay for the drinks of any woman who befriends them; that's the start of the scenario. Women travellers shouldn't expect hassle-free drinking anywhere.

Nightclubs About the best of a dire bunch are the *Caesar* at the Sheraton and *Black House* at the Hyatt Regency. They generally get swinging from about 11 pm to 3 am. Entry costs Dr120/150 during the week/weekend and drinks are much the same price.

A new place, and less easy to categorise, is the *Cage* disco in Centre 2000. It's popular with the young; entry is around Dr100 (but it varies depending on the day of the week).

Gay male travellers should head for *Le Village* and *Armstrong's*, in the Corniche, although don't expect anything too exciting. The latter place is better for a drink.

Bars The city centre is riddled with drinking establishments, usually under the guise of cafes, bars, brasseries or even pharmacies. Almost all are spit-and-sawdust places, and attract a male-only clientele (plus prostitutes) that can be a little rough around the edges (this is a port after all).

Le Marignan (beside the restaurant of the same name) is one such place, a classic, but no good for women. *Au Petit Poucet* (*Blvd Mohammed V*), is more refined. It's a die-hard relic of 1920s France and a good, low-key bar with a restaurant next door. Saint-Exupéry, the French author and aviator, used to spend time here between mail-flights south across the Sahara on the Toulouse to Chile service.

Just around the corner, the fine *Sphinx Brasserie* is spacious, friendly and has a good atmosphere, but is a bit of a male preserve.

Somewhat more refined are the bars in the larger hotels, which also stay open later but are very expensive. In *Bar Casablanca* in the Hyatt Regency a beer is going to cost

you Dr70, though there's a happy hour (6.30 to 7.30 pm) when the second drink's free.

Considered to be the hottest bar in town among the affluent, trendy set, is the *Villa Fadango* (☎ 398508) on Rue Hubert-Giron, close to the Restaurant Croc Magnon in the Corniche. It's a very popular Latino-type bar serving up shots of tequila and Mexican beer. You'll need to be snappily dressed to get past the bouncers. Also in the Corniche try *Le Balcon*, which is a little more laid back.

Arts Venues The *Villa des Arts* (☎ 295087, @ vi.art@atlasnet.net.ma, 30 Blvd Brahim Roudani) often hosts exhibitions (international and Moroccan) sponsored by the Institut Français (see Cultural Centres earlier in this chapter). This wonderful converted Art Deco house is close to Parc de la Ligue Arabe and is open from 11 am to 7 pm Tuesday to Saturday. The entry fee is Dr10.

Complex Cultural Sidi Belyout (28 Rue Léon L'Africain) near the CTM bus station is a theatre with a small exhibition space for paintings. The theatre seats 200 and plays are usually in Arabic. There are occasionally music recitals and dance performances. You can buy tickets an hour before performances. Shows usually start at 9 pm.

Cinemas There are about half a dozen cinemas around the city centre. The *Cinema Lynx* (☎ 220229, 50 Ave Mers Sultan), although not the largest, is considered the best in town. It's spacious and comfortable with an excellent sound system. Tickets cost Dr25/30/50 for seats in the *orchestre/balcon/club* (close to orchestre/balcony/standard). You can often catch films recently released in the West, but there are no guarantees on whether it has been cut or just dubbed into French.

Cheaper is *Cinéma Rialto* (*Rue Salah ben Bouchaib*). It's a classic cavernous Art Deco cinema, showing a mix of Indian action flics and movies from the Western world.

Shopping

In Casablanca prices for craft goods are high and vendors seem unwilling to lower their prices dramatically. There's better shopping to be had elsewhere, but the Exposition Nationale d'Artisanat (☎ 267064), 3 Ave Hassan II, has three floors of crafts and has some good quality stuff for fixed prices. If nothing else it'll give you an idea of prices to pay in the medina. It's open daily 8.30 am to 12.30 pm and 2.30 to 8 pm.

In the medina, the busiest shopping areas are along Rue Chakab Arsalane and Rue de Fès. Such craft stalls as there are, can mostly be found outside the city walls (along Blvd Houphouet Boigny) and, just inside, on Rue Mohammed al-Hansali (which quickly changes its name to Rue de Fès).

Otherwise you could try the Tour des Habous or the area around the Royal Palace, south of the centre. Quality can be variable in these places and hard bargaining is definitely the order of the day. If you want a new watch, these are the places to get it. Along with dope, watches seem to be the main illegal product on offer, and you're bound to be offered a good many 'Rolexes' during even a cursory visit.

For anyone with more than a passing interest in Moroccan music, a good place for LPs, cassettes and CDs is Le Comptoire Marocain de Distribution de Disques (☎ 369153), 26 Ave Lalla Yacout, close to the Cinema Lux. It has a substantial range of most types of traditional Arab and Berber music. Also good is Disques GAM (☎ 268954), 99 Rue Abderrahhman Sehraoui, with a big stock of second-hand vinyl.

Getting There & Away

Air From Casablanca's Mohammed V international airport (30km south-east of the city), there are regular connections to most countries in Western Europe, as well as to West Africa, Algeria, Tunisia, Egypt, the Middle East and North America.

Internally, the vast majority of Royal Air Maroc's (RAM) flights go via Casablanca, so you can get to any destination directly from Casablanca. For instance, there are three to five daily flights to Agadir (Dr929, one hour), five weekly flights to Fès (Dr578, 50 minutes), at least two daily flights to Marrakesh (Dr648, 50 minutes) and a daily flight to Tangier (Dr688, one hour). For more information on flights see

the Getting There & Away and Getting Around chapters earlier in this book.

Airlines flying into and out of Mohammed V international airport include:

Aeroflot (☎ 206410) 47 Blvd Moulay Youssef
Air Afrique (☎ 318379) 10th floor, Tour des Habous, Ave des FAR
Air Algerie (☎ 266995) 1 Rue el-Amraoui Brahim
Air France (☎ 294040) 15 Ave des FAR
Air Mauritanie (☎ 314136) 110 Rue Allah ben Abdellah
Alitalia (☎ 314181) 17th floor, Tour des Habous, Ave des FAR
British Airways (☎ 229464) 7th floor, Centre Allah ben Abdellah, Rue Allah ben Abdellah
EygptAir (☎ 315564) 6th floor, Tour des Habous, Ave des FAR
Iberia (☎ 279600) 17 Ave des FAR
KLM-Royal Dutch Airlines (☎ 203222) 6 Blvd Houphouet Boigny
Lufthansa Airlines (☎ 312371) 9th floor, Tour des Habous, Ave des FAR
Royal Air Maroc (☎ 311122) 44 Ave des FAR
Sabena (☎ 313280) 7th floor, Tour des Habous, Ave des FAR
Swissair (see Sabena)
Tunis Air (☎ 293452) 10 Ave des FAR

Bus – CTM The flash CTM bus station (☎ 449224 for information) is on Rue Léon L'Africain, behind Hôtel Sheraton. It's a pleasant, reasonably efficient place with a cafe and left-luggage counter (open from 8 am to midnight daily; Dr10 for 24 hours). There are daily CTM departures to:

destination	cost (Dr)	duration (hours)	no of services
Agadir	140	9	4
Beni Mellal	55	4	3
El-Jadida	25	1½	6
Essaouira	100	7	3
Laayoune	315	24	3
Marrakesh	65	4	8
Meknès	63	4	hourly from 6.15 am to 10 pm
Rabat	30	1	hourly from 6 am to 10 pm
Sefrou	85	5	one at 3 pm
Tangier	110	6	5
Taza	110	7½	6
Tetouan	110	7	3

In addition, there are buses to Safi via El-Jadida (Dr65, four hours), Fès via Meknès (Dr80, 5 hours) and Oujda via Taza (Dr165, 10½ hours, two services).

CTM (☎ 458000) also operates international buses to Belgium, France, Germany, Italy and Spain from Casablanca (see Land in the Getting There & Away chapter).

Bus – Other Companies Gare Routière Ouled Ziane is the new bus station for almost all non-CTM services. It's a thoroughly modern-looking affair, bright and almost tranquil (for the moment!). The only drawback is its distance from the city centre. The 4km trip costs Dr10 by taxi or take bus No 10 from Blvd Mohammed V opposite the market. There's a left-luggage office (Dr5 for 12 hours storage), information booth and cafe in the main building.

At the front of the building are 30 ticket windows, each given over to a separate company. Below are the edited highlights:

No 4 Tetouan (Dr73) six daily, mostly between 7 pm and 1 am
No 5 Tangier (Dr70) every 30 minutes
No 6 Ouezzane (Dr45) nine daily; Chefchaouen (Dr60) 9.45 am and 4.45 pm
Nos 7 & 8 Rabat/Kenitra (Dr18 to Dr20/Dr25 to Dr30) numerous 1st- and 2nd-class buses to both destinations
No 9 Oujda (Dr130), Nador (Dr120), Al-Hoceima (Dr140) and Fès (Dr58 to Dr70; 1st and 2nd class); all evening departures
No 13 Er-Rachidia (Dr119) mostly night buses
No 21 Marrakesh (Dr44) frequent services between noon and midnight
No 23 Ouarzazate (Dr100) six per day; Zagora (Dr130) five evening buses; Tinerhir (Dr130) two night buses
No 24 Tiznit (Dr110) frequent day-time services
Nos 25 & 27 Agadir (Dr100) and Essaouira (Dr60) services from 5 am to 11.30 pm
No 26 Safi (Dr48) very frequent services

Also on Route Ouled Ziane, but more than 1km closer to town, is the SAT bus station (☎ 444470). SAT runs national and international buses of a similar standard to CTM, but fares are slightly cheaper.

Train Casablanca has five train stations. Most departures are from Casa-Voyageurs train station, 4km east of the city centre. The station is a Dr15 taxi ride from the centre or catch bus No 30, which runs all the way down Mohammed V and costs Dr3. The Casa-Port train station is a few hundred metres north-east of Place des Nations Unies, the most convenient place to be, but trains from here only run as far as Kenitra to the north-east and Mohammed V international airport to the south-east. The other stations, 'Ain Sebaa, Nouvelle Medina and Mers Sultan, are out in the suburbs and so are of little interest to travellers.

Both main stations have left-luggage facilities. Casa-Voyageurs charges Dr10 for 24-hour storage. Casa-Port charges Dr2.50 per 24 hours per item, but you must have a padlock on your bag or pack.

Services All long-distance trains run from Casa-Voyageurs (except trains to Rabat and Kenitra, which go from Casa-Port, see following). Second-class fares in the various classes are shown below.

There's now only one cheap *ordinaire* service per day to Marrakesh (Dr56, departing 4.55 am), Oujda (Dr152, Dr202 for a couchette, departing 10.30 pm) and Tangier (Dr87, departing 12.15 am). All other services, including the shuttle trains between Kenitra and Mohammed V international airport, are standard *rapide* trains.

Destinations serviced by rapide and ordinaire trains include Marrakesh (Dr73, 3¼ hours, seven trains daily), Fès (Dr94, 4½ hours, eight trains daily) via Meknès (Dr78, 3½ hours), Oujda (Dr197, 10 hours, two trains daily) via Taza (Dr130, seven hours), and Tangier (Dr114, 5¾ hours, two trains daily). For Safi (Dr93, five hours, one train daily) change at Benguérir.

All trains running to Oujda call at Meknès and Fès and all trains heading to the north stop at Rabat. However, the quickest and easiest way to get to Rabat (Dr27, one hour) is by the express shuttle trains that run from the Casa-Port train station to Kenitra (Dr38, 1½ hours, at least hourly services). These operate from around 7 am to midnight and bypass the Casa-Voyageurs train station.

Taxi *Grand taxis* (shared long-distance taxis) to Rabat (Dr27), and some to Fès (Dr50 to Dr60) leave from Blvd Hassan Seghir, near the CTM bus station. There are also grand taxis to Rabat departing from Place de Nations Unies. Many grand-taxi stops for other destinations are on the outskirts of town, so are not terribly useful.

Car & Motorcycle The following business are among the 50 or so car rental agencies in Casablanca. Many of the smaller agencies are concentrated around Ave des Far and Blvd Mohammed V. They often employ runners to bring in business – follow some of them and you could end up with a much better deal.

The airport is a great place to rent a car. The offices are cheek-by-jowl, and you can beat prices right down (by more than 50% in the low season) by playing one offer against another.

Avis (☎ 312424, 311135) 19 Ave des FAR; (☎ 339072) Mohammed V international airport
Budget (☎ 313124) Tour des Habous, Ave des FAR; (☎ 539157) Mohammed V international airport
Europcar (☎ 313737) Tour des des Habous, Ave des FAR; (☎ 314069) 44 Ave des FAR; (☎/fax 339161) Mohammed V international airport
Hertz (☎ 484710) 25 Rue Araibi Jilali; (☎ 339181) Mohammed V international airport
National (☎ 472550) 5 Ave des FAR; (☎ 539716) Mohammed V international airport

If you do rent a car, be aware of Casablanca's horrendous parking problems. It's very difficult to find a space in the city centre between 8 am and 6 pm. The car park next to the British cemetery charges Dr20 for a day, Dr15 for a night.

The parking meters around the city centre charge Dr2 per hour (2 hours maximum stay). They operate from 8 am to noon and 2 to 7 pm except on Sunday, public holidays and during festivals.

Getting Around
To/From the Airport You can get from Mohammed V international airport to Casablanca by train (Dr30, 2nd class, 27 to 40 minutes). Trains are comfortable and reliable; there are 12 services between 6.15 am and 10.45 pm, all of which continue on to Rabat (Dr55) and eight of which go as far as Kenitra (Dr60). The trains leave from below the ground floor of the airport terminal building.

From Casa-Port train station to the airport, the first service leaves at 5.15 am and the last leaves at 8.45 pm (all services go via Casa-Voyageurs train station).

The grand taxis that meet travellers at the airport late at night can be any old van/car that is pressed into service by very unofficial taxi drivers. A taxi between the airport and the city centre costs around Dr200.

Bus The main local bus station is on Place Oued al-Makhazine, west of the centre. There is even a faded route map posted up here. Other buses go from Place de la Concorde and No 30 leaves from Blvd Ziraoui. Some useful city routes are:

No 2 Blvd Mohammed V to Casa-Voyageurs train station. Walking out of the train station continue straight ahead and cross the road into Place al-Yassir, from where you can catch it into the city centre.
No 4 Along Rue Strasbourg and down Ave Lalla Yacout to Nouvelle Medina.
No 5 From the bus station to Place de la Victoire.
No 9 From the bus station to 'Ain Diab and the beaches.
No 10 From Place de la Concorde, along Blvd Mohammed V to Gare Routière Ouled Ziane (heading into town this can be caught from the dual carriage-way in front of the bus station, but you're better off taking a petit taxi).
No 15 From the bus station heading north to the Hassan II Mosque.
No 30 From Blvd Ziraoui to Casa-Voyageurs train station via Ave des FAR and Blvd Mohammed V.

Taxi There's no shortage of red *petit taxis* (metered local taxis) in Casablanca. Expect to pay Dr10 for a ride in or around the city centre. The minimum fare is Dr5. Most drivers use the meter without question, but if they refuse to, just get out of the cab. Prices rise by 50% after 8 pm.

There are plenty of petit-taxi stands around town.

NORTH ATLANTIC COAST

AROUND CASABLANCA
Mohammedia
☎ 03

About 30km north-east of Casablanca lies the local resort town of Mohammedia, which also doubles as the centre of Morocco's petrol industry – the SAMIR oil refinery is one of the country's busiest ports. The two might seem incompatible, but Mohammedia, which until the 1960s was little more than a decaying fishing village (then known as Fedala), manages to keep the two activities apart, not that sunbathing next to an oil refinery is everyone's cup of tea. However, the northern beaches are not bad.

At the height of summer, the place tends to fill to bursting point with Casablancans, but out of season it's very quiet, just a little shabby and has the same bizarre attraction that many tatty, purpose-built seaside resorts seem to have.

In the town itself, the walls of an old kasbah still stand and it's worth wandering around, though there is nothing much to see. The town has an unusually high number of good restaurants to choose from and one of the best golf courses in the country (a favourite of the late King Hassan II).

It's an easy day trip from Casablanca and not hard to find your way around.

Information The main post office is on Ave Mohammed Zerktouni, a couple of blocks in from the beach. Several banks have branches in Mohammedia. BMCI (with ATM) is closest to the train station, just opposite the kasbah on Ave des FAR.

If the banks are closed, you can change money in the Sabah Hôtel.

Cyber Centre is at the back of Café Glacier du Centre at 6 Ave des FAR (Dr15 per hour); it's open from 9 am to 9 pm.

Hammams The Hammam Essaada is conveniently located close to the cheaper hotels. It's through the unmarked door on the corner of Blvd Bir Anzarane and Rue al-Mansour ed-Dahbi, and is open from 6.30 am to 9 pm to both men and women (in separate parts). A bath costs Dr6. You may like to try the local shampoo and soap, which you can buy here.

MOHAMMEDIA

PLACES TO STAY
- 5 Hôtel Hager; Pâtisserie
- 16 Sabah Hôtel
- 23 Hôtel Ennasr

PLACES TO EAT
- 2 Restaurant du Port
- 3 Restaurant Bec Fin
- 4 Diner Grill
- 6 Restaurant Sans Pareil
- 7 Boulangerie du Port
- 9 Café el-Fath
- 27 Pizzeria Eurosnack

OTHER
- 1 Sailing Club
- 8 Libre Service Grand Mamouth
- 10 Market
- 11 Total Petrol Station
- 12 Ranch Club
- 13 Church
- 14 Post Office
- 15 BMCE
- 17 Mosque
- 18 Gendarmarie Royal
- 19 Pharmacie du Marghreb
- 20 Labo Couleur el-Jamahir; Telephones; Fax
- 21 Pressing Blancherie Modern
- 22 Royal Air Maroc
- 24 Telephones
- 25 Cyber Centre (Café Glacier du Centre)
- 26 BMCI
- 28 Hammam Essaada
- 29 Petrom Petrol Station
- 30 Telephones
- 31 Bus No 900 to Casablanca
- 32 Telephones

Places to Stay Decent accommodation is limited. The overpriced *Hôtel Ennasr*, on Rue Abdarrahmane Sarghini, has singles/doubles for Dr100/200. The cell-like rooms are very clean.

By far the best is the new, clean and bright *Hôtel Hager* (☎ 325921, *Ave Ferhat Hachad*). Singles/doubles with bath and phone cost Dr220/264 (rooms with added TV and heating cost Dr270/294). It's good value and well deserving of its two stars. There's a restaurant downstairs and an excellent patisserie next door.

If the dark corridors and cigarette-burnt carpet don't put you off, you could try the *Sabah Hôtel* (☎ 321451, *42 Ave des FAR*). Rooms costs Dr409/554 with breakfast (add about 20% in high season). There's a happy hour in the 'Irish Bar', (the Irish connection being a lonely bottle of Jameson's) between 7 and 8 pm.

Places to Eat & Drink The waterfront is lined with cafes, and there are a few standard hole-in-the-wall places on Ave des FAR and around the train station. There's also a collection of decent restaurants at the north end of Rue de Fès. Not surprisingly, fish is the theme.

Pizzeria Eurosnack (Rue al-Mansour ed-Dahbi), near the kasbah, is a favourite with the locals and does good, cheap fare such as hamburgers for Dr10 to Dr24 and pizzas for Dr65 to Dr90.

The *Diner Grill* (☎ 310436) on Ave Ferhat Hachad is a simple place serving reasonable fish dishes for around Dr30.

The *Restaurant Bec Fin* has become rather upmarket after moving premises. Seafood dishes hover around the Dr100 mark, but the place now seems a little out of favour.

Probably the best place in town is *Restaurant du Port* (☎ 322466, *1 Rue du Port*). It specialises in Mediterranean cuisine. Mains cost between Dr80 to Dr160; it's closed on Monday. Not far away, close to the Hôtel Hager, is *Restaurant Sans Pareil* (☎ 322855), which specialises in French cuisine (with a touch of Spanish) and is also excellent. It charges much the

same as du Port. You'll need to make a reservation for both places in high season.

A good place for cakes, doughnuts and excellent chocolate croissants is the *Boulangerie du Port* on Rue Tafilalet. Dough-based items can be taken around the corner to *Café el-Fath*. The patisserie is open from 6 am to 1 pm and 3 to 8 pm daily.

There's also a good food market close by and the *Libre Service Grand Mamouth* general store is also a well-stocked booze emporium.

For ice cream, head for the *Glacier Étoile de Mer* or *Café le Voilier Vert* on the seafront, or the *Pâtisserie Glacier Forces Armées* on Ave des FAR.

For a little nightlife, try the *Ranch Club* on Ave Mohammed Zerktouni. It costs Dr60 (drinks Dr40 to Dr50), plays a kind of 'Europop' and is open from around 10 pm to 2.30 am.

Getting There & Away Coming from Casablanca your best bet is the train, which runs roughly every half hour during the day (Dr12, 2nd class, 25 minutes). Alternatively, bus No 900 links Casa-Port train station and the square in front of Mohammedia train station (Dr6.50, departing every eight minutes between 6 am and 8.45 pm). Grand taxis also ply this route (Dr8).

Getting Around Petit taxis are lime-green. A couple of buses run down to the beach from the roundabout in front of the train station.

RABAT
☎ 07

The modern capital of Morocco has had something of a roller-coaster history, climbing at one point to the status of imperial capital only to descend later to the level of a backwater village, before finding favour again. The great walls enclose a largely modern city, but there remain several quarters to remind you of Rabat's rich past, including Salé – home to the corsairs – across the river Bou Regreg.

There is enough to keep the sightseer occupied for a few days, and the atmosphere

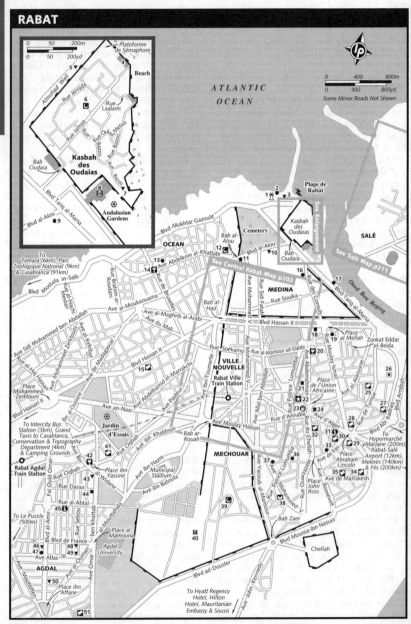

RABAT

ATLANTIC OCEAN

Plateforme de Sémaphore

Beach

Rue Jerrada

Rue Laalami

Almohad Wall

Rue Jamaa

Rue Ouel Metaa

Rue Bazo

Kasbah des Oudaias

Bab Oudaia

Andalusian Gardens

Blvd Tariq al-Marsa

Blvd al-Alou

To Temara (6km), Parc Zoologique National (9km) & Casablanca (91km)

Blvd Mostafa as-Saïh

Blvd Mokhtar Gazoulit

OCEAN

Ave Abdelkrim al-Khattabi

Bab al-Alou

Cemetery

Blvd al-Alou

Kasbah des Oudaias

Bab Oudaia

Plage de Rabat

SALÉ

See Salé Map p211

Oued Bou Regreg

Rue Brahim ar-Roudani

See Central Rabat Map p202

MEDINA

Rue Sidi Fatah

Rue Mohammed V

Rue Souika

Rue de Consuls

Blvd Tariq al-Marsa

Ave al-Moukaouama

Ave al-Maghrib al-Arabi

Ave du Mali

Bab al-Had

Rue Soékarno

Rue Mohammed V

Blvd Hassan II

Ave Sidi Mohammed ben Abdallah

Ave Mohammed Zerktouni

Ave de Madagascar

Blvd Hassan II

Ave al-Kebiat

Place Mohammed Zerktouni

Blvd Hassan II

Ave Abdelhamid el-Marrakchi

Ave Pasteur

Rue al-Mansour ad-Dahbi

Ave Mohammed V

VILLE NOUVELLE

Rabat Ville Train Station

Rue Patrice Lumumba

Rue d'Annaba

Ave Allal ben Abdallah

Ave Abderrahman

Place de l'Union Africaine

Rue Oqba

Ave an-Nasr

Ave Ibn Toumerte

Ave Moulay Hassan

Bab ar-Rouah

Place ibn Yassine

Rue Ibn Khaldoun

Rue Ibn Hazm

MECHOUAR

Rue d'Alger

Rue de Tunis

Ave Fal Ould Oumar

Place Mohammed Zerktouni

To Intercity Bus Station (3km), Grand Taxis to Casablanca, Conservation & Topography Department (4km) & Camping Grounds

Rabat Agdal Train Station

Rue Daraa

Rue al-Abtal

To Le Puzzle (500m)

Blvd de l'Amir ben Khattab

Blvd de France

AGDAL

Place ibn Affane

Ave Atlas

Ave Maachtala

Municipal Stadium

Ave Ibn Batouta

Place al-Mamouna

Agdal University

Rue al-Moultahida

Ave Yacoub al-Mansour

Ave Patrice Lumumba

Rue Mohammed

Place Abraham Lincoln

Ave de Fes

Ave Ouarzazate

Place John Ross

Ave de Marrakesh

Ave Roosevelt

Bab Zaer

Bab Zaer

Chellah

Blvd Moussa ibn Nassair

Blvd ad-Douster

Ave John Kennedy

To Hyatt Regency Hotel, Hilton Hotel, Mauritanian Embassy & Soussi

Place de l'Union Africaine

Zankat Eddar el-Beida

Place Mellah

Ave Moulay Ismail

Blvd Abi Raqraq

To Hypermarché Marjane (200m), Rabat-Salé Airport (12km), Meknès (140km) & Fès (200km)

Some Minor Roads Not Shown

RABAT

PLACES TO STAY
9 Hôtel des Oudaias
11 Hôtel Darna
18 Hôtel Bou Regreg
21 Hôtel La Tour Hassan
24 Hôtel Sofitel Diwan

PLACES TO EAT
3 Borj Eddar;Restaurant de la Plage
5 La Caravelle
7 Café Maure
10 Restaurant Dinarjat
43 Restaurant Chez el-Ouazzani
46 L'Entrecôte
48 Pizza Hut
49 Au Vert Gallant
50 McDonald's

OTHER
1 Lighthouse
2 Oudayas Surf Club
4 Carpet Factory
6 Kasbah Mosque
8 Musée des Oudaia
12 Mosque
13 Universmatic Services
14 Church
15 French Consulate
16 Carpet Souq
17 Ensemble Artisanal
19 Garages & Car Mechanics
20 Jour et Nuit Nightclub
22 Préfecture de Police
23 Shell Petrol Station
25 British Embassy
26 Le Tour Hassan; Mohammed V Mausoleum
27 Italian Embassy; Instituto Italiano di Cultura
28 Dutch Embassy
29 Algerian Embassy
30 Tunisian Embassy
31 Ministère du Tourisme
32 Spanish Consulate
33 American Language Center (Annexe)
34 US Embassy
35 Belgian Embassy
36 American Language Center; American Bookshop
37 British Council
38 Post Office
39 Ahl al-Fas Mosque
40 Royal Palace
41 French Embassy
42 Elysee Bar & Brasserie
44 Voyages Schwartz (AmEx)
45 ONMT Tourist Office; Boulangerie Pâtisserie al-Abtal
47 Pharmacy ibn Sina
51 Canadian Embassy

is relaxed enough to encourage some to stay a little longer. In contrast to the great tourist attractions of the interior, such as Fès and Marrakesh, there is virtually no sign of hustle and hassle here, not even in the souqs.

The new city is comparatively quiet and, although its people appear as cosmopolitan as their counterparts down the coast in Casablanca, Rabat lacks the gritty, big-city edge of its economic big brother.

History

Apart from two brief spells as imperial capital, Rabat has been the capital of Morocco only since the days of the French protectorate. However, as far back as the 8th century BC, indigenous people had a settlement in the area of the necropolis of Chellah. They were followed by the Phoenicians and the Romans, who successively patrolled the coast and set up outposts of their empires.

The Roman settlement, called Sala Colonia, was built along the river of the same name (today's Bou Regreg, which has since altered its course). Like Volubilis, it lasted long after the empire's fall and became the seat of an independent Berber kingdom.

The settlement's fate is obscure enough to have given rise to varying stories about

what happened next. It appears the people of Sala Colonia embraced Islam on the arrival of the Arabs in the late 7th century AD, but with unorthodox modifications.

The first Moroccan dynasties, the Idrissids and Almoravids, largely neglected Sala Colonia and, as its river port silted up, the town declined.

By the 10th century, the new town of Salé had sprung up on the north bank of the river. Its inhabitants, of the Zenata tribe (although some sources attribute the rise of the new town to the people of the old town), built a *ribat* (fortress-monastery) on the present site of Rabat's kasbah, as a base for fighting a rival and heretic tribe south of the river. Whether Sala Colonia had already been emptied of its population by then, or whether the process was accelerated by the fighting, is unclear.

Things changed with the arrival of the Almohads in the 12th century. They put an end to the fighting and built a kasbah on the site of the ribat. Their intention was to make it the jumping-off point for campaigns against the Christian Reconquista in Spain.

It was under Yacoub al-Mansour (the Victorious) that Rabat enjoyed a brief peak of glory. After successful campaigns in Spain,

Ribat al-Fatah, 'Victory Fortress', was to become a great capital. Al-Mansour had extensive walls built, added the Bab Oudaia gate to the kasbah and began work on what was intended to be the greatest mosque in all of the Muslim west, if not in all of the Islamic world.

Al-Mansour's death in 1199 brought an end to these grandiose schemes. The great Hassan Mosque, overlooking the bridge across the Oued Bou Regreg, was never completed – all that remains today are the impressive, squat (and incomplete) minaret (Le Tour Hassan) and some columns that have since been re-erected on the site. The city lost all significance quickly thereafter.

Rabat's fortunes began to change in the 17th century with the arrival of Muslim refugees from Christian Spain. At the same time, the cities of Rabat and Salé received a colourful injection of Christian renegades, Moorish pirates, freebooters and multinational adventurers.

The two cities flourished as those whom English chroniclers called the Sallee Rovers (or corsairs) set about a campaign of brazen piracy that saw them venture as far as the coast of America for Spanish gold and the coast of Cornwall, southern England, to capture Christian slave labour.

Although the first Alawite sultans curtailed their activities, no sultan ever really exercised control over the corsairs, who continued plundering European shipping until well into the 19th century, by which time Europe's wishes were becoming writ in Morocco.

Sultan Mohammed ben Abdallah briefly made Rabat his capital at the end of the 18th century, but with little appreciable effect on its destiny.

France decided to shift the capital of its protectorate, established in 1912, from Fès to Rabat. The new capital was on the coast and therefore easily supplied and defended. It was also far from the hornet's nest of political intrigue and potential unrest of Fès or Marrakesh – long the traditional choices for capital. Since independence (in 1956), Rabat has remained the seat of government and home to the king.

Orientation

Rabat is best approached by rail, since Rabat Ville train station lies on the city's main thoroughfare – the wide, palm-lined Ave Mohammed V. Arrival by bus is inconvenient, as the intercity bus station lies a good 5km outside the centre.

All the main administrative buildings and many of the hotels lie on, or just off, Ave Mohammed V, although there are others further afield. The main embassy area is east of the centre around Place Abraham Lincoln and Ave de Fas (or Fès as it sometimes appears); see Embassies & Consulates in the Facts for the Visitor chapter for addresses.

The medina is divided from the *ville nouvelle* (new town) by the wide and busy Blvd Hassan II, which follows the line of the medina walls to Oued Bou Regreg. The river also separates the twin cities of Salé and Rabat. They may share a river and an airport, but are separate entities with their own colour of petit taxis, and separate train and bus stations. Whereas Rabat is cosmopolitan, Salé is often regarded as conservative. Only the medina of Salé is of interest to travellers.

Maps The Cartography Division of Morocco's Conservation & Topography Department (☎ 295034, fax 295549) has moved to a grand government complex on Ave Hassan II, near the Centre de Transfusion Sanguine, 4km south-west of the city centre. It stocks a range of topographical Moroccan maps and town plans, but thanks to security concerns, obtaining them is not always easy, though far from impossible. See under Information in the Trekking chapter for more details.

Information

Tourist Offices ONMT (☎ 730562) on Rue al-Abtal in Agdal, to the south-west of the city (bus No 3 from Blvd Hassan II will drop you outside) is one of Morocco's main tourist offices, though desk staff seem to have little to offer beyond the usual brochures. However, it's worth persevering and, when pushed, staff can be very helpful. The office is open from 8.30 to noon and 3 to 6.30 pm weekdays.

There's also a tourist office at 22 Ave d'Alger, east of the ville nouvelle, but though they'll chat to you, it's really an administrative centre for the Ministère du Tourisme only.

Visa Extensions Should you want to extend your visa, go to the Préfecture de Police (Police Headquarters; Service des Étrangers) on Rue Hussein I just off Place al-Joulane in the centre (see Visas & Documents in the Facts for the Visitor chapter for further details).

Money Numerous banks (with ATMs) are concentrated along Ave Mohammed V and the parallel Ave Allal ben Abdallah. The Wafa Bank, BMCE (by far the busiest), BMCI and Crédit du Maroc banks have small, separate bureau de change booths. The one at the BMCE on Ave Mohammed V is open daily 8 am to 8 pm. There's also a useful BMCE bureau de change at Rabat Ville train station.

Post & Communications The post office, on the corner of Rue Soékarno and Ave Mohammed V, is open from 8.30 am to noon and 3 to 6.45 pm weekdays. Poste restante is on the left in the main post office building. To collect mail you need to show your passport as proof of identity and there's a small charge for each letter collected. *Colis postaux* (parcel post) and *Poste Rapide* (EMS) are in a separate office, to the right of the main entrance.

There are numerous *téléboutiques* (privately run phone offices) and Internet cafes dotted around town. Internet access is commonly Dr10 per hour. Wave Cyber Cafe at 53 Ave Allal ben Abdallah is young and hip and open all hours, while INT Plus on Ave Mohammed V (probably the best choice) is open daily from 10 am to 10 pm – the entrance is rather tucked away beside a clothes shop. Librairie Livre Service bookshop, in the city centre, has a good Internet cafe, but it's only open standard shop hours (see Bookshops & Newsstands for contact details).

Travel Agencies A good place for cheap flights to African destinations is Africa Voy-

ages (☎ 709647), 28 Ave Allal ben Abdallah, but CAP Tours around the corner (☎ 733571, fax 731878, e Captours@sis.net.ma), on the corner of Rue Tanta and Rue Dimachk Damas, is a sharper operation. It is an agent for numerous airlines and can make ferry reservations. It is open 8.30 am to noon, 2.30 to 7 pm and on Saturday mornings.

Carlson Wagonlits (☎ 709625) is nearby on Ave Moulay Abdallah.

Voyages Schwartz (☎ 681569), the agency for AmEx, is south-west of the centre in Agdal on the corner of Ave Omar ben Khattab and Rue Daraa. It runs a wide range of tours across Morocco.

Bookshops & Newsstands The English Bookshop (☎ 706593), near Rabat Ville train station at 7 Zankat Alyamama, is run by the friendly Mohammed Belhaj and stocks a good selection of mainly second-hand English and American novels, some guides, language books and dictionaries. Mohammed will also buy books from you for between 20 and 30% of what he can sell them on for. The bookshop is open from 9 am to noon and 3 to 7 pm Monday to Saturday.

The American Bookshop (☎ 768717), part of the American Language Center, has a smaller, but a little more astute collection of new books, including English-language fiction, guidebooks, travel books and English-Arabic dictionaries. In addition, it has a modest, but very interesting, stand on Morocco, which includes writing on social, anthropological, historical and religious issues. There's also some feminist writing by Moroccan authors, and in this field it's one of the best sources in the country. It's open from 9.30 am to 12.30 pm and 2.30 to 7.30 pm weekdays, plus 10 am to noon and 1.30 to 5.30 pm Saturday.

Rabat has the best bookshops in Morocco for Francophone readers. There are several along Ave Mohammed V in the centre. Editions La Porte Librairie aux Belles Images (☎ 709958) has numerous coffee-table books and a good second-hand section. Librairie Livre Service (☎ 724495), 46 Ave Allal ben Abdallah, is mainly aimed at students, but also stocks a few guidebooks on

Morocco (including hiking and wildlife guides), coffee-table books and a large selection of French novels.

Numerous French newspapers and magazines are available at newsstands scattered around the ville nouvelle. The newsstands along Ave Mohammed V are the best hunting grounds. Limited other foreign press is also available at these stands, though the one beside the medina car park on Blvd Hassan II seems particularly good for Spanish, German, US and UK papers. The various cultural centres also have foreign newspapers and magazines.

Film & Photography There are plenty of places along Ave Mohammed V that sell photographic supplies and develop film. One that's recommended is the Photolab Photomagic, on the corner of Ave Mohammed V and Rue Ghazza.

Rabat Ville train station has a passport photo booth (Dr20 a go).

Cultural Centres In order to use the facilities at the cultural centres you usually need to pay for membership, though the occasional discreet day visit is usually possible.

British Council (☎ 760836, fax 760850) just south of the centre at 34 Rue Tanger. As well as a library, which holds a stock of some 14,000 books and periodicals, it has a program of lectures and exhibitions. The library is open from 2 to 6.45 pm Monday, 11 am to 6.45 pm Tuesday to Friday and 9 am to 1.45 pm Saturday. Web site: www.britishcouncil.org.ma

Centro Cultural Español (☎ 708738) 5 Zankat Madnine, next to the Spanish embassy. Open from 9 am to 1 pm and 3 to 6 pm weekdays.

Goethe Institut (☎ 706544) 7 Rue Sana'a. Open from 10 am to 7 pm weekdays. There is a library; art and photography exhibitions are held here and there's a stylish cafe, Le Weimar Club Restaurant (see Ville Nouvelle under Places to Eat later in this section).

Institut Français (☎ 701122) 2 Rue al-Yanboua, just south of Rabat Ville train station. It puts on films, theatrical performances and lectures, and has a library, which is open 2.30 to 7 pm Tuesday and from 10 am to noon Wednesday to Saturday.

Istituto Italiano di Cultura (☎ 720852) 2 Zankat al-Aghouat, near Place de l'Union Africaine,

east of the city centre. Its library is open from 9 am to noon Monday, Wednesday and Friday.

Laundry Universmatic Services (☎ 726485) is a self-service laundry just off Ave Abdelkrim al-Khattabi on Rue Istambul in Ocean, just west of the ville nouvelle. An 8kg load costs Dr25 to wash and about Dr15 to dry. Powder is Dr5 scoop. It's open daily 8.30 am to 9 pm.

Medical Services & Emergencies The Pharmacie du Nuit (night chemist) is on Rue Moulay Rachid, opposite Théâtre Mohammed V in the centre. It's open from 9.30 pm to 7.30 am. Town pharmacies open at night and on weekends on a rotational basis, the rota is posted in French and Arabic in all pharmacy windows.

In Agdal, to the south-west Polyclinique de Rabat (☎ 204914, 206161), 8 Rue de Tunis, is a reasonable private hospital.

SAMU (☎ 737373) is a private ambulance service, while SOS Médecins (☎ 202020) has doctors on call 24 hours a day. Doctors will come to your hotel if required (for around Dr300).

Medina

The walled medina is far less interesting than those in Fès, Meknès and Marrakesh, and dates only from the 17th century. It's still worth a stroll, and there is no hustling to worry about.

About the most interesting medina street is **Rue Souika**. Starting out from the corner of Rue Sidi Fatah and heading north-east, you will find mainly food, spice and general stores until you reach the area around the Great Mosque.

From here to the Rue des Consuls (so called because foreign diplomats lived here until 1912), you are in the Souq as-Sebbat, where jewellery is the main item for sale.

If you continue past the Rue des Consuls you end up in a **flea market** before emerging at the river. Most of the stuff in the flea market is junk, but you never know what a rummage might turn up.

If you head north along the Rue des Consuls on the way to the kasbah, you will find

The Evil Eye

The power of the evil eye is a potent force in the minds of many Moroccans. A symbolic means of warding it off is to show the open palm of the hand, fingers pointing upwards. This 'hand of Fatima' (the Prophet's daughter) can frequently be spotted as stickers, painted on doors or as jewellery.

In the herb and spice markets you may come across another force enlisted to avert the evil eye: the chameleon (al-boua). Many believe that these harmless insect-eaters possess considerable magical powers. To restore the fidelity of a straying husband a wife may conceal chameleon meat or bones in his food. If Moroccans feel they've been struck by misfortune from a spiritual source beyond their control, one option is to throw a chameleon into a small, wood-fired oven and walk around it three times. If the chameleon explodes, the evil has been averted, but if it just melts down to goo, they're still in trouble. Not that either outcome is any consolation to the hapless chameleon.

yourself surrounded on all sides by carpet and **rug shops**, along with the occasional leatherwork, *babouche* (leather slipper) or copperwork place. On Thursday women gather here to sell their hand-woven rugs and carpets. There are some bargains to be had, but get there early before the carpet dealers.

The street ends in a fairly broad, open area that leads up the hill to the kasbah. In the days of the Sallee Rovers, this was the site of the **slave auctions**.

Kasbah des Oudaias

The Kasbah des Oudaias, built on the bluff overlooking the estuary and the Atlantic Ocean, dominates the surrounding area and can be seen from some distance. It is unfortunate that a much-used city circular road runs right past the entrance. You can only guess at the long-term damage done to the buildings by the passing traffic.

The main entry point is the enormous Almohad gate of **Bab Oudaia**, built in 1195.

This is one of the few places in Rabat where you will encounter 'guides'. It's completely unnecessary to take one. Once through the gate, there's only one main street, Rue Jamaa, so it's difficult to get really lost.

Most of the houses here were built by Muslim refugees from Spain. There are great views over the estuary and across to Salé from what is known as the Plateforme du Sémaphore, at the end of Rue Jamaa. On your left as you head towards the viewpoint is the oldest **mosque** in Rabat, built in the 12th century and restored in the 18th.

From just inside Bab Oudaia you can turn to your right (south-east) and walk down to a passage running more or less parallel to Rue Jamaa. Enter the passage and on your right is a 17th-century palace built by Moulay Ismail. It now serves as part of the **Musée des Oudaia** (Museum of Moroccan Arts). To get tickets, however, you have to proceed a little further south into the **Andalusian Gardens** (actually laid out by the French during the colonial period).

Built into the walls of the kasbah are two small galleries that form part of the museum. The entrances to the galleries lead off from the central gardens. The northernmost of these contains a small display of traditional musical instruments and the ticket desk for the whole museum, while the second gallery houses a display of traditional costumes.

Back up in Moulay Ismail's palace (which later became a *medersa* – theological college), two of the four galleries are devoted to Fès ceramics and one to jewellery. The last has been decked out as a traditional, high-class Moroccan dining and reception room. Tickets cost Dr10, and the galleries are open from 9 am to noon and 3 to 5 pm (6 pm in high season). The gardens stay open later.

Le Tour Hassan & Mausoleum of Mohammed V

Rabat's most famous landmark is Le Tour Hassan, which overlooks the bridge across the Oued Bou Regreg to Salé. Construction of this enormous minaret – intended to be the largest and highest in the Muslim world – was begun by the Almohad sultan Yacoub al-Mansour in 1195, but abandoned on his death some four years later.

Meant to reach a height of more than 60m, it only made it to 44m. The tower still stands, but little remains of the adjacent mosque, which was all but destroyed by an earthquake in 1755. Only the re-erected, shattered pillars testify to the grand plans of Al-Mansour.

On the same site is the Mausoleum of Mohammed V, in which the present king's grandfather and now father (the late Hassan II) are laid to rest. Built in the traditional Moroccan style and richly decorated, the tomb of these kings is located below ground in an open chamber. Above, visitors enter a gallery from which they can see the tomb below. Admission is free, but you must be dressed in a respectful manner.

Chellah

Beyond the city walls, in the south of the city at the end of Ave Yacoub al-Mansour at the junction with Blvd ad-Douster, are the remains of the ancient Roman city of Sala Colonia. It's enclosed by the walls of the necropolis of Chellah, built here by the Merenids in the 13th century. The city of Rabat had by this time fallen on hard times, and this pretty spot south of the city gates was as close as the Merenids came to taking an interest in it.

The construction has a defensive air about it, which is no coincidence. The sultan who completed it, Abu al-Hassan Ali, was intent on protecting his dynasty from possible attack or interference.

After entering through the main gate, you are pretty much obliged to follow a path heading diagonally away from the gate. You can see what little remains of the Roman city, but it is all fenced off. Around you, fig, olive, orange and banana trees, as well as all sorts of other vegetation, prosper amid the tombs and koubbas (domed shrines). It's also a haven for birds and butterflies too.

At the bottom of this short walk are the remains of a mosque. A couple of fairly half-hearted would-be guides hang about here – you're in no way obliged to take up their offers. Penetrate further into the mosque, where a couple of tombs stand in front of a chunk of wall. Here lie Abu al-Hassan Ali and his wife.

As you enter the site, on the far right are the tombs of local venerated saints, and a walled pool. Infertile women come here with peeled boiled eggs to feed the eels that dwell in the murky waters of the pool.

You will have already noticed a minaret topped by a stork's nest (hardly anything here isn't topped by a stork's nest). At one point this was a small medersa that functioned as an endowment of Abu al-Hassan Ali. You can make out where the students' cells were on either side of the building, as well as the mihrab (prayer niche) at the end opposite the minaret.

This peaceful, half-overgrown monument of Chellah is open daily from 8.30 am until 6 pm (5 pm in winter). Entry costs Dr10.

Archaeology Museum

Although dusty and under-funded this is a good museum dealing with the country's ancient past. It's tucked away close to the Hôtel Chellah at 23 Rue al-Brihi Parent, off Rue Moulay Abdel Aziz.

The ground floor is given over to displays of implements and other finds from the oldest known civilisations in Morocco. Some of the material dates back 350,000 years to the Stone Age period.

In a courtyard to the right are some prehistoric rock carvings. On the 2nd floor you can see finds from Morocco's history, from the Roman era to the Middle Ages with explanations in French and Arabic.

In a separate building is the highlight of the collection, the Salle des Bronzes, though at the time of writing many pieces were on extended loan to France. Most of the ceramics, statuary and implements in bronze and other metals date from the period of Roman occupation and were found at Volubilis, Lixus and Chellah. There are various bronze plates with Latin texts, including a 'military diploma' awarded by the emperor to a local worthy. Don't miss the beautiful head of Juba II. This is in complete contrast to the unforgiving realism of Cato the Younger's bust, complete with good Roman nose, stubborn brow and sticking-out ears.

The museum is open daily (except Tuesday) from 9 to 11.30 am and from 2.30 to 5.30 pm. Entry costs Dr10.

Royal Palace

Of the four remaining Almohad gates in Rabat's city walls, by far the most impressive is Bab ar-Rouah (Gate of the Winds), which forms the north-west corner of the walls around the Royal Palace complex.

There are several entrances into the palace grounds. The main one is off Ave Moulay Hassan, a little way inside Bab ar-Rouah. It takes you south towards the *mechouar* (parade ground), on the east side of which is the Ahl al-Fas (People of Fès) Mosque.

All the palace buildings, which were built in the last century, are off-limits, so you're not likely to be tempted to hang around here for long. However, it makes a pleasant enough walk on the way from the centre of town out towards Chellah.

Musée Nationale des PTT

There is a small and much-ignored postal museum on Ave Mohammed V in the centre that has a collection of stamps and first-day covers going back to pre-protectorate days. Entry is free, and the museum is open weekdays during office hours.

Surfing

Oudayas Surf Club (☎ 260683, fax 260684), housed in a beautiful, stylish building above the breakers of the Atlantic coast, between the kasbah and the lighthouse, opened in June 1999. Apparently, King Mohammed VI was out jet-skiing when a local surfer managed to bend his ear about the lack of facilities for young local surfers. One thing led to another and the King became the founding member (and president) of Oudayas Surf Club.

Nonmembers can use the cafe for Dr15 per day (this includes a free soft drink), while full membership is Dr1250. Surfing courses cost Dr160 for two hours and includes use of equipment.

While there are some good waves to be had right in front of the club house, a lot of club meetings and tuition sessions take place near Temara, 6km south of Rabat.

Places to Stay – Budget

Camping The nearest camping ground is *Camping de la Plage* (☎ 844566), in from the beach at Salé; it's well signposted from the Salé end of the bridge over the Oued Bou Regreg. It's open all year and costs Dr15 per adult, Dr8 per child (under 12), Dr12/22 for small/large tents, plus Dr12/25/35 per car/camper van/bus. It also charges Dr10 for power and water and hot showers cost Dr7. There's very little shade, but it seems reasonably secure. There's a small cafe (they will rustle up a tajine for Dr50) and the supermarket nearby sells alcohol.

There are several more camping grounds on the road south towards Casablanca. The first of them is the *Palmeraie*, about 15km south of Rabat, on the beach at Temara. Another 10km south, near Ech-Chiahna Plage, are two others: *Camping Gambusias* (☎ 749142) and *Camping Rose Marie* (☎ 749251). Both are OK and the locations are pleasant enough.

Hostels The *Youth Hostel* (☎ 725769, 43 Rue Marassa) is opposite the walls of the medina. It's a pleasant place with an attractive and verdant courtyard, and costs Dr27 per night (Dr32 without a card) in dormitory accommodation. There are cold showers, but no cooking facilities. The hostel is open from 8 to 10 am, noon to 3 pm and 6.30 to 10.30 pm.

Hotels – Medina There are several basic budget hotels on or just off the continuation of Ave Mohammed V as it enters the medina. Few make any concessions to creature comforts (like showers) and an extra dollar or two will buy you better accommodation outside the medina.

One of the cheapest is the *Hôtel Chaab* (☎ 731351), in the first lane inside the medina wall between Blvd Mohammed V and Rue Sidi Fatah. It's based around a pleasant covered courtyard. Basic singles/doubles cost Dr30/50.

Close by, *Hôtel du Centre* charges about Dr80/160. Rooms are clean, with table, chair and washbasin; there are separate showers and toilets, but it's overpriced.

CENTRAL RABAT

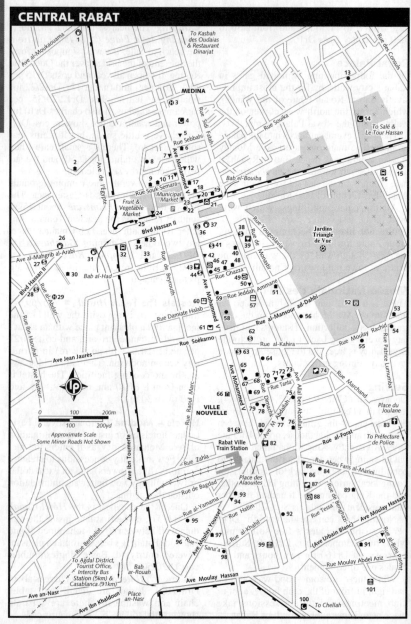

CENTRAL RABAT

PLACES TO STAY
- 2 Youth Hostel
- 6 Hôtel Maghreb
- 9 Hôtel France
- 10 Hôtel d'Alger
- 17 Hôtel Dorhmi;
  Banque Populaire
- 18 Hôtel du Centre
- 19 Hôtel Chaab
- 30 Hôtel d'Alsace
- 33 Hôtel Mamounia
- 34 Hôtel Majestic
- 35 Hôtel Petit Vatel
- 40 Hôtel Capitol
- 47 Hôtel Splendid; Chez
  Thami Music Store
- 48 Hôtel de la Paix
- 51 Hôtel Royal
- 53 Grand Hôtel
- 68 Hôtel Central
- 69 Hôtel Balima
- 76 Hôtel Velleda
- 89 Hôtel les Oudayas
- 91 Hôtel Chellah
- 93 Hôtel d'Orsay
- 97 Hôtel Bélère

PLACES TO EAT
- 5 Restaurant Taghazout
- 7 Restaurant de la Libération
- 11 Café Restaurant
  Afrique du Nord
- 12 Café de la Jeunesse
- 20 Restaurant el-Bahia
- 23 Pizza Rica
- 24 Pâtisserie Salon de Thé Bami
- 25 Cheap Fish Restaurants
- 42 Pâtisserie 4 Saison
- 50 Pâtisserie Majestic
- 65 Taki Fried Chicken
- 71 La Dolche Vita

- 72 La Mamma;
  Restaurant Equinox
- 77 McDonald's
- 78 La Petit Beure Dar Tajine
- 85 Pâtisserie Lina
- 86 City VIPS
- 90 Restaurant La Koutoubia
- 94 Restaurant La Clef

OTHER
- 1 Mobil Petrol Station
- 3 Douches
  Modernes
- 4 Mosque
- 8 Douches
  (Men Only)
- 13 Carpet Souq
- 14 Great Mosque
- 15 Shell Petrol Station
- 16 Main Local Bus Station;
  Grand Taxis to Fès,
  Meknès & Salé
- 21 Petit Taxi Stand
- 22 Newsstand
- 26 Total Petrol Station
- 27 Crédit Agricole
- 28 BMCI Bank (ATM)
- 29 Bains Douches
- 31 Shell Petrol Station
- 32 Bus Nos 3, 17 & 30
- 36 Wafa Bank (ATM)
- 37 Total Petrol Station
- 38 Crédit du Maroc (ATM)
- 39 Amnesia Nightclub
- 41 BMCE (ATM)
- 43 Bar L'Alsace
- 44 BMCE (ATM)
- 45 Photolab Photomagic
- 46 INT Plus
- 49 Librairie Livre
  Service

- 52 Théatre Mohammed V
- 54 Europcar
- 55 Pharmacie de Nuit
  (Night Pharmacy)
- 56 Ministry of Culture
- 57 Cinéma du 7éme Art
- 58 Ministry of Information
- 59 Librairie aux
  Belles Images
- 60 Cinéma Renaissance
- 61 Main Post Office
- 62 Bank al-Maghreb
- 63 Société Generale
- 64 Mini Marché
  du Centre
- 66 Chambres des
  Représentants
- 67 Air France
- 70 CAP Tours
- 73 Africa Voyages
- 74 German & Spanish
  Embassies; Centro
  Cultural Español
- 75 Carlson Wagonlits
- 79 International
  Language Centre
- 80 Royal Air Maroc
- 81 BMCI Bank (ATM)
- 82 Henry's Bar
- 83 St Pierre Cathedral
- 84 Avis
- 87 French Consulate
- 88 Wave Cyber Cafe
- 92 Hertz
- 95 English Bookshop
- 96 Goethe Institut;
  Le Weimar Club Restaurant
- 98 Institut Français
- 99 Musée Nationale des PTT
- 100 Sunna Mosque
- 101 Archaeology Museum

Hôtel France (☎ 723457, 46 Rue Souk Semara), opposite the fruit & vegetable market, is a basic but adequate place; some rooms look on to a courtyard with enormous banana trees. Singles cost Dr30 to Dr35 and doubles/triples cost Dr50/60.

Hôtel d'Alger (☎ 724829, 34 Rue Souk Semara), nearby, is about the best deal in the lower half of this category. Rooms are quite large, clean and quiet and look on to a pleasant courtyard, but there are no showers. Singles/doubles/triples/quads cost Dr35/70/90/110 respectively.

A little more expensive, but one of the best in this area, is *Hôtel al-Maghrib al-Jadid* (☎ 732207, fax 202583, 2 Rue Sebbahi). It's clean and bright and geared up for travellers. Singles/doubles/triples cost Dr50/80/90. A hot shower costs Dr5, a cold one Dr2.

Right up at the kasbah end of the medina is a quiet little place, the *Hôtel des Oudaias* (☎ 732371, 132 Blvd al-Alou). Though not top value for money (Dr60/100 for basic rooms, with hot showers Dr12 extra; doubles with bath cost Dr120) it's in a pleasant location and they have a nice tearoom downstairs.

A little more expensive is the **Hôtel Darna** (☎ 736787, 24 Blvd al-Alou) just north of the centre. It's a shabby hotchpotch of a hotel and could be cleaner, but rooms come with shower or, if you're lucky, full bathroom. They cost Dr80/120. Reception is in the busy cafe downstairs.

The best by a mile at the higher end of this category, and well located, is the friendly, family-run and immaculate **Hôtel Dorhmi** (☎ 723898, 313 Ave Mohammed V), above the Banque Populaire close to the main southern entrance of the medina. Singles/doubles/triples cost Dr80/100/150 (hot showers cost Dr7).

Hotels – Ville Nouvelle West of Bab al-Had, on the south-west corner of the medina, there is a small clutch of hotels on and around Blvd Hassan II. The area is nothing special, but it's close enough to the action if you are having trouble getting a bed elsewhere.

A good cheapie is the **Hôtel d'Alsace** (☎ 722611, Derb Guessoussn) although the toilets can get a bit smelly. It's a quiet place on just off Blvd Hassan II; most (basic) rooms look onto a cool internal courtyard. Rooms cost Dr45/80/110. Hot showers are Dr10.

Back inside the city walls, a couple of places along Blvd Hassan II are worth considering. To reach the **Hôtel Petit Vatel** (☎ 723095) go through a dark corridor and up some stairs. The clean, basic rooms cost Dr50/70 and hot showers are Dr5.

A block south is the **Hôtel Mamounia** (☎ 724479, 10 Rue de la Mamounia). Despite the uninviting entrance and the climb up to the 3rd floor, it's a peaceful, bright and clean place. Simple singles go for Dr50, doubles/triples cost Dr90/120. Some rooms have balconies; hot showers cost Dr5.

Long a popular budget place, but now considerably more expensive and not such good value, is the **Hôtel Central** (☎ 707356, 2 Zankat al-Basra). Spacious, well-maintained and clean singles/doubles/triples with washbasin and bidet go for Dr80/110/140. Rooms with a shower cost Dr100/136/172. Hot showers cost Dr10 (mornings only).

A little more expensive for singles, but a rival for value in doubles, is the **Hôtel Velleda** (☎ 769531, 106 Ave Allal ben Abdallah), it's on the 4th floor (with a lift) and has good views. It's a tidy, bright place offering fairly spacious rooms with showers (and some with toilet as well) costing Dr120/165. Hot water is available from 8 pm to 8 am, but it's more warm than hot in the morning.

Then there's the one-star **Hôtel Capitol** (☎ 731236, 34 Ave Allal ben Abdallah), which has rooms without shower for Dr88/108. Rooms with shower are Dr105/140, and with shower and bathroom are Dr137/160. Most rooms are large, clean and light and have a balcony. There is also a lift and a restaurant.

The nearby **Hôtel Splendid** (☎ 723283, 8 Rue Ghazza) is rather good and designed around a pleasant courtyard. There are some great rooms with renovated bathrooms for Dr150/175, but rooms without showers and toilets are not so great value at Dr97/118.

A few doors along the same road is **Hôtel de la Paix** (☎ 732031). Reasonable rooms without shower cost Dr90/135, rooms with private toilet and shower go for Dr160/200/250 – a little overpriced.

Further afield, opposite the Jardins Triangle de Vue, is the **Grand Hôtel** (☎ 727285, 19 Rue Patrice Lumumba). Reasonable rooms go for Dr97/122; self-contained rooms cost Dr150/175 (breakfast costs Dr28). It has a lift and the somewhat seedy Bar Manhattan.

Places to Stay – Mid-Range

For those in search of a tad more comfort, there are a few decent two-star possibilities, mostly in the city centre.

The **Hôtel Royal** (☎ 721171, fax 725491, 1 Rue Jeddah Ammane), has comfortable rooms furnished with 1940s/50s polished wood furniture. Clean singles/doubles with shower and toilet cost Dr186/241 (including breakfast). There is piping hot water all day. Try to get a room with views over the park.

Near the train station is the **Hôtel d'Orsay** (☎ 202277, 11 Ave Moulay Youssef). It's quite an attractive place and good value. It has just 31 rooms. Five singles/doubles without shower cost Dr120/150 (communal showers are Dr12). The other singles/doubles/triples with shower, toilet and satellite TV cost Dr211/264/300.

Further north, along Ave Mohammed V, is the huge *Hôtel Balima* (☎ 707755, fax 707450). It's a pleasant place with a lift; comfortable, but characterless, self-contained rooms with TV and phone cost Dr324/394. It's an extra Dr75 for a third person.

Hôtel Bou Regreg (☎ 720414) is near the local city bus station, on the corner of Rue an-Nador and Blvd Hassan II. It has large, clean self-contained rooms with phone and TV for Dr324/394. The hotel has a lift, restaurant and cafe.

Hôtel les Oudayas (☎ 707820, fax 708235, 4 Rue Tobrouk) is OK, but is showing its age. Self-contained rooms with TV and phone cost Dr256/313.

The recently renovated *Hôtel Majestic* (☎ 722997, 121 Blvd Hassan II) is now a very good choice in the middle-price bracket. Large, reasonably furnished, rooms with bath (some with balconies) cost Dr189/223/286. Try for one at the front with views of the medina. There's a small salon de thé.

Places to Stay – Top End
The two four-star hotels in Rabat are not very special. The *Hôtel Bélère* (☎ 709689, fax 709801, 33 Ave Moulay Youssef), which must have got its four stars out of a cracker, charges Dr342/434/563 for singles/doubles/triples. A little better is *Hôtel Chellah* (☎ 701051, fax 706354, 2 Rue d'Ifni), north of the Archaeological Museum, with singles/doubles for Dr589/808.

The five-star hotels are much better. In town, but just east of the centre, the new, modern and very stylish *Hôtel Sofitel Diwan* (☎ 262727, fax 262424, Place de l'Union Africaine) is an excellent choice. Doubles cost upwards of Dr1800.

Heading north, the *Hôtel La Tour Hassan* (☎ 721491, fax 725408, 26 Ave Abderrahman Annegai) is arguably the best all-round five-star hotel in town. Rooms cost upwards of Dr914/1064. It has all the facilities you'd expect, plus a good bar and disco.

Out in the swish suburb of Souissi, south of the city centre, is the *Hilton* (☎ 675656, fax 671492). Rooms start at Dr2700.

Places to Eat
Restaurants Rabat is a cosmopolitan place, the seat of government and home to hundreds of wealthy Moroccans and expats. Consequently, there are a number of excellent, if expensive, restaurants all over the city and in the upmarket suburb of Agdal. But those on a budget need not despair as there are a number of cheap eateries in the medina.

Medina Perhaps cheapest of all is the collection of small restaurants under a common roofed area directly opposite the Hôtel Majestic, on the medina side of Blvd Hassan II. In some of them you can get fried fish along with the usual chips and salad, although you will probably be offered more standard meat or fish tajines for Dr15. For a full meal, you are looking at around Dr25.

Equally cheap are the restaurants close to the market on Ave Mohammed V. At *Café de la Jeunesse (305 Ave Mohammed V)* you can get a more-than-sufficient meal of tajine and chips, plus a soft drink, for Dr31. You can be close to the action at ground level or eat upstairs. However, the tajines across the street at *Café Restaurant Afrique du Nord* probably have the edge (Dr25) and the harira soup (Dr3.50) is often good. Both places are popular with locals at lunch time.

Just up the road at the *Restaurant de la Libération (256 Ave Mohammed V)* is another good, though slightly more expensive place. Meat or fish, chips and veg costs Dr29 and it does delicious couscous on Friday for Dr29.

Built into the medina walls is the pleasant *Restaurant el-Bahia* (☎ 734504, Blvd Hassan II). You can sit in the Moroccan-style interior upstairs, in a shaded courtyard or outside on the terrace. It's also quite good value: tajine costs Dr32, brochettes Dr35 and pastilla for three people Dr225.

For a splurge in one of the traditional Moroccan palace restaurants, you could try the *Restaurant Dinarjat* (☎ 704239, 6 Rue Belgnaoui) in the heart of the medina, opposite the cemetery. It was built as a private house at the end of the 17th century and is decorated in the Andalusian palace style. Main courses, including couscous and tajine cost around Dr140, but with 10% service charge and 20% tax, it soon adds up. The restaurant is licensed (a bottle of wine costs Dr70) and there are *spectacles* (traditional entertainment) in the evening. It's open every day for lunch and in the evenings from 8 pm, but it's best to reserve in advance. A lantern-bearing guide will be sent to pick you up from the medina entrance, just south of the Hôtel des Oudaias nearby on Blvd al-Alou, and lead you for the last bit of the journey. Some people complain that the experience is better than the food.

Ville Nouvelle On Zankat Tanta, *Equinox Snack* is open daily between 8.30 am and 11 pm. It's decorated in 1980s style (if that's not a contradiction) and is a friendly, relaxed place for women travellers. Unremarkable mains cost upwards from Dr50 and salads from Dr27. The set menus are better value starting at Dr70.

The *Restaurant La Koutoubia (10 Rue al-Brihi Parent)* is a colourful place with a fragile-looking, mock Andalusian extrusion at the entrance. The house speciality is tajine and couscous; there's a good selection, although it's a bit on the pricey side (Dr70). Beer/wine is also available for Dr14/70 per bottle.

A block behind the Hôtel Balima is a cluster of good, but a little more expensive, restaurants. *La Petit Beure Dar Tajine (☎ 731322, 8 Rue Damas)* is licensed and open Monday to Saturday; good couscous with vegetables or tajine costs Dr70.

For a romantic night out, you could try the candlelit *La Mamma (☎ 707329, 6 Zankat Tanta)*, next to Equinox Snack, which has been run by the same Italian-French family since 1964. It's an atmospheric, informal place and very popular with expats and wealthy locals. The restaurant is decorated in an Italian style, with wooden beams and old candlelit tables; there's an open pizza oven and slabs of meat sizzle on a grill. Pizzas (all for Dr50) are excellent, but fresh pasta (starting at Dr45) and some meat dishes (Dr60 to Dr90) are also served. It's open daily from 11.30 am to 3 pm and 8 pm to 1 am.

Restaurant Chez el-Ouazzani (☎ 779297, Sahat ibn Yassine) on the edge of Agdal district is a great place for brochettes. The lovely *zellij* (tilework) and cedar ceilings are genuine, and the place is packed with locals. Brochettes are usually the only thing on offer, and a dozen with chips will cost you Dr70, soup is Dr5 and salad is Dr10. It's a lively place and open every day for lunch and dinner (until 10.30 pm).

The best place for an excellent selection of traditional Moroccan fare is the *Restaurant La Clef (☎ 701972, Ave Moulay Youssef)*, just south of Rabat Ville train station, a couple of doors down from the Hôtel d'Orsay. It makes a half-hearted effort to look traditional with mock zellij tilework and plaster mouldings, but is a pleasant, relaxing little place. It does an excellent value, three-course dinner for Dr55. Main courses, if ordered separately, cost around Dr45. There's also salads for Dr11 to Dr20 and omelettes from Dr11. If you fancy an apéritif before dinner, there's a local bar downstairs, or you can have beer/wine with your meal for Dr14/71 per bottle. In summer, you can sit outside on the little terrace. It might be a good idea to make a reservation during this period, as the restaurant is popular.

Le Weimar Club Restaurant (☎ 732650, 7 Rue Sana'a) in the Goethe Institut is already a favourite of well-heeled locals and expats. The German-French and Mediterranean cuisine is excellent, for example the chicken in cream and bacon (yes bacon!) sauce (Dr46), and pizzas (around Dr45) are some of the best in town. There's live music on Friday night and the restaurant (and bar) is open until at least midnight.

There is a number of chic, French-style restaurants in Rabat with good reputations, although price-wise you're talking around Dr250 per head. *L'Entrecôte (☎ 671108, 74 Blvd al-Amir Fal Ould Omar)* in Agdal, is a good place where main dishes cost around Dr95. Not far away on the corner of Ave Atlas and Rue Sebou is the *Au Vert Gallant (☎ 674247)*. It has an excellent reputation but you'll be looking at spending about Dr350 per person. Both restaurants are in the wealthy Agdal district, some way from the town's centre; you'll need to get a petit taxi.

Outside the Centre The **Restaurant de la Plage** (☎ 723148) and the **Borj Eddar** (☎ 701501) serve fish and other seafood down by the Plage de Rabat, catering to well-heeled Rabatis and tour groups. Main courses start at Dr110. To get to them, just follow Blvd Tariq al-Marsa past the kasbah. The former, while closed in winter, keeps a cafe open all year. Just outside the kasbah on the north-east corner is the pleasant **La Caravelle** (☎ 738844). It is licensed and open daily for lunch from noon to 3 pm and dinner from 6.30 pm. Tajine and seafood mains go for Dr65.

Cafes Rabat is crawling with cafes (mainly European-style), which are great places for a morning croissant and coffee; most of these are women-friendly. Some of them double as bars (see under Entertainment later).

In the old part of town, the most pleasant cafe by far is the **Café Maure** in the Kasbah des Oudaias on the far side of the Andalusian Gardens. It's a calm and shady spot looking out over the estuary to Salé, and is a favourite with young Moroccan courting couples. They serve coffee and mint tea (Dr5), soft drinks (Dr6) and a small selection of excellent Moroccan pastries (Dr6). Try the *doigts de jeunes filles* (little girls' fingers) or the *bracelets aux amandes* (almond bracelets). Prices are posted up on a board, so keep a tally as the waiters can be a bit 'absent-minded'. The cafe is open every day from 9 am to 5.30 pm – often longer hours in summer.

Back in town, the **Cafeteria du 7éme Art** is a popular spot for evening coffee.

Fast Food There are several **McDonald's** in town, including one on Ave Moulay Abdallah. A Big Mac Chicken costs Dr23, a cheese burger Dr9.90.

Nearby, with much more character, is **La Bidoche** where decent burgers cost from Dr14. They also do brochettes for Dr15.

The **City VIPS** (☎ 202840, 47 Ave Allal ben Abdallah), is another popular fast-food joint (with abrupt 1980s decor); hamburgers cost Dr19 and pizzas cost Dr23.

Taki Fried Chicken (281 Ave Mohammed V) is a wonderful rip-off of the real thing and there's a reasonable choice: roast chicken and chips costs Dr30, soft drinks are Dr8.

Pizza Rica, on the edge of the medina, does decent pizzas to eat in or take away from around Dr50. La Mamma restaurant operates **SOS Mamma** (☎ 707329), an excellent pizza delivery service.

A couple of **Pizza Huts** have recently opened in town (try the one at 107 Ave Fal Ould Oumeir in the Agdal district) although they're expensive at Dr69 for a small pizza.

Patisseries & Ice-Cream Parlours If you haven't had much joy with the ONMT tourist office in Agdal, the **Boulangerie Pâtisserie al-Abtal**, almost next door, should make up for it. It does good ice cream and outstanding cakes and patisseries.

The **Pâtisserie Lina** (45 Allal ben Abdallah) is a fashionable (expensive) place around tea time and good for breakfast. It has a great selection of sweets, including more unusual French-style treats such as very rich chocolate cake. It's a tranquil place for women travellers, nonsmoking and open daily from 6.30 am to 9.25 pm. A rival in the town centre is the excellent **Pâtisserie Majestic** on the corner of Rue Jeddah and Ave Allal ben Abdallah. It's also nonsmoking and women-friendly. Great for cakes, its bread is top notch too.

A cheaper option is **Pâtisserie Salon de Thé Bami**, just inside the medina, beside the indoor fruit and vegetable market. It's a relaxing place with good bread, some savouries and a fine selection of French and Moroccan sticky cakes. Consume these delicacies outside on the busy terrace or in the large nonsmoking area indoors, which is more women-friendly.

Pâtisserie 4 Saisons, on Ave Mohammed V, is a popular spot for breakfast; downstairs is a bit of a male preserve but upstairs is popular with a younger crowd.

For an ice-cream fix, head straight for **La Dolche Vita** on Rue Tanta. It's owned by the Benenatis, the same family which has the pizzeria La Mamma next door. The 43 or so flavours are home-made in the traditional Italian style and are delicious. Cones cost Dr7 and a tub Dr12. It's open daily from 7.30 to 1 am, and makes a great late stop on a warm night.

Self-Catering For self-caterers the grocery stalls around the indoor fruit and vegetable market are a good bet (there's also a booze emporium), though food is cheaper on the stalls close to Bab el-Bouiba and along Rue Souika.

Mini Marché du Centre on Rue Dimachk stocks a small selection of groceries and a good selection of alcohol. It's open daily from 8.30 am to 1 pm and 3 to 8 pm.

Hypermarché Marjane is just off the road to Salé, and if it hasn't got it, you probably can't buy it in Morocco. It's open daily from 7 am to 7 pm.

Entertainment
Nightclubs There's a good choice of nightclubs in Rabat, some of which are attached to the more expensive hotels, and they're all popular with well-heeled young people. The music is standard international disco fare. They normally charge Dr60 for entry (which includes the first drink) and the same amount for subsequent drinks. Most clubs are open from around 11 pm (though at weekends they don't get going until around midnight) and go on until 2, 3 or 4 am. You'll need to be suitably dressed in trousers, or preferably a suit, to get in.

Some of the better nightclubs include the disco at the *Hôtel Balima* (see Places to Stay – Mid-Range), *5th Avenue* and *Van Gough's* in the Agdal area, plus the sweaty *Amnesia (Rue de Monastir)* just south of the medina. The latter attracts a mix of people, can be sleazy, but can also be fun. It's done out like an American bar complete with American trains, trucks and even an aeroplane suspended from the roof. It plays a Western mix of music. Entry is Dr60 during the week (free to women) and Dr100 during the weekend. Expats seem to favour Van Gough's these days.

Gay places are, as usual, rather limited, but you could try the nightclub *Jour et Nuit*, just east of the centre on Ave Abderrahman, the terrace of the *Hôtel Balima* in the early evening, or *Amnesia*.

Bars A very popular place for a drink, particularly around pre-dinner time, is the pleasant terrace of the *Hôtel Balima*, which also serves uninspired and expensive food. *Elysee Bar & Brasserie*, out past the French embassy near Place ibn Yassine, is popular and reasonably women-friendly – the patio is a good spot for a quiet evening drink.

Henry's Bar is a classic little bar ideally placed (opposite Rabat Ville train station) for a restorative daytime Stork. *Bar de l'Alsace* on Ave Mohammed V is not bad either, but both places close early.

The most upmarket places are out of the city centre in Agdal. *Le Puzzle (☎ 670030, 79 Ave ibn Sina)* has a good bar attached to the smart restaurant (where mains start at Dr70), and karaoke and rock & blues evenings on Wednesday and Sunday evening, when local beer is half-price (it's usually Dr35 a bottle).

Cinemas & Theatres Rabat has a wide choice of cinemas; the best is *Cinéma du 7éme Art (Ave Allal ben Abdallah)*, which shows a range of films and costs Dr15. There are two showings daily between 3 and 9 pm. The nearby *Cinéma Renaissance* is firmly mainstream and has four showings a day between 3 and 9.30 pm; tickets cost Dr15/20 depending on where you sit. The *Royal (Rue Jeddah Ammane)*, near the hotel of the same name, is reputed to be a hashish den and is best avoided. The French-language newspapers also advertise what's on around town.

The *Théatre Mohammed V* puts on a wide variety of performances, ranging from classical music recitals to dance and the occasional lighthearted play (usually in Arabic).

Shopping
Rabat is well known for its carpets (see the special colour section 'Moroccan Arts & Crafts'). If you're interested in buying one, first try the Ensemble Artisanal (☎ 730507),

Blvd Tariq al-Marsa, by the Oued Bou Re-greg. It's open 9 am to noon and 2.30 to 6.30 pm and has its very own Banque Populaire bureau de change. There is also a carpet factory in the kasbah.

Rue des Consuls, not far from the kasbah, is one of the best places for purchases, particularly around the upper end. On Tuesday and Thursday mornings, the whole place becomes a kind of carpet souq, with local women bringing their wares into the city to sell. Try to get there early.

For traditional Moroccan and Arabic music, try the Chez Thami music store, 22 Rue Ghazza, close to Hôtel Splendid. It also has a small Western selection. It sells mainly cassettes, though there are a few CDs.

The front lobby of the Ministry of Culture on Rue Gandhi, just around the corner from the Theatre Mohammed V, is a good place to buy some excellent anthologies of varying styles of Moroccan music (see Music under Arts in the Facts about Morocco chapter).

Getting There & Away

Air RAM (☎ 709766) and Air France (☎ 707066) are both on Ave Mohammed V near Rabat Ville train station and both have flights twice daily to Paris (around Dr4600 return) from Rabat-Salé airport, 10km north-east of town (Dr100 in a grand taxi). The tiny airport is not used for internal flights. However, Casablanca's Mohammed V international airport is linked to Rabat by an express rail service (Dr55, 1½ hours).

Bus The intercity bus station *(gare routière)* is inconveniently situated about 5km south-west of the city centre on the road to Casablanca. Fortunately, there are local buses (No 30 is the most convenient) and petit taxis (about Dr15) into the centre. There is a left-luggage service at the station (Dr5 per item per day); it's open from 7 am to 9 pm.

All the various bus companies have their offices in this cylindrical building. There are 13 ticket windows, stretching around to the left of the main entrance to the CTM and Eurolines window (interrupted by a cafe on the way). CTM has buses to:

destination	cost (Dr)	duration (hrs)	no of services
Agadir	166	12	
Casablanca	30	1½	6
Chefchaouen	65	5	
El-Jadida	55	3½	
Er-Rachidia	133		
Essaouira	130	8	
Fès	55	3½	7
Marrakesh	94	5½	
Nador	141	9½	
Ouarzazate	155	10	
Oujda	141	9½	
Safi	95	5½	
Tangier	83	5½	6
Taroudannt	185		
Tetouan	80		
Tiznit	186	10½	

Tickets with cheaper companies for these and many more destinations can be bought from the following ticket windows, though touts are sure to 'advise' of the most imminent departures:

No 1 Ouezzane (Dr30), Chefchaouen (Dr45), Tetouan (Dr56) and Tangier (Dr60)
No 2 Meknès (Dr30), Fès (Dr50), Taza (Dr70) and Oujda (Dr100)
No 3 Er-Rachidia (Dr110), Erfoud (Dr110), Tinerhir (Dr130) and Zagora (Dr150)
No 4 Larache (Dr40), Asilah (Dr50) and Tangier (Dr60)
Nos 7 & 8 El-Jadida (Dr35), Marrakesh (Dr60 to 70), Safi (Dr70), Essaouira (Dr80), Ouarzazate (Dr110) and Agadir (Dr115)
No 9 Not in use
No 10 Mohammedia (Dr12) and Casablanca (Dr18)
No 11 international ticket office for buses to Europe: Madrid (Dr645), Barcelona (Dr1070) and Paris (Dr1220)
Nos 12 & 13 Agadir (Dr110), Tiznit (Dr130) and Taroudannt (Dr130)

If you arrive by bus from northern destinations, check that you can be dropped off in town, otherwise you could save yourself some time by alighting at Salé and taking a local bus (Dr3) or grand taxi (Dr3) into central Rabat.

Train This is the best way to arrive in Rabat, as Rabat Ville train station is in the centre of town, on Ave Mohammed V at Place des Alaouites. (Don't get off at Rabat Agdal train station to the west of the city.) Within the station there's an information booth (open daily 7 am to 7 pm); BMCE bureau de change; offices for Budget (☎ 705789); and a Supratours office (☎ 208062) open weekdays 8.30 am to noon and 2.30 to 6 pm, and Saturday mornings.

The left-luggage counter charges Dr10 per item per 24 hours, but items must be locked.

Services There are more than 20 trains between Rabat Ville train station and Casablanca every day (Dr27). About half are shuttle services that link Casablanca's Mohammed V international airport, via Casablanca's Casa-Port train station, with Rabat (Dr55, 1½ hours) and the other half are long-distance rapide services, though these usually only stop/leave from Casa-Voyagers train station. In addition there are two late-night cheap ordinaire services.

The first connecting service to Casablanca from Rabat is at 3.45 am and the last leaves Rabat at 10.30 pm. In the opposite direction, services commence at 6.15 am (from Casa-Port train station) and finish at 12.15 am.

On all long-distance routes there's one late-night ordinaire train among the rapide services. Destinations include Fès (Dr54/69 for 2nd class ordinaire/rapide, 3½ hours, eight services daily) via Meknès (Dr41/53, 2½ hours); Tangier (Dr67/87, 4¾ hours, three services); and Marrakesh (Dr76/99, 4½ hours, eight services).

There are trains to Oujda (Dr174/134, 9 hours, three services) and couchettes are available on the ordinaire service (Dr264, 2nd class).

Taxi Grand taxis leave for Casablanca (D27) from just outside the intercity bus station. Other grand taxis can be found between the city's main local bus station and the Hôtel Bou Regreg on Blvd Hassan II. They leave for Fès (Dr55), Meknès (Dr40) and Salé (Dr3).

You can't take petit taxis between Rabat and Salé because they come under separate city jurisdictions.

Car & Motorcycle The following are among the car rental agencies in Rabat:

Avis (☎ 769759) 7 Rue Abou Faris al-Marini
Budget (☎ 705789) Rabat Ville train station, Ave Mohammed V
Europcar (☎ 722328) 25 Rue Patrice Lumumba
Hertz (☎/fax 709227) 46 Ave Mohammed V
National (☎ 722731) on the corner of Rue du Caire and Rue Ghani

There's a car park at the edge of the medina close to the junction of Blvd Hassan II and Ave Mohammed V. Pay the guardian around Dr5 per day to keep an eye on your car.

City centre parking restrictions apply from 8 am to noon and 2 to 7 pm Monday to Saturday. Tickets (from meters) cost Dr1 for 30 minutes up to a maximum of 2½ hours for Dr5. If you get your wheels clamped it costs Dr20 to have the clamps removed.

Getting Around

Bus The main city bus station is on Blvd Hassan II. Tickets cost around Dr3 (hold on to them for inspection). Useful bus routes that depart from here include:

Nos 2 & 4 Bab Zaer for Chellah
No 16 Salé (get off after passing under the railway bridge)
Nos 37 & 52 From the intercity bus station into central Rabat.

Useful buses that depart from near Bab al-Had include:

No 3 Agdal (and right past the tourist office)
Nos 17 & 30 Past Rabat's intercity bus station and the map office; No 17 goes on past the zoo to Temara

Taxi A ride around town in a blue petit taxi will cost about Dr10, though the meters seem to go around pretty quickly. It's about Dr15 to the intercity bus station from the centre of town. There's a petit taxi stand near the entrance of the medina on Blvd Hassan II.

SALÉ
☎ 07

Although just across the estuary from Rabat the whitewashed city of Salé has a distinct character. Little within the city walls seems to

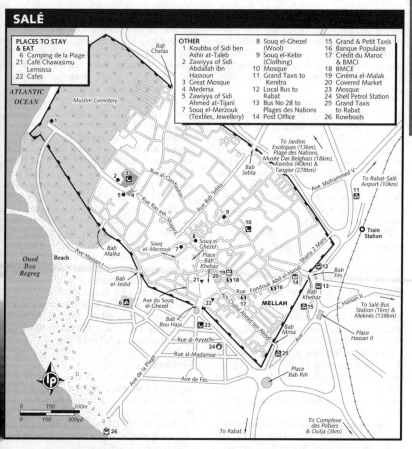

SALÉ

PLACES TO STAY & EAT
6 Camping de la Plage
21 Café Chawasimu Lemsissa
22 Cafes

OTHER
1 Koubba of Sidi ben Ashir at-Taleb
2 Zawiyya of Sidi Abdallah ibn Hassoun
3 Great Mosque
4 Medersa
5 Zawiyya of Sidi Ahmed at-Tijani
7 Souq el-Merzouk (Textiles, Jewellery)
8 Souq el-Ghezel (Wool)
9 Souq el-Kebir (Clothing)
10 Mosque
11 Grand Taxis to Kenitra
12 Local Bus to Rabat
13 Bus No 28 to Plages des Nations
14 Post Office
15 Grand & Petit Taxis
16 Banque Populaire
17 Crédit du Maroc & BMCI
18 BMCE
19 Cinéma el-Malak
20 Covered Market
23 Mosque
24 Shell Petrol Station
25 Grand Taxis to Rabat
26 Rowboats

have changed over the centuries and it is difficult to escape the feeling that Salé has been left by the wayside while Rabat forges ahead.

With a long history of action independent from central authorities, Salé is also a strongly traditional enclave amid the comparative liberalism of its sister city.

These two elements are best symbolised by the presence here of Abdessalam Yassine, who heads the Al-Adl wal-Ihsan (Justice & Charity) religious movement. He is here under house arrest and has long been considered a threat to the king and the central government.

Salé is not the most interesting of towns and can seem pretty grubby and worn out. It's also a bit difficult to find your way around, but it's worth persevering for the beautiful medersa in the medina.

History

The origins of the town are little known, but Salé rose as Sala Colonia, south of the Oued Bou Regreg, sank into obscurity. The Almohads took control of the area in the 12th century, putting an end to local warring and establishing neighbouring Rabat as a base for expeditions to Spain.

Salé's walls were not built until the following century. The Merenids, who otherwise took little interest in either Salé or Rabat, built them after a raid in 1260 by Spanish freebooters. A canal was dug from the river to Bab Mrisa to allow safe access for shipping.

Salé subsequently entered its most prosperous period, establishing trade links with Venice, Genoa, London and the Netherlands. It was this position as a trading city on the coast that led to Salé and Rabat becoming home to the Sallee Rovers (see History under Rabat) in the 16th century. Both cities prospered from the Sallee Rovers' pirate activities, and an influx of Muslim refugees from Spain in the 17th century only improved matters.

The end of pirating in the 19th century, in conjunction with Rabat's promotion to capital city under the French, left Salé to turn in on itself.

Orientation & Information

The town's sights can be seen in half a day. The medina's main point of access is Bab Bou Haja, on the south-western wall, which opens onto Place Bab Khebaz. From here it's a short walk to the souqs, although getting from these to the Great Mosque through the somewhat complicated system of narrow alleyways and arches can be tricky. You may need to ask some of the local people for directions.

An easy approach to the Great Mosque is along the road on the outside of the city walls, through Borj Nord Ouest or along the road that runs inside the city walls past Bab Bou Haja and Bab Malka.

Various banks (closed at weekends, but with ATMs) and the post office can be found on Rue Fondouk Abd el-Handi close to Bab Fès.

Great Mosque & Medersa

These are two of the most interesting buildings in Salé. The Great Mosque, built during Almohad times, is out of bounds to non-Muslims. However, the medersa no longer functions as such and is open to non-Muslim visitors.

Constructed in 1333 by Sultan Abu al-Hassan Ali, the mosque is a superb example of Merenid artistry and, although smaller, is certainly equal to Fès' Medersa Bou Inania. It follows a formula that is familiar to those who have seen Merenid medersas: the walls display a zellij base topped by intricately carved stucco and elegant cedar wood work (see the special section 'Moroccan Architecture' in the Facts about Morocco chapter).

Students once occupied the small cells around the gallery. A narrow flight of stairs leads onto a flat roof above the cells, from where there are excellent views of Salé and across to Rabat. Entry to the medersa costs Dr10 and the guardian who shows you around will expect a small tip (they don't get many visitors, so their income is limited).

Beware of a notorious *faux* (unofficial) guide who hangs around here. He may pretend that he has just seen off a potential assailant or troublesome faux guide on your behalf, and will expect you to allow him to guide you around the medersa (and show your gratitude with a large tip afterwards).

Photography is allowed inside the medersa and from the roof. It's open daily from 9 am to noon and 2.30 to 6 pm.

Shrines

At the back of the Great Mosque is the **Zawiyya of Sidi Abdallah ibn Hassoun**, the patron saint of Salé. Revered by many Moroccan travellers (in much the same way as St Christopher is among Christians), this respected Sufi died in 1604 and his religious fraternity is located here.

Sidi Abdallah ibn Hassoun is the object of an annual pilgrimage and procession through the streets of Salé on the eve of Mouloud, the Prophet's birthday. On this day, local fishers dress in period costume, while others carry decorated candles and parade through the streets, ending up at the marabout's shrine.

The Zawiyya of Sidi Abdallah ibn Hassoun is one of three shrines in Salé. The other two are the **Zawiyya of Sidi Ahmed at-Tijani**, on the lane that runs between the mosque and medersa, and the white **Koubba of Sidi ben Ashir at-Taleb** (the Doctor), in the cemetery north-west of the mosque.

Souqs

The souqs are connected to the Great Mosque via Rue Ras ash-Shajara (also known as Rue de la Grande Mosquée), along which rich merchants in previous times constructed their houses.

There are three souqs in all, but perhaps the most interesting of them is the **Souq el-Ghezel**, the Wool Market. Here under the shade of trees you can watch wool being bought and sold with the aid of scales suspended from a large tripod, as it has been for centuries.

Close by is the **Souq el-Merzouk**, where textiles, basketwork and jewellery are made and sold. A little further out is the Souq el-Kebir, featuring second-hand clothing and household items.

Places to Stay & Eat

Hotel options are limited in Salé, and those that are available tend to be basic. Unless you want to stay at *Camping de la Plage* (see Places to Stay – Budget under Rabat), there seems little point in staying here. There's a much better choice of accommodation in Rabat.

There are plenty of hole-in-the-wall cafes in the souqs and surrounding streets, as well as the area just south of Place Bab Khebaz, where refreshments and good, cheap meals can be found (*Café Chawasimu Lemsissa* is pretty good). It's worth calling into one or more of them to soak up the unhurried atmosphere of this timeless place.

Getting There & Away

Bus Salé's main bus station, the destination for most buses from Rabat, is some way away from the medina. Take bus No 16 from Rabat and get off after passing under the railway bridge and walk west to Bab Fès and the medina.

Returning, No 16 services pass by Bab Fès as do No 28 Rabat-bound services from Bouknadel and the Plage des Nations (going the other way the No 28 stops at Salé bus station). Fares cost Dr3.

Train It's possible also to take the train to Rabat, but buses or grand taxis are probably the simplest options. The train fare from Kenitra is Dr13.

Taxi Probably the easiest way to get to Salé medina is to pick up a taxi in Rabat close to the local bus station on Blvd Hassan II. From Salé there are departures from Bab Mrisa (Dr3 one way). Note that Salé's beige petit taxis are not permitted to cross into Rabat.

Grand taxis for Kenitra leave from a lot just north of the train station (Dr11).

Boat Small rowboats go across the Oued Bou Regreg from just below the mellah in Rabat to Salé and back. They operate all day, leaving when full. It costs locals Dr1, but you'll probably find yourself paying more.

On the far side, simply follow the rest of the people up the rise to Bab Bou Haja.

AROUND RABAT & SALÉ
Complexe des Potiers, Oulja

This pottery and craft cooperative 3km south-east of Salé produces a wide range of ceramics, basketwork and furniture. The quality is really quite good and it's a relaxed place with a bookshop, cafe and refreshment stalls. The clay comes from a rich seam in the surrounding hills (you'll see it on the left as you drive in). The tajine dishes are thrown and turned on kick wheels, raw glazed then fired once in enormous kilns using thinnings (twigs and leaves) from nearby eucalyptus forests. A firing takes 15 hours and reaches 900°C. Finer domestic pottery is fired in gas kilns provided by a joint Moroccan and Canadian initiative designed to reduce environmental degradation and air pollution.

To get there take a petit taxi from Salé (Dr12) or catch bus No 35 or 53 to/from Salé (Dr3).

Jardins Exotiques

About 13km north of Rabat on the road to Kenitra, the Jardins Exotiques are as much a monument to one man's persistent eccentricity as anything else.

Created in 1951 by one M François, a horticulturist, the gardens contain a sampling of flora (in themed gardens) from all over the world.

Popular with courting couples and cats (both often seen scurrying into the undergrowth) they appear a little disappointing at first, but get steadily better as winding paths lead you further into them. François spent a lot of time roaming the forests of Africa. His conclusion on his own efforts was that, 'it is poetry that recreates lost paradises; science and technology alone are not enough'.

The gardens are open from 9 am to 5.30 pm and entry costs Dr5 (children Dr3). Have the exact change ready, as the fellow in the ticket booth does not have any. The best time to visit is between March and April.

You can reach the gardens on the No 28 bus, which can be caught from Ave Moulay Hassan in Rabat; it goes via the bus station in Salé and past Bab Fès, the main gate at Salé medina. Ask to be let off at the Jardins Exotiques – there's a fading sign on the left-hand side of the road, but the palm trees are a better clue.

Musée Dar Belghazi

Almost exactly 17km from both Rabat and Kenitra is the Musée Dar Belghazi (☎ 07-822178, ℮ belghazi@maghrebnet.net.ma).

Entry to this, the first private museum in Morocco, is expensive (Dr50), but if you're keen on traditional Moroccan art and craft, it's not to be missed.

The museum's ethnographic collection, housed in an old *riad* (traditional lavish town house), has been amassed by the Belghazi family over three generations and contains some stunning examples of Andalusian, Jewish Moroccan and Islamic art. With some 4000 items, the museum claims to be the largest in Africa, and pieces are sent to international exhibitions all over the world. There are few, if any, state museums with such a collection.

On view are 17th-century carpets; exquisitely carved wooden pieces, such as minbars (pulpits), doors, cupolas and ceilings dating from as early as the 10th century; exceptional pottery and embroidery from Fès; and miniature copies of the Quran. Look out for the tiny antique kaftans made for brides as young as 12 years old. Captions are in English and French.

If you're really fired up by the exhibits, the reserve collection can be viewed for another Dr50. It's worth it. If you're lucky you may get a guided tour from Mr Belghazi himself, a master craftsman in his own right (he produced minbars for Casablanca's Hassan II Mosque) and an impassioned connoisseur. The museum is open every day from 8.30 am to 6 pm.

At the time of writing there were plans to open a traditional Moroccan restaurant here.

Plage des Nations

This beautiful beach is clean and far better and more exclusive than those at Rabat, Mohammedia or Salé. However, be a bit wary of coming here alone and watch out for strong waves (it's a popular surf spot) and currents when swimming.

Above the beach, *Hotel Firdaous* (☎ 07-822131) has a pool, cafe, bar and restaurant, and good singles/doubles for Dr459/598. The 1970s-style interiors are classic (though the rooms have been upgraded), with the bar and restaurant areas still replete with original, well-maintained, fixtures and fittings. Not many of these places are left, so check it out.

Bus No 28 from Rabat and Salé will take you to the turn-off for Plage des Nations which is opposite Musée Dar Belghazi 5km north of the Jardins Exotique. From the main highway a 2km-long sealed road leads down to the beach, which is also known as Sidi Bouknadel (not to be confused with the nearby town of Bouknadel).

Parc Zoologique National

The Parc Zoologique National, 9km south of Rabat on the road to Temara, is a clean, well kept place with over 90 species of mammals, 25 species of reptiles and 160 bird species. The zoo covers 50 hectares and most animals have a fair amount of room, but an unfortunate and depressed few are housed in rather cramped cages. The zoo runs captive-breeding programs for several endangered species including the bald ibis, Dame Mohr gazelle, addex antelope and scimitor horned oryx. The 18 lions are extremely special, being 80% Barbary in their genetic make up.

There are snack stands, a reasonable cafe and games for the kids. The zoo is open Monday to Saturday from 9.30 am to 6 pm and on Sunday and holidays from 9 am to 6 pm; entry is Dr3/9 for children/adults. Parking costs Dr3.

Bus Nos 17, 41 and 45 take about 20 minutes from Rabat city centre. Bus No 17 leaves from a side street off Blvd Hassan II, just inside Bab al-Had. Ask to be let off at the zoo (the stop is just past Prince Moulay Abdallah sports stadium).

From the main road, you have to walk a few hundred metres off to the left (east), as the entrance is at the back. You'll notice a shantytown spilling over close to the zoo entrance.

Forest of Mamora

For travellers with their own vehicle, the enormous cork and eucalyptus forests of Mamora – which dominate the area north-east of Rabat – provide an excellent escape from the city and a cool spot for a picnic.

There is abundant wildlife in the region, including wild boar, although much of the area forms part of a protected royal hunting reserve.

Forest of Zaer

South of Rabat is the picturesque area known at the Forest of Zaer. One particularly scenic road route follows the P22 around 30km south of Rabat to the little village of Aïn el-Aouda. If you want to make a circuit of it, you could continue on for another 10km until you reach the tiny S216 road to Merchouch, signposted to the right.

At Merchouch, you should bear right again onto the S106 towards Sidi Bettache and Ben Slimane, which takes you through green valleys and impressive gorges. There are also some good views to be had before starting the descent to the main road for Rabat or Casablanca.

If you're keen on birds, you may prefer to take the S208 back towards Rabat. The road begins at Sidi Bettache and heads northwards through a region that has become well known in ornithological circles for its rich bird life.

The area considered to be most favoured is around the hunting lodge about 15km south of the village of Sidi-Yahya. The extensive areas of cork-oak and scrub support larks, black-headed bush-shrikes, black-shouldered kites and double-spurred francolins. More commonly seen are spotted flycatchers and white storks.

There are plenty of other possibilities for motor excursions, particularly around the town of Ben Slimane.

Keep a look out for wild boar crossing the path in front of you when you're walking or driving in this area.

KENITRA
☎ 07 • pop 100,000

About 40km north of Rabat lies the French-built town of Kenitra. The country's sixth largest port, it was known until 1958 as Port Lyautey.

It's a sprawling town of no particular interest, but the nearby Plage Mehdiya and nature reserve of Lac de Sidi Bourhaba make stopping here worthwhile.

Information

The post office is on Ave Hassan II. Some banks have ATMs and most have foreign-exchange facilities, but all are only open weekdays.

The best Internet cafes (Dr10 per hour, open daily until late) are Dali Net, 47 Rue Maamora, and Millennium Palace, 315 Ave Mohammed V.

Places to Stay

The friendly *Hôtel Marignan* (☎ 363424) near the train station offers the best value. Clean, decent singles/doubles cost Dr40/60 and with three/four people sharing, Dr60/80 (some rooms have cold showers).

About five minutes' walk east of the centre is *Hôtel de la Poste* (☎ 379982, 307 Blvd Mohammed V). Clean, reasonably furnished singles/doubles with hot shower cost Dr60/150.

In the mid-range, *Hôtel La Rotonde* (☎ 371401, 60 Ave Mohammed Diouri) offers singles/doubles/triples with bath for Dr150/177/217. It's a clean, friendly place with a choice of bars, a free nightclub and a restaurant.

Near the town hall is the slightly fancier **Hôtel Mamora** (☎ *371775, fax 371446)*; rooms with bath, TV and phone go for Dr322/391. The hotel has a lift, and there's a restaurant, bar and disco (Dr50 for non-guests, open 11 pm to 3 am). The pool is open to nonguests for Dr40.

Places to Eat

You'll find a few simple eateries and cafes in the town centre, especially along Ave Mohammed Diouri. **Snack Zagadirte** is

open daily from 11.30 am till about midnight and serves good fast food. A decent hamburger/sausages and chips with a rice starter costs Dr15.

If you're pining for a Western breakfast, search for **El-Dorado** *(64 Ave Mohammed Diouri)*. It doubles as a bar and also has a good choice of mains (Dr46 for steak and chips; Dr 16 for salad *niçoise*).

Pâtisserie Mona Lisa *(80 Ave Mohammed Diouri)* is the best patisserie in town. It's a cool, relaxed place and open daily from 6 am to 8.30 pm.

L'Eté Indien, closer to the train station on Ave Mohammed Diouri, is a popular spot for morning coffee.

Entertainment

Mama's Club, **Le Village** and **007** are all slightly sleazy, seedy nightclubs and clustered around the junction of Blvd Mohammed V and Ave Mohammed Diouri. **El-Dorado** is a good place for a beer, or you could try the discos in the big hotels. Good luck.

Getting There & Away

The easiest way to get to Kenitra is by train (get off at the southern 'Kenitra' station not Kenitra Medina). Second-class fares include Rabat (Dr12), Souk el-Arba du Rharb (Dr34), Casablanca (Dr39), Meknès (Dr41), Fès (Dr58), Asilah (Dr62) and Tangier (Dr76).

CTM buses going to Souk el-Arba du Rharb (Dr23), Larache (Dr43), Chefchaouen (Dr53), Tangier (Dr70) and Tetouan (Dr72) leave once or twice a day from their office in the centre of town. Far more frequent (and cheaper) are the departures from the main bus station at the eastern end of Blvd Mohammed V; grand taxis to numerous destinations also leave from here.

AROUND KENITRA
Plage Mehdiya
☎ 07

Plage Mehdiya is a pleasant, cafe-lined beach 7km west of Kenitra, which is very popular in summer. Before reaching the beach itself there's a useful-looking surf break where Atlantic waves are channelled

---

KENITRA

Oued Sabou

0 — 100 — 200m
0 — 100 — 200yd

To Lac de Sidi Bourhaba,
Plage Mehdiya (7km)
& Mehdiya

Rue Souq el-Baladia

Ave Mohammed Diouri

Blvd Imam Ali

Ave Al Istiqla

To Millenium
Palace (100m),
Hôtel de la
Poste (250m),
Bus Station (500m)
& Tangier

Rue Amira Aicha

To Rabat
(40km)

Rue Reine Elizabeth

Ave Hassan II

Ave Mohammed V

To Rabat

Rue Mohammed Abdouh

Rue Mohammed Amrawi

To Train Station,
Hôtel Marignan
& L'Eté Indien

PLACES TO STAY		6 Pharmacy
5 Hôtel La Rotonde		10 Telephones
15 Hôtel Mamora		11 Banque Populaire
		12 Dali Net
PLACES TO EAT		13 Town Hall
7 El-Dorado Restaurant		14 Agip Petrol Station
8 Pâtisserie Mona Lisa		16 Post Office
9 Snack Zagadirte		17 Pressing (Laundry)
		18 Wafa Bank
OTHER		19 Telephone Office
1 Bus Nos 9 & 15;		20 BMCE (ATM)
Grand Taxis to Mehdiya		21 Total Petrol Station
and Plage Mehdiya		22 BMCI
2 Police		23 Cinéma Palace
3 Crédit du Maroc		24 CTM Office
4 Mobil Petrol Station		& Bus Station

into the estuary. Above the beach is the main village of Mehdiya and the ruins of a kasbah built by Moulay Ismail (though everyone from the ancient Carthaginians to the US Marines seem to have occupied the site at some time). It's a quiet place to explore and a path (on the southern side of ruins) leads down to the Café Restaurant Belle Vue and the beach road that runs south (left) for 2km into the centre of Plage Mehdiya. (Note that after only 300m is the turning for Lac de Sidi Bourhaba, an excellent bird sanctuary – see later in this section).

Places to Stay & Eat *Camping International* (☎ 388148) is large and geared up for the summer hordes, with good facilities including hot showers and a cafe. It costs Dr15 per person, per tent and per car. Caravans cost Dr20 and motorcycles Dr10.

The new *Auberge de Jeunes* has recently opened close to the grand taxi rank and bus stop. Prices look set to be around Dr50 per person.

The rather gloomy *Hôtel Atlantique* (☎ 388116) down the beach has doubles without/with bath (Dr150/200). Looking on the bright side, local *chanteuses* (singers) perform exuberantly in the downstairs bar until the wee hours of the morning.

If you plan to hang around a few days and want to hire a basic apartment (Dr150 per day), contact Driss at the Restaurant Le Dauphin (see following).

The best restaurant in the area is the licensed *Café Restaurant Belle Vue* (☎ 388366), overlooking the port, next to the steps leading up to the kasbah. Good salads cost Dr20 and main courses (mostly fish) cost from Dr50 to Dr100 (plus tax).

Closer to the beach, and a cheaper option (though it's -simply a cafe in winter), is *Restaurant Le Dauphin* (☎ 350895). Main courses cost around Dr35 and there are good fruit juices for Dr5.

Getting There & Away The frequent local bus No 9 from Kenitra terminates at the kasbah in Mehdiya village (Dr2.40) high above the harbour, while the hourly bus No 15 bypasses the village, travelling below the kasbah to Plage Mehdiya (Dr3.40), 7km from Kenitra. Catch both buses from the corner of Rue du Souk el-Baladia and Ave Mohammed Diouri in Kenitra. Regular grand taxis also leave from here (Dr4) to both destinations.

Lac de Sidi Bourhaba

The large, freshwater Lac de Sidi Bourhaba is a kilometre or so inland from Plage Mehdiya. It's a beautiful place and in spring the hillsides are covered in fragrant white broom. The marsh, lake and scrub habitats provide some of the best bird-watching in the country.

Covering an area of more than 200 hectares, the lake serves as a refuelling stop for many thousands of birds migrating between Europe and sub-Saharan Africa. Many species choose to winter or nest here – among them a number of rare or endangered species. This has earned the lake international recognition and it's one of Morocco's very few protected areas. More than 200 species of birds have been seen here – almost half of Morocco's total complement. This is one of the last places on earth where you can still see large numbers of marbled duck, distinguished by the dark patch around its eyes. Other birds to look out for include the beautiful marsh owl (seen most often at dusk), the crested coot and the black-shouldered kite.

Unfortunately, the information centre (☎ 07-747209) on the northern side of the lake is frequently closed, only opening for pre-booked groups. The guided walks and binocular hire service are now also a thing of the past. However, the construction of a new hide below the centre suggests that all is not lost, and it's probably worth phoning ahead to see what the state of play is. A network of trails still exists, though birders are advised to push up west away from the car park and information centre where picnickers and unthinking visitors have left mountains of rubbish and have vandalised the picnic furniture.

The best time to visit the sanctuary is between the months of October and March.

The turn-off to the lake is well signposted from the beach road to Plage Mehdiya,

300m past the Café Restaurant Belle Vue. If you're on foot the lake is a pleasant 3.3km walk from the turn-off.

MOULAY BOUSSELHAM
☎ 07

The little fishing village of Moulay Bousselham is 44km north-west of Souk el-Arba du Rharb and around 40km due south of Larache. During the summer months, it becomes a low-key beach resort, popular with Moroccans and a handful of European windsurfers. In late June or July, the town hosts an important annual *moussem* (festival) held in honour of the town's namesake, the 10th-century Egyptian saint who is commemorated in one of the koubbas that line the slope down to the sea.

Moulay Bousselham is little more that a one-street town with a post office and several téléboutiques, but no bank.

Merdja Lerga Lagoon

From December to January the Merdja Lerga lagoon to the south-east of the town attracts thousands of migrant birds, including wildfowl, waders and flamingos, making it one of the best areas for bird-watching in Morocco. Boat trips to see the greater flamingos in the lagoon are easily arranged, but if the tide is out you'll be a long way away from the birds.

If you're keen to see rarer species it's worth contacting Hassan Dalil – ask at Café Milano. The cafe has a detailed log book which is updated by birders from all over the world. Hassan can generally locate the species you're interested in and he speaks French and adequate English, as well as a little German and Spanish. His charges are Dr200/300 for a half/whole day (Dr100/200 if you're on your own). A rowboat will cost another Dr100 and a motor boat around Dr50 per hour. Boats generally accommodate a maximum of five people and trips are arranged in two sessions: from around dawn until noon; and from 3 pm to dusk. The best time for bird activity in the lagoon is just after dawn.

The lagoon is a good place to look for the slender-billed and Audouin's gulls and African marsh owl. Shelduck, teal, and numerous terns are frequently seen as are marsh harriers and peregrine falcons.

The greatest drawcard, attracting birders from around the world, was the slender-billed curlew. Unfortunately, and possibly as a result of the severe drought in 1995, the last sighting was in March 1995 and the species is now considered extinct in Morocco.

Hardcore birders may also want to explore the attractive lake of **Merdja Khaloufa**, about 8km east of Moulay Bousselham, which offers good views of a variety of wintering wildfowl.

Places to Stay & Eat

Camping Caravaning International de Moulay Bousselham is on the left about 500m before the entrance to the town. It's a beautiful spot but the facilities are shabby and mosquitoes are a problem in the summer. It costs Dr12 per person, Dr20 per tent and Dr10/30 per car/caravan, and hot showers are Dr6.

The *Hôtel Le Lagon* (☎ 432650), also close to the town's entrance, charges Dr200 for doubles (no singles) with (occasional) hot shower. An extra bed costs Dr60. The rooms are OK if you squint a bit and they have terraces with great views of the lagoon. The hotel has a pool and serves soft drinks and coffee.

The most comfortable accommodation is *Villa Villanora* (☎ 432071) on the seafront at the far north end of town. It's run by a British brother and sister. Their six rooms are homely and meals are eaten with the family. Singles/doubles with shared bath cost Dr200/400, including breakfast. It's a good idea to make a reservation. There's also an art gallery and an Internet cafe (summer only).

If you're here for a few days (particularly outside high season), ask at the cafes about renting an *apartment*. For example, Said Chtairi (☎ 432412), at the Restaurant Ocean in the middle of the main street near where the grand taxis stop, has two reasonable apartments; the first (for a maximum of four) costs Dr150 per day and the second (for up to eight people) costs Dr250.

La Maison des Oiseaux (☎ 673903, [e] gedmunson@ras.edu.ac.ma) has seven bedrooms and can arrange bird guides and the like. Accommodation is on a bed and breakfast basis. Check out their Web site on www.multimania.com/moulaybousselham.

Take your pick from the string of *cafes* along the main street. They all have menu boards displayed out front and most offer mains (usually fresh fried fish) for around Dr35 and salads for around Dr13. There are several small general stores and the market is directly behind the main street.

Getting There & Away
Regular grand taxis (Dr10) and a few buses (Dr8) link Moulay Bousselham with the little town of Souk el-Arba du Rharb, which is easily reached from Kenitra or Larache – it has a train station catering for five trains in either direction.

Alternatively, catch an express bus between Kenitra and Larache along the new motorway (Dr25, although you may be charged full fare) and get dropped at the Moulay Bousselham turn off from where you can catch a grand taxi the last 8km (Dr5).

LARACHE
☎ 09
Most people come to Larache to visit the Roman ruins of Lixus, 4.5km north of town, but it's worth staying a night or two for the town's own sake. Bigger and scruffier than Asilah, and with a more substantial fishing port, Larache is actually quite a tranquil place where, other than the odd chancer, you'll have few hassles. Some people here speak a bit of Spanish and you may come across some disarming English accents, especially in summer when Moroccans living in London return to Larache for a holiday.

The old medina was once walled, but its kasbah and ramparts are now ruined. What remains intact in Larache is the old medina, a fortress known as the Casbah de la Cigogne and a pocket-sized, Spanish-built citadel that houses the Musée Archéologique.

The medina, a tumble-down affair, is worth exploring. The heart of the ville nouvelle is Place de la Libération (formerly Plaza de España), a typical example of colonial Spanish urban planning.

The whitewashed town, inside the medina and out, is dominated by one other colour – the blue used on doors and window frames.

Although it's a long time since the Spanish left, the social institution of the evening stroll lives on. Between 5.30 and 9 pm, everyone emerges from the woodwork to promenade, drink coffee or beer, play cards and talk about the day's events. Not so Spanish, however, is the fact that by 10 pm the streets are virtually empty.

Information
At the north end of Blvd Mohammed V are a cluster of banks, most of which accept cash and travellers cheques. Some have ATMs.

The post office has telephones, is on the same street and is open normal office hours. There are some cardphones outside and numerous téléboutiques dotted around town.

There's a *douche* (public shower) next door to the Pension Amal on Ave Abdallah ben Yassine.

The Moussem of Moulay Abdeslam ben M'chich Alama is held in the village of Beni Arous near Larache in May/June.

Musée Archéologique
The tiny archaeological museum contains a small collection displayed over two floors with explanations in Arabic and French. Most of the artefacts are from the nearby Roman ruins of Lixus (see Around Larache, later), including ceramics, utensils and the like from Phoenician and Roman times.

The building itself is a former Spanish citadel and bears the arms of Charles V above the main door. It's worth a look-in if you're passing, but seems to open erratically. It should open daily from 9 am to noon then 3 to 6 pm (closed Tuesday). Entry costs Dr10.

Old Town
The only intact fortification here is the **Casbah de la Cigogne**, which was built by the Spaniards under Philip III in the 17th century. However, it is out of bounds to visitors.

The old town walls and ruined **kasbah** (the Qebibat) constructed by the Portuguese in the 16th century, while not out of bounds,

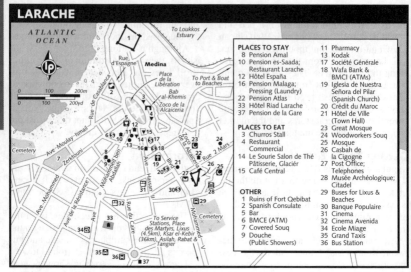

LARACHE

PLACES TO STAY		11 Pharmacy
8 Pension Amal		13 Kodak
10 Pension es-Saada;		17 Société Générale
Restaurant Larache		18 Wafa Bank &
12 Hôtel España		BMCI (ATMs)
16 Pension Malaga;		19 Iglesia de Nuestra
Pressing (Laundry)		Señora del Pilar
22 Pension Atlas		(Spanish Church)
33 Hôtel Riad Larache		20 Crédit du Maroc
37 Pension de la Gare		21 Hôtel de Ville
		(Town Hall)
PLACES TO EAT		23 Great Mosque
3 Churros Stall		24 Woodworkers Souq
4 Restaurant		25 Mosque
Commercial		26 Casbah de
14 Le Sourie Salon de Thé		la Cigogne
Pâtisserie, Glacièr		27 Post Office;
15 Café Central		Telephones
		28 Musée Archéologique;
OTHER		Citadel
1 Ruins of Fort Qebitat		29 Buses for Lixus &
2 Spanish Consulate		Beaches
5 Bar		30 Banque Populaire
6 BMCE (ATM)		31 Cinema
7 Covered Souq		32 Cinema Avenida
9 Douche		34 Ecole Miage
(Public Showers)		35 Grand Taxis
		36 Bus Station

are made dangerous by the possibility of falling masonry.

The old cobbled **medina**, on the other hand, is alive and well and, although not comparable with the medinas of the imperial cities, is worth exploring. Few people will hassle you and there are excellent photographic possibilities. The medina has the feel of a typical, living Moroccan medina – there are few tourist trappings.

As you enter the medina by the large, unmistakable Hispano-Moorish arch (**Bab al-Khemis**) on Place de la Libération, you come immediately into a colonnaded market square, the **Zoco de la Alcaiceria**, built by the Spaniards during their first occupation of Larache in the 17th century. It is the busiest part of the medina, full of vendors.

You can also get into the heart of the medina through a similar arch opposite the Bab al-Khemis and turn past the Pension Atlas down Rue 2 Mars, which will take you through, among other things, the **woodworkers souq**.

Beaches

The nearest beaches are a 7km journey from Larache, across the other side of the

Loukkos Estuary. You can take a small boat across the estuary from the port, but beware of chancers rowing you around in circles to extract more money. To avoid this hassle take the hourly (during June to August) No 4 bus from opposite the Casbah de la Cigogne to the beach (Dr2.50).

Throughout the year, local red and blue buses, which are often unnumbered, will drop you at the turn-off just before Lixus (Dr2.50), from where it's a 3km walk to the beach.

There are a number of simple restaurants at the beach, offering the usual range of seafood.

Places to Stay – Budget

There's a good choice of budget accommodation in Larache.

Inside the medina there are at least three extremely basic places. About the best of these is the **Pension Atlas** (☎ 912014, 154 Rue 2 Mars), close to the Zoco de la Alcaiceria, which charges Dr20/50 for small, moderately clean singles/doubles. Really though, you're better off staying in the ville nouvelle.

Next to the bus station is **Pension de la Gare** (☎ 913030); basic clean rooms with a washbasin cost Dr35/70, but there's no hot water.

The bulk of the other cheapies are on or near Ave Mohammed ben Abdallah. *Pension es-Saada* (☎ 913641, 16 Ave Mohammed ben Abdallah), close to Place de la Libération, has pleasant, clean rooms, some with balconies, for Dr30 per person. The rooms on the ground floor can be a bit noisy.

Perhaps the top of the lot is the *Pension Amal* (☎ 912788, 10 Ave Abdallah ben Yassine), which has smallish, but very clean rooms for Dr40/65. Hot showers cost Dr6.

Places to Stay – Mid-Range & Top End

Pension Malaga (☎ 911868, 4 Rue de Salé) has hot water and small but decent singles/doubles, some with balconies, for Dr60/100. It also has one double with bath (and towels) for Dr120.

Once *the* place to stay during Spanish colonial times, the two-star *Hôtel España* (☎ 913195, fax 915628), which fronts onto Place de la Libération, is faded, but still exudes an air of grandness. Clean and well-maintained rooms with TV, phone and heating (some have balconies) cost Dr165/195 with bath and Dr100/150 without. Add 10% in summer.

The only top-end hotel in town is the three-star *Hôtel Riad Larache* (☎ 912626, fax 912629, Ave Mohammed ben Abdallah). Apparently once the private home of a French noble family, it's now part of the Kasbah Tours Hotels chain. Set in spacious, somewhat neglected grounds, with swimming pool, tennis courts and private parking, the hotel offers large, self-contained rooms for Dr334/504 (including breakfast and dinner). As well as a beer garden, there's a bar and restaurant that offers fairly pricey meals.

Places to Eat

The cheapest eateries are the little places around Place de la Libération and the Zoco de la Alcaiceria (inside the medina), which serve very edible Spanish-style fare.

One of the best of them is *Restaurant Commercial*, on your right just before you enter the Zoco through Bab al-Khemis. For around Dr25 you can get a plate of seafood, and a decent salad for Dr4.

The *Restaurant Larache*, on Mohammed ben Abdallah next door to the Pension es-Saada, serves a range of mains including reasonable seafood for around Dr25.

Still popular since the days of the Spanish are *churros*, a kind of doughnut traditionally eaten for breakfast. There's a *churros stall* selling them in the late afternoon (around 5 pm) three doors down from Bab al-Khemis.

The best cafe-type places for breakfast are *Salon de thé Lacoste* opposite the Hôtel España on Ave Mohammed ben Abdallah and the nearby *Le Sourier Salon de Thé, Pâtisserie, Glaciér* next to Hôtel España on Ave Hassan II. Both have a good selection of patisseries and (in summer) ice cream.

There are various cafes and bars around Place de la Libération and along Ave Hassan II and Blvd Mohammed V. A popular spot for that caffeine fix is the *Café Central*, its long bar and general air a reminder of the days of the Spanish protectorate. Opposite is a lively little *bar* (with a rather discrete entrance).

A good and reasonably civilised place for a drink is the beer garden at the *Hôtel Riad Larache*. Beers are Dr15; it's very quiet during the low season.

Getting There & Away

Larache is most easily reached by bus. CTM and several private lines run buses through here. Booking is not always possible, so turn up in the morning and get the first service you can.

CTM buses include services to Tangier (Dr29, four services); Fès (Dr61, three services) via Meknès; Casablanca (Dr82, three services) via Kenitra (Dr43) and Rabat (Dr56); and Tiznit (Dr238) via Marrakesh (Dr143) and Agadir (Dr212).

Cheaper non-CTM buses also cover these destinations (and more), and with greater frequency. Destinations include Asilah (Dr10), Ouezzane (Dr20), Tetouan (Dr20), Fnideq on the Ceuta frontier (Dr25) and Kenitra (Dr30).

Grand taxis run from just outside the bus station. The standard run is to Ksar el-Kebir

(Dr10), but you may also get a taxi north to Asilah if you get in early (Dr10).

AROUND LARACHE
Lixus

The Roman ruins of Lixus are 4.5km north of Larache, on a hillock overlooking the Loukkos Estuary and the Larache-Tangier highway. Although not as substantial or as well excavated as those at Volubilis (see the special section 'Volubilis' in the Middle Atlas & the East chapter), they are definitely worth an hour or so.

There's no entry fee and the site is not enclosed, so you're at liberty to wander around on your own. Inevitably, some local unemployed youths will offer their services as guides, but they know very little about the remains.

It's a pity Lixus has been allowed to decay to the degree that it has. Were it in Europe, it would no doubt be regarded as an important national monument. On the other hand, there is something exhilarating about finding this place in its overgrown state, largely unprettied by human hands. In winter, your only companions will be the wind and the odd goat. Sole women travellers may find this a bit disconcerting and are advised to avoid coming here alone during the low season.

History Lixus was originally occupied by prehistoric, sun-worshipping people. A number of stones left in the vicinity of the citadel suggests that they had some knowledge of astronomy and mathematics, but more is known of the Phoenicians who set up a colony here, known as Liks, in about 1000 BC. The colony was essentially a trading post and commerce was principally in gold, ivory and slaves.

Though the Phoenician Atlantic colonies fell to the Carthaginians in the 6th century BC, gold remained the focus of trade. Indeed, some historians claim that as a result of explorations in West Africa by the Carthaginian Hanno (see the boxed text 'Hanno the Navigator' under History in the Facts about Morocco chapter), Carthage is said to have been able to monopolise the trade in gold from West Africa and to keep its source a secret.

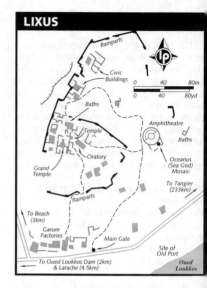

LIXUS

[Map labels: Ramparts, Civic Buildings, Baths, Temple, Amphitheatre, Baths, Oratory, Oceanus (Sea God) Mosaic, Grand Temple, To Tangier (233km), Ramparts, To Beach (3km), Garum Factories, Main Gate, Site of Old Port, To Oued Loukkos Dam (2km) & Larache (4.5km), Oued Loukkos]

Whatever Hanno's intentions, by the time Carthage fell to the Romans in 146 BC Lixus was a key trading base. Shortly after the ascension of Emperor Claudius in AD 42, Lixus entered its second period of importance as the nature of its exports changed from gold to salt, olives, *garum* (an aromatic fish paste), and wild animals for the various amphitheatres of the empire.

Lixus rapidly declined following the Roman withdrawal north under Diocletian, but was not finally abandoned until some time in the 5th century AD, when the Roman Empire fell apart.

Things to See Small paths criss-cross the site but the main gravel track starts at the main gate in the green railings just beyond the garum factories alongside the highway. This leads you up the hill side past a number of minor ruins to the **public baths** and **amphitheatre**. Restoration has been done on these and they're undoubtedly the most impressive of the ruins here.

Also to be found is a **mosaic** of Oceanus (the Greek Sea God) – the only such mosaic to be seen at Lixus. Unfortunately, as it's been exposed both to the elements and to local vandalism only the god's hair entangled in a lobster's legs and claw remains to be seen. Mosaics found at Lixus' Grand Temple depicting Helios, Mars and Rhea, the three Graces, and Venus with Adonis are all exhibited in the Archaeology Museum in Tetouan, with some bronze statuettes (see Tetouan in the Rif Mountains section of the Mediterranean Coast & the Rif chapter).

Continuing on to the top of the hill, you come to the **citadel** where most of the civic buildings were located, including the main temple and associated sanctuaries, an oratory, more public baths and what remains of the city walls and ramparts. The **view** over the Loukkos Estuary is excellent from here, but most of the antiquities are in an advanced state of decay and there's been some woefully amateurish restoration done on them.

Getting There & Away To get here take bus No 4 or 5 from outside the Casbah de la Cicogne. Some local red and blue buses are unnumbered so make sure to ask for Lixus and ask to be dropped outside the main gate (Dr2.50). A petit taxi is more expensive at around Dr15, depending on how hard you haggle.

Oued Loukkos Dam

If you have your own transport, you may want to explore further east of Lixus towards the Oued Loukkos Dam, which is excellent for bird-watching. The area attracts a very good selection of ducks and waders. Keep an eye out also for the spoonbills, glossy ibis and little bustards. To get there follow the sign just after the bridge over the Loukkos Estuary, around 2km north of Larache on the main road south.

Ksar el-Kebir

In Almoravid and Almohad times, the 'Great Castle', 36km south-east of Larache on what was previously the main road to Rabat, was a comparatively important base. It was near here, too, that the Battle of the Three Kings was fought in 1578, costing the lives of the king of Portugal and two Moroccan sultans.

Today there are few physical reminders of its past, but the town does boast one of the largest weekly souqs of the region every Sunday. If you're in the area, it's definitely worth a visit – just head for the bus station.

There is also Sufi music festival here in June.

If you want to stay, *Hôtel Ksar al-Yamama (☎ 907960, 8 Ave Hassan II)* offers spotless and comfortable singles/doubles (some with small balconies) for Dr89/116 and Dr116/133 with hot shower. There's a reasonable tearoom downstairs.

The town is a few kilometres off the old Rabat-Tangier road, but is easily reached by grand taxi (Dr10) or bus (Dr8) from Larache or Souk el-Arba du Rharb.

ASILAH
☎ 09

The port of Asilah lies 46km south of Tangier. Small it may be, but for over two millennia it has had a tumultuous history far out of proportion to its size.

The first settlers were the Carthaginians, who named the port Zilis. Next were the Romans. Forced to deal with a population that had backed the wrong side during the Punic Wars, Rome decided to move the inhabitants to Spain and replace them with Iberians.

Asilah featured again in the 10th century, when it held Norman raiders from Sicily at bay. In the following century it became the last refuge of the Idrissids.

The town's most turbulent period, however, followed the Christian victories over the forces of Islam on the Iberian peninsula in the 14th and 15th centuries.

In 1471 it was captured by the Portuguese, and the walls around the city date from this period, although they have been repaired from time to time.

In 1578 King Dom Sebastian of Portugal chose Asilah as the base for an ill-fated crusade, which resulted in his death and the subsequent passing of Portugal (and its Moroccan possessions) into the hands of Spain (see the boxed text 'Battle of the Three Kings', later).

Asilah was captured by the Moroccans in 1589, lost again to the Spanish and then was recaptured by Moulay Ismail in 1691. In the 19th century, as a result of pirate attacks on

The Battle of Three Kings

Dynasties wouldn't be true to their nature without dynastic quarrels, but one that began in 1574 in Morocco was destined for quite a Shakespearian end.

When Mohammed al-Mutawwakil took the reins of Saadian power in 1574, on the death of his father, he contravened the family rule that the eldest *male* in the family should succeed, not the eldest *son*. Al-Mutawwakil's uncle, Abdel Malik, then in Algiers and an ally of the Ottoman Turks, decided to rectify the situation and, after two victories with the help of Turkish troops in 1576, Abdel Malik succeeded in evicting his nephew.

Al-Mutawwakil fled and asked Philip II of Spain to help him regain power. Philip declined in what turned out to be a very astute move, and sent Al-Mutawwakil to King Dom Sebastian of Portugal.

Promised a virtual protectorate over Morocco in exchange for his help, Dom Sebastian could not resist. Abdel Malik went to considerable lengths to dissuade Dom Sebastian, offering Portugal a Moroccan port of its choice, but to no avail.

When, in 1578, the Portuguese army of some 20,000 landed in northern Morocco, Abdel Malik gathered a force of 50,000 to meet it. On 4 August, caught in marshy territory near Ksar el-Kebir, Dom Sebastian was routed. He and Al-Mutawwakil drowned trying to flee across the Oued Makhazin (hence the Arab name of the battle) and Abdel Malik died of an illness that had long plagued him, although some say it was a heart attack.

Ahmed al-Mansour succeeded in Morocco, but in Portugal there was no heir. Philip II of Spain became the biggest winner of all, swallowing Portugal into his empire.

its shipping, Spain sent in the navy to bombard the town and early this century, Asilah was used as a base by one of the most colourful bandits ever produced by the wild Rif Mountains: Er-Raissouli.

Shortly after the end of WWI Er-Raissouli was forced to abandon Asilah, and within a few years had lost everything.

Asilah found its niche in the late 20th century as a bijou resort town. Money has been poured into gentrifying houses within the city walls by affluent Moroccans, the government and Europeans. A large new harbour suitable for the small local fishing fleet and pleasure yachts was almost complete at the time of writing and there's a sophisticated annual cultural festival. Consequently, the streets gleam with whitewash, ornate wrought-iron adorns windows, and chic craft shops have sprouted along virtually every alley.

A little further north along the beaches, camping resorts have mushroomed to cater to legions of European summer holidaymakers. Other than the medina, the beaches to the north of town are the main attraction of Asilah. During the summer months they are awash with tourists from Europe. A whole service industry has grown up to cater for the needs of these people, including camping grounds, restaurants, discos and the like. It's a smaller-scale version of Agadir at this time of year and you can meet people from as far afield as Brisbane and Bremen.

Despite the changes mass tourism has brought (including the arrival of a band of touts and guides), it is worth staying in Asilah for a while, especially in the low season, when there are hardly any tourists around.

Information

Money The BMCE and Banque Populaire, both on Place Mohammed V, will change cash and travellers cheques and issue cash advances on credit cards, but beware of big commissions and bad rates. Cash can be changed at Wafa Bank and Crédit Agricole, also on Place Mohammed V. At the time of writing there were no ATMs.

Post & Communications The post office, which also has telephones, is on the eastern side of town, just off the Tangier-Rabat road. It is open during regular office hours. There are few public phones in town (and no public cardphones), but numerous téléboutiques.

Other Services The best place for a good scrub is the Bain Maure hammam close to the police station. It costs Dr6 and is open

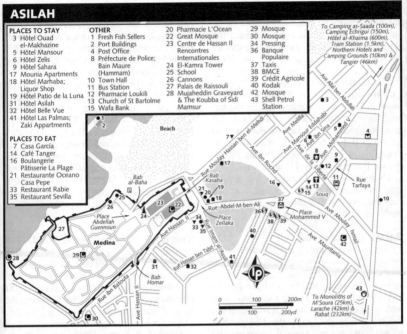

ASILAH

PLACES TO STAY
3 Hôtel Ouad el-Makhazine
5 Hôtel Mansour
6 Hôtel Zelis
9 Hôtel Sahara
17 Mounia Apartments
18 Hôtel Marhaba; Liquor Shop
19 Hôtel Patio de la Luna
31 Hôtel Asilah
32 Hôtel Belle Vue
41 Hôtel Las Palmas; Zaki Appartments

PLACES TO EAT
7 Casa García
14 Café Tanger
16 Boulangerie Pâtisserie La Plage
21 Restaurante Oceano Casa Pepe
33 Restaurant Rabie
35 Restaurant Sevilla

OTHER
1 Fresh Fish Sellers
2 Port Buildings
4 Post Office
8 Préfecture de Police; Bain Maure (Hammam)
10 Town Hall
11 Bus Station
12 Pharmacie Loukili
13 Church of St Bartolme
15 Wafa Bank

20 Pharmacie L'Ocean
22 Great Mosque
23 Centre de Hassan II Rencontres Internationales
24 El-Kamra Tower
25 School
26 Cannons
27 Palais de Raissouli
28 Mujaheddin Graveyard & The Koubba of Sidi Mamsur

29 Mosque
30 Mosque
34 Pressing
36 Banque Populaire
37 Taxis
38 BMCE
39 Crédit Agricole
40 Kodak
42 Mosque
43 Shell Petrol Station

from 5 to 11 am and 7 pm to midnight for men, and from 11 am to 7 pm for women.

There are a couple of *pressings* (laundries) on Ave Hassan II.

Almost opposite Bab Kasaba is Pharmacie l'Ocean, while the bigger Pharmacie Loukili is on Ave Mohammed V near the bus station.

There is guarded parking (Dr10 per 24 hours) outside Bab al-Baha, near the port.

Dangers & Annoyances If hoteliers are to be believed, faux guides are playing an increasing role in the accommodation business. Apparently, unwary travellers led off buses into the depths of the medina with tales of amazing luxury at rock-bottom prices have often been ripped off in shabby hovels.

Centre de Hassan II Rencontres Internationales & El-Kamra Tower
This beautiful gallery space and conference centre (check out the ceiling above the reception) forms the focus of the annual International Cultural Festival. Artists, musicians and performers from across the world have displayed, played, demonstrated and congregated here, between mid-July and mid-August, since 1978. There's a strong element of Spanish and Islamic talent, and numerous workshops and public art demonstrations take place. A three-day horse festival (including a Moroccan *fantasia* or musket-firing cavalry charge) starts towards the end of the festival.

For the rest of the year a revolving exhibition of international painting and sculpture (open 8 am to 12.30 pm and 3 to 6.30 pm) is housed in the centre's gallery and nearby tower. **El-Kamra Tower** is a renovated Portuguese fortification on Place Abdellah Guennoun. Entrance is free. For more information call ☎ 417065 or fax 417360.

Ramparts & Medina
The impressive 15th-century Portuguese ramparts are largely intact, partly as a result

of modern restoration work. Access is limited, since many private houses abut them. Of the two prongs that jut out into the ocean, only the south-western one can be visited and affords great views, providing plenty of photographic opportunities.

The bright medina is worth a wander. You'll notice a lot of cheery **murals** on many of the houses painted during the annual International Cultural Festival. Of more historical note is the **Bab Homar** (also known as Bab al-Jebel or, to the Spaniards, Puerta de la Tierra), topped by the much-eroded Portuguese royal coat of arms.

There are a few old cannons left just inside the seaward wall, although you can only see them from a distance – access has been cut off by another thick wall.

Palais de Raissouli

Undoubtedly one of the town's most interesting sights (also known as Raissouli Palace or Palace of Culture), this beautifully preserved, three-storey building was constructed in 1909 and includes a main reception room with a glass-fronted terrace overlooking the sea. It was from this terrace that Er-Raissouli forced convicted murderers to jump to their deaths onto the rocks 30m below.

Once open to the public the palace, in the medina, is now used exclusively for cultural events and workshops. You may just get a look-in during the festival, but it's hard to get an idea of the sumptuousness of Er-Raissouli's life at the height of his power (see the boxed text 'Er-Raissouli').

Places to Stay – Budget

Camping For campers, there are a number of well-equipped camping grounds along the beach north of town. The nearby top-end hotels have useful facilities for campers (see Places to Stay – Top End).

The first two you come across, a few hundred metres north of town, are among the best. The first one, *Camping as-Saada* (☎ *417317*) charges Dr10 per person/tent/car and Dr20 per caravan/camper van. Cell-like rooms go for Dr100/150 in low/high season.

Camping Echrigui (☎ *417182*) is the better of the two. Camping charges are slightly higher, but facilities much better (including a cafe-cum-restaurant and grocery store). Other than shaded pitches, accommodation ranges from self-contained apartments (Dr100/250 in low/high season) to tiny huts highly suited to amorous couples (Dr60/100).

Closer to the Mohammed V Bridge, which lies about 10km north of Asilah, are at least three more Atlantic coast camps: *L'Océan*, *Atlas* and *Hôtel Sahara*. They tend to be pretty full in summer and at Easter, as they are often block-booked by tour groups from Europe. At other times of the year, you'll virtually have them to yourself. They all have guarded camping facilities, shower and toilet blocks, and restaurants and bars. They all charge around the same rates as Camping Echrigui.

Hotels The *Hôtel Marhaba* (☎ *417144*), overlooks Place Zellaka close to Bab Kasaba, the main entrance to the medina, and is a quiet, pleasant place to stay. Singles/doubles with washbasin cost Dr50/100. Hot showers cost Dr5. Ask for a room at the front; those at the back can be a bit poky. There's a liquor shop next door.

Hôtel Asilah (☎ *417286),* just off Ave Hassan II, is one of the best-value deals in town. Small but clean rooms without shower cost Dr35/70; rooms with shower cost Dr100/120. Communal hot showers are Dr7. It may be closed in low season.

Further up the price scale is the very well-maintained *Hôtel Sahara* (☎ *417185, 9 Rue Tarfaya).* Singles/doubles/triples cost Dr98/126/186. Showers are Dr5.

Places to Stay – Mid-Range

Hotels Probably best value is *Hôtel Las Palmas* (☎ *418756, 9 Rue Imam al-Assili).* It has clean, rather soulless singles/doubles with shower for Dr100/150 (Dr50 more in high season). Ask about using their kitchen.

Hôtel Belle Vue (☎ *417747)* offers adequate doubles with shared facilities for Dr100/200 (low/high season).

A good bet is *Hôtel Mansour* (☎ *417390, fax 417533, 49 Ave Mohammed V).* It's a cosy little place with spotless rooms, with shower, toilet and TV from Dr112.50/225.

Er-Raissouli

The Palais de Raissouli, built for the man himself in 1909

Moulay Ahmed ben Mohammed er-Raissouli (or Raisuni) began his career in the late 19th century as a petty mountain bandit, but soon progressed to murder on such a scale that the whole countryside around Tangier and Tetouan lived in fear of him.

At this time, however, he had been made pasha (governor) of Asilah, which was to become his main residence and base. In 1899, when Er-Raissouli was 23 years old, the sultan lost patience (or summoned up the nerve to act against the 'pasha') and had him arrested and jailed in Mogador (modern Essaouira) for several years.

When he was released he returned home, but was soon back at his kidnapping and banditry. His most profitable game proved to be the kidnapping of westerners. He and his band held various luminaries to ransom, including US businessman Ion Perdicaris, who was ransomed in 1904 for US$70,000.

In return for promising good conduct, Er-Raissouli was made governor of the Tangier region. His conduct, however, was anything but good and by 1907 the European powers were sufficiently worried by his antics that they compelled the Moroccan government to attack him. It did, but failed to capture him. Things were looking grim for Er-Raissouli, but in 1909 Moulay Abd al-Hafiz became sultan, and Er-Raissouli ź whose influence over the Rif tribes was still great ź proclaimed his allegiance to the new sultan immediately. In return he was made governor of most of north-west Morocco, with the exception of Tangier.

Spain, which took control of the north under the deal that cut Morocco up into protectorates in 1912, tried to make use of Er-Raissouli to keep order among the Rif tribes. Madrid invested considerable money and military hardware in the effort, but in vain. Er-Raissouli as often as not used the arms against the Spanish, inflicting several stinging defeats.

Having obtained promises from Germany that he would be made sultan after WWI, he found himself at loggerheads with everyone when Germany lost the war in 1918. The Spaniards forced him to flee Asilah, but for the following few years he continued to wreak havoc in the Rif hinterland.

The final irony was his arrest and imprisonment at the beginning of 1925 by a Rif rebel with a slightly broader political outlook, Abd al-Krim. Er-Raissouli, who had submitted to the medical attention of a Spaniard, stood accused of being too closely linked to the Spanish! He died on 10 April 1925 of natural causes.

Cheaper rooms are also available. There is a restaurant and competent travel agency (☎ 416272) attached. The manager and staff are very helpful.

A rather characterless place, but with spacious and comfortable rooms, is the *Hôtel Ouad el-Makhazine* (☎ *417090, fax 417500, Ave Melilla*). Rooms with bath and phone cost Dr224/260 in high season, Dr174/210 in low season. The hotel has a pool, which is open to nonguests for Dr25 per day.

Apartments Though many people have bought houses in the medina and converted them into holiday homes, finding one of these places to rent is not easy, despite whatever faux guides may tell you (see Dangers & Annoyances). However, a few legitimate companies do operate and can offer good deals for long stays. Book well in advance.

Zaki Apartments (☎ *417497, 14 Rue Imam al-Assili*) have an office next door to the Hôtel Las Palmas and their large, comfortable apartments with terraces are close by. Apartments for two/four/seven people cost Dr190/205/450 in low season rising to Dr320/510/750 in high season.

Mounia Apartments (☎ *417815, 14 Rue Moulay Hassan ben el-Mehdi*) have better appointed and better-looking apartments for two/four/six people down close to the harbour for Dr225/360/450 in low season, Dr375/600/750 in high season.

Both sets of apartments have reasonable gas cookers and water heaters.

Places to Stay – Top End

A great place to stay if you've a little spare cash is the Spanish-run *Hôtel Patio de la Luna* (☎ *416074, 12 Place Zellaka*). It's next door to Hôtel Marhaba, and is the same intimate size, but leagues above in terms of style, class (and price). Gorgeous singles/doubles with bath cost Dr150/300. Book ahead as it's popular with well-heeled mid-30s Europeans.

Hôtel Zelis (☎ *417069, fax 417098, 10 Ave Mansour Eddahabi*) is a big, brash new place, more reminiscent of a city hotel, but with good views from the front rooms. Rooms are Dr300/363 in low season and Dr400/463 in high season. There's also a pool but nonguests can only use it if they eat in the restaurant.

The three-star, 110-room *Hôtel al-Khaima* (☎ *417428, fax 417566*) is about 600m north of town to the right of the main road. Singles/doubles/triples cost Dr287/351/462 in low season and Dr387/451/562 in high season. Add Dr8 per person for tax. Breakfast costs Dr45. The hotel has a restaurant, pool and disco.

Out near the camping grounds by the Mohammed V Bridge are a couple of other hotels, the *Hôtel Club Solitaire* and the *Atlantis*, which are more important for the pools, restaurants and discos they offer campers than for their accommodation. If you would like to stay here, prices are in the same league as Hôtel al-Khaima.

Places to Eat

The *Café Tanger* (*52 Ave Mohammed V*), is a good place for coffee, fruit juice and toast in the morning. It's clean and comfortable, and in summer it has air-con. It's open every day from 6 am to 8 pm.

The *Boulangerie Pâtisserie La Plage* (*Ave ibn Rochd*) is unnamed but has a blue awning. It does a good breakfast (Dr12) and has some fine-quality pastries, including croissants and some heavenly almond tarts. It's a great place for preparing a beach picnic as they will prepare sandwiches for you to take away.

For main meals about the cheapest option is the string of restaurants and cafes on Ave Hassan II. They're simple, pretty basic places specialising in fish dishes. Main courses such as fish tajine, brochettes and paella (rice and seafood dish) cost around Dr30. The *Restaurant Rabie* is one of the better ones, but you could pick any one of a dozen.

Slightly more expensive are the Spanish restaurants of *Restaurante Oceano Casa Pepe* (☎ *417395, 8 Place Zallaka*) across from Bab Kasaba, and *Casa García* (☎ *417465, 51 Rue Moulay Hassan ben el-Mehdi*). There's not a great deal to choose between them, as both are licensed and specialise in Spanish-style fish dishes (most around Dr50), from octopus and eels to shrimps and barnacles.

Also good value is *Restaurant Sevilla*, (☎ *418501, 18 Rue Imam al-Assili*). It's BYO and serves fish dishes and some tasty traditional Moroccan fare for Dr25 to Dr45.

Entertainment

The bar in *Hôtel Ouad el-Makhazine* is locally regarded as the most pleasant place for a drink. It's open every day from 11 am to midnight and a beer will cost you Dr15.

The most popular discos are those north of the centre at the *Hôtel al-Khaima* and, on Saturday, the *Hôtel Club Solitaire*. Entry costs Dr50 at both discos.

For a quiet tipple at your hotel, there is a small liquor shop next to the Hôtel Marhaba near Bab Kasaba.

Getting There & Away

Bus Your best bet for getting to and from Asilah is the bus. All buses leave from the same station on Ave de la Liberté. CTM, with the only ticket office, has a few services to Tangier (Dr15); Fès (Dr72) via Meknès (Dr57); Casablanca (Dr110) via Rabat (Dr83); Nador (Dr175); Oujda (Dr175); and Tiznit (Dr260) via Marrakesh (Dr154) and Agadir (Dr237).

Cheaper non-CTM buses to Tangier and Casablanca leave roughly every half hour from 6.30 am to 8 pm. A number of southern-bound services (both CTM and non-CTM) stop at Larache and there are also plenty of non-CTM services to Meknès, Fès, Tetouan and Ouezzane. You can pay on the bus.

Train This is the inconvenient way to get to Asilah, as the station is 1.5km north of town, but it's possible to get 2nd-class fares on ordinaire and rapide train services to Tangier (Dr11/13), Rabat (Dr57/74), Casablanca (Dr76/99) and Fès (Dr61/78).

Taxi Grand taxis to Tangier from Place Mohammed V cost Dr12 and, if you get there early enough in the day, you might be able to get one to Larache (also for Dr12).

To/From the Airport Tangier's airport is only 26km north of here, so taking a taxi from Asilah (Dr130) may save you a lot of time and energy in Tangier.

AROUND ASILAH

The ancient and little-understood **Monoliths of M'Soura** (a stone circle) stand on a desolate patch of ground some 25km (by road) south-east of Asilah. The stones range from 50cm to 6m in height and some historians believe they surround the tomb of a noble, perhaps dating back to Punic times.

To get to the site you must first reach the village of Souq Tnine de Sidi el-Yamani, off highway P37, which branches east off the main Tangier-Rabat road. From here, 6km of bad *piste* (unsealed track) road leads north to the site. You need a good vehicle, and a local guide would help.

The area just north of Asilah is a popular spot for wintering **birds**, including huge populations of common cranes (up to one thousand have been reported at one time) and a good number of birds of prey, including black kites, lesser kestrels and, particularly, the great bustard. They often can be spotted from the main road around Briex and the Mohammed Bridge, about 10km north of Asilah.

Mediterranean Coast & the Rif

From those two bastions of Spanish tenacity, the enclaves of Ceuta and Melilla, to the cosmopolitan hustle and hassle of Tangier and the contrasting laid-back ambience of Chefchaouen in the Rif Mountains, northern Morocco offers a diverse range of experiences for the independent traveller.

East of Chefchaouen, the Rif presents a wealth of trekking opportunities and a spectacular mountain-crest trip through a wild and rugged area given over to intense kif (marijuana) cultivation. Those who brave the hustlers will be rewarded by the views and by a couple of modest Mediterranean resorts where the Rif makes a rare concession and gives way to beaches at Saidia and Al-Hoceima.

Mediterranean Coast

TANGIER
☎ 09

For more than 2500 years people have inhabited this strategic point on the strait separating Europe from Africa. And just about every race or power that ever had any interests in this corner of the Mediterranean has left its mark. The world-weary port has seen them all come and go: Phoenicians, Romans, Visigoths, Arabs, Portuguese, British and Spaniards among others. For some 40 years under the dubious control of an international council, Tangier (Tanja to the locals) today is like an ageing libertine – propped up languidly at a bar, he has seen it all.

In the days legendary author William Burroughs called Interzone (when Tangier was part of an official 'international zone'), every kind of questionable activity was carried out. Smugglers, money launderers, currency speculators, gunrunners, prostitutes and pimps formed a good part of the local and foreign population – Tangier (often erroneously called Tangiers) flourished.

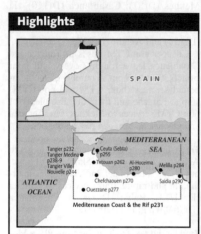

Highlights

SPAIN

MEDITERRANEAN SEA

Tangier p232
Tangier Medina p238-9
Tangier Ville/ Nouvelle p244
Ceuta (Sebta) p255
Tetouan p262
Al-Hoceima p280
Melilla p284

ATLANTIC OCEAN

Chefchaouen p270
Ouezzane p277
Saidia p290

Mediterranean Coast & the Rif p231

- Hanging loose in the pretty and laid-back town of Chefchaouen, with its blue-washed houses set against dramatic mountains

- Beating the hassle and hustle of Tangier and enjoying the vibrant, unique atmosphere of a city steeped in history

- Driving east from Tangier to Cap Malabata to take in the picturesque sheer cliffs, isolated beaches and tiny villages

- Trekking in the wild, spectacular and still untamed Rif Mountains

- Exploring the gritty, Hispano-Moorish city of Tetouan and its unique medina

! Telephone numbers in Morocco have changed. For new codes and complete numbers, see the boxed text 'Changes to Telephone Numbers' on page 89.

Since its incorporation into the rest of independent Morocco in 1956, the city has lost much of its attraction and was long neglected by the government of Hassan II. Drug trafficking (including a growing contribution from South American cocaine barons) and people smuggling (see the boxed text 'Immigrants' later) have become

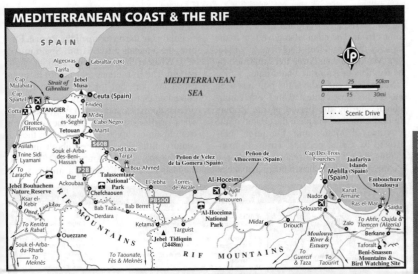

MEDITERRANEAN COAST & THE RIF

huge money-spinners, which many claim accounts for the number of new, vacant multistorey buildings (money has to be laundered somehow).

However, the economic development of northern Morocco, with Tangier at its centre, is now a government priority. In addition, the European Union (EU) plans to fund huge infrastructure programs in the region, including a coast road from Tangier to Nador, and hopes that increased economic opportunities will reduce the area's dependence on drug production. There's also optimism in some circles that the new king's affinity for the city will help speed up its development; some large-scale infrastructure projects are already under way. Most noticeable is the motorway to Casablanca (that's still a few kilometres short of Tangier) and a new industrial zone close to the airport – there's also talk of creating North Africa's biggest container port in this area while Africa's biggest (allegedly) casino is being built near Cap Malabata, east of the city.

Little of this may be obvious to travellers passing through, but they are soon aware of what makes the place tick – money. From shoeshine boys up, everyone is on the make, and for the small-time hustlers in this city of half a million, the main trade is in tourists, especially those newly arrived from Europe. The Brigade Touristique has cracked down on Tangier's legendary hustlers, particularly in the medina, but the city is far from hassle free (see Dangers & Annoyances later) and remains difficult for first-time visitors; many can't wait to get out. But if you give it time, take the place head on and learn to handle the hustlers and con artists, you'll find it a likeable, lively place that's never for a minute dull. Tangier is a unique city – hardly truly Moroccan, nor European, nor even African and the nightlife here, though rough at times, is lively and vibrant. Stay a few days and absorb the atmosphere of this mongrel creation.

History

Tangier has been coveted for millennia as a strategic site commanding the Strait of Gibraltar. The area was settled by the ancient Greeks and Phoenicians, for whom it was a trading port, and its early days are shrouded in myth. Paradise on earth, the Garden of the Hesperides, supposedly lay nearby.

It was here that Hercules slew the giant Antaeus and fathered a child, Sophax, by the giant's widow, Tinge – no prizes for guessing where the city's original name, Tingis, comes from. The name also gave rise to the name of the citrus fruit tangerine, a variant on a Mediterranean citrus tree imported by the Romans or Arabs at a later date.

Since those early days, the port has been one of the most contested in the Mediterranean. During the period of the Roman Empire, Diocletian made it the capital of the province of Mauretania Tingitana, garrisoned by Celtic peoples' (from Roman-colonised Britain) cavalry. Not long after, it became part of the Christian Episcopal See

of Spain, and in fact may have been the seat of the bishops.

Following the break-up of the Roman Empire, the Vandals arrived from Spain in AD 429. Whether they ever took Tangier is uncertain. The Byzantines took an erratic interest in the port, but for the most part they contented themselves with their strongly fortified outpost at Ceuta. Apart from them, and scant reports suggesting that the Visigoths from Spain occupied it for a time in the 7th century, little was recorded about the area until the arrival of the Arabs in AD 705. This may have been partly due to a smallpox epi-

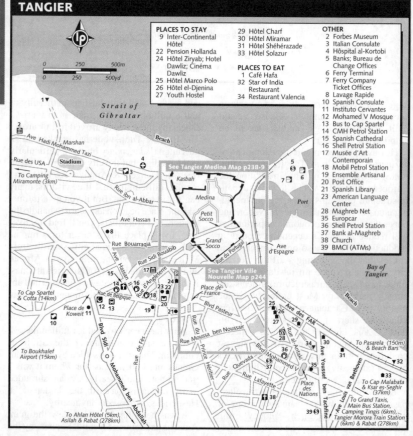

TANGIER

PLACES TO STAY
9   Inter-Continental Hôtel
22 Pension Hollanda
24 Hôtel Ziryab; Hôtel Dawliz; Cinéma Dawliz
25 Hôtel Marco Polo
26 Hôtel el-Djenina
27 Youth Hostel
29 Hôtel Charf
30 Hôtel Miramar
31 Hôtel Shéhérazade
33 Hôtel Solazur

PLACES TO EAT
1   Café Hafa
32 Star of India Restaurant
34 Restaurant Valencia

OTHER
2   Forbes Museum
3   Italian Consulate
4   Hôspital al-Kortobi
5   Banks; Bureau de Change Offices
6   Ferry Terminal
7   Ferry Company Ticket Offices
8   Lavage Rapide
10 Spanish Consulate
11 Instituto Cervantes
12 Mohamed V Mosque
13 Bus to Cap Spartel
14 CMH Petrol Station
15 Spanish Cathedral
16 Shell Petrol Station
17 Musée d'Art Contemporain
18 Mobil Petrol Station
19 Ensemble Artisanal
20 Post Office
21 Spanish Library
23 American Language Center
28 Maghreb Net
35 Europcar
36 Shell Petrol Station
37 Bank al-Maghreb
38 Church
39 BMCI (ATMs)

Immigrants

Alongside the lucrative business of drug-running in northern Morocco, there is the commerce in people, many of whom come from sub-Saharan Africa.

Moroccan and Spanish boat captains charge these people as much as US$1000 per person to smuggle them into Spain (an enormous sum for the average Moroccan worker). Often the boats are so small and overcrowded that they don't make it – bodies of those who have risked all and lost, frequently wash up on the Spanish and Moroccan coasts. It's a sick local joke in Tangier that there are no pedalos to hire along the city's long stretch of beach.

The Petit Socco (also known as the Zoco Chico or Socco Chico) in the heart of Tangier, long *the* place for transactions of the greatest diversity, is one of the centres for organising this nasty trade. Well-heeled West Africans with cellphones and designer labels are willing customers, but there are other less affluent people willing to sign themselves into virtual slavery in order to get into Europe, where they then have a huge debt to pay.

The Spanish government, under pressure from the EU, is getting increasingly tough in its stance on illegal immigration, but with little success judging by how difficult it is to get a cheap room in Tangier now.

demic that swept through Europe and North Africa not long after the Byzantines left the scene, but continual warfare between the indigenous Berber tribes and the conquering Arabs would not have helped.

Once Arab supremacy had been established, it passed between various factions eventually passing to the Almohads in 1149. When the Almohad regime reached its nadir, the city elected to be ruled by the Hafsids of Tunis, but passed to Merenid control shortly afterwards in 1274.

Following the victories of the Christian armies in the Iberian peninsula, the Portuguese attempted to take Tangier in 1437. Unsuccessful at first, they finally made it in 1471, only for the city to pass to Philip II of Spain in 1580 when Spain and Portugal were united. It reverted to Portugal when that country regained its independence, but was then passed to England in 1661 as part of Catherine of Braganza's dowry to Charles II.

The English were not to remain long. Tangier was besieged by Moulay Ismail in 1679 and the English abandoned the city seven years later (after destroying the port and most of the city), following a dispute between parliament and the king in which the former refused to fund the reinforcement of the garrison in Tangier.

The Moroccans were left in control until the mid-19th century, when Tangier became the object of intense rivalry between the French, Spanish, Italians, British and Germans. The situation was partially resolved by the Treaty of Algeciras in 1906, whereby the British were bought off with Egypt and the Italians with Libya, leaving the remaining three European powers intriguing for the spoils.

The status of the city was finally resolved only in 1923, when Tangier and the surrounding countryside was declared an 'international zone' controlled by the resident diplomatic agents of France, Spain, Britain, Portugal, Sweden, Holland, Belgium, Italy and the USA. Even the Moroccan sultan was represented by an agent, although the latter was appointed by the French resident-general (by this time France and Spain had divided Morocco into protectorates). In fact, much of the administration of Tangier had been in European and American hands since the late 19th century, and their hold had been progressively tightened by the Treaties of Madrid (1880) and Algeciras.

Tangier was to remain an international zone until a few months after Morocco's independence in 1956, it was then reunited with the rest of the country (although it was some years before all its economic and financial privileges were removed). In the meantime it became one of the most fashionable Mediterranean resorts, renowned for its high-profile gay scene and popular with freebooters, artists, writers, exiles and bankers. However, it was also an infamous haven for paedophiles.

Each of the countries represented in Tangier maintained its own banks, currency

Ibn Battuta

Sheikh Abu Abdallah Mohammed bin Abdallah bin Mohammed bin Ibrahim al-Lawati became known as the 'voyager of Islam' and is arguably Tangier's most famous son, though little-known in the West. Born in 1304 in the bustling port city of Tangier, Ibn Battuta, as he became known, spent 30 years criss-crossing the Muslim world from one end to the other. There is a saying in the East that he who travels much comes to know more than he who lives long.

No sooner were his studies over than, in 1325, Ibn Battuta set off for Egypt. 'I left Tangier, my birthplace, on the 2nd of Rajab in the year 725 (14 June 1325)…I decided to leave behind my friends, men and women, and abandoned my home as birds leave the nest…'

His adventures took him on several pilgrimages to Mecca and the holy places in Arabia, and then beyond, across Iraq and Iran into India and China. On his initial journey, after crossing North Africa and visiting Syria, he made his first pilgrimage to Mecca in 1326. He did so again the following year, after travelling to Mosul in Iraq and Esfahān, Shīrāz and Tabrīz in Iran. In the following years he explored the east coast of Egypt, the Arabian coast and the Gulf before heading into Anatolia and touring Asia Minor. He spent seven years at the court of the sultan at Delhi in India before setting off again in 1342. From there he headed south for the Maldives and travelled on as far as Sumatra. He supposedly ended up in Peking (now Beijing) at one point but his own accounts seem shaky at best.

In 1349 he was back in his native territory, staying in Fès, but only after more travels into the Sudan, Niger, Mali and Muslim Spain did he finally stay put and dictate his adventures; the manuscript of which now lies in the Bibliothèque Nationale de Paris. Appropriately enough, one of the ferries plying the Strait of Gibraltar between Morocco and Spain today bears his name.

MARTIN HARRIS

and post offices, and took a share in the policing of the city. Banks, in particular, made fortunes out of manipulating the currency markets. All this ended in 1956, but the legend of notoriety lingers on.

Orientation

Generally speaking, the small medina climbs up the hill to the north-east of the city, while the *ville nouvelle* (new town) surrounds it to the west, south and southeast. The square known as the Grand Socco (officially renamed Place du 9 Avril 1947) is the centre of things and the link between the medina and the ville nouvelle. Rue Semmarine leads off the Grand Socco almost immediately into Rue as-Siaghin, which takes you east to the modest central square inside the medina – the Petit Socco (also known as the Socco Chico, and officially Place Souq ad-Dakhil).

The kasbah occupies a dominant position on top of the cliff in the north-western corner of the medina.

East of the medina lie the port and ferry terminal. A little to the south of the port is the CTM bus station.

At the heart of the ville nouvelle is Blvd Pasteur and Blvd Mohammed V, a compact area close to the medina. It contains the main post office, banks, some of the consulates, many of the restaurants and bars and the bulk of the mid-range and top-end accommodation.

Further south at the end of Ave Louis van Beethoven, on Place Jamia el-Arabia, is the *gare routière* (main bus station) and *grand taxi* (long-distance taxi) rank. About 6km to the south-east, past the old bull ring, is Tangier Morora, now the city's only train station. While the main bus station is a 40-minute walk from the Grand Socco and the bulk of the cheap hotels, the train station is a Dr10 *petit taxi* (local taxi) ride away.

Further out, to the north-west, is the Marshan, a modestly elevated plateau where the rich once maintained (and in some cases still maintain) their palatial villas. Dominated by 'the Mountain', it has a prominent place in the legends surrounding the colourful band of expatriates who lived here.

Information

Tourist Offices The Délégation Régionale du Tourisme (☎ 948050) at 29 Blvd Pasteur in the ville nouvelle, has the usual limited range of brochures. The staff are helpful (if pushed) and speak several languages including English, French and Spanish. The office is open from 8.30 am to noon and 2.30 to 6.30 pm weekdays. This is the place to arrange official guides for the medina, although the quality of guides varies greatly.

Money There are plenty of banks along Blvd Pasteur and Blvd Mohammed V in the ville nouvelle.

The BMCE on Blvd Pasteur has ATMs. It also has an exchange booth where you can change cash or travellers cheques and get cash advances on Visa and MasterCard. The booth is open from 10 am to 2 pm and 4 to 8 pm daily.

Out of bank hours try the El-Minzah hotel. Voyages Schwartz handles American Express (AmEx) problems (see Travel Agencies following).

Post & Communications The main post office is on Blvd Mohammed V in the ville nouvelle and is open from 8.30 am to noon and 2.30 to 6.30 pm weekdays, and Saturday morning. For poste restante (c/o Tangier Principle 90000) head to the third counter in from the right. The parcel counter is around the back of the building (turn left out the main entrance then left again down a small side street). Beware of hustlers inside the post office who'll point out the obvious and then demand money for 'helping' you while staff turn a blind eye.

There are numerous *téléboutiques* (privately owned phone services) dotted about the town. Most have fax services.

There are several cafes in the ville nouvelle. Most charge Dr10 per hour and are open from 10 am to 10 pm. Quality varies, but recommended are Maghreb Net on Rue al-Antaki (with fast new machines); Cyber Cafe Mam Net on Rue Allal ben Abdellah; and Cyber Café Adam on Rue ibn Rochd.

Travel Agencies In the ville nouvelle, Carlson Wagonlits (☎ 331024), 91 Rue de la Liberté and Voyages Schwartz (☎ 330372), 54 Blvd Pasteur – also the AmEx agent – are competent and open standard business hours.

Bookshops In the past 100 years Tangier has welcomed more than its fair share of literary figures, novelists and writers. Much of the more recent literary life has been based around Paul Bowles who brought many Moroccan writers to Western readers (see the boxed text 'Paul Bowles' later). Bowles was one of a set of writers who came to the city during the 'Interzone years' and a number of books have been written about this period of history (see Books in the Facts for the Visitor chapter for more information). Many of these titles can be found in Tangier.

By far the city's best bookshop is the Librairie des Colonnes (☎ 936955), 54 Blvd Pasteur, in the ville nouvelle. It keeps largely Francophone literature with a reasonable selection of English novels. The shop was

Paul Bowles

Perhaps the best-known foreign writer who lived in and wrote about Morocco, was the controversial American author Paul Bowles, who died in Tangier in 1999 aged 88. Living in Tangier and thoroughly immersed in Morocco's literary scene for 50 years, Bowles did a tremendous amount to bring Moroccan authors to English-speaking audiences.

Bowles was born in New York in 1910. Somewhat directionless after leaving school, he spent time at art college and university, but perhaps more significant were the trips he made to Europe and the influential artist and intellectual friends he made there. In 1931, on Gertude Stein's rather off-beam advice, he stopped writing and went briefly to Tangier before devoting the next 15 years of his life to music composition and criticism.

In 1937 he married Jane Sydney Auer. They married a year later, but they were never a conventional couple – he was an ambivalent bisexual and she was an active lesbian. After WWII he returned to creative writing and to Tangier where he was visited by the likes of Allen Ginsberg and William Burroughs.

During the 1950s he began taping, transcribing and translating stories by Moroccan authors, in particular Driss ben Hamed Charhaki (also known by the pseudonym Larbi Layachi) and Mohammed Mrabet.

Books by Bowles include *The Sheltering Sky* (1949), a bleak and powerful story of an innocent American couple who arrive in North Africa shortly after WWII and try to put their relationship back together, and *Let It Come Down* (1952) a thriller set in Tangier. *Their Heads Are Green* (1963) and *Points in Time* (1982) are excellent collections of travel tales.

There is a definite dark undercurrent to some of his writing, which is almost gothic at times, though his autobiography *Without Stopping* (nicknamed Without Telling) sheds a little light on a few dark corners of his life.

founded in the interwar years and was taken over by the prestigious French publisher Gallimard. It was run for a long time by two French women, Yvonne and Isabelle Gerofi, who played host to pretty well all the high and low-life of European Tangier.

Another good option is Librairie Dar Baroud (☎ 931143) at the Hôtel Continental, which stocks a good range of English books on Morocco and translations of Moroccan authors.

Film & Photography Studio Flash (☎ 931399), 79 Rue de la Liberté, is probably the best photography shop in town and has a good selection of print and slide film. It was a decent one-hour developing service and does camera repairs.

Cultural Centres The Institut Français (☎ 942589, fax 940937, e institut-tanger@diplomatie.fr), 41 Rue Hassan ibn Wazzane, puts on a good variety of films and exhibitions. It also helps organise a number of Tangier's cultural festivals. Many of the institute's events are held in Galerie d'Exposition Delacroix, 86 Rue de la Liberté. The gallery is open 11 am to 1 pm and 4 to 8 pm daily except Monday, while the main part of the institute is open Tuesday to Saturday.

The Spanish are also well represented with the Instituto Cervantes and its Biblioteca Española (☎ 932001, fax 947630), 99 Blvd Sidi Mohammed ben Abdallah. The library was founded in 1941 and has a varied collection of material on Tangier (some in English), as well as Moroccan, Spanish and Gibraltarian phone books. The complex is open from 10 am to 1 pm and 3 to 7 pm Tuesday to Friday, and Saturday morning.

Laundry Lavage Rapide at 106 Ave Hassan I is a self-service laundrette charging Dr15 for 7kg of washing and Dr20 to tumble dry. It's open from 9 am to 1.30 pm and 3 to 7 pm daily (closed Friday afternoon).

Pressing du Détroit on Rue el-Jarraoui in the ville nouvelle takes 24 hours and charges Dr10 for trousers, Dr8 for a shirt.

Medical Services & Emergency The Depôt de Nuit (night pharmacy), opposite the Cinéma Paris and down the Galerías Fès on Rue de Fès in the ville nouvelle is open from 9 pm to 9 am every night.

The police can be contacted in an emergency on ☎ 19 and the fire brigade on ☎ 15. There's a 24-hour doctor service (☎ 333300) should you have a medical emergency, but according to local diplomats, Tangier is the worst Moroccan city in which to get sick.

Dangers & Annoyances Despite considerable improvements in recent years thanks to the Brigade Touristique, Tangier is still home to some of the most adept hustlers and pickpockets in the country. See also the boxed text 'Prepare for Tangier' in the Getting There and Away chapter.

Arriving by Boat In particular, those arriving by ferry will meet a barrage of multilingual 'friends' and 'guides'.

Expect a whole repertoire of colourful stories too – that your hotel is full, closed or in ashes after a fire; that the medina is unsafe for foreigners; that all taxis, buses and trains are on strike; and that the only way you will possibly survive all this is under your new friend's protection. The best way to deal with this is to arrive well prepared and above all, with a good sense of humour.

Before disembarking, try to change your money on the boat and decide exactly where you're headed, or you'll find yourself being led to any number of hotels, banks or places you didn't want to go to, *and* having to pay for it. Some hustlers will follow you anyway in order to try to claim commission on your hotel room; if that fails, they will then renew their offers for services every time you emerge from the hotel.

After disembarking, the best approach is to look blase, claim that you already know the city, politely decline the offers for assistance and take a cab to your hotel. Petit (Dr10) and grand taxis (around Dr30) can be found below the ferry terminal, but make sure the driver doesn't let anyone else get in with you.

Departing by Boat Catching the ferry *from* Tangier is no picnic either. There are numerous ticket offices and travel agents close to the Port Gate in Tangier and if you come here on foot you'll be approached by touts intent on dragging you into one or other of them. They may well bustle you about and act as your guide to the ferry terminal, or simply try to sell you a set of bongos and 'something special' for the journey. All these characters want is money, so if you're not feeling overly generous, watch out for them or take a petit taxi to the terminal building.

Once inside the Port Gate things ease off, but there are still a lot of people around pretending to be officials of one sort or another. Keep hold of your ticket and if you're in any doubt about the time of departure of your ferry, check at the ticket office. Don't hand over your ticket or passport to anyone until you're right inside the customs area. Keep an eye on your belongings at all times.

On the Train Tangier Morora train station (5km from the city centre) poses no problems at all (at the time of writing), but we've had reports of hassle on the train itself. One popular scam is for a friendly, well-dressed man to pretend to save you from a nasty, aggressive hustler. Your 'saviour' then tells you of the dangers the big, bad cities that are teeming with deranged, aggressive guides. However, luckily, you could see the 'real Morocco' by visiting his village where there just happens to be a gathering of his Berber tribe. Don't allow yourself to be coerced off the train – Asilah is a popular disembarkation point for these con artists.

Grand Socco

The Grand Socco was once as full of life as the Djemaa el-Fna in Marrakesh, with makeshift shops, snake charmers, musicians, storytellers and food stalls filling the night air with cacophonous activity. It's still a busy place, especially on Thursday and Sunday, when Riffian peasants come to market, and the area comes alive.

MEDITERRANEAN COAST & THE RIF

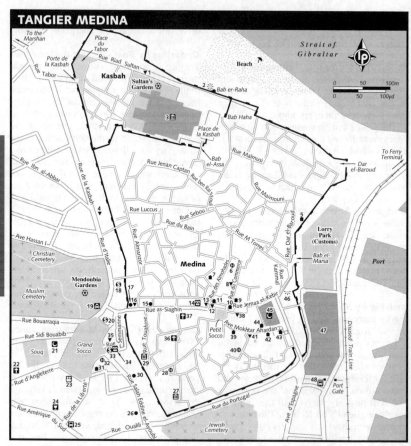

TANGIER MEDINA

Medina

You enter the medina from the Grand Socco by Rue Semmarine and quickly veer right onto Rue as-Siaghin. This was once Tangier's main gold market (some jewellery stores remain), located on the northern flank of the *mellah* (old Jewish quarter).

On your right, you soon pass the Spanish **Church of the Immaculate Conception** (closed), built in 1880 when Spaniards made up one-fifth of the city's population. A few doors down is what used to be the residence of the *naib* (sultan's agent) who was the point of contact between the Moroccan

leader and European legations until 1923. From here you emerge on to the **Petit Socco**.

Gone are the days when William Burroughs could cheerfully write of the endless stream of louche offers from young boys and men around the Petit Socco. There's nothing quaint or romantic about paedophilia, but the busy little square is a great place to sit over a mint tea, watch the world go by and contemplate its colourful past. And sleaze remains close to the surface. You'll have plenty of offers for 'something special, my friend' and a few of the cheap pensions overlooking the square double as brothels.

TANGIER MEDINA

PLACES TO STAY
5 Hôtel Continental
7 Pension Agadir
9 Hôtel Larache
10 Pension Becerra
11 Pension Mauritania
31 Hôtel du Grand Socco
39 Pension Palace
42 Hôtel Olid
43 Pension Victoria; Hammam
44 Hôtel Mamora;
 Pressing (Laundry)

PLACES TO EAT
1 Café Détroit
4 Hamadi
8 Café Andalus
12 Café Central
13 Tingis Café

16 Restaurant Mamounia Palace
35 Pâtisserie Charaf
38 Cheap Snack Bar
41 Restaurant Ahlan

OTHER
2 Lookout
3 Dar el-Makhzen Museum
6 Hammam
14 Telephones
15 Shamalabo Photo Shop
17 Pharmacy Anegax
18 Crédit du Maroc
19 Grand Taxis
20 BMCE (ATM)
21 Mosque
22 St Andrew's Church
23 Cinéma Rif
24 Dean's Bar

25 Local Bus Terminal
26 Covered Market
27 Old American
 Legation Museum
28 Hammam
29 Musée de la
 Fondation Lorin
30 Covered Market
32 Hammam
33 Banque Populaire
34 Telephones
36 Spanish Church
37 Church of the Immaculate
 Conception
40 Douche
45 Great Mosque
46 Viewpoint
47 Customs and Port Buildings
48 CTM Bus Station

It's perhaps difficult to imagine now, but at the end of the 19th century the Fuentes was one of Tangier's luxury hotels. At that time there was little more to the town than the medina and, as the Europeans became more influential, the city's administration was established here, including the Spanish postal service and the main banks.

If you head down Ave Mokhtar Ahardan (formerly Rue de la Poste), you will probably find it hard to believe that some of the little pensions here were classy hotels squeezed in among such important offices as the Spanish Legation and French post office. (From here you can descend a series of stairways and walk down to the port.) The grand era came to an end as the ville nouvelle was built and the administration was transferred out of the medina in the early 20th century.

At the end of Rue Jemaa el-Kebir (formerly Rue de la Marine) you come to a small belvedere overlooking the port. You could easily miss the **Great Mosque** on the corner. The building itself is of little interest, but it's said to have been the site of a Roman temple and at one time housed a church built by the Portuguese.

From the Petit Socco, Rue des Almohades (formerly Rue des Chrétiens) takes you north, past some very determined shopkeepers, to the kasbah.

Kasbah The kasbah is on the highest point of the city and isolated from the rest of the medina by its walls. If you follow Rue M Torres, stick to the wide streets and continue uphill, you will reach Place de la Kasbah and Dar el-Makhzen, the former sultan's palace, which is now a good **museum** devoted to Moroccan arts. As with many museums in Morocco, the building is as attractive and interesting as the exhibits.

The palace was built by Moulay Ismail in the 17th century and enlarged by later sultans, including Moulay Hafid – the last sultan to live here in 1912, along with his four wives and 40 concubines. The private apartments were arranged around an inner courtyard, and still contain beautiful examples of carved wood ceilings and doors, *zellij* (tilework) and *muqarnas* (plasterwork).

Displayed in the salons are good examples of Moroccan crafts, including musical instruments, pottery (from Fès and Meknès), textiles (including Berber kilims and embroidery from Chefchaouen), leatherwork, metalwork and weapons.

There is also a small archaeological collection. Most of the exhibits come from Volubilis, including the well-preserved Roman mosaic, Voyage of Venus.

Before leaving the museum, take a stroll around the **Sultan's Gardens** designed in the

Andalusian fashion with a central fountain and citrus and pomegranate trees providing welcome shade. The museum is open from 9 am to 12.30 pm and 3 to 5.30 pm. On Friday it's open from 9 to 11.30 am and it's closed Tuesday. Entry is Dr10.

If you feel in need of a refreshment, the **Café Détroit** on the 2nd floor in the walls can be reached through these gardens. It was set up by Brion Gysin, the 1960s writer and friend of the Rolling Stones, and was called The Thousand & One Nights. It became famous for the trance musicians who played here in the 1960s and released a record produced by Brian Jones. Musicians still occasionally play here, but it has become a bit of a tourist trap. It's open from 10 am to 2 pm, and although the views through the grubby windows are good, the tea is expensive.

Quite a few of the houses inside the kasbah are owned by wealthy foreigners, only some of whom live here for much of the time. Just outside the kasbah is the **Calle Amrah**, where expatriate American author Paul Bowles bought himself a small house in 1947.

Not far away was the **Sidi Hosni Palace** where Barbara Hutton, the Woolworths heiress, lived and gave some of her grandest parties. It's said that when things were going well she had an annual income of US$3 million, but when she died in 1979 in Los Angeles, she had less than US$4000 in the bank.

Old American Legation Museum The Old American Legation is an intriguing relic of the international zone. The five-storey building has been built up over two centuries from a small stone building that was a gift to the USA in 1821 by Sultan Moulay Suleyman. Morocco was the first nation to politically acknowledge the USA, and the diplomatic mission to Morocco was located here from 1821 to 1956.

It now houses a fascinating collection of antique maps, furniture and 17th- to 20th-century paintings, prints and drawings. A few of the highlights are work by Delacroix, Oskar Kokoschka and the intimate engravings by the Scottish artist James McBey.

There's an excellent research library dedicated to the Maghreb and a general English-language library for students, where you'll see some great old photos featuring the likes of Churchill, Roosevelt and de Gaulle.

A few hours in the museum is time very well spent, though if you arrive unannounced you may find that only a French-speaking guide is available.

To get there turn into Rue du Portugal from Rue Salah Eddine el-Ayoubi and enter the medina at the first gate on your left, it's a little way down Zankat America, after the dogleg turn.

Open from 10 am to 1 pm and 3 to 5 pm weekdays, you'll need to knock on the door. Appointments can be made (☎ 935317). A small shop sells books in English and copies of the collection. Entry is free but donations are greatly appreciated.

Musée de la Foundation Lorin Housed in an unlikely looking building, this museum (fax 334696, ⓔ lorin@tangeroise.net.ma) at 44 Rue Touahine contains a wonderful collection of photographs, posters and prints of Tangier from 1890 to 1960. Featured in this remarkable illustration of Tangier's history are Winston Churchill, James McBey, King Mohammed V and other local characters from the era such as Caid McLean, Emily Keene and her husband the sherif of Ouezzane (see also St Andrew's Church later). Photos of these figures are interspersed with street scenes and French newspaper clippings. Upstairs there's a display of work by young art students.

It's signposted on the right from Rue Touahin and is open from 11 am to 1 pm and 3.30 to 7.30 pm daily except Saturday. Entry is free, but a donation would be appreciated.

Ville Nouvelle

The core of the ville nouvelle, largely unchanged since its heyday in the 1930s, is worth a wander. The area around Place de France and Blvd Pasteur, with its cafes and patisseries, still retains something of that decade's glamour.

The aptly named **Terrasse des Paresseux** (Idlers' Terrace) just up from the Place de France, provides lovely panoramic views of the port, Gibraltar and Spain. It's a favourite spot with the locals who come for an evening promenade.

A remnant of the days when Spaniards formed the largest non-Moroccan community in Tangier is the **Gran Teatro de Cervantes**, in a side street off Rue Salah Eddine el-Ayoubi (also known as Rue de la Plage). Opened in 1913, the theatre enjoyed its heyday in the interwar years. You can't miss the dazzling Art Deco facade, but the building has long been in decline.

Virtually across the road stands the closed and crumbling **Grand Hôtel Villa de France**. Delacroix stayed here in 1831 while he sketched Tangier. The French impressionist painter, Henri Matisse, was also a guest in the early 1900s – his imagination captured and his brush driven by the African light.

St Andrew's Church

There has been a small English church in Tangier as far back as the 1660s, when England occupied the city for a 20-year period. The present church, St Andrew's, is on Rue d'Angleterre, just outside the medina and was built in 1894 on ground donated by Sultan Moulay al-Hassan. It was consecrated in 1905.

The caretaker, Mustapha Chergui, will be pleased to show you around the beautiful building (Matisse painted a marvellous picture of it), which was constructed in the Moroccan style with the Lord's Prayer in Arabic around the chancel arch.

In the church is a plaque to the memory of Emily Keene, an English woman who married the sherif of Ouezzane and spent many years of her life introducing vaccination to the people of northern Morocco.

Others buried here include Walter Harris, the British journalist who chronicled Tangier's goings-on from the late 19th century (in the church there's a plaque with a rather appropriate inscription), and 'Caid' McLean, a military adviser to the sultans who, like Harris, was at one time imprisoned and held to ransom by the Rif bandit Er-Raissouli.

This wonderful church is open to all denominations, but depends on voluntary contributions for its upkeep. If you'd like to make a donation contact the Diocese in Europe (London ☎ 020-7976 8001, [e] diocesan.office@europe.c-of-e.org.uk).

There is a story that the **Great Mosque** on Place de Koweit was built after a rich Arab Gulf sheikh sailed by Tangier and noticed that the cathedral's spire overshadowed all the minarets of Tangier. Shocked, he paid for the mosque and now the spire plays second fiddle to the new minaret.

Musée d'Art Contemporain

Housed in the former British consulate on Rue d'Angleterre, this gallery displays examples of Moroccan art, mainly from the 1980s and early '90s.

There is work on display by the contemporary Moroccan painters Abdallah Hariri and Farid Belkahia. Chaibia Tallal has an interesting painting of vibrant, bright abstract figures and Fatima Hassan is one of the few female painters represented.

The paintings are unfortunately suffering in the humid atmosphere, but the gallery is certainly worth a visit. It's open from 9 am to 12.30 pm and 2 to 6 pm Wednesday to Monday. Entry is Dr10.

Forbes Museum

Unfortunately the Forbes Museum, owned by the family of the American tycoon Malcolm Forbes (of *Forbes Magazine*), who died in 1990, has now closed. The museum claimed to have the largest collection of toy soldiers in the world, an 'army' of 120,000 miniatures, and dioramas depicting all sorts of unrelated conflicts, from the Battle of the Three Kings (1578) to the Green March (1975).

There is still hope that the museum will re-open in the future.

Beaches

The beaches of Tangier, although not bad, are hardly the best in Morocco. They're relatively clean, but in some areas raw sewage is pumped into the sea. They are used for football matches at weekends and in the evening. The beach bars strung along the sand have changing cabins (officially compulsory), showers, deck chairs, and food and drink.

The much reduced presence of the European gay population still frequents certain bars, some of which can be fun in summer. As with many beaches in Morocco, women will not feel at ease sunning themselves here and it's not a great place for an evening stroll – muggings are common.

Language Courses

At Tangier's American Language Center (☎ 933616), 1 Rue M'sallah, you may be able to arrange private Arabic tuition (about Dr120 per hour), while English speakers might be able to pick up some work.

Special Events

In May a very successful **Theatre Festival** is held at venues all over town.

In high season an **Arabic**, **French and Spanish book fair** is held in the grounds of the Institut Français. Many Moroccan authors, as well as authors who write about Morocco, attend and give readings.

For information on these and other cultural events, inquire at the French and Spanish cultural centres (see under Information earlier).

Hammams & Public Showers

There are several *hammams* (traditional bathhouses) near the medina around the Petit Socco, including one close to the Pension Victoria on Ave Mokhtar Ahardan. There is another at 80 Rue des Almohades. Both cost Dr5 and are open from 8 am to 8 pm.

There's a public shower, Douche Cléopatra, just by the Hôtel Valencia on Rue Salah Eddine el-Ayoubi. A shower costs Dr5.

Places to Stay – Budget

Outside high season, you shouldn't have trouble finding a room in Tangier. As in most Moroccan cities, you have the choice between the medina and the ville nouvelle. The hotels in the ville nouvelle have the edge on comfort and are a good bet for the new arrival. At the time of writing many of the cheapest hotels in the medina were booked out by well-heeled West African migrants looking for a way into Europe (see the boxed text 'Immigrants' earlier).

Most of the traditional Moroccan-style hostelries are in the medina around the Petit

Socco and on Ave Mokhtar Ahardan, which connects the Petit Socco with the port area.

If you arrive by ferry, many of the cheap hotels are within easy walking distance. However, the port can still be a hive of hustlers and hassle, so you may well feel like taking a taxi (see Dangers & Annoyances earlier).

Camping The most convenient and reliable of Tangier's camp sites is *Camping Miramonte* (☎ 947504), 3km west of the city centre, high above Jews' Bay. Also known as *Camping Marshan*, it's a pleasant site set in lush grounds, but a little isolated – don't leave your valuables unattended. The restaurant and cafe has great views over the bay and swimming pool, but the food and drink are not up to much and prices seem to fluctuate. Take a petit taxi from the town centre for about Dr7. If you're driving, turn left off Ave Hassan II on to Rue des USA then first right (having passed a beautiful mosque on your left), and weave down a narrow street to a huge, grey, metal gate. Camping costs Dr15 per adult, Dr10 for children, plus Dr10 to pitch a tent and Dr10/15/20 for a car/caravan/bus. Hot showers cost Dr10 and electricity Dr8. The single/double rooms with bathroom are nice enough but well overpriced at Dr200/250.

The other site is *Camping Tingis* about 6km east of the town centre. At the time of writing it looked to be in terminal decay, but may open its rusting doors in high season.

Hostels The *Youth Hostel* (☎ 946127, 8 Rue al-Antaki) is just up past Hôtel el-Djenina. It's a nicely laid out place and very clean, though there have been complaints from women travellers. A dorm bed will cost you Dr27 with a HI card (Dr29.50 without). Hot showers are an extra Dr5. The hostel is open from 8 to 10 am and noon to 9 pm.

Hotels – Medina There are plenty of cheap pensions to choose from here. Most are basic and you won't get much more than a bed and shared bathroom facilities, although some have hot water (for a small extra charge). The absence of showers in some of the hotels is not a huge problem, as there are various hammams around the Petit Socco.

Prices vary slightly and you're looking at Dr30 to Dr50 for singles and Dr60 to Dr100 for doubles. Standards vary considerably from room to room as well as from place to place.

One of the best places on the Petit Socco is the *Pension Mauritania* (☎ *934677, Rue as-Siaghin)*. The entrance is just off the Socco. Clean rooms with washbasin cost Dr35 to Dr45 per person. The cold showers are free. Some of the rooms have small balconies overlooking the square. This hotel is popular with gay travellers.

Pension Agadir (☎ *938084)* off Rue des Almohades is a friendly, busy place based around a covered courtyard, but it only has single cell-like rooms for Dr35 (Dr40 in high season). Hot showers cost Dr5.

Across the Petit Socco from the sleazy Fuentes, *Pension Becerra* (☎ *932369)* has singles/doubles/triples for Dr30/50/70. It's clean, but has a slightly dicey air about it.

Close by is *Hôtel Larache* (☎ *940138)*, which charges Dr40 for a room and Dr20 for an extra bed. The showers are cold. It's a tiny, basic place but friendly enough.

Ave Mokhtar Ahardan has a load of accommodation. In the budget range, two of the best options are *Pension Palace* (☎ *936128)* at No 2 and *Hôtel Olid* (☎ *931310)* at No 12. The Palace's rooms are small but clean, and many of them front on to a quiet courtyard. Singles/doubles without shower cost Dr40/80 (Dr10 for a hot shower) and doubles with a shower go for Dr120. The Olid has seen better days, but is fairly clean and most rooms (Dr40/80) come with a cold shower.

One of the best of the others along Ave Mokhtar Ahardan is at No 22, *Pension Victoria* (☎ *931299)*. It has reasonably clean and pleasant good-value rooms set around a rather garish fountain and covered courtyard for Dr30/60 with cold shared showers. It's a peaceful, straightforward place.

Hôtel du Grand Socco (☎ *933126)* is just outside the medina on the square of the similar name. Basic rooms with shared bathroom cost Dr50/80/120. Some rooms have balconies and great views of the square. It's

a good location but the hotel is as shabby as hell.

Hotels – Ville Nouvelle First up are the unrated hotels and pensions along Rue Salah Eddine el-Ayoubi. Most are no better than the cheapies in the medina and some are decidedly characterless. Most offer basic accommodation with shared bathroom and toilet facilities for Dr30 to Dr40 for singles and Dr50 to Dr60 for doubles. Some have hot water.

Heading up from the waterfront you strike several in a row on the left-hand side – they seem to improve as you climb. Good value and straight down the line is *Pension Le Détroit* (☎ *934838)*, which offers clean, but smallish singles/doubles for Dr40/60 (Dr50/80 in high season). Hot showers are Dr8.

Pension Miami (☎ *932900, 126 Rue Salah Eddine el-Ayoubi)* offers clean decent singles/doubles/triples, some with balcony, for Dr50/80/120. Shared hot showers cost Dr10. However, it can be a little unwelcoming.

If none of these appeal, or you just want to be a bit further away from the medina walls, you could try some of the places along Ave d'Espagne. One of the best-value options is *Hôtel l'Marsa* (☎ *932339)* at No 92, which has clean and comfortable rooms for Dr50 per person, although some look straight out over the cafe, which can be noisy. Hot showers are Dr7.

Just up the little lane heading uphill next to Hôtel L'Marsa you'll find the basic but adequate *Pension Majestic* (☎ *937246, 33 Rue ibn Zohr)*. The rooms have washbasins, but are a bit dingy. They cost Dr30/60 (Dr50/100 in high season). Hot showers cost Dr5.

Hôtel Magellan (☎ *372319)* is a little further up and away from the fray. The slightly shabby but clean rooms are good value at Dr40/80 and some have views. Hot showers cost Dr10.

Further up around to the left, you strike two good hotels opposite each other. *Hôtel ibn Batouta* (☎ *939311, 8 Rue Magellan)*, offers clean, recently renovated rooms with

MEDITERRANEAN COAST & THE RIF

TANGIER VILLE NOUVELLE

PLACES TO STAY
3 El-Minzah;
   Restaurant el-Korsan
15 Pension Miami
16 Pension Le Détroit
19 Pension Majestic
20 Hôtel l'Marsa;
   Restaurant l'Marsa
31 Hôtel Astoria
34 Pension Atlal &
   Hôtel al-Hoceima
42 Hôtel Lutetia
47 Hôtel el-Muniria;
   Tanger Inn
48 Hotel Biarritz
49 Hôtel Magellan
50 Hôtel ibn Batouta
51 Hôtel Panoramic
   Massilia
52 Hôtel Rembrandt
54 Hôtel de Paris
58 Hôtel Atlas

67 Hôtel Tanjah-Flandria;
   Le Palace Disco
74 Hôtel Chellah

PLACES TO EAT
1 Restaurant
   Populaire Saveur
7 Pâtisserie
   La Española
10 Café de Paris
12 Sandwich Genève
13 Sandwich Cervantes
17 Afrika; Hassi Baida
25 Brahim Abdelmalik
   Fast Food
29 La Pagode
32 San Remo
33 Excel Food
36 Café Metropole
40 Romero's
55 Pâtisserie le
   Petit Prince

59 Pizzeria Piazza Capri
60 Rubis Grill
62 Casa Pepé
71 Pâtisserie
   Rahmouni
72 The Pub
82 Churros Stall
89 Café Oslo;
   Pizzeria Oslo

OTHER
2 Studio Flash
4 British Airways
5 Carlson Wagonlits
6 Galerie d'Exposition
   Delacroix
8 Telephones; Fax
9 French Consulate
11 Gran Teatro de
   Cervantes
18 Douche
   Cléopatra
21 Terrasse des
   Paresseux
22 Pharmacy

23 Royal Air Maroc
24 Pressing du
   Détroit
26 Negrescu
27 Depôt de Nuit
   (Night Pharmacy)
28 Cinéma Paris
30 Stop Pressing
35 BMCE (Late Bank
   & ATMs)
37 Synagogue
38 SUM Informatique
39 Délégation
   Regionale
   du Tourisme
   (Tourist Office)
41 Telephone; Fax
43 Budget
44 Limadet Boat
   Ticket Office
45 Studios Samar
46 Church
53 Scott's
56 Scott's
57 Cinéma
   Mauritania

61 Danish Consulate
63 Librairie des
   Colonnes
64 Avis
65 Voyages Schwartz
66 Téléboutique
68 Crédit du Maroc
69 Cinéma Flandria
70 Cyber Café Adam
73 Institut Français
75 Cinéma Goya
76 Pharmacy du Lycée
77 Cyber Café
   Mam Net
78 Cinéma Roxy
79 London Pub
80 Telephone; Fax
81 Pressing Dallas
83 Pharmacy
84 Banque Populaire
85 Wafa Bank
86 Cady & Douka
87 Hertz
88 Main Post Office
90 British & Belgian
   Consulates

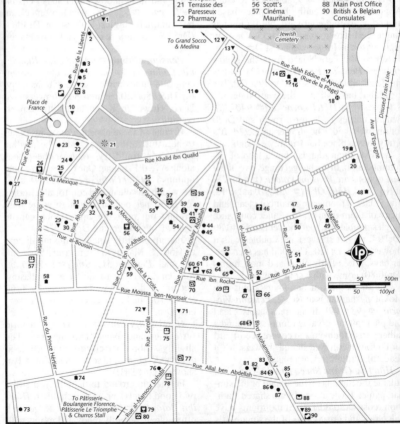

shower for Dr120/200. The cafe terrace has excellent views and is popular but the drinks are often overpriced.

Hôtel el-Muniria (☎ 935337), opposite, is showing its age but remains an excellent choice. Clean rooms with hot showers go for Dr110/130. There's a lingering nostalgic air of the 1950s, when Jack Kerouac and Alan Ginsberg stayed here, while William Burroughs wrote *The Naked Lunch* in room No 9.

Close by and also with good views (if you can get a front room) is *Hôtel Panoramic Massilia* (☎ 935015) on the corner of Rue ibn Joubair and Rue Targha. Fairly run-down but reasonably clean rooms with shower, toilet and hot water (in the morning) cost Dr50/100 (Dr70/130 in high season).

A less pleasant bolt hole is *Hotel al-Hoceima* (☎ 933063, 2 Rue al-Moutanabi). Basic rooms cost Dr70/120 (Dr10 for a hot shower) and doubles with shower cost Dr140.

For the truly desperate, there are a few more south of Rue Moussa ben-Noussair, but you shouldn't need them.

Places to Stay – Mid-Range

Medina If you prefer a modicum of luxury but still want to stay in the medina then try the two-star *Hôtel Mamora* (☎ 934105, 19 Ave Mokhtar Ahardan*). Good, clean singles/doubles with shower (and some have toilets) cost Dr147/180 (Dr197/230 in high season). Some rooms have beautiful views out to the sea over the Great Mosque, though an early morning wake-up call is guaranteed.

Perched above the port is the *Hôtel Continental* (☎ 931024, fax 931143, 36 Dar el-Baroud*). the pick of the middle crop. It's a charmingly eccentric hotel full of atmosphere (if a little ragged around the edges) and was used for some scenes in the film version of Paul Bowles' *The Sheltering Sky*. The terrace is a great place to relax and watch the activity of the port. Rooms cost Dr161/210 (Dr186/240 during high season), including an unexceptional breakfast. It's very popular (so book ahead) and well signposted.

Ville Nouvelle There are a few possibilities at the lower end of this scale where a

single will cost a little more than Dr140. *Pension Hollanda* (☎ 937838, 139 Rue Hollanda*) is in a pleasant shady spot in a backstreet behind the French consulate. It charges Dr100/150 for simple, clean, singles/doubles. Three rooms come with shower (cold) for no extra charge, and two rooms (Nos 3 and 11) have nice balconies. There's also space for parking.

A little more accessible and a good choice is *Hôtel Astoria* (☎ 937202, 10 Rue Ahmed Chaouki*). It has a lift and is a pleasant and straightforward place. Single/double/triple rooms, with showers, cost Dr134/165/230.

Hôtel de Paris (☎ 931877, 42 Blvd Pasteur*) is virtually opposite the tourist office. Clean, comfortable rooms with shower cost Dr177/216 (Dr227/266 in high season).

Just up from the port, though not in the most salubrious location, is *Hôtel Biarritz* (☎ 932473, 102–4 Ave d'Espagne*). For Dr161/212 you can get comfortable, spacious old rooms with shower. Some rooms overlook the sea.

In the heart of the ville nouvelle are some more expensive alternatives to Hôtel de Paris. *Hôtel Astoria* (☎ 937201, 10 Rue Ahmed Chaouki*) is good and easy-going. Reasonable rooms with showers cost Dr109/140 in low season and Dr136/180 in high season.

The pleasant *Hôtel Lutetia* (☎ 931866, 3 Rue du Prince Moulay Abdallah*) has parking facilities and a bar. Rooms with shower and toilet cost Dr102/126 (Dr24 more during high season).

Hôtel Atlas (☎ 936435, fax 933095, 50 Rue Moussa ben Noussair*) offers clean, bright rooms with bathroom and TV for Dr243/302. (Add around Dr35 during high season). However, it's a little out of the way and has a slightly odd air about it.

Heading into what most people would consider the top range is *Hôtel Chellah* (☎ 324457, fax 943346, 47–49 Rue Allal ben Abdellah*), a multistorey building decorated à la Maroccan. Comfortable, clean rooms with bathroom, phone and TV start at Dr287/351 (add Dr100 for high season). The hotel has a pool that is usually open to nonguests (Dr25/40 per child/adult).

The following places are away from the heart of the ville nouvelle. At the junction of Ave des FAR and Ave Youssef ben Tachfine is *Hôtel Miramar (☎ 941715)*. It's definitely on the tatty side, but it's clean and the staff are friendly. Rooms (some with views) with private shower and toilet cost Dr120/153/211 (Dr145/178/236 in high season).

Where Rue al-Antaki heads up from Ave d'Espagne (and where Ave d'Espagne becomes Ave des FAR) is the pleasant *Hôtel Marco Polo (☎ 941124, fax 942276)*, run by Germans. The rooms are so clean they smell of disinfectant. This hotel used to be popular with gay travellers and its bar and restaurant still seem to serve as a meeting point. It charges Dr189/217 and some rooms have terraces and good views.

Next door is the good-value, well-put together, two-star *Hôtel el-Djenina (☎ 942244, fax 942246, 8 Rue al-Antaki)*. Decent, clean rooms with phones (and some with balconies) go for Dr177/216 (Dr230/266 in high season), and there's a restaurant and bar.

If you can afford it try the pricey, two-star *Hôtel Charf (☎ 943340, 25 Rue al-Farabi)*. The self-contained rooms are very good and have magnificent views, as does the 4th-floor bar and restaurant. Rooms are Dr177/216 (add Dr50 in high season).

Places to Stay – Top End

With a tourist trade the size of Tangier's, there's plenty of top-end hotels to choose from, though only a few are worth the cash.

An excellent option is *Hôtel Rembrandt (☎ 937870, fax 930443)* at the junction where Blvd Pasteur becomes Blvd Mohammed V. It's a friendly place with a bit of style and singles/doubles cost Dr375/475 (add Dr100 to each in high season).

Across the road, *Hôtel Tanjah-Flandria (☎ 933279, fax 934347)* offers all the mod cons including sauna (Dr30) for Dr639/729 (there's a 40% reduction in winter).

A line of multistorey hotels has been thrown up along Ave des FAR. One of these unexceptional four-star joints is *Hôtel Solazur (☎ 940164, fax 945286)*. It has recently been given a face-lift and charges upwards of Dr630/774.

Further along Ave des FAR towards town and much the same, is the four-star *Hôtel Shéhérazade (☎ 940803, fax 940801)*. It has rooms for Dr380/542.

The *Intercontinental Hotel (☎ 936053, fax 937945)* near Place de Koweit has a pool and nightclub. Rooms cost Dr592/758 (Dr702/869 in high season).

Hôtel Dawliz (☎ 331812, fax 331823, 42 Rue de Hollande) offers rooms for Dr519/688 (Dr619/788 in high season). The hotel is uninspired but there are stunning panoramic views of the Bay of Tangier. Many of the units in the adjoining complex remain unfilled, but there's a bank, two restaurants, a McDonald's, the Bar Daliah, Salon de Thé Iris and a car park (Dr2 per hour).

The only top-end hotel in Tangier worth its salt is *El-Minzah (☎ 935885, fax 934546,* e *elminzah@tangeroise.net.ma, 85 Rue de la Liberté)*. It's a well-maintained reminder of the 1930s, when it was patronised by anyone who was anyone (and lots of people who thought they were someone) in the transient and not-so-transient European community. In 1931 the US businessman Ion Perdicaris, who at one point spent an uncomfortable spell as a prisoner of Er-Raissouli, the Rif bandit, converted what had been the Palmarium casino into the hotel. It's beautifully conceived, being built along the lines of a Moroccan palace and was once the mansion of a certain Lord Bute. During WWII, as Tangier turned into a viper's nest of spies and mercenaries of all types, the hotel catered for a mainly American clientele. The excellent amenities include a swimming pool, fitness centre and a babysitting service. Golf, horse-riding and tennis are all possible in grounds nearby. Singles cost from Dr1015 to Dr1365 and doubles from Dr1330 to Dr1630. Add Dr200 per room in high season.

Places to Eat

Restaurants Tangier has a range of restaurants for all budgets.

Medina There are several cheap eating possibilities in and around the Petit Socco, in between the cafes. **Restaurant Ahlan (8 Ave Mokhtar Ahardan)** is reasonable value with decent *tajine* (meat and vegetable stew), couscous and kebabs going for around Dr25. A bowl of *harira* (spicy lentil soup) will set you back just Dr4. It's a clean, pleasant restaurant and is open from 10 am to 10 pm daily.

Café Andalus (7 Rue Commerce) is a little hole-in-the-wall, sawdust-on-the-floor place that serves up some great cheap meals. Beautifully weighted liver, peas and chips is Dr35. Sword fish is Dr45.

Further north on the same road, *Restaurant Sose* is also worth a try for solid Moroccan fare.

There are a few *food stalls* at the bottom of the steps at the end of Ave Mokhtar Ahardan and around the Grand Socco. They serve up fried fish and one or two other things for a few dirham.

On Rue as-Siaghin is the more expensive *Restaurant Mamounia Palace* (☎ 935099), which offers the usual 'Moroccan feasts' in sumptuous surroundings. It's expensive (there are two set menus for Dr100), but there's a great view over the medina from the top salon. It's open from 10 am to 10 pm daily and mainly caters for tour groups. Don't miss the nougat seller whose *stall* is diagonally opposite the Mamounia. A bag big enough to give you jaw cramp is Dr4.

Another Moroccan palace restaurant is *Hamadi* (☎ 934514, 2 Rue de la Kasbah), just outside the medina walls. The food is not bad and reasonably cheap (Dr40 to Dr45 for a main course), but watch out for the 20% tax. They normally have musicians and you can get a beer or wine with your meal for Dr20/70.

Ville Nouvelle Two good, cheap places are the *Sandwich Cervantes* and *Sandwich Genéve* close to each other on Rue Salah Eddine el-Ayoubi, just south of the Jewish cemetery. They are both popular with the locals, have seating and charge around Dr10 for a large roll filled with meat, or fish and salad. *Brahim Abdelmalik Fast Food* on the corner of Rue du Mexique and Rue el-Jarraoui is a similar deal; half a baguette filled with *kefta* (seasoned minced lamb) and salad costs Dr15.

Down Rue Salah Eddine el-Ayoubi towards Ave d'Espagne are two reasonably priced licensed restaurants, *Afrika* (No 83) and, next door, *Hassi Baida*. Both offer set meals for around Dr50, main courses start at around Dr30, salads for around Dr11 and a bowl of soup for Dr10 (add 10% for tax). The Hassi Baida also offers options for vegetarians. Both are open until 11 pm daily.

Perhaps the best value of all is the *Restaurant Populaire Saveur* (☎ 336326) down the steps from Rue de la Liberté. This excellent little fish restaurant serves authentic Moroccan food and eating here is a real experience for travellers. It's a local favourite and reasonably priced (around Dr40 for a main course). It's open for lunch and is closed Friday.

If you're desperate for Western-style fare there's *Excel Food* on the corner of Blvd Pasteur and Rue Ahmed Chaouki. It serves burgers and chips for Dr35 a throw, while *Pizzeria Piazza Capri* (☎ 937221, 2 Rue de la Croix) does good pizza for around Dr18 to Dr30. It's open from 11.30 am to 11.30 pm daily, and has a free delivery service.

For grilled meat or fish, you could try the *Rubis Grill (3 Rue ibn Rochd)* where mains start at around Dr60. It's decorated like a hunter's lodge and is a cosy place for a beer (Dr15) and tapas during the winter.

The stretch of Rue du Prince Moulay Abdallah around the corner from the tourist office is laden with eating possibilities. *Romero's*, at No 12, has a bar and is not a bad choice. The service is impeccable and the food homely and satisfying (excellent desserts). Mains cost from Dr50 to Dr75, with great seafood paella for Dr65. Half a bottle of red will cost you Dr45, but don't forget the 10% tax.

Restaurant Valencia close to the beach on Ave Youssef ben Tachfine is also worth a try. They specialise in seafood. Mains start at Dr50 and salads around Dr20.

The Pub (5 Rue Sorolla) caters for local drinkers and homesick Brits hungry for pub grub. Chalked up on the blackboard you'll find favourites such as scampi and chips, liver and onions and even shepherd's pie, all for Dr50 to Dr60.

MEDITERRANEAN COAST & THE RIF

Popular with locals and expats is the Italian restaurant **San Remo** (☎ 938451, 15 Rue Ahmed Chaouki). Fish and meat dishes go for around Dr100 and pizzas start at Dr35.

If you're craving Asian food, try the pleasant **La Pagode** (☎ 938086, 3 Rue al-Boussiri), just off Ave du Prince Héritier. Main dishes cost around Dr70 and a bottle of wine from Dr75 (add 20% tax). It's closed Monday.

Restaurant l'Marsa (☎ 932339, 92 Ave d'Espagne) is near the hotel of the same name. It has a very pleasant terrace and offers reasonable set menus for Dr70, pizza from Dr23 to Dr43 and salads from Dr14. It's also a great place for a coffee, milkshake or, in summer, home-made ice cream.

For a big splurge, you could try **Restaurant el-Korsan** (☎ 935885) in El-Minzah hotel. It serves expensive but high quality Moroccan food (main courses cost around Dr130) and there's usually traditional dancing in the evening.

Star of India (☎ 944866, Ave des FAR) opposite Hôtel Solazur is apparently the only Indian restaurant in Morocco. Specialising in cuisine of the Punjab and Goa, there are a variety of set vegetarian and nonvegetarian menus (Dr45 up to Dr85). Otherwise, a biryani will cost you Dr100.

Cafes There are some excellent cafes in Tangier. A few are a bit rough around the edges and in general they're more male dominated than those in Rabat or Casablanca, dedicated to the serious business of coffee drinking and lengthy conversation with barely a spare thought for small niceties like patisseries.

In the heart of the medina, **Café Central** on the Petit Socco was a favourite hang-out for William Burroughs and others. **Tingis Café**, opposite, is another good spot to watch the world go by.

Blvd Pasteur in ville nouvelle is lined with elegant, European-style cafes with tables spilling out onto the pavement. **Café Metropole** is a classic coffee drinkers' retreat. The ageing *grande dame* of Tangier coffee society is **Café de Paris**, where you're likely to have an odd assortment of

characters for company: remnants of the Spanish population, genteel Moroccans and the occasional northern European.

Hidden away in a tiny street behind the stadium is **Café Hafa**, set in shaded, terraced gardens overlooking the Strait of Gibraltar. It's a simple but delightful place to while away the hot afternoon. Cats snooze among the flower pots. It was a favourite of writers and beatniks and remains a popular place with locals who come for a quiet smoke.

Patisseries & Ice-Cream Parlours In the medina, **Pâtisserie Charaf** (28 Rue Semmarine) just off the Grand Socco, is a great place to retreat from the crowds and bustle for delicious almond croissants and coffee.

In the ville nouvelle, **Pâtisserie Rahmouni** (35 Rue du Prince Moulay Abdallah) is run by Hassan Rahmouni and his family who pride themselves on high quality, traditional Moroccan pastries.

Pâtisserie Boulangerie Florence (33 Rue al-Mansour Dahabi) has a good selection of both French and Moroccan pastries, sweet as well as savoury, including *pastilla* (pigeon pie). They also sell freshly baked bread. It's a good place to prepare a picnic.

Pâtisserie Le Triomphe (30 Ave Lafayette), close by, does delicious ice cream in summer. Opposite the patisserie on the same street, there's a stall selling *churros* (doughnuts) in the early morning, which are traditionally eaten for breakfast.

More central is **Pâtisserie le Petit Prince** (34 Blvd Pasteur), which has an excellent selection of sweet and savoury pastries. The house speciality is *polvorone*, a kind of powdery, cinnamony shortbread. It also does fruit juice and ice cream in summer.

On Rue de la Liberté you find **Pâtisserie La Española**, a popular and relaxing women-friendly retreat.

Café Oslo (41 Blvd Mohammed V) is a very civilised, but expensive, cafe. It's a great place to read the local papers or to eat breakfast. *Croque madam* (fried eggs and bread) go for Dr12. Upstairs, the restaurant serves mains from around Dr70. It's open from 5 am to midnight daily. Pizza is avail able next door at *Pizzeria Oslo*, a place run by the same people.

Self-Catering The liquor store *Casa Pepé (9 Rue ibn Rochd)* in the ville nouvelle stocks a decent selection of delicatessen foods such as French and Spanish salami, pâté and cheese. It's an excellent place to stock up for a picnic.

You can buy good, fresh produce from the market stalls in the medina, just off the Grand Socco.

Entertainment

Bars Anyone who has read about Tangier will have come across *Dean's Bar (Rue Amérique du Sud)*, south of the Grand Socco. Hardly a westerner of any repute did not prop up this bar at some time. It's a bit of a dump now, but may be worth a drink if you've steeped yourself in Tangier mythology. Women will feel uncomfortable here.

For something a little more upmarket, or if you're thirsting for a Heineken (Dr30), try *The Pub (5 Rue Sorolla)* in the ville nouvelle. It styles itself on a typical English pub and is open from noon to 3 pm and 6 pm to 2 am; closed Sunday.

An excellent place for a civilised drink is the well-stocked *London Pub (15 Rue al-Mansour Dahabi)*, also in the ville nouvelle, which has live music most nights, though it's often covers of Western pop songs played on a synthesiser. Draught beer starts at Dr25 and there's excellent tapas. It's by far the best bet for women too – any problems ask for Youssef, the owner!

Next to Hôtel el-Muniria, *Tanger Inn* is a tiny place and lovingly maintained – one of the last reminders of the Interzone days. As such it's a bit of a tourist ghetto but worth investigating for the nostalgia of Ginsberg photographs and the like. It's open from 9 pm to about 1 am (3 am if there are plenty of people) daily.

Many of the mid-range and top-end hotels have bars. *Le Caid's Piano Bar* in El-Minzah hotel is good for an expensive tipple (spirits/cocktails for around Dr50/60). It's open from 9 pm to 1 am. The *Wine Bar* in the same hotel is a great place if you fancy

tasting some Moroccan wine; they have a selection of about 20 sold by the bottle or glass.

Negrescu, on the corner of Rue de Mexique and Ave du Prince Héritier, is a clean and calm bar with an adjacent restaurant.

Chico's Pub (10 Rue de Soroya) has the feel of a piano bar, though it is very subdued. There's an extensive and expensive selection of liquor.

The Pilo (Rue de Fès), just past the Rue du Mexique intersection, is a relaxed place with high ceilings and 1950s decor. There's plenty of excellent tapas; the two large windows upstairs overlook Ave Mexique and all the people cruising in the twilight hours.

Radio Bar (Rue du Prince Moulay Abdallah) provides a glimpse of the seedier side of Tangier but there's decent live music.

The Carousel (Ave Khalil Metrane), a block up from Ave Mexique, serves some reasonable Western food and has a nice (if sleazy) bar with a decent selection of beer.

Hotel Chellah (Rue Allal ben Abdellah) has a nice bar with amazing artisanal work and live music. The disco (high season only) starts hopping around midnight.

Close by is *Juana del Arco*, a small local bar with friendly patrons.

Nightclubs Entry for all the nightclubs is Dr100; drinks usually cost Dr40 to Dr50.

Morocco Palace (Rue du Prince Moulay Abdallah) is decorated with excellent artisanal work throughout and popular live music (mostly contemporary Arabic music covers). It's a bit sleazy and there's supposedly a belly-dancer late Friday and Saturday night.

Pasarela (Ave des FAR) in the southeastern part of the ville nouvelle is a large complex with several bars, an attractive garden and outdoor swimming pool. The music is a Western mix. It's open from 11.30 pm to 3 am.

Another popular place is the *Olivia Valere* nightclub in the Ahlan Hôtel, about 5km outside the city on the road to Rabat. *Le Palace* disco (Dr50) in the Hôtel Tanjah-Flandria is open from 9 pm to 3 am. The entrance is next to Cyber Café Adam.

Gay Venues The gay scene is not what it once was. The few places sustaining any reputation as meeting places for gays include *Scott's* nightclub on Rue al-Moutanabi (open from 11 pm until 2 am), and sometimes the *Tanger Inn*.

You can also try the cafes around the Petit Socco, and particularly *Café Central*, and *Café de Paris* in the ville nouvelle. During the summer months, certain bars along the beach, including *Macumba*, *Miami Beach* and *Coco Beach* are a much better bet.

Cinema The best cinema in town is *Cinéma Dawliz* in the Istiraha complex beside the Hôtel Ziryab just south of the medina. It shows a mixture of Bollywood and Hollywood. The *salles* (halls) are air-conditioned and entry is Dr20.

Shopping

Tangier is not the best place for souvenir hunting. The variety is quite wide, but the quality can be variable and prices are inflated to catch the hordes of unwary day-trippers. As in all Moroccan towns, the best bargains are to be found in the medina – spend some time looking around and be prepared to haggle hard.

Ensemble Artisanal, the government-backed arts and crafts centre on Rue de Belgique, makes a good first stop to get an idea of the range and quality of craft available and the maximum prices to offer.

Parfumerie Madini (☎ 934388), in the medina at 14 Rue Sebou, is run by the Madini family. They have passed down the secrets of the trade – the distillation of essential oils – through 14 generations. The little shop attracts Muslims from all over the world and is definitely worth the olfactory experience. Madini is said to be capable of reproducing perfectly any scent you care to give him. To get there, walk east from the Grand Socco down Rue as-Siaghin, take the first left after passing Rue Touahine (the Shamalabo Photo Shop is on the corner) and follow the signs (also keep a look out for the wonderful spice shops along here).

Getting There & Away

Air Royal Air Maroc (RAM; ☎ 979501, fax 932681) has an office on Place de France in the ville nouvelle. All RAM's internal flights from Tangier go via Casablanca (Dr688 one way). RAM also has direct international flights to Amsterdam, Brussels, London, Madrid and Paris. British Airways has an office on Rue de la Liberté and flies to London Gatwick three times a week. Iberia (☎ 936178/9), 35 Blvd Pasteur, flies to Madrid daily. Regional Airlines (☎ 02-538080 in Casablanca) flies to Malaga at least once a day. See under Air in the Getting There & Away chapter for further details on flying to Tangier from Spain.

There is also a Lufthansa office in town (☎ 931327) in the ville nouvelle at 7 Rue du Mexique.

Bus – CTM The CTM bus station and office is beside the port entrance – you'll probably encounter a few chancers hanging around so take care. All international services start/stop here along with most long-distance buses. Many also pass through the main non-CTM gare routière, on Place Jamia el-Arabia, about 2km from town.

There are five departures for Casablanca from 11 am to midnight (Dr110, seven hours); they stop at Rabat (Dr83, 5½ hours) and Kenitra (Dr70, four hours). One bus departs for Marrakesh (Dr165, 11 hours) at 4.30 pm, travelling on to Agadir (Dr237, 15 hours) and Tiznit (Dr260). Buses to Fès (Dr85, six hours) leave at noon, 3, 7 and 9 pm, stopping at Asilah (Dr15, one hour), Larache (Dr29,

Reddy-Made

One of the most common sights in the herb and spice souqs throughout Morocco is the large pyramids of a deep, olive-green powder.

The crushed leaves of the henna plant are greatly valued for their health-giving properties and women use it for the care and beautification of their skin and hair. Mixed with egg, milk or the pulp of fruit, it's applied to the hair to lend it a vibrant reddish tone, much admired by Berber women.

2½ hours) and Meknès (Dr70, five hours). At noon a bus leaves for Ouezzane (Dr39, five hours) via Tetouan (Dr16, one hour) and Chefchaouen (Dr33, 3½ hours). Departures for Nador (Dr175, 10 hours) are at 9 pm and for Oujda (Dr175, 12½ hours) at 7 pm.

Bus – Other Companies Cheaper bus companies operate from the main bus station. Very regular departures leave for the destinations mentioned above, along with services to Fnideq (Dr19), a small town 3km from the Ceuta border, Al-Hoceima (Dr80) and local destinations.

The main bus station can be busy, but pretty hassle-free. The left-luggage facility is open from 5 am to midnight and charges Dr4 per item for 24 hours. Take a petit taxi for Dr10.

Train There is now only one train station operating in Tangier – Tangier Morora – about 5km south-east of town (the Tangier Gare train station in the centre of town is no longer used). It's a quiet and peaceful little place, but keep your guard on the train itself (see Dangers & Annoyances earlier). A petit taxi from the town centre should cost around Dr10 (if the driver uses the meter).

Four trains depart daily from Tangier Morora train station. The 7.15 am and 4.30 pm services go as far as Casa-Voyageurs in Casablanca; the 10.30 am only goes as far as Sidi Kacem (where you can get connections as far as Marrakesh or east to Oujda via Meknès and Fès); whereas the 10.30 pm *ordinaire* service (with couchettes) goes as far as Marrakesh. Some 2nd-class fares include Rabat (Dr87, five hours), Casa-Voyageurs in Casablanca (Dr74, six hours), Meknès (Dr77, four hours), Fès (Dr93, five hours), Taza (Dr128, seven hours) and Oujda (Dr197, 11 hours).

The ordinaire service to Marrakesh takes about 10 hours and costs Dr193/274 in 2nd/1st class with a couchette, Dr143/214 without. If you're shooting straight through Tangier, the same service up from Marrakesh on the overnight train arrives in Tangier early enough (6 am) to avoid some of the hassles associated with catching the ferry to Spain,

though you may need to buy your ticket in the ferry terminal itself (not always easy at weekends) or in advance from a travel agent.

Grand Taxi Grand taxis leave from a lot next to the main bus station. The main destinations are Tetouan (Dr20), Asilah (Dr20), Larache (Dr30), Fnideq (Dr25) and the Ceuta border (Dr28).

Car The following are among the car rental agencies in Tangier:

Avis (☎ 933031) 54 Blvd Pasteur
Budget (☎ 948060) 7 Rue du Prince Moulay Abdallah
Cady Loc (☎ 322207) 3 Rue Allal ben Abdellah
Europcar (☎ 941938) 87 Blvd Mohammed V
Hertz (☎ 332210) 36 Blvd Mohammed V

If your French is up to it, you can get information on the current state of the roads (important in winter when roads east towards Tetouan and Chefchaouen are often closed) from the Services des Travaux Publiques on ☎ 711717.

There is reasonably secure parking next to the Hôtel Dawliz for guests and non-guests. It costs Dr2 per hour, Dr12 per day, Dr15 per night and Dr22 for 24 hours.

Boat If you're heading to Spain or Gibraltar by boat you can buy tickets from the company ticket booths below the ferry terminal, in the ferry terminal building (though this is unreliable, especially on weekends), or from virtually any travel agency around town.

There are ferries to Algeciras, Málaga and Cadiz (Spain), Gibraltar and Sète (France). Occasionally there are also ferries to Tarifa in Spain. For more details see under Sea in the Getting There & Away chapter.

There are several money changing booths in the port area, but no ATMs.

Getting Around
To/From the Airport The tiny Boukhalef airport is 15km south-east of town. Take a cream-coloured grand taxi to/from Tangier (about Dr70) or Asilah (Dr130).

There's no direct bus service but the main road between Asilah and Tangier passes the airport and it's a 1km walk from the turn-off (not recommended for arrivals!).

Bus There's no local bus station and very few local buses. The best place to catch them is in front of the Mohammed V mosque at Place de Koweit.

Petit Taxi Petit taxis are an ultra-marine colour with a yellow stripe down the side. The metered price for a standard journey around town is about Dr6. Fares go up by 50% after 8 pm.

AROUND TANGIER
Cap Spartel

Just 14km west of Tangier lies Cap Spartel, the north-western extremity of Africa's Atlantic coast, marked by a lighthouse and fish restaurant. It's a dramatic drive from Tangier.

If you're keen on **birds** the area around Cap Spartel is a great place for watching flocks of birds migrating to Europe in late March to early April, or returning to Africa from Europe in October. The most impressive of the migrants are the large raptors such as the black kites and booted eagles, but white storks also make the trip along with more than 200 other species.

Below Cap Spartel, the beach Plage Robinson stretches off to the south. The **Grottes d'Hercule** (about 100m from Hôtel Robinson) are 4km away. Since the 1920s these have been quarried for millstones, worked by prostitutes and used as a venue for private parties by rich celebrities from Tangier. There is usually a small entry fee (Dr10) for entering the chambers, but there's a good view overlooking the Atlantic from one of the windows. The caves have long been something of a tourist attraction and there are several rather overpriced cafes around the entrance to the grotto.

About 1km inland on a rough farm track are the remains of a tiny Roman settlement, **Cotta**. Like the more important town of Lixus further south, it was a centre for producing *garum* – a kind of fish-paste delicacy much prized by the Romans. Walk about 200m down the road (which continues 7km south-east to the main Tangier-Rabat high-

way) past the camp site on the left and you'll find a track with a barrier. Ignore the latter and proceed down the track – the scattered ruins are about 800m in front of you.

Places to Stay & Eat You can stay at *Hôtel Robinson* (☎ 372345, cell ☎ 01-377920) near the caves or *Camping Robinson*. The former is pleasant enough, but pricey, with rooms with bathroom for Dr332 in low season and quite a bit more in high season. The camp site is a bit spartan, but OK, and costs Dr15 per person, Dr20 per tent and per car, and Dr10 for electricity. Guests can use the hotel showers for Dr10. Simple meals are available. Fishing tackle can be hired from the shop in Hôtel Robinson, and both golf and riding excursions can be organised to nearby clubs.

Restaurant Mirage (☎ 333332) by the grotto is rather overpriced and charges around Dr90 for fish dishes, but there are good views across the sea from the restaurant's terrace. Alcohol is very expensive and so are the rooms here (Dr1800 per double), though it's one of the best hotels in the region.

Getting There & Away If you have your own transport, from Tangier take Rue de Belgique, cross Place de Koweit and head west for La Montagne, an exclusive suburb of royal palaces and villas. The road beyond here to Cap Spartel is heavily wooded.

By public transport, the cheapest option is to take a bus from outside the Mohammed V mosque, though the service was uncertain at the time of writing and appears to only run on Sunday during high season.

The alternative is to take a grand taxi for about Dr7 a seat or charter a grand taxi (around Dr150) for the round trip. Try the rank in front of St Andrew's Church.

Cap Malabata & Ksar es-Seghir

The bay east of Tangier has recently seen the development of new tourist complexes, including a Club Med and what has been heralded as Africa's biggest casino. The beaches are excellent and a much better choice than those of Tangier. It's a good place to spend an afternoon, and there are some decent cafes and restaurants around if you fancy a bite of lunch.

At Cap Malabata, a curious Gothic folly, Chateau Malabata and the lighthouse are the main features. There are wonderful views of Tangier and the strait. Bus No 15 comes here from the Grand Socco in Tangier.

Ksar es-Seghir, 37km east of Tangier, is a small fishing port still largely surrounded by high Portuguese walls and dominated by the remains of a castle. It's a picturesque place and its good, unspoilt beaches attract locals in the summer. The town makes a very pleasant day trip from Tangier. The No 15 bus also runs past here.

Road to Ceuta

If you have your own transport, the drive south from Ksar es-Seghir along the wild and hilly 'coast' road to Fnideq and Ceuta is an attractive alternative route if you are thinking of heading to Tetouan and Chefchaouen from Tangier, although it will add a couple of hours to the trip.

The road climbs up to **Jebel Musa**. Like Cap Spartel to the west, in spring or autumn this is a great place to watch migrating birds. These birds use the thermal currents that rise up from the Jebel Musa and Gibraltar peaks to reach a good height before crossing the strait between Africa and Europe.

CEUTA (SEBTA)
☎ 956 • pop 70,000

Jutting out east into the Mediterranean, the 19 sq km peninsula that is Ceuta has been a Spanish enclave since 1640. One-third of the population may be 'Spanish Muslims', but there's no question that Ceuta is a small corner of Mediterranean Europe in Africa. The place has an Andalusian feel to it and remains, officially, part of that Spanish province. The pleasant, relaxed and well-kept city centre is home to numerous busy cafes and bars and you can also buy beer in

MEDITERRANEAN COAST & THE RIF

Spanish Morocco

For hundreds of years Spain has controlled the two North African enclaves of Ceuta and Melilla. It has also controlled five islets that have served as military bases and prisons: the three Jaafariya Islands off Ras el-Mar (also known as Cap de l'Eau), about 25km west of Saidia; the Peñon de Alhucemas, just off the coast near Al-Hoceima; and the Peñon de Velez de la Gomera, some 50km west of the same town.

Moroccan independence in 1956 brought no change, as Spain claims a historical right to the enclave that was first ruled as part of Andalusia by the Umayyads (Moorish occupiers of Spain) in AD 931. The subsequent Christian reconquest does not, apparently, dilute these claims. Curiously, Spain does not recognise any such historical British right to control Gibraltar, which was seized in 1704, and drawing parallels between the two does not amuse the locals. Morocco has made several half-hearted attempts to have the enclaves returned, however, but Rabat is not keen to rock the boat as Spain is an increasingly important trading partner.

By the end of 1993 a process of granting Spain's regions a large degree of political autonomy was complete, except in the enclaves, which were still waiting to have their statutes approved.

In March 1995 a change to Spanish *Ley Organica* (Constitutional Law) gave Melilla limited self-government without legislative powers.

Moroccans fear that complete autonomy would mean Rabat could no longer negotiate the enclaves' future with Madrid, but would have to talk directly to the enclaves' political leaders, who will have no interest in restoring Moroccan rule.

Indeed, many of the enclaves' Muslim inhabitants, mostly of Rif Berber origin, would themselves regard such a transfer with mixed feelings.

Because of its distance from Ceuta, Melilla has been included in the East Coast section later in this chapter. Entering either of the enclaves can be a bit of a culture shock, and some Spanish is just about essential.

McDonald's, but the presence of so many Muslims (often treated as 2nd-class citizens) gives Ceuta a very different feel.

Ostensibly the peninsula is devoted to the military (almost half of it is owned by the army), duty-free shopping and a lot of very shady cross-border commerce. Although Spanish citizens get huge tax breaks for residing in Ceuta (and Melilla), the enclave's uncertain – economic rather than political – future has led some to migrate to the Spanish mainland. It remains to be seen how the EU Free Trade agreement will affect Ceuta's economic viability once the profit in smuggled goods disappears, but considerable amounts of money are still being invested in the place, not least by Spanish shipping lines that now use fast catamarans almost exclusively on routes to the mainland.

Much maligned by guidebooks, and long used merely as a port of entry for Morocco, Ceuta does in fact have a few things to offer and is keen to detain many of the travellers planning to just pass through. And this it can do successfully for a couple of days, especially for those with travel-fatigue or Morocco-bound vehicle owners who can take advantage of the duty-free status and stock up with booze and fuel. However, Ceuta is certainly not a cheap town by Moroccan standards, so some travellers may still prefer to catch an early ferry from Algeciras in Spain and push straight on from Ceuta to Tetouan or Chefchaouen in the same day.

Don't forget that Ceuta (and Melilla) keep Spanish not Moroccan time, which is two hours ahead of Morocco in summer and one hour ahead at other times.

History

Ceuta's Arabic name, Sebta, stems from the Latin Septem. Two heroes of Greek mythology, Hercules and Ulysses, are both supposed to have passed through here, but more certainly it served as one of the Roman Empire's coastal bases.

The city later passed into the control of the Byzantine Empire and, in AD 931, was taken by the Arab Umayyad rulers of Muslim Spain. In 1083 it fell to the Almoravids and remained under direct Moroccan control

until 1309, when James II of Aragon took it. In 1415 Portugal grabbed Ceuta and, when Portugal and Spain united under one crown in 1580, it passed by default to Spain.

When the two countries split in 1640, Ceuta remained Spanish, as it has ever since.

Orientation

Most of the hotels, restaurants and offices of interest are gathered around the narrow spit of land linking the peninsula to the mainland. The port and ferry terminal are a short walk to the west.

Information

Tourist Offices There's just one tourist office (☎ 956 501401), close to the end of Ave Muelle Cañonero Dato, beside the fishing dock. It's open 8 am to 7 pm on weekdays and 9 am to 2 pm Saturday. A brochure, good map and an accommodation list are available, and there's a public phone outside.

Money There are plenty of banks along the main street, Paseo de Revellín, and its continuation, Calle Camoens. It's sometimes possible to buy Moroccan dirham (hotels are good places to try), but there's no real need as you can easily change cash at the border where you'll get a better rate of exchange.

Most banks are open from 8.15 am to 2.30 pm, while some open on Friday from 5 to 7.30 pm. Outside business hours you can change money at many travel agents and the more expensive hotels. The ATMs of most Spanish banks support a bewildering number of debit- and credit-card systems including Visa, Plus, Electron, MasterCard, Cirrus, Maestro, Eurocheque and Servired.

Most banks in Ceuta also charge about 1% commission on travellers cheques, with a minimum of 650 ptas per transaction.

At the border you'll find a few informal moneychangers on both sides (these guys are only useful if you've some leftover dirham/pesetas) and branches of the BMCE and Banque Populaire (which change cash only) on the Moroccan side.

Post & Communications You won't miss the Correos y Telégrafos (main post

CEUTA (SEBTA)

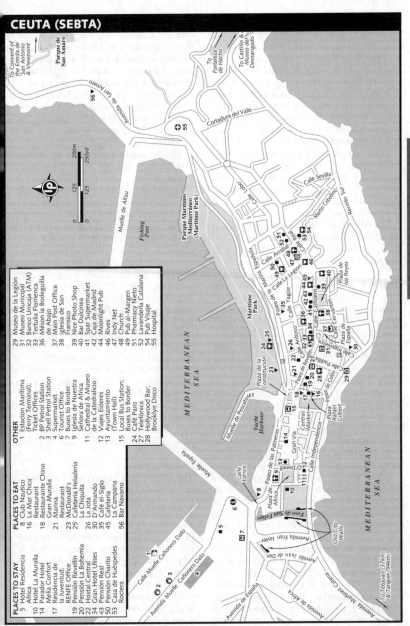

MEDITERRANEAN COAST & THE RIF

PLACES TO STAY
5 Hotel Residencia
   Africa
10 Hotel La Muralla
14 Parador Hotel
17 Melia Confort
   Residencia de
   la Juventud;
   RENFE Office
19 Pensión Revellin
20 Pensión La Bohemia
22 Hostal Central
34 Gran Hotel Ulises
43 Pensión Real
50 Pensión Charito
53 Casa de Huéspedes
   Rociera

PLACES TO EAT
8 Club Nautico
16 La Mar Chica
   Restaurant
18 Restaurante Chino
   Gran Muralla
21 Marina
   Restaurant
23 McDonald's
25 Cafetería Heladería
   La Chiquita
26 La Jota
30 D'Armando
35 Café el-Siglo
45 Cafetería
   La Campana
56 Bar Navarro

OTHER
1 Estación Marítima
   (Ferry Terminal);
   Ticket Offices
2 BP Petrol Station
3 Shell Petrol Station
4 Supermarket
6 Tourist Office
7 Buses to Border
9 Iglesia de Nuestra
   Señora de Africa
11 Cathedral & Museo
   de la Catedralicio
12 Viajes Eideres
13 Ayuntamiento
   (Town Hall)
15 Local Bus Station;
   Buses to Border
24 Café París
27 Telefónica
28 Hollywood Bar;
   Brooklyn Disco

29 Museo de la Legión
31 Museo Municipal
32 Banco Unicaja (ATM)
33 Tertulia Flamenca
36 Mesón la Bodeguilla
   de Abajo
37 Main Post Office
38 Iglesia de San
   Fransico
39 Nice Photo Shop
40 Bar Dulcinea
41 Spar Supermarket
42 Caja de Madrid
44 Moonlight Pub
46 Rives
47 Indy Net
48 Church
49 Pub al-Margen
51 Pharmacy Nieto
52 Lavandería Catalana
54 Pub Visaje
55 Hospital

office) – it's the big yellow building on Plaza de España, a square just off Calle Camoens, in the centre of town. For letters it's open from 8 am to 8 pm weekdays with some limited services available 9.30 am to 2 pm on Saturday. Spanish public servants take the siesta seriously, so it may be hard to get anyone's attention from 2 to 4 pm.

Like the rest of Spain, all telephone numbers, even if dialled from within Ceuta, must now be prefixed with the STD code ☎ 956.

There are plenty of both blue and green public phones around. They accept coins, phonecards (available in *tabacs* – tobacconist and newsagencies) and credit cards. Direct overseas dialling is possible and cheaper than in Morocco.

The only place offering Internet access is Indy Net Cafe at 6 Isabel Cabral, but at 700 ptas per hour it's three times the price of Moroccan Internet cafes.

Other Services If you desperately need some washing done head to Lavandería Catalana (☎ 956 519581), 41 Calle Real. However, it'll cost you a couple of thousand pesetas and take at least 24 hours.

Hospital de la Cruz Roja can be reached on ☎ 956 528400.

Duty Free Ceuta is a duty-free zone, although nothing seems extravagantly cheap. If you are heading to mainland Spain, duty of 10% to 14% may be slapped on items worth more than 6840 ptas. Going to Morocco, the main attraction is petrol. At the time of writing diesel cost 67 ptas a litre, super 88 ptas and unleaded 78 ptas.

If you want to stock up on goodies there are big supermarkets on Ave Muelle Cañonero Dato and a number of shops on Paseo de Revellín worth a browse. The petrol stations close to the port are open from 7 am to 11 pm.

Dangers & Annoyances Many people enter Morocco via Ceuta to avoid the touts who hang around in Tangier, but the Ceuta-Morocco border is not completely hustler-free – some travel all the way from Tetouan especially to meet the ferry disembarkations. Also watch out for suspiciously over-friendly

ferry passengers. However, Ceuta itself is a breeze compared to Tetouan (and decidedly more pleasant than Algeciras!), but certain Spanish citizens are not beyond reproach – women travellers can attract considerable attention from bored military conscripts.

The process of crossing between Ceuta and Morocco is often subject to long, bureaucratic delays. If you are driving, try to arrive at the frontier either early in the morning or late at night.

The Spaniards barely take any notice of you leaving, but are more meticulous if you're arriving.

On the Moroccan side, you must collect, fill in and re-present a yellow card at the passport window and, if you have a car, a green one at the vehicle registration window (beware of touts who try to sell you these free cards). If you have hired a car in Morocco, you will be required to show proof of authorisation to take the vehicle out of the country.

If there's more than one of you travelling, you can save a lot of time by sending one person (preferably female!) ahead to collect the forms while the other queues. A smile, good humour and, even better, a greeting in Arabic at the window and at the barriers, will speed things up miraculously.

Car crime is also an issue in Ceuta. Take all valuables out of your car and use a secure car park. Parking around town is restricted to a maximum of two hours (110 ptas), use the kerb-side machines, but the underground car park next to the maritime park charges 125 ptas for one hour and 1100 ptas for 12 hours.

Museums

The **Museo de la Legión** at the southern end of Paseo de Colón is perhaps the most intriguing of the few museums in Ceuta. It's dedicated to and run by the Spanish Legion, an army unit set up in 1920 that played a pivotal role in Franco's republican army at the beginning of the Spanish Civil War. Most of the Legion's actions have been in North Africa; the Rif War of 1921–26 was the most disastrous campaign.

The museum is beautifully kept, (there's not a speck of dust in sight), and full of memorabilia of battles right up to the recent

Bosnia conflict. There's a large collection of medals, some uniforms, bloodstained flags and frightening weapons, but perhaps the most interesting and poignant are the old, informal photos.

The museum is open from 10 am to 1.30 pm weekdays, and from 10 am to 1.30 pm and 4 to 6 pm Saturday. Entry is free (but they like to see your passport or driving licence) and you get a guided tour.

The **Museo Municipal**, which contains a tiny room with local archaeological finds from Palaeolithic times on, is on the corner of Paseo del Revellín and Calle Ingenieros. It's open from 10 am to 1 pm and 5 to 8 pm (7 pm to 9 pm in high season) weekdays and 10 am to 2 pm Saturday.

The **Museo de la Catedralicio** in the cathedral (☎ 956 519659) has a small collection of ecclesiastical paraphernalia and paintings, but opens erratically. At the time of writing it was open from 11.30 am to 1 pm Tuesday, Friday (Martes and Viernes in Spanish) and public holidays.

The **Museo del Desnarigado** is a small military museum at the Castillo del Desnarigado on the south-eastern tip of the peninsula. It's open from 11 am to 2 pm and 4 to 6 pm on weekends and public holidays only.

Parque Marítimo del Mediterráneo

The Parque Marítimo del Mediterráneo (Maritime Park) is a huge new complex on the seafront, complete with manufactured beach, pools and waterfalls, bridges, sculptures and even a mock castle.

It was designed by the Catalonian architect, César Manrique, and was opened in May 1995. There is a casino in the park, several restaurants, a children's playground, cafes and bars, and changing rooms for the pools. It's an agreeable, though rather expensive, place to while away an afternoon.

Entry costs and opening hours vary wildly depending on the day and season of the year. In high season you're looking at around 800 ptas per adult and 350 ptas per child. At peak times the complex is open from 10 am to 8 pm and then 9 pm to 1 am. In low season it's likely only to be open

from 11 am to 8 pm. The swimming pools are open from May to September only.

The casino, plus many of the cafes and bars, have separate street entrances. If you're feeling lucky or like losing cash quickly, the casino is open from 1 pm to 5 am daily.

Peninsula

If you've three hours to spare, it's easy to walk around the peninsula (the hourly No 4 bus from Plaza Constitucíon goes part of the way), which is topped by Monte Hacho, said by some to be the southern Pillar of Hercules (Jebel Musa, west of Ceuta, is the other contender; Gibraltar is the northern pillar). From the **Convent of the Ermita de San Antonio** there is an excellent view towards Gibraltar.

The convent, originally built in the 17th century and reconstructed in the 1960s, is the venue for a large festival held annually on 13 June to mark St Anthony's day.

Monte Hacho is crowned by the **Fortaleza de Hacho**, a fort first built by the Byzantines and added to since by the Moroccans, Portuguese and Spanish.

Castillo del Desnarigado on the south-eastern end of the peninsula was built as a coastal battery in the 19th century, but there are remnants of earlier Spanish and Portuguese fortifications.

City Walls

The most impressive leftovers of the city walls (west of Plaza de Africa) and the navigable, walled moat of **Foso de San Felipe** date back to Almohad times, although they were largely reconstructed by the Spaniards at the end of the 17th century.

Places to Stay

Finding somewhere to stay in Ceuta can be a nightmare, especially if you're arriving late in the day from Morocco and haven't been able to reserve a room – to do so requires an international telephone call (and some Spanish). By 1 pm many of the best-value rooms have often been snapped up, but if you're having trouble finding one, pick up the accommodation list from the tourist office.

In mid-March, when the annual carnival is held, a decent room can be impossible to find.

Obviously, for those coming from Spain, booking a place at least a couple of days in advance is no problem.

The prices below are subject to 3% tax.

Places to Stay – Budget

Residencia de la Juventud (☎ 956 515148) is not an HI hostel and, at 3400/4000/ 5400 for singles/doubles/triples, is hardly cheap. It's nevertheless often full. Tucked away on Plaza Rafael Gilbert, it opens in the early morning and late afternoon (no precise time). Go up the stairs off Paseo de Revellín by the Restaurante Chino Gran Muralla. The hostel is on your right as you enter the square; ring the doorbell. Hot showers are included and there's a washing machine.

There is no shortage of inexpensive *fondas* (inns) and *pensiónes* or *casas de huéspedes* (guesthouses) some of which are identifiable by the large blue-and-white 'F' or 'CH' on the entrances, while others are very easily missed. No-one seems to go in for serious signage at the cheaper end of the market.

The cheapest of these is the small and friendly *Pensión Charito* (☎ 956 513982, 5 Calle Arrabal), on the 1st floor about a 15-minute walk along the waterfront from the ferry terminal. The only indication that it's a guesthouse is the 'Chambres' sign, and the 'CH' sign on the wall. Basic singles/doubles cost 1500/2000 ptas. There are no hot showers. Occasionally, travellers have found it closed without explanation.

Conveniently situated in the centre, *Pensión Revellín* (☎ 956 516762, 2 Paseo de Revellín) is on the 2nd floor of the building opposite the Banco Popular Español. The doorway is in the middle of the busy shopping street and, again, can be identified by the 'CH' sign. Rooms cost 1200/2200 ptas, and hot showers (300 ptas) are available in the morning. It's definitely seen better days, and is not amazingly friendly, but the rooms are clean.

Further east, a few doors down from the Caja de Madrid bank, *Pensión Real* (☎ 956 511449, 1 Calle Camoens) offers basic but clean rooms for 3000/4000 ptas in winter and 3500/4500 ptas in high season. Hot showers are included and there's a washing machine here.

Above the intersection of Calle Real and Calle Arrabal is *Casa de Huéspedes Rociera* (☎ 956 513559), another possibility. Rooms go for 2000/3000 ptas.

If you can afford a little more, one of the best deals in town is *Pensión La Bohemia* (☎ 956 510615, 16 Paseo de Revellín) on the 1st floor (look for the small sign in the shopping arcade). It charges 2000/4000 ptas for good rooms. They're fresh and clean and there are piping-hot showers (free) in a shared bathroom.

Places to Stay – Mid-Range

Conveniently located near the ferry terminal, but overpriced and unwelcoming, is *Hotel Residencia Africa* (☎ 956 509467, fax 956 507527, 9 Ave Muelle Cañonero Dato). In low season it has singles/doubles for 5500/8500 ptas, but in high season prices go up to 7000/10,500 ptas. Credit cards are accepted and they ask these prices with a straight face.

Gran Hotel Ulises (☎ 956 514540, fax 956 514546, 5 Calle Camoens) is slightly better value, but still pricey at 7200/9270 ptas in low season and 10,300/12,360 ptas in high season.

You're much better off getting a room at the two-star *Hostale Central* (☎ 956 516716, Paseo del Revellín). This new place has small rooms (some of which overlook the street) with bathroom, hot water on demand and TVs for 3600/6000 ptas. Prices increase by around 20% in high season.

Places to Stay – Top End

Just east of the square is *Hotel Meliá Confort* (☎ 956 511200, fax 956 511501, e melia .confort.ceuta@solmelia.es, 3 Calle Alcalde Sánchez Prados). Run by the Sol Meliá group, it's mainly a business hotel and has conference facilities, an indoor pool and the like. Basic singles/doubles start at 11,750/ 14,900 ptas. However, cheaper weekend and low-season deals may be available.

The premier establishment is the comfortable, but rather characterless, four-star *Parador Hotel La Muralla* (☎ 956 514940, fax 956 514947, 15 Plaza de Africa). Mostly a 1970s creation, some rooms are converted munitions stores of the Foso de San Pelipe, hence the status as part of the Parador chain of hotels. Rooms with bath and balcony in low season will set you back 12,000/15,200 ptas, and 15,000/16,500 ptas in high season. It has a restaurant, bar, parking and swimming pool.

Places to Eat

Restaurants There are a few cheap tapas and snack bars along Calle Real to the east of the centre. Closer to Plaza de la Constitución, on a side street connecting the Paseo de Revellín and Marina Española is *Marina Restaurant*. Raciones (main courses) start at around 700 ptas while the three-course *menú de la casa* (fixed-price menu) will set you back 1500 ptas. The Marina is a fairly popular local bar with a fine selection of tapas.

The restaurant *Club Nautico* (☎ 956 514440, Calle Edrisis) is a simple, but decent place above the sailing club and overlooking the fishing port. The *menú de la diá* (daily set menu) is 1300 ptas, but some of the luscious fish dishes will set you back this much on their own. There are a couple of vegetarian options and a decent wine list.

Also recommended for good, slightly cheaper, fresh fish is *Bar Navarro* out on Ave de San Amaro, past the fishing port.

Restaurante Chino Gran Muralla (☎ 956 517602, 4 Plaza de la Constitución) is the cheaper option of Ceuta's two Chinese restaurants. Fixed menus start at 950 ptas, rising to 3200 ptas for three people. Mains start at 585 ptas.

Close to the Museo de la Legión is *D'Armando* (☎ 956 514749, 25 Paseo Colón), a reasonable Italian restaurant and a local favourite for pizza (from 500 ptas), salads, meat and pasta dishes (from around 850 ptas). If you arrive much after 9.30 pm, you'll probably have to queue to get in.

More low-budget is *La Mar Chica* (Plaza Rafael Gilbert). A cheap, local bar first and foremost, it does some reasonable lunchtime paella and fish dishes for 600 ptas.

Cafes The *Cafetería La Campana* (15 Calle Camoens) is probably the best place in town for breakfast (around 350 ptas for coffee, a

juice and *tostada* or toast). It also does reasonably priced cakes, pastries, snacks and tapas and a 975 ptas menú de la diá, which is rather good. It's a very popular place with the local office workers and is open all day. The *La Campana cafe* (Paseo del Revellín), down from Hostal Central, is also good.

Coming third in the breakfast stakes is *La Jota* on the corner of Calle Mendez Nuñez and Calle Antioco. It also has a good selection of tapas and ice cream and is open from 8 to 1 am daily.

The new *Cafetería Heladería La Chiquita* at the edge of the maritime park, serves up good ice cream and delicious waffles on a pleasant terrace by the pool. It also does snacks such as hot dogs and hamburgers – if you're craving fast food – though prices are quite high.

There are also a number of sophisticated *cafes* (and bars) just off Millán Astray, on the road that leads down the hill to the left behind the Spar supermarket.

Entertainment

Bars & Pubs There's no shortage of bars and pubs in Ceuta, and many are a far cry from the male-dominated drinking establishments of Morocco. At a normal bar/cafe a *caña* (small glass) of beer, costs around 250 ptas. However, be advised that negotiating the Morocco-Ceuta border with a stinking hangover is not a pleasant experience.

Bar Dulcinea (Calle Sargento Coriat) is popular with an older and quite sophisticated crowd. Not far away on Millán Astray, *Mesón la Bodeguilla de Abajo* attracts a good crowd, though it's only about 20 stools long and four stools deep – it also has some good tapas.

Heading (or rolling) down the hill is *Cafe el-Siglo*, which is an excellent place for coffee or brandy (or both) at almost any time of the day or night.

Café Paris at the edge of the maritime park is a trendy and rather expensive, place for a drink. It gets busy after midnight, especially on weekends, and a bottle of beer is 400 ptas, a cola 300 ptas. It's open from 4 pm to 4 am daily (6 am on weekends). An entry charge of 800 ptas sometimes applies after midnight.

MEDITERRANEAN COAST & THE RIF

A more alternative crowd can be found at the small *Pub al-Margen (Calle Fernández Mendoza)*, where the beer's cheaper and gin and tonics (500 ptas) generous.

If you're into Spanish dancing, try *Tertulia Flamenca (3 Plaza Teniente Ruiz)* below the guesthouse Casa de Huéspedes Tiuna. It's a flamenco club with a lively bar and there's usually dancing every Friday and Saturday. However, it's for members only, so some diplomacy is required to gain entry here.

Nightclubs If you're after a late night, the disco *Rives* is Ceuta's most fashionable. It starts up around midnight and keeps going 'for as long as you can'. Entry costs around 800 ptas and drinks are not much less. You'll find it off Calle Real, down some steps to the right.

Moonlight Pub (Calle Camoens) has a kind of beer garden-cum-disco out the back. Other places you might try include *Hollywood Bar* and *Brooklyn Disco* on Calle Padilla, or *Pub Visaje*, which has a disco next door at Martin Cebollino.

Getting There & Away

Morocco Bus No 7 runs up to the border every 10 minutes from Plaza de la Constitución (75 ptas, 20 minutes). Look for the 'Frontera del Tarajal' sign on the front of the bus. If you arrive by ferry and want to head straight for the border, there's a bus stop near Calle Edrisis, up past the tourist office and opposite the ramparts.

On the Moroccan side of the border, there's often a separate channel for foreign passport holders. Further on, just beyond the banks, is the place to hang out for a grand taxi to Tetouan or Tangier. However, taxis to Fnideq, a small town 3km south of the border are more regular. From this small town there are plenty of grand taxis and buses to Chefchaouen, Tetouan and Tangier. You may be pressured into hiring the whole taxi all the way to Chefchaouen. If you're in a group this is a good option, but you'll have to bargain hard (aim for around Dr250) and watch out for dicey-looking characters quoting suspiciously reasonable

fares (such as Chefchaouen, via the carpet shops and kif dens of Tetouan for Dr200).

Coming the other way, it's important to remember that many bus services advertised as heading to Ceuta actually terminate in Fnideq, leaving you an extra grand taxi ride to the *frontera* (border). It's therefore easier to take a grand taxi to Ceuta the whole way from Tetouan. A seat should cost you around Dr15, but incoming travellers are often asked for more.

Mainland Spain The *estación marítima* (ferry terminal) is west of the town centre on Calle Muelle Cañonero Dato, and there are frequent fast ferry (hydrofoils mostly) and regular ferry departures to Algeciras, plus a twice daily fast ferry to Málaga. However, the flash way to leave the African mainland is to use the regular helicopter service between Ceuta and Málaga airport! See Spain under Air in the Getting There & Away chapter for details.

You can purchase train tickets to European destinations at the RENFE office on Plaza Rafael Gilbert, or at one of the travel agencies dotted about town – Viajes Eideres (☎ 956 524656, ⓔ eideres@teleline.es), on Plaza de Africa, can be recommended. Some agencies, including many in the ferry terminal, also sell Eurocoach (Málaga departures mostly) and Enatcar (the main Spanish coach company) bus tickets.

There's about one bus an hour between the ferry terminal and the centre of town (about 800m), but there are usually a few taxis outside the terminal.

The Rif Mountains

TETOUAN
☎ 09

Taken over in 1912 as a Spanish protectorate, and for more than 40 years the capital of the protectorate, Tetouan is unique for its mixed Hispano-Moroccan look and feel.

The medina, a conglomeration of cheerfully whitewashed and tiled houses, shops and religious buildings set against the brooding Rif Mountains, shows off its Andalusian heritage. The Spaniards added the new part of town where even now you can buy a *bocadillo* (sandwich) and more people speak Spanish than any other foreign language.

Unfortunately, for both travellers and Tetouan's shopkeepers, the town is quite a painful introduction to Morocco (most visitors come from Ceuta). Although not as bad as it once was, Tetouan is an active hive of touts, *faux* (unofficial) guides, pickpockets and hustlers. The bus station seems to be the main focus for devious activity and can be a thoroughly unpleasant place. There have also been reports of a serious drug problem in the town, and wandering around the medina at night is a definite no-no – you can stumble across some decidedly inhospitable individuals.

Many visitors simply stop here to change buses and push on, which is a shame, because the medina is a fascinating Unesco World Heritage site, there are some good museums, and even the modern part of the city contains some wonderful examples of Spanish colonial architecture and, although neglected, is worth a quick look.

History

Tetouan's ancient predecessor was Tamuda, a Mauretanian city founded in the 3rd century BC. Destroyed in the 1st century AD after a local revolt, the Romans built a fortified camp in its place, the unremarkable remnants of which are visible about 5km from the modern town.

In the 14th century the Merenids created the town of Tetouan as a base from which to control rebellious Rif tribes, but the city was destroyed by Henry III of Castille in 1399.

Reoccupied in the 15th and 16th centuries by Muslim and Jewish refugees from Granada, who were led initially by Sidi Ali al-Mandari, Tetouan prospered. Part of that prosperity was due to the skills new arrivals brought with them, but in part it was due to piracy, to which the Spanish put an end by blockading Tetouan's port at Martil. They succeeded in stopping the piracy, but legitimate trade suffered too.

Moulay Ismail built Tetouan's defensive walls in the 17th century, and the town's trade links with Spain improved and developed on and off until 1859, when Spanish forces occupied it for three years during a punitive campaign against Rif tribes aimed, it was said, at protecting Ceuta.

In 1913 the Spanish made it the capital of their protectorate, which they only abandoned in 1956 when Morocco regained independence.

Orientation

The medina makes up about two-thirds of the city centre. The ville nouvelle is where you'll find the hotels, banks, most of the restaurants and cafes, bus station and taxi stands. From a compact centre the town sprawls into the surrounding valleys and hillsides.

Many streets, called 'calles', still advertise the town's Spanish heritage, but this is changing as, alongside Arabic, French takes over as Morocco's semi-official second language.

Information

Tourist Office The Délégation Régionale du Tourisme (☎ 961916) is at 30 Calle Mohammed V, near the corner of Rue Youssef ben Tachfine. The staff are helpful, try hard and can arrange guides for the medina.

The office is open from 8.30 am to noon and 2.30 to 6.30 pm Monday to Thursday. On Friday, it's open from 8.30 am to 11.30 am and 3 to 6.30 pm.

Money There are plenty of banks along Calle Mohammed V. BMCE has a branch with a separate *bureau de change* (foreign exchange bureau) on Place Moulay el-Mehdi, open 8 am to 8 pm weekdays and 10 am to 2 pm and 6 to 8 pm weekends.

Post & Communications The post office is on Place Moulay el-Mehdi, and is open from 8.30 am to noon and 2.30 to 6.30 pm weekdays, and from 8.30 to 11 am Saturday.

There are several Internet cafes in the ville nouvelle. Most charge Dr10 per hour. Good ones that are open daily are Cyber Primo next to the BMCE on Place Moulay el-Mehdi and World Vision at 8 Salah Eddine al-Ayoubi.

TETOUAN

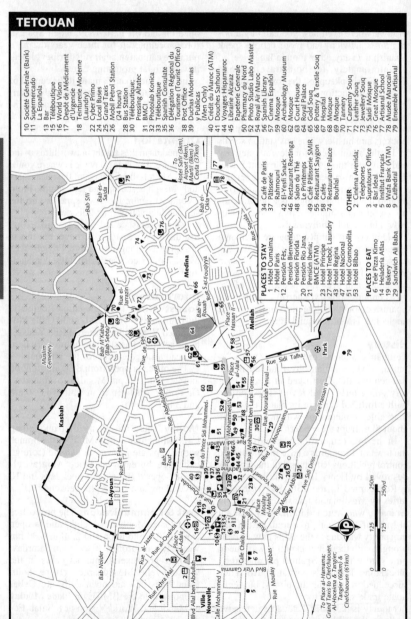

10 Société Générale (Bank)
11 Supermercado
   La Española
13 Bar
15 Téléboutique
16 World Vision
17 Depôt de Médicament
   d'Urgencie
18 Teinturerie Moderne
   (Laundry)
22 Cyber Primo
24 Local Buses
25 Grand Taxis
26 Mobil Petrol Station
   (24 hours)
28 Bus Station
30 Téléboutique;
   Pressing Aliatec
31 BMCE
32 Photolab Konica
33 Téléboutique
35 Spanish Consulate
36 Délégation Regional du
   Tourisme (Tourist Office)
38 Post Office
39 Duchas Modernas
   y Publicas
   (Men Only)
40 Crédit du Maroc (ATM)
41 Douches Sarhoun
44 Voyages Hispamaroc
45 Librairie Alcaraz
50 Papeterie Generale
51 Pharmacy du Nord
52 Photo Studio Labo Master
53 Banque Populaire du Maroc
54 Spanish Library
57 Cinema Español
59 Mosque
60 Archaeology Museum
62 Mosque
63 Court House
64 Royal Palace
65 Gold Souq
66 Pottery & Textile Souq
67 Hospital
68 Mosque
69 Mosque
70 Tannery
71 Carpentry Souq
72 Leather Souq
73 Jewellery Souq
75 Saïdi Mosque
76 Great Mosque
77 Artisanal School
78 Musée Marocain
79 Ensemble Artisanal

PLACES TO STAY
1 Hôtel Oumaima
7 Hôtel Paris
12 Pension Fès;
   Pension Bienvenida;
   Pension Florida
20 Pension Rio Jana
21 Pension Iberia;
   BMCE (ATM)
23 Hotel Principe
27 Hotel Trebol; Laundry
43 Hotel Nacional
47 Hotel Regina
51 Hotel Cosmopolita
51 Hotel Bilbao

PLACES TO EAT
6 Tele Pizza Kimo
14 Heladería Atlas
19 Bakery
29 Sandwich Ali Baba

34 Café de Paris
37 Pâtisserie
   Rahmouni
42 El-Yesfi Snack
46 Restaurant Restinga
48 Salon du Thé
   Le Printemps
49 Café Pâtisserie SMIR
55 Restaurant Saygon
58 Cafés
74 Restaurant Palace
   Bouhlal

OTHER
2 Cinema Avenida;
   Telephones
3 Supratours Office
4 Bar Ideal
5 Institut Français
8 Wafa Bank (ATM)
9 Cathedral

Beware the Man on a Camel

Dream interpretation in Morocco forms an important part of life.

The snake in dreams is considered a herald of good fortune. A man on a camel augurs imminent death; a man on a mule, riches. To dream of a thief means good fortune and safety.

But dreams of corn, of grapes or of beans are omens of disaster.

MICK WELDON

Travel Agencies RAM (☎ 961577) is on Place al-Jala, while Voyages Hispamaroc (☎ 964224, fax 963821), a fairly switched-on travel agency, is on Calle Mohammed V.

Bookshops Librairie Alcaraz Papeterie Generale on Calle Mohammed V has a reasonable range of Moroccan history books in French.

Film & Photography The Photo Studio Labo Master on Calle Mohammed V is probably the best place to buy film and have it developed. The Photolab Konica on Rue Youssef ben Tachfine is another good one.

Laundry Pressing Altatec is at the back of a téléboutique on Rue Mourakah Anual.

Medical Services & Emergencies The night pharmacy, Dépôt de Médicament d'Urgencie (☎ 965902), 7 Ave al-Wamda, is open from 9 pm to 9 am. The police can be called on ☎ 19.

Parking The car park close to Bab Tout charges Dr8 for 12 hours, Dr4 for 4 hours.

Medina & Around

Place Hassan II Surrounded by three mosques and four modern minarets, Place Hassan II links the medina to the ville nouvelle. This is the heart of the town and the place has traditionally served as the city's meeting place – there are a couple of cafes that are good for relaxing and people-watching. Heading west, Calle Mohammed V is a pedestrian zone right up to Place Moulay el-Mehdi, and is lined with shops, cafes, restaurants and the odd hotel.

The main entrance into the medina is Bab er-Rouah (Gate of the Winds), to the right of the former Spanish consulate. The medina is an industrious, bustling place, and you'll see much just by wandering around. It's quite unlike the great medinas further south, as the Spaniards had a hand in some of the building in the 19th century. In any case, most of its inhabitants from the 16th century on were refugees from what had been Muslim Spain.

There are some 20 mosques within the medina, of which the Great and Saidi Mosques stand out. As is usual in Morocco, non-Muslims are not allowed to enter.

The north-eastern area of the medina, north of Bab el-Okla, was the upmarket end of town. Some of the fine houses built by the city's residents in the last century still stand here and several have been turned into carpet showrooms and extravagant tea-rooms. You'll probably stumble across them yourself, but there are plenty of touts around who will gladly escort you, particularly to the carpet shops.

Although the shopkeepers don't do a roaring tourist trade here, wood and leatherwork are two local artisanal specialities – there's still a tannery up by Bab M'Kabar (Bab Sebta). You'll also come across other shops dedicated to the tourist trade, selling copper and brassware, *babouches* (traditional leather slippers) and a limited selection of souvenirs. If you're interested in Tetouan carpets, go first to the Artisanal school (see following) just east of Bab el-Okla to get an idea of what to look for.

Musée Marocain Also known as the Musée Ethnographique, this place has an interesting collection of traditional clothing, musical instruments, jewellery, carpets, arms and household implements. The museum is built in a bastion in the town wall and cannons are still in place in the garden.

Look out for the Jewish wedding robes beautifully embroidered with gold thread, and the very elaborate iron door knockers and key hole covers. Captions are in French and Arabic. Ask the guardian if you can get onto the terrace where there are good views of the Rif Mountains.

The museum is open from 8 am to noon and 3 to 5 pm daily (closed Tuesday). The entry fee is Dr10. It's easy to find, walk through Bab el-Okla to inside the medina, turn immediately left, and you reach the entrance after 200m.

Artisanal School Opposite Bab el-Okla is the artisanal school, where children are taught traditional art and crafts. Girls learn carpet-weaving and boys are taught the intricate art of plaster-carving, brasswork and the making of enamel zellij (ask to be taken to the main ceramic section close to Bab es-Saida).

The school has around 40 pupils; the youngest are 10 years old. After seven or eight years under a master craftsman, the students will sit the diploma in their chosen craft and eventually, if they are successful, open their own studio.

The 14 or so studios around the courtyard offer an excellent and fascinating opportunity to see Moroccan artisans at work, and to appreciate the intensity of labour and high skill still required for many of these ancient professions.

The pupils' work is on display (but not for sale) in a palatial exhibition room – which is worth a visit in itself. The school is open from 8 am to noon and 2.30 to 5.30 pm weekdays. Entry is Dr10.

Archaeology Museum The small archaeology museum just off Place al-Jala is well worth a visit. In the entrance hall you're greeted by a striking mosaic of the Three Graces from the Roman ruins of Lixus. A room on the ground floor houses more artefacts from Lixus, including a good collection of Roman coins, some bronze statuettes and two mosaics depicting Venus and Adonis, and Venus being discovered asleep by Mars.

There's a wonderful, peaceful garden filled with old Iberian and Jewish gravestones, more mosaics and some 16th century Arab stone tablets found in the Andalusian cemetery in Tetouan.

It's open from 8.30 am to noon and 2.30 to 6.30 pm Monday to Thursday. On Friday it's open from 8.30 to 11.30 am and 3.30 to 6.30 pm (closed weekends). Entry costs Dr10.

Ensemble Artisanal On Ave Hassan II, south of the town walls, you'll find the large government-sponsored emporium of Moroccan arts and crafts. It's not a bad place to get an idea of the upper range of prices of Moroccan crafts without the pressure of souq sales tactics. It's open from 9 am to 12.30 pm and 3.30 to 6.30 pm weekdays.

Hammams & Public Showers

The public shower Douches Modernas y Publicas on Rue Youssef ben Tachfine (opposite El-Yesfi Snack) is for men only. On the same street at No 3 is the Douches Sarhoun, open to both men and women (upstairs). All these places cost around Dr5.

Places to Stay – Budget

Camping The nearest camp site is by the beach at Martil, about 8km north-east of town (see Around Tetouan following). There's also a site to the north, not far from Club Med, about halfway between Tetouan and the Ceuta border.

Hotels There are plenty of cheap, very basic pensions available in Tetouan, most of which charge from Dr50 for a single. Standards vary considerably, so have a good look around.

Some of the pensions could be straight out of Spain, with their wrought-iron balconies overlooking the street. Others are flophouses or straight-out brothels. The *Pensión Fès*, *Pensión Bienvenida*, *Pensión Florida* and *Pensión Rio Jana* all fall into the latter two categories.

Hôtel Cosmopolita (☎ 964821, *3 Rue du Prince Sidi Mohammed*) is good value. It's very clean and tidy with nice furniture and good balconies. Singles/doubles/triples go for Dr35/70/105. A hot shower costs Dr7.

Also excellent value is *Pensión Iberia* (☎ 963679, *5 Place Moulay el-Mehdi*) above the BMCE. There are only a few rooms and it has a homey atmosphere. Room Nos 10, 11 and 12 have great views over the square, but the terrace is just as good if you're not in luck. Spotless rooms with shared bathroom cost Dr40/70. Hot showers are an extra Dr5.

Hotel Bilbao (☎ 964114, *7 Calle Mohammed V*) is reasonably straight forward if a little eccentric. Rooms with washbasin and cold shower cost Dr51/52/73. The rooms at the front are the best.

Hotel Trebol (☎ 962018) close to the bus station is also good value. Reasonable rooms cost Dr31/52 or Dr41/62 with a cold shower. Another good choice is *Hotel Príncipe* (*20 Rue Youssef ben Tachfine*); reception is in the downstairs cafe. Clean rooms are Dr60/74/120, or Dr70/100/150 with shower.

Hotel Nacional (☎ 963290, *8 Rue Mohammed ben Larbi Torres*) has dingy singles/doubles for Dr61/77, or Dr71/90 with shower and toilet. It has a slight air of seediness but is a fall-back option.

Places to Stay – Mid-Range & Top End

The entrance to *Hotel Regina* (☎ 962113, *8 Rue Sidi Mandri*) is opposite Bank Magreb. It's attached to an intimidating cafe, but the rooms are OK and there's a lift. Singles/doubles/triples with shower cost Dr90/123/160.

More expensive *Hôtel Paris* (☎ 966750, *11 Rue Chakib Arsalane*) has rooms with hot shower and toilet for Dr166/188 (Dr200/236 in high season). It's nothing special and the rooms are a bit gloomy. Parking in their garage costs Dr30 a night.

Straight down the line and probably the best in this category is *Hôtel Oumaima* (☎ 963473, *10 Rue Achra Mai*). Clean rooms with bathroom and phone cost Dr166/198 (Dr200/246 in high season).

Hotel Safir (☎ 970177, *fax 970692*) on the road to Ceuta is hardly worth heading 3km

out of town for, but it does have a pool, tennis courts and a bar. Rooms cost Dr380/484 (rising to Dr410/530 in high season) – bath plug not necessarily included.

Places to Eat

Restaurants An excellent place for a cheap snack is *Sandwich Ali Baba* (*19 Rue Mourakah Annual*). Create a sandwich of choice for Dr4 to Dr8 or sit at the back for salads (Dr8), harira (Dr3) and tajine (Dr15).

El-Yesfi Snack (*Rue Youseff ben Tachfine*) does great baguette sandwiches with various meats, potato salad, chips and salad for Dr16. It's open until 11.30 pm daily.

For delicious, good-value food try *Restaurant Saygon* (*2 Rue Mohammed ben Larbi Torres*) – or Saigon – which despite its name, serves mainly Moroccan dishes. You can get a big bowl of chunky harira soup for Dr4.50, followed by a huge serving of couscous, *brochettes* (skewered meat) or paella for around Dr27. It's a friendly place and there's seating in a tranquil gallery upstairs.

Also good is *Restaurant Restinga*, which you get to through a small alley off Calle Mohammed V. You can eat inside or in the courtyard. The staff are friendly and serve much the same fare as the Saygon; the big plus, however, is that they serve beer here. A bottle of Heineken costs Dr15.

Those seeking Western-style fast food can get quick gratification at *Tele Pizza Kimo* (☎ 968159, *37 Calle Chakib Arsalan*). It's a tiny place close to Hôtel Paris. Hamburgers cost Dr8 and good pizzas start at Dr18 (free deliveries are available).

For a splurge, *Restaurant Palace Bouhlal* in the medina is about the best place. It serves a decent four-course set lunch (including couscous) for Dr100. It's attractively decorated in the traditional way and popular with groups who come for the 'spectacles' (musicians and dancing). If you want to avoid them, come around 2 pm. The restaurant is open from 10 am to 5 pm daily. To get here, look for the large iron gates in a tiny alley off the route around the Great Mosque. You'll probably need to ask a local for directions. Pop your head into the spice shop near the entrance, it's a tourist trap but worth a look.

MEDITERRANEAN COAST & THE RIF

Patisseries & Cafes Generally considered the best in town and with a delicious selection of Moroccan and French goodies is the *Café Pâtisserie SMIR (17 Calle Mohammed V)*. There's a seating area upstairs where you can have breakfast. It's also a relaxing place for women travellers looking for a bit of peace and quiet. It's open from 6 am to 9.15 pm daily. If you're appreciative enough, Hassan, the unsmiling but charming manager, is quite likely to give you a little something *pour goûter* (to try).

An excellent spot to watch the world go by over a coffee is *Café de Paris (Place Moulay el-Mehdi)*. More sophisticated is *Le Printemps Salon du Thé (Rue Mohammed ben Larbi Torres)*; it's a great place to relax and read the papers.

Pâtisserie Rahmouni (10 Youssef ben Tachfine) has a sister shop in Tangier. The Rahmouni family has established a reputation for high-quality, traditional (largely Moroccan) sweets. It's open to 11 pm daily and there's a coffee and juice bar at the back.

If you're after ice cream, try *Heladería Atlas* on Rue Achra Mai.

Self-Catering There is a mass of fresh fruit and veg for sale in the medina close to the gates of Bab el-Okla and Bab er-Rouah. More *stalls* line Rue du Prince Sidi Mohammed. Numerous hole-in-the-wall general *stores* are dotted around town and *Supermercado La Española* next to Heladería Atlas on Rue Achra Mai, sells alcohol.

Entertainment

For a drink you could try the bar in Hôtel Safir, though it's not cheap. The alternatives are the *Ideal Andalusia*, facing Cinéma Avenida, or an unmarked bar opposite the Wafa Bank on Calle Mohammed V, but these are the usual men-and-prostitutes-only, spit-and-sawdust places.

Getting There & Away

Air This tiny airport only deals with internal flights. One-way to Casablanca costs Dr623 (or Dr249 if you are a student or under 25). The only other destination is Al-Hoceima (Dr322 one way).

Bus The bus station is at the junction of Rue Sidi Mandri and Rue Moulay Abbas.

CTM has buses to Chefchaouen (Dr16.50, 1½ hours, five per day); Tangier (Dr13, one hour, twice daily); Casablanca (Dr105, about seven hours) via Rabat (Dr80, about five hours) at 6.30 am and 10.30 pm, plus a *rapide* bus (stopping only at Rabat) at 11 pm. There are also buses to Fès at 11.30 am and 1.45 pm (Dr68, five hours); for Ouezzane (Dr33, four hours) catch the 11.30 am service.

Buses for Al-Hoceima (Dr70, about eight hours) leave at 5, 7 and 9 am and 10 pm, and for Nador (Dr100, about 11 hours) at 5 am and 7 pm.

There are regular non-CTM departures for all these destinations and more including Oujda (Dr120), Larache (Dr20), Meknès (Dr59) and Marrakesh (Dr130).

Local buses for Fnideq (Dr5), Cabo Negro (Dr3), Martil (Dr2.50) and other local destinations leave from Rue Moulay Abbas.

Train There is no train station at Tetouan, but the Office National des Chemins de Fer (ONCF) runs two daily Supratours buses to Tnine Sidi Lyamani, just south of Asilah, at 6.30 am and 3.40 pm to link up with trains to and from Tangier. Some one-way fares are Casablanca (Dr118.50), Fès (Dr98.50) and Marrakesh (Dr192.50). The Supratours office (☎ 967559) is on Rue Achra Mai near the Cinéma Avenida.

Grand Taxi Grand taxis leave from all over town, but two taxi ranks seem to be the most useful.

For Ceuta, Martil, Cabo Negro and M'diq, taxis leave frequently from Rue Moulay Abbas, close to the bus station. A seat to the Spanish border (Ceuta) costs Dr15. Although the border is open 24 hours, there's little transport between about 7 pm and 5 am. On the Spanish side of the border, the No 7 public bus runs every 30 minutes or so to the city centre (75 ptas). Local grand taxis to the beach at Martil cost Dr3.50.

Grand taxis to Chefchaouen (Dr20) and Tangier (Dr20) leave frequently from a taxi rank on Place al-Hamama, about 1km out of town towards Tangier. If you are arriving from Chefchaouen or Tangier, the grand taxis usually drop you closer to the town centre.

Getting Around
You'll need to take a grand taxi to or from the airport 4km away. It should cost Dr20, but around Dr50 is more likely.

Petit taxis are yellow and a ride around town should not be more than about Dr6.

AROUND TETOUAN
Martil & Cabo Negro
About 8km north-east of Tetouan is the beach town of Martil. Once Tetouan's port and home to pirates, it's altogether quieter now (despite the huge new university) but has a reasonable beach and some pleasant waterfront cafes.

Walking along the seafront in Martil is a rather desolate experience in low season when, without the summer crowds, there's not much to see except shabby buildings and rubbish on the beach. However, many Moroccan families have summer houses here and it's in July and August that the place really comes to life.

Further north up the coast is Cabo Negro (or Ras Aswad in Arabic), a headland jutting out into the Mediterranean that's clearly visible from Martil. There is a well-established package tourist resort here with discos, bars, restaurants and all the rest of it.

Places to Stay & Eat The closest camp site to Tetouan is *Camping Martil*, but it's not well-maintained. It costs Dr6 per person and per car, and Dr10 per tent. Cold showers are available and electricity costs an extra Dr3.

As Martil is so close to Tetouan, there's hardly any need to stay here, but you could try *Charaf Pensión*, by the main mosque, or *Hôtel Nuzha* (☎ 979232, 9 Rue Miramar). In high season the Charaf charges a fairly hefty Dr70/90/120/160 for singles/doubles/triples/quads with a washbasin, while at the Nuzha singles/doubles with hot showers go for Dr60/120.

A more upmarket place is *Hotel Etoile de la Mar* (☎ 979276, Ave Moulay al-Hassan), which has modern rooms for Dr179/259/339, including breakfast.

Getting There & Away You can catch a local bus back to Tetouan from outside the main mosque in the centre of town.

M'diq
About 15km north of Tetouan, just south of the sprawling tourist resorts that make up Restinga-Smir, is the small fishing port of M'diq. Fishing is the lifeblood of this small community, the hassles are few and the pace of life is slow.

The port, with its boat-building, fishing fleet and hordes of expectant cats, is well worth a visit, and there's a good stretch of beach north of town. To the south of town rises the headland of Cabo Negro. A *moussem* (festival) is held here in July. There are a few reasonable places to stay and this is a good stopover if you're late leaving Ceuta.

Places to Stay & Eat *Hotel La Playa* (☎ 975166) is the budget option in M'diq. Basic doubles/triples go for Dr150/180. There are no singles and most rooms have a toilet and shower. There's a bar and restaurant downstairs.

More expensive is the *Hotel Narijiss* (☎ 975841) at the southern end of town. Slightly rough, singles/doubles with bathroom, phone and satellite TV cost Dr150/200 in low season and Dr175/250 in high season – not bad value.

At the top end of the scale, at the northern end of town with ocean views, is the four-star *Golden Beach Hotel* (☎ 975077, fax 975096). Deceptively shabby at first glance, the rooms with bathroom are well-kept and well-equipped. There's a pool and rooms go for Dr291/404 during low season and Dr451/724 in high season for half board.

There's a string of *cafes* and cheap eateries opposite the Catholic church in the centre of town, but the best food in town (at around Dr100 per head) is to be had at the restaurant of the *Royal Yachting Club du M'diq*, down by the port. It's a private club, so book in advance. *Restaurante del Puerto* (☎ 663872) close by is a cheaper alternative.

Getting There & Away A large number of grand taxis and buses travelling between

Tetouan and Fnideq (3km short of the border with Ceuta) pass through the town.

CHEFCHAOUEN
☎ 09

This delightful town set in the Rif Mountains has long been a favourite with travellers. It's relatively hassle-free, the air is cool and clear, there's more kif than you can poke a stick at, and the town is clean, small and manageable. Once the domain solely of bleary backpackers, all grades of tourist now enjoy the town, which has made it a relatively prosperous place and led to the creation of more upmarket restaurants, hotels and boutiques.

History
The town was originally called Chaouen (meaning the 'Peaks'), referring to the Rif Mountains surrounding the town. Under Spanish occupation the spelling changed to Xauen and in 1975 the town was renamed Chefchaouen (meaning 'Look at the Peaks').

Founded by Moulay Ali ben Rachid in 1471 as a base from which the Rifian Berber tribes could launch attacks on the Portuguese in Ceuta, the town prospered and grew considerably with the arrival of Muslim and Jewish refugees escaping persecution in Granada in 1494. It was these refugees who built the whitewashed houses with tiny balconies, tiled roofs and patios (with a citrus tree planted in the centre), giving the town its distinctive Hispanic flavour. However, the pale blue wash now so typical was introduced in the 1930s by the Jews – previously windows and doors had been painted green, a traditional Muslim colour.

The town remained isolated, and almost xenophobic, until occupied by Spanish troops in 1920. The Spaniards were surprised to hear the Jewish inhabitants still speaking a variant of medieval Castilian. In fact, Christians were forbidden entry to the town before Spanish occupation and only did so on pain of death. Two managed to do so in disguise – the French adventurer Charles Foucauld in 1883 and, five years later, the British wanderer and journalist Walter Harris (disguised as a Jew).

The Spanish were briefly thrown out of Chefchaouen by Abd al-Krim between 1924 and 1926 during the Riffian War, but soon returned to stay until independence in 1956.

Orientation
The new bus station is a 20-minute hike south-west of the town centre, which is downhill when you leave, but a rather steep incline on arrival. The main street in the ville nouvelle is Ave Hassan II. At Bab al-'Ain it swings south and follows the medina wall around towards Oued Ras el-Maa, taking the name of Rue Tarik ibn Ziad at this extension. If pavement of a street in the medina is painted then it's a dead end.

Information
Money The BMCE (no ATM) and the Banque Populaire are both on Ave Hassan II. You can change cash and travellers cheques and get cash advances on Visa and MasterCard at both banks. They are open from 8.15 to 11.30 am and 2.15 to 4.30 pm Monday to Thursday (Friday from 8.15 to 11.15 am and 2.45 to 4.45 pm).

The Crédit Agricole on Plaza Uta el-Hammam will change cash only.

Post & Communications The post office is on Ave Hassan II, about 50m west of the Bab al-'Ain entrance to the medina. It's open from 8.30 am to 12.15 pm and 2.30 to 6.30 pm Monday to Saturday (on Friday it's closed for noon prayers from 12.30 pm to 3 pm). There are coin and cardphones outside – phonecards can be bought inside.

There are several téléboutiques around town.

The Internet Cafe Sefiani Network, opposite the Mobil petrol station on Ave Tarik Tetouan, charges Dr30 per hour. Groupe Chaouni Info, 91 Ave el-Moukawama, charges D10 to Dr20 per hour (weekends are cheapest). Both places are roughly open 9 am to 9 pm.

Newsstands & Bookshops There's a newsstand opposite the BMCE on Ave Hassan II, which normally sells French newspapers and magazines.

Kif in the Rif Mountains

kif, *n*. another name for marijuana. C20: from Arabic *kayf*, pleasure

The smoking of kif is an ancient tradition in northern Morocco. In the Rif Mountains, from Chefchaouen to Ketama and beyond, its cultivation is widespread – some villages grow nothing else – and tolerated until another crop can be found that grows as successfully or profitably.

Hashish, which is essentially compressed kif, is a stronger, modern (1960s) invention developed for export. Whereas an old goatherd in the mountains will break out his kif pipe should you stop to chat, hashish is favoured by younger, more westernised Rifians.

Discreet possession and use is also, in practice, tolerated. Travellers should never be tempted, however, to buy more than small quantities for personal use. Never travel in possession with it, avoid buying it in Tetouan and Tangier, and mistrust all dealers: many double as police informers. See also under Dangers & Annoyances in the Facts for the Visitor chapter.

The Librairie Al-Nahj, next to Pâtisserie Magou on Ave Hassan II, has a small collection of books including the odd publication in French, English, Spanish and occasionally German.

Other Services There is no Syndicat d'Initiative. If you're after local and trekking information and tours of the medina your best bet is to contact Abdeslam Mouden (the President of the Association Randonnée et Culture) who can be reached at Casa Hassan hotel or at home on ☎ 02-113917.

The hospital is on Ave al-Massira al-Khadra, while the well-stocked Farmacia Utaa Hammam is just off Plaza de Makhzen to the west.

You can safely park your car in front of the Hotel Parador; there's no charge but a tip would seem appropriate.

Water is drinkable from the tap, it's piped straight off the mountain, in fact the Spanish were bottling and selling it in the 1930s.

Market

The market near Plaza Mohammed V is the centre of attention on Monday and Thursday, when merchants come from all over the Rif to trade. The emphasis is on food and second-hand clothes, although there are sometimes a few interesting souvenirs.

Medina

The old medina is small, uncrowded and easy to find your way around. For the most part, the houses and buildings are a blinding blue-white colour and, on the northern side especially, you'll still find a few tiny ground-floor rooms crowded with weaving looms. Previously it was silk that was woven (the mulberry trees in Plaza Uta el-Hammam are a legacy of these times), but most of the weaving done now is of wool, one of the area's biggest products.

There is also a fair smattering of tourist shops, particularly around Plaza Uta el-Hammam and Plaza de Makhzen – the focal points of the old city.

Plaza Uta el-Hammam & Kasbah The shady, cobbled Plaza Uta el-Hammam is dominated by the red-hued walls of the kasbah and the striking Great Mosque. The cafes that ring the square are a great place to sit and relax, especially in the early evening.

Behind the north-east corner of the square is a **funduq** (caravanserai), Chefchaouen's ancient accommodation and stabling block, long-used by pilgrims and travellers and still full on market days. A look inside is like a glance back in time.

The **kasbah** was built by Moulay Ali ben Rachid and was restored in the 17th century by Moulay Ismail to defend the town against unruly Berber tribes, as well as outsiders such as the Spaniards. For a time it was Abd al-Krim's headquarters.

The walls enclose a **garden** and to the right of the kasbah entrance are the cells used during Spanish occupation – complete

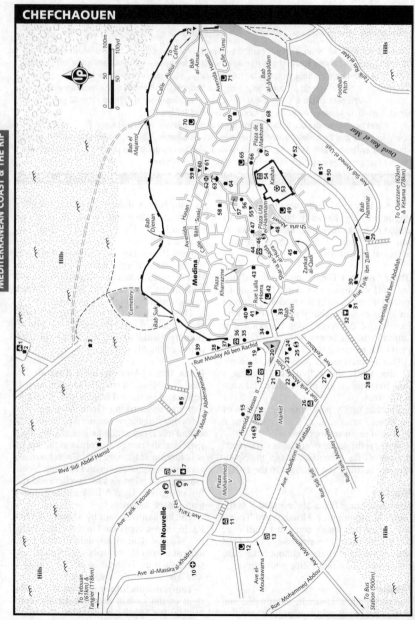

CHEFCHAOUEN

CHEFCHAOUEN

with neck chains at floor level. To the left is a small **museum** containing a collection of traditional arms, instruments, textiles and some old photos of the town and people in traditional costumes. It also houses a small Andalusian studies centre. You can climb up a couple of storeys onto the roof for some good views of the town.

A small **gallery** displaying work by international and local artists is tucked away in the right-hand corner of the kasbah. It can be reached through the kasbah or free of charge through a door opposite the Great Mosque.

The kasbah is open from 9 am to 1 pm and 3 to 6.30 pm daily, and entry costs Dr10.

Next to the kasbah is Chefchaouen's **Great Mosque**, built in the 15th century by the son of the town's founder, Ali ben Rachid. It has an unusual octagonal tower. Non-Muslims cannot enter.

Plaza de Makhzen The Plaza de Makhzen is the lesser of the two town squares; instead of cafes, it has mostly tourist shops. How-ever, on market days you still get people squatting under the tree selling bundles of mint and vegetables grown in the district.

If you take the lane heading north-east from the square, you'll eventually come out at Bab al-Ansar. There's a shady cafe where men busy themselves drinking tea and playing dominoes while women do the washing in the Ras el-Maa below. From here it's a 15-minute walk to the ruined mosque overlooking the town. It was built by the Spanish, just before the Rif War (1921–26), but the local population refused to use it.

Trekking

The Rif Mountains, bordering the Moroccan coast for about 200km, are the highest peaks in the north. Though rarely reaching above 1800m, they are also the best watered and offer very attractive mountain scenery for the hiker. Cedars dominate the hillsides close to Chefchaouen, while forests of pine and holm oak grow on the higher slopes. Trekking opportunities here are good enough to draw even the most sloth-like backpacker away from the cafes and roof terraces of Chefchaouen. See the Rif Mountains section in the Trekking chapter for further details.

Special Events

There is a modest festival of Andalusian music and culture in September and a poetry festival in May. The Moussem of Sidi Allal al-Hadh is held in September.

Hammams & Public Showers

There's an old hammam next to Pensión La Castellana just off Plaza Uta al-Hammam. It's supposed to cost Dr5, but travellers have been turned away or charged much more. More reliable, though new and concrete, is Douches Barakat up the hill from Plaza Uta al-Hammam. They charge Dr5; women get their turn between noon and 8 pm, men at all other times.

Places to Stay – Budget

If you've arrived from Tetouan, you'll find the standard of accommodation considerably better and cheaper here. There are plenty of places around, but in peak periods especially, they can all fill up fairly quickly. It's a good idea to make a reservation, or arrive here early, but if you're really stuck many places will let you sleep on the roof terrace for Dr15.

In winter it can get very cold and few hotels have heating. Bring a sleeping bag and ask for lots of extra blankets.

Camping & Hostels Right up on the side of the hill behind the Hotel Asma on Rue Sidi Abdelhamid is *Camping Azilan* and the *Auberge de Jeunesse* (☎ 986979 for both). They're open all year, are in a pleasant location and are a good option if you have your own vehicle. Otherwise it's a steep 30-minute walk by the road (follow the signs to the Hotel Asma), or a 15-minute scramble up the hill through the cemetery; you shouldn't attempt the latter on a Friday, as the locals don't take kindly to it.

Camping Azilan is popular and reasonably well maintained. There's a small cafe and with a couple of hours warning they'll rustle up a tajine for Dr25. Camping costs

Dr7 per person (Dr3 for children under 10) plus Dr10/20 per small/large tent. If you're content to sleep under the stars it will cost you Dr10. The charge for vehicles is Dr5 per motorcycle, Dr10 per car, Dr20 for a caravan or 4WD and Dr30 for a bus or camper van. Electricity or water cost Dr10 and there are hot showers for Dr10.

A bunk-bed in the Auberge de Jeunesse hostel costs Dr15. It's extremely basic, so bring your own bedding. There are cold showers and a kitchen.

Hotels The cheapest places are the pensions in the medina. Mostly they are OK, if a little gloomy and claustrophobic at times.

Pensión La Castellana (☎ 986295, 4 Sidi Ahmed el-Bouhali), just off the north-eastern end of Plaza Uta el-Hammam, is an excellent travellers hang-out, with singles/doubles for Dr30/60, including hot showers. It's been renovated, but it retains a great atmosphere and is probably better value than ever, though some rooms are a little small. The roof terrace is a popular place to crash in high season (Dr15 including a shower) – the panoramic views are great. There's also a guests kitchen.

Also popular with travellers, and charging the same for similar facilities, is *Hotel Andaluz* (☎ 986034, Rue Sidi Salem). The upper-floor rooms are lighter and airy.

Another place travellers zero in on is *Pensión Mauritania* (☎ 986184, 15 Zankat Qadi Alami), which charges Dr20/30 per person for a small or large bed. Hot showers are Dr5. The rooms are a bit dark and cell-like, but the staff are friendly and there's an attractive, traditional lounge area. Breakfast costs Dr10.

Also good value is the pleasant *Pensión Znika* (☎ 986624, 4 Rue Znika) north of the kasbah. Rooms are clean, light and airy and cost Dr30 per person, hot showers included.

North-east of Plaza de Makhzen is *Hotel Hamra* (☎ 986362, 39 Rue ibn Askar). It's a quiet place away from the bulk of the tourist trade and has clean, reasonable rooms decorated in the traditional style with arched doorways and wooden ceilings. The rooms cost Dr30/60 and a hot shower is Dr5.

Up from the Bab al-'Ain along Rue Lalla Horra and easily missed is *Hotel Abie*

Khancha (☎ *986879*). Rooms cost Dr40/60. Some doubles have bathrooms and some are gloomy, so choose well. There's a great roof terrace and rough old pool table.

Places to Stay – Mid-Range

Just inside the Bab al-'Ain is *Hotel Bab el-Ain* (☎ *986935, 77 Rue Lalla Horra*). Comfortable singles/doubles with shared showers cost Dr41/82, and those with bathroom cost Dr51/102. Get here early for the best rooms. The terrace is a wonderful spot.

Outside the medina is *Hotel Salam* (☎ *986239, 39 Ave Hassan II*). It's basic and a bit dusty, but has hot water and a restaurant serving a reasonable set menu for Dr50. Small rooms (some with good views south) are Dr40/80.

Hotel Marrakesh (☎ *987113*) virtually next door to the Salam is a friendly place offering rooms for Dr50/80 (Dr80/120 with bathrooms). The rooms are on the small side, but are modern, clean and comfortable. Six have views.

Hotel Rif (☎ *986982, 29 Rue Tarik ibn Ziad*) just below the city walls has largish rooms for Dr50/80 and Dr87/120 with hot showers. Try to get a room with views of the valley. There's also a tearoom and licensed restaurant.

There are a couple of hotels to the northwest of town on Blvd Sidi Abdel Hamid, which loops up to the Hotel Asma. *Hotel Ahrazem* (☎ *987384*) has small, pleasant rooms for Dr35/70 (hot showers cost Dr5) and a double with shower costs Dr90. Most rooms are set around an internal courtyard, and a couple have great views.

Just on from the Ahrazem is *Residencia La Estrella* (☎ *986526*). The hotel is made up of four basic apartments that can be rented for Dr500 a day (they accommodate up to 10 people). If you just want a room, these cost Dr40/80. There are hot showers and a kitchen.

Places to Stay – Top End

Hotel Madrid (☎ *987496, Ave Hassan II*) is just out of the mid-range bracket. Clean singles/doubles/triples with shower, phone and heater cost Dr180/261/364. It's popular with

tours, though outside high season you can negotiate prices down about 25%.

The cheapest of the genuine top-end hotels is the ageing *Hotel Asma* (☎ *986002*), a huge, concrete beast lurking above the cemetery. Singles/doubles with bathroom, phone and heater cost Dr255/312. There's a bar and a pricey restaurant. The views are good, but you're some way from town.

More expensive is the four-star *Hotel Parador* (☎ *986324, fax 987033*) on Plaza de Makhzen inside the medina. It costs Dr317/396 for rooms in low season and 398/498 in high season. The hotel has its own bar, restaurant and swimming pool (Dr50 for nonguests) and good views down the Ras el-Mar Valley.

Casa Hassan (☎ *986153, fax 988196*) up from Plaza Uta al-Hammam is the more discerning upmarket choice. The nice double rooms off the gallery that overlooks Restaurant Tissemlal are a little noisy (Dr250 for half board), the four suites on the enclosed floor above have a real touch of class. Beautifully furnished rooms (a wood-burning stove eases the chill of winter evenings) with bathroom cost Dr500 to Dr550 per double for half board. There's a great roof terrace.

Places to Eat

Restaurants For a really cheap feed (about Dr3) you could wait until after 4.30 pm and get a bowl of harira, chick pea soup or freshly cooked snails from one of the *stalls* in Plaza Uta el-Hammam or outside Bab al-'Ain.

Near the Pensión Valencia, *Restaurant Granada* is run by a cheery character who cooks a variety of dishes at reasonable prices (brochettes and couscous are both Dr18).

Almost opposite and popular with travellers and locals is *Restaurant Chez Fouad*. Prices are a little higher than the Granada, but the food is good and portions generous. Look out for the bakery below the restaurant, where local women bring their daily bread, sweets and biscuits to be baked.

A favourite with the locals is *Restaurant Assaada*, just inside the Bab al-'Ain and up to the left. It's a friendly little place that has mastered the art of doing simple things well and usually serves one sort of tajine per day for around Dr18.

Outside the medina, up the hill from the Bab al-'Ain, are two good-value eateries: *Restaurant Moulay Ali Berrachid* and *Restaurant Zouar*. They are simple, reasonable places and charge Dr3 for harira soup, Dr5 for salads, Dr7 for omelettes and Dr20 for mains of tajine, brochettes or fish.

On Rue Tarik ibn Ziad, the street leading up to Plaza de Makhzen, is *Restaurant Chefchaouen*. It's a very laid-back place, the service is good and it serves up a set menu of the usual Moroccan fare (soup, tajine or couscous and fruit) for Dr45.

Salon Aladin just up from Plaza Uta el-Hammam is a traveller-friendly place with a chilled atmosphere and delicious food (including vegetarian options). Tajine costs Dr25 and excellent pastilla is Dr35, though the three-course set menu (Dr45) is best value of all.

If you're looking for a more upmarket place, and one with a slightly more imaginative menu (lemon chicken for example), head to *Restaurant Tissemlal* (☎ 986153, 22 Rue Targui), the restaurant in Casa Hassan. The beautifully conceived restaurant is justifiably popular, with the three-course Dr50 set menu excellent value.

There's little choice for a splurge, but you could try the *restaurant* at Hotel Parador. The three-course *menu touristique* costs Dr130 and the four-course *menu gastronomique* is (Dr150). Wine costs from Dr60 a bottle.

Cafes & Patisseries Sitting outside one of the many *cafes* on Plaza Uta el-Hammam is a popular local and tourist pastime. All these places serve drinks and basic meals (tajine, salad and a drink for Dr25) throughout the day, though there's little to choose between them. However, at the time of writing *Cafe Mounir* was a fine place to have breakfast.

The interiors of a few of these cafes also double as full-on kif smoking dens, though games of dominoes and cards are still played with great energy. These places are worth a peek, but women will not be made to feel welcome.

The *Pâtisserie Magou* (10 Ave Hassan II) is open from 7 am to 10 pm daily and has a reasonable range of patisseries to take away.

Across the road is the pleasant, shady terrace of *Pâtisserie Diafa*. There's not much to choose between them, though the terrace of the Diafa is a lovely place to start the day – a full breakfast (coffee, orange juice and croissant or toast and jam) will cost you Dr11. It's open from 7 am to midnight daily.

After about 4 pm numerous tiny *stands* can be found around Plaza Uta el-Hammam and Bab al-'Ain selling piles of freshly baked goodies.

Self-Catering The *market* is excellent for fresh fish, meat, fruit and vegetables. In addition, the *stalls* on Plaza Kharrazine, and small shops on the road between Plaza Uta el-Hammam and Bab al-'Ain, supply all kinds of local foods including delicious (goats) butter, ewes cheese and fragrant mountain honey. Add a fresh hob of *dial makla* (a type of bread) and you have all the ingredients for a heavenly picnic.

If you're keen on olives, the Monday and Thursday markets are a great place to indulge yourself. At the market, you'll find a whole range: the black ones are from the north of the country, the green are from the west and the brown are from the Atlas.

Entertainment

At the edge of kif country, Chefchaouen is as laid-back a place as you could imagine. There's no cinema, no nightclub and only one bar, *Bar Oum-Rabiá* (Ave Hassan II), which closes at 10 pm.

Some of the larger hotels also serve alcohol, including the *Hotel Parador*. The terrace, with its panoramic views, is a pleasant place for a beer (Dr15) or two.

Cafe Castilo just before Plaza de Makhzen, has a football table; book-swapping seems to be a popular traveller pastime – it seems that almost every traveller in town has a book they want to swap.

Getting There & Away

Bus Chefchaouen can be an easy place to get into, but a difficult one to get out of.

Many of the buses passing through the town are through-services from elsewhere and are often full on arrival. It's therefore a very good idea to make a free reservation a day in advance (at least three days before during public holidays). You'll have to go in person to the station and collect the ticket.

The bus station is a relaxed place about a 20-minute walk south-west of the town centre. CTM and all other buses leave from here.

CTM has a bus to Casablanca (Dr90, six hours) via Ouezzane (Dr18, 1½ hours), Souk el-Arba du Rharb (Dr32, three hours), Kenitra (Dr53, nearly four hours) and Rabat (Dr65, five hours) at 7 am. There are buses to Fès (Dr52, 4½ hours) via Ouezzane, at 1 and 3.30 pm.

CTM departures to Nador (Dr88, 10½ hours) via Ketama (Dr21, two hours) and Al-Hoceima (Dr51, seven hours) leave at 6.30 am and 8.30 pm.

The easiest place to get to from Chefchaouen is Tetouan (Dr18, 1½ hours), with departures at noon, 3, 4 and 7 pm. The 3 pm bus heads on to Tangier (Dr33, three hours).

Other companies are represented at four other windows. The timetables are generally posted up outside and are quite easy to follow. There are a handful of departures to Fès and Meknès spread throughout the morning and afternoon; services to Casablanca (via Rabat and Kenitra) at 6 and 9.15 am; regular departures to Fnideq (Dr22), from 6 am to 1.30 pm; and very frequent services to Tangier, Tetouan and Ouezzane.

For Oued Laou (Dr15, 1½ hours) catch the daily bus heading to El-Jebha (Dr40, 5½ hours) that leaves at 1.30 pm. It returns from Oued Laou around 7 am the following day.

There's also a bus at 1 pm to Ksar el-Kbir (Dr30), which may be of interest.

Taxi Grand-taxi drivers, well used to backpackers looking for a cheap ride, often dismiss the possibility of any *collectif* (shared) grand taxis to Fès or other further-flung destinations, but make inquiries locally. Getting one to neighbouring towns is straightforward.

There are two collection points for long-distance grand taxis. For journeys north and west, they depart from just beyond the Plaza Mohammed V. Destinations include the most common journey to Tetouan (Dr25), Ceuta (Dr35) and Tangier (Dr50).

For trips south or east – Ouezzane (Dr25), Rabat (Dr75) and Fès (Dr100) – head to Ave Allal ben Abdallah. Arrive early for all trips, especially for infrequent, long-distance journeys, when you might have to head for Ouezzane first (it's a bigger transport hub).

Grand taxis also leave from just south of the market. These are for local destinations like Dar Ackoubaa (Dr5), the turning for Oued Laou. Petit taxis huddle by Hotel Parador and below the market.

THE COAST NORTH & EAST OF CHEFCHAOUEN

The Mediterranean coastline north of Chefchaouen is far off the beaten track and stunning. In fact, just the journey from Oued Laou, which lies 44km south-east of Tetouan, along the S608 to El-Jebha is a worthwhile excursion.

Heading south-east from Oued Laou, the coastline is dotted with police observation stations keeping an eye on kif smuggling. The rolling foothills of the Rif Mountains drop away to cliffs and tiny black-sand beaches.

There's little in the way of accommodation in the villages south-west of Oued Laou, but if you ask around in the cafes someone will put you up.

Oued Laou

Oued Laou, sprawled out along the wide bay, is the biggest town in the area and unexceptional apart from its beautiful, octagonal tiled mosque. However, it's easy-going and has a big, vibrant Saturday souq 4km inland.

Places to Stay & Eat Oued Laou's *Camping Oued Laou* (☎ 993995) seems reasonably secure and well shaded, but facilities aren't great. They charge Dr7 per person and per tent plus Dr10/20 for a car/van. There are also three small, unexceptional bungalows (Dr150 per double).

Both hotels in Oued Laou are on Blvd Massira one block in from the beach. *Hôtel*

Restaurant Oued Laou has hot showers and pleasant, simple rooms (sleeping three people) for Dr100. Roof terrace space is Dr20.

Hôtel Restaurant Laayoune is cheaper (Dr40 per person), but has cold showers.

Numerous *cafes* are dotted about town and along the beachfront, some serve brochettes, tajine or fish for around Dr25. There's no bar.

Getting There & Away If you're driving from Chefchaouen turn off the P28 at Dar Ackoubaa 11km north of Chefchaouen and follow the 8304 for 42km to Oued Laou. It's a wonderful drive past the large hydroelectric dam and through rolling hills and the stunning Laou Gorge. Coming from Tetouan, the S608 hugs the dramatic coastline for 134km to El-Jebha.

A daily bus leaves Chefchaouen at 1.30 pm and arrives at Oued Laou around 3 pm (Dr15). This bus continues on to El-Jebha (Dr40). A returning service leaves El-Jebha at 5.30 am passing through Oued Laou at 7 am.

There's a 7 am departure from Tetouan to Oued Laou (Dr10) and El-Jebha (Dr 40). A 2 pm returning service passes through Oued Laou at around 6 pm.

In Oued Laou buses drop you at the Zig petrol station (past the market), leaving a 45-minute walk or Dr5 grand taxi ride to town.

Grand taxis also run from the souq area in Oued Laou to Tetouan (Dr15) and Chefchaouen (Dr20) and up to Dar Ackoubaa (Dr15), the junction on the P28 north of Chefchaouen.

Less formal transport runs along the coast; market days are the best days to travel.

Targa to Ketama

Targa, 17km south of Oued Laou, is a striking little village with an illustrious history of piracy and a wonderful stone fort that sits atop a large outcrop of black stone. There's also a small 13th-century mosque, a weaving cooperative, two general stores and a few cafes.

About 18km south-east of Targa in the wide valley of **Oued Bouchia**, are the twin villages of **Steha** (an administrative centre) and **Bou-Ahmed**. They are set back from the coast and are the end point for a long-distance trek from Chefchaouen. There's a souq on Tuesday.

From here the road winds 52km to **El-Jebha**, essentially a fishing village (with lighthouse) of Spanish design. It's interesting but shabby, and the last stop before the P8500 climbs up through the Rif to **Ketama** (see later). Kif dealers can be a hassle here, but there are a number of beautiful bays close to the town and the Tuesday souq is also an attraction.

The EU is planning to fund the entire upgrade of the S608 from Tetouan to extend it to Nador, but no work has begun. See Getting There & Away under Oued Laou, earlier.

OUEZZANE
☎ 07

Lying in the plains at the southern edge of the Rif, Ouezzane (pronounced **wa**-za-neh) is another town to which Andalusian refugees, many of them Jews, fled in the 15th century. Muslims regard it as a holy city, with a *zawiyya* (fraternity based around a saint's mausoleum) dedicated to the memory of Moulay Abdallah ben Brahim, one of several contenders for supremacy in the chaotic Morocco of the early 18th century. His moussem is celebrated in late March.

Jews also make an annual pilgrimage (around May) to visit the tomb of Rabbi Amrane ben Diwan, an Andalusian 'miracle worker' who died in about 1780 and whose tomb is 9km north-west of Ouezzane off the Rabat road, in the Jewish cemetery of Azjem.

The town was also home to Emily Keene and her husband the sherif of Ouezzane, Sherif Si Absellam, who married in the late 19th century causing much scandal and gossip – he divorced his three wives to marry Emily who was a Christian. Emily is buried in St Andrew's Church in Tangier (see St Andrew's Church under Tangier earlier in this chapter).

Orientation

The small medina, the southern half of which forms the old Jewish quarter, lies to the south-east. North of the medina are the

Mosque of the Zawiyya (also known as the Green Mosque) and the Moulay Abdallah Sherif Mosque.

If you enter the Bab ash-Shurfa, the main gate in the south-eastern corner of the square, you'll find yourself walking through the metalworkers market and soon after across into the woodworkers market. Another good access point is along Rue Abdallah ben Lamlih, which leads off into the medina near Hotel Marhaba.

There are a few places where rugs and the like can be bought, but this medina is not geared up to satisfy the tourist desire for trinkets. Much of the stuff produced and sold here seems to be for Moroccan consumption. With so few travellers coming through, you could well strike a good bargain for a carpet or piece of painted furniture.

You're bound to meet the town's two or three guides on your wanderings.

Information

Wafa Bank (it cashes travellers cheques and does credit card advances) and the post office lie on the main road leading north off Place de l'Indépendance. Banque Populaire is on the square.

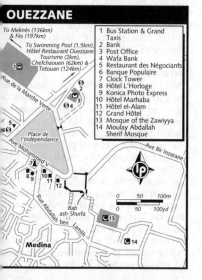

OUEZZANE

To Meknès (136km)
& Fès (197km)

To Swimming Pool (1.5km),
Hôtel Restaurant Ouezzane
Tourisme (2km),
Chefchaouen (62km) &
Tetouan (124km)

Rue de la Marche Verte

Place de
l'Indépendance

Ave Mohammed V

Ave Bir Inzarane

Bab
ash-Shurfa

Rue Abdallah ben Lamlih

Medina

1 Bus Station & Grand Taxis
2 Bank
3 Post Office
4 Wafa Bank
5 Restaurant des Négociants
6 Banque Populaire
7 Clock Tower
8 Hôtel L'Horloge
9 Konica Photo Express
10 Hôtel Marhaba
11 Hôtel el-Alam
12 Grand Hôtel
13 Mosque of the Zawiyya
14 Moulay Abdallah Sherif Mosque

0   50   100m
0   50   100yd

There's a public swimming pool just off Ave Hassan II (high season only).

On Thursday there's a large souq just north of the bus station.

Places to Stay & Eat

There's no camp site in town, despite what a character called Samir may tell you – he'll simply lead you to an empty piece of ground up from the hotel (and charge you for it).

Of the four hotels clustered around the clock tower at the southern end of Place de l'Indépendance, *Hôtel el-Alam* (☎ 907182) is probably the best bet. It has basic but clean singles/doubles/triples around a courtyard on the top floor for Dr35/50/70. Room Nos 1 to 4 have wonderful views of the mountains.

The cafe at the *Grand Hôtel* (☎ 907096) is a pretty good place to pass the time, plus there are plenty of cavernous, basic rooms for Dr30/60/90 below it. There's a communal hot shower (Dr5).

Hotel Marhaba also has a cafe and the rooms upstairs are basic but functional for Dr30/45. Cheapest of all is *Hôtel L'Horloge* with rooms for Dr15/30/45. The rooms are a bit pokey, but some have views and it's not bad for the price.

Around 2km from the centre, just off the Chefchaouen road, is the more expensive *Hôtel Restaurant Ouezzane Tourisme* (☎ 907154, 30 Place Lalla Amina). Rooms are pretty simple (they've changed little since 1946), but the beds and linen are new and it's a friendly and relaxed place. Rooms go for Dr80/94/126 and most have bathrooms. There's also a small car park. A tajine in the restaurant costs around Dr33.

There are numerous cafes and snack stands on the square. The cheapest food (brochettes) is to be had at the bus station, while *Restaurant des Négociants* is good for a drink and game of pool. For a fine view of the northern plains, head through Bab ash-Shurfa and keep going for 200m to *Café Bellevue*, which is below the Moulay Abdallah Sherif Mosque.

Getting There & Away

Bus Ouezzane is a bit of a crossroads and if you are losing hope of getting out of

Chefchaouen to head south, it might be worth trying your luck here. However, the earlier you start the better – there are virtually no buses after 5 pm.

Two dusty lots next to each other on Rue de la Marche Verte function as the bus station (which has a left-luggage facility; Dr3 for six hours) and grand taxi stand.

There is one CTM bus daily to Casablanca (Dr74), Rabat (Dr48) and Fès (Dr36). There are frequent non-CTM buses from 7.30 am to 5.30 pm to Meknès and Fès (both Dr30), Chefchaouen (Dr15) and Kenitra (Dr25), and other services to Casablanca (Dr55), Tetouan (Dr30) and Tangier (Dr50).

Grand Taxi Grand taxis run regularly to Chefchaouen (Dr25), Fès (Dr50) and Kenitra (Dr35). Other long-distance destinations may be possible (Rabat or Tangier), but inquire beforehand and turn up very early in the morning. All departures are more frequent on market day (Thursday).

KETAMA
☎ 09

Instead of heading south out of the Rif from Chefchaouen towards Ouezzane and on to the coast or the Middle Atlas, you could turn east and plunge into the heart of the Rif and on to a couple of minor Mediterranean resorts.

Buses head right across to Al-Hoceima and Nador via Ketama, and ride along what is virtually the backbone of the Rif. This slowly becomes more barren before dropping back down to the coast. It's among the most breathtaking road trips in Morocco.

You could stop in Ketama, but you could be inviting hassles. This is the centre of kif country and it will be assumed you've come to buy a load, which might have unpleasant consequences (see Dangers & Annoyances in the Facts for the Visitor chapter). However, though the town is universally regarded as a pain for travellers, the surrounding mountains offer some great trekking. Jebel Tidiquin (2448m), the highest mountain in the Rif Mountains, lies about 30km to the south-east. You are well advised to bring a trekking guide from Chefchaouen (see the

Rif Mountains section of the Trekking chapter if you're heading up here).

Hotel Tidighine in the town centre is a fading upmarket hotel once patronised by Spanish walkers and cross-country skiers and is your best bet should you choose to stay.

AL-HOCEIMA
☎ 09 • pop 90,000

Set on a bay at one of the rare points along the coast where the Rif drops away and makes a little room for beaches, Al-Hoceima is a relaxed and largely modern town. Founded in 1920 by a Spanish officer, General Sanjuro it was known initially as Villa Sanjuro.

The fact that the Rif rebel Abd al-Krim had, from 1921 to 1926, one of his main bases only 10km away at Ajdir, shows how tenuous Spain's hold over this part of its protectorate was after 1912.

Al-Hoceima only began to grow in the wake of Moroccan independence. The Spanish influence remains but all new construction is resolutely cheap North African-style

The main attractions are the couple of small beaches, making Al-Hoceima a pleasant stop while en route east or west through the Rif. In high summer it fills up with Moroccan holiday-makers and even some European charter tourists. What attracts the latter is hard to guess; although it's a pleasant enough place to rest, it's hardly one of the Mediterranean's great package resorts.

Orientation

Most of the banks, better hotels and restaurants are on or near Calle Mohammed V the main road in from Nador. Just east of this road, as you enter the town proper, is the old village centre, with the budget hotels and eateries, as well as all transport.

Apart from the town beach, Plage Quemado, there are a couple of quieter beaches just out of town on the Nador road. From some vantage points you can see the Spanish controlled islet of Peñon de Alhucemas off the coast. It may look pretty, but it has served mainly as a prison and military base.

The town holds a modest festival at the end of July or in the first week of August; ask the tourist office for details.

Road Rules in Kif Country

Driving in the Rif has its own set of rules. This is one of the biggest hashish smuggling areas in the world and the police, who have numerous road blocks set up across the region, can get a little inquisitive should they stumble across a European-registered vehicle on some minor road in the Rif. In fact, foreign-registered vehicles commonly get stopped at road blocks and their drivers grilled on the suspicion of being international dope fiends. Even though this can become deeply annoying be calm, have all your documentation handy and put a smile on your face.

The 100km or so of winding tarmac road between Ketama and Chefchaouen in the heart of Kif country will take you along one of the most dramatic routes in Morocco.

Unfortunately, the scenery does not provide the only spectacle; equally dramatic and certainly more memorable is the sudden appearance of the kif dealers, who pop up on the side of the road waving enormous bales of kif or freeze-block–sized lumps of hashish. Occasionally dealers will try the same enticing tactics from vehicles and may pursue you with tooting horns and flashing lights. It's not a good idea to stop, not for anyone.

Information

Money There are plenty of banks (with ATMs) along Calle Mohammed V where you can change cash and travellers cheques on weekdays. Both the BMCE and BMCI will do cash advances on Visa and MasterCard. The larger hotels will change cash.

Post & Communications The post office (with cardphones outside) is on Calle Mouly Idriss Alkbar, a few blocks west of Calle Mohammed V.

For cheap Internet access go to Club Computer Club Al-Hoceima, 46 Rue Tetouan, where the cost is Dr6 an hour. It's open 4 to 9 pm daily plus 10 am to noon at weekends. Also try PC Rif Net near the stadium.

Other Services The Délégation Régionale du Tourisme (☎ 981185) is on Calle Tariq on Ziad. It's a helpful place open from 8.30 am to noon and 2.30 to 6.30 pm weekdays.

There's a photo lab opposite Hotel al-Khouzama. Nikor Voyageurs (☎ 840065) and Ketama Voyages (☎ 985120) on Calle

Mohammed V are two fairly competent travel agents.

Beaches

The town beach, **Plage Quemado**, is OK, but unfortunately the large ugly hotel of the same name forms the main backdrop. Better are the small beaches at **Cala Bonita** (where there's a camp site), before the southern entry into town, and **Plage Sebadella**, about a 2km walk to the northwest. **Plage Espalmadero**, 4km from the centre of town along the road to Nador, and **Plage Asfiha**, 5km further on, are OK, and usually fairly quiet. Local buses to Ajdir and Imzouren run by the turn-offs for both beaches (Dr2). They leave from just past the Mobil petrol station at the southern end of Calle Mohammed V.

Hammams & Public Showers

The Baño Popular, a block east of Calle Mohammed V, is open to women from 10 am to 5.30 pm, and to men from 6 to 9.30 am and 5.30 to 10.30 pm. It costs Dr5.

MEDITERRANEAN COAST & THE RIF

MEDITERRANEAN COAST & THE RIF

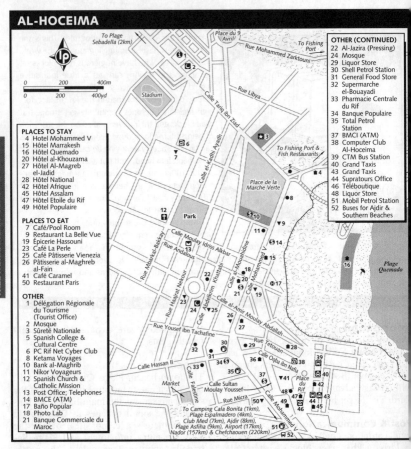

AL-HOCEIMA

To Plage Sebadella (2km)

Place du 9 Avril
To Fishing Port
Rue Mohammed Zarktouni

Stadium

Rue Libya

Calle Tariq Ibn Ziad

To Fishing Port & Fish Restaurants

Place de la Marche Verte

Calle el-Kadhi Ayadh

Park

Calle Moulay Idriss Alkbar

Rue Andalous

Rue Mbarkai Bakkay

Rue Haajrat Nekour

Calle Abdelkrim Khattabi

Calle al-Mouahidine

Calle Mohammed V

Plage Quemado

Rue Yousef ibn Tachafine

Calle al-Amir Moulay Abdallah

Rue Tetouan

Calle Hassan II

Calle Falestine

Calle Ogba ibn Nafia

Place du Rif

Market

Calle Sultan Moulay Youssef

Rue Micra

To Camping Cala Bonita (1km),
Plage Espalmadero (4km),
Club Med (7km), Ajdir (8km),
Plage Asfiha (9km), Airport (17km),
Nador (157km) & Chefchaouen (220km)

PLACES TO STAY
4 Hotel Mohammed V
15 Hôtel Marrakesh
16 Hôtel Quemado
20 Hôtel al-Khouzama
27 Hôtel Al-Magreb el-Jadid
28 Hôtel National
42 Hôtel Afrique
45 Hôtel Assalam
47 Hôtel Etoile du Rif
49 Hôtel Populaire

PLACES TO EAT
7 Café/Pool Room
9 Restaurant La Belle Vue
19 Épicerie Hassouni
23 Café La Perle
25 Café Pâtisserie Vienezia
26 Pâtisserie al-Maghreb al-Fain
41 Café Caramel
50 Restaurant Paris

OTHER
1 Délégation Régionale du Tourisme (Tourist Office)
2 Mosque
3 Sûreté Nationale
5 Spanish College & Cultural Centre
6 PC Rif Net Cyber Club
8 Ketama Voyages
10 Bank al-Maghrib
11 Nikor Voyageurs
12 Spanish Church & Catholic Mission
13 Post Office; Telephones
14 BMCE (ATM)
17 Baño Popular
18 Photo Lab
21 Banque Commerciale du Maroc

OTHER (CONTINUED)
22 Al-Jazira (Pressing)
24 Mosque
29 Liquor Store
30 Shell Petrol Station
31 General Food Store
32 Supermarche el-Bouayadi
33 Pharmacie Centrale du Rif
34 Banque Populaire
35 Total Petrol Station
37 BMCI (ATM)
38 Computer Club Al-Hoceima
39 CTM Bus Station
40 Grand Taxis
43 Grand Taxis
44 Supratours Office
46 Téléboutique
48 Liquor Store
51 Mobil Petrol Station
52 Buses for Ajdir & Southern Beaches

Places to Stay – Budget

Camping About 1km from the town centre just off the road to Ajdir, *Camping Cala Bonita* (☎ 980301) is on probably the prettiest little beach in Al-Hoceima. Shaded 'family' pitches go for a flat fee of Dr50 and unshaded terrace pitches for the 'young and single' go for Dr35. Prices are for four people. Facilities are basic (cold showers only) and the pitches are really packed together, but there's a bar and restaurant close by.

Hotels There are loads of budget hotels close to Place du Rif, but they still fill midsummer.

A good, reliable choice is *Hôtel D'Afrique* (☎ 983065, 20 Blvd el-Alaouiyine). Clean basic singles/doubles with washbasins cost Dr40/50 (Dr50/60 in high season). A hot shower is Dr10.

Hotel Assalam (☎ 981413, 10 Rue Sama Rif) offers spartan but bright and airy rooms for Dr40/60 (hot showers cost Dr10).

For the desperate there's *Hôtel Populaire* (☎ 985750), which has basic singles/doubles/triples for Dr40/50/60.

Hôtel Rif (☎ 982268, 13 Calle Sultan Moulay Youssef) offers singles with wash basin for Dr30 (Dr50 in high season) and doubles/triples with hot showers for Dr60/70. It's an austere place but the rooms are OK.

Places to Stay – Mid-Range

About the cheapest of the mid-range hotels is *Hôtel Marrakesh* (☎ 983025, 106 Calle Mohammed V) set above a male-dominated cafe. Slightly shabby singles/doubles with showers and sea glimpses cost Dr120/141.

More expensive is *Hotel al-Khouzama* (☎/fax 985669), just off Calle Mohammed V. Nice, tidy singles/doubles/triples (some with TV) go for Dr199/236/295. There's a very popular cafe and a pool room.

Closer to public transport is *Hôtel National* (☎ 982681, 23 Rue Tetouan). Slightly shabby rooms with bathroom, phone and heater cost Dr199/236/330.

On Place du Rif is a curious Art Deco building, *Hôtel Etoile du Rif* (☎ 840848). Pleasant, clean rooms with toilet, shower and phone cost Dr141/161. It's a well-run place and the pick of the crop with a popular cafe and a quiet *salon de thé* (gentile cafe).

Not markedly better and considerably pricier, is *Hôtel al-Maghreb el-Jadid* (☎ 982504, 56 Calle Mohammed V). Rooms with bathroom and heater go for Dr212/266/362 (add 10% for high season). The hotel has a lift, and a bar and restaurant in high season.

If you've got a little more money to throw around, *Hotel Mohammed V* (☎ 982233, fax 983314), which overlooks Plage Quemado, has rooms with bathroom, phone, TV and balcony for Dr328/413. There's a lift, a restaurant and bar, but you pay for the location.

Hotel Quemado (☎ 983315, fax 983314), on the beach, was closed at the time of writing, but check it out if you're here.

Club Med (☎ 802013, fax 802014), about 7km out of town, past Ajdir, is down a track off the Ketama-Nador road. It's an altogether grander affair, with all the usual facilities and is a popular place. You'll need to book at least a week in advance (it's only open from May to August when package tourists are flown in from Europe). It costs a *little* more than the Camping Cala Bonita.

Places to Eat

Restaurants There are numerous little restaurants serving up the usual fare for about Dr25 around Place du Rif. Excellent by any standards is the tiny *Cafe Caramel*. It's a bright, friendly place serving tajine for Dr20, salad for Dr5 and harira for Dr3.

On a good day you're in for a treat at the slightly quirky *Restaurant Paris* (21 Calle Mohammed V), but be sure to check the prices before ordering so you won't be charged 'tourist prices' later. Main courses cost around Dr35 and three-course set menus go for Dr58 or Dr68 with a choice of chicken, beef or fish. Given some notice, they can run you up a vegetarian option too.

Restaurant La Belle Vue, also on Calle Mohammed V, justifies its name with a good view, but only serves food in high season.

There's a cluster of fish restaurants at the port. Fish courses are between Dr20 and Dr60 (the cheapest options are often the best). The fresh, simple food at *Restaurant Escorpio* is a good choice, while at *Club Nautique* you can get beer or wine with your meal.

You could try one of the better hotels; *Hotel Mohammed V* has a menu touristique (Dr135) or menu gastronomique (Dr150).

Patisseries & Self-Catering The *Pâtisserie al-Maghreb al-Fain* (Calle Mohammed V) is OK for breakfast (omelettes Dr10), while *Café La Perle* on the roundabout off Rue Haajrat Nekour has an agreeable terrace and serves good juices (Dr6). A more sophisticated choice, *Café Pâtisserie Venezia*, has a peaceful seating area upstairs.

The market on Calle Falestine is open Sunday and Tuesday. On Monday there's a souq that sells just about everything out at Imzouren. The souq is the preserve of women until 9 am, after which men are allowed.

Many small, general food stores are dotted around town. *Épicerie Hassouni* on Calle Mohammed V and *Supermarche el-Bouayadi* on Calle Abdelkrim Khattabi are good. There are two well-stocked liquor stores.

Entertainment

The *bar* at Hotel Mohammed V is not bad and the terrace has excellent views over

Plage Quemado. A beer will cost you Dr18. The hotel also puts on a beach disco from 10 pm to 2.30 am. Entry is Dr50 (including your first drink).

Cheaper (Stork beer is Dr15), is the bar in *Club Nautique* down by the fishing port. It's a sophisticated looking place, often with an unsophisticated but entertaining crowd.

Getting There & Away
Air RAM has weekly flights from the Al-Hoceima airport (17km to the south-east) to Tetouan (Dr324) and Casablanca (Dr734). RAM has a weekly flight to Amsterdam (Dr4050 one way, Dr4800 return) and to Brussels in high season. Thanks to Club Med, in high season there are also charter flights from France, Spain and Germany.

Bus All the bus companies have offices on or near Place du Rif.

CTM has daily buses to Nador at 5.30 am and 12.30 pm (Dr37, 3½ hours) and to Tangier (Dr85, eight hours) at 10 pm – this service goes via Tetouan (Dr70, seven hours). Additional buses for Tetouan leave at 1 and 10 pm. Only the 1 pm bus travels via Chefchaouen (Dr55, about 5½ hours), but on the others you could be dropped at Derdara (the turn-off to Ouezzane) then pick up local transport into Chefchaouen (8km).

Buses for Casablanca (Dr160, more than 10 hours) leave at 6.30 am and 8 pm. These travel via Taza (Dr47, less than four hours), Fès (Dr82, five hours), Meknès (Dr98, 5½ hours) and Rabat (Dr136, 6½ hours).

Supratours (☎ 981100) on Place du Rif is open from 7 am to 10 pm daily. A coach departs for Taza at 8 pm connecting with the overnight train to Fès (Dr82), Meknès (Dr88), Rabat (Dr128), Casablanca (Dr148) and Marrakesh (Dr204). Apparently, there's no connecting bus meeting the trains at Taza so you'll need to get a bus or taxi to Al-Hoceima.

There are numerous other small companies serving all the above destinations. There are five services to both Nador and Tetouan, plus two morning services for Oujda (Dr58, about six hours) and buses to Taza (Dr35) at 5 am and 1.30 pm.

Grand Taxi The best time to try to get a grand taxi is the morning. They line up a block east of the Place du Rif. The most popular destinations are Taza (Dr55) and Nador (Dr50), though taxis to Fès (Dr100) or Tetouan (Dr150) are possible.

The East Coast

MELILLA
☎ 952 • pop 70,000
With about 70,000 inhabitants, a third of whom are Muslims of Rif Berber origin, Melilla (pronounced Meh-**lee**-ya) is marginally smaller and visibly less affluent than its Spanish sister enclave to the west, Ceuta.

The presence of 10,000 Spanish troops provides a boost to the local economy, but Melilla lives mainly on contraband trade. Anything up to 80% of the goods that arrive in the enclave end up not only in Morocco, but countries throughout north-west Africa. The free-trade agreement between Morocco and the EU, under which all trade barriers will be abolished by 2012, looks set to devastate this business. While Ceuta, a more convenient point of entry into North Africa, may be able to ride out the economic storm, Melilla could be in deep trouble – it already has an unemployment rate higher than any city in the EU.

Relations between the Muslim population (worst hit by unemployment) and the rest of the inhabitants are strained. The ill-feeling bubbled over into violent protests in the 1980s when new citizenship laws threatened to leave many Muslims in limbo without proper papers.

Spaniards in the enclave also worry that the Muslims will one day push for the enclave to be handed over to Morocco. Most of the Muslims say this is rubbish, that as Rif Berbers they owe no allegiance to the Moroccan king and that in any case they would prefer to be under Spanish rule. Other Spaniards fear that, with their big families, the Muslims will eventually outnumber the Christians and gain power. Melilla may be uncompromisingly Spanish in look and feel, but it lives under a cloud of uncertainty.

History

The port and peninsula of Melilla have been inhabited for more than 2000 years. The Phoenicians and Romans both counted it among their network of Mediterranean coastal bases – it was then known as Rus-sadir. After the departure of the Romans, the city fell into obscurity until it was captured by Abd ar-Rahman III of Cordoba.

In 1496 it was taken by a Spanish raiding party and has remained in Spain's hands ever since, although Abd al-Krim's rebels came close to taking the town during the Rif War in 1921. It was from here that Franco launched the Spanish Civil War in 1936.

Melilla's excellently preserved medieval fortress gives the city a lingering fascina-tion. Right up until the end of the 19th cen-tury virtually all of Melilla was contained within these massive defensive walls.

Orientation

Plaza de España is the heart of the new part of town, most of the hotels are in the grid of streets leading to the north-west of the plaza. In the same area you'll find the banks and most of the restaurants and bars.

East of Melilla la Vieja lies the estacíon marítima (ferry terminal); the frontier with Morocco is a 20-minute bus ride south, over the trickle of effluent known as the Río de Oro.

Information

Tourist Offices The Officiana du Turismo (☎ 952 675444) in the Palicio de Congresos y Exposiciones on Calle Fortuny. It's staf-fed from 9 am to 3 pm weekdays. The help-ful staff only have leaflets in Spanish. For more information in Spanish check its Web site: www.melilla.500.com.

Money You'll find several banks (whose ATMs accept numerous types of cards) along or near Ave de Juan Carlos I Rey. The Cen-tral Hispano on Plaza de España is as good as any. Banks buy and sell dirham at a slightly inferior rate to that found in Morocco, but as good as anything you'll get from the Moroc-can dealers in the streets. Money dealers hang about Plaza de España and the ferry port.

There's a Banque Populaire on Morocco's side of the border (it accepts cash only).

Post & Communications The *correos y telégrafos* (post office) on Calle Pablo Vallescá is open from 8.30 am to 8.30 pm weekdays and Saturday 9.30 am to 2 pm.

There are numerous téléboutiques and public phones that accept coins and cards (available from tabacs). Some téléboutiques offer Internet access (350 ptas per hour). There are two near Calle Ejercito Espanol.

To phone Melilla from outside Spain, dial ☎ 0034. The ☎ 952 code must be di-alled at all times, even when you're calling from within Melilla.

Film & Photography A good general photography shop is Photo Imperio (☎ 952 670948) at 3 Ave de Juan Carlos I Rey.

Duty Free Melilla is a duty-free zone, so if you're driving it's worth filling up here. Petrol is about one-third cheaper than in Morocco or Spain (super 92.5 ptas, normal 81.9 ptas, diesel 65.5 ptas).

The Supersol supermarket, on the road to the frontier, is open from 10 am to 10 pm daily. It's good for booze (a litre of Johnny Walker costs 1375 ptas) and cheap tents (7000 ptas).

Medical Services & Emergencies Ur-gencias Sanitarias (☎ 952 674400) at 40 Al-varo de Bazan is a night pharmacy that is open 5 pm to 9 am Monday to Saturday and all day Sunday and public holidays.

The Hospital Comarcal (☎ 952 670000) is near Plaza de Toros.

Local police can be called on ☎ 092.

Other Services Remember that Melilla is two hours ahead of Morocco during sum-mer and one hour ahead at other times.

You can buy basic camping equipment from Deportes Garnica (☎ 952 681898), 8 General Pareja.

Melilla la Vieja

Melilla la Vieja (Old Melilla) is well worth exploring. Perched over the Mediterranean,

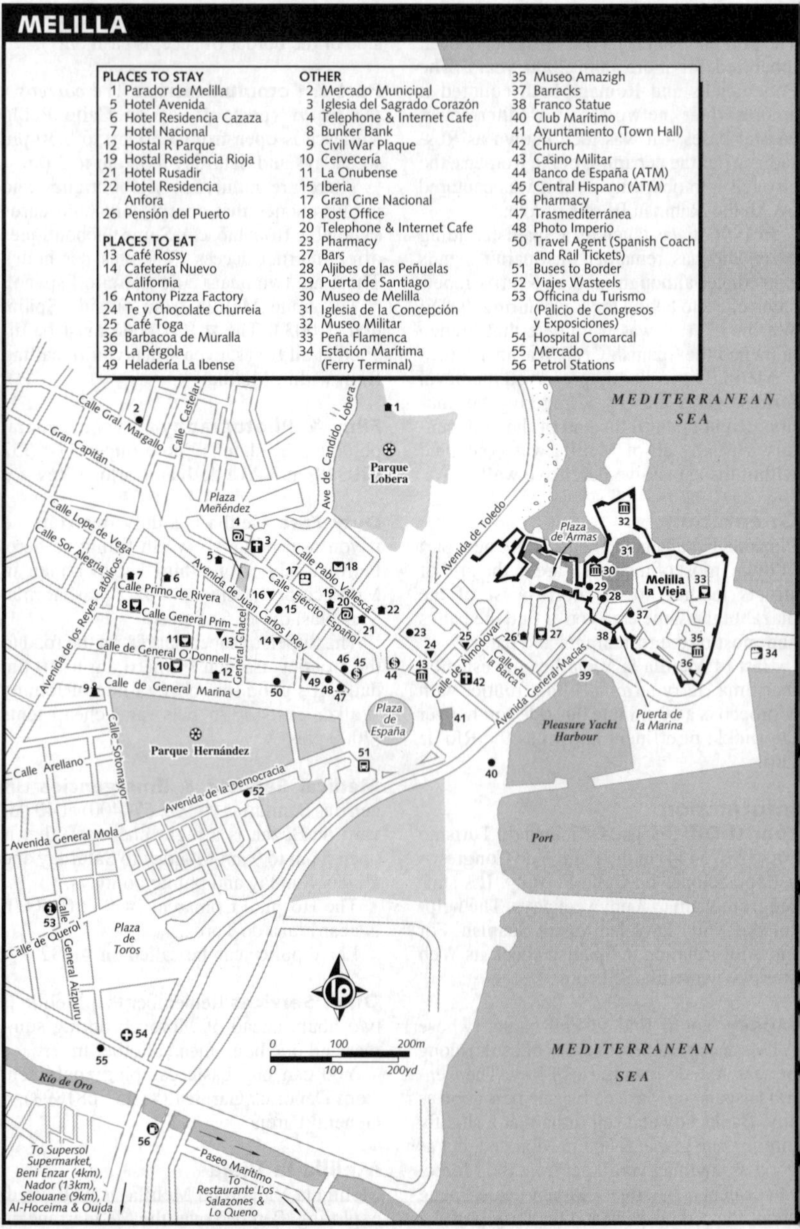

MELILLA
PLACES TO STAY
1 Parador de Melilla
5 Hotel Avenida
6 Hotel Residencia Cazaza
7 Hotel Nacional
12 Hostal R Parque
19 Hostal Residencia Rioja
21 Hotel Rusadir
22 Hotel Residencia Anfora
26 Pensión del Puerto
PLACES TO EAT
13 Café Rossy
14 Cafetería Nuevo California
16 Antony Pizza Factory
24 Te y Chocolate Churreia
25 Café Toga
36 Barbacoa de Muralla
39 La Pérgola
49 Heladería La Ibense
OTHER
2 Mercado Municipal
3 Iglesia del Sagrado Corazón
4 Telephone & Internet Cafe
8 Bunker Bank
9 Civil War Plaque
10 Cervecería
11 La Onubense
15 Iberia
17 Gran Cine Nacional
18 Post Office
20 Telephone & Internet Cafe
23 Pharmacy
27 Bars
28 Aljibes de las Peñuelas
29 Puerta de Santiago
30 Museo de Melilla
31 Iglesia de la Concepción
32 Museo Militar
33 Peña Flamenca
34 Estación Marítima (Ferry Terminal)
35 Museo Amazigh
37 Barracks
38 Franco Statue
40 Club Marítimo
41 Ayuntamiento (Town Hall)
42 Church
43 Casino Militar
44 Banco de España (ATM)
45 Central Hispano (ATM)
46 Pharmacy
47 Trasmediterránea
48 Photo Imperio
50 Travel Agent (Spanish Coach and Rail Tickets)
51 Buses to Border
52 Viajes Wasteels
53 Officina du Turismo (Palicio de Congresos y Exposiciones)
54 Hospital Comarcal
55 Mercado
56 Petrol Stations
MEDITERRANEAN SEA
Calle Gral. Margallo
Calle Castelar
Gran Capitán
Ave de Candido Lobera
Parque Lobera
Plaza Meñéndez
Calle Lope de Vega
Calle Sor Alegria
Avenida de Juan Carlos I Rey
Calle Pablo Vallescá
Calle Ejército Español
Calle Primo de Rivera
Calle General Prim
Calle de General O'Donnell
Calle de General Marina
C General Chacel
Avenida de los Reyes Católicos
Avenida de Toledo
Plaza de Armas
Melilla la Vieja
Calle de Almodovar
Calle de la Barca
Avenida General Macías
Puerta de la Marina
Pleasure Yacht Harbour
Plaza de España
Calle Sotomayor
Parque Hernández
Calle Arellano
Avenida de la Democracia
Avenida General Mola
Calle de Querol
Calle General Aizpuru
Plaza de Toros
Port
MEDITERRANEAN SEA
0 100 200m
0 100 200yd
Río de Oro
Paseo Marítimo
To Supersol Supermarket, Beni Enzar (4km), Nador (13km), Selouane (9km), Al-Hoceima & Oujda
To Restaurante Los Salazones & Lo Queno

it's a good example of the kind of 16th and 17th century fortress stronghold the Portuguese (and in this case the Spaniards) built along the Moroccan littoral. At the time of writing considerable reconstruction and maintenance work was being done. When complete it should open up a network of tunnels that run under the castle and lead out to the ocean.

The main entrance to the fortress is **Puerta de la Marina** on Ave General Macías (you'll also see a monument to Franco here).

Just up from Puerta de la Marina are the **Aljibes de las Peñuelas**, an impressive pair of renovated cisterns. A film about the cisterns and the fort is shown across the square. Entry to both is 200 ptas.

Museo de Melilla has a good collection of historical and architectural drawings, Phoenician and Roman ceramics and coins, and numerous models and archaeological finds. It has a great terrace overlooking the city, a library and downstairs a small contemporary art galley. Entry is free.

Museo Amazigh at Cuesta de Florentina displays some Moroccan artefacts and archaeological finds but it's nothing really special. Entry is free.

All the museums are open from 10 am to 2 pm and 5 to 9.30 pm (4.30 to 8.30 pm in winter) Tuesday to Saturday and 10 am to 2 pm Sunday.

Also worth a look is the **Iglesia de la Concepción**, with its gilded reredos (decorative hanging) and shrine to Nuestra Señora la Virgen de la Victoria (the patroness of the city).

If you continue up Calle de la Concepción you reach the **Museo Militar**, perched high over the Mediterranean. It's stuffed full of exhibits from the Spanish military in Melilla with flags, uniforms, busts of Franco and Alfonso XII (1886–1914), the hoof of Alfonso's horse, plus a chilling collection of weapons ranging from bayonets to AK47s and rocket launchers. It's open 10 am to 2 pm Tuesday to Sunday and entry is free.

New Town

Construction of the new part of town, to the west of the fortress, was begun at the end of the 19th century. It was laid out by Don Enrique Nieto who, following Gaudí's lead, is considered by some to have made Melilla Spain's 'second modernist city', after Barcelona. This is rather on the generous side and the general decay of the city has not helped the case, but the classic Spanish architecture is still in stark contrast with Moroccan towns like Nador, nearby.

A walk around can be an instructive lesson in the city's more recent past. A statue on Ave de Juan Carlos I Rey and a plaque opposite the Parque Hernández on Calle de General Marina celebrate 7 July 1936, the day Franco began the campaign against the government in Madrid, with the cry of 'Viva España'.

Beaches

There's a string of beaches south of the Río de Oro to the border. They're quite clean, but nothing special – you'd be better off heading for mainland Spain or into Morocco.

Special Events

The town is buzzing with a sailing regatta in the second week of August and the annual fiesta in September. There's also an international bikers' meet in July.

Places to Stay – Budget

If you're coming from Morocco, you'll know you've arrived in Europe when you look for a place to stay. There are no bargains to be had (prices rise by around 15% in high season and Easter week) and many places fill up quickly so book ahead if possible.

The cheapest option is *Pensión del Puerto* (☎ 952 681279) set just back from Ave de General Macías. A bed should cost 1500 ptas, the shared bathrooms are new and clean, but the place is a little rough around the edges.

The family-run *Hostal Residencia Rioja* (☎ 952 682709, 10 Calle Ejército Español) has bright, basic singles/doubles with shared hot showers for 3100/4100 ptas.

An alternative is *Hostal R Parque* (☎ 952 682143) fronting the Parque Hernández. Slightly dingy rooms with phone and bathroom cost 3000/5500 ptas.

The small **Hostal Residencia Cazaza** (☎ 952 684648, 6 Calle Primo de Rivera) offers reasonable rooms with shower and TV for 3500/5500 ptas.

A block west is **Hotel Nacional** (☎ 952 684540, fax 952 684481, 10 Calle Primo de Rivera). It has pleasant rooms with bathroom, air-con, phone and TV for 4990/6985 ptas.

Also up on the price scale is **Hotel Avenida** (☎ 952 684949, fax 952 683226, 24 Ave de Juan Carlos I Rey). It has rooms with bathroom for 4503/7176 ptas.

Places to Stay – Mid-Range & Top End

The rather institutional **Hotel Residencia Anfora** (☎ 952 683340, 8 Calle Pablo Vallescá) offers rooms with bathroom, minibar, air-con and TV for 6860/10,640 ptas.

The pleasant **Hotel Rusadir** (☎ 952 681240, fax 952 670527, 5 Calle Pablo Vallescá) has a bar and restaurant. Rooms with air-con, TV, phone and minibar cost 9800/12,900 ptas.

Parador de Melilla (☎ 952 684940, fax 952 683486) off Ave de Candido Lobera, is top of the tree with great views over the Mediterranean. The exterior is concrete and modern and the rooms stylish. Rooms start at 8800/12,000 ptas.

Places to Eat

Restaurants The best area to search for good cheap bocadillos and the like is along Calle Castelar, not far from the mercado municipal (food market).

There are countless bars and the odd restaurant where you can get a meal in the streets around Ave de Juan Carlos I Rey. The popular **Antony Pizza Factory** (☎ 952 684320, 1 Calle Cándido) serves good pizza for 575 ptas to 950 ptas and pasta for 675 ptas.

A restaurant with a good reputation for seafood is **Restaurante Los Salazones** (☎ 952 673652, 15 Calle de Alcaudete) off the Paseo Marítimo (closed Monday). The set menu (three courses and wine) costs 2500 ptas, mains go for 600 to 1500 ptas.

For a treat, you can't beat the **Barbacoa de Muralla**, at Calle Fiorentina in the southernmost corner of Melilla la Vieja. The three-course set menu is 4000 ptas.

Cafes A popular meeting place for young and old alike is **Cafetería Nuevo California** (Ave de Juan Carlos I Rey), which serves good coffee and snacks. **La Pérgola**, set on the pleasure yacht harbour, is a great place for a drink in the late afternoon. It has a large terrace and a pool table; table football and board games are available.

The small **Cafe Rossy** (Calle General Prim) is a good place for breakfast and is very popular with women. Great bocadillos (with delicious ham) go for 250 ptas. Order at the bar as there's no waiter service.

For a cheap traditional breakfast of churros and thick hot chocolate, head for **Te y Chocolate Churreia**.

The nearby **Café Toga** (Plaza de Don Pedro de Estopiñán) is a pleasant little bar serving tapas and sandwiches during the day.

Heladería La Ibense on Calle General O'Donnell is the best place in town for ice cream with more than 20 flavours (cones cost around 125 ptas and cups 225 ptas). In winter, there are hot waffles (150 ptas) covered in chocolate or cream – or both! It stays open late – from 10 am to about 4 am daily.

Entertainment

Evenings out in Melilla seem to have more to do with bars and tapas than cheap restaurants. And some of the tapas are excellent, just keep drinking!

There are two fantastic bars opposite each other on Calle de General O'Donnell. The attractive **La Onubense** serves an excellent selection of classic tapas including callos (tripe) and the speciality bollito de Pringá (a kind of meatball). Equally good is the **Cervecería**, a larger place done out in a Gaudíesque fashion by the Melillan architect Carlos Baeza. Both are open from 7.30 pm to about 2 am.

If you're looking for something different you could try **Peña Flamenca**, a folk music club inside the fortress.

As far as discos and disco-pubs (a Spanish speciality) go, **Lo Queno** on the Carretera de Alfonso XIII west of the football stadium, is the biggest and best in town.

Marachas (30 Mar Chia) south towards the border plays Salsa music and has a friendly atmosphere. *Bunker Bank (14 Calle General Prim)* is recommended by locals for gay travellers. All nightclubs are open from around 11 pm to 4 am; entry is usually free and drinks cost about 450 ptas.

Getting There & Away

There are several travel agencies that can book train and coach tickets for Spain. Some offices are on Calle de General Marina.

Air Binter Mediterraneo, a subsidiary of Iberia, Spain's national carrier, has an office on Ave de Juan Carlos I Rey. There are direct daily flights to Granada, Málaga, Madrid and Almería (see under Air in the Getting There & Away chapter).

A taxi (☎ 952 683621) to the airport is around 1000 ptas.

Bus & Taxi Local buses (catch the No 2 marked 'Aforos') run between Plaza de España and the Beni-Enzar border post (75 ptas) about every half hour from around 7.30 am to 10 pm. From where the buses stop, it's about 150m to Spanish customs and another 200m to Moroccan customs.

No 19 (often unmarked) Moroccan buses go to Nador (Dr2.20), which is a large transport hub (see Nador following). To catch them, walk away from the border post and straight over the crossroads.

Grand taxis (Dr4) to Nador are tucked away in a lot to the right of the cross road.

Border Crossings Before entering Morocco, fill in a white form and get your passport stamped at the booth. Crossing the border here is less confusing (and less hassle) than at Ceuta. Spanish checks seem largely cursory, but the Moroccans can hold things up for quite a while. If you're driving into Morocco, remember to retain the green customs slip, which you must present when you (and your vehicle) leave the country.

When leaving Morocco, fill in a yellow form and get your passport stamped. Some nationalities require visas to enter Spain (see Embassies & Consulates in the Facts

for the Visitor chapter) and if they don't stop you here, they will when you try to move on to the mainland.

Boat Only Trasmediterránea operates ferry and hydrofoil services out of Melilla. Buy your tickets at the Trasmediterránea office (☎ 952 690902) on Plaza de España, open from 9 am to 1 pm and 5 to 7 pm weekdays, and 9 am to noon Saturday, or direct at estación marítima (☎ 952 690170).

Ferries leave every night except Sunday for Málaga and Almería (see Sea in the Getting There & Away chapter).

Passport and customs checks at Melilla (although technically you're travelling inside Spain) can delay departure considerably.

NADOR
☎ 06

Nador is a sprawling town set on a lagoon 13km south of Melilla and is earmarked for development as a business centre – the EU plans to fund a coast road from Tetouan to Nador, which it hopes will boost commerce. Nador is a relaxed, modern city and a gentle introduction to Morocco if it is your first stop.

Luckily, most transport (to a huge number of destinations) is located in one of two places, which makes arriving and leaving comparatively painless. There is also a ferry port, though connections are few. Should you get stuck and have to stay overnight, there's no shortage of hotels of all classes. Many of them are near the bus and grand taxi lots.

Information

There's a tourist office (☎ 606518) of sorts at 80 Blvd ibn Rochd and a Spanish consulate (☎ 606136, fax 606152) at 12 Rue Mohammed Zerktouni.

You can surf the Internet (afternoon only) at PCNord-Nadornet opposite Lycee Ablkaim Khattabi just off Ave Sidi Mohammed. Access costs Dr12 an hour.

Nador is established on a strict grid system. The central street is Ave Hassan II, with the main bus station at its southern end. It's bisected by Ave Mohammed V, which runs east to west – long-distance buses leave from the western end.

Places to Stay & Eat

Heading west out of the bus station and up Ave des FAR you will see **Hôtel Anoual** (☎ 602828, 16 Rue 20) on your left, across the dusty patch of ground used by the buses headed for the border. Reasonable singles/doubles with showers cost Dr128/146 (30% less in low season).

More spartan, rougher and cheaper are **Hotel Nador** (☎ 606071) and **Hotel el-Khattabi** (☎ 330390) opposite each other on Rue 22, which is the road before (and parallel to) Rue 20. They both offer singles/doubles/triples with showers for Dr50/70/105.

Heading south from Place Municipale along Rue ibn Roched you'll come across **Hotel La Marche Verte** (☎ 606721, 106 Rue ibn Roched) on the right. It's a clean and tidy place with doubles for Dr60 (hot showers Dr5).

Almost opposite is **Hôtel ibn Khaldoun** (☎ 607042, 91 Rue ibn Roched), which is OK but nothing special. Rooms cost Dr58/75/100 or Dr70/95/120 with shower.

For quick service and good value go to one of the eateries along Ave Hassan II close to the main bus station. **Restaurant Central** and **Restaurant Canaria** are a good bet; they both serve chicken and chips (Dr20), fish and chips (Dr30), salad (Dr5) and soup (Dr3.50). A pleasant (though expensive) spot for a coffee is **El-Club**, which juts out into the lagoon east of the main market.

Getting There & Away

Air There are direct weekly flights to Amsterdam (Netherlands), Brussels (Belgium), Dusseldorf and Frankfurt (Germany). One-way fares with RAM are all Dr4054. There are flights to Casablanca three times a week.

Bus Departures are divided between two set points: the gare routière down by the lagoon south of the city centre and Rue General Meziane off Place Municipale to the west of the city centre. CTM has offices in both places, but only its 8.30 pm express service to Casablanca (Dr165, 11 hours) via Rabat (Dr141, 9½ hours) leaves from Rue General Meziane. Between 5 and 10 pm numerous Casablanca-bound express buses belonging

to other reputable, slightly cheaper companies leave from the same area. Many go via Fès and Meknès as well as Taza.

The gare routière is a relaxed sort of place – the touts look suspiciously like university students. From here CTM has services to Tangier (Dr175, 12 hours; departs at 7 pm), via Taza (Dr57), Fès (Dr90) and Meknès (Dr106). Buses for Tetouan (Dr100, 9½ hours), leave at 9.30 am and 6 pm and go via Chefchaouen (Dr88, eight hours). There's a bus to Oujda (Dr25, 2½ hours) at 9 am and two buses to Al-Hoceima (Dr37, three hours).

Cheaper bus companies also run these routes and many more. There are buses every 30 minutes to Fès during the morning, hourly services to Al-Hoceima and half-hourly services to Oujda and Selouane. Other useful services include eight daily buses to Ras el-Mar (Dr15) via Kariat Arkmane (Dr5); and to Saidia (Dr17, departing at 11.30 am); Er-Rachidia (Dr115, 4.30 pm); and Figuig (Dr90, 9.15 am).

The No 19 buses for Beni Enzar (the Melilla border) leave from outside the main bus station. They're often unnumbered and run between about 7 am and 7 pm (Dr2.20).

Train The Supratours office (☎ 607262) on Ave Sidi Mohammed organises a bus to Taourirt to catch connecting trains to Casablanca (Dr198.50) and Tangier (Dr196.50). The bus leaves Nador at 8 pm daily and returns from Taourirt at 5.30 am.

Alternatively, catch a bus (Dr20) or grand taxi (Dr35) to/from Taourirt.

Taxi The grand taxi rank is next to the main bus station and a large number of destinations are catered for – there are taxis to Oujda (Dr35), Saidia (Dr35), Kariat Arkmane (Dr7) and Selouane (Dr3.50), Al-Hoceima (Dr50), Taza (Dr55), Fès (Dr100) and Meknès (Dr120).

Grand taxis to Beni Enzar (the Melilla border) cost Dr4.

If you need a cab around town catch a red petit taxi; an average journey shouldn't cost more than Dr5. There's a taxi rank outside the bus station.

Football pitch in Talassemtane National Park (top); kif plantations above the Oued Farda Gorges (middle left); farm in the hills outside Chefchaouen (middle right); sleepy cats and snowcapped mountains, Chefchaouen (bottom left); typical suburban alley and blue door, Chefchaouen (bottom right)

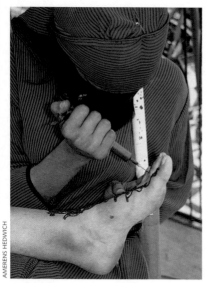

Under the tip of the henna pen

Entering the Medersa Bou Inania, Fès

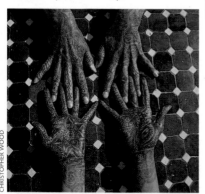

Henna tattoos with the evil eye ward off danger.

Kufic script in the Medersa Bou Inania, Meknès

Applying a magic potion, Fès

AROUND NADOR
☎ 06

If you are driving, watch the stretch of road from Melilla to Nador. It's notorious for police controls, where heavy fines (up to Dr400) are levied on the spot for the slightest incursion. Don't break the 40km/h town speed limit by even 1km/h.

Selouane
About 24km south of Melilla and 11km south of Nador is the unremarkable little town of Selouane, but for those who enjoy a splurge, the place might still be worth a stop.

Restaurant Brabo (☎ 609033, 110 Ave Mohammed V) next to the Banque Populaire is considered one of the best restaurants in northern Morocco. It's run by a Moroccan man and his Belgian wife, and they do all the cooking. Main fish and meat courses from an extensive menu cost around Dr100 (wine from around Dr75). If you're very lucky, you might even get a Belgian chocolate with your coffee. The restaurant is open from noon to 4 pm and from 8 pm to midnight every day (except Sunday evening and Monday).

East from Nador
Bird-watchers and travellers wanting to get off the beaten track may want to head east from Nador along the reasonable 8101 road. It follows the coast to Ras el-Mar and Moulouya Estuary 12km west of Saidia.

About 25km from Nador, at the far eastern end of the **lagoon**, is the town of **Kariat Arkmane**. The lagoon and surrounding salt marsh attracts various sea and wading birds, including greater flamingo, and various terns and gulls, despite considerable habitat destruction. The only accommodation is at the beach 1km from the second half of the town (the marsh divides the two). The camp site is a bit of a sandpit (pitches cost around Dr50) but *Résidence L' Amite* (☎/fax 360103) has tidy, new apartments that sleep at least four for Dr400. If you block out the rubbish the beach is fairly nice and there are a couple of pleasant cafes and restaurants. Catch a bus (Dr5) or grand taxi (Dr8) from Nador and ask to be dropped at the turn-off to the beach.

Further west is **Ras el-Mar**, whose vast beach is a popular weekend spot with Moroccan families during summer. There's an active fishing port here and a walk up to the lighthouse at the headland will give you a reasonable view of the Spanish-owned **Jaafariya Islands** just off the coast (but inaccessible from Morocco), which is said to support the Mediterranean's largest seabird colony, plus some monk seals. Populations of Audouin's gull breed on the island and osprey nest in the coastal cliffs nearby – these fish-eating raptors are hugely impressive in flight. To the west of this little town is the Moulouya Estuary which is also very rich in bird life (see Around Saidia later in this section). The town has a few basic *cafes* that serve grilled fish, but no accommodation. Catch the bus from Nador (Dr15) or a grand taxi (Dr8) or bus (Dr5) from Berkane.

SAIDIA
About 2km short of the Algerian border (you can't cross here) is the small seaside town of Saidia, a friendly easy-going place. Out of season it's very quiet and there's little to do other than enjoy the long sandy beach and crystal-clear water, but in high season (and at weekends) it's packed with Moroccans, especially during August's traditional music festival.

Places to Stay & Eat
Camping al-Mansour (☎ 625165) is about 1km from the town centre on the road to Moulouya Estuary. It's well kept with good facilities (Dr20 per person, Dr20 per car and Dr30 per a site, including electricity). Nice bungalows sleeping up to five people cost Dr300 (rising to Dr500 in high season).

Saidia's hotels are all on the expensive side and some open only in high season (mid-June to the end of August) when you should book in advance. The cheapest option is *Hôtel Bar Bleu* (☎ 625097) on Blvd Laayoune. It's a straightforward place above a popular cafe with cold showers and clean, basic rooms with washbasins for Dr50/100 a single/double.

Not so good and more expensive is *Hotel el-Kalaa* (☎ 625123) next door. Rooms

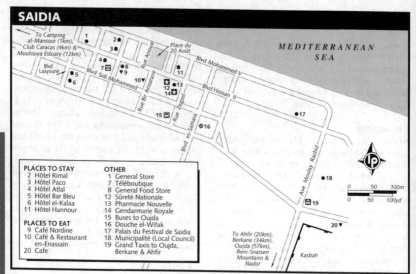

SAIDIA

PLACES TO STAY	OTHER
2 Hôtel Rimal	1 General Store
3 Hôtel Paco	7 Téléboutique
4 Hôtel Atlal	8 General Food Store
5 Hôtel Bar Bleu	12 Sûreté Nationale
6 Hôtel el-Kalaa	13 Pharmacie Nouvelle
11 Hôtel Hannour	14 Gendarmerie Royale
	15 Buses to Oujda
PLACES TO EAT	16 Douche el-Wifak
9 Café Nordine	17 Palais du Festival de Saidia
10 Café & Restaurant	18 Municipalité (Local Council)
en-Enassain	19 Grand Taxis to Oujda,
20 Cafe	Berkane & Ahfir

with bathroom go for Dr80/120 with cold water only.

Hôtel Paco (☎ 625110) charges Dr120/160 (Dr160/200 in high season) for pleasant rooms (some have showers). *Hôtel Hannour* (☎ 625115) only offers doubles with bathroom for Dr190.

Hôtel Rimal has great sea views, and charges around Dr200/250.

The friendly three-star *Hôtel Atlal* (☎ 625021, fax 625022, 44 Blvd Hassan II) has a bar, cafe and reasonable licensed restaurant serving mains for Dr70, the set menu is Dr112. Large, well-kept rooms with TV, phone and balcony go for Dr272/339.

Cheap eats, tea and coffee can be had in the shade outside the kasbah, but most drinking and eating activity takes place around Place du 20 Août. *Café Nordine* is a good place for breakfast and *Cafe & Restaurant en-Enassain* is popular in the evening for light snacks and meals; harira goes for Dr6, brochettes are Dr15.

About 3km west of town set on a beautiful piece of beach is the *Club Caracas Club*, which was almost completed at the time of writing. It's an upmarket place with a swimming pool, bar and restaurant that serves ex-

pensive food. Omelettes go for Dr15, salad is Dr35 and fish dishes cost from Dr60 to Dr80. There's a popular disco and jet skis can be hired for Dr50 for 10 minutes.

Getting There & Away

Saidia is easily reached from Berkane by grand taxi (Dr7) or bus (Dr5). You can get to Oujda by grand taxi (Dr20) or bus (Dr11.50) leaving at 6 am and 1.50 pm (there are more on Sunday and in high season). Buses leave Nador (Dr17) for Saidia at 11.30 am. Infrequent grand taxis to Nador cost (Dr35).

AROUND SAIDIA

About 12km west of town, past the new apartment complexes and the pleasure boat marina, is the **Moulouya Estuary**. This area is rich in lagoon and salt marsh bird habitats that are readily accessible. The mudflats attract a mixture of waders, sandpipers, curlews and plovers – similar habitats occur on the western side of the river, but Saidia makes a better base. Expect to pay around Dr180 when hiring a grand taxi for a full bird-watching session.

South of Saidia are the scenic **Beni-Snassen Mountains**. The S403 leads across the range from the Nador-Berkane road through the hill village of Taforalt to the main Taza-Oujda road. Plenty of public transport runs along it, but if you want to explore the heart of the area, which is criss-crossed by numerous small roads and tracks, you need either plenty of time, your own transport or to hire a grand taxi.

Two of the region's highlights are **La Grotte de Chameau** (Cave of the Camel), 13km south of Berkane, and the **Zegzel Gorge** (which is really a whole series of gorges) about 1km further north. Both are best accessed via Taforalt. La Grotte de Chameau is an amazing and untamed sec-tion of caves and tunnels complete with sta-lagmites (one of which looks like a camel), stalactites and hot springs. Adventurous ex-plorers need strong torches and an air of caution – it's easy to get lost.

Taforalt has *cafes* but no accommodation, though it's a good place to hire grand taxis for a tour of the caves and gorges about 8km to the east. The village is most easily reached from Berkane and Oujda on Wednesday and Sunday (market days). At other times your best bet is to get to Berkane early and pick up onward transport from there.

Michelin's Morocco (959) map is the best reference to the region.

MEDITERRANEAN COAST & THE RIF

Middle Atlas & the East

MIDDLE ATLAS & THE EAST

A visit to the Middle Atlas region can take in such diversities as skiing in the mountains of Ifrane, exploring the Roman ruins at Volubilis, trekking in the Middle Atlas, wandering the labyrinthine medina of Fès and visiting Moulay Ismail's huge palace at Meknès.

From Fès, the route to the Algerian border leads through Taza, a historically strategic pass, and the once prosperous border town of Oujda. The barren road south from Oujda is the easiest route to the frontier oasis of Figuig, reputedly the hottest place in Morocco.

MEKNÈS
☎ 05

The city of Meknès is known as the Versailles of Morocco. Had the enormous building projects of the Alawite sultan, Moulay Ismail, survived the ravages of time, then this metaphor might not seem so extravagant.

Encircled by the rich plains below the Middle Atlas, Meknès is blessed with a hinterland abundant with cereals, olives, wine, citrus and other agricultural products that remain the city's economic backbone.

Although the tour programs rank it third behind Marrakesh and Fès, Meknès was once the heart of the Moroccan sultanate, and its buildings impressively reflect this heritage. It is also quieter, smaller and more hassle-free than the other two and has a habit of imperceptibly growing upon you. It's worth at least a couple of day's exploration, which should include a trip to the Roman ruins of Volubilis and the hilltop tomb of Moulay Idriss.

History

The Berber tribe of the Meknassis (hence the name Meknès) first settled here in the 10th century AD. Under the Almohads and Merenids, Meknès medina was expanded and some of the city's oldest remaining monuments were built. The city fell with the Merenids but the accession to power of Moulay Ismail in 1672 (on the death of his brother and founder of the Alawite dynasty, Moulay ar-Rashid) yanked it back from obscurity.

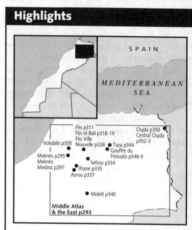

Highlights

Fès p311
Fès el-Bali p318-19
Fès Ville
Volubilis p305
Nouvelle p326
Meknès p295
Meknès
Medina p297
Sefrou p334
Ifrane p335
Azrou p337
Oujda p350
Central Oujda p352-3
Taza p344
Gouffre du
Friouato p348-9

● Midelt p340

**Middle Atlas
& the East p293**

- Taking a step back in time in the Fès medina, one of the world's last remaining medieval cities

- Marvelling at the Unesco World Heritage site at Volubilis, the best preserved Roman ruins in the country

- Searching the cedar forests near laid-back Azrou for a glimpse of Barbary apes

- Exploring hassle-free Meknès, the most imperial of cities

! ● Telephone numbers in Morocco have changed. For new codes and complete numbers, see the boxed text 'Changes to Telephone Numbers' on page 89.

Ismail reigned for 55 years and made the city his capital, endowing it with an enormous palace complex (never completed) and 25km of imposing walls with monumental gates. That he could to devote so much to construction was partly due to his uncommon success in subduing all opposition in Morocco and keeping foreign meddlers at bay (see the boxed text 'Moulay Ismail' later).

His death in 1727 also struck the death knoll for Meknès, which again became a backwater, as his grandson Mohammed III (1757–90) moved to Marrakesh. The 1755 earthquake that devastated Lisbon also dealt Meknès a heavy blow and, as so often happened in Morocco, its monuments were subsequently stripped for buildings elsewhere. It's only in the past few decades, as tourist potential has become obvious, that any serious restoration attempts have taken place.

In 1912 the arrival of the protectorate revived Meknès as the French made it their military headquarters. The army was accompanied by French farmers who settled in the fertile land nearby. After independence most properties were recovered by the Moroccan government and leased to local farmers.

Orientation

The valley of the (usually dry) Oued Bou Fekrane neatly divides the old medina and the French-built *ville nouvelle* (new town). Moulay Ismail's tomb and imperial city are south of the medina.

Train and CTM bus stations are in the ville nouvelle, as are most offices and banks. The more expensive hotels and most of the better restaurants are also there.

Buses and *grand taxis* (long-distance taxis) use a station on the west side of the medina. The cheap hotels, camping ground and sights are in the medina.

It's a 20-minute walk from the medina to the ville nouvelle, but there are regular (and crowded) local buses and urban grand taxis.

Information

Tourist Offices The Délégation Régionale du Tourisme (☎ 524426) is next to the main post office and both face Place de France (or Place Administrative). A simple city map and glossy brochure are available; it's open from 8.30 am to noon and 2.30 to 6.30 pm Monday to Thursday and from 8.30 am to 11.30 am and 3 to 6.30 pm Friday.

The Syndicat d'Initiative (☎ 520191) is in the Palais de la Foire, but is not that useful.

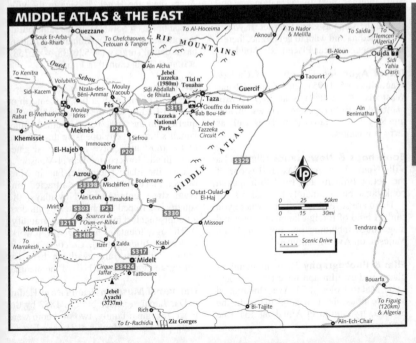

MIDDLE ATLAS & THE EAST

Money There are banks both in the new town (mainly on Ave Hassan II, Ave Mohammed V and Blvd Allal ben Abdallah) and old town (on Rue Sekkakine), with a good number and range of ATMs.

BMCE's main branch on Ave des FAR in the ville nouvelle, opposite the Hôtel Excelsior, operates an out-of-hours *bureau de change* (foreign exchange office) that's open from 10 am to 2 pm and 4 to 8 pm daily.

Post & Communications The main post office is in the ville nouvelle facing Place de France. It's open normal hours. The phone office, in the same building, is open from 8.30 am to 9 pm daily. The parcel office is around the corner to the left.

There is another large post office on Rue Dar Smen in the medina.

Club Internet, next to the Hôtel Continental on Ave des FAR in the ville nouvelle, has Internet access for Dr10 per hour; it's open daily till late. Nearby are Winword Internet, next to Pizza Fongue, and Drugstore Internet near the post office; both charge the same as Club Internet. If you're in the medina and want to get online, there's an Internet cafe near Place Lalla Aouda.

Travel Agencies The office of Carlson Wagonlits (☎ 521995) is at 1 Zankat Ghana. Wasteels (☎ 523062) is at 45 Ave Mohammed V. Both represent airlines, including Royal Air Maroc (RAM) as well as ferry companies.

Bookshops & Newsstands Librairie La Ville Nouvelle on Ave Hassan II is one of the better French- and English-language bookshops, but it's mainly for students.

There are several newsstands where you can get hold of foreign-language press and magazines, including one opposite Hôtel Majestic on Ave Mohammed V.

Film & Photography There are plenty of places to buy film and have it developed. Labo Macro Color at 21 Ave Mohammed V, ville nouvelle, is a good place. In the medina, try Studio el-Almal on 131 Rue Rouamzine.

Cultural Centres The Institut Français (☎ 524071) is on the corner of Ave Moulay Ismail and Rue Farhat Hachad in the ville nouvelle. It has a program of films and lectures and a small library but access to the institute and library is limited to its students. If you want to try and get in it's open from 9 am to noon and 3 to 7 pm Monday to Saturday.

Laundry In the medina, Pressing el-Fath at 46 Rue Rouamzine is open from 10.30 am to 8.30 pm daily (Friday until 1 pm only).

In the ville nouvelle, Atlas Pressing at 26 Blvd Allal ben Abdallah is open from 8 am to 8 pm Monday to Saturday.

Medical Services There are three hospitals in Meknès. The most central, Hôpital Moulay Ismail is actually a military hospital. The night pharmacy and a Red Cross post are on the southern side of the town hall.

If you want to see a doctor, Dr Abdelilah Mechti has a surgery (☎ 515885) at 8 Zankat Accra, near the Hôtel de Nice in the ville nouvelle. He can be contacted in emergencies at home (☎ 530024). In the same building on the 2nd floor, Dr Mohammed Dahani has a dental surgery (☎ 526838, ☎ 527587 at home). Both trained in France.

Medina

The heart of the medina lies to the north of Place al-Hedim, with the *mellah* (old Jewish quarter), to the west. To the south, Moulay Ismail's imperial city opens up through one of the most impressive monumental gateways in all Morocco, the Bab el-Mansour.

Like the Place Djemaa el-Fna in Marrakesh, Place el-Hedim once attracted itinerant street entertainers. Nowadays, the square is stripped of character by modern attempts (against local wishes) to 'grandify' it. The ugly fountains no longer even work, collecting litter instead. *Calèches* (horse-drawn carriages) are available here for petit/grand tours (Dr60/120) of the medina.

Dar Jamaï Museum Near Place el-Hedim is Dar Jamaï, a palace built in 1882 by the powerful Jamaï family, two of whom were viziers to Sultan Moulay al-Hassan I.

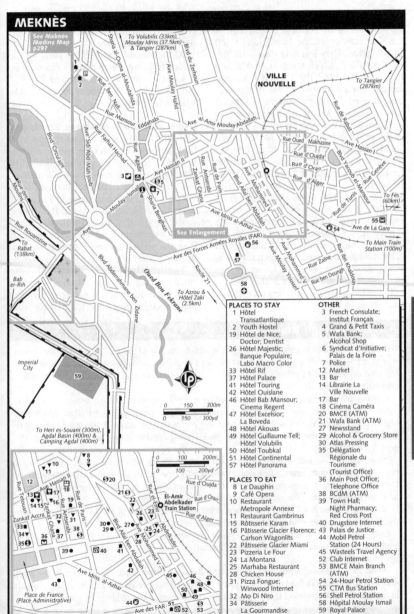

MEKNÈS

PLACES TO STAY
1 Hôtel
  Transatlantique
2 Youth Hostel
19 Hôtel de Nice;
  Doctor; Dentist
26 Hôtel Majestic;
  Banque Populaire;
  Labo Macro Color
33 Hôtel Rif
37 Hôtel Palace
41 Hôtel Touring
42 Hôtel Ouislane
46 Hôtel Bab Mansour;
  Cinema Regent
47 Hôtel Excelsior;
  La Boveda
48 Hôtel Akouas
49 Hôtel Guillaume Tell;
  Hôtel Volubilis
50 Hôtel Toubkal
51 Hôtel Continental
57 Hôtel Panorama

PLACES TO EAT
8 Le Dauphin
9 Café Opera
10 Restaurant
  Metropole Annexe
11 Restaurant Gambrinus
15 Rôtisserie Karam
16 Pâtisserie Glacier Florence;
  Carlson Wagonlits
22 Pâtisserie Glacier Miami
23 Pizzeria Le Four
24 La Montana
25 Marhaba Restaurant
28 Chicken House
31 Pizza Fongue;
  Winwood Internet
32 Mo Di Niro
34 Pâtisserie
  La Gourmandise

OTHER
3 French Consulate;
  Institut Français
4 Grand & Petit Taxis
5 Wafa Bank;
  Alcohol Shop
6 Syndicat d'Initiative;
  Palais de la Foire
7 Police
12 Market
13 Bar
14 Librairie La
  Ville Nouvelle
17 Bar
18 Cinéma Caméra
20 BMCE (ATM)
21 Wafa Bank (ATM)
27 Newsstand
29 Alcohol & Grocery Store
30 Atlas Pressing
35 Délégation
  Régionale du
  Tourisme
  (Tourist Office)
36 Main Post Office;
  Telephone Office
38 BCdM (ATM)
39 Town Hall;
  Night Pharmacy;
  Red Cross Post
40 Drugstore Internet
43 Palais de Justice
44 Mobil Petrol
  Station (24 Hours)
45 Wasteels Travel Agency
52 Club Internet
53 BMCE Main Branch
  (ATM)
54 24-Hour Petrol Station
55 CTM Bus Station
56 Shell Petrol Station
58 Hôpital Moulay Ismail
59 Royal Palace

When the sultan died in 1894, in following with the fickle political atmosphere of the Moroccan court, the Jamaï family fell into disgrace. They lost everything, including the palace, which went to Al-Maidani al-Glaoui. In 1912 the French commandeered it for a military hospital. Since 1920 it has housed the Administration des Beaux Arts and one of Morocco's best museums.

As usual, the museum building is as interesting as the exhibits, which include traditional ceramics, jewellery, rugs, textiles, embroidery and woodwork. Keep an eye out for the silver *sebsi* (pipe) for smoking kif and the beautiful, 17th century cedar minbar (pulpit). There are also some decorative ankle bracelets. (Fully decked out for a ceremony, a woman might traditionally carry up to 20kg of jewellery). The *koubba* (domed sanctuary) upstairs is furnished as a traditional *grand salon* (cushioned or carpeted room for entertaining guests) complete with luxurious rugs and cushions. There is also a Berber tent.

The exhibits are well put together; explanations are in French, Arabic and English.

The museum's Andalusian garden and courtyard is a shady, peaceful spot amid overgrown orange trees.

At the time of research the building was closed for some much needed renovations. It's open from 9 am to noon and 3 to 6.30 pm Wednesday to Monday (except public holidays). Entry costs Dr10.

Great Mosque & Medersa Bou Inania

The Great Mosque is closed to non-Muslims, but you can enter the *medersa* (theological college), which was built in the 14th century during the reign of the Merenids.

Completed in 1358 by Bou Inan (after whom a more lavish medersa in Fès is also named), the Meknès version of the Quranic school is typical of the exquisite interior design that distinguishes Merenid monuments. (See the special section 'Moroccan Architecture' in the Facts about Morocco chapter).

The standard *zellij* (tilework) base, stucco middles and carved olive wood top of the interior walls (only the ceiling is made of cedar) are here in all their elegance.

A Walk Through the Souqs

The easiest route into the souqs is through the arch to the left of the Dar Jamaï Museum. If you plunge in here, you will quickly find yourself in amid **carpet shops**. As you walk notice the *qissariat* (covered markets) off to either side. A couple of these are devoted to textiles and carpets, which are noisily auctioned off.

Keeping more or less to the lane you started on and heading north, you will emerge at Rue Najarine. Here the carpets give way to textiles and to the **slipper souq**: quite a few shops specialising in *babouches* (slippers). Follow the street west and veer with it left into Rue Sekkakine to reach an exit, Bab Berrima, in the west wall of the medina. Virtually opposite is the Qissariat ad-Dahab, the gold & jewellery souq.

If you take the exit and follow the lane north hugging the city wall on the outside, you'll pass a colourful **spices & nuts souq**, a **flea market** and, a bit further to the west, Meknès' **tanneries** (see the colour boxed text 'Tanneries' in the Central Morocco chapter for more information). All are a bit more interesting than the carpentry and steel shops on the interior.

To the north-west is a Muslim cemetery and the tomb and **Koubba of Sidi ben Aissa**, who gave rise to one of the more extreme religious fraternities in Morocco.

Enter the city again at Bab el-Jedid, the inside of which is a small musical instrument souq. Turning left up Rue el-Hanaya, the fruit & vegetable market opens up in front of you – a cheap place to get your groceries.

Eventually, continuing north, you arrive at the **Berdaine Mosque** and, just beyond it, the city's northernmost gate, **Bab Berdaine**. You could then proceed back down Rue Zaouia Nasseria (which becomes Rue Souika) passing tailors to reach the Great Mosque and Medersa Bou Inania.

MEKNÈS MEDINA

PLACES TO STAY
33 Hôtel Nouveau
34 Hôtel de Meknès
35 Hôtel Regina
36 Hôtel Agadir
47 Hôtel de Paris
52 Hôtel Maroc

PLACES TO EAT
14 Food Hall
17 Cafés
27 Snack Bounana
30 Restaurant Bab Mansour;
   Fruit Juice Bars
31 Restaurant Économique
40 Restaurant Zitouna
44 Doughnut Shop;
   Snack Shops
45 Café Mamounia
53 Collier de la Colombe

OTHER
1 Berdaine Mosque
2 Hammam (Men Only)
3 Fruit & Vegetable Market
4 Koubba of Sidi ben Aissa
5 Musical Instrument Souq
6 Flea Market
7 Tanneries
8 Spices & Nuts Souq
9 Main Bus Station
10 Grand Taxis
11 Local Buses
12 Petit Taxis
13 Calèches
15 Wafa Bank
16 Pharmacy el-Fath
18 Telephones
19 Banque Populaire
20 BMCE
21 Gold & Jewellery Souq
22 Carpet Shops

23 Dar Jamaï Museum
24 BMCI
25 Slipper Souq
26 Textile Souq
28 Medersa Bou Inania
29 Great Mosque
32 Banque Populaire (ATM)
37 Post Office
39 Haberdashers Souq
39 Mansour Palace
41 Hammam
42 Mosque
43 Pressing el-Fath
46 Public Swimming Pool
48 Douche (Men Only); Hammam
49 BMCE
50 Crédit du Maroc
51 Studio el-Almal
55 Mausoleum Moulay Ismail
56 Carpet Shops

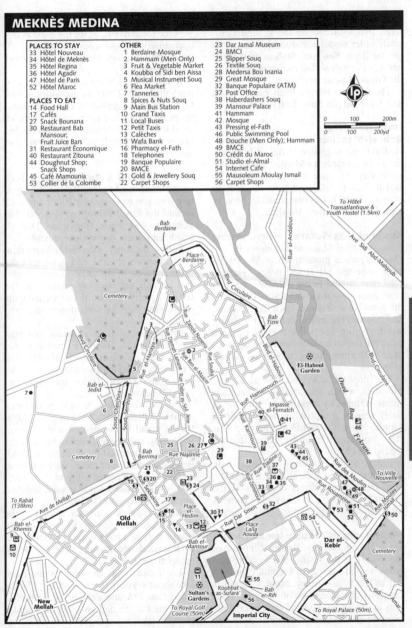

MIDDLE ATLAS & THE EAST

Students aged eight to 10 years once lived two to a cell on the ground floor, while older students and teachers lived on the 1st floor. You can climb on to the roof and see the green-tiled roof and minaret of the Great Mosque next door.

The medersa is open from 9 am to noon and 3 to 6.30 pm daily. Entry is Dr10.

Imperial City

Bab el-Mansour The focus of Place el-Hedim is the huge gate of Bab el-Mansour, the main entrance to Moulay Ismail's imperial city. The gate is well preserved with lavish (faded) zellij and inscriptions right across the top. It was completed by Moulay Ismail's son, Moulay Abdallah.

Koubbat as-Sufara' After passing through Bab el-Mansour and along the *mechouar* (parade ground) where Moulay Ismail inspected his famed Black Guard, a road runs around to the right. On the right is an open grass area with a small building, the Koubbat as-Sufara', once the reception hall for foreign ambassadors. It's hardly worth visiting, but beside it is the entrance to an enormous underground granary complete with vents that open onto the surface of the lawn.

The popular story has this as a huge prison in which thousands of Christians (most captured by corsairs operating out of Salé) were held captive as slave labour on Moulay Ismail's building schemes. This story has largely been discredited, but the legend dies hard.

Entry to the vaults and reception hall, open from 9 am to noon and 3 to 6 pm daily, costs Dr10. Almost directly opposite are the Sultan's Gardens, part of Moulay Ismail's imperial city complex; these are off-limits.

Mausoleum of Moulay Ismail Through the imposing gateway, Bab er-Rih (Gate of the Wind), is the resting place of the man who elevated Meknès to becoming the capital in the 17th century. Moulay Ismail is generally considered one of the greatest figures in Moroccan history, and perhaps because of this non-Muslims are allowed into the sanctuary (although only Muslims can visit the tomb itself). Make the most of this opportunity; the mausoleum is peaceful and beautifully displays Moroccan architecture and craftsmanship.

It's open from 9 am to noon and 3 to 6 pm Saturday to Thursday and entry is free. Opposite are a number of craft and carpet shops belonging to a cooperative. There's a good selection of Meknassi specialities, but prices are fairly high and salesmen are persistent.

Heri es-Souani & Agdal Basin If, back on the main road before Bab er-Rihr, you turn left, you have about a 20-minute walk around the Royal Palace (no visitors). The complex was once known as Dar el-Makhzen (House of the Government).

Follow the street to the end and turn right (you have no choice) and head past the main entrance of the palace (on the right) and beyond the camping ground (on the left). Virtually in front of you are the quite impressive Heri es-Souani granaries and vaults.

The storerooms are immense and brilliantly designed. There are small windows in the walls and water was circulated below the floor to keep temperatures cool and air circulating. The wells for drawing water can still be seen.

The first few vaults have been restored, but the stables, which once housed 12,000 horses, stand in partial ruin with no roof, seemingly stretching forever. Such is the atmosphere here that the place ties with Aït Benhaddou as one of the country's favourite film sets and poster subjects.

It is open from 9 am to noon and 3 to 6 pm daily. Entry costs Dr10.

Another doorway further around to the Agdal Basin leads upstairs to a rooftop cafe, from where you have sweeping views both back towards the Royal Palace and of the Agdal Basin below.

The basin is an enormous stone-lined lake about 4m deep that was once fed by the Oued Bou Fekrane and served as both a reservoir for the Sultan's Gardens and a pleasure lake.

Moulay Ismail

Moulay Ismail, the second sultan of the Alawite dynasty (which still rules today), marked his ascent to power at the age of 25 in 1672 in an unforgettable manner. As a warning to unruly tribes, he sent the heads of 10,000 slain enemies to adorn the walls of the two great imperial capitals, Fès and Marrakesh. He had presumably collected these earlier during battles against insurgents in the north of Morocco.

It was the beginning of a particularly gruesome period of rule, even by Moroccan standards, but Moulay Ismail is one of the few Moroccan sultans ever to get the whole country under his control. His cruelty was legendary, and the cheerful ease with which he would lop off the heads of unfortunate servants who displeased him, or labourers not working hard enough, probably contributed much to his hold over the country.

His first 20 years of rule were taken up with bloody campaigns of pacification. It is difficult to know just how much blood was spilt, but more than 30,000 people are said to have died at his hands alone.

The core of his military success lay in the infamous Black Guard. Having brought some 16,000 slaves from sub-Saharan Africa, Moulay Ismail guaranteed the continued existence of his elite units by providing the soldiers with women and raising their offspring for service in the guard. By the time of his death, the Black Guard had grown tenfold and resembled a huge family whose upkeep was paid for by the treasury.

In addition to quelling internal rebellion, he chased the Portuguese and English out of Asilah, Larache, Mehdiya and Tangier. Spain managed to hang on to Ceuta, Melilla and Al-Hoceima in spite of unrelenting sieges. Moulay Ismail disposed of the Ottoman Turk threat from Algeria, securing a stable eastern frontier with a string of fortifications centred on Taza, and established a virtual protectorate over modern Mauritania.

A contemporary of Louis XIV of France (the Sun King), Moulay Ismail was at least partly inspired by descriptions of Versailles when he planned the construction of his imperial palace and other monuments in Meknès. For decades he tried to secure an alliance with France against Spain, but continued attacks by the corsairs of Salé on French merchant shipping effectively scuppered his hopes.

Although both monarchs bestowed presents on each other, Louis XIV stopped short of acceding to Moulay Ismail's request to marry his illegitimate daughter, the Princess of Conti. Not that the sultan was in need of more female company – it is reckoned he had 360 to 500 wives and concubines (depending on which source you believe) and 800 children by the time he died.

To carry out his building plans, he needed plenty of labour, and it is said he used 25,000 Christian prisoners as slave labour in Meknès, in addition to 30,000 common criminals. Not one to do things by halves, his Heri es-Souani (Great Stables) could house 12,000 horses.

Activities

Club Farah D'Equitation (☎ cell 01-134951) has horse riding for Dr75/125 per child/adult.

The nine-hole, 2707m, par 36, Royal Golf Course (☎ 530753) is one of Morocco's more scenic courses with prime position near the Agdal Basin.

Special Events

One of the largest *moussems* (festival in honour of a saint) in Morocco takes place in May/June at the Koubba of Sidi ben Aissa just outside the medina walls during the Islamic month of Mouloud. Once devotees would cheerfully digest anything from glass to snakes; nowadays, although you'll still come across the entranced, you're only likely to see the hardcore stuff in photos displayed around town. Still, it's a busy festival with fantasias, fairs and the usual singing and dancing.

Hammams & Public Showers

There are several *hammams* (traditional bathhouses) in the medina. You'll find one down an alley near Hôtel de Paris. Look for the 'Douche' and 'Bain' signs. The showers are for men only (7 am to 9 pm). The baths are open to men from 7 am to 1 pm and 8 pm to midnight, and open to women from 1 to 8 pm.

Places to Stay

Most of the cheapest places are clustered together in the old city along Rue Dar Smen and Rue Rouamzine. The ville nouvelle also has a few cheapies as well as the mid-range to more expensive choices.

Unfortunately, apart from the Hôtel Transatlantique, none of the hotels listed have inspiring views, and few even have terraces. Plenty do have balconies or large windows – most are on busy roads so if you're a light sleeper you might want to request a room at the back.

Places to Stay – Budget

Camping There is a good, shady camping ground near the Agdal Basin south of the imperial city. It's a long walk to *Camping Agdal* (☎ 551828) and a taxi from the train or bus stations will cost about Dr12. Camping costs Dr12/17 per child/adult, Dr10 to pitch a tent, Dr17 for a car or caravan (Dr20 for a camper van), Dr7 for a hot shower and Dr10 for electricity. There is a food store, bar, restaurant and cafe on site.

Hostels The *Youth Hostel* (☎ 524698) is close to the large Hôtel Transatlantique in the ville nouvelle, about 1km north-west of the centre. It's clean and reasonably well kept and is in a quiet residential area. In summer (June to September), it's open from 8 to 9 am, noon to 4 pm and 6 to 10 pm. During the rest of the year, it's open from 8 to 10 am, noon to 3 pm and 6 to 10 pm (10 am to 6 pm Sunday). A dorm bed costs Dr40. There are also family rooms for three and four people, which cost Dr30 per person. Hot showers cost an extra Dr5, and there is a communal kitchen and washing room. You can also have meals here (breakfast costs Dr15, lunch or dinner Dr60).

Hotels – Medina It may look unpromising at first but *Hôtel Maroc* (☎ 530075, Rue Rouamzine) is one of the better places. Singles/doubles for Dr60/120 are quiet and clean with a washbasin and window that opens onto a flowered courtyard. The (cold) showers and toilets are reasonably well maintained.

Along Rue Dar Smen are a cluster of good cheapies. A good choice, *Hôtel Regina* (☎ 530280, Rue Dar Smen) is a biggish place with rooms around a central, covered courtyard. Singles/doubles/triples/quads cost Dr60/90/120/150 and hot showers are Dr5. *Hôtel Agadir* (Rue Dar Smen) has basic rooms around a wooden courtyard painted green for Dr40/70. *Hôtel de Meknès* (Rue Dar Smen) has grim rooms with washbasins but they're clean and fairly spacious; they cost Dr30/60. There are no showers. Nearby, opposite the Banque Populaire, is *Hôtel Nouveau* (☎ 533139). It's OK, if a little dusty with peeling walls. Rooms are Dr30/50.

Not quite as good as Hôtel Regina, the older *Hôtel de Paris* (58 Rue Rouamzine) has large rooms for Dr30/60. There are no showers but the hammam is nearby so it's not a bad deal.

Hotels – Ville Nouvelle Probably the cheapest place, and the hardest to get into (if you don't speak Arabic), is *Hôtel Guillaume Tell* (☎ 521203, 51 Rue de la Voûte), down an alleyway next to Hôtel Volubilis. The rooms are cell-like, but reasonably clean, and cost Dr20/30 for singles/doubles.

One of the best, although it's right on a busy junction, is *Hôtel Toubkal* at the southern end of Ave Mohammed V. Rooms with a balcony onto the street or windows onto a central courtyard are large, clean, bright and a reasonable Dr50/90. A hot shower costs Dr5.

Across the road, *Hôtel Continental* (☎ 525471, 92 Ave des FAR) also has nicely furnished, large, bright rooms; some with a balcony and shower are Dr109/141, others with bathroom are Dr137/162.

The one-star *Hôtel Touring* (☎ 522351, 34 Blvd Allal ben Abdallah) is clean, though a bit dark, gloomy and frayed around the edges. Rooms cost Dr70/95 or Dr106/134 with shower and toilet.

Hôtel Panorama (☎ 522737) just off Ave des FAR has big bright rooms with balcony looking onto the quiet street below. Rooms with bathroom are Dr80/125.

Hôtel Excelsior (☎ 521900, 57 Ave des FAR) has clean rooms with large windows that might remind you of your bedroom back at your parents' house. They cost Dr65/88, or Dr121/140 with shower.

Also good value and with a bit of character is **Hôtel Majestic** (☎ 522035, fax 527427, 19 Ave Mohammed V, **e** majestic.hotel@ excite.fr). Large rooms come with washbasin and bidet and some have a balcony. Singles/doubles/triples cost Dr112/150/217, Dr150/180/257 with shower, and Dr189 /225/292 with bathroom. It also has a nice 1st-floor terrace for breakfast.

Places to Stay – Mid-Range
The following places are in the ville nouvelle.

At the lower end of this category is the two-star **Hôtel Palace** (☎ 514158, 11 Zankat Ghana), which has recently had a lick of paint. Singles/doubles have windows onto a flowered courtyard and cost a good-value Dr144/174. The restaurant here is little more than a smoky bar.

Also good value, **Hôtel de Nice** (☎ 520318, 10 Zankat Accra) has clean rooms with bathroom for Dr185/217. You're not allowed to take alcohol into the rooms.

Hôtel Ouislane (☎ 521743, 54 Blvd Allal ben Abdallah) has clean but rather gloomy rooms with bathroom for Dr185/217. There's a rowdy and popular bar attached.

Hôtel Volubilis (☎ 525082, 45 Ave des FAR) is older although it does have a lift. Large rooms with bathroom go for Dr185/ 217. Alcohol is banned from the rooms so you'll have to make do with the dodgy bar downstairs.

Two three-star places are found within a stone's throw of each other. **Hôtel Bab Mansour** (☎ 525239, fax 510741, 38 Rue el-Emir Abdelkader), a 'hotel for businessmen', is clean and modern with lifts and somewhat sterile rooms for Dr280/342. It also has a bar and nightclub with floorshows. Quieter, with a bit more Moroccan character is **Hôtel Akouas** (☎ 515967, fax 515994, 27 Rue el-Amir Abdelkader). It's a modern, comfortable place and there is access to office facilities and a decent bar, a restaurant and a terrace. Rooms cost Dr280/342/453 and are good value, ask to see a few.

Places to Stay – Top End
The four-star **Hôtel Rif** (☎ 522591, fax 524428, Zankat Accra) is a huge and typical city hotel with a concrete square design. It has a swimming pool (Dr30 for nonguests), restaurant, bar and air-con throughout; singles/doubles cost Dr402/503 with bathroom. The hotel organises tours such as a half-day to Volubilis and Moulay Idriss (Dr200) and a half-day city tour (Dr100).

North-west of the centre, **Hôtel Transatlantique** (☎ 525050, fax 520057, Rue el-Merinyne) is one of those places where you can imagine you're back in the good old colonial days. At least you can in the traditional half, there's also a modern half with rooms neatly separated between the two. There are even two pools, as well as tennis courts and extensive gardens with views over the medina. Rooms with air-con and all other creature comforts cost Dr590/750. It's a good place for a swim (Dr100 for nonguests) or a sunset drink – the bar is quite classy (and pricey).

Places to Eat
Medina If you are staying in the medina, there are a few simple restaurants along Rue Dar Smen. Two of the best are **Restaurant Économique**, at No 123 and, at No 127, **Restaurant Bab Mansour**. Tajine (meat and vegetable stew) costs around Dr25. Alongside are a couple of good fruit-juice bars (Dr4 to Dr6 for a glass). There's also a mass of cheap-eat stalls spilling out in the lanes just outside the Bab el-Jedid.

Another option is **Snack Bounana** in a square near the medersa. You can get all the usual fare and the square, complete with cafe, is almost relaxing.

If you want a 'good' restaurant try **Collier de la Colombe** (☎ 555041, 67 Rue Driba). It's a modern place trying to look old, but it needn't try anything as the view over the river to the ville nouvelle is unparalleled. It has set menus (Moroccan and international) with mint tea and patisseries for Dr75 and Dr95 as well as trout for Dr80 and other mains for Dr70.

A palace-type place is **Restaurant Zitouna** (44 Jamaa Zitouna), which is located in the heart of the medina and geared almost exclusively towards the large tour groups that are herded through. If crowds are your thing, the set menus cost Dr110 to Dr170.

Café Mamounia (Rue Rouamine) is also not bad, and just down from it is a *doughnut shop* selling freshly fried *sfinj* – a light, deep-fried doughnut great for dunking in coffee. You buy a few at a time and they are tied together with a strand of palm frond. Get there before 11 am (it opens at 5 am), or they'll be sold out.

The *cafes* on Place el-Hedim in the medina are good for people-watching. Before plunging into the heart of the old medina from Place el-Hedim, you might want to take a look at the *food hall* west of the square. The displays are a sight in themselves.

Ville Nouvelle There are a few cheap eats and *rotisseries* along Ave Mohammed V. Also cheap are the little *restaurants* around the corner from the Hôtel Majestic on the roads leading to the train station. A filling meal costs about Dr30.

One place that stands out is *Rôtisserie Karam (2 Zankat Ghana)* near the corner of Ave Hassan II. The food is cheap and good; filled rolls cost from Dr12 and tajine, *brochettes* (skewered meat) cost Dr23 to Dr25. There are a few tables upstairs where you can take your food, if you can find a place. There are a few similar places lined up alongside – take your pick.

If you're after Western-style fast food, by far the best place in town is trendy *Mo Di Niro (14 Rue Antserabi)* – look for the Coca-Cola machine outside. It serves decent hamburgers with chips (Dr14.50 to Dr21.50), salads, pizzas (Dr40 to Dr90) and milkshakes; there's even a nonsmoking area. Along the same vein is *Chicken House (Ave Mohammed V)* – it's all neon lights and Formica.

If you're after cheap pizza (Dr20 to Dr25), head to *Pizza Fongue (Zankat Accra)*.

Pizzeria Le Four (Rue Atlas) is suitably Italian with dark timber and whitewashed walls. The attached bar is the same and pleasant for a drink. Excellent pizzas served on wooden platters cost Dr34 to Dr46. The onion soup (Dr40) is almost a meal in itself.

Meat dishes, pasta and salads (Dr22 to Dr45) are also available, as are wine (Dr45) and beer (Dr14). Watch out for the 14% taxes. It's a popular place with trendy locals.

Opposite, *La Montana* is another licensed place with a whole range of Moroccan, French and Italian dishes and a popular bar downstairs.

For traditional Moroccan food, many choose *Restaurant Metropole Annexe* (☎ 525223, 11 Rue Charif Idrissi), around the corner from the junction of Ave Hassan II and Ave Mohammed V. A set menu costs Dr90, mains start at Dr50. The food is good and the restaurant has a touch of atmosphere and is licensed.

Next door, on the corner, is *Restaurant Gambrinus*. It's simple and better value than the Metropole, and is also very popular with the locals. The food is good – the set menu costs Dr70 (mains around Dr40).

A couple of cheaper options are *Marhaba Restaurant*, a tiled place on Ave Mohammed V, and *La Boveda* next to the Hôtel Excelsior; both have tajine for Dr30.

The licensed *Le Dauphin* (☎ 523423, 5 Ave Mohammed V) is pleasant enough and has a reputation for its seafood. It's not cheap though – mains cost between Dr60 and Dr110. The entrance is through a garden, which is beyond a side door down a street off Ave Mohammed V.

There is a *market* in the ville nouvelle as well as a shop selling alcohol.

The ville nouvelle, especially on and around Ave Mohammed V, is full of cafes and patisseries – some of the best in Morocco. *Café Opera (7 Ave Mohammed V)* has an upstairs section, which is women-friendly. For very early starters, *Pâtisserie Glacier Miami (15 Ave Mohammed V)* serves almond croissants from 4 am (until 9.30 pm) daily.

If you fancy something else sweet and sticky, follow the smell of baking to *Pâtisserie Glacier Florence (Zankat Ghana)*. A breakfast of orange juice, chocolate croissant and coffee/tea costs Dr12. Try a Moroccan *jus d'amande* (almond juice) here. For more lovely sweets, head for the *Pâtisserie La Gourmandise (8 Rue Tetouan)* near the Hôtel Rif.

Entertainment

There appear to be more bars in Meknès (they're all the ville nouvelle) than any other Moroccan city. Unfortunately for lone women they're mostly very seedy affairs. They're largely grouped around Blvd Allal ben Abdallah, although most hotels and restaurants also have bars.

The bars at the restaurants *La Coupole* and *Pizzeria Le Four* (see Places to Eat – Ville Nouvelle) are two of the better places. Try the *Hôtel Transatlantique* at sunset. If you prefer to take away your drink try the *alcohol & grocery store* on Blvd Allal ben Abdallah.

A popular disco is that in *Hôtel Bab Mansour* (see Places to Stay – Mid-Range earlier). Entry and drinks each cost Dr50 during the week and Dr70 at the weekend.

There are some cinemas around town, but choose carefully because many screen pornography.

Getting There & Away

Air There is a small airstrip just outside Meknès, but no scheduled flights.

Bus The CTM station is on Ave des FAR about 500m east of the junction with Ave Mohammed V. The main bus station is just outside Bab el-Khemis, west of the medina. There is a left-luggage office (Dr5 per item per 24 hours), a cafe and phone office. The timetables are in Arabic only but as always there will be someone nearby to help you out.

Services The following departures are from the CTM station but most also stop at the main bus station. There are seven daily departures to Casablanca (Dr63, four hours) and Rabat (Dr37, four hours) between 7 am and 10 pm; eight buses go to Fès (Dr15, one hour) between 10.30 am and 11 pm; one bus goes to Er-Rachidia (six hours), Rissani (eight hours) and Erfoud at 10 pm; two buses go to Ifrane (one hour) and Azrou (1½ hours); three buses go to Tangier (Dr68, five hours); and three go to Taza (Dr49, three hours). One bus goes to Agadir and Marrakesh (nine hours) at 7pm; and two buses leave daily for Nador (Dr106) and Al-Hoceima (Dr97).

There are international departures from the CTM station to Spain (Dr900) at noon on Monday, Wednesday and Friday.

The following services leave from the numbered windows in the main bus station:

No 5 Rabat (13 daily), Casablanca (10 daily)
No 6 Tangier (five daily), Tetouan (four daily), Chefchaouen (four daily), Ouezzane (four daily)
No 7 Fès (five daily), Taza (five daily), Sefrou (two daily), Oujda (eight daily), Nador (eight daily)
No 8 Moulay Idriss (hourly from 7 am to 6 pm)
No 9 Marrakesh (two daily)

Train The most convenient train station is El-Amir Abdelkader (☎ 516135), one block from and parallel to Ave Mohammed V, where all trains stop.

A total of nine trains go to Fès (2nd-class fare on *ordinaire/rapide* service Dr13/16, one hour), four of which continue to Oujda (Dr93/121, 6½ hours), and at least nine go to Casablanca (Dr62/80, 4½ hours) via Rabat (Dr41/53, 2¼ hours). There are five direct services to Marrakesh (Dr116/151, seven hours) and five for Tangier (Dr59/77, five hours).

Taxi Grand taxis leave from a dirt lot between Bab el-Khemis and the main bus station, just west of the medina. You can't miss it. They also leave from outside the Institut Français (east of the medina) and other points around town.

There are regular departures to Beni Slimane (Dr18), Chefchaouen (Dr55), Fès (Dr16), Moulay Idriss (for Volubilis, Dr7), Ouezzane (Dr40), Rabat (Dr40) and Sidi Kacem (Dr12).

Getting Around

Bus There are local buses running between the medina and the new city, but these are invariably crowded and difficult to fight your way onto.

Useful routes include the No 2 (Bab el-Mansour to Blvd Allal ben Abdallah, returning to the medina along Ave Mohammed V) and No 7 (Bab el-Mansour to the CTM bus station).

Grand Taxi Urban grand taxis (silver-coloured Mercedes-Benz with black roofs) link the ville nouvelle and the medina (Dr5).

A pale-blue coloured *petit taxi* (local taxi) from the main bus station to El-Amir Abdelkader train station costs Dr15.

AROUND MEKNÈS
Moulay Idriss

Moulay Idriss, about 4.5km from Volubilis (see the special section 'Volubilis' later in this section), is named after Morocco's most revered saint, a great-grandson of the Prophet Mohammed and the founder of the country's first real dynasty.

Moulay Idriss fled Mecca in the late 8th century AD in the face of persecution at the hands of the then recently installed Abbasid Caliphate, which was based in Baghdad. Idriss settled at Volubilis, where he managed to convert the locals to Islam and made himself their leader. From there he went on to establish Morocco's first imperial dynasty.

Moulay Idriss is an attractive town, nestled in a cradle of verdant mountains, and for Moroccans it's a place of pilgrimage. The place has been open to non-Muslims for the past 70 years or so. You still cannot visit any of the mosques or shrines and you are not supposed to stay overnight.

Saturday is market day and is a more lively time to be in Moulay Idriss; it's also the easiest day to get here.

Walking Tour Although the twin-hill town is a veritable maze of narrow lanes and dead ends, it is not hard to get around to the few points of interest.

The first is the **Mausoleum of Moulay Idriss**, the object of veneration and the reason for the country's greatest annual moussem in late August. A huge pilgrimage for many, including the royals, it is accompanied by fantasias, markets, singing and dancing.

From the main square (where buses and grand taxis arrive), walk up the street that starts to the left of the bus ticket booths. This brings you into the main street, which is lined on both sides by cafes and cheap-food stands; those on the right overlook the square from which you have just emerged. Proceed

straight down this street and under the arch – the number of guides (which are unnecessary) and tourist groups should reassure you that you're getting warm. About 50m on to your left you'll see a three-arched gateway. Go through it and continue straight ahead – you'll soon come up against the barrier that marks the point beyond which non-Muslims may not pass. Moulay Ismail built the mausoleum that stands here today, although various additions have since been made.

You can now head left into the maze of streets and try to find your way to a couple of vantage points that give you a good **panoramic view** of the mausoleum, the town and the surrounding country – plenty of guides will offer to help.

If you don't feel like being guided, there is an alternative. Head back to the beginning of the main street, which you reached coming up from the main bus stop square. Looking again in the direction of the mausoleum, you'll notice a side street heading uphill to your left and signposted 'Municipalité'. Follow it, and just before the Agfa photo shop on the left take the cobbled street to the right. As you climb up you'll notice the only **cylindrical minaret** in Morocco. The green tiles spell out in stylised script the standard Muslim refrain: *la illah illa Allah* (there is no god but Allah). Proceed another 200m and you're close to the viewpoint. This is where you have to ask a local for the *grande* or *petite terrasse* – this should produce no problem. The terraces provide vantage points high above the mausoleum and a good part of the town.

Places to Eat There is nowhere to stay in Moulay Idriss. The main battery of cheap restaurants and cafes is in the main street above the bus station.

The best restaurant in town (even with a minor international gastronomy award) is *Restaurant Baraka (22 Aïn Smen-Khiber)*, which has two excellent though pricey menus for around Dr100. Main courses are available for around Dr65.

There are a few *cafes* on the square and its approaches.

[Continued on page 310]

IMPRESSIVE PORTALS

As with most of Morocco's great artistic expressions, the best of the *maallem's* (woodworker's) art is reserved for mosques and *medersas* (religious schools). The feature most characteristic of Moroccan woodwork is the door.

Throughout Morocco you can see huge doors with elaborate detailing, decorated with an ornamental vocabulary that includes calligraphy, geometrical motifs and the ubiquitous talismanic images. Hands of Fatima, ancient fertility symbols, star patterns and necklaces are often carved into doors as protection against djinn (evil spirits). This is particularly true of the massive doors to *agadirs* (fortified granaries), which were built to protect lives and possessions during times of fierce tribal warfare.

Metalwork also features on Moroccan doors, which are often studded with iron and nails made of brass. Traditionally, iron door handles were found on the doors of poorer rural people, while those in brass and bronze, often in the shape of Fatima's hand, adorned the doors of the urban wealthy.

Another common feature of Moroccan doors is the colour blue. Doors and shutters are painted in shades of eye-catching blue in keeping with traditional practice (believed to originate in ancient Egypt) of using the colour to ward off evil spirits.

Martin Hughes

Inset: Door with padlock and decorative iron studs, Fès (photo by Christopher Wood)

Right: The simple door at the Mausoleum of Moulay Ismail, Meknès

CHRISTOPHER WOOD

CHRISTOPHER WOOD

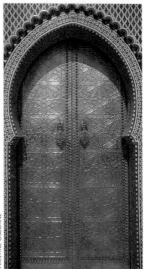

CHRISTINE OSBORNE

DUSHAN COORAY

Top left: Traditional blue door, Chefchaouen

Top right: The glistening guest entrance to the magnificent Dar el-Makhzen (Royal Palace), Fès

Bottom: The finely decorated entrance with azure blue tiles and traditional blockwork, Royal Palace, Meknès

VOLUBILIS

About 33km north of Meknès is Volubilis (Oualili in Arabic), the largest and best-preserved Roman ruins in Morocco. It was declared a Unesco World Heritage site in December 1997. Volubilis, which can be combined with a visit to the nearby town of Moulay Idriss, is an easy day trip from Meknès and shouldn't be missed, even if you're not normally into Roman remains.

History

Volubilis dates largely from the 2nd and 3rd centuries AD, although excavations have revealed that the site was originally settled by Carthaginian traders in the 3rd century BC.

One of the Roman Empire's most remote outposts, it was annexed in about AD 40. According to some historians, Rome imposed strict controls on what could, or could not, be produced in its North African possessions, according to the needs of the empire. One result was massive deforestation and the large-scale planting of wheat. The sweep of largely treeless plains around Volubilis certainly validates such a thesis.

Volubilis' population of Berbers, Greeks, Jews and Syrians continued to speak Latin and practise Christianity right up until the coming of Islam. Unlike Lixus, to the north-west, which was abandoned shortly

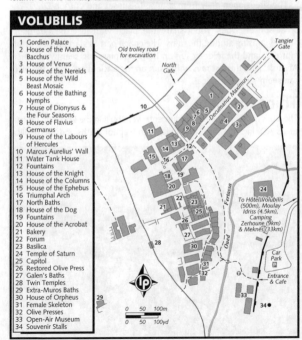

VOLUBILIS

1 Gordien Palace
2 House of the Marble Bacchus
3 House of Venus
4 House of the Nereids
5 House of the Wild Beast Mosaic
6 House of the Bathing Nymphs
7 House of Dionysus & the Four Seasons
8 House of Flavius Germanus
9 House of the Labours of Hercules
10 Marcus Aurelius' Wall
11 Water Tank House
12 Fountains
13 House of the Knight
14 House of the Columns
15 House of the Ephebus
16 Triumphal Arch
17 North Baths
18 House of the Dog
19 Fountains
20 House of the Acrobat
21 Bakery
22 Forum
23 Basilica
24 Temple of Saturn
25 Capitol
26 Restored Olive Press
27 Galen's Baths
28 Twin Temples
29 Extra-Muros Baths
30 House of Orpheus
31 Female Skeleton
32 Olive Presses
33 Open-Air Museum
34 Souvenir Stalls

Old trolley road for excavation

Tangier Gate
North Gate

Decumanus Maximus

To Hôtel Volubilis (500m), Moulay Idriss (4.5km), Camping Zerhoune (9km) & Meknès (33km)

Car Park

Entrance & Cafe

0 50 100m
0 50 100yd

Inset: Detail of a mosaic (photo by Joyce Connolly)

after the fall of the Roman Empire, Volubilis continued to be inhabited until the 18th century, when its marble was plundered for the building of Moulay Ismail's palaces in Meknès.

Information

At the time of writing, less than half of the 40 hectares comprising the site of Volubilis had been excavated. A Moroccan-French team of archaeologists is working on the site, and new and exciting discoveries are made every day.

Explanatory panels (in Arabic, English, French and Spanish) offer brief descriptions of the main sights, and eventually a museum will open displaying the objects unearthed here (many are currently in the archaeology museum in Rabat). Brochures and books should also be available soon. In the meantime, if there are several people in your group, or you can find others, you might want to share a guide. They do good 45- to 60-minute tours for Dr80 to Dr100.

Otherwise, you are free to wander at will and absorb the sights. A guard with a whistle theoretically discourages people from wandering over the ruins, yet the sight of visitors stepping over the ropes for a snapshot with the mosaics remains disarmingly common ź please don't join them.

The site is open daily from sunrise to sunset and entry is Dr20. The best time to visit is during the early morning (ideally just after sunrise) or at sunset, when you'll share the place with just the guardian's donkey grazing among the ruins. The coach parties start arriving in late morning, and the midday sun on the open plain can seem very fierce. At dusk, with the last rays of the sun on the ancient columns, the place can seem almost magical.

Things to See

The site's most impressive monuments were built in the 2nd and 3rd centuries AD, including the triumphal arch, capitol, baths and the basilica.

CHRISTINE OSBORNE

Bottom: The foundation of a Roman house stand starkly against the treeless plain surrounding Volubilis.

The most attractive features without doubt are the stunning mosaics, made even more so by the fact that they have been left *in situ* (in the orginal position), although this has caused their colours to fade.

The better known monuments are in the northern part of the site, although it's more convenient to start in the south. Once over the Oued Fertassa, the path from the entrance takes you through the residential quarter. This part of the site is fairly unremarkable apart from some **oil presses** and the remains of a **female corpse** (thought to be Muslim as she was buried facing Mecca) entombed in one of the walls.

The **House of Orpheus**, a little higher up and identifiable by the three pine trees growing in the corner, was a sumptuous mansion for one of the city's wealthier residents. It has two mosaics, one representing the Orpheus myth and the other the chariot of Amphitrite.

The basilica, capitol and 1300-sq-metre **forum** are, typically, built on a high point. The **capitol** dates back to AD 218; the **basilica** dedicated to the trilogy of Jupiter, Juno and Minerva lies to the north.

On the left, just before the Triumphal Arch, are a couple of roped-off **mosaics**. One depicts an athlete being presented with a trophy for winning a *desultor* race, a competition in which the rider had to dismount and jump back on his horse as it raced along. Opposite these mosaics are the remains of an aqueduct and fountain.

The marble **triumphal arch** on the decumanus maximus road, built in AD 217 in honour of Emperor Caracalla and his mother, Julia Domna, used to be topped with a bronze chariot. The arch was reconstructed in the 1930s, and the mistakes made then were rectified in the 1960s.

The **decumanus maximus** stretches up the slope to the north-east. The houses lining either side of the road contain the best **mosaics** on the site. The first house on the far side of the arch is known as the **House of the Ephebus** and contains a fine mosaic of Bacchus in a chariot drawn by panthers.

Bottom: The numerous mosaics at Volubilis are a testament to the high level of artistry reached by their creators.

JOYCE CONNOLLY

VOLUBILIS

CHRISTOPHER WOOD

Next along is the **House of the Columns** (so named because of its colonnaded facade ź note the differing styles of the columns, which include spirals), and adjacent to this is the **House of the Knight** with its incomplete mosaic of Bacchus and Ariadne.

Behind these houses you can still see the trolley tracks laid to cart away excavated material. The size of the pile of waste moved to uncover the site is astonishing ź there's a sizable artificial hill out there.

In the next couple of houses are excellent mosaics entitled the *Labours of Hercules* and *Nymphs Bathing*. However, the best collection on the whole site is in the **House of Venus**, one block further up and one block to the right. Although some of the house is roped off, there is a viewing platform built along the southern wall that gives you a good vantage point over the two best mosaics ź the *Abduction of Hylas by the Nymphs* and *Diana Bathing*.

The decumanus maximus continues up the hill to the Tangier Gate, past the uninteresting Gordien Palace, which used to be the residence of the city's administrators.

Places to Stay & Eat

Camping Zerhoune (☎ 05-517756) 9km from Volubilis (14km from Meknès) is a pleasant, shady and well-run place with a swimming pool and a cafe and restaurant. It costs Dr15 per adult, Dr10 per child, Dr10 to pitch a tent and Dr7 per car (Dr20 for a caravan or camper van). The pool is open from June to August only and a swim costs Dr10/15 per child/adult.

The only hotel in the area is the four-star *Hôtel Volubilis* (☎ 05-544405, fax 636393), about 500m beyond the site entrance coming from Meknès. It's an extremely pleasant and tranquil place with a pool, a tennis court, two restaurants and a bar. It charges Dr625 for doubles with balcony, bathroom, TV, fridge and telephone. Rooms with a view cost Dr825. If you want to have just one night of luxury in Morocco,

Top: The Arch of Caracalla

this might be the place for it. The set menu in its ***Berber tented restaurant*** costs Dr160 (mains from Dr90). If you can't afford a room or a meal here, then you could always come for coffee and cake. There is a very pleasant, shaded terrace with wonderful views of the ruins and the plain stretching below.

There is also a ***cafe*** by the entrance to the site, which offers a set menu for around Dr70.

Getting There & Away

To get here from Meknès take one of the infrequent buses (Dr6) or a more frequent grand taxi (Dr7) from the main bus station outside Bab el-Khemis. Get off at the turn-off to Moulay Idriss. From there it's about a 30-minute walk - extremely pleasant when it's not too hot ź and follow the turn-off to the left for 'Oualili' (the local word for Volubilis).

Getting back, the best thing to do is to try to hitch a lift with the many tourist coaches, minibuses or private vehicles heading back to Meknès, or Moulay Idriss (a good hour's walk) from where you can catch a bus or grand taxi to Meknès. Don't leave it too late in the afternoon however, as transport tends to dry up.

The last option is to get a group together and a hire a grand taxi for half a day. You should pay no more than Dr300 for this.

Bottom: Corinthian capitals are the silent sentinels of 2000 years of history at Volubilis.

DUSHAN COORAY

[Continued from page 304]

Getting There & Away Frequent grand taxis (Dr7) leave from outside the Institut Français, just west of Meknès' centre, and hourly buses (Dr6) leave from the bus station in Meknès every hour from 7 am to 6 pm. Note that it can be extremely difficult getting out of Moulay Idriss after about 3 pm. The occasional bus stops here en route to or from such places as Casablanca.

If you have your own transport, you might consider continuing to Fès via Nzala-des-Béni-Ammar, or to Meknès via the village of El-Merhasiyne. Both routes have wonderful views and eventually join back up with the main roads. As the road surfaces are very rough, unless you have a 4WD these drives are really only possible in summer.

FÈS

☎ 05 • pop 1,000,000

The oldest of the imperial cities, Fès is arguably the symbolic heart of Morocco. Founded shortly after the Arabs swept across North Africa and Spain, it soon became the religious and cultural centre of Morocco. All the great dynasties left their mark on it, but the city owes much of its magnificence to the people who fuelled its cosmopolitan population. In the early days, thousands of families from Muslim Spain came, followed by Arabs from the east. Berbers too have moved here, yet Fès retains a distinctly Arab identity.

Long considered the centre of Islamic orthodoxy, its allegiance, or at least submission, has always been essential to Morocco's rulers. Even when it was not the official capital, Fès could not be ignored and never really ceased to be considered the northern capital.

With such symbolic importance attached to their city, Fassis (the people of Fès) are conscious of the power they wield. The city continues to act as a barometer of popular sentiment – Morocco's independence movement was born here, and when there are strikes or protests, they are always at their most vociferous here.

The medina of Fès el-Bali (Old Fès) is one of the largest living medieval cities in the world – with the exception of Marrakesh, Cairo and Damascus, there is nothing remotely comparable.

Its narrow winding alleys and covered bazaars are crammed with every conceivable sort of workshop, restaurant, meat and market, as well as mosques, medersas and extensive dye pits and tanneries – a veritable assault on the senses.

But Fès is a city in trouble. Its million or so inhabitants are straining it to the utmost, and the old city, some experts have warned, is slowly falling apart. Unesco has done a lot to stop this deterioration, and in 1997 the World Bank loaned Fès US$75 million for restoration of the medina and improvements to waste disposal and traffic management.

In spite of the hordes of tourists that pile through, Fès gives the impression of living largely in the centuries-old traditions that have shaped it and still represents an experience you are unlikely to forget.

The ville nouvelle and its chic, cafe-lined avenues provide a jarring contrast. Sipping coffee and watching the passers-by along Blvd Mohammed V, you could just about be forgiven for thinking you're in southern France. In sync, the young Fassis have cast aside the trappings of their parents' lives, adopting fashions and lifestyles more readily identified with the West. However, many remain without work and the smart, clean ville nouvelle disguises the sad lot of the poorer people living on the periphery.

History

There is some dispute over who founded Fès. Some say that in 789 AD, Idriss I, who founded Morocco's first imperial dynasty, decided Oualili (Volubilis) was too small for the role of capital and began work on a new one here. Others claim his son was responsible and just as his father is venerated in the village of Moulay Idriss, so the memory of Idriss II is perpetuated in his *zawiyya* (religious fraternity based around a shrine) in the heart of Fès el-Bali.

In any event, a town was well established here by 809. The town's name is believed to come from the Arabic word for 'axe', and one tale relates that a golden pickaxe was unearthed here at the start of construction.

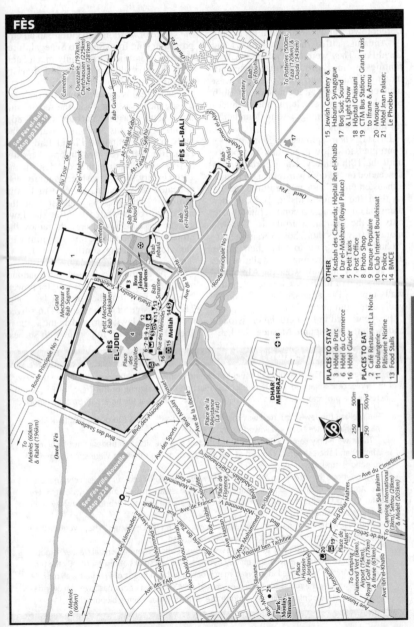

FÈS

FÈS EL-BALI

FÈS EL-JDID

DHAR MEHRAZ

To Meknès (60km), Ouezzane (197km), Meknès, Chefchaouen (225km), & Tetouan (281km)

To Meknès (60km) & Rabat (196km)

To Meknès (60km)

To Camping Diamond Vert (6km), Royal Golf Fès (17km) & Ifrane (61km)

To Fès International Airport (15km), Ifrane & Sefrou

To Potteries (500m), Taza (120km) & Oujda (343km)

To Camping International (3km), Sefrou (28km) & Midelt (203km)

See Fès el-Bali Map pp318-19

See Fès Ville Nouvelle Map p326

Bab Guissa
Bab el-Mahrouk
Bab Bou Jeloud
Bab el-Hadid
Bab el-Ftouh
Bab el-Jdid
Bab Smarine
Bab Jebala

At-Talâa al-Kebir
At-Talâa as-Sebir

Oued Fès
Oued Fès

Route du Tour de Fès
Route Principale No 1
Route Principale No 1

Grand Mechouar & Bab Segma
Petit Mechouar & Bab Dekkaken
Place des Alaouites

Bou Jeloud Gardens
Shara Moulay Suleiman

Ave de la Liberté
Ave de la Liberté
Blvd des Saadiens
Blvd des Alaouites
Bab Moulay Youssef

Rue des Mérinides
Mellah
Place de la Résistance (La Fiat)

Ave des Sports
Blvd Chefchaouni
Ave Abdallah Chefaouni
Ave Mohammed es-Slaoui
Ave Arabe Saoudite
Rue Hassan
Blvd Mohammed V
Place de Florence
Ave Mohammed V
Ave de France
Rue Arabe
Ave des Almohades
Rue Chengir
Ave Omar ben el-Khattab
Blvd Tariq ibn Ziad
Ave Mohammed ben Abdallah
Rue Jamal ben el-Jarrah
Ave Obaid bnou el-Kari
Place Hussein de Jordanie
Ave des FAR
Ave Youssef ben Tachfine
Ave Mohammed Slimane
Rue Moulay Slimane
Park Moulay Slimane
Ave Hassan II
Blvd Abdallah
Place des Atlas
Place du 11 Janvier
Ave du Cimetière
Ave Sidi Brahim
Blvd Dhar Mahres
Ave tbn el-khatib
Ave de Sefrou

0   250   500m
0   250   500yd

PLACES TO STAY
3 Hôtel du Parc
5 Hôtel du Commerce
16 Hôtel Glacier

PLACES TO EAT
2 Café Restaurant La Noria
11 Boulangerie
   Pâtisserie Nisrine
13 Food Stalls

OTHER
1 Kasbah des Cherarda; Hôpital Ibn el-Khatib
4 Dar el-Makhzen (Royal Palace)
5 Petit Taxis
8 Post Office
9 Photo Shop
10 Banque Populaire
11 Club Internet Boulkhissat
12 Police
14 BMCE
15 Jewish Cemetery & Habaim Synagogue
17 Bori Sud; Sound & Light Show
18 Hôpital Ghassani
19 CTM Bus Station; Grand Taxis to Ifrane & Azrou
20 Mosque
21 Hôtel Jnan Palace; Le Phoebus

The city started modestly enough as a Berber town, but then 8000 families fleeing Al-Andalus settled the east bank of the Oued Fès. They were later joined by Arab families from Kairouan (Qayrawan) in modern Tunisia, who took over the west bank creating the Kairaouine quarter. Both brought a religious, cultural and architectural heritage, forming a solid foundation for future greatness.

Idriss II's heirs split the kingdom, but Fès continued to enjoy peace and prosperity until the 10th century, when Berber tribes descended on the civil war-torn and famine-exhausted city. Chaos reigned until the arrival of the Almoravids in 1070. Under them the city became second in importance only to the capital, Marrakesh. The Almoravid stay was short, however, as the Almohad dynasty rose to take their place around 1154, destroying the walls of the city as they went. Only when the Almohads were assured of the Fassis, loyalty were the walls replaced – large sections of today's walls date from this period.

Fès continued to be a crucial crossroads and, with the Kairaouine Mosque and University already well established, it became *the* centre of learning and culture in an empire stretching from Spain to Senegal. It recovered its political status only much later, with the arrival of the Merenid dynasty around 1250.

The Merenids are acclaimed for their exquisite medersas, but it was the second sultan, Abu Youssef Yacoub (1258–86), paranoid about his subjects' loyalty, who built the self-contained Fès el-Jdid (New Fès), filling it with loyal troops – mostly Syrian and Christian mercenaries. In the 14th century, Fès' Jewish community was relocated here, creating the first mellah in Morocco. The records suggest that the move was orchestrated to offer the Jews greater protection, and they did enjoy the protection of the sultan, repaying him with their loyalty during conflict. Few Jewish families remain in Fès today.

As the Merenids collapsed, the Saadians and the Fès-based Wattasids vied for power. The latter won, but they did not last long. The successive Saadian rule was short-lived too, and the Alawites arrived on the scene in 1664. Fès remained important with succes-

The 1912 Insurrection

The insurrection of 17–19 April 1912 caught the French somewhat by surprise, although in the wake of the violence it appeared a fairly predictable reaction to the signing of the Treaty of Fès, which ushered in the protectorate. Several French journalists were in Fès at the time. *L'Illustration* reported:

The Mellah, the Jewish quarter, was the first to be sacked – still a Moroccan tradition. How many corpses have been swallowed up in its ruins?

There were only some 1400 to 1500 troops to bring the situation under control, colonial infantry and sharpshooters camped at Dar Debibagh, some of whom were still engaged in operations around Sefrou.

Throughout the afternoon the struggle between the rebels and our soldiers continued in the streets. By nightfall, all the Europeans who had escaped the insurgents' assaults were safe. Our officers and non-commissioned officers had many an occasion to display their courage and sangfroid...

The following day, however, the rebels dared attack Dar Debibagh. They were pushed back, but Captain Bourdonneau was mortally wounded.

It was only on the 18th that the uprising was brought under control; General Dalbiez's troops, called in from Meknès, arrived and quickly overcame the last sparks of resistance...By the time General Moinier had arrived at a forced march beneath the ramparts of Fès, it was all over.

Losses among the rebels have been estimated at 800 dead. For our part, we can only deplore the deaths of nine civilians...Among the military, it has been a bloodbath.

Fès in the 19th Century

Entering Fès el-Bali today is like stepping into a time warp back to the Middle Ages, not so different from the city discovered by Edmondo De Amicis on a diplomatic visit from Italy in the 1880s. He described his experiences in *Morocco: Its People & Places* and had this to say about Fès:

The first impression is that of an immense city fallen into decrepitude and slowly decaying. Tall houses, which seemed formed of houses piled one upon the other, all falling to pieces, cracked from roof to base, propped up on every side, with no opening save some loophole in the shape of a cross; long stretches of street, flanked by two high bare walls like the walls of a fortress; streets running uphill and down, encumbered with stones and the ruins of fallen buildings, twisting and turning at every thirty paces; every now and then a long covered passage, dark as a cellar, where you have to feel your way; blind alleys, recesses, dens full of bones, dead animals, and heaps of putrid matter; the whole steeped in a dim and melancholy twilight. In some places the ground is so broken, the dust so thick, the smell so horrible, the flies so numerous, that we have to stop to take breath.

In half an hour we have made so many turns that if our road could be drawn it would form an arabesque as intricate as any in the Alhambra. Here and there we hear the noise of a mill, a murmur of water, the click of a weaver's loom, a chanting of nasal voices, which we are told come from a school of children, but we see nothing…We approach the centre of the city; people become more numerous; the men stop to let us pass, and stare astonished; the women turn back, or hide themselves; the children scream and run; the larger boys growl and shake their fists at a distance…We see fountains richly ornamented with mosaics, arabesque doors, arched courts…We come to one of the principal streets, about six feet wide, and full of people who crowd about us…There are a thousand eyes upon us; we can scarcely breathe in the press and heat, and move slowly on, stopping every moment to give passage to a Moor on horseback, or a veiled lady on a camel, or an ass with a load of bleeding sheep's heads.

To the right and left are crowded bazaars; inn courtyards encumbered with merchandise; doors of mosques through which we catch a glimpse of arcades and figures prostrate in prayer…The air is impregnated with an acute and mingled odour of aloes, spices, incense and kif; we seem to be walking in an immense drug-shop. Groups of boys go by with scarred and scabby heads; horrible old women, perfectly bald and with naked breasts, making their way by dint of furious imprecations against us; naked, or almost naked, madmen, crowned with flowers and feathers, bearing a branch in their hands, laughing and singing…We go into the bazaar. The crowd is everywhere. The shops, as in Tangier, are mere dens opened in the wall…We cross, jostled by the crowd, the cloth bazaar, that of slippers, that of earthenware, that of metal ornaments, which altogether form a labyrinth of alleys roofed with canes and branches of trees…

Essentially, the only way in which Fès has changed since then is that the moderate affluence Fassis now enjoy has enabled them to restore many of the buildings and clean up the streets. However, that hasn't radically altered the atmosphere; Fès is still worlds apart from anything you will find north of the Strait of Gibraltar.

sive sultans residing here to maintain control over the north.

During the 19th century, as central power crumbled and European interference increased, the distinction between Marrakesh and Fès diminished with both effectively serving as capitals of a fragmented country.

Fès retained its status as the 'moral' capital however, and it was here, on 30 March 1912, that the treaty introducing the French and Spanish protectorates over Morocco was signed. Less than three weeks later, rioting and virtual revolt against the new masters served as a reminder of the city's volatility.

The French may have moved the political capital to Rabat, but Fès remains a constituency to be reckoned with. The Istiqlal (Independence) Party of Allal al-Fassi was established here, many of the impulses towards ejecting the French originated here, and the city was the scene of violent strikes and riots in the 1980s.

Orientation

Fès can be neatly divided into three distinct parts: Fès el-Bali, Fès el-Jdid and the ville nouvelle. The first two of these form the medina, while the last, to the south-west, is the administrative area constructed by the French in 1916. (That Moroccan cities did not experience the wholesale colonial destruction and rebuilding characterised in Algeria is largely due to General, later Marshal, Lyautey.) Nowadays, the city's expanding population has filled out the ville nouvelle and spread to the hillsides in an arc stretching principally to the north and south.

Fès el-Bali is the area of most interest to visitors. Its walls encircle an incredible maze of approximately 9400 twisting alleys, blind turns and souqs. Finding your way around here, at least at first, can be difficult, but you can always pay an eager kid a couple of dirham to guide you to a familiar landmark.

The wall has a number of spectacular gates, with Bab Bou Jeloud in its south-western corner providing the main entrance to the medina – a cluster of cheap pensions lies nearby.

Next to Fès el-Bali is the Merenid city of Fès el-Jdid, which houses the mellah and Dar el-Makhzen (Royal Palace). There are another couple of hotels here.

The ville nouvelle is laid out in typical French colonial style with wide, tree-lined boulevards, squares and parks. Here you'll find most restaurants and hotels, as well as the post office, banks and most transport connections.

It lacks the atmosphere of the medina, but pulses to the rhythm of modern Morocco and is where you'll stay if you're looking for something other than a cheapie.

There are frequent local buses connecting the ville nouvelle with the medina (a 10-minute journey), so there's no great disadvantage in staying here. It is also possible to walk between the two – allow about 30 minutes from Place de Florence to Bab Bou Jeloud.

Information

Tourist Offices The tourist office is tucked away in a building on Place de la Résistance. It has listings and a good range of brochures. There is also a Syndicat d'Initiative (☎ 623460, fax 654370) on Place Mohammed V. Both offices open from 8.30 am to noon and 2.30 to 6.30 pm weekdays.

Guides In spite of what you'll hear, a guide is not necessary for the medina, although having one by your side will stop others hassling you and you'll get from site to site quicker. Hiring an official guide for a half-day (Dr120) is adequate to give you an introduction to Fès el-Bali, though a whole day (Dr150) will do the city more justice.

Your hotel or the tourist office can arrange an official guide. Two female guides that speak English, French and German, Amina Zakkari (☎ cell 01-351171) and Hakima Hayani (☎ cell 01-356032) can be contacted directly.

Money Most of the banks with ATMs are in the ville nouvelle around Blvd Mohammed V. In the medina the Société Générale does cash advances and exchanges travellers cheques – the others tend to be limited to cash transactions.

Out of hours try one of the bigger hotels, such as the Sheraton, for foreign exchange.

Post & Communications The main post office, on the corner of Ave Hassan II and Blvd Mohammed V in the ville nouvelle, is open from 8.30 am to 6.45 pm weekdays, and Saturday from 8 to 11 am. Poste restante is at window No 9 and the parcels office is on the Ave Hassan II side. The phone office on the Blvd Mohammed V side is open from 8.30 am to 9 pm daily. There is another post office in the medina near the Dar Batha Museum. DHL (☎ 652031) has a representative at the Sheraton Hôtel.

There is Internet access all over the ville nouvelle and a few around the medina; most places charge Dr10 per hour. Those in the ville nouvelle are generally cheaper and more reliable with faster access.

Travel Agencies The Carlson Wagonlits agency (☎ 622958, fax 624436) behind the Grand Hôtel in the ville nouvelle is open business hours; it can book flights and ferries.

Bookshops & Newsstands Close to Place de la Résistance in the ville nouvelle, the bookshop at 68 Ave Hassan II is a good place to buy international papers. Alternatively, try the stand across from the police station on Blvd Mohammed V, also in the ville nouvelle.

There are a few other decent bookshops catering largely to students. Librairie Papeterie du Centre opposite the central market in the ville nouvelle has French- and English-language books.

Film & Photography There are quite a few places around the ville nouvelle and well-trodden parts of the medina where you can buy film. For developing in the ville nouvelle, try Photomagic Kodak on Blvd Mohammed V, or Labo Couleur Florence (☎ 620449) at 52 Ave Hassan II.

Cultural Centres The Institut Français (☎ 623921) at 2 Rue Loukiki in the ville nouvelle puts on films, lectures and occasional classes in Arabic.

Laundry Pressing Nationale at 47 Ave Mohammed es-Slaoui, just off Place Mohammed V in the ville nouvelle, is open daily.

Medical Services If you need to visit a doctor, Dr Annie Burg has a surgery (☎ 650647) at 13 Rue Imam Ali, close to the French consul's residence in the ville nouvelle. If you have dental problems, you can visit Mr Leblond (☎ 624030) at 91 Blvd Mohammed V. Both are French and recommended by the

American Language Center. You will need to make an appointment, unless it's urgent.

The night pharmacy (☎ 623380) is on Blvd Moulay Youssef in the north of the ville nouvelle. One of the biggest hospitals is the Hôpital Ghassani (☎ 622776) in the Dhar Mehraz district, east of the ville nouvelle.

Dangers & Annoyances Fès' notorious *faux guides* (unofficial guides; see Touts, Guides & Hustlers under Dangers & Annoyances in the Facts for the Visitor chapter) were once a big problem. The situation has definitely improved with the introduction of a Brigade Touristique: plain-clothed policemen who patrol the medina and tourist areas, and arrest suspect faux guides at random.

High unemployment forces many to persist. Some hang about Fès train station (so arrive knowing exactly where you're headed), hotels and strategic points approaching Fès el-Jdid and Bab Bou Jeloud in Fès el-Bali – tell them you're staying at one of the cheap hotels just inside the gate. Others will shadow you around the medina but if you persevere, you should generally be left alone.

Drivers should note a Fès speciality: motorised hustlers and guides on the approach roads to the city offering to guide you to a hotel, they can be very persistent. See the boxed text 'Interview with a Faux Guide' later in this section for one faux guide's story.

Fès el-Bali

Thanks to the surrounding cemeteries and the enlightened siting of the ville nouvelle, nothing has been built immediately outside the walls of Fès el-Bali (Old Fès). Within, about 9400 streets and lanes twist and turn their way through the original medina. Finding your way around can be confusing, but it's a delightful way to get lost and found. As you become disoriented remember this 'rule': threaded through the labyrinth are a few main streets that will eventually bring you to a gate or landmark. Just follow the crowds.

The easiest stretch is from Bab Bou Jeloud downhill on either At-Talaa al-Kebir or At-Talaa as-Seghir to the Kairaouine Mosque. Heading back, follow the other route (and the throng) back uphill. Similarly, if you want to

Interview with a Faux Guide

Ahmed is one of 10 children; he has four brothers and five sisters. They live with their mother and aunt in the medina of Fès.

Ahmed's father, a bus driver, had a heart attack one morning in 1987 at the age of 46. Ahmed, aged 15, was the eldest, so he left school in order to help his mother. He had hoped to learn the woodcarver's trade, but Dr700 had to be found each month to pay the rent.

Sometimes he helped his uncle who owned a clothes stall in the medina. Occasionally he sold cigarettes or ran errands for his neighbours and friends. Then he got to know the tourists who gave him sweets and pens, and began guiding them through the medina when they got lost. Sometimes he'd get tips as well which he'd take home to his family.

Spurred on by his mother, he learnt to repeat what the official guides told the tourists – the history, the places, the stories. Later, and encouraged by his progress, he began to borrow basic school language books from his cousin, Ali. Things began to improve for the family. The best times, he remembers, were always in June, July and August when he could find work among the tourists all day and sometimes in the evening too. Then the new law came and they weren't allowed to guide any more.

Ahmed was caught by the police one day leading a German tourist to the Medersa Bou Inania in Fès. He got three months in prison. Many of his friends – the older ones – have now given up guiding. It's the shock, he says, 'C'est la mort là', and doesn't want to talk about it. Ahmed will continue, he says, he can take it – he's still young, and so are his brothers and sisters who need him. What else will he do, anyway? He's never learned any other profession and there are no jobs. Prison won't kill him and, if it does, at least he's done his duty and taken care of his family.

get towards the Hôtel Palais Jamaï and the northern gates, keep heading *up* to the north of the Kairaouine Mosque.

It takes at least a couple of days to get around and appreciate the sights. And, interesting as they are, mosques and medersas contribute only in part to the city's attractions. You're much more likely to find Fès by following your senses through the crowded bazaars, pausing to watch something of interest, negotiate a sale, or relax with a mint tea and take it all in. Listen out for the mule driver's cry *'barek'* (look out), or you may be knocked off your feet by some urgent load. The animals wear special shoes made of car tyres, which help them get a grip on the steeper slopes, but don't help their legs much.

Like any Moroccan medina, Fès el-Bali's houses are interspersed with craft guilds and souqs. It is also replete with fascinating old buildings, mostly religious and closed to non-Muslims. And because this part of the city is so compact, little can be seen of them from the outside. No-one particularly minds if you discreetly peer through the doorways, but that's the limit.

The medina's souqs are virtually empty on Thursday afternoon and Friday.

Walking Tours There are three parts to the following walking tour: the walk into the medina, the exit north and the eastern exit.

Into the Medina This route takes you from Bab Bou Jeloud to the Kairaouine Mosque, from where there are a few options for exiting the medina. It should take an hour or two, depending on the number of distractions.

Unlike much of the rest of the city walls and gates, the main entry, **Bab Bou Jeloud**, is a recent addition, built in 1913. Pass through it and you come upon a cluster of cheap hotels and cafes – a hive of activity and a great place to sit and people-watch.

Head down the left side of Bank Commerciale du Maroc (BCdM) towards the minaret of **Medersa Bou Inania**, built by Bou Inan between 1350 and 1357. Take an opportunity to appreciate Merenid building style at its most perfect.

Opposite the entrance to the medersa is a famous **water clock** designed by a clock-maker and part-time magician. Unfortunately, it has been covered up for restoration for some years now – maybe they just don't have the magic to get it going again.

Turn right out of the medersa and continue down for about 150m to a **fountain** on your left and a little further on a **hammam**, which precedes one of the medina's 300 or so mosques, the **Gazleane Mosque**.

At-Talaa al-Kebir continues right down to Medersa el-Attarine, but changes its name along the way. At the Gazleane Mosque it is known as the Qanitra Bou Rous. About 100m further down, at an unmistakable dogleg (there is another **hammam** on the left), it becomes Ash-Sherabliyin (the slippermakers); the **mosque** you pass on the right another 200m or so further down has taken the same name.

Another 100m on, At-Talaa as-Seghir (the parallel artery from Bab Bou Jeloud) joins this street to take you through an unassuming gate, beyond which it makes a slight incline into the **Souq el-Attarine** (a spice market).

Just past the gate on the left is **Dar Saada** a restaurant-cum-carpet warehouse, and a useful landmark.

Virtually across the road and down a short narrow alley is the **henna souq**, where you can pick up some hair dye or get a temporary tattoo. Moroccan women decorate their hands and feet with henna for particular events, such as weddings.

Heading west again into the jumble of back lanes and small squares south of At-Talaa as-Seghir and Ash-Sherabliyin junction is **Souq an-Nejjarine** (Carpenters Souq). Here, **Place an-Nejjarine** is dominated by one of the city's most beautiful fountains and an impressive *funduq* – caravanserai for travelling merchants who would store and sell their goods below and take lodgings on the floors above. It has recently been transformed into the **Nejjarine Museum of Wooden Arts & Crafts** (see after Walking Tours later in this section) complete with a great rooftop cafe (you must pay entry to the museum to get to it).

From Place an-Nejjarine, a lane leads off the south-east corner to the women-only gateway of **Zawiyya Moulay Idriss II**, identifiable by its green-tiled roof. The son of the founder of Morocco's first dynasty, and almost as highly revered as his father, Moulay Idriss II is often credited with founding the city of Fès. It is more likely that Moulay Idriss I was responsible, but there is no doubt that it was his son who brought the city to life – many make pilgrimages here.

To get to the main entrance of the zawiyya from Dar Saada head a few metres east into Souq el-Attarine and take the first alley to the right. Both entries usually have bars across them marking the point beyond which non-Muslims may not pass – don't pass if you're non-Muslim.

The street that continues straight through the northern edge of Souq el-Attarine leads to the **Medersa el-Attarine** (see after Walking Tours later in this section).

Emerging from the medersa, turn left. You'll see Rue Bou Touil on the left with a few snack stalls. The walls of the great **Kairaouine (Qayrawin) Mosque and University** stretch ahead of you on the left-hand side of this street (the qissaria opens up to the right).

The mosque is said to hold 20,000 people, while the university, built between 859 and 862, has for centuries been a highly regarded centre of Muslim learning, surpassed only by the Al-Azhar in Cairo.

Built by Fatma bint Mohammed ben Feheri for fellow Tunisian refugees it was enlarged in 956 by the Almoravid sultan Ali ben Youssef. The Almohads and Saadians also contributed some detail. The buildings house one of the finest libraries in the Muslim world, and there are usually 300 students in residence. Unfortunately, non-Muslims may not enter, and it's so hemmed in by other buildings that little can be seen from outside. You can follow the walls right around and occasionally sneak a peek inside, especially on Friday when all seven doors are opened.

Proceeding along the university walls, you emerge on another small square, **Place as-Seffarine** (Brassmakers Square). With the university walls (and the entrance to its library) still on your left, there is a small **medersa** with a studded cedar door, named after the square, on your right. Built in 1280, it is the oldest in Fès, but is in an advanced state of disrepair. Across the main

FÈS EL-BALI

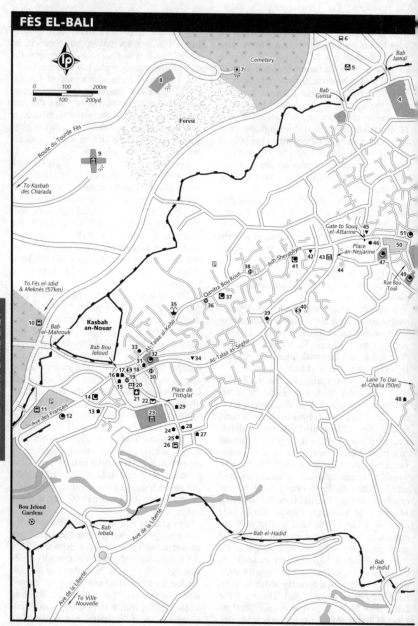

Cemetery

Bab Jamaï

Bab Guissa

Forest

Route du Tourde Fès

To Kasbah des Charada

To Fès el-Jdid & Meknès (57km)

Gate to Souq el-Attarine

Place an-Nejjarine

Ash-Sherabliyin

Qanitra Bou Rous

Rue Bou Touil

Kasbah an-Nouar

Bab el-Mahrouk

Bab Bou Jeloud

At-Talaa al-Kebir

At-Talaa as-Seghir

Lane To Dar el-Ghalia (50m)

Place de l'Istiqlal

Ave des Français

Bou Jeloud Gardens

Bab Jebala

Ave de la Liberté

Bab el-Hadid

Bab el-Jedid

To Ville Nouvelle

FÈS EL-BALI

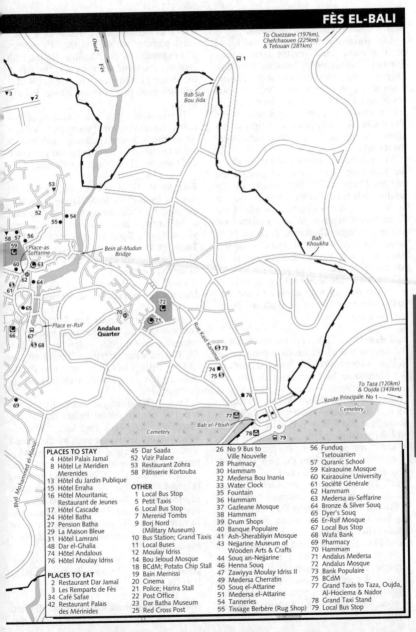

To Ouezzane (197km),
Chefchaouen (225km)
& Tetouan (281km)

Oued Fès

Bab Sidi
Bou Jida

Bab
Khoukha

Bein al-Mudun
Bridge

Place-as
Seffarine

Place er-Rsif

Andalus
Quarter

Rue Kaid Kadmar

To Taza (120km)
& Oujda (343km)

Route Principale No 1

Cemetery

Bab el-Ftouh

Cemetery

Blvd Mohammed el-Alaoui

MIDDLE ATLAS & THE EAST

PLACES TO STAY
4 Hôtel Palais Jamaï
8 Hôtel Le Meridien
   Merenides
13 Hôtel du Jardin Publique
15 Hôtel Erraha
16 Hôtel Mouritania;
   Restaurant de Jeunes
17 Hôtel Cascade
24 Hôtel Batha
27 Pension Batha
29 La Maison Bleue
31 Hôtel Lamrani
48 Dar el-Ghalia
74 Hôtel Andalous
76 Hôtel Moulay Idriss

PLACES TO EAT
2 Restaurant Dar Jamaï
3 Les Remparts de Fès
34 Café Safae
42 Restaurant Palais
   des Mérinides

45 Dar Saada
52 Vizir Palace
53 Restaurant Zohra
58 Pâtisserie Kortouba

OTHER
1 Local Bus Stop
5 Petit Taxis
6 Local Bus Stop
7 Merenid Tombs
9 Borj Nord
   (Military Museum)
10 Bus Station; Grand Taxis
11 Local Buses
12 Moulay Idriss
14 Bou Jeloud Square
18 BCdM; Potato Chip Stall
19 Bain Mernissi
20 Cinema
21 Police; Harira Stall
22 Post Office
23 Dar Batha Museum
25 Red Cross Post

26 No 9 Bus to
   Ville Nouvelle
28 Pharmacy
30 Hammam
32 Medersa Bou Inania
33 Water Clock
35 Fountain
36 Hammam
37 Gazleane Mosque
38 Hammam
39 Drum Shops
40 Banque Populaire
41 Ash-Sherabliyin Mosque
43 Nejjarine Museum of
   Wooden Arts & Crafts
44 Souq an-Nejjarine
46 Henna Souq
47 Zawiyya Moulay Idriss II
49 Medersa Cherratin
50 Souq el-Attarine
51 Medersa el-Attarine
54 Tanneries
55 Tissage Berbère (Rug Shop)

56 Funduq
   Tsetouanien
57 Quranic School
59 Kairaouine Mosque
60 Kairaouine University
61 Société Générale
62 Hammam
63 Medersa as-Seffarine
64 Bronze & Silver Souq
65 Dyer's Souq
66 Er-Rsif Mosque
67 Local Bus Stop
68 Wafa Bank
69 Pharmacy
70 Hammam
71 Andalus Medersa
72 Andalus Mosque
73 Bank Populaire
75 BCdM
77 Grand Taxis to Taza, Oujda,
   Al-Hociema & Nador
78 Grand Taxi Stand
79 Local Bus Stop

street leading east off the square (away from the Kairaouine) is a **hammam**.

Still following the mosque walls and heading north you'll see the 14th century **Funduq Tsetouanien** (Tetouan Funduq). Originally the preserve of businessmen from Tetouan, for centuries it served as a hotel and warehouse for travelling merchants. You're free to wander the carpet shop it now houses and if you ask nicely and offer a tip you can climb onto the roof for limited views over the mosque.

You can now continue along the walls of the Kairaouine back to where you started and head back to Bab Bou Jeloud, ideally taking At-Talaa as Seghir. On the way, you could get off the beaten track south of the Kairaouine University to have a quick look at the **Medersa Cherratin**, built in 1670 under Moulay ar-Rashid, the first of the Alawites. It is not as interesting as its Merenid precursors.

You could then head back up the hill and wind the day up with a visit to the **Dar Batha Museum** (see after Walking Tours later in this section).

Exit East If you're having too much fun in the medina and want to explore further east to Bab el-Ftouh, take the lane just north of the Kairaouine Medersa to reach Fès' famous **tanneries**; (see the colour boxed text 'Tanneries' in the Central Morocco chapter for more information) take the left fork after about 50m and follow your nose. You will probably be directed through a leather shop to a platform overlooking the tanners' pits, from where you will get the best view but may also be asked to donate to a 'workers' fund'. Try to get here in the morning, when the pits are awash with coloured dyes.

From the tanneries, take the lane back to the fork and turn left to reach the Bein al-Mudun (Between the Cities) bridge over the Oued Fès and into the **Andalus Quarter**.

From the bridge, head more or less straight until you reach an arch. Once through the arch (you emerge on a small square), turn to the left. Straight ahead is the women's entrance to the **Andalus Mosque** and, shortly before on the right, the entrance to the **Medersa es-Sahriji**. The main entrance to the mosque, founded as a small local place of worship in the 9th century and expanded by the Almohads in the 13th century, is around the corner to the left of the women's entrance. The Merenids also left their mark here with decoration and a library.

If you want to leave the medina at this point, return to the small square, turn left and follow the wide street heading south-east. It leads to Bab el-Ftouh, where you can catch local bus No 12 or 18 to the ville nouvelle.

Exit North An alternative way out of the medina from Place as-Seffarine is to take the main lane heading south of the Medersa as-Seffarine, where you will quickly find yourself in the **Dyers Souq** by the Oued Fès. There are two small bridges over the fairly filthy-looking stream, whose water is used in the dyeing process.

From the wide square by the **Er-Rsif Mosque** you can get the No 19 bus back to the ville nouvelle.

If you want to reach **Bab Guissa** in the northern medina, take the street just on the western side of the gate to Souq el-Attarine. Stick to the wider streets and keep going *up* and you really can't go wrong – you should pass a little square with a cinema on its northern side.

From Bab Guissa you can easily see the late 19th-century **Hôtel Palais Jamaï** (see Places to Stay – Top End later). What is now a luxury hotel was built by the Grand Vizier to Moulay al-Hassan I, Sidi Mohammed ben Arib al-Jamaï, who fell from grace with the rise of Sultan Abd al-Aziz. (He and his brother also had a palace built in Meknès, on Place el-Hedim, which now houses a museum.) Set in lush gardens, the former palace is a wonderful place to have refreshment – if you can afford Dr20 for a cup of coffee!

You can pick up local bus No 10 and petit taxis to the ville nouvelle from outside Bab Guissa.

Medersa Bou Inania Built by the Merenid sultan Bou Inan between 1350 and 1357, this

Ibn Khaldun

Although Fès cannot count him as one of its own, Ibn Khaldun, one of the Arab world's greatest thinkers, was one of many luminaries attracted to Morocco's centre of learning, where he studied in the Kairaouine University.

Considered the greatest of Arab historians, Ibn Khaldun developed the first philosophy of history not based on religion. Called the *Muqaddimah* (Introduction to History), his book is regarded as a classic. The 20th century historian Toynbee has called it 'a philosophy of history which is undoubtedly the greatest work of its kind that has ever yet been created by any mind in any time or place'. Ibn Khaldun also wrote a definitive history of Muslim North Africa.

Born in Tunisia in 1332 he spent his formative years there, but by the age of 23, after completing his studies at the Kairaouine, he had become a secretary to the sultan of Fès. After having been imprisoned for two years on suspicion of being involved in a palace rebellion, Ibn Khaldun moved to Granada, then Bejaia, Tlemcen, Biskra and Fès before ending up back in Granada.

In 1375 he gave up the world of business and politics and retired to the village of Frenda in Algeria where, under the protection of the local emir, he spent four years writing the *Muqaddimah*.

He spent the latter years of his life teaching at the Kairaouine's eastern counterpart, the Al-Azhar in Cairo. He died in 1406.

is said to be the finest of the theological colleges constructed by the Merenids. The zellij, *muqarna* (plasterwork) and woodcarving is stunning, and should not be missed.

There are excellent views over the nearby water clock from the roof. Those parts of the medersa already restored display a degree of skill that proves the Moroccans have lost none of the talents for which they are renowned.

Different from others you may have seen already, the medersa has an elaborate mosque complete with a minaret. Medersas usually have some form of prayer hall, what Muslims would still call a masjid (mosque), but it's normally of modest dimensions perhaps with a simple mihrab (niche indicating the direction of Mecca). Some explain that the medersa required a larger-scale mosque of its own because there was none other nearby at the time. As this little mosque is still in use, non-Muslims may not pass the barrier marked by a tiny tributary of the Oued Fès.

Near Bab Bou Jeloud, the medersa is open from 8 am to 5 pm (except at prayer times); entry costs Dr10.

Medersa el-Attarine Built by Abu Said in 1325, this medersa has the traditional patterns of Merenid artisanship. Halls for teaching and a modest masjid flank the central courtyard. The zellij base, stucco work and cedar wood at the top of the walls and the ceiling is every bit as elegant as the artistry of the Medersa Bou Inania.

It's in the heart of the medina and is open from 9 am to noon and 2 to 5 pm daily. Entry costs Dr10.

Andalus Medersa Built in 1321, the basic structure of this college is simple, but the inside is richly decorated and there are good views from the roof. Much of the structure lay in ruins until fairly recently, and restoration work continues.

It is in the east of the medina in the Andalus Quarter and is open daily from 8.30 am to noon and 3 to 5 pm. Entry is Dr10.

Nejjarine Museum of Wooden Arts & Crafts Opened in 1998, this museum is in a beautifully panelled and restored funduq. With displays of everything wooden, largely dating from the 19th century onwards, it offers an opportunity to examine some intricately carved detail close up. Artefacts in rooms around a courtyard include domestic tools, musical instruments, babies' cots and chairs, minbars, wedding furniture, Berber locks and chests. The museum itself is very attractive and the terrace cafe has good views over the surrounding rooftops.

Right on Place an-Nejjarine, the museum opens from 10 am to 6 pm daily; entry costs Dr10.

MIDDLE ATLAS & THE EAST

Dar Batha Museum One place you should not miss is the Dar Batha Museum, now the Musée du Batha (also known as the Museum of Moroccan Arts) on Place de l'Istiqlal.

Built as a Hispano-Moorish palace more than 100 years ago by Moulay al-Hassan and Moulay Abd al-Aziz, it houses an excellent collection of historical and artistic artefacts, including fine wood-carving, zellij work and sculpted plaster, much of it from ruined or decaying medersas.

There is also some fine Fassi embroidery, colourful tribal carpets and a well-known ceramic collection dating from the 14th century to the present. It's a great place to see some of the famous blue pottery of Fès – some of the exhibits number among the best of their kind in the country. The cobalt glaze responsible for the colour is developed from a special process discovered in the 10th century.

As usual, the exhibit's explanations are in Arabic and French only. The attractive Andalusian-style garden outside offers temporary respite from the bustle and noise of the medina. The museum is open from 8.30 am to noon and 2.30 to 6 pm Wednesday to Monday. Entry costs Dr10.

Fès el-Jdid

Fès el-Jdid (New Fès) has some spectacular buildings, the old Jewish quarter and, although less interesting than Fès el-Bali, is much easier to explore.

The entrance to **Dar el-Makhzen** (Royal Palace) on Place des Alaouites is a stunning example of modern restoration. The palace grounds' 80 hectares are covered with palaces, pavilions, medersas, mosques and pleasure gardens; an Arab League conference was hosted here. It was once possible to visit the palace with permission from the tourist office, but this is no longer the case unless you have political or cultural clout.

South of the palace is the old **mellah**, the Jewish quarter. Few Jews live here now, but their houses, with windows and balconies looking into the streets, are in marked contrast to Muslim practices.

In the south-west corner of the mellah is the fascinating **Jewish Cemetery & Habarim Synagogue**, where the sea of white tombs is almost blinding. The larger tombs (including one that looks like a train) are for rabbis. One of the tombs is for the martyr Solica, a 14 year-old-girl who refused to convert to Islam and the advances of the Governor of Tangier and subsequently had her throat slit.

The synagogue is now a museum with a whole mishmash of articles left behind after the Jewish exodus, and some good photo and postcard displays. Genealogists with family ties to Fès are welcome to access the detailed records that have been researched here. The cemetery and museum are open from 7 am to sunset Sunday to Friday and you're bound to be guided and asked for a donation.

Towards the northern end of Sharia Moulay Suleiman (formerly Grande Rue de Fès el-Jdid), lined with shops and stalls but lacking the atmosphere of Fès el-Bali, is the **Petit Mechouar**. The parade ground for the sultan's troops fronts the enormous Merenid gate of **Bab Dekkaken**, once the main palace entrance.

Between it and Bab Bou Jeloud are the well-maintained and relaxing **Bou Jeloud Gardens** (or Jnan Sebil), through which flows the Oued Fès, still the city's main source of water.

North of Bab Dekkaken is the **Grand Mechouar**, leading up to Bab Segma. The western wall of the Grand Mechouar was

Mellah

The word *mellah* (from the Arabic for salt) appears to have referred to the area of Fès el-Jdid to which the city's Jewish population was transferred under the Merenids. Some say it was watered by a salty tributary of the Oued Fès, whereas others describe something more along the lines of a salty swamp.

According to a more colourful explanation, the area in which the Jews lived derived its name from a job Jews were assigned by the Muslim city authorities – salting the heads of criminals, rebels and the like before they were hung up to adorn the city's gates and walls.

Whatever the reason, the word eventually took on the same meaning in Morocco as 'ghetto' in Europe: the Jewish quarter.

once the royal arms factory, but it now serves as a carpet factory.

North of the Medina

For a spectacular overview of Fès, head through the Grand Mechouar and Bab Segma and walk left around the old **Kasbah des Cherarda**, built in the 17th century to house Berbers but now home to secondary schools, a university and hospital. From the kasbah follow the road behind the cemetery up to **Borj Nord**. Alternatively, you can scramble up one of the tracks that leads up the hill further east. Like its counterpart on the southern side of the city (Borj Sud), Sultan Ahmed al-Mansour built Borj Nord in the late 16th century to monitor the potentially disloyal populace of Fès.

Borj Nord now houses a military museum: mainly endless rows of muskets, rifles and cannons, many taken from Riffian rebels in 1958. It's open 8.30 am to noon and 2.30 to 6.30 pm Wednesday to Monday. Entry is Dr10.

Further up are the **Merenid Tombs**, dramatic in their advanced state of ruin although little remains of their fine original decoration. The views over Fès are spectacular and well worth the climb; unfortunately the best times to visit (early morning and sunset) are also the dodgiest – don't come alone.

Activities

Fès Royal Golf (☎ 665210) is a nine-hole course (3168m, par 36) set in the rolling countryside about 17km south of town.

Language Courses

The American Language Center (☎ 624850, fax 931608, e alif@fesnet.net.ma) and its affiliated Arabic Language Institute (same ☎/fax, e alifmbox.azure.net) are at 2 Rue Ahmed Hiba in the ville nouvelle, near the youth hostel.

This is one of the few places in Morocco set up for the systematic teaching of Arabic to foreigners. Staff can also organise accommodation for you in its residence (from Dr65 per night), with a family (from Dr600 per week) or in an apartment (from Dr1500 per month).

Courses are for three/six weeks and cost from Dr4150/7800 (Dr4350/8200 in summer), though private tuition can also be arranged (Dr165 per hour); the group rate is cheaper.

If you're interested in teaching English, look up the International Language Centre rep, Mme Bassou (☎ 641408) at 15 Blvd el-Joulan.

Special Events

The Fès Festival of World Sacred Music held during June/July each year bills itself as a festival of world music with an international cast from all corners of the globe as well as Morocco. Performances are held in venues as diverse as Volubilis, Dar Batha Museum and the Salle de la Prefecture. The program is available early in the year from tourist outlets, the secretariat (☎ 740535, fax 633989, e fesfestival@fesnet.net.ma) or on the festival Web site: www.fezfestival.org.

In September the town is packed for the Moussem of Moulay Idriss II when a large procession leads to his tomb.

Hammams & Public Showers

There are hammams galore in the medina, plenty of them near hotels. Bain Mernissi at Bab Bou Jeloud in Fès el-Bali is open to men from 6 am to 1 pm and 9 pm to midnight; to women from 1 to 9 pm. A bath/massage costs Dr7/15.

In the ville nouvelle, the modern Douche el-Fath (in the lane behind the CTM hotel) is open to men from 6 am to 8.30 pm and women from 8 am to 8 pm.

Places to Stay – Budget

The most colourful places to stay, where you'll be woken in the early hours by the call to prayer, are the cheapies clustered around Bab Bou Jeloud in Fès el-Bali. They're basic and the shower situation is grim (none in the following places listed unless stated otherwise), but there are hammams.

Where you stay will also depend on the season and time of day you arrive. In summer, when many of the smaller hotels tend to fill up quickly, there's little point in heading to Fès el-Bali if it's getting late. If this is the case, or you simply don't want to be quite so close to the action, you could try the places around Fès el-Jdid.

Also, in summer many of the cheapies in the medina inflate their prices, and you end up paying the same as you would for better accommodation in the ville nouvelle. At the same time singles are almost impossible to find – hoteliers make more by letting them out as doubles and triples.

Because there is such a demand for accommodation, Fès hotel managers can be quite arrogant and in some cases aggressive – don't expect too warm a welcome after your long bus or train ride.

Camping There are two camping grounds outside the city. *Camping Diamant Vert* (☎ 608369) at 'Ain Chkef, some 6km south of town off the Ifrane road, sits at the bottom of a valley through which a clean stream runs. There's plenty of shade, a swimming pool and disco. Camping costs Dr20 per adult (Dr10 for children), Dr15 for a car, Dr20 for a caravan and Dr15 to pitch a tent. Bus No 17 to 'Ain Chkef (from Place de Florence in the ville nouvelle) will get you close to the camping ground. You can pick it up in the ville nouvelle from Place de l'Atlas, near the mosque.

The second place is the rather more luxurious *Camping International* (☎ 731439, fax 731554) about 3km south of town close to the stadium on the Sefrou road. It's well maintained and set in large gardens with a swimming pool (open May to October), tennis courts, restaurants, a bar and shops. It's good for children, who have their own pool, play park and organised activities such as swimming lessons. Each camping block has its own showers, and use of a kitchen. It costs Dr20/40 per child/adult, Dr30 for a tent, and Dr15/30/40 for a motorcycle/car/caravan. Bus No 38 from Place d l'Atlas in the southwest of the city comes past here.

Hostels The *Youth Hostel* (☎ 624085, 18 Rue Abdeslam Serghini) in the ville nouvelle is a small, clean place with a tiled courtyard, TV lounge and hot showers. It costs members Dr45/55 each in dormitory/twin-bed accommodation with breakfast (non HI-members pay Dr50/60). They also do meals for groups on request. The hostel is open from 8 to 10 am, noon to 3 pm and 6 to 10 pm daily.

Hotels – Fès el-Bali Most of the budget places are near or around Bab Bou Jeloud.

One of the cheapest, *Hôtel Erraha* (☎ 633226), is just inside Bab Bou Jeloud. It has clean but tatty and cell-like singles/doubles for Dr30/60 and a terrace. Some rooms actually overlook the gate.

Hôtel du Jardin Publique (☎ 633086) close by, down an alley after the mosque, has large and clean rooms for Dr35/60; a couple have balconies.

Just inside the bab is *Hôtel Mouritania* (☎ 633518, 20 Rue Serrajine), which charges Dr40 per person for clean, cell-like rooms; the bonus is the hot showers (Dr10).

Next door, *Hôtel Cascade* (☎ 638442) remains popular and has simple rooms for Dr40/60. There are two roof terraces with good views and usually a trickle of hot water. This is probably the worst hotel for hassle from guides – you won't even be out of your taxi with your backpack before someone is offering to guide you there (even though it's clearly visible from the medina gate!).

Closer to the Medersa Bou Inania is *Hôtel Lamrani* (☎ 634411), the nicest place in the area, although the manager can be stroppy. It has spotless rooms overlooking the medina for Dr90/120; a night under the stars on the terrace costs Dr20.

If you're desperate for a cheapie, you could look at the very basic hotels along Rue Kaid Khammar in the Andalus Quarter in the east. Not many tourists venture this way and you'll need to take care alone at night. *Hôtel Moulay Idriss* and *Hôtel Andalous* (☎ 648262) both have very basic rooms for Dr30/50.

Back among the tourists and near the museum, *Pension Batha* (☎ 741150, fax 741159, 8 Sid Lkhayat Batha) is a small place with rooms for Dr60/80, with breakfast.

Hotels – Fès el-Jdid The *Hôtel du Parc* (☎ 941698, Rue de Fès Jdid) off Sharia

Moulay Suleiman is a bit shabby, but reasonably clean and a cheap deal at Dr30/50. Singles/doubles with a view over the nearby gardens or ramparts are Dr50/80.

Closest to the ville nouvelle and a good deal is *Hôtel du Commerce* (☎ 622231, *Place des Alaouites*). It has pleasant rooms, four opening onto a terrace overlooking the palace, for Dr40/60.

Around the corner, *Hotel Glacier* (*9 Place du Commerce*) is a small pastel pink-and-blue place down an alley. Basic rooms (a couple have wrought-iron balconies) start at Dr35.

Hotels – Ville Nouvelle The central *Hôtel Renaissance* (☎ 622193, *29 Rue Abdel el-Khattabi*) is an old, rather dark, cavernous place but remains a popular cheapie. The clean singles/doubles/triples, some with balcony, cost Dr50/80/120 and there's a cold, shared shower and terrace.

Brighter and cleaner, *Hôtel du Maghreb* (☎ 621567, *25 Ave Mohammed es-Slaoui*) has rooms with brass beds and a balcony for Dr50/80/120; a hot shower is Dr7.

Closer to the student area, *Hôtel Savoy* (☎ 620608, *Blvd Abdallah Chefchaouni*) has reasonably clean, airy rooms with washbasins and there are (usually) hot showers. Rooms cost Dr50/70/90/120. Around the corner, *Hôtel Volubilis*, not to be confused with the more expensive hotel of the same name further south on Ave Allal ben Abdullah, is brightly decorated with rooms from Dr30 per person. Those on the terrace and with balconies for Dr70 are better.

The reasonably clean and secure *Hôtel Central* (☎ 622333, *50 Rue Brahim Roudani*) has rooms with shower, bidet, washbasin and balcony for Dr89/106/159.

Hôtel du Pacha (☎ 652290, *32 Ave Hassan II*) overlooks the city's main tree-lined boulevard. The exterior promises more than the Dr80/120 rooms with bathroom and balcony deliver, but it's OK.

Hôtel Royal (☎ 624656, *36 Rue du Soudan*) has rooms with piping hot showers for Dr96/132 and rooms with a shower and toilet for Dr120/150.

Close to the train station, *Hôtel Kairouan* (☎ 623590, *84 Rue du Soudan*) has spacious rooms with big clean beds and a shower for Dr120/150, but the loos are a bit smelly.

The two-star *Hôtel Lamdaghri* (☎ 620310, *10 Rue Abasse el-Massadi*) is modernish, central and reasonably quiet. Clean rooms with showers are Dr124/168. The hotel also has a dining area on the 1st floor and a seedy bar next door.

Places to Stay – Mid-Range
The only medina choice in this category, overlooking the Dar Batha Museum, is a good one. *Hôtel Batha* (☎ 741077, *fax 741078, Place Batha*) has value singles/doubles with bathroom for Dr193/243. It also has a bar and restaurant, and a pool in its attractive whitewashed garden courtyard. Apparently the rooms at the front can get affected by fumes from the busy road outside.

In the ville nouvelle, the pleasant *Hôtel Amor* (☎ 623304, *31 Rue Arabie Saoudite*) has bright, clean rooms with bathroom for Dr160/190, as well as a restaurant and bar.

Hôtel Olympic (☎ 932682, *fax 932665, 5 Blvd Mohammed V*) around the corner from the central market has clean rooms for Dr218/276/340 with bathroom.

Moving up to the three-star range, the *Grand Hôtel* (☎ 932026, *fax 653847, Blvd Abdallah Chefchaouni*) is an older colonial place with a bit of traditional decoration with a salon and fountain. Rooms with bathroom are Dr215/251. It also has basement parking.

Hôtel de la Paix (☎ 625072, *fax 626880, 44 Ave Hassan II*) has characterless, but quiet and comfortable rooms for Dr260/330/419.

The modern tour-group style *Hôtel Splendid* (☎ 622148, *fax 654892, 9 Rue Abdel el-Khattabi*) has large and comfortable air-con rooms with TV for Dr275/361 (including breakfast). It also has a small swimming pool, a bar and good restaurant.

Closeish to the CTM bus station but still in the ville nouvelle, *Nouzha Hôtel* has tiling and murals endowing it with character. It also has restaurants, a bar, a nightclub, a panoramic terrace and rooms that cost Dr270/320.

Right by the train station is *Hôtel Ibis Moussafir* (☎ 651902, *fax 651909*). One of

FÈS VILLE NOUVELLE

PLACES TO STAY
4 Hôtel Ibis Moussafir
11 Hôtel Kairouan
19 Hôtel Amor
22 Hôtel Royal
25 Hôtel de la Paix
31 Hôtel Menzah Zalagh
32 Hôtel Menzah Zalagh
    Annexe
38 Hôtel du Pacha
41 Hôtel Sofia
49 Hôtel Olympic
51 Hôtel Savoy;
    Hôtel Volubilis;
    Avis
52 Youth Hostel
62 Grand Hôtel
67 Hôtel Lamdaghri
71 Hôtel Renaissance
72 Hôtel Splendid
74 Hôtel du Maghreb
75 Hôtel Central
81 Nouzha Hôtel
83 Hôtel CTM
86 Sheraton Hôtel
87 Hôtel Volubilis

PLACES TO EAT
12 La Cheminée
18 Venisia
21 Sandwich Bajelloul
23 American Donuts
29 Pâtisserie Glacier
    Zegzouti; L'Empire Cinema
45 La Medaille
47 Café Renaissance
48 24-Hour Cafe/Restaurant
50 Restaurant Fish Friture
61 Restaurant Sicilia
64 Restaurant Le Chamonix
68 Restaurant du Centre;
    Dentist
69 Pâtisserie L'Entente
76 Al-Khozama
79 Restaurant Pizzeria Chez
    Vittorio; Banque Populaire

OTHER
1 Supratours
2 Grand Taxis
   to Meknès
3 Petit Taxis; Local Buses
5 Public Swimming Pool
6 Night Pharmacy
7 Local Buses
8 Tourist Office
9 Cyberclub
10 Institut Français
13 Budget
14 La Gare Supermarket
15 Shell Petrol Station
16 Mosque
17 Hertz
20 BMAO; BMCE
24 BCdM
26 Labo Couleur Florence
27 ABN-AMRO
28 Royal Air Maroc
30 Bookshop
33 Wafa Bank (ATM)
34 Europcar;
    Europ Assistance
35 Main Post &
    Telephone Office
36 Police
37 Bank al-Maghrib
39 Club Internet
40 Bar Cala Iris
42 French Consulate
43 Newsstand
44 Wafa Bank (ATM)
46 Photomagic Kodak
53 American Language
    Center
54 Petrol Station
55 Librairie Papeterie
    du Centre
56 Supermarket
57 Surgery
58 Catholic Church
59 Petit Taxis
60 Syndicat d'Initiative
63 Carlson Wagonlits
65 Coin Net
66 Petit Taxis
70 BMCE (ATM)
73 Astor Cinema
77 Cinéma Rex
78 Pressing Nationale
80 Pharmacy
82 Shell Petrol Station
84 Internet Cafe
85 Douche
    el-Fath
88 Ensemble Artisanal

a chain of hotels, its rooms, with all mod cons, cost Dr275/345 plus taxes.

Places to Stay – Top End

Medina If you have the money, then the swankiest choice in town is *Hôtel Palais Jamaï* (☎ 634331, fax 635096, ⓔ cresa@palais.jamai.co.ma). Once the pleasure dome of a late 19th-century grand vizier to the sultan, it's set in a lush Andalusian garden. Doubles in the new wing have the views and start at Dr1800, while those in the old palace have more character and a bigger Dr2300 price tag. Suites start at Dr5000 on the medina side and reach a whopping Dr18,000 for the Royal Suite in the old palace. Along with Marrakesh's Mamounia, this is a jewel of another epoch. The hotel has a swimming pool (on a lovely terrace above the medina), fitness centre, restaurants (see Places to Eat – Palace Restaurants), bar and hammam (Dr180 with massage).

For the same kind of money you forfeit facilities such as swimming pool for personalised service in a lavish and a bit more tasteful than usual 18th-century palace. *Dar el-Ghalia* (☎ 634167, fax 636393, 13/15 Ross Rhi, ⓔ Darelghalia@fesnet.net.ma), off the beaten track in the Andalus Quarter, has individually designed and named suites starting at Dr900 for a single rising to Dr6800 for a three-bedroom suite. Its restaurant *Dar Tagine* is well regarded and you can eat your couscous (Dr120) on the hotel terrace overlooking the medina.

Following the same luxury formula and still in Fès el-Bali but much more central is *La Maison Bleue* (☎ 636052, fax 740686, 2 Place de Batha, ⓔ maisonbleue@fesnet .net.ma). A beautifully restored *riad* (traditional lavish town house) it also has a highly regarded restaurant. Suites range from Dr1500/1700 for singles/doubles to Dr3000. Dinner will set guests/nonguests back another Dr450/500 (including drinks).

Ville Nouvelle In the four-star category *Hôtel Volubilis* (☎ 623098, fax 621125, Ave Allal ben Abdullah), not to be confused with the more central budget place, has a lovely garden and pool; the rooms with a balcony are air-conditioned. The only drawback is that it's not really within quick strolling distance of anything except the Ensemble Artisanal. Single/double rooms cost Dr635/755.

A good choice, with wonderful views across Fès el-Bali from its gardens, pool and rooms, is *Hôtel Menzeh Zalagh* (☎ 625531, fax 651995, Rue Mohammed Diouri). Large rooms in the main hotel or in the annexe across the road cost Dr750/950 plus tax. There are also suites for Dr1650/2650 and nonguests can use the pool for Dr40.

More interesting and near the Merenid tombs on the north-west side of Fès el-Bali is *Hotel le Meridien Merinides* (☎ 645226, fax 645225) with its sweeping panorama of Fès el-Bali. The swimming pool and two restaurants have fantastic views and it's a good spot for a sunset drink. Air-con rooms start at Dr1100/1300.

The *Sheraton Hôtel* (☎ 930909, fax 620486, Ave des FAR) has rooms ranging from Dr1400/1700 to Dr10,000 for a suite. It, of course, has a pool, bars, restaurants and a 24-hour coffee shop.

Places to Eat

Medina In the medina the choice is limited to snack bars, basic restaurants or palace restaurants catering to tourist groups.

The restaurants around Bab Bou Jeloud in Fès el-Bali, where you can watch the passing cavalcade, remain among the most popular. Although the quality-price relationship is not always good, a reassuring number of Moroccans eat here. *Restaurant des Jeunes* (near Hôtel Mouritania), is also basic like the others, but cheap and quick.

There are also some great-value *snack stands*, including those serving *harira* (spicy lentil soup) and potato chips, around here. For around Dr12 you can get a huge sandwich stuffed with all sorts – easily a satisfying lunch. (There are similar snack places along Sharia Moulay Suleiman in Fès el-Jdid.) Also around the Bab Bou Jeloud are plenty of cafes, but a better option is to grab a pastry and head into the medina along At-Talaa as-Seghir to *Café Safae*, which serves good coffee.

If you get hungry down around the Kairaouine Mosque in the heart of Fès el-Bali, there is a small huddle of cheap-food stands between it and Medersa el-Attarine. Also here, the small *Pâtisserie Kortouba* is a good place for an energy boost while sightseeing.

Café Restaurant La Noria next to an old waterwheel in the Bou Jeloud Gardens is a great place to start the day or retreat from the noise and bustle of the streets. As well as serving coffee it also does main courses such as couscous (Dr40) or omelettes and salads (Dr20). It's open from 6 am to 9 pm daily.

Boulangerie Pâtisserie Nisrine opposite the Royal Palace in Fès el-Jdid is good for a cuppa or snack.

Palace Restaurants The medina is dotted with a few restaurants housed in old palaces and the like offering extravagant Moroccan meals in grand, traditional surroundings. Many also offer stage shows, including Moroccan music and oriental dancing, in an attempt to recreate the atmosphere of *The Thousand and One Nights*, and one extravagant evening along these lines is worth the experience. Some of these restaurants are among the best in Morocco.

Atmosphere-wise, they're at their best in the evening and when reasonably well patronised. In the winter, they are often very cold and very empty. If it's just you, the expensive menu and some desultory singing can seem rather depressing.

The set menus consist of the usual brochettes, tajine and couscous fare but this may be the time to try something a bit fancier such as *trid* (fried dough stuffed with egg and meat and covered in cinnamon and sugar), *m'choui* (whole roast lamb), *dalaa* (chops) or pigeon tajine. Also recommended is the Moroccan salad, generally a selection of separate dishes such as spiced carrots, lentils, beans, eggplant and olives.

Les Remparts de Fès (☎ 637415, fax 633945, 2 Arset Jiar el-Guissa) in the north of Fès is close to Palais Jamaï. It has a la carte lunches and dinner menus accompanied by music and belly-dancing for Dr260 to Dr510. It also boasts an enclosed room with panoramic views.

One of the cheapest (and least used by the tourist group circuit) is the nearby *Restaurant Dar Jamaï* (☎ 635685, 14 Funduq Lihoudi Zenjfour). It's a small, pleasant and friendly place with the 'bonus' of no entertainment. A three-course set menu costs Dr100 and alcohol is available.

Dar Saada (☎ 633343, 21 Souq el-Attarine) in the heart of the medina has good-value set menus (including a superb couscous) for Dr135 or Dr220. Open for lunch only, it serves alcohol and is a great place for sampling the less standard dishes, which cost from Dr90 (plus tax).

The easy-to-find *Restaurant Palais des Mérinides* (☎ 634028, 36 Chrablyne) is on a main thoroughfare. Set menus cost Dr170 and Dr190 and main courses are Dr90. Entertainment is provided on request only – to avoid the groups come in the evening.

Restaurant al-Fassia in the Hôtel Palais Jamaï is well known both for its beautiful decor and the quality of food. There's a terrace overlooking the medina and a choice of French or Moroccan cuisine accompanied by a belly-dancing show. Its reputation and popularity with well-heeled tourists has kept prices high (Dr390 per person for food alone).

Close to the tanneries, *Vizir Palace* (☎ 635546, 35 Derb Touil Blida) is a carpet shop and restaurant combo with menus from Dr160 to Dr200. Open for lunch only, it's popular with tour groups.

Nearby and better value with less crowds, *Restaurant Zohra* (☎ 637699, 3 Derb Ain Nass Blida) has tasty menus for Dr70, Dr90 and Dr120.

La Maison Bleue and the restaurant at *Dar el-Ghalia* are a couple of other places suitable for a real splurge (see Places to Stay – Top End).

Ville Nouvelle There are a few *cheap eats* and *creameries* (dairies) on or just off Blvd Mohammed V, especially around the central market.

A decent place very popular with the locals is *Sandwich Bajelloul* (2 Ave Saoudia). It has a good selection of meat, including liver and sausages, which they grill in front of you.

Among the cafes and shops on Ave de France are a couple of hamburger joints. *Venisia* is extremely popular. It has a good range of fish as well as the usual meats and sausages for sandwiches, brochettes, and good chips.

Restaurant Le Chamonix off Blvd Mohammed V offers reasonable fare including pizza and a set menu for Dr50.

Al-Khozama (☎ 622377, 23 Ave Mohammed es-Slaoui) is a pleasant place with an indoor terrace. Its menu costs Dr60 and there are crepes (Dr35) and pizza and pasta (Dr35). It's open from 7 am to 11 pm daily.

Restaurant Fish Friture (☎ 940699, 138 Blvd Mohammed V) is a bright and friendly fish and Moroccan restaurant, decorated in Mediterranean style. It serves very tasty food (Dr35 to Dr70). It's air-conditioned and has a terrace around a fountain.

Another restaurant with a good reputation for fish is *Nautilas* in the Hotel de la Paix on Ave Hassan II. Dishes cost from Dr55 to Dr80 and a *menu gastronomique* is Dr135.

If you're after a drink with your meal, try *Restaurant du Centre* (105 Blvd Mohammed V). There's no sign – look for the menu outside and the rowdy bar next door. It has good, simple Moroccan fare (menu for Dr80) that washes down nicely with a wine or beer (Dr18).

Further south, another place with a good reputation is *Restaurant Pizzeria Chez Vittorio* (☎ 624730, 21 Rue Brahim Roudani). Decorated in a Tuscan style, it's licensed and has salads from Dr25, and pasta and pizza dishes from Dr45.

Restaurant Sicilia (☎ 626565, 4 Blvd Abdallah Chefchaouni) opposite the Syndicat d'Initiative is a chain-restaurant style place that does pizza from Dr20 to Dr35 and self-serve salads from Dr12 to Dr20. It's a good place for vegetarians and takeaway. It's open daily from noon to midnight.

La Cheminée (☎ 624902, 6 Ave Lalla Asma) is a popular, yet tranquil and civilised little place with air-con and waiters in bow ties. It serves good French-Moroccan dishes for Dr70 to Dr90.

Another French-Moroccan place is *La Medaille* (☎ 620183, 24 Rue Laarbi Karrat). With live music and a good menu (Dr150) as well as superb mains, it's a good licensed place with a touch of ambience.

Night owls and midnight munchers will be glad to know there is a *24-hour cafe/restaurant* near the central market.

Cafes, Tearooms & Patisseries There is no shortage of cafes, *salons de thé* (gentile cafes) and patisseries, especially along Blvd Mohammed V in ville nouvelle. Buy some croissants or cakes then settle down at an outdoor table and watch the morning slide by.

Café Renaissance has the best fruit juices in town (Dr5 to Dr9), and is popular with students. It's open from 7.30 to 2.30 am daily.

One of the best in town is *Pâtisserie L'Entente* (83 Blvd Mohammed V). It's very civilised with plenty of seating, including a pleasant section upstairs. It's open 6 am to 9 pm daily.

There are also several patisseries and fruit-juice bars in a row just outside the central market, some with seating.

Cafe Patisserie Glacier Peacock (29 Ave Mohammed es-Slaoui) is very popular with a good (but not cheap) selection of cakes and sundaes. It also has Internet access (Dr15 per hour) at the back of its upstairs section.

Pâtisserie Glacier Zegzouti (Ave Hassan II) sells ice cream in summer and has a discreet upstairs section if you want privacy.

American Donuts (Place de Florence) obviously serves doughnuts as well as crepes and waffles.

Self-Catering For fresh fruit and veg, spices, nuts, olives or a parcel of delicious dates, you can't beat the *central market*.

There is a *La Gare* supermarket not far from the train station that sells food and alcohol from 8.30 am to 12.30 and 3 to 9 pm. Another east of the central market has better food supplies but no alcohol; fortunately there's an alcohol store nearby, opposite Hôtel Olympic.

Entertainment

Bars There are quite a few bars scattered around the ville nouvelle. They are generally male-only, spit-and-sawdust places that can get a bit rowdy towards the end of a night's drinking. Take your pick; the European-style *Bar Cala Iris (Ave Hassan II)* is a good place to start as are the hotel bars. The *Oasis Bar* in the Sheraton Hôtel has a happy hour from 7 to 8 pm. The *bar* at Hotel Menzah Zalagh has a happy hour at the same time.

Nightclubs Some of the bigger hotels have nightclubs or discos. Entry generally costs around Dr50 to Dr100, drinks are around Dr80, and decent dress is expected, but after going to all that effort you often find they are little more than glorified versions of the bars, except with mirror balls.

Most are open from 10.30 pm to 3 am Tuesday to Sunday. Considered the best are *Le Phoebus* in the Hôtel Jnan Palace, and the discos in the hotels *Volubilis* and *Sofia* in the ville nouvelle and *Hôtel le Meridien Mérinides* near Fès el-Bali.

Sound & Light Show Morocco's first sound and light show is well done with the usual laser, sound and even water effects. Images are projected on to the walls of the Borj Sud near Bab el-Ftouh in the southeast of Fès el-Bali (where it's based) and onto the medina below.

Recounting 12 centuries of Fès' history, the nightly show lasts 45 minutes. Performances start at 9.30 pm (15 February to May), 10 pm (June to August) or 7.15 pm (September to 15 November).

There's commentary in English, French and Spanish, but only two are possible per night – make sure you sit on the appropriate side for your language. You can check the schedule and buy tickets at the tourist office, Syndicat d'Initiative (Jardin Public in the ville nouvelle), larger hotels (don't let them charge commission on it) or by phoning ☎ 629371. Entry is an expensive Dr200, but if you can afford it, it's an entertaining evening.

Cinemas The best cinema in town is *L'Empire Cinema (60 Ave Hassan II)* near Pâtisserie Glacier Zegzouti in the ville nouvelle. It has sessions at 3.30 and 9 pm with tickets

for Dr12/17/25 *orchestre/balcon/club* (close to screen/balcony/standard).

Shopping

Fès always has been, and still is, the artisanal capital of Morocco. The choice of crafts is wide, quality is high, and prices are about half of those in Marrakesh and Tangier. As usual, it's best to seek out the little shops off the main tourist routes (principally the At-Talaa al-Kebir and At-Talaa as-Seghir in Fès al-Bali). If you head for the craftsmen's workshops rather than the boutiques you'll find much cheaper prices. You'll also learn more about the crafts themselves and the range of quality available.

The Ensemble Artisanal next to the top-end Hôtel Volubilis on Ave Allah ben Abdullah is open from 9.30 am to 12.30 pm and 2.30 to 6.30 pm daily, and is one of the best of its kind in Morocco. As usual, it's a good first stop to get your eye in regarding quality and price, although it's a bit of a trek from town.

There is an ever-increasing number of beautifully restored riads used as carpet showrooms. Even if you're not interested in buying, they do offer a good opportunity to feast your eyes on the fabulous range of rugs available in some spectacular settings. While showing their wares, salesmen will explain the different features of the building to you and they will always throw in a free mint tea. Of course there will be pressure to buy, but as long as you're firm it really is worth the chance to appreciate the talented work that went into building (and restoring) these mansions. Finding them is easy – they're everywhere and you will be guided to at least one on any foray into the medina.

If you're after some of Fès' famous blue-and-white pottery, or just want to see the different processes, the best place to head are the potteries, about 500m east of Bab el-Ftouh. Get a petit taxi to take you there; negotiate a price in advance and ask them to wait for you (it's difficult to find another back and it's a long walk).

For all kinds of perfumed oils and scents, try the area around the henna souq (close to Zawiyya Moulay Idriss II in the heart of Fès

MIDDLE ATLAS & THE EAST

The Carpet-Buying Ritual

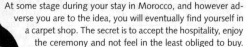

At some stage during your stay in Morocco, and however adverse you are to the idea, you will eventually find yourself in a carpet shop. The secret is to accept the hospitality, enjoy the ceremony and not feel in the least obliged to buy. Many of the larger stores, particularly in the bigger cities, are housed in former palaces and your brief sojourn will also provide you with a wonderful opportunity to admire one.

Just inside the shop you will be met by the manager (probably Mohammed, Ahmed or Hassan). Well groomed and multi-lingual, he will welcome you ceremoniously to his unique and superlative country, town and store. You will then be led to a seat, positioned almost throne-like at one end of the room and the obligatory glass of mint tea will soon arrive. Next you'll receive the all-you-ever-wanted-to-know-about-carpets lecture.

MICK WELDON

Five to 10 minutes later, Ahmed, Mohammed or Hassan will be addressing you with newly found respect, sharing his opinions and seeking yours, as if from one great carpet connoisseur to another.

Unsatisfied and impatient with the rugs so far shown, and certain of your unusual, appreciative abilities, he will demand that the real stock – even his own private collection – be brought out before you. Attendants, silent and slipper-shod, will wait for the cue (anticipation is all) to send them unrolling in a flourish before you.

Carefully calculated to contrast dramatically with the tired, motley wares that came before, these 'unique, rare and genuinely antique carpets' cannot fail to impress. Carpet after carpet will be bared before you (your host now almost in a frenzy of lyrical appreciation) until a veritable sea of colour, pattern and design seems ready to overwhelm you.

All the while you will be scrutinised intently. The slightest comment, the hint of a smile, a lingering gaze, will give you away at once, and a whole range of similar-styled rugs will be unleashed in a torrent before you. Smelling blood, your host will go in for the kill. As the ceremony nears the end, you will be treated to the full repertoire of the famous Moroccan sales techniques, generally regarded as the most skilled, sophisticated and effective in the world. But that's a whole other story.

el-Bali). The map identifies more souqs that specialise in other goods.

Getting There & Away

Air Fès airport (☎ 674712) is at Saiss, 15km to the south. RAM (☎ 625516) has an office at 54 Ave Hassan II in the ville nouvelle. There are daily flights to Casablanca (Dr512, 50 minutes) and twice-weekly flights to Paris (two hours). Regional Air Lines (☎ 02-538080 in Casablanca) has services between Fès and Casablanca.

Bus – CTM CTM buses (☎ 732384) depart from the bus station outside Bab el-Mahrouk,

just west of Fès el-Bali, and call in at the CTM bus station on Blvd Dhar Mahres, in the southern ville nouvelle, half an hour later. In high season it's a good idea to buy tickets in advance, particularly on the Fès-Tangier and Fès-Marrakesh runs. The table on the next page shows some of the bus services.

Heading south, there are buses to Er-Rachidia, Erfoud, Rissani and Ouarzazate at 5.30, 7 and 9 pm. Buses to Agadir, Laayoune, Smara and Dakhla leave at 6 am and 7.30 and 9 pm.

Bus – Other Companies Non-CTM buses also depart from the bus station next

CTM Bus Services

destination	cost (Dr)	duration (hours)	departures
Al-Hoceima	64	7	noon & 1 am
Casablanca	78	5	8 services;
via Rabat	54	3½	6.30 am to
via Meknès	15	1	12.30 am
Marrakesh	123	9	noon &
via Beni Mellal	68	6	12.30 am
Nador	89		1 & 2 am
Oujda	89	2	noon & 12.30 am
Tangier	82	6	10.30 am, 5.30 pm & 12.40 am
Taza	30	2	noon, 6 pm, 11 pm & 1am
Tetouan	68	5	7.30 am, 10.30 am & 11.30 pm

to Bab el-Mahrouk and reservations can be made for popular runs. There are frequent (at least eight daily) runs to Beni Mellal, Casablanca, Chefchaouen, Er-Rachidia, Marrakesh, Meknès, Oujda, Rabat, Tangier and Tetouan. Fares are a little cheaper than on CTM buses. Buses for Rissani leave at 6.30 am, 10 am and 10 pm. There's a bus to Ouarzazate at 9 pm and a bus to Tinerhir at 6.30 pm. Buses to Agadir leave between 2 and 7 pm. Locally there are several departures to Azrou (Dr18, two hours), Ifrane (Dr14, 1¾ hours), Moulay Yacoub (Dr7, one hour), Sefrou (Dr6, one hour) and Taza (Dr25, two hours). There are international departures from the CTM station to Spain on Monday, Wednesday and Friday.

Train The train station (☎ 930333) is in the ville nouvelle, a 10-minute walk north-west of Place de Florence. There are 24-hour left luggage facilities, a newsstand and cafe (where they cheekily bring you stuff you haven't ordered – just send it back).

There are at least eight daily ordinaire/rapide departures to Casablanca (Dr74/96, 5½ hours), all of which stop at Rabat (Dr54/

69, 3½ hours) and Meknès (Dr13/16, one hour). There are five direct runs each to Marrakesh (Dr130/168, about eight hours) and Tangier (Dr72/93, five hours). Direct trains for Oujda (Dr79/104, six hours) via Taza (Dr27/35, two hours) leave four times daily.

Grand Taxi Most grand taxis leave from the front of the bus station, although there are additional ranks around town. Destinations include Azrou (Dr23), Casablanca (Dr85), Ifrane (Dr20), Meknès (Dr16), Ouezzane (Dr50) and Rabat (Dr55).

Other taxis leave from around Bab el-Ftouh in the south-east of Fès el-Bali for Taza (Dr30), and for Sefrou (Dr8) from Place de la Résistance in the ville nouvelle.

Car The following are among the car rental agencies in Fès:

Avis (☎ 626746) 50 Blvd Abdallah Chefchaouni
Budget (☎ 940092) ville nouvelle;
(☎ 940092) airport
Europcar (☎ 626545) 41 Ave Hassan II
Hertz (☎ 622812) ville nouvelle;
(☎ 651823) airport
Tourvilles (☎ 626635) 15 Rue Houmn Fetouaki

The Grand Hôtel on Blvd Abdallah Chefchaouni, has reasonably secure car-parking facilities and charges Dr10/20 for guests/nonguests for 24 hours.

Getting Around

To/From the Airport There is a regular bus service (No 16) between the airport and the train station (Dr4). Otherwise you'll have to get a grand taxi (Dr80) – even though it's only 15km they're virtually impossible to beat down to less than Dr80.

Bus Fès has a fairly good local bus service, although the buses are like sardine cans at certain times of the day, and are notorious for pickpockets. Useful routes include:

No 2 Bab Smarine (Fès el-Jdid) via Ave Hassan II (ville nouvelle) to Hay Hussein
No 9 Place de l'Atlas (ville nouvelle) via Ave Hassan II to Dar Batha Museum (Fès el-Bali)

No 10 Train station via Bab Guissa (northern Fès el-Bali) to Bab Sidi Bou Jidda (north-eastern Fès el-Bali)

No 12 Bab Bou Jeloud via Bab Guissa to Bab el-Ftouh (all in Fès el-Bali)

No 17 Blvd Tariq ibn Ziad to 'Ain Chkef

No 18 Bab el-Ftouh to Dar Batha Museum (both in Fès el-Bali)

Nos 19 & 29 Ave Hassan II (ville nouvelle) via Bab el-Jedid (southern Fès el-Bali) to Place er-Risf (central Fès el-Bali)

No 47 Train station to Bab Bou Jeloud (Fès el-Bali)

No 50 Bab Smarine (Fès el-Jdid) via Ave Hassan II (ville nouvelle) to Soukarin

Taxi The drivers of the red petit taxis generally use their meters without any fuss. Expect to pay about Dr10 from the train or CTM station to Bab Bou Jeloud. There is a surcharge after 9.30 pm. Only grand taxis go out to the airport.

AROUND FÈS
Sefrou
☎ 05

At just 30km south-east of Fès, Sefrou is an easy day trip, but with little accommodation it's a dubious overnight stop. About the size of Chefchaouen, the picturesque Berber town is well worth visiting. With the exception of the odd Fès-trained 'guide' hanging about near the bus station, you will be left to wander the compact medina in peace. Sefrou once boasted one of Morocco's largest Jewish communities and it was here that Moulay Idriss II lived while planning Fès.

The walled medina and mellah straddle the Oued Aggaï, across which there are a number of bridges. The best points of entry or exit are Bab Taksebt, Bab Zemghila and Bab Merba. The town walls that stand today were built in the 19th century.

Along the banks of the river is a small park with a duck pond and a good children's playground. Further afield, about 1.5km from town, there's a pleasant walk through a gorge to a waterfall. Follow the signposts from Ave Moulay Hassan around to the right of Al-Qala' (a semi-walled *ksar* or fortified stronghold) and along the river to the waterfall.

There is a market on Thursday and, at the end of June, the annual Cherry Festival has music, sports and the crowning of the Cherry Queen.

The main post office and the BMCE bank are on Blvd Mohammed V.

Places to Stay There is a rather neglected *camping ground* on the hill overlooking the town. It's a long, steep walk (take a taxi), but a pleasant spot with toilets and cold showers; it costs Dr10 per person, tent or car. If you continue a little further up the hill there's a brilliant viewpoint over Sefrou and the plains below.

The cheapest hotel in town is the unmarked *Hôtel Frenaie* (☎ 660030) on the Fès road. It's difficult to find (look for the green flagpoles and arch) and is basic with a cold shower and singles/doubles for Dr70/100. There's a communal area (although there's unlikely to be anyone to commune with) and a cafe.

The two-star *Hôtel Sidi Lahcen el-Youssi* (☎ 683428, Rue Sidi Ali Bouserghine), the only other option, is set in pleasantly overgrown gardens. It has rooms with hot shower and balcony for Dr165/200. There's heating in winter and a restaurant, a modest nightclub and a swimming pool (open from May to September; nonguests pay Dr15).

Places to Eat There's a good choice of small, cheap *snack bars* on either side of the covered market and at Bab Merba.

The only restaurant in town is *Restaurant Café Oumnia* up near Blvd Mohammed V. Also a cafe, the restaurant section is above a smoky card den. It does limited set menus from Dr35.

There's a string of *cafes* and a *bar* along Blvd Mohammed V, and the excellent *Pâtisserie Halou* is hidden away down a street just off it.

Getting There & Away Regular buses (Dr5, one hour) and grand taxis (Dr8) run between La Fiat in Fès and Sefrou. Grand taxis also go to Immouzer des Ida Outanane (Dr10), from where you can pick up others for Azrou.

MIDDLE ATLAS & THE EAST

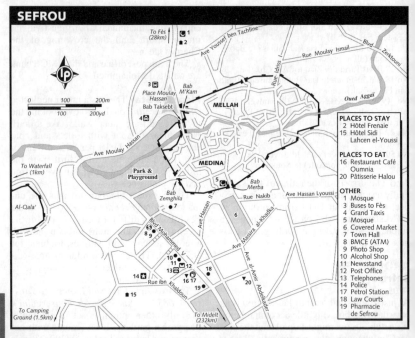

SEFROU

PLACES TO STAY
2 Hôtel Frenaie
15 Hôtel Sidi
     Lahcen el-Youssi

PLACES TO EAT
16 Restaurant Café
     Oumnia
20 Pâtisserie Halou

OTHER
1 Mosque
3 Buses to Fès
4 Grand Taxis
5 Mosque
6 Covered Market
7 Town Hall
8 BMCE (ATM)
9 Photo Shop
10 Alcohol Shop
11 Newsstand
12 Post Office
13 Telephones
14 Police
17 Petrol Station
18 Law Courts
19 Pharmacie
     de Sefrou

Moulay Yacoub
☎ 05

The hot springs at Moulay Yacoub, 20km from Fès, provide therapeutic 54°C waters pumped from 1500m below ground that are reputed to be good for skin complaints and rheumatism. The village has a real resort feel to it, with more Moroccans than overseas tourists flocking here to treat their ailments.

There are two options depending on your budget and hygiene standards. The public hammam is a pool fed by the hot springs. Segregated into male and female sections, the usual hammam etiquette applies and entry costs Dr5. The water is not that clean but you can have a (recommended) shower or (another) hammam after your dip.

The second option is the high tech, sci-fi looking Moulay Yacoub Hot Springs (☎ 694066, fax 694065). A very swish operation, it has rheumatology, gynaecology and dermatology treatments ranging from Dr80 for one-off bath treatments to Dr2700

for 18-day medically supervised treatments. Towels are supplied – bring your bathers – and packages with accommodation at the four-star Hotel Moulay Yacoub (see Places to Stay later) can be arranged. The clinic is open from 9 am to 6 pm Tuesday to Sunday and has a cafe on site.

To find the public pool follow your nose and the people carrying buckets down the hill, past the cafes and the souvenir, hammam and food stands. The road to the hot springs leads from the top of the hill; if you're walking it's better to head down through the village past the public pool. Look for the green-tiled roof.

Places to Stay There are quite a few places to stay and these are mainly at the top end of the range with facilities such as a TV, fridge and phone, as well as views over the rooftops and valley. *Hotel de la Paix*, right by the pool, is the cheapest option and has basic singles/doubles with none of the above for Dr70/100. A more luxurious option is *Hotel Fadoua* (☎ *694098, fax 694050)* overlooking the old pool (public hammam) with rooms for Dr300. *Hotel Moulay Yacoub* (☎ *694035, fax 694012)* at the top of the hill has rooms for Dr520/650 and bungalows for four/six people for Dr520/740.

Getting There & Away There are regular buses (Dr6) and grand taxis (Dr7) between the station halfway down the hill in Moulay Yacoub and the main bus station in Fès.

Middle Atlas

IFRANE
☎ 05 • elevation 1650m

Just 17km short of Azrou south on highway P24 from Fès is Ifrane, where you would be hard pressed not to do a double-take and wonder whether you'd just left Morocco.

Built by the French in the 1930s as an alpine-style resort, the town's red-tiled roofs, partly obscured by trees and lake-studded parklands, transport you to another place. Outside the uncertain winter ski season and summer weekends, when the affluent flock here to escape the heat of the big cities, the place has a quiet, academic air courtesy of an English-language university. The town and parks are lovely to walk around and provide a relaxing break.

Many of the grander villas are actually company hotels – the post office, Banque Populaire and CTM bus company are some that have 'hotels' here for staff holidays – and more are being jerry-built.

The tourist office (☎ 566822) is in a little hut on the corner of Ave Prince Moulay Abdallah and Ave des Tilleuls. Open the usual hours, staff are helpful and can suggest good local excursions.

Things to See & Do
Dominated by holm oak and cedar forests, the countryside surrounding Ifrane is pleasant for **hikes** or picnics.

The focus of town, at its northern end, is **Al-Akhawayn University**, a squeaky clean

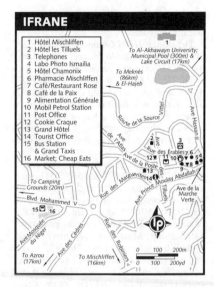

IFRANE

1 Hôtel Mischliffen
2 Hôtel les Tilluels
3 Telephones
4 Labo Photo Ismailia
5 Hôtel Chamonix
6 Pharmacie Mischliffen
7 Café/Restaurant Rose
8 Café de la Paix
9 Alimentation Générale
10 Mobil Petrol Station
11 Post Office
12 Cookie Craque
13 Grand Hôtel
14 Tourist Office
15 Bus Station
   & Grand Taxis
16 Market; Cheap Eats

To Al-Akhawayn University;
Municipal Pool (300m) &
Lake Circuit (17km)

To Meknes
(86km)
& El-Hajeb

To Camping
Grounds (20m)

To Azrou
(17km)

To Mischliffen
(16km)

0   100   200m
0   100   200yd

educational establishment for Morocco's elite. Founded in 1995 by Morocco's King Hassan II and King Fahd of Saudi Arabia with aims such as promoting religious tolerance between faiths, it's something of a showpiece. The car parks are full of flash cars and the kids sport designer labels and never leave home without their cellphones – it's definitely the Moroccan equivalent of Beverly Hills 90210 (without the sex and drugs – probably). Lessons (in English) are based on the American system and there are US staff and exchange students. The campus grounds are well tended and contain a mosque, a synagogue, a coffee shop and a store with junk food and a good selection of English-language fiction. There's also nightly entertainment such as movies, theatre and concerts.

Places to Stay & Eat
Other than the *camping grounds* just west of the bus station on Blvd Mohammed V, there is no budget accommodation in Ifrane. Camping in this pleasant, leafy spot costs Dr7 per person, Dr8 per car, Dr5 to pitch a tent or Dr20 per camper van.

In the centre of town, *Hôtel les Tilluels* is about the cheapest option in Ifrane with singles/doubles for Dr250/316, and a restaurant and bar.

The similar *Hôtel Chamonix* (☎ *566028, fax 566826, Ave de la Marche)* has rooms for Dr257/300 and a restaurant.

The *Grand Hôtel* (☎ *566203, fax 566407, Ave de la Poste)* was being renovated at the time of research. Built in 1941, it's Ifrane's 'character' hotel with a bar and restaurant. It's worth checking out though it's bound to be even more expensive than the previous hotels.

Top of the range is the five-star *Hôtel Mischliffen* (☎ *566607, fax 566623)* in pine gardens. Overlooking and dominating the north of town, it has singles/doubles/triples for Dr500/650/780, apartments for Dr1500 or suites from Dr2000. It has a large restaurant serving Moroccan or international dishes (the set menu costs Dr150), a pool and a nightclub open from 11 pm to 2 am.

Cookie Craque (Ave des Tilleuls) is excellent for breakfast (Dr17) or for preparing a picnic. It has a wonderful choice of sweets and savouries (Dr5 to Dr15) and ice cream in summer. It's open from 7 am to 10 pm daily and has an adjoining restaurant serving pizza (Dr30 to Dr49) and the like.

Down in the market area next to the bus station are a few cafes and cheap eats with tajine, brochettes etc and fresh produce.

Café/Restaurant Rose (☎ *566215, 7 Rue des Érables)* is a simple place with a good set menu for Dr60 (main courses cost around Dr45). There is couscous on Friday.

Popular with students, *Café de la Paix* in the centre of town, has a good selection of dishes (mains around Dr40) accompanied by a tasty tomato sauce.

Getting There & Away

The main bus and grand taxi station is next to the market, west of the town centre.

CTM buses leave for Marrakesh (Dr108, eight hours) via Beni Mellal (5½ hours) at 7.30 am, Meknès (1¾ hours) at 8 am and Fès (Dr20, two hours) at 2 pm.

Other non-CTM services run to Agadir (departing at 7 and 8 pm), Azrou (30 minutes, six daily), Beni Mellal (three daily), Casablanca (1 am), Demnate (9.30 am), Fès

(hourly from 5.30 am to 7 pm), Marrakesh (three daily), Oujda (1 pm), Rabat (five daily) and Rissani (three daily).

Grand taxis run to Azrou (Dr6), Sefrou (Dr17.50), Fès (Dr18), Meknès (Dr20) and Midelt (Dr45). They will also take you to Dayet Aoua lake (see Lake Circuit later) for Dr9.50.

AROUND IFRANE
Lake Circuit

For those with their own sturdy vehicle, there is an attractive **Lake Circuit** (Tour Touristique des Lacs), which starts at a turn-off 17km north of Ifrane. The five lakes are spread along the 100km or so between the P24 and P20, and attract large numbers of birds (when there's been enough rain), as do the surrounding woodlands. Keep an eye out in particular for raptors, including booted eagles, black and red kites and Egyptian vultures.

Dayet Aoua, the first lake on the circuit, is a particularly good spot for wildlife, attracting significant numbers of ducks and waders. Sightings of crested coot are common and, if you're lucky, you may see woodpeckers, treecreepers and nuthatches, particularly among the trees around the south-eastern end of the lake.

There are several very pleasant picnic areas dotted around the lake. If you've come without provisions, head for *Hôtel Restaurant Chalet du Lac* (☎ *663197)* on the northern edge of the lake. It's run by a mother and daughter from Toulouse in France, and they are renowned for their cooking. Politicians and statesmen come from as far afield as Rabat; look out for the enormous cars parked outside. If you can stretch to it, the menu gastronomique for Dr170 makes a great splurge. It's a pleasant, very peaceful place and has wonderful views overlooking the lake. If you want to wake up to these views, rooms without bathroom cost Dr168/177.

Mischliffen

If you want to ski at nearby Mischliffen, which is the main ski station of the Middle Atlas and 20km south of Ifrane, you can hire equipment at Hôtel Chamonix in Ifrane. This costs Dr100 per day for the whole kit (don't expect the latest technology) and Dr40 for sledges.

The season runs from January to early March, but conditions can be very unreliable. The runs are quite good though short (lifts cost Dr3 per ride), and apart from a couple of *cafes* and nice views, there's precious little to do. In summer it's a popular place with walkers who have their own transport. Grand taxis make their way out here.

AZROU
☎ 05

The green-tiled rooftops of central Azrou contrast with Ifrane, and this Berber town is a cheerful, hassle-free little place. Surrounded by pine and cedar forests, it's a good spot to wind down after the pressure-cooker of Fès.

The lively Tuesday market is held below the clump of stone that gives the town its name (Azrou means 'Rock') to the west of town. Beyond that there's not much to do, except wander the streets and surrounding countryside soaking up cool mountain air and searching for Barbary apes.

A visit to the Ensemble Artisanal on Blvd Mohammed V is worthwhile. Here you can find work in cedar wood and wrought iron, as well as excellent Berber carpets typical of the Middle Atlas.

Orientation & Information

There is no tourist office in Azrou, but hotels can help with information on local treks. Mountain guides can be hired (Dr150 per day), along with full camping gear, mules and even a cook (Dr75 per day). Permits for fishing local trout streams and lakes can also be obtained at hotels from July to September.

You can change money at the BMCE or Banque Populaire on Place Mohammed V; both have ATMs. The post office is next to the Banque Populaire, just east of the square.

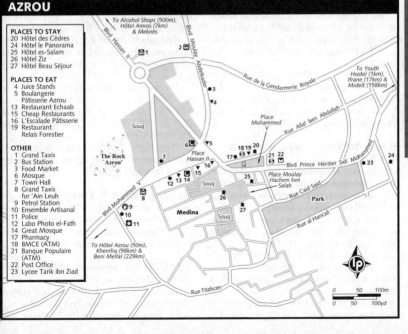

AZROU

MIDDLE ATLAS & THE EAST

PLACES TO STAY
20 Hôtel des Cèdres
24 Hôtel le Panorama
25 Hôtel es-Salam
26 Hôtel Ziz
27 Hôtel Beau Séjour

PLACES TO EAT
4 Juice Stands
5 Boulangerie Pâtisserie Azrou
13 Restaurant Echaab
15 Cheap Restaurants
16 L'Escalade Pâtisserie
19 Restaurant Relais Forestier

OTHER
1 Grand Taxis
2 Bus Station
3 Food Market
6 Mosque
7 Town Hall
8 Grand Taxis for 'Ain Leuh
9 Petrol Station
10 Ensemble Artisanal
11 Police
12 Labo Photo el-Fath
14 Great Mosque
17 Pharmacy
18 BMCE (ATM)
21 Banque Populaire (ATM)
22 Post Office
23 Lycee Tarik ibn Ziad

To Alcohol Shops (500m), Hôtel Amros (7km) & Meknès

Blvd Hassan II

Blvd Moulay Abdelkader

To Youth Hostel (1km), Ifrane (17km) & Midelt (158km)

Rue de la Gendarmerie Royale

Souq

The Rock 'Azrou'

Place Hassan II

Place Mohammed V

Rue Allal ben Abdallah

Blvd Prince Héritier Sidi Mohammed

Place Moulay Hachem ben Salah

Blvd Mohammed V

Souq

Medina

Souq

Park

Rue Caid Said

Rue al Hancali

To Hôtel Azrou (50m), Khenifra (98km) & Beni Mellal (229km)

Rue Titahcen

0   50   100m
0   50   100yd

There's a night pharmacy at the bus station. The cheaper hotels and most restaurants are around Place Mohammed V, as are the banks and post office. The bus and taxi stations are a five-minute walk to the north, beyond the big new mosque.

Places to Stay – Budget

Though OK in summer, these places don't make a great choice in winter. There's no heating and blankets are in very short supply.

The cheapest place to stay is the *Youth Hostel* (☎ 563933) north-east of town overlooking the valley. A dorm bed costs Dr20 and you must be a HI member. The showers are cold and there's no kitchen, but it's clean. The hostel is open from noon to 3 pm and 6 to 10 pm and is signposted from the Midelt road, 1km east of the town centre.

Of the little places around Place Moulay Hachem ben Salah, the cheapest is *Hôtel Beau Séjour* (☎ 563272), with rooms ranging from Dr25 to Dr75. Try for a room with a balcony overlooking the square. Hot showers cost Dr7.

The second-best is the *Hôtel es-Salam* (☎ 562562) where reasonably clean small/large doubles with a bit of character cost Dr30/80. Hot showers are Dr8 and there's a terrace.

The showerless *Hôtel Ziz* (☎ 562362) just off the square is the last choice in this category. Ask for a room with a window; the others are very cell-like. Basic, but spotless, singles/doubles cost Dr40/70.

Places to Stay – Mid-Range & Top End

The one-star *Hôtel des Cèdres* (☎ 562326, Place Mohammed V) has large, comfortable and spotless singles/doubles/triples for Dr74/103/159. Rooms have a washbasin, heating, a table and chairs and a balcony overlooking the square and cafe below. A steaming shower costs Dr10.

Just as good, *Hôtel Azrou* (☎ 562116, fax 564273, Route de Khenifra) is about 50m from the centre of town. It has spotless and pleasant rooms with a balcony for Dr74/103, or Dr109/140 with shower. It often has rooms when the Cèdres doesn't,

and prices are negotiable. It also has a bar (open until 10 pm), restaurant, small ivy-covered terrace and guarded parking.

Hôtel le Panorama (☎ 562010, fax 561804) has rooms (heated in winter) for Dr280/342/453 with shower and toilet. The alpine lodge-style hotel is in a quiet wooded spot, a short stroll east of town, and can help arrange trekking and skiing; it also has its own bar and restaurant.

About 7km out on the road to Meknès is the four-star *Hôtel Amros* (☎ 563663, fax 563680). Although a bit remote, it has great views, a pool, tennis courts, restaurants, a bar and nightclub and can organise activities and provide trekking information. Rooms cost Dr398/506/660 but staff may try to talk you into a half-board arrangement.

Places to Eat

There is no shortage of cheap eats in Azrou – a couple are scattered through the medina and along the road to the bus station. The *restaurants* opposite the new mosque usually have huge pots of steaming harira (Dr2) and grills by their entrances. You can get a filling meal and drink for less than Dr30.

Restaurant Relais Forestier (Place Mohammed V) has a fixed menu for Dr65 and main courses, including trout and vegetarian options, but it closes early.

There are numerous *cafes* and a few juice stands on Blvd Moulay Abdelkader. A good place for coffee is *Boulangerie Pâtisserie Azrou*, but *L'Escalade Pâtisserie* nearby has better cakes.

There are a couple of *shops* that sell alcohol north-west of the centre on Blvd Hassan II (towards Meknès).

Getting There & Away

Azrou is a crossroads, with one axis heading north-west to south-east from Meknès to Er-Rachidia, and the other north-east to Fès and south-west to Marrakesh.

Bus CTM has departures to Beni Mellal (Dr63, 4½ hours, departing at 8 am), Casablanca (Dr87, 7.30 am), Fès (Dr19, three hours, 2 pm), Marrakesh (Dr103, seven hours, 8 am), Meknès (Dr16, 2½ hours, 7.30

and 9 am), Midelt (two hours, 8 am) and Rissani (11 pm).

Other companies have buses to Agadir (departing at 7.30 pm), Beni Mellal (nine daily), Casablanca (three daily), Ifrane (Dr15), Marrakesh (seven daily – book ahead), Meknès (seven daily), Rabat (seven daily), Rissani (four daily), Tangier (9 am) and Tetouan (2.30 am). There are also frequent daily departures to Fès and Er-Rachidia.

There are international departures to Belgium (Wednesday), France (Wednesday) and the Netherlands (Wednesday and Saturday).

Grand Taxi Regular grand taxis for Fès (Dr24), Meknès (Dr20), Khenifra (Dr23), Ifrane (Dr6), Sefrou (Dr22) and Midelt (Dr35) leave from near the bus station.

SOUTH OF AZROU

If you want to see some **Barbary apes** head north-east towards Ifrane for 10km, then take the track to the right that leads up to a patch of cedars.

If you have your own transport, there's a good drive from Azrou that takes you through some of the best of the Middle Atlas greenery. A forest lane takes you the 20km to the Berber village of **'Ain Leuh** where, on Wednesday, there's a souq that attracts market-goers from around the region, particularly from the semi-nomadic Beni m'Guid tribe.

Leave Azrou by the Midelt road and take the first right (the S3398). Once in 'Ain Leuh, you could continue south into the heart of the Middle Atlas along the S303 – be warned that some of the tracks here are difficult and impassable in or after foul weather. A little further on (signposted to the left around 25km south of the village) are some impressive **waterfalls** at the **Sources de l'Oum-er-Rbia** – a good spot for a picnic.

Along the road to Midelt, the volcanic lake **Aguelmane Sidi Ali**, formed in an extinct crater, makes a pleasant stop where you can swim and camp. Continuing along the road, around 5km before it joins the main P21 road to Midelt, you'll go through the tiny Berber village of **Itzer**. It's a great place to pick up a Berber carpet, particularly at the large weekly markets on Monday and Thursday.

MIDELT
☎ 05

Lying almost at the centre of Morocco between the Middle and the High Atlas mountains, Midelt is a kind of no-man's land between the north and the south. Of little interest in itself, the town makes a convenient stopping point on the principal route south from Fès, Meknès and Azrou to Er-Rachidia and the south. It's also a useful base from which to explore both mountain ranges.

The town consists of little more than one main street (Ave Mohammed V, which later becomes Hassan II), a modest souq and a number of oversized restaurants, which cater to the well-heeled tourist buses whistling through on their way south. As there's nothing to see, you're unlikely to be hassled by would-be guides. More common, though largely targeting the tour parties, are the energetic mineral and fossil sellers or the carpet-shop touts.

There are a couple of banks but no ATMs. The post office is in the south of town.

Places to Stay
Camping Municipal (☎ 580581) is southeast of town. It's a bit untidy and there are few facilities, but it's cheap and friendly. Camping costs Dr2 per person and per tent, Dr2.50 for a car and Dr3 for a caravan.

The best budget hotel is *Hôtel Boughafer* (☎ 583099) opposite the municipal market. Small and clean singles/doubles cost Dr35/70 (hot showers Dr10), Dr100/120 with bathroom. Ask for a front room with a big window. There is also a restaurant that has set menus for Dr45 and a roof terrace.

Hôtel Atlas (☎ 582938, 3 Rue Mohammed el-Amraoui) is close to the main square. Although basic and on the small side, the rooms are spotless and cost Dr60/90/150 for two/three/four people. A hot shower costs Dr10, there's a pleasant terrace and the family running this place is lovely.

Hôtel Roi de la Biére (☎ 582675, Ave des FAR) has no beer, but it does have modern rooms for Dr100, or Dr150 with shower.

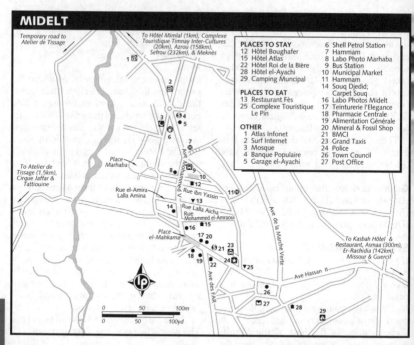

MIDELT

Temporary road to
Atelier de Tissage

To Hôtel Mimlal (1km), Complexe
Touristique Timnay Inter-Cultures
(20km), Azrou (158km),
Sefrou (232km), & Meknès

To Atelier de
Tissage (1.5km),
Cirque Jaffar &
Tattiouine

Place
Marhaba

Rue el-Amira
Lalla Amina

Rue ibn Yassin

Rue Lalla Aicha
Rue
Mohammed el-Amraoui

Place
el-Mahkama

Ave Mohammed V

Ave de la Marche Verte

Ave Hassan II

Ave des FAR

To Kasbah Hôtel &
Restaurant, Asmaa (300m),
Er-Rachidia (142km),
Missour & Guercif

0   50   100m
0   50   100yd

PLACES TO STAY
12 Hôtel Boughafer
15 Hôtel Atlas
22 Hôtel Roi de la Bière
28 Hôtel el-Ayachi
29 Camping Muncipal

PLACES TO EAT
13 Restaurant Fès
25 Complexe Touristique
   Le Pin

OTHER
1 Atlas Infonet
2 Surf Internet
3 Mosque
4 Banque Populaire
5 Garage el-Ayachi
6 Shell Petrol Station
7 Hammam
8 Labo Photo Marhaba
9 Bus Station
10 Municipal Market
11 Hammam
14 Souq Djedid;
   Carpet Souq
16 Labo Photos Midelt
17 Teinturerie l'Elegance
18 Pharmacie Centrale
19 Alimentation Générale
20 Mineral & Fossil Shop
21 BMCI
23 Grand Taxis
24 Police
26 Town Council
27 Post Office

Hôtel el-Ayachi (☎ 582161, fax 583321, *Rue d'Agadir*) has a colonial air about it with lots of dark wood and large windows. Rooms with bathroom cost Dr274/330/400. The hotel has a pleasant garden, a bar that's open to 11 pm, and a licensed restaurant in a Berber tent that serves both Moroccan and international food. The set menu costs Dr118.

About 3km south of the centre is the **Kasbah Hôtel & Restaurant Asmaa** (☎ 580405, fax 580408). The building is a pretty hideous version of a kasbah, but it's pleasantly decorated and very comfortable inside, with differently coloured salons arranged around a central fountain. Rooms cost Dr250/320 and there's a roof terrace, pool and licensed restaurant with a set menu for Dr95 (mains cost Dr50). Pony trekking can be arranged here.

Places to Eat
Apart from the hotel restaurants, the best place in town by far is the **Restaurant Fès**

(*Rue Lalla Aicha*). It's run by a Berber family and Fatima, the grandmother who oversees the cooking, has earned quite a following. The excellent set menu costs Dr65, main courses like the delicious tajine *á sept legumes* (with seven beans) are Dr50 to Dr60 and a bowl of hearty harira is Dr3.

There are quite a few **restaurants** and **cafes** along the main road. **Complexe Touristique Le Pin** (*Ave Hassan II*) is one of the most pleasant and has garden seating.

There is a small **municipal market** near the bus station and alcohol is available at the **Alimentation Général** opposite Hotel Roi de la Bière.

Shopping
Carpets are probably Midelt's greatest asset. The quality is high and the attractive geometric designs are distinctive to the Berber tribes of the surrounding Middle Atlas region. Be wary of the town's boutiques however, which are accustomed to the 10-minute

shoppers of the coach parties. Prices are high, there's pressure to buy and any so-called 'antique' carpets will never be more than 10 to 15 years old. The carpet souq, in the Souq Djedid area off Ave Mohammed V, is the best place to head. There is a special carpet market here every Sunday.

Also well worth a visit is the Atelier de Tissage run by some charitable French Franciscan sisters in a convent about 1.5km out of town. Every three years, 20 or so local Berber women are taken on for apprenticeship, during which time they learn the trades of embroidery, weaving and sewing. The fruits of their training form a very small exhibition and some items are for sale. Prices are high, but so is the quality. The studio is open from 8 to 11.45 am and 2 to 5 pm every day except Friday and Sunday. At the time of writing, a bridge connecting the convent road with the town road had been washed away. Vehicle access was from a road to the right just before another bridge at the northern entrance to the town. Look out for the 'Kasbah Myriem' sign.

If you're into minerals or fossils, there is a shop opposite the Hôtel Roi de la Bière on the road to Er-Rachidia. It's a good place to get an idea both of the quality available, and maximum prices to pay the street vendors.

Getting There & Away

Bus The bus station is off the main street, Ave Mohammed V, and it's quite a transport hub. CTM runs buses to Casablanca (Dr117, eight hours) departing at 11 and 11.30 pm. Services depart for Beni Mellal (Dr47, 4½ hours) at 2 and 11.30 pm; Erfoud (Dr61, 5½ hours); Rissani (Dr68, six hours) at 2 am; Er-Rachidia (Dr40, three hours) at 2, 3 and 3.30 am; Meknès (Dr92, four hours) via Azrou (Dr33, two hours) at 7 am and 11 pm; and Rabat (Dr70, six hours) at 11 pm.

Other buses cover the same routes more frequently, plus Sefrou (Dr35) at 2 am, Oujda at 6 am and Nador at 7.30 am and 9 pm. Twelve daily buses to Fès (Dr44.50, 4½ hours) leave between 5 am and 5 pm.

Grand Taxi The grand taxi rank is down a little lane close to the police station, just off Ave Hassan II. Departures are quite frequent, but it's best to arrive early in the morning.

Destinations include Azrou (Dr35), Er-Rachidia (Dr40), Erfoud (Dr60), Fès (Dr60), Meknès (Dr55), Rissani (Dr70) and Sefrou (Dr60).

Car Garage el-Ayachi on Ave Mohammed V is supposedly the best garage in the region, and a good place to sort out minor problems before continuing further south.

EXCURSIONS FROM MIDELT

For those with their own vehicle (for those without, see Complexe Touristique Timnay Inter-Cultures following), there are some excellent excursions that will take you into the heart of the Middle Atlas. The roads are rough and only negotiable during the drier months from around May to October. It's a good idea to check the state of the roads before setting off. Some routes, such as the Cirque Jaffar, are best attempted by 4WD vehicles.

The 79km **Cirque Jaffar** to the south-west of Midelt is the best-known excursion. The road winds through the foothills of Jebel Ayachi (3737m), the highest mountain in the eastern High Atlas, and will give you a glimpse of traditional Berber villages, wild mountain scenery and some spectacular views.

The circuit is well signposted from Midelt, starting just off the S3424 to Tattiouine, passing via Miktane and Aït Oum Gam, looping back to the Midelt-Azrou road. You should allow almost a day for the circuit.

If you want to climb **Jebel Ayachi**, you can drive or take a taxi to Tattiouine. From a point just beyond the village near the springs there's a mule track, which leads up to the summit. It's not a difficult climb, and the descent can take you via cedar forests and various mountain villages, though you'll probably need a guide.

Other routes you might follow include the S317 road to **Ksabi**, which will take you through the **Moulouya Gorges** and some old mines about 15km north of Midelt.

An area particularly noted for its **birds** are the plains a few kilometres south of the village of **Zaïda** on the main Midelt-Meknès route. The place has become synonymous among ornithologists for a rare species of bird: Dupont's lark. Other birds more commonly spotted include species of finch, other larks and sandgrouse. The Complexe Touristique Timnay Inter-Cultures is a useful source of information for bird-watchers.

Complexe Touristique Timnay Inter-Cultures

About 20km to the north of Midelt, just before the village of Zaïda on the main Meknès road, is the Complexe Touristique Timnay Inter-Cultures (☎/fax 583434). It's well signposted and is built in the style of a kasbah, so it's easy to spot. The centre was the result of a joint Moroccan-Belgian venture set up in 1990 by a group of teachers with the aim of 'initiating visitors into the culture and lifestyle of the nomads and sedentary people of the mountains'.

It's very pleasant and peaceful, and the Berber manager runs the place efficiently, seriously and enthusiastically. It's especially good for those keen to learn more about the local people and landscape.

The complex includes a well-equipped camping ground, bungalows, tents, restaurant, cafe, grocery store and swimming pool (open from March to the end of August). It's an excellent source of information for the region, with knowledgeable staff and guides and a few reference books on the birds and flora of the region. Mountain bikes can be hired (Dr30/50 per half/whole day) and so can horses.

Camping costs Dr18 per person, Dr15 for a car, Dr15 per tent, Dr25 for a camper van and Dr10 for electricity. Basic bungalows (with a simple bathroom) can be rented for Dr30/50 per child/adult. From March to August you can spend the night under one of the large Berber tents for Dr15 per person. If you really want to get to know the locals, you can stay *en famille* (with a family) on a Berber farm for Dr50 per person.

The centre is becoming better known, so it's a good idea to make a reservation, particularly during high season, and for longer trips.

For those without their own vehicle, the centre can organise an airport pick-up; call them to discuss this. Alternatively, hire a grand taxi from Midelt.

Organised Tours The centre can organise excursions whether they be on foot, with mountain bikes, with mules and a cook, in 4WDs or on bivouacs. The most regular trips take from a half-day to two days, but there are also one week to 15-day circuits, and longer trips that could take you right across the Atlas Mountains or deep into the desert.

Shorter trips include various excursions to nearby lakes and cedar forests, the Outat Gorges (Dr120, half-day), the Mougger Saffen Gorges (Dr300, full day), the Cirque Jaffar (Dr300, full day), the Tadroute Canyon (Dr380, full day) and the Berber villages in the upper valley of Taâraârt (Dr415, two days). All prices are per person and include meals. If the thought of an organised tour doesn't appeal, you can hire a guide, some mules and take off on your own on bivouac. Guides cost from Dr200 to Dr300 per day and mules Dr100 per day.

The East

TAZA
☎ 05

Despite its tempestuous history, Taza is quiet these days and relatively unused to tourists, although there are many locals willing to act as guides for those who do visit. It may be worth a stop if you are passing through the area, if only for the views and the crumbling fortifications.

If you have your own transport, there's a superb drive around Jebel Tazzeka, taking in a visit to the Gouffre du Friouato – one of the most incredible open caverns in the world – and Tazzeka National Park.

History
The fortified citadel of Taza is built on the edge of an escarpment overlooking the only feasible pass between the Rif Mountains and the Middle Atlas. It has been important throughout Morocco's history as a garrison

town from which to exert control over the eastern extremities of the country.

The Taza Gap, as it is known, has provided the traditional invasion route for armies moving west from Tunisia and Algeria. The Romans and the Arabs entered Morocco via here, and the town itself was the base from which the Almohads, Merenids and Alawites swept down into Fès to conquer lowland Morocco and establish their dynasties.

All Moroccan sultans had a hand in fortifying Taza. Nevertheless, their control over the area was always tenuous because the fiercely independent and rebellious local tribes were always willing to exploit any weakness in the central power in order to overrun the city.

Never was this more the case than in the first years of the 20th century, when 'El-Rogui' (the Pretender to the Sultan's Throne), Bou Hamra, held sway over Taza (although he was based largely in Selouane, 24km south of Melilla) and most of northeastern Morocco (see the boxed text 'Bou Hamra').

The French occupied Taza in 1914 and made it the main base from which they fought the prolonged rebellion by the tribes of the Rif Mountains and Middle Atlas.

Orientation

Arriving by local bus or train, you'll find yourself on the main Fès-Oujda road, a short taxi ride from Place de l'Indépendance. This is the heart of the ville nouvelle where you'll find the banks, main post office and most hotels and restaurants. If you arrive by CTM bus, you're in luck because the office is right near this square.

The medina is 2km to the south. Local buses (Dr1.50) and petit taxis (Dr4) run regularly between the ville nouvelle and medina.

Information

Most banks are represented in Taza, BMCE and Wafa Bank, both in the ville nouvelle, have ATMs.

The main post and phone offices (open normal office hours) are in the ville nouvelle; there's another post office up the hill in the medina. There's an Internet place, Stibnet, behind Hôtel de la Poste.

There are several photo shops where you can buy or develop print film.

Bou Hamra

Bou Hamra (the Man on the She-Ass), or Jilali ben Driss as he came into the world, was one of a host of colourful and violent characters who strode across the Moroccan stage at the turn of the 19th and 20th centuries when central power evaporated and the European powers prepared to take greater control.

Born in 1868 in the Jebel Zerhoun area, he became a minor government official in Fès. In 1894, he was jailed for forgery, but managed to escape to Algeria six years later.

In for a penny, in for a pound, Bou Hamra decided on a more ambitious fraud – claiming with conviction to be Sultan Abd al-Aziz's elder brother Mohammed. He acquired his nickname by dint of his custom of travelling around on a she-donkey and staked a claim in eastern Morocco as the legitimate pretender to the throne – El-Rogui. As the British journalist Walter Harris wrote, Bou Hamra had learned 'a few conjuring tricks' – but surely the best was having himself proclaimed sultan in Taza in 1902.

Another character of a different style, Er-Raissouli, who at this time held sway in the Tangier area of northern Morocco, placed an each-way bet by signing a deal with Bou Hamra recognising him as sultan. In the end he needn't have worried, for in 1908 the real Mohammed stood up and the Rif tribes that had backed Bou Hamra turned on him.

He soon fell into the hands of the new sultan, Moulay Abd al-Hafiz. Bou Hamra was paraded around the country for a month in a 1m-high cage on the back of a camel before being thrown to the lions of the sultan's menagerie in Fès in March 1909.

TAZA

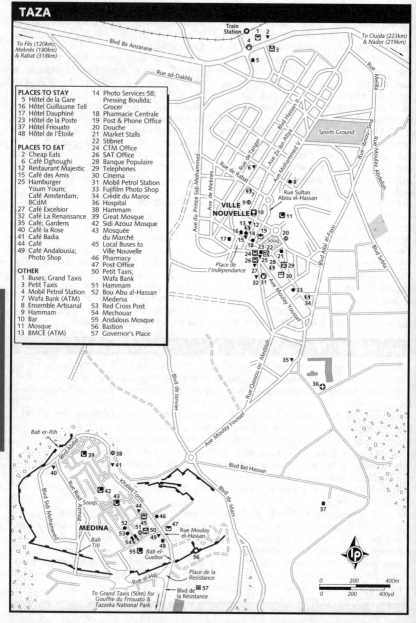

PLACES TO STAY
5 Hôtel de la Gare
16 Hôtel Guillaume Tell
17 Hôtel Dauphiné
23 Hôtel de la Poste
37 Hôtel Friouato
48 Hôtel de l'Étoile

PLACES TO EAT
2 Cheap Eats
6 Café Dghoughi
12 Restaurant Majestic
15 Café des Amis
25 Hamburger
    Youm Youm;
    Café Amsterdam;
    BCdM
27 Café Excelsior
32 Café La Renaissance
35 Café; Gardens
40 Café la Rose
41 Café Badia
44 Café
49 Café Andalousia;
    Photo Shop

OTHER
1 Buses; Grand Taxis
3 Petit Taxis
4 Mobil Petrol Station
7 Wafa Bank (ATM)
8 Ensemble Artisanal
9 Hammam
10 Bar
11 Mosque
13 BMCE (ATM)

14 Photo Services 58;
    Pressing Boulida;
    Grocer
18 Pharmacie Centrale
19 Post & Phone Office
20 Douche
21 Market Stalls
22 Stibnet
24 CTM Office
26 SAT Office
28 Banque Populaire
29 Telephones
30 Cinema
31 Mobil Petrol Station
33 Fujifilm Photo Shop
34 Crédit du Maroc
36 Hospital
38 Hammam
39 Great Mosque
42 Sidi Azouz Mosque
43 Mosquée
    du Marché
45 Local Buses to
    Ville Nouvelle
46 Pharmacy
47 Post Office
50 Petit Taxis;
    Wafa Bank
51 Hammam
52 Bou Abu al-Hassan
    Medersa
53 Red Cross Post
54 Mechouar
55 Andalous Mosque
56 Bastion
57 Governor's Place

Medina

Most of the medina walls, which are about 3km in circumference, date from the time of the Almohads (12th century). Having withstood so many sieges, they are ruined in parts. There's also a bastion built by the Saadians in the 16th century, just where the walls jut out to the east of the medina.

The most interesting section of wall is the **Bab er-Rih** (Gate of the Wind), from where there are superb views over the surrounding countryside. You can see the wooded slopes of Jebel Tazzeka and before that, across the Oued Taza, the terraced gardens and dry ravines of the foothills of the Rif Mountains. Looking north over the ville nouvelle you'll see the Rif Mountains in the distance.

Not far from here is the **Great Mosque**, begun by the Almohads in 1135 and added to by the Merenids in the 13th century. Non-Muslims are not allowed to enter, and it is difficult to get much of an impression from the outside of the building. From here the main thoroughfare, known variously as Rue Kettanine, Rue Nejjarine, Rue Koubet and Rue Sidi Ali Derrar, stretches down to the far end of the medina. With many examples of richly decorated doorways and, occasionally, windows high up in the walls guarded by old, carved cedar screens, this is perhaps the most interesting part of town.

The **souqs** and qissaria are about halfway down the street, around the Mosquée du Marché. Some offer mats and carpets woven by the Beni Ouarain tribe in the surrounding mountains, and are virtually bereft of tourist shops. It's a great chance to observe the workings of a typical Berber market. The weekly market is held on Friday.

While in this part of the city, don't miss the minaret of the **Mosquée du Marché**, which is perhaps unique in Morocco in that its upper part is wider than its base.

Right at the end of the main street, close to the **mechouar**, is the **Andalous Mosque**, constructed in the 12th century.

Nearby is a **ruined house** once occupied by Bou Hamra, and the Merenid **Bou Abu al-Hassan Medersa**. It may be possible to gain entry to the latter if you ask around and enlist the help of a guide.

Places to Stay

Unless stated, none of the budget places have showers – luckily there's a choice of hammams – and their cleanliness is variable.

In the medina about the only choice is the fairly basic *Hôtel de l'Étoile* (☎ 270179), opposite the post office. It's a cheerful Spanish-run place with a central pink courtyard. Rooms with fireplaces and brass beds start at Dr35.

Down on the main Fès-Oujda road, more or less in front of the train station, is *Hôtel de la Gare* (☎ 672448). It has cheap and not overly inviting singles/doubles/triples for Dr48/64/99, and substantially better rooms with shower for Dr75/95/130. It's convenient for transport, but not much else.

The remaining budget options are near Place de l'Indépendance in the ville nouvelle. The cheapest is *Hôtel Guillaume Tell* (☎ 672347), which offers simple and reasonably clean rooms for Dr40/60. There are cold communal showers .

Just off Ave Moulay Youssef is *Hôtel de la Poste* (☎ 672589), which has small, but clean and comfortable rooms with balcony for Dr48/64.

Hôtel Dauphiné (☎ 673567), a two-star hotel west of Place de l'Indépendance, is an attractive colonial building that's clean and comfortable with large balconies overlooking the square. Rooms with hot shower and toilet cost Dr130/165. The hotel has a TV lounge, a decent restaurant and a lively bar; cots for babies are available.

The only top-end hotel in Taza is *Hôtel Friouato* (☎ 672593, fax 672244), an ugly place in dilapidated grounds awkwardly located between the ville nouvelle and medina. The rooms themselves with shower and toilet for Dr240/275 are OK. The hotel has a bar, a restaurant, a nightclub, a pool (nonguests can use it for Dr30) and tennis courts.

Places to Eat

While there are no real restaurants in the medina, there are numerous small stands where you can pick up a snack, and there is plenty of fresh produce in the souqs.

Café Badia is quite a basic place for coffee but it does have a good terrace with sweeping views of the town and countryside. There are a couple of other options by the main square including *Café Andalousia*, opposite the post office, which also has a terrace.

North of the ville nouvelle, there is a series of cafes and cheap-eat places by the grand taxis on the Fès-Oujda road (Blvd Bir Anzarane).

In the centre of the ville nouvelle, probably the best choice for a meal remains *Restaurant Majestic (Ave Mohammed V)*. It's a bit basic, but popular with locals for harira, tajines, brochettes or chicken.

Around the corner from Hôtel de la Poste is *Hamburger Youm Youm*, which does decent burgers, eggs and chips. A couple of doors down is *Café Amsterdam*, a pleasant place for breakfast where there's a Dutch-speaking owner.

Boulangerie Pâtisserie du Palais (65 Blvd Allal ben Abdullah), better known by the locals as Pâtisserie Mahfoud (after the proprietor), has pastries that are considered to be the best in town.

There are *market stalls* and a *covered market* selling food supplies just north of the cinema.

Getting There & Away

Bus The CTM bus office is next to Hôtel de la Poste on Place de l'Indépendance.

Buses run to Casablanca (Dr109, 7½ hours) via Fès (Dr31, two hours), Meknès (Dr49, three hours) and Rabat (seven hours), departing Taza at 7 and 10 am and 11 pm. Another bus to Fès leaves at 2.45 and 10 pm; the latter continues to Tangier. There's a bus to Al-Hoceima and Oujda at 2.45 pm.

Opposite the CTM office is the SAT office with a 1.30 am service to Oujda and 10.30 am service to Fès. It also has international services to France, Italy and Spain.

All other buses to the same destinations plus Nador (Dr57) gather near or pass by the grand taxi rank on the Fès-Oujda road. As there is no organised bus station as such, it can be a bit chaotic. The best bet is to turn up as early as you can and choose between the buses and grand taxis – taking whichever leaves first.

Train The train is generally a more reliable and comfortable option. There are four daily trains to Casablanca (Dr101/131, seven hours) via Fès (Dr27/35, two hours), Meknès (Dr40/52, three hours) and Rabat (Dr81/105, 5½ hours). Four daily trains go to Tangier (Dr98/128, eight hours) and three to Oujda (Dr54/69, 3¼ hours). Fares are for ordinaire/rapide services.

Grand Taxi Most grand taxis leave from the main Fès-Oujda road, near the train station. They depart fairly regularly for Fès (Dr30).

You can also catch a grand taxi to Oujda (Dr50) throughout the day, but the morning is best. Taxis go to Nador and Al-Hoceima (Dr50) less regularly.

Grand taxis to Gouffre du Friouato cavern (Dr30) leave from a lot just south of the Governor's Palace.

AROUND TAZA
Jebel Tazzeka Circuit

If you have your own transport (hitching isn't really feasible), you can make an interesting day trip around Jebel Tazzeka, southwest of Taza, taking in the Cascades de Ras el-Oued (waterfalls), Daïa Chiker (lake bed) the Gouffre du Friouato (cavern), and the gorges of the Oued Zireg. Most hotels in Taza have a free map and information on the Jebel Tazzeka Circuit.

Though the road (S311) is sealed and good the whole way, it's very narrow and twisty in parts. Unaccustomed to meeting any other traffic, grand taxis helter-skelter down them – take care, especially outside summer. If you don't have your own transport it would be worthwhile getting a small group together and hiring a taxi for the day.

Having negotiated the long, winding road up from Taza onto the plateau, you'll find yourself in a different world. It's almost eerie in its apparent emptiness, with small patches of farmland, a few scattered houses and, closer to Jebel Tazzeka itself, dense coniferous forests.

There are superb views from several points, including the semi-derelict hamlet of Bab Bou-Idir.

If you're coming from Fès, take the right turn signposted for Bab Bou-Idir. This road curves around and under the main highway to head south.

The First Leg The **Cascades de Ras el-Oued** are the first stop. Shortly before you reach Daïa Chiker plateau, you'll see a sign on your left for Ras el-Mar (headwater). The waterfalls are here, but they are really only worth a stop after the winter rains. By the summer they have usually slowed to a trickle.

A little beyond the cascades is the entry to **Tazzeka National Park**, which has picnic areas, walks, toilets, camping and an eco-museum.

After this the road flattens out, you take a right fork and have on your left the odd depression of the **Daïa Chiker**. The lake bed is usually pretty dry, but the earth is good and is used for grazing and crops. Daïa Chiker is a geological curiosity associated with fault lines in the calciferous rock structure. It is connected to a subterranean reservoir, the water of which is highly charged with carbon dioxide. Depending on the season and the state of affairs in the subterranean reservoir, the surface of the lake can change dramatically.

The nearby **Grottes du Chiker** (caves) at the northern end of the lake have been explored and are said to give access to a 5km-long underground river, but they are not open to casual visitors.

Gouffre du Friouato A little further along, the Gouffre du Friouato is signposted off to the right. You can drive up or take a steep, 20-minute walk to the entrance. It is the main attraction of this circuit and a must-see at any time of the year.

This vast cavern is said to be the deepest and possibly the most extensive in the whole of North Africa. It was first explored in 1935 and has only been partially explored to date – no-one has ever reached the end of the chamber.

The main part plummets vertically some 100m to a floor below, from where various chambers break off and snake away to who knows where. There are 520 rather precipi-

tous steps (with handrails) leading you to the floor of the main cavern (this is quite strenuous on the climb back up). At the bottom of the steps there's a hole through which you drop to start exploring the more interesting chambers 200 more steps below. You'll need your own torch (flashlight). Some of the stalactite formations are extraordinary.

Speleologists have made explorations to a depth of 300m and it is believed a fossil river runs another 500m below. Among the most spectacular chambers are the **Salle de Lixus** and the **Salle de Draperies** (this will take around 2½ hours to reach).

Entry to the cave is Dr3. Mostapha, the guardian of the caves, has a torch if you don't and though his guided tours seem pricey at Dr100, he is honest and reliable and there is no-one who knows the caves better than he. His longest exploration of the caves was with a party of Germans with whom he emerged 28 hours later!

There is quite a bit of climbing and clambering to do, so wear shoes or trainers with a good grip and be prepared to get pretty grubby. If you have your own torch, you're free to explore the caves on your own (but be wary), and if you don't re-emerge, Mostapha will come and look for you anyway. The caves are open from 8 am to 6, 7, or 8 pm, depending on the number of visitors.

Back to Taza As you leave Daïa Chiker lake behind, the road begins to climb again into coniferous forests past **Bab Bou-Idir**. This must have once been a beautiful retreat with its tiled alpine-style houses, but it appears to have been largely abandoned – weekend picnickers notwithstanding. Along the way you can catch good views of the snowcapped Atlas Mountains.

About 8km past Bab Bou-Idir, a poor track branches 9km off to the right (north). If you can get your car up the incline, you'll find the TV relay station at the top of **Jebel Tazzeka** (1980m) and wonderful views all around, particularly to the Rif Mountains in the north and the Middle Atlas in the south.

The main road continues around for another 38km back to the main Fès-Taza road at Sidi Abdallah de Rhiata. On the way you

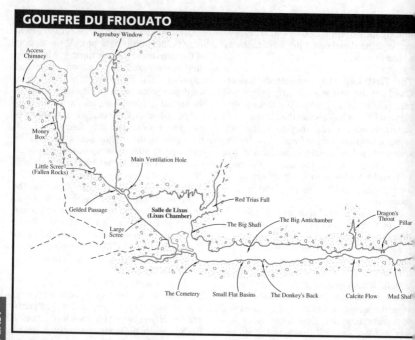

GOUFFRE DU FRIOUATO

Pagroubay Window

Access Chimney

Money Box

Little Scree (Fallen Rocks)

Main Ventilation Hole

Gelded Passage

Salle de Lixus (Lixus Chamber)

Large Scree

Red Trias Fall

The Big Shaft

The Big Antichamber

Dragon's Throat

Pillar

The Cemetery

Small Flat Basins

The Donkey's Back

Calcite Flow

Mud Shaf

will wind your way around hairpin bends through some dense woodland and then down through the pretty **gorges** of the Oued Zireg.

From the intersection at Sidi Abdallah de Rhiata, you can take the main highway back east to Taza, pausing at **Tizi n'Touahar** on the way for some more views.

OUJDA
☎ 06 • pop 250,000
Oujda, the largest town in eastern Morocco is a sprawling, modern city that is still reasonably affluent, if only judging by the number of Mercedes-Benz cars and the sophistication of the cafes along the main street. Though there is little to detain the traveller very long, it's a pleasant, relaxed and hassle-free place to put your feet up after heading down from the Rif Mountains, or for those on their way south to Figuig and the Sahara. An added attraction is the Mediterranean beach town of Saidia only 58km away (see the East Coast in the Mediterranean Coast & the Rif chapter).

The town's size is due to its position close to the Algerian border. In the past, floods of Algerian visitors (often buying up products unavailable at home for resale) passed through the town, but the closure of the Algerian border in 1995 put an end to all that. Some smuggled goods still find their way into town, but many businesses have suffered since 1995. Worst hit are the numerous mid-range hotels that were thrown up between 1989 and 1995, the brief period when the border with Algeria was open. Many are struggling to survive and most official prices (good value already) will tumble should you show any sign of staying elsewhere – such is the desire to please. The few westerners who stay in the town can sometimes be rather saddening.

History
The site of Oujda has long been important as it lies on the main axis connecting Morocco with the rest of North Africa (the Ro-

GOUFFRE DU FRIOUATO

Cross-Section

0   20   40m
0   20   40yd

Grand Chimney

Salle de Draperies

Micro Stalagmite Salle

Balcony

Letterbox

Duck Pond & Skating Rink

Shafts

Access Passage Below

Parapet

Adame Blanche's Bathtub

Fallen Rock

Soldier's Shaft

Infiltrations

mans built a road through here). Like Taza, it has occupied a key position in controlling the east and was often seen as a vital stepping stone for armies aiming to seize control of the heartland around Fès.

The town was founded by the Meghraoua tribe in the 10th century and it remained independent until the Almohads overran it in the 11th century. All the subsequent dynasties have left their mark on its fate.

Under the Merenids, however, Algerian rulers based in Tlemcen took the town on several occasions, and in the 17th century it fell under the sway of the Ottoman administration that had set up in Algiers.

Moulay Ismail put an end to this in 1687, and Oujda remained in Moroccan hands until 1907 when French forces in Algeria crossed the frontier and occupied the town in one of a series of 'incidents'. The protectorate was still five years away, but the sultan was powerless to stop it.

The French soon expanded the town,

which has since swelled in size as provincial capital and in its role as the main gateway for commerce with Algeria. Its industrial role rests on mining, particularly zinc, which is carried out further to the south.

Orientation

Although quite large, only the centre of Oujda is of any interest to travellers. The main street is Blvd Mohammed V, along or near which you'll find banks, the post and tourist office, and many of the better budget and mid-range hotels and restaurants.

About a five-minute walk to the west along Blvd Zerktouni is the Oujda train station. A further 15 minutes to the south-west, across Oued Nachef, is the main *gare routière* (bus station). Also here, on the road to Taza, are grand taxis for Taza and Fès.

Information

Tourist Offices The tourist office (☎ 685631) is on Place du 16 Août 1953 at

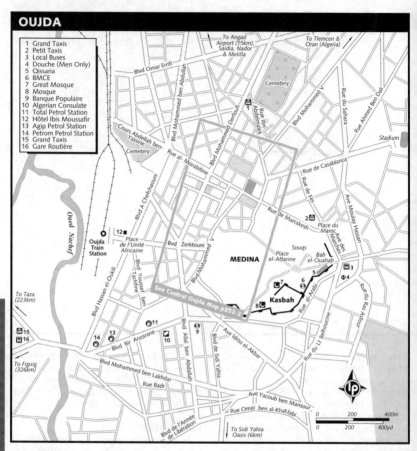

OUJDA

1 Grand Taxis
2 Petit Taxis
3 Local Buses
4 Douche (Men Only)
5 Qissaria
6 BMCE
7 Great Mosque
8 Mosque
9 Banque Populaire
10 Algerian Consulate
11 Total Petrol Station
12 Hôtel Ibis Moussafir
13 Agip Petrol Station
14 Petrom Petrol Station
15 Grand Taxis
16 Gare Routière

See Central Oujda Map p352-3

the junction with Blvd Mohammed V. As well as the usual brochures it has good accommodation and restaurant lists and a photocopied pamphlet explaining a little about the town (in French). The English-speaking staff are helpful.

It's open 8.30 am to noon and 2.30 to 6.30 pm weekdays.

Money Most of the Moroccan banks have branches in Oujda and almost all have ATMs.

Wafa Bank, Crédit du Maroc and BMCE on Blvd Mohammed V have separate bureau de change offices. However, the latter two are only open during summer. The BMCE and Banque Populaire are your best bet for changing travellers cheques.

Post & Communications The main post office is on Blvd Mohammed V. It's open from 8.30 am to 12.15 pm and 2.30 to 6 pm weekdays and 8 am to noon Saturday and there's a counter for poste restante. The parcel office is to the right of the main entrance.

The phone office, in the right-hand side of the post office building, is open daily from 8.30 am to 9 pm. You can buy (and use) phonecards here.

The best place in town for Internet access is Alf@Net above a *téléboutique* (privately operated phone office) on Blvd Mohammed V. It charges Dr13 per hour, but the machines and connections are as fast as you like (big screens and swivel chairs too). It's sometimes open 24 hours a day. Acrosys Maroc, opposite Hotel Simon on Rue Tarik ibn Ziad, offers fast Internet access for Dr10 per hour and is open from 9 am to 1 am daily. On Blvd Zerktouni, Espace Net is another option.

Travel Agencies Carlson Wagonlits (☎ 682520, fax 681968) is on Blvd Mohammed V.

Film & Photography A reasonable place to buy and develop film is Labo Express Provincial (☎ 706479) just back from Blvd Mohammed V.

Laundry The Central Pressing is opposite Hôtel du 16 Août on Rue de Marrakesh.

Medical Services The night pharmacy opposite the CTM bus station is open 8.30 pm to 8.30 am.

Medina

Although hardly the most fascinating of medinas, Oujda's old centre warrants a bit of a stroll at least. The most animated part is the area inside and outside the eastern gate, **Bab el-Ouahab**. Also known as the Gate of Heads – local pashas (governors) had a habit of having the heads of criminals and renegades hung here – it is full of food stalls, beggars, shoppers and all the noise and bustle of a typical North African market.

Plunging in deeper you'll find clothes shops; a few hotels and the **Great Mosque**, built in the 14th century by the Merenids.

Hammams & Public Showers

You can take a shower at the Douche Balima on Blvd Mohammed Derfoufi. The Douche Moderne close to Hôtel Afrah is open to men only. Both places cost Dr6.

There is a hammam (Dr5) and public shower (Dr6) for women on a side road north-east of the post office.

Places to Stay – Budget

There are several fairly simple hotels along Rue de Marrakesh that charge about Dr20/40 for singles/doubles, usually with shared cold showers. They are adequate without being stunning.

A prince among cheap hotels, is the large, well-run *Hôtel al-Hanna* (☎ 686003, 132 Rue de Marrakesh). Spotless, pleasant rooms with washbasin cost Dr40/60. There's a communal hot shower. Try to get one of the rooms upstairs as the lower floors are a little gloomy.

Nearby, but not quite as good as al-Hanna, is *Hôtel du 16 Aout* (☎ 684197, 128 Rue de Marrakesh). Basic rooms with washbasins go for Dr35/70 and there are shared hot showers.

Hôtel Lahlou (☎ 683894, 95 Rue el-Mazouzi) is a good choice in the heart of the medina, and has hot showers.

Another good hunting ground for cheap hotels is the pedestrian zone off Blvd Mohammed V, and the area nearby.

Hotel l'Oasis (☎ 683214) just off Blvd Mohammed V is a simple, clean place charging Dr40 per person (or Dr60 for a couple). The beds are a bit hammock-like but it's OK. There are cold showers.

A little tatty around the edges, but good value is *Hôtel Isly* (☎ 683928, 26 Rue Ramdane el-Gadhi). Clean and bright singles/doubles go for Dr30/60. There are cold showers.

A little more money will get you a considerably better deal. *Hôtel Simon* (☎ 686304, 1 Rue Tarik ibn Ziad) has lovely, large rooms with cold showers, washbasins and (in some of them) wrought-iron balconies for Dr70/90. The toilets may not be any good and the bar can get noisy, but it's definitely a place full of character.

Better value is *Hôtel Afrah* (☎ 686533, 15 Rue de Tafna), which has been attractively done out and offers comfortable, spotless rooms with bathrooms (cold water only) for Dr50/100.

Not far away is one of the best budget deals in Oujda, the one-star *Hôtel Royal* (☎ 682284, 13 Blvd Zerktouni). It charges Dr77/98 for rooms without shower (Dr5 for a hot shower in the communal bathroom) and Dr120/141 with shower and toilet (with hot water more or less all day). It's a little austere, but the rooms are very well kept and you can negotiate a cheaper deal. The hotel also has guarded parking (Dr12 a night).

Places to Stay – Mid-Range
The mid-range hotels have been hardest hit by the closure of the Algerian border. A few struggle on but many have closed.

A reasonable choice is *Hôtel Angad* (☎ *691451, Rue Ramdane el-Gadhi),* which offers unexceptional but clean singles/doubles with bathroom, hot water and TV for Dr80/120.

Pretty good value normally is the modern, three-star *Hôtel des Lilas* (☎/fax *680840, Rue Jamal ed-Din el-Afghani).* The rooms are smallish, but very comfortable. They have a bathroom, satellite TV and telephone and cost Dr120/180. However, at the time of writing the hotel had no hot water. Underground parking is available.

Places to Stay – Top End
There are few hotels in the three-star bracket and up. West of the centre on Place de l'Unité Africaine, the *Hôtel Ibis Moussafir* chain (☎ *688200, fax 688208)* has one of its standard and fairly reliable hotels for people who want to be near train stations. It's not the best one in the family, but it's your best bet if you've got the cash. Modern, well-kept singles/doubles (with satellite TV etc) cost Dr305/380.

Hôtel Oujda (☎ *684093, fax 685064, Blvd Mohammed V)* charges Dr266/327 for rooms with bathroom, TV and phone. It's a hotel down on its luck and many of the furnishings have remained unchanged since the 1970s.

Both hotels have swimming pools, which nonguests can use for Dr50.

Places to Eat
The cheapest place for snack food is at the *stalls* inside Bab el-Ouahab at the easternmost point of the medina, providing you have a taste for broiled sheep heads, deep-

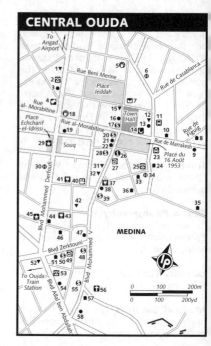

fried intestines and very large bags of snails. Fortunately, you can also find slightly more mundane meals like soup and omelettes. There's also an excellent selection of fresh fruit and vegies here.

Next up the scale are the sandwich joints on Blvd Mohammed Derfoufi, north of the Institut Français. One of the most popular is *Sandwich Sindibad,* which serves mostly *kefta*-based (lamb mince) sandwiches for around Dr10.

Restaurant Nacional on the corner of Blvd Zerktouni and Blvd Allal ben Abdallah is a great little place for lunch or an early dinner. On offer are tasty, well-seasoned lamb chops (Dr25) and roast chicken (Dr20).

There are several cheap eateries close to Place du 16 Août 1953 and *Restaurant Baraka* is particularly good; local women eat upstairs. Salad, roast chicken and chips goes for Dr30.

Restaurant Brasserie de France (☎ *685987, 87–89 Blvd Mohammed V)* is a

CENTRAL OUJDA

PLACES TO STAY		OTHER			
8	Hôtel du 16 Août	2	Telephones	26	Tourist Office
10	Hôtel al-Hanna	3	Pharmacie Nouvelle	27	Alf@Net
24	Hôtel Isly	4	Institut Français; French	28	BMCI (ATM); BCME (ATM)
33	Hôtel Afrah		Consulate	29	Police
35	Hôtel Lahlou	5	Shell Petrol Station	30	Douche Balima
36	Hôtel Simon	6	Douche (Women Only)	34	Douche Moderne
44	Hôtel Al Fajr		& Hammam		(Men Only)
46	Hôtel des Lilas	7	Post & Phone Office	37	Hôtel la Concorde
51	Hôtel Royal	9	Central Pressing	38	Labo Express Provincial
57	Hôtel Oujda	11	CTM Bus Station	39	Bank el-Maghrib
		13	Night Pharmacy	40	Cinéma Royal
PLACES TO EAT		14	Mosque	41	Bar
1	Sandwich Sindibad	16	Hertz	43	Bar Chanteclair
12	Restaurant Baraka	17	Wafa Bank (ATM)	45	Sûreté Nationale
15	Café Le Trésor	18	Agip Petrol Station	47	Pharmacie L'Orientale
31	Pâtisserie Colombo	19	Maison de la Presse	48	Société Générale (ATM)
32	Brasserie Restaurant		(French Newspaper Stand)	49	Espace Net
	de France	20	Crédit du Maroc (ATM)	50	Banque Populaire
42	Restaurant le Comme	21	Carlson Wagonlits; Europcar	53	Telephones; Fax
	Chez Soi	22	Pharmacie Ben Bakhti	54	Pharmacie Le Paris
52	Restaurant	23	Petit Taxis	55	BCM (Bank)
	Nacional	25	Téléboutique	56	Église St Louis
				58	Royal Air Maroc

safe, more upmarket choice with good service. French-style mains go for Dr60 to Dr70. Better value is the three-course *menu de la jour* (menu of the day – Dr90). A beer costs Dr20 and half a bottle of wine is Dr40.

Restaurant Le Comme Chez Soi (☎ 686079, 8 Rue Sijilmassa) is a step above the de France in terms of price and quality. It specialises in French cuisine and has good fish dishes.

There is no shortage of good cafes all over the ville nouvelle and in the area around the medina. The more upmarket, and most popular, are those on Blvd Mohammed V. Most cafes and patisseries are open from around 5 am to 9 pm.

Café Le Trésor does a breakfast of coffee, orange juice and *pain au chocolate* (chocolate croissant) for Dr9. Women travellers may appreciate the more secluded upstairs seating area.

Pâtisserie Colombo and *Café la Defense* are a little more expensive, but offer an excellent selection of cakes.

Entertainment

Bars are not difficult to find, but most are of the seedy spit-and-sawdust variety (beers for around Dr14). Those at the bigger hotels are a little better, though sometimes they only provide a higher class of sleaze; the entertaining bar at *Hôtel Oujda* is excellent in this respect.

The bar at *Hôtel Ibis Moussifir* is a straighter sort of place (beers cost around Dr18), while the one in the *Hôtel la Concorde* is dingy and cheap without being too dicey.

Getting There & Away

Air Oujda's Angad airport is 15km north of the town, just 400m east of the road to Ahfir and Saidia. It's a Dr50 grand taxi ride, though buses to Ahfir, Berkane or Saidia can drop you on the main road for a tenth of the price.

RAM (☎ 710000), which has an office beside Hôtel Oujda on Blvd Mohammed V, has one or two direct flights to Casablanca daily (Dr884, 1¾ hours). Regional Airlines has two flights per weekday to Casablanca (Dr1125). All other internal flights, with both airlines, go via Casablanca.

There are also twice weekly flights to Paris, France (Dr3054) and weekly direct flights to Marseille, France (Dr2954); Brussels, Belgium (Dr4054); and Amsterdam,

Netherlands (Dr4054). The Brussels flight connects with a service to Dusseldorf, Germany (Dr4054).

Bus – CTM CTM has a small office east of the town hall servicing one daily express bus (departing at 8.30 pm) to Casablanca (Dr165, 10½ hours) via Taza (Dr50, four hours), Fès (Dr80, six hours), Meknès (Dr100, seven hours) and Rabat (Dr141, 9½ hours).

All other buses, including CTM's other services, leave from the gare routière across Oued Nachef on the south-western edge of town, about a 15-minute walk from the train station or a petit taxi ride (around Dr6). The left-luggage counter is open from 5 am to 9 pm daily and charges Dr5 per item per day.

Other departures are at 11 am and 7 pm to Taza (Dr50) and Fès (Dr80). The 11 am bus continues to Meknès (Dr100, about seven hours), Rabat (Dr120) and Casablanca (Dr130, 12 hours). The 7 pm bus goes on to Tangier (Dr175, 11½ hours) via Larache (Dr151, 8½ hours). A bus to Nador (Dr25, 2½ hours) leaves at 1 pm.

For Al-Hoceima, Chefchaouen and Tetouan change at Nador or Fès.

Bus – Other Companies Other bus companies operate services to numerous other destinations. All express Casablanca services leave from one of three bus offices just east of the town hall; all others leave from the gare routière south-west of the town. SAT and Trans Ghazala bus companies, both close to the CTM office, have five evening services and two dawn services to Casablanca (Dr130) between them.

Around 15 buses a day run to Fès (Dr66), though the bulk of these are in the early morning and late evening; many go on to Meknès (Dr78). There are at least five to Taza (Dr40), seven to Figuig (Dr66) and Bouarfa (Dr49), around 20 to Nador (Dr25), seven to Al-Hoceima (Dr58), three to Er-Rachidia (Dr100), numerous services to Berkane (Dr10) and four or five (in summer, two or three in winter) to Saidia (Dr11).

There are also two daily buses to Tangier (Dr130, the best one leaves at 3 pm) via Chefchaouen (Dr110) and Tetouan (Dr120).

Train Oujda train station is fairly close to the centre of town, at the western end of Blvd Zerktouni. The left-luggage counter is open from 6 am to 10 pm and charges Dr10 per item per day.

There are three departures for Casablanca per day including one evening ordinaire service that has both 2nd- and 1st-class sleepers (Dr202/Dr287). The rapide train has one class of sleeping carriage (Dr298 to Casablanca). There is also one direct daily service to Tangier (Dr152 for 2nd-class ordinaire, Dr197 for 2nd-class rapide). All these trains call at Taza (Dr54/69 ordinaire/rapide, four hours), Fès (Dr79/104, 6½ hours) and Meknès (Dr93/121, 7½ hours).

There are no longer services to Bouarfa.

Grand Taxi Grand taxis to Taza (Dr50) and occasionally to Fès (Dr90; though more often than not you'll have to change at Taza) leave fairly regularly from outside the main bus station.

Grand taxis to Nador (Dr35), Saidia (Dr20), Ahfir (Dr10) and Berkane (Dr15) congregate around the corner of Rue ibn Abdelmalek and Blvd Mohammed Derfoufi, north of the centre.

Car The following rental agencies can be found in Oujda:

Avis (☎ 703922) Angad airport
Budget (☎ 681011) Train station and Angad airport
Europcar (☎/fax 704416) Carlson Wagonlits, Blvd Mohammed V
Hertz (☎ 683802) Immeuble el-Baraka Bldg, Blvd Mohammed V
Oro Car (☎ 710756) Blvd Mohammed V

To Algeria With the closure of the Algerian border, previously existing services have stopped. In the past, buses ran there every half-hour, as well as trains and grand taxis. Should the border re-open, bus and grand taxi services should quickly resume.

AROUND OUJDA
Sidi Yahia Oasis
About 6km south of Oujda medina is the oasis of Sidi Yahia and a shrine to the man

Christians know as John the Baptist, but whom both Muslims and Jews revere as a prophet. It's said that John is buried here, though no-one is sure where exactly. It's a peaceful, shady place surrounded by urban sprawl and a wasteland littered with plastic bags. There are numerous snack stalls and cafes clustered around the entrance to the shrine. The inside of the shrine is off-limits to non-Muslims but you are free to wander around the outside, which is decorated with carved Arabic script and beautiful tilework. The annual moussem held in September is one of the bigger celebrations of this type in the country and is well worth a look.

Frequent No 1 buses (Dr2) leave from the square outside Bab el-Ouahab or you can charter a petit taxi for about Dr12.

BOUARFA
☎ 06

The 376km journey south from Oujda to Figuig is long, hot and, for the most part, monotonous. Figuig itself warrants a visit – particularly for those who see the desert routes through the Sahara as the main attraction of Maghreb travel – but the towns on the way down from Oujda do not.

The administrative and garrison town of Bouarfa is no exception, and the only thing that separates it from the others is the fact that it serves as a minor transport hub for the south-eastern corner of Morocco.

Should you get stuck here, the best accommodation bet is *Hôtel Tamlalte*, on the town's main street and about 100m from the bus station. Singles/doubles are clean and basic and cost Dr30/60. There are no showers, but there are washbasins in the rooms. A few *cafes* and *snack stands* are scattered around town.

There are six buses daily to Oujda (Dr49.50) and four to Figuig (Dr21). Heading west to Er-Rachidia (Dr53) there is a bus around noon.

FIGUIG
☎ 06

Some 200,000 palm trees are fed by artesian wells in this oasis on the edge of the Sahara. Figuig was once the last stop before crossing

---

Sand Baths

Anyone suffering from rheumatism may want to consider being buried up to their neck in the baking hot sands of the desert while they're in Morocco.

A famous doctor in Figuig came up with this form of treatment as a very effective way of drawing dampness out of the body. It can be dangerous (several people died doing this in Merzouga in 1993) and must be carefully supervised.

The time spent buried (head poking out, one presumes) is just a few minutes, but overall treatment usually takes place over several days. Despite the very real possibility of being cooked alive, sand baths seem to be growing in popularity.

---

the Sahara for Moroccan pilgrims heading to Mecca, and until the closure of the Algerian border in 1995, was the second border post after Oujda. Like Oujda, the local economy has suffered heavily; most hotels have closed.

Figuig's greatest charm is as a place to simply unwind. It would be hard to find a more laid-back place, although in summer this is mainly due to the oppressive heat.

The main road from Bouarfa goes through the oasis and on to Beni Ounif, on the Algerian side of the frontier.

There is a Banque Populaire, post and phone office set back off the main road, Blvd Hassan II.

There's a hammam next to the now-defunct Hôtel Sahara.

Things to See & Do

However, if you do come all this way, there is a surprising amount of interest in the town. There are seven **ksour** (fortified strongholds), each of which surrounds an area of palmeraie. Over the centuries the inhabitants of the ksour have remained independent of each other and have ferociously fought against each other for water and grazing land. The major ksour to see are El-Oudahir, the administrative part of town; Zenaga, the largest ksar with a platform affording good views over the walls, a particularly good cafe and the pink mosque; El-Hammam el-Foukanni, with hot springs; and El-Maiz, the prettiest quarter with houses with broad verandas.

There is a souq held every Friday at Figuig. On Sunday, after the first prayer, but before sunrise, the unusual **Souq de Jellaba** takes place, which is for the old people of Figuig only.

Places to Stay & Eat

A lack of accommodation is the biggest problem for the traveller to Figuig.

On the road to the Algerian border and recently renovated, *Camping du Diamant Vert* (☎ 899309) has doubles with bathroom for Dr120. The attached hotel also has a pool, restaurant and terrace.

Figuig Hotel (☎ 899309) in the centre, has accommodation in rooms and Berber tents as well as the best views in town.

Other basic options include *Hôtel el-Meliasse* and *Maison des Jeunes (Blvd Hassan II)* opposite Café La Paix.

There are no proper restaurants in Figuig, just a couple of *cafes* and *snack stands*. The best place for food is a small *cafe* opposite the bus office. It does a reasonable tajine each day for Dr20 to Dr25 (anything else will have to be ordered in advance), and is a good place for breakfast. It's open from 6 am to 10.30 pm.

Café La Paix (Blvd Hassan II) is good for coffee.

Getting There & Away

Bus There are buses to Oujda (Dr68, seven hours) at 2, 5, 6, 7 and 8 am every day. They all stop at Bouarfa and from there you can connect with the Er-Rachidia bus (10 hours).

To Algeria Should the border reopen, it's 3km from Figuig to the Moroccan customs, another 1km to Algerian customs and a further 3km to the first Algerian town, Beni Ounif.

MIDDLE ATLAS & THE EAST

Central Morocco

The central region of Morocco has to be one of the most exciting and romantic destinations in the entire country. The biggest drawcard is the ochre-coloured city of Marrakesh. Founded almost 1000 years ago, it is one of the great cities of the Maghreb and is home to its most perfect Islamic monument, the Koutoubia Mosque.

Marrakesh is above all a city of drama. Its spectacular setting against the snowcapped High Atlas Mountains lingers long in the mind of most travellers, and the famous Djemaa el-Fna square provides perhaps the greatest open-air spectacle in the world.

Just an hour away are the High Atlas foothills of the Ourika Valley and the wilder territory around Jebel Toubkal, barely visited except by animals and Berber shepherds.

Once over the High Atlas, you're into the sub-Sahara, a vast, open landscape shot through with the lush river valleys of the Dadès, Drâa and Ziz Rivers.

Crowded with *palmeraies* (oasis-like areas) and overlooked by imposing red-earth kasbahs and starry desert skies, the valleys were once caravan routes linking Morocco with the riches of the Sahara proper, and brought gold and slaves from West Africa.

Apart from exploring the river valleys, there's good walking and climbing in the stunning ochre-coloured Dadès and Todra Gorges, and serious trekking possibilities among the jagged blue-black peaks of the Jebel Sarhro (see the Trekking chapter). In the far south-east, the alluring Saharan sand dunes of Merzouga are not to be missed.

About 30km south of Agdz, the A6956 runs to the small town of Tazzarine, from where the A3458 cuts across to the oases of the Tafilalt (the last stop on the long caravan journeys) via the Jebel Sarhro mountain range. This is part of a handy scenic loop that enables you to return west through the Dadès Valley (the 'Road of a Thousand Kasbahs') and the Todra and Dadès Gorges, or vice versa. To really do the trip justice (and take in the Drâa Valley), allow at least five days.

Highlights

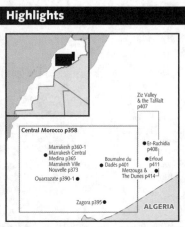

- Jostling with the crowds in Marrakesh's Djemaa el-Fna – a microcosm of Morocco where you'll see it all

- Plunging into the rock pools of Cascades d'Ouzoud and the 100m of cascading water

- Belching camels and welcoming Tuaregs create the sounds at Merzouga, but it's the dunes with their vivid ever-changing colours that steal the show

- Wishing upon every *ksar* (fortified stronghold) in Aït Benhaddou's huge kasbah complex will bring you a long and fruitful life

- Wondering at Todra Gorge's stunning, 300m ochre-coloured cliffs cut into the High Atlas

! Telephone numbers in Morocco have changed. For new codes and complete numbers, see the boxed text 'Changes to Telephone Numbers' on page 89.

When driving, beware of the false hitchhiker syndrome. A few less-than-honest Moroccans work popular roads looking for tourists to take home in 'gratitude' for the lift – but they then start the hard-sell on carpets. Don't fall for the pretend car breakdown, either.

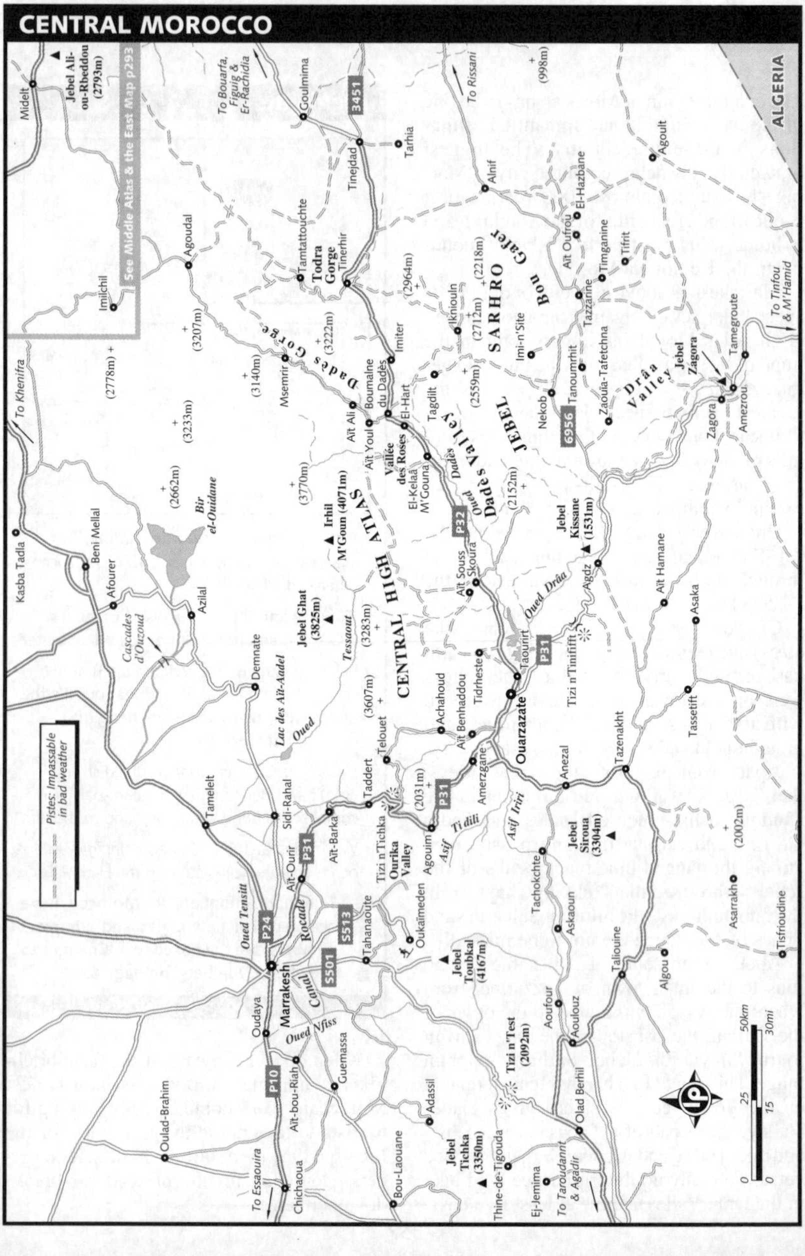

CENTRAL MOROCCO

CENTRAL MOROCCO

See Middle Atlas & the East Map p293

ALGERIA

Midelt
Jebel Ali-ou-Rheddou (2793m)
(2778m) +
To Khenifra
Imilchil
Agoudal
(3207m)
Imi-n-Tanoute
Goulmima
3451
Tineghad
Tarhia
To Rissani
Agoult
(998m)
To Bouarfa, Figuig & Er-Rachidia
Tamtattouchte
Todra Gorge Tinerhir
Iknioun
(2964m)
Alnif
El-Hazbane
Aït Ouffrou
Timganne
Tifilt
To Tinfou & M'Hamid
Tamegroute
Jebel Zagora
Zagora
Amezrou
Draa Valley
Zaouïa-Tafetchna
Nekob
Tanoumrhit
6956
Imi-n-Site
(2559m)
Tazzarine
Bou Gafer
JEBEL SARHRO
(2712m)
(2218m)
Msemrir
(3222m)
Dadès Gorge
Imiter
Aït Ali
El-Hart
Tagdilt
Boumalne du Dadès
Aït Youl
Vallée des Roses
El-Kelaâ M'Gouna
Dadès Valley
Oued Dadès
(2152m)
Jebel Kissane (1531m)
Agdz
Oued Drâa
Aït Hamane
Asaka
Aït Hamane
(3140m)
(3233m)
(2662m)
Bir el-Ouidane
Cascades d'Ouzoud
(3770m)
Irhil M'Goun (4071m)
Jebel Ghat (3825m)
CENTRAL HIGH ATLAS
Tessaout
(3283m)
Aït Souss Skoura
P32
Tizi n'Tinififft
P31
Tamelelt
Kasba Tadla
Beni Mellal
Afourer
Azilal
Demnate
Lac des Aït-Aadel
Oued
(3607m)
Telouet
Achahoud
Tidreshte
Aït Benhaddou
Taddert
P31
Amerzgane
Ouarzazate
Tizi n'Tichka
Sidi-Rahal
Aït-Barka
(2031m)
Agouim
Tizi n'Tichka
Ourika Valley
Oukaïmeden
Asif Tidili
Asif Ifni
Amerzgane
Anezal
Tazenakht
Tasselift
(2002m)
Tisfrioudine
Marrakesh
Tahanaoûte
Jebel Toubkal (4167m)
Jebel Siroua (3304m)
Askaoun
Tachokchte
Anezal
Taliouine
(2002m)
Asarrakh
Oudaïa
Guemassa
Adassil
Jebel Tichka (3350m)
Tizi n'Test (2092m)
Aoufour
Aoulouz
Algou
Canal
Oued Nfiss
Oued Tensift
Aït-bou-Rliah
Aït-Ourir
P10
Ej-Jemima
Thine-de-Tigouda
Olad Berhil
To Taroudannt & Agadir
Oulad-Brahim
Bou-Laouane
Chichaoua
To Essaouira

Pistes: impassable in bad weather

P24 P31 S513 S501 P10

0 25 50km
0 15 30mi

Spring and autumn are the best times to explore the area; the midsummer heat will have you sweating your socks off. However, spring is also sandstorm season so don't set off into the desert without preparing for it adequately, and allow a few days there to ensure you actually get to see the dunes, rather than a face full of sand.

MARRAKESH

☎ 04 • pop 1.5 million

Basking in the clear African light of the south, Marrakesh has an entirely different feel from its sister cities to the north. It remains unmistakably more African than cosmopolitan Casablanca, more Moroccan than sanitised Rabat, and more Berber than proud and aloof Fès.

Positioned on an important crossroads, Morocco's fourth-largest city is still regarded as the southern capital, and as such attracts merchants and traders from the surrounding plains, High Atlas and the Sahara.

Just as the colour blue is synonymous with Fès, green with Meknès and white with Rabat, red has become the colour of Marrakesh. A local Berber legend has it that when the Koutoubia was planted in the city's heart, it poured so much blood that all the walls, houses and roads turned this colour. Today the red of the earth walls surrounding the medina and its flat-roofed houses is that of still-raw scars and at dusk, in the last rays of the setting sun, you could almost believe the blood is flowing again as the walls of the city turn crimson. Don't miss it.

The best time to visit is undoubtedly early spring. If you can, avoid Marrakesh during the sticky months of July and August.

History

Founded in 1062 by the Almoravid sultan Youssef bin Tachfin, Marrakesh was to become one of the Islamic world's most important artistic and cultural centres. Using much of the wealth plundered during the Almoravid conquest of Spain, he continued extending and beautifying the city. When he died in 1106, he could do so content in the knowledge that he had not only consolidated control of Morocco and Spain, but he had also bequeathed an urban jewel to his successors.

However, Marrakesh's heyday came under Youssef's son, Ali, born to a Christian slave mother. As well as palaces and baths, Ali commissioned construction of the extensive *khettara* (underground irrigation canals), which still supply the city's gardens. Meanwhile, inside the city's red stone and earthen ramparts, artisans from Muslim Spain were busy erecting the first of the refined, Andalusian-style buildings that were to grace the city.

Sadly, much was razed by the Almohads in 1147, although the walls and the gateway to Ali's huge palace were spared. The city was rebuilt shortly afterwards and again artisans from Andalusia were responsible for much of the construction. Marrakesh was to remain the capital until the collapse of the Almohad dynasty in 1269, when the conquering Merenids decided to rule from Fès.

With the rise to power of the Saadians in the 16th century, Marrakesh again became the capital. Prior to this, times had been hard; the Portuguese tried to capture it in 1515, and then famines crippled it and the surrounding countryside. Now the city prospered again and the *mellah* (Jewish quarter), the huge Mouassine Mosque and the Ali ben Youssef Medersa were built. A customs house for the Christian colony that had emerged was also established.

One of the more outstanding of the Saadian sultans, Ahmed al-Mansour – known as 'the Golden One' because of his riches, largely accumulated in his 'conquest' of Timbuktu – left his mark with the exquisite El-Badi Palace and the long-hidden Saadian tombs.

Again, the golden days were soon followed by chaos and decadence as the Saadians' successors, the Alawites, moved the capital to Meknès. Marrakesh could not be ignored, however, and while Moulay Ismail was responsible for tearing apart the El-Badi Palace for building materials, his successor, Sidi Mohammed ben Abdallah, poured resources into rebuilding or restoring the walls, kasbah, palaces, mosques and *mechouars* (royal parade grounds), as well

CENTRAL MOROCCO

MARRAKESH

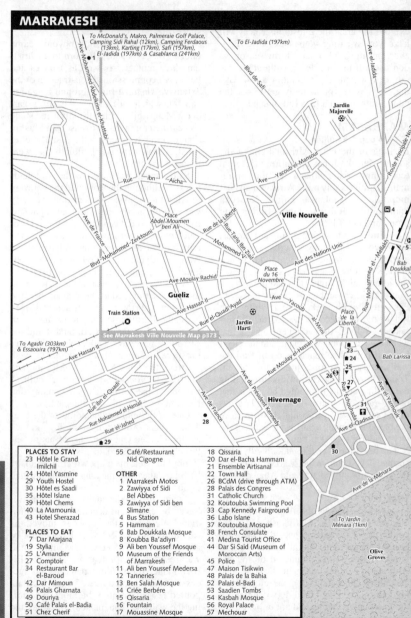

To McDonald's, Makro, Palmeraie Golf Palace, Camping Sidi Rahal (12km), Camping Ferdaous (13km), Karting (17km), Safi (157km), El-Jadida (197km) & Casablanca (241km)

To El-Jadida (197km)

Ave Mohammed Abdelkrim el-Khattabi

Ave el-Jadida

Blvd de Safi

Jardin Majorelle

Route Principale No-24

Rue ibn Aicha

Ave Yacoub el-Mansour

Ville Nouvelle

Ave de France

Place Abdel.Moumen ben Ali

Rue de la Liberté

Rue Tariq Ibn Ziad

Blvd Mohammed 'Zerktouni'

Mohammed V

Ave des Nations Unis

Rue Mohammed el - Mellah

Bab Doukkala

Ave Moulay Rachid

Place du 16 Novembre

Gueliz

Ave Yacoub al-Mrin

Ave Hassan II

Rue el-Quadi Ayad

Place de la Liberté

Train Station

Jardin Harti

Bab Larissa

See Marrakesh Ville Nouvelle Map p373

To Agadir (303km) & Essaouira (197km)

Ave Hassan II

Rue Ibn el-Quadi

Rue Mohammed el-Hansali

Rue el-Jahed

Ave de France

Rue Moulay el-Hassan

Ave du Président Kennedy

Hivernage

Rue Echouhada

Ave el-Yarmouk

Ave el-Qadissa

To Jardin Ménara (1km)

Ave de la Ménara

Olive Groves

PLACES TO STAY	55 Café/Restaurant	18 Qissaria
23 Hôtel le Grand	Nid Cigogne	20 Dar el-Bacha Hammam
Imilchil		21 Ensemble Artisanal
24 Hôtel Yasmine	**OTHER**	22 Town Hall
29 Youth Hostel	1 Marrakesh Motos	26 BCdM (drive through ATM)
30 Hôtel es Saadi	2 Zawiyya of Sidi	28 Palais des Congres
35 Hôtel Islane	Bel Abbes	31 Catholic Church
39 Hôtel Chems	3 Zawiyya of Sidi ben	32 Koutoubia Swimming Pool
40 La Mamounia	Slimane	33 Cap Kennedy Fairground
43 Hotel Sherazad	4 Bus Station	36 Labo Islane
	5 Hammam	37 Koutoubia Mosque
PLACES TO EAT	6 Bab Doukkala Mosque	38 French Consulate
7 Dar Marjana	8 Koubba Ba'adiyn	41 Medina Tourist Office
19 Stylia	9 Ali ben Youssef Mosque	44 Dar Si Said (Museum of
25 L'Amandier	10 Museum of the Friends	Moroccan Arts)
27 Comptoir	of Marrakesh	45 Police
34 Restaurant Bar	11 Ali ben Youssef Medersa	47 Maison Tisikwin
el-Baroud	12 Tanneries	49 Palais de la Bahia
42 Dar Mimoun	13 Ben Salah Mosque	52 Palais el-Badi
48 Palais Gharnata	14 Criée Berbère	53 Saadien Tombs
49 Douriya	15 Qissaria	54 Kasbah Mosque
50 Café Palais el-Badia	16 Fountain	56 Royal Palace
51 Chez Cherif	17 Mouassine Mosque	57 Mechouar

CENTRAL MOROCCO

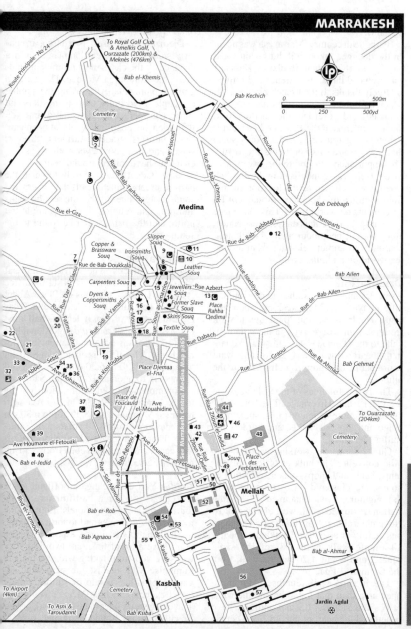

MARRAKESH

Route Principale- No 24

To Royal Golf Club
& Amelkis Golf,
Ourzazate (200km) &
Meknès (476km)

Bab el-Khemis

Bab Kechich

0   250   500m
0   250   500yd

Cemetery

Rue Assouel

Rue de Bab-Tarhzout

Rue de Bab-Khemis

3

Medina

Bab Debbagh

Rue el-Gza

Rue de Bab-Debbagh

Remparts

12

Slipper
Souq

11

Copper &
Brassware
Souq

Ironsmiths
Souq

9

7

Rue de Bab Doukkala

8

10

Leather
Souq

Bab Ailen

6

Carpenters Souq

15

Jewellers
Souq

Rue Azbezt

Rue de- Bab Ailen

Dyers &
Coppersmiths
Souq

14

13

Former Slave
Souq

Place
Rahba
Qedima

16

Skins Souq

17

Rue Soua as-Smarine

20

18

Textile Souq

Rue Dabach

Rue Issettyine

22

Rue Sidi el-Yamani

Rue Dar el-Glaoui

Rue Fatima Zahra

Rue Sidi el-Yamani

Rue Mouassine

19

Graoui

Rue Ba-Ahmad

21

Place Djemaa
el-Fna

Bab Gehmat

33

Sebti

34   35

Rue

32

Rue Abbes

36

Ave Mohammed V

Rue el-Koutoubia

Place de
Foucauld

Ave
el-Mouahidine

To Ouarzazate
(204km)

37

38

Cemetery

39

44

Ave Houmane el-Fetouaki

45

46

41

40

43

42

47

48

Bab el-Jedid

Souq

49

Place
des
Ferblantiers

Ave Houmane- el-Fetouaki

Rue Riad Zitoun el-Jedid

Bab Agnaou

Rue Sidi Mamoun

Rue Riad Zitoun el-Kedim

51

50

Mellah

Blvd el-Yarmouk

Bab er-Rob

52

54

53

Bab Agnaou

55

Rue de la Kasbah

Bab al-Ahmar

To Airport
(4km)

Kasbah

56

To Asni &
Taroudannt

Cemetery

Bab Ksiba

57

Jardin Agdal

See Marrakesh Central Medina Map p365

CENTRAL MOROCCO

as creating new gardens (such as the Jardin Ménara).

By the 19th century, Marrakesh was again on the decline, although it did regain some prestige in 1873 when Moulay al-Hassan I was crowned there. Its current good fortune is largely thanks to the French protectorate, which built the *ville nouvelle* (new city), revitalised and resettled the medina (old town), and created the Place de Foucauld.

Increasing tourism in Marrakesh since then has ensured its continued prosperity. The importance attached to the city by Morocco itself was symbolised in April 1994, when it was chosen as the location for the final signing of the international GATT agreements on world trade. This took place in the impressive Palais du Congress which, along with its neighbouring five-star hotels, continues to attract delegates from around the world on a regular basis.

Orientation

As in Fès and Meknès, the old city and the ville nouvelle of Marrakesh are about the same size. It takes about 30 minutes to walk from the centre of activity in the ville nouvelle to the Djemaa el-Fna, the main square in the heart of the old city, so you may want to use public transport to get from one to the other.

The two main areas of the ville nouvelle are Gueliz and Hivernage. The latter contains little more of interest than some midrange and top-end hotels, and borders the Jardin Ménara.

Gueliz forms the working centre of the ville nouvelle. The bulk of offices, restaurants, cafes and shops, plus a collection of hotels, are clustered on or near the main thoroughfare, Ave Mohammed V. The train station is situated south-west of Place du 16 Novembre along Ave Hassan II. The main bus station is near Bab Doukkala, about a 10-minute walk north-east of the same square, and about a 20-minute walk from the Djemaa el-Fna.

The medina walls enclose a far more open area than that found behind the walls of Fès and Meknès. It is not until you have penetrated the heart of the old city, Djemaa el-Fna, that you reach the traditional maze of souqs and twisting alleys.

Djemaa el-Fna itself is a large, irregularly shaped open area dominated from a distance by the city's most prominent landmark, the Koutoubia Mosque. There are no grand monuments overlooking the jumble of people, food stalls, tourists, hustlers and snake charmers who give it life, but you will soon be beguiled by its atmosphere. For centuries, traders, farmers, thieves, slaves and just about every other possible character have milled around here.

Most budget hotels are clustered in the narrow streets branching off the eastern and south-eastern sides of the square. The souqs and principal religious buildings are to the north, and the palaces can be found to the south.

Information

Tourist Offices The Office National Marocain Tourisme (ONMT) office (☎ 436131, fax 436057) is on Place Abdel Moumen ben Ali in the ville nouvelle. It has the usual range of glossy leaflets and a list of classified hotels and *riad* (traditional lavish town house) accommodation, but not much else. The office is open from 8.30 am to noon and 3.30 to 6.30 pm weekdays and from 9 am to noon and 3 to 5 pm Saturday.

For more localised information, try the tourist bureau (☎ 430886) at 170 Ave Mohammed V (open from 8.30 am to 6.30 pm weekdays and from 8.30 am to noon Saturday). There is a separate medina tourist office near La Mamounia (open from 8.30 am to noon and 3 to 6 pm weekdays).

Guides You can arrange an official guide for Dr120/150 for a half/full day at the tourist office or bigger hotels. Entry to the monuments, taxi rides and so forth are extra.

The benefits of a guide, especially if you don't have a lot of time, are two-fold: they can save you from taking wrong turns and immunise you against the persistent advances of other would-be guides. Many travel agencies such as Ménara Tours (see Travel Agencies later in this section), organise city tours for around Dr200 per person.

Money You should have no trouble changing money and there are plenty of banks with ATMs both in the ville nouvelle and medina. There is even a branch of the BCdM with a drive-through ATM facility in Hivernage.

Most banks, including the Bank al-Maghrib (Banque du Maroc) on the Place Djemaa el-Fna, will change cash and travellers cheques.

American Express (AmEx) is represented by Voyages Schwartz (☎ 436600, 436603) on the 1st floor of Immeuble Moutaouakil, at 1 Rue Mauritania in the ville nouvelle. It is supposed to be open from 9 am to 1 pm daily, though there never seems to be anyone there.

Post & Communications The main post office is on Place du 16 Novembre in the ville nouvelle. It's open the usual hours and poste restante is at window No 6. There is a parcel office around the corner on Ave Hassan II. The rather small phone office is to the left of the main entrance and is open from 8.30 am to 9 pm daily.

There's another post office, flanked by phones, on the Djemaa el-Fna.

There's a DHL office (☎ 437647) at Residence el-Mouhandiz, 133 Ave Abdelkrim el-Khattabi.

There are heaps of Internet cafes in the Gueliz and the medina (marked on the maps) charging between Dr15 and Dr20 an hour.

Travel Agencies The bulk of the travel agencies, and Royal Air Maroc (RAM), are around Ave Mohammed V, west of Place du 16 Novembre in Gueliz.

These include the Carlson Wagonlits agency (☎ 431687, fax 624436) at 122 Ave Mohammed V, Ménara Tours (☎ 446654, fax 446107) at 41 Rue de Yougoslavie, and Atlas Voyages (☎ 841913).

Bookshops For books in English, about the best option is the American Language Center bookshop (see Cultural Centres later), which has a range of English literature and titles on Morocco.

The best bookshop in town for French speakers is the Librairie Amor (☎ 447997) at 19–21 Ave Mohammed V in the ville nouvelle.

International newspapers can be bought from stands around town, including one opposite Hôtel Mandalay in Gueliz and another in front of Hôtel CTM on Djemaa el-Fna.

Libraire d'art, next to L'Entrecote restaurant, has a fabulous selection of art and travel books in French and English and is a good place for a browse.

Film & Photography There are several places along Ave Mohammed V where you can buy film and get it processed.

Two photo labs with good reputations are Labo Islane (☎ 444691), close to the Hôtel Islane at 279 Ave Mohammed V; and Felix Labo, at 133 Ave Mohammed V in the ville nouvelle.

Cultural Centres The Institut Français (☎ 446930, e ifm@mbox.azure.net) is in the ville nouvelle, off Route de la Targa, close to the Victor Hugo school. It's an active, well-run place, which, apart from French classes, organises a range of films, plays, lectures and the like which are open to all. The library houses a good collection of books on Islam and the Arab world.

The institut is open from 8.30 am to noon and 2.30 to 6.30 pm Tuesday to Sunday (to 10 pm Tuesday). There's an annexe near Djemaa el-Fna handy for ticket sales. This is open from 3 to 7 pm Monday to Saturday.

There's a branch of the American Language Center (☎ 447259, e alc@iam.net.ma) in the ville nouvelle at 3 Impasse du Moulin. The center's main activity is holding English classes for Marrakshis – it begins recruiting staff for the start of the academic year (September) in spring. You'll need a curriculum vitae (resume), photos and a contact telephone number to apply for work. It also has notices recruiting extras for any US-backed films that may be shooting around Morocco.

Otherwise, the centre organises the occasional film and lecture, and has a small library. It is open from 9 am to noon and 3 to 7 pm weekdays and from 9 am to noon on Saturday.

Medical Services There are night pharmacies on Rue Khalid ben el-Oualid (☎ 434275), just off Place de la Liberté in the ville nouvelle (a doctor is also permanently available) and next to Club Med on Place Djemaa el-Fna. Also on Place Djemaa el-Fna is a Red Cross clinic for emergencies. Ambulances can be called on ☎ 443724.

Church Services The Catholic church (built in 1926) is in the ville nouvelle, south of Ave Yacoub al-Mrinis. The church itself is a nice example of the European interpretation of Moroccan architecture. Mass is celebrated at 6.30 pm daily, with an extra service at 10.30 am Sunday.

The Protestant church (☎ 431479) in Hivernage doesn't have a minister, so services are held once monthly only.

Dangers & Annoyances Marrakesh has long been a magnet for travellers, and during the early 1960s and 1970s formed a part of the hippie trail, along with Istanbul, Kabul and Kathmandu. Hot on the hippies' heels were hordes of package tourists armed with much more money but far less time. In a city with little money and a large population with nothing but time on its hands, this onslaught gave birth to the rise and rise of Morocco's most unpleasant phenomenon, the *faux guide* (informal guide; see the boxed text 'Green, Gauche & Gullible' in the Facts for the Visitor chapter).

Recent laws have significantly reduced, but not yet eliminated, the problem of the faux guides, and as long as unemployment remains at such high levels, they will probably never be entirely eradicated. The majority hang about the main entrances to the souqs on Djemaa el-Fna. Once inside the souqs proper, you should be left alone. If you end up with someone more persistent who follows you in, remember that their main interest is in making a commission on articles sold to you in the souqs (and you really shouldn't pay them more than about Dr25 for two or three hours).

First-time visitors may find the souq 'experience' rather overwhelming. If you wish to purchase something, prepare yourself for some extreme hard-sell. Shop owners size up their potential clients early on, and it is claimed they have a sliding scale of prices according to how much cash and how little sense they credit you with. Some of them can get quite nasty if you don't want to buy.

Try and remain polite, calm and firm and remember you're the customer and are under no obligation to buy anything. That said, don't spend a lot of time in any one shop unless you are seriously interested; otherwise, you may well be in for a very wearing, some would even say traumatic, experience.

The combination of hustlers and heavy-sell has had an adverse effect on the city's tourism. According to a government study, 94% of first-time visitors to Marrakesh never come back for seconds! This is one of the lowest rates for a city in the entire world.

The best approach is to do what the Moroccans do – ignore unwanted attention entirely – and above all keep your sense of humour.

As if the hard-sell wasn't bad enough, time-share operators have been spotted around such touristy areas as Jardin Majorelle. Don't get sucked in by the 'Wow, you've won a holiday' routine unless you're actually interested in investing in holidays for life.

Djemaa el-Fna

The focal point of Marrakesh is the Djemaa el-Fna, a huge square in the medina, and the backdrop for one of the world's greatest spectacles. According to the author Paul Bowles, without it, Marrakesh would be just another Moroccan city. Other than the souqs, this is where everything happens and you'll find yourself drawn back time after time.

Although it's lively at any hour of day (look out for the Berber acrobats around 4 pm), it comes into its own with the setting of the sun. Then the curtain goes up on rows and rows of open-air food stalls smoking the immediate area with mouth-watering aromas. Jugglers, storytellers, snake charmers, magicians, acrobats and benign lunatics consume the remaining space, each surrounded by jostling spectators who listen and watch intently, or fall about laughing before moving on to the next act. Naturally, tourists are soon singled out and cajoled into joining in; however, few (Moroccans included) get away without paying a few dirham for the show.

In between the groups of spectators, diners, shoppers and tourists, weave hustlers, thieves, knick-knack sellers and the occasional glue-sniffing kid. On the outer edges, kerosene lanterns ablaze, are the fruit and juice stalls. Beyond them, hunched on the ground with their eye-catching wares spread before them are the herbalists poised to prescribe a potion for whatever ails you.

It is a scene that, to one extent or another, was played out in the great squares of many Moroccan cities. Unfortunately, TV and modernisation has killed off much of it elsewhere. The curtain threatened to fall here too, with the proposal of a car park to take its place. Fortunately, the powers that be agreed that the show must go on and the medieval pageantry was saved.

Many believe that it is the tourists who fuel the activity in the Djemaa el-Fna. This may be true in the case of the water sellers and snake charmers, but it doesn't explain the crowds around the storytellers. Few tourists understand the marvels or lunacies they are recounting, to the obvious delight of locals.

Once you've wandered the stalls, take a balcony seat in a rooftop cafe or restaurant (see Places to Eat) to absorb the spectacle at a more relaxing and voyeuristic distance.

Souqs

Just as the Djemaa el-Fna is famous for its energy and life, the souqs of the Marrakesh medina are renowned for their variety of high-quality crafts, as well as a fair amount of rubbish and a lot of hassle.

The streets here are just as labyrinthine as in Fès and every bit as busy. But then as abruptly as they started, the shops selling arts and crafts come to an end at the Ali ben Youssef Mosque, making the hard-sell part of the medina comparatively compact.

It might be a good idea to engage a guide for your first excursion into the medina's

MARRAKESH CENTRAL MEDINA

PLACES TO STAY
5 Hôtel el-Kennaria
6 Hôtel Mimosa
7 Hôtel/Cafe/Restaurant de France
8 Résidence de la Place
15 Hôtel CTM
26 Hôtel Ali; Internet Cafe
29 Hôtel Ichbilia
31 Hôtel Central Palace
32 Hôtel Afriquia
33 Hôtel Essaouira
34 Hôtel Medina
35 Hôtel Chellah
36 Hôtel Gallia
37 Hôtel Souria
39 Hôtel el-Atlal
40 Hôtel Sahara
46 Hôtel la Gazelle
51 Hôtel de Foucauld
56 Grand Hôtel du Tazi

PLACES TO EAT
3 Café Restaurant Chez Chegrouni
4 Restaurant le Marrakchi
9 Quissaria Food Stalls
10 Argana
11 Juice Stands
12 Central Market
14 Café Glacier
25 Pâtisserie Mik Mak
30 Pâtisserie des Princes
41 Snack Sahara
45 Restaurant el-Bahja

OTHER
1 BCdM
2 Qessabin Mosque
13 Red Cross Clinic
16 Banque Populaire
17 Pharmacy
18 Hammam
19 Crédit du Maroc (ATM)
20 Bank al-Maghrib
21 Petit Taxis
22 Night Pharmacy
23 Calèche Stand
24 Post & Phone Office
27 Newsstand
28 Wafa Bank
38 Bain Polo (Hammam)
42 Bicycle Hire
43 Banque Populaire
44 Cinéma Mabrouka
47 BMCE (ATM)
48 Institut Français
49 Petrol Station
50 Local Buses
52 BMCI (ATM)
53 Petrol Station
54 Cyber Internet
55 Internet Cafe

CENTRAL MOROCCO

souqs and monuments. This is not to say that you really need one. However tortuous the lanes become, the first rule of navigation applies – keep to the main streets and you will always emerge, eventually, at a landmark or city gate. As you wander through the various souqs there are plenty of opportunities to watch artisans at work fashioning slippers, weaving rugs, dyeing textiles and hammering metals.

Most of the shops in the souqs have stickers displaying the fact that they accept AmEx, Diners Club, Visa and MasterCard, as well as many other more obscure credit cards.

The main entrance to the souqs is along Rue Souq as-Smarrine, behind the potters souq on Djemaa el-Fna and flanked mainly by **textiles** shops and souvenir stalls. Inside the main entrance, and to the left, is the first **qissaria** (covered market).

Just before Rue Souq as-Smarrine forks into Rue Souq al-Kebir and Rue Souq al-Attarine, a narrow lane to the right leads to the Place Rahba Qedima, a small square given over mainly to **carpet** and **sheepskin** sales. There are also **apothecary** stalls on the southern edge with all kinds of ingredients for magical potions – check out the caged iguanas. To the north of the square is the carpet souq, also known as the **Criée Berbère**. It was in this area that slaves were auctioned off to the highest bidders until the French put a stop to the trade in 1912.

Back on Rue Souq as-Smarrine, you could take either fork. Both more or less lead to the Ali ben Youssef Mosque and Medersa.

If you take the left fork, you will pass **spice** and **perfume** shops before reaching the **dyers** souq, where colourful skeins hang overhead. Continuing, you end up among **carpenters** and **blacksmiths**, who rely little on tourists and therefore pay them little attention. With a little luck, you'll emerge at either the mosque or the Koubba Ba'adiyn.

Along the right fork, you'll first encounter **jewellers**, then more **qissariat**, stocked with westernised goods, which give way to **leatherwork** and **babouche** (leather slipper) shops.

An alternative route back to the Djemaa el-Fna could take you to the west via the

Remedies and Cures

Pre-Islamic folklore is still widespread in Morocco. A trip to a good spice market in any souq will bear that out. In cages, stuffed or dried, you'll find an extraordinary collection of amphibians, reptiles, bird and mammals. What to do with them?

For 'syphilis of the throat and mouth, swallow the ashes of a crow which has been knocked down and stunned, then cremated in a new cooking pot'.

Syphilis used to be so widespread in Morocco that there is a saying: 'He who doesn't have syphilis in this world will have it in the next'.

Mouassin Mosque and the **coppersmiths** souq.

Mosques, Medersas & Koubbas

Like their counterparts elsewhere in Morocco, the mosques and working *medersas* (theological colleges) in Marrakesh are generally closed to non-Muslims. Those inside the medina are so hemmed in by other buildings that little can be seen from the outside.

Koutoubia Mosque The only mosque that has a perspective you can really appreciate, and the one you are most likely to encounter first, is the Koutoubia, across the other side of Place de Foucauld, south-west of the Djemaa el-Fna. It is also the tallest (70m) and most famous landmark in Marrakesh, visible for miles in any direction.

Constructed by the Almohads in the late 12th century on the site of a previous 11th-century Almoravid mosque, it features the oldest and best preserved of their three most famous minarets – the others are the Tour Hassan in Rabat and the Giralda in Seville (Spain). The name (from *koutoub* or *kutub*, Arabic for books) comes from a booksellers' market that once existed around the mosque.

The Koutoubia minaret is a classic of Moroccan-Andalusian architecture; its features are mirrored in many other minarets throughout the country, but not one of these matches the Koutoubia's for sheer size.

When first built, the Koutoubia was covered with painted plaster and brilliantly coloured *zellij* (tilework), but this decoration has all disappeared. What can still be seen, however, are the decorative panels, which are different on each face and practically constitute a textbook of Islamic design.

The views from the summit would be incredible, if non-Muslims were allowed to climb up there. Compensation lies in the attached paved and flowered gardens, which everyone is free to wander around, although there is very little shade. The excavations here are from the original mosque and Almoravid kasbah.

Koubba Ba'adiyn After a stroll up through the souqs, the first monument open to non-Muslims (although it was closed at the time of research) that you'll probably reach is one of the smallest Marrakesh has to offer, but (restoration aside) about the oldest.

Although most of Almoravid Marrakesh was destroyed by the zealous Almohads who succeeded them, the koubba, thought to have been an ablutions block for the nearby mosque, is a rare exception. Built in the early 12th century, it is a small but elegant display of Muslim decorative invention, much of which appears to have been developed during the construction of this structure.

Signposted on a small square in front of the Ali ben Youssef Mosque, entrance to the koubba is Dr10 and the guardian will want to show you around. He'll probably dig up a friend to 'guide' you to the Ali ben Youssef Medersa too, although it's just around the corner.

Ali ben Youssef Mosque The largest of the mosques inside the medina is the Ali ben Youssef Mosque, first built in the second half of the 12th century by the Almoravid sultan of the same name.

It's the oldest surviving mosque in Marrakesh, but the building itself is fairly recent, as it was almost completely rebuilt in the 19th century in the Merenid style in response to popular demand.

When first constructed it was about twice its present size, but it was severely damaged when the Almoravids were overthrown by the Almohads. It was later restored by both the Almohads and the Saadians. The mosque is closed to non-Muslims.

Ali ben Youssef Medersa Next to the Ali ben Youssef Mosque is the medersa of the same name, a beautiful and still peaceful and meditative place with some stunning examples of stucco decoration.

The medersa is the largest theological college in the Maghreb and was built by the Saadians in 1565 (and much restored in the 1960s). Heading east from the koubba, simply follow the mosque walls around to the left, and you'll come to the entrance of the medersa on your right.

Although all Moroccan medersas at least loosely follow a similar ground plan (see the special section 'Moroccan Architecture' in the Facts about Morocco chapter), the Ali ben Youssef is not only bigger, but also quite different in layout.

You walk down a corridor and turn right onto the central courtyard, entering where you find yourself facing the masjid (mosque). Like virtually every other great medersa on view to non-Muslims, this was built under the Merenids and is typical of the style of those times, with intricate stucco decoration combined with a zellij base and crowned by carved cedar.

Go back to the corridor and take the entrance opposite the courtyard. Two sets of stairs lead up to students' cells. As usual, they are small and bare. It's hard to imagine how, as is claimed, they crammed as many as 900 people into these rooms!

The big difference between their arrangement here and that in other medersas is that many of them are clustered around seven small and charming 'minicourtyards'. Moreover, a few look out on to the street – somewhat of an exception to the general rule of Moroccan and Andalusian architecture.

The medersa, which is undergoing renovation, is open from 9 am to 6 pm daily, and entry costs Dr10.

Mouassine Mosque The other big mosque in the medina is the Mouassine Mosque, built in the 16th century by the Saadians on land formerly occupied by the Jewish community.

Its most notable features are the three huge doorways and the intricately carved cedar ceilings. The fountain attached to this mosque still survives and is quite elaborate, with three sections: two for animals and one for humans. The mosque is closed to non-Muslims.

Ben Salah Mosque Of the other mosques in the medina, the Ben Salah Mosque (also known as the Ben Salah Zawiyya) is the most prominent; its brilliant green-tiled minaret can be seen from afar. It was built by the Merenid sultan Abu Said Uthman between 1318 and 1321. Again, it's closed to non-Muslims.

Zawiyyas In the north-western zone of the medina are two *zawiyyas* (locations of religious fraternities) dedicated to two of the seven saints claimed by Marrakesh. Pilgrimage to the tombs of all seven is, in the popular mind at any rate, the equivalent of a pilgrimage to Mecca (a considerably more arduous undertaking for Moroccans).

North of the Sidi ben Slimane Zawiyya is that of Sidi Bel Abbes, the most important of the seven saints. Entry to the sanctuaries is forbidden to non-Muslims.

Palaces & Environs
Palais el-Badi The most famous of the palaces of Marrakesh is the Palais el-Badi, south of Place Djemaa el-Fna. Built by Ahmed al-Mansour between 1578 and 1602, at the time of its construction it was reputed to be one of the most beautiful in the world (and was known as 'the Incomparable'). It included marble from Italy and other precious building materials from as far away as India.

The enormous cost of building the palace was met largely from the ransom the Portuguese were forced to pay out following their disastrous defeat at the hands of the Saadians in 1578 in the Battle of the Three Kings.

Unfortunately, the palace is now largely a ruin, having been torn apart by Moulay Ismail in 1696 for its materials, which were used to build his new capital at Meknès.

What remains is essentially a huge square surrounded by devastated walls enclosing a sunken orange grove and a number of modern concrete pools. When you're inside by the orange grove, you'll notice a large structure to the west. This is the Koubba al-Khamsiniyya, which was used as a great reception hall on state occasions and was named after its 50 marble columns.

Proceed south towards the walls of the Royal Palace (which is closed to visitors) and you'll find yourself in a confusing maze of underground corridors, storerooms and dungeons. For lovers of dark places, there's a bit of potential exploring to do – bring a torch (flashlight).

The Palais el-Badi is open to the public from 8.30 to 11.45 am and 2.30 to 5.45 pm daily, except on certain religious holidays. Entry costs Dr10. You're free to wander around on your own, although guides will initially hassle you to engage their services. The palace is also the venue for the annual Folklore Festival, usually held in June.

The easiest way to get to the palace is to take Ave Houmane el-Fetouaki down from the Koutoubia Mosque to Place des Ferblantiers, where the ramparts begin, and you'll see a large gate. Go through this and turn right. The entrance and ticket booth are straight ahead.

Palais de la Bahia The Palais de la Bahia was built towards the end of the 19th century, over a period of 14 years, as the residence of Si' Ahmed ben Musa (also known as Bou Ahmed), the Grand Vizier of Sultan Moulay al-Hassan I.

On Bou Ahmed's death it was ransacked, but much has since been restored. It's a rambling structure with fountains, living quarters, pleasure gardens and numerous secluded, shady courtyards, but it lacks architectural cohesion. This in no way detracts from the visual pleasure of the place and there's a noticeable difference between the peace, quiet and coolness inside the palace and the heat, noise and chaos in the streets outside.

The Palais exemplifies the priority of privacy in Muslim architecture. You will often

AMERENS HEDWICH

CHRISTOPHER WOOD

CHRISTOPHER WOOD

Middle Atlas rooftop views: the Mausoleum of Moulay Idriss dominates the town of Moulay Idriss (top); the village of Midelt lies in foothills between the Middle Atlas and the High Atlas (middle); the complex sprawl of the imperial city of Fès from the Borj Sud (bottom)

Marrakesh moments: the red hue of houses has become synonymous with the central Moroccan city of Marrakesh (top left); Berber dancers take a break (top right); the focal point of Marrakesh, the lively Djemaa el-Fna is an open square by day and impromptu concert arena by night (bottom)

find that the multiple doorways linking various parts of the palace are so placed that you often can't see much past the open doorway, creating the impression of a series of separate and unconnected zones within the whole.

You can only visit part of the palace, as some of it is still used by the royal family and to house maintenance staff. You will be taken through a series of rooms, among them the vizier's sleeping quarters (he had separate ones for snoozing during the day and evening) and various courtyards set aside for his wives and concubines. The four wives each had a room arranged around a courtyard. The sleeping quarters for the rather more numerous concubines were also gathered around a (separate) courtyard.

The palace is open from 8.30 to 11.15 am and 2.30 to 5.45 pm daily and from 8.30 to 11.30 am and 3 to 5.45 pm Friday. Entry is free, but you must take and pay a guide.

To get there (orientation is easiest from the Palais el-Badi), go back to the Place des Ferblantiers, and keep following Ave Houmane el-Fetouaki away from the budget hotel area and around to the left (north). You'll soon come to the entrance, set in a garden, on your right.

Dar Si Said Further north of the Palais de la Bahia and again off to the right (it's signposted), the Dar Si Said, which now houses the **Museum of Moroccan Arts**, is well worth a visit.

Sidi Said, Bou Ahmed's brother, built what became his town house at about the same time as the grand vizier's palace was constructed. Today, the museum houses one of the finest collections in the country, including jewellery from the High Atlas, the Anti Atlas and the extreme south; carpets from the Haouz and the High Atlas; oil lamps from Taroudannt; blue pottery from Safi and green pottery from Tamegroute; and leatherwork from Marrakesh.

As you enter, you will see a series of doors typical of the richer High Atlas and Anti Atlas houses. At the end of this corridor is the oldest exhibit in the museum: an old marble basin dating back to about 1000,

brought to Marrakesh from Spain by Ali ben Youssef.

Next up are some delightful medieval precursors of the Ferris wheel for tiny tots.

The central garden and courtyard is flanked by rooms housing displays of heavy southern jewellery in silver, traditional women's garments, household goods, old muskets and daggers.

On the next floor is a magnificently decorated room; its characteristic stucco and zellij capped by a stunning carved and painted cedar ceiling. From here, the signs lead you upstairs again and then down through various rooms dominated by rug and carpet displays. All the explanations are, unfortunately, in Arabic and French only.

It's open from 9 to 11.45 am and 2.30 to 5.45 pm Monday, Wednesday, Thursday, Saturday and Sunday; and from 9 to 11.30 am and 3 to 5.45 pm Friday. Entry costs Dr10.

Museum of the Friends of Marrakesh Inaugurated in March 1997, the Omar Benjelloun Foundation's museum is housed in a beautifully restored 19th-century riad with some very impressive zellij work. Not only does the house have a serene central courtyard with fountains around which galleries display artworks, it also allows the visitor an insight into household features such as the original *hammam* (traditional bathhouse).

Displays include clothing, maps, manuscripts, jewellery, arms, ceramics and old currency, and there is also a gallery dedicated to changing contemporary art exhibitions.

Entry costs Dr10/20 for children/adults and the museum is open from 9 am to 6.30 pm daily. There is also a courtyard cafe and a gift shop selling a good selection of art books, posters and postcards.

Maison Tiskiwin En route to the Dar Si Said is Maison Tiskiwin (☎ 443335), the house of Bert Flint, a Dutch art lecturer and long-time resident of Morocco.

Open to the public as a small museum, it has displays of basketwork, lots of carved Berber doors and locks, carpets, jewellery and textiles. You're reminded you're in a home by cosy lounge areas and delicious cooking smells, and it's a pleasant retreat. Entry costs Dr10 and it's open from 9.30 am to 12.30 pm and 3 to 6.30 pm daily. If the big wooden door is closed during these times, simply knock on it to be let in.

Mellah

The old Jewish quarter, established in the 16th century, is just south of the Palais de la Bahia. Much neglected and now populated mainly by Muslims, it still has quite a different look from the rest of the city.

The main entrance is off Place des Ferblantiers through the qissaria, and if you want to visit any of the small synagogues (one is still in use), you'll need a local guide.

Saadian Tombs

Alongside the Kasbah Mosque is this necropolis, started by the Saadian sultan Ahmed al-Mansour in the late 1500s. Unlike the Palais el-Badi, another of al-Mansour's projects, the tombs escaped Moulay Ismail's depredations – possibly because he was superstitious about plundering the dead. Instead he sealed the tombs and, as a result, they still convey some of the opulence and superb artistry that must also have been lavished on the palace.

Although the mad sultan Moulay Yazid was laid to rest here in 1792, the tombs essentially remained sealed following Moulay Ismail's reign. They were not 'rediscovered' until 1917 when General Lyautey, his curiosity awakened by an aerial survey of the area, ordered the construction of a passageway down into the tombs. They have since been restored.

The mausoleum is divided into three small halls. There are 66 Saadians, including al-Mansour, his successors and their closest family members, buried under the two main structures, and there are more than 100 buried outside the buildings. The halls at either end contain tombs of children. The central Hall of the Twelve Columns is held to be one of the finest examples of Moroccan-Andalusian decorative art. Among the columns of Italian marble are the tombs of Ahmed al-Mansour, his son and grandson. The elegant little mausoleum, set further in, houses the tomb of al-Mansour's mother.

The tombs are signposted down a narrow alleyway at the southern edge of the Kasbah Mosque. After buying your ticket, you follow a very narrow passage that opens onto the main mausoleum.

The tombs are open from 8 am to noon and 2.30 to 7 pm (6 pm in winter) daily, except Friday morning. Entry costs Dr10 and you're allowed to wander around at will – it doesn't take long. If you prefer, a guardian will accompany you and explain what you are looking at. A tip will be expected.

Tanneries

The tanneries are out by Bab Debbagh, at the north-eastern end of the medina and a reasonably straightforward walk from the Ali ben Youssef Mosque.

If you have trouble finding them, just ask for the road to the gate or take up the offer of one of the young lads hanging around the entrance to the medersa to guide you there. They will also no doubt follow you around the tanneries explaining the process (see the colour boxed text 'Tanneries' in this chapter) and will be keen to get you into a leather shop in the hope of earning some commission; otherwise, expect to pay a tip.

Gardens

A slightly more pleasant olfactory experience is provided by the several beautiful gardens, which are laid out around the city. As well as those detailed following, the gardens at La Mamounia (see Places to Stay later) and Jardin Harti offer cool respite.

Jardin Ménara About a 2km walk from the Koutoubia Mosque, along Ave de la Ménara, the Jardin Ménara is the most easily reached of Marrakesh's green spaces. Although it is quite popular with Marrakshis, it is generally a peaceful place to escape the summer heat and bustle of the city.

The centrepiece of what is basically a more organised continuation of the olive groves immediately to the east, is a large still pool backed by a pavilion built in 1866 (you'll see pictures of it in most of the tourist literature). What is now open to the public was once the exclusive preserve of sultans and high ministers.

Jardin Agdal Stretching for several kilometres south from the Royal Palace, the vegetation is more varied here than in the Jardin Ménara and there are several pavilions.

To get there (a bicycle would be ideal), take the path that runs south from the southwestern corner of the mechouar in front of the Royal Palace.

Jardin Majorelle & Museum of Islamic Art Now owned by the French coutourier Yves Saint-Laurent, these cool gardens were laid out by the French painter Jacques Majorelle, who lived here from 1922 to 1962. In among the cacti and bamboo is a deep-blue villa, now housing the museum. The museum has one of those typical Moroccan collections that you'd love to scoop up and take home to decorate your house with. Exhibits, including carpets, wedding curtains, belts, jewellery and manuscripts are labelled in Arabic and French with the odd explanation in English. There's also a 'Kasbahs of the Atlas' exhibition of Majorelle's work.

The gardens, in the ville nouvelle, are open from 8 am to noon and 2 to 5 pm daily (3 to 7 pm in summer). Children, dogs and picnics are not allowed, and they're a bit edgy about 'professional-looking' cameras. Entry to the gardens and museum are Dr15 each.

Golf

You may catch a glimpse of some royalty at the 18-hole (6200m, par 72) Royal Golf Club (☎ 404705), but apart from that a round here seems overpriced. Across the road, the 18-hole Amelkis (6214m) boasts views to the mountains and water features, although it lacks the shade of the Royal. On the road to Casablanca, the 18-hole (6214m, par 72) Palmeraie Golf Palace (☎ 301010) is also shaded with good water features.

Karts & Quad Bikes

Locaquad offers quad-bike trips across 50km of *piste* (unsealed track), through palmeraies and stopping for tea en route. Pilots/passengers pay Dr340/440 and the half-day tour can be booked through the Hôtel Ibis Moussafir.

If you feel like a bit of Grand Prix action, there is a karting circuit (☎ 448163) 17km out on the Safi road.

Swimming

If you fancy a dip, there are a couple of options. The Koutoubia and municipal pools are the cheaper alternative, but it can get very overcrowded and women travellers should be warned that it is almost exclusively the reserve of adolescent male Moroccans. Pools open from June to September only. The second option is the hotels. The Hôtel Ibis Moussafir (see Places to Stay – Mid-Range) charges Dr50 per day to nonguests.

Organised Tours

It is possible to organise tours down the Drâa Valley, into the Atlas Mountains or to the Atlantic coast through agents in Marrakesh. Many organise a range of activities for groups (generally a minimum of four people), and although they cost more than doing it on your own, they are very useful if you've got limited time.

Hôtel Ali (see Places to Stay – Budget) offers good deals for the budget traveller with limited time, although doing it yourself will always be cheaper. It organises day trips to the Cascades d'Ouzoud and two- to four-day trips to Zagora, Merzouga (including the obligatory camel trip into the dunes) and the Todra and Dadès Gorges. The four-day trip taking in all of the previously mentioned costs Dr950; you provide your own drinks and lunch.

The hotel is also a good source of information on High Atlas trekking. Staff can suggest trekking routes from places such as Asni and Imlil, and help find you a guide (state approved). The National Association of Moroccan Mountain Guides (Angamm) can be contacted through them.

Hôtel de Foucauld can help organise mountain-bike excursions, 4WD trips and cross-country skiing.

Ménara Tours (see Travel Agencies earlier in this section) offers day trips to the Ourika Valley (Dr275); Asni, Ouirgane and

Tahanaoute (Dr275); Telouet in the High Atlas (Dr500); and the Cascades d'Ouzoud (waterfalls; Dr450). If you're keen to get off the beaten track, Ménara's 4WD vehicles can take you to more remote, far-flung areas (Dr800). Prices are per person and don't include meals.

Another agency with a good reputation is Pampas Voyages (☎ 431052, fax 446455) in Gallerie Jassim on Ave Mohammed V. It specialises in tailor-made tours of a longer duration into the Atlas Mountains and the Drâa Valley. Among other things, it can organise excursions into the desert with *meharis* (a kind of extra-speedy dromedary!) and bivouacs. Otherwise, it may be worth trying the package-tour operators found in the building next to Hôtel Hasna.

Special Events

If you're in Marrakesh in June (the dates change), inquire about the two-week Festival of Folklore (☎ 446114, e fnap.aga@ucam.ac.ma), which is held in the Palais el-Badi. It's an all singing and folk-dancing extravaganza, performed by some of Morocco's best troupes. Representatives from all over the country congregate to perform and party and there are exhibitions, theme nights and academic meetings. Also during the festival is the opportunity to witness the famous fantasia, a charge of Berber horsemen, which takes place each sunset outside the ramparts near Bab el-Jedid. You often see pictures of it in the tourist literature. Details of the festival can be found at this Web site (French-only): www.ucam.ac.ma/FNAP-AGA

At other times of the year you can relive the whole festival experience at Chez Ali (see Entertainment later in this section).

It's not quite a festival, but if you enjoy watching athletics, you might want to be around at the end of January for the annual Grand Prix de Hassan II Marathon which finishes at the Djemaa el-Fna.

Hammams

There are a couple of hammams a few minutes' walk south of Djemaa el-Fna. The most popular hammam in town is the Dar el-Bacha at 20 Rue Fatima Zohra; it's open for men from 7 pm to midnight, and for women from noon to 7.30 pm.

Places to Stay – Budget

Camping There is no longer any camping within the city limits but if you have your own transport, you can consider *Camping Sidi Rahal* (☎ 436785), 12km out on the El-Jadida road; or *Camping Ferdaous* (☎ 313167), 13km out on the Casablanca road, which has a pool and charges Dr13 per adult and Dr12/17 per tent/caravan.

Hostel The *youth hostel* (☎ 447713, Rue el-Jahed) is close to the train station, so could be a good first stop. Other than that it's a bit far from the action. You'll need your HI membership card; beds cost Dr14, hot showers are Dr5, and it has a small kitchen. It's open from 8 to 9 am and noon to 11 pm daily.

Hotels – Medina Most of the cheapest accommodation can be found immediately south of the Djemaa el-Fna and east of Rue de Bab Agnaou, where there are scores of reasonably priced hotels, most of them signposted from the square. Many have rooms around bright and colourful courtyards and terraces to soak up the sun and views. Apart from that, their cleanliness and the shower situation, there's often not much difference between them.

Prices vary little, and in summer most hike up their prices according to demand, so you could end up paying more than you would for a better room in a classified hotel. If you have your heart set on a particular hotel, it's worth calling ahead, as they fill up pretty quickly. Some will let you sleep on their terraces for around Dr25. At the time of research, many places were refurbishing or upgrading, so don't be surprised if you find some listed here are improved upon.

One of the best rock-bottom places is *Hôtel Afriquia* (☎ 442403, 45 Quartier Sidi Bouloukat). It charges Dr40/70/110 for basic singles/doubles/triples but has a fantastic courtyard with orange trees and a psychedelically tiled and tiered terrace with panoramic views (including some over the square).

MARRAKESH VILLE NOUVELLE

PLACES TO STAY
2 Residence el-Hamra
3 Résidence al-Bahja
5 Hôtel Kenzah;
   Club Sherazad
6 Residence Gomassine
8 Hôtel al-Bustan
10 Hôtel des Voyageurs
20 Hôtel des Ambassadeurs
21 Hôtel Oasis
   et Negociants
26 Hôtel Amalay
27 Hôtel Oudaya
30 Hôtel Tachfine;
   Mirador
42 Hôtel Toulousain
67 Hôtel Ibis Moussafir
71 Hôtel Farouk
74 Hôtel Hasna
79 Hôtel le Marrakech

PLACES TO EAT
7 Dragon d'Or
11 La Jacaranda
12 Boulangerie Pâtisserie
   Hilton; Boule de Neige

15 La Sirene
17 Fener Sarl
18 Brasserie le Petit Poucet
28 Restaurant Chez
   Jack'Line
34 Charly Cabana
39 Le Liberty's
41 Restaurant le Catanzaro
43 Market
48 Oliveri
49 La Trattoria
52 Pâtisserie al-Jawda
53 Jeff de Bruges
55 Virginia Mekong
59 Restaurant Sindibad
64 Rotisserie de la Paix
65 Bagatelle
70 Villa Rose
75 Restaurant al-Fassia
81 Pizza Hut; Bank
84 Puerto Banus

OTHER
1 Hospital
4 American Language
   Center

9 Tourist Cars; Budget
13 Shell Petrol Station
14 Al-Moutamid
16 BCdM (ATM)
19 Somardis Supermarket
22 Supermarket
23 Shell Petrol Station
24 Libraire Armor
25 Artisanal Marocain
31 Cinéma Le Colisée
32 CTM Booking Office
33 Cyber Colisee
35 BMCE (ATM)
36 ABN-AMRO;
   L'Entrecote;
   Libraire d'Art
37 Europcar
38 Nouvelles Frontieres
40 Dentist
44 Hertz
45 Carlson Wagonlits
46 ONMT Tourist Office
47 Ménara Tours
50 Atlas Voyages
51 Avis; Felix Labo

54 Palais de l'Alimentation
56 Voyages Schwarz
57 Wafa Bank (ATM)
58 Tourist Bureau
60 Mosque
61 Main Post
   & Phone Office
62 Gallerie Jassim;
   Pampas Voyages
63 Royal Air Maroc;
   Car Hire
   Companies
66 Supratours
68 Shell Petrol Station
69 Municipal Theatre
72 Panerea Pub Club
73 Tour Operators
76 Cybernour Internet
77 Night Pharmacy
78 Disco Diamant Noir;
   El-Morocco
80 Le Star's House
82 Mosque
83 Eglise des
   Saints-Martyrs
85 Police

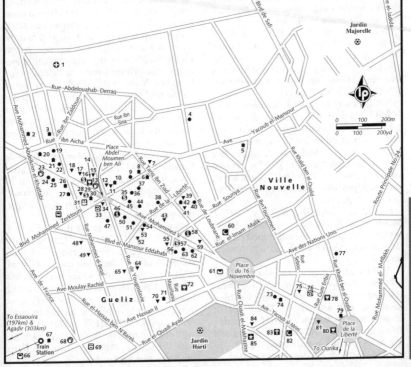

Hôtel Central Palace (☎ 440235, fax 442854, 59 Quartier Sidi Bouloukat) has basic rooms with washbasin around a large courtyard for Dr50/100; doubles with shower cost Dr120. At the time of research a cafe was being constructed on the large terrace; this has good views onto Djemaa el-Fna and to the Atlas. There's also a snack bar and an annexe, so getting a room should be easy.

A short way down from the Djemaa el-Fna, between Rue Zitoune el-Qedim and Rue de Bab Agnaou is *Hôtel el-Atlal* (☎ 427889), with bright and clean (if small) rooms upstairs for Dr60/100. Ask for a room off the street. A hot shower costs Dr10.

Nearby is *Hôtel Souria* (☎ 426757, 17 Rue de la Recette), with clean rooms around a cool and tranquil courtyard overlooked by stuffed animals, or on the cheerful rooftop terrace. Rooms start at Dr60/100 and hot showers are Dr10. The friendly female owners are also more than happy to share their small kitchen with guests.

Hôtel Chellah (☎ 442977, 14 Derb Sekaya), just off Rue Zitoune el-Qedim, has large, clean rooms around a courtyard, which with its orange trees and salons is a nice place to chill out. Rooms cost Dr40/80 plus Dr10 for a hot shower.

Not far away is *Hôtel Essaouira* (☎/fax 443805, 3 Quartier Sidi Bouloukat). With a terrace cafe and clean rooms, it's a good place to meet other travellers, although it gets full fast and bathroom facilities are limited. You pay from Dr35/70 for a room, and a cold/hot shower is Dr3/5. To reach it, the best approach is from the east from Rue Zitoune el-Qedim.

Next door, *Hôtel Medina* (☎ 442997, 1 Quartier Sidi Bouloukat) is a similar design but not quite as nice. It's still a good choice; clean rooms cost Dr40/80 and hot showers are Dr5.

At the eastern edge of the square, *Hôtel Mimosa* (☎ 426385, 16 Rue des Banques) has singles/doubles/triples around a tiled courtyard with fountain for Dr40/70/110; doubles with bathroom are Dr160. There's also a terrace with views to the square and it's a bit off the usual tourist track. Be warned they lock the door at 1 am.

Further along, *Hôtel el-Kennaria* (☎ 390228, 10 Rue el-Kenneria) has no real views, but it does have clean rooms around a modern courtyard for Dr40/60.

Three hotels that are a little more expensive, but can be recommended, are within a stone's throw of the Djemaa el-Fna, and offer more comfort than the run-of-the-mill cheapies.

Hôtel Ichbilia (☎ 390486, 1 Rue Bani Marine) has clean and comfortable (if you don't mind the colour mauve) rooms for Dr60/120. The showers are hot in the mornings. Try to get a room upstairs, as the street can be noisy.

Further north, and one of the best places in this category, is *Hôtel Ali* (☎ 444979, fax 440522, e kotelali@hotmail.com, Rue Moulay Ismail). It's very efficiently run, with everything the traveller needs: Internet, restaurant, cafe, car rental, tours, laundry service, baggage storage and mountaineering advice. The terrace restaurant has views over the square, Place de Foucauld and the Atlas. It's also excellent value, with rooms for Dr85/120/180 with bathroom (and sometimes semi-private terrace or balcony) and breakfast. You can also sleep in the dorm or on the roof terrace for around Dr40 (Etudiants et Association Dortour members get a free breakfast thrown in). Try to get a room around the back, as the rooms on the street can be a bit noisy.

Back on Rue Bani Marine, *Hôtel la Gazelle* (☎ 441112, fax 445537) is a good place with rooms for Dr60/100. Room 80 on the top floor opens onto the terrace, which has good views to the square, mosque and mountains.

If you want to be in the thick of it, you could try *Hôtel CTM* (☎ 442325) on the southern edge of Djemaa el-Fna. The bus company of the same name used to be here, so there's plenty of parking space below (Dr10/20 per day/overnight). Rooms with breakfast on the terrace (the only time you'll get up here without having to buy a drink) cost Dr68/104/158, or Dr93/132/187 with bathroom. The front rooms look out onto the square; the others face the fairly unspectacular courtyard.

At the other side of the square, *Hôtel de France* (☎ 442319) has views for a much cheaper Dr40/60. The staff are a bit surly and facilities are basic but you really can't beat the views.

Hotels – Ville Nouvelle There are no unclassified pensions and not too many cheap hotels in the ville nouvelle. The few that exist can be found around Ave Mohammed V, west of Place du 16 Novembre.

Handy for the train station, *Hôtel Farouk* (☎ 431989, 66 Ave Hassan II) has good singles/doubles/triples with showers for Dr70/100/130. There's also a restaurant and it organises excursions.

The one-star *Hôtel des Voyageurs* (☎ 447218, 40 Blvd Mohammed Zerktouni) has rooms (some with balconies) for Dr83/140. It's a bit frayed around the edges (cracked toilet seats and so forth), but it's clean.

Another good and very reasonable place is *Hôtel Toulousain* (☎ 430033, 44 Rue Tariq ibn Ziad), a nice, calm and cool place with a wonderful old palm tree in the courtyard. It has rooms without shower for Dr80/100, or Dr105/135 with; those on the 1st floor are better than the ground floor. There's also parking.

Slightly more expensive is the gloomier *Hôtel Oasis et Negociants* (☎ 447179, 50 Ave Mohammed V), which has rooms without a shower for Dr110/155, or Dr130/190 with a shower.

Places to Stay – Mid-Range

Medina *Hôtel Gallia* (☎ 445913, fax 444853, 30 Rue de la Recette) is one of the most pleasant hotels in the medina area, with a tree-filled courtyard. Singles/doubles with shower cost Dr210/270. It has central heating in winter and the entire place is scrubbed from top to toe daily. It is often booked out, especially during holidays and on weekends, so make a reservation or arrive early.

On a par, *Hôtel Sherazade* (☎/fax 429305, 3 Derb Djama) is a riad decorated in traditional style and run by a Moroccan-German couple. Rooms cost from Dr125/175; those with bathroom range from Dr160/190 to Dr310/360. There are also mini-apartments available from Dr310 for two. Breakfast costs Dr30 and set meals are Dr70 to Dr90. Take the westernmost lane from Djemaa el-Fna and it's up the third lane to the left.

Grand Hôtel du Tazi (☎ 442787, fax 442152), on the corner of Rue Bab Agnaou and Ave el-Mouahidine, is so long that from some rooms it could almost be quicker to get to the Koutoubia pool than to the hotel's small pool. Rooms with shower, toilet, TV and phone are Dr246/293. All have balconies; ask for a room away from the street if you want peace. There is also a bar and restaurant (guests receive a 20% discount), roof terrace and parking.

A little further away but with a better vista is the cavernous *Hôtel de Foucauld* (☎ 443499, fax 441344, Ave el-Mouahidine). Although some of the rooms can be noisy and a tad small, they're clean, nicely decorated and comfortable, and not bad value at Dr173/232 with breakfast, or Dr144/174 without. Rooms have a shower and toilet. Ask for one away from the street if you want a quiet night. The hotel has a tiny pool and a popular traditional-style restaurant hung with carpets. If it's full, you may be directed to its Hivernage annexe.

Heading west towards Bab Larissa and the ville nouvelle, there's a good two-star place, *Hôtel Islane* (☎ 440081, 440083, fax 440085, 279 Ave Mohammed V). Rooms are modern and comfortable, and some have balconies facing the Koutoubia. There's a rooftop restaurant, cafe, gift shop and parking. Rooms with bathroom, heating, TV and phone cost Dr214/275, including breakfast.

Ville Nouvelle The bulk of the mid-range hotels are outside the medina, mostly in Gueliz, with a couple closer to the medina boundary in the Hivernage area. There are a lot of them, especially in the three- and four-star category.

One of the cheapest is *Hôtel Yasmine* (☎ 446200, fax 447386, Place de la Liberté), which is a bit run-down but does have a pool, garden, bar and parking. Singles/doubles/triples/quads are Dr163/232/319/406, including breakfast.

CENTRAL MOROCCO

Hôtel al-Mouatamid (☎ 448855, 94 Ave Mohammed V) is getting on a bit. It has a bar downstairs and another on its top floor. Rooms with balcony are Dr177/206/276.

Hôtel du Pacha (☎ 431327, fax 431326, 33 Rue de la Liberté) is an older style place with a cool central courtyard. Air-con rooms with balcony are Dr204/249/324.

Another place with a bit of character and reasonable rooms is *Hôtel des Ambassadeurs* (☎ 447159, Ave Mohammed V). With a restaurant and bar next door, it's in a lively part of Gueliz; more good eateries and cafes are nearby. Biggish rooms with bathroom and small balcony cost Dr260/280.

Also on Ave Mohammed V, the three-star *Hôtel Amalay* (☎ 431367, fax 431554) and, along the road, *Hôtel Tachfine* (☎ 447188, fax 437862), are largish, anonymous places. Both charge Dr303/366 and have bars and restaurants but no pool.

Heading back down towards the medina, the three-star *Hôtel le Grand Imilchil* (☎ 447653, fax 446165, Ave Echouhada) charges Dr315/402 for rooms with balcony. The pool and gardens here are on the small side but it has a bar and restaurant.

Hôtel Oudaya (☎ 448751, fax 435400, e oudaya@iam.net.ma, 147 Rue Mohammed el-Beqal) is a nice choice, with a terrace overlooking the small tiled courtyard with pool, and a hammam. Rooms with air-con are pretty good value at Dr320/386.

Hôtel Hasna (☎ 449972, fax 449994, 247 Ave Mohammed V) has spotless rooms (with terrible paintings, satellite TV and phone) for Dr369/449. There is a very small pool, a hammam and pleasant Moroccan restaurant complete with *poofahs* (cushioned seating).

Closer to the medina and in a quiet setting is *Hôtel de la Ménara* (☎ 436478, fax 447386), overlooking Place de la Liberté. A modernish place, it's done out in traditional style and has spacious rooms with balconies. It charges Dr365/486, including breakfast, and there's a good pool, tennis courts, bar, restaurant and gardens.

If you arrive on a late train, you might well want to spend a night at the three-star *Hôtel Ibis Moussafir* (☎ 435929, fax 435936), beside the station. It's a reliable, modern choice and has a small pool set in a peaceful (as long as there's no train passing) garden with willow trees and birds. Rooms cost Dr329/428/596 and the restaurant has one/two/three-course meals for Dr59/79/99.

Although it's a cavernous and characterless tour-group place, *Hôtel al-Bustan* (☎ 446810, fax 446813, 66 Blvd Mohammed Zerktouni) has a big pool, albeit in a concrete courtyard, restaurant and bar. When you consider this, the rooms for Dr207/266/366 with breakfast are pretty good value.

Holiday Residences Apart from Club Med on the Djemaa el-Fna, there are a couple of residences offering long-term lets of fully equipped flats. They are good for families or groups planning a longer stay; the tourist office has a complete list.

On the Djemaa el-Fna is *Résidence de la Place* (☎ 425174). It is the least appealing of the residences, but the position can't be beaten. Tatty and rather run-down single/double apartments cost Dr125/150, although they accommodate up to six. Two have wonderful balconies overlooking the square (light sleepers may well prefer something on the courtyard out the back). For those who don't get the views, there is a terrace cafe and restaurant.

An altogether more upmarket place is *Résidence el-Hamra* (☎ 448423, fax 446986, 26 Ave Mohammed V) in Gueliz. It offers single/double/family (two adults and three children) apartments with kitchen, lounge, TV and phone for Dr312/374/524. Reductions are available for stays longer than 15 days.

Residence Gomassine (☎ 433086, fax 433012, 71 Blvd Mohammed Zerktouni) has singles/doubles with kitchen for Dr300/400, or Dr300 for a double without. Larger apartments with a Moroccan salon and kitchen for five/six/seven/eight people are also available for Dr700/770/870/950.

Places to Stay – Top End

Medina While there aren't that many hotels within the medina itself, many Europeans (and Moroccans) have invested in riads, tastefully restoring them to their former glory. Many have been set up as B&Bs

and were being classified at the time of research. Contact the tourist office for a list.

With all the comforts of home, plus a few more, some are available as weekly rentals. Agences Immobileres manages them and rates start at around Dr2000/4000 per week for four/eight people. Some agencies to contact include *Mustapha Belkahia* (☎ *446601, fax 446607, 55 Blvd Zerktouni), Chez l'Artisant Cherif* (☎ *426675, 50 Souq el-Kimakhine); and Jalila Belkhil* (☎ *429133, or* ☎ *01 43 25 98 77 Silvana Saint German in Paris,* e *silva@easynet.fr).

Just before La Mamounia is *Hôtel Chems* (☎ *444813, fax 440547, Ave Houmane el-Fetouaki),* a four-star hotel down a quiet side street. Singles/doubles with aircon and balcony or terrace overlooking its secluded garden with pool are Dr400/500. There's also a restaurant, bar and tennis courts, and it's very convenient for the main sights minus the hassle.

On Ave Houmane el-Fetouaki, just inside Bab el-Jedid, is the jewel in the crown of the city's hotels, *La Mamounia* (☎ *444409, fax 444660,* e *resa@mamounia. com)* – though at five-star 'luxe', you'd want to be on an expense account to stay.

Built between 1925 and 1929 for the (French-controlled) Moroccan railways, it was the favoured destination of well-heeled Europeans, many of them taking a break from the decadence of Tangier. Guests as diverse as Winston Churchill (who came for the climate and to indulge in his hobby of painting) and Eric von Stroheim have passed through.

Renovated in 1986, it has lost some of its charm, but jetsetters still patronise it. Rooms start at Dr2000 for a single in low season and finish at Dr30,000 for a three-room suite in high season (add Dr200 for breakfast).

Between 10 am and 4 pm the hotel opens its doors to the riff-raff, allowing them (well, us) an opportunity to wander the cool lobby and lush and sedate gardens. You may have to dress for the occasion, as sneakers and shorts are not allowed; 'bouncers' in Fès hats enforce the dress code at the door.

Ville Nouvelle There are many four- and five-star hotels aimed at tour groups and delegates; lots of them are on Ave de France (near the Palais du Congress) and further out of town on the road to Casablanca. The tourist office has the full list.

The four-star *Hôtel Kenzah* (☎ *448330, fax 435386, Ave Yacoub el-Mansour)* is pretty good value, with comfortable singles/doubles for Dr436/557. There's a pool, bars, restaurants, fitness club and nightclub.

The huge *Hôtel le Marrakech* (☎ *434351, fax 434980)* near Place de la Liberté charges Dr500/600 for rooms and Dr55 for breakfast. It has a large pool, restaurants, boutiques, bars and plenty of tour groups.

If you're planning on bringing your toy dog with you, the five-star *Hôtel es-Saadi* (☎ *448811, fax 447644)* is the place for you. Rooms cost Dr1500/1700; the dog pays Dr80.

Places to Eat
Cheap Eats There are plenty of places to fill a rumbling stomach without putting a hole in your wallet.

Medina Palace restaurants may try to create a Moroccan experience with musicians and dancers but the liveliest, cheapest and most entertaining place to eat remains the *Djemaa el-Fna*.

By the time the sun sets, much of the square is taken over by stalls, each specialising in certain cuisine and vying for your custom. At one you can pick up kebabs with salad, while at another it's fish and chips Moroccan style or even snails and sheep heads. Almost as soon as you've ordered, it's in front of you with a range of accompaniments including chips, salad, eggplant and fried chillies. You can eat your fill for Dr25 or less and wash it down with a Dr3 orange juice from a nearby juice stand.

If you're a bit hesitant about eating at the stalls (there's little to worry about) there are other cheap eats around. Offering pretty much the same fare for the same price are the stalls in the *Quissaria* on the other side of the juice stands.

To the north-east, *Café Restaurant Chez Chegrouni (4–6 Djemaa el-Fna)* is popular and probably the best cheap restaurant, though its terrace is at ground level. Salads cost Dr5 and mains, such as a great *tajine kefta* (lamb and vegetable stew), are Dr25.

At the southern end of the square, by all those hanging carpets, is a small group of *restaurants* and *cafes* that offer cheap meals, and some even have small terraces.

If you've had your fill of the square, you could try the small restaurants on Rue Bani Marine and Rue de Bab Agnaou. *Snack Sahara*, for example, offers a filling tajine for Dr24, although you can still hear the square from its outdoor seating and terrace. Down by Hôtel la Gazelle, *Restaurant el-Bahja* has good set menus from Dr40 or sandwiches and grills. It's a simple, clean place that's very popular with the locals.

If you want to enjoy the Marrakesh atmosphere on a smaller scale, head to Place des Ferblantiers, which has *snack stalls*, *fish fryers* and *cafes* in the style of Djemaa el-Fna. Behind the *food market*, *Chez Cherif* has good salads that are stuffed into sandwiches. The only cheap restaurant, *Cafe Palais el-Badia*, has a terrace overlooking Palace el-Badi, making it a top spot for a drink or light meal.

Ville Nouvelle There are any number of places to eat in the ville nouvelle; a good collection is concentrated on or around Ave Mohammed V and Blvd Mohammed Zerktouni.

For bottom-rung local food, you'll find a group of *hole-in-the-wall* places on Rue ibn Aicha, where a solid meal of *brochettes* (skewered meat), chips and salad will cost about Dr25.

La Sirene might not have the best location, right next to a petrol station, but it makes the best of it with undersea decor and mermaids. Even better, a filling plate of fried fish, salad and chips is Dr30.

If you fancy a bit of fast food, *Star Food* has burgers (Dr16) and sandwiches (Dr18) and it also does breakfast for Dr24.

Restaurant Sindibad has a good selection of Moroccan favourites, pizzas and salads and is a popular place for breakfast. It looks like a Parisian cafe and has a nice terrace, but its appearance belies its prices, which are very reasonable.

Fener Sarl (72 Ave Mohammed V) has *shwarma* sandwiches (similar to a kebab) with garlic sauce for Dr18.

For something a bit more substantial, *Hôtel Farouk* has a good menu for Dr50. *Hôtel Oasis et Negociants* also has menus for Dr60 (four courses) plus 10% service, and beer for Dr11. See Places to Stay – Budget for the locations of both hotels.

If you're desperate to fill up on greens, you could try *Pizza Hut* (☎ 431980, 6 Ave Mohammed V), which has a good self-serve salad bar for Dr42 per visit. Pizzas cost from Dr39 to Dr139, and it does deliveries.

Restaurants If sitting down while you munch away is more your style, then there are a multitude of places that will satisfy even the fussiest eaters.

Medina There are plenty of restaurants with terraces overlooking the frenzied chaos of Djemaa el-Fna. *Argana* (you can't miss the bright neon sign) has three set menus for Dr80/90/130. It is also a patisserie and *glacier* (ice-cream parlour) so those with a sweet tooth should be happy.

Other good choices are *Cafe/Restaurant de France*, which has a set menu for Dr90, and *Résidence de la Place*, with two set menus for Dr55/100.

Off the square (but with views of it from the terrace, where lunch is served) and deservedly popular with travellers is *Hôtel Ali*. If you fancy a pig-out, wait until 6.30 pm, when you can load up your plate as many times as you like from the ground-floor restaurant's pots of Moroccan fare, vegetables, salad, fruit and dessert for Dr60 (Dr50 for hotel guests). There's often a musician valiantly attempting to drown out the glare of the fluorescent lighting and provide that 'authentic' touch.

Completely detached from the visual feast and atmosphere of the Djemaa are a couple of hotel restaurants, popular with tourists, that serve large helpings of good food, albeit for a bit more cash (or credit). *Hôtel de Foucauld* has a buffet for Dr100, which includes a good selection of vegetable dishes. The *Grand Hôtel du Tazi* has a licensed restaurant attached to its bar (beer costs Dr20) – good for a pre- or post-dinner drink – and a good buffet with great salads for Dr90. Both try to re-create the palace atmosphere but don't succeed.

From Dr100 to Dr150 per person, you could eat at the rooftop restaurant in the *Hôtel Islane*. It has the best view of the Koutoubia, though the traffic below can be a bit noisy. Serving traditional Moroccan as well as Italian food, it has pizzas for Dr40 to Dr50, and Moroccan specialities from Dr60.

A good stop for lunch while sightseeing is *Café Restaurant Nid Cigogne*, a tiered terrace with lounges overlooking the Kasbah Mosque and Saadien Tombs. The set menu is Dr120, but you can simply pop up for a coffee and take a few snaps of the storks nesting opposite.

Ville Nouvelle In a small mall on Blvd Mohammed Zerktouni, *L'Entrecote* has pizzas from Dr35 to Dr45 and pasta for Dr45. A set menu costs Dr110, children's menus are Dr50 and an express menu made up of three courses is Dr70. It's licensed, with beer/ wine for Dr18/90. Open Monday to Saturday for lunch and dinner, it accepts credit cards.

Rotisserie de la Paix (☎ 433118, 68 Rue de Yougoslavie) has a large garden courtyard, is licensed and serves up seafood, kebabs, salads, tajine and pizza from Dr45 to Dr100.

Charly Cabana (☎ 305017, 39 Blvd Mohammed Zerktouni) is licensed, with international dishes accompanied by the occasional jazz or country rendition.

Peurto Banus (☎ 446534, Rue ibn Hanbal) is a Spanish-influenced and licensed restaurant with courtyards. Dishes include gazpacho (Dr45), trout (Dr95) and paella (Dr75 per person – minimum two).

L'Amandier (☎ 446093, Ave Echouhada) is a cottage-style villa in gardens with a cool verandah and attentive staff. Allow Dr100 for mains and Dr25 for a glass of wine; it also has a good dessert/ice-cream selection.

Nearby, *Comptoir* (☎ 437702, Ave Echouhada) is a restaurant-boutique with a garden courtyard and sister establishment in Paris. The waiting staff are suitably chic

and the menu has interesting choices, such as tandoori and lemon brochettes for Dr120.

Restaurant al-Fassia (☎ 434060, 232 Ave Mohammed V) has a good reputation for its traditional Moroccan cuisine. It's a very attractive place with a cool, peaceful garden and two cushioned pavilions. There is a good set menu for Dr120 which is served only at lunch time; otherwise, it's a la carte, with main courses for about Dr95. It's open from noon to 2.30 pm and 7.30 to 11 pm daily.

La Trattoria (☎ 432641, 179 Rue Mohammed el-Beqal) is an extraordinary, palatial place behind a large gate that's unlocked by a Quasimodo-type figure. The open log fire and the dachshund curled up beside it make it a very homely place in winter. Pasta/meat/fish dishes cost from Dr60/70/120, and it's licensed.

Bagatelle (☎ 430274, 101 Rue de Yougoslavie) serves good French food for around Dr80. There's not much atmosphere in the restaurant itself, but there's a lovely garden outside covered by a canopy of vines. It's open daily, except Wednesday.

Restaurant Chez Jack'Line (☎ 447547, 63 Ave Mohammed V) is a place full of character done out like a French bistro. Look out for the 24-year-old parrot, who seems as much in charge of the place as Madame Jack'Line herself. The place does very good three-course set menus for Dr80. A la carte main courses are around Dr70. It serves Italian and French-style food and is open daily.

The French restaurant *La Jacaranda* (☎ 447215, 32 Blvd Mohammed Zerktouni) serves dishes such as frogs legs, calf brains and duck. It does good lunch/dinner menus for Dr105/180 with a good selection of fish, and beef/fish fondues for Dr140/150.

If you feel like something Asian, head for the *Dragon d'Or* (☎ 430617, 10 Blvd Mohammed Zerktouni), a tacky Asian restaurant with menus for Dr120. *Virginia Mekong* (Rue Mauritania) also serves oriental cuisine, including duck for Dr50.

Villa Rosa (☎ 430832, 64 Ave Hassan II) is a posh licensed place with Italian (Dr60 to Dr100) and French (Dr315) food served inside or in its courtyard. It has seafood from Dr70 upwards and wine from Dr70.

Virtually all the bigger hotels have at least one restaurant. *La Mamounia* (see Places to Stay – Top End) has five rather expensive places (Dr600 for set menus). Meals are sometimes accompanied by a show of one sort or another. Don't forget to dress for the occasion.

Palace Restaurants Marrakesh offers some very good fine-dining opportunities in lavish surrounds. A splurge in a palace restaurant is pricey but you will be treated to the best Moroccan cuisine and some form of entertainment, whether it be of the belly-dancing or unobtrusive classical music variety.

Some places are difficult to find and at others a reservation may be required – if you have your heart set on visiting a particular restaurant, call ahead. Otherwise, many places are signposted from the main sights. Feel free to have a look around them and check out the menu for unlisted goodies.

Restaurant le Marrakchi (☎ 443377, 52 Rue des Banques) offers views over Djemaa el-Fna from behind the comfort of large glass windows. It's great to be sheltered from the wind but you pay for it with menus ranging from Dr220 to Dr420, although the food is worth it. Naturally, it's licensed and there's music and belly-dancing.

Dar Mimoun (☎ 443348, 1 Derb ben Amrane) has lovely salons around a tree shaded courtyard. Although its menu is pricey (Dr350), mains start at a reasonable Dr60 and you can get *harira* (spicy lentil soup) for Dr8. It's also a *salon de thé* (gentile cafe) and sometimes does breakfast – a great place to start (or end) the day.

For a complete blow-out in lavish surroundings, try *Dar Marjana* (☎ 445773, fax 429152, 15 Derb Sidi Ali Tair) down an alley is open only upon reservation. Considered one of the best restaurants in Marrakesh, it has hosted the likes of actors Dustin Hoffman and Isabelle Adjani.

Another similar place, frequented by the royal family, is *Yacout* (☎ 382929, fax 382538, 79 Sidi Ahmed Soussi). It was designed by the American architect Bill Willis and is an extraordinary place, complete with illuminated terrace, beautiful fountain and

pool. Reservations are necessary and fixed menus are a smooth Dr600 (including aperitifs and wine). It's open from 8.30 pm to midnight. Ask someone to guide you here.

Restaurant Bar el-Baroud (☎ 426009, 275 Ave Mohammed V), past the Hôtel Islane, serves French-influenced traditional food in intimate surrounds. There's entertainment, and the menu costs Dr400. Main courses cost Dr150 and a bottle of wine is Dr90. Credit cards are accepted, and it's open Tuesday to Sunday.

Stylia (☎ 440505, fax 445837, 34 Rue Ksour) is another lavish place serving 'Haute Gastronomie Marocaine' in 15th-century surrounds. For many, it's the best place in Marrakesh. To get there, get a *petit taxi* (local taxi) to drop you off at Rue Sidi el-Yamani (the restaurant is signposted off Rue Fatima Zohra). Open from 8 pm daily, you can arrange for a doorman to collect and guide you through the dark winding streets.

On the lane leading to the museum, *Palais Gharnata* (☎ 389615, 5–6 Derb al-Arsa) is a very plush 14th-century palace tastefully decorated in red and gold and strewn with rose petals. Lunch/dinner costs Dr300/500 including alcohol, and there's music in the evening. Its celebrity diners have included two James Bonds and one Bo Derek.

They boast that housewives prepare the fare at *Douirya* (☎ 403030, 14 Derb J'Did), which faces Place des Ferblantiers. Another restored minipalace, it's very classy, with menus for Dr320/380 and wine for Dr100.

Cafes, Patisseries & Glaceries The most interesting cafes are, of course, gathered around Djemaa el-Fna – and you could spend a day doing a crawl of them and taking in the different vistas of the square. *Hôtel CTM*, *Argana*, *Café de France* and *Café Glacier* (where you place your order before going through a turnstile) have good terraces and service can be excruciatingly slow.

Pâtisserie Mik Mak, next door to Hôtel Ali near Place Djemaa el-Fna, has a good selection of Moroccan and French-style cakes at reasonable prices.

Nearby, the smarter *Pâtisserie des Princes* (32 Rue de Bab Agnaou) has a good selection of cakes and pastries and some ice cream. It's a cool, peaceful place and is good for breakfast.

Ave Mohammed V in the ville nouvelle is the other part of town that usually attracts a people-watching crowd of caffeine addicts.

Boule de Neige (30 Place Abdel Moumen ben Ali) is a cafe serving continental (Dr30) and American (Dr50) breakfasts, the latter comprising the former plus fried or scrambled eggs and yogurt. Open from 6.30 am to midnight daily, it also has Moroccan bread and oil, as well as that Western favourite, Corn Flakes (Dr15). The cafe also has ice cream and cakes, which can be enjoyed on the roof terrace.

Le Liberty's (☎ 436416, 23 Rue de la Liberté) has a nice garden at the back (though overlooked by a horrendous multi-storey building); it's open from 6.30 am to midnight. It also does a good Moroccan breakfast of crepes etc for Dr15, salads from Dr13 and sandwiches from Dr10.

A well-known place in Marrakesh is the *Boulangerie Pâtisserie Hilton*, opposite the Café de la Renaissance in the ville nouvelle. It is a veritable feast for your eyes, as well as your palate and nose, and sells a wide selection of traditional Moroccan sweet and savoury things, including chicken *pastilla* (pie; Dr10). It's open from 4 am to 11.30 pm daily.

The best ice-cream parlour in town is *Oliveri (9 Blvd el-Mansour Eddahbi)* in the ville nouvelle. Its sister is in Casablanca, and both are well known for their home-made ice cream. It also sells good milk shakes (Dr16), fruit juices (Dr5.50) and ice-cream cakes. You can also have breakfast here.

For real indulgence, visit *Jeff du Bruges* chocolatier, just off Ave Mohammed V.

Self-Catering The *Somardis* supermarket on Rue ibn Aicha in the ville nouvelle is a reasonable place to stock up on supplies you might find hard to get elsewhere – like Corn Flakes. It also sells alcohol. *Palais de l'Alimentation (Ave Mohammed V)* also sells alcohol. If you want to completely stock up, try *Makro*, a huge supermarket about 4km out on the road to Casablanca.

For fresh produce there are *markets* in the ville nouvelle and Djemaa el-Fna.

Entertainment

Bars As with most towns in Morocco, most of the bars in Marrakesh are filled with prostitutes plying their business. That's not to say women can't go out on their own, they just have to be a bit judicious about it.

Possibly the most popular bar in town (and the most pick-uppy) is the *Mirador* at the top of the Hôtel Tachfine (see Places to Stay – Mid-Range). It also boasts the best view in town, but a drink is compulsory. It's open from 9 am to 11 pm and you need to ring the bell by the lift (elevator) in order to call the lift porter. The cafe on the ground floor of the same building is a great Art Deco relic and a good place for a beer (inside) or coffee (outside).

Almost opposite, another rooftop place, a bar at the top of *Al-Moutamid* (same lift rules apply), has views just as good and is almost worth the trip to see the glamorous prostitutes patiently lined up waiting for custom.

In the medina, *Grand Hôtel du Tazi* (see Places to Stay – Mid-Range) has a small bar that is a good place to hook up with other travellers.

Obviously, the big hotel bars with their happy hours are fairly safe places for a drink – albeit with muzak and sterilised atmosphere, and of course their higher-class prostitutes.

Nightclubs If you want to party on, many hotels in the ville nouvelle have nightclubs, and there are more independent of hotels. As elsewhere, the usual entry fee varies between Dr50 and Dr100, which includes the first drink. Each drink thereafter costs at least Dr50. Most offer the predictable standard fare of contemporary Moroccan pop music mixed with the usual disco.

A good place to start the night with a bit of local flavour and live music is *Club Bustane*, which closes at midnight. It is open during the day, however, and entry is free.

Club Sherazad, behind Hôtel Kenzah, is a good choice that kicks off around midnight with a couple of hours of the best folk music you'll hear, closely followed by disco.

As far as regular discos go, one of the most popular is *Diamant Noir* in the Hôtel le Marrakech. *Le Star's House*, next door to the Café Jet d'Eau, is also popular and is open until the early hours.

Cinema The plushest cinema in Marrakesh is *Le Colisée* (☎ 448893, *Blvd Mohammed Zerktouni*) in the ville nouvelle. Seats in the stalls/balcony are Dr20/30 (Dr5 less on Monday), and the sound and comfort are excellent. Women customarily sit in the balcony.

There are three screenings a day at 3, 7 and 9.30 pm; check the paper *L'Economie* for listings. Films are dubbed into French.

Folkloric Shows Several upmarket restaurants, some in the bigger hotels, put on entertainment involving local tribal singing and dancing. These include *El-Morocco* at Hôtel le Marrakech for Dr145 per person. Inquire at the tourist office for others.

Chez Ali (☎ 307730, [e] *chezali@cybernet. net.ma*) re-creates the entire Marrakesh festival complete with an enactment of a fantasia (musket-firing cavalry charge) and dinner for Dr400 (including pick-ups and drop-offs) nightly from 8 pm to midnight. Book through hotels or tourist offices, but don't let them rip you off with commission.

Casino You can also try La Mamounia *casino*, complete with gaming machines, blackjack tables and roulette wheels. It's open to all, but a jacket and tie are required for men, and smart skirts for women. Moroccan garb is out. It's open from 9 pm to late. Drinks are in the range of Dr100 to Dr200.

Shopping

As in most of the major Moroccan cities, the Ensemble Artisanal, on Ave Mohammed V in the ville nouvelle, is a sensible first stop to get an idea of the maximum prices to offer for souvenirs once you are rummaging around in the souqs. It's better for sampling the quality of merchandise than for purchasing. It's also a good place to watch artisans at work.

If you can't face bargaining in the souqs, there are various other fixed-price craft shops along Ave Mohammed V. One with quite a large selection of goods at prices which aren't too extortionate is the Artisanal Marocain at No 27.

Many shops have notices posted in their windows listing a number (☎ 308430 ext 360) to call if you feel you've been unfairly treated in a purchase, either on price or quality of the goods. This is definitely worth doing, if you have a serious and fair cause for complaint. Believe it or not, any potential damage caused to the tourism industry is taken very seriously.

Getting There & Away

Air Ménara airport (☎ 447865) is 6km south-west of town.

RAM (☎ 446444, fax 446002) at 197 Ave Mohammed V has daily flights to and from Casablanca (Dr437, 40 minutes), where you can pick up connections, and a direct daily flight to Agadir (Dr437, 35 minutes).

RAM direct international flights go to Geneva (Dr6054, three hours) once weekly, and London (Dr6659, 3½ hours) and Paris (Dr5644, 2¼ hours) twice weekly. Other carriers include British Airways, with twice weekly flights to London; Air France, with daily services to Paris; and Iberia, with weekly flights to Granada and Málaga.

Bus The main bus station (☎ 433933), from which the majority of buses leave, is just outside the city walls by Bab Doukkala, a 20-minute walk or Dr15 taxi ride from Djemaa el-Fna. The main building is big with many booths covering all sorts of local and long-distance destinations. There are left-luggage facilities (Dr4 per item per day; open 24 hours), cafes, toilets and touts.

Window No 10 is the CTM booking desk; it also has a booking office on Blvd Mohammed Zerktouni in Gueliz, and some buses stop there, too. It has buses to the destinations shown in the table on the next page.

Buses also go to Meknès (Dr132), M'Hamid (Dr100, 7 am), Safi (Dr37), Tangier (Dr166), Tan Tan (Dr170), Tinerhir, Dadès, Todra (5 am) and Zagora (Dr82, eight hours).

destination	price (Dr)	duration (hours)	departures
Agadir	70	4½	four daily
Beni Mellal	53	3½	three daily
Casablanca	65	3½	four daily
Essaouira	40	3	6 am
Er-Rachidia	103	10	4.45 am
Fès	130	8	6.30 am & 9 pm
Laayoune	250	16	5 pm
Ouarzazate	65	5	four daily
Rabat	84	5½	8 am & 2.30 pm
Taroudannt	91	6½	4.30 pm
Tiznit	80	6	11.30 pm

You can get tickets for local bus lines at the following windows:

window	destination	departures
No 1	Beni Mellal	hourly from 4 am to 9 pm
No 2	Rabat (via Casablanca)	hourly from 5 am to 9 pm
No 3	Asni (for Jebel Toubkal)	hourly
No 4	Safi	nine daily
No 5	El-Jadida line	hourly from 6 am to 4 pm
No 6	Ouarzazate	2 & 5 pm
No 7	Essaouira	eight daily
No 18	Azilal	8.30 am & 3.30 pm

Other regular buses leave from a variety of signposted windows to Agadir, Casablanca, Demnate, Fès, M'Hamid (via Er-Rachidia), Oualidia, Sidi Ifni, Taroudannt and Zagora.

Buses to villages on the north side of Jebel Toubkal, including Ourika and Asni (Dr8), leave when full from a dirt patch on the southern side of the medina outside Bab er-Rob.

There are international departures from the CTM office to Paris (Dr1000) and Madrid (Dr900) on Monday and Friday. There are also buses to London (see Land in the Getting There & Away chapter).

Train The train station (☎ 447703) is on Ave Hassan II, south-west of Place du 16 Novembre. Take a taxi or No 8 bus into the centre. It has left-luggage open to 7.30 pm daily.

There are eight trains to Casablanca (Dr58/76 for 2nd class *ordinaire/rapide*, three hours) and Rabat (Dr76/99, four hours).

There are five direct trains to Fès (Dr130/168, eight hours) via Meknès (Dr116/151, seven hours), and one to Safi (Dr49/63, 4½ hours; change at Benguérir). Overnight trains to Tangier (Dr143) leave once daily and couchettes can only be booked on the day of departure.

Supratours The office of Supratours (☎ 776520) is by the train station. Buses leave from here for Agadir (Dr70, four hours, three daily), Essaouira (Dr45, 2¼ hours, once daily), Tan Tan (Dr158.50, 10 hours, once daily), Laayoune (Dr253.50, 14 hours, once daily), Smara (Dr202, 23 hours, once daily) and Dakhla (Dr389, 25 hours, once daily).

Grand Taxi Standard *grand taxis* (shared taxis) to Ourika (Dr5), Asni (Dr10, one hour) and other nearby High Atlas destinations depart from outside Bab er-Rob near the Royal Palace. Taxis to other destinations leave from the main bus station.

Car & Motorcycle Local car rental companies often offer more competitive deals, with quoted rates starting at around Dr500 per day, or Dr400 per day with a minimum of three days. However, you should be able to negotiate a 10% to 20% discount in the high season and a 30% to 40% discount in the low season (October to mid-December and mid-January to end of February). Most hotels have a car rental agency representative and you can play them off against each other to get better rates. Other car rental agencies in Marrakesh include:

Avis (☎ 433727, fax 449485) 137 Ave Mohammed V
Budget (☎ 437483) 68 Blvd Mohammed Zerktouni; (☎ 438875) Airport
Europcar (☎ 431228, fax 432769) 63 Blvd Mohammed Zerktouni
Goldcar (☎ 431377) Hôtel Semiramis Méridien, Route de Casablanca
Hertz (☎/fax 434680) 157 Ave Mohammed V; (☎ 447230) Airport
Tourist Cars (☎ 448457) 64 Blvd Mohammed Zerktouni

Marrakesh Motos (☎ 448359) at 31 Route de Casablanca next to the Goodyear garage, rents both mountain and ordinary bikes for Dr20/30 per half/full day. Scooters cost Dr150/250 and motorcycles (50cc and up) are Dr350 per day. It's open from 8.30 am to 7 pm daily (except Sunday afternoon).

Getting Around
To/From the Airport A petit taxi from Marrakesh to the airport (6km) should be Dr50, but you'll need to establish the fare before getting in. Bus No 11 runs irregularly to Djemaa el-Fna.

Bus Local buses (☎ 494269) run from opposite Hôtel de Foucauld, near Djemaa el-Fna, to the following destinations:

Nos 1 & 20 Ave Mohammed V, Gueliz
Nos 3 & 10 Bab Doukkala, main post office, train station, Douar Laskar
No 8 Bab Doukkala, main post office, train station, Douar Laskar
No 11 Ave Menara, airport
No 14 train station

Taxi The creamy-beige petit taxis around town cost about Dr10 per journey, but insist that the meter be used. From the train station to the Djemaa el-Fna, the official fare is Dr10 but you'll rarely get away with less than Dr15.

Bicycle Various hotels rent bicycles. Among them are Hôtel de Foucauld (Dr30/60 per half/full day), but you're not supposed to take them outside the medina. Hôtel Ali also rents bicycles for Dr30/40. There is also bicycle hire for Dr70 per day at the place opposite Bain Polo.

In the ville nouvelle are several bicycle-hire places on street corners close to the main hotels.

Calèche Calèches (horse-drawn carriages) are a pleasant way to get around, and can work out cheaper than a taxi. Posted inside the carriage are the official fares: Dr9 for a straightforward trip from A to B 'intramuros' (within the medina walls) and Dr12 for the same 'extramuros' (outside the medina walls). Otherwise, it's Dr60 an hour for pottering around the sights. If you're interested in a bit of horse-drawn romance, they're based at the south-western side of Djemaa el-Fna and inside Bab Doukkala.

AROUND MARRAKESH
Cascades d'Ouzoud & Azilal
☎ 03

About 167km north-east of Marrakesh are Morocco's best waterfalls; they're well worth the effort of getting there. If you have a car, it's an easy enough proposition as a day trip; otherwise, you might have to be prepared to stay overnight in the area – not a bad option.

The drive up passes through irrigated landscapes with the Atlas to the south, and you can do a circuit to include **Demnate** – a bustling walled town with Sunday market. If you've come this far, it's worth detouring another 6km to the east to **Imi-n-Ifri**, a natural bridge over a gorge. Crows sail overhead and it's possible to clamber down into the gorge and pass under the formation. There is a *cafe* overlooking the gorge and a seasonal *auberge*. About 7km further is the two-hectare excavation site of **Iroutane** (see the boxed text 'A Missing Link' later).

The drive between Ouzoud and Afourer, which brings you to the main Marrakesh–Beni Mellal road, is another treat, especially the views of the lake formed by the **Bin el-Ouidane Dam**.

The three-tiered falls (*ouzoud* is Berber for olives, and refers to the cultivation of olive trees in the area) drop 110m into the river below, where plastic bags and bottles bob against the spray. Plenty of local and international tourists visit, and the line of souvenir stalls down to the boats that ferry you across the river (for a few dirham) are proof of their popularity. Fortunately, as yet it is all on a modest and pretty laid-back scale.

It is possible to walk along the course of the river to the **Gorges of Oued el-Abid**, and as you continue downstream there are small, clean pools offering a great opportunity for a swim. An easy destination is the village of **Tanaghmelt**, known as Mexican village, on the wooded slopes of the hills 2km beyond the waterfalls.

Places to Stay & Eat Interspersed between the souvenir stands on the tiers surrounding the falls are several *cafes* with shady *camp sites*. Facilities are limited but it's a beautiful place to pitch a tent, and you're looking at about Dr2 per person, or sometimes nothing if you eat on site.

Directly above the falls and overlooking the valley are two basic hotels. *Hôtel Salam* and *Hôtel Cascades* are very basic with rooms and not much else for Dr60.

Les Cascades Hôtel (☎ 459658) is a tasteful and upmarket riad. It retains character, with a salon, restaurant and terrace where you can have breakfast (Dr50) with a view. The rooms have some stylish features and bathrooms, and cost Dr400/500 for a single/double.

There's also accommodation in Azilal, the local transport hub, but if you have time, it's better to head straight to the falls. Choices there include the cheap and cheerful *Hôtel Tissa* for Dr30 per person, or heated comfort at *Hôtel Assounfou* (☎ 459220, fax 458442), which has doubles with bath for Dr220. Both are on the main road through town, as are *restaurants* and *cafes*.

Getting There & Away If you're coming from Marrakesh, it would be preferable to get transport direct to Azilal, which has a CTM station on the main road through town. Two buses a day run from the Bab Doukkala bus station and cost Dr40. From Azilal, there are daily morning and afternoon departures to Marrakesh. There's one daily bus service to Beni Mellal (Dr20).

There are also grand taxis between Marrakesh and Azilal for Dr60 and others between Azilal and Ouzoud for Dr12. If you're returning to Azilal don't leave it too late in the day.

Beni Mellal
☎ 03

About 200km north-east of Marrakesh, the small but ever-expanding town of Beni Mellal makes a good stopover point. Though not particularly attractive in itself, the town has a good range of accommodation and is well placed for those interested in treks into the Middle Atlas and (for the adventurous) the High Atlas.

The Aït Bou Goumez Valley, to the south-west of Beni Mellal, beyond Azilal, provides access to Irhil M'Goun (4071m), the second-highest peak in the country. Guides and mules can be found in Beni Mellal and it's also possible to arrange 4WD expeditions there.

The main street, Ave Mohammed V, runs off the P24 to Marrakesh through the centre of the town and is intersected by Ave Hassan II and Ave des FAR. The medina is south of Ave Mohammed V and the bus station is north of it, about a 10-minute walk down Ave des FAR.

A huge market sprawls all the way up the hill, from the bus station to Ave Mohammed V, each Tuesday.

The tourist office (☎ 483981) is on Ave Hassan II, south of Ave Mohammed V. There are heaps of banks, most with ATMs and money-changing facilities, including Banque Populaire opposite the bus station. There are a couple of Internet places, including Sphinx Internet (just inside the western medina gate) and Hansali Internet (opposite Hôtel es-Saada) in the medina, charging Dr8 per hour.

Worth a visit are the **spring** within gardens and **Kasbah de Ras el-Aïn** on the hills to the south of town.

A cotton harvest festival is held here in March.

Places to Stay & Eat There are plenty of hotels in town, including a cluster opposite the bus station. Of these, *Hôtel Zidania* (☎ 481898, Ave des FAR) has the best rooms with bathroom for Dr133/154 a single/double.

Closer to the action of the medina, *Hôtel es-Saada* (☎ 482991, 129 Rue Tarik ibn Ziad) just off Ave Mohammed V, has small singles/doubles/triples for Dr30/50/70, a public douche downstairs and a terrace.

On the southern side of the medina, *Hôtel Marhaba* (☎ 483991, 58 Place de la Liberté) has reasonable rooms overlooking the terrace, which overlooks the square, for Dr40/70/90. Hot showers cost Dr5. On the

A Missing Link

In 1987, while exploring the plains of Azilal, a keen-eyed team of foreign geologists spotted bones jutting out of a remote hillside near the village of Wawmdane. After several months of careful excavation palaeontologists were rewarded with a complete skeleton belonging to a giant dinosaur named *Atlasaurus Imelakei* (Giant Lizard of the Atlas), which roamed the area more than 165 million years ago.

Having been trapped in a bend in a stream, the carcass became entombed and preserved in river refuse such as branches and sand. An important find, filling in a missing link of the Middle Jurassic period, the remains complete the genealogical picture of plant-eating dinosaurs.

The logistics of the excavation were tricky – the 15m-long creature is believed to have originally weighed more than 22½ tonnes, with its heart alone accounting for one tonne and a brain towering 6m above the ground. While the majority of the bones were brought down from the hillside by mule, some were so heavy (more than 500kg each), they needed to be hauled out by helicopter.

A complete fossil of this size is rare and there is evidence to suggest that a further wealth of diverse remains lie beneath the Moroccan landscape awaiting discovery. Unfortunately there are few resources to look for, protect and conserve these archaeological wonders. Many of those that are found end up in foreign markets whereas others are left to crumble into dust or are damaged by inexperienced workers.

While there's little left to see at the original site, the rebuilt fossil may soon be seen in the Archaeology museum in Rabat, with a full replica on display in Paris' Natural History Museum in France.

---

opposite side of the square, *Hôtel el-Fath* *(15 Place de la Liberté)* is similar, with rooms for Dr35/60/75.

Back in the medina, *Hôtel Tasmmet* *(☎ 421313, Blvd Ahmed el-Hansali)* has doubles for Dr100, or Dr160 with shower. The bathrooms smell a bit damp but they come with towels.

There are many cheap *cafe-restaurants* along Ave Mohammed V and *food stalls* around the medina. The restaurant at *Auberge du Vieux Moulin (Ave Mohammed V)* serves good French and Moroccan meals, but it's mainly an extension of the attached bar.

There's a nice shaded *cafe* with roof terrace opposite Hôtel es-Saada; you can pick up something tasty at *Patisserie el-Manzah* nearby.

Getting There & Away CTM buses leave from the main bus station, with some calling in at its office on Ave Mohammed V. Daily buses leave for Azilal (Dr20, 1½ hours) at 4 pm; Casablanca (Dr55, four hours) at 6 am and 1 pm; Er-Rachidia at 11.30 pm; Fès (Dr68, six hours) at 10 am, 11 pm and midnight; Marrakesh (Dr53, 3½ hours) at 12.30 and 3 pm; Midelt (Dr50, four hours) at 8 am;

and Rabat (Dr60) at 5 am. Regular local buses cover the same routes, plus Meknès, Nador, Demnate, Er-Rachidia, Safi, Essaouira and El-Jadida.

Grand taxis leave from Ave Mohammed V opposite the Hôtel des Voyageurs and from the bus station.

Ourika Valley
☎ 04

Skiers and trekkers (in spring and summer only) alike head down the Ourika Valley, to the east of Jebel Toubkal. The main options as bases are the ski resort of Oukaïmeden (virtually deserted outside the November to April snow season) or the village of Setti Fatma further east.

During spring **Oukaïmeden** is beautiful. In addition to long treks, you can explore the immediate vicinity of the resort in search of rock carvings (see *Gravures Rupestres du Haut Atlas* by Susan Searight & Danièle Hourbette). The Club Alpin Français (CAF) offers good trekking advice, including some on a route through to Toubkal. You're likely to see good bird life in the area.

Oukaïmeden boasts the ski lift at the highest altitude in Africa (3273m), but at the time of research it was closed. There was also no snow, causing further bad luck for the valley following severe floods in August 1995 – these resulted in the loss of hundreds of lives.

The most reliable months for skiing are February to April. There are seven runs ranging from good nursery slopes to a black run. Lessons are available for Dr150/250 per half/full day for individuals and Dr15/25 per half day for children/adults in a group class. Lift passes (should the ski lift be working) cost Dr30/50 per half/full day and equipment hire (there are several outlets in the town) is about Dr70 per day.

There are waterfalls at **Ourika**, which is best combined with a trip to its Monday market.

Setti Fatma, 24km away along a poor road, is the site of an important four-day *moussem* (festival in honour of a holy man) in August when a fair and market are set up at the Koubba of Setti Fatma. There is good walking locally, with seven waterfalls around town, and it is a good starting point for treks further afield (see the Trekking chapter).

Places to Stay & Eat On the way to Oukaïmeden are two fairly expensive hotels. Around 42km out of Marrakesh, the modern, box-like *Hôtel Ourika* (☎ 120999) has singles/doubles/triples with balconies for Dr262/327/412. There's a pool, restaurant and good views.

Auberge de Ramuntcho (☎ 484521, fax 484522), 50km from Marrakesh and a short way along the Setti Fatma turn-off, is a smallish place with a great terrace overlooking the river, a bar, restaurant and doubles for Dr250. Half-board is Dr300 per person.

In Oukaïmeden, the very good *CAF refuge* (☎ 319036, fax 319020, 60137) has dormitory beds, hot showers and a well-equipped kitchen. Rates are Dr24 for CAF members, Dr36 for HI members and Dr48 for nonmembers. You'll need your own sleeping bag.

The dated but comfortable *Hôtel de L'Angour – Chez JuJu* (☎ 319005, fax 448378) charges Dr240 per person for rooms with full board during the ski season. Cheaper dorm accommodation is also available. The hotel has a bar and restaurant, and this place received rave reviews from several travellers.

At the top end of the scale, *Hôtel Kenzi Louka* (☎ 319080, fax 319088) is a huge place with an indoor pool and spa (non-guests can use it for Dr50), hammam, fitness centre, nightclub, two restaurants, terraces and a bar. The interior is open plan, with rooms off balconies overlooking the bar, which has a great fireplace creating the apres-ski atmosphere. Rooms with all facilities are Dr750/900. The hotel also has tours and a range of activities available.

Tattoos

Quite separate from henna decorations, many Arab and Berber women (sometimes men, too) have permanent tattoos. The simple stylised designs, usually applied during a ceremony, are found on the face, hands, ankles and elsewhere on the body. The tradition resulted from the belief that the body orifices were vulnerable to the evil eye.

Tattoos also indicate a woman's social group as well as its systems and values. Girls are often tattooed to mark their entry into adulthood; designs also communicate whether a woman is married or not.

Some tattoos are placed to enhance the sensuality of the female body, others are believed to have healing powers – special tattoos placed on a woman's back are thought to prevent infertility.

Berber tattoo design

There are several other hotels which are only open during the winter. There are no shops in Oukaïmeden, so bring any provisions you require with you – you can buy them in the valley en route.

In Setti Fatma, the best place to stay is the *Hôtel Tafoukt*, which has rooms with shower and toilet for Dr90/127. There are a handful of basic cafe-restaurants which rent out rooms for about Dr40/60.

Getting There & Away Out of season there is little or no transport to Oukaïmeden from Marrakesh (75km), although you should be able to charter a grand taxi.

Otherwise, you could take a bus or grand taxi as far as Aghbalou (there are basic rooms to rent here) or Ourika (Dr20) and try hitching up the mountain. Buses to Setti Fatma leave from Bab er-Rob in Marrakesh (Dr10) at 11 am and 1 pm.

To the Tizi n'Test
☎ 04

About 15km south of Asni (see the High Atlas section in the Trekking chapter for information on this town), **Ouirgane** is a pretty spot which makes an attractive place to stop for a night or two. Market day is Thursday.

The French-run *Au Sanglier Qui Fume* (*☎ 485707, fax 485709*) has doubles for Dr250, but they may insist on half board for Dr510. It has a swimming pool (nonguests pay Dr50) and rooms are heated in winter. You can camp in the grounds for Dr20 each.

Heading south to Tin Mal, along the pretty Oued Nfiss and just past a couple of **kasbahs** (you can't miss the one on the left, perched up on a rocky outcrop), travellers with their own transport should take the time to stop at one of only two mosques in Morocco which non-Muslims can enter.

Built in 1156 by the Almohads in honour of Mohammed ibn Tumart, the dynasty's 'founding father' and spiritual inspiration, **Tin Mal Mosque** has recently been restored. The building, all a soft rose-coloured pink, contains some beautifully decorated archways. From the outside it looks inviolate; inside the immense doors it has a feeling of great tranquillity and openness.

On Friday the mosque is used for prayer, but on other days the guardian will be happy to show you around (a tip is expected). If you climb up to the minaret, you may also be lucky enough to see the resident owl that sleeps in the rafters.

Over the next 30km, the road winds its way rapidly up to the pass known as **Tizi n'Test** – at 2092m, it's one of the highest in the country.

The views are breathtaking from numerous points along the way, but if you are driving, note that heavy cloud and mist often cuts vision to near zero at the top of the pass and during the descent on the Taroudannt side. In winter it is quite possible that you'll find the road blocked by snow, so be prepared.

THE TWO ROADS TO OUARZAZATE

About 50km south-east of Marrakesh, the P31 to Ouarzazate crosses the Oued Zat (Le Coq Hardi, a hotel and restaurant of long standing, sits by the bridge) and soon after begins to climb towards the village of Taddert. Around here you'll see oak trees, walnut groves and oleander bushes.

After Taddert, the road quickly climbs and the landscape is stripped of its green mantle. The **Tizi n'Tichka** is higher than the Tizi n'Test to the west, but probably less spectacular. (Don't be surprised to be confronted by locals urgently waving pieces of amethyst and other semi-precious minerals at you as you round the hairpin bends.) Once over the pass, however, a remarkable scene is unveiled: the lunar landscape of the Anti Atlas and the desert beyond, obliterating memories of the green behind you.

An alternative route to Ouarzazate is via **Telouet** (a recommended destination in its own right) and the former main caravan route to Mali, the evidence of which can be seen in the features of the people you'll encounter. The turn-off to the village is a few kilometres beyond the pass, from where it's another 21km to the east (watch out in winter, as the narrow road can be snowbound).

Telouet is dominated by a **kasbah** that once served as a palatial residence and headquarters of the powerful Glaoui tribe.

Until Morocco gained independence in 1956, the Glaouis were virtually given a free hand in central Morocco by the French administration, in return for support for the protectorate. It's possible to visit the kasbah, a few rooms of which have been preserved, for a small fee. Wednesday is market day.

There are two hotels, the better of which, *Auberge Telouet* (☎ 04-890717), has prime position (and a Berber tented eating area) at the turn-off to, and overlooking, the kasbah. The second, *Chez M Bennouri*, is up a rough road through the souq. Both charge around Dr25 per person and offer meals. There's a daily bus to Marrakesh at 7 am.

The route beyond Telouet is rewarding, although the stream of 4WDs passing through ensures you're accompanied by kids chanting their 'stylo, bonbon, dirham' chorus. Those with a sturdy vehicle (or a couple of days to spare on foot or mountain bike) could follow the rough piste south from Telouet to Aït Benhaddou and back to the P31.

About 5km before Aït Benhaddou, the road hits the broken (but passable in the dry) bridge over the Oued Ounila. About 1.5km north-east of the bridge stands yet another Glaoui kasbah, that of **Tamdaght**. It is not as spectacular as the Aït Benhaddou complex, but comparatively little visited.

Aït Benhaddou
☎ 04

Aït Benhaddou, 32km from Ouarzazate, is one of the most exotic and best preserved kasbahs in the entire Atlas region. This is hardly surprising, since it has had money poured into it as a result of being used for scenes in as many as 20 films, notably *Lawrence of Arabia* and *Jesus of Nazareth*.

Much of the village was rebuilt for the filming of the latter. Its fame lives on, but the population has dwindled.

The main access is by the Auberge la Baraka, head down past the souvenir stalls and you'll see the kasbah on the other side of the Oued Ounila. Usually no more than a trickle with a ramp and stepping stones to cross it, the river can flow more strongly in early spring. The main entrance to the kasbah complex is a little way upstream (you'll

know you've found it when you see more souvenir stalls).

One of the locals may half-heartedly hassle you to engage him as a guide, but this is not really necessary. Simply wander at will through the alleys. A few locals make a few dirham by showing you their houses, which often have a few 'artefacts' strewn around them. Most of the untended structures are littered with garbage, but the overall effect remains impressive and worthwhile. From the upper reaches of the kasbah there are magnificent views of the surrounding palmeraie and, beyond, the unforgiving *hammada* (stony desert).

Places to Stay & Eat There are a few places to stay, and there is a lot to be said for doing so rather than bedding down in Ouarzazate.

By the roadside, in the centre, *Auberge la Baraka* (☎ 890305, fax 886273) has clean and basic doubles with shower for Dr60, or Dr100 with toilet. It also has a cosy restaurant, from where Berber music emanates.

Further along the road *Auberge Etoile Filante d'or* (☎ 890322, fax 886113) has sparkly bed sheets, proper toilets and hot water. There's a terrace where you can sleep for Dr20, and breakfast in the restaurant is Dr20.

The *Auberge el-Ouidane* (☎ 890312), signposted from the road, has better rooms with showers, and some have views across to the kasbah.

Next door, the *Hôtel Restaurant la Kasbah* (☎ 890302, fax 883787) has rooms overlooking the pool, which overlooks the kasbah, with half board for Dr220/360 a single/double. Rooms in the main building cost Dr160/260 with half board or Dr100/130 for room only.

All these places offer meals. There's another *restaurant*, which has a unique location on the kasbah side of the river and offers an alternative vista.

Getting There & Away To get there from Ouarzazate, drive or take a bus along the main road to Marrakesh to the signposted turn-off (22km); Aït Benhaddou is another

9km down a good bitumen road (stop at the signs for the hotels). Occasionally, local buses travel to Aït Benhaddou from Ouarzazate, but it's a lot easier to get there by grand taxi (Dr20).

Otherwise, ask around among tourists in the restaurants or hotels. Hitching is difficult.

OUARZAZATE
☎ 04 • pop 30,000
Ouarzazate (pronounced **War**-zazat) was created by the French in 1928 as a garrison and regional administrative centre. Before that, all there was around here was the Glaoui kasbah of Taourirt at the eastern end of the modern town. Now something of a boom town, except for the kasbah, it's a pretty quiet and nondescript place.

Nevertheless, the Moroccans have been hard at work promoting Ouarzazate as a big destination, or at least as a launching pad for excursions along the Drâa and Dadès Valleys. It has also become the film centre of Morocco, and many productions, including *The Sheltering Sky,* have been shot in the area. There are often parts as extras available during shootings – check hotel noticeboards and American Language Centers.

The movie industry and government promotion explains the sparkling luxury hotels that continue to spring up; however, regular flights from Paris and Casablanca only just keep them half full. Ouarzazate does have other drawcards, albeit outside of town, which more than justifies the trip. The weather also appeals to package tourists who are happy to soak up the sun and sand so far away from the sea. You will need some warm clothes in winter, as bitterly cold winds often whip down off the snow-covered High Atlas and can do so well into spring.

Information
Tourist Office The Délégation Régionale du Tourisme (☎ 882485, fax 885290) is helpful and centrally located on Blvd Mohammed V, opposite the post office.

It's open from 8.30 to noon and 2.30 to 6.30 pm weekdays. These hours are sometimes extended during summer.

Money There are at plenty of banks in town. The main Banque Populaire on Rue de la Poste is open standard hours weekdays and from 3 to 6 pm Saturday and from 9 am to 1 pm Sunday.

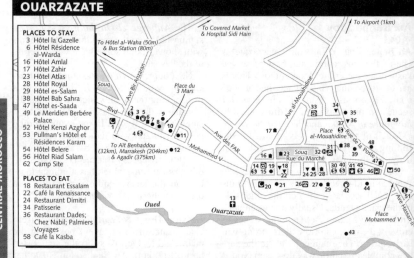

OUARZAZATE

PLACES TO STAY
3   Hôtel la Gazelle
6   Hôtel Résidence al-Warda
16 Hôtel Amlal
17 Hôtel Zahir
23 Hôtel Atlas
28 Hôtel Royal
29 Hôtel es-Salam
38 Hôtel Bab Sahra
47 Hôtel es-Saada
49 Le Meridien Berbère Palace
52 Hôtel Kenzi Azghor
53 Pullman's Hôtel et Résidences Karam
54 Hôtel Belere
56 Hôtel Riad Salam
62 Camp Site

PLACES TO EAT
18 Restaurant Essalam
22 Café la Renaissance
24 Restaurant Dimitri
34 Patisserie
36 Restaurant Dades; Chez Nabil; Palmiers Voyages
58 Café la Kasba

To Covered Market & Hospital Sidi Hain
To Airport (1km)
To Hôtel al-Waha (50m) & Bus Station (80m)
Souq
Place du 3 Mars
Blvd
Ave Bir Anzarah
Ave al-Mouahidine
Place al-Mouahidine
Ave des FAR
To Aït Benhaddou (32km), Marrakesh (204km) & Agadir (375km)
Mohammed V
Souq
Rue du Marché
Rue de la Poste
Oued
Ouarzazate
Place Mohammed V
Ave Hassan II

For cash advances on your credit card, go to the very efficient Crédit du Maroc at the western end of town on Blvd Mohammed V, on the corner of Ave Bir Anzaran. It's open during standard banking hours.

Post & Communications Both the post office and phone office on Rue de la Poste are open normal working hours.

There are a few cardphones outside. There are plenty of *téléboutiques* (privately operated telephone service) around town with telephone and fax services.

There are a couple of Internet options, including Info-Ouarzazate near the Hôtel Amlal, which charges Dr15 per hour; First Net, which charges Dr10 per hour, is north of the town centre.

Travel Agencies RAM (☎ 885102) is at 1 Blvd Mohammed V. Palmiers Voyages on Rue de la Poste is an agent for RAM and also has Visa advance and change facilities. There are plenty of other agencies, including Ksour Voyages (☎ 882840) on Place 3 Mars, where you can book flights, hire bicycles and organise trips to destinations such as Telouet, Skoura, the Todra Gorge and Zagora.

Bookshops Belmsaggam bookshop opposite Cafe des Voyages stocks a range of French books and a few English titles (including LP books). The téléboutique opposite Restaurant Dimitri has a selection of foreign newspapers and magazines.

Medical Services There are two hospitals, one (☎ 882444) east of the tourist office on Blvd Mohammed V and the other out past the covered market. There's a medical centre and a night pharmacy (☎ 882490) on Blvd Mohammed V.

Things to See & Do

The only place worth visiting in Ouarzazate itself is the **Taourirt Kasbah** at the eastern end of town, off Blvd Mohammed V. During the 1930s, in the heyday of the Glaoui chiefs, this was one of the largest kasbahs in the area. It housed numerous members of the Glaoui dynasty, along with hundreds of their servants and workers. Unesco has carefully restored sections of the building.

The 'palace' that the Glaouis occupied consists of courtyards, living quarters, reception rooms and the like, and is open from 8 am to noon and 3 to 6.30 pm daily.

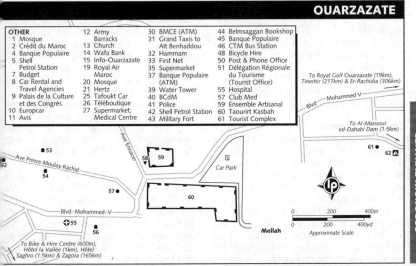

OUARZAZATE

OTHER
1 Mosque
2 Crédit du Maroc
4 Banque Populaire
5 Shell Petrol Station
7 Budget
8 Car Rental and Travel Agencies
9 Palais de la Culture et des Congrés
10 Europcar
11 Avis
12 Army Barracks
13 Church
14 Wafa Bank
15 Info-Ouarzazate
19 Royal Air Maroc
20 Mosque
21 Hertz
25 Tafoukt Car
26 Téléboutique
27 Supermarket; Medical Centre
30 BMCE (ATM)
31 Grand Taxis to Aït Benhaddou
32 Hammam
33 First Net
35 Supermarket
37 Banque Populaire (ATM)
39 Water Tower
40 BCdM
41 Police
42 Shell Petrol Station
43 Military Fort
44 Belmsaggan Bookshop
45 Banque Populaire
46 CTM Bus Station
48 Bicycle Hire
50 Post & Phone Office
51 Délégation Régionale du Tourisme (Tourist Office)
55 Hospital
57 Club Med
59 Ensemble Artisanal
60 Taourirt Kasbah
61 Tourist Complex

Entry costs Dr10. You can take on a guide if you want to know what each of the now empty rooms was used for.

There are some good views over the rest of the kasbah and the Oued Ouarzazate which, like the Oued Dadès, spills into the **Al-Mansour ed-Dahabi Dam** to the southeast which then becomes the Oued Drâa.

Opposite the entrance to the kasbah is another building in the same style, which houses the **Ensemble Artisanal**. Here you can find stone carvings, pottery and woollen carpets woven by the region's Ouzguita Berbers. It's open from 8.30 am to noon and 1 to 6 pm weekdays and from 8.30 am to noon Saturday.

There are plenty of other craft shops around the kasbah area, which makes for some pretty interesting wanders. Don't expect to pick up any bargains – Club Med is virtually next door and there are direct flights to Ouarzazate from Paris!

After visiting the kasbah you will probably be accosted by someone wanting to show you the old **mellah** (Jewish quarter) and synagogue. You don't really need a guide to explore the alleys but finding specific sights is difficult. It's also possible to walk all the way down to the dam, the waters of which now encircle a highly photogenic kasbah.

Activities

Quad Adventure Ouarzazate (☎ 884024) offers quad-biking around the local pistes and palmeraies.

Royal Golf Ouarzazate (☎ 882653), 19km east of town, is a nine-hole course (3150m; par 36) overlooking Al-Mansour ed-Dahabi.

Special Events

In March/April of each year the Marathon des Sables, a seven-day footrace across the desert, originates and finishes in Ouarzazate. If you're crazy enough to consider taking part, check out the organiser's Web site: www.saharamarathon.co.uk.

A bit more civilised and relaxing event, Symphonies of the Desert, occurs in June. The tourist office can provide details of the philharmonic orchestra performances that are staged in the desert outside of town.

Within Ouarzazate itself, the moussem of Sidi Daoud is held in August.

Places to Stay – Budget

Camping You'll find a *camp site* (signposted) next to the so-called Tourist Complex (basically a zoo and swimming pool) off the main road out of town towards Tinerhir, about 3km from the bus station.

There is some shade, and it's beside the Oued Ouarzazate. It also has a grocery store and restaurant. It costs Dr6/10 per car/person, Dr7 to pitch a tent and Dr10 for electricity.

Hotels There are effectively only six budget hotels in Ouarzazate, so if you arrive late, you may have to pay for something more expensive if they're all full (which does happen).

One of the best is *Hôtel Royal* (☎ 882258, 24 Blvd Mohammed V), with all sorts of rooms for all sorts of prices. Small singles start at Dr30 and doubles are Dr72, or Dr92 with shower. The beds are comfortable, the linen is clean and the showers are hot. Like most here it has three-day tours taking in the Dadès Valley, Todra Gorge and Merzouga for Dr1200.

Opposite, *Hôtel es-Salam* (☎ 882512) has large and bright singles/doubles/triples for Dr41/82/93, or Dr61/102/133 with bathroom. The hotel also offers basic cooking facilities and there are supplies for sale; there are cosy lounges and a terrace but the manager can be a bit over-friendly.

Another decent choice is *Hôtel Atlas* (☎ 882307, 13 Rue du Marché). Clean rooms cost Dr36/67, or Dr46/82 with private shower. There's a terrace and restaurant.

A few cheapies around the market square, handy for the bus station, include the clean *Hôtel al-Waha* (☎ 886666), which has rooms for Dr45/65.

About 1km out of town on the Zagora road is an excellent deal, *Hôtel la Vallée* (☎ 854034, fax 854043). It's beside the palmeraie, which its good (unlicensed) Berber-tented restaurant overlooks. The pool is tucked away within the hotel courtyard, and pleasant rooms with bathroom cost Dr120/200.

About 500m further out on the right is *Hôtel Saghro* (☎ 854135, fax 854709). It also has a pool but it's not as good or well located as La Vallée. Rooms are cheaper though, at Dr100/150.

The best one-star hotel is *Hôtel Amlal* (☎ 884030, fax 884600, e hotelamlal@ yahoo.fr), a block north of Blvd Mohammed V. It's modern and clean, and comfortable singles/doubles/triples/quads with bathroom cost Dr100/130/170/210. There is guarded parking out the front.

Hôtel Bab Sahra (☎ 884722, fax 884465, Place al-Mouahidine), near the water tower, has decent-sized, comfortable rooms for Dr50/80, or Dr80/120 with shower.

Hôtel es-Saada (☎ 883231, 12 Rue de la Poste) has small rooms with just as small bathrooms for Dr108/128/170. It's worth a look just for the plastic flowers and huge posters of a tropical New York skyline.

Places to Stay – Mid-Range
Just by Place du 3 Mars on Blvd Mohammed V, *Hôtel Résidence al-Warda* (☎ 882344) offers large but tatty and stark mini-apartments with up to five beds, bathroom, kitchen (unequipped) and balcony for Dr150/200 for two/three people.

The run-down, motel-style *Hôtel la Gazelle* (☎ 882151, fax 884727, Blvd Mohammed V) seems to be living off a worn-out reputation. Rooms with bathroom cost Dr127/159. It has a restaurant, basic bar, pool and enclosed parking in the front courtyard.

Hôtel Zahir (☎ 885740, fax 884837, Ave al-Mouahidine), north-west of the market, has spotless rooms with bathroom for Dr128/156. A suite for four to six people with TV and heating costs Dr300. The hotel has a restaurant and there is a cafe/patisserie next door.

Places to Stay – Top End
There are plenty of options in the four- and five-star brackets, most of which can be found on Ave Prince Moulay Rachid. Predominantly geared towards the package tourist, they can be a bit cavernous but they blend quite well into the environment with their kasbah style designs.

The *Hôtel Riad Salam* (☎ 883335, fax 882766), off Blvd Mohammed V, is one of the nicest and cheapest. The rooms are modern and the hotel boasts two restaurants (one of them is usually the stage for folkloric music performances and the like), a sauna and a tennis court. The mosaic-tiled pool is in very serene gardens and some rooms, which cost Dr308/390 for a single/double, look onto smaller courtyards.

Hôtel Belere (☎ 882803, fax 883145) has a huge foyer, a biggish piano bar and rooms for Dr600/800, or suites for Dr1000/1500. *Hôtel Kenzi Azghor* (☎ 886501, fax 886353, Ave Prince Moulay Rachid) has a great terrace overlooking town, loads of sports, kid-friendly facilities and a good bar. Rooms start at Dr359/468 plus taxes.

More expensive is *Le Meridien Berbère Palace* (☎ 883105, fax 883071), a sumptuous place with hammam, bar and boutiques. Standard rooms cost Dr900, and there are apartments for Dr1500.

Pullman's Hotel et Résidences Karam (☎ 882225, fax 882642, Ave Prince Moulay Rachid) has many facilities, including the Byblyos nightclub, a hammam and bars. Rooms cost Dr660/770.

Places to Eat
Restaurant Essalam, between Blvd Mohammed V and Rue du Marché, has a good selection of the old favourites and a roof terrace.

Just as good, and cheaper, is the *Café la Renaissance*, just around the corner on Blvd Mohammed V, where you can tuck into a big plate of brochettes, chips and salad for around Dr30. The restaurant attached to the *Hôtel Atlas* also serves reasonably priced basic meals.

In the evening there are cheap *food stalls* along Rue du Marché. There are more cheap and cheerful places to eat by the bus station.

The restaurant at *Hôtel la Vallée* is worth going to for well-prepared, moderately priced Moroccan dishes in pleasant surroundings. There's often music here as well.

Restaurant Dimitri (☎ 887346, 22 Blvd Mohammed) once served as a petrol station, general store, dance hall, telegraph office and just about everything else besides. The atmosphere is very relaxing and it has a good range of both Moroccan, French and Italian dishes. A full meal (with wine) will set you back about Dr170. The place is often packed to the hilt with tourists.

There are a couple of restaurants along Rue de la Poste, including *Restaurant Dades*, which does pizzas for Dr25; and *Chez Nabil*, which has menus for Dr40/50.

Plenty of the bigger hotels have expensive restaurants.

There's a cluster of cafes around the middle of Blvd Mohammed V. *Café la Kasba* is in a slightly better spot, with a view of the Taourirt Kasbah. You'll find a good *patisserie* on Rue de la Poste, and an *ice-cream* place on Place du 3 Mars.

You can pick up fresh local produce in the small *market* off Rue du Marché. The *supermarket* on Blvd Mohammed V carries an excellent range of alcohol and toiletries. Another *supermarket* with fresh cheese, meat and vegetables can be found behind the water tower.

The *market*, with loads of fresh produce, is held near the bus station on Friday.

Getting There & Away
Air Taourirt airport (☎ 882348) is 1km north of town. RAM has direct flights to Casablanca (Dr557, one hour) daily, and to Paris (Dr3402, 3½ hours) twice weekly. Air France also has a weekly service to Paris.

Bus The bus station is about 1km northwest of the town centre. CTM (☎ 882427) has a station on Blvd Mohammed V, close to the post office. It has buses to Agadir (Dr86, seven hours) via Taroudannt (Dr70, 5½ hours) at noon; Casablanca (Dr120, 8½ hours) at 9.45 pm; M'Hamid (Dr52.50, seven hours) via Zagora (Dr35, four hours) at 4 am and 12.30 pm; Marrakesh (Dr49, four hours) at 8.30, 10 and 11 am and noon; and Er-Rachidia (Dr65.50, nine hours) via Boumalne du Dadès (Dr24.50) and Tinerhir (Dr35, 3½ hours) at 10.30 am.

Local companies have run services to the same destinations plus Fès (Dr142) and Skoura (Dr11).

Grand Taxi Grand taxis also leave from the bus station to Agdz (Dr25), Marrakesh (Dr100), Skoura (Dr12), Tinerhir (Dr50) and Zagora (Dr45). Local grand taxis to Aït Benhaddou (Dr20) leave from Place al-Mouahhidine.

Car & Motorcycle Since the Drâa Valley route down to Zagora and beyond to M'Hamid is such a spectacular and interesting journey, it's worth considering car rental before you leave Ouarzazate (from Dr400 per day), although it's not as cheap here as it is in Marrakesh. With your own vehicle, you'll be able to stop wherever you like to explore the *ksar* (fortified strongholds) or take photographs.

In a bus or shared taxi you'll simply speed through all these places, catch only fleeting glimpses and probably arrive in Zagora feeling disappointed. Ouarzazate agencies include:

Avis (☎ 884870) corner of Blvd Mohammed V and Rue A Sehraoui
Europcar (☎ 882035) Place du 3 Mars
Hertz (☎ 882084) 33 Blvd Mohammed V
Tafoukt Car (☎ 882690) 88 Rue Errachidia

Getting Around
If you opt to stay south of the river you may want to hire a bicycle from the Bike & Hire Centre to the south of the bridge; it also rents quad bikes. In town there is another place with bicycles for around Dr70 per day on Rue de la Poste.

If you're not that energetic, there are petit taxis to ferry you around town.

Drâa Valley

From Ouarzazate the P31 leads you southeast along the magical Drâa Valley, a long ribbon of technicoloured palmeraies, kasbahs and busy Berber villages. One of the longest rivers in Morocco, the Drâa originates in the High Atlas and winds its way through mountains and desert sands before it finally reaches the Atlantic at Cap Drâa, just north of Tan Tan. The water generally stops at M'Hamid (it last flowed all the way to the sea following freak floods in 1989).

The fertile palmeraies that it feeds are crammed with date palms, olive and almond groves and citrus trees. The richest section of the valley lies between Agdz and Zagora, a stretch of about 95km. Beyond Zagora, a minor road takes you a further 96km south to the tiny village of M'Hamid, just 40km short of the Algerian border.

AGDZ
☎ 04

About 20km south-east of Tizi n'Tinififft, Agdz (pronounced Ag-a-dez) is basically a one-road town with a **palmeraie**, a **kasbah** and views of the weird-looking **Jebel Kissane**. It makes a decent base for walks through the Drâa and has petrol, a post office and telephones as well as several souvenir shops.

Carpets adorn Ave Mohammed V, the main road through town, which leads to the main square, Place de la Marché Verte, before heading off to the right and southwards towards Zagora.

Camping Kasbah-Palmeraie is, as the name suggests, near the kasbah, about 4km north of the square.

There are a couple of cheapies on Place de la Marché Verte. *Hôtel Restaurant Draa* (☎ 843153) has big, simple rooms with double beds for Dr35/70 a single/double – the terrace has good views over the square, the palmeraie and kasbah. *Hôtel des Palmiers* (☎ 843127) has cleaner, brighter rooms for Dr60/90 (slightly more if you want a window facing the street).

Kissane Hôtel (☎ 843044, fax 843259), at the Ouarzazate end of town, offers more comfortable singles/doubles/triples with balcony for Dr150/230/310. The hotel has a cafe, restaurant and pool.

There are plenty of *restaurants* and *snack stands* on the square.

CTM, SATAS and several other buses stop here en route between Ouarzazate and Zagora. Sometimes you can get on, sometimes you can't. Otherwise, occasional grand taxis go to Ouarzazate and Zagora – Dr30 for either.

ZAGORA
☎ 04 • pop 15,000

Like Ouarzazate, Zagora is largely a recent creation, dating from French colonial times, when it was set up as an administrative post.

Nevertheless, the oasis has always been inhabited, and it was from this area that the Saadians began their conquest of Morocco in the 16th century. Moroccan rulers long before them passed through here too, and there are vestiges of an Almoravid fortress atop Jebel Zagora.

There are plenty of interesting places to explore in the vicinity and the town does

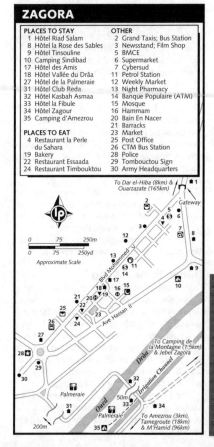

ZAGORA

PLACES TO STAY	OTHER
1 Hôtel Riad Salam	2 Grand Taxis; Bus Station
8 Hôtel la Rose des Sables	3 Newsstand; Film Shop
9 Hôtel Tinsouline	5 BMCE
10 Camping Sindibad	6 Supermarket
17 Hôtel des Amis	7 Cybersud
18 Hôtel Vallée du Drâa	11 Petrol Station
27 Hôtel de la Palmeraie	12 Weekly Market
31 Hôtel Club Reda	13 Night Pharmacy
32 Hôtel Kasbah Asmaa	14 Banque Populaire (ATM)
33 Hôtel la Fibule	15 Mosque
34 Hôtel Zagour	16 Hammam
35 Camping d'Amezrou	20 Bain En Nacer
	21 Barracks
PLACES TO EAT	23 Market
4 Restaurant la Perle du Sahara	25 Post Office
19 Bakery	26 CTM Bus Station
22 Restaurant Essaada	28 Police
24 Restaurant Timbouktou	29 Tombouctou Sign
	30 Army Headquarters

To Dar el-Hiba (8km) & Ouarzazate (165km)

Gateway

0   75   250m
0   75   250yd
Approximate Scale

Blvd Mohammed V

To Camping de la Montagne (1.5km) & Jebel Zagora

Ave Hassan II

Oued Drâa

Irrigation Channel

Palmeraie

Palmeraie

To Amezrou (3km), Tamegroute (18km) & M'Hamid (96km)

50m

200m

have its moments, particularly when a dust storm blows up out of the desert in the late afternoon and the lighting becomes totally surreal. Zagora is also where you'll see that somewhat battered sign reading 'Tombouctou 52 jours' (by camel caravan).

Although little more than an oversized village, Zagora has more than its fair share of expensive hotels and is a good place to rest up before heading into the desert proper.

There's a large market on Wednesday and Sunday, when fruit (dates are the big commodity down here), vegetables, herbs, hardware, handicrafts, sheep, goats and donkeys are brought in to be sold.

If you are here over the period of Mouloud (see Public Holidays & Special Events in the Facts for the Visitor chapter), try to see the moussem of Moulay Abdelkader, which brings the town to life.

Information

There's a Banque Populaire and a BMCE along Blvd Mohammed V, open during normal banking hours. The post office is at the southern end of the street. There are phones here. Cybersud, on Ave Hassan II, is the place for Internet access, but it's pricey (Dr25 per hour).

Limited international newspapers are available at the newsstands near the market.

If you need medicine, there is a night pharmacy opposite Bank Populaire.

There are hammams south of Blvd Mohammed V, around a small market area.

Things to See & Do

The spectacular **Jebel Zagora**, which rises up across the other side of the river, is worth climbing for the views – if you have the stamina and set off early in the morning. Halfway up are the ruins of an 11th-century Almoravid fortress to explore, but the modern-day fort at the summit remains off-limits. It's also possible to drive up to a viewpoint – follow the piste beyond Camping la Montagne.

The beautiful, extensive **palmeraies** are within easy reach, particularly those close to the hotels and camp sites at the southern end of town.

It seems like everyone in Zagora has a camel for hire and it's possible to arrange **camel treks** of up to a week or so through shops and accommodation. Prices start at about Dr200 per person per day – check if you need to supply your own drinking water and bedding.

Places to Stay – Budget

Camping Campers have a choice of three good sites all with some form of shade.

Camping d'Amezrou, about 200m past the Hôtel la Fibule along the dirt track that runs alongside the irrigation channel, has a couple of Berber tents set up around the site. It costs Dr10 per person, Dr5 for a car, Dr15 to pitch a tent and Dr10 for electricity. Hot showers cost Dr5. The setting, although out of town, is attractive and close enough to hotel restaurants.

Also over this side of town is *Camping de la Montagne*, at the foot of Jebel Zagora. Follow the signpost off to the left after La Fibule. It's about 1.5km down the dirt track from here. There are toilets and plenty of shade. Cold drinks are available, but you're advised to bring your own food. It costs Dr10 per person and Dr5 for a tent. Hot showers are free.

Camping Sindibad (☎ 847553), off Ave Hassan II, is central and surrounded by palm trees, with a tented restaurant and small pool. It costs Dr5/10 per child/adult, Dr10 per tent and Dr5 for a hot shower. There are also a couple of basic singles/doubles for Dr35/50.

Hotels There are two hotels next to each other on Blvd Mohammed V. The better of the two, if you can get a front room, is *Hôtel Vallée du Drâa* (☎ 847210). Singles/doubles cost Dr45/66 with shared bathroom, Dr69/85 with shower and Dr77/90 with bathroom. It's clean and friendly and has its own restaurant.

Almost next door is *Hôtel des Amis* (☎ 847924) with basic singles/doubles/triples with shower for Dr35/60/75. Rooms without showers, but with the bonus of a balcony overlooking the main road, cost Dr50.

Hôtel la Rose des Sables (☎ 847274, Ave Hassan II) has better rooms, also with shower but no balcony, for Dr50/70. There's also a good restaurant.

The popular one-star *Hôtel de la Palmeraie* (☎ 847008, fax 847878, Blvd Mohammed V) has rooms with bathroom for Dr110/150/190. The main attraction is the pool, and the fly-blown bar attracts some intriguing characters.

Places to Stay – Mid-Range

It can be worth your while booking ahead in high season for the following places, which are often full. On the other hand, you may well be able to get hefty reductions on room rates in low season.

The two best places to stay in Zagora are south of town by the river and palmeraies. *Hôtel Kasbah Asmaa* (☎ 847599, fax 847527) is a pleasant, welcoming two-star hotel designed to resemble a Berber ksar. There is a lovely garden, as well as an outdoor tea salon and a good restaurant. In high season rooms are Dr250 per person. In the warmer months you can sleep in the nomad tents set up around the courtyard for Dr50.

Just 50m up the road is the very relaxing two-star *Hôtel la Fibule* (☎ 847318), which has its own shady garden, bar, pool and excellent restaurant. The rooms with showers and toilets are in traditional Berber style. Doubles with breakfast cost Dr180, or Dr360 with shower. Half-board rates from Dr180 per person are available

If these places are full, the next best option is *Hôtel Zagour* (☎ 846178, fax 847451), a new place on the piste leading to Jebel Zagora. It has clean singles/doubles for Dr180/250.

Dar el-Hiba (☎ 847805), 8km north of Zagora, is quite unique. A renovated kasbah tucked away among the ksar, it's basic but clean with mud walls and a few Berber features. It costs Dr150 per person half board and you won't see many other tourists. It's signposted from the main Zagora road. The toilets and showers are clean but you have to go outside and across the alley to get to them.

Places to Stay – Top End

The cheapest place to stay in this category is also the nicest, with a large pool surrounded by Berber tents. Singles/doubles at *Hôtel Riad Salam* (☎ 847400, fax 847551) cost Dr485/545 plus taxes but the location by the Ouarzazate exit leaves a lot to be desired. There are also suites for Dr900/1300.

Hôtel Tinsouline (☎ 847252, fax 847042, e tinsouli@iam.net.ma) has a pool, hammam, bar and restaurant, but is rather characterless. Rooms with bathroom cost Dr530/650 and suites accommodating four cost Dr1950.

Top of the line is *Hôtel Club Reda* (☎ 847079, fax 847012), in the palmeraie next to the Oued Drâa Rooms cost a steep Dr660/770 but the hotel has all the amenities you would expect, including a bar, restaurant and tennis courts.

Places to Eat

All the hotels have their own restaurants, and it's probably true to say that they all try hard to produce tasty Moroccan dishes, the cheaper ones for around Dr30. Offering much the same are quite a few basic and popular restaurants, including *Restaurant Essaada*, *Restaurant la Perle du Sahara* and *Restaurant Timbouktou*, all along Blvd Mohammed V.

Hôtel de la Palmeraie has a decent licensed restaurant with meals for around Dr70. For excellent food in pleasant surroundings, head to the restaurants at the *Hôtel Kasbah Asmaa* and *Hôtel la Fibule*. A three-course meal with wine or beer will cost upwards of Dr100.

There's fresh produce at the main entry to the *market*, a *supermarket* at the northern end of town with limited supplies (no alcohol) and a *bakery*.

Getting There & Away

Bus The CTM bus station is at the southwestern end of Blvd Mohammed V, and the main bus and grand taxi lot is at the northern end.

There's a daily CTM bus to Ouarzazate (Dr35, four hours) at 7 am. Starting in M'Hamid it comes past Hôtel la Fibule at about 6.30 am, so if you're staying around there, you can flag it down en route, before continuing through to Marrakesh (Dr79, eight hours). The return bus for M'Hamid leaves at 4 pm (Dr18, three hours).

Other companies have at least one run a day (either morning or around 9 pm) to Casablanca (Dr139), Erfoud (Dr70, at 7.45 am), Er-Rachidia (Dr80), Marrakesh (Dr90), Meknès (Dr155) Ouarzazate (Dr35), Rabat (Dr150) and Rissani (Dr60) via Tazzarine (Dr30).

Grand Taxi Grand taxis are more regular early in the morning. Destinations include Agdz (Dr30), Ouarzazate (Dr80), M'Hamid (Dr25), Rissani (Dr90) and Tazzarine (Dr40).

SOUTH OF ZAGORA
Amezrou
Across the Oued Drâa, about 3km south of Zagora, is the village of Amezrou. It has an interesting old mellah, which still produces silver jewellery. Jews lived here for centuries and formerly controlled the silver trade, but they all took off for Israel after 1948, leaving the Berbers to carry on the tradition.

If you look like you might buy something, the locals will be willing to show you the entire process. Because the village is so close to Zagora, local children will leap on you, offering to be guides, but it's fairly low-key hassle. Elsewhere in the palmeraie life goes on much as it always has. It's well worth spending a day wandering through the shady groves along the many tracks that dissect it.

The dates grown here are reputedly the best in Morocco, but times have been getting harder because of Bayoud disease, a fungal disease that attacks and kills the palms.

Tamegroute
Further south, about 18km from Zagora, is Tamegroute. For many centuries, right up until recent times, the town was an important religious and educational centre whose influence was felt throughout the Drâa region and into the desert beyond.

Tamegroute consists of a series of interconnected ksar, at the centre of which is the zawiyya and its famous library.

The **library** (signposted on the main road as 'Librairie Coranique') houses a magnifi-

cent collection of illustrated religious texts, dictionaries and astrological works, some of them on gazelle hides. The oldest texts date back to around the 13th century. Most of them are kept on shelves behind glass doors, but others are displayed in glass cases.

They're beautifully illustrated, and visitors are allowed into the outer sanctuary and the library in the morning and late afternoon (it's generally closed from noon to 3 pm). You'll be expected to leave a donation for the upkeep of the place. The zawiyya remains a pilgrimage site for people needing charity and hoping to be cured of their ills.

There's also a small **pottery factory** in the village, which is worth a look for its distinctive green glazed products, and a Saturday **souq**. There is no shortage of local people willing to act as guides, should you need one.

Hôtel/Restaurant Riad Nacir, on the left-hand side as you enter town from Zagora, has basic singles/doubles for Dr30/60.

Tinfou Dunes
About 5km south of Tamegroute you can get your first glimpse of the Sahara. Off the road to the left are a number of isolated sand dunes. If you've never seen sandy desert and do not intend to head to Merzouga, Tinfou is a pleasant spot to take a breather and enjoy a taste of the desert.

There's no village as such here, but there are a couple of attractive accommodation options. *Hôtel Repos du Sables* (π/fax 04-848566) is a kasbah with simple but comfortable and individually styled rooms costing Dr50 per person. It has a relaxed ambience, enhanced by the artworks of the owners that surround the main courtyard. The food is also very good (about Dr45) and there is a trio of monkeys to provide entertainment. There are camels parked outside that can take you to the dunes at sunset for Dr150.

Sitting further back from the road, the very comfortable but characterless three-star *Porte au Sahara* (π 04-848562, fax 847002) is also in the kasbah style. The hotel offers spacious singles/doubles, all with balcony and bathroom, for Dr380/480, including breakfast. There's also a fully licensed restaurant and a hammam.

M'Hamid
☎ 04 • pop 2000

Most people who come to Zagora try to make it to the end of the road at M'Hamid, about 96km to the south. The attraction again is the journey itself. The road south of Tinfou soon crosses the Drâa and leaves it behind to cross a vast tract of implacable hammada. After crossing a low pass you hit the village of **Tagounite**, which has a couple of cafes, including *Es-Saada* and *Sahara*, and some persistent guides.

A few more kilometres takes you over the dramatic Tizi Beni Selmane pass, from which the oases of the Drâa again come into view. The village and kasbah of **Oulad Driss** make a picturesque stop before the final run into M'Hamid.

There's not an awful lot happening in M'Hamid. **Jew's Dunes**, a section of sandy desert, is 10km to the north-east. This is where overnight camel treks (from Dr200 per person) end up; if you have a sturdy vehicle, preferably a 4WD, you can drive out there and camp among the dunes (you'll need a guide to lead you across the hammada).

There are a couple of small craft shops and a Monday market in M'Hamid. About 3km beyond M'Hamid are the remains of the old village, which was destroyed during a 1970s Polisario attack.

Places to Stay & Eat Once you're at Oulad Driss, on the approach to M'Hamid, there is a smattering of camp sites with rooms, and Berber tents set up for the bus loads of tourists that come here for camel treks. Isolated from town, they all have restaurants and you should be able to convince a bus driver to drop you off en route.

One of the first you come to is *Carrefour des Caravanes (☎ 848665)*, which has its own dunes and charges Dr10 each per person, van or tent. There are a few basic rooms for Dr50, but a better option is to stay in its Berber tents for Dr20 per person; there's also a pool.

Across the road, but without the dunes, is *Bivouac Mille et Une Nuits (☎ 847061, fax 847922)*, which has a tiled hammam, small pool and tented accommodation for Dr70 per person, or Dr120 with dinner and breakfast.

In M'Hamid, *Hôtel Restaurant Sahara (☎ 848009)* has grubby facilities for Dr25 per person and shared cold showers. The hotel cafe is pleasant and serves decent meals.

Auberge al-Khaima is about 500m over the river to the left as you enter town. Rather

---

Morocco's Travelling Acrobats

For hundreds of years, the remote region of Tazeroult in southern Morocco has been the traditional birthplace of Morocco's most famous acrobats, the sons of Sidi Hamed ou Moussa.

Taking their name from their patron saint, this Berber brotherhood of acrobats travels throughout the country, and is known for its spectacular and highly dangerous tumbling routines. At the beginning of this century, its reputation spread abroad, and the troupe wandered as far as America. Soon there was hardly a circus in Europe which didn't lay claim to a Berber among its troupe.

The origin of the acrobats is believed to lie in a distant warrior tradition. Originally, members of this Berber clan were famous marksmen and agile warriors, greatly in demand above all for the accuracy of their aim. Acting as armed escorts or bodyguards for pilgrims or travellers, they were also recruited to fight in the tribal wars of the Anti Atlas.

Some have claimed that the immense human pyramids, now a major feature of the Berber repertoire, were devised in battle to scale the walls of fortified mountain kasbahs. The complicated tumbles may have formed part of a martial arts training, rather like karate or judo does for many soldiers today.

What is certain is that in times of peace these marksmen toured Morocco putting on demonstrations of their skills. This is the tradition that continues up to the present day. Djemaa el-Fna in Marrakesh hosts daily afternoon performances of the Berber acrobats, and remains the starting point for the majority of Europe's circus tumblers.

characterless rooms and Berber tents cost Dr25 per person, and there's a hammam.

Getting There & Away There's a daily CTM bus from Zagora (Dr18; originating in Marrakesh and passing through Ouarzazate) to M'Hamid around 4 pm; it returns at 6 am in summer and 5 am in winter. If you're lucky, you may be able to get a lift with other tourists or in one of the rare grand taxis.

If you don't have your own transport and just want to make a day trip from Zagora, it comes down to hiring a taxi. The usual charge is up to Dr400 for the day, although this is negotiable.

Dadès Valley & the Gorges

Heading roughly east of Ouarzazate, the Dadès Valley threads its course between the mountains of the High Atlas to the north and the rugged Jebel Sarhro range to the south. The biggest oases and the line of kasbahs that give this route its nickname, 'Valley of a Thousand Kasbahs', begin just before the town of Skoura.

Further along the valley, the beautiful Dadès and Todra Gorges, also lined with palmeraies, cut back up into the High Atlas. From here rough pistes lead all the way over to the Middle Atlas.

SKOURA
☎ 04

Skoura is situated 39km east of Ouarzazate and can be visited on a day trip from there. The oases here contain a collection of impressive kasbahs.

One of the most easily accessible is the **Kasbah ben Moro**, just off the main road, 2km before you reach town. Its owners, who live next door, use it mainly for animals and storage, but will open it up for a small fee. There's not a lot to see inside, but from the top there are great views of the palmeraie and another kasbah, **Amerdihl**, which is owned by a wealthy Casablanca family and cannot be visited.

If you want to stay, *Hôtel Palmerie* (☎ 852208 through the téléboutique), in the centre of town, is a basic place with rooms for Dr30. There are a few restaurants, cafes and snack stands and a market on Monday.

The odd bus passes through from Ouarzazate and Tinerhir (Dr10), but a grand taxi from Ouarzazate (Dr12) is a better option.

EL-KELAÂ M'GOUNA
☎ 04

Another 50km up the valley, marked by balancing rocks at its entrance, the small town of El-Kelaâ M'Gouna is a famous rose-water production centre which celebrates its harvest in May with a colourful rose festival, where rose petals rain down on dancers. There are banks, restaurants and, of course, rose-water shops along the main road through town and you can visit one of the **rose-water factories**. Market day is Wednesday.

A cooperative here produces **traditional daggers**. You can buy them at a much lower price than through merchants in larger cities. If you ask around in the small town, someone will point you in the right direction.

If you have decent transport, a 40km meander through the **Vallée des Roses** makes a pleasant loop north of M'Gouna. In spring the entire area is awash with pink Persian roses and it's a stunning area for walking.

If you want to stay, *Hôtel du Grand Atlas*, on the main street, has basic rooms with washbasin for Dr45 per person.

A much better option is *Rosa Damaskina* (☎ 836913, fax 836969), 4km before you enter town. With a terrace overlooking the river, it has an excellent restaurant (no alcohol) and kasbah views. Basic doubles/triples/quads cost Dr129/188/288; or Dr169/228 for doubles/triples with bathroom. The rooms have hotplates and heating and you can also sleep in its Berber tent for Dr25 per person.

Overlooking town, the four-star *Les Roses de Dadès* (☎ 836336) has great views, especially from the pool, over the river to the mountains. It's getting a bit ragged round the edges but has the advantage of the only bar in town. Rooms cost Dr250/300/400.

TANNERIES

Tanneries provide perhaps the greatest illustration of how resolutely some parts of Morocco have clung to practices developed in medieval times. Moroccan leather, and more particularly the Fassi leather produced in Fès, has for centuries been highly prized as among the finest in the world. One type of leather, a soft goatskin used mainly in bookbinding, is itself known (naturally enough) as *morocco*.

At the tanneries of Marrakesh and Fès, little has changed in centuries. Skins are still carried by donkey to the tanner's souq, tanning and dyeing vats are still constructed from mud brick and tile, the (strictly male) tannery workers are still organised according to medieval guild principles, and their health and safety practices are also scarily old-fashioned.

Along with being one of Morocco's (and the world's) oldest arts, with a history that stretches back at least 7000 years, leather-making is undoubtedly also one of its smelliest. Rank odours abound at the tanneries of Fès el-Bali, and the delicate tourist who comes to view the work here will be offered a sprig of mint to hold to the nose and take the edge off the pong.

Among the exotic ingredients that add to the heady brew are pigeon poo, cow urine, fish oils, animal fats and brains, chromium salts and sulphuric acids.

Inset: Leather drying, Taroudannt (photo by Amerens Hedwich)

Right: Workers plunge hides into vats of dyes, Fès

CHRISTOPHER WOOD

Many travellers say that not only do they find the smell almost unbearable, but they also feel uncomfortably voyeuristic about viewing from the roof terraces the tannery workers tending the skins in the souq down below.

Still, a visit to the tanneries on the outskirts of the medinas of Fès and Marrakesh is right up there on the must-see list.

Carolyn Papworth

MARK DAFFEY

IZZET KERIBAR

Top: Fresh livestock hide waiting for preparation before auction, Chouara Tannery, Fès

Left: Drying coloured hides after tanning, Fès

BOUMALNE DU DADÈS
☎ 04

At a fork in the road 24km north-east of El-Kelaâ M'Gouna, the left branch takes you up the stunning Dadès Gorge, while the main road continues over the river to the hillside town of Boumalne du Dadès.

Though you may want to press on up to the gorge, Boumalne itself is a pleasant, laid-back place and has a reasonable choice of accommodation. Market day is Wednesday.

There's a Banque Populaire on Ave Mohammed V, which is open during normal hours. The post office is up the hill. There are photo and craft shops, and trekking guides can be found at Café des Fleurs or through the accommodation options in town. There's a hammam for men and women down the stairs next to the CTM office.

The hammada and grassy plains immediately to the south of Boumalne offer some rewarding **bird-watching** opportunities. Take the piste leading off the main road beyond town south towards the village of Tagdilt and Vallée des Oiseaux (Valley of the Birds) to look for larks, wheat-ears, sandgrouse, buzzards and eagle owls. Auberge le Soleil Bleu has details of the latest spottings.

Places to Stay

About the first place you come across in the lower end of the town is *Hôtel Adrar* (☎ 830355) with basic, clean singles/doubles from Dr40/50. Next door, *Hôtel Bougafer* has rooms with a bit more character for the same price, as well as a terrace and salon.

Up the hill, *Auberge le Soleil Bleu* (☎/fax 830163) has clean and cosy rooms with shower for Dr70/120 (Dr140 per person half board). You can pitch a tent for Dr10 per person, or sleep on the roof terrace for Dr30.

Next to the Shell petrol station, *Hôtel Vallée des Oiseaux* (☎/fax 830764) has reasonable rooms for Dr50/80, or Dr105/120 with shower and toilet. The hotel has a restaurant, and a Berber tent and model kasbah in its garden.

Hôtel al-Manader (☎ 830172), to the right on Ave Mohammed V, the main road uphill, has a great spot overlooking the valley. Rooms without shower are Dr60/80 and rooms with shower and balcony are Dr80/120.

Virtually next door, and following the same design with the same vista, *Hôtel Restaurant Chems* (☎ 830041, fax 831308) has a pleasant restaurant and terrace cafe.

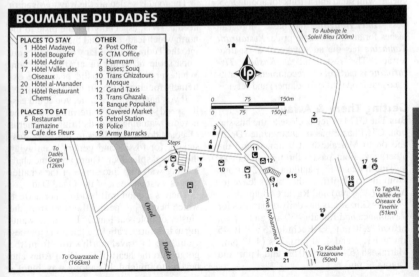

BOUMALNE DU DADÈS

PLACES TO STAY
1 Hôtel Madayeq
3 Hôtel Bougafer
4 Hôtel Adrar
17 Hôtel Vallée des Oiseaux
20 Hôtel al-Manader
21 Hôtel Restaurant Chems

PLACES TO EAT
5 Restaurant Tamazine
9 Cafe des Fleurs

OTHER
2 Post Office
6 CTM Office
7 Hammam
8 Buses; Souq
10 Trans Ghizatours
11 Mosque
12 Grand Taxis
13 Trans Ghazala
14 Banque Populaire
15 Covered Market
16 Petrol Station
18 Police
19 Army Barracks

To Auberge le Soleil Bleu (200m)

0   75   150m
0   75   150yd

To Dadès Gorge (12km)

Steps

Oued Dadès

To Ouarzazate (166km)

Ave Mohammed V

To Tagdilt, Vallée des Oiseaux & Tinerhir (51km)

To Kasbah Tizzaroune (50m)

CENTRAL MOROCCO

Half-board rates are Dr170 per person and the food is quite good. At the time of research a pool was being constructed.

Kasbah Tizzarouine (☎/fax 830256), along a short stretch of piste past Chems, is a great kasbah-style complex with wonderful valley views. Half board, in comfortable rooms with bathroom, costs Dr300 per person. Just as comfortable are its troglodytes (cave rooms) built into the rock overlooking the valley. They too have bathroom and nice furnishings for Dr250 per person. Alternatively, you can sleep in nomad-style tents for Dr200. Camping is also possible for Dr25 per person. The hotel has an excellent restaurant and terraces and is a good place to enjoy local Berber music.

The only other mid-range choice is *Hôtel Madayeq* (☎ 830261, fax 830131), the weird-looking building dominating the hill. Rooms will set you back Dr225/375 plus taxes. The hotel is a bit gloomy but has a swimming pool, bar (the only place in town where you can buy alcohol) and expensive restaurant.

Places to Eat
For cheap eats, the restaurant below *Hôtel Adrar* serves a filling meal of tajine or brochettes with salad and a drink for about Dr35. Other restaurants nearby compete for business. *Hôtel Bougafer* has basic Moroccan dishes for about the same price. *Restaurant Tamazine* has the advantage of a 1st-floor terrace. The restaurant at *Kasbah Tizzarouine* is particularly recommended for its excellent food (Dr80 for dinner) and service.

Getting There & Away
Bus The CTM office is close to the bus station. CTM has a bus to Ouarzazate (Dr25) and on to Marrakesh at 9 am. Going the other way, a bus passes through on its way to Tinerhir and Er-Rachidia at 12.30 pm. From the same office other buses leave for Agadir (8.30 pm) and Rabat (7.30 pm).

Trans Ghizatours has daily departures for Casablanca and Rabat (9.30 am and 4 pm), Erfoud (2.30 pm), Er-Rachidia (5 and 10.45 am and 1, 2 and 4.30 pm), Fès (4.30 pm), Marrakesh (6, 7 and 8.30 am and 4 pm) and Zagora (2 pm).

Trans Ghazala has one departure at 6.15 pm for Ouarzazate, Marrakesh, Casablanca and Rabat.

Grand Taxi, Truck & Minibus You may have to wait a while for a grand taxi to fill up; the fare to Ouarzazate is Dr40, Dr15 to Tinerhir, Dr10 to Aït Oudinar, at the start of the gorge, and Dr15 to the Vallée des Oiseaux. There are also minibuses and trucks heading out to local towns from the bus station.

THE DADÈS GORGE
The drive up to the gorge is pleasant, taking you past almond and fig trees, some fabulous rock formations and impressive kasbahs and ksar.

The road snakes up in a leisurely fashion inside the wide walls of the gorge for about 25km to Aït Oudinar. Here the gorge narrows abruptly and the river flows right by the roadside.

About 2km further, the road winds up inside the main canyon in a series of hairpin bends. After a few kilometres of this, the road flattens out again as you leave the best of the scenery behind you.

The road is sealed all the way to **Msemrir** (63km), beyond which you will definitely need a 4WD, especially for the piste to the north which leads east, and then south, down into the Todra Gorge. Many of the pistes are impassable in winter or after heavy rain. Whatever the weather, the pistes are extremely rough and the driving is very slow.

If you have plenty of time, you could easily spend several days pottering about in the gorge – watching nomads bring vast herds of goats down the cliffs to the river, fossicking for fossils and generally enjoying the natural splendour. There are some challenging walks up into some of the smaller gorges west and east of the Oued Dadès.

There's a good trail heading north-west, which begins just across the river from the cluster of hotels at Km27. For those wanting to trek further afield, a tempting journey would be to travel northwards from the gorge into the heart of the High Atlas and beyond to Imilchil. It's a long way, but it's feasible if you combine days of walking with the occasional ride on local transport (there is a slow but regular and reliable market circuit of trucks and minivans).

Almost all the hotels in the gorge and in Boumalne du Dadès can put you in touch with guides who know the area well. You can also hire bicycles (Dr70 per day) and in the summer it's possible to go **rafting**.

Places to Stay & Eat

The choice of places to stay in the gorge is growing rapidly, and most of what's on offer is really good value. As well as offering a range of rooms, nearly all will let you sleep on their terrace or salon (bring a sleeping bag), or camp by the river for around Dr5 or sleep on the terrace or salon for Dr10. If you prefer the comfort of your own basic room, expect to pay around Dr30 per person, which includes hot showers. Hotels also have information on trekking, and guides eager to take you to the top of the gorge from about Dr100 per day.

They also have their own restaurants, but there's nothing to stop you trying out another hotel's grub. However, most hotels offer half-board rates and dinner is often accompanied or followed by Berber music, so there may not be much incentive to leave.

There is very little in the way of shops in the gorge, so if you want to self-cater, it's best to bring your own supplies.

The first hotel at Km14 is the basic **Café Mirguirne**, which has a terrace looking down the valley and rooms for Dr50. It also offers trekking trips with overnight camping at the nearby Sidi Boubar Gorge, which has springs and rock pools.

Another 1km further on, **Hôtel Restaurant Kasba** overlooks the fantastic rock formations on the other side of the valley. It's an interesting little place with small balconies, and is constructed in a mixture of modern and traditional styles with rooms for Dr60, or Dr120 with bathroom.

At Km25 is the village of Aït Oudinar, where you'll find the **Auberge des Gorges du Dadès** (☎ 831710) perched over the river. There are simple rooms for Dr40/60 (shared hot showers) or rooms with bath-

room for Dr100/140. Breakfast is included in the price. Most rooms, especially the more expensive ones, overlook the river.

A bit further up, **Chez Pierre** (☎ 830267) is a tasteful auberge with a sumptuous menu. It's the one place in the gorge that serves cake. Half board is Dr360 per person.

The main cluster of hotels is at Km27. **Hôtel Restaurant Camping du Peuplier** has four basic rooms (three with shower) for Dr50.

Next up is **Hôtel la Gazelle du Dadès** (☎ 831719, fax 830131), which has a very pleasant rooftop terrace. Rooms with a shower are Dr30/60 (Dr80 with a view). They are clean and there is hot water.

Next door, **Hôtel la Kasbah de la Vallée** (☎/fax 831717) has four basic rooms for Dr60 and more with shower and toilet for Dr80/120/150 for singles/doubles/triples.

A little further up is the simple **Hôtel Tisdrine** (☎ 831745, fax 830145), which offers doubles for Dr45, or Dr80 with shower.

Closer to the narrowest part of the gorge, and on the river, is **Hôtel Atlas Berbere** (☎ 831742). Built in earthen kasbah style, it's the nicest in the bunch here, with beautifully decorated rooms for about the same price as the Tisdrine.

Next door, **Hôtel le Vieux Chateaux du Dadès** (☎ 831719, fax 830131) has clean, bright rooms (a few with balconies) for Dr50, or Dr120 with bathroom.

Just beyond the most dramatic stretch of the gorge, by the river, is **Hôtel Berbere de la Montagne** (☎ 830228) offering comfortable rooms with shower for Dr80 and free couscous on Friday. Still further are two more simple places: **Hôtel Taghia**, which has rooms for up to three people for Dr40, and **La Kasbah des Roches**, a bright little cafe offering two rooms that sleep two or three for Dr40.

Getting There & Away

If you happen to be around at the right time, you may be able squeeze into one of the Berber lorries that ply between Boumalne and outlying villages on market days (Friday and Saturday in Msemrir; Wednesday in Boumalne).

Grand taxis and minibuses run from the grand taxi lot in Boumalne (Dr10) and you can ask to be dropped at your chosen hotel. To return, simply wait by the road and flag down a passing vehicle. Hiring a taxi for a half-day trip into the gorge should cost around Dr150.

Alternatively, you could get up to the gorge by a combination of hitching and walking. The energetic could combine the Dadès and Todra Gorges by crossing between the two (a two- to three-day walk).

TINERHIR
☎ 04

About 51km north-east of Boumalne du Dadès is the bustling town of Tinerhir, which has spread quite a way beyond the boundaries of the original town. Essentially a mining town, it is also the launching pad for trips up into the Todra Gorge.

The highway is known as Ave Mohammed V as it passes through the town on the way to Er-Rachidia. There are banks with ATMs, a couple of petrol stations and several restaurants along here.

You'll find a branch of the BCME and the post office on Ave Hassan II, a block in to the south. Tougdha Internet, next to the Ziz petrol station on Ave Mohammed V, charges Dr15 per hour. Most of the town's hotels and restaurants can be found on or near Ave Hassan II.

Immediately north and south-east of the town are some lush **palmeraies** dotted with kasbahs and ksour that are well worth exploring. An enormous souq is held about 2km west of the centre on Sunday and Monday.

Places to Stay – Budget
About 2.5km west of the town centre, *Camping Ourti* (☎ 833205) is awkwardly located and exposed. Camping costs Dr12 per person, Dr10 to pitch a tent and Dr12 for a caravan. If the pool is in use, a swim costs Dr10. There are also basic rooms for Dr35 a person.

There is a handful of budget hotels virtually in a row on Ave Hassan II. *Hôtel Salam* (☎ 835020), next to the CTM office, has basic singles/doubles for Dr30/60. There is a hot shared shower.

Hôtel el-Houda (☎ 834613, 11 Rue Moulay Ismail), just off Ave Hassan II, has clean rooms for a negotiable Dr30/60.

Hôtel Alqods (☎ 834605), at the end of the block, has bright rooms around a covered courtyard for Dr30/60, but the noise from the downstairs cafe can get a bit much.

A better bet is *Hôtel l'Oasis* (☎ 833670, Ave Mohammed V), next to the Total petrol station. It has a restaurant and perfectly clean, comfortable rooms for Dr40/80.

Hôtel el-Fath (☎ 834806, 56 Ave Hassan II) has clean rooms for Dr60/70, a terrace and a salon overlooking the gardens.

Places to Stay – Mid-Range
Overlooking the gardens, *Complexe Touristique Todra* (☎ 834249, fax 834565, Ave Hassan II) has plenty of ageing, dark wood-panelling and colonial furniture. There's a pleasant balcony terrace and a bar and restaurant. There's a choice of three rooms ranging from Dr72/95 to Dr205/260 a single/double.

Back behind Ave Hassan II, near the central market area, is the popular *Hôtel de l'Avenir* (☎/fax 834599). Very pleasant singles/doubles/triples cost Dr60/100/130, including breakfast in the sociable restaurant area. Trekking can also be organised here.

Hôtel Tomboctou (☎ 834604, fax 833505, Ave Bir Anzarane) is a beautiful old kasbah. Appropriately decorated and comfortable en suite rooms with fan cost Dr250/300/350. Rooms without bathroom are Dr89/156/200 and half-board rates are available. There's a pool in the serene courtyard, an excellent restaurant with international dishes and good information on the area with hand-drawn maps for sale (covering the nearby gorges and as far afield as Merzouga). Mountain trekking and bicycle trips can also be organised.

Hôtel Kenzi Bougafer (☎ 833280, fax 833282) is a modern three-star hotel on the road to Ouarzazate, opposite Camping Ourti. The location isn't great, but the rooms are fine and cost Dr460/570.

The four-star *Hôtel Sargho* on top of the hill overlooking town was being renovated

Places to Eat

The best place to look for cheap food is the market area south of Ave Hassan II. There are loads of simple little *food stalls* here.

There are a few simple restaurants on Ave Hassan II, including *Café des Amis*, which serves excellent brochettes. You'll find more choices along Ave Mohammed V.

Café Centrale and *Restaurant Essaada* are both good for simple Moroccan standards. Slightly fancier are *Restaurant la Kasbah* and the restaurant at *Hôtel l'Oasis*, both of which offer three-course meals for around Dr70.

The restaurant at *Hôtel de l'Avenir* serves a very good paella (two hours' notice required) and the one at the *Tomboctou* is good for a licensed splurge.

Getting There & Away

Bus Buses leave from the Place Principale, off Ave Mohammed V in the centre of town.

CTM has a couple of buses that pass through Tinerhir on their way east and west. Only 10 seats are set aside for passengers boarding at Tinerhir. At 2 pm a bus goes to Er-Rachidia (two hours). At 8 am a bus passes through on its way to Marrakesh (10 hours) via Ouarzazate (five hours). Another bus leaves for Ouarzazate at 2.30 pm. Otherwise, several private buses also leave from the same area to the same destinations.

Local buses cover the same destinations plus Agadir, Casablanca, Fès, Meknès, Midelt, Tangier and Zagora.

Grand Taxi Grand taxis to Ouarzazate (Dr45) and Er-Rachidia (Dr35) leave from the eastern end of the gardens, near Hôtel al-Qods. This is also the place to hunt for occasional transport (taxis, lorries or pick-up trucks) up the Todra Gorge (Dr10) and beyond.

THE TODRA GORGE
☎ 04

Only 15km from Tinerhir, at the end of a valley thick with palmeraies and Berber villages, is the magnificent Todra Gorge. A massive fault in the plateau dividing the High Atlas from the Jebel Sarhro, with a crystal-clear river emerging from it, the gorge rises to 300m at its narrowest point.

It's best in the morning, when the sun penetrates to the bottom of the gorge, turning the rock from rose pink to a deep ochre. In the afternoon it gets very dark and, in winter, bitterly cold.

Climbing is becoming increasingly popular on the vertical rock face of the gorge. There are some sublime routes here (French grade 5), some of them bolted. Pillar du Couchant, near the entrance to the gorge, offers classic long climbs; hotels can provide further information but the guides with the most experience tend to predominantly speak Spanish.

As the base of the main gorge can be explored quite quickly, those with more time might like to wander further afield. About a 30-minute walk beyond the main gorge is the **Petite Gorge**, aptly named and better for novice climbers with some good short routes.

A more strenuous choice would be to walk a three-hour loop from one side of the gorge to the other. The walk starts after leaving the main gorge – as the road heads right, take the track leading up the hill to the left. It's well defined for most of the route, as it is used by donkeys and mules. Head to the pass and from there ascend south-east to the next pass. You can deviate off the main route to look over the rim of the gorge but be careful, as the winds get mighty powerful up here. From the second pass descend to the village of **Tizgui**, from where you can walk back through the **palmeraies** to the gorge. The palmeraies to the south of here are covered in ruined kasbahs, and photographic opportunities abound.

A network of difficult pistes links the sporadic villages here in the High and Middle Atlas, many of which are snowbound in winter. You could spend weeks exploring them, but you should bear in mind that you'll be far away from banks, post offices and even basic health services most of the time, so come prepared. The hotels in Tinerhir and the gorge can put you in touch with local guides.

CENTRAL MOROCCO

Places to Stay & Eat

Along the road to the gorge, about 9km from Tinerhir, is a line of camp sites. They're all in the palmeraies and have showers and toilets. There's a small shop that sells basic supplies across the road from *Auberge de l'Atlas* (☎/fax 834209), the first of the camp sites. L'Atlas is very good, but marginally more expensive than the other two. It costs Dr7/10 per child/adult, Dr15 for a car or tent and Dr20 for a camper van. There are also doubles/triples for Dr90/140, a restaurant and Berber tent area.

Next is *Camping le Lac* (☎ 834215) which has no *lac* (lake) and is quite spartan. Camping costs Dr8 per person, Dr15 per van, Dr10 per tent and Dr10 for electricity. The site also has six basic rooms for Dr60 and a restaurant. The third *Camping Les Poissons Sacre* does have a lake and charges similar prices.

There are a couple of auberges and camping places en route to the gorge, but the five options within and closer to the gorge are worth the extra travel. All offer the option of sleeping in salons or terraces from Dr25 per person and have restaurants serving good food (but no alcohol). There's Berber music in all.

Hôtel Restaurant Yasmina (☎ 834207, fax 833013) is the most expensive, with half board in rooms with showers for Dr110/200 a single/double. You can sleep in the tent or on the roof for Dr50 half board – not bad. The hotel has bicycles for hire, a téléboutique and an open fire in the cafe. *Hôtel Restaurant les Roches* (☎ 834814, fax 833611) offers double rooms for Dr100, or Dr150 with shower. It too has cheaper salon and roof accommodation. Both places offer good deals to 'poor students'.

You can get good food in both places, the latter of which serves lunches to an average of 300 bus tourists per day.

If these two are full or are a bit too sanitised for you, *Hôtel el-Mansour* (☎ 834213), just before the entrance to the gorge proper and with a Berber tented cafe outside, has basic rooms for Dr50. Next door, *Hôtel Etoile des Gorges* (☎ 835158) offers similarly basic rooms from Dr50 to Dr70.

There's a decent and cheap tented terrace restaurant here.

The most basic place is *Hôtel la Vallée* (☎ 835580), which has smelly rooms overlooking the palmeraie for Dr60.

Getting There & Away

See the previous Tinerhir entry for transport to the gorge.

At the top of the gorge, **Tamtattouchte** has basic accommodation at *Auberge Baddou* for Dr60 and is the place to turn off to the west for the long loop south through to the Dadès Gorge. The more ambitious might consider making their way further up into the Atlas Mountains. A combination of souq lorries, 4WD taxis and hiking could take you north to Aït Hani, from where you could push on over the Tizi Tirherhouzine towards Imilchil.

IMILCHIL

In the heart of the Middle Atlas, the small village of Imilchil is known for its September moussem, a kind of tribal marriage market where the women do the choosing. Though somewhat less tribal and a lot more touristy than it once was, it's a big event attracting merchants, singers and dancers, as well as would be brides and grooms. It's very colourful with the flirtatious girls in their elaborate jewellery and the strutting boys in their white *jellabas* (flowing garments) hung with knives. On the sidelines, groups of parents huddle together arranging marriage contracts and dowries. The dates of the festival are posted at tourist offices throughout the country and there are many organised tours from the large cities.

At other times Imilchil remains quiet and is a good base for trekking; there are several experienced mountain guides based here.

During the festival the area is covered in tented accommodation; otherwise, there are just two basic *hotels* and several *cafe/restaurants*.

To get to Imilchil from Marrakesh, head north-east by bus or a series of grand taxis to Kasba Tadla. From there you need to get another grand taxi to El-Ksiba. Here you may have to wait to get something for Aghbala. The turn-off for Imilchil is near Tizi n'Isly, about 10km before Aghbala. From there, 61km of piste leads south to Imilchil. Around here you will have to rely on souq lorries – market days in Imilchil are Friday and Sunday.

If you have plenty of time, it's also possible to get to Imilchil (a breathtaking 160km by souq lorries or 4WD) from Boumalne du Dadès or Tinerhir.

Ziz Valley & the Tafilalt

The Ziz Valley leads down from the small town of Rich to the end of the road at Merzouga. The route to Er-Rachidia is spectacular, reminiscent of Monument Valley. The main highlight is the **Ziz Gorges**, stretching from the French-built **Tunnel du Légionnaire**, 20km south of Rich. This magnificent route through palm-fringed towns and ksar passes a series of dams, including the **Barrage Hassan Adakhil**, the turquoise blue of which is visible from the main highway. These and an irrigation system were built after massive flooding of the Oued Ziz in the late 1960s. Thanks to these measures the region is now relatively prosperous – Er-Rachidia is the place where the locals nicknamed one of their new suburbs Dallas!

If you have your own transport you can detour to the 17th-century Berber village of **Amjouj** (along the piste to the left, 100m before the bridge over the Oued Ziz, just before the reservoir), stop for a bit of trout fishing or enjoy the therapeutic properties of the **hot springs** 1km or so before the tunnel. Whatever your mode of transport, this trip is best appreciated during daylight.

Beyond Er-Rachidia the road heads past the fertile Source Bleue de Meski before heading deep into the desert and dunes of Merzouga. The Tafilalt was one of the last areas to succumb to French control under the protectorate, its tribes putting up sporadic resistance until 1932. Two years later, Morocco was officially considered 'pacified'. To make sure this state of affairs did

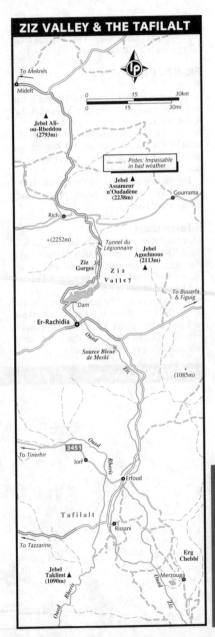

ZIZ VALLEY & THE TAFILALT

not change, Erfoud was built as an administrative and garrison town to keep a watchful eye on the Tafilalt tribes.

ER-RACHIDIA
☎ 05

At the crossroads of important north-south and east-west routes across Morocco, Er-Rachidia (named after the first Alawite leader, Moulay ar-Rashid) was originally built by the French as an administrative and military outpost. A fairly large army garrison is still maintained here.

Depending on where you're coming from, Er-Rachidia can be a relaxing place to stay for a day or two.

Information

There are at least four banks in town, including a BMCE on Place Moulay Hassan and a Banque Populaire near the main street heading out to Erfoud. They both have ATMs.

The post office is on Blvd Mohammed V on a service lane. The phone office, to the left of the post office, is open from 8.30 am to 9 pm daily. There are a few cardphones outside. As elsewhere, Er-Rachidia has a fair scattering of téléboutiques.

Discover Internet and Galaxienet, both near the covered market, charge Dr10 per hour. There is another Internet cafe near the bus station.

There is a night pharmacy (☎ 572695) by the bus station.

There are hammams opposite the bus station and by the main mosque.

Places to Stay

The three cheapest places are all extremely basic and just off Place Moulay Hassan. All have cold communal showers.

At the western end of the square in a side street is the **Hôtel Royal**. Singles/doubles with big windows are Dr40/60. Slightly better is the **Hôtel Z'toun** (e soul_22@usa.net, Rue Abdallah ben Yassine), with rooms for Dr30/50 and a terrace overlooking the square.

Better is **Hôtel Restaurant Rennaissance** (☎ 572633, 19 Rue Moulay Youssef) with simple rooms that sleep one or two for Dr50 and rooms with shower that sleep two or three for Dr80. They will probably try and talk you into half board for Dr100 per person.

The best choice in town by far is **Hôtel M'Daghra** (☎ 574047, fax 790864, 92 Rue M'Daghra) on a busy street leading to the

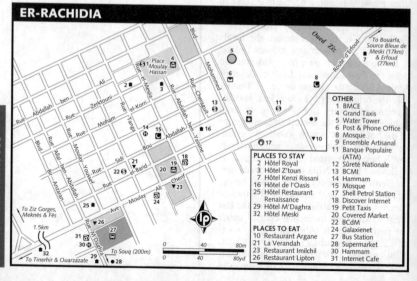

ER-RACHIDIA

OTHER
1 BMCE
4 Grand Taxis
5 Water Tower
6 Post & Phone Office
8 Mosque
9 Ensemble Artisanal
11 Banque Populaire (ATM)
12 Sûreté Nationale
13 BCMI
14 Hammam
15 Mosque
17 Shell Petrol Station
18 Discover Internet
19 Petit Taxis
20 Covered Market
22 BCdM
24 Galaxienet
27 Bus Station
28 Supermarket
30 Hammam
31 Internet Cafe

PLACES TO STAY
2 Hôtel Royal
3 Hôtel Z'toun
7 Hôtel Kenzi Rissani
16 Hôtel de l'Oasis
25 Hôtel Restaurant Rennaissance
29 Hôtel M'Daghra
32 Hôtel Meski

PLACES TO EAT
10 Restaurant Argane
21 La Verandah
23 Restaurant Imilchil
26 Restaurant Lipton

To Bouarfa, Source Bleue de Meski (17km) & Erfoud (77km)

To Ziz Gorges, Meknès & Fès
1.5km

To Tinerhir & Ouarzazate

To Souq (200m)

To Tinehir & Ouarzazate

market. Comfortable, clean rooms with guaranteed hot showers cost Dr131/158.

The one-star *Hôtel de l'Oasis* (☎ 572519, *fax 570126, Rue Sidi Bou Abdallah*) is a good choice, with bright and clean rooms with bathroom for Dr125/148. The hotel has its own bar and restaurant.

A bit cheaper is *Hôtel Meski* (☎ 572065, *Ave Moulay Ali Cherif*) on the Fès road. Clean, bright rooms with phone and bathroom cost Dr96/122; there's a restaurant and pool.

The only top-end hotel is the four-star *Hôtel Kenzi Rissani* (☎ 572186, fax 572585, Route d'Erfoud) just across the Ziz bridge. Rooms cost Dr560/700, and although the hotel is a bit sanitised it does have all the amenities you would expect, including bar, restaurant and swimming pool.

Places to Eat

One of the most popular places to eat is *Restaurant Imilchil*, opposite the covered market. It has a good selection of tajines etc, indoor and outdoor seating and a rooftop terrace cafe. In much the same league is the busy *Restaurant Lipton*, across the main road from the Hôtel Restaurant Renaissance.

Restaurant Argane, down the road by the side of the Ensemble Artisanal, has good roast chicken; *La Verandah*, by the mosque, does burgers and other snacks.

For a splurge, try a meal at the licensed *Restaurant Oasis*, which is attached to the hotel of the same name. There's a very good but pricey restaurant at *Hôtel Kenzi Rissani*.

For breakfast, there are a couple of good *cafes* on Rue M'Daghra, down by the bus station. You'll also find hole-in-the-wall snack sellers down here.

Those wishing to put their own meals together should have a look around the *covered market*, where a wide variety of very reasonably priced food is available.

There's a good *supermarket* on Rue M'Daghra for stocking up on supplies. Further down this road is the *souq*, which has fresh produce as well as household goods.

Getting There & Away

Bus All buses operate out of the central bus station, which is on Rue M'Daghra. CTM (☎ 572024) has a daily departure to Marrakesh (Dr110.50, 10 hours) at 5.45 am via Tinerhir (three hours) and Ouarzazate (Dr65.50, six hours). It also runs two buses to Meknès (Dr80, six hours) at 7.30 and 10 pm and one to Rissani (Dr18, three hours) at 5 am via Erfoud.

Quite a few other bus companies have services running more frequent services to the same destinations plus Azrou (Dr113); Bouarfa (Dr50, five hours); Casablanca (Dr120, 10 hours), via Meknès and Rabat (8½ hours) at 5.30 and 9 pm; and Fès (Dr78.50, 8½ hours).

Grand Taxi Most grand taxis leave from Place Moulay Hassan. Destinations include Azrou (Dr75), Erfoud (Dr16), Fès (Dr100) and Meknès (Dr100).

AROUND ER-RACHIDIA
Source Bleue de Meski

The source, about 17km south of Er-Rachidia, is a wonderful natural spring spilling into a swimming pool.

On weekends, heat-plagued locals from Er-Rachidia flock here in droves; otherwise, it's pretty quiet. It's a swimming stop (Dr5) that's well-recommended for the hot and sweaty traveller passing by.

Women should note that there is the usual crowd of Moroccan men ready to ogle while you swim. If you really like the place, you can stay longer at *Camping Source Bleue de Meski* for Dr10 per person, tent or car. There's a cafe and a few souvenir shops.

The spring is about 1km west of the main road and signposted. From Er-Rachidia, any bus or grand taxi to Erfoud or Aoufous can drop you off at the turn-off. When leaving, you should be able to flag down a grand taxi or hitch from the main road.

ERFOUD
☎ 05 • pop 7000

Erfoud is a fairly quiet place. There is a range of accommodation and it's a useful staging point from which to head into the desert. Sunrise excursions to the Erg Chebbi dunes near Merzouga are becoming part of the standard traveller menu, so you are

The Tuareg

While travelling in the south of Morocco you'll hear much about the famous Tuareg (pronounced twah-reg) nomads of the central Sahara. Thought to be of Berber origin, they migrated south a thousand or more years ago and played a central role in the great caravan routes linking Morocco to the Sahara and West Africa. If not trading, they were raiding.

Robbery was considered an honourable occupation and they were renowned for their bravery and their fierce raids on camel caravans. They would also attack the villages of other tribes, stealing crops and livestock and enslaving the inhabitants.

The French put an end to much of this activity by restricting nomadic movement and abolishing slavery (although in remoter parts of Niger it persisted until the 1960s). Without their slaves, the Tuareg eventually turned to herding and had to move south to the desert's rim in search of greener pastures. Today, only a few still follow their traditional nomadic lifestyle.

Tuaregs can be recognised by their light-coloured skin and grey or blue eyes, often the only feature showing through the distinctive blue *taguelmoust* (shawl or scarf) that the men wear wrapped around the head to keep out the desert winds and sand. Tuareg are often called 'blue men' because indigo was used to dye their robes and was also rubbed onto the skin as protection from the sun.

Though Muslim, the customs of the Tuareg are distinct from those of the Arabs. Tuareg women enjoy a freedom and status unheard of in the Muslim world. The Tuareg are one of the few matrilineal ethnic groups in West Africa. Tuareg women do not wear veils, can own property, maintain it separately from their husbands during marriage, keep their social status while marrying into a lower caste, and divorce their husbands.

likely to be resolutely hassled by touts and guides on arrival.

In October there is a large festival held to celebrate the date harvest, with dancing, music and, of course, tastings.

The main street, Ave Mohammed V, is intersected by Ave Moulay Ismail (which leads to the highways) at the post office.

Information

The post and phone offices are on the corner of Ave Mohammed V and Ave Moulay Ismail. They, like the four banks in town (no ATMs), are open during standard office hours. Téléboutiques dotted around town keep longer hours.

Two Internet places on Ave Moulay, El-Hassane and Navigation Internet, charge a whopping Dr30 per hour.

There are hammams for men and women behind Hôtel Sable d'Or.

Dunes

Most hotels will do their best to get you on a sunrise excursion to Erg Chebbi for a hefty fee.

It's better to stay near Merzouga (see Merzouga & the Dunes later in this chapter) but if you do want to whiz out there and back from Erfoud, a taxi can pick you up at 3 or 4 am and have you back by 10 am. It should cost around Dr300 – finding other travellers to make up numbers shouldn't be too difficult.

Places to Stay – Budget

Camping Erfoud, next to the river, is just a 10-minute walk from the bus area. It's fairly basic, however, and there is little shade. It costs around Dr10 per person, the same to pitch a tent or Dr20 to park a caravan.

Hôtel Merzouga (☎ 576532, 114 Ave Mohammed V) has clean, basic singles/doubles for Dr60/80 (with showers ingeniously installed over the toilets!) and a terrace. *Hôtel Saada*, in the Total petrol station, is much the same; rooms with shower cost Dr50/100.

Hôtel la Gazelle (☎ 576028, Ave Mohammed V) has bright rooms on a quiet street for Dr74/85; Dr86/110 with shower (hot water in the evening). The hotel has a decent basement restaurant.

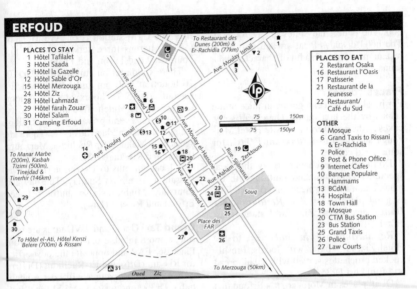

ERFOUD

PLACES TO STAY
1 Hôtel Tafilalet
3 Hôtel Saada
5 Hôtel la Gazelle
12 Hôtel Sable d'Or
15 Hôtel Merzouga
24 Hôtel Ziz
28 Hôtel Lahmada
29 Hôtel farah Zouar
30 Hôtel Salam
31 Camping Erfoud

PLACES TO EAT
2 Restarant Osaka
16 Restaurant l'Oasis
17 Patisserie
21 Restaurant de la Jeunesse
22 Restaurant/ Café du Sud

OTHER
4 Mosque
6 Grand Taxis to Rissani & Er-Rachidia
7 Police
8 Post & Phone Office
9 Internet Cafes
10 Banque Populaire
11 Hammams
13 BCdM
14 Hospital
18 Town Hall
19 Mosque
20 CTM Bus Station
23 Bus Station
25 Grand Taxis
26 Police
27 Law Courts

Places to Stay – Mid-Range

The cheapest (and best value) mid-range place is **Hôtel Lahmada** (☎ 576980, fax 576097, Ave Moulay Ismail). The rooms, all with bathroom and most with balcony, are spotless and cost Dr121/140/187 for singles/doubles/triples. The hotel also has a Moroccan-Italian restaurant and a terrace.

Hôtel Sable d'Or (☎ 576348, Ave Mohammed V) has comfortable singles/doubles with shower, toilet, table and chair, and 24-hour hot water for Dr133/154. There's a cafe downstairs, a rooftop terrace with great views and a good, cheap restaurant on the 1st floor.

Hôtel Ziz (☎ 576154, fax 576811, 3 Ave Mohammed V), just around the corner from the bus area, has clean rooms with bath for Dr250/320. The hotel has a relaxing courtyard salon and one of the few bars in town.

Hôtel Farah Zouar (☎/fax 576230) on the corner of the Rissani and Tinerhir roads is worth considering. Rooms cost Dr170/220 (or Dr300 for a comfortable suite for four with TV). Like most, it has its own restaurant.

Places to Stay – Top End

The nicest place to stay, if you don't mind being 500m out on the road to Tinerhir, is **Kasbah Tizimi** (☎ 576179, fax 577375, e katizimi@iam.net.ma). Built in traditional kasbah style around a leafy courtyard, the hotel has cool, comfortable singles/doubles with bathroom for Dr250/300; suites are Dr515. It has a restaurant, pool and bar.

The three-star **Hôtel Tafilalet** (☎ 576535, fax 576036, Ave Moulay Ismail) has fully equipped rooms for Dr410/510. The newer rooms on the far side of the swimming pool are superb and feature a large, sunny balcony, a comfortable bedroom and a separate dining area, all floored with local earthen tiles. The old rooms are nowhere near as attractive. This place has its own bar (avoid the basement bar, which is a bit seedy) and restaurant (breakfast is Dr50). The hotel also runs a cheap place just south of Merzouga village.

Outside town, on the road to Rissani, are two four-star and tour-group places next to each other. **El-Ati Hôtel** (☎ 577372, fax 577086) has a bit more character and spacious rooms for Dr500/650. **Hôtel Kenzi Belere** (☎ 578190, fax 578192) has rooms with minibar for Dr700/900. Both have bars, pools and restaurants.

Top of the line is **Hôtel Salam** (☎ 576665, fax 576426), across from Hôtel Farah Zouar.

Rooms around the courtyard pool are Dr450/560. The better riad suites are Dr700/800. The hotel displays local art and also has a restaurant, a bar with a bit of character and a sauna.

Places to Eat

For breakfast you can get fresh juice at the stands by the taxi ranks. Then grab some cakes at the *patisserie* opposite Hôtel Merzouga and head to *Restaurant l'Oasis* for some good coffee.

Don't miss the chance to try the local speciality *kalia*, minced mutton with tomato, onion and 44 spices served in a tajine. A good place to try it is *Restaurant des Dunes*, next to the Ziz petrol station past Hôtel Tifilalat.

Restaurant/Café du Sud, next to the Hôtel Ziz, is popular with locals. Freshly cooked brochettes served with salad, bread and fruit cost Dr35.

Of all places in Morocco, it's Erfoud that has a Moroccan-Japanese restaurant! *Restaurant Osaka* (☎ 578045, *Ave Moulay Ismail*) has the usual Moroccan fare and kalia, as well as miso soup, a Japanese paella and rice dishes.

The extremely friendly *Restaurant de la Jeunesse* (*Ave Mohammed V*) has good Moroccan dishes for reasonable prices.

The restaurant at *Hôtel la Gazelle* has a comfortable Moroccan-style dining room where you can get a three-course evening meal for about Dr40.

Another place worth trying is the restaurant at *Hôtel Sable d'Or*, which offers a range of dishes from Dr30.

Of the restaurants in the top-end hotels, the most inviting choice is the one in the very pleasant *Kasbah Tizimi*.

The *souq* at the southern end of town sells fresh produce.

Shopping

Erfoud is full of shiny black fossilised marble, which is quarried nearby in the desert. You can buy pieces in several shops around town and watch it being cut at Manar Marbre, the factory between town and Kasbah Tizimi.

Getting There & Away

Bus The CTM station is on Ave Mohammed V. It runs three services to Fès (11 hours) at 7 and 11 am and 11 pm.

There's a direct bus to Meknès (Dr110, 10 hours) at 8.30 pm and another via Er-Rachidia (Dr15, 1½ hours) at 8 am. A noon service runs to Midelt (five hours).

There are several private bus lines, all of which leave from Place des FAR. There are services to Meknès, Er-Rachidia, Merzouga (Dr13) and Rissani (Dr5).

A local bus runs to Tazzarine (Dr30) via Rissani at 10 am on Sunday, Tuesday and Thursday. Minibuses also shuttle between Erfoud and Rissani (Dr4).

Grand Taxi Grand and 4WD taxis are, as a rule, a more reliable bet. They leave from Place des FAR and opposite the post office for Rissani (Dr6) and Er-Rachidia (Dr16).

A 4WD to Merzouga will cost a negotiable Dr300 one way or Dr600 for a full-day's hire – you'll find them lined up outside the main hotels.

RISSANI
☎ 05

In the heart of the Tafilalt, the small town of Rissani is in a sense the end of the road, where the Ziz Valley peters out into the hot 'nothingness' of stone and sand.

It was from Rissani that the Filali (from whom the ruling Alawite dynasty is descended) swept north to supplant the Saadians as the ruling dynasty in Morocco. It did not happen overnight; the founder of the dynasty, Moulay Ali ash-Sharif, began expanding his power in the early 17th century in a series of small wars with neighbouring tribes. His sons continued a slow campaign of conquest, but only in 1668 was Moulay ar-Rashid recognised as sultan.

It was his brother and successor, Moulay Ismail, who later became the uncontested ruler of Morocco, and underlined his power by establishing a new capital at Meknès.

The centre of town is quite small and manageable, with most travellers needs flanking the northern edge of the souq. A pleasant, shady market place in the south-eastern corner of town, its souq becomes a bustling hive of activity every Sunday, Tuesday and Thursday.

There is a post and phone office, at the northern end of the medina walls, and plenty of téléboutiques. The Micro Stop Internet cafe, about 50m north of Hôtel Panorama, charges Dr30 per hour but also offers the same deal for two people (ie, Dr15 each).

There is a Banque Populaire opposite the souq and a BCDM next to the CTM office (no ATMs).

There are a few carpet and jewellery shops in Rissani worth a look, including the Maison Toureg, on the road to Merzouga, and Maison du Sud, just inside the market gateway.

Circuit Touristique

This 21km loop around the palmeraies south of Rissani (on fairly rough stretches of road) takes you through villages past several ruined ksar and some barely visible ruins of the fabled city of Sijilmassa.

From the centre of Rissani head north from the souq then follow the signposts to the west. En route you'll pass a ruined ksar, from where there are good views. About 2km to the south-east is the zawiyya (closed to non-Muslims) of Moulay Ali ash-Sharif.

Just nearby, and worth a look, are the 19th-century ruins of the Ksar d'Akbar, which once housed disgraced or unwanted members of the Alawite dynasty.

About 1km or so further on is the Ksar Oulad Abdelhalim, built for Sultan Moulay Hassan's elder brother around 1900. There is still a substantial amount of beautiful decoration remaining.

The road continues past another group of ksar, some of which are still inhabited by members of the Filali. Just before you reach Rissani are the ruins of Sijilmassa, once the capital of a virtually independent Islamic principality adhering to the Shiite 'heresy' in the early days of the Arab conquest of North Africa.

Uncertainty reigns over exactly when Sijilmassa was founded, but by the end of the 8th century it was playing a key role on the trans-Saharan trade routes. Internal feuding led to its collapse in the 14th century and

Sijilmassa itself has fallen into ruin; there's little to indicate its past glories except for two decorated gateways and a few other structures.

Places to Stay & Eat

The cheapest place in town, *Hôtel el-Filalia* (☎ 575103, fax 774071) is basic but adequate. Next to the CTM office, it has singles/doubles with shower for Dr40/70 and a terrace.

Hôtel Restaurant Panorama (**e** hotel_panorama@caramail.com) is in the thick of the action at the eastern side of the market. It has a good terrace where you can enjoy the local version of pizza – a huge round of bread stuffed with meat, eggs and spices – which is pricey (Dr100 for five) but good. The OK rooms cost Dr35/60.

Better is *Hôtel Sijilmassa* (☎/fax 575042, Place al-Massira al-Khadra), near the post office. It's clean and comfortable, with spacious rooms with shower and toilet for Dr92/150. There's a rooftop terrace with great views and a restaurant in the basement.

About 3km out along the road to Erfoud is the welcoming *Hôtel Kasbah Asmaa* (☎ 774083, fax 575494). Comfortable rooms with bathroom cost Dr250/320. There is a swimming pool, a good restaurant and bar. Naturally, the hotel can organise trips to the dunes.

There are a number of simple *restaurants* and *snack stands* fronting the market where you can eat cheaply and well.

Getting There & Away

Buses and grand taxis leave from the area in front of the Hôtel el-Filalia, although at the time of research a new bus station was being built out on the road to Erfoud. CTM has a bus to Meknès (Dr115, eight hours) via Erfoud (1½ hours) and Er-Rachidia (Dr20, three hours) at 8 pm. Other companies schedule three departures to Fès via Erfoud (Dr5) at 6 and 10 am and 11.30 pm (this last one via Sefrou).

A bus also leaves for Casablanca via Erfoud at 8 pm. Minibuses make the trip regularly on market days.

Grand taxis (Dr6.50) are probably the best bet. A red-and-white camionette leaves for Merzouga (Dr20) and the dunes from near the taxi area at 2 pm daily.

4WD taxis run between Rissani and Merzouga on market days, and also cost about Dr20 per person. Departures are uncertain and depend on demand.

MERZOUGA & THE DUNES
☎ 05

About 50km south of Erfoud is the tiny village of Merzouga and nearby the famous **Erg Chebbi**, Morocco's only genuine Saharan *erg* – one of those huge, drifting expanses of sand dunes that typify much of the Algerian Sahara.

It's a magical landscape, which deserves much more than just a sunrise glimpse. The dunes themselves are fascinating, changing colour from pink to gold to red at different times of the day. It is a great place to appreciate the immense, clear desert sky. For film buffs, the 1990s horror/action film, *The Mummy,* was filmed here.

For bird-watchers, this is the best area in Morocco for spotting many desert species, including desert sparrows, Egyptian nightjars, desert warblers, fulvous babblers and blue-cheeked bee-eaters.

Sometimes in spring a shallow lake appears north-west of Merzouga, attracting flocks of pink flamingos and other water birds.

Merzouga itself is tiny but it does have téléboutiques, general stores, a mechanic and, of course, a couple of carpet shops.

Places to Stay & Eat

Simple auberges, most built in similar kasbah style, flank the western side of Erg Chebbi to the north and south of the villages of Merzouga and Hassi Labied. Basic but comfortable singles/doubles cost about Dr30/60 and you can usually sleep on or in the roof, salon or Berber tent for about Dr25 to Dr30 per person.

All have views of the dunes and offer food (including the local kalia), Berber music in the evenings and some form of sand toy (snowboard, skis etc) and/or bicycles. Showers are usually shared but hot. It's worth noting that the largest dunes are alongside both villages.

You can arrange camel treks from most hotels. Asking prices can be high, but should cost from around Dr100 for a couple of hours to Dr200 to Dr300 per night with meals. As usual, they all congregate in the same spot for the first night – if you had a romantic notion of just you, the dunes and the stars, you'd be better off taking a two-day trip.

The places to the north of Merzouga tend to offer more comfort, with bathrooms attached to the still-simple rooms; luxuries like fridges may not exist.

In Hassi Labied, *Auberge Kasbah des Dunes* (☎ 577287, fax 577303) has rooms for Dr60, or Dr80 with bathroom. It also has an amazing fountain in its restaurant.

Opposite the palmeraie, heading north out of Hassi Labied, *l'Oasis* (☎ 01-739041) has singles/doubles for Dr50/80 and a pleasant courtyard.

La Source (☎ 552202), also by the palmeraie, has basic singles/doubles/triples with

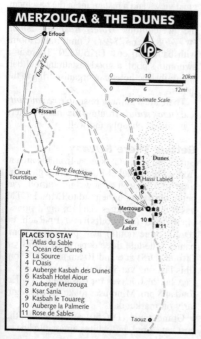

MERZOUGA & THE DUNES

Erfoud

Oued Ziz

0   10   20km
0   6   12mi
Approximate Scale

Rissani

Ligne Électrique

Circuit Touristique

Dunes
1
2
5
3
4
Hassi Labied
6
7
Merzouga   8
9
Salt   10
Lakes   11

Taouz

PLACES TO STAY
1 Atlas du Sable
2 Ocean des Dunes
3 La Source
4 l'Oasis
5 Auberge Kasbah des Dunes
6 Kasbah Hotel Aiour
7 Auberge Merzouga
8 Ksar Sania
9 Kasbah le Touareg
10 Auberge la Palmerie
11 Rose de Sables

CENTRAL MOROCCO

nice touches like radios and books for Dr50/75/100.

Ocean des Dunes is a very clean but basic place with nice salon-type seating outside its Dr50 rooms.

Atlas du Sable (☎ 577037) is a bit far from the dunes, stuck in the hot hammada. It has two restaurants and large family rooms. A simple double costs Dr70, while singles/doubles/triples/quads with bathroom cost Dr100/120/150/180.

Kasbah Hôtel Aiour is a clean place with a large arched restaurant area and blue-and-yellow decor. Close to the dunes, rooms with bathroom are Dr90/150.

Places in Merzouga include the *Auberge Merzouga* (*book through Hôtel Tifalalet in Erfoud*), the large pink place in front of the larger dunes, which serves beer and puts on nightly entertainment for the tourists. Half-board rates are Dr200 per person.

Moving south and next along, with local character compromised by typically French chic, is *Ksar Sania* (☎ 577414, fax 577230). The hotel offers the area's most comfortable doubles from Dr70 to Dr180, and the restaurant has a French menu for Dr90 (cheaper individual dishes are available).

Next, *Kasbah le Touareg* (☎/fax 577215) is another slightly upmarket place, with colourful rooms for Dr100. The more basic rooftop rooms are in the turrets, with the front two having excellent dune views for Dr60.

A super chilled-out place is *Auberge la Palmerie*, with pink rooms, not facing the dunes, for Dr50/60/80/100.

The last place down the line is *Rose de Sables* (☎ 577145). The interior is aptly pink and a bit cavernous but the turret rooms look onto the dunes for Dr70. More comfortable rooms on the ground floor cost Dr100. The restaurant serves Berber pizza (Dr65) on request.

Getting There & Away

You can get out here by public transport, drive down yourself or arrange a tour from Erfoud. The pistes can be rough (and getting stuck in sand is a real possibility), but a Renault 4 can make it down, winding across rough, black hammada.

Without your own transport Merzouga is most accessible from Rissani. A red-and-white camionette leaves the taxi place at 2 pm daily (Dr20, 1½ hours). The bus departs from Café du Sud in Merzouga between 7.30 and 9.30 am.

There are also 4WD taxis (Dr20) between the two on market days (Sunday, Tuesday and Thursday), although there's no timetable as such and demand can vary enormously.

If you're driving your own car from Rissani, you are advised to engage a local guide (about Dr180 but they may try and steer you towards their family auberge), since the route is not as straightforward as that from Erfoud.

The drive from Erfoud takes just over an hour and if you follow the line of telegraph poles you can't really go wrong. A bus leaves Erfoud between 3 and 4 pm and returns from Merzouga at 7.30 am. Apart from the 'sunrise tours', the only other option is to charter a 4WD taxi for about Dr300. You'll find them lined up outside all the large hotels in Erfoud. Alternatively, you can try and hitch a ride with some fellow tourists.

South Atlantic Coast

From Casablanca, the Atlantic coast stretches 350km south-west to Essaouira, a popular windsurfing spot and one time hippie Mecca, before dropping south to Agadir. From there it sweeps south-west for 300km to the tiny town of Tarfaya, just north of the Western Sahara. Between these towns are beaches galore, some stunning wild coastlines and prime bird-watching opportunities.

Reminders of Europe's long history of interference on the Moroccan seaboard abound. Azemmour, El-Jadida, Essaouira and Agadir were all once European military and commercial bridgeheads, and all but Agadir retain architectural evidence of this. Agadir, the country's premier beach resort, is where modern Europeans, in the guise of package tourists, choose to invade the country today.

Stretching hundreds of kilometres south of Tarfaya to the Mauritanian border is the disputed territory of Western Sahara. Occupied by Morocco when the Spaniards left in 1975, it's a vast, desolate and lightly populated tract of *hammada* (stony desert). Its people are mainly fishermen, work-hungry Moroccans, and soldiers. The latter are here to keep an eye on the rebel group, Polisario, and also to maintain Morocco's claim on the area (which neighbouring Mauritania has never relinquished).

EL-JADIDA
☎ 03 • pop 150,000
The historic centre of this quiet, relaxed town is one of the best-preserved examples of Portuguese military architecture in Morocco. The rambling lanes, impressive ramparts and elegant old cistern of the small Cité Portugaise (Portuguese fortress) are well worth a visit.

During the summer months, Moroccan city dwellers flock to El-Jadida for the beaches; at other times the town has an open, hassle-free air, making it a pleasant enough place to spend a couple of days.

The Moussem of Moulay Abdallah, one of Morocco's best festivals with parades

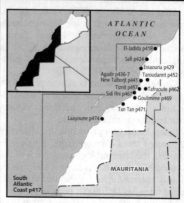

Highlights

- Joining everyone else at Essaouira – fortunately the Portuguese fortifications and townsfolk continue to bear the onslaught graciously

- Going sick on beer, burgers and speaking your native tongue in Agadir – don't forget to sing 'push pineapple, shake a tree'

- Bartering for *babouches* (leather slippers) in Tafraoute then beating a track to one of the Berber villages just a short stroll away

- Gazing at the sea for hours in the former Spanish town of Sidi Ifni – if the pace is still too fast head for nearby Mirhleft

- Travelling to the end of the road in the Western Sahara: though there's almost nothing there, it has space and genuine hospitality

! Telephone numbers in Morocco have changed. For new codes and complete numbers, see the boxed text 'Changes to Telephone Numbers' on page 89.

and fantasias, is held at the saint's tomb 11km from here, in August. This village also has the ruins of a 12th century fortified monastery.

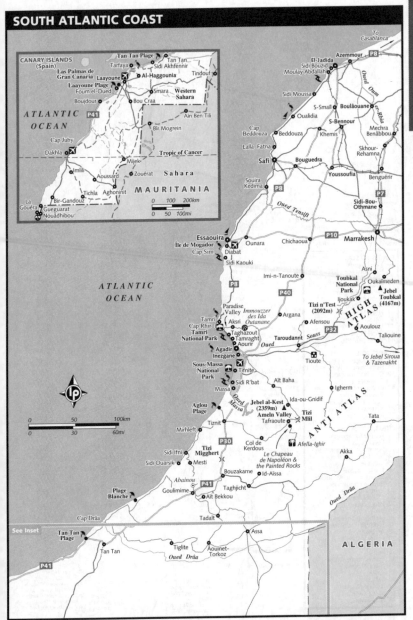

SOUTH ATLANTIC COAST

SOUTH ATLANTIC COAST

EL-JADIDA

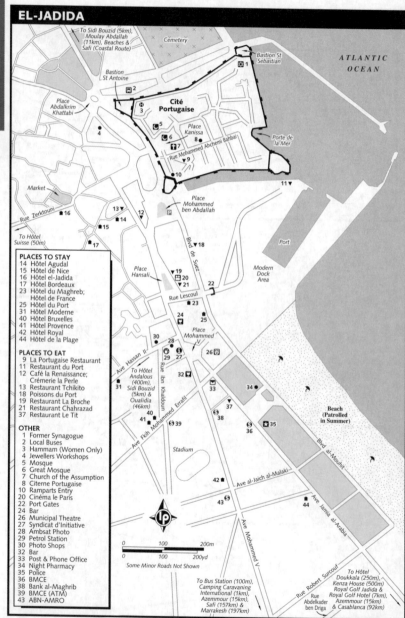

To Sidi Bouzid (5km),
Moulay Abdallah
(11km), Beaches &
Safi (Coastal Route)

Cemetery

Bastion St Antoine

Bastion St Sébastian

ATLANTIC OCEAN

Place Abdalkrim Khattabi

Cité Portugaise

Place Kanissa

Porte de la Mer

Market

Rue Zerktouni

To Hôtel Suisse (50m)

Place Mohammed ben Abdallah

Rue Mohammed Ahchemi Bahbai

Port

Blvd de Suez

Place Hansali

Modern Dock Area

Rue Lescoul

Ave Hassan II

Place Mohammed V

To Hôtel Andalous (400m), Sidi Bouzid (5km) & Oualidia (46km)

Rue ibn Khaldoun

Rue Mohammed Errafii

Ave Fkih Mohammed

Beach (Patrolled in Summer)

Stadium

Blvd al-Mouhit

Ave al-Jaïch al-Malaki

Ave Jamia al-Arabia

Ave Mohammed V

Rue Robert Surcouf

Rue Abdelkader ben Driga

To Bus Station (100m),
Camping Caravaning
International (1km),
Azemmour (15km),
Safi (157km) &
Marrakesh (197km)

To Hôtel
Doukkala (250m),
Kenza House (500m),
Royal Golf Jadida &
Royal Golf Hotel (7km),
Azemmour (15km)
& Casablanca (92km)

0   100   200m
0   100   200yd
Some Minor Roads Not Shown

PLACES TO STAY
14 Hôtel Agudal
15 Hôtel de Nice
16 Hôtel el-Jadida
17 Hôtel Bordeaux
23 Hôtel du Maghreb;
   Hôtel de France
25 Hôtel du Port
31 Hôtel Moderne
40 Hôtel Bruxelles
41 Hôtel Provence
42 Hôtel Royal
44 Hôtel de la Plage

PLACES TO EAT
9 La Portugaise Restaurant
11 Restaurant du Port
12 Café la Renaissance;
   Crémerie la Perle
13 Restaurant Tchikito
18 Poissons du Port
19 Restaurant La Broche
21 Restaurant Chahrazad
37 Restaurant Le Tit

OTHER
1 Former Synagogue
2 Local Buses
3 Hammam (Women Only)
4 Jewellers Workshops
5 Mosque
6 Great Mosque
7 Church of the Assumption
8 Citerne Portugaise
10 Ramparts Entry
20 Cinéma le Paris
22 Port Gates
24 Bar
26 Municipal Theatre
27 Syndicat d'Initiative
28 Ambsat Photo
29 Petrol Station
30 Photo Shops
32 Bar
33 Post & Phone Office
34 Night Pharmacy
35 Police
36 BMCE
38 Bank al-Maghrib
39 BMCE (ATM)
43 ABN-AMRO

History

The Portuguese founded Mazagan, as El-Jadida used to be known, in 1513 on the site of an old Almohad fortress. In those days Portugal was building up a maritime trading empire that would stretch across the globe as far as China and Japan.

Mazagan was to become Portugal's main Atlantic entrepot in Morocco and it held on to the town until 1769, when, following a siege by Sultan Sidi Mohammed ben Abdallah, the Portuguese were forced to evacuate the fortress.

Before leaving, the Portuguese mined the ramparts and, at the last moment, blew the fort to smithereens, taking with them a good part of the besieging army.

The walls of the fortress lay in ruins until 1820, when they were rebuilt by Sultan Moulay Abd ar-Rahman. The Moroccans who took over the town preferred to settle outside the walls of the fortress.

The medina inside the walls was largely neglected until the mid-19th century, when it was recolonised by European merchants (particularly the Portuguese). A large and influential Jewish community became established at this time, controlling trade with the interior, particularly Marrakesh. Contrary to common Moroccan practice, these Jews were not confined to the *mellah* (Jewish quarter of the medina), but mixed with the general populace.

Tourism, sardine fishing and a prosperous agricultural hinterland have made contemporary El-Jadida an animated and growing commercial centre, and this is reflected in its clean look and busy atmosphere.

Orientation

El-Jadida faces north-east onto the Atlantic, and the protection this affords partly accounts for the town's suitability as a port. The Cité Portugaise is at the north-western end of town.

The focal point of the town is the pedestrianised Place Hansali – you'll find the post office, banks, tourist office and some of the hotels in the cluster of streets to the south of it. The bus station is about 1km south-east of here.

There's a market area to the west of the Cité Portugaise. Most cafes lie to the south between the beach and Ave Mohammed V.

Information

Tourist Offices There is a Syndicat d'Initiative opposite Place Mohammed V, which is open from 9 am to 12.30 pm and 3 to 7 pm Thursday to Tuesday. It offers photocopied information and details on local beaches.

Money Several banks have branches here, including the BMCE, BMCI and the Bank al-Maghrib; most have ATMs.

Post & Communications The post and phone offices are together, on the block bounded by Ave Mohammed V and Ave Jamia al-Arabia near Place Mohammed V. They open from 8.30 am to noon and 2.30 to 6 pm weekdays. You'll find a few cardphones outside, on Ave Jamia al-Arabia.

Internet Village and Kenza, both in Kenza House at the southern end of town, charge Dr15 per hour for Internet access.

Medical Services There's a night pharmacy (☎ 355252) at 10 Ave Jamia al-Arabia.

Cité Portugaise

There are two entrance gates to the fortress, almost right next to each other, the southernmost opens onto the fort's main street, Rue Mohammed Ahchemi Bahbai, which ends at the Porte de la Mer. This is where ships used to discharge their cargo in the Portuguese era – it now appears to be where the drains discharge their sewage.

About halfway down the main street is the famed **Citerne Portugaise** (Portuguese Cistern). Although the Romans built water collection and storage cisterns similar to this, it remains a remarkable piece of architecture and engineering that has stood the test of time and is still functional. Visitors are invariably impressed by the dramatic and beautiful effect created by the reflection of the roof and 25 pillars in the water covering (or almost covering) the floor. This hasn't escaped the attention of various film directors. The best known of these is perhaps Orson Welles, who used the cistern in his acclaimed *Othello*. The cistern is open from 9 am to 1 pm and 3 to 6 pm daily. Entry costs Dr10.

You can take a pleasant stroll all the way around the **ramparts** of the Cité Portugaise – simply walk up onto them by the Porte de la Mer or enter through the large door at the end of the tiny cul-de-sac to the right of the fortress entrance (if it's locked, the man with the key won't be far away). You can get back down to ground level at Bastion St Antoine.

The Portuguese built several churches within the medina, but unfortunately, they are all closed. You can see the principal one, the **Church of the Assumption**, to the left as soon as you enter the main gateway. Even if it were possible to visit all of the churches, you'd see little of their original features, since they were taken over and used for secular purposes long ago. Even the **Great Mosque**, adjacent to the Church of the Assumption, was once a lighthouse.

Just inside the Bastion St Sebastian, on the extreme northern seaward side, you can enter a former synagogue, but there is little to see.

Beaches

There are beaches to the north and south of town, although those to the north occasionally get polluted by oil. They're pleasant enough in low season, but can get very crowded during July and August, when they are also patrolled. If El-Jadida isn't quite the pristine beach you were looking for, try **Sidi Bouzid**, 5km to the south – it's quieter with clearer waters and cleaner sands.

Activities

One of the newest royal golf courses, the 18-hole Royal Golf Jadida (☎ 352251) 6274m, par 72, is just off the beach 7km north of town.

In El-Jadida, there is good surfing by the jetty and a beach break. Out of town at Sidi Bouzid there are shore and right point breaks.

Hammams & Public Showers

There's a small *hammam* (traditional bathhouse) for women just near the Bastion St Antoine in the north-west corner of the Cité Portugaise.

Other hammams can be found around town – ask your hotel for the nearest one.

Places to Stay

Because this is a seaside resort, you will have to be prepared to pay much higher prices in the summer when hotels fill up quickly – it's probably worth booking ahead. Unfortunately, few places offer sea frontage but still there are some good options, especially in the cheaper area to the south-west of the Cité Portugaise, which with its winding lanes has the most character.

Places to Stay – Budget

Camping About a 15-minute walk southeast of the bus station – follow the signs from Ave Mohammed V or Ave Jamia al-Arabia – *Camping Caravaning International* (☎ 342755, *Ave des Nations Unies*) is quite well shaded. Camping costs Dr14 per person, Dr8.50 per car and Dr16 per tent. Electricity costs an extra Dr14/16 per tent/caravan. It also has equipped but damp two- and four-bed self-contained bungalows from Dr140/260.

A free *camp site*, manned during the summer, operates at Sidi Bouzid – the tourist office in El-Jadida has details.

Hotels There are a bunch of cheapies in the lanes west of the fortress. The most basic – and we mean basic – is *Hôtel Agudal*, with beds in small, bare rooms for Dr40 a head. The charm of this place lies in the fact that the rooms are centred around an overgrown banana-palm filled courtyard.

Hôtel de Nice (☎ 352272, *15 Rue Mohammed Smiha*) nearby has clean and bright singles/doubles/triples for Dr40/55/75, although some rooms are tiny.

The best of the three is *Hôtel Bordeaux* (☎ 373921, *47 Rue Moulay Ahmed Tahiri*), whose pleasant small rooms are gathered around a spotlessly whitewashed, covered courtyard. There is continuous hot water and rooms cost Dr41/57.

In the busier local market area, *Hôtel el-Jadida* (☎ 340178, *Rue Zerktouni*) has rooms with basins, bidets and big beds, but no showers (a hammam is next door) for Dr31/45/61.

Hôtel Suisse (☎ *342816, 147 Rue Zerktouni*) is south-west of the Cité Portugaise, making it quite a trek from the bus station. However, once there the garden cafe and restaurant offers a good place to recover. Airy rooms with cold/hot shower start at Dr70/100.

Two budget deals just off Place Hansali are owned by the same guy and share the same rooftop. *Hôtel du Maghreb* and *Hôtel de France* (☎ *342181)* have enormous rooms with high wooden ceilings, some of which look out over the port to sea. They cost Dr41/57. Another even more basic seafacing option is *Hôtel du Port* (☎ *342701, Blvd de Suez)*, with rooms for Dr30/45.

Another decent choice is *Hôtel Moderne* (☎ *343133, 21 Ave Hassan II)*. Rooms with washbasin and bidet cost Dr60/75, but some are small.

The one-star *Hôtel Bruxelles* (☎ *342072, 40 Rue ibn Khaldoun)* offers clean rooms with bathroom for Dr75/120. Some have balconies and there's a parking garage next door.

Hôtel Royal (☎ *941100, 108 Ave Mohammed V)* is handy for the bus station and offers the nicest option in this range. Its big, bright rooms are standard but the hallways are traditionally decorated and it has a (seedy) bar with a pleasant open courtyard. Rooms without shower cost Dr62/80, those with shower are Dr98/116.

Also within reasonable distance of the bus station and sea-facing, the friendly *Hôtel de la Plage* (☎ *342648, Ave Jamia al-Arabia)* has clean rooms for Dr50/60/75.

Places to Stay – Mid-Range & Top End

El-Jadida's only mid-range hotel, *Hôtel Provence* (☎ *342347, fax 352115, 42 Ave Fkih Mohammed Errafil)* was undergoing renovations at the time of research. A popular choice with a licensed restaurant, bar and parking, it's worth checking out.

At Sidi Bouzid 5km out of town, *Motel Club Hacienda* (☎ *348311)* has self-contained bungalows, complete with TV, which sleep up to four. Set within lush gardens, there's a cafeteria and swimming pool and staff speak English. Doubles start at Dr300.

Back in El-Jadida, *Hôtel Andalous* (☎ *343745, fax 351690, Blvd Docteur de la Lanouy)* is becoming a bit run down, but there's no detracting from the splendour of the open courtyard with its bar. Once the palace of a local *pasha* (high official in the Ottoman Empire), the place was converted into a spacious hotel in 1980. Full of exquisite Moroccan tiles and hectares of intricate plasterwork, the hotel has comfortable salons and singles/doubles with everything (one even has a pasha-sized bed) costing from Dr250/300. It's a little out of the way – follow the orange 'hotel' signs up Ave Hassan II from the city centre.

Hôtel Doukkala (☎ *343737)* on the ocean side of Ave Jamia al-Arabia is a rather grim concrete bunker of a hotel. It does, however, have all the amenities you would expect of a four-star establishment, including a swimming pool, and is the only place in town with real ocean frontage. Rooms cost from Dr293/347.

Seven kilometres to the north of town, the *Royal Golf Hotel* (☎ *354141, fax 353473)* is a new top-end place right on the ocean with a golf course, five restaurants, three bars, tennis courts, a hammam and a pool.

Places to Eat

Being a port, there's plenty of seafood to be had as well as the usual Moroccan and French fare.

For fishy snacks try *Poissons du Port*, basically a large hole in the port wall, or *Restaurant Tchikito*, in a side lane a short walk north-west of Place Hansali. The former sells fresh catch while the latter fries up filling takeaway meals of fresh fish to eat with the fingers and accompanied by a plate of ear-busting chillies.

Much more upmarket is the licensed *Restaurant du Port* (☎ *342579)* at the northern end of the dock area overlooking the ramparts of the fortress. An excellent three-course meal costs around Dr100. To get there enter through the port gate and follow the signs.

Restaurant La Broche (*Place Hansali)* is a kitsch but homely, family-run place that offers a range of Moroccan and French meals for around Dr45. *Restaurant Chahrazad*, on the other side of the Cinéma Le Paris, has similar prices and the food is just as good. Both have pavement seating for people-watching.

Despite its prime location within the walls of the Cité Portugaise, *La Portugaise Restaurant* serves inexpensive meals and drinks.

Serving seafood and other fare is the *Restaurant Le Tit*, behind the post office. The food, albeit more expensive than other places, is good but beware: along with its liquor license comes a crowd of Moroccan drinkers, which can make it a bit smoky.

It's worth taking a trip out to Sidi Bouzid to the licensed *Restaurant Le Blue*, which serves a full menu from its tiered terraces overlooking the beach. Allow around Dr100 per head.

A whole string of *cafes* with uninterrupted sea views and a sunset promenade of locals and tourists lines the seafront on Blvd al-Mouhit. *Café la Renaissance* and *Crémerie la Perle*, both at the top of Place Hansali, also offer great people-watching opportunities.

Should you want to self-cater, the *market* area around Rue Zerktouni has plenty of fruit and vegetable stalls and small grocery shops.

Getting There & Away

The bus station is south-east of town on Ave Mohammed V, a 15-minute walk from the Cité Portugaise. You can leave your gear here for Dr3 – you'll need to show ID.

CTM runs services to and from Casablanca (Dr35, 1½ hours), Marrakesh (Dr40, four hours), Safi (Dr25, 2 hours) and Essaouira (Dr69, five hours).

There are local buses to Casablanca (every 20 minutes), Rabat (nine daily), Oualidia (three daily), Safi (seven daily), Essaouira (six daily) and Marrakesh (hourly) as well as other local and further afield destinations. In summer, buses to Casablanca and Marrakesh should be booked at least one day ahead.

Regular local buses to Sidi Bouzid (Dr2.10) and Azemmour leave from the northern side of the Cité Portugaise.

Grand taxis (shared taxis) gather on the side street near the bus station south of town.

AROUND EL-JADIDA
Azemmour
☎ 03

While in El-Jadida, it's worth taking a break from the beach to explore this little-visited fortress town 15km to the north-east.

Here you'll find another monument to those energetic seafaring people, the Portuguese. Although they only stayed in Azemmour for a short while (1513–41) it was sufficient for them to build a fortress alongside the banks of the wide Oued Oum er-Rbia. One of Morocco's largest rivers, it rises in the Middle Atlas and empties into the sea about 1km downriver from Azemmour. The best views of the fortress and crumbling, whitewashed medina are from the bridge across the river.

Azemmour once had a thriving Jewish community, but since the community's exodus to Israel, the houses have fallen into ruin – all too often, only their facades remain. However, there is still a synagogue, which is in reasonable shape, with lettering in Hebrew and Roman script above the door saying 'Rabbi Abraham Moul Niss'.

The fortress ramparts are open to visitors – the main entry is on the inside to the left after you enter from Place de Souq. You could also enter by a door on the open square at the extreme north-eastern tip of the fort, but you might have to wait for the guardian to arrive with the keys.

There's nothing much of interest in the new part of town, but you can visit the beach (Haouzia), about 30 minutes' walk from Place du Souq (signposted). When the wind's not howling, it's not a bad spot and surfers may find some waves on outgoing-to-low tides. Bird-watchers should head for the dunes at the mouth of the river.

Market day is Tuesday.

Places to Stay & Eat There are at least two basic hotels in El-Jadida: *Hôtel de la Victoire* (☎ 347157, 308 Ave Mohammed V), where a single room without shower costs Dr31; and *Hôtel Moulay Bouchaib*, up the hill from the Victoire to the left of the mosque.

Café el-Manzeh (Place du Souq) is the most pleasant of a string of cafes on the main road. There are a few by the beach, as well as the moderately priced *La Perle (☎ 347905)*, a restaurant that opens in summer.

Getting There & Away Local buses link El-Jadida with Place de Souq in Azemmour (Dr3) every half hour. Grand taxis (Dr5) leave from the market area west of town.

OUALIDIA
☎ 03

Midway to Safi from El-Jadida, Oualidia is an attractive, relaxed seaside fishing village, most of which is sandwiched between the sea and a lagoon. A growing cluster of holiday bungalows overlook the lagoon, which is famous for its oysters, good swimming (stay in the calm waters of the lagoon) and windsurfing (you can hire equipment in the summer). Bird-watching opportunities include flamingos, Mediterranean and Audouin's gulls, godwits, stilts and terns.

For more bird-watching nearby, the coastal lagoons, creeks and saltpans that begin at Sidi Moussa, north towards El-Jadida, are a great spot as cormorants, ducks, gulls, terns and waders can be found here. It also has a beach break that is good for surfing. South of Oualidia, Cap Beddouza is another rich habitat with a variety of other water birds.

A post office, CTM office, grand taxis, market stalls and cafes can be found on the main road on the escarpment above the lagoon. To get to the beach, head down the road by the side of the post office.

Places to Stay & Eat
Thirty kilometres north of Oualidia at Sidi Moussa, *Villa La Brise (☎ 346917)* is an 'unrated' hotel looking out over the Atlantic. Singles/doubles cost Dr49/64, or Dr67/95 with shower. The hotel has a restaurant, bar and swimming pool.

In Oualidia, the cheapest option is *Camping Oualidia*, tucked behind the dunes not far from the lagoon. Two people in a camper van pay Dr36 and a bit less with a tent.

On the road down to the beach from the main road to the village, signposted off to the right, is the chic *L'Hippocampe (☎ 366108, fax 366461)*. It has rooms with bathroom set in a terraced garden, those at the back have lagoon views. There's also a good restaurant and pool, both overlooking the lagoon beach, and if you can afford Dr75 for a plate of fish it's a recommended place for a meal or drink. Half-board rates are Dr550/850 for one/two people.

Complexe Touristique Chems (☎ cell 01-711838), right on the edge of the lagoon, has small bungalows (for five with fully equipped kitchen) from Dr300 and doubles with a shower, almost right on the beach, for Dr200. It's a bit dilapidated, but you can't beat those views. It also has a licensed restaurant.

On the beach, *Motel A l'Araignee Gourmande (☎ 366144)* is a French-style villa with a Moroccan salon, Bavarian-style bar and views over the lagoon. Rooms cost Dr200/350 and half board costs Dr300/400.

The *restaurant* at Motel A l'Araignee Gourmande and *Les Roches* opposite Complexe Touristique Chems have excellent seafood. Or you could buy some of the day's catch from an angler in town and cook it.

Getting There & Away
Local buses (Dr15, 1½ hours) and grand taxis (Dr20) run at irregular times between Oualidia and El-Jadida and Safi; they leave from near the post office on the main road. CTM also has an office here and there is a daily early morning bus (Dr16) in either direction.

SAFI
☎ 04

Largely a modern fishing port and industrial centre, Safi (also known as Asfi) sits on the Atlantic coast in a steep crevasse formed by the Oued Chabah. Its industrial side is pretty obvious if you arrive from the north. A lot of Morocco's raw phosphate rock and fertilisers pass through here, the latter produced in chemical plants south of the town. As well as this, its sardine fleet is one of the biggest in the world, although the canning

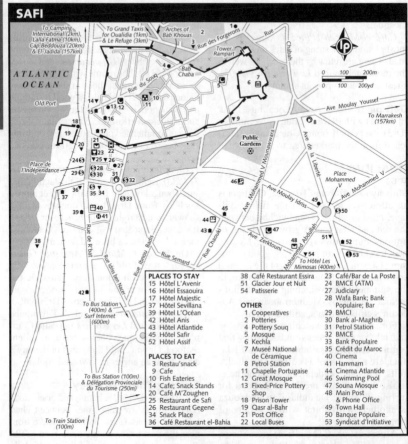

SAFI

PLACES TO STAY
15 Hôtel L'Avenir
16 Hôtel Essaouira
17 Hôtel Majestic
37 Hôtel Sevillana
39 Hôtel L'Océan
42 Hôtel Anis
43 Hôtel Atlantide
45 Hôtel Safir
52 Hôtel Assif

PLACES TO EAT
3 Restau'snack
9 Cafe
10 Fish Eateries
14 Cafe; Snack Stands
20 Café M'Zoughen
25 Restaurant de Safi
26 Restaurant Gegene
34 Snack Place
36 Café Restaurant el-Bahia
38 Café Restaurant Essira
51 Glacier Jour et Nuit
54 Patisserie

OTHER
1 Cooperatives
2 Potteries
4 Pottery Souq
5 Mosque
6 Kechla
7 Museé National
  de Céramique
8 Petrol Station
11 Chapelle Portugaise
12 Great Mosque
13 Fixed-Price Pottery
  Shop
18 Prison Tower
19 Qasr al-Bahr
21 Post Office
22 Local Buses
23 Café/Bar de La Poste
24 BMCE (ATM)
27 Judiciary
28 Wafa Bank; Bank
  Populaire; Bar
29 BMCI
30 Bank al-Maghrib
31 Petrol Station
32 BMCE
33 Bank Populaire
35 Crédit du Maroc
40 Cinema
41 Hammam
44 Cinema Atlantide
46 Swimming Pool
47 Souna Mosque
48 Main Post
  & Phone Office
49 Town Hall
50 Banque Populaire
53 Syndicat d'Initiative

industry has declined from the peaks it reached under the French protectorate.

The city centre has a lively walled medina and souq, with battlements dating from the brief Portuguese occupation. Safi is also well known for its traditional potteries, and even if you are not interested in buying any souvenirs, it is worth walking around the pottery souq to see the artisans at work.

History

Safi's natural harbour was known to the Phoenicians, and was probably used by the Romans. Founded in the 12th century by the Almohads, the city became an important religious and cultural centre.

Involvement with Europe didn't really begin until the Portuguese arrived in 1508. They built a fortress, using Essaouira as their base, but despite its monumental proportions (as with all Portuguese military installations), they didn't stay long, abandoning it in 1541.

In the late 17th century the French established a consulate at the port and signed trading treaties with the indigenous rulers. By the 19th century, however, the port had faded into insignificance.

Its revival came in the 20th century, with the expansion of the fishing fleet and the construction of a huge industrial complex.

Orientation

The bus and train stations are 1km to the south of the town centre.

A post office and the bulk of cheaper hotels and restaurants are just inside the medina walls; many banks are on or near Place de l'Indépendance.

Cafes, the more expensive hotels and the main post office, the Syndicat d'Initiative are up the hill to the east and around Place Mohammed V.

Information

Tourist Offices The Délégation Provinciale du Tourisme (☎ 622496, fax 624553) is on Rue Imam Malek, a short walk south of the bus station. It's open from 8.30 am to noon and 2.30 to 6.30 pm weekdays.

The Syndicat d'Initiative (☎ 464553), on a lane just south of Place Mohammed V, is open from 9 am to noon and 3 to 6.30 pm weekdays.

Money The BMCE and BMCI banks have branches on Place de l'Indépendance; other banks can be found on the parallel road next to the cemetery, and there are quite a few ATMs. There's a Banque Populaire on Place Mohammed V.

Post & Communications The phone section of the main post office, near Place Mohammed V, is open daily from 8 am to 9.45 pm. There are also cardphones outside the post office just south of the medina's walls.

Surf Internet, south of the bus station on Rue el-Kennedy, has Internet access for Dr15 per hour.

Qasr al-Bahr

Overlooking the Atlantic and in impressively good shape is the main fortress erected by the Portuguese to enforce their short-lived control here. Built not only to protect the port, but also to house the town governor, the 'Castle on the Sea' was restored in 1963.

There are good views from the south-west bastion, as well as a number of old Spanish and Dutch cannons dating from the early 17th century.

Just to the right of the entrance is the prison tower. The prisoners went to the bottom, but you can climb to the top for views across the medina – you might want to bring a torch (flashlight) to help you up and down the dark stairs. Visiting hours are 8.30 am to noon and 2.30 to 6 pm; entry costs Dr10. Access is via the underpass just to the north of the fort.

Medina

Across the street from the Qasr al-Bahr lies the walled medina. Dominating its eastern end is the **Kechla**, a massive defensive structure with ramps, gunnery platforms and living quarters. Just outside the Kechla, the **Musée National de Céramique**, a moderately interesting display of pottery from Safi, Fès and Meknès, and offers great views over town. Entry costs Dr10.

Coming through the medina you can climb up onto the ramparts for a good view of the potteries by heading up the tower rampart in the north-west corner.

Inside the medina are the remains of the so-called **Chapelle Portugaise**, which would have become Safi's cathedral had the Portuguese remained; as it turned out, they stayed only long enough to complete the choir and there's only one room. To get to it, head up Rue du Souq (the main thoroughfare through the medina) and turn right just after the **Great Mosque**. It's signposted to the right of the wooden door about 100m down the alley. It's Dr10 to get in but only really worth it if you're a big fan of Portuguese chapels.

Potteries

Just inside the medina, on the right-hand side of Rue du Souq is a pottery shop displaying the more popular wares complete with a price tag. Further on, shortly before Rue du Souq leads out of the medina, you'll notice, off to your left, the colourful **pottery souq**. The shopkeepers in both places are pretty low-key, and little inclined to bargain. Take the time to look at the different shops and prices then head out of the medina by

Bab Chaba to see if you can't strike a better deal at the potteries and cooperatives.

Outside the gate, to the left, you'll see an enormous series of arches; they look as though they were an aqueduct at one time, but in fact were probably associated with the defensive walls of the medina. Straight ahead, on the hill opposite Bab Chaba, you can't miss the earthen kilns of the potteries.

Opinions vary wildly on the quality of the ceramics produced here. Some of the many cooperatives devote themselves to the production of the green tiles that top many important buildings throughout the country, while many others manufacture a wide range of bowls, platters, vases, candlesticks and the like.

You can wander at will and are likely to be beckoned to watch the potters at work. Apart from the ancient wood-fired kilns, you can watch the busy workers moulding clay for tiles and utensils, designing and glazing.

If you're collared by a guide, buying a small item or two from their cooperative will save you forking out the usual guide's tip (not that there's anything to stop you paying a tip as well).

Places to Stay – Budget
Camping About 2km north of town, just off the coast road to El-Jadida, is *Camping International*. It's a reasonable site, and much cooler than the town below in the hot summer months. It charges Dr9/9/12 per tent/car/person, Dr10 for a hot shower and Dr20 to use the pool. Get a taxi up here from the centre or bus station.

Hotels There's a fair choice of budget hotels in Safi, most of them clustered around the port end of Rue du Souq and along Rue de R'bat. Many are used by Moroccans who come to work here during the week.

Inside the medina itself, *Hôtel Essaouira* (☎ 464800) has comparatively small and nicely tiled singles/doubles, which although a bit gloomy have big windows onto the courtyard for Dr30/60. There's a terrace and warm showers are Dr5.

Hôtel L'Avenir nearby (☎ 462657) is a good place charging Dr30/60. The rooms,

some with sea views and all with toilets, are set around a bright courtyard. It has a noisy cafe and restaurant and there are good views from the roof.

The best value is the *Hôtel Majestic* (☎ 464011, fax 462490), right next to the medina wall. It offers very clean, large singles/doubles/triples with washbasin for Dr40/70/110; gas-heated showers are Dr5. The best rooms look out onto the Qasr al-Bahr and the ocean (and the noisy freight railway line).

On the south side of Place de l'Indépendance you can get yourself a tiny room for Dr30/60 in *Hôtel Sevillana* (*Impasse ben Hassan*); hot showers are Dr7.

Considerably better than the Sevillana, but not up to the Majestic's standard, is the female-managed *Hôtel L'Océan* (☎ 464207, *Rue de R'bat*). The rooms for Dr50/70 are quite OK, and there is a hot shower (Dr5) on each floor.

Places to Stay – Mid-Range
The only mid-range hotel close to the centre is the two-star *Hôtel Anis* (☎ 463078, *Rue de R'bat*), where you can get a comfortable single/double with private shower and toilet for Dr135/159. It has limited parking for Dr10 and interesting old photos of Safi.

Other mid-range hotels are higher up in the city, around Place Mohammed V. Rooms at *Hôtel Assif* (☎ 622311, fax 621862, *Ave de la Liberté*) are well decked-out, with heating, telephone and bathroom for Dr200/250. There's a good restaurant here.

Hôtel Les Mimosas (☎ 623208, fax 625955), south-east of the centre, consists of two block-like buildings either side of Rue ibn Zeidoun. Rooms cost Dr185/217 and there's a sauna, restaurant, bar and nightclub, the Golden Fish.

Places to Stay – Top End
There are two four-star hotels in Safi, both with great views over the medina and industrial port area; the cheaper is *Hôtel Atlantide* (☎ 462160, fax 464595, *Rue Chaouki*) charging Dr279/340 for singles/doubles. It has a bar, a restaurant, a pool and grand French character.

Its more expensive counterpart up the road, *Hôtel Safir* (☎ 464299, *Ave Zerktouni*) seems to have opted for a Japanese ambience. Rooms here cost Dr420/550 plus taxes. Amenities include restaurants, a bar, a nightclub, a pool and tennis courts.

Places to Eat

Restaurants The real treat in Safi is sampling the seafood in the pokey little *fish eateries* tucked away behind Chapelle Portugaise. A meal of fresh fish with chips, salads and drinks costs about Dr20. In the evening you'll find a few *snack stands* set up at the port end of Rue du Souq. Offerings include tiny bowls of snails.

Café Restaurant el-Bahia, which takes up the whole south side of Place de l'Indépendance, has a cafe downstairs and a slightly fancier restaurant upstairs. A fairly ordinary meal will cost around Dr50.

On the other side of Rue de R'bat, behind the Crédit du Maroc bank, is a small *snack place* open until late. A good-sized serving of chicken, rice, salad and bread costs Dr25. *Restaurant de Safi* (*Rue de la Maraine*), off Place de l'Indépendance, does brochettes (skewered meat) and chicken for about the same. *Restaurant Gegene*, on the same street, has a wider selection of dishes and is a little more expensive.

The only real alternatives to these places are the *restaurants* in the bigger hotels, such as the *Hôtel Assif*, up by Place Mohammed V, in the swankier part of town.

Le Refuge (☎ 464354) is a very good fish restaurant a few kilometres north of Safi on the coast road to El-Jadida. It's closed on Monday and is a little pricey, but is possibly *the* choice restaurant in the area. You'll need your own car or a taxi to get there.

Cafes & Patisseries There is no shortage of cafes along Place de l'Indépendance and Rue de R'bat and, though it's nothing special, *Café M'Zoughen* makes the best choice for breakfast. *Restaurant Essira*, a short walk along the beach road south of the centre, is the best choice on the place with views out over the ocean. Another pleasant option is the shaded *cafe* on Ave Moulay

Youssef just outside the entrance to the medina. *Restau'snack* on the edge of the potteries has a good shaded terrace where you can enjoy a light snack or coffee before or after your shopping expedition.

You'll find plenty more cafes up around Place Mohammed V, a selection of ice creams at *Glacier Jour et Nuit* and a good *patisserie* next door to Café Oukaïmeden.

Entertainment

You can get a soothing ale in *Café/Bar de La Poste* (*Place de l'Indépendance*), and a couple of other cafes serve alcohol inside although they're definitely male-dominated. Otherwise, you're obliged to try the bars in the bigger hotels.

The *Golden Fish*, in Hôtel Les Mimosas south-east of the centre, is one of those dodgy nightclubs prevalent throughout the country.

Getting There & Away

Bus Most of the CTM buses stopping in Safi originate elsewhere, so consider booking in advance. CTM has one daily service to Agadir (Dr66, 6½ hours) departing at 10 am; six services to Casablanca (Dr65, four hours); three services to El-Jadida (Dr40, two hours); and one daily service each for Essaouira (Dr38, 2½ hours) departing at 9 pm; Marrakesh (Dr37) at 7 am; Oualidia (Dr16, 1½ hours) at 6.15 am; and Tiznit (10 hours) at 10 am.

Other operators have daily departures for Agadir, Casablanca, El-Jadida, Essaouira, Marrakesh, Rabat, Tan Tan, Taroudannt and Tiznit.

Train A daily 7.30 am train to Rabat (Dr79, six hours) via Casablanca (Dr53.50, 4½ hours) connects with a service to Marrakesh (Dr48, four hours) at Benguérir.

Getting Around

Both the bus station on Ave Président Kennedy and the train station on Rue de R'bat are quite some way from the centre of town; local bus No 7 and *petit taxis* (local taxis; 9(Dr5) go to the centre from both places (Place de l'Indépendance).

AROUND SAFI

The beaches in the immediate vicinity of Safi are not much chop, so you need to go a little further afield. To the north you have the choice of **Lalla Fatna** (10km) and **Cap Beddouza** (20km). In summer there are local buses from Place de l'Indépendance and grand taxis to both. The coast road along the first 40km or so north of Safi is particularly breathtaking in parts.

About 30km to the south is **Souira Kedima**, populated by Moroccan summer holiday bungalows. This place is not special, whatever anyone in Safi may tell you. However, shortly before it, after you've cleared the Maroc Phosphore plant, there are a couple of wild and woolly Atlantic beaches that beg to be stopped at – if the wind dies down.

ESSAOUIRA

☎ 04

Essaouira (pronounced Esa-wera) is the most popular of the coastal towns, both with independent travellers and with an ever-increasing number of day-tripping package tourists. The town has a magnificent beach that curves for kilometres to the south, and its relaxed atmosphere is in complete contrast to other cities.

Essaouira is also Morocco's best-known windsurfing centre, and increasingly promotes itself as 'Windy City, Afrika'. Indeed, the Atlantic winds can be powerful, which is good news for windsurfers, but (for much of the year) bad news for sunbathers!

The fortifications of the old city are a mixture of Portuguese, French and Berber military architecture, and their massiveness lends a powerful mystique to the town. Inside it's all light and charm. You'll find narrow lanes, whitewashed houses with blue-painted doors, tranquil squares, pleasant cafes and artisans in tiny workshops beavering away at fragrant thuya wood. Many Europeans and artists, enchanted by the place, have invested in medina properties and the expat influence is evident throughout the town.

The snug, fortified harbour, immediately south-west of the medina, is a hive of activity, with nets laid out on the quayside, fishing boats unloading their catch, traditional wooden boats being built and fresh seafood sizzling on outdoor grills.

The Île de Mogador, south-west across the bay, is known for its Eleonara's falcons, which come here to breed during summer.

Essaouira's reputation is spreading, and its tranquillity can be stretched to breaking point in summer. If you intend to visit during high season, it's worth booking a room ahead. Also, while it is a relatively laid-back place, travellers should be prepared for a certain amount of hustling.

History

As far back as the 7th century BC, Phoenician sailors had discovered this part of the Moroccan coast, and it is believed that the Carthaginians and Romans followed in their footsteps. The main evidence lies in the little offshore islands, which were celebrated as a site for murex (a type of mollusc), the secretion of which was used in the manufacture of purple dyes (popular with the Romans) – hence their name: the Purple Isles (Îles Purpuraires or Île de Mogador).

It was the Portuguese who established a commercial and military bridgehead here towards the end of the 15th century, which they named Mogador. They lost it in 1541 and the coastal town subsequently fell into decline.

Most of what stands today is the result of a curious experiment. In 1765, Sultan Sidi Mohammed ben Abdallah hired a French architect, Théodore Cornut, to design a city suitable for foreign trade. Renamed Essaouira, it became an open commercial link between Timbuktu and Europe until the French protectorate was established in 1912, when it was rebaptised Mogador and lost much of its importance. With independence, in 1956, it again became Essaouira.

Orientation

Essaouira is pretty compact. The walled town is split into the mellah, medina and kasbah where most hotels, restaurants, cafes, banks and shops are concentrated, although new hotels are sprouting up all the time, especially towards the southern end of the beach.

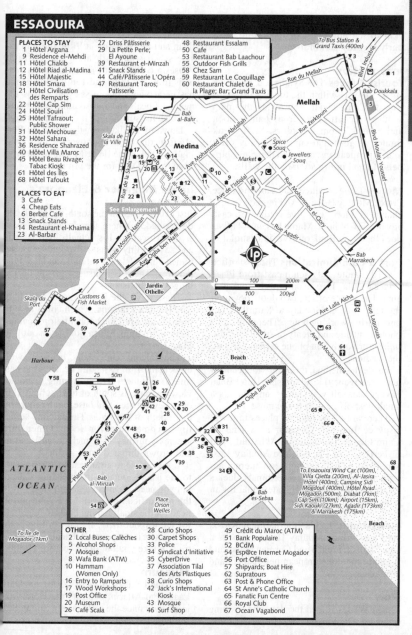

ESSAOUIRA

PLACES TO STAY
1 Hôtel Argana
9 Residence el-Mehdi
11 Hôtel Chakib
12 Hôtel Riad al-Madina
15 Hôtel Majestic
18 Hôtel Smara
21 Hôtel Civilisation des Remparts
22 Hôtel Cap Sim
24 Hôtel Souiri
25 Hôtel Tafraout; Public Shower
31 Hôtel Mechouar
32 Hôtel Sahara
36 Residence Shahrazed
40 Hôtel Villa Maroc
45 Hôtel Beau Rivage; Tabac Kiosk
61 Hôtel des Îles
68 Hôtel Tafoukt

PLACES TO EAT
3 Cafe
4 Cheap Eats
6 Berber Cafe
13 Snack Stands
14 Restaurant el-Khaima
23 Al-Barbar

27 Driss Pâtisserie
29 La Petite Perle; El Ayoune
39 Restaurant el-Minzah
41 Snack Stands
44 Café/Pâtisserie L'Opéra
47 Restaurant Taros; Patisserie

48 Restaurant Essalam
50 Cafe
53 Restaurant Bab Laachour
55 Outdoor Fish Grills
58 Chez Sam
59 Restaurant Le Coquillage
60 Restaurant Chalet de la Plage; Bar; Grand Taxis

OTHER
2 Local Buses; Calèches
5 Alcohol Shops
7 Mosque
8 Wafa Bank (ATM)
10 Hammam (Women Only)
16 Entry to Ramparts
17 Wood Workshops
19 Post Office
20 Museum
26 Café Scala

28 Curio Shops
30 Carpet Shops
33 Police
34 Syndicat d'Initiative
35 CyberDrive
37 Association Tilal des Arts Plastiques
38 Curio Shops
42 Jack's International Kiosk
43 Mosque
46 Surf Shop

49 Crédit du Maroc (ATM)
51 Bank Populaire
52 BCdM
54 Esp@ce Internet Mogador
56 Port Office
57 Shipyards; Boat Hire
62 Supratours
63 Post & Phone Office
64 St Anne's Catholic Church
65 Fanatic Fun Centre
66 Royal Club
67 Ocean Vagabond

To Bus Station & Grand Taxis (400m)

Mellah

Bab al-Bahr

Skala de la Ville

Medina

Spice Souq

Jewellers Souq

Market

Rue du Mellah

Rue Zerktouni

Blvd Moulay Youssef

Bab Doukkala

Blvd Industrie

Rue de la Skala

Derb Laâlouj

al-Attarin

Ave Mohammed ben Abdallah

Ave de l'Istiqlal

Rue Mohammed el-Qory

Ave Mohammed ben Nafi

Place Prince Moulay Hassan

Ave Oqba ben Nafi

Jardin Othello

See Enlargement

Rue Agadir

Bab Marrakech

0   100   200m
0   100   200yd

Skala du Port

Customs & Fish Market

Harbour

ATLANTIC OCEAN

To Île de Mogador (1km)

Blvd Mohammed V

Ave Lalla Aicha

Rue Laqouas

Ave el-Moukaouama

Beach

0   25   50m
0   25   50yd

Bab al-Minzah

Place Orson Welles

Place es-Sebaa

Bab es-Sebaa

Ave Oqba ben Nafi

To Essaouira Wind Car (100m), Villa Qietta (200m), Al-Jasira Hôtel (400m), Camping Sidi Mogdoul (500m), Hôtel Ryad Mogador (500m), Diabat (7km), Cap Sim (10km), Airport (15km), Sidi Kaouki (27km), Agadir (173km) & Marrakesh (175km)

Beach

The bus station and grand taxis are about 1km to the north-east of the centre, in a fairly raggedy part of town.

Information

Tourist Offices The Syndicat d'Initiative (☎ 475080) is within the town walls at 10 Rue de Caire, about 50m inside the main southern gate. It's open from 9 am to noon and 3 to 6.30 pm weekdays. Staff speak limited English and can only really offer tourist publications, although there are snippets of local information on the walls.

Money There are three banks around Place Prince Moulay Hassan. All are good for exchange and most can give credit card cash advances. Crédit du Maroc has an ATM, as does the Wafa Bank on Ave de l'Istiqlal.

Post & Communications The post office is a 10-minute walk south-east from Place Prince Moulay Hassan on Ave el-Moukaouama. The phone office, two doors down on the left, is open Monday to Saturday, but only during working hours. There are cardphones outside and plenty of small *téléboutiques* (privately run phone offices) around the medina.

Inside the medina, the *tabac* (tobacconist and newsagency) kiosk outside Hôtel Beau Rivage can sell you stamps, and there's a small post office next to the museum.

There are a few Internet places in town: Esp@ce Internet Mogador at 8 Rue de Caire (above Téléboutique Akhardid), and CyberDrive on Place Prince Moulay Hassan, charge Dr20 per hour for Internet access and have a fair few terminals. Jack's International Kiosk has one terminal for an expensive Dr30 per hour.

Newsstands Jack's International Kiosk, on Place Prince Moulay Hassan, stocks a few English, French and German books and a good range of European newspapers and magazines.

Port

Orson Welles filmed the dramatic opening shots of *Othello* on the ramparts of Es-saouira. Heading north from Place Prince Moulay Hassan you can gain access to both them and the **Skala de la Ville**, the impressive sea bastion built along the cliffs. It houses a collection of European brass cannons from the 18th- and 19th-centuries and has great views out to sea and across the medina. Locals and tourists alike gather here to watch the sun disappear over the horizon.

Down by the harbour, the **Skala du Port** offers picturesque views over the busy fishing port and of the Île de Mogador, but you have to pay Dr10 for the privilege.

Île de Mogador & Eleanora's Falcons

Just off the coast to the south-west is the Île de Mogador, where there's another massive fortification. It's actually two islands and several tiny islets – also known as the famed Purple Isles of antiquity and Îles Purpuraires. There is a disused prison on the biggest of the islands.

These days, the islands are a sanctuary for **Eleanora's falcons**, which come here to breed from April to October before making their incredible return journey south to Madagascar.

The falcons can easily be seen with binoculars from Essaouira beach – the best time to spot them is early evening. (Another viewing place is south of town, about 1km or so beyond the lighthouse, on the shore by the mouth of the river. The falcons sometimes come here for food. Other bird species you may spot include gulls, terns and Brown-throated sand martins.)

It is possible to arrange a boat trip across to the islands outside the breeding season, but you need to obtain a permit (free) from the port office; once you have your permit head for the small fishing boats to negotiate for the trip out there. If you can't be bothered to sort it out yourself, Fanatic Fun Centre will take you out in its boat for Dr300.

Museum

The small museum (☎ 475300) on Dar Laalouj al-Attarin, opposite the Hôtel Majestic, was once the residence of Sultan Sid Mohammed ben Abdallah's governor. I displays jewellery, costumes, weapons, musical instruments and tapestries. There's a section explaining the signs and symbols used by local craftspeople and some interesting photographs of the town taken at the turn of the century. It's open from 8.30 am to 6 pm Wednesday to Monday and entry is Dr3/10 for children/adults.

St Anne's Catholic Church
The beautifully kept, light-filled Catholic church on Ave el-Moukaouama, just south of the post office, offers mass alternately in French, English, Dutch and German on Sunday at 10 am.

Beaches & Water Sports
The beach stretches some 10km down the coast to the sand dunes of Cap Sim. Free entertainment in the form of soccer and basketball matches often takes place at the top end of the beach. Further south, across the Ksar River, you'll pass the ruins of an old fortress and pavilion partially covered in sand. The beach is windy and has a strong current but is excellent for windsurfing. If you're alone, don't wander too far from town as attacks have been reported.

Along the shore, Fanatic Fun Centre, Royal Club and Ocean Vagabond rent windsurfing equipment (Dr120 per hour or Dr150 with instructor) and surf boards (Dr40 per hour). Equipment standards vary so shop around. Ocean Vagabond also offers fly surfing (using a kite to propel yourself) in the summer.

Special Events
The Essaouira Festival is a week-long musical event held in June. There are concerts on Place Prince Moulay Hassan and other venues throughout town. International, national and local performers provide music ranging from Gnaoua (see Music under Arts in the Facts about Morocco chapter for an explanation) to jazz and there are simultaneous art exhibitions. It's huge and some events run right through the night. For dates and line-ups check out the (French-language) festival Web site: www.festival-gnaoua.co.ma.

Hammams & Public Showers
There are plenty of small hammams hidden about town; there's one for women across the road from the Hôtel Chakib, in the centre of the medina.

Places to Stay
Most places to stay are within the walls of the fort and medina with some of the more popular budget hotels being well situated near the ramparts and on Place Prince Moulay Hassan. If you arrive later in the day, don't be surprised to find them full. All have terraces of varying sizes, which are likely to be the only places you'll get the sea view most advertise. Meals, more commonly breakfast, can usually be served there, providing sanctuary from both the masses below and the wind.

New, higher-class hotels are opening at the southern end of town, allowing for more of a beach-based stay.

Upon arrival at the bus station you are likely to be 'welcomed' by groups of locals offering to rent you rooms in their houses or apartments. Both are reasonable options, with the former costing about the same as a room in a budget hotel. There are some pretty swanky apartments around (ideal for artists) with all the comforts of home. These can be relatively expensive, but reasonable if there are enough people. Other apartments are advertised around town and at Jack's International Kiosk (e apartment@essouira.com).

Places to Stay – Budget
Camping The best *camp site* is near Diabat (see Diabat under Around Essaouira later) about 7km out of town.

Camping Sidi Mogdoul (☎ 472196), 400m out on the Agadir road, is quite a stark compound with no shade (till the saplings mature). It costs Dr9 per person, Dr15 per camper van, Dr10 for electricity and Dr22 to pitch a tent – although you'd be better off bush-camping elsewhere. Hot showers are available for Dr8 and the facilities are new and clean.

Hotels A few of these places can be quite damp, which helps keep things cool during summer but can make them cold at other times – it's worth having a bit of a look around to find the best option.

The best sea views are from the terraces of the *Hôtel Civilisation des Remparts* (☎ 475110, 18 Rue ibn Rochd) and *Hôtel Smara* (☎ 475655, 26 Rue de la Skala). Both have basic singles/doubles around covered courtyards for Dr60/80, including use of a shared shower, which you must pay extra for. Smara has a few well-sought-after rooms with sea views for Dr100 and two terrace rooms for Dr120. Both it and the Hôtel Civilisation des Remparts serve breakfast on their terraces.

Hôtel Beau Rivage (☎/fax 475925), overlooking Place Prince Moulay Hassan, is clean and there are cafes and patisseries just outside the front door. Simple rooms at the back of the hotel cost Dr60/90. The same with private shower are Dr120, or Dr180 with a small balcony overlooking the square.

Hôtel Majestic (☎ 474909, Darb Laalouj al-Attarin) charges Dr50/100 for bright, airy rooms with shared shower (Dr5). They also have a 'penthouse' room with bathroom for Dr150. The hotel terrace affords one of the highest panoramas in Essaouira.

Cheap and cheerful places that will do if there's nothing else available include *Hôtel Chakib* (☎ 472291), in towards the middle of the medina, and *Hôtel Argana* (☎ 475975), just outside Bab Doukkala, east of the medina. Both charge Dr40/70 with shared bathroom and are ordinary, but acceptable.

Residence Shahrazed (☎ 472977, fax 476436, 1 Rue Youssef el-Fassi), near the Syndicat d'Initiative, charges Dr120/200 for singles/doubles with bathroom, or Dr100 for a double without. It has a large communal area downstairs and offers bicycle hire.

The one-star *Hôtel Tafraout* (☎ 476276, 7 Rue de Marrakesh) off Rue Mohammed ben Abdallah is clean, comfortable and very welcoming. Rooms without bathroom cost Dr99/148, those with bathroom cost Dr149/248.

Hotel Souiri (☎ 475339, 37 Darb Laalouj al-Attarine) is a good option, with clean rooms, some looking out onto the action on the street below. The terrace is predomi-

nantly used by those in the rooftop apartment (Dr600 for four with salon and kitchen) but you can still use both it and the salon with TV, stereo and book exchange downstairs. Rooms with breakfast cost Dr95/120 without bathroom, or doubles with bath are Dr250. It accepts credit cards (for a fee).

Places to Stay – Mid-Range

The huge two-star *Hôtel Sahara* (☎ 472292, Ave Oqba ben Nafii) has garish decor and a mixed bag of rooms with bathroom for Dr150/200.

Just next door, *Hôtel Mechouar* (☎ 475828, fax 784827) has nicer bright, clean rooms with bathroom for Dr150/250. While the rooms are modern, downstairs its 18th-century history is evident in its cosy bar and licensed restaurant serving Moroccan and French fare – a very civilised place for a drink or meal.

Hôtel Cap Sim (☎ 785834, 11 Rue ibn Rochd, e capsimhotel@hotmail.com) has clean rooms with breakfast for Dr150/225; with bathroom they're Dr250 a double. There's a lounge downstairs and the hotel's hot water supply is solar powered.

Al-Jasira Hôtel (☎ 475956, fax 476074, 18 Rue Moulay Ali Cherif, e aljasira@iam .net.ma) in the Quartier des Dunes has large bright and clean rooms, some with terraces, from Dr200/350. It also has a Moroccan restaurant.

Places to Stay – Top End

Practically right on the beach, the three-star *Hotel Tafoukt* (☎ 784504/5, fax 784416, 58 Blvd Mohammed V) has unsurpassed views to the Île de Mogador with rooms starting from Dr288/306 including breakfast. The hotel has an expensive restaurant and bar.

Residence el-Mehdi (☎ 475943, fax 475943, 15 Rue Sidi Abdesmih, e rmehdi @iam.net.ma), a 19th-century town house restored with a contemporary look, is a tasteful place with a restaurant and bar. The staff are very obliging and will dash out to buy fresh ingredients for any special meals you may request. Singles/doubles cost from Dr250/352 and it also has double apartments for Dr600.

If you fancy yourself as a bit of a rock star and want to treat yourself while in Essaouira, try *Hôtel Riad al-Madina* (☎ 475907, fax 475727, 9 Darb Laalouj al-Attarin). Originally a local pasha's villa, it's been frequented by the likes of Jimi Hendrix, Frank Zappa, Leonard Cohen and Jefferson Airplane. Painstakingly restored to its original 18th-century splendour, it has a beautiful central courtyard, restaurant and sauna. Split-level rooms, all with bathroom, TV and telephone, cost Dr432/664; for a real splurge, the Suite Royale is Dr2364.

Hôtel Villa Maroc (☎ 476147, fax 472806, 10 Rue Abdallah ben Yassine, e villa.maroc@casanet.net.ma), just inside the inner city walls, comprises two renovated 18th-century houses. It has been exquisitely decorated – there are several intimate salons where you can sip mint tea and gaze at antiques and at bowls brimming with rose petals – and has only a dozen or so rooms (some with four-poster beds). Rooms cost Dr510/610 plus taxes. The villa also has an excellent restaurant (about Dr150 per head). You'll need to book for both accommodation and meals.

Back at the more sanitised international scale, the four-star *Hôtel des Îles* (☎ 472329, fax 472472, Blvd Mohammed V) is of a similar era to the Tafoukt, but is closer to the medina. It is equipped with two bars, restaurants, pool and all you would expect (eg, minibar, robes and baskets of fruit). Rooms start at Dr500/640 for basic singles/doubles and rise to Dr2000 for the main suite.

Hôtel Ryad Mogador (☎ 783555, fax 783556) at the Agadir end of town is a new place with a huge swimming pool, fitness club and tennis courts. Singles/doubles/triples set around the pool in Andalusian gardens start at Dr650/800/1100.

Villa Qietta (☎ 783281, fax 783421, 86 Blvd Mohammed V) is a B&B converted from a family home. All suites have terraces with views and there are some pretty appealing options. With cool lounges and sunny terraces, all within a short stroll of the beach, it rivals many of its medina counterparts. Rooms are Dr488/588, while garden/sea-view suites are Dr1280/1450.

Places to Eat

Cheap Eats The best place for breakfast is the terrace of your hotel or a *cafe* on Place Prince Moulay Hassan. For the former, your hotel should be able to sort you out with bread, coffee etc; for the latter you can order an omelette, grab a pastry or two en route or simply wait for one of the boys who parade around town with pastries and biscuits to pass by while you sip your coffee.

For simple snacks and cheap hole-in-the-wall-type food, there are a few places along Ave Mohammed ben Abdallah, Rue Zerktouni and just inside Bab Doukkala. Back on Place Prince Moulay Hassan, two **snack stands** sell excellent baguettes stuffed with meat, salad and just about anything else for around Dr15.

Possibly the best cheap eats are en route to the port, at several **outdoor fish grills** offering a fabulous selection of the day's catch. Meals cost from Dr25 and make an excellent alfresco lunch.

A **Berber cafe**, just off the main drag conveniently close to the **fresh produce stalls**, will prepare your own personal *tajine* (meat and vegetable stew) – just take along the ingredients a few hours before you want to eat. There's also a *fish market* at the port.

Restaurants On Place Prince Moulay Hassan, *Café/Pâtisserie L'Opéra*, which spills out in front of the Hôtel Beau Rivage, serves some very good cheap meals. Not quite as popular but nearly as good is *Restaurant Essalam*, where you can pick up an excellent set menu for Dr40.

A bit pricier, *Restaurant Taros*, upstairs opposite Banque Populaire, is traditionally decorated, and has a terrace and live music to accompany its Moroccan dishes.

Moving away from the square, *La Petite Perle* and *El-Ayoune*, both located on Rue el-Hajelli, are cosy little salon-styled places with live music where you can eat your fill for about Dr40.

The licensed *Restaurant al-Baba*, just by the Hôtel Tafraout, offers a small range of authentic Italian dishes (no pizza though) at reasonable prices. Look for the sign with a camel sporting a fez.

Restaurant el-Minzah (*Ave Oqba ben Nafii*) has tasty set menus for about Dr70. Sit on the terrace outside and watch the changing colours of the medina ramparts.

With a more formal and tour-group atmosphere, the licensed *Restaurant el-Khaima* is set back on a small square off Darb Laalouj al-Attarin. Mains cost about Dr60, and they offer two set menus for Dr80 and Dr180.

Chez Sam is a long-standing institution known for its seafood, although many have written in to say that it's overrated. Still, it overlooks the harbour at the far end of the port and you can choose a la carte (about Dr100 a head including wine) or take one of the two set menus (Dr70 or Dr170). It's open daily for lunch and dinner. *Restaurant Le Coquillage*, also on the port, also specialises in seafood. Prices are on a par with Chez Sam.

Back on Place Prince Moulay Hassan, *Restaurant Bab Laachour* also offers a range of seafood; you're looking at about Dr70 for a meal. It has a good terrace overlooking the square and ramparts.

Also good for seafood is the licensed *Restaurant Chalet de la Plage*, which is on the beach, outside the medina walls. It offers four-course meals for Dr90; mains range from Dr50 to Dr90.

Cafes & Patisseries The most popular and relaxing places for a hot drink are the *cafes* on Place Prince Moulay Hassan. Some people spend the better part of a day here, slowly shifting from cafe to cafe with the moving sunlight. There are plenty of patisseries around the square, including *Driss Pâtisserie* (which also has a hidden seating area) and another below Restaurant Taros, with a good range of croissants and other pastries to get the day going. You can buy them here to take to a cafe.

The *seafront cafes* sell ice cream and are good choices for an outdoor beverage – as long as the sea breeze isn't blowing too hard.

The seashell-decorated *cafe* outside Bab Doukkala has refreshing fruit cocktails and great views over the ocean.

Entertainment

Quite apart from enjoying a drink over dinner in the licensed restaurants or listening to live music in the smaller places, Essaouira has a few night-time alternatives.

Almost a mandatory prelude to any night in Essaouira is finding a good spot to watch the fishing fleet come in at sunset; hotel terraces are ideal and there are a couple of *alcohol shops* at the entrance to the medina that can sell you your favourite tipple.

If you'd rather a bar with a view, head for the terrace of the small place to the east of Restaurant Chalet de la Plage: it looks like a toilet from the outside but it's a bar – honest. Local drinkers gather here or at the bars in the *Hôtel Mechouar* or *Hôtel Tafoukt*.

Hôtel des Îles has a choice of bars: one out by the pool; another, the rather kitsch *Orson Welles Bar* decorated with the same three pieces of memorabilia, upstairs; or the piano bar with large TV and piped piano music, out the front. The latter two are open till 11 pm.

There's no alcohol at *Café Scala* at the northern end of Place Prince Moulay Hassan but it does have Berber music jamming sessions in its back room every couple of nights.

Shopping

Beneath the ramparts of the Skala de la Ville are dozens of wood-carving workshops overflowing with exquisite marquetry work made from local fragrant thuya wood. The craftsmen, who toil away until the last fading light of dusk, are very accommodating, so you can watch them without too much pressure. The work is reputedly the best in Morocco although the wood itself is an endangered species.

A better souvenir option is a painting by one of the many artists who live in Essaouira. As a huge number of artists are drawn here, the works available are diverse and plentiful. Association Tilal des Arts Plastiques is an interesting workshop and salesroom for up-and-coming Essaouira artists. It's run by Hamid Boutali, the artist of satirical cartoon postcards sold around town and further afield.

Carpet and rug shops, as well as bric-a-brac, jewellery and brassware shops, are clustered together in the winding streets between Place Prince Moulay Hassan and Ave Oqba ben Nafii. The beautifully decorated skin lamps sold all over town are some of the best on offer in Morocco.

In the heart of the medina, up towards the mellah, you'll find a spice souq selling all sorts of medicinal herbs and spices, as well as perfumes and dyes. The nearby jewellery souq is worth a look.

There are also a few surf shops dotted around should you be running low on sexwax or board shorts.

Getting There & Away

Air Essaouira's airport (☎ 476709) is 15km north of town. Royal Air Maroc (RAM) has services to Casablanca (Dr350, one hour).

Regional Air Lines flies to Agadir on Saturday and Casablanca on Sunday.

Bus The bus station (☎ 784764) is about 400m to the north-east of the medina. It's easy to find – head past the second-hand market. It's probably better to get a petit taxi if you're arriving/leaving late at night.

CTM is at window No 7. There is a bus to Safi (Dr29, 2½ hours) departing at 10.30 am; Casablanca (Dr100, 6½ hours) via El-Jadida (Dr40.50, 4½ hours) at midnight; and Marrakesh (Dr40, three hours) at 5 pm. The 12.30 pm bus to Agadir (Dr37, four hours) continues to Tiznit (Dr57, six hours).

Plenty of other companies run to the same destinations as well as Taroudannt (windows 3 & 6) at 8.30 am and 12.30 and 8 pm; Tan Tan at 9.30 pm; and Rabat at 8 am and 10 pm.

Supratours (☎ 472317) runs buses from its office, near Bab Marrakech, to Marrakesh train station at 6.10 am and 4 pm (Dr45, 2½ hours) and Agadir (Dr55, three hours).

Local buses to Diabat and Sidi Kaouki leave from Bab Doukkala.

Grand Taxi The grand taxi rank is next to the bus station. The fare to Agadir (or Inezgane) is around Dr50.

Getting Around

The No 7 bus to Sidi Kaouki passes the airport; a taxi to the airport should cost Dr100.

The blue petit taxis are a good idea for getting to and from the bus station (about Dr10) but they can't enter the medina. An alternative is to chuck your luggage into a cart at the bus station and let the guy pushing it take you directly to your chosen accommodation. You can also take a ride around town in one of the *calèches* (horse-drawn carriages) that gather just outside Bab Doukkala (Dr60 per hour).

Cars can be hired from Essaouira Wind Car (☎ cell 01-347134), on Rue Princesse Lalla Amina just off the beach, for Dr350 per day.

You can hire bicycles from Residence Shahrazed for Dr30 per day.

AROUND ESSAOUIRA
Diabat

Close to Cap Sim, inland about 1km through sand dunes and scrub, is the Berber village of Diabat, which became a legend among hippies in the 1960s after a visit by Jimi Hendrix.

It subsequently became a dope-smoking colony similar to those on the beaches of Goa (in India), but was cleared by the police in the mid-1970s following the murder of several hippies by local junkies. These days it has returned to tranquillity, and although there's little to see many still make the pilgrimage up here to boast that they've had a smoke at Jimmy's house.

Driving from Essaouira, take the coast road for Agadir, and turn up the *piste* (dirt track) just after the bridge about 7km out of town. There is a small camp site next door – though fairly basic, it's a much better alternative to the camp site in Essaouira.

A local bus runs up here from Essaouira regularly.

Sidi Kaouki

About 27km south of Essaouira is a surfing and windsurfing spot that is fast growing in popularity. A local bus ride away from Essaouira, this excellent stretch of stony sand is backed by a basic camp site, a couple of hotels and small stalls serving tajine, seafood and snacks. It's the perfect place to tackle some waves, sit around a camp fire and relax a few days away.

Auberge de la Plage (☎ 473383) has basic singles/doubles for Dr150/250, or Dr350 a double with bathroom. Try for the rooftop room that is bright and airy with good views of the beach and mountains. The auberge also offers horse riding along the beach for Dr150 per hour.

Residence el-Karam is a bit cheaper with nice enough rooms for Dr120/220 with breakfast, or Dr80/180 without.

To get to Sidi Kaouki, local bus No 5 to the beachfront at Sidi Kaouki leaves Bab Marrakech in Essaouira just under every two hours (Dr6).

AGADIR
☎ 08

Agadir is a modern city, having been completely rebuilt after a devastating earthquake in 1960; this was a double tragedy as it occurred in a decade responsible for so much ugly architecture. Sitting by a vast sweep of protected beach with an average 300 days of sunshine per year, the town has been specifically developed as a resort for short-stay package tourists from Europe, who arrive daily by the planeload in search of sun, sand and a sanitised version of the mysteries of the Barbary Coast.

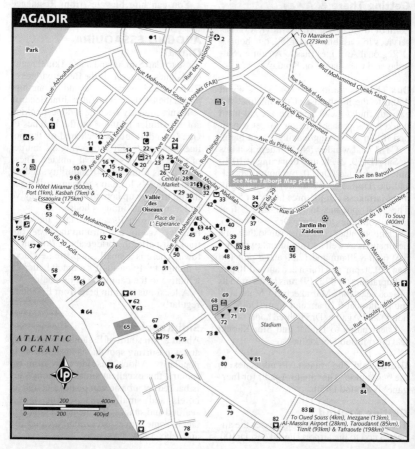

The reek of Ambre Soleil and the rustle of *Paris Match*, *Der Spiegel* and the *Sunday Times* fill the air. Not that it's unpleasant – it's just that it could be any resort town on the northern Mediterranean coast. It's also incredibly popular with Moroccans drawn here by its cosmopolitan air and the opportunity to escape the restraints of everyday life.

Agadir's high tourist profile often leads people to forget its growing importance as a commercial and fishing port – a big chunk of Morocco's sardine catch now comes through Agadir, and arriving from the north you can hardly fail to notice the sprawling port facilities.

Although the town can be expensive, it's well placed for trips south-east into the Anti Atlas and north-east into the High Atlas (a two-hour drive from Agadir and you're into some pretty mountain countryside), as well as further south towards the Western Sahara.

Bird-watchers will find a rewarding estuarine area busy with bird life just a few kilometres south of town.

History

Little is known of Agadir's distant past, but in 1505 an enterprising Portuguese mariner decided to build himself a fort, Santa Cruz de Cap de Gué, a few kilometres north of the modern city.

Sold to the Portuguese government eight years later, it became a busy centre of commerce, visited by Portuguese, Genoese and French merchants. Retaken by the Moroccans in 1541 and subsequently used as the

AGADIR

PLACES TO STAY	6	Budget	42	Town Hall; Night Pharmacy
5	Camp Site	7	Hertz	44	Bank Populaire Bureau de
11	Hôtel Petit Suede	8	Naviganet 2000;		Change
18	Hôtel Sud Bahia		Hôtel Oasis	45	Air France
41	Atlantic Hôtel	9	BMCE (ATM)	46	Car & Motorcycle Hire
43	Hôtel Kamal	10	BMCI (ATM)	47	Travel Agencies
50	Hôtel Aladin	12	Royal Air Maroc	48	Moroccan Institute of
51	Hôtel Anezi	13	Mosque		Management
64	Iberotel Tafoukt	14	Banque Populaire	49	Royal Tennis Club
73	Hôtel Transatlantique	17	Sports Evasion Maroc		of Agadir
79	Résidence Club La Kasbah	19	Atlas Tours	52	Sheraton Hotel; Shem's
84	Hôtel Les Cinq Parties du	20	Newsstand		Casino
	Monde	21	Supratours	53	Syndicat d'Initiative
		23	Crédit du Maroc (ATM)	54	Public Swimming Pool
		24	Bar	57	Children's Rides
PLACES TO EAT	25	Alcohol Shop	59	Banque Populaire
15	Restaurant la Tour de Paris	26	Cinéma Rialto	60	Orient Express Toy Train
16	Restaurant Darkoum	28	Crown English	61	Jimmy's
22	Disney Burger		Bookshop	65	Tafoukt Complex; The Pub
27	Restaurant Seoul	30	Uniprix Supermarket; Cafe;	66	L'Oasis Beach
29	Italian Restaurants		Wafa Bank (Bureau de	67	Hôtel al-Medina Palace;
55	All-Night Snack Vans		Change)		Laundry
56	Restaurant Jour et Nuit	31	Délégation Régionale du	68	Municipal Theatre
58	Restaurant Le Nil Bleue		Tourisme	69	Musée Municipal
62	Johara	32	ABN-AMRO	74	Newsstand
63	Oliveri Pistache; Taco Loco	33	Main Post	75	Le Central
70	La Truite		& Phone Office	76	Massira Travel
71	Fish Friture	34	Clinique al-Massira	77	Hôtel Beach Club;
72	Pizza Hut; Fuji Film Shop	35	St Anne's Catholic Church		Flamingo
81	McDonald's	36	Synagogue Beth-El	78	Newsstand
		37	New Labocolour	80	El-Paradiso; Hôtel Argana
OTHER	38	AgadirNet; La Verandah	82	Alhambra Cabaret
1	American Language Center		Pâtisserie	83	Royal Palace
2	Hôpital Hassan II	39	Saawa Supermarket	85	Local Bus Station
3	Museum; Jardin de Olhão	40	Alcohol Shop		& Grand Taxis
4	Protestant Church				

main outlet for products (especially sugar cane) from the Souss region, it slowly began to decline, and was finally eclipsed by the rise of Essaouira in the late 18th century.

In 1911, shortly before Morocco became a French protectorate, Germany, miffed over French and British plans to keep North Africa to themselves, took gun-boat diplomacy to the limit by sending the warship *Panther* to make noises off the Agadir coast.

The city survived that drama but on 29 February 1960, just four years after Morocco gained independence, it was flattened by an earthquake, which killed 15,000 people. The town has since been completely rebuilt, and continues to grow as Morocco's top beach resort. In 2000, Mohammed VI scheduled his first official visit to coincide with the quake's 40th anniversary. For one month the city commemorated the disaster with the opening of new public buildings, events such as women's soccer matches and earthquake education seminars under the slogan 're-building a town, uniting a nation'.

Orientation

Agadir's bus stations and most of the budget hotels are in a small area called New Talborjt in the north-east of the town. From here it's about a 20-minute walk down to the beach, which is lined with cafes, restaurants and hotels. Most of the banks and the main post office are between the beach and Ave du Prince Moulay Abdallah.

Information

Tourist Offices The Délégation Régionale du Tourisme (☎ 846377, fax 846378) is on the upper level of the central market area, just off Ave Sidi Mohammed. It's open from 8.30 am to noon and 2.30 to 6.30 pm Monday to Thursday and 8.30 to 11.30 am and 3 to 6.30 pm on Friday.

The office also has an information desk at Al-Massira airport (☎ 839077), which is open daily.

The Syndicat d'Initiative (☎ 840307), on Blvd Mohammed V, is almost opposite the junction with Ave du Général Kettani. Here you can pick up *Agadir*, a small brochure with useful information such as lists of car-

hire companies, restaurants and the like. It also has a noticeboard with bus timetables, lists of pharmacies and doctors, and details of market days in surrounding towns. It's open from 9 am to noon and 3 to 6 pm weekdays. During summer it's also open on the weekend.

Money Most banks have branches here with ATMs; Banque Populaire and Wafa Bank on Blvd Hassan II have *bureaus de change* (foreign exchange offices) that are open out of normal hours. The larger hotels can also change cash and travellers cheques.

Crédit du Maroc (☎ 840188), on Ave des Forces Armées Royales (FAR), represents American Express (AmEx) and has a bureau de change open daily from 9.30 am to 1 pm and 2.30 to 7 pm.

There is also an ATM at Al-Massira airport.

Post & Communications The main post and phone office, on Ave du Prince Moulay Abdallah, is open from 8.30 am to 6.45 pm weekdays. There is another post office on Rue du 29 Février in the budget hotel area in New Talborjt.

The phone office is in the main post office. It's open daily from 8 am to 9 pm.

There are a few Internet options, including Futurenet, opposite the mosque in New Talborjt; Naviganet 2000 at 1 Rue Hyber Girode; and AgadirNet, on the 4th floor of a building on Blvd Hassan II. They all charge between Dr10 and Dr15 per hour.

Travel Agencies Atlas Tours (☎ 841913) at 50 Blvd Hassan II represents the major airlines and can organise tours.

Bookshops The Crown English Bookshop, a couple of doors down from the tourist office in the central market, has a pretty good selection of new and second-hand English books.

There are several newsstands with a fair selection of European and international papers (usually a day or two late) and magazines. The larger hotels have stands in their driveways and there's a good selection at the stand near the corner of Blvd Hassan II and Ave des Forces Armées Royals (FAR).

Film & Photography You can buy and have film developed in several places that represent Kodak and other well-known brands. New Labocolor, on Ave du Prince Moulay Abdallah, is one of the nearest to New Talborjt. Fuji film can be bought at the shops by Pizza Hut and the Saawa supermarket on Blvd Hassan II.

Laundry There is a coin-operated laundrette at the Hôtel al-Medina Palace on Blvd du 20 Août. It's open from 9 am to 5 pm Monday to Saturday. Most hotels will do laundry (pricey) and there are pressings (dry cleaners) in Talborjt and other areas.

Medical Services Clinique al-Massira (☎ 843238), on Ave du Prince Moulay Abdallah, and Clinique de la Residence (823682) in Talborjt are large, established clinics. Hôpital Hassan II (☎ 841477) is a large modern facility out on the Marrakesh road. The main tourist office also posts a list of doctors and pharmacies.

There's a night pharmacy (☎ 820349) near the town hall.

Church Services The Catholic Church, St Anne's, on Rue de Marrakesh has services on Saturday at 6.30 pm and Sunday at 10 am and 7 pm. The Protestant church at 2 Rue de Chouhada has weekday services. There's also Synagogue Beth-El on Ave du Prince Moulay Abdallah.

Musée Municipal

This small, recently opened museum contains very good displays of jewellery, carpets and other Berber arts and crafts. On three levels, the exhibits are nicely presented, although signs are in French and Arabic only. The staff, though, speak English and are helpful. It's open from 9 am to 1 pm and 3 to 6 pm daily; entry is free and it has a small garden.

Vallée des Oiseaux

This pleasant strip of parkland running between Blvd Hassan II and under Blvd Mohammed V to Blvd du 20 Août contains a tiny aviary, a zoo and a children's playground. Entry is Dr3/5 for children/adults and it's open from 9.30 am to 12.30 pm and 3 to 7 pm Wednesday to Sunday.

Kasbah

What's left of the old kasbah is up the hill to the north-west of the town. An inscription from 1746 still adorns the gateway, exhorting visitors to 'fear God and honour your king'.

The fort was built in 1540 overlooking the former Portuguese emplacement and was restored and regarrisoned in 1752 in case Portugal decided to make a comeback.

The ramparts were partially restored after the 1960 earthquake, but nothing remains within. The grassy area below the kasbah, known as Ancienne Talborjt, covers the remains of Agadir's medina. Thousands of people lie here where they died when the quake hit.

It's a long, hot walk up to the kasbah – it's a better idea to get a taxi up and walk back down.

Jardin de Olhão

These rather odd-looking gardens mark the twinning of Agadir with the Portuguese town of Olhão, and commemorate the 'historical ties' that have so often had Morocco and Portugal at loggerheads. In 2000 a small museum was opened within the gardens displaying an exhibition of traditional costumes. Cool and relaxing, the gardens are open daily.

Beaches

Agadir's main claim to fame is its fine crescent beach, which usually remains unruffled when the Atlantic winds are blustering elsewhere. It's very well kept and you can wander at will along the sands without being hassled – although single females are still likely to be pestered by boys who are there for the exotic scenery and football matches. In the fenced-off areas of the main beach hotels you are supposed to pay a fee for use of the beach, deckchairs, umbrellas and the like. In practice you can generally plonk your towel down anywhere. During peak periods the beach is patrolled by lifeguards (there is a strong undertow) and mounted police.

Activities

Most of the larger hotels have organised activities. Hôtel Beach Club, towards the southern end of the beach, rents out pedalos, jet skis, surf skis, windsurfing equipment and surfboards (you really have to head to the northern beaches for the good breaks) but it isn't cheap. A surfboard will set you back Dr100 an hour and a wetsuit will be another Dr30. An hour on a surf ski (which usually means paddling around) costs Dr150.

Further south along the beach you'll find people with horses, camels and quad bikes for hire. Prices, again, are high. Ranch REHA (☎ 847549), 17km out on the Essaouira road, and Royal Club Equestre, on the Ait Melloul road, are two places offering horse treks.

Massira Travel (see Organised Tours later) and Sports Evasion Maroc (☎ 840122), next to the Hôtel Sud Bahia, organise ocean-fishing trips, including shark fishing. The latter also offers horse-riding and scuba diving.

Cruises along the coast are as active or inactive as you want them to be. There are plenty of yachts and catamarans that generally head towards the northern beaches. Half-day cruises cost around Dr250 and they can be booked through agencies, hotels or the yacht club (☎ 843708) at the port.

If you fancy taking to the dunes and pistes on quad bikes and can afford Dr500 for one to two people, contact the Iberotel Tafoukt.

If you fancy a round of golf there are shuttles from the main hotels to the Royal Golf Club (☎ 831278) on the Ait Melloul road and Golf les Dunes (☎ 834690) on Impasse Oued Souss.

Agadir is a family resort and has many facilities specifically for the young. These include a small group of kiddie rides on the promenade, including a bucking bronco. The Jardin ibn Zaidoun has play parks within its gardens, as does the Vallée des Oiseaux (see earlier).

The larger hotels have organised activities for children and can offer babysitting services (for a fee). Taking the kids out at night should create no major problems as most places to drink are also restaurants – of course the clubs will be off limits.

Swimming Pools

There's a public pool behind the Syndicat d'Initiative, at the top end of the beach. Most mid-range and all top-end places have swimming pools, although they rarely allow nonguests to use them – if you're cheeky enough you can always just swan in. Because they're in top-end hotels and are so protected they tend to offer a bit more privacy from stares than the usual Moroccan hotel pools.

Language Courses

The American Language Center (☎ 821589) has a branch at 6 Impasse de Baghdad, north of the city centre.

The Moroccan Institute of Management (☎ 823356, fax 823335), on Blvd Hassan II, operates as a representative for the International Language Centre.

Organised Tours

Agadir is a thriving centre for locally organised tours, mostly aimed at those charter-flight tourists in Morocco for a week or two who are anxious to do more than bake in the sand. Hotels and package-tour companies, with agencies clustered around the intersection of Blvd Hassan II and Ave des Forces Armées Royales (FAR), offer a whole range of options. Local companies, including Massira Travel (☎ 840075), at 25 Blvd du 20 Août, usually offer slightly cheaper choices.

Principal destinations include Marrakesh, Taroudannt, Tafraoute and Immouzzer des Ida Outanane. Organised tours range from Dr180 for a half day at Immouzzer des Ida Outanane to Dr1400 for a full day trundling about in a 4WD. It's much cheaper and less restrictive to organise trips yourself, especially as there are good and comfortable buses to the principal destinations. For example, if you take an organised day trip to Marrakesh you'll be leaving just as things in Djemaa el-Fna are getting interesting, whereas if you do it under your own steam you can choose a later departure or stay overnight. For more remote destinations such as Immouzzer des Ida Outanane it's worth renting a car, which also allows you to stop off at Berber villages and less populated beaches. (See Getting There & Away later for car rental agencies, and individual destination entries for more information about beaches).

Half-day tours of Agadir, including a trip up to the kasbah, are Dr85. An alternative way to see the 'sights' is to hop on the 'Orient Express' toy train that toots its way around town stopping at the main hotels. The round trip (Dr18) starts from Blvd du 20 Août but you can flag it down en route.

Special Events
In December Agadir plays host to the Southern Folk Arts Festival, which features performances and exhibitions. The beach and ocean are perfect for sports events such as the Jet Ski Tournament held in May, as well as surfing competitions. The tourist office has details of events, which are also advertised locally.

Hammams & Public Showers
There are hammams to be found around the budget hotel area (see the New Talborjt map), including two off Rue Allal ben Abdallah.

Places to Stay – Budget
Camping There are heaps of signs around town prohibiting camping – unusual in Morocco – so it's fortunate that Agadir's *camp site* (☎ 846683), just off Blvd Mohammed V on the port side of town, although pretty stony, is livable. Within walking distance of both the beach and town centre, it has a shop, snack bar, phones and a safe. Camper vans predominate but camping is possible for Dr5 per person and Dr10/15 per car/tent.

Hotels In high season, you must get into Agadir early in the day (or book ahead) if you want to be sure of a room. If you arrive late, you may have to pay through the nose at an expensive hotel. By standards elsewhere, you pay more for less here.

Most of the budget hotels and a few of the mid-range hotels are in the slightly sleazy, but pretty compact, area off Rue Ya-

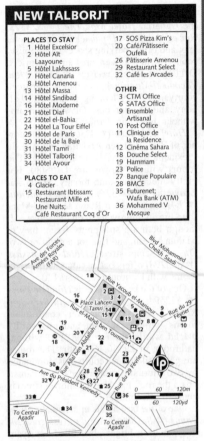

NEW TALBORJT

PLACES TO STAY	
1	Hôtel Excelsior
2	Hôtel Aït Laayoune
5	Hôtel Lakhssass
7	Hôtel Canaria
8	Hôtel Amenou
13	Hôtel Massa
14	Hôtel Sindibad
16	Hôtel Moderne
21	Hôtel Diaf
22	Hôtel el-Bahia
24	Hôtel La Tour Eiffel
25	Hôtel de Paris
30	Hôtel de la Baie
31	Hôtel Tamri
33	Hôtel Talborjt
34	Hôtel Ayour

PLACES TO EAT	
4	Glacier
15	Restaurant Ibtissam; Restaurant Mille et Une Nuits; Café Restaurant Coq d'Or

17	SOS Pizza Kim's
20	Café/Pâtisserie Oufella
26	Pâtisserie Amenou
29	Restaurant Select
32	Café les Arcades

OTHER	
3	CTM Office
6	SATAS Office
9	Ensemble Artisanal
10	Post Office
11	Clinique de la Residence
12	Cinéma Sahara
18	Douche Select
19	Hammam
23	Police
27	Banque Populaire
28	BMCE
35	Futurenet; Wafa Bank (ATM)
36	Mohammed V Mosque

coub el-Mansour (see the New Talborjt map). The all-night bus activity and prostitution ensures that most hotel receptions are open 24 hours so don't worry too much about arriving late.

Two of the cheapest places have prime position on Place Lahcen Tamri, but are less than salubrious. *Hôtel Canaria* (☎ 846727) has very basic singles/doubles/triples for Dr55/80/115 with shared shower; *Hôtel Massa* offers pretty much the same deal for musty cell-like rooms.

Across from the mosque, *Hôtel La Tour Eiffel* (☎ 823712, Rue du 29 Février), has small depressing rooms for the same price as the Canaria. *Hôtel Moderne* (☎ 823373, *Rue el-Mahdi ben Toummert*), is in a quieter spot and offers parking space. Dirty, musty rooms with shower are an overpriced Dr110/120. *Hôtel Excelsior* (☎ 821028, *Rue Yacoub el-Mansour)* has small rubber-treed courtyards. Tatty looking rooms with balcony and shower cost Dr97/110; rooms without shower are Dr68/87.

Hôtel de la Baie (☎ 823014), on the corner of Rue Allal ben Abdallah and Ave du Président Kennedy, is a mixed bag. The rooms without shower are Dr65/80. For pretty much the same money, *Hôtel Aït Laayoune* (☎ 824375) and *Hôtel Amenou* (☎ 841556), both on Rue Yacoub el-Mansour, are an improvement on the above. Although both are still pretty basic, they're neat and clean, and fine for a night or two. On the same street, *Hôtel Lakhssass* (☎ 822798) offers better value, with bright rooms with bathroom for Dr80/120.

One of the better places is *Hôtel de Paris* (☎ 822694, *fax 824515, Ave du Président Kennedy)*. It has clean and very comfortable rooms (with washbasin and awkwardly placed wardrobe) for Dr90/110 without bathroom, or Dr140/160 with. The rooms are gathered around courtyards dominated by two enormous rubber trees. You can sit up on the roof, too. The hot shower (free) is generally steaming.

One of the best hotels in the area is *Hôtel Tamri* (☎ 821880, *1 Ave du Président Kennedy)*, with a bright plant-filled courtyard and rooms with bathroom for Dr80/100.

Hôtel Diaf (☎ 825852, *Rue Allal ben Abdallah)* has clean, decent rooms. You pay Dr100/110 for rooms with private bathroom; Dr74/140 without (hot water is available in the morning and evening).

Places to Stay – Mid-Range

Hotels There are three hotels on Rue de l'Entraide, just on the beach side of Ave du Président Kennedy in New Talborjt. The cheapest is the *Hôtel Itrane* (☎ 822959), which charges Dr121/140 for singles/doubles but is often full. The two-star *Hôtel Ayour* (☎ 824976, *fax 842474)* at No 4, is a modern

establishment with a roof terrace. Rooms with TV, phone and bathroom are OK at Dr189/223. More expensive still, but with more of a Moroccan flavour, *Hôtel Talborjt* (☎ 841832, *fax 840396)* offers pleasant, carpeted rooms, some overlooking lush gardens. They cost from Dr207/244.

Hôtel Petite Suede (☎ 840779, *fax 840057)* is a fairly tranquil place just off Ave du Général Kettani that's closeish to the beach. For Dr136/195, the comfortable rooms with bathroom and balcony are good value. There's also a book exchange and baggage storage.

Back up in the heart of New Talborjt are two slightly fancier hotels.

Hôtel Sindibad (☎ 823477, *fax 842474)* has pleasant rooms with TV, phone and balcony overlooking the activity on Place Lahcen Tamri for Dr184/216. It also has a bar, restaurant, money-changing facilities (cash only), a small pool and sun terraces where the sunbaking Scandinavians contrast starkly with the *jellabas* (flowing garments) below.

Another comfortable place in Talborjt, and one of the better in this range, is *Hôtel el-Bahia* (☎ 822724, *fax 824515, Rue el-Mahdi ben Toummert)*. Again, rooms have a phone and TV, and in winter are centrally heated. The cheapest rooms cost Dr110/140. Rooms with shower cost Dr150/180, while those with full bathroom and private terrace are Dr180/220.

A fine two-star place, the *Atlantic Hôtel* (☎ 843661/2, *fax 843660, Blvd Hassan II)* is clean and comfortable, with boiling-hot water. Rooms cost Dr198/225. Breakfast is available in the pleasant, leafy courtyard. Better still is *Hôtel Aladin* (☎ 843228, *fax 846071, Rue de la Jeunesse)*, with a pool and restaurant. Rooms with balconies cost Dr240/283.

Hôtel Kamal (☎ 842817, *fax 843940, Blvd Hassan II)* has perfectly acceptable rooms with bathroom for Dr292/357. It's a package place so has a pool, bar etc.

Hôtel Les Cinq Parties du Monde (☎ 845484, *Blvd Hassan II)* is a modern hotel near the local bus and grand taxi ranks. Under normal circumstances there'd be no reason to stay in this particularly ugly part of town, but if you're having trouble elsewhere, or arrive in town late, it's OK for a night. Rooms cost Dr188/234.

Not that appealing from the outside, *Hôtel Sud Bahia* (☎ 840782, fax 846386, *Rue des Administrations Publiques)* charges Dr226/312, including breakfast. Inside it has a busy package atmosphere with the expected facilities and the rooms are in reasonable shape.

Hôtel Miramar (☎ 840770), at the western end of Blvd Mohammed V, is a small older place – in fact, the only hotel to survive the earthquake – offering just a few rooms (some with sea views) for Dr237/275, including breakfast. It has a secluded sun terrace, a bar and a well-regarded restaurant with a set menu for Dr105.

Residences Residences are good options if you want to do your own cooking and can be cheap if there's a group of you; they usually offer swimming pools.

Residence Tislit (☎ 842527, fax 822580) has apartments with kitchen and bathroom for Dr250/300/350/ 450 for one/two/three/four people. The Vietnamese Restaurant La Tonkinese is downstairs for the days you don't fancy cooking.

Residence Fleurie (☎ 843624, fax 844274, *Rue de la Foire)* is an ageing place with a pool and currency exchange facilities that plays host to organised biking holidays. Rooms with kitchen and TV cost Dr256/300 for singles/doubles.

Places to Stay – Top End
You will find no shortage of expensive hotels in Agadir. The bulk of them are inhabited by block-booked charter groups, which generally get a considerable discount on the normal individual prices. Places in this category are more likely to increase their rates in high season (March to April, July to August, October, and mid-December to mid-January). If you want this kind of hotel, it's a good idea to hunt around the beachside places to see what kind of deal you can come up with.

Hôtel Anezi (☎ 840714, fax 840713, *Blvd Mohammed V)* has villa-style accommodation as well as standard singles/doubles for Dr470/600. It's a large place with four restaurants, bars, a nightclub, pools and secure parking.

A newish, swankier four-star hotel is the *Hôtel Transatlantique* (☎ 842110, fax 842076, *Blvd Mohammed V)*, where rooms start at Dr438/557. Places like the *Résidence Club La Kasbah* (☎ 823636) cost more like Dr1100/1460.

The most central place with beach frontage is the four-star *Iberotel Tafoukt* (☎ 840986, fax 840971, *Blvd du 20 Août)* – all other places on the beach spread south of here. Rooms are set around the central garden and pool (which is big enough to hold a small galleon) and cost Dr750/920 on a half-board basis or Dr535 per room. There are organised activities, sports, a kids' club (plus kids' menus and babysitting), a fitness room, restaurants and bars. The rooms themselves have balcony, bar fridge, satellite TV, air-con and a safe.

Places to Eat
Agadir is crawling with burger joints, snack bars, restaurants and cafes – many, but by no means all, are on the expensive side – offering something for every nationality (Italian is the most popular cuisine on offer but you'll also find German, Danish and oriental options to name but a few).

Don't leave it too late – Moroccan foodies are no night owls and a lot of restaurants stop serving food by 10 pm, although they often stay open later for drinks.

Cheap Eats & Snacks A number of cheap restaurants and sandwich bars can be found around the bus stations and they're reasonable value, serving almost anything from seafood, tajines and couscous to roast dinners.

New Talborjt has a smattering of places with a choice of sitting inside or at tables in the open air. The food is very good and portions are large. Prices are reasonable as they compete for your business, with three-course menus for Dr35. These places are also good for a coffee. A group on Place Lahcen Tamri, *Restaurant Ibtissam*, *Restaurant Mille et Une Nuits* and *Café Restaurant Coq d'Or*, are very popular with travellers and night strollers from the tourist district in search of a change.

Restaurant Select, by the hotel of the same name, does a solid range of old favourites, and you can eat well for about Dr20. Similar in style is **Café les Arcades** on Ave du Président Kennedy.

La Truite, near the Municipal Theatre, bills itself as an Irish bar but really it's just a restaurant that sells cheap beers. It also does breakfast for Dr25, which includes eggs along with the standard bread and spreads.

The fact that there are direct charter flights from Ireland could have inspired **Oliveri Pistache**, fronting the Al-Madina centre, which has baked spuds with heaps of fillings for Dr22.50. There aren't any flights from Mexico, but **Taco Loco** next door is popular for its pricier Tex-Mex fare.

You can pick up a 'Big Mick' burger at **Disney Burger** near the Supratours office or if you'd rather the genuine article there's a **McDonald's** near the stadium.

For cheap, ultra-fresh fish in less-than-salubrious surroundings, head to the entrance of the port where there are dozens of cheap **fish stalls**. Meals cost from Dr20. Tucked behind them is a popular place (full of locals rather than tourists) serving fish tajine. The stalls are open for lunch and dinner. If you don't want to trek all the way to the port try the **Fish Friture** opposite the museum, which fries up similarly priced fish throughout the day and evening.

To the north of the public swimming pool are **all-night snack vans** serving up post-pub food. If you prefer to sit (and drink) while you midnight-munch try the 24-hour **Restaurant Jour et Nuit**, nearby on the beachfront. The **snack stands** near the bus stations also stay open most of the night catering for late bus departures/arrivals.

SOS Pizza Kim's (☎ 846866, 6 Rue de Tarfaya) in Talborjt has a great range of pizzas from around Dr65 (enough for four), which they will deliver anywhere within Agadir for free. Open from 11.30 am to 3 pm and 5 to 11 pm (midnight on Saturday), they also do lasagne, salads and drinks; if you're here for long enough you get your 10th pizza free. There's also a **Pizza Hut** (☎ 847709)

near the Municipal Theatre, which has a restaurant section and delivery service.

Restaurants The tourist office can supply you with a list of the classier restaurants but it's a better idea to cruise the main strips till something takes your fancy, especially as many offer their own interpretation of entertainment to accompany dinner. Places to look include the large hotels, Blvd du 20 Août, the central market and the beachfront. All of the following restaurants are licensed.

If you came to Morocco to try Moroccan food and you want to treat yourself, try **Johara** (845353, Blvd du 20 Août), which is the closest thing you're going to get to the palace restaurants found in Marrakesh or Fès. Tastefully decorated with the requisite veranda and featuring traditional entertainers, as opposed to crooners, it has a set menu for Dr260, which includes *pastilla* (pigeon pie). A bit cheaper, **Restaurant Darkoum** (Ave du Général Kettani), near Hôtel Sud Bahia and with waiters adorned in impeccable white robes and red fezzes, is similar.

Restaurant la Tour de Paris (Blvd Hassan II) is a well-regarded restaurant near Ave du Général Kettani. The mainly French menu is tempting and the food is of a reasonably high standard, but it is pricey, costing a minimum of Dr170 per person.

The restaurant in the **Hôtel Miramar** (Blvd Mohammed V), overlooking the port, has an excellent reputation for its seafood and a view across the road to the beach. Right on the beachfront, **Restaurant Le Nil Bleue** also has a good choice of fishy dishes.

Further along the promenade is **Le Côte d'Or**, which serves a diverse range of fairly reasonable dishes and has plenty of outdoor seating, allowing you to watch the passing strollers and vendors selling everything and anything from cigarettes to model ships.

There are a few Asian restaurants, including the Vietnamese **La Tonkinese**, just where Ave Sidi Mohammed runs into Blvd Mohammed V. If you feel like trying some Korean food, you could investigate **Restaurant Seoul**, upstairs in the central market, a few doors down from the tourist office.

Cafes & Patisseries There are plenty of cafes where you can relax from the rigours of Agadir beach life or ease into the day with coffee and pastries.

Café/Pâtisserie Oufella, opposite Hôtel Diaf on Rue Allal ben Abdallah in New Talborjt, has a good range of patisseries, as does *Pâtisserie Amenou* near Hotel de Paris. For ice cream, stop by the *glacier* outside the Hôtel Sindibad.

La Verandah Pâtisserie, opposite the Royal Tennis Club of Agadir, is a chic place with a good and tempting range of sweet and savoury treats; it is very popular with Agadir's smart set.

The *cafe* next to the Uniprix supermarket on Blvd Hassan II is one of the few such places to serve beer as well as coffee.

Self-Catering The large *Uniprix supermarket*, on the corner of Blvd Hassan II and Ave Sidi Mohammed, sells everything from cheese and biscuits to beer, wine and spirits. A bit less crowded with souvenir hunters is the *Saawa supermarket* further south along Blvd Hassan II. There are also other smaller supermarkets in the main tourist areas.

The *souq* has piles of fresh produce as well as spices and olives etc. Saturday and Sunday are general market days. If you want to cook your own fresh seafood head to the *fish market* at the port.

Entertainment

If you want alcohol to take away, there are plenty of supermarkets dotted around the centre with good choices of beers, wines and spirits.

Bars & Nightclubs You can get a beer (and wine and spirits) at a lot of beachfront and main road restaurants and cafes. Otherwise, there are countless bars to choose from in the bigger hotels (which have happy hours between 5-ish and 8-ish each night), as well as some Moroccan male-dominated bars on the periphery of the tourist areas. Although you'll see plenty of advertising for the likes of Guinness and Lowenbrau, draught beers are generally limited to Flag and Heineken. The bottled beers on offer

are surprisingly diverse and there's the usual range of saucy-sounding cocktails to test.

Many establishments try to attract the punters by offering karaoke or crooning entertainers keen to get you singing and clapping along – the standards of both are questionable and you'll have to be a Celine Dion or Elton John fan to fully appreciate them.

There is a club scene and you'll find even numbers of Moroccans and tourists jostling on the dance floors, although the music remains firmly geared towards Moroccan taste. Entry to the clubs, which are generally attached to hotels, ranges from Dr60 to Dr100 but includes a drink – thereafter you'll be paying top dollar.

No-one really ventures into the clubs until after midnight, so it's a good idea to check out the bars beforehand. *The Pub*, on the 10th floor of *Hôtel Anezi*, the huge neon writing of which can be seen from the beachfront, has a magnificent panoramic view providing a great place to watch the sunset, although the 'entertainment' can be a bit much.

The Irish bar in the Tafoukt complex, also named *The Pub*, has a bit more of a pub atmosphere, with tempting rows of taps representing the best of British and Irish beers. Unfortunately, they only distribute the usual Moroccan draughts.

L'Oasis Beach at the southern end of the main beach is one of the few places where you can actually drink with the sand between your toes. Also an average restaurant, the party moves indoors for karaoke entertainment at sunset. It also hosts a raucous beach party on Saturday night.

For all-night drinking there's the 24-hour *Restaurant Jour et Nuit* on the beachfront.

Popular nightclubs include *Flamingo*, in the Hôtel Beach Club at the southern end of the beach, and *El-Paradiso* at the Hôtel Argana. *Jimmy's* on Blvd du 20 Août is quite kitsch, with booths done up like cars, and attracts most of the gay crowd. *Le Central*, attached to the restaurant and karaoke bar of the same name, is another busy venue.

For glitzy tourist-oriented entertainment you could try the *Alhambra Cabaret*, at Hôtel Sahara on Blvd du 20 Août.

Theatre & Cinemas The *Muncipal Theatre*, an outdoor amphitheatre on Blvd Mohammed V, plays host to Moroccan artists and is the venue for cultural events year-round. Look for advertising around town or in the tourist offices for forthcoming events. Place de l'Esperance occasionally hosts similar (free) events.

Alliance Franco-Marocaine (☎ 841313, 5 Rue Yahchech) puts on films, theatre and lectures – mainly in French. You can pick up its program in the Syndicat d'Initiative.

There are also a few cinemas scattered about town, including *Cinéma Sahara* on Place Lahcen Tamri in New Talborjt, serving up Chuck Norris and porn, and *Cinema Rialto* just off Ave du Prince Moulay Abdallah near the central market area, with more run-of-the-mill Western stuff.

Casinos *Shems Casino* at the Sheraton Hotel offers the chance to either recoup the cost of your trip or cut it short!

Shopping

Agadir is not a great place to pick up souvenirs. Most of what's on offer is trucked in from other parts of the country, and the steady stream of package tourists, unaware of what's on offer elsewhere in the country, keep prices up on low quality goods.

The Ensemble Artisanal at Rue du 29 Février, open 9 am to 1 pm and 3 to 7 pm, and the Uniprix supermarket both sell handicrafts at fixed prices. There are plenty of souvenir shops in the central market and in other supermarkets.

Agadir souq is a large, walled market in the south-east of town. It also has souvenir stalls, clothing, food and household goods as well as a second-hand area outside the western gate of the souq – this is a good place to experience some Moroccan atmosphere.

Getting There & Away

Air The new Al-Massira airport (☎ 839003), 28km south-east of Agadir, is the destination for many European charter flights. The airport bank (cash and travellers cheques only) and car-hire offices are open business hours. A couple of restaurants and the tourist information are open daily. Take the Tafraoute road and allow at least half an hour to drive there.

RAM (☎ 840793) has an office on Ave du Général Kettani. To connect to other Moroccan towns you have to change at Casablanca (Dr944, 50 minutes), which is served by frequent daily services.

A weekly direct flight serves Dakhla (Dr1269, two hours), another weekly direct flight services Marrakesh (Dr437, ½ hour) and three a week serve Laayoune (Dr817, one hour).

Regional Air Lines (☎ 02-538080 in Casablanca) has services to Casablanca daily, Laayoune on weekdays and Las Palmas in the Canary Islands daily.

RAM has a few direct international flights, including four a week to Paris, France (Dr5974, 3½ hours); two to Las Palmas (Dr3219, 1¼ hours) in the Canary Islands; and one to Zurich, Switzerland (Dr6384, 3½ hours). Air France has five flights per week to Paris.

Bus Although a good number of buses and grand taxis serve Agadir, there is a huge bus and taxi station in the nearby town of Inezgane. It is quite possible that you'll end up here – check before you buy your ticket if you don't want the unnecessary expense and delay involved in getting between the two towns. Should you need them, there are plenty of grand taxis (Dr4) and local buses (Dr3) to take you from one to the other.

In Agadir, buses stop at their respective company offices along Rue Yacoub el-Mansour, a small street in New Talborjt.

CTM has buses to Casablanca (Dr140, 10 hours) at 8.30 am and 1.30, 10 and 11 pm. The 10 pm bus goes on to Rabat (Dr166, 12 hours) and the 11 pm service continues to Tangier (Dr237, 14 hours). Buses for Marrakesh (Dr70, four hours) leave at 5, 8.30 and 11am and 3 and 7.30 pm. Buses for Essaouira (Dr40, four hours) and Safi (Dr65, six hours) leave at 7.30 and 11.30 am; the first bus continues to El-Jadida (Dr91, nine hours). There are buses for Tiznit (Dr21, two hours) at 6.30 am and 4 pm. A bus for Tafraoute leaves at 3 am (Dr57, five hours). At 11.30 pm there's a bus to Laayoune (Dr204, 11 hours), which continues to Smara. The Dakhla bus (Dr325.50, 19 hours) leaves at 8 pm, and there's a bus for Taroudannt (Dr29, 2½ hours) at 9.30 am.

SATAS and about 10 other smaller companies have several more buses serving the same destinations a bit more regularly.

International buses leave twice per week for destinations in France and Spain.

Supratours (☎ 841207) has an office at 10 Rue des Orangiers, just off Ave des Forces Armées Royales (FAR). There are four daily services to Marrakesh train station (Dr80, four hours) and a 7 pm bus for Essaouira (Dr55, three hours). Two daily buses head south to Dakhla (19½ hours), Goulimime (four hours), Laayoune (11 hours), Smara (9½ hours) and Tan Tan (six hours).

Car & Motorcycle Some very good deals on car and motorcycle hire are to be found in Agadir, but you will have to hunt around and be prepared to bargain. It is well worth checking out local agencies, which quote Dr700 per day, but there's still room for haggling, especially in low season.

Near the big hotels you'll find a series of booths that rent out motorcycles and scooters (the average charge for a motorcycle is about Dr200 per day). There are at least 40 car rental outlets to choose from, many of them on Blvd Hassan II. The main agencies include:

Avis (☎ 841755) Blvd Hassan II; (☎ 839244) airport
Budget (☎ 844600) Blvd Mohammed V
Europcar (☎ 840203) Bungalow Marhaba, Blvd Mohammed V
Hertz (☎ 840939) Bungalow Marhaba, Blvd Mohammed V; (☎ 839071) airport

Grand Taxi Grand taxis to Tiznit (Dr23), Inezgane (Dr4) and Taghazout (Dr10) leave from the local bus and grand taxi ranks.

Getting Around
To/From the Airport Airport transport is just a little complicated. Local bus No 22 runs from the airport car park to Inezgane (Dr4)

every 40 minutes or so until about 9 pm. From Inezgane you can change to buses No 5 and 6 for Agadir (Dr3), or take a taxi (Dr4).

Grand taxis between the airport and Agadir should not cost more than Dr150/200 during day/night.

Otherwise, many travellers have stories of simply walking onto tour and hotel buses with other passengers – since most of them are generally on package tours, it's unlikely any questions will be asked.

Bus The main local bus station is a block in from Blvd Hassan II, where grand taxis also depart, at the southern end of town. Buses No 5 and 6 go to Inezgane. The green-and-white No 12 goes to Taghazout (Dr6).

Taxi The orange petit taxis run around town; prices are worked out by meter and there are signs in hotels detailing the rates around town.

Bicycle There are several stands set up around the big hotels near the beach that rent out bicycles for Dr20 per hour.

AROUND AGADIR
Northern Beaches
If you're looking for less-crowded beaches than those at Agadir, and for fellow independent travellers (most with their own transport), then head north of Agadir. There are beautiful sandy coves every few kilometres.

Most of the beaches closer to Agadir have been colonised by Europeans who have built their winter villas here. King Fahd of Saudi Arabia has a palace here and funded the building of a new road along this stretch. Further north, this gives way to a sea of camper vans, but by the time you are 20km to 30km north of Agadir, you might find something resembling space and even peace and quiet.

Local bus No 12 from the bus and grand taxi stop (this also stops outside the Sheraton) in Agadir runs up the coast to Taghazout (Dr6) and beyond.

Aourir The first village of any size you pass is Aourir (Banana Village), about 12km north of Agadir, which has several cheap roadside cafes and restaurants (including one called *Enaama*!), dozens of banana stalls and a market on Wednesday.

Hotel Littoral (☎ *08-314726, fax 314357,* e *hotellittoral@casanet-a.net.ma*) on the main road has singles/doubles/triples, all with balcony or terrace, for Dr218/274 and suites (for three/four people) or apartments (for four/five people) for Dr496/696. It's a nice, new, tastefully decorated place with a restaurant and cafe. All prices include breakfast.

Tamraght A few kilometres beyond is Tamraght, with the *Hotel Riad Imourane* (☎ *08-314345, fax 576365*). Back off the road, the location isn't ideal but the place is nice, it's set around a central garden courtyard with kitsch ornaments. There's a restaurant and salon and the rooms, costing Dr140/180, are imaginatively decorated.

Taghazout About 6km further on is Taghazout, a laid-back spot popular with surfers – the serious guys get to spots such as Killer Point, La Source and Anka Point to the north, while the not so serious only get as far as the appropriately named Hash Point at the northern end of the village.

There are no banks in Taghazout and the only Internet access costs Dr50 per hour.

There's a large and fairly ugly *camp site* just behind the group of restaurants and cafes along the southern beach. It's usually crammed with camper vans, more of which dominate the surrounding beaches. You can also rent basic private rooms in the village or stay at *Auberge Taghazout* right on the seafront or *Residence Atlantique* (☎ *08-200068*), just off it but with sea views, for Dr50/100 and Dr80/100 respectively for singles/doubles. There are plenty of eateries and cafes, including *Cafe Panorama* at the southern end of the village, and more on the main road and beachfront – those to the south are the places to head for a cold beer.

Further North To get to peaceful and largely unspoiled beaches, you need to continue northwards. Those around 27km north of Agadir are better. You can find a few

other attractive spots just south and north of **Cap Rhir** (easily identified by its shipwreck). The surf spot known as Boilers, a reef break, is just south of the lighthouse.

About 12km beyond Cap Rhir the road turns inland to **Tamri**. The lagoon here is reported to be the most reliable site in Morocco for spotting the very rare bald ibis. Other birds you may see include Abhhudouin's gulls, Barbary falcons, Lanner falcons and passerines. For surfers, it's worth continuing another 4km north to find an excellent beach break.

Immouzzer des Ida Outanane

This thoroughly recommended side trip from Agadir through the stunning **Paradise Valley**, a popular yet not necessarily safe camping spot, and along its palm-tree lined river, takes you about 60km north-east of Agadir to the High Atlas foothills.

The waterfalls *(cascades)*, for which Immouzzer des Ida Outanane is best known, flow most strongly between February and August – at other times irrigation control reduces them to little more than a trickle, but the curtain of spray dropping into the clear blue pool remains impressive. The locals are keen to perform, and dive from ledges high above the plunge pool, especially on Thursday when there's almost a queue of tourists vying for a viewpoint.

There is a second set of falls, known simply as the 'second falls', nearby. Any villager will be glad to take you there, telling you along the way how Jimi Hendrix is responsible for the peace/love symbol carved in the rock.

From March to April the area is filled with white almond blossom, there is a honey harvest (including a festival) in July and around late November you may be lucky enough to witness the olive harvest. At this time the groves are alive with villagers who climb up into the trees to shake the olives from the branches.

Places to Stay & Eat About halfway along the road to Immouzzer des Ida Outanane from the coastal turn-off is the family-run *Hôtel Tifrit* (☎ *08-826044*) set right by the river. Very clean rooms with separate

Ode to The Olive

In Islam the olive tree is associated with virility and with light, and is also associated with the Prophet. The gnarled, silvery-green-leafed olive trees growing on the rocky hill-sides of Morocco have been there since Palaeolithic times. And the oil they produce is arguably the best in the world. A feast in Morocco can simply be a round of fresh bread, a bowl of virgin olive oil and a big blue sky.

Nothing of the olive is wasted. The first 'virgin' pressing is used for marinades and dressings; the second and third are used for cooking; the fourth pressing is used in the manufacture of soaps, shampoos and beauty products; the pulp is used for fertiliser; and the stones provide a lubricating oil. The wood is carved into bowls.

For oil the olives are allowed to ripen fully on the trees. The olives you can buy – green, violet, deep red and black – are picked earlier. They are conserved in marinades flavoured with preserved lemons and herbs, bitter oranges or fiery hot red peppers. You'll often find them in tajines, where the added delight is fishing them out from the rich sauce with your fingers.

shower and half board cost Dr240 per person. The hotel has a pleasant terrace onto the river, a restaurant and a swimming pool.

Further along, in the village of **Aksri**, 15km from Immouzzer des Ida Outanane, is the *Restaurant a la Bonne Franquette* (☎ 08-823191), a welcoming little place that serves good, reasonably priced French fare and cake. To the left of it, the **Promenade Dos D'ane**, a one-hour circuit through plantations, offers a good opportunity to work off, or build up to, that lunch. If you'd rather take a picnic on the walk, the cafe nearby will rustle something up for you.

In Immouzzer des Ida Outanane the only 'real' accommodation is the expensive *Hôtel des Cascades* (☎ 08-826016, fax 821671), which has large singles/doubles/triples with terrace or balcony from Dr365/457/626. Even if you splurged at lunch time it's worth repeating the treat here in the evening, as the restaurant, though pricey, is

highly recommended. There's a terrace overlooking the valley, fireplaces, tennis courts and a swimming pool. There's also a path leading down through the olive groves to the cascades.

There's a *restaurant/cafe* near the cascades, which has a couple of basic and well overpriced rooms for Dr50/70. You can also *camp* nearby. There's some excellent walking – the cafe can help plan treks of up to a week.

Getting There & Away One local bus a day leaves Agadir for Immouzzer des Ida Outanane (2½ hours) from the local bus and grand taxi ranks at around 2 pm (departure times vary so ask around the day before).

You may have to wait until the following day for the bus back, although hitching isn't too difficult. The best time to get up here is Thursday, which is market day.

See Organised Tours under Agadir earlier for details of coach tours to Immouzzer des Ida Outanane.

Inezgane

Inezgane, 13km south of Agadir, is one of the biggest transport hubs for the whole region. It's not a tourist destination at all, but some travellers enjoy stopping off here rather than in Agadir for that very reason. A big market is held in the area next to the bus station on Tuesday.

There are plenty of hotels about. *Hotel Louz* (☎ 08-331843), a large place on the main bus square, has modern singles/doubles with bathroom and small salons for Dr75/130. It also has a TV lounge and a restaurant.

Hotel Hagounia (☎ 08-832783, 9 Ave Mokhter), back on the main road, has rooms with bathroom and balcony for Dr138/160.

You'll find dozens of cheap cafes/restaurants around the main square. Even cheaper are the *restaurants familiers* (small, family-run restaurants) in the side streets between Blvd Mohammed V and Blvd Moulay Abdallah. The *Café/Restaurant Saâda*, on Blvd Moulay Abdallah opposite the stadium, is a particularly pleasant and well located place.

There are plenty of buses going in all possible directions from here and most buses to/from Agadir also stop here. The bus station is just off the Agadir-Tiznit road and there are CTM and Supratours offices on the approach to the station.

Loads of grand taxis to Essaouira (Dr50), Tiznit (Dr23) and Taroudannt (Dr23) also gather here, as well as less regular taxis for Goulimime (Dr60) and Tan Tan (Dr70).

Adding to the organised chaos are regular local buses (Dr3) and grand taxis (Dr4) to Agadir and Al-Massira airport.

Souss-Massa National Park

Stretching south from Agadir for about 60km west of the main P30 highway, this national park contains some rare wildlife treats and a phenomenal variety of bird life, especially around the tidal creeks and lagoons of Oued Massa and Oued Souss.

The region is a diverse one, made up of cliffs, sand dunes, farmland and forests. Among the species of mammals present are the shy Egyptian mongoose, the increasingly rare common otter and the Eurasian wild boar. In the north of the park is a large fenced area containing Dawker's gazelle, adak, red-necked ostrich and Arabian oryx. However, the biggest attraction is probably three colonies of the rare bald ibis in the park (see the boxed text 'The Bald Ibis'). Small groups of osprey are commonly seen during March and September, as are the colonies of pochard and greater flamingo that spend the winter here. The flamingos spend their time over winter in the salt marshes and lagoons on and around the Oued Massa to the south of the park.

The **Oued Souss Estuary** lies a few kilometres south of Agadir (signposted off the Inezgane road). At the river mouth you're likely to see oystercatchers, plovers, godwits, curlews, herons, spoonbills, flamingos, gulls and terns, to name but a few.

Just to the north of the river mouth is the Royal Palace (there's another in Agadir). You can't visit the king, of course, but the floodlit perimeter of the palace is apparently a good place for watching red-necked nightjars!

Oued Massa lies some 40km further south of Oued Souss. There are car parks, a bird hide and a nature trail close to the estuary. Vast reed beds line the banks of the Oued Massa, along with various species of indigenous euphorbia, and tamarisk with its unmistakable pink flowers. Some of the species to be seen in the area include black-bellied sandgrouse, bald ibis, marbled duck, glossy ibis, cranes, little crake, warblers, black-headed bush shrike, brown-throated sand martin, flamingos, herons and even Bonelli's eagles.

There's a small hotel in the village of Massa a couple of kilometres away, while just north of the river is the tiny village of **Sidi R'bat**. There's nothing much here, (there are rumours of a small hotel opening) but along with having a good beach break for surfing, the village makes two interesting claims. According to one story, this is where the biblical Jonah is supposed to have been spewed up by the whale. And Uqba bin Nafi, the first

The Bald Ibis

A revered religious icon in ancient Egypt, hunting and habitat destruction has reduced the bird's status to an endangered species. Despite being regarded as a dinner delicacy in the Middle Ages, in the 17th century the northern bald ibis *(Geronticus eremita)* or waldrapp was still widespread in Central Europe, North Africa and the Middle East. However, climatic change in North Africa and the Middle East led to more frequent droughts and reduced feeding areas; human-related habitat loss and pesticide use also took their toll. By the mid-20th century the wild population of these birds was reduced to tiny colonies in Turkey, Morocco and Algeria.

Morocco's Souss-Massa National Park protects three vital breeding colonies with around 220 closely monitored birds. It is vital that visitors do not approach these signposted areas. There are many more habitats where the birds can be seen.

The good news is that bald ibis are breeding so well in captivity that there are plans to reintroduce the birds to Italy and Spain.

Arab commander to penetrate Morocco (in the 7th century) supposedly rode his horse triumphantly into the sea here. At the time of writing, the small camp site at Sidi R'bat was closed; if you're thinking of heading down here, it's worth checking with the tourist office in Agadir to see if it has reopened.

From Agadir, 4WD tours head into the park, but a 2WD (or grand taxi) will get you to all the major sites. For up-to-date information pop into the new Souss-Massa National Park headquarters (☎ 837949, [e] ibsi@casanet-a.net.ma), 800m off the main Agadir-Inezgane P30 highway on the road to the Oued Souss estuary.

Working closely with Eaux et Forêts (the government ministry responsible for national parks), the international bird conservation nongovernmental organisation Birdlife International has done much to help set up the park, and in the coming few years it's likely that Souss-Massa will become Morocco's first national park to charge for entry. The only blot on the landscape is Club Med's desire to build a holiday complex at Tifnite, currently a beautiful little fishing village about 30km south of Agadir.

TAROUDANNT
☎ 08

Surrounded by magnificent, crenellated red-mud walls and with the snowcapped peaks of the High Atlas beckoning beyond, Taroudannt looks every inch a traditional Berber market town. The French never tacked on a ville nouvelle here, which gives the impression that things have changed little in the past hundred or so years.

The town souqs are well worth a browse (though, as everywhere, you'll need to be prepared for a certain amount of hustling) and the small tanneries outside the walls make an interesting stop.

Taroudannt is a fairly easy day trip from Agadir (85km) and also makes a good base for travellers interested in trekking up into the little-explored western High Atlas.

History
As far back as 1056, Taroudannt was overrun by the Almoravids at the beginning of

their conquest of Morocco. It played only a peripheral role in the following years until, in the 16th century, the newly emerging Saadians made it their capital for about 20 years. This dynasty was responsible for the construction of the old part of town and the kasbah; most of the rest dates from the 18th century.

The Saadians eventually moved on to Marrakesh, but not before the fertile Souss Valley, in which the city stands, had been developed into the country's most important producer of sugar cane, cotton, rice and indigo – valuable items of trade along the trans-Saharan caravan routes.

The city narrowly escaped destruction in 1687 at the hands of Moulay Ismail after it became the centre of a rebellion opposing his rule. Instead, Ismail contented himself with the massacre of its inhabitants.

It regained some of its former prominence when one of Moulay Abdallah's sons was proclaimed sultan here at the end of the following century, but his reign during this, one of the more turbulent periods in Moroccan history, was brief.

Taroudannt was to remain a centre of intrigue and sedition against the central government well into the 20th century, and indeed played host to the Idrissid el-Hiba, a southern chief who attempted to rebel after the Treaty of Fès (introducing French protectorate rule) was signed in 1912.

Orientation
Unlike many Moroccan towns of the same size and importance, Taroudannt was never chosen as a French administrative or military centre. Consequently, there is no 'European' quarter of wide boulevards and modern buildings.

The cheaper hotels are all on or near the two central squares: Place al-Alaouyine (often called by its former Berber name, Place Assarag); and Place an-Nasr (formerly Talmoqlate). You'll find banks, restaurants and a small post office clustered in this area.

Most of the buses and grand taxis terminate just outside the southern gate of the medina, Bab Zougan.

SOUTH ATLANTIC COAST

TAROUDANNT

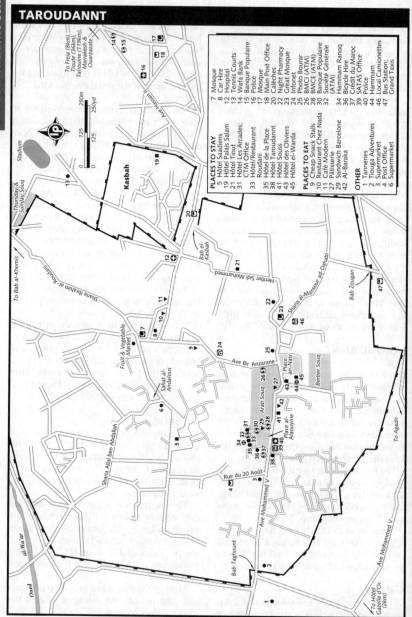

To Freja (8km), Tioute (36km), Taliouine (19km), Marrakesh & Ouarzazate

Stadium

Kasbah

Thursday & Sunday Souq

To Bab al-Khemis

Ave Hassan II

Bab el-Kasbah

Héritier Sidi Mohammed

Sharia Ibrahim ar-Roudani

Fruit & Vegetable Market

Sahat al-Andalous

To Bab el-Khemis

Sharia Allal ben Abdallah

Ave Bir Anzarane

Place an-Nasr

Arab Souq

Berber Souq

Sharia al-Mansour ad-Dahabi

Bab Zougan

Place al-Alaouyine

Rue du 20 Août

Ave Mohammed V

Ave Mohammed V

To Agadir

To Hôtel Gazelle d'Or (2km)

Bab Taghount

al-Wa'ur

Oued

250m
250yd

0 125
0 125

PLACES TO STAY
15 Hôtel Saadiens
19 Hôtel Palais Salam
21 Hôtel Tiout
31 Hôtel les Arcades;
  CTM Office
33 Hôtel/Restaurant
  Roudani
35 Hôtel de la Place
38 Hôtel Taroudannt
41 Hôtel des Oliviers
43 Hôtel Souss
45 Hôtel el-Warda

PLACES TO EAT
9 Cheap Snack Stalls
10 Restaurant Chez Nada
11 Café Modern
27 Pâtisserie
29 Sandwich Barcelone
42 Al-Baraka

OTHER
1 Tanneries
2 Tiouga Adventures
3 Supermarket
4 Post Office
6 Supermarket
7 Mosque
8 Car Hire
12 Hospital
13 Tennis Courts
14 Wafa Bank
16 Banque Populaire
16 Police
17 Mosque
18 Main Post Office
20 Calèches
22 Night Pharmacy
23 Great Mosque
24 Infonet
25 Photo Bourar
26 BMCI (ATM)
28 BMCE (ATM)
30 Banque Populaire
32 Société Générale
  (ATM)
34 Hammam Ranoq
36 Bicycle Hire
37 Crédit du Maroc
39 RATAS Office
40 Hammam
44 Local Camionettes
46 Bus Station;
47 Grand Taxis

Information

Money The BMCE and Banque Populaire have branches and ATMs on Place al-Alaouyine, and there is a BMCI on Ave Bir Anzarane. All are good for changing cash and travellers cheques. The BMCE also does cash advances.

Post & Communications The main post and phone office is off Ave Hassan II, to the east of the kasbah and south of the Agadir-Marrakesh highway. There is a smaller post office on Rue du 20 Août, north-west of Place al-Alaouyine.

Infonet, north of Place an-Nasr, is not that well signposted – look for a big wooden door and go to the 1st floor – Internet access costs Dr10 per hour.

Newsstands The stand outside Hôtel Palais Salam has a good selection of international newspapers and magazines.

Film & Photography You can buy film and have it developed within 30 minutes at Photo Bourar, a Fuji outlet on Ave Mohammed V, near Place an-Nasr.

Medical Services There is a night pharmacy on Heritier Sidi Mohammed and a hospital by the kasbah.

Ramparts

Taroudannt's ramparts can be explored on foot, but it's better to hire a bicycle, or go by calèche. One nice idea advertised in the tourist literature is to take a moonlit ride around the walls. The calèches gather just inside Bab el-Kasbah, the main squares and other prominent spots. A one-way trip costs Dr10 while 1½-hour tours are Dr35.

Souqs

The Arab souq, to the east of Place al-Alaouyine, is relatively small, but some of the items for sale are of high quality; limestone carvings and traditional Berber jewellery are featured (the town is populated mainly by Chleuh Berbers).

This jewellery has been influenced by the tribes of the Sahara, as well as by the Jews; the latter were a significant part of the community until the late 1960s. Only the core of the market is devoted to crafts and souvenirs – the rest serves as the Roudanis' (people of Taroudannt) shopping centre.

One shop worth visiting is that of Lichir el-Houcine (☎ 852145), 36 Souq Semata, which has an extensive array of items ranging from carpets and fabulous jewellery to antique couscous platters. Lichir considers himself a serious antiques dealer, and as a result may be a tougher bargainer than others. As always, the best advice is to take your time to look around for what you want.

Taroudannt's Berber souq extends south of Place an-Nasr and you'll no doubt have a few guides wanting to usher you this way. Although there are a few stalls selling carpets and jewellery, this market deals mainly in fruit, vegetables, spices and ordinary household goods.

Both markets offer the usual tourist fare as well as a good range of leather shoes and sandals made from the product of the nearby tanneries.

On Thursday and Sunday a large market for people in the surrounding countryside spreads out just outside Bab al-Khemis (which means Thursday Gate) near the north-east corner of town. It is interesting for the spectacle rather than for the goods (mainly household supplies and second-hand gear), but you need to get there early.

Tanneries

There are tanneries here similar to those at Fès, but they're much smaller. Head west out of Bab Taghount and turn left, then continue for about 100m and take the first right (signposted).

You'll find lamb, sheep and goatskin rugs (prices start at about Dr100), soft leather bags and traditional red and yellow slippers for sale here. The people working in the tanneries are generally happy to give visitors a tour and a brief explanation of the process involved in getting to the rug stage.

Kasbah

The walls around the kasbah date mainly from the time of Saadian rule in Taroudannt, and the area is worth a little stroll, though there are no sights as such inside its walls. Walled off as it is from the rest of the city, it seems almost like a separate little town.

Trekking

Taroudannt is the only sizable town within striking distance of the western High Atlas region, which is relatively little-visited. The walking here is less demanding than in the Toubkal region, the climate is wetter and the vegetation more lush.

It is, however, well off the beaten track. There are no official refuges in this area, let alone hotels or even towns. Though there are plenty of Berber villages up in the mountains, anyone thinking of trekking up here should be prepared to camp and will have to carry all necessary supplies, including detailed maps, food, and water purification tablets. There are a number of guides in town. See the Trekking chapter for further details.

Places to Stay – Budget

There are many hotels around or close to Place al-Alaouyine, and there's not a huge difference in quality or price. They're all basic with roof terraces providing good people-watching opportunities. The only budget option with hot showers (free) is Hôtel/Restaurant Roudani, but there are hammams aplenty, including Hammam Ranoq, just behind Place al-Alaouyine.

One of the cheapest and most basic places right on the square is *Hôtel de la Place*. Tiny rooms cost Dr40; more roomy doubles with views over the square are Dr50. The terrace is tiny and the toilet is terrible.

On the other side of the lane is *Hôtel/ Restaurant Roudani* (☎ 852219). The best rooms are on the large terrace, but unlike those on the lower floor they don't have showers. Singles/doubles, shower or not, cost Dr40/80. *Hôtel Les Arcades*, virtually next door, costs the same and is on a par with Hôtel de la Place.

Just off the square, heading towards Place an-Nasr, you'll find the *Hôtel Souss*. The top-floor rooms open onto the terrace, which is also a cafe overlooking the street; these and the 1st-floor rooms cost Dr30/50.

Closer to Place an-Nasr is *Hôtel des Oliviers* (☎ 852021) which is the cleanest and most modern place around here. Rooms cost Dr50/60 and although it has a terrace the views are limited.

Hôtel el-Warda (☎ 852763), the place with all the *zellij* (tilework) terraces overlooking Place an-Nasr, has basic singles/ doubles/triples with washbasin and (cold) shower for Dr30/50/70.

By far the best deal, if your budget can stretch to it, is one of the city's institutions, *Hôtel Taroudannt* (☎ 852416). Although fading, it has a unique flavour, from the tree-filled courtyard surrounded by terraces to the colonial dining room, where you can get moderately priced and good French and Moroccan food. Wallpapered rooms cost Dr70/ 90, Dr80/100/120 with private shower, and Dr100/120 with bath and toilet.

Places to Stay – Mid-Range

Hôtel Tiout (☎ 850341, Ave Heritier Sidi Mohammed) is a modern place with decent, clean rooms and comfortable beds. Singles/doubles all with bathroom, and some with a balcony looking onto the hotel car park, cost Dr195/250.

The two-star *Hôtel Saadiens* (☎ 852589, fax 852118, Borj Oumansour), used by some adventure travel groups, is clean and comfortable with a pool (nonguests pay Dr30), rooftop restaurant (open for dinner only), *salon de thé* (gentile cafe) and secure parking. It offers B&B for Dr165/210 or half board for Dr235/350.

Places to Stay – Top End

The four-star *Hôtel Palais Salam* (☎ 852501, fax 852654) is right inside the ramparts, in the kasbah by the main Agadir-Marrakesh road. Access is from outside the walls, not through the kasbah. One of the best of the Salam chain, the building started life as a pasha's residence in the 19th century. Set in luxuriant and very romantic gardens with a bar, restaurants, parking, hammam, fitness centre, swimming pool and tennis courts, it offers standard singles/doubles for Dr500/ 600 or better rooms in the towers or gardens from Dr780/900.

A couple of kilometres south-west of town is the incredibly exclusive *Hôtel Gazelle d'Or* (☎ 852039, fax 852737, ⓔ gazelle@ marocnet.net.ma). Built in 1961 by a Belgian baron, it has 40 bungalows set in extensive gardens and all the amenities you would expect, right down to the tennis courts, horseriding and even croquet. A bungalow for two with half board costs Dr3800, while the same in a suite is Dr8500. Frequented by rich Brits, this is one of Morocco's top establishments and advance booking is compulsory.

Places to Eat

There are quite a few small *cheap snack stalls* along Ave Mohammed V, near the Hôtel Souss, where you can get traditional food such as tajine, *harira* (spicy lentil soup) and salads.

The *restaurants* on the ground floors of the hotels on Place al-Alaouyine offer goodvalue set menus. *Hôtel/Restaurant Roudani* does the usual favourites including generous helpings of brochettes, chips and salad for Dr30.

Sandwich Barcelone, also on Place al-Alaouyine, is one of the few places with fixed prices on display where you can get a very good, fat baguette stuffed with *kefta* (seasoned minced lamb), chips and salad for Dr15.

If you want a break from the centre of town, *Restaurant Chez Nada* on the main street leading towards Bab el-Kasbah has a good terrace with a bit of shade and good views over the surrounding flower-filled gardens, a 1st-floor restaurant and a groundfloor cafe. The menu costs Dr70 with free tea and the option of mineral water instead of dessert.

Further south, *Al-Baraka (Ave Bir Anzarane)* is a small place, but offers very good fish (fresh from Agadir), chicken and brochettes along with the usual accompaniments.

In the evening, head for the colonial-style restaurant at the *Hôtel Taroudannt*. The menu here includes the old Moroccan reliables, but people looking for a change may want to opt for one of the French dishes – they do a pretty good steak. Main courses cost about Dr40 to Dr60.

A fair bit pricier, but very good, are the licensed French and Moroccan restaurants at the *Hôtel Palais Salam*. Mains cost from Dr40 to Dr110 and you can eat inside or outside at one of the secluded spots in the gardens – ideal for romantics.

Hôtel Saadiens has a moderate terrace restaurant where you can dine within view of the alluring Atlas Mountains.

There's no end to the *cafes* scattered about Taroudannt's winding streets. The terraces on Place al-Alaouyine are best for breakfast and are well placed for a pleasant morning of people-watching.

There are also a couple of upstairs *terraces* on Place an-Nasr for mint tea and mountain views, as well as a *patisserie* near the entrance to the Arab souq that has a wide selection of Moroccan cookies.

Café Modern, near Restaurant Chez Nada, has a good range of refreshing fruit cocktails, ideal for cooling down on hot sticky days.

Travellers wanting to put together their own picnic foods won't have any problems in Taroudannt – the *markets* are brimming with fresh produce from the fertile Souss Valley. In addition to the twice weekly market, there's also a *fruit & vegetable market* east of Hôtel Saadiens and plenty of *grocery shops* around the main squares.

Getting There & Away

Bus CTM has an office in Hôtel Les Arcades on Place al-Alaouyine. Services include an 11.30 am departure for Ouarzazate (Dr70, 5½ hours) and an 8 pm service to Casablanca (Dr150, 10 hours) via Agadir (Dr30, 2½ hours) and Marrakesh (Dr91, 6½ hours).

SATAS has an office next door to the Hôtel Taroudannt, also on the square. Services include a 7.30 am departure to Tata (Dr40, five hours) and a 12.30 pm service to Ouarzazate (five hours).

Local buses going to Marrakesh via the Tizi n'Test, and to Agadir and other destinations leave throughout the day.

All buses leave from outside Bab Zougan, the southern gate.

Grand Taxi Grand taxis also gather by Bab Zougan. Apart from small towns in the area around Taroudannt, the main destination is Inezgane (for Agadir), and sometimes Agadir itself. Either way, the fare is Dr23.

A place in a grand taxi to Tata costs Dr60 and to Marrakesh the fare is Dr100. The pea-green taxis go to local villages and the Western Sahara, blue ones go further afield. *Camionettes* (pick-up trucks) for outlying Berber villages leave from a lot near the Great Mosque.

Getting Around

It's highly unlikely that you'll need one of the white petit taxis, but if you do, they gather at Place an-Nasr.

You can hire bicycles (Dr5 per hour) from a workshop on Place al-Alaouyine.

Another possibility is touring around town in a calèche. They gather just inside Bab el-Kasbah or can be found trotting around town. A 1½-hour tour costs around Dr35.

AROUND TAROUDANNT
Tioute

Some 36km to the south-east of Taroudannt lie the impressive ruins of the kasbah of Tioute. Part of the kasbah has been turned into an expensive restaurant, but there's nothing to stop you simply enjoying the views over the *palmeraies* (oases) and village below. Scenes for *Ali Baba & the Forty Thieves*, starring Yul Brynner, were shot here in 1952.

Without your own transport, you'll have to organise a taxi to take you out there from Taroudannt.

If driving, take the main road towards Marrakesh for about 8km, turn right and cross the *oued* (riverbed) just before the village and ruined kasbah of **Freija** (which itself makes a good bicycle trip from Taroudannt). From here it's another 21km down the S7025 towards Igherm before you hit a turn-off to the right. After 5km, this reverts to a 2km stretch of piste where you're bound to be befriended by a guide.

Taliouine & Jebel Siroua

If you intend heading on to the southern oasis valleys from Taroudannt and don't want to go over the High Atlas to Mar-

rakesh, you can continue eastwards along the P32 via the villages of Taliouine and Tazenakht. From there the road heads north to join the main Marrakesh-Ouarzazate road not far from the turn-off to Aït Benhaddou. This route may be particularly worthwhile for travellers interested in trekking up **Jebel Siroua** (3304m), an isolated volcanic peak to the south of the High Atlas at the eastern edge of the Anti Atlas (see the Anti Atlas section in the Trekking chapter).

Taliouine is a pretty village where saffron is grown – there is a cooperative you can visit. Taliouine's market day is Monday. *Auberge Souktana*, a couple of kilometres east of the village on the main road, is very popular with travellers. In summer it's possible to sleep on the auberge's roof terrace or camp in its grounds; it also serves good meals and is a good base for treks to Jebel Siroua.

There are buses passing through Taliouine from both Taroudannt and Ouarzazate, but they may not always have seats available. There is a daily morning bus service to Marrakesh. Grand taxis head west to Oulad Behril where you can change for Taroudannt, and east to Tazenakht (Dr20) where you can change for Ouarzazate (Dr23).

TIZNIT
☎ 08

In an arid corner of the Souss Valley at the very end of the Anti Atlas, Tiznit appears like an old town, with its 6km of encircling red, mud walls. In fact, it's a fairly recent creation, but still worth a short stay if you've come this far. It's also not a bad staging point for Sidi Ifni, on the coast, and is the main departure point for Tafraoute, to the east.

History

Although there was a settlement of sorts here previously (see Source Bleue under Things to See & Do), the town dates mostly from 1881. In that year it was chosen by Sultan Moulay al-Hassan as a base from which to assert his authority over the rebellious Berber tribes of the Souss Valley and Anti Atlas.

He was only partly successful in this quest; it wasn't until the 1930s – 20 years after Spain and France had divided Mo-

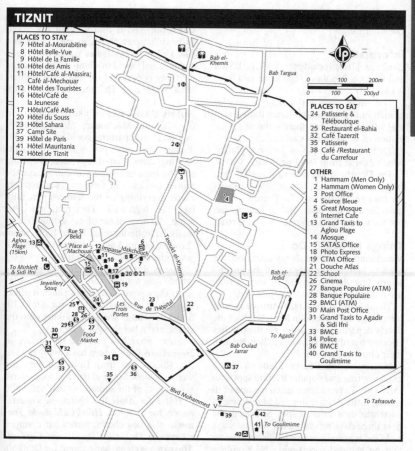

TIZNIT

PLACES TO STAY
7 Hôtel al-Mourabitine
8 Hôtel Belle-Vue
9 Hôtel de la Famille
10 Hôtel des Amis
11 Hôtel/Café al-Massira;
Café al-Mechouar
12 Hôtel des Touristes
16 Hôtel/Café de
la Jeunesse
17 Hôtel/Café Atlas
20 Hôtel du Souss
23 Hôtel Sahara
37 Camp Site
39 Hôtel de Paris
41 Hôtel Mauritania
42 Hôtel de Tiznit

PLACES TO EAT
24 Patisserie &
Téléboutique
25 Restaurant el-Bahia
32 Café Tazerzit
35 Patisserie
38 Café /Restaurant
du Carrefour

OTHER
1 Hammam (Men Only)
2 Hammam (Women Only)
3 Post Office
4 Source Bleue
5 Great Mosque
6 Internet Cafe
13 Grand Taxis to
Aglou Plage
14 Mosque
15 SATAS Office
18 Photo Express
19 CTM Office
21 Douche Atlas
26 Cinema
27 Banque Populaire (ATM)
28 Banque Populaire
29 BMCI (ATM)
30 Main Post Office
31 Grand Taxis to Agadir
& Sidi Ifni
33 BMCE
34 Police
36 BMCE
40 Grand Taxis to
Goulimime

rocco between themselves – that the tribes were finally 'pacified'.

In the first decade of the 20th century, Tiznit became a base for the resistance against the 1912 treaty that turned Morocco into a French and Spanish protectorate. The resistance was led by El-Hiba, an Idrissid chief from Mauritania who was regarded as a saint and credited with performing miracles.

El-Hiba had himself proclaimed sultan at Tiznit's mosque in 1912, and he succeeded in uniting the tribes of the Anti Atlas and the Tuareg in what proved to be a vain effort to dislodge the French. Ejected from

Tiznit, and at one point forced to move to Taroudannt, El-Hiba pursued the campaign of resistance until his death in 1919.

Orientation

Within the medina, Place al-Machouar is where you'll find the jewellery souq, most buses and the cheap hotels. Heading out of the medina through the main gate – known as Les Trois Portes (Three Gates) – you reach the main grand taxi rank, the post office, banks, restaurants and a food market.

The camp site and mid-range to top-end hotels can be found at the southern end of town, coming out of the walls through Bab Oulad Jarrar.

Information

Banks in Tiznit include the BMCE, BMCI and Banque Populaire. The latter two have ATMs.

The main post office and a smaller branch in the medina are open during normal office hours and there's the usual selection of téléboutiques around town.

There are a couple of Internet places, which charge from Dr12 per hour.

The Douche Atlas, down a side alley near Impasse Idakchouch, has separate showers for men and women (Dr5). There's a hammam for men just inside Bab el-Khemis and one for women 200m further down the road.

Things to See & Do

Wandering around the sleepy interior of the town or hunting for bargains in the just-as-sleepy **jewellery souq** can be fun, despite the pretty low-key hassle to 'just look'.

The minaret at the **Great Mosque** is reminiscent of those found in Mali. Souls of the dearly departed supposedly use the perches sticking out of its mud walls to help them in their climb to paradise.

Nearby is the **Source Bleue**, a pretty mucky spring and popular bathing spot with local kids. Legend has it that a woman of ill repute, Lalla Zninia, stopped to rest here at what was then a desert spot. She spent the next three days repenting her wicked ways and God was so impressed with her fervour that he showed forgiveness by having a spring gush beneath her feet. Her name was thus given to the village that preceded Moulay al-Hassan's 19th-century fortress town.

It's possible to climb onto sections of the city walls, which have 29 towers and nine gates. From Bab Targua for instance, you get a great view into the lush **palmeraie** where there is another natural spring, used as a laundry by local women.

Things liven up a little on Tuesday and Thursday, which are market days.

The Moussem of Sidi Ahmed at the end of August is a large, primarily religious, festival.

Places to Stay – Budget

Camping You'll find a *camp site* about halfway between the main roundabout and Bab Oulad Jarrar. It has patches of shade and is mainly used by camper vans. It costs Dr10 per person and car and Dr16 per caravan. Water costs Dr2 and electricity Dr15.

Hotels Many travellers like the hotels right on Place al-Machouar, although early morning bus departures could interrupt your dreams. Most other places have both rooms looking onto something interesting and rooftop terraces where you can escape the tourist hordes – in fact you escape pretty much everything as the terraces generally have very high walls. They're all much the same, and none of the places within the city walls have bathrooms. Some have warm showers, others don't – so Tiznit could be a good place to try a hammam.

One of the best hotels, *Hôtel Belle-Vue* (☎ 862109, fax 861622, 101 Rue du Bain) is off the square. A cheerful place, it offers big, clean singles/doubles for Dr40/70. Some have large windows looking onto the street, and a hot shower is Dr5.

Many travellers stay on the square at *Hôtel/Café Atlas*, which has a lively restaurant. Rooms cost from Dr40 and there are warm showers. Some of the front rooms have good views of the square, but that's about it.

Hôtel des Amis has cheap and cheerful rooms for Dr40/60. *Hôtel/Café de la Jeunesse* also has cheap, somewhat cramped rooms for Dr25/50. The *Hôtel/ Café al-Massira* has clean, basic rooms for Dr30/60.

Hôtel des Touristes (☎ 862186), at the northern end of the square, has decent-sized, spotless rooms for Dr60/90. The gas-powered shower is hot and free.

In addition to the Belle-Vue, there are half a dozen or so other cheapies along Rue du Bain. *Hôtel al-Mourabitine* (☎ 862755), at the end of the street, is not bad. Smaller rooms cost Dr20/40, but they have bigger and more pleasant rooms at the front for Dr50/70. The hotel is up on the 1st floor with a little cafe. There is a warm shower.

A bit closer to the square, *Hôtel de la Famille* (☎ 862156) and *Hôtel du Souss* have acceptable, but grubby, rooms for Dr20/40. There's no shower in either. Charging the same, the poky *Hôtel Sahara* (☎ 862498) is a bit further from Place al-Machouar. Rooms have clean double beds and little else.

Hôtel Mauritania (☎ 862072), on the road to Goulimime, has good value singles/doubles/triples with private shower and toilet for Dr60/80/100. The hotel also has a bar and restaurant.

Places to Stay – Mid-Range & Top End

The only mid-range hotel in town is the two-star *Hôtel de Paris* (☎ 862865, Blvd Mohammed V) by the roundabout. Singles/doubles are comfortable and clean and cost Dr138/164 with shower, toilet and balcony. There is solar-powered hot water and the hotel has a TV lounge and restaurant.

Tiznit's top hotel is the three-star *Hôtel de Tiznit* (☎ 862411, fax 862119, Rue Bir Inzaran), which is also close to the main roundabout. Rooms with hot water and phone cost from Dr253/319 and look out onto a secluded courtyard, which is where you find the bar, restaurant and pool. There's also parking and a nightclub.

Places to Eat

Restaurant el-Bahia, next to the cinema on Blvd Mohammed V, does excellent sandwiches and French fries. For something more substantial you can bring your own fresh ingredients to *Café Tazerzit*, near the market, and have a very cheap meal cooked for you.

The restaurants in *Hôtel Mauritiania*, *Hôtel de Paris* and *Hôtel de Tiznit* are worth trying in the evening if you want a more comfortable option. The first two are quite reasonably priced.

The air-con *Café/Restaurant du Carrefour*, opposite Hôtel de Paris, offers well-prepared Moroccan dishes and is a great place for breakfast. Ideal for hot, sticky days, it also has a chilled drinking water fountain.

Quite a few of the hotels on the main square have cafes offering food. One of the most popular is the *Hôtel/Café Atlas*.

There's plenty of choice, but the best place for coffee and patisseries on the square is *Café al-Mechouar*, close to Hôtel al-Massira.

There are a few other cafes about town. At Les Trois Portes there's a patisserie-cum-téléboutique – ideal for calling home and crying poor while you tuck into a cream cake.

Those who want to prepare their own meals should go to the covered *market*, behind Banque Populaire, which has an excellent selection of meat, vegetables, fruit (fresh and dried) and other foodstuffs.

Shopping

The best time to look at the silver jewellery souq (which reputedly has some of the best stuff in the south, if not in all of Morocco), is when the package-tour buses have left (mid to late afternoon). It then reverts to normality and is a much more pleasant place to hang around and explore.

Jewellery is not only made here, but is bought to be traded for tribal jewellery in the Saharan regions further south. You may be lucky enough to see some of these pieces before they're sold on to merchants in the big northern cities.

If you're not heading to Tafraoute or Taroudannt then Tiznit is probably the next best place to buy *babouches* (leather slippers) and sandals.

Getting There & Away

Bus All buses leave from Place al-Machouar. CTM buses for Agadir (Dr21, two hours) leave at 11 am and 8.30 pm. A service to Casablanca (Dr98.50, 13 hours) via Agadir (Dr21, 1½ hours), Essaouira (Dr43, six hours), Safi (Dr64.50, eight hours) and El-Jadida (Dr83.50, 10 hours) leaves at 5.30 am.

A 1st-class bus leaves for Tangier (Dr260, 16 hours) via Agadir, Marrakesh (Dr95, seven hours), Casablanca (Dr154, nine hours) and Rabat (Dr184, 10½ hours) at 9 pm.

CTM also runs a service to Goulimime (2½ hours) and Tafraoute (Dr32, four hours) at 5 am.

There are plenty of other buses leaving from the early morning until evening to Agadir, Casablanca, Goulimime (Dr25), Marrakesh, Ouarzazate, Sidi Ifni, Tafraoute, Tan Tan and Tata.

Berber Jewellery

The tribal jewellery of Morocco is among the most beautiful in Africa. The traditional assemblage necklaces made in the southern oasis valleys are particularly striking, with some of the more exquisite featuring talismans of silver, pink coral, amazonite, amber, Czech glass and West African ebony beads.

The urban tradition of jewellery-making in Morocco has been heavily influenced by Arab culture and uses gold or gilded silver. Rural jewellery has been influenced by Moorish Spain, but still essentially reflects the Berber animistic beliefs that pre-date Islam.

Berber jewellery is always made of silver (gold was considered to be evil); in the case of necklaces the silver is used in combination with other materials. It serves a much wider purpose than simple adornment, identifying clan, symbolising wealth, reflecting cultural traditions and acting as a source of supernatural and religious power for the wearer.

A woman will receive jewellery from her mother until she marries. Her future husband will commission pieces made by his mother or sister and these will be kept by her as dowry and added to throughout her life. Necklaces are important, but she will also have bracelets, fibulas (elaborate brooches, often triangular-shaped, used for fastening garments), anklets, earrings and headdresses. Some pieces will be worn every day, but the finest will be worn for festivals, pilgrimages, funerals and so on.

The protective, medicinal and magical properties of jewellery are extremely important. The assemblage necklaces will contain charms bought from magicians or holy men for all sorts of purposes, including protection from the evil eye, warding off disease and accidents, and easing childbirth.

Silver is believed to cure rheumatism; coral symbolises fertility and is thought to have curative powers; amber is worn as a symbol of wealth and to protect against sorcery (it's also considered an aphrodisiac and a cure for colds); amazonite and carnelian stones are used in divining fortunes; and shells traded from East Africa symbolise fertility.

Talismans feature stylised motifs of animals, suns, moon and stars, which all have various supernatural powers. A common symbol to ward off the evil eye is the hand of Fatima, the daughter of the prophet Mohammed. Any depiction of the hand (which represents human creative power and dominance) or of the number five is believed to have the same effect as metaphorically poking the fingers into the evil eye with the words *khamsa fi ainek* (five in your eye).

Jewellery features numerous representations of the number five – as dots, lines, stars, crosses and as groups of five elements placed together.

Grand Taxi Grand taxis to Sidi Ifni (Dr20) and Agadir (Dr20) leave from the main grand taxi rank, opposite the post office in the western part of town. Taxis occasionally go to Tafraoute (Dr35).

For Goulimime (Dr30), and possibly for Tan Tan, there are grand taxis from a stand opposite the Hôtel Mauritania.

Taxis to Aglou Plage (Dr5) leave from another stand, on Blvd Mohammed V by the city walls.

AROUND TIZNIT
Aglou Plage
About 15km from Tiznit lies Aglou Plage, which has a reasonable beach and good surf, though you'll come across the occa-sional glass and plastic bottle, as well as other rubbish. Most of the time it's deserted and, when Atlantic winds start blustering, it's a wild and woolly sort of place.

There's a walled *camp site* at the entrance to the village, but it's stony and has no shade whatsoever. Camping at the site (open only in summer) costs next to nothing.

It's possible to stay in caves near the beach with all the comforts of home (people do live in them); ask around when you arrive. Local buses and grand taxis run from Tiznit (Dr5).

Mirhleft
☎ 08

Around 40km south-west of Tiznit, on the coastal road to Sidi Ifni, is the seaside village of Mirhleft, an increasingly popular spot with travellers looking for a good beach (along a turn-off from the northern end of town) and some peace and quiet. There's a ruined fort behind the village, a smaller beach with some dramatic rocks and a few cafes to the south. There is a post office and petrol station (but no banks).

There are five basic hotels here, all of which are on the main street off the highway. *Hôtel du Sud* (☎ 719024) has bright, clean singles/doubles for Dr30/50 (as well as a good cafe/restaurant downstairs) and a large rooftop terrace. Other places in town include *Hotel Atlas*, *Hotel Farah* and *Hôtel Tafkout*. They all have similar rates (around Dr25 per person) and facilities; most have cafes that serve up some of the tonnes of fresh fish that end up here.

If you get caught up in Mirhleft, it's also possible to rent houses for as little as Dr600 a month; ask around at the cafes.

Local buses and grand taxis between Tiznit and Sidi Ifni stop in Mirhleft.

THE TIZNIT-TATA-TAROUDANNT CIRCUIT
☎ 08

The small town of Tata makes a good stopover point on an excellent and little-travelled route that takes you 300km south-east of Tiznit through a series of desert oases then up over the Anti Atlas another 200km to Taroudannt.

Tata itself is a sleepy place with one colonnaded main street and everything painted in pastel shades of blue, pink and yellow. There's a petrol station as you come in from the west. The post office and Banque Populaire are central – just off Ave Mohammed V.

There are basic *hotels* along Ave Mohammed V and by the bus station with cheap rooms from Dr20 per person, as well as cafes and restaurants.

Hôtel de la Renaissance (☎ 802225, Ave des FAR), which runs into Ave Mohammed V, has clean, plain singles/doubles with bathroom for Dr100/150. It also has a pleasant restaurant.

Just before town, coming in from the west, *Hôtel les Relais des Sables* (☎ 802301) has comfortable, but quite small, rooms with bathroom for Dr230/280. The hotel has a small swimming pool, flower-filled courtyards, a bar and a restaurant.

Several *cafe/restaurants* along Ave Mohammed V offer simple Moroccan dishes.

You'll find buses and taxis towards the end of the town in a small square off Ave Mohammed V. SATAS has daily departures to Tiznit (Dr69, seven hours) and Taroudannt (Dr40, five hours). There's no shortage of grand taxis.

THE TIZNIT-TAFRAOUTE-AGADIR CIRCUIT

The village of Tafraoute, which is tucked away in the Anti Atlas, can be reached by road from either Tiznit (107km) or Agadir (198km). A circuit taking in all three is the ideal way of doing the trip – unfortunately buses to Tafraoute only go via Tiznit, so you do need your own transport for this.

From **Tiznit**, the road east to Tafraoute starts off ordinarily enough across gentle farming country, until it reaches Oued Assaka. From here it winds up into the mountains, which in the late afternoon light take on every hue imaginable – from soft pinks and mauves to golden browns. (If you are travelling by bus there are departures from Tiznit to coincide with this light show.)

Sprinkled about the hills are precarious Berber pisé (mud brick) villages (most of the Berbers in this region are Souss Chleuh), surrounded by the cultivated terraces that are worked all through the day – mostly by the women.

At 1100m you cross the stunning **Col de Kerdous** and from here you hardly lose altitude for the remainder of the run into Tafraoute. *Hôtel Kerdous* (☎ 08-862063, fax 600315) is perched in a former kasbah right on the pass. There are extraordinary views on all sides, but especially towards Tiznit. The hotel has two restaurants, a bar and double rooms for Dr650. It's worth stopping here for an expensive drink or meal (set menu is Dr120) just for the outlook.

The route to Agadir is just as fascinating. Leaving Tafraoute (see following), the road passes through the eastern half of the

Ameln Valley and over Tizi Mlil before doubling back on itself for the trip north-west to Agadir. The land is generally much gentler and more heavily cultivated on this run, but the road passes through plenty of villages – often little clusters of houses, sometimes in the most unlikely places.

The most remarkable spot along the way is Ida-ou-Gnidif, perched on a solitary hill-top back from the highway, about 40km south of Aït Baha. From Aït Baha the road flattens out, and the final stretch up to Agadir is of little interest.

TAFRAOUTE
☎ 08

Nestled in behind the enchanting Ameln Valley is the village of Tafraoute, itself un-spectacular, but extremely relaxed – the perfect base for days of hiking in the sparkling pink mountains, tranquil valleys, rich palmeraies and Berber villages around it.

Unsurprisingly, tourism is on the in-crease in Tafraoute, which may well be good news for many locals, as for centuries this strikingly beautiful area has allowed its inhabitants to eke out only the barest of liv-ings. Apart from almond, argan and palm trees, along with limited wheat and barley cultivation, there's not much to the local economy and the region has a long history of emigration. This has resulted in a large percentage of men leaving their families in Tafraoute to spend their working lives over-seas – something that is evident in the big cars with foreign numberplates around town.

Towards the end of February the villages around Tafraoute celebrate the almond har-vest with all night singing and dancing; the festivities move from village to village and therefore last several days (see Ameln Val-ley under Around Tafraoute later).

Information
There are two banks in Tafraoute – BMCE and Banque Populaire; the latter is open on market day (Wednesday) only. The post of-fice is on Place Mohammed al-Khamis and has pay phones; there are a couple of téléboutiques as well. There's a hammam behind the old mosque and another one south-east of the centre.

A lively souq takes place just by the Hôtel Salam on Monday and Wednesday.

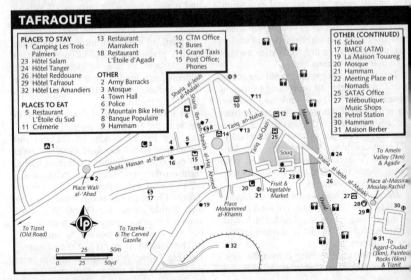

TAFRAOUTE

PLACES TO STAY
1 Camping Les Trois Palmiers
23 Hôtel Salam
24 Hôtel Tanger
26 Hôtel Reddouane
29 Hôtel Tafraout
32 Hôtel Les Amandiers

PLACES TO EAT
5 Restaurant L'Étoile du Sud
11 Crémerie
13 Restaurant Marrakech
18 Restaurant L'Étoile d'Agadir

OTHER
2 Army Barracks
3 Mosque
4 Town Hall
6 Police
7 Mountain Bike Hire
8 Banque Populaire
9 Hammam
10 CTM Office
12 Buses
14 Grand Taxis
15 Post Office; Phones

OTHER (CONTINUED)
16 School
17 BMCE (ATM)
19 La Maison Touareg
20 Mosque
21 Hammam
22 Meeting Place of Nomads
25 SATAS Office
27 Téléboutique; Music Shops
28 Petrol Station
30 Hammam
31 Maison Berber

Trekking

Several local people have set themselves up as guides to the area around Tafraoute offering mountain-biking and trekking trips either up Jebel al-Kest (2359m) or along the palm-filled gorges leading towards the bald expanses of the southern Anti Atlas. Stay in Tafraoute a few days, go on some hikes around the countryside, and you'll find it hard to leave. Spring and autumn are the best seasons for walking – summer is roastingly hot. See Around Tafraoute later and the Trekking chapter for further details.

There are quite a few climbing opportunities around Tafraoute. A small craft shop, Meeting Place of Nomads, in the souq area has copies of routes and maps put together by climbers who have passed this way.

Places to Stay – Budget

Camping Les Trois Palmiers is set in a small stony compound – all the palm trees are outside the walls – but it's still not a bad little place and has patches of shade. It costs Dr6/10 per child/adult, Dr10 to pitch a tent, Dr7.50 for a car and Dr7 for a hot shower. There are also two basic double rooms, which cost Dr50, and one room for four people, which costs Dr100.

Since there are only five hotels in town, it may be worthwhile booking ahead. The two cheapest places are just opposite each other towards the eastern end of town. Of these, *Hôtel Tanger* (☎ 800033) is the more basic, offering singles/doubles for Dr25/45 – a hot shared shower costs (Dr7). This place has a pleasant (as long as the wind is blowing the right way from the oued) 1st-floor terrace restaurant.

On the other side of the road, *Hôtel Red-douane* (☎ 800066) has rooms from Dr35, with hot shower included. There is a sun terrace, and the restaurant downstairs is a popular hang-out.

The best option is the *Hôtel Tafraout* (☎ 800060, Place al-Missira Moulay Rachid). Rooms are huge, modern, clean and cost (Dr40/80). Some overlook the square below and all are comfortable. The gas-heated shared showers are free and steaming hot. There's also a terrace.

Places to Stay – Mid-Range & Top End

Hôtel Salam (☎ 800026, fax 800448) has been rebuilt after 'blowing up' some years ago. Large, comfortable rooms with shower cost Dr115/150. There are a few basic rooms for Dr50, but there's no shared shower. The hotel has a pleasant terrace and a salon de thé overlooking the market square below.

The only remaining option in Tafraoute is *Hôtel Les Amandiers* (☎ 800088, fax 800343), which sits on the crest of the hill overlooking the town and has some pretty impressive views. Self-contained rooms with TV and phone cost Dr311/522 plus taxes. Aimed at package tourists, the hotel has a swimming pool (nonguests may use it for Dr35) in a spectacular boulder setting, as well as a bar, restaurant and shaded parking.

Places to Eat

Both the cheaper hotels have their own reasonably priced restaurants – you can eat your fill for about Dr25, but as they both overlook the river you may not enjoy it too much if the wind is blowing the wrong way. *Restaurant Marrakech*, on a road up to the main square is about the same without the wafts.

Restaurant L'Etoile d'Agadir, near the post office, is popular with the locals and has filling meals from Dr25.

The best restaurant if you have a bit of money to spare is the licensed *Restaurant L'Etoile du Sud* (Sharia Hassan at-Tani) opposite the post office. The Dr80 set menu, although not offering much choice, is tasty. The interior is done up as a traditional Moroccan salon, and the atmosphere is laid-back. You can also eat under the similarly decorated tent outside.

For an ice cream you could try the *cremerie* opposite the CTM office, which will also cook you up a tajine if you supply the ingredients – available from the fruit & vegetable market behind the souq daily. It also has cheese (the hard stuff) and other stores can help with the rest of your picnic supplies.

Shopping

There are, as usual, a couple of carpet shops in town. If you fancy a pair of traditional leather slippers (yellow for men, red for women) Tafraoute is the place to buy them. You'll find dozens of slipper shops around the market area in the centre of town (pay no more than Dr60).

Local women selling argan and olive oil gather here to target the tourists coming in on tour buses.

Getting There & Away
Bus The bus offices are along Sharia al-Jeish al-Malaki.

There is a CTM service to Casablanca (14 hours) via Tiznit (Dr30, three hours), Agadir (Dr52, five hours) and Marrakesh (10 hours) at 7 pm. A couple of other companies cover the same destinations plus Rabat. Local buses for Tiznit leave at 4 am and 7 am.

Grand Taxi The occasional grand taxi goes to Tiznit in the morning (Dr35). Otherwise, 4WD taxis do the rounds of various villages in the area, mostly on market days. If there are any to be had, they hang around Place Mohammed al-Khamis or Sharia al-Jeish al-Malaki.

Getting Around
You can hire mountain bikes for Dr70 per day from La Maison Touareg and other souvenir shops around town. If you're exploring the surrounding area you may want to take a puncture repair kit as there are thorns all over.

AROUND TAFRAOUTE
Le Chapeau de Napoléon & the Painted Rocks
The village of **Agard-Oudad**, a few kilometres out of Tafraoute, is famous for its distinctive rock formation known as Le Chapeau de Napoléon (Napoleon's Hat) and its **painted rocks** – the work of Belgian artist Jean Veran who has done similar things in places such as the Sinai in Egypt.

In this case Veran had a collection of the smooth, rounded boulders peculiar to this patch of the mountains spray-painted in shades of blue and red in 1984. In true Moroccan style, the rocks have a faded air – the paint has chipped and they would benefit from another visit from Jean and his spray

gun. However, they remain impressive against the landscape.

To walk out to the painted rocks, take the road to Agard-Oudad, which follows the river through lush greenery. On the way you'll see **Le Chapeau de Napoléon** rising above Agard-Oudad. Take the signposted right branch into the village and follow the piste to the square, where there's a mosque. From here, veer right and then left to get around the mosque, and follow the piste, power lines and river out into the countryside. A couple of kilometres further on you'll come to some pale-blue rocks on the left-hand side – keep going and follow the piste bearing left to another set, which includes a large blue boulder with a purple rock atop. Beyond is an even larger display of painted rocks.

If you're driving, head past Oulad Agard and follow the signs to a turn-off about 5km beyond the village. Follow the couple of kilometres of piste and leave the car where the piste peters out. About 100m on, you arrive at a good viewpoint over the rocks.

The Carved Gazelle
To get to this beautiful and apparently ancient carving, take the road for Tazzeka on your right as you pass the Hôtel Les Amandiers. The road climbs up a hill from here, you need to get in behind this hill and leave it to your left. You'll see a simple drawing of an animal on a rock. The carving is on the top side of a fallen rock right in front of this one. The walk from Tafraoute should take about 20 minutes.

Ameln Valley
Tafraoute lies in a basin, largely surrounded by craggy gold-pink rocks and cliffs. To the north-west lies one such ridge, on the other side of which runs the Ameln Valley (Ameln is the name given to the local tribe of Chleuh Berbers). From Tafraoute there are some rock formations clearly visible that look like a lion's head. North again of the valley is a mountain range dominated by **Jebel al-Kest**. La Maison Tuareg sells a reasonable map of the area (Dr12).

The Agadir road takes you to the valley, which is lined by picturesque Berber villages,

Wandering through the 300m-high walls of the Todra Gorge (top left); a boy on a bicycle keeps watch at a kasbah in the Drâa Valley (top right); Berber women wash clothes in an oasis below an abandoned village near Er-Rachidia (middle right); the seemingly endless Merzouga dunes (bottom)

Essaouira's beach, Morocco's windsurfing centre, curves for kilometres along the south Atlantic coast.

Wooden boats and the fishing fleet idle in Essaouira's port.

The Anti Atlas, on the edge of the Sahara Desert.

Enchanting Tafraoute in the Anti Atlas

some of them only partly inhabited. Four kilometres out of Tafraoute, the road forks, the right branch turning off eastwards out of the valley towards Agadir. The other proceeds west down the valley. You could take either and hike for days, going directly from village to village through barley fields or following narrow goat tracks and irrigation channels.

One of the most visited of the villages is **Oumesnat**, a few kilometres after the fork and off to the left along a short piste. The main attraction here is the **Maison Traditionelle**. Blinded as a young man in Tangier, Si Abdessalam decided to open up his three-storey house (some 400 years old). He and his son will give you a tour of every nook and cranny for which they expect a small consideration – it's worth every dirham.

Another popular village is **Anameur**, with a natural spring, 10km west of Oumesnat.

Taghdichte, between Oumesnat and Anameur, is used by adventure-travel groups (mainly English and German) as a base for ascents of Jebel al-Kest (an all-day walk/ scramble, but not a difficult climb).

Further west, before the village of Aït Omar, there's an unmarked piste, opposite a well, that leads to **Tirnmatmat**. Small adventure groups also base themselves here, and with good reason. The village sits in a lovely spot – there are some rock carvings along the riverbed (the local kids will lead you there) and good walking in all directions.

Excursions to Afella-Ighir

From Tafraoute there are a couple of routes that take you south to the pretty oasis of

Berber Houses

Traditional building methods throughout the Atlas Mountain villages had, until recently, changed little over the centuries. Prosperous mountain Berbers now use more modern techniques, but many subsistence farmers and their families continue to employ age-old methods.

The typical house is flat-roofed and made of pisé, rammed earth or clay. A decent house has three or four floors. Argan-wood beams and palm fronds are typically used for the ceilings between each floor.

The bottom floor is basically for the animals. Cows and the like are kept in a dark area, to reduce the number of flies. Scraps are dropped through a hole in the ceiling from the kitchen above – a natural form of waste disposal. Farming tools are also kept on this floor, along with utensils for making flour and for grinding coffee and argan nuts for oil. If there is a toilet, it's down here.

A better house has a stairway or ladder up to the next floor, both inside and out. Visitors thus have no reason to see the bottom floor. The kitchen might occupy the main floor-space on this level. Gathered around it are what amount to corridors. One (the biggest) is the family dining room, while the rest serve as bedrooms. Occasionally, on festive occasions these rooms host women (there is traditionally, although not always, strict segregation of the sexes if men from outside the immediate family are visiting, whatever the reason).

A ramp leads up to the next floor, most of which is occupied by the most sumptuous room in the house, where the men usually eat with guests or take tea. Here you take your shoes off before walking on the mats, and all the silver teaware is brought out. On the same floor or above is the inevitable open terrace – especially important in the summer, when it can be far too hot to sleep inside.

The models vary (sometimes the 2nd and top floors are reversed), but the basic formula remains pretty much the same.

Some of these houses have been standing for hundreds of years, but only in a very loose sense. Habitation of villages has historically been cyclic. Berber villages were, until early this century, regularly exposed to epidemics and subject to raids by enemy tribes, and as a result were often abandoned, sometimes for generations. Where the population was severely reduced, the excess houses stood empty and slowly began to crumble. In better days, these same old houses would be reoccupied, the top floors rebuilt and so the cycle begun again.

Afella-Ighir. You could cover most of it in a 4WD (a Renault 4 will do it too), but it's preferable to drive part of the way, then leave the car and do a circuit on foot or mountain bike.

The road south of **Agard-Oudad** takes you roughly 15km over a mountain pass (sometimes snowed over in winter) to **Tlata Tasrite**. From here it is possible to take several pistes that drop into lush palm-filled valleys, and do a loop of about 30km to 40km through to the Afella-Ighir oasis and back up to Tlata Tasrite.

At **Oussaka**, about 9km south of Souq al-Had, there are ancient animal carvings. More can be seen 8km further on at **Tasselbte**. It would be best to talk to a guide (see Around Tafraoute in the Anti Atlas section of the Trekking chapter) about the latter part of this hike. On market days 4WD taxis sometimes do the run to various villages of this area.

ID-AÏSSA & TAGHJICHT

A worthwhile side excursion along the way to Tata is to the magnificent *agadir* (fortified granary) at Id-Aïssa, north-east of the village of Taghjicht, 35km from Bouzakarne.

The well-preserved agadir sits high above the village, seemingly growing straight from the rocky mountain. Ali, the friendly local caretaker, will take you up on foot, or by donkey if you prefer. The main door to the agadir remains locked and must be opened with a massive wooden Berber key.

There are no facilities in the village, which has a market on Sunday, but you can *camp* by the river nearby, or there's a mid-range *hotel* and *restaurant* in Taghjicht from where you can negotiate a grand taxi to Id-Aïssa.

SIDI IFNI
☎ 08 • pop 15,000
Known to some simply as Ifni, this quirky town is at the heart of the former Spanish Sahara. Shrouded for much of the year in an Atlantic mist, this haunting and short-lived coastal outpost of Spanish imperial ambitions (the Spanish originally christened it Santa Cruz del Mar Pequeña) has a decaying but fascinating air about it.

The town dates largely from the 1930s and features an eclectic mix of Spanish Art Deco and traditional Moroccan styles.

The fabulous balustraded esplanade is crumbling, the *calles* (streets) are half-empty, but even so this sleepy town attracts a surprising number of visitors who return year after year to soak up the atmosphere and enjoy the unhurried pace of life here.

The people here live mainly from small-scale fishing; most of the catch is sold in Agadir.

A moussem is held here in the second week of June.

History
After the Spanish-Moroccan war of 1859, which Morocco lost (just 14 years after a defeat at the hands of a French army from Algeria), Spain obtained the enclave of Sidi Ifni by treaty. Quite what they were going to do with it seems to have been a question in a lot of Spanish minds, because they did not take full possession until 1934.

By the 1950s, some 60% of the town's population was Spanish, but under pressure from the UN, Spain agreed to cede the enclave back to Morocco in 1969. Morocco had sealed off its land borders three years before. Only a few Spanish families now remain.

Information
There's just one bank in town, the Banque Populaire, on Ave Mohammed V (away from the heart of the old Spanish town), where you can change cash and cheques. The post office is also on Ave Mohammed V (the letter box outside is still marked 'Correos').

Things to See & Do
Apart from wandering around the old Spanish part of town, the heart of which is Place Hassan II (formerly Plaza de España), there's precious little to do here. The beaches are largely deserted, though a little littered. If the whim takes you it's possible to go out fishing with the locals.

Don't miss the **church** just off the main plaza, the **former Spanish consulate**, the **lighthouse**, and the **house** in the form of a ship on the edge of the cliff next to the

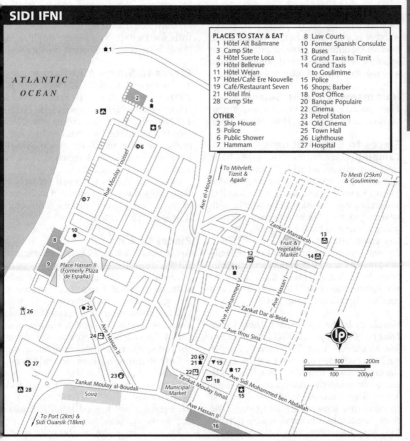

SIDI IFNI

PLACES TO STAY & EAT
1 Hôtel Ait Baâmrane
3 Camp Site
4 Hôtel Suerte Loca
9 Hôtel Bellevue
11 Hôtel Wejan
17 Hôtel/Café Ere Nouvelle
19 Café/Restaurant Seven
21 Hôtel Ifni
28 Camp Site

OTHER
2 Ship House
5 Police
6 Public Shower
7 Hammam
8 Law Courts
10 Former Spanish Consulate
12 Buses
13 Grand Taxis to Tiznit
14 Grand Taxis to Goulimime
15 Police
16 Shops; Barber
18 Post Office
20 Banque Populaire
22 Cinema
23 Petrol Station
24 Old Cinema
25 Town Hall
26 Lighthouse
27 Hospital

ATLANTIC OCEAN

Rue Moulay Youssef

To Mihrleft, Tiznit & Agadir

To Mesti (25km) & Goulimime

Zankat Marrakesh

Fruit & Vegetable Market

Place Hassan II (Formerly Plaza de España)

Ave el-Houria

Ave Mohammed V

Ave Hassan I

Zankat Dar al-Beida

Ave Ifrou Sina

Ave Hassan II

Zankat Moulay al-Boudali

Souq

Zankat Moulay Ismail

Municipal Market

Ave Sidi Mohammed ben Abdallah

Ave Hassan II

To Port (2km) & Sidi Ouarsik (18km)

0   100   200m
0   100   200yd

Hôtel Suerte Loca. The **central gardens** on Place Hassan II occasionally hosts exhibitions of art and music.

Walking south along the beach you'll come to the port; just offshore is an old land-sea conveyor that was used to take cargo from ships to the old Spanish port. The new port is further south.

On Sunday a large, animated **souq** takes place in front of the abandoned airfield south of town.

For a glimpse into the past, you might visit Hassan Aznag, the second **barber** on Ave Mohammed V heading south, who has

a collection of Spanish photos and magazines from the 1930s to the 1960s.

If you're happier soaking up the sun on a terrace, you could pick up some beads at the Hôtel Suerte Loca shop and fashion yourself some souvenir **jewellery**.

There's also some OK **surfing** here – you can borrow boards off the locals. Paragliding is popular in the area, the hotels have information.

Each 30 June there are **celebrations** commemorating Sidi Ifni's return to Morocco.

You can make several **excursions** into the countryside from Sidi Ifni. One hike takes you 18km south, along coastal track, to **Sidi Ouarsik**, a fishing village with a good beach. Another is to **Mesti**, a Berber village 25km towards Goulimime. Hôtel Suerte Loca can organise 4WD trips, incorporating some walking, to these and other nearby areas.

Hammams & Public Showers
There are male and female hammams just up the road just south of the Hôtel Suerte Loca.

Places to Stay – Budget
Camping There are two cheap but basic patches of ground set aside for campers, but they're really only good for people with camper vans. The first, south of the hospital, has small areas of garden and is popular with returning tourists, but is still pretty cheerless (camper van plus two costs Dr15). The second *camp site (☎ 780707, fax 875366),* downhill from Hôtel Suerte Loca, is little more than a car park (and the focus of stares from above) but is right on the beach. Two plus camper van costs Dr25 and it also has a couple of apartments from Dr130.

Hotels By far the best option is *Hôtel Suerte Loca (☎ 875350, fax 780003),* at the end of Rue Moulay Youssef. This friendly family-run hotel is divided into two wings, one considerably newer than the other. The older rooms are perfectly comfortable, and some have balcony access. Singles/doubles cost Dr50/80 (hot showers are Dr6 extra). The clean, bright rooms in the new wing (Dr120/155) have bathrooms plus balconies overlooking the beach. It's also possible to sleep under the Berber tent on the roof. There is a small collection of novels and the like to lend to guests, a good restaurant (excellent breakfast and crepes), live music when it's busy, a terrace for sunbathing and a shop next door selling crafts at reasonable fixed prices.

If Hôtel Suerte Loca is full (which is quite possible, particularly at Christmas), there are a few standard Moroccan cheapies scattered around Ave Mohammed V. *Hôtel Ifni*, near the bank, is as good as any, with very basic rooms and cold showers for Dr20 a head. *Hôtel Wejan*, further up Ave Mohammed V, offers the same. *Hôtel/Café*

Ere Nouvelle (☎ 875298, 5 Ave Sidi Mohammed ben Abdallah) has rooms with no frills for Dr30/60 (go for the brighter top floor), a terrace and a decent restaurant.

Places to Stay – Mid-Range
The two-star *Hôtel Bellevue (☎ 875072, fax 780499, 9 Place Hassan II)* has comfortable singles/doubles with bathroom from Dr150/182, some have sea views while others look onto the plaza. The hotel has two bars and a restaurant; unfortunately the terrace seems to have been specifically designed to block the sunset, but you can see the beach.

Down on the beach itself, *Hôtel Ait Baâmrane* was being renovated at the time of research, but should make a good choice if only for the location.

Places to Eat
Apart from a few small cafe/restaurants on Blvd Hassan II and others dotted about the town, the only choices are really the hotel restaurants. *Hôtel Suerte Loca* is particularly good value – they'll cook up whatever you feel like eating for a reasonable price, including freshly caught fish and any number of Spanish and Moroccan specialties, but you will need to order in advance.

Café/Restaurant Seven, around the corner from the post office, does a pretty good chicken and chips. There are also roadside *snack stands* along Ave Mohammed V in the evenings and a good small *fish place* next to the market's public toilets.

There's a busy *fish market* open from 5 to 8 pm at the municipal market and a *fruit & vegetable market* walled in behind Zankat Marrakesh.

There are grocery shops along Ave Mohammed V.

Getting There & Away
Buses depart from along Ave Mohammed V. There are early morning departures to Agadir (Dr36, 3½ hours), Goulimime (Dr18, 1½ hours), Marrakesh (Dr85, 8½ hours) and Tiznit (Dr18, 2½ hours). There are other afternoon departures to Tiznit but the most reliable way to and from Sidi Ifni is by grand taxi. These leave from a couple of dirt lots

around the corner from the northern end of Ave Hassan I and cost Dr20 a head to either Tiznit or Goulimime. A place in an (irregular) taxi to Agadir costs Dr40.

GOULIMIME
☎ 08

The most striking thing about Goulimime (pronounced Gooly-meem), the dusty little town that proclaims itself the 'Gateway to the Sahara', is the bold crimson colour of almost all the buildings. Overlooking the town are the ruins of Caid Dahman Takri's palace. Apart from that, and the chance to see a variety of desert bird life in the surrounding area, Goulimime doesn't have a great deal to offer the traveller and is the last town on the 'tourist circuit'.

Once upon a time, 'blue men' came in from the desert every week to buy and sell camels at a souq just outside town. In the evenings, the women would perform the mesmerising *guedra* dance to the beat of drums of the same name. About the only time you're likely to see any of this is during the moussem and camel fair held here at the start of June.

Still, this is what the package tourists pile into Goulimime for on Friday night and Saturday – they must leave sorely disappointed. Economic considerations have long since rendered the camel market obsolete. There is a large souq held every Saturday a couple of kilometres outside town, along the Route de Tan Tan. You'll see plenty of fruit here and quite a lot of overpriced souvenirs, but very few camels. Be prepared for some insistent hustlers and touts around Goulimime.

Bird-watchers may like to look out for a variety of desert bird species off the main road heading south of Goulimime. Birds that have been seen around here include warblers, wheateaters, sandgrouse and larks, as well as eagles, buzzards and falcons.

There are four banks in Goulimime, but they get incredibly busy and you may have to queue for ages – bring cash with you. The post office is near the mosque between the two main roundabouts.

There's a hammam next to the mosque.

Places to Stay

See Fort Bou Jerif later for camping options around Goulimime. There are five cheap hotels to choose from in town, the best of which is the new *Hôtel Tinghir* (☎ 871638), next to the CTM office. Clean singles/doubles cost Dr35/70 and a hot shower is Dr6. There's a decent cafe/restaurant downstairs.

Hôtel Bir Anazarane and *Hôtel Oued Dahab*, both on the roundabout opposite Banque Populaire, have very basic rooms for around Dr20/35. There is no shower in the Bir Anazarane and a cold one in the Dahab.

Further down Blvd Mohammed V you'll find the similarly priced *Hôtel la Jeunesse* and *Hôtel L'Ere Nouvelle*. The latter has a warm communal shower.

The one-star *Hôtel Salam* (☎ 872057), with a bar and restaurant, is the best mid-range choice but it's usually booked by the UN, making a room near impossible to get.

Also used by the UN but more likely to have vacancies, the newish *Bahia Hôtel*

GOULIMIME

PLACES TO STAY
1 Bahia Hôtel
5 Hôtel Tinghir
10 Hôtel Salam; Internet
13 Hôtel Oued Dahab
14 Hôtel Bir Anazarane
19 Hôtel L'Ere Nouvelle
20 Hôtel la Jeunesse

PLACES TO EAT
8 Café Le Diamant Bleue
9 Café de la Poste
15 Rotisserie al-Jawda
16 Rotisserie el-Menara
24 Café Ali Baba
25 Café Paloma

OTHER
2 Wafa Bank
3 Studio Colour
4 CTM Office; Cafe
6 Post Office
7 Petrol Station
11 Hammam
12 Mosque
17 Banque Populaire
18 BCdM
21 BMCE
22 Caid Dahman Takri's Palace Ruins
23 Grand Taxis to Asrir; Petit Taxis

To Buses & Grand Taxis (400m)
To Camel Market (2km) & Tan Tan (131km)
To Agadir (93km) & Tiznit (107km)
To Abainou (15km), Fort Bou Jerif (40km), Sidi Ifni (44km) & Plage Blanche (122km)

Ave Abaynou
Ave Hassan I
Route de Tan Tan
Blvd Mohammed V

0   50   100m
0   50   100yd

(☎ 772178, 31 Ave Abaynou) is a maze-like building with noisy courtyard-facing rooms and a roof terrace, it also has a restaurant. Rooms are a bit cell-like and therefore overpriced at Dr150/180.

Places to Eat

There are a couple of good rotisseries near the Hôtel Bir Anazarane – it's a toss-up between *Rotisserie al-Jawda* and *Rotisserie el-Menara*. A filling meal of chicken, chips and salad costs around Dr30 at both.

Something more like a restaurant, and with the usual Moroccan fare, is the *Café de la Poste*, opposite the post office. A full meal here costs about Dr50.

Similar food is on offer at the *Café le Diamant Bleue* and in the cafe below the *Hôtel Tinghir*. There's a reasonably priced restaurant, as well as the town's only (stark and seedy) bar, at the *Hôtel Salam*.

The most pleasant cafes are *Café Ali Baba* and *Café Paloma*, both with terraces, about 500m south of the main roundabout.

Getting There & Away

Bus The CTM office and station is on the Agadir road. The main bus and grand taxi stations are about 1km north of the town centre.

CTM has several daily buses to Agadir (Dr45, 4½ hours) departing at 8 pm and one to Casablanca (Dr178, 14 hours) via Marrakesh (Dr118, 9½ hours) at 8 pm. There's a 12.30 am run to Dakhla (Dr266, 15½ hours) via Laayoune (Dr140, seven hours) and a 6.30 am bus to Tan Tan (Dr34, three hours).

There are plenty of local buses to the same destinations, offering reasonable alternatives and more regular choices.

Grand Taxi Grand taxis leave from behind the bus station north-east of the centre. You can get a taxi to Sidi Ifni (Dr20), Tiznit (Dr30), Tan Tan (Dr36), Inezgane (Dr52) and Laayoune (Dr130). Grand taxis to Asrir leave from a spot south of the centre.

AROUND GOULIMIME
Fort Bou Jerif

Well worth getting to if you have your own transport is *Fort Beau Jerif* (fax 08-873039), a wonderful oasis of civilisation in the desert about 40km north-west of Goulimime (the last 5km is rough piste).

Built near a ruined military fort and run by a very welcoming French couple, Fort Bou Jerif has motel/hotel-style doubles for Dr150/300, hot communal showers, plenty of camping space (Dr20), a room for groups, beds in comfortable nomad tents (Dr30), a superb restaurant (Dr160 for a set menu) and good French wine.

Fort Bou Jerif also offers 4WD trips to **Plage Blanche**, a little-visited and unspoiled stretch of beach 80km further south of the fort, as well as donkey treks in the area.

Abainou

About 15km north of Goulimime, on the road to Sidi Ifni, is the tiny oasis village of Abainou, where you can bathe in hot springs. There are separate round bathing pools for men and women. Entry costs Dr5. The water is said to be very beneficial, especially for the skin. There's a basic camp site here, which costs Dr5 per person, Dr5 for a car and Dr3 for a tent.

Hôtel Abainou is a fairly comfortable place with doubles (and cold communal showers) for Dr100 including breakfast. The hotel has a restaurant and bar. There are a couple of simple cafes in the village too.

Aït Bekkou

About 17km south-east of Goulimime, Aït Bekkou is a pleasant oasis village – you'll probably see more camels here than in Goulimime on a Saturday, but don't fall for the old 'Berber market, today only' story.

From Goulimime you can get grand taxis as far as Asrir (Dr6), but you may well have to hitch the remaining 7km of piste to Aït Bekkou. Alternatively, you could hire a taxi for the day.

If you want to stay overnight, the midrange *Hôtel Tighmert* has clean, comfortable rooms.

TAN TAN
☎ 08 • pop 50,000

Taking the road south-west from Goulimime, you soon get the feeling you're head-

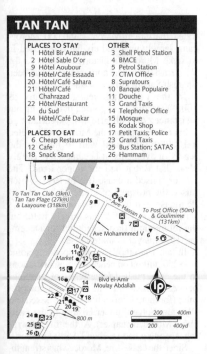

TAN TAN

PLACES TO STAY	OTHER
1 Hôtel Bir Anzarane	3 Shell Petrol Station
2 Hôtel Sable D'or	4 BMCE
9 Hôtel Aoubour	5 Petrol Station
19 Hôtel/Café Essaada	7 CTM Office
20 Hôtel/Café Sahara	8 Supratours
21 Hôtel/Café	10 Banque Populaire
Chahrazad	11 Douche
22 Hôtel/Restaurant	13 Grand Taxis
du Sud	14 Telephone Office
24 Hôtel/Café Dakar	15 Mosque
	16 Kodak Shop
PLACES TO EAT	17 Petit Taxis; Police
6 Cheap Restaurants	23 Grand Taxis
12 Cafe	25 Bus Station; SATAS
18 Snack Stand	26 Hammam

To Tan Tan Club (3km),
Tan Tan Plage (27km)
& Laayoune (318km)

Ave Hassan II
To Post Office (50m)
& Goulimime
(131km)

Ave Mohammmed V

Market

Blvd el-Amir
Moulay Abdallah

800 m

0   200   400m
0   200   400yd

ing well into the unknown – few travellers get this far.

The 125km of desert highway is impressive in parts, but this is harsh hammada rather than the soft, sandy type of dunes. Breaking up the monotony, the road also crosses several rivers, including the Oued Drâa, which is usually dry this far away from its sources.

You could drive through the main street of Tan Tan and not realise you had missed most of the town, which spreads south of the highway (known as Blvd Hassan II within the town boundaries).

Tan Tan is in what was once part of Spanish-occupied Morocco, an area known under the Spaniards as Tarfaya, which stretched south to the border of the former Spanish Sahara, a colony Spain abandoned only in 1975 (see Tarfaya in the Western Sahara section later).

The Tarfaya zone was handed over in 1958, two years after independence.

There's nothing much to do in Tan Tan, although it has quite a busy air about it. There's a fairly high army and police presence due to the proximity of the disputed Western Sahara. If you are heading south, it makes a convenient overnight stop.

Information
There's a BMCE bank next to the Shell petrol station, where Ave Mohammed V runs into Blvd Hassan II, and a Banque Populaire on the first square heading down Ave Mohammed V away from Blvd Hassan II.

The post office is east along Blvd Hassan II. There's a telephone office on the main square and several téléboutiques scattered around town. Tan Tan's weekly souq takes place on Sunday.

In June the Moussem of Sidi Mohammed Ma el-Ainin is a religious festival where the guedra dance is performed.

Places to Stay & Eat
There are plenty of cheap hotels in Tan Tan, so you should have no trouble finding a bed. The best hotel around the bus station square, south of the centre, is the *Hôtel/Café Dakar* (☎ 877245). Singles/doubles cost Dr50/60, or Dr80/100 with shower.

The others here, and in the side lanes heading north along Ave Mohammed V, are basic places costing about Dr30 to Dr40 per person. Most offer cold showers at best, but can direct you to a hammam (there's one near the bus station).

There are several more such hotels on the main square. Here you can try the *Hôtel/Restaurant du Sud*, *Hôtel/Café Chahrazad*, *Hôtel/Café Sahara* or *Hôtel/Café Essaada*. They all have cafes or restaurants downstairs. The *Hôtel Aoubour*, on Ave Hassan II, is more convenient for people with their own transport, but it's no great shakes.

Hôtel Bir Anzarane (☎ 877834), west along Ave Hassan II, has rooms for Dr50 per person (shared hot showers), but is well overpriced.

The best hotel in town by a long chalk is the new *Hotel Sable D'or* (☎ 878069, *Ave Hassan II*). Enormous rooms with bathroom and some with balcony cost Dr100/150.

There's a terrace, comfy beds and good hot showers.

Another option for a similar price, *Tan Tan Club* (☎ 878895), on the road to Laayoune, has large, clean rooms. There's a reasonable restaurant (though the same food in town will cost a lot less) and a popular cafe.

Getting There & Away

Bus All buses leave from the bus station, about 1km south of the main central square.

CTM and SATAS are the best companies operating buses from here, although a lot of the services are 'through-runs' from other towns. There are plenty of local buses. Services include Laayoune (Dr100, four hours), Casablanca (Dr170, 16 hours), Agadir (Dr70, 7½ hours) and Marrakesh (Dr170, 12 hours).

Grand Taxi Grand taxis to Laayoune, Tan Tan Plage (Dr10) and, occasionally, Tarfaya leave from a small square off Blvd el-Amir Moulay Abdallah. Others, for Goulimime (Dr36), Tiznit, Inezgane and Agadir (Dr70), leave from a lot by the bus station.

AROUND TAN TAN
Tan Tan Plage

About 27km west of Tan Tan is the beach of the same name. It's a rather uninspiring little spot, with a few cafes among the scruffy housing and public buildings. With the main business being fish exports, the port area does nothing to improve the atmosphere on the beach.

Western Sahara

What the Moroccan tourist brochures refer to as the Saharan provinces largely comprise the still-disputed territory of the Western Sahara. This covers the former Spanish colonies of Spanish Sahara and part of Tarfaya.

Abandoned by Spain in 1975, Morocco and Mauritania both raised claims to the sparsely populated desert territory, but the latter soon bailed out. This left Rabat to fight the rebel group, Polisario, which had contributed to Madrid's decision to abandon the phosphate-rich region in the first place.

In November 1975 King Hassan II orchestrated the Green March – 350,000 Moroccans, largely unarmed civilians, marched in to stake Morocco's historical claims to the Western Sahara. The border of what had been Spanish Sahara ran just south of Tarfaya.

In the following years, as many as 100,000 troops were poured in to stamp out resistance. As Polisario lost Algerian and Libyan backing, and the Moroccans erected a 1600km-long sand wall to hamper the rebels' movements, it became increasingly clear that Rabat had the upper hand. The UN organised a cease-fire in 1991, which raised the prospect of a referendum to settle the issue of the Western Sahara region's status. The cease-fire has largely held, but the referendum (last scheduled for December 1999) is yet to materialise.

In late 1996 the UN, after spending some US$250 million on peace-keeping operations in the area, pushed for a series of meetings between parties in a bid to reach a compromise (for more information see the boxed text 'Western Sahara' under History in the Facts about Morocco chapter). At the time of writing, spending had reached US$400 million.

Since the cease-fire, Morocco has strengthened its hold on the territory, pouring money into infrastructure projects and expanding the city of Laayoune. Moroccans from the north have been enticed to move down by the prospect of employment and tax-free living (hence the cheap petrol – the first of the Atlas Sahara petrol stations is just outside Tarfaya and about 240km south of Tan Tan). To all intents and purposes, Morocco appears to have succeeded in its claim to the territory, largely due to the world community being too preoccupied by crises elsewhere and foreign diplomats questioning the legitimacy and practicality of Polisario's independence demands. Despite this, Western Saharans maintain an independent air, patiently awaiting the referendum and referring to Morocco as a separate country. The people also look different, with the women wearing sari-like material wrapped around them and the men wearing the blue robes of the nomads.

Although there have been outbreaks of violence (which do continue on a small scale) the area is pretty safe and the presence of the UN means that many people speak English as well as Spanish and French.

Apart from the endless police roadblocks and checks (where foreigners must fill in a form stating their nationality, profession, destination etc), going south to Dakhla is now a routine affair, and it has been possible to cross into Mauritania in convoy since the running of the 1994 Paris-Dakar rally.

As part of a drive to attract Moroccans into the Western Sahara, many items are tax free. This includes petrol, which costs a couple of dirham less per litre than is the case elsewhere in the country.

Although there are plenty of téléboutiques available for national calls, international calls can only be made from government telephone offices and top-end hotels (at premium rates).

TAN TAN TO TARFAYA

The 235km drive from Tan Tan to Tarfaya takes you across a relatively monotonous stretch of desert highway. The road, however, is reasonably good and traffic is relatively light – just the occasional lorry and pale yellow or Saharan-blue taxis stuffed with turbaned passengers.

Along the route you'll see angler's huts perched on the cliff tops (many of these anglers sell their catch by the roadside) and further south, herds of camels wandering slowly through the hammada.

Around 150km south-west of Tan Tan is the tiny roadside village of **Sidi Akhfennir**, which has a string of mechanics workshops and several cafes serving fish straight from the sea. The area just north of Tarfaya is extremely scenic, with wild, untouched beaches and a series of shipwrecks clearly visible from the road.

The raggedy little coastal town of **Tarfaya** is unlikely to hold anyone's attention for long. Near Cap Juby, it was the second-largest town in the Spanish-controlled zone of the same name, but started life late in the 19th century as a minor British trading post.

The population of the surrounding area is largely nomadic, and the town itself boasts a small fishing industry.

Possibly the most interesting thing about the town is the unusual building stuck well out from the beach amid the breakers. Known as **Casamar** (from *casa del mar*, house in the sea), it was once a British trading house.

Otherwise, there is a monument to the French pilot and writer Antoine de Saint-Exupéry (perhaps best known for his children's story *The Little Prince*), one of several aviators who, in the interwar years, used the town as a stopover on the French air-mail service between Toulouse and Dakar. In fact he used Tarfaya as the setting for another of his books, *The Sand and the Stars*.

At the time of writing, Tarfaya's only hotel was closed; there are, however, plenty of places to pitch a tent or park a camper van. There are a few simple *cafes* offering standard Moroccan meals.

There are occasional buses and grand taxis linking Tarfaya to Tan Tan and Laayoune, but they are infrequent; the CTM bus whizzes by without stopping.

LAAYOUNE
☎ 08 • pop 120,000

Laayoune (also known as Al-'Uyun), was once a neglected Spanish administrative town, but has been transformed out of all recognition since the Moroccans took it back in 1975. Although you'll still see the odd street name posted as a 'calle', little evidence of the Spanish presence remains. With the population mostly outsiders – it is Morocco's showpiece in the Western Sahara.

The 115km road south from Tarfaya is unexciting, cut by the occasional dry riverbed and occasionally awash with sand. There are few beaches to speak of, with the desert simply dropping away in sheer cliffs into the ocean below. About 65km north of Laayoune, in the Tah depression (55m below sea level), there is a monument commemorating both a visit this far south by Sultan Moulay al-Hassan I back in 1885 (probably on an expedition to punish unruly tribes and extract taxes) and Hassan II's 'return' on a visit 100 years later.

There is not an awful lot to see in Laayoune itself, although the atmosphere is odd enough to make a stay of a day or two

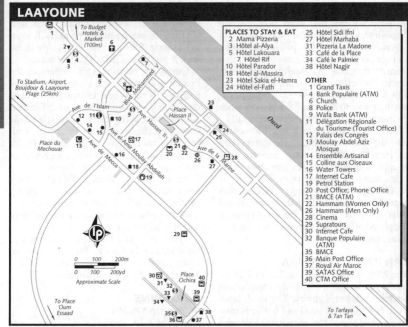

LAAYOUNE

PLACES TO STAY & EAT
2 Mama Pizzeria
3 Hôtel al-Alya
5 Hôtel Lakouara
7 Hôtel Rif
10 Hôtel Parador
18 Hôtel al-Massira
23 Hôtel Sakia el-Hamra
24 Hôtel el-Fath
25 Hôtel Sidi Ifni
27 Hôtel Marhaba
31 Pizzeria La Madone
33 Café de la Place
34 Café le Palmier
38 Hôtel Najgir

OTHER
1 Grand Taxis
4 Bank Populaire (ATM)
6 Church
8 Police
9 Wafa Bank (ATM)
11 Délégation Régionale
   du Tourisme (Tourist Office)
12 Palais des Congrès
13 Moulay Abdel Aziz
   Mosque
14 Ensemble Artisanal
15 Colline aux Oiseaux
16 Water Towers
17 Internet Cafe
19 Petrol Station
20 Post Office; Phone Office
21 BMCE (ATM)
22 Hammam (Women Only)
26 Hammam (Men Only)
28 Cinema
29 Supratours
30 Internet Cafe
32 Banque Populaire
   (ATM)
35 BMCE
36 Main Post Office
37 Royal Air Maroc
39 SATAS Office
40 CTM Office

worthwhile. In any case, whether you're heading north or south, the distances involved are such that you'll almost have no choice but to sleep over for at least a night.

Orientation

Although the town's showpiece is the shiny new Place du Mechouar (where bored youths hang about at night), there is no really obvious centre. It's a very up and down town with the practical considerations, such as post and phone offices, banks and most hotels, somewhere along or near Ave Hassan II. There is a collection of budget hotels at the north-west end of town downhill in a lively market area.

Buses gather at offices along Ave de Mecca. Grand taxis north are on a square at the north-west end of Ave Hassan II, with several other stations scattered about town.

Information

Tourist Offices The Délégation Régionale du Tourisme (☎ 891694, fax 891695) is just

back from Ave de l'Islam, virtually across the road from the Hôtel Parador. It's open from 8.30 to 11.30 am and 2 to 6 pm weekdays. Apart from a couple of brochures, it has little to offer, but staff are anxious to please.

Money The BMCE has a branch on Place Hassan II, next to the post office. There is a Banque Populaire and a couple of other banks with ATMs up from the intersection of Ave Hassan II and Blvd Mohammed V. Other branches are dotted around town.

Post & Communications The post and phone offices are lumped together at the south-eastern end of Ave Hassan II, and are open from 8.30 am to noon and 2 to 6 pm weekdays (the phone office also opens Saturday and Sunday). There is another post office at Place Ochira and numerous téléboutiques. However, international calls can only be made from the phone office or top-end hotels.

There are a couple of Internet places in town, the first is near Hôtel Parador and the other next to Pizzeria la Madone, both charge Dr20 per hour.

Things to See & Do

The **Colline aux Oiseaux**, on the hill between the tourist office and Ave de Mecca, is a small aviary with some quite spectacular parrots and other birds. Unfortunately it's almost always shut.

The little domed workshops next to it house the **Ensemble Artisanal**. Mostly inhabited by silversmiths tinkering away, there is minimum pressure to buy.

Quite a few football matches are held at the **stadium** north-west of town, check locally to see who's playing. Otherwise it's fun just wandering around town. Then there's the kilometres of **dunes**, clearly visible from several vantage points in and around the city, spreading north and west of Laayoune. To get in among them, take a 4WD off the road to Tarfaya (the top-end hotels can organise trips). There are a few coastal lagoons with prolific **bird life** among the dunes north of town.

About 25km out along the road south-west to Boujdour and Dakhla is **Laayoune Plage**, a reasonable little beach. There is a simple camp site and Club Med has a few rooms for anglers. Apart from that, a few houses in the village of **Foum el-Oued** (a couple of kilometres inland) and the nearby port, there's nothing else here. There is a bus in summer but you may need to hire a taxi to get out here, or join the hitchers at the Boujdour road from Laayoune, near the stadium.

Hammams & Public Showers

There are hammams for men and women on Ave de la Marine, just east near the BMCE bank.

Places to Stay

All places in the top-end and mid-range categories may be block-booked by the UN – if you don't want to end up in a budget place, call ahead. At the budget end, you will probably find most of the guests are soldiers or policemen – there are a lot of them about.

Places to Stay – Budget

There is a simple *camp site* with minimal facilities at Laayoune Plage (see Things to See & Do).

All the hotels in this range charge around Dr31/42 for singles/doubles; some have good views across the (dry) river with a few dunes in sight. A number of them are quite basic and the best cleaning facility you can hope for is a cold, salty bore-water shower – luckily there are hammams nearby.

A collection of hotels on Ave Maître Salem Bida, out near the market north-west of the centre, includes *Hôtel La Victoire*, *Hôtel Atlas*, *Hôtel Tafilalet*, *Hôtel Inezgane* and *Hôtel Errimal Eddahabia*.

Similar places near Place Hassan II include *Hôtel Sakia el-Hamra*, *Hôtel el-Fath* and *Hôtel Sidi Ifni*. *Hôtel Rif*, near the church, has very clean rooms and great views.

Slightly better is *Hôtel Marhaba (Ave de la Marine)* on the continuation of Ave Hassan II. The rooms are clean and have a table, chair and wardrobe, but the mattresses are rather thin. There's a cafe and restaurant downstairs.

Places to Stay – Mid-Range & Top End

From the Hôtel Marhaba there is a huge leap in prices. The cheapest is *Hotel al-Alya* (✆ 890246, Rue Kadi el-Khalaoui) with singles/doubles for Dr120/150, but they're not really worth the extra cash.

Much better (and pricier still) is the *Hôtel Lakouara* (✆ 893378, Ave Hassan II). Rooms with private bathroom cost Dr291/355.

The least expensive of the top-end places is the *Hôtel Nagjir* (✆ 894168) on Place Ochira. Comfortable rooms cost Dr385/496 and the hotel has a restaurant.

The two top hotels, with bars, restaurants and pools, are *Hôtel al-Massira* (✆ 994848, fax 890962) and *Hôtel Parador* (✆ 892814). Both have all the facilities of expensive hotels, the latter with more character, and cost Dr800/950 and Dr900/1100 respectively.

Places to Eat

The cheapest (and probably best) place to hunt for food is around the budget hotel and market area. There are plenty of small *stalls* and simple *restaurants* selling the usual meat dishes, salads and good local fish. Dr25 should get you a filling meal.

There are a couple of pleasant cafes, *Café de la Place* and *Café le Palmier* on Place Ochira, and plenty of others scattered about town. *Pizzaria la Madone (☎ 993252, 141 Ave Chahid Bouchraya)* does good salad and pizzas and will deliver. *La Mama Pizzeria* also does pizza.

Getting There & Away

Air RAM (☎ 894071) has an office at 7 Place Ochira, next to the Hôtel Nagjir. It has six direct weekly flights to Casablanca (Dr1729, 1½ hours), three to Agadir (Dr817, one hour), two to Dakhla (Dr634, one hour) and two to Las Palmas (Dr1664, 45 minutes) in the Canary Islands.

Regional Air Lines (see the Getting Around chapter) has weekday services to Agadir.

Bus CTM, SATAS and Supratours are all on Ave de Mecca.

CTM has a bus to Dakhla at 8 am (Dr140.50, nine hours) and Agadir (Dr204, 11½ hours) via Tan Tan (3½ hours) and Tiznit at 4, 6 and 8 pm. The 4 pm bus continues to Casablanca (Dr325, 19 hours) via Marrakesh (Dr262, 15 hours).

Supratours has daily buses to Marrakesh (Dr262, 16 hours) at 3, 5.15 and 9.15 pm, Dakhla (Dr140.50) at 7.20 am and Smara (nine hours) at 1 pm.

Grand Taxi Grand taxis to Tan Tan, Goulimime and Inezgane (for Agadir) leave from a rank at the north-western end of Ave Hassan II. You might even be able to get one right through to Marrakesh.

Taxis to Boujdour, Smara and Dakhla leave from another lot (ask for the 'station taxis Boujdour') on the southern periphery of town. A red-and-white petit taxi there will cost you Dr5.

SMARA

About 240km east of Laayoune (245km south of Tan Tan) lies what the Office Na-

tional Marocain Tourisme (ONMT) brochure bluntly calls 'A Historic City'. The original town was established here on a Saharan caravan route a century ago. There's really very little left of the old town, except for the mosque. Kofi Annan visited Smara (also known as As-Smara) in November 1998 during his trip to try to resolve the Western Sahara conflict.

There are banks, a post office and a few hotels largely full of Moroccan soldiers and UN observers. Buses and taxis run between Smara, Laayoune and Tan Tan.

DAKHLA
☎ 08

Established by the Spanish in 1844 and formerly called Villa Cisneros, Dakhla (also known as Ad-Dakhla) is just north of the Tropic of Cancer on the end of a sandy peninsula stretching out 40km from the main coastline.

It's a very long, lonely 542km drive from Laayoune through endless hammada, and only worth the effort if you are making an attempt to get into Mauritania.

The place is crawling with soldiers, but with the threat posed by Polisario receding, there is little sense of danger.

Dakhla is easy to get around, with most hotels and cafes situated around the market. The place has a bit of a name for ocean fishing, and it's not a bad spot to take a surfboard either.

The tourist office (☎ 898388), at 1 Rue Tiris, is to the east of the CTM office and there are a couple of banks, including BMCE, on Blvd Mohammed V (no ATMs).

There are mechanics around town who can service vehicles before the trek south.

Places to Stay & Eat

There's a *camp site* 7km north of Dakhla that costs Dr10 per person plus charges for a car and tent. There are plenty of cheap hotels in town, but they can often be full of soldiers.

You'll find quite a few hotels near the market area, including the *Hôtel Sahara* and the *Hôtel Bahia*, which has a bar next door and sea views. Both have clean, basic rooms for around Dr30 per person. The nicest option, with complete sea frontage, is *Hôtel Miramar (☎ cell 01-612298)*. Rooms here are basic and cost Dr30 person, or Dr100 for a double with toilet and sea view. The hotel also has a restaurant looking out to sea and can be reached by turning down the road next to Hôtel Doums.

Dakhla's top hotel, the three-star *Hôtel Doums (☎ 898046, fax 898045, Ave el-Waha)*, has ordinary singles/doubles with shower, toilet and balcony for Dr230/280.

There are eateries throughout the market, a nice *cafe* with pagodas overlooking the seafront and a *restaurant* at Hôtel Miramar. There's also *Bar Juan*, next door to the Bahia, for bored overlanders to while away the hours – it also sells takeaway alcoholic drinks.

Getting There & Away

The airport is on the outskirts of town and a taxi to a hotel should cost Dr4. RAM (☎ 897049) on Ave des PTT, has three flights a week to Casablanca, one of them stopping in Agadir and two in Laayoune.

CTM, Supratours and SATAS have daily buses to Laayoune (Dr141, nine hours), Tan (Dr240, 13½ hours), Agadir (Dr380, 18 hours) and Marrakesh (Dr387, 25 hours) – tickets should be booked ahead.

Grand taxis cover the same destinations.

Mauritania Since the beginning of 1994, the border with Mauritania has, as far as Rabat is concerned, been open.

There are no buses doing this run, so you need to arrange transport (which would have to be good to cope with travelling on the Mauritanian side of the frontier). Once this is done you have to get a permit from the military in Dakhla (they won't be difficult to find if you ask around). Finally, you have to wait until a convoy (usually leaving Tuesday and Friday) of at least half a dozen vehicles is assembled. It is then escorted (in case of an attack by Polisario) 363km (five hours) to the frontier (through a minefield).

It is possible to have a Mauritanian visa issued in Rabat, but you are strongly advised to get one before arriving in Africa. French citizens can get a visa at the border when they enter Mauritania.

See under Land in the Getting There & Away chapter for more on the crossing into Mauritania.

Trekking

Morocco is truly blessed with great mountainous areas, many of which only see a handful of travellers every year and some remain almost totally unexplored by foreigners. The possibilities are endless and the scale of the challenges vary from strolls through the cedar forests of the Middle Atlas to gruelling climbs up long, steep, rocky slopes in the High Atlas. When December snows turn Jebel Toubkal (4167m), North Africa's highest peak, into a playground for winter mountaineers, Jebel Sarhro, at the edge of the Sahara, offers a completely contrasting trekking experience in a landscape of mud bricks, arid plateaus and sculptural rock formations. To the north, routes through the Rif Mountains should entice even the most laid-back traveller away from the cafes of Chefchaouen.

Not every trekking area or mountain range is covered in this chapter, but it will give you a taste of the trekking options in Morocco. After all, if you find yourself say, in the Beni-Snassen Mountains (south-east of Saidia), there is nothing to stop you finding a guide or a man with a mule and heading into the hills.

One of the undoubted highlights of trekking here are the village encounters with Berber people. Well off the tourist trail, their genuine hospitality and generosity is a highlight for many trekkers. Having a guide who can translate will enhance the experience.

PLANNING
When to Walk
With the right clothing and equipment you can trek in Morocco year-round, though spring and early autumn are the most pleasant times (see When to Trek in The High Atlas section). However, there are a couple of things to remember. December to mid-April is the best time to trek in the Jebel Sarhro. After the beginning of May the temperatures soar, water sources dry up and the arid land becomes the domain of snakes and scorpions. There's little water from then until December. Jebel Toubkal, and many of the peaks and high passes in the High

Highlights

* Exploring the wonderful rock formations of Bab n'Ali in the Jebel Sarhro
* Splashing through the deep water-filled gorges in the M'Goun Massif
* Experiencing the friendliness of remote Berber villages in the Atlas Mountains
* Watching Barbary apes in the cedar forests of the Rif Mountains
* Arriving at the summit of Jebel Toubkal, the highest mountain in North Africa

! Telephone numbers in Morocco have changed. For new codes and complete numbers, see the boxed text 'Changes to Telephone Numbers' on page 89.

Atlas, can be covered in snow until mid-June.

Unless you are well equipped for winter trekking (with crampons, ice axes etc) then it's impossible to walk Toubkal and Sarhro in one trip. If you want to do both, November would be your best bet for this, though the snows have often started to fall on Jebel Toubkal and the Sarhro will still be very hot. Most companies run Sarhro trips when Toubkal is snowed out.

TREKKING AREAS

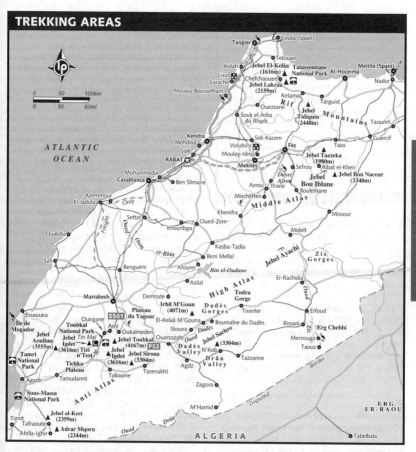

TREKKING

Dangers & Annoyances

Altitude sickness, caused by lack of oxygen, is a possibility at heights above 3000m. Symptoms can include headaches, nausea, dizziness, a dry cough and insomnia. Symptoms usually abate as you acclimatise, but if they persist or worsen you must descend immediately. Be sure to drink plenty of water, walking at a slow, steady pace will help the body acclimatise (see Environmental Hazards under Health in the Facts for the Visitor chapter for more information).

Be very wary of dogs you encounter; they seem to be particularly vicious around homesteads (see Rabies under both Predeparture Planning and Less Common Diseases under Health in the Facts for the Visitor chapter). Often the action of stooping down to pick up a stone is enough to ensure that dogs keep their distance. You are unlikely to be attacked, but if they are looking mean, face them as you back away from their territory and do not run. Try to intimidate them by shouting, throwing stones or waving a big stick.

Clubs

The Royal Moroccan Ski and Mountaineering Federation (☎/fax 02-474979), Le Ministère

The Treks & Maps

The treks covered in this chapter are hot off the boots of either Lonely Planet authors or experienced guides in the region. The Toubkal Massif, Imlil to Setti Fatma and Rif Mountains treks have been trekked personally by LP authors. The other treks suggested in this chapter are based on specialist trekking books as well as recommendations from experienced guides and trekking companies.

Special trekking route lines and symbols have been used on the maps throughout this chapter. Refer to the map legend at the back of the book for the list of trekking symbols.

de la Jeunesse et Sport, Parc de la Ligue Arabe (PO Box 158999), Casablanca, runs three basic refuges (see Accommodation later in this section) and can provide information for trekkers, climbers and skiers (*ski randonnée* or ski trekking seems to be a particular passion).

The Club Alpin Français (CAF; ☎ 02-270090, fax 297292), 1 Rue Aknoul, off Blvd Ziaoui, BP 6178, Casablanca, has five refuges in the Toubkal area, but it is not a great source of trekking information for non-members. See its Web site (www.clubalpin.com) for information in French.

Maps

Morocco is covered by a 1:100,000 and 1:50,000 topographical map series. However, some of the 1:50,000 series is unavailable to the public (coverage of the Jebel Sarhro, eastern High Atlas and Middle Atlas is patchy) and due to the restrictions placed upon map purchase travellers exploring wide areas are advised to stick to the 1:100,000 series.

The Conservation & Topography Department in Rabat (see Orientation under Rabat in the North Atlantic Coast chapter) stocks a range of topographical Moroccan maps and town plans.

However, security concerns mean that it's only possible to buy three maps at a time, and only of *some* areas – major trekking areas are usually among these. For additional maps, or maps covering suppos-

edly sensitive areas, you'll need to make a written request (in French), explaining who you are and why you want maps.

At this stage you can request as many maps as you like, but prepare for some requests to be turned down. A panel meets on Friday, so you'll get a decision on Friday afternoon or (more likely) Monday morning.

Most maps cost Dr70 a sheet. The office is open from 9 to 11.30 am and 3 to 5.30 pm weekdays. You must bring your passport for ID and be prepared for disappointment.

If you get no joy in Rabat, photocopied maps are sometimes available at Hôtel Ali in Marrakesh (see Guides & Mules later in this section for contact details) or in Imlil.

Alternatively, 1:200,000 Russian military survey maps printed in Cyrillic script are topographically accurate and cover the whole country. However, these can take six months to get hold of (from good map shops worldwide).

Useful specialist travel map and bookshops around the world include Stanford's (☎ 020-7836 1321, e sales@stanfords.co.uk), 12–14 Long Acre, London WC2E 9LP, Web site: www.stanfords.co.uk; Rand McNally in New York (☎ 212-758 7488), 150E, 52nd St or in San Francisco (☎ 415-777 3131), 595 Market St; Mapland (☎ 03-9670 4383), 372 Little Bourke St in Melbourne; or The Travel Bookshop (☎ 02-9241 3554), 20 Bridge St in Sydney. In Paris, see Ulysse (☎ 01 43 25 17 35), 26 rue Saint-Louis-en-Île, 75004 or Au Vieux Campeur (☎ 01 53 10 48 27), 2 rue de Latran, 75005.

Often the best source of maps, plus detailed information on trekking in Morocco generally, is Atlas Mountains Information Services (☎ 01592-873546), 26 Kirkcaldy Rd, Burntisland, Fife, Scotland KY3 9HQ.

Also in the UK, the map room of the Royal Geographical Society (☎ 020-7591 3050), 1 Kensington Gore, London SW7 2AR, has loads of Moroccan maps and is open to the public. Check its Web site: www.rgs.org.

Books

The Moroccan tourist office, Office National Marocain Tourism (ONMT), publishes an

Trekking in the High Atlas will give you an aerial view of lush farm terraces from Tizi n'Tichka (top); walks along the desolate ridge near Tizi n'Tichka (middle); and a perspective from more than 3000m at Tizi n'Ouanoums (3600m) in the Toubkal Massif (bottom).

Park your mule and enjoy a cup of mint tea at Bivi Thé, Tizi n'Tamatert in the Toubkal Massif.

Assif n'Timellite in the High Atlas is covered in snow until mid-July.

Useful Trekking Words

The following words will be helpful for your treks in Morocco. For definitions of other words, see the Glossary at the back of this book.

Key: (A) is for Arabic, (B) is for Berber.

adfel (B) – snow
adrar (B) – mountain, (plural idraren)
afella (B) – summit
agdal (B) – pasture (also aougdal)
aghbalu (B) – water spring
'ain (A) – water spring
aman (B) – water
anzar (B) – rain
argaz (B) – man
asserdoun (B) – mule
assif (B) – watercourse, river
azaghar (B) – plane, plateau (also izwghar)
azib (B) – temporary summer settlement (plural azerbane)
brhel (A) – mule
châba (B) – ravine
ifri (B) – cave
iferd (B) – lake
kerkour (B) – cairn
taddart (B) – house
talat (B) – dried up ravine or watercourse
tamada (B) – lake
tigm (B) – house
tizi (B) – col or pass

extremely useful booklet every year called *The Great Trek Through the Moroccan Atlas*. It contains a list of guides for various regions in the High and Middle Atlas, including Toubkal; lists of *gîtes* (trekkers accommodation), huts, refuges and the like and the names of their owners; a table of official prices for guides, mules, muleteers and porters; and a list of village market days. Recommended maximum fares on some of the public transport routes also appear. Marrakesh tourist office has the most reliable stock, but other major tourist offices should be able to help. French copies are usually available, but German and English translations are also made. Moroccan tourist offices abroad hold stock.

ONMT also publishes *Grauvres Rupestres du Haut Atlas* (which looks at the rock art of Plateau du Yagour, north-east of Setti Fatma), *Randonnées Pédestres Dans le Massif du Mgoun* and *Ski Dans le Haut Atlas de Marrakesh*. These are only available sporadically. Try the main tourist offices, bookshops in Marrakesh or the Club Alpin Français.

Most available trekking books concentrate on the High Atlas. These include Robin Collomb's *Atlas Mountains*, Michael Peyron's *Great Atlas Traverse*, Karl Smith's *The Atlas Mountains: A Walker's Guide* and Richard Knight's new *Trekking in the Moroccan Atlas*. The latter two have some coverage of the Jebel Sarhro (though Richard Knight's book is better than Smith's). Peyron's book, which is divided into two volumes (volume one covers the Toubkal region), is seen as the definitive text.

Mountaineers concentrating on the high peaks around Toubkal may appreciate *Le Massif du Toubkal* published in French by Belvisi/Edisud. *Trekking in Africa – A Guide to the Finest Routes* by Stefano Ardito, *Le Haut-Atlas* by André Fougerolles (published in French) are both coffee-table-hybrid books. *Le Haut-Atlas* is now a little out of date but it illustrates some wonderful trekking expeditions in the High Atlas.

What to Bring

Camping & Survival Gear A good tent opens up endless trekking possibilities and strong (well broken-in) walking boots are by far the best footwear. A waterproof and windproof outer layer is essential in any season. Light, baggy, cotton trousers and long-sleeve shirts are best in summer (June to August) but prepare for very cold weather during winter (November to March) throughout the country; outside the height of summer pack warm clothing, a woollen hat and gloves for the High Atlas. In summer, even at 1800m, it's cold enough at night to require a fleece or jumper. Likewise you'll need a sun hat, sunglasses and plenty of sunscreen year-round.

From autumn through to early spring (September to early April) a four-season sleeping bag is required for the High Atlas and Jebel Sarhro – temperatures as low as -10°C are not unknown at this time. In lower mountain ranges, and even in high summer, a bag comfortable at 0°C is advised. A thick sleeping mat or thin foam mattress is a good idea since the ground is extremely rocky.

Anyone attempting peaks over 3000m between November and May should have experience with winter mountaineering and be equipped with crampons, ice axes, snow shovels and other essential equipment.

Multi-fuel stoves that burn anything from aviation fuel to diesel are ideal. Methylated spirits is very hard to get hold of, but kerosene is available. Pierce-type butane gas canisters are available, but not recommended because of environmental reasons.

Bring a basic medical kit and a supply of water purification tablets or a mechanical purifier – all water should be treated unless you take it at the very source.

Accommodation

CAF has five refuges in the Toubkal/Oukaïmeden area, but officially bookings must be made in advance through its office in Casablanca (see Clubs under Information earlier in this section) or (a better bet) through Oukaïmeden Refuge (☎ 04-319036, fax 319020), PO Box 60137, Oukaïmeden. However, in practice you can usually find out if space is available at the other refuges in the Toubkal region by asking down in Imlil, though be warned that refuges are often packed full in July and August. Members of CAF and other affiliated and recognised alpine clubs and organisations get the cheapest price for a bed, followed by HI members and then everyone else. Children between 5 and 15 years get a 50% reduction.

The Royal Moroccan Ski and Mountaineering Federation has refuges at Oukaïmeden, on the south face of Irhil M'Goun and in the Jebel Bou Iblane in the Middle Atlas, 60km south of Taza.

However, the bulk of trekking accommodation in the High and Middle Atlas are gîtes or the homes of local people. In the Rif and little-walked Anti Atlas, gîtes are uncommon and a tent is essential.

Gîtes provide basic accommodation, often offering little more than a foam mattress in an empty room or on a roof terrace or balcony. They have basic bathrooms and toilets (cold showers only) and can usually rustle up a *tajine* (meat and vegetable stew) given enough notice. Accommodation is around Dr30 per person and a tajine for two would be about Dr50.

Food

Other than powdered milk, dried fruit and the occasional sachet of soup, dehydrated rations are not widely available in Morocco (try the hypermarkets in major cities) and you're well-advised to bring these from home.

If you want to rely on local foods then a diet of chocolate, tuna or sardines, bread and processed cheese is likely. By taking a mule you have the option to take bulkier, heavier (and more satisfying) local foodstuffs.

You may be able to buy bread, eggs and vegetables in some mountain villages, but don't count on it. Meals can be arranged in some villages (Dr30 per person is standard), though this shouldn't be relied upon. Basic supplies (eg, tinned tuna and tea) are available in some villages. See also Equipment & Supplies later in the High Atlas section.

Change money in the nearest major town and ensure that you have plenty of small notes. Suitable gifts to carry with you include foods such as dried fruits, Chinese gunpowder tea and sugar (preferably in large chunks).

Guides & Mules

Given the unavailability of good maps, guides are just about essential for sustained treks in most walking areas in Morocco. Mules to carry all your gear can easily be hired. Obviously, from a navigational point of view, those with considerable experience reading maps in mountain regions will not need a guide, but should seriously consider engaging one anyway. A guide will be your translator, chaperone (so *faux guides* – unofficial guides – won't come near you), deal-getter and vocal guidebook. They'll know people throughout the area, which will undoubtedly result in invitations for tea and food and greater experiences of Berber life. Never walk into the mountains on your own and remember a flash-looking English-speaking faux guide from Marrakesh is no substitute for a local mountain guide who knows the area like the back of his hand.

ONMT publishes a list of all official mountain guides in *The Great Trek Through the Moroccan Atlas*. There is a *bureau des guides* (guide office) in Imlil and at other trailheads you should be able to pick up a trained, official guide. Many guides for the High Atlas and Jebel Sarhro can also be contacted at the Hôtel Ali (☎ 04-444979, fax 433609, e kotelali@hotmail.com) in Marrakesh. Official guides have been trained in mountain craft, including first aid, and in times of uncertain weather or an emergency official guides will be better than some cheap local you picked up along the way. They all carry official photo identity cards – always ask to see it.

Some official guides specialise in canyoning, rock climbing, mountaineering and ski trekking. All guides speak French and a few speak English, Spanish and German.

Mules (and the odd donkey) are widely used in Morocco for transporting goods through the mountains. If you are relying on heavy local supplies or are in a large group, hiring a mule (which can carry the loads of four people) makes good sense. However, some routes are not suitable for mules, though detours (for the mule) are often possible. If high passes are covered in snow, porters may have to be used in place of mules (one porter can carry 18kg).

Check the current rates in *The Great Trek Through the Moroccan Atlas*. At the time of writing, the rate for official guides was Dr200 a day and Dr250 for specialist guides (eg, ski trekking or rock climbing). However, away from the Toubkal area many guides charge Dr250 a day.

A mule costs between Dr85 and Dr100 a day, and porters from Dr70 to Dr100 a day, depending on the season and the difficulty of the terrain. A cook would want Dr70 a day.

These rates apply to a normal working day, per guide *not* per person, and do not include food and accommodation expenses (though guides get free accommodation in refuges and gîtes). If you embark on a linear route you'll also be expected to pay for the return journeys of the people you employ.

'All-inclusive' deals where the guide provides all food and accommodation for a flat fee per person may be offered, but they are hardly ever a good deal (expect a diet of three-day-old bread, tinned sardines and La Vache Qui Rit cheese).

Before departure negotiate all fees (a 10% tip at the end is standard), and ask where accommodation will be sought, whether tents will need to be shared (most guides have tents or bivvy bags), what food is to be carried (plus your guide's food preferences) and the division of food and equipment between the group.

Don't hesitate to check the credentials of a would-be guide, and don't feel pressured to engage the services of the first person who comes along.

Organised Treks

There are now numerous foreign and Moroccan operators offering trekking tours in Morocco. Many concentrate on the High Atlas, but some bigger companies provide tours that get people trekking well off the beaten track. In fact, for areas like the Jebel Sarhro, some of these companies offer tours as cheap or almost as cheap as you could organise yourself (not including the price of the flight).

Marrakesh is the best place to find local tour operators (see Organised Tours under Marrakesh in the Central Morocco chapter). See also Organised Tours in the Getting There & Away chapter for foreign operators.

RESPONSIBLE TREKKING
Responsible Tourism

Morocco's mountainous regions are dotted with small villages and as the country's potential as a walking destination has only been lightly tapped, many remote regions are extremely susceptible to the cultural and environmental impact of tourism. Many travellers return home warmed and heartened by the hospitality of the Berber people and as the number of visitors increases, so does the pressure on the inhabitants. In response, travellers should adopt certain codes of behaviour.

TREKKING

Dress code is very important (see Dos & Don'ts under Society & Conduct in the Facts about Morocco chapter), especially in the deeply conservative societies of the hill tribes. Inside the villages, travellers should wear buttoned shirts (rather than T-shirts that are seen by villagers as underwear) and, above all, trousers (rather than shorts) for both men and women. The importance of dress in the villages cannot be overemphasised (as many a frustrated and embarrassed trekking tour leader will affirm). An effort to respect this tradition will bring greater rewards for the traveller, not least by way of hospitality and assistance.

In remote villages the drinking of alcohol is seen as offensive – don't do it.

As in other parts of Morocco, cameras can cause offence and, in some cases, upset people, particularly when pointed at women.

Invitations for tea and offers of food are common in the mountains, and by taking a guide (who may open yourself to even more offers of genuine hospitality. While these offers are unconditional, an offer of tea or some of your own food will be appreciated –it is worth bearing in mind that the mountain economy is one of basic subsistence farming and in outlying villages there may be little surplus food. It's therefore important to be generous when buying provisions for yourself and guides.

In order to avoid aggravating the persistent and serious problem of overgrazing in many of the regions, sufficient fodder (barley) for all baggage mules and donkeys should be brought. It is a good idea to inquire carefully about this before setting off.

Rubbish

Carry out all your rubbish, never bury it and don't burn it (Western-style packaging never burns well). Your guide may be happy to bag up all your rubbish then hurl it over a cliff, but if you've carried it in, then you can carry it out – this includes orange peel and cigarette butts. Empty packaging weighs very little anyway and should be stored in a dedicated rubbish bag. Make an effort to carry out rubbish left by others.

Discourage the presence of wildlife by not leaving food scraps behind you. Place gear out of reach and tie packs to rafters or trees.

Minimise the waste you'll carry out by taking minimal packaging and repackaging in reusable containers when appropriate.

Don't rely on bought water in plastic bottles. Disposal of these bottles is creating a major problem in Morocco. Use iodine drops or purification tablets instead.

Human Waste Disposal

Contamination of water sources by human faeces can lead to the transmission of hepatitis, typhoid and intestinal parasites such as giardiasis and amoebas. This is a particular problem in more populated trekking areas.

Where there is a toilet, please use it. Where there is none, bury your waste. Dig a small hole 15cm (6 inches) deep and at least 100m from any watercourse. Consider carrying a lightweight trowel for this purpose. Cover the waste with soil and a rock. Use toilet paper sparingly, burn it when possible or bury it with the waste. In snow, dig down to the soil; otherwise, your waste will be exposed when the snow melts.

Washing

Don't use detergents or toothpaste in or near watercourses, even if they are biodegradable.

For personal washing, use biodegradable soap at least 50m away from the watercourse. Disperse the waste water widely to allow the soil to filter it fully before it finally makes its way back to the watercourse.

Use a scourer, sand or snow to wash cooking utensils rather than detergent. Again, make sure you're 50m from any watercourse.

Erosion

Hillsides and mountain slopes, especially at high altitudes, are prone to erosion. Stick to existing tracks and avoid short cuts that bypass a switchback. If you blaze a new trail straight down a slope, it will turn into a watercourse with the next heavy rainfall and eventually cause soil loss and deep scarring.

If a well-used track passes through a mud patch, walk through the mud: walking around the edge will increase the size of the patch.

Avoid removing the plant life that keeps topsoils in place.

Low-Impact Cooking & Camping

Don't depend on open fires for cooking. The cutting of wood for fires in Morocco has caused widespread deforestation. Ideally, cook on a lightweight multi-fuel or kerosene stove and avoid those powered by disposable butane gas canisters.

Ensure that you fully extinguish a fire after use. Spread the embers and douse them with water. A fire is only truly safe to leave when you can comfortably place your hand in it.

When camping, minimise your impact on the environment by not removing or disturbing the vegetation around your camp site – vegetation at high altitude is highly sensitive. However, in the High Atlas your camp sites are likely to simply be flat rocky areas.

The High Atlas

The highest mountain range in North Africa, the High Atlas runs diagonally across Morocco, from the Atlantic coast north-east of Agadir all the way to northern Algeria, a distance of almost 1000km. In Berber they're called Idraren Draren (Mountains of Mountains). There are several summits higher than 4000m and more than 400 above 3000m. The Toubkal region contains all the highest peaks of the High Atlas, and is the most frequently visited area of the High Atlas – it's only two hours from Marrakesh and is easily accessible by public transport.

The area is bordered by the Tizi n'Test to the west and the Tizi n'Tichka to the east, the two mountain passes that lead to Marrakesh. In the western High Atlas, the beautiful Tichka Plateau and uncrowded valleys are a great attraction, while the M'Goun Massif, some 260km east of Marrakesh, offers some fantastic, challenging trekking through a gorge-scarred landscape, including the ascent of Irhil M'Goun (4071m), Morocco's second highest mountain and the highest in the massif.

Climbers may appreciate the gorges surrounding this peak, while the cliffs of Taza-

ghart in the Toubkal Massif are deservedly popular. However, the Todra Gorge in the south-east of the High Atlas arguably provides the best rock climbing in the country.

Ski-trekking is becoming popular around Jebel Toubkal and Jebel Azourki (3682m) in the M'Goun Massif, though the season is short (late December to early February).

Although wild and harsh, the area has long been inhabited by the Atlas Berbers. Their flat-roofed, earthen villages cling tenaciously to the mountain sides while irrigated terraced gardens and walnut groves flourish below. The entire area is crisscrossed with well-used mule trails – some of which undoubtedly carried ancient trade caravans and pilgrims between the Sahara and the northern plains.

NATURAL HISTORY

Spectacularly rugged and sparsely vegetated, the mountains are characterised by terraced cliffs, enormous escarpments, deep gorges and flat-topped summits. The deeply dissected range exposes a thick sequence of sedimentary and volcanic rocks intersected with granite intrusions. The predominant rock is Jurassic limestone and the oldest rocks are the 610 million-year-old granites and granodiorites of the Ourika region (near Setti Fatma). Some minor glaciation also took place around 45,000 years ago.

The incredibly green, terraced and irrigated mountainsides of these valleys are a breathtaking sight. For generations local people have used systems of small channels (*targa* in Berber), to move irrigation water from rivers and streams.

In the lower valleys, almonds and apricots are grown along with subsidiary crops of carob, quince, pomegranates, apples, cherries and figs. Vegetable plots include potatoes, carrots, turnips, onions, lentils and beans. In October much of the terraces are ploughed for barley, which is harvested in late May or June. Walnuts are also a major crop in higher villages and are harvested in late September.

Overgrazing, agriculture and the collection of wood for fuel has had a tremendous impact on the vegetation of the High Atlas and much of the indigenous vegetation has

TREKKING

disappeared. In the sub-alpine zone (2400m to 3200m) you'll see thickets of Spanish juniper *(Juniperus thurifer)* – thick, gnarled trees often blasted into extraordinary shapes by the wind; higher up many 'hedgehog plants' – spiny, domed bushes adapted to dry conditions that burst into flower for a short time in the spring. Herbs such as lavender, rosemary and thyme are common.

Big mammals are not common in the High Atlas, though mouflons (a mountain sheep with big horns), wild boars and gazelles are found in some areas. Wildlife includes Moorish geckos, Iberian wall lizards and painted frogs. Birds of the sub-alpine zone include crimson-winged finches and Moussier's redstarts and, in wooded areas, Levaillant's green woodpeckers. Crows are omnipresent and you'll sometimes catch a glimpse of majestic raptors such as lammergeiers, Egyptian vultures and golden eagles.

Small snakes are quite common but they are often dispatched by guides before you get a chance to look at them.

WHEN TO WALK

It's possible to trek throughout the year in the High Atlas, though temperatures can drop below freezing above 2000m between November and May when snow covers the higher peaks and passes. Therefore April to late June is the ideal time to visit. In spring (April to May) alpine flowers will be in bloom and daytime temperatures are pleasantly warm.

Midsummer guarantees long daylight hours and snow-free passes, but in the lower valleys temperatures can be extremely hot and water non-existent. Rivers have maximum flow in autumn (November) and in late spring (April or May) after the winter snows have melted. Though many rivers are reduced to a trickle by midsummer, the area can be subject to flash flooding in summer after tremendous thunderstorms. In August 1995, an unusually heavy rainstorm caused massive flooding and extensive damage in both the Mizane and Ourika Valleys.

Despite the heat, July and August are also the busiest months for visitors to both Marrakesh and the High Atlas.

Jebel Toubkal can be ascended in winter if you have winter climbing experience and full alpine gear.

Toubkal Circuit via Lac d'Ifni

Duration 7–9 days
Distance 66.5km
Standard medium to hard
Start/Finish Imlil village
Highest Point Jebel Toubkal (4167m)
Nearest Large Town Marrakesh
Accommodation camping, village gîte & mountain refuges
Public Transport yes
Summary Easily accessible from Marrakesh, this circuit around Jebel Toubkal, North Africa's highest peak (which can be climbed), passes through a variety of landscapes ranging from lush, cultivated valleys and Berber villages to forbidding peaks and bleak high passes. This is a demanding trek due to long, gruelling climbs and rocky terrain, and unless you're highly experienced, a guide is essential.

Apart from majestic peaks and fabulous views, this route offers a fascinating glimpse into High Atlas village life with sections of the trek following rich river valleys that have been intensively cultivated for centuries. Imlil, in the heart of the Mizane Valley, is the most popular trailhead in Morocco (the base of Jebel Toubkal is only a four- or five-hour trek south from here). Transport is good and businesses are geared up for trekkers. There's accommodation and guides, making it the best launching point for treks in the area. However, despite the reasonable popularity of the circuit, walkers are unlikely to encounter many other trekkers and the tourist atmosphere of Imlil is soon left behind.

Tents and camping gear are required, though some stages offer the option of staying in basic village accommodation or mountain refuges (gîtes). Since the trek is fairly strenuous, you could include an extra rest day, though there are options for cutting the trek short. Indeed, if the following seems too much, there is always the simple and popular two-day ascent of Toubkal from Imlil (see the Jebel Toubkal Ascent later in this section).

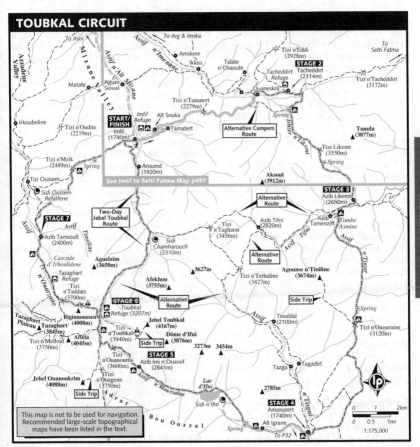

TOUBKAL CIRCUIT

This map is not to be used for navigation. Recommended large-scale topographical maps have been listed in the text.

1:175,000

Most of the route is above 2000m with several high passes over 3000m. The ascent of Jebel Toubkal takes place on the sixth day, allowing five days of acclimatisation.

The circuit detailed below has been described as a spring or summer walk. Numerous other trekking routes to the east, south, west and north emanate from this outline.

PLANNING
Days Required

The walk described later requires a minimum of eight days, but the circuit could easily be shortened or lengthened. From Azib Likemt

it's possible to head west to Sidi Chamharouch (on the main Imlil-Toubkal route) via Tizi n'Tagharat (3465m), thus creating a three-day circuit from Imlil (spending the second night at Azib Tifni) or saving a day on the way to Toubkal. By missing out the trek over Tizi n'Taddate to the Tazaghart Refuge after ascending Toubkal, you'd save two days. Likewise there are many options for extending the trek, either by peak bagging or exploring side routes (such as the Tazaghart Plateau). Experienced mountain guides (and experienced trekkers) can customise routes to suit time, ability and conditions.

Maps & Books

The 1:50,000 sheet map *Jebel Toubkal* covers the whole Toubkal Circuit. Occasionally you can get hold of the clearer and more accurate 1994 edition.

For exploration further east to Oukaïmeden, you'd be advised to get hold of the 1:100,000 sheet map *Oukaïmeden-Toubkal* (which also covers the circuit). Sheets *Amizmiz* and *Tizi n'Test* (both 1:100,000) cover routes west to Ijoukak and Tin Mal on the Tizi n'Test road.

These topographical maps of the Toubkal region (UK£16 for a set of four) can usually be found at Stanford's in London (see Maps under Information earlier in this section).

Permits

No permits are required for walking in the High Atlas, though CAF refuges must be booked in advance. Current advice suggests that this is best done via the very good *CAF Refuge* (☎ 04-319036, fax 319020) in Oukaïmeden. You could try the Toubkal Refuge warden's two unreliable cellphones (☎ 01-655133, 01-624981). The CAF Web site has full details (in French), check it out at www.clubalpin.com.

Always obtain permission from landowners before setting up camp anywhere near a village.

Equipment & Supplies

Although basic food supplies are available in Imlil, it's best to bring some from Marrakesh – there'll be more variety and prices will be lower. Bread, eggs, meat and some fresh fruit and vegetables can be picked up in Imlil and from some villages along the route. A large weekly souq is held in Asni (at the turn-off to Imlil) every Saturday, so some fresh food supplies could be obtained there.

Petrol, diesel and kerosene can be bought in Asni, but if you have to use pierce-type gas canisters, buy them in Marrakesh.

Anyone attempting Toubkal or any of the other 3000m-plus peaks between November and May should have experience with winter mountaineering. A limited number of crampons (Dr40), ice axes (Dr15) and skis (Dr150) can be hired in Imlil (all fees are per day).

Guides & Mules

You don't need a guide if you just want to ascend Toubkal, but if you're going further afield then you will need to engage one and possibly also a mule to cart your gear. Imlil is by far the best place to do this. There is a small bureau des guides on the village square that has a list of official guides, complete with mugshots. In the past few years, several young Moroccan women have succeeded in breaking into the previously all-male world of mountain guiding, but their services, and those of English-speaking and specialist guides, are in high demand. In addition, guides work in rotation, so if you have specific needs, try to organise a guide in advance – of the 60 official guides based in the Toubkal area, only 10 or so may be in Imlil at any one time.

It's rarely a problem to organise mules, but trekkers should be aware that these animals are unable to cross Tizi n'Ouanoums east of Lac d'Ifni, or Tizi n'Taddate between the Toubkal and Tazaghart refuges. Lengthy detours will need to be made and you may be left to carry one day's kit and food. Talk this through with your guide and muleteer.

Those starting from the Ourika Valley could ask for Lahcen Izahan at the Café Azagya, about 2km before the village of Setti Fatma (on the Marrakesh side), who also knows the Atlas like the back of his hand.

Allow a day or so to hire a guide and make the required trekking arrangements.

NEAREST TOWNS
Asni

The roadside village of Asni is only really worth a stop if you're around for the large Saturday souq (don't miss the barbers with their fold-away salons) or in need of a *hammam* (traditional bathhouse) after a long dusty trek. The large numbers of tourists and travellers of all types coming through here over the years have turned it into a minor den of iniquity.

Stay overnight if you must, but don't organise anything that even sounds like a trek. It may have been OK once, but there are now some very cheeky people ripping serious amounts of money off innocent travellers.

If you want to stay the night at Asni there is a **Youth Hostel** at the far end of the village, which has clean beds for Dr20 a night. You'll need your own sleeping bag.

There are several roadside *cafes* outside the entrance to the market, which serve cheap Moroccan dishes.

Buses and taxis leave here for Bab er-Rob in Marrakesh. You can also pick up the odd bus heading the other way to Ouirgane and Ijoukak. See Getting There & Away under Imlil later in this section for details of the Asni to Imlil leg.

Imlil
☎ 04

In 1996 Imlil was the scene of positive excitement when Martin Scorcese turned up with a massive film crew to shoot scenes for his movie *Kundun* about the life of the Dalai Lama. The snow-covered High Atlas doubled as Himalayan peaks and the kasbah on the hill north of the village was made to look like a Tibetan Buddhist temple. The 'India-Tibet border' was halfway down the Imlil road.

Places to Stay & Eat At Imlil, the trailhead, there are several accommodation options. The **CAF Refuge** in the village square offers basic dorm-style accommodation for Dr24 (CAF members), Dr39 (HI members) and Dr52 (nonmembers), plus there's a common room with an open fireplace, cooking facilities (Dr5 for use of gas), cutlery and crockery. You can camp here for Dr12 per tent plus Dr6 per person. Bookings for refuges elsewhere in the region cannot be made from here.

Café Aksoual on the main street virtually opposite the CAF has fairly basic rooms for Dr30. The showers are cold.

Hôtel el-Aïne (☎ 485625) offers good deals on rooms: Dr40 per person for comfortable, bright rooms gathered around a tranquil courtyard. Hot showers are included, but prices rise in midsummer. You can sleep on the roof in summer for Dr10 (plus Dr10 per hot shower) and apartments are available from Dr100. *Café de la Source* below the hotel serves some reasonable food.

Café Soleil (☎ 485622) on the village square also charges Dr40 per person for a foam mat on the floor (hot showers included). The *restaurant* on the terrace overlooking the river offers good tajines and the like.

There are a number of small restaurants all offering standard Moroccan meals from around Dr30. *Café Imouzar* just off the square has cheap, excellent eats.

Hôtel Etoile de Toubkal (☎ 485618) charges Dr90/136/190/280 for reasonable singles/doubles/triples/quads with balcony – some have bathroom. Below is a *restaurant* offering a set menu for Dr70 and main courses of Moroccan fare for Dr40 to Dr50. There's a pleasant little cafe next door – *Le Jardin d'Imlil*. The hotel and the cafe are owned by the same people who can change money and rent basic winter mountaineering equipment.

There's also a *bakery* and quite a few small *grocery shops* well-stocked with basic goods such as dried fruit, nuts, olive oil, instant coffee, tins of sardines, processed cheese, powdered milk and biscuits. You can buy cigarettes in the village, but not alcohol. You'll need to carry food with you when trekking, so you can either stock up here, or in Marrakesh where provisions are cheaper and more plentiful.

Discovery Ltd, a UK company that specialises in small group trips to the High Atlas, has restored **Kasbah du Toubkal** (☎ 485611, fax 485636, e kasbah@discover.ltd.uk) on the hill above Imlil. Beds are available in three large rooms that have dorm space on mezzanine floors above comfortable Moroccan-style *salons* (rooms) for Dr300 per person, full board. Luxurious double rooms are Dr600 per person full board. Meals here are excellent.

Just out of Imlil on the road to Ouaneskra are two other places. The first is the simple and friendly *Gîte d'Etape* (☎ 485616). A bed here will cost you Dr30 per person (hot showers Dr10). *Demi-pension* (half board) is Dr80.

Next up is *Chez Jean Pierre* (☎/fax 485609), which is far more hotel-like and has four simple, clean rooms and a recommended restaurant. Half board costs Dr135 per person.

TREKKING

Getting There & Away The Toubkal area of the High Atlas is just over 60km south of Marrakesh, from where you'll glimpse the snowcapped peaks in winter. Frequent local buses (Dr10, 1½ hours) and *grand taxis* (shared taxis; Dr15, one hour) leave when full from Bab er-Rob in Marrakesh (the city gate near the Saadian Tombs south of the medina) to the village of Asni, 47km south of Marrakesh along the S501 (this road continues over the Tizi n'Test to Taroudannt and then on to Agadir). Local pick-up trucks travel the final 17km between Asni and Imlil (Dr15 to Dr20, one hour), the trailhead for Jebel Toubkal and this circuit.

The dirt road to Imlil is in very poor condition so it's slow going (about one hour). The scenery, however, is spectacular, as the road climbs steadily up into the fertile Mizane Valley. If you're lucky, the journey from Marrakesh to Imlil will take two hours.

Around Imlil

Aroumd A 30-minute walk south of Imlil is the village of Aroumd, which is surrounded by extensive orchards and terraced fields. Several trekking companies use Aroumd as a base for group treks around the Toubkal area. Accommodation options here include village rooms and the French-run *Atlas Gîte* (☎ *04-449105* in Marrakesh) where doubles with bathroom cost around Dr60 per person. The French cooking here is said to be excellent. There is also a *camp site*, a small *hotel*, the *Café Residence* (which has hot showers as well as a restaurant), and a couple of *cafes*. For more on Aroumd see Stage 1: Imlil to Toubkal Refuge under the Jebel Toubkal Ascent later in this section.

THE TREK
Stage 1: Imlil to Tacheddirt
3½–4½ hours, 9.5km, 560m ascent

Much of the first day's walk follows the 4WD track that links Imlil (1740m) to the village of Ouaneskra, 2km west of Tacheddirt (2300m). Follow the track up through the centre of Imlil. At the top of the village take the left-hand fork (the right-hand fork continues to the village of Aroumd, a 45-minute walk south of Imlil) which soon

bends left, crosses the river (Assif n'Aït Mizane) then climbs gently eastwards before zig-zagging up to Aït Souka.

After an hour or so, just past a young pine plantation, a fairly well-defined but rocky path heads east, skirting the village of Tamatert, while the dirt road follows a slightly longer, more gentle route to the north. The path continues eastward for about 15 minutes, passing through another small pine grove and crossing the road, before climbing steeply north-east to the pass, Tizi n'Tamatert (2279m). The walk up takes 30 to 45 minutes. At the pass is *Bivi Thé*, a weather-beaten tin shed where you can buy soft drinks and mint tea. To the north-east are great views of Tizi n'Eddi (2928m), the pass that leads to the ski resort of Oukaïmeden, and Tizi n' Tacheddirt (3172m), north-east of which is the beautiful Ourika Valley.

The path rejoins the dirt road at Tizi n'Tamatert and from here it's an easy 45-minute walk to the village of **Ouaneskra**. All along this stretch are very pretty views across the valley to the neat Berber houses and lush terraces of Talate n'Chaoute, Tamguist and Ouaneskra. There are two gîtes in Ouaneskra and a nice little restaurant, but since the second stage of this walk makes for a fairly long day, it's best to have lunch here then carry on to **Tacheddirt** (2km) along the well-defined mule trail.

There's a basic *CAF Refuge* in Tacheddirt that sleeps 23 people.

The best place to *camp* is on the mule track close to Irhzer n'Likemt (a stream and reliable water source) due south of Tacheddirt. This is the starting place for the next day's climb up to Tizi Likemt. Therefore after crossing Tizi n'Tamatert campers may wish to traverse along the southern side of the valley (tracks lead the way) thus bypassing Ouaneskra and Tacheddirt altogether.

Stage 2: Tacheddirt to Azib Likemt
4½–5 hours, 9km, 1200m ascent, 900m descent

From Tacheddirt you can either head straight down and across the Assif n'Imenane (river) then up past the camp site or wind around the head of the valley on a more gentle route to the start of the climb. Either way, leave Tacheddirt as early as possible for the two- to three-hour walk up to Tizi Likemt (3550m). Though the better part of the walk is in shadow, it's a hard climb (especially for the unclimbitised!) with a very steep scree slope towards the top ('the grandfather of all Atlas scree slopes' according to climber Michael Peyron). It's a killer.

From close to the camp site a well-defined rocky path heads up the centre of the gully on the east side of the river bed (though it crosses over twice) climbing for about 50 minutes before bearing left (south-east) up to the col. From the top of the Tizi Likemt there are good views of Oukaïmeden; it's also possible to get a glimpse of Jebel Toubkal.

The path leading down the other side (south-east) is quite rocky; you'll pass a semi-permanent water source on the left after 30 minutes. After about another hour the first of the irrigated pastures above Azib Likemt are reached. *Azibs* are summer settlements and Azib Likemt (2650m) is occupied from the first week of May to the last week of October during which time local people grow crops on the irrigated terraces and fatten their cattle in lush summer pastures. Their rudimentary stone dwellings, the well-worked terraces and sheer natural beauty of the valley provides an amazing vista.

You may well be offered shelter or a place to pitch your tent in Azib Likemt, but failing this, walk through the terraces down to the Assif Tifni (river), cross, turn right and then walk upstream to a group of large boulders where there is some flat ground close to the river to pitch your tent.

Stage 3: Azib Likemt to Amsouzert

7–9½ hours, 15.2km, 470m ascent, 1380m descent

This direct route south to Amsouzert is a relatively gentle route and offers contrasting landscapes, peak bagging and ridge walking. From Azib Likemt the well-worn trail leads south up the mountainside from behind the camp site and into the tremendous gorge formed by the Assif n'Tinzer. Well above the river's eastern bank the trail snakes above the

thundering Tombe Asmine waterfall (and alternative camp site) before descending close to the river. Follow the river for the next two hours, past stunning cliffs and through wide pastures, until an obvious track leads up the side of the valley to Tizi n'Ououraine (3120m) as it is on the 1:50,000 maps, or Tizi n'Ouarai (3120m).

There are some tremendous views of the eastern face of Toubkal, Dôme d'Ifni (3876m) and the rest of the jagged Toubkal massif. By way of contrast, Agounss n'Tiniline (3674m; see the side trip later in this section) 90 minutes away to the northwest and other lesser peaks and ridges to the east are softer and rounded – there's huge potential for sustained ridge walking or a long circuit back to Azib Likemt from Tizi n'Ououraine.

Continuing over the col where the trail traverses around the head of the valley to a spur and cross-roads of trails. Heading southwest, a trail leads down the ridge to Tagadirt (after 50m there's a fantastic viewpoint looking south to Jebel Siroua and the Ifnouan Plateau), but turn left (south-east) and follow the mule track south. Traverse around the head of another valley and then along the side of a spur finally gaining the ridge after about 90 minutes. Lac d'Ifni is visible to the west. After a further 15 minutes, just before two pointed outcrops, the path forks. Turn right and continue descending slowly south to a large cairn (another good viewpoint). Descend south-west, then west down the end of the spur to arrive in Amsouzert (1740m) in 50 minutes.

Amsouzert is a relatively large, prosperous village (with one mosque and half a dozen satellite dishes at last count) spread on both sides of the river. If you're planning a rest day this is an excellent place to take it. Next to the school you'll find an outdoor tea shop shaded by an enormous walnut tree – you may be able to camp here (Dr20 per tent). *Gîte Himmi Omar* charges Dr30 per person for a bed, either on two cracking roof terraces or in a couple of rooms. Expect to pay around Dr30 for a tajine. There's a cold shower; renovations and extensions were taking place at the time of writing.

Above the village just below the track to Lac d'Ifni is *Hotel Igroute*, which looks quite good, but was incomplete at the time of writing. It's likely to cost Dr40 per person.

There are a number of small *shops* in Amsouzert and a couple of *cafes* near the village school just west of the river. There's also early morning transport to the Taroudannt-Ouarzazate P32 road with connections for Marrakesh (Dr75) and Ouarzazate (Dr80). About 3km south of Amsouzert is another village, Imlil, which hosts a weekly souq on Wednesday (not to be confused with the Imlil trailhead on the northern side of the range).

Alternative Routes From Azib Likemt there's a popular two-day route to Amsouzert, firstly west beside the Assif Tifni to Azib Tifni (2820m) then south over Tizi n'Terhaline (3427m) and down the Assif n'Tisgui Valley via Tazga. These valleys are achingly beautiful and the route is well worth considering if you have the time.

In addition, as a short cut to Jebel Toubkal, from Azib Tifni it's possible to take the route up and over Tizi n'Tagharat (3456m) or Tizi n'Terhaline (3247m) to **Sidi Chamharouch**, a small village two hours north of the Toubkal Refuge (see Jebel Toubkal Ascent later in this section for details about Sidi Chamharouch).

Side Trip: Agounss n'Tiniline From Tizi n'Ououraine the easiest side trip is the straightforward 1½-hour trek up to Agounss n'Tiniline (3674m), which lies to the northwest. The summit is reached after crossing a number of lesser peaks and affords tremendous views of the Toubkal ridge.

Stage 4: Amsouzert to Azib Imi n'Ouassif

5½–6 hours, 10.5km, 1100m ascent

Unfortunately for those with mules, your beasts of burden will not be able to make it more than 2km west of Lac d'Ifni. You will have to make arrangements to send them around to Toubkal via Sidi Chamharouch and you'll have to carry your necessary kit to Azib Imi n'Ouassif, over Tizi n'Ouanoums to Toubkal Refuge.

From Amsouzert, follow the level, wellused 4WD track that heads north-west towards Lac d'Ifni above the north side of the river. The path takes you through the villages of Ibrouane, Takatert and Tisgouane before reaching Aït Igrane where *Gîte Blaïde* offers basic accommodation for Dr30. Opposite, *Camping Toubkal* is a flat, shady but stony site with a rudimentary shower (cold) and toilet block. There's also a tiny 'shop' and cafe.

Follow the 4WD track that follows the riverbed north-west out of Aït Igrane and then, at the end of the river valley where the vegetation ends abruptly and the 4WD track crosses the river (there's a spring to the north) and then turns sharp left, pick up the narrow, rocky mule path that leads around the north side of Lac d'Ifni. The landscape for the next hour is incredibly sharp, rocky, barren and inhospitable. The climb is steep at first and finally descends to the north-eastern corner of Lac d'Ifni (2295m), a surprisingly large, and very welcome, expanse of still, green water. The walk to the lake should take two to three hours. On the small beach on the northern shore are a few stone shelters not far from the lake side where you can seek shade – they make a good spot for a leisurely lakeside lunch. The ground is rocky and there is no vegetation to speak of, but the lake is safe – and very refreshing – to swim in.

Villagers from the surrounding area gather at Lac d'Ifni for a three-day *moussem* (festival) in honour of a local marabout (saint) every October. His tomb sits in splendid isolation high above the south-eastern corner of the lake. A track leads around from the northeast shore of the lake up to the tomb.

From the north-western side of the lake, a long trudge (about 1km) leads across the wide, dry part of Lac d'Ifni before climbing steeply up towards Tizi n'Ouanoums. Once clear of the lake, the path climbs up through a rocky gorge, keeping to the south side of the river. It's a hot, sweaty climb in the afternoon sun – relieved somewhat by the cooling sound of running water. About 3.5km and a 1½ to two hour trek from the lake, you'll reach Azib Imi n'Ouassif (2841m; marked on the 1:100,000 map by altitude only), situated at a crossroads of dramatic gorges. After this point the path climbs steeply to Tizi n'Ouanoums. There are some small waterfalls (freezing even in the height of summer) nearby. You'll find several flat (but rocky) areas for pitching tents as well as natural shelters in the surrounding cliffs; these have probably been used by local shepherds for centuries.

Stage 5: Azib Imi n'Ouassif to Toubkal Refuge

3–4 hours, 4km, 759m ascent, 393m descent

The path to Tizi n'Ouanoums (3600m) is immediately to the north-west of the camp site, leading up into a particularly rocky, rugged landscape. It's a steep, demanding climb pretty much the entire way, but the views from the top down Assif n'Moursaïne, which is hemmed in by the jagged ridges of Adrar bou Ouzzal and Ouimeksane, are spectacular. The path crosses the river several times after leaving the camp and the col is reached after 1½ to two hours (a stone shelter and water source is an hour away). Even in midsummer, it's likely to be cold and blustery at the top with a fair bit of snow in shady crevices.

Coming down the other side (where there's lots of treacherous loose rock and snow until July) you can see Jebel Toubkal and, to the west, the path up to Tizi n'Melloul (3750m), from where it's possible to reach the Tazaghart (formerly known as Lépiney) Refuge. After the descent, the track levels out and heads due north to the Toubkal Refuge (3207m) reached about two hours after leaving Tizi n'Ouanoums.

Toubkal Refuge (formerly known as Neltner) was totally rebuilt in 1999 and has a capacity for more than 80 people. There are hot showers (Dr10), flush toilets, a kitchen (Dr7 per hour for gas) and a generator. Meals are available and there's a small shop selling chocolate, cola, biscuits and other limited supplies. Bring your own bedding. The warden has two, rather unreliable, cellphones (☎ 01-655133, 01-624981), though it's best to make a reservation (see Accommodation under Information earlier in this chapter). Beds cost Dr64 per person for non-CAF members, Dr48 for HI members and Dr32 for CAF members. Prices rise by 50% in winter.

You can *camp* downstream from the refuge (Dr12 per tent, Dr6 per person) or pick a spot 20 minutes south of the refuge on flat areas of pasture. The latter is preferable, but you won't have access to the refuge facilities.

It's likely that you'll reach the refuge before lunch. There are a number of options for the afternoon including the three or four hour trudge down to Imlil, if you want to avoid climbing Jebel Toubkal (a six to seven hour round trip which should be attempted the next morning at first light – see Stage 2 of the Jebel Toubkal Ascent); tackling Stage 6: Toubkal Refuge to Azib Tamsoult, the gruelling climb up and over to the Tazaghart Refuge, which lies at the head of the Azzadene Valley; or an ascent of Jebel Ouanoukrim which is best attempted straight after descending from Tizi n'Ouanoums (see Side Trip later). However, the best option (especially if you've got three days of trekking ahead of you) is to rest all day to prepare to climb Jebel Toubkal the following morning.

If you've sent your mules around from Amsouzert (a taxing diversion via Sidi Chamharouch for man and beast) and intend to carry on to the Tazaghart Refuge you should send your mules on the day you climb Toubkal. However, arguably you could release your mules once you've been resupplied at the Toubkal Refuge or indeed at Lac d'Ifni (with two high passes ahead that mules cannot climb and supplies run down this may be the wiser course of action). You will have to pay for the time your mules and muleteers spend returning to Imlil.

Side Trip: Jebel Ouanoukrim Ascent

The final stages of the circuit are fairly demanding, but for those with incurably itchy feet it's possible to spend the afternoon climbing Jebel Ouanoukrim (4088m, five to six hours return), the second-highest mountain in the region. If you're mega-fit and want to have a bash at it after descending from Tizi n'Ouanoums, once you hit the river turn left and head south up the valley. It's a good idea to take a guide or get some advice before setting off for this peak. Take the valley path back beyond the turn-off to Tizi n'Ouanoums and continue to climb up to Tizi n'Ouagene (3750m); from there follow the ridge to the summit.

Stage 6: Toubkal Refuge to Azib Tamsoult

5½–6 hours, 6km, 493m ascent, 1300m descent
From the refuge, pick up the mule track that heads north-west then gently climbs north across the slope. Pass the first jagged, narrow gully and then from a position high above a stream, turn left along a ridge west into the second. Keep to the southern side of the gully initially, but the rough trail soon switches to the northern side and the route becomes rough, requiring considerable scrambling.

After about 80 minutes, and having passed a couple of flat areas (just about OK for a mountain bivvy) and a spring, you'll reach a wide and rather difficult scree slope (it's unpleasant to climb with a heavy pack). Follow the rough zig-zagging trail up to a small cliff face to the north-east and then turn left and traverse across to the rocky and exposed Tizi n'Taddate (approx 3700m). To the left of the col is Biginnoussen (4008m), while straight ahead the trail traverses the head of Assif Timellite to another col (this area is covered in snow until mid-July). From this second col is a steep, tricky descent down the northern side of the narrow, rocky gully. Some scrambling is required for the first hour until the cliffs part, leaving a simple descent to the small, but homely, *Tazaghart Refuge* (3000m), sitting beside a stunning waterfall.

Unfortunately the guardian is based in Azib Tamsoult (an 80 minute-walk north) so the key can be obtained from the tiny shop on the main trail to Imlil, north of the main village. You'll probably find the place closed unless you've made a reservation. There are places for 20 people. CAF members pay Dr32, HI members Dr48 and nonmembers Dr64. Campers can pitch tents beside the refuge or on flat ground above the falls.

The refuge is mostly used by climbers attempting the cliffs of Tazaghart (3845m), the summit of which is accessible to trekkers (who will not regret the chance to explore the wonderful Tazaghart Plateau to the west).

Tizi n'Melloul (3750m), south-east of Tazaghart Refuge, not only offers a harder route to/from the Toubkal Refuge, but also provides access to Afella (4045m), to the south-east of the pass, and access to the jagged ridge leading north to Biginnoussen.

The route down to Azib Tamsoult (approx 2400m) is straightforward. Shortly after passing the impressive **Cascade d'Irhoulidene**, vegetation and tree cover increase. Five minutes' walk from the base of the falls is a pleasant wooded area, ideal for camping. The village is 10 to 15 minutes' walk north.

Stage 7: Azib Tamsoult to Imlil

4½–5 hours, 6km, 89m ascent, 749m descent
This descent to Imlil is straightforward and could be tacked onto the end of Stage 6.

From the vegetable patches of Azib Tamsoult, with the Assif n'Ouarzane down to the left, a clear mule track that traverses along the eastern forested slopes of the valley is clearly visible to the north. Head towards it through the village and over the stream and stay on it, avoiding left forks into the valley. Climbing slightly steadily north-east with Tizi Oussem due west, you arrive at Tizi n'Mzik (2489m), where there's a possible camp site. Imlil is a 90-minute descent along a well-worn mule track – a spring to the right of the trail is passed after 20 minutes.

Jebel Toubkal Ascent

Duration 2 days
Distance 22km
Standard medium to hard
Start/Finish Imlil village
Highest Point Jebel Toubkal (4167m)
Nearest Large Town Marrakesh
Accommodation camping or mountain refuges
Public Transport yes
Summary The ascent of Jebel Toubkal is the most popular walk in the High Atlas – the views are magnificent. The route is straightforward and (outside winter) easily achieved without mountaineering experience or a guide. However, it should not be taken lightly as the trek up the scree slope is hard, trekkers can be struck down with altitude sickness and the mountain's climate can be extreme.

Having the distinction of being the highest mountain in North Africa means that Jebel Toubkal (4167m) sees several hundred visitors every year, through both summer and winter. It's a challenging walk rather than a climb, and anyone in good physical condition can get to the summit. Toubkal is, however, subject to an extreme climate, it's rugged, rocky and famous for its long, steep slopes of scree (small stones). The severe looking deep brown, red and almost black rocks of Toubkal are all volcanic; the andesites and rhyolites are intensely fractured and bedded together to form unusually loose masses. The summit is also high enough to make mild altitude sickness a possibility, so care should be taken to ascend slowly and steadily.

Many people opt for this quick two-day trek, but the large region around Jebel Toubkal offers endless possibilities for longer walks (see the Toubkal Circuit earlier).

The route described here is the standard two-day walk undertaken by most visitors to Jebel Toubkal, but there are plenty of variations. An ascent of Toubkal can be combined with satellite peaks and many (very fit) people squeeze in an ascent of Ouanoukrim as well. Those wanting a slightly more leisurely pace might want to consider stopping an extra night on the route between Imlil and the Toubkal Refuge (either camping or lodging the night at Sidi Chamharouch).

Stage 1: Imlil to Toubkal Refuge

4–6 hours, 10km, 1467m ascent

Leave Imlil (see Imlil earlier in this section for general information) as early as possible for the walk up to the Toubkal Refuge. It's not a particularly steep climb, but it is a remorseless uphill trek all the way and can be very tiring if you haven't done any previous warm-up walks or spent time acclimatising. Follow the dirt track that leads through Imlil towards Aroumd (see Aroumd earlier in this section) and at the top of the village turn left onto a mule track that wends its way up through walnut groves and past the Kasbah du Toubkal.

Beyond the kasbah, the path zig-zags steeply upwards to rejoin the road at the Aroumd Plain.

Once past Aroumd cross the broad, stony flood plain and on the other side follow the well defined mule trail above the east side of the Assif Reraya to the hamlet and shrine of Sidi Chamharouch (see the boxed text 'The King of the Djinn'). Sidi Chamharouch (2310m) is just under halfway between Imlil and the Toubkal Refuge. Soft drinks are available here and beyond the marabout are a couple of nice cascades and pools. Lunch here or choose a quieter spot further along the trail towards the refuge.

After crossing the river by the bridge at Sidi Chamharouch, the rocky path veers away from the river for a couple of kilometres and zig-zags above the valley floor before levelling off a bit and rejoining the course of the river. The refuge is visible for a good hour or so before you reach it, situated immediately below the western flank of Jebel Toubkal (see Toubkal Circuit earlier in this section for details).

Stage 2: The Ascent

6 hours, 12km, 960m ascent & descent

Two cwms (valleys formed by past glacial activity) run down the western flank of Toubkal and are divided by the west-north-west ridge leading down from the summit. The southern cwm is the more usual route

The King of the Djinn

The straggly hamlet at Sidi Chamharouch, the halfway mark between Imlil and the Toubkal Refuge, is not really a traditional Berber village but rather the result of the 'service industry' that has grown up around the important shrine here. The enormous white-painted boulder next to the shrine (closed to non-Muslims) is said to have crashed down from the mountains, entombing Sidi Chamharouch, who is widely believed to be the 'King of the Djinn'. Tradition tells that Sidi Chamharouch roamed the hills as a dog during the day and then changed into a man at night before returning to his house in Aroumd. People from throughout the country visit the site seeking cures for various illnesses, particularly mental disturbances.

Dorinda Talbot

TREKKING

and starts immediately below the refuge. Set off as early as possible to avoid climbing in the sun, and carry water, snacks and warm clothing – a strong, bitter wind often blows across the summit. After a one-day trek up from Imlil you will not be ideally acclimatised and altitude sickness is a possibility. Be sure to walk at a steady, slow pace. If you do experience more than mild symptoms, such as severe headache and vomiting, descend immediately.

Cross the river behind the refuge and head eastwards to the clearly visible scree slope. Start to climb on the well-defined path that moves to the left of the slope, cross a 'field' of boulders before following the straightforward path that zig-zags up to Tizi n'Toubkal (3940m) straight ahead on the skyline. From there, the path turns left (north-east) and follows the ridge to the summit (4167m). Provided there is no heat haze, you should be rewarded by superb views in all directions, especially early in the morning. Allow 2½ to 3½ hours to reach the top.

Stick to the same route coming down, bearing left when the refuge comes into view. The descent should take two to 2½ hours.

Imlil to Setti Fatma

Duration 3 days
Distance 30km
Standard easy to medium
Start Imlil village
Finish Setti Fatma
Highest Point Tizi n'Tacheddirt (3172m)
Nearest Large Town Marrakesh
Accommodation camping & gîtes
Public Transport yes
Summary A superb – and relatively leisurely – three-day walk through some of the most spectacular country in the High Atlas. The route includes only one rocky high pass, which is followed by a long descent into the upper Ourika Valley, a heavily cultivated area where countless green terraces and shady walnut groves cascade down the steep mountainsides.

Although this walk doesn't include the highest peaks of the High Atlas, it does give a good taste of everything the mountains have to offer – high windswept passes, wild and rocky landscapes and a glimpse into a way of life that has changed little in centuries. The walk travels across varied terrain and through a dozen or more Berber villages, some of which are still waiting to be connected to electricity.

There's nothing to stop interested visitors staying an extra night or two in the mountain villages and there are innumerable side trips that can be added on to the trek.

In many ways, it's a more rewarding trek than the more popular route up Toubkal. The trailhead is only two hours from Marrakesh and is easily accessible by public transport.

PLANNING

This walk can be done comfortably in three days, but (for the very fit) is feasible in two. Plenty of side trips and variations are possible, especially around Timichi. If planning a longer stay, you'll need to bring extra supplies. This area of the High Atlas is covered by the 1:100,000 *Oukaïmeden-Toubkal* government survey sheet.

Setti Fatma has several small and fairly basic hotels (*Hôtel Tafoukt* has hot showers), and plenty of *cafes*. See also Stage 3: Timichi to Setti Fatma later in this section. Buses and taxis travel pretty frequently between Setti Fatma and Bab er-Rob in Marrakesh (67km). Buses cost Dr10. Taxis take about 1½ hours, buses a bit longer.

THE TREK
Stage 1: Imlil to Ouaneskra
3–3½ hours, 7km, 560m ascent
The first section of this trek is almost the same route as for the first day of the Toubkal Circuit (see Stage 1: Imlil to Tacheddirt earlier). Once at Tizi n'Tamatert it's an easy 45-minute walk to the village of Ouaneskra. All along this stretch are very pretty views across the valley to the neat Berber houses and lush terraces of Talate n'Chaoute, Tamguist and Ouaneskra. There are two well-run *gîtes* in Ouaneskra, one at either end of the village, and where you stay will

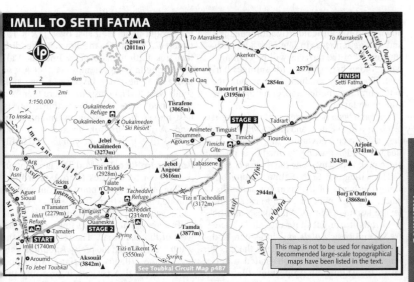

IMLIL TO SETTI FATMA

To Marrakesh

To Marrakesh

Agourii (2011m)

Akerker

Iguenane

Aït el Oaq

2577m

2854m

Taourirt n'Ikis (3195m)

FINISH Setti Fatma

0 — 2 — 4km
0 — 1 — 2mi
1:150,000

Oukaïmeden Refuge

Oukaïmeden

Oukaïmeden Ski Resort

To Imska

Tisrafene (3065m)

STAGE 3

Tadrart

Animeter Timguist

Tinoummer Agouns

Timichi

Timichi Gîte

Tiourdiou

Arjoût (3741m)

Jebel Oukaïmeden (3273m)

Tizi n'Eddi (2928m)

Jebel Angour (3616m)

Labassene

3243m

Arg

To Asni

Ikkiss

Talate n'Chaoute

Tacheddirt Refuge

Tizi n'Tacheddirt (3172m)

2944m

Borj n'Oufraou (3868m)

Aguer Sioual

Tizi n'Tamatert (2279m)

Tamguist

Tacheddirt (2314m)

Ouaneskra

STAGE 2

Tamda (3877m)

Imlil Refuge

Tamatert

START
Imlil (1740m)

Aroumd

To Jebel Toubkal

Tizi-n'Likemt (3550m)

Spring

Spring

Aksouâl (3842m)

See Toubkal Circuit Map p487

This map is not to be used for navigation. Recommended large-scale topographical maps have been listed in the text.

TREKKING

---

probably depend on which particular gîte your guide has family connections to. Both charge around Dr30 per person and the same for evening meals. There are cold showers, but you can ask for a kettle of warm water.

Alternatively, you could continue 2km on to Tacheddirt where there's a *CAF Refuge* that sleeps 23 people.

A possibility for the afternoon is to explore the Imenane Valley, another heavily cultivated valley dotted with Berber villages, which stretches from Ouaneskra and Tacheddirt north-west towards Asni.

Stage 2: Ouaneskra to Timichi
6–7 hours, 12km, 900m ascent, 1300m descent
Follow the well-used mule path out of Ouaneskra and on to the village of Tacheddirt, which boasts a vast area of beautifully terraced fields. On the far side of the village the track begins to climb steadily up to Tizi n'Tacheddirt (3172m); the pass is visible the entire way. The rocky path keeps to the left-hand side of the river bed, zig-zagging steeply up towards the south face of Jebel Angour (3616m) for the last half hour or so. From the exposed and windy pass there's an exhilarating and very long descent (at least

three hours) down to Timichi. Look for a sheltered spot for lunch 30 minutes' or so walk beyond Tizi n'Tacheddirt.

The path continues down past ancient, gnarled juniper trees and around the sloping eastern flank of Angour where sheep and goats graze from early spring. Though fairly well defined, the trail is very rocky and at times clings precariously to the mountainside. The colour of the landscape gradually changes from a pale coffee colour to red and then to green. Finally, the cascading terraces of Labassene come into view; head for the huge old walnut tree standing guard outside the village and take the path that leads past the village houses. The path veers north-east from here and Timichi is just another 2km further on.

The friendly Timichi *gîte* is on the south side of the river, opposite the village proper (the terrace is a great place from which to watch village activities). A bed costs around Dr30 and basic meals are available.

Stage 3: Timichi to Setti Fatma
3–4 hours, 11km, 370m descent
Cross the riverbed and turn right to follow the long, easy trail that runs high above the

valley. There are fantastic, birds-eye views down onto the intricate irrigation channels and village terraces. In late May and early June many of the terraces will be crammed with golden barley ready for summer harvest. The valley gradually opens out, the path climbing higher and clinging to the bare mountainsides.

The path becomes increasingly rocky as it heads into Setti Fatma and after a while joins the road that cuts down into the village – instead of plodding along the road, it is possible to pick your way along the river's course.

The village of **Setti Fatma**, strung out along the banks of the river for some distance, is a very popular place to escape the severe summer heat of Marrakesh and on weekends it can get quite crowded. There are several basic *hotels* and *cafes* here and in the foothills east of the village there is a series of six or seven much-visited waterfalls. In August an important four-day moussem takes place in Setti Fatma (see Ourika Valley under Around Marrakesh in the Central Morocco chapter).

OTHER WALKS AROUND TOUBKAL
Oukaïmeden
Between the Imenane and the Ourika Valleys is Oukaïmeden, Morocco's premier ski resort. There's good day walking up here in spring and summer and the area is also known for its prehistoric rock carvings and bird life. The most obvious walk would be an ascent of Jebel Oukaïmeden (3273m). The *CAF Refuge (☎ 04-319036, fax 319020, PO Box 60137 Oukaïmeden)* is a good source of information (see Ourika Valley in the Central Morocco chapter for other information on the region). Make sure you have good topographical maps and, preferably, a guide.

Winter Treks
The Toubkal region can be bitterly cold in winter with snow not uncommon in Imlil. However, if you stick below about 2400m (the snow line), stay on the major local routes, and are prepared for blizzard conditions and sub-zero temperatures, there's nothing to stop you enjoying some great trekking.

Imlil Circuit A pleasant three- or four-day trek would be to head east over Tizi n'Tamatert (2279m) to **Ouaneskra** or **Tacheddirt**, then trek north-west down the Imenane Valley staying in village homes in either **Arg** or **Imska**. The next day involves a long trek south-west to Tizi Oussem, where there's a comfortable *gîte*. This long (third) day is best broken in two by an overnight camp stop. A four-hour trek up and over Tizi n'Mzik (2489m) will take you back to Imlil.

Asni or Imlil to Tin Mal The next option is a five- or six-day trek from Asni or Imlil to Tin Mal. If you plan to continue to Taroudannt from here, it's ideal.

The starting place, **Imi Ourhlad**, is about halfway between Asni and Imlil, just to the west of the main road. The route takes you south-west through the pretty **Agoundis Valley** via the villages of **Tiziane**, **Tizgi** and **Ameslane**. Tizi Ameslane is probably the highest point of the trek at 2059m. From here you wend your way down the valley to **Ijoukak** on the Tizi n'Test road. You'll find grocery shops, basic *cafes*, *rooms* to rent and a hammam. Market day in is Wednesday.

From Ijoukak you're within striking distance (8km south-west) of the beautiful Tin Mal Mosque. Local buses stop at Ijoukak en route between Taroudannt and Marrakesh – check the times with the locals.

Imlil to Tagadirt A third short winter trek, which covers a good range of terrain, takes you from Imlil to Tizi Oussem and then further west towards the **Ouigane Valley** and the **Nfis Gorges**. Three or four days of fairly easy trekking will take you to the seldom-visited **Plateau du Kik** via **Tassa Ouirgane**, Tizi Ousla and the village of **Tagadirt**. From the plateau, you can return to Asni.

WESTERN HIGH ATLAS – TICHKA PLATEAU
Trekking in the western High Atlas is arguably less taxing than in the central regions, but nevertheless provides some truly excellent trekking in a beautiful landscape. The high pastures of the Tichka Plateau are undoubtedly a highlight, but there are more

than enough peaks to keep the most energetic peak-bagger occupied. And in this area you're unlikely to meet any other trekkers.

In spring the Tichka Plateau is a mass of wildflowers. This stunning route is also blessed with passages along the Oued Nfis that pass through oak forests and gorges.

Hiring guides and mules can be a problem in the area. If you're coming from Marrakesh then sort this out at Hôtel Ali (see Places to Stay – Budget under Marrakesh in the Central Morocco chapter) before setting off. If you're in Taroudannt (only 85km from Agadir) there are also guides available here, but some are dubious operators.

The Treks

Access is possible from the west of the range via Imi n'Tanoute, **Timesgadiouine** or **Argana** on the Agadir-Marrakesh road or from **Taroudannt** to the south. If you come from the west, head (along dirt roads) for **Afensou** (not to be mistaken with another village to the south), which has a mine nearby (ensuring a flow of transport) and a Thursday souq. However, Souk Sebt Talnakant, which is closer to Timesgadiouine and Argana, is an alternative more western, trailhead.

From Taroudannt south, things are a little easier as *camionettes* (pick-up trucks) ply the route beside the Oued Ouaar up to Imoulas (with a Sunday souq) and up to Tagmout and Souk Tnine-Tigouga (Monday souq).

From **Imoulas** there's a rather energetic route up to Jebel Aoulime (3555m; also known as Jebel Tinergwet 3551m on many maps) to the north-east, but also plenty of scope for multi-day circuits via Afensou and Souk Tnine-Tigouga. However, arguably the best idea is to head east through the Tichka Plateau. Jebel Toubkal may be a 13-day trek away, but five or six days will get you to Tin Mal and the Tizi n'Test road. From the top of the Tizi n'Test you can ascend Jebel Igdet (3616m), the highest peak of the western High Atlas.

CENTRAL HIGH ATLAS – M'GOUN MASSIF

The central High Atlas, dominated by the M'Goun Massif, offers great scope for trekkers, arguably more so than the Toubkal area. This area of the High Atlas is more remote; the rock is sedimentary and forms dramatic ridges and escarpments. Erosion has carved some tremendous gorges with deep red and orange walls. Some can be walked and/or waded through (they're sometimes waist deep), while others should not be attempted without considerable climbing or canyoning skills. These gorges are a highlight of the area.

Planning

To the north of the dominant peak of Irhil M'Goun (4071m) is the Aït Bou Goumez Valley, a place of striking Berber architecture and lush irrigated fields. It's the launching point for many treks. Access is via Azilal (which has regular transport to Marrakesh) from where reasonably regular transport heads to Aït Mohammed. Transport into the Aït Bou Goumez Valley is then by camionette or truck, but most traffic leaves early in the morning. Sunday is the best day to travel as there's a big souq in **Tabant**, the principal settlement in the valley and launching point for many a trek. There's accommodation and some supplies here and mules can be arranged.

Guides are best arranged in **Azilal** where there is a bureau des guides though you could contact Mustapha Ahitass at the Hotel Dades (☎ 03-458245) on Rue Marrakesh. He's highly competent and experienced.

There are gîtes throughout the range while the 1:100,000 survey sheets *Zawyat Ahannsal*, *Qalat M'Gouna*, *Azilal* and *Skoura* cover the major trekking areas. West Col Productions produces a 1:100,000 *Mgoun Massif* map and guide which, although devoid of contours, is a good trail reference and useful for planning.

The Treks

One popular seven-day route from Tabant is as follows:

Head south-east on a testing 1000m climb to Tizi n'Aït Imi (2905m) before descending to **Tighremt n'Aït Ahmed** (2235m) on the banks of the **Assif M'Goun** for the night. The next day the trail follows the

TREKKING

TREKKING

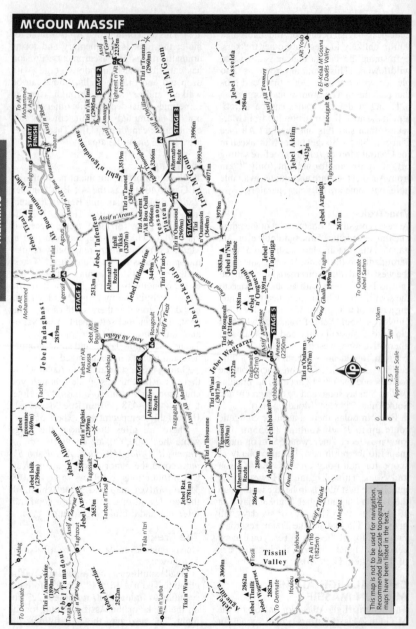

M'GOUN MASSIF

To Ait Mohammed & Azilal

START/ FINISH ▲

Tabant

Agoudin

Imi n'Talat

STAGE 1 ▲

Agersif ▲

To Ait Mohammed

Jebel Tadaghast
2819m ▲

Jebel Titzal 3041m ▲   Aït Bou Gomez Imelghas

Assif n'Rbat

Assif n'Igoudamene

Ait Bou Goumez

Jebel Tignousti

Assif n'Ait Boua Goumene

Assif n'Arous

3519m ▲

Tizi n'Tanout (3074m)

Tizi Asdrent n'Ait Bou Oulli (3066m)

Jebel Tafentent

2513m ▲

Ichil n'Ikkis (3207m) ▲

Alternative Route ▲

Jebel Tiftaniwine
3449m ▲

Tizi n'Taziyt

Jebel Tarkeddid

Oued Tassoul

Tizi n'Ait Imi (2905m)

Assif Amougr

Tissaout Plateau

Tizi n'Oumsoud (2969m)

STAGE 4 ▲

Tizi n'Oumassine (2969m)

Assif M'Goun 2235m ▲

Tighremt n'Ait Ahmed

Tizi n'Tounza (2960m)

STAGE 2 ▲

STAGE 3 ▲ Irhil M'Goun

Tizi n'Oulilimt

Jebel 3266m ▲   3996m ▲

Irhil M'Goun
3993m ▲
4071m ▲
3978m ▲

Jebel Asselda
2984m ▲

To El-Kelaâ M'Gouna & Dadès Valley

Assif Aït Toumert

Taouglait

Jebel Aklim
3432m ▲

Tighouzzirine

Jebel Azguigh
2617m ▲

To Ouarzazate & Jebel Sarhro

Oued Ghalb   Taghra
1989m ▲

To Aït Youb

Jebel n'Nig Oumassine
3883m ▲

Jebel Tazrp n'Ouguert
3991m ▲

Jebel Tajouija

3381m ▲

STAGE 5 ▲

Amezri (2250m)

Tizi n'Oulaum 2767m ▲

Rougoult

Assif n'Tuzi

Assif Aït Mallal

Sebt Aït Mallal

Abachkou

Tarbat n'Ait Moussa

STAGE 6 ▲

Alternative Route ▲

Tazagalt

Assif Aït Mallal

Tizi n'Rougoult (3216m)

Tizi n'Wani
3272m ▲

Jebel Waqraraz
3017m ▲

Tasgaiwalt (2521m)

Assif Ameskane

Ichbbakene

Tacht

Jebel Igoumane 2469m ▲

Jebel Isilk (2396m) ▲

Jebel Alimmu
2586m ▲

Tizi n'Tighist 2399m ▲

Tagassalt

Taghzout

Tarbat n'Tirsal

Jebel Azegza
2665m ▲

Assif n'Zawya

Jebel Amerzaz
2522m ▲

Tizi n'Amarskine (890m)

Jebel Tamadout

Targa

Assif n'Zawya

To Demnate

Adlag

Imi n'L'arba

Tizi n'Wawat

Jebel Asuedid
3060m ▲

Jebel Timilit 2862m ▲
Jebel Waquersst 2882m ▲

To Demnate

Tizi n'Iblouzene

Tignousti 3819m ▲

Jebel Rat
3781m ▲

2809m ▲

Aghoulid n'Ichbbakene

2864m ▲

Alternative Route ▲

Oued Tassaout

Tissili Valley

Fakhour

Ifoulou

Aït Ali n'Ito (1825m)

Assif n'Tiflicht

Megdaz

10km

5

2.5

5mi

0

Approximate Scale

This map is not to be used for navigation. Recommended large-scale topographical maps have been listed in the text.

Assif n'Oulilimt up to another camp site, before tackling the climb south up to the Irhil M'Goun ridge on the third stage. From beside the 3993m-high peak turn west along the ridge to the 4071m-high summit, then two further peaks before descending to Tizi n'Oumassin (3640m; sometimes known as Tizi n'Iqandoul). Descend north and camp on the Tessaout Plateau (2897m).

Well-equipped canyoners and climbers can attempt to trek downstream along the Oued Tessaout and through dramatic gorges, but the 10m- and 20m-descents are easier climbs from the other direction. The trekkers' route keeps high above the gorge to the north before reaching Tizi N'dern (3200m), then Amezri (2250m) for a night in a gîte.

Days five and six are spent heading north through Rougoult to Sebt Aït Bou Wlli and then north-east to Agerssif on the edge of the Aït Bou Goumez Valley, which you follow east to Tabant on the seventh day.

Variations to this route are numerous. From the Tessaout Plateau you could trek north back into the Aït Bou Goumez Valley, bagging the peaks of Ighil n'Ikkis (3207m) and Ighil n'Igoudamene (3519m) on the way. Or you could lengthen the trek to 11 or 12 days and head west from Amezri for two days then up the Tissili Valley before returning north-east to Tabant via the peaks of Jebel Rat (3781m) and Tignousti (3819m) and the large village of Abachkou.

More radical alternatives include a circuit of Jebel Rat and a complete traverse of the range from Aït Mohammed to El-Kelaâ M'Gouna (a handy launching point for treks into the Jebel Sarhro) or Dadès Gorge.

EASTERN HIGH ATLAS – JEBEL AYACHI

About 30km south-west of Midelt, Jebel Ayachi (3737m) is the highest mountain in the eastern High Atlas. In fact it's really a 45km-long ridge culminating in Ichichi n'Boukhlib, the 3737m-high peak. It's a pretty simple climb, usually starting from Tattiouine (where guides and mules are available); there is occasional transport to Midelt. From a point just beyond the village near the springs, there's a mule track, which leads up the Oued Ikkis Valley to the summit. It's not a difficult climb and after the ascent there are a number of routes down. Cedar forests and mountain villages wait to be explored. However, realistically you're looking at two days with a bivvy high in the Ikkis Valley before the final ascent.

The best time to trek is spring (April to May) and autumn (September to November). Snow lingers above 3400m until July. Michael Peyron's *Great Atlas Traverse* is a good guide, but for further information drop in at Complexe Touristique Timnay Inter-Cultures (☎/fax 583434), 20km north-west of Midelt (see Excursions from Midelt in the Middle Atlas chapter).

The Middle Atlas

As far as trekking is concerned, the limestone plateaus, cedar-covered hills and rounded peaks and ridges of the Middle Atlas are rather undiscovered. The area is criss-crossed by a network of thin tarmac roads and, if you have time on your hands, local transport can get you to most places – eventually. See the Middle Atlas & the East chapter for further information about this region.

PLANNING

Winter is not the ideal time to be wandering around the Middle Atlas. Spring is the best season and you'll need a tent for most of the routes.

Volume Two of Michael Peyron's *Great Atlas Traverse* covers trekking and skitrekking possibilities in the area. For maps, the 1:100,000 sheets *Al-Hajeb, Azrou, Sefrou* and *Boulmane* cover the eastern Middle Atlas and sheets *Ribat al-Khayr, Berkine, Imouzzer Marmoucha* and *Missour* the western side.

THE TREKS

The ski resort of Mischliffen south of Ifrane has good infrastructure and is popular with day-trekkers in summer. If you want more than a gentle stroll contact the tourist office in Ifrane for information on guides and routes.

TREKKING

The cedar-covered hillsides and 2000m-high peaks south of **Azrou** (the habitat of Barbary apes) offer some great potential for long-distance treks, though the Berber village of **'Ain Leuh** to the south-west is probably a better launching point. A trek that encompasses the impressive waterfalls at Sources de l'Oum-er-Rbia and volcanic lake Aguelmane Sidi Ali is a good option. In Azrou, Hôtel Le Panorama and Hôtel Amros can both provide information on guides, mules and routes.

However, some of the most impressive trekking regions in the Middle Atlas are the Jebel Bou Iblane ridge 60km south of Taza and the area around Jebel Bou Naceur (3340m) a further 20km south-east. Some efforts have been made to develop skiing infrastructure north-east of Jebel Bou Iblane, where the Royal Moroccan Skiing and Mountaineering Federation (☎/fax 02-474979) runs *Tafferte Refuge* (1957m), but otherwise the area is untouched. Heading east from the refuge there is some good ridge walking and a simple trek to the summit of Moussa ou Salah (3190m).

South-east towards the Sahara is Jebel Bou Naceur, the arid pinnacle of the Middle Atlas. This is a target of intrepid peak-baggers, but exploring the Mansour Valley between Bou Iblance and Bou Naceur and the forests and valleys around Bou Iblane is probably more rewarding.

To reach the area by public transport you're probably best starting from Boulemane or coming via Ribat el-Kheir off the Fès-Taza road.

The Rif Mountains

The northernmost mountain range in Morocco, the Rif is not high on most people's list of Moroccan trekking destinations, largely due to the region's notoriety as an area of drug production. This is a shame as the region is blessed with some magnificent ranges, peaks, gorges and valleys, and large tracts of cedar and fir forest populated by Barbary apes. Although kif production takes up about 90% of cultivatable land east

of Chefchaouen, there's little reason for trekkers to feel threatened, especially if you take a guide.

NATURAL HISTORY

Some of the Rif peaks above 1500m are cloaked in a rare cedar, *Abias maroccana,* a variant of the Spanish species *Abies pinsapo* and a relict of a colder age. On the limestone mountains, which are almost bright white in places, are areas of holm and cork oak, pine and wild olive. Birds to look out for include golden eagles, black shouldered kites and buzzards, while wild boars and Barbary apes (known locally as *mgou*) are common in some areas. Locals also maintain that there are wolves in the hills, which may also hide mountain goats and a small species of gazelle. The bigger rivers are also said to contain trout.

Creatures to beware of (and not get bitten by) include the red scorpion (the pain from its bite lasts around two hours) and the *faire à cheval* viper, so called because of the horseshoe-like mark on its head.

One of the most beautiful areas in the region is contained within Talassemtane National Park, which the European Union (EU) is keen to see improved for tourism, which may provide an alternative to kif growing.

PLANNING

You can trek year-round in the Rif Mountains, though it can be bitterly cold between November and March (snow is not uncommon). It can rain at any time between autumn (late September) and summer (June), while during high summer it is fiercely hot, even on the peaks, and some water sources and courses dry up.

You'll need a tent and a decent sleeping bag at all times except summer and light waterproofs are also advisable.

Most food and fuel supplies can be obtained in Chefchaouen (see the Rif Mountains section in the Mediterranean Coast & the Rif chapter for further information). Abdeslam Mouden (☎ 02-113917) is president of the local Association Randonnée et Culture and can organise trekking guides. Con-

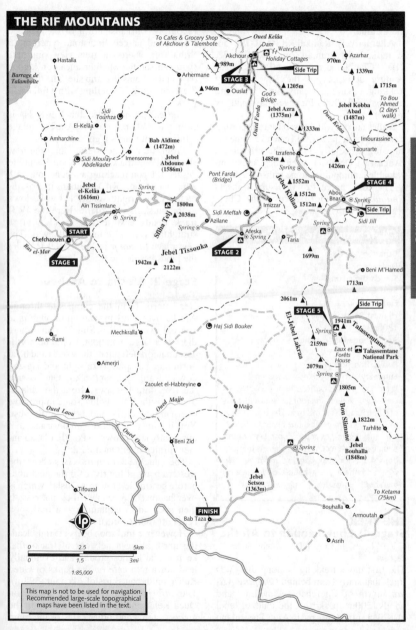

THE RIF MOUNTAINS

To Cafes & Grocery Shop of Akchour & Talembote

Oued Kelâa

Dam

Waterfall

Holiday Cottages

Akchour

989m

STAGE 3

Side Trip

Azarhar

970m

▲1339m

▲1715m

Arhermane

946m

Ouslaf

God's Bridge

▲1205m

Jebel Azra (1375m)

Jebel Kobba Abad (1487m)

To Bou Ahmed (2 days' walk)

Hastalla

Barrage de Talambolte

Sidi Tourhza

El-Kelâa

Amharchine

Bab Aïdime ▲(1472m)

Imensorme

Jebel Abdoune ▲(1586m)

▲1333m

Oued Farda

Oued Kelâa

Imourassine

Taouarte

Sidi Moulay Abdelkader

Pont Farda (Bridge)

Izrafene

1485m ▲

Jebel Kilaa

▲1552m

▲1426m

STAGE 4

Jebel el-Kelâa ▲(1616m)

Aïn Tissimlane

Spring

1800m

2038m

Sidi Meftah

Azilane

Imizzar

▲1512m

▲1512m

Abou Bnar

Spring

Side Trip

Sidi Jill

Chefchaouen

START

Râs el-Mar

STAGE 1

Spring

Afeska

Spring

Taria

Spring

Jebel Tissouka

STAGE 2

1942m ▲

▲2122m

▲1699m

Beni M'Hamed

▲1713m

2061m ▲

Side Trip

STAGE 5

▲1941m Talassemtane

Mechkralla

Haj Sidi Bouker

El-Jebel Lakraa

Spring

2159m ▲

Eaux et Forêts House

Talassemtane National Park

Aïn er-Rami

Amerjri

Zaoulet el-Habteyine

2079m ▲

Spring

599m

Oued Majjo

Majjo

1805m

Bou Slimane

▲1822m

Tarhlite

Oued Laou

Oued Ouara

Beni Zid

Spring

Jebel Bouhalla (1848m)

Tifouzal

Jebel Setsou (1363m)

To Ketama (75km)

FINISH

Bab Taza

Bouhalla

Armoutah

Asrih

N

0   2.5   5km

0   1.5   3mi

1:85,000

This map is not to be used for navigation. Recommended large-scale topographical maps have been listed in the text.

TREKKING

tact him through the Casa Hassan hotel in the medina.

Alternatively, Radikal Rif (☎ 01-798156, ✉ radikalrif@caramail.com), PO Box 72, 91000 Chefchaouen, offers all sorts of adventure activities in the Rif including trekking, caving and canyoning. Rates are reasonable (Dr3000 for seven days and six nights).

Mules are not widely used for transporting trekkers' kit in the Rif, and can take some organising especially during the kif harvest (August to October) when there are more valuable commodities to be transported.

The government 1:50,000 survey sheets *Chaouen* and *Bab Taza* cover the Chefchaouen to Bab Taza trek.

Chefchaouen to Bab Taza

Duration 4–5 days
Distance 53km
Standard medium
Start Chefchaouen
Finish Bab Taza
Highest Point Sfiha Telj Pass (approximately 1800m)
Accommodation camping & holiday cottages
Public Transport yes
Summary An enjoyable and reasonably relaxed trek through *kif* (cannabis) country, it's well-worth leaving the roof terraces and cafes of Chefchaouen for this trek. There are a couple of long hard climbs, but beautiful forest, long snaking gorges and the hospitality of the people is ample recompense. There is tremendous scope for peak-bagging and other side trips and there are a couple of interesting marabouts en route.

THE TREK
Stage 1: Chefchaouen to Afeska
5½–6½ hours, 14.5km, 1200m ascent, 600m descent

The first day's trekking is along the 4WD track that starts from behind *Camping Azilan*, north of Chefchaouen medina, and winds 1200m up, skirting the south of Jebel el-Kelâa (1616m) past Aïn Tissimlane

(where there's a spring), to a high pass (about 1800m) just north of the wooded slopes and jagged limestone outcrops of Sfiha Telj. There's a great viewpoint here (you can see the Mediterranean on a good day) and a fantastic camp site. The three- to 3½-hour climb is gruelling with a full backpack.

The easiest access to Jebel el-Kelâa is from the 4WD track above Aïn Tissimlane – this ascent makes a good day-walk.

From the pass head east along the now shaded 4WD track, which soon begins to descend. Upon reaching a T-junction, with a fine view of the Rif Mountains in most directions, turn right (south) and walk down to the outskirts of **Azilane**. Here the 4WD track bends east to **Afeska** (1200m) a straightforward 40-minute walk away. The best place to *camp* in the hamlet is under the pines beside the football pitch.

Stage 2: Afeska to Akchour
3½–4½ hours, 10km, 859m descent

Head north from the camp site through Afeska over a stream and up through pine and oak woodland to Sidi Meftah, where there is a large marabout. Continue northeast then fork left out of the woods and head north along a spur. Turn right and zig-zag down towards Imizzar (963m). Once beside the river turn left away from the village, then cross the river, below some impressive overhanging cliffs and head north-west. You'll join a well-worn mule track that eventually leads down to Pont Farda, an ancient bridge over Oued Farda.

The mule track then traverses above the western bank of the river for the next hour before bearing left towards **Ouslaf**, which is overshadowed by a giant rock buttress. It then goes on to explain how a trail soon bears off right (north).

However, a trail soon bears off right leading north along a network of tracks that keep to the higher ground and eventually lead down to a cafe on the banks of Oued Kelâa, on the outskirts of **Akchour** (398m). The *cafe* is about 100m from a dam on Oued Kelâa and 800m south-east from the grocery stores and other cafes of the main centre of Akchour village. It does some good, cheap meals (a *room* for trekkers was being added at the time of writing).

Just behind the dam is a wide deep (and cold) pool ideal for swimming, while just upstream, where the Oued Kelâa and Oued Farda meet, are some pleasant camping spots. East of here on the Oued Kelâa are well-equipped holiday *cottages* (Dr90 per person or Dr300 full-board; book through Radikal Rif in Chefchaouen – see Planning earlier).

Akchour has a reasonable *shop*, a couple of *cafes* and morning and evening transport to Chefchaouen (more on market days). There's more frequent transport from Tal-embote, about 2km further along the road. It's best to travel on a Tuesday when it's market day in Talembote; it's often a matter of paid hitchhiking on some occasions. For most journeys you'll need to change vehicles (mostly grand taxis, camionettes or converted vans) and change vehicles in Dar Ackobah (a T-junction on the P28 about 10km north of Chefchaouen). The whole journey should cost around Dr15.

Side Trip: God's Bridge
1½ hours, 3km return

This short side trip up the Oued Farda to the magnificent geological feature called God's Bridge is a must for travellers, though it's a real scramble in places. If you don't mind getting wet up to your thighs, things are a lot easier.

Pass the dam on its southern side and bear right up the river, which is crossed twice in 45 minutes before reaching God's Bridge. The red stone arch is stunning in the sunlight and now stands some 25m above the river that as an underground water-course eroded the rock to form it.

Return by the same route, though there's an impressive waterfall about 100m upstream of the holiday cottages on the Oued Kelâa.

Stage 3: Akchour to Pastures above Abou Bnar
4½–6 hours, 12km, 977m ascent

Head upstream, passing to the north of the dam and then turn right across the bridge over the Oued Kelâa. Take the obvious

track that heads south-east up the spur emanating from Jebel Azra (1375m), eventually passing below the peak (it's an extra 20-minute scramble to the summit) after two hours' walking.

There are no reliable water sources between here and Izrafene so fill up before you leave. The views across the steep gorges and jagged mountains towards the Mediterranean from the ridges and summit are spectacular.

The trail then heads south into more rolling, hilly country over a small col (the trail bearing left here leads east to Taourarte and then to Bou Ahmed on the coast) and south into the village of Izrafene. Head south through the village and along the hillside to a spring. Replenish your water supplies and then continue south into and along a narrow valley, before picking up a trail that leads east up the hillside to a ridge where the path forks. Turn left, walk 20m and then turn right onto a trail that heads south-east to Abou Bnar via a saddle shaded by holm oak. Continue south-east through the village to a river and grassy area south of the marabout of Sidi Jil (a possible *camp site*).

You can either camp here or, after visiting the marabout that lies further to the south-east, head west along a 4WD track that follows the river to a second, beautiful and more secluded *camp site* on an area of flat pasture (1325m) south-west of Abou Bnar – there's a spring close by.

Alternative Routes If supplies are required then there's a small shop in Beni M'Hamed, south of Abou Bnar. From Sidi Jil a trail winds south around the head of the Oued Tijidda Valley to the village, though it's also possible to drop down to it from the camp site south-west of Abou Bnar. Either way, it's best to make the trip as part of Stage 4 (see following).

Stage 4: Pastures above Abou Bnar to Talassemtane National Park
2–2½ hours, 6km, 352m ascent

From the camp site south-west of Abou Bnar, walk back to the 4WD track. Turn left crossing the river and walk into the pine woodland. Ignore a turn-off on the left and turn right at the T-junction (a left turn will take you down into Beni M'Hamed) and just keep trekking south as the track gradually keeps climbing until east of El-Jebel Lakraa (2159m) about 1½ hours after setting out. You will have gone by en route a number of passes and some stunning viewpoints.

Ignore an old 4WD track that heads east and keep heading south, descending now, for 10 minutes until a turn on the left leads to the house of the Eaux et Forêts guardian for Talassemtane National Park. A warm and highly knowledgeable man, he welcomes trekkers and allows them to camp in his compound.

Side Trips The short walking day allows plenty of time to explore and watch wildlife. Talassemtane National Park is where you are most likely to see Barbary apes.

An excellent afternoon wildlife walk takes you north back along the 4WD track up from the guardian's house to a clearing and junction. Turn right and follow the track east into mgou country – you can stumble across troops of these tail-less apes from here on in. The track bends south giving great views out across the valley to the long ridge of Jebel Taloussisse (2005m) before turning briefly east again. Here a trail on the right leads south over the spur of Talassemtane (1941m) to a football pitch (strange, but true) on an area of flat land. From here it's possible to make a rocky traverse west back to the camp site.

Alternatively, there's El-Jebel Lakraa (2159m) to be climbed. The best approach is from the north of the mountain, trekking along the ridge to descend down one of the stream gullies south-east of the summit. However, there's no fixed path and it's a scramble in places. Allow around 3½ hours return.

Stage 5: Talassemtane National Park to Bab Taza
2½–3½ hours, 13.5km, 825m descent
This simple day walk is a steady descent south-west along the 4WD track to Bab Taza. After turning left out of the Eaux et Forêts

compound and descending for 30 minutes a pleasant grassy clearing (and alternative camp site) is reached. Some amazing cave systems are found in this area and close to the camp site is **Grotte Tikhobaie**, which is 140m deep. Climbing equipment and caving experience are required.

The trail then swings through a wide pasture and the cork woodland of Jebel Setsou (1363m) before arriving in Bab Taza, about 2½ hours after setting out. There are numerous cafes in the small town and regular grand taxis to Chefchaouen (Dr10) from the western end of town.

OTHER WALKS IN THE RIF
Chefchaouen to the Mediterranean
This popular five-day, one-way trek basically follows the first 2½ stages of the Chefchaouen to Bab Taza trek described previously, before heading north-east to the tiny fishing village of Bou Ahmed. You'll need the survey sheets *Chaouen*, *Bab Taza*, *Talembote* and *Bou Hammed*. See the Rif Mountains section in the Mediterranean Coast & the Rif chapter for more information on this area.

Jebel el-Kelaâ
Towering over Chefchaouen, Jebel el-Kelaâ (1616m) is an inviting peak and can be easily climbed in one day. The route follows the 4WD track taken on the first day of the Chefchaouen to Bab Taza walk. The best route is to head up west of Chefchaouen past Aïn Tissimlane and then, at the top of the zig-zags, traverse back west along the mountain to a saddle and then up to the summit. Descend back east to the saddle and then head north down into a cluster of villages on the other side of the mountain. El-Kelaâ, one of these villages, has 16th century grain stores and a mosque with a leaning minaret. A number of simple tracks lead back to Chefchaouen.

Jebel Tissouka & Sfiha Telj Ridge Walk
Both these mountains look deservedly impressive from Chefchaouen and this trek (a

climb and scramble in places) should certainly not be attempted alone; taking a guide is advisable. The trek will take a good 10 hours.

From Chefchaouen, walk past the Spanish Mosque on the mule track south to Mechkralla. About 800m before the village a track leads north-east straight up towards the lower peak (1942m) of Jebel Tissouka. Head east to the true summit (2122m) then north along the ridge to Sfiha Telj (2038m). From here there's a very rocky and jagged section to the pass and 4WD track back to Chefchaouen.

Jebel Tidiquin

Though Ketama, 99km east of Chefchaouen, is a troublesome place, it is the launching point for treks up Jebel Tidiquin (2448m), the Rif's highest mountain. You are well advised to bring a guide from Chefchaouen for the climb, which is best approached from Tleta-Ketama, a tiny place 9km south-west of Ketama. From here, a track of sorts climbs west some 1000m to the rounded summit.

The region east and south-east of the mountain is untouched trekking country, though asking for maps of this region leads to raised eyebrows.

The Anti Atlas

The last mountain range before the Sahara, the arid pink and ochre-coloured mountains of the Anti Atlas are rarely explored by trekkers. Tafraoute is the ideal launching point with the quartzite massif of Jebel al-Kest (2359m), the 'Amethyst Mountain' lying about 10km to the north, and the twin peaks of Adrar Mqorn (2344m) 10km to the south-east. The arid, jagged mass of the peaks are in stark contrast to the irrigated valleys and oasis.

At the eastern end of the Anti Atlas is Jebel Siroua, a dramatic volcano that offers an excellent and varied long-distance trek. See Tafraoute and Jebel Siroua in the South Atlantic Coast chapter for more information on this region.

AROUND TAFRAOUTE
Planning

Several local people offer guiding services and a number of foreign adventure travel companies use the area. English-speaker Mohammed Sahnoun Ouhammou (☎ 08-800547) specialises in treks and mountain-bike trips in and around the Afella-Igir oasis south of Tafraoute. Abid Ahdaj (☎ 08-800210 at Maison Touareg), from the village of Taska offers much the same service; as does Abdoulah Brahim (also of the Maison Touareg and based in Tafraoute from October to April); he can also provide logistical support.

Jebel al-Kest and the approaches from Tafraoute are covered by the 1:50,000 map sheets *Had Tahala* and *Tanalt,* while the whole area is covered by 1:100,000 sheets *Annzi, Tafrawt, Foum al-Hisn* and *Taghjijt.*

Other than the odd small store you won't find many supplies in the area and mules are not commonly used in the Anti Atlas.

Despite the occasional snowfall on the high passes and peaks, the Anti Atlas is best walked at the end of winter – late February is ideal. Day-time temperatures may be 20°C, but at night it can drop below freezing. Accommodation can be found in the villages, but having a tent is an advantage.

There are also quite a few climbing opportunities around Tafraoute. A small craft shop in the souq area, Meeting Place of Nomads, has copies of routes and maps put together by climbers who have passed this way.

The Treks

Running roughly east to west south of Jebel al-Kest, sits a row of villages in the Ameln Valley. Diverted springs irrigate terraced arable lands and orchards, while each village is linked to the next by a network of paths and irrigation channels. The highest village in the valley, Taghdichte, is the launching point for a day ascent of Jebel al-Kest. It's a tough scramble, and the ascent is best seen as part of a gentle trek east through the valley from, say, Timertmat (where there are some excellent day walks) to Oumesnat (both villages lie just off the 7148 road). This is an enchanting area to explore.

South-east of Tafraoute the possibilities are equally exciting. Adrar Mqorn is a hard (but worthwhile) scramble. Due south of its twin peaks a gorge and pass lead though *palmeraies* (oasis-like areas) to the oasis of Afella-Ighir. There is plenty to explore.

JEBEL SIROUA

Some way south of the High Atlas at the eastern edge of Anti Atlas is the isolated volcanic peak of Jebel Siroua (3304m). Isolated villages, tremendous gorges, a tricky final ascent and some dramatic scenery all make this an excellent seven- to eight-day trek.

Planning

Guides, mules and advice can be obtained at *Auberge Souktana*, a couple of kilometres east of Taliouine on the main road. The 1:100,000 sheet *Taliwine* and 1:50,000 *Sirwa* maps cover the route.

In winter it can be fiercely cold in the region and the best time to trek is spring. See Taliouine & Jebel Siroua in the Central Coast section in the South Atlantic Coast chapter for further information.

The Trek

From Taliouine a dirt trail heads east up the Zagmouzine Valley to Tagmout and then north-east, ascending the summit on the morning of the fourth day. Descending into the gorges for the night, Tagouyamt is reached on the fifth day. You'll find limited supplies here and someone may offer to put you up, though there's a good place to camp in the amazing Tislit Gorge. After reaching Ihoukarn you can either head south to the P32 Taliouine-Ouarzazate road at Tizi n'Taghatine (and pick up passing transport) or keep truckin' west towards Taliouine.

Jebel Sarhro Range

The starkly beautiful Jebel Sarhro range of mountains continues the line of the Anti Atlas, rising up between the High Atlas and Dadès Valley to the north and the sub-Sahara that stretches away to the south.

Little-visited and totally undeveloped (for the tourist market), it offers a landscape of flat-topped mesas, deep gorges and twisted volcanic pinnacles softened by date palms and almond groves. It's wild, arid, isolated nomad country. The great warriors of the south were the Aït Atta people of this region and their last stand against the French took place here, on Jebel Bou Gafer, in 1933.

PLANNING

You could set out from the towns of El-Kelaâ M'Gouna or Boumalne du Dadès (see the Dadès Valley & the Gorges section in the Central Morocco chapter), north of the range, but the ideal place to start from is the village of N'Kob, 67km south-east of Agdz. This village has basic *cafes* and *rooms* to rent and there are rock carvings nearby. Market day in N'Kob is Sunday – the day you'll find most local transport heading that way. You can hire mules in N'Kob, but you will probably be better off organising guides at the Hôtel Ali in Marrakesh or at El-Kelaâ M'Gouna.

Occasional transport runs to and from the provincial town of Ikniouln at the northern edge of the range to Boumalne du Dadès, where a market is held on Wednesday.

Jebel Sarhro is a winter trekking destination and a number of foreign tour operators run good-value trips here. The ideal times to trek are spring, when there is still water around and night-time temperatures no longer fall well below zero, or late autumn when you may see Berber clans moving their camps down from the higher mountains. Summer is scorchingly hot (more than 35°C), water sources disappear, and snakes and scorpions are two a penny. Dehydration is common at any time of the year.

All supplies should be bought beforehand in Ouarzazate or Marrakesh (N'Kob is OK for tea, tinned fish, biscuits and bread) and carried for the duration, though you'll come across eggs, dates, almonds, bread and tinned fish in the villages. In this environment, and with the amount of water that must often be carried, mules are a worthy investment.

The paved A6956 heading east to Rissani from near Agdz skirts the southern edge of the range. Mid-way along this route is the

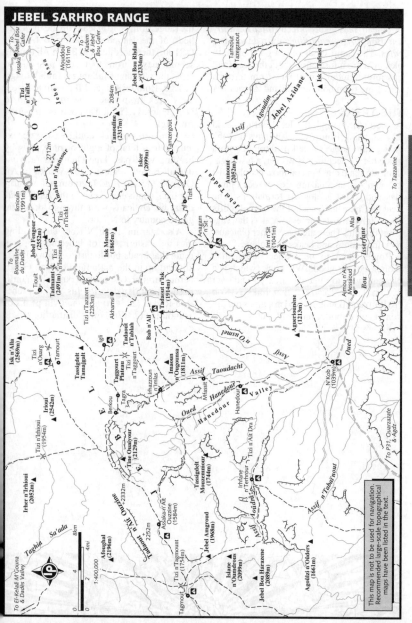

JEBEL SARHRO RANGE

This map is not to be used for navigation.
Recommended large-scale topographical
maps have been listed in the text.

small town of **Tazzarine**, which has the simple, clean, reasonably priced *Hôtel/Restaurant Bougaffer*, *camping* and a few basic *cafes*. The camp site here is a good place to pick up more information about the area (and possibly a guide). Local buses run through Tazzarine from both Erfoud and Zagora.

THE TREKS

A good trek through the Jebel Sarhro could take anything from five to 20 days and the choices are endless – talk it through with a guide before deciding. However, a few highlights do stand out. First on most people's list is Bab n'Ali, an amazing area of rock pinnacles and weird geological formations. The Tete de Chamaux (Head of the Camel) cliffs above Igli are also impressive, as is the Taggourt Plateau. There are many other plateaus, rock formations and peaks to explore.

Routes tend to be longer rather than shorter, but the good 4WD track (which is a pleasant two- to three-day trek up and over 2283m Tizi n'Tazazert) that links N'Kob (1039m) and Ikniouln (1991m), gives the option of some shorter one-way routes.

One five-day loop on the western side of the range from N'Kob leads up the dry river beds of the Hanedour Valley to **Mfassit** (1210m) then north-east to **Bab n'Ali** (on the second day). From there it's possible to cross the plateau of **Tadaout n'Tablah** to **Igli** village. Both N'Kob and Ikniouln are two-days' trek from here. The route south to N'Kob across Tizi n'Taggourt is an option from Igli.

From Igli the trek could easily be extended to a total of eight or nine days by heading west past Tine Ouaiyour (a wonderful raised plateau) to Assaka n'Aït Ouzzine (1584m) and **Tagmout** before turning back south-east down to the **Assif Aoûdraz**, which leads west through dramatic gorge country to N'Kob.

Also starting from N'Kob, but heading into the eastern side of Jebel Sarhro, is a route that heads north-east to Imi n'Sit, Tizlit and up to the battlefield of Bou Gafer, before turning west back to Ikniouln. You'll need at least five days for this trek, but Jebel Bou Rhdad (2334m) and the twin peaks of Tamouline (2317m) offer distractions.

Language

MOROCCAN ARABIC

Moroccan Arabic *(darija)* is a dialect of the standard language, but is so different in many respects as to be virtually like another tongue. It's the everyday language that differs most from that of other Arabic-speaking peoples. More specialised or educated language tends to be much the same across the Arab world, although pronunciation varies considerably. An Arab from Jordan or Iraq will have little trouble discussing politics or literature with an educated Moroccan, but might have difficulty ordering lunch.

The influence of French is seen in some of the words that Moroccan Arabic has adopted. An example is the use of the French word for 'coach' (intercity bus), *car*.

The spread of radio and TV has increased Moroccans' exposure to and understanding of what is commonly known as Modern Standard Arabic (MSA). MSA, which has grown from the classical language of the Quran and poetry, is the written and spoken lingua franca (common language) of the Arab world, and in fact not so far removed from the daily language of the Arab countries of the Levant. It's the language of all media and the great majority of modern Arabic literature.

Foreign students of the language constantly face the dilemma of whether first to learn MSA (which could mean waiting some time before being able to talk with shopkeepers) and then a chosen dialect, or simply to acquire spoken competence in the latter.

If you do take the time to learn even a few words and phrases, you will discover and experience much more while travelling through the country. Just making the attempt implies a respect for local culture that Moroccans all too infrequently sense in visitors to their country.

If you'd like a more comprehensive guide to the Arabic spoken in the Maghreb, get a copy of Lonely Planet's *Moroccan Arabic phrasebook*.

Pronunciation

Pronunciation of Arabic can be tongue-tying for someone unfamiliar with the intonation and combination of sounds. Pronounce the transliterated words slowly and clearly.

This language guide should help, but bear in mind that the myriad rules governing pronunciation and vowel use are too extensive to be covered here.

Vowels

a	as in 'had'
e	as in 'bet'
i	as in 'hit'
u	as in 'put'

A macron over a vowel indicates that the vowel has a long sound:

ā	as the 'a' in 'father'
ī	as the 'e' in 'ear', only softer
ō	as the 'o' in 'note'
ū	as the 'oo' in 'food'

Long vowels are also sometimes transliterated as double vowels, eg, 'aa' (ā), 'ee' (ī), 'oo' (ū).

Consonants

Pronunciation for all Arabic consonants is covered in the alphabet table on the following page. Note that when double consonants occur in transliterations, both are pronounced. For example, *hammam* (bath), is pronounced 'ham-mam'.

For those who read some Arabic, it's worth noting that the Moroccans have added a letter for the hard 'g' (as in *Agadir*) – a *kaf* ('k' in transliterations) with three dots above it.

Other Sounds

Arabic has two sounds that are very tricky for non-Arabs to produce, the 'ayn and the glottal stop. The letter 'ayn represents a

The Arabic Alphabet

Final	Medial	Initial	Alone	Transliteration	Pronunciation
ﺍ			ﺍ	ā	as the 'a' in 'father'
ﺐ	ﺒ	ﺑ	ﺏ	b	as in 'bet'
ﺖ	ﺘ	ﺗ	ﺕ	t	as in 'ten' (but the tongue touches the teeth)
ﺚ	ﺜ	ﺛ	ﺙ	th	as in 'thin'; also as 's' or 't'
ﺞ	ﺠ	ﺟ	ﺝ	zh	as the 's' in 'measure'
ﺢ	ﺤ	ﺣ	ﺡ	H	a strongly whispered 'h', almost like a sigh of relief
ﺦ	ﺨ	ﺧ	ﺥ	kh	a rougher sound than the 'ch' in Scottish *loch*
ﺪ			ﺩ	d	as in 'den' (but the tongue touches the teeth)
ﺬ			ﺫ	dh	as the 'th' in 'this'; also as 'd' or 'z'
ﺮ			ﺭ	r	a rolled 'r', as in the Spanish word *caro*
ﺰ			ﺯ	z	as in 'zip'
ﺲ	ﺴ	ﺳ	ﺱ	s	as in 'so', never as in 'wisdom'
ﺶ	ﺸ	ﺷ	ﺵ	sh	as in 'ship'
ﺺ	ﺼ	ﺻ	ﺹ	ş	emphatic 's' *
ﺾ	ﻀ	ﺿ	ﺽ	ḑ	emphatic 'd' *
ﻂ	ﻄ	ﻃ	ﻁ	ţ	emphatic 't' *
ﻆ	ﻈ	ﻇ	ﻅ	ẓ	emphatic 'z' *
ﻊ	ﻌ	ﻋ	ﻉ	'	the Arabic letter 'ayn; pronounce as a glottal stop – like the closing of the throat before saying 'Oh oh!' (see Other Sounds on p.511)
ﻎ	ﻐ	ﻏ	ﻍ	gh	a guttural sound like Parisian 'r'
ﻒ	ﻔ	ﻓ	ﻑ	f	as in 'far'
ﻖ	ﻘ	ﻗ	ﻕ	q	a strongly guttural 'k' sound; often pronounced as a glottal stop
ﻚ	ﻜ	ﻛ	ﻙ	k	as in 'king'
ﻞ	ﻠ	ﻟ	ﻝ	l	as in 'lamb'
ﻢ	ﻤ	ﻣ	ﻡ	m	as in 'me'
ﻦ	ﻨ	ﻧ	ﻥ	n	as in 'name'
ﻪ	ﻬ	ﻫ	ﻩ	h	as in 'ham'
ﻮ			ﻭ	w	as in 'wet'; or
				ū	long, as the 'oo' on 'food'; or
				aw	as the 'ow' in 'how'
ﻲ	ﻴ	ﻳ	ﻱ	y	as in 'yes'; or
				ī	as the 'e' in 'ear', only softer; or
				ay	as the 'y' in 'by' or as the 'ay' in 'way'

Vowels Not all Arabic vowel sounds are represented in the alphabet. See Pronunciation on p.511.

*Emphatic Consonants Emphatic consonants are similar to their nonemphatic counterparts but are pronounced with greater tension in the tongue and throat.

sound with no English equivalent that comes even close. It is similar to the glottal stop (which is not actually represented in the alphabet) but the muscles at the back of the throat are gagged more forcefully – it has been described as the sound of someone being strangled. In many transliteration systems 'ayn is represented by an opening quotation mark, and the glottal stop by a closing quotation mark. To make the transliterations in this language guide easier to use, we have not distinguished between the glottal stop and the 'ayn, using the closing quotation mark to represent both sounds. You should find that Arabic speakers will still understand you.

Transliteration

It's worth noting here that transliteration from the Arabic script into English – or any other language for that matter – is at best an approximate science.

The presence of sounds unknown in European languages and the fact that the script is 'defective' (most vowels are not written) combine to make it nearly impossible to settle on one universally accepted method of transliteration. A wide variety of spellings is therefore possible for words when they appear in Latin script – and that goes for places and people's names as well.

The whole thing is further complicated by the wide variety of dialects and the imaginative ideas Arabs themselves often have on appropriate spelling in, say, English

The Transliteration Dilemma

TE Lawrence, when asked by his publishers to clarify 'inconsistencies in the spelling of proper names' in *Seven Pillars of Wisdom* – his account of the Arab Revolt in WWI – wrote back:

Arabic names won't go into English. There are some 'scientific systems' of transliteration, helpful to people who know enough Arabic not to need helping, but a washout for the world. I spell my names anyhow, to show what rot the systems are.

(words spelt one way in Jordan may look very different again in Lebanon, with strong French influences); not even the most venerable of Western Arabists have been able to come up with a satisfactory solution.

While striving to reflect the language as closely as possible and aiming at consistency, this book generally spells place, street and hotel names and the like as the locals have done. Don't be surprised if you come across several versions of the same thing.

Greetings & Civilities

When Arabic speakers meet, they often exchange more extensive and formalised greetings than westerners are used to. Any attempt to use a couple (whether correctly or not) won't go astray.

When addressing a man the polite term more or less equivalent to Mr is *asīdī* (shortened to *sī* before a name); for women the polite form of address is *lalla*, followed by the first name. You may be addressed as 'Mr John' or 'Mrs Anne'. To attract the attention of someone on the street or a waiter in a cafe, the expression *shrīf* is commonly used.

Hello.	*ssalamū 'lekum* (lit: 'peace upon you')
Goodbye.	*bessalama*
Goodbye.	*m'a ssalama* ('with peace')
Good morning.	*ṣbah lkhīr*
Good evening.	*mselkhīr*
Please.	*'afak/'afik/'afakum* (to m/f/pl)
Thank you (very much).	*shukran (bezzef)*
You're welcome.	*la shukran 'la wezhb*
Yes.	*īyeh/na'am*

(*na'am* can also mean 'I'm sorry, could you repeat that, please')

Yes, OK.	*wakha*
No.	*la*
No, thank you.	*la, shukran*
Excuse me.	*smeh līya*
How are you?	*labas* or *kīf halek?*
Fine, thank you.	*labas, barak llāhū fīk*
Fine, praise God.	*bekhīr, lhamdū llāh*

Pronouns

I	*ana*
you (sg)	*nta/nti* (m/f)
he/she	*hūwa/hīya*
we	*hna*
you (pl)	*ntūma*
they	*hūma*

Useful Words & Phrases

Who?	*shkūn?*
Why?	*'alesh?*
How?	*kīfash?*
Which?	*ashmen?*
Where?	*fīn?*
Is there ...?	*wash kein ...?*
What's that?	*ash dak shī?*
If God wills.	*ensha'llāh*
Go ahead/Come on!	*zid!*

big/small	*kabīr/saghīr*
open	*meHlūl*
closed	*masdūd*
now	*daba*

Do you speak (English)?	*wash kat'ref (neglīzīya)?*
What do you call this?	*'ah katsmiw hada/ hadi?* (m/f)
I understand.	*fhemt*
I don't understand.	*mafhemtsh*

Small Talk

What's your name?	*shnū smītek?*
My name is ...	*smītī ...*
How old are you?	*shHal f'amerek?*
I'm (25).	*'āndī (khamsa ū'ashrīn) 'am*
Where are you from?	*mnīn nta/nti/ntūma?* (m/f/pl)

I'm/We're from ...	*ana/hna min ...*
America	*'amrīka*
Australia	*ustralya*
Canada	*kanada*
England	*anglatira*
France	*fransa*
Germany	*almānya*
Italy	*'itālīya*
Japan	*el-zhaban*
The Netherlands	*hulanda*
Spain	*isbanya*

Sweden	*sswīd*
Switzerland	*swīsra*

Getting Around

When does the ... leave/arrive?	*wufūqash keikhrezh/ keiwṣul ...?*
boat	*lbabūr*
bus	*ṭṭubīs*
intercity bus	*lkar*
train	*tran*

Where is (the) ...?	*fīn kein ...?*
bus station	*mheṭṭa dyal ṭṭōbīsat*
ticket office	*maktab lwerqa*
train station	*lagār*

street	*zenqa*
city	*medīna*
village	*qerya*
bus stop	*blaṣa dyal ṭṭōbīsat*
station	*mheṭṭa*

What's the fare?	*shhal taman lwarka?*
Which bus is going to ...?	*ashmen kar ghādī til ...?*
Is this bus going to ...?	*wash had lkar ghādī l ...?*
How many buses per day go to ...?	*shhal men kar kaymshī l ... fenhar?*
Please tell me when we arrive at ...	*'afak īla wṣelna l ... gūlhalīya*

I want to pay for one place only.	*bghīt nkhelleṣ blāṣāwaheda*
Stop here please.	*wqef henna 'afak*
Please wait for me.	*tsennanī 'afak*
Is this seat free?	*wash had lblāṣā khawīya?*
Where can I hire a bicycle?	*fīn yimkin li nkri bshklit?*

address	*'unwān'*
air-conditioning	*klīmatīzasīyun*
airport	*maṭar*
camel	*zhmel*
car	*ṭumubīl*
daily	*yawmīyyan*
donkey	*hmar*
horse	*'awd*
number	*raqem*
ticket	*werqa*

Directions

How do I get to ...?	kīfesh ghādīnuwṣul l ...?
How far?	bshhal b'eid?
left/right	līser/līmen
here/there	hna/hunak
next to	hedda
opposite	'eks
behind	men luy
north	shamel
south	zhanūb
east	sherq
west	gherb

Around Town

Where is (the) ...?	fīn kein ...?
bank	shī bānka
barber	shī hellaq
beach	laplazh
... embassy	ssifāra dyal ...
market	lmarshei
mosque	zhame'
museum	al-matHaf
old city	lmdīna lqdīma
palace	al-qasr
pharmacy	farmasyan
police station	lkūmīsarīya
post office	lbūsṭā
restaurant	riṣtura/maṭ'am
university	zhamī'a
zoo	hadīqa delhayawa

I want to change ...	bghīt nṣerref ...
some money	shī flūs
travellers cheques	shek sīyahī

Accommodation

Where is a hotel?	fīn kein shī ūṭel
Can I see the room?	wash yemkenlī nshūf lbīt?
How much is a room for one day?	bash hal kein gbeit l wahed nhar
This room is too expensive.	had lbīt bezzaf ghalī
This room is good.	had lbīt mezyana

bed	namūsīya
blanket	bṭṭānīya
camp site	shī mukheyyem

Signs

ENTRY	مدخل
EXIT	خروج
TOILETS (Men)	حمام للرجال
TOILETS (Women)	حمام للنساء
HOSPITAL	مستشفى
POLICE	الشرطة
PROHIBITED	ممنوع

full	'amer
hot water	lma skhūn
key	sarūt
room	bīt
sheet	īzar
shower	dūsh
toilet	bīt lma
youth hostel	'ūberzh, dār shshabab

Shopping

Where can I buy ...?	fīn ghādī neshrī ...?
How much?	bshhal?
That's very expensive.	ghalī bezzaf
enough	kafī
Do you have ...?	wash 'andkom ...?
Can I pay by credit card?	wash nkder nkhelleṣ bel kart kredī?
stamps	ttnaber
newspaper	zhārida

Time

What time is it?	shal fessa'a?
When?	fūqash//īmta?

today	lyūm
tomorrow	ghedda
yesterday	lbareh
morning	feṣsbah
afternoon	fel'shīya
evening	'shīya
day/night	nhar/fellīl
week/month/year	l'ūsbū'/shshhar/l'am

Emergencies

Help!	*'teqnī!*
Help me please!	*'awennī 'afak!*
Call the police!	*'ayyet 'la lbūlīs!*
Call a doctor!	*'ayyet 'la shī tbīb!*
Thief!	*sheffar!*
I've been robbed.	*tsreqt*
Where's the toilet?	*fīn kein lbīt lma?*
Go away!	*sīr fhalek!*
I'm lost.	*tweddert*

after	*men b'd*
on time	*felweqt*
early	*bekrī*
late	*m'ettel*
quickly	*bizerba/dghīya*
slowly	*beshwīya*

Days

Monday	*nhar letnīn*
Tuesday	*nhar ttlat*
Wednesday	*nhar larb'*
Thursday	*nhar lekhmīs*
Friday	*nhar zhzhem'a*
Saturday	*nhar ssebt*
Sunday	*nhar lhedd*

Months

In Moroccan Arabic the names of the months are virtually the same as in English and sound very similar:

January	*yanāyir*
February	*fibrāyir*
March	*māris*
April	*abrīl*
May	*māyu*
June	*yunyu*
July	*yulyu*
August	*aghustus/ghusht*
September	*sibtimbir/shebtenber*
October	*uktūbir*
November	*nufimbir/nu'enbir*
December	*disimbir/dijenbir*

Arabic Numbers

Arabic numerals are simple enough to learn and, unlike the written language, run from left to right across the page.

Due to the fact that it was colonised by France, Morocco uses standard Western numerical systems rather than those normally associated with Arab countries.

0	*sifr*
1	*wahed*
2	*zhūzh*
3	*tlata*
4	*reba'a*
5	*khamsa*
6	*setta*
7	*seb'a*
8	*tmenya*
9	*tes'ūd*
10	*'ashra*
11	*hdāsh*
12	*tnāsh*
13	*teltāsh*
14	*rba'tāsh*
15	*khamstāsh*
16	*settāsh*
17	*sbetāsh*
18	*tmentāsh*
19	*tse'tāsh*
20	*'ashrīn*
21	*wahed ū'ashrīn*
22	*tnein ū'ashrīn*
30	*tlatīn*
40	*reb'īn*
50	*khamsīn*
60	*settīn*
70	*seb'īn*
80	*tmanīn*
90	*tes'īn*
100	*mya*
200	*myatein*
225	*myatein ūkhamsa ū'shrīn*
300	*teltmya*
400	*rba'mya*
1000	*alf*
2000	*alfein*
3000	*telt alf*

Ordinal Numbers

first	*lūwwel*
second	*tanī*
third	*talet*
fourth	*rabe'*
fifth	*khames*

FRENCH

The most commonly spoken European language in Morocco is French, so if the thought of getting your tongue around Arabic is too much, it would be a good investment to learn some French.

An inability on the part of westerners to speak French is seen by some French-speaking (and therefore at least bilingual) Moroccans as the height of ignorance.

The following words and phrases should help you communicate on a basic level in French:

Greetings & Civilities

Hello/Good morning/Good day.	*Bonjour.*
Goodbye.	*Au revoir/Salut.*
Good evening.	*Bonsoir.*
(Have a) good evening!	*Bonne soirée!*
Good night.	*Bonne nuit.*
Please.	*S'il vous plait.*
Thank you.	*Merci.*
You're welcome.	*De rien/Je vous en prie.*
Yes.	*Oui.*
No.	*Non.*
No, thank you.	*Non, merci.*
Excuse me.	*Excusez-moi/Pardon.*
How are you?	*Comment allez-vous/ Ça va?*
I'm well, thanks.	*Bien, merci.*

Useful Words & Phrases

I	*je*
you	*vous*
he/she	*il/elle*
we	*nous*
they	*ils/elles* (m/f)
Why?	*Pourquoi?*
now	*maintenant*
Is/Are there ...?	*(Est-ce qu')il y a ...?*
big/small	*grand/petit*
open/closed	*ouvert/fermé*
Do you speak English?	*Parlez-vous anglais?*
I understand.	*Je comprends.*
I don't understand.	*Je ne comprends pas.*

Small Talk

What's your name?	*Comment vous appelez-vous?*
My name is ...	*Je m'appelle ...*
How old are you?	*Quel âge avez-vous?*
I'm 25.	*J'ai vingt-cinq ans.*
Where are you from?	*D'ou êtes-vous?*
I'm from ...	*Je viens ...*
We're from ...	*Nous venons ...*
America	*de l'Amérique*
Australia	*de l'Australie*
Canada	*du Canada*
England	*de l'Angleterre*
Germany	*de l'Allemagne*
Italy	*de l'Italie*
Japan	*du Japon*
The Netherlands	*des Pays Bas*
Spain	*de l'Espagne*
Sweden	*du Suède*
Switzerland	*de la Suisse*

Getting Around

I want to go to ...	*Je veux aller à ...*
What is the fare to ...?	*Combien coûte le billet pour ...?*
When does the ... leave/arrive?	*À quelle heure part/arrive ...?*
bus	*l'autobus*
intercity bus	*le car*
train	*le train*
boat	*le bateau*
ferry	*le bac*
Where is the ...?	*Ou est ...?*
bus station for ...	*la gare routière pour ...*
train station	*la gare*
ticket office	*la billeterie/le guichet*
street	*la rue*
city	*la ville*
village	*le village*
bus stop	*l'arrêt d'autobus*
Which bus goes to ...?	*Quel autobus/car part pour ...?*
Does this bus go to ...?	*Ce car-là va-t-il à ...?*

How many buses per day go to ...?	Il y a combien de cars chaque jour pour ...?
Please tell me when we arrive in ...	Dites-moi s'il vous plaît à quelle heure on arrive ...
Stop here, please.	Arrêtez ici, s'il vous plaît.
Please wait for me.	Attendez-moi ici, s'il vous plaît.
May I sit here?	Puis-je m'asseoir ici?
Where can I rent a bicycle?	Ou est-ce que je peux louer une bicyclette?

address	adresse
air-conditioning	climatisation
airport	aéroport
camel	chameau
car	voiture
crowded	beaucoup de monde
daily	chaque jour
donkey	âne
horse	cheval
number	numéro
ticket	billet
Wait!	Attendez!

Directions

How far is ...?	À combien de kilomètres est ...?
left/right	gauche/droite
here/there	ici/là
next to	à côté de
opposite	en face
behind	derrière
Which?	Quel?
Where?	Ou?
north	nord
south	sud
east	est
west	ouest

Around Town

Where is the ...?	Ou est ...?
bank	la banque
barber	le coiffeur
beach	la plage
embassy	l'ambassade
market	le marché
mosque	la mosquée
museum	le musée
old city	le centre historique
palace	le palais
pharmacy	la pharmacie
police station	la police
post office	la poste
restaurant	le restaurant
university	l'université
zoo	le zoo

I want to change ...	Je voudrais changer ...
money	de l'argent
travellers cheques	des chèques de voyage

Accommodation

Where is the hotel?	Ou est l'hôtel?
May I see the room?	Peux-je voir la chambre?
How much is this room per night?	Combien est cette chambre pour une nuit?
Do you have any cheaper rooms?	Avez-vous des chambresmoins chères?
That's too expensive.	C'est trop cher.
This is fine.	Ça va bien.

bed	lit
blanket	couverture
camp site	camping
full	complet
hot water	eau chaude
key	clef or clé
roof	terrasse
room	chambre
sheet	drap
shower	douche
toilet	les toilettes
washbasin	lavabo
youth hostel	auberge de jeunesse

Shopping

Where can I buy ...?	Ou est-ce que je peux acheter ...?
How much?	Combien?
How much does it cost?	Ça coûte combien?
more	plus
less	moins
too much	trop cher

Emergencies – French

Call the police!	*Appelez la police!*
Call a doctor!	*Appelez un médecin!*
Help me please!	*Au secours/*
	Aidez-moi!
Thief!	*(Au) voleur!*

Do you have ...?	*Avez-vous ...?*
stamps	*des timbres*
a newspaper	*un journal*

Time

What is the time?	*Quelle heure est-il?*
At what time?	*À quelle heure?*
When?	*Quand?*
today	*aujourd'hui*
tomorrow	*demain*
yesterday	*hier*
morning	*matin*
afternoon	*après-midi*
evening	*soir*
day/night	*jour/nuit*
week/month/year	*semaine/mois/an*
after	*après*
on time	*à l'heure*
early	*tôt*
late	*tard*
quickly	*vite*
slowly	*lentement*

Days

Monday	*lundi*
Tuesday	*mardi*
Wednesday	*mercredi*
Thursday	*jeudi*
Friday	*vendredi*
Saturday	*samedi*
Sunday	*dimanche*

Months

January	*janvier*
February	*février*
March	*mars*
April	*avril*
May	*mai*
June	*juin*
July	*juillet*
August	*août*
September	*septembre*
October	*octobre*
November	*novembre*
December	*décembre*

Numbers

0	*zéro*
1	*un*
2	*deux*
3	*trois*
4	*quatre*
5	*cinq*
6	*six*
7	*sept*
8	*huit*
9	*neuf*
10	*dix*
11	*onze*
12	*douze*
13	*treize*
14	*quatorze*
15	*quinze*
16	*seize*
17	*dix-sept*
18	*dix-huit*
19	*dix-neuf*
20	*vingt*
21	*vingt-et-un*
22	*vingt-deux*
30	*trente*
40	*quarante*
50	*cinquante*
60	*soixante*
70	*soixante-dix*
80	*quatre-vingts*
90	*quatre-vingt-dix*
100	*cent*
101	*cent un*
125	*cent vingt-cinq*
200	*deux cents*
300	*trois cents*
400	*quatre cents*
1000	*mille*
2000	*deux milles*

first	*premier*
second	*deuxième*
third	*troisième*
fourth	*quatrième*
fifth	*cinquième*

Food Terms

English	Arabic	French	English	Arabic	French
Vegetables & Pulses			kidneys	kelawwi	rognons
artichoke	qūq	artichaut	lamb	lehem ghenmee	agneau
cucumber	khiyaar	concombre	liver	kebda	foie
garlic	tūma	ail	meat	lehem	viande
green beans	lūbeeya	haricots verts			
haricot beans	fasūliya	haricots blancs	**Fruit**		
lentils	'āds	lentilles	apple	teffah	pomme
lettuce	khess	laitue	apricot	meshmash	abricot
mushroom	feggī	champignons	banana	banan/moz	banane
olives	zītoun	olives	dates	tmer	dattes
onion	besla	oignon	figs	kermūs	figues
peas	zelbana bisila	petits pois	fruit	fakiya	fruits
potatoes	batatas	pommes de terre	grapes	'eineb	raisins
tomato	mataisha tamatim	tomate	orange	līmūn	orange
vegetables	xôdra	légumes	pomegranate	remman	grenade
			watermelon	dellah	pastèque
Fish					
anchovies	shton	anchois	**Miscellaneous**		
cod	lamūrī	morue	bread	khubz	pain
lobster	lāngos	homard	butter	zebda	beurre
sardine	serdīn	sardine	chips	ships	frites
shrimp	qaimrūn	crevette	cheese	fromaj	fromage
sole	sol	sole	eggs	bayd	œufs
tuna	ton	thon	oil	zit	huile
whiting	merla	merlan	pepper	filfil/lebzaar	poivre
			salt	melha	sel
Meat			soup	chorba	potage
beef	begrī	bouef	spicy lentil soup	harira	...
camel	lehem jemil	chameau	sugar	sukur	sucre
chicken	farūj/dujaj	poulet	yogurt	zabadī/laban/danūn	yaourt

BERBER

There are three main dialects commonly delineated among the speakers of Berber, which in a certain sense also serve as loose lines of ethnic demarcation.

In the north, in the area centred on the Rif, the locals speak a dialect that has been called Riffian and is spoken as far south as Figuig on the Algerian frontier. The dialect that predominates in the Middle and High Atlas and the valleys leading into the Sahara goes by various names, including Braber or Amazigh.

More settled tribes of the High Atlas, Anti-Atlas, Souss Valley and south-western oases generally speak Tashelhit or Chleuh.

The following phrases are a selection from the Tashelhit dialect, the one visitors are likely to find most useful:

Greetings & Civilities

Hello.	la bes darik (m)
	la bes darim (f)
Hello (response).	la bes
Goodbye.	akayaūn arbī
Please.	barakalaufik
Thank you.	barakalaufik
Yes.	eyeh
No.	oho
Excuse me.	semhī
How are you?	menīk antgīt?
Fine, thank you.	la bes, lhamdulah

Good.	*īfulkī/īshwa*	the pass	*tizī*
Bad.	*khaib*		
See you later.	*akrawes dah inshallah*	Is it near/far?	*īs īqareb/yagūg?*
		straight	*nīshan*

Basics

		to the right	*fofasīnik*
Is there ...?	*īs īla ...?*	to the left	*fozelmad*
big/small	*mqorn/īmzī*		

Numbers

today	*zig sbah*
tomorrow	*ghasad*
yesterday	*īgdam*
Do you have ...?	*īs darūn ...?*
a lot/little	*bzef/īmīk*
food	*tīremt*
mule	*aserdon*
somewhere to	*kra lblast mahengwen*
sleep	
water	*amen*
How much is it?	*minshk aysker?*
no good	*ūr īfulkī mqorn/īmzī*
too expensive	*nuqs emīk*
give me	*fīyī*
I want ...	*rīh ...*

1	*yen*
2	*sīn*
3	*krad*
4	*koz*
5	*smūs*
6	*sddes*
7	*sa*
8	*tem*
9	*tza*
10	*mrawet*
11	*yen d mrawet*
12	*sīn d mrawet*
20	*ashrīnt*
21	*ashrīnt d yen d mrawet*
22	*ashrīnt d sīn d mrawet*
30	*ashrīnt d mrawet*
40	*snet id ashrīnt*
50	*snet id ashrīnt d mrawet*
100	*smūst id ashrīnt/mīya*

Getting Around

I want to go to ...	*rīh ...*
Where is (the) ...?	*mani hīla ...?*
village	*doorwar*
river	*asīt*
mountain	*adrar*

Glossary

This glossary is a list of Arabic (A), Berber (B), French (F) and Spanish (S) terms you may come across in Morocco. For a list of trekking terms, see the boxed text 'Useful Trekking Words' in the Trekking chapter.

agadir (B) – fortified communal granary
aid (A) – feast (also *eid*)
ain (A) – water source, spring
aït (B) – family (of), often precedes tribal and town names
akhbar (A) – great
Al-Andalus (A) – Muslim Spain and Portugal
Allah (A) – God
Almohads – puritanical Muslim group (1130–1269), originally Berber, which arose in response to the corrupt Almoravid dynasty
Almoravids – fanatical Muslim group (1054–1160) that ruled Spain and the Maghreb
'ashaab (A) – herbal remedies
auberges de jeuness (F) – youth hostels

bab (A) – gate
babouches – traditional leather slippers
bain (F) – see *hammam* and *douche*
baksheesh (A) – tip
bali (A) – old
baraka (A) – divine blessing or favour
Barbary – European term used to describe the North African coast from the 16th to 19th centuries
basilica – type of Roman administrative building; later used to describe churches
Bedouin (A) – desert dweller of Arabia; later used to denote nomadic Arab tribes
beni (A) – sons of, often precedes tribal name (also 'banu')
Berbers – indigenous inhabitants of North Africa
bidonville (F) – slum area, especially in Casablanca
borj (A) – fort; literally, tower (also 'burj')
brochette (F) – kebab; skewered meat

burnous (A) – traditional full-length cape with a hood, worn by men throughout the Maghreb

caid – see *qaid*
calèche (F) – horse-drawn carriage
caliph – successor of Mohammed; ruler in the Islamic world
calle (S) – street
camionette (F) – Berber pick-up truck
capitol – main temple of Roman town
caravanserai – large merchant's inn enclosing a courtyard, providing accommodation and a marketplace
cascades (F) – waterfall
chergui (A) – dry, easterly desert wind (also known as *sirocco*)
col (F) – mountain pass (see *tizi*)
Compagnie de Transports Marocaine (F) – CTM; national bus company
corniche (F) – coastal road
couscous – semolina, staple food of North Africa

dar (A) – a traditional town house
Délégation Régionale du Tourisme (F) – tourist office
douar (A) – word generally used for village in the High Atlas
douche (F) – public showers (see *hammam*)

Eaux et Forêts (F) – government ministry for national parks, forests, lakes and rivers
eid (A) – feast (also *aid*)
Ensemble Artisanal – government handicraft shop
erg (A) – sand dunes

fantasia – military exercise featuring a cavalry charge now performed for tourists
Fatimids – Muslim dynasty (909–1171) which defeated the Aghlabid dynasty; descendants of the Prophet's daughter Fatima and her husband, Ali (see *Shiites*)
faux guides – unofficial or informal guides
forum – open space at centre of Roman towns

foum (A) – usually mouth of a river or valley (from Arabic for mouth)

funduq (A) – caravanserai (often used to mean hotel)

gardiens de voitures (F) – car park attendants

gare routière (F) – bus station

ghar (A) – cave

ghurfa (A) – room

gîte (F) – hiker's accommodation

glaoua – rug with combination of flatweave and deep fluffy pile (also *zanafi*)

grand taxi (F) – (long-distance) shared taxi

guerba (B) – water bag made from the skin of a goat or sheep, seen hanging on the side of many Saharan vehicles

guichets automatiques (F) – automated teller machine (ATM)

haj (A) – pilgrimage to Mecca; hence 'haji', one who has made the pilgrimage

hammada – stony desert

hammam (A) – Turkish-style bathhouse with sauna and massage; also known by the French word *bain* (bath) or *bain maure* (Moorish bath)

hanbel – see *kilim*

harem (A) – (literally) a sacred or forbidden area; the family living area of a house or palace, primarily the domain of women

harira (A) – soup or broth with lentils and other vegetables

heddaoua (B) – wandering Berber minstrels

hejira (A) – the flight of the Prophet Mohammed from Mecca to Medina in AD 622; the first year of the Islamic calendar

hijab (A) – veil and women's head scarf

hôtel de ville (F) – town hall

ibn (A) – son of (also 'bin', 'ben')

Idrissids – Moroccan dynasty who reigned from AD 800–1080

iftar (A) – the breaking of the fast at sundown during Ramadan; breakfast (also 'ftur')

imam (A) – Muslim cleric

Interzone – the name (coined by author William Burroughs) for the period 1923–56 when Tangier was controlled by nine countries; notable for gun-running, prostitution, currency speculation and smuggling

Itissalat al-Maghrib (A) – public telephone office (see also *téléboutique*)

jamal (A) – camel

jami' (A) – Friday mosque (also 'djemaa', 'jama', 'jemaa' or 'jamaa')

jardin (F) – garden

jebel (A) – hill, mountain (sometimes 'djebel' in former French possessions)

jedid (A) – new (sometimes spelled 'jdid')

jellaba (A) – flowing men's garment, usually made of cotton

jezira (A) – island

kasbah (A) – fort, citadel; often also the administrative centre (also *qasba*)

khutba – Friday sermon preached by the imam of a mosque

kif (A) – marijuana

kilim – flatwoven blankets or floor coverings (also *hanbel*)

koubba (A) – sanctuary or shrine (also *qubba;* see also *marabout*)

ksar (A) – fortified stronghold (also *qasr;* plural 'ksour')

Maghreb (A) – west (literally, where the sun sets); used to describe the area covered by Morocco, Algeria, Tunisia and Libya

majoun (A) – sticky paste made of crushed seeds of the marijuana plant

marabout (A) – holy man or saint; also often used to describe the mausolea of these men, which are places of worship in themselves and sites of festivals or *moussems*

masjid (A) – another name for a mosque, particularly in a *medersa* (see also *jami'*)

mechouar (A) – royal assembly place

medersa (A) – college for teaching theology, law, Arabic literature and grammar; widespread throughout the Maghreb from the 13th century (also 'madrassa')

medina (A) – old city; used these days to describe the old Arab part of modern towns and cities

mellah (A) – Jewish quarter of medina

mihrab (A) – prayer niche in the wall of a mosque indicating the direction of Mecca (the *qibla*)

minbar (A) – pulpit in mosque; the *imam* delivers the sermon from one of the lower steps because the Prophet preached from the top step

moulay – ruler

Mouloud (A) – Islamic festival period properly named Mawlid an-Nabi, but known as Mouloud in the Maghreb

moussem – pilgrimage to *marabout* tomb; festival in honour of a *marabout*

muezzin (A) – mosque official who sings the call to prayer from the minaret

musée (F) – museum

nuit pharmacy (F) – night pharmacy (also *pharmacie de garde*)

ONMT (F) – Office National Marocain Tourisme, national tourist body, usually has offices called Délégation Régionale du Tourisme

oued (A) – riverbed, often dry (sometimes 'wad' or 'wadi')

oulad (A) – sons (of), often precedes tribal or town name

palais de justice (F) – law court

palmeraie (F) – oasis-like area around a town where date palms, vegetables and fruit are grown

pasha – high official in Ottoman Empire (also 'pacha')

patisserie (F) – cake and pastry shop

pensión (S) – guesthouse

petit taxi (F) – local taxi

pharmacie de garde (F) – late-night pharmacy (also *nuit pharmacy*)

pisé (F) – building material made of sun-dried clay or mud

piste (F) – poor unsealed tracks, often requiring 4WD vehicles

place (F) – square, plaza

plage (F) – beach

plat du jour (F) – daily special (in a restaurant)

pressing – laundry

qaid (A) – local chief, loose equivalent of mayor in some parts of Morocco (also 'caid')

qasba (A) – see *kasbah*

qasr (A) – see *ksar*

qebibat (A) – cupola

qibla (A) – the direction of Mecca, indicated in a mosque by a *mihrab*

qissaria (A) – covered market sometimes forming commercial centre of a medina (plural qissariat)

qubba (A) – see *koubba*

Quran (A) – sacred book of Islam

Ramadan (A) – ninth month of the Muslim year, a period of fasting

ras (A) – headland

refuge (F) – mountain hut, basic hikers' shelter

reg (B) – stony desert

riad – traditional, lavish town house

ribat (A) – combined monastery and fort

rotisseries (F) – roast chicken fast-food outlets

Saadians – Moroccan dynasty (1500s)

saha (A) – square (or French *place;* plural 'sahat')

salon de thé (F) – gentile cafe

sebkha (A) – saltpan

sharia (A) – street

shariaa (A) – Islamic law

shedwi – flatwoven rug of black and white beads

sherif (A) – descendant of the Prophet

Shiites – one of two main Islamic sects, formed by those who believe the true *imams* are descended from Ali (see also *Sunnis*)

sidi (A) – honorific (like Mr; also 'si')

sirocco (A) – easterly desert wind (also known as *chergui*)

skala (A) – fortress

souq (A) – market

Sufism – mystical strand of Islam; adherents concentrate on their inner attitude in order to attain communion with God

Sunnis – one of two main Islamic sects, derived from followers of the Umayyad caliphate (see also *Shiites*)

Syndicat d'Initiative (F) – government-run tourist office

tabac (F) – tobacconist and newsagency

tajine (A) – stew, usually with meat as the main ingredient

tapas (S) – various kinds of savoury snacks traditionally served in Spanish bars

tariq (A) – road, avenue
téléboutique (F) – privately operated telephone service
télécarte (F) – phonecard
tizi (B) – mountain pass (French *col*)
tour (F) – tower
Tuareg – nomadic Berbers of the Sahara; they are among several Berber tribes known as the Blue Men because of their indigo-dyed robes, which gives their skin a bluish tinge

Umayyads – Damascus-based Muslim dynasty (AD 661–750)

ville nouvelle (F) – new city; town built by the French, generally alongside existing towns and cities of the Maghreb

vizier – another term for a provincial governor in the Ottoman Empire, or adviser to the sultan in Morocco

wali (A) – Islamic holy man or saint
Wattasids – Moroccan dynasty of the 15th century
wilaya (A) – province

zanafi – see *glaoua*
zankat (A) – lane, alley (also 'zanqat')
zawiyya (A) – religious fraternity based around a *marabout*; also, location of the fraternity (also 'zaouia')
zeitouna (A) – olive tree or grove
zellij (A) – ceramic tiles used to decorate buildings

Acknowledgments

THANKS

Many thanks to the travellers who used the last edition and wrote to us with helpful hints, useful advice and interesting anecdotes:

Leanne Abbott, James & Emma Abel, Lina Abirafeh, Amanda Abrams, Eli & Muriel Abt, Chris D Adam, Manny Albam, Carie Allen, Justin Anderson, Craig Andrews, Said Azouagh, J Bailey, Alan Balchin, Gordon Balderston, Roy Ball, Luigina Baratto, Helen Barr, Peter Barsony, Alan Bartlett, Caroline Bassiti, Ingrid Bauwens, Ugo Bechini, Hakim Benmoussa, Janet Berdai, Ruth Bereson, Michael Bergeron, M Beverley, Yuval Bitan, Claire Bondin, Helga Boom, Audrey & Roy Bradford, Taco Brandsen, Megan Brayne, Joel Brazy, Timothy Brennan, Jeremy Brock, Mick Broekhof, Rosemary & John Brown, Andrew Bruce, Jerome Brugger, Christine Brunier, Lin Bryan, Ian Burley, Lachlan Burnet, Lisa Cameron, Joseph Caputo, S Carapiet, Michele & Pete Card, Nicholas Carson, B Casselden, Helen Catley, Stephen Chalkley, Paul Champman, Jacky Chan, Christine Chapuzet, Michael Clark, R Clau, Michele Claus, Katja Clement, Louise Cooke, Juliette Coopey, Hannah Copping, Carlos Cortijo, Geoff Cosson, Catherine Couture, Emmanuelle Crane, B Crawford, Paolo Criscuoli, Clare Crowley, Maggie Cruickshank, Michael Cummins, Mrs Cunningham, Claire Darwin, Roy Davey, Dave Davidson, Christine Dawson, David de Vries, Carrie Deere, Peter Deleu, Roland Deme, Klaus DeWinter, Peter Dhondt, Marilyn & Barrie Dickson, Carlo Donzella, Rob Doumaid, Jake Doxat, Johannes Ebeling, Chris Eddy, Kate Edwards, Hassan El Hadiou, E Elena Hall, J Ellis, Bavastrello Enrico, Kate Esson, the Estradas, Daniel Evans, Tom Fearnahough, Isabel Fernandez, Alicia Fernandez Ugarte, Michael Finn, Victor Fiorillo, B Fisher, Astrid Fleming, Svenningsen Flemming, Brita Flinner, David French, Deidre Galbraith, Peter Gardiner, Adam Gaubert, Astrid Gauffin, Peter Geerts, Peter Geukes, John Gilroy, Nicolas Godfrin, Ilana Gordon, Connor Gorry, A Graves, Peter Gray, JW Grayson, Christina Grillanda, Andrew Grossman, Mark Grump, Josef Gugler, Anne Gundry, Bromwyn Gunner, Wade Guthrie, Mickey Gutman, Kevin H, Andrew Hague, Peter Hahn, Claudia Hammett, Del Harding, Ulrike Haring, Danette Harrigan-Wilson, Fred Harshbarger, Camilla Hayes, Nick Heiden, Rory Hensey, Dusty Henson, Jean Francis Heond, Colman Higgins, Yasuko Higuchi, Sarah Hildran, Prof Peter Hillman, AP Hilton, Kurt M Hoffman, Brian Holmes, Malcolm Holmes, Raya & Andrew Hook, Sydney Hope, Janet Howell, Andy Howes, Serge Hubers, Kate Hungerford, Geroge Hunker, Nerrida Hunt, Paul Husken, R Hussain, Paula Hutt, Boaz Inbal, Tim Ives, Stephen Jakobi, Bridgett James, Anton Jansen, Jennifer M Jasper, Sabine Jefferies, Sheila Jefferson, Geraint Jenkins, Vemund Jensen, Hans Jochen Baethge, P Jones, Peter de Jong, Onno Fabery de Jonge, Tse Ka Ho,

Yasmin & Steve Kappel, Eric Kaufmann, Joshua Kaufmann, Sarah Kayson, Tim Kearley, Ursula Kennedy, Melissa Kerr, Paul Kingsworth, Steffen Knauss, Martin & Silke Kossmann, D Kudera, DeEtha Kundera, Ali Laamirni, W Labi, Knut Larsson, Gaston Latex, Andrew Lee, Michael Levin, Dr CM Leyland, Joakim Lidgren, Hariet Little, Kathryn Loosemore, Glen Lorentzen, Matthew Low, George H Lower, Edith Luray, Claudia Manke, Lothar Manke, Jon Marks, Lee Marshall, Gede Matyas, Amihai Mazar, Christine Mcbride, Joanne McCormick, Daniel McCrohan, Gregory McElwain, Sarah McGuire, Mark McHugh, Allison McKenzie, A Meinerzag, Natja Mellendorf, Clare Mercer, Isabelle Metayer, Steve Michmerhuizen, Robin Miller, T Mills, Robert D Mitchell, Don Moore, Mauro Moroni, Adrian Morrice, Ada Mulhern, Jorg Muller, Thomas Murphy, Richard Murray, Tarig & Lesley Musa, Koenraad Muylaert, Marc N, Imani Nabili, R & J Naiman, Peter Nankivell, Daniel Navas, Jane & Peter Nelmes, Frank Nemek, Daniela Neu, Quyen Ngo, Subylle & Ralf Niekisch, Phil & Mike Nolan, Helena Ohlund, Doug Oldfield, Glen Oliff, Glenn Ord, Teresa Pannone, Danic Parenteau, Annie & Anthony Pascoe, Robert Patterson, Benjamin Pearman, Antoine Pekel, Meredith Perish, P Phillips, David & Pauline Pickles, Marlou Pijnappel, Anastasia Plazzotta, Jorg A Polzer, Stuart Poole, Hanco Poot, Catherine Powell, Greg Powell, Holly Prior, Lucy Proud, Michele Puliti, John Pyle, A Quinn, JD Rabbit, Morten Rasmussen, Michael Raue, Stuart Rigby, William Ring, Guiseppe Riva, Kristi Robison, Frank Rogers, Jason Rogers, Wilko J Roggenkamp, Jason Rothman, Patricia Rothman, Christopher Ruane, Jonathan Ruck, Harvey & Laurie Ruskin, Victor Sadilek, CT Sartain, Frank Schaer, Frank Schmidt, Sebastian Schmitz, Sarit & Erez Schwarz, Jill A Scopazzi, Peter Shanks, Betty Sheets, Ernest Shenton, Yvonne Sherwood, Dominique & Pieter Shipster, Adam Simmons, Brad Simmons, Basil Singer, Hanna Sjerps, Simon Skerritt, Oystein Skjeveland, Biljana Skoric, Brooks Slaybaugh, Hans Slempkes, Iain Smith, Nick Smith, Jason Snyder, Birgitta Steen, Flemming Svenningsen, John Swepston, Eszter Szira, Thomas Tallis, David & Aneta Thackray, Michael Thogersen, Bentham Thompson, David Thuis, Manisha Tiwari, Rene van Eijk, J Van Klinlen, Luk Van Sand, Peter van Schellebeck, Pierre Vanderhout, Tom Verlent, Jan Vermazen, JDR Vernon, Veeke Verstraete, Gerry Vinson, Dre Visscher, Rob Voncken, Ali Wale, Gina Wales, Anna Walters, Michael Ward, Elixabeth Wardle, Jurjen van der Weg, Elizabeth Wells, Hans Werink, S Whitehead, Philip Wibaux, I William Zartman, Angie Williams, Teresa Wolf, A Wolff, Pam Wood, Chris Woodbridge, Mourad Yaakoubi, Alison Yates, Thelma Zarb, Liesbeth Zuidema.

LONELY PLANET

You already know that Lonely Planet produces more than this one guidebook, but you might not be aware of the other products we have on this region. Here is a selection of titles that you may want to check out as well:

Africa on a shoestring
ISBN 0 86442 663 1
US$29.99 • UK£17.99

Healthy Travel Africa
ISBN 1 86450 050 6
US$5.95 • UK£3.99

Europe on a shoestring
ISBN 1 86450 150 2
US$24.99 • UK£14.99

Mediterranean Europe
ISBN 1 86450 154 5
US$27.99 • UK£15.99

French phrasebook
ISBN 0 86442 450 7
US$5.95 • UK£3.99

Read This First: Africa
ISBN 1 86450 066 2
US$14.95 • UK£8.99

West Africa
ISBN 0 86442 569 4
US$29.95 • UK£17.99

Moroccan Arabic phrasebook
ISBN 0 86442 586 4
US$5.95 • UK£3.99

The Blue Man
ISBN 1 86450 000 X
US$12.95 • UK£6.99
*not available in Australia

Tunisia
ISBN 1 86450 185 5
US$16.99 • UK£10.99

World Food Morocco
ISBN 1 86450 024 7
US$11.95 • UK£6.99

Available wherever books are sold

LONELY PLANET

ON THE ROAD

Travel Guides explore cities, regions and countries, and supply information on transport, restaurants and accommodation, covering all budgets. They come with reliable, easy-to-use maps, practical advice, cultural and historical facts and a rundown on attractions both on and off the beaten track. There are over 200 titles in this classic series, covering nearly every country in the world.

 Lonely Planet Upgrades extend the shelf life of existing travel guides by detailing any changes that may affect travel in a region since a book has been published. Upgrades can be downloaded for free from **www.lonelyplanet.com/upgrades**

For travellers with more time than money, **Shoestring** guides offer dependable, first-hand information with hundreds of detailed maps, plus insider tips for stretching money as far as possible. Covering entire continents in most cases, the six-volume shoestring guides are known around the world as 'backpackers bibles'.

For the discerning short-term visitor, **Condensed** guides highlight the best a destination has to offer in a full-colour, pocket-sized format designed for quick access. They include everything from top sights and walking tours to opinionated reviews of where to eat, stay, shop and have fun.

CitySync lets travellers use their Palm™ or Visor™ hand-held computers to guide them through a city with handy tips on transport, history, cultural life, major sights, and shopping and entertainment options. It can also quickly search and sort hundreds of reviews of hotels, restaurants and attractions, and pinpoint their location on scrollable street maps. CitySync can be downloaded from **www.citysync.com**

MAPS & ATLASES

Lonely Planet's **City Maps** feature downtown and metropolitan maps, as well as transit routes and walking tours. The maps come complete with an index of streets, a listing of sights and a plastic coat for extra durability.

Road Atlases are an essential navigation tool for serious travellers. Cross-referenced with the guidebooks, they also feature distance and climate charts and a complete site index.

LONELY PLANET

ESSENTIALS

Read This First books help new travellers to hit the road with confidence. These invaluable predeparture guides give step-by-step advice on preparing for a trip, budgeting, arranging a visa, planning an itinerary and staying safe while still getting off the beaten track.

Healthy Travel pocket guides offer a regional rundown on disease hot spots and practical advice on predeparture health measures, staying well on the road and what to do in emergencies. The guides come with a user-friendly design and helpful diagrams and tables.

Lonely Planet's **Phrasebooks** cover the essential words and phrases travellers need when they're strangers in a strange land. They come in a pocket-sized format with colour tabs for quick reference, extensive vocabulary lists, easy-to-follow pronunciation keys and two-way dictionaries.

Miffed by blurry photos of the Taj Mahal? Tired of the classic 'top of the head cut off' shot? **Travel Photography: A Guide to Taking Better Pictures** will help you turn ordinary holiday snaps into striking images and give you the know-how to capture every scene, from frenetic festivals to peaceful beach sunrises.

Lonely Planet's **Travel Journal** is a lightweight but sturdy travel diary for jotting down all those on-the-road observations and significant travel moments. It comes with a handy time-zone wheel, world maps and useful travel information.

Lonely Planet's eKno is an all-in-one communication service developed especially for travellers. It offers low-cost international calls and free email and voicemail so that you can keep in touch while on the road. Check it out on **www.ekno.lonelyplanet.com**

FOOD & RESTAURANT GUIDES

Lonely Planet's **Out to Eat** guides recommend the brightest and best places to eat and drink in top international cities. These gourmet companions are arranged by neighbourhood, packed with dependable maps, garnished with scene-setting photos and served with quirky features.

For people who live to eat, drink and travel, **World Food** guides explore the culinary culture of each country. Entertaining and adventurous, each guide is packed with detail on staples and specialities, regional cuisine and local markets, as well as sumptuous recipes, comprehensive culinary dictionaries and lavish photos good enough to eat.

LONELY PLANET

OUTDOOR GUIDES

For those who believe the best way to see the world is on foot, Lonely Planet's **Walking Guides** detail everything from family strolls to difficult treks, with 'when to go and how to do it' advice supplemented by reliable maps and essential travel information.

Cycling Guides map a destination's best bike tours, long and short, in day-by-day detail. They contain all the information a cyclist needs, including advice on bike maintenance, places to eat and stay, innovative maps with detailed cues to the rides, and elevation charts.

The **Watching Wildlife** series is perfect for travellers who want authoritative information but don't want to tote a heavy field guide. Packed with advice on where, when and how to view a region's wildlife, each title features photos of over 300 species and contains engaging comments on the local flora and fauna.

With underwater colour photos throughout, **Pisces Books** explore the world's best diving and snorkelling areas. Each book contains listings of diving services and dive resorts, detailed information on depth, visibility and difficulty of dives, and a roundup of the marine life you're likely to see through your mask.

LONELY PLANET

OFF THE ROAD

Journeys, the travel literature series written by renowned travel authors, capture the spirit of a place or illuminate a culture with a journalist's attention to detail and a novelist's flair for words. These are tales to soak up while you're actually on the road or dip into as an at-home armchair indulgence.

The new range of lavishly illustrated **Pictorial** books is just the ticket for both travellers and dreamers. Off-beat tales and vivid photographs bring the adventure of travel to your doorstep long before the journey begins and long after it is over.

Lonely Planet **Videos** encourage the same independent, tough-minded approach as the guidebooks. Currently airing throughout the world, this award-winning series features innovative footage and an original soundtrack.

Yes, we know, work is tough, so do a little bit of deskside dreaming with the spiral-bound Lonely Planet **Diary**, the tearaway page-a-day **Day-to-Day Calendar** or a Lonely Planet **Wall Calendar**, filled with great photos from around the world.

Chasing Rickshaw

TRAVELLERS NETWORK

Lonely Planet Online. Lonely Planet's award-winning Web site has insider information on hundreds of destinations, from Amsterdam to Zimbabwe, complete with interactive maps and relevant links. The site also offers the latest travel news, recent reports from travellers on the road, guidebook upgrades, a travel links site, an online book-buying option and a lively traveller's bulletin board. It can be viewed at **www.lonelyplanet.com** or AOL keyword: lp.

Planet Talk is a quarterly print newsletter, full of gossip, advice, anecdotes and author articles. It provides an antidote to the being-at-home blues and lets you plan and dream for the next trip. Contact the nearest Lonely Planet office for your free copy.

Comet, the free Lonely Planet newsletter, comes via email once a month. It's loaded with travel news, advice, dispatches from authors, travel competitions and letters from readers. To subscribe, click on the Comet subscription link on the front page of the Web site.

LONELY PLANET

Mail Order

Lonely Planet products are distributed worldwide. They are also available by mail order from Lonely Planet, so if you have difficulty finding a title please write to us. North and South American residents should write to 150 Linden St, Oakland, CA 94607, USA; European and African residents should write to 10a Spring Place, London NW5 3BH, UK; and residents of other countries to Locked Bag 1, Footscray, Victoria 3011, Australia.

INDIAN SUBCONTINENT Bangladesh • Bengali phrasebook • Bhutan • Delhi • Goa • Healthy Travel Asia & India • Hindi & Urdu phrasebook • India • Indian Himalaya • Karakoram Highway • Kerala • Mumbai (Bombay) • Nepal • Nepali phrasebook • Pakistan • Rajasthan • Read This First: Asia & India • South India • Sri Lanka • Sri Lanka phrasebook • Tibet • Tibetan phrasebook • Trekking in the Indian Himalaya • Trekking in the Karakoram & Hindukush • Trekking in the Nepal Himalaya
Travel Literature: The Age of Kali: Indian Travels and Encounters • Hello Goodnight: A Life of Goa • In Rajasthan • A Season in Heaven: True Tales from the Road to Kathmandu • Shopping for Buddhas • A Short Walk in the Hindu Kush • Slowly Down the Ganges

ISLANDS OF THE INDIAN OCEAN Madagascar & Comoros • Maldives • Mauritius, Réunion & Seychelles

MIDDLE EAST & CENTRAL ASIA Bahrain, Kuwait & Qatar • Central Asia • Central Asia phrasebook • Dubai • Hebrew phrasebook • Iran • Israel & the Palestinian Territories • Istanbul • Istanbul City Map • Istanbul to Cairo on a shoestring • Jerusalem • Jerusalem City Map • Jordan • Lebanon • Middle East • Oman & the United Arab Emirates • Syria • Turkey • Turkish phrasebook • World Food Turkey • Yemen
Travel Literature: Black on Black: Iran Revisited • The Gates of Damascus • Kingdom of the Film Stars: Journey into Jordan

NORTH AMERICA Alaska • Boston • Boston City Map • California & Nevada • California Condensed • Canada • Chicago • Chicago City Map • Deep South • Florida • Great Lakes • Hawaii • Hiking in Alaska • Hiking in the USA • Honolulu • Las Vegas • Los Angeles • Los Angeles City Map • Louisiana & The Deep South • Miami • Miami City Map • New England • New Orleans • New York City • New York City City Map • New York City Condensed • New York, New Jersey & Pennsylvania • Oahu • Out to Eat – San Francisco • Pacific Northwest • Puerto Rico • Rocky Mountains • San Francisco • San Francisco City Map • Seattle • Southwest • Texas • USA • USA phrasebook • Vancouver • Virginia & the Capital Region • Washington DC • Washington, DC City Map • World Food Deep South, USA • World Food New Orleans
Travel Literature: Caught Inside: A Surfer's Year on the California Coast • Drive Thru America

NORTH-EAST ASIA Beijing • Beijing City Map • Cantonese phrasebook • China • Hiking in Japan • Hong Kong • Hong Kong City Map • Hong Kong Condensed • Hong Kong, Macau & Guangzhou • Japan • Japanese phrasebook • Korea • Korean phrasebook • Kyoto • Mandarin phrasebook • Mongolia • Mongolian phrasebook • Seoul • Shanghai • South-West China • Taiwan • Tokyo
Travel Literature: In Xanadu: A Quest • Lost Japan

SOUTH AMERICA Argentina, Uruguay & Paraguay • Bolivia • Brazil • Brazilian phrasebook • Buenos Aires • Chile & Easter Island • Colombia • Ecuador & the Galapagos Islands • Healthy Travel Central & South America • Latin American Spanish phrasebook • Peru • Quechua phrasebook • Read This First: Central & South America • Rio de Janeiro • Rio de Janeiro City Map • Santiago • South America on a shoestring • Santiago • Trekking in the Patagonian Andes • Venezuela
Travel Literature: Full Circle: A South American Journey

SOUTH-EAST ASIA Bali & Lombok • Bangkok • Bangkok City Map • Burmese phrasebook • Cambodia • Hanoi • Healthy Travel Asia & India • Hill Tribes phrasebook • Ho Chi Minh City • Indonesia • Indonesian phrasebook • Indonesia's Eastern Islands • Jakarta • Java • Lao phrasebook • Laos • Malay phrasebook • Malaysia, Singapore & Brunei • Myanmar (Burma) • Philippines • Pilipino (Tagalog) phrasebook • Read This First: Asia & India • Singapore • Singapore City Map • South-East Asia on a shoestring • South-East Asia phrasebook • Thailand • Thailand's Islands & Beaches • Thailand, Vietnam, Laos & Cambodia Road Atlas • Thai phrasebook • Vietnam • Vietnamese phrasebook • World Food Thailand • World Food Vietnam

ALSO AVAILABLE: Antarctica • The Arctic • The Blue Man: Tales of Travel, Love and Coffee • Brief Encounters: Stories of Love, Sex & Travel • Chasing Rickshaws • The Last Grain Race • Lonely Planet Unpacked • Not the Only Planet: Science Fiction Travel Stories • Lonely Planet On the Edge • Sacred India • Travel with Children • Travel Photography: A Guide to Taking Better Pictures

Index

Text

Bold indicates maps.

Boxed Text & Special Sections

MAP LEGEND

CITY ROUTES

Freeway	Freeway	Lane	Lane	Pedestrian Street	
Highway	Primary Road	On/Off Ramp		Stepped Street	
Road	Secondary Road	Unsealed Road		Tunnel	
Street	Street	One-Way Street		Footbridge	

TRANSPORT

Train
Underground Train
Ferry

REGIONAL ROUTES

Tollway, Freeway
Primary Road
Secondary Road
Minor Road

BOUNDARIES

International
State
Disputed
Fortified Wall

TREKKING FEATURES

4WD Track
Mule Track/Path
Scenic Drive
Described Route

HYDROGRAPHY

River, Creek
Lake
Dry Lake; Salt Lake
Spring; Rapids
Waterfalls

AREA FEATURES

Building
Park, Gardens
Market
Sports Ground
Beach
Cemetery
Oasis
Plaza

POPULATION SYMBOLS

✪ CAPITAL	National Capital	● CITY	City	● Village	Village
◉ CAPITAL	State Capital	● Town	Town		Urban Area

MAP SYMBOLS

● Place to Stay	▼ Place to Eat	● Point of Interest
Airfield; Airport	Embassy	Mosque	Shopping Centre
Anchorage	Fountain	Museum	Ski Field
Bank	Golf Course	National Park	Surf Beach
Battle Site	Hammam	Parking	Swimming Pool
Border Crossing	Hazard	Pass; Spot Height	Taxi; Transport
Bus Station/Stop	Hospital	Petrol	Telephone
Camp; Caravan Park	Internet Cafe	Picnic	Tomb
Castle	Islamic Monument	Police Station	Tourist Information
Cave	Lighthouse; Lookout	Post Office	Trail Head
Church	Monument	Pub or Bar	Windsurfing
Cinema; Theatre	Mountain	Ruins	Zoo; Bird Sanctuary

Note: not all symbols displayed above appear in this book

LONELY PLANET OFFICES

Australia
Locked Bag 1, Footscray, Victoria 3011
☎ 03 8379 8000 fax 03 8379 8111
email: talk2us@lonelyplanet.com.au

UK
10a Spring Place, London NW5 3BH
☎ 020 7428 4800 fax 020 7428 4828
email: go@lonelyplanet.co.uk

USA
150 Linden St, Oakland, CA 94607
☎ 510 893 8555 TOLL FREE: 800 275 8555
fax 510 893 8572
email: info@lonelyplanet.com

France
1 rue du Dahomey, 75011 Paris
☎ 01 55 25 33 00 fax 01 55 25 33 01
email: bip@lonelyplanet.fr
www.lonelyplanet.fr

World Wide Web: www.lonelyplanet.com *or* AOL keyword: lp
Lonely Planet Images: lpi@lonelyplanet.com.au